UNITED STATES TREATIES IN FORCE 2007 WITH INDEX

UNITED STATES TREATIES IN FORCE 2007 WITH INDEX

UNITED STATES DEPARTMENT OF STATE

Nova Science Publishers, Inc.
New York

For permission to use material from this book please contact us:
Telephone 631-231-7269; Fax 631-231-8175
Web Site: http://www.novapublishers.com

LIBRARY OF CONGRESS CATALOGING-IN-PUBLICATION DATA

Available Upon Request
ISBN 978-1-60456-115-9

Published by Nova Science Publishers, Inc. ✢ New York

Contents

Foreword

Treaties in Force is prepared by the Department of State for the purpose of providing information on treaties and other international agreements to which the United States has become a party and which are carried on the records of the Department of State as being in force as of its stated publication date, January 1, 2007.

The electronic edition of *Treaties in Force* may be updated periodically throughout the year on the Treaty Affairs webpage. It is presented in Adobe Acrobat PDF format, which allows text searches and printing of individual pages or the entire document.

(A print edition of *Treaties in Force* is published annually in limited quantities to meet the needs of certain users who are not able to consult the on-line version. The print edition lists only those treaties on record at the time of publication as being in force for the United States on January 1 of each year. Because the print edition is updated only annually, the electronic edition, in most cases, will better reflect the current status of U.S. treaties and international agreements.)

Arrangement

Treaties in Force is arranged in two sections. **Section 1, presented here,** includes bilateral treaties and other international agreements listed by country or other international entity with subject headings under each entry. Arrangements with territorial possessions of a country appear at the end of the entry for that country. In some cases, treaties and international agreements applicable to a territory prior to its independence are included in the entry for that country on the basis of its assumption of treaty obligations upon becoming independent, as noted at the beginning of the entry for that country. For convenience, some treaties and agreements concluded with countries whose name or statehood status has changed continue to be listed under the name in use at the time the agreement was concluded, if the title of the treaty or agreement has not been formally amended.

Section 2 lists multilateral treaties and other international agreements to which the United States is a party, arranged by subject. The electronic edition of *Treaties in Force* no longer furnishes a comprehensive list of parties to most agreements, because the depositary is the authoritative source for a current list of parties and information on other matters concerning the status of the agreement, and status information often changes. Instead, information is provided on the depositary for the agreement in question, and contact information, including an Internet site is provided for the depositary where available. (The print edition of *Treaties in Force* will continue to list the parties to a multilateral agreement as of January 1 of that year.)

Scope

Treaties in Force uses the term "treaty" in the generic sense as defined in the Vienna Convention on the Law of Treaties, that is, an international agreement "governed by international law, whether embodied in a single instrument or in two or more related instruments and whatever its particular designation." The term "treaty" as a matter of U.S. constitutional law denotes international agreements made by the President with the advice and consent of the Senate in accordance with Article II, section 2 of the Constitution of the United States. In addition to such "treaties", this publication covers international agreements in force that have been concluded by the Executive (a) pursuant to or in accordance with existing legislation or a prior treaty; (b) subject to congressional approval or implementation, and/or (c) under and in accordance with the President's constitutional powers.

Treaties in Force includes those treaties and other international agreements entered into by the United States which, as of the specified date, had not expired by their own terms, been denounced by the parties, replaced or superseded by other agreements, or otherwise definitely terminated. Certain agreements, particularly those concerned with World War II and the immediate postwar period, which contain continuing provisions or which have not been clearly terminated in their entirety are included even though operations under the agreements may have ceased. The absence of a listing for a particular agreement should not be regarded as a determination that it is not in force.

Searching **Treaties in Force**

To search the documents, select either individual PDFs or the One File PDF. Once in Adobe Acrobat, select the search button on the tool bar. This will open the Acrobat search function where you can do basic or advanced searches of the document.

If you have questions or comments about *Treaties in Force*, please e-mail the Office of Treaty Affairs at treatyoffice@state.gov.

A

AFGHANISTAN

AGRICULTURAL COMMODITIES

Agricultural commodities agreement, with exchanges of notes.

Signed at Kabul May 22, 1965.

Entered into force May 22, 1965.

16 UST 1078; TIAS 5849; 579 UNTS 29.

Agricultural commodities agreement with exchange of notes.

Signed at Kabul December 22, 1966.

Entered into force December 22, 1966.

17 UST 2229; TIAS 6161; 681 UNTS 123.

Agricultural commodities agreement with annex.

Signed at Kabul July 19, 1967.

Entered into force July 19, 1967.

18 UST 1766; TIAS 6322; 692 UNTS 345.

Related agreements

July 2, 1968 (19 UST 5413; TIAS 6523; 707 UNTS 111).

February 1 and March 15, 1969 (20 UST 520; TIAS 6660; 707 UNTS 120).

March 27, 1971 (22 UST 538; TIAS 7096; 792 UNTS 229).

August 23, 1971 (22 UST 2181; TIAS 7262).

February 21, 1973 (25 UST 245; TIAS 7793; 944 UNTS 73).

Agricultural commodities agreement, with minutes of understanding.

Signed at Kabul August 8, 1976.

Entered into force August 8, 1976.

27 UST 3740; TIAS 8390.

Agricultural commodities agreement, with minutes of understanding.

Signed at Kabul December 28, 1977.

Entered into force December 28, 1977.

29 UST 3321; TIAS 9014; 1124 UNTS 129.

CULTURAL RELATIONS

Agreement concerning cultural relations.

Exchange of notes at Washington June 26, 1958.

Entered into force June 26, 1958.

9 UST 997; TIAS 4069; 321 UNTS 67.

DEFENSE

Agreement relating to the deposit by Afghanistan of ten percent of the value of grant military assistance furnished by the United States.

Exchange of notes at Kabul May 24 and June 29, 1972.

Entered into force June 29, 1972; effective May 24, 1972.

23 UST 1219; TIAS 7389.

Agreement regarding grants under the Foreign Assistance Act of 1961, as amended, or successor legislation, and the furnishing of defense articles, defense services and related training, including pursuant to the United States International Military and Education Training Program (IMET), from the United States of America to the Afghanistan Interim Administration.

Exchange of notes at Kabul April 6 and 13, 2002.

Entered into force April 13, 2002.

NP

Agreement regarding the status of United States military and civilian personnel of the U.S. Department of Defense present in Afghanistan in connection with cooperative efforts in response to terrorism, humanitarian and civic assistance, military training and exercises, and other activities.

Exchange of notes September 26 and December 12, 2002 and May 28, 2003.

Entered into force May 28, 2003.

TIAS

Acquisition and cross-servicing agreement, with annexes.

Signed at Doha and Kabul January 22 and February 16, 2004.

Entered into force February 16, 2004.

TIAS

ECONOMIC AND TECHNICAL COOPERATION

General agreement for technical cooperation.

Signed at Kabul February 7, 1951.

Entered into force February 7, 1951.

2 UST 592; TIAS 2210; 132 UNTS 265.

Amendment

January 2 and 24, 1952 (3 UST 4683; TIAS 2624; 177 UNTS 341).

Agreement relating to a loan for the purchase of wheat and flour for famine relief in Afghanistan.

Exchange of notes at Washington January 8, 1953.

Entered into force January 8, 1953.

4 UST 2941; TIAS 2896.

Agreement providing development assistance to Afghanistan.

Exchange of notes at Kabul June 23, 1956.

Entered into force June 23, 1956.

7 UST 2047; TIAS 3606; 271 UNTS 295.

Agency for International Development

September 19, 2005 (NP).
September 19, 2005 (NP).
September 19, 2005 (NP).
September 30, 2005 (NP).
September 30, 2005 (NP).
September 30, 2005 (NP).
April 6, 2006 (NP).
April 6, 2006 (NP).
April 6, 2006 (NP).
May 11, 2006 (NP).
May 11, 2006 (NP).
June 28, 2006 (NP).
June 28, 2006 (NP).
June 28, 2006 (NP).
September 18, 2006 (NP).
September 18, 2006 (NP).
September 30, 2006 (NP).

EDUCATION

Agreement for financing certain educational exchange programs.

Signed at Kabul August 20, 1963.

Entered into force August 20, 1963.

14 UST 1218; TIAS 5421; 488 UNTS 41.

FINANCE

Agreement relating to investment guaranties under section 413(b)(4) of the Mutual Security Act of 1954; as amended.

Exchange of notes at Kabul June 5 and 9, 1957.

Entered into force June 9, 1957.

8 UST 2507; TIAS 3972; 307 UNTS 97.

Investment incentive agreement.

Signed at Kabul April 17, 2004.

Entered into force April 17, 2004.

TIAS

GENERAL RELATIONS

Provisional agreement in regard to friendship and diplomatic and consular representation.

Signed at Paris March 26, 1936.

Entered into force March 26, 1936.

49 Stat. 3873; EAS 88; 5 Bevans 1; 168 LNTS 143.

INFORMATIONAL MEDIA GUARANTIES

Agreement providing for an informational media guaranty program.

Exchange of notes at Kabul January 26 and February 15, 1961.

Entered into force February 15, 1961.

12 UST 378; TIAS 4726; 406 UNTS 235.

INTERNATIONAL CRIMINAL COURT

Agreement regarding the surrender of persons to the International Criminal Court.

Signed at Washington September 20, 2002.

Entered into force August 23, 2003.

TIAS

NARCOTIC DRUGS

Agreement concerning the prohibition of opium poppy cultivation in the project area of the Central Helmand drainage project (phase II).

Signed at Kabul August 29, 1977.

Entered into force August 29, 1977.

29 UST 2481; TIAS 8951.

Agreement concerning the prohibition of opium poppy cultivation in the project area of the integrated wheat development project.

Signed at Kabul September 29, 1977.

Entered into force September 29, 1977.

29 UST 2479; TIAS 8950.

Letter of agreement on police, justice and counternarcotics programs.

Signed at Kabul February 19, 2003.

Entered into force February 19, 2003.

TIAS

PEACE CORPS

Agreement relating to the establishment of a Peace Corps program in Afghanistan.

Exchange of notes at Kabul September 6 and 11, 1962.

Entered into force September 11, 1962.

13 UST 2100; TIAS 5169; 461 UNTS 169.

PUBLICATIONS

Agreement relating to the exchange of official publications.

Exchange of notes at Kabul February 29, 1944.

Entered into force February 29, 1944.

58 Stat. 1393; EAS 418; 5 Bevans 3; 106 UNTS 247.

RELIEF SUPPLIES AND PACKAGES

Agreement relating to duty-free entry and defrayment of inland transportation charges on relief supplies and packages to Afghanistan.

Exchange of notes at Kabul April 29 and May 29, 1954.

Entered into force May 29, 1954.

5 UST 1533; TIAS 3030; 234 UNTS 3.

Amendment

December 27, 1960 and January 12, 1961 (12 UST 52; TIAS 4673; 402 UNTS 319).

TELECOMMUNICATIONS

Agreement for the establishment and operation of United States radio transmitting facilities in Afghanistan, with annexes.

Signed at Washington October 3, 2002.

Entered into force October 3, 2002.

TIAS

Amendment

May 4, 2006.

AFRICAN DEVELOPMENT BANK

ECONOMIC AND TECHNICAL COOPERATION

Agency for International Development

June 30, 1976 (28 UST 6963; TIAS 8698).

FINANCE

Cooperation agreement.

Signed at New York May 29, 1986.

Entered into force May 29, 1986.

TIAS 11363.

AFRICAN UNION

DEFENSE

Agreement regarding grants under the Foreign Assistance Act of 1961, as amended, or successor legislation, and the furnishing of defense articles, related training and other defense services from the United States of America to the African Union.

Exchange of notes at Addis Ababa August 27 and September 6, 2004.

Entered into force September 6, 2004.

TIAS

ALBANIA

AVIATION

Air transport agreement, with annexes.

Signed at Washington September 24, 2003.

Entered into force April 5, 2004.

TIAS

CLAIMS

Agreement on the settlement of certain outstanding claims, with agreed minute.

Signed at Tirana March 10, 1995.

Entered into force April 18, 1995.

TIAS 12611.

Amendment

November 18, 2005 and April 27, 2006.

DEFENSE

Agreement regarding grants under the Foreign Assistance Act of 1961, as amended, and the furnishing of defense articles, related training and other defense services from the United States to Albania.

Exchange of notes at Tirana April 27 and May 6, 1994.

Entered into force May 6, 1994.

TIAS 12272.

Agreement concerning the status of U.S. military personnel and civilian employees of the Department of Defense who may be present in Albania in connection with the Search and Rescue (SAREX) joint military exercise.

Exchange of notes at Tirana January 17 and 24, 1995.

Entered into force January 24, 1995.

NP

Security agreement.

Signed at Washington October 16, 1995.

Entered into force October 16, 1995.

TIAS 12244.

Acquisition and cross-servicing agreement, with annexes.

Signed at Tirana November 8, 2000.

Entered into force November 8, 2000.

TIAS

Agreement regarding grants under the Foreign Assistance Act of 1961, as amended, and the furnishing of defense articles, related training and other defense services from the United States to Albania.

Exchange of notes at Tirana October 15 and December 4, 2002.

Entered into force December 4, 2002.

TIAS

Supplementary agreement to the "Agreement among member countries of the North Atlantic Treaty and other participating states in the Partnership for Peace regarding the status of their forces" on the status of the forces of the United States of America in the Republic of Albania.

Signed at Tirana March 31, 2004.

Entered into force August 19, 2004.

TIAS

DIPLOMATIC RELATIONS

Memorandum of understanding concerning the re-establishment of diplomatic relations.

Signed at Washington March 15, 1991.

Entered into force March 15, 1991.

TIAS 12428.

ECONOMIC AND TECHNICAL COOPERATION

Agreement concerning economic, technical and related assistance.

Signed at Tirana June 10, 1992.

Entered into force June 10, 1992.

TIAS 12456.

EMPLOYMENT

Agreement relating to the employment of dependents of official government employees.

Exchange of notes at Washington August 30 and September 30, 1993.

Entered into force September 30, 1993.

TIAS

EXTRADITION

Treaty of extradition.

Signed at Tirana March 1, 1933.

Entered into force November 14, 1935.

49 Stat. 3313; TS 902; 5 Bevans 22; 166 LNTS 195.

FINANCE

Investment incentive agreement.

Signed at Washington November 19, 1991.

Entered into force March 18, 1993.

TIAS 12441.

INTERNATIONAL CRIMINAL COURT

Agreement regarding the surrender of persons to the International Criminal Court.

Signed at Tirana May 2, 2003.

Entered into force July 7, 2003.

TIAS

INVESTMENT

Treaty concerning the reciprocal protection of investment, with annex and protocol.

Signed at Washington January 11, 1995.

Entered into force January 4, 1998.

TIAS

MAPPING

Basic exchange and cooperative agreement for topographic mapping, nautical and aeronautical charting and information, geodesy and geophysics, digital data and related mapping, charting and geodesy materials.

Signed at Tirana March 25, 1994.

Entered into force March 25, 1994.

NP

PACIFIC SETTLEMENT OF DISPUTES

Arbitration treaty.

Signed at Washington October 22, 1928.

Entered into force February 12, 1929.

45 Stat. 2728; TS 770; 5 Bevans 14; 92 LNTS 217.

Treaty of conciliation.

Signed at Washington October 22, 1928.

Entered into force February 12, 1929.

45 Stat. 2732; TS 771; 5 Bevans 17; 92 LNTS 223.

PEACE CORPS

Agreement concerning the program of the Peace Corps in the Republic of Albania.

Signed at Tirana July 22, 2003.

Entered into force October 9, 2003.

TIAS

POSTAL MATTERS

Convention for the exchange of money orders.

Signed at Washington June 18, 1932.

Entered into force October 1, 1932.

NP

Express mail agreement, with detailed regulations.

Signed at Tirana and Washington June 26 and July 15, 1996.

Entered into force September 15, 1996.

NP

TRADE AND COMMERCE

Agreement concerning most-favored-nation treatment and passports.

Exchange of notes at Tirana June 23 and 25, 1922; operative July 28, 1922.

Foreign Relations, 1925, Vol. I, p. 511; 5 Bevans 9.

Agreement on trade relations, with exchange of letters.

Signed at Washington May 14, 1992.

Entered into force November 2, 1992.

TIAS 12454.

VISAS

Agreement relating to waiver of passport visa fees for nonimmigrants.

Exchange of notes at Tirana May 7, 1926; operative June 1, 1926.

5 Bevans 12.

WEAPONS

Agreement concerning cooperation in the area of the prevention of proliferation of weapons of mass destruction, and the promotion of defense and military relations.

Signed at Washington May 12, 2003.

Entered into force May 12, 2003.

TIAS

Agreement concerning the safe, secure and ecologically sound destruction of chemical weapons.

Signed at Tirana and Washington November 9 and December 30, 2004.

Entered into force December 30, 2004.

TIAS

Amendments

September 21 and 27, 2005.

March 8 and April 4, 2006.

August 22 and September 5, 2006.

ALGERIA [1]

NOTE

1 For the "Declarations of the Government of the Democratic and Popular Republic of Algeria ..." initialed at Algiers January 19, 1981, see IRAN — CLAIMS.

AGRICULTURAL COMMODITIES

Agricultural commodities agreement with exchange of notes and related agreement.

Signed at Algiers February 23, 1966.

Entered into force February 23, 1966.

17 UST 551; TIAS 6002; 592 UNTS 117.

CONSULS

Consular convention.

Signed at Washington January 12, 1989.

Entered into force July 30, 1997.

TIAS

CULTURAL RELATIONS

Agreement on cultural cooperation.

Signed at Algiers June 2, 1987.

Entered into force October 3, 1988.

TIAS 12016; 2244 UNTS 33.

DEFENSE

Agreement with respect to articles and services provided from the Government of the United States of America to the Government of Algeria pursuant to the Trans Sahara Counterterrorism Initiative.

Exchange of notes at Algiers March 20, May 31 and June 20, 2006.

Entered into force May 31, 2006.

TIAS

ECONOMIC AND TECHNICAL COOPERATION

Agreement establishing the United States-Algerian Joint Commission for economic, technical and technological cooperation.

Signed at Washington April 17, 1985.

Entered into force April 17, 1985.

TIAS 11998.

FINANCE

Investment incentive agreement.

Signed at Washington June 22, 1990.

Entered into force December 4, 1990.

TIAS 12075.

Agreement regarding the consolidation and rescheduling or refinancing of certain debts owed to, guaranteed by or insured by the United States Government and its agencies, with annexes.

Signed at Algiers December 15, 1994.

Entered into force February 8, 1995.

NP

Agreement regarding the consolidation and rescheduling of certain debts owed to, guaranteed by, or insured by the United States Government and its agencies, with annexes.

Signed at Algiers March 27, 1996.

Entered into force June 24, 1996.

NP

INTERNATIONAL CRIMINAL COURT

Agreement regarding the surrender of persons to international tribunals.

Exchange of notes at Algiers April 6 and 13, 2004.

Entered into force April 13, 2004.

TIAS

JUDICIAL ASSISTANCE

Agreement for mutual assistance in connection with the investigation of activities of International Systems and Controls Corporation and International Telephone and Telegraph Company, their affiliates and subsidiaries.

Exchange of letters at Washington May 22, 1980.

Entered into force May 22, 1980.

32 UST 1411; TIAS 9780; 1234 UNTS 339.

Related agreement

December 18, 1980 (32 UST 4491; TIAS 9960; 1266 UNTS 378).

POSTAL MATTERS

International express mail agreement, with detailed regulations.

Signed at Algiers and Washington June 25 and July 26, 1994.

Entered into force September 1, 1994.

NP

SCIENTIFIC COOPERATION

Memorandum of understanding concerning scientific and technical cooperation in the earth sciences, with annexes.

Signed at Algiers February 21, 2000.

Entered into force February 21, 2000.

TIAS

ANDORRA

EDUCATION

Memorandum of understanding on the Fulbright Exchange Program.

Signed at Andorra November 29, 2000.

Entered into force January 8, 2002.

TIAS

ANGOLA

DEFENSE

Agreement concerning the provision of training to military and related civilian personnel of foreign countries under the United States International Military Education and Training (IMET) Program.

Exchange of notes at Luanda September 21, 1995 and January 24, 1996.

Entered into force January 24, 1996.

NP

ECONOMIC AND TECHNICAL COOPERATION

Economic, technical and related assistance agreement.

Signed at Luanda April 9, 1996.

Entered into force April 9, 1996.

TIAS 12741.

FINANCE

Investment incentive agreement.

Signed at Luanda July 27, 1994.

Entered into force August 18, 1994.

TIAS 12189.

INTERNATIONAL CRIMINAL COURT

Agreement regarding the surrender of persons to international tribunals.

Signed at Washington May 2, 2005.

Entered into force October 6, 2005.

TIAS

POSTAL MATTERS

International express mail agreement, with detailed regulations.

Signed at Luanda and Washington December 29, 1993 and October 17, 1994.

Entered into force December 1, 1994.

NP

ANTIGUA AND BARBUDA

On November 1, 1981 Antigua and Barbuda became an independent state. In a note dated November 4, 1981 to the Secretary-General of the United Nations, the Deputy Prime Minister and Minister of Foreign Affairs made a statement reading in part as follows:

"I have the honour to inform you that Antigua and Barbuda became an independent nation on 1st November, 1981, and is now ready to participate with other nations in fulfilling obligations under international law with respect to treaties to which this Government succeeded upon independence.

However, it is necessary to examine in depth such treaties to ascertain whether or not under customary international law any may have lapsed. Until this has been done the Government of Antigua and Barbuda wish:

(a) that it be presumed that each Treaty has been legally succeeded to by Antigua and Barbuda; and

(b) that future action be based on the presumption in (a) above.

You will be notified in due course of those treaties this Government regards as having lapsed and those treaties which this Government wishes to terminate. Notice of lapse or termination in an appropriate form will also be given to the country or countries that is or are party to those treaties."

AVIATION

Agreement between the United States and the United Kingdom concerning air services, with annexes and exchange of letters.

Signed at Bermuda July 23, 1977.

Entered into force July 23, 1977.

28 UST 5367; TIAS 8641.

Amendments

April 25, 1978 (29 UST 2680; TIAS 8965).

December 4, 1980 (33 UST 655; TIAS 10059).

August 19 and October 7, 1991 (TIAS 11794).

CONSULS

Consular convention between the United States and the United Kingdom.

Signed at Washington June 6, 1951.

Entered into force September 7, 1952.

3 UST 3426; TIAS 2494; 165 UNTS 121.

DEFENSE

Agreement regarding United States defense areas and facilities in Antigua, with annex, memorandum of understanding and agreed minute.

Signed at Washington December 14, 1977.

Entered into force January 1, 1978.

29 UST 4183; TIAS 9054; 1135 UNTS 3.

Amendments and extensions

December 4, 1985 and February 5 and 26, 1986.

October 28, 1988.

January 19, 1999.

August 23, 2004.

Agreement concerning the provision of training related to defense articles under the United States International Military Education and Training (IMET) Program.

Exchange of notes at St. John's December 7 and 10, 1981.

Entered into force December 10, 1981.

33 UST 4411; TIAS 10311.

Agreement regarding articles, services, and associated training transferred to the Government of Antigua and Barbuda for antinarcotics purposes.

Exchange of notes at Bridgetown and St. John's November 13 and 25, 1998.

Entered into force November 25, 1998.

TIAS

ECONOMIC AND TECHNICAL COOPERATION

General agreement for economic, technical, and related assistance.

Signed at St. John's June 17, 1983.

Entered into force June 17, 1983.

35 UST 1523; TIAS 10742; 2006 UNTS 335.

EMPLOYMENT

Agreement relating to the employment of dependents of official government employees.

Exchange of notes at Bridgetown and St. John's December 23, 1997 and January 27, 1998.

Entered into force January 27, 1998.

TIAS

EXTRADITION

Extradition treaty.

Done at St. John's June 3, 1996.

Entered into force July 1, 1999.

TIAS

FINANCE

Agreement relating to investment guaranties.

Signed at St. John's October 9, 1968.

Entered into force October 9, 1968.

19 UST 6060; TIAS 6567; 702 UNTS 253.

INTERNATIONAL CRIMINAL COURT

Agreement regarding the surrender of persons to the International Criminal Court.

Exchange of notes at Washington September 29, 2003.

Entered into force September 29, 2003.

TIAS

JUDICIAL ASSISTANCE

Treaty on mutual legal assistance in criminal matters, with exchange of notes.

Signed at St. John's October 31, 1996.

Entered into force July 1, 1999.

TIAS

NARCOTIC DRUGS

Agreement concerning maritime counter-drug operations.

Signed at St. John's April 19, 1995.

Entered into force April 19, 1995.

TIAS 12763.

Amendments

June 3, 1996 (TIAS 12763).

September 30, 2003.

PEACE CORPS

Agreement relating to the establishment of a Peace Corps program in Antigua.

Exchange of notes at Bridgetown and Antigua December 19 and 28, 1966.

Entered into force December 28, 1966.

18 UST 25; TIAS 6195; 681 UNTS 137.

PEACEKEEPING

Agreement for the furnishing of commodities and services in connection with the peacekeeping force for Grenada.

Exchange of notes at Bridgetown and St. John's November 30, 1983 and January 27, 1984.

Entered into force January 27, 1984.

35 UST 4334; TIAS 10934; 2015 UNTS 127.

Related agreement

December 16, 1985 and January 28, 1986 (TIAS 11172; 2126 UNTS 155).

POSTAL MATTERS

Convention for the exchange of postal money orders with Antigua.

Signed at Antigua December 5, 1956 and at Washington March 22, 1957.

Entered into force December 1, 1957.

11 UST 1425; TIAS 4482.

PROPERTY

Convention between the United States and the United Kingdom relating to the tenure and disposition of real and personal property.

Signed at Washington March 2, 1899; applicable to Antigua June 17, 1901.

31 Stat. 1939; TS 146; 12 Bevans 246.

Supplementary convention relating to the tenure and disposition of real and personal property of March 2, 1899.

Signed at Washington May 27, 1936.

Entered into force March 10, 1941.

55 Stat. 1101; TS 964; 5 Bevans 140; 203 LNTS 367.

TAXATION

Agreement for the exchange of information with respect to taxes.

Signed at Washington December 6, 2001.

Entered into force February 10, 2003.

TIAS

TELECOMMUNICATION

Agreement between the United States and the United Kingdom relating to the reciprocal granting of authorizations to permit licensed amateur radio operators of either country to operate their stations in the other country.

Exchange of notes at London November 26, 1965; applicable to Antigua December 11, 1969.

16 UST 2047; TIAS 5941; 561 UNTS 193.

Agreement between the United States and the United Kingdom extending to certain territories the application of the agreement of November 26, 1965 relating to the reciprocal granting of authorizations to permit licensed amateur radio operators of either country to operate their stations in the other country.

Exchange of notes at London December 11, 1969.

Entered into force December 11, 1969.

20 UST 4089; TIAS 6800; 732 UNTS 334.

Memorandum of understanding providing for a radio relay facility in Antigua for relaying Voice of America programs to areas in the Caribbean.

Signed at St. John's September 12, 1980.

Entered into force September 12, 1980.

33 UST 1541; TIAS 10130; 1560 UNTS 409.

Arrangement relating to radio communications between amateur stations on behalf of third parties.

Exchange of notes at St. John's April 30 and May 24, 1982.

Entered into force June 23, 1982.

34 UST 1103; TIAS 10395; 1566 UNTS 117.

TRACKING STATIONS

Agreement between the United States and the United Kingdom concerning the establishment and operation of a space vehicle tracking and communications station on Antigua.

Exchange of notes at Washington January 17 and 23, 1967.

Entered into force January 23, 1967.

18 UST 112; TIAS 6207.

TRADE-MARKS

Declaration by the United States and the United Kingdom affording reciprocal protection to trade-marks.

Signed at London October 24, 1877.

Entered into force October 24, 1877.

20 Stat. 703; TS 138; 12 Bevans 198.

ARGENTINA

AGRICULTURAL COMMODITIES

Agreement providing for the sale and purchase of cottonseed oil, etc.

Signed at Washington April 25, 1955.

Entered into force April 25, 1955.

6 UST 1085; TIAS 3247; 251 UNTS 283.

Amendments

April 11 and 22, 1958 (9 UST 543; TIAS 4032; 316 UNTS 380).

September 19 and November 26, 1962 (13 UST 2621; TIAS 5230; 462 UNTS 344).

Agricultural commodities agreement to finance the sale to Argentina of edible oils and/or fat.

Signed at Buenos Aires December 21, 1955.

Entered into force December 21, 1955.

6 UST 6077; TIAS 3459; 240 UNTS 329.

Amendment

September 19 and November 26, 1962 (13 UST 2621; TIAS 5230; 462 UNTS 344).

Agricultural commodities agreement with exchanges of notes.

Signed at Washington June 12, 1959.

Entered into force June 12, 1959.

10 UST 1068; TIAS 4246; 347 UNTS 59.

AGRICULTURE

Agreement for cooperation in the fields of agriculture, livestock and forestry.

Signed at Washington May 20, 1981.

Entered into force May 20, 1981.

33 UST 1971; TIAS 10161.

Extension

November 17, 1986.

ATOMIC ENERGY

Agreement providing for a grant to assist in the acquisition of certain nuclear research and training equipment and materials.

Exchange of notes at Buenos Aires September 9, 1959 and May 23, 1960.

Entered into force May 23, 1960.

11 UST 1628; TIAS 4508; 377 UNTS 3.

Agreement providing for equipment to be used in nuclear research and training programs at La Plata University, Argentina.

Exchange of notes at Buenos Aires November 8, 1962 and November 30, 1963.

Entered into force November 30, 1963.

14 UST 1907; TIAS 5504; 505 UNTS 131.

Agreement for cooperation concerning peaceful uses of nuclear energy, with annex and agreed minute.

Signed at Buenos Aires February 29, 1996.

Entered into force October 16, 1997.

TIAS 12730.

Implementing arrangement for technical exchange and cooperation in the area of peaceful uses of nuclear energy.

Signed at Buenos Aires October 16, 1997.

Entered into force October 16, 1997.

TIAS

Arrangement for the exchange of technical information and cooperation in regulatory and safety research matters.

Signed at Buenos Aires and Rockville January 8 and 18, 2002.

Entered into force January 18, 2002.

TIAS

AVIATION

Air transport services agreement, with annexes.

Signed at Buenos Aires October 22, 1985.

Entered into force provisionally October 22, 1985; definitively December 29, 1986.

TIAS 11262.

Amendment

October 26 and November 24, 2000.

Agreement relating to the reciprocal acceptance of airworthiness certifications.

Exchange of notes at Buenos Aires June 22, 1989.

Entered into force June 22, 1989.

TIAS 11669; 2190 UNTS 383.

COMMERCE

Treaty of friendship, commerce and navigation.

Signed at San Jose July 27, 1853.

Entered into force December 20, 1854.

10 Stat. 1005; TS 4; 5 Bevans 61.

CONSULS

See COMMERCE

COPYRIGHT

Copyright arrangement. Exchanges of notes at Buenos Aires April 28, July 28, August 28, and September 3, 1934; operative August 23, 1934.

5 Bevans 72; 160 LNTS 57.

DEFENSE

Agreement relating to a military assistance program.

Exchange of notes at Buenos Aires May 10, 1964.

Entered into force May 10, 1964.

15 UST 719; TIAS 5594; 527 UNTS 77.

Armed forces cooperative projects agreement.

Exchange of notes at Buenos Aires May 5, 1970.

Entered into force May 5, 1970.

21 UST 1297; TIAS 6881; 752 UNTS 25.

Agreement relating to the deposit by Argentina of ten percent of the value of grant military assistance furnished by the United States.

Exchange of notes at Buenos Aires April 4 and June 8, 1972.

Entered into force June 8, 1972.

23 UST 1324; TIAS 7414.

Memorandum of understanding on the exchange of officers between the U.S. Marine Corps and the Argentine Marine Corps.

Signed at Washington October 7 and December 3, 1987.

Entered into force December 3, 1987.

TIAS 11559.

Memorandum of understanding on the exchange of service personnel between the United States Navy and Argentine Navy and on the general conditions which will apply to the exchange of such personnel.

Signed at Washington July 13, 1992.

Entered into force July 13, 1992.

NP

Agreement concerning exchange of research and development information, with appendix.

Signed at Washington July 22, 1998.

Entered into force July 22, 1998.

TIAS

Amendment

October 17, 2000.

Agreement concerning security measures for the protection of classified information.

Signed at Washington January 12, 1999.

Entered into force January 12, 1999.

TIAS

Acquisition and cross-servicing agreement, with annex.

Signed at Miami and Buenos Aires January 11 and 15, 1999.

Entered into force January 15, 1999.

TIAS

Memorandum of understanding concerning the inter-American naval telecommunications network.

Signed October 9 and November 8, 2006.

Entered into force November 8, 2006.

TIAS

ECONOMIC AND TECHNICAL COOPERATION

General agreement for a program of technical cooperation.

Signed at Buenos Aires June 3, 1957.

Entered into force June 3, 1957.

8 UST 811; TIAS 3840; 291 UNTS 61.

Agreement concerning the establishment of an Americas Fund and Administering Commission.

Signed at Buenos Aires September 27, 1993.

Entered into force September 27, 1993.

TIAS 12507.

EDUCATION

Agreement for financing certain educational exchange programs.

Signed at Buenos Aires August 21, 1963.

Entered into force August 21, 1963.

14 UST 1236; TIAS 5423; 488 UNTS 61.

Amendment

January 18 and March 20, 2000.

EMPLOYMENT

Agreement relating to the employment of dependents of official government employees.

Exchange of notes at Buenos Aires May 28 and December 15, 1986.

Entered into force December 15, 1986.

TIAS 11414.

ENVIRONMENTAL COOPERATION

Agreement for cooperation in the Global Learning and Observations to Benefit the Environment Program, with appendices.

Signed at Buenos Aires June 28, 1995.

Entered into force June 28, 1995.

TIAS 12671.

EXTRADITION

Treaty on extradition.

Signed at Buenos Aires June 10, 1997.

Entered into force June 15, 2000.

TIAS; 2159 UNTS 129.

FINANCE

Agreement relating to investment guaranties under section 413(b)(4) of the Mutual Security Act of 1954, as amended.

Signed at Buenos Aires December 22, 1959.

Entered into force provisionally December 22, 1959; definitively May 5, 1961.

12 UST 955; TIAS 4799; 411 UNTS 41.

Agreement regarding the consolidation and rescheduling of certain debts owed to, guaranteed by or insured by the United States Government and its agencies, with annexes.

Signed at Buenos Aires April 8, 1986.

Entered into force May 19, 1986.

NP

Swap agreement between the United States Treasury and the Central Bank of the Argentine Republic/Government of the Argentine Republic, with related letter and amendment.

Signed at Washington and Buenos Aires February 23, 1988.

Entered into force February 23, 1988.

TIAS

Swap agreement between the United States Treasury, the Central Bank of the Argentine Republic/Government of the Argentine Republic, with memorandum of understanding.

Signed at Washington and Buenos Aires October 19, 1988.

Entered into force October 19, 1988.

TIAS

Agreement regarding the consolidation and rescheduling or refinancing of certain debts owed to, guaranteed by, or insured by the United States Government and its agencies, with annexes.

Signed at Buenos Aires December 14, 1989.

Entered into force January 22, 1990.

NP

Agreement regarding the consolidation and rescheduling of certain debts owed to, guaranteed by, or insured by the United States Government and its agencies, with annexes.

Signed at Buenos Aires December 5, 1990.

Entered into force January 16, 1991.

NP

Agreement regarding the consolidation and rescheduling or refinancing of certain debts owed to, guaranteed by or insured by the United States Government and its agencies, with annexes.

Signed at Washington December 6, 1991.

Entered into force February 10, 1992.

NP

Agreement regarding the consolidation and rescheduling of certain debts owed to, guaranteed by or insured by the United States Government and its agencies, with annexes.

Signed at Washington January 13, 1993.

Entered into force March 8, 1993.

NP

Agreement regarding the reduction of certain debts related to foreign assistance owed to the Government of the United States and its agencies, with appendices.

Signed at Washington and Buenos Aires January 13 and 15, 1993.

Entered into force February 14, 1993.

NP

INVESTMENT

Treaty concerning the reciprocal encouragement and protection of investment, with protocol.

Signed at Washington November 14, 1991.

Entered into force October 20, 1994.

TIAS

Amendment

August 24 and November 6, 1992.

JUDICIAL ASSISTANCE

Treaty on mutual legal assistance in criminal matters, with attachments.

Signed at Buenos Aires December 4, 1990.

Entered into force February 9, 1993.

TIAS

MAPPING

Agreement relating to cooperation and mutual assistance in cartography and geodesy, with annex.

Signed at Buenos Aires July 11, 1983.

Entered into force July 11, 1983.

35 UST 1310; TIAS 10730; 1578 UNTS 91.

Agreement concerning nautical cartography and geodesy, with annexes.

Signed at Buenos Aires and Fairfax November 28, 1990 and June 18, 1991.

Entered into force June 18, 1991.

NP

Basic exchange and cooperative agreement concerning geospatial information and services cooperation, with annex.

Signed at Buenos Aires March 5, 2001.

Entered into force March 5, 2001.

NP

MARITIME MATTERS

Agreement relating to the transfer to Argentina of certain United States naval vessels.

Exchange of notes at Washington January 4 and 8, 1951 with memorandum of understanding dated January 11, 1951.

Entered into force January 8, 1951.

3 UST 2735; TIAS 2442; 165 UNTS 89.

Memorandum of understanding regarding certain maritime matters.

Signed at Buenos Aires March 31, 1978.

Entered into force January 30, 1979.

30 UST 1054; TIAS 9239; 1152 UNTS 227.

MISSIONS, MILITARY

Agreement for a United States Air Force Mission to the Argentine Republic.

Signed at Buenos Aires October 3, 1956.

Entered into force October 3, 1956.[1]

7 UST 2571; TIAS 3652; 279 UNTS 13.

Amendment

October 16, 1959 (10 UST 1978; TIAS 4363; 361 UNTS 358).

Agreement relating to the appointment of officers to constitute a United States Army Mission to Argentina.

Signed at Buenos Aires August 2, 1960.

Entered into force August 2, 1960.

11 UST 1964; TIAS 4546; 384 UNTS 105.

Amendment

January 8 and June 7, 1962 (13 UST 1376; TIAS 5098; 458 UNTS 354).

NOTE

1 Article 17 suspended by agreement of November 27, 1972 (24 UST 279; TIAS 7550).

NARCOTIC DRUGS

Memorandum of understanding on cooperation in the narcotics field.

Signed at Buenos Aires September 15, 1972.

Entered into force September 15, 1972.

23 UST 2620; TIAS 7450; 852 UNTS 97.

NAVIGATION

Treaty for the free navigation of the rivers Parana and Uruguay.

Signed at San Jose de Flores July 10, 1853.

Entered into force December 20, 1854.

10 Stat. 1001; TS 3; 5 Bevans 58.

PEACE CORPS

Agreement establishing a Peace Corps program in Argentina.

Exchange of notes at Buenos Aires July 18 and August 30, 1991.

Entered into force August 30, 1991.

TIAS 12102.

POSTAL MATTERS

Agreement for the exchange of insured parcel post packages.

Signed at Buenos Aires February 28 and at Washington April 8, 1939; operative October 1, 1938.

53 Stat. 2223; Post Office Department print; 198 LNTS 55.

International express mail agreement, with detailed regulations.

Signed at Buenos Aires and Washington September 4 and 26, 1980.

Entered into force January 1, 1981.

33 UST 2509; TIAS 10193; 1529 UNTS 269.

Memorandum of understanding concerning the operation of the INTELPOST field trial, with details of implementation.

Signed at Washington August 24 and October 12, 1982 and Buenos Aires September 16, 1982.

Entered into force November 1, 1982.

TIAS 10526; 1777 UNTS 355.

PUBLICATIONS

Agreement relating to the exchange of official publications.

Exchange of notes at Buenos Aires September 30 and October 17, 1939.

Entered into force October 17, 1939.

54 Stat. 1855; EAS 162; 5 Bevans 83; 201 LNTS 273.

SCIENTIFIC COOPERATION

Agreement for scientific and technical cooperation.

Signed at Buenos Aires April 7, 1972.

Entered into force August 11, 1972.

23 UST 2534; TIAS 7442; 852 UNTS 77.

SEISMIC OBSERVATIONS

Agreement on scientific and technical cooperation for a global telemetered seismograph network.

Signed at Reston and San Juan December 28 and 29, 1987.

Entered into force December 29, 1987.

TIAS 12054.

SOCIAL SECURITY

Agreement relating to the payment of old-age, survivors, and disability benefits to beneficiaries residing abroad.

Exchange of notes at Buenos Aires September 15, 1972.

Entered into force September 15, 1972.

23 UST 2660; TIAS 7458; 852 UNTS 91.

SPACE COOPERATION

Agreement for cooperation in the civil uses of space.

Signed at Buenos Aires August 6, 1991.

Entered into force August 6, 1991.

TIAS 12214.

Extension

August 2, 2001.

Memorandum of understanding concerning the SAC-B Astrophysics Engineering Demonstration Mission.

Signed at Buenos Aires August 6, 1991.

Entered into force August 6, 1991.

TIAS 12212.

Memorandum of understanding concerning the Scientific Applications Satellite-C Earth Observation Mission.

Signed at Washington October 28, 1996.

Entered into force October 28, 1996.

TIAS

Memorandum of understanding concerning the flight of the SAC-A Mission on the Shuttle.

Signed at Buenos Aires October 16, 1997.

Entered into force October 16, 1997.

TIAS

Memorandum of understanding for cooperation on the Aquarius/SAC-D mission.

Signed at Buenos Aires March 2, 2004.

Entered into force March 2, 2004.

TIAS

TAXATION

Agreement for relief from double taxation on earnings derived from operation of ships and aircraft.

Exchange of notes at Washington July 20, 1950.

Entered into force July 20, 1950.

1 UST 473; TIAS 2088; 89 UNTS 63.

TECHNOLOGY TRANSFER

Memorandum of understanding on the transfer and protection of strategic technology.

Signed at Buenos Aires February 12, 1993.

Entered into force February 12, 1993.

TIAS 12487.

TELECOMMUNICATION

Agreement relating to the reciprocal granting of authorizations to permit licensed amateur radio operators of either country to operate their stations in the other country.

Exchange of notes at Buenos Aires March 31, 1967.

Entered into force April 30, 1967.

18 UST 361; TIAS 6243; 636 UNTS 95.

Agreement relating to radio communications between amateur stations on behalf of third parties.

Exchange of notes at Buenos Aires March 31, 1967.

Entered into force April 30, 1967.

18 UST 365; TIAS 6244; 636 UNTS 103.

Agreement concerning the provision of satellite facilities and the transmission and reception of signals to and from satellites for the provision of satellite services to users in the United States of America and the Argentine Republic, with protocol.

Signed at Washington June 5, 1998.

Entered into force June 5, 1998.

TIAS

TOURISM

Agreement on the development and facilitation of tourism.

Signed at Buenos Aires September 25, 1990.

Entered into force September 25, 1990.

TIAS 12420.

TRACKING STATIONS

Agreement relating to a cooperative program for the optical satellite tracking station at Villa Dolores, Argentina.

Exchange of notes at Buenos Aires March 16, 1962.

Entered into force March 16, 1962.

13 UST 1385; TIAS 5100; 454 UNTS 3.

TRADE

See also COMMERCE

Trade agreement with exchanges of notes.

Signed at Buenos Aires October 14, 1941.

Entered into force provisionally November 15, 1941; definitively January 8, 1943.

56 Stat. 1685; EAS 277; 5 Bevans 102; 119 UNTS 193.

Agreement relating to the effectiveness of United States schedules to the trade agreement of October 14, 1941.

Exchange of notes at Buenos Aires July 24, 1963.

Entered into force July 24, 1963.

14 UST 1046; TIAS 5402; 487 UNTS 183.

Amendment

December 18 and 27, 1967 (18 UST 3102; TIAS 6402; 693 UNTS 370).

Agreement relating to the status of the trade agreements of October 14, 1941 and July 24, 1963.

Exchange of notes at Buenos Aires August 3 and 8, 1966.

Entered into force August 8, 1966.

17 UST 1223; TIAS 6086.

Amendment

December 18 and 27, 1967 (18 UST 3102; TIAS 6402; 693 UNTS 370).

Agreement concerning trade in women's and girls' wool trousers, with attachment.

Exchange of notes at Buenos Aires May 14 and 31, 1991.

Entered into force May 31, 1991.

NP

VISAS

Agreement relating to the reciprocal waiver of nonimmigrant passport visa fees.

Exchange of notes at Buenos Aires April 15, 1942; operative June 1, 1942.

56 Stat. 1578; EAS 266; 5 Bevans 117; 103 UNTS 307.

ARMENIA

For agreements prior to December 31, 1991, see UNION OF SOVIET SOCIALIST REPUBLICS.

ATOMIC ENERGY

Agreement on cooperative thermal-hydraulic code applications and maintenance research and severe accident research, with addendum.

Signed at Rockville and Yerevan February 11 and 24, 2004.

Entered into force February 24, 2004; effective May 31, 2003.

TIAS

DEFENSE

Acquisition and cross-servicing agreement, with annexes.

Signed at Yerevan April 26, 2004.

Entered into force October 29, 2004.

TIAS

ECONOMIC AND TECHNICAL COOPERATION

Agreement regarding cooperation to facilitate the provision of humanitarian and technical economic assistance.

Signed at Yerevan December 15, 1992.

Entered into force December 15, 1992.

TIAS 12483.

Millennium challenge compact, with annexes.

Signed at Washington March 27, 2006.

Entered into force September 29, 2006.

TIAS

EMPLOYMENT

Agreement on employment of dependents of members of diplomatic missions and consular posts.

Exchange of notes at Yerevan September 20 and December 30, 2005.

Entered into force October 16, 2006.

TIAS

FINANCE

Investment incentive agreement.

Signed at Washington April 2, 1992.

Entered into force April 2, 1992.

TIAS 12451.

INTERNATIONAL CRIMINAL COURT

Agreement regarding the surrender of persons to the International Tribunals.

Signed at Yerevan October 16, 2004.

Entered into force March 17, 2005.

TIAS

INVESTMENT

Treaty concerning the reciprocal encouragement and protection of investment, with annex.

Signed at Washington September 23, 1992.

Entered into force March 29, 1996.

TIAS

PEACE CORPS

Agreement concerning the program of the Peace Corps in Armenia.

Signed at Washington September 24, 1992.

Entered into force September 24, 1992.

TIAS 12082.

SCIENTIFIC COOPERATION

Agreement on science and technology cooperation.

Signed at Washington February 28, 1997.

Entered into force February 28, 1997.

TIAS

TRADE

Agreement on trade relations, with related exchanges of letters.

Signed at Washington April 2, 1992.

Entered into force April 7, 1992.

TIAS

WEAPONS

Agreement concerning cooperation in the area of counterproliferation of weapons of mass destruction.

Signed at Washington July 24, 2000.

Entered into force November 25, 2002.

TIAS

ASIAN DEVELOPMENT BANK

FINANCE

Agreement relating to the United States contribution to the Multi-Purpose Special Fund of the Asian Development Bank.

Signed at Manila April 19, 1974.

Entered into force April 19, 1974.

25 UST 1672; TIAS 7903.

Amendment

December 23, 1974 and April 1, 1975 (26 UST 897; TIAS 8074).

ASSOCIATION OF SOUTHEAST ASIAN NATIONS (ASEAN)

AGRICULTURE

Agreement regarding the establishment of an ASEAN Agricultural Development and Planning Center.

Exchange of notes at Kuala Lumpur June 28, 1980.

Entered into force June 28, 1980.

32 UST 1371; TIAS 9778; 1234 UNTS 399.

ECONOMIC AND TECHNICAL COOPERATION

Agreement concerning cooperation in economic development, education, culture, and narcotics.

Signed at Denpasar and Kuala Lumpur July 2 and October 24, 1979.

Entered into force October 24, 1979.

TIAS

AUSTRALIA

AEROSPACE DISTURBANCES

Agreement concerning the transfer to the Australian National University of the facility for research on aerospace disturbances at Amberley, Queensland.

Exchange of notes at Canberra January 31 and February 26, 1975.

Entered into force February 26, 1975.

26 UST 446; TIAS 8043; 992 UNTS 139.

ATOMIC ENERGY

Agreement for cooperation regarding atomic information for mutual defense purposes.

Signed at Washington July 12, 1957.

Entered into force August 14, 1957.

8 UST 1339; TIAS 3881; 290 UNTS 139.

Agreement concerning peaceful uses of nuclear energy, with annex and agreed minute.

Signed at Canberra July 5, 1979.

Entered into force January 16, 1981.

32 UST 3227; TIAS 9893; 1217 UNTS 211.

Memorandum of understanding concerning the acceptance by the United States Government of spent fuel from the HIFAR research reactor, with attachment.

Exchange of notes at Canberra October 30, 1997.

Entered into force October 30, 1997.

TIAS

Agreement for cooperation concerning technology for the separation of isotopes of uranium by laser excitation, with annexes, agreed minute and related exchange of letters.

Signed at Washington October 28, 1999.

Entered into force May 24, 2000.

TIAS; 2117 UNTS 243.

Agreement concerning the application of non-proliferation assurances to Australian uranium to be transferred to the United States of America for enrichment and retransfer to Taiwan, with annex.

Exchange of notes at Washington July 31, 2001.

Entered into force May 17, 2002.

TIAS; 2208 UNTS 497.

Memorandum of understanding for cooperation and the exchange of unclassified information in nuclear regulatory affairs, with addenda.

Signed at Rockville September 8, 2003.

Entered into force September 8, 2003.

TIAS

AVIATION

Air transport agreement.[1]

Signed at Washington December 3, 1946.

Entered into force December 3, 1946.

61 Stat. 2464; TIAS 1574; 5 Bevans 170; 7 UNTS 201.

Amendments

December 22, 1987 (TIAS 11922; 1571 UNTS 480).

March 23, 1989 (TIAS 11990; 1820 UNTS 495).

February 22, 1994 (TIAS 12174; 1820 UNTS 468).

Related agreement

March 23, 1989 (TIAS 11989).

Air service agreement relating to facilities at Eagle Farm and Amberley, Queensland.

Signed at Canberra March 10, 1947.

Entered into force March 10, 1947.

61 Stat. 3843; TIAS 1732; 5 Bevans 181; 10 UNTS 89.

Agreement relating to the reciprocal acceptance of airworthiness certifications.

Exchange of notes at Washington December 24, 1974 and June 11, 1975.

Entered into force June 11, 1975.

26 UST 1665; TIAS 8126; 1006 UNTS 241.

NOTE

1 Applicable to all territories.

CONSULS

Convention to regulate commerce (article IV) between the United States and the United Kingdom.

Signed at London July 3, 1815.

Entered into force July 3, 1815.

8 Stat. 228; TS 110; 12 Bevans 49.

DEFENSE

Mutual defense assistance agreement.

Exchange of notes at Washington February 1 and 20, 1951.

Entered into force February 20, 1951.

2 UST 644; TIAS 2217; 132 UNTS 297.

Mutual weapons development program agreement.

Signed at Washington August 23, 1960.

Entered into force August 23, 1960.

11 UST 2089; TIAS 4565; 388 UNTS 232.

Agreement concerning the status of United States forces in Australia with protocol.

Signed at Canberra May 9, 1963.

Entered into force May 9, 1963.

14 UST 506; TIAS 5349; 469 UNTS 55.

Agreement relating to the establishment of a United States naval communication station in Australia.

Signed at Canberra May 9, 1963.

Entered into force June 28, 1963.

14 UST 908; TIAS 5377; 475 UNTS 331.

Amendments

July 12, 1968 (19 UST 5445; TIAS 6527; 660 UNTS 401).

March 21, 1974 (27 UST 2667; TIAS 8338).

November 24, 1982 (TIAS 10610).

May 8, 1992 (1680 UNTS 494).

Memorandum of arrangement between the United States, Australia, and the United Kingdom to cover re-entry experiments in Australia (Project Sparta), with exchanges of notes.

Signed at Canberra March 30, 1966.

Entered into force March 30, 1966.

17 UST 350; TIAS 5984; 593 UNTS 261.

Agreement relating to the establishment of a joint defense space research facility.

Signed at Canberra December 9, 1966.

Entered into force December 9, 1966.

17 UST 2235; TIAS 6162; 607 UNTS 83.

Extensions and amendments

October 19, 1977 (29 UST 2759; TIAS 8969).

November 16, 1988 (TIAS 12266).

June 4, 1998 (2171 UNTS 89).

Agreement relating to the establishment of a joint defense space communications station in Australia.

Signed at Canberra November 10, 1969.

Entered into force November 10, 1969.

20 UST 3097; TIAS 6788; 729 UNTS 17.

Extension and amendment

November 16, 1988 (TIAS 12267).

Memorandum of understanding regarding the exchange training program of units from both forces.

Signed at Washington November 4, 1976.

Entered into force November 4, 1976.

28 UST 8237; TIAS 8757; 1095 UNTS 91.

Agreement relating to operation of United States military flights through RAAF Base Darwin.

Exchange of notes at Canberra March 11, 1981.

Entered into force March 11, 1981.

33 UST 1300; TIAS 10112.

Memorandum of understanding concerning the exchange of service personnel between the U.S. Marine Corps and the Royal Australian Air Force.

Signed at Washington April 13, 1984.

Entered into force April 13, 1984.

TIAS 11131.

Memorandum of understanding on logistic support, with annexes.

Signed at Washington and Canberra March 30 and April 23, 1985.

Entered into force April 23, 1985.

TIAS 12052.

Memorandum of arrangement relating to the provision of NOMAD aircraft and related services, with attachment.

Signed at Washington April 2, 1987.

Entered into force April 2, 1987.

TIAS 11317.

Memorandum of understanding concerning exchange of service personnel between the U.S. Marine Corps and the Australian Army.

Signed at Canberra and Washington August 31 and September 16, 1987.

Entered into force September 16, 1987.

TIAS 11550.

Agreement concerning cooperation in defense logistic support.

Signed at Sydney November 4, 1989.

Entered into force November 4, 1989.

TIAS; 1571 UNTS 167.

Amendment and extension

August 7, 2000 and July 30, 2001.

Agreement concerning defense communications services, with annexes.

Signed at Canberra November 6, 1989.

Entered into force November 6, 1989.

TIAS 12268; 1571 UNTS 189.

Agreement concerning Navstar Global Positioning System.

Signed at Washington February 7, 1991.

Entered into force February 7, 1991.

TIAS 12269; 1642 UNTS 299.

Agreement concerning cooperation in radar activities, with project arrangements.

Signed at Salisbury March 3, 1992.

Entered into force March 3, 1992.

TIAS 12270; 1679 UNTS 251.

Arrangement for the exchange of military personnel between the Royal Australian Navy and the U.S. Coast Guard.

Signed at Washington July 27, 1992.

Entered into force July 27, 1992.

NP

Agreement concerning the exchange of electronic warfare officers between the Department of Defense of the United States and the Department of Defense of Australia, with annexes.

Signed at Washington August 26, 1992.

Entered into force August 26, 1992.

NP

Agreement concerning cooperative and collaborative research, development and engineering, with appendix.

Signed at Washington October 21, 1994.

Entered into force October 21, 1994.

TIAS 12271; 1856 UNTS 291.

Agreement concerning the establishment of certain mutual defense commitments.

Exchange of notes at Sydney and Canberra December 1, 1995.

Entered into force December 1, 1995.

TIAS 12704; 1945 UNTS 263.

Memorandum of understanding for the production of the offboard active decoy Nulka, with annexes.

Signed at Washington June 25, 1996.

Entered into force June 25, 1996.

TIAS 12771.

Agreement concerning defense communications services, with annexes.

Signed at Washington October 14 and 30, 1998.

Entered into force July 13, 1999.

TIAS; 2076 UNTS 343.

Agreement concerning acquisition and cross-servicing, with annexes.

Signed at Canberra December 9, 1998.

Entered into force September 22, 1999.

TIAS; 2117 UNTS 185.

Agreement concerning security measures for the protection of classified information, with exchange of notes.

Signed at Canberra June 25, 2002.

Entered into force November 7, 2002.

TIAS; 2208 UNTS 481.

Agreement concerning the cooperative framework for system development and demonstration of the joint strike fighter.

Signed at Washington October 31, 2002.

Entered into force November 14, 2002.

TIAS

Memorandum of understanding for test and evaluation program cooperation.

Signed at Washington and Canberra April 14 and 23, 2003.

Entered into force April 23, 2003.

TIAS

Memorandum of understanding concerning ballistic missile defense, with attachment.

Signed at Washington July 7, 2004.

Entered into force July 7, 2004.

TIAS

Memorandum of understanding for the cooperative development, production and support of the combat control system AN/BYG-1 tactical subsystem, with annexes.

Signed at Washington and Canberra November 5 and 18, 2004.

Entered into force November 18, 2004.

TIAS

Memorandum of understanding for the loan of defense advanced global positioning system receiver (DAGR).

Signed at Arlington and Canberra March 4 and 7, 2005.

Entered into force March 7, 2005.

TIAS

Agreement concerning cooperative and collaborative research, development and engineering project arrangement on the Australia/United States phased array radar (AUSPAR) project, with annexes.

Signed at Canberra and Washington April 11 and 21, 2005.

Entered into force April 21, 2005.

TIAS

Memorandum of understanding regarding assignment of liaison officers to headquarters, United States Strategic Command, with annex.

Signed at Omaha and Canberra April 28 and June 22, 2005.

Entered into force June 22, 2005.

TIAS

Memorandum of understanding concerning collaboration on tactile missile design, development, test and evaluation, with annexes.

Signed at Washington and Canberra August 3 and September 1, 2005.

Entered into force September 1, 2005.

TIAS

Memorandum of understanding concerning the mutual exchange of military satellite communications services and support, with attachment.

Signed at Offutt and Canberra September 9 and 26, 2005.

Entered into force September 26, 2005.

TIAS

Information exchange annex to the memorandum of information exchange of April 18, 1997 concerning surface ship air warfare, with attachments

Signed October 4, 2005.

Entered into force October 4, 2005.

TIAS

Information exchange annex to the memorandum of information exchange of April 18, 1997 concerning surface ship undersea warfare, with attachments

Signed October 4, 2005.

Entered into force October 4, 2005.

TIAS

Information exchange annex to the memorandum of information exchange of April 18, 1997 concerning surface ship surface warfare, with attachments.

Signed at Canberra October 4, 2005.

Entered into force October 4, 2005.

TIAS

Research, development, test and evaluation annex (Annex A) to the memorandum of understanding of July 7, 2004 concerning ballistic missile defense, with attachment.

Signed at Canberra October 4, 2005.

Entered into force October 4, 2005.

TIAS

Memorandum of understanding concerning Joint Combined Training Center (JCTC).

Signed at Adelaide November 18, 2005.

Entered into force November 18, 2005.

TIAS

Memorandum of understanding concerning defense communications services, with annexes and appendices.

Signed at Canberra and Arlington December 16, 2005 and March 30, 2006.

Entered into force March 30, 2006.

TIAS

Memorandum of understanding concerning cooperation on future design, development, test and evaluation for the soldier combat system, with annexes and appendix.

Signed at Brisbane October 25, 2006.

Entered into force October 25, 2006.

TIAS

ECONOMIC AND TECHNICAL COOPERATION

Agreement relating to training and other technical services to be furnished by the Bureau of Reclamation, Department of the Interior, in connection with proposed projects of the Australian Snowy Mountains Hydroelectric Authority.

Exchange of notes at Washington November 16, 1951.

Entered into force November 16, 1951.

3 UST 2836; TIAS 2456; 168 UNTS 75.

EDUCATION

Agreement for financing certain educational and cultural exchange programs.

Signed at Canberra August 28, 1964.

Entered into force August 28, 1964.

15 UST 1689; TIAS 5643; 510 UNTS 201.

Amendments

May 12, 1967 (18 UST 493; TIAS 6255; 638 UNTS 300).

February 20 and 21, 1992 (TIAS 12449; 1680 UNTS 502).

EMPLOYMENT

Agreement relating to employment of dependents of official government employees, with related notes.

Exchange of notes at Canberra November 5 and 9, 1984.

Entered into force November 9, 1984.

TIAS 11138.

ENERGY

Memorandum of understanding relating to coal information exchange in the areas of health, safety and environment.

Signed at Canberra October 24 and 25, 1978.

Entered into force November 23, 1978.

30 UST 2208; TIAS 9328.

ENVIRONMENTAL COOPERATION

Memorandum of understanding for cooperation in the Global Learning and Observations to Benefit the Environment (GLOBE) Program, with appendices.

Signed at Canberra April 21, 1995.

Entered into force April 21, 1995.

TIAS 12634.

EXTRADITION

Treaty on extradition.[1]

Signed at Washington May 14, 1974.

Entered into force May 8, 1976.

27 UST 957; TIAS 8234.

Amendment

September 4, 1990 (1736 UNTS 344).

NOTE

1 Applicable to all territories.

FISHERIES

Agreement concerning fishing by United States vessels in waters surrounding Christmas Island and Cocos/Keeling Islands pursuant to the treaty on fisheries between the United States and certain Pacific Island states.

Exchange of notes at Port Moresby April 2, 1987.

Entered into force April 2, 1987.

TIAS 11295.

JUDICIAL ASSISTANCE

Procedures for mutual assistance in administration of justice in connection with the Lockheed Aircraft Corporation matter.

Signed at Washington September 13, 1976.

Entered into force September 13, 1976.

27 UST 3424; TIAS 8372.

Treaty on mutual assistance in criminal matters, with related exchange of notes.

Signed at Washington April 30, 1997.

Entered into force September 30, 1999.

TIAS; 2117 UNTS 157.

Memorandum of understanding for the sharing of information on lost and stolen passports, with annex.

Signed at Washington and Canberra March 4 and 14, 2005.

Entered into force March 14, 2005.

TIAS

LEND-LEASE

Agreement relating to the principles applying to the provision of aid in the prosecution of the war.

Exchange of notes at Washington September 3, 1942.

Entered into force September 3, 1942.

56 Stat. 1608; EAS 271; 5 Bevans 146; 24 UNTS 195.

Agreement on settlement for lend-lease, reciprocal aid, surplus war property, and claims.

Signed at Washington June 7, 1946.

Entered into force June 7, 1946.

60 Stat. 1707; TIAS 1528; 5 Bevans 164; 4 UNTS 237.

Agreement relating to the investment of a portion of the trust account established under the lend-lease settlement agreement of June 7, 1946, and the education agreement of November 26, 1949.[1]

Exchange of notes at Canberra July 9 and August 25, 1952.

Entered into force August 25, 1952.

5 UST 650; TIAS 2954; 229 UNTS 262.

NOTE

1 November 26, 1949 agreement (TIAS 1994) superseded by agreement of August 28, 1964 (TIAS 5643). See under EDUCATION.

MAINTENANCE

Agreement for the enforcement of maintenance (support) obligations.

Signed at Canberra December 12, 2002.

Entered into force December 12, 2002.

TIAS; 2208 UNTS 469.

MAPPING

Cooperative mapping agreement. Approved by Australia March 6, 1947 and by the United States April 4, 1947.

Entered into force April 4, 1947.

5 Bevans 183.

Agreement concerning cooperative development of the digital chart of the world.

Signed at Washington June 22, 1990.

Entered into force June 22, 1990.

1598 UNTS 263.

Memorandum of understanding concerning geospatial information and services cooperation, with annexes.

Signed at Bethesda and Canberra March 27 and 31, 2000.

Entered into force March 31, 2000.

NP

MARITIME MATTERS

Agreement relating to the furnishing of certain supplies and services to naval vessels.

Exchange of notes at Canberra December 19 and 31, 1956.

Entered into force January 26, 1957.

8 UST 9; TIAS 3729; 266 UNTS 89.

Amendment

March 28, 1963 (14 UST 347; TIAS 5319; 474 UNTS 338).

METEOROLOGY

Agreement concerning the conduct of a program known as the Equatorial Mesoscale Experiment, with related letter.

Exchange of notes at Canberra January 5, 1987.

Entered into force January 5, 1987.

TIAS

PACIFIC SETTLEMENT OF DISPUTES

Treaty amending in their application to Australia certain provisions of the treaty for the advancement of peace between the United States and the United Kingdom signed at Washington September 15, 1914.

Signed at Washington September 6, 1940.

Entered into force August 13, 1941.

55 Stat. 1211; TS 974; 5 Bevans 143.

PATENTS

Agreement to facilitate the interchange of patent rights and technical information for defense purposes, with exchange of notes.

Signed at Washington January 24, 1958.

Entered into force January 24, 1958.

9 UST 5; TIAS 3974; 307 UNTS 105.

Agreement approving the procedures for reciprocal filing of classified patent applications.

Exchange of notes at Washington September 13 and October 2, 1961.

Entered into force October 2, 1961.

12 UST 1359; TIAS 4857; 421 UNTS 318.

POSTAL MATTERS

Parcel post agreement and detailed regulations of execution.

Signed at Melbourne May 16 and at Washington May 27, 1952.

Entered into force August 1, 1952.

3 UST 4305; TIAS 2580; 178 UNTS 113.

Memorandum of understanding for the exchange of international express mail, with details of implementation.

Signed at Washington and Victoria June 5 and 16, 1981.

Entered into force July 1, 1981.

33 UST 3872; TIAS 10266; 1543 UNTS 89.

PROPERTY

Conventions between the United States and the United Kingdom applicable to Australia from April 3, 1902:

Convention relating to tenure and disposition of real and personal property.

Signed at Washington March 2, 1899.

TS 146; 31 Stat. 1939; 12 Bevans 246.

Supplementary convention extending the time within which notifications may be given of the accession of British colonies or foreign possessions to the convention of March 2, 1899.

Signed at Washington January 13, 1902.

Entered into force .

TS 402; 32 Stat. 1914; 12 Bevans 261.

Supplementary convention relating to the tenure and disposition of real and personal property.

Signed at Washington May 27, 1936 by the United States, the United Kingdom, Australia, and New Zealand.

Entered into force March 10, 1941.

55 Stat. 1101; TS 964; 5 Bevans 140; 203 LNTS 367.

SCIENTIFIC COOPERATION

Agreement relating to the establishment, maintenance and operation of a solar observatory at Learmonth, Western Australia.

Exchange of notes at Canberra October 14 and 27, 1977.

Entered into force October 27, 1977.

29 UST 2747; TIAS 8968.

Agreement concerning the use of Australian facilities by the National Aeronautics and Space Administration (NASA) for balloon flights for scientific purposes.

Exchange of notes at Canberra June 15 and 19, 1992.

Entered into force June 19, 1992.

TIAS 12458; 1698 UNTS 393.

Agreement concerning the use of Australian facilities by the National Aeronautics and Space Administration for the conduct of scientific balloon flights for civil research purposes.

Exchange of notes at Canberra February 16, 2006.

Entered into force February 16, 2006.

TIAS

SEISMIC OBSERVATIONS

Agreement regarding the management and operation of the joint geological and geophysical research station at Alice Springs, Australia.

Exchange of notes at Canberra February 28, 1978.

Entered into force March 2, 1978.

29 UST 3040; TIAS 8995; 1120 UNTS 67.

Amendment

February 17, 1984 (35 UST 4421; TIAS 10946).

SOCIAL SECURITY

Agreement on social security, with administrative arrangement.

Signed at Canberra September 27, 2001.

Entered into force October 1, 2002.

TIAS; 2208 UNTS 435.

SURPLUS PROPERTY

Agreement regarding disposal of United States Government excess property in Australia.

Exchange of notes at Canberra November 9, 1973.

Entered into force November 9, 1973.

24 UST 2280; TIAS 7750; 938 UNTS 375.

TAXATION

Convention for the avoidance of double taxation and the prevention of fiscal evasion with respect to taxes on gifts.[1]

Signed at Washington May 14, 1953.

Entered into force December 14, 1953.

4 UST 2264; TIAS 2879; 205 UNTS 237.

Convention for the avoidance of double taxation and the prevention of fiscal evasion with respect to taxes on the estates of deceased persons.[1]

Signed at Washington May 14, 1953.

Entered into force January 7, 1954.

5 UST 92; TIAS 2903; 205 UNTS 277.

Convention for the avoidance of double taxation and the prevention of fiscal evasion with respect to taxes on income.

Signed at Sydney August 6, 1982.

Entered into force October 31, 1983.

35 UST 1999; TIAS 10773.

Amendment

September 27, 2001.

NOTE

1 Applicable to Norfolk Island.

TELECOMMUNICATION

Agreement relating to the reciprocal granting of authorizations to permit licensed amateur radio operators of either country to operate their stations in the other country.

Exchange of notes at Canberra June 25, 1965.

Entered into force June 25, 1965.

16 UST 973; TIAS 5836; 541 UNTS 155.

Arrangement relating to radio communications between amateur stations on behalf of third parties.

Exchange of notes at Canberra May 21 and 26, 1982.

Entered into force June 25, 1982.

34 UST 1109; TIAS 10396; 1566 UNTS 133.

Agreement concerning the agreement of December 16, 1988 and January 20, 1989, and the transfer to the Government of Australia of the high frequency diplomatic radio communications facility in Uriarra.

Exchange of notes at Canberra December 19, 1994 and March 22, 1995.

Entered into force March 22, 1995.

TIAS 12201.

TERRORISM

Agreement for combating terrorism research and development, with annex.

Signed at Washington May 17, 2006.

Entered into force May 17, 2006.

TIAS

TRACKING STATIONS

Agreement providing for the establishment and operation in Australia of a tracking station in connection with the transit navigational satellite program.

Exchange of notes at Canberra June 5, 1961.

Entered into force June 5, 1961.

12 UST 789; TIAS 4779; 409 UNTS 279.

Agreement providing for the continuation of a cooperative program facilitating space flight operations.

Exchange of notes at Canberra May 29, 1980.

Entered into force May 29, 1980; effective February 26, 1980.

32 UST 1417; TIAS 9781; 1217 UNTS 237.

Amendments and extensions

January 17 and May 2, 1990 (TIAS 12413; 1571 UNTS 548).

August 4, 2000 (TIAS; 2171 UNTS 139).

TRADE AND COMMERCE

Agreed record of conclusions within the context of the multilateral trade negotiations with exchange of letters clarifying conclusions, and related letters of February 4 and March 26, 1980.

Done at Washington March 29, October 22 and 26, 1979.

Entered into force March 31, 1980.

32 UST 5233; TIAS 9975.

Agreement relating to cooperation on antitrust matters.

Signed at Washington June 29, 1982.

Entered into force June 29, 1982.

34 UST 388; TIAS 10365; 1369 UNTS 43.

Framework for arrangement on steel trade liberalization, with appendices, and related letters.

Exchange of letters at Washington March 9, 1990.

Entered into force March 9, 1990.

TIAS; 1679 UNTS 161.

Agreement on mutual antitrust enforcement assistance, with annex.

Signed at Washington April 27, 1999.

Entered into force November 5, 1999.

TIAS; 2117 UNTS 203.

United States–Australia free trade agreement, with annexes and related exchange of letters.

Signed at Washington May 18, 2004.

Entered into force January 1, 2005.

TIAS

VISAS

Agreement relating to the reciprocal waiver of visa fees for nonimmigrants.

Exchange of notes at Canberra February 10, 1950.

Entered into force February 10, 1950; operative March 1, 1950.

1 UST 457; TIAS 2082; 51 UNTS 167.

Agreement concerning reciprocal changes in immigration regulations relating to nonimmigrant visas.

Exchanges of notes at Canberra July 29 and August 9, 17 and 20, 1955.

Entered into force August 20, 1955; operative September 1, 1955.

6 UST 6225; TIAS 3472; 268 UNTS 133.

Agreement relating to the relaxation of nonimmigrant visa requirements.

Exchange of notes at Canberra March 13, June 1 and August 19, 1959.

Entered into force August 19, 1959.

11 UST 2049; TIAS 4561; 388 UNTS 183.

WEAPONS

Agreement amending the agreement of January 25, 1962 regarding the mutual weapons development data exchange concerning weapons of mass destruction threat reduction technologies.

Signed at Washington August 14, 2006.

Entered into force August 14, 2006

TIAS

WEATHER STATIONS

Agreement providing for the construction and operation of a weather station on Nauru Island.

Exchange of notes at Canberra February 19 and 25, 1958.

Entered into force February 25, 1958.

9 UST 266; TIAS 4001; 317 UNTS 153.

AUSTRIA

AGRICULTURAL COMMODITIES

Agreement providing for emergency relief for Hungarians in Austria.

Exchange of notes at Vienna May 10, 1957.

Entered into force May 10, 1957.

8 UST 709; TIAS 3825; 283 UNTS 33.

Agreement relating to the utilization of counterpart funds to provide assistance for Austrian program of permanent refugee housing.

Exchange of notes at Vienna August 9 and October 3, 1961.

Entered into force October 3, 1961.

12 UST 1651; TIAS 4879; 426 UNTS 187.

Amendment

May 18 and June 14, 1962 (13 UST 1306; TIAS 5084; 459 UNTS 314).

AVIATION

Agreement for reciprocal acceptance of certificates of airworthiness for imported aircraft.

Exchange of notes at Washington April 30, 1959.

Entered into force April 30, 1959.

10 UST 796; TIAS 4219; 343 UNTS 41.

Memorandum of agreement relating to the provision of flight inspection services.

Signed at Washington and Vienna March 10 and June 22, 1978.

Entered into force June 22, 1978; effective April 1, 1978.

30 UST 288; TIAS 9200.

Air services agreement, with annexes.

Signed at Vienna March 16, 1989.

Entered into force June 2, 1989.

TIAS 11265.

Amendment

June 14, 1995 (TIAS 11503).

CLAIMS

Agreement regarding settlement for war accounts and claims incident to the operations of United States forces in Austria from April 9, 1945 to June 30, 1947, inclusive.

Signed at Vienna June 21, 1947.

Entered into force June 21, 1947.

61 Stat. 4168; TIAS 1920; 5 Bevans 380; 67 UNTS 89.

Agreement providing for settlement of certain claims under article 26 of the Austrian State Treaty of May 15, 1955.

Exchange of notes at Vienna May 8, 15 and 22, 1959.

Entered into force May 22, 1959.

10 UST 1158; TIAS 4253; 347 UNTS 3.

Agreement concerning the Austrian Fund "Reconciliation, Peace and Cooperation" (Reconciliation Fund).

Signed at Vienna October 24, 2000.

Entered into force December 1, 2000.

TIAS; 2162 UNTS 3.

Agreement relating to the agreement of October 24, 2000 concerning the Austrian Fund "Reconciliation, Peace and Cooperation" (Reconciliation Fund), with attachment.

Exchange of notes at Vienna January 23, 2001.

Entered into force June 6, 2001.

TIAS; 2170 UNTS 279.

COMMERCE

Treaty of friendship, commerce and consular rights.

Signed at Vienna June 19, 1928.

Entered into force May 27, 1931.

47 Stat. 1876; TS 838; 5 Bevans 341; 118 LNTS 241.

Supplementary agreement to the treaty of friendship, commerce and consular rights of June 19, 1928.

Signed at Vienna January 20, 1931.

Entered into force May 27, 1931.

47 Stat. 1899; TS 839; 5 Bevans 372; 118 LNTS 259.

CONSULS

See COMMERCE

CUSTOMS

Agreement regarding mutual assistance between the customs services of the United States and Austria.

Signed at Vienna September 15, 1976.

Entered into force July 3, 1978.

29 UST 1011; TIAS 8863.

Amendment

April 2, 1986.

DEFENSE

Agreement relating to the purchase by Austria of certain military equipment, materials and services.

Exchange of notes at Washington August 9, 1957.

Entered into force August 9, 1957.

8 UST 1241; TIAS 3875; 288 UNTS 299.

Acquisition and cross-servicing agreement, with annexes.

Signed at Patch Barracks and Vienna March 15, 2000.

Entered into force March 15, 2000.

TIAS

ECONOMIC AND TECHNICAL COOPERATION

Economic cooperation agreement and supplementary note.

Signed at Vienna July 2, 1948.

Entered into force July 2, 1948.

62 Stat. 2137; TIAS 1780; 5 Bevans 404; 21 UNTS 29.

Amendments

October 21 and November 30, 1949, and February 20, 1950 (1 UST 145; TIAS 2020; 79 UNTS 288).

January 16 and March 7, 1951 (2 UST 1315; TIAS 2283; 141 UNTS 372).

May 11 and 15, 1951 (2 UST 2569; TIAS 2380; 139 UNTS 79).

October 15 and December 6, 1952 (3 UST 5300; TIAS 2731; 185 UNTS 322).

EDUCATION

Agreement for financing certain educational exchange programs.

Signed at Vienna June 25, 1963.

Entered into force June 25, 1963.

14 UST 957; TIAS 5386; 479 UNTS 223.

ENVIRONMENTAL COOPERATION

Agreement for cooperation in the Global Learning and Observations to Benefit the Environment (GLOBE) Program, with appendices.

Signed at Vienna April 20, 1995.

Entered into force April 20, 1995.

TIAS 12631.

EXTRADITION

Extradition treaty.

Signed at Washington January 8, 1998.

Entered into force January 1, 2000.

TIAS

FINANCE

See also PROPERTY

Agreement relating to the funding of the indebtedness of Austria to the United States.

Signed at Washington May 8, 1930; operative January 1, 1928.

Treasury Department print; 5 Bevans 365.

Agreement modifying the debt funding agreement of May 8, 1930.

Signed at Washington September 14, 1932; operative July 1, 1931.

Treasury Department print; 5 Bevans 376.

Agreement relating to guaranties authorized by Section 111(b)(3) of the Economic Cooperation Act of 1948, as amended.

Exchange of notes at Washington February 14 and 16, 1952.

Entered into force February 20, 1952.

3 UST 3874; TIAS 2516; 177 UNTS 299.

Amendment

October 23, 1958 (9 UST 1345; TIAS 4127; 336 UNTS 336).

Agreement regarding certain bonds of Austrian issue denominated in dollars, with annex and protocol.

Signed at Washington November 21, 1956.

Entered into force September 11, 1957.

8 UST 1457; TIAS 3903; 290 UNTS 181.

Counterpart settlement agreement, with related exchange of notes of March 10 and 28, 1961.

Signed at Vienna March 29, 1961.

Entered into force July 12, 1962.

13 UST 1838; TIAS 5133; 459 UNTS 45.

Agreement to supplement the counterpart settlement agreement of March 29, 1961.

Signed at Vienna April 30, 2004.

Entered into force August 1, 2004.

TIAS

GENERAL RELATIONS

Treaty establishing friendly relations.

Signed at Vienna August 24, 1921.

Entered into force November 8, 1921.

42 Stat. 1946; TS 659; 5 Bevans 215; 7 LNTS 156.

JUDICIAL ASSISTANCE

Treaty on mutual legal assistance in criminal matters, with attachments.

Signed at Vienna February 23, 1995.

Entered into force August 1, 1998.

TIAS; 2029 UNTS 153.

MUTUAL SECURITY

Agreement relating to the assurances required under the Mutual Security Act of 1951.

Exchange of notes at Vienna December 14, 1951 and January 5, 1952.

Entered into force January 5, 1952.

3 UST 4525; TIAS 2600; 179 UNTS 73.

NARCOTIC DRUGS

Arrangement for the direct exchange of information regarding the traffic in narcotic drugs.

Exchange of notes at Vienna April 10 and July 24, 1931.

Entered into force July 24, 1931.

5 Bevans 373.

OCCUPATION COSTS

Agreement relating to occupation costs of United States forces in Austria subsequent to June 30, 1947.

Signed at Vienna June 21, 1947.

Entered into force July 1, 1947.

61 Stat. 4171; TIAS 1921; 5 Bevans 383; 67 UNTS 99.

PACIFIC SETTLEMENT OF DISPUTES

Arbitration treaty.

Signed at Washington August 16, 1928.

Entered into force February 28, 1929.

45 Stat. 2752; TS 776; 5 Bevans 353; 88 LNTS 95.

Treaty of conciliation.

Signed at Washington August 16, 1928.

Entered into force February 28, 1929.

45 Stat. 2756; TS 777; 5 Bevans 356; 88 LNTS 101.

POSTAL MATTERS

Agreement for collect-on-delivery service.

Signed at Vienna November 8 and at Washington December 11, 1929; operative December 1, 1929.

46 Stat. 2427; Post Office Department print.

Parcel post convention.

Signed at Vienna February 16 and at Washington March 1, 1928; operative March 1, 1928.

45 Stat. 2468; Post Office Department print.

Agreement relating to international express mail with memorandum of understanding.

Exchange of letters at Washington and Vienna August 6 and September 4, 1986.

Entered into force February 2, 1987.

TIAS 11391.

PROPERTY

Agreement concerning the disposition of certain United States property in Austria.

Signed at Vienna September 26, 1955.

Entered into force September 26, 1955.

7 UST 223; TIAS 3499; 272 UNTS 31.

Agreement regarding the return of Austrian property, rights and interests, with schedule and annex.

Signed at Washington January 30, 1959.

Entered into force May 19, 1964.

15 UST 439; TIAS 5577; 511 UNTS 145.

PUBLICATIONS

Agreement for the exchange of official publications.

Exchange of notes at Washington March 11 and 23, 1949.

Entered into force March 23, 1949.

63 Stat. 2434; TIAS 1927; 5 Bevans 422; 43 UNTS 127.

RELIEF SUPPLIES AND PACKAGES

Agreement relating to duty-free entry of relief goods and packages and standard packs and for defrayment of transportation charges.

Exchange of notes at Vienna February 3 and 11, 1949.

Entered into force February 11, 1949.

63 Stat. 2420; TIAS 1922; 5 Bevans 419; 79 UNTS 113.

Amendment

July 1 and 31, 1952 (3 UST 5042; TIAS 2685; 181 UNTS 326).

SOCIAL SECURITY

Agreement on social security, with administrative arrangement.

Signed at Vienna July 13, 1990.

Entered into force November 1, 1991.

TIAS 12037.

Amendment

October 5, 1995 (TIAS 12696; 1974 UNTS 470).

TAXATION

Convention for the avoidance of double taxation and the prevention of fiscal evasion with respect to taxes on estates, inheritances, gifts and generation-skipping transfers.

Signed at Vienna June 21, 1982.

Entered into force July 1, 1983.

TIAS 10570.

Convention for the avoidance of double taxation and the prevention of fiscal evasion with respect to taxes on income, with memorandum of understanding.

Signed at Vienna May 31, 1996.

Entered into force February 1, 1998.

TIAS; 2009 UNTS 309.

TELECOMMUNICATION

Agreement relating to the operation of amateur radio stations.

Signed at Vienna November 21, 1967.

Entered into force December 21, 1967.

18 UST 2878; TIAS 6378; 634 UNTS 43.

TRADE

See also COMMERCE

Arrangement within the context of the multilateral trade negotiations concerning agricultural products, and related letters of January 30 and April 14, 1980.

Done April 12 and October 17, 1979.

Entered into force January 1, 1980.

32 UST 5257; TIAS 9977; 1265 UNTS 235.

Agreed record of discussions and memorandum of understanding within the context of the multilateral trade negotiations concerning the Austrian motor vehicle tax, and related letters of January 30 and April 14, 1980.

Done at Geneva April 11, 1979.

Entered into force January 1, 1980.

32 UST 5225; TIAS 9974; 1265 UNTS 227.

VISAS

Agreement relating to the waiver of passport visas and passport visa fees.

Exchange of notes at Vienna June 10 and 28 and July 12, 1949.

Entered into force July 12, 1949; operative July 15, 1949.

63 Stat. 2740; TIAS 1988; 5 Bevans 426; 84 UNTS 291.

AZERBAIJAN

For agreements prior to December 31, 1991, see UNION OF SOVIET SOCIALIST REPUBLICS.

DEFENSE

Memorandum of understanding on humanitarian demining and training.

Signed at Baku August 4, 2000.

Entered into force August 4, 2000.

TIAS

DIPLOMATIC PROPERTIES

Agreement concerning the acquisition and retention of diplomatic and consular properties in the United States of America and the Republic of Azerbaijan.

Signed at Baku March 5 and April 21, 1999.

Entered into force June 8, 1999.

TIAS

ECONOMIC AND TECHNICAL COOPERATION

Agreement regarding cooperation to facilitate the provision of assistance.

Signed at Baku May 11, 2000.

Entered into force August 21, 2000.

TIAS

EMPLOYMENT

Agreement relating to the employment of dependents of official government employees.

Exchange of notes at Washington February 10 and March 8, 1995.

Entered into force March 8, 1995.

TIAS 12608.

FINANCE

Investment incentive agreement.

Signed at Washington September 28, 1992.

Entered into force January 17, 1995.

TIAS

INTERNATIONAL CRIMINAL COURT

Agreement regarding the surrender of persons to the International Criminal Court.

Signed at Washington February 26, 2003.

Entered into force August 28, 2003.

TIAS

INVESTMENT

Treaty concerning the encouragement and reciprocal protection of investment, with annex.

Signed at Washington August 1, 1997.

Entered into force August 2, 2001.

TIAS

NUCLEAR MATERIAL

Implementing arrangement for cooperation in the prevention of illicit trafficking in nuclear and other radioactive material.

Signed at Baku December 8, 2005.

Entered into force December 8, 2005.

TIAS

PEACE CORPS

Agreement concerning the program of the Peace Corps in the Republic of Azerbaijan.

Signed at Baku October 8, 2003.

Entered into force February 3, 2004.

TIAS

TRADE

Agreement on trade relations, with exchanges of letters.

Signed at Washington April 12, 1993.

Entered into force April 21, 1995.

TIAS

WEAPONS

Agreement concerning cooperation in the area of counterproliferation of weapons of mass destruction and defense activities.

Signed at Washington September 28, 1999.

Entered into force May 7, 2003.

TIAS

Agreement concerning cooperation in preventing the proliferation of weapons of mass destruction.

Signed at Baku January 2, 2004.

Entered into force January 2, 2004.

TIAS

Amendments

September 29 and October 28, 2004.

August 1 and 26, 2005.

Agreement concerning cooperation in the area of prevention of proliferation of technology, pathogens and expertise that could be used in the development of biological weapons.

Signed at Baku and Washington May 6 and June 6, 2005.

Entered into force June 6, 2005.

TIAS

Amendment

June 12 and 23, 2006.

B

THE BAHAMAS

On July 10, 1973 The Bahamas became an independent state. In a note dated July 10, 1973 to the Secretary-General of the United Nations, the Prime Minister made a statement reading in part as follows:

"I have the honour, further to inform you that the Government of the Commonwealth of The Bahamas, conscious of the desirability of maintaining existing legal relationships, and conscious of its obligations under international law to honour its treaty commitments, acknowledges that many treaty rights and obligations of the Government of the United Kingdom in respect of The Bahamas were succeeded to by the Commonwealth of The Bahamas upon Independence by virtue of customary international law.

Since, however, it is likely that in virtue of customary international law certain treaties may have lapsed at the date of Independence of the Commonwealth of The Bahamas, it seems essential that each treaty should be subjected to legal examination. It is proposed, after this examination has been completed, to indicate which, if any, of the treaties which may have lapsed by customary international law the Government of the Commonwealth of The Bahamas wishes to treat as having lapsed.

It is desired that it be presumed that each treaty has been legally succeeded to by the Commonwealth of The Bahamas and that action be based on this presumption until a decision is reached that the treaty should be regarded as having lapsed. Should the Government of the Commonwealth of The Bahamas be of the opinion that it has legally succeeded to a treaty, and wishes to terminate the operation of the treaty, it will in due course give notice of termination in the terms thereof."

AVIATION

Agreement between the United States and the United Kingdom relating to air services.

Signed at Bermuda February 11, 1946.

Entered into force February 11, 1946.

60 Stat. 1499; TIAS 1507; 12 Bevans 726; 3 UNTS 253.

Agreement on preclearance for entry into the United States, with annex.

Signed at Nassau April 23, 1974.

Entered into force April 23, 1974.

25 UST 646; TIAS 7816.

Related agreement

December 28, 1977 and January 10, 1978 (29 UST 4645; TIAS 9072).

Memorandum of agreement for the provision of assistance in developing and modernizing the civil aviation infrastructure of The Bahamas.

Signed at Washington and Nassau December 14, 1998 and January 8, 1999.

Entered into force January 8, 1999.

TIAS

CONSULS

Consular convention between the United States and the United Kingdom.

Signed at Washington June 6, 1951.

Entered into force September 7, 1952.

3 UST 3426; TIAS 2494; 165 UNTS 121.

CUSTOMS

Agreement between the United States and the United Kingdom relating to the prevention of abuses of customs privileges at certain leased naval and air bases.

Exchange of notes at Washington January 18 and February 21, 1946.

Entered into force February 21, 1946.

61 Stat. 2637; TIAS 1592; 12 Bevans 739; 6 UNTS 137.

DEFENSE

Arrangement between the United States and the United Kingdom relating to naval and air bases.[1]

Exchange of notes at Washington September 2, 1940.

Entered into force September 2, 1940.

54 Stat. 2405; EAS 181; 12 Bevans 551; 203 LNTS 201.

Agreement between the United States and the United Kingdom regarding leased naval and air bases, and exchanges of notes.[1]

Signed at London March 27, 1941.

Entered into force March 27, 1941.

55 Stat. 1560; EAS 235; 12 Bevans 560; 204 LNTS 15.

Agreement between the United States and the United Kingdom amending articles IV and VI of the leased bases agreement of March 27, 1941.[1]

Exchange of notes at Washington July 19 and August 1, 1950.

Entered into force August 1, 1950.

1 UST 585; TIAS 2105; 88 UNTS 273.

Agreement between the United States and the United Kingdom concerning a long-range proving ground for guided missiles to be known as "The Bahamas Long Range Proving Ground", and exchange of notes.[1]

Signed at Washington July 21, 1950.

Entered into force July 21, 1950.

1 UST 545; TIAS 2099; 97 UNTS 193.

Amendment

July 17, 1967 (18 UST 1657; TIAS 6308; 619 UNTS 330).

Agreement between the United States and the United Kingdom regarding the establishment by the United States of a high altitude interceptor range in connection with the operation of the Bahamas Long Range Proving Ground.[1]

Exchange of notes at Washington February 24 and March 2, 1953.

Entered into force March 2, 1953.

4 UST 429; TIAS 2789; 172 UNTS 257.

Agreement between the United States and the United Kingdom providing for regular use by civil aircraft of certain facilities in the Bahama Islands Long Range Proving Ground for guided missiles.[1 2]

Exchange of notes at Washington July 11 and 22, 1955.

Entered into force July 22, 1955.

6 UST 3783; TIAS 3379; 218 UNTS 384.

Amendment

December 6, 1956 and January 4, 1957 (8 UST 1; TIAS 3727; 266 UNTS 396).

Agreement between the United States and the United Kingdom amending the agreement for the establishment of the Bahamas Long Range Proving Ground by extending the flight testing range.[1]

Exchange of notes at Washington April 1, 1957.

Entered into force April 1, 1957.

8 UST 493; TIAS 3803; 288 UNTS 364.

Agreement between the United States and the United Kingdom for the establishment of oceanographic research stations in the Bahama Islands.[1]

Signed at Washington November 1, 1957.

Entered into force November 1, 1957.

8 UST 1741; TIAS 3927; 299 UNTS 167.

Amendment

May 12, 1960 (11 UST 1405; TIAS 4479; 372 UNTS 364).

Agreement between the United States and the United Kingdom concerning the establishment in the Bahama Islands of a long range aid to navigation station.[1]

Signed at Washington June 24, 1960.

Entered into force June 24, 1960.

11 UST 1587; TIAS 4502; 377 UNTS 63.

Agreement between the United States and the United Kingdom for the establishment of an Atlantic Undersea Test and Evaluation Center in the Bahama Islands, with agreed minutes.[1 3]

Signed at Washington October 11, 1963.

Entered into force October 11, 1963.

14 UST 1431; TIAS 5441; 483 UNTS 3.

Agreement between the United States and the United Kingdom relating to the transfer of certain real estate on Eleuthera Island to the United States Navy with annexes.[1]

Exchange of notes at Nassau August 9, 1971 and February 17, 1972.

Entered into force February 17, 1972.

23 UST 155; TIAS 7286.

Understanding between the United States and the United Kingdom relating to the use by Bahamian organizations of certain land at the United States Navy Base, Georgetown, Great Exuma Island, with map and schedule.[1]

Exchange of notes at Nassau June 19, September 12 and November 2, 1972.

Entered into force November 2, 1972.

23 UST 3688; TIAS 7514.

Agreement relating to the continuance of United States military rights in the Bahamas as well as existing maritime practices.

Exchange of notes at Nassau July 10 and 20, 1973.

Entered into force July 20, 1973; effective July 10, 1973.

24 UST 1783; TIAS 7688.

Agreement concerning United States defense facilities in The Bahamas, with annex, agreed minute, exchanges of notes and implementing arrangement, with maps.

Signed at Washington April 5, 1984.

Entered into force April 5, 1984; effective January 26, 1983.

TIAS 11058; 2034 UNTS 189.

Amendment and extensions

August 20, 1987, January 25, February 3 and 23, 1988.

January 27, February 6, July 27 and August 11, 1992.

September 22 and October 7, 1992.

Agreement concerning the provision of training related to defense articles under the United States International Military Education and Training (IMET) Program.

Exchange of notes at Nassau March 11 and May 6, 1985.

Entered into force May 6, 1985.

TIAS 11103.

Implementing arrangement to the agreement of April 5, 1984, relating to United States defense facilities, concerning the provision of sites for United States defense purposes.

Signed at Nassau January 25 and March 10, 2000.

Entered into force March 10, 2000.

TIAS

NOTES

1 Continues to apply *mutatis mutandis* by virtue of the agreement relating to the continuance of U.S. military rights in the Bahamas as well as existing maritime practices, effected by exchange of notes at Nassau July 10 and 20, 1973 (TIAS 7688).

2 Paragraph 2(2) superseded by agreements between the United States and the United Kingdom of June 11, 1971 (TIAS 7446) and December 12, 1979 (TIAS 9711).

3 See also agreement of April 5, 1984 under UNITED KINGDOM — DEFENSE.

EMPLOYMENT

Agreement relating to the employment of dependents of official government employees.

Exchange of notes at Nassau April 7 and 8, 2005.

Entered into force April 8, 2005.

TIAS

EXTRADITION

Extradition treaty.

Signed at Nassau March 9, 1990.

Entered into force September 22, 1994.

TIAS

FINANCE

Agreement on investment insurance and guaranties.

Exchange of notes at Nassau April 5, 1983 and September 27, 1984.

Entered into force September 27, 1984.

TIAS 10997; 2021 UNTS 333.

JUDICIAL ASSISTANCE

Treaty on mutual assistance in criminal matters.

Signed at Nassau June 12 and August 18, 1987.

Entered into force July 18, 1990.

TIAS

Agreement correcting the text of the treaty on mutual assistance in criminal matters of June 12 and August 18, 1987, with attachments.

Exchange of notes at Nassau January 27 and February 4, 1988.

Entered into force February 4, 1988.

TIAS

NARCOTIC DRUGS

Agreement for the interdiction of narcotics trafficking.

Signed at Nassau March 6, 1985.

Entered into force March 6, 1985.

TIAS 11123; 2120 UNTS 75.

Agreement on the control of narcotic drugs and psychotropic substances, with appendix.

Signed at Nassau February 17, 1989.

Entered into force February 17, 1989.

TIAS 11602; 2190 UNTS 363.

Agreement concerning a cooperative shiprider and overflight drug interdiction program.

Exchange of notes at Nassau May 1 and 6, 1996.

Entered into force May 6, 1996.

TIAS 12750.

POSTAL MATTERS

Money order agreement.

Signed at Washington June 22 and at Nassau July 7, 1921; operative August 1, 1921.

NP

Agreement concerning the exchange of parcel post, and regulations of execution.

Signed at Nassau October 29 and at Washington December 21, 1936; operative November 1, 1936.

50 Stat. 1472; Post Office Department print; 176 LNTS 411.

International express mail agreement, with detailed regulations.

Signed at Nassau and Washington June 24 and July 17, 1985.

Entered into force September 9, 1985.

TIAS 11153; 2126 UNTS 177.

Memorandum of understanding concerning the INTELPOST service, with details of implementation.

Signed at Nassau and Washington September 15 and October 7, 1987.

Entered into force November 1, 1987.

TIAS 11544.

PROPERTY

Convention between the United States and the United Kingdom relating to tenure and disposition of real and personal property.

Signed at Washington March 2, 1899; applicable to the Bahamas February 9, 1901.

31 Stat. 1939; TS 146; 12 Bevans 246.

Supplementary convention relating to the tenure and disposition of real and personal property.

Signed at Washington May 27, 1936.

Entered into force March 10, 1941.

55 Stat. 1101; TS 964; 5 Bevans 140; 203 LNTS 367.

SHIPPING

Agreement relating to jurisdiction over vessels utilizing the Louisiana Offshore Oil Port.

Exchange of notes at Nassau September 23 and October 5, 1982.

Entered into force October 5, 1982.

35 UST 3842; TIAS 10888; 2014 UNTS 451.

SOCIAL SECURITY

Agreement relating to United States participation in the national insurance scheme of The Bahamas, with related note.

Exchange of notes at Nassau October 27, 1976, May 6 and September 23, 1977.

Entered into force September 23, 1977; effective October 7, 1974.

29 UST 2423; TIAS 8946.

TAXATION

Agreement concerning the reciprocal exemption from income tax of income derived from the international operation of ships and aircraft.

Exchange of notes at Washington June 26 and July 16, 1987.

Entered into force July 16, 1987.

TIAS 11276; 2174 UNTS 371.

TELECOMMUNICATION

Agreement between the United States and the United Kingdom relating to the reciprocal granting of authorizations to permit licensed amateur radio operators of either country to operate their stations in the other country.

Exchange of notes at London November 26, 1965; applicable to the Bahamas December 11, 1969.

16 UST 2047; TIAS 5941; 561 UNTS 193.

Agreement between the United States and the United Kingdom extending to certain territories the application of the agreement of November 26, 1965 relating to the reciprocal granting of authorizations to permit licensed amateur radio operators of either country to operate their stations in the other country.

Exchange of notes at London December 11, 1969.

Entered into force December 11, 1969.

20 UST 4089; TIAS 6800; 732 UNTS 334.

Agreement relating to pre-sunrise operations of certain standard broadcasting stations.

Exchange of notes at Nassau January 30 and September 4, 1974.

Entered into force September 4, 1974.

25 UST 2478; TIAS 7929.

TRADE-MARKS

Declaration by the United States and the United Kingdom affording reciprocal protection to trade-marks.

Signed at London October 24, 1877.

Entered into force October 24, 1877.

20 Stat. 703; TS 138; 12 Bevans 198.

WEATHER STATIONS

Agreement relating to the continuation of a cooperative meteorological program in the Bahama Islands with memoranda of arrangement.

Exchange of notes at Nassau October 14, 1982 and August 25, 1983.

Entered into force August 25, 1983; effective July 2, 1982.

35 UST 3570; TIAS 10868; 2014 UNTS 457.

BAHRAIN

AVIATION

Civil aviation security agreement.

Signed at Manama November 15, 1992.

Entered into force November 15, 1992.

TIAS 11912.

Air transport agreement, with annexes.

Signed at Washington May 24, 1999.

Entered into force July 6, 2001.

TIAS

DEFENSE

Agreement relating to the status of personnel of the Administrative Support Unit in Bahrain.

Exchange of notes at Manama June 28, 1977.

Entered into force June 28, 1977.

28 UST 5312; TIAS 8632.

Agreement regarding grants under the Foreign Assistance Act of 1961, as amended, and the furnishing of defense articles, related training and other defense services from the United States to Bahrain.

Exchange of notes at Manama July 18 and August 8, 19 and 29, 1992.

Entered into force August 29, 1992.

TIAS

Agreement concerning the deployment of United States forces, with exchange of letters.

Signed at Manama January 13, 1991.

Entered into force January 13, 1991.

TIAS 12236.

Cross servicing agreement, with annexes.

Signed at Washington January 20, 1994.

Entered into force January 20, 1994.

TIAS 12259.

Amendments

November 17, 2001.

November 21, 2003 and January 6, 2004.

Agreement concerning mutual aid in fire protection.

Signed October 29 and December 1, 2004.

Entered into force December 1, 2004.

TIAS

ENVIRONMENTAL COOPERATION

Agreement for cooperation in the Global Learning and Observations to Benefit the Environment (GLOBE) Program, with appendices.

Signed at Manama June 16, 2001.

Entered into force June 16, 2001.

TIAS

FINANCE

Investment incentive agreement.

Signed at Manama April 25, 1987.

Entered into force April 25, 1987.

TIAS 12091.

INVESTMENT

Treaty concerning the encouragement and reciprocal protection of investment, with annex.

Signed at Washington September 29, 1999.

Entered into force May 30, 2001.

TIAS

PEACE CORPS

Agreement relating to the establishment of a Peace Corps program in Bahrain.

Exchange of notes at Manama April 24 and June 12, 1973.

Entered into force June 12, 1973.

24 UST 1762; TIAS 7684.

Agreement between the United States and the United Kingdom for the establishment of an Atlantic Undersea Test and Evaluation Center in the Bahama Islands, with agreed minutes.[1 3]

Signed at Washington October 11, 1963.

Entered into force October 11, 1963.

14 UST 1431; TIAS 5441; 483 UNTS 3.

Agreement between the United States and the United Kingdom relating to the transfer of certain real estate on Eleuthera Island to the United States Navy with annexes.[1]

Exchange of notes at Nassau August 9, 1971 and February 17, 1972.

Entered into force February 17, 1972.

23 UST 155; TIAS 7286.

Understanding between the United States and the United Kingdom relating to the use by Bahamian organizations of certain land at the United States Navy Base, Georgetown, Great Exuma Island, with map and schedule.[1]

Exchange of notes at Nassau June 19, September 12 and November 2, 1972.

Entered into force November 2, 1972.

23 UST 3688; TIAS 7514.

Agreement relating to the continuance of United States military rights in the Bahamas as well as existing maritime practices.

Exchange of notes at Nassau July 10 and 20, 1973.

Entered into force July 20, 1973; effective July 10, 1973.

24 UST 1783; TIAS 7688.

Agreement concerning United States defense facilities in The Bahamas, with annex, agreed minute, exchanges of notes and implementing arrangement, with maps.

Signed at Washington April 5, 1984.

Entered into force April 5, 1984; effective January 26, 1983.

TIAS 11058; 2034 UNTS 189.

Amendment and extensions

August 20, 1987, January 25, February 3 and 23, 1988.

January 27, February 6, July 27 and August 11, 1992.

September 22 and October 7, 1992.

Agreement concerning the provision of training related to defense articles under the United States International Military Education and Training (IMET) Program.

Exchange of notes at Nassau March 11 and May 6, 1985.

Entered into force May 6, 1985.

TIAS 11103.

Implementing arrangement to the agreement of April 5, 1984, relating to United States defense facilities, concerning the provision of sites for United States defense purposes.

Signed at Nassau January 25 and March 10, 2000.

Entered into force March 10, 2000.

TIAS

NOTES

1 Continues to apply *mutatis mutandis* by virtue of the agreement relating to the continuance of U.S. military rights in the Bahamas as well as existing maritime practices, effected by exchange of notes at Nassau July 10 and 20, 1973 (TIAS 7688).

2 Paragraph 2(2) superseded by agreements between the United States and the United Kingdom of June 11, 1971 (TIAS 7446) and December 12, 1979 (TIAS 9711).

3 See also agreement of April 5, 1984 under UNITED KINGDOM — DEFENSE.

EMPLOYMENT

Agreement relating to the employment of dependents of official government employees.

Exchange of notes at Nassau April 7 and 8, 2005.

Entered into force April 8, 2005.

TIAS

EXTRADITION

Extradition treaty.

Signed at Nassau March 9, 1990.

Entered into force September 22, 1994.

TIAS

FINANCE

Agreement on investment insurance and guaranties.

Exchange of notes at Nassau April 5, 1983 and September 27, 1984.

Entered into force September 27, 1984.

TIAS 10997; 2021 UNTS 333.

JUDICIAL ASSISTANCE

Treaty on mutual assistance in criminal matters.

Signed at Nassau June 12 and August 18, 1987.

Entered into force July 18, 1990.

TIAS

Agreement correcting the text of the treaty on mutual assistance in criminal matters of June 12 and August 18, 1987, with attachments.

Exchange of notes at Nassau January 27 and February 4, 1988.

Entered into force February 4, 1988.

TIAS

NARCOTIC DRUGS

Agreement for the interdiction of narcotics trafficking.

Signed at Nassau March 6, 1985.

Entered into force March 6, 1985.

TIAS 11123; 2120 UNTS 75.

Agreement on the control of narcotic drugs and psychotropic substances, with appendix.

Signed at Nassau February 17, 1989.

Entered into force February 17, 1989.

TIAS 11602; 2190 UNTS 363.

Agreement concerning a cooperative shiprider and overflight drug interdiction program.

Exchange of notes at Nassau May 1 and 6, 1996.

Entered into force May 6, 1996.

TIAS 12750.

POSTAL MATTERS

Money order agreement.

Signed at Washington June 22 and at Nassau July 7, 1921; operative August 1, 1921.

NP

Agreement concerning the exchange of parcel post, and regulations of execution.

Signed at Nassau October 29 and at Washington December 21, 1936; operative November 1, 1936.

50 Stat. 1472; Post Office Department print; 176 LNTS 411.

International express mail agreement, with detailed regulations.

Signed at Nassau and Washington June 24 and July 17, 1985.

Entered into force September 9, 1985.

TIAS 11153; 2126 UNTS 177.

Memorandum of understanding concerning the INTELPOST service, with details of implementation.

Signed at Nassau and Washington September 15 and October 7, 1987.

Entered into force November 1, 1987.

TIAS 11544.

PROPERTY

Convention between the United States and the United Kingdom relating to tenure and disposition of real and personal property.

Signed at Washington March 2, 1899; applicable to the Bahamas February 9, 1901.

31 Stat. 1939; TS 146; 12 Bevans 246.

Supplementary convention relating to the tenure and disposition of real and personal property.

Signed at Washington May 27, 1936.

Entered into force March 10, 1941.

55 Stat. 1101; TS 964; 5 Bevans 140; 203 LNTS 367.

SHIPPING

Agreement relating to jurisdiction over vessels utilizing the Louisiana Offshore Oil Port.

Exchange of notes at Nassau September 23 and October 5, 1982.

Entered into force October 5, 1982.

35 UST 3842; TIAS 10888; 2014 UNTS 451.

SOCIAL SECURITY

Agreement relating to United States participation in the national insurance scheme of The Bahamas, with related note.

Exchange of notes at Nassau October 27, 1976, May 6 and September 23, 1977.

Entered into force September 23, 1977; effective October 7, 1974.

29 UST 2423; TIAS 8946.

TAXATION

Agreement concerning the reciprocal exemption from income tax of income derived from the international operation of ships and aircraft.

Exchange of notes at Washington June 26 and July 16, 1987.

Entered into force July 16, 1987.

TIAS 11276; 2174 UNTS 371.

TELECOMMUNICATION

Agreement between the United States and the United Kingdom relating to the reciprocal granting of authorizations to permit licensed amateur radio operators of either country to operate their stations in the other country.

Exchange of notes at London November 26, 1965; applicable to the Bahamas December 11, 1969.

16 UST 2047; TIAS 5941; 561 UNTS 193.

Agreement between the United States and the United Kingdom extending to certain territories the application of the agreement of November 26, 1965 relating to the reciprocal granting of authorizations to permit licensed amateur radio operators of either country to operate their stations in the other country.

Exchange of notes at London December 11, 1969.

Entered into force December 11, 1969.

20 UST 4089; TIAS 6800; 732 UNTS 334.

Agreement relating to pre-sunrise operations of certain standard broadcasting stations.

Exchange of notes at Nassau January 30 and September 4, 1974.

Entered into force September 4, 1974.

25 UST 2478; TIAS 7929.

TRADE-MARKS

Declaration by the United States and the United Kingdom affording reciprocal protection to trade-marks.

Signed at London October 24, 1877.

Entered into force October 24, 1877.

20 Stat. 703; TS 138; 12 Bevans 198.

WEATHER STATIONS

Agreement relating to the continuation of a cooperative meteorological program in the Bahama Islands with memoranda of arrangement.

Exchange of notes at Nassau October 14, 1982 and August 25, 1983.

Entered into force August 25, 1983; effective July 2, 1982.

35 UST 3570; TIAS 10868; 2014 UNTS 457.

BAHRAIN

AVIATION

Civil aviation security agreement.

Signed at Manama November 15, 1992.

Entered into force November 15, 1992.

TIAS 11912.

Air transport agreement, with annexes.

Signed at Washington May 24, 1999.

Entered into force July 6, 2001.

TIAS

DEFENSE

Agreement relating to the status of personnel of the Administrative Support Unit in Bahrain.

Exchange of notes at Manama June 28, 1977.

Entered into force June 28, 1977.

28 UST 5312; TIAS 8632.

Agreement regarding grants under the Foreign Assistance Act of 1961, as amended, and the furnishing of defense articles, related training and other defense services from the United States to Bahrain.

Exchange of notes at Manama July 18 and August 8, 19 and 29, 1992.

Entered into force August 29, 1992.

TIAS

Agreement concerning the deployment of United States forces, with exchange of letters.

Signed at Manama January 13, 1991.

Entered into force January 13, 1991.

TIAS 12236.

Cross servicing agreement, with annexes.

Signed at Washington January 20, 1994.

Entered into force January 20, 1994.

TIAS 12259.

Amendments

November 17, 2001.

November 21, 2003 and January 6, 2004.

Agreement concerning mutual aid in fire protection.

Signed October 29 and December 1, 2004.

Entered into force December 1, 2004.

TIAS

ENVIRONMENTAL COOPERATION

Agreement for cooperation in the Global Learning and Observations to Benefit the Environment (GLOBE) Program, with appendices.

Signed at Manama June 16, 2001.

Entered into force June 16, 2001.

TIAS

FINANCE

Investment incentive agreement

Signed at Manama April 25, 1987.

Entered into force April 25, 1987.

TIAS 12091.

INVESTMENT

Treaty concerning the encouragement and reciprocal protection of investment, with annex.

Signed at Washington September 29, 1999.

Entered into force May 30, 2001.

TIAS

PEACE CORPS

Agreement relating to the establishment of a Peace Corps program in Bahrain.

Exchange of notes at Manama April 24 and June 12, 1973.

Entered into force June 12, 1973.

24 UST 1762; TIAS 7684.

BARBADOS

On November 30, 1966 Barbados became an independent state. In a note dated February 10, 1967 to the Secretary-General of the United Nations, the Prime Minister and Minister of External Affairs made a statement reading in part as follows:

"I have the honour to inform you that the Government of Barbados, conscious of the desirability of maintaining existing legal relationships, and conscious of its obligation under international law to honour its treaty commitments, acknowledges that many treaty rights and obligations of the Government of the United Kingdom in respect of Barbados were succeeded to by Barbados upon independence by virtue of customary international law.

2. Since, however, it is likely that by virtue of customary international law certain treaties may have lapsed at the date of independence of Barbados, it seems essential that each treaty should be subjected to legal examination. It is proposed after this examination has been completed, to indicate which, if any, of the treaties which may have lapsed by customary international law the Government of Barbados wishes to treat as having lapsed.

3. It is desired that it be presumed that each treaty has been legally succeeded to by Barbados and that action be based on this presumption until a decision is reached that it should be regarded as having lapsed. Should the Government of Barbados be of the opinion that it has legally succeeded to a treaty and wishes to terminate the operation of the treaty, it will in due course give notice of termination in the terms thereof."

AVIATION

Air transport agreement, with exchange of letters.

Signed at Bridgetown April 8, 1982.

Entered into force April 8, 1982.

34 UST 439; TIAS 10370.

CONSULS

Consular convention between the United States and the United Kingdom.

Signed at Washington June 6, 1951.

Entered into force September 7, 1952.

3 UST 3426; TIAS 2494; 165 UNTS 121.

Agreement continuing in force between the United States and Barbados the consular convention of June 6, 1951 between the United States and the United Kingdom.

Exchange of notes at Bridgetown September 14, 1972 and May 10, 1973.

Entered into force May 10, 1973.

24 UST 1803; TIAS 7693.

DEFENSE

Agreement concerning the provision of training related to defense articles under the United States International Military Education and Training (IMET) Program.

Exchange of notes at Bridgetown March 6 and April 3, 1980.

Entered into force April 3, 1980.

32 UST 960; TIAS 9743; 1234 UNTS 321.

ECONOMIC AND TECHNICAL COOPERATION

General agreement for economic, technical and related assistance.

Signed at Bridgetown September 14, 1983.

Entered into force September 14, 1983.

35 UST 2943; TIAS 10829; 1590 UNTS 153.

EXTRADITION

Extradition treaty.

Signed at Bridgetown February 28, 1996.

Entered into force March 3, 2000.

TIAS

FINANCE

Agreement relating to investment guaranties.

Signed at Bridgetown March 11, 1968.

Entered into force March 11, 1968.

19 UST 4692; TIAS 6463; 698 UNTS 87.

JUDICIAL ASSISTANCE

Treaty on mutual legal assistance in criminal matters, with forms.

Signed at Bridgetown February 28, 1996.

Entered into force March 3, 2000.

TIAS

METEOROLOGY

Agreement between the United States and the United Kingdom providing for a tropical meteorological research program (including Project Harp) in Barbados.

Exchange of notes at Bridgetown January 7 and 15, 1963.

Entered into force January 15, 1963.

14 UST 109; TIAS 5276; 466 UNTS 181.

NARCOTIC DRUGS

Agreement concerning cooperation in suppressing illicit maritime drug trafficking.

Signed at Bridgetown June 25, 1997.

Entered into force October 11, 1998.

TIAS

Agreement regarding articles, services and associated training transferred to the Government of Barbados for anti-narcotics purposes.

Exchange of notes at Bridgetown November 13, 1998 and June 30, 1999.

Entered into force June 30, 1999.

TIAS

PEACE CORPS

Agreement relating to the establishment of a Peace Corps program in Barbados.

Exchange of notes at Bridgetown May 10 and June 8, 1982.

Entered into force June 8, 1982.

34 UST 1257; TIAS 10413.

PEACEKEEPING

Agreement for the furnishing of commodities and services in connection with the peacekeeping force for Grenada.

Exchange of notes at Bridgetown November 25, 1983 and January 12, 1984.

Entered into force January 12, 1984.

35 UST 4245; TIAS 10922; 2015 UNTS 115.

POSTAL MATTERS

Convention for the exchange of postal money orders.

Signed at Washington September 27 and at Bridgetown November 30, 1933, operative October 1, 1933.

NP

Agreement for the exchange of parcels by parcel post, and detailed regulations.

Signed at Washington September 13 and at Bridgetown August 14, 1939.

Entered into force November 1, 1938.

54 Stat. 1838; Post Office Department print; 199 LNTS 375.

International express mail agreement, with detailed regulations.

Signed at Hamburg June 27, 1984.

Entered into force October 1, 1984.

TIAS 11006; 2021 UNTS 343.

Memorandum of understanding concerning the operation of the INTELPOST service, with details of implementation.

Signed at Bridgetown and Washington October 18 and 26, 1989.

Entered into force February 15, 1990.

TIAS 11704.

PROPERTY

Convention between the United States and the United Kingdom relating to the tenure and disposition of real and personal property.

Signed at Washington March 2, 1899; applicable to Barbados February 9, 1901.

31 Stat. 1939; TS 146; 12 Bevans 246.

Supplementary convention relating to the tenure and disposition of real and personal property.

Signed at Washington May 27, 1936.

Entered into force March 10, 1941.

55 Stat. 1101; TS 964; 5 Bevans 140; 203 LNTS 367.

TAXATION

Agreement for the exchange of information with respect to taxes.

Signed at Washington November 3, 1984.

Entered into force November 3, 1984

TIAS 11203; 2143 UNTS 277.

Convention for the avoidance of double taxation and the prevention of fiscal evasion with respect to taxes on income, with exchange of notes.[1]

Signed at Bridgetown December 31, 1984.

Entered into force February 28, 1986.

TIAS 11090; 2120 UNTS 197.

Protocol amending the convention for the avoidance of double taxation and the prevention of fiscal evasion with respect to taxes on income signed December 31, 1984, with exchange of notes and understandings.[1]

Signed at Washington December 18, 1991.

Entered into force December 29, 1993.

TIAS

Second protocol amending the convention of December 31, 1984, as amended, for the avoidance of double taxation and the prevention of fiscal evasion with respect to taxes on income.

Signed at Washington July 14, 2004.

Entered into force December 20, 2004.

TIAS

NOTE

1 With reservation.

TELECOMMUNICATION

Agreement relating to the reciprocal granting of authorizations to permit licensed amateur radio operators of either country to operate their stations in the other country.

Exchange of notes at Bridgetown September 10 and 12, 1968.

Entered into force September 12, 1968.

19 UST 5994; TIAS 6553; 702 UNTS 175.

TRADE-MARKS

Declaration by the United States and the United Kingdom affording reciprocal protection to trade-marks.

Signed at London October 24, 1877.

Entered into force October 24, 1877.

20 Stat. 703; TS 138; 12 Bevans 198.

WEATHER STATIONS

Agreement relating to a cooperative program for operation and maintenance of a rawinsonde station at Seawell Airport, Barbados.

Exchange of notes at Bridgetown October 13, 1975.

Entered into force October 13, 1975; effective July 1, 1970.

26 UST 2557; TIAS 8174; 1028 UNTS 37.

BELARUS

For agreements prior to December 31, 1991, see UNION OF SOVIET SOCIALIST REPUBLICS.

CUSTOMS

Agreement regarding cooperation and mutual assistance between their customs services.

Exchange of notes at Minsk January 14, 1994.

Entered into force January 14, 1994.

TIAS 12531.

DEFENSE

Agreement concerning the provision of material and services for the establishment of a continuous communications link, with annexes.

Signed at Minsk January 15, 1993.

Entered into force January 15, 1993.

TIAS

EMPLOYMENT

Agreement relating to the employment of dependents of official government employees.

Exchange of notes at Washington June 14 and July 26, 1996.

Entered into force July 26, 1996.

TIAS 12786.

FINANCE

Investment incentive agreement.

Signed at Minsk June 24, 1992.

Entered into force June 24, 1992.

TIAS 12460.

POSTAL MATTERS

International express mail agreement, with detailed regulations.

Signed at Minsk and Washington September 21 and November 8, 1993.

Entered into force January 1, 1994.

NP

TRADE AND COMMERCE

Agreement on trade relations.

Exchange of notes at Minsk January 6 and February 16, 1993.

Entered into force February 16, 1993.

TIAS 12488.

Memorandum of understanding concerning the establishment of annual quantitative limits on imports into the United States of fiberglass fabrics in category 622, women's wool coats in category 435 and women's wool trousers in category 448.

Signed at Washington January 10, 2003.

Entered into force January 10, 2003.

NP

Amendment

May 13, 2004 (NP).

WEAPONS

Agreement concerning emergency response and the prevention of proliferation of weapons of mass destruction.

Signed at Washington October 22, 1992.

Entered into force October 22, 1992.

TIAS

Amendments and extensions

April 29, 1993.

July 22, 1993.

October 1 and 22, 1997.

January 14 and 21, 1998.

Agreement concerning the conversion of military technologies and capabilities into civilian activities.

Signed at Washington July 22, 1993.

Entered into force July 22, 1993.

TIAS

Agreement concerning the environmental restoration of former Strategic Rocket Forces facilities and sites to promote the prevention of proliferation of weapons of mass destruction.

Signed at Washington July 22, 1993.

Entered into force July 22, 1993.

TIAS

Agreement concerning the disposal of the remnants of dismantled conventional military equipment, with annex.

Signed at Minsk August 12, 1994.

Entered into force August 12, 1994.

TIAS

Agreement concerning the elimination of strategic offensive arms.

Signed at Minsk June 23, 1995.

Entered into force June 23, 1995.

TIAS

Agreement concerning control, accounting and physical protection of nuclear material to promote the prevention of nuclear weapons proliferation.

Signed at Minsk June 23, 1995.

Entered into force June 23, 1995.

TIAS

BELGIUM

ATOMIC ENERGY

Agreement for cooperation on the use of atomic energy for mutual defense purposes.

Signed at Brussels May 17, 1962.

Entered into force September 5, 1962.

13 UST 1995; TIAS 5157; 461 UNTS 3.

Agreement relating to severe nuclear accident research.

Signed at Washington and Brussels March 29 and April 18, 1983.

Entered into force April 18, 1983; effective February 10, 1983.

TIAS 10692.

Arrangement for the exchange of technical information and cooperation in nuclear safety matters, with addenda.

Signed at Rockville March 10, 2005.

Entered into force March 10, 2005.

TIAS

AUTOMOTIVE TRAFFIC

Agreement regarding the facilitation of road travel in the United States for holders of Belgian driving permits and in Belgium for holders of United States driving permits.

Exchange of notes at Brussels February 4 and 12, 1971.

Entered into force February 12, 1971.

22 UST 1525; TIAS 7172; 806 UNTS 281.

AVIATION

Agreement relating to the reciprocal acceptance of airworthiness certifications.

Exchange of notes at Brussels February 12 and May 14, 1973.

Entered into force May 14, 1973.

24 UST 1720; TIAS 7675.

Air transport agreement.

Exchange of notes at Washington October 23, 1980.

Entered into force October 23, 1980.

32 UST 3515; TIAS 9903; 1275 UNTS 103.

Amendments

September 22 and November 12, 1986.

November 5, 1993 and January 12, 1994.

Memorandum of agreement concerning assistance in developing and modernizing Belgium's civil aviation infrastructure.

Signed at Washington and Brussels June 19 and July 30, 1998.

Entered into force July 30, 1998.

TIAS

CLAIMS

Agreement relating to reciprocity on indemnification for war damages to private property.

Exchanges of notes at Brussels December 5, 1949, March 17 and December 1, 1950, and March 12, 1951.

Entered into force March 12, 1951.

2 UST 943; TIAS 2248; 93 UNTS 109.

COMMERCE

Convention in addition to the treaty of July 17, 1858, with annexed declaration.[1]

Signed at Brussels May 20, 1863.

Entered into force June 27, 1864.

13 Stat. 647; TS 22; 5 Bevans 468.

Treaty providing for the extinguishment of the Scheldt dues.

Signed at Brussels July 20, 1863.

Entered into force June 27, 1864.

13 Stat. 655; TS 23; 5 Bevans 471.

Treaty of friendship, establishment and navigation, with protocol.

Signed at Brussels February 21, 1961.

Entered into force October 3, 1963.

14 UST 1284; TIAS 5432; 480 UNTS 149.

NOTE

1 Articles I and IV remain in force perpetually; remaining articles terminated July 1, 1875 with termination of 1858 treaty (12 Stat. 1043; TS 20; 5 Bevans 454).

CONSULS

Consular convention with exchanges of notes.

Signed at Washington September 2, 1969.

Entered into force January 5, 1974.

25 UST 41; TIAS 7775.

CUSTOMS

Arrangement relating to the granting to diplomatic and consular personnel, on a reciprocal basis, of exemption from duties and import taxes on merchandise imported for their personal use.

Exchange of notes at Brussels February 26 and May 28, 1948.

Entered into force May 28, 1948.

5 Bevans 670.

Agreement regarding mutual assistance between customs services.

Signed at Brussels June 26, 1991.

Entered into force May 1, 1993.

TIAS 12111.

DEFENSE

See also MUTUAL SECURITY

Mutual defense assistance agreement.

Signed at Washington January 27, 1950.

Entered into force March 30, 1950.

1 UST 1; TIAS 2010; 51 UNTS 213.

Agreement concerning export licenses for goods bought in the Belgo-Luxembourg Economic Union for common defense effort under the offshore procurement program.

Exchange of notes at Brussels June 18, 1953.

Entered into force June 18, 1953.

4 UST 1; TIAS 2760; 222 UNTS 3.

Agreement relating to offshore procurement with exchange of notes.

Signed at Brussels September 2, 1953.

Entered into force July 22, 1954.

5 UST 1311; TIAS 3000; 200 UNTS 127.

Agreement approving the standard offshore procurement contract with Belgium.

Signed at Brussels November 19, 1953.

Entered into force July 22, 1954.

5 UST 1334; TIAS 3001; 233 UNTS 310.

Amendment

May 13 and July 19, 1954 (5 UST 2254; TIAS 3085; 237 UNTS 342).

Agreement relating to the disposal of redistributable and excess property furnished in connection with the mutual defense assistance program.

Signed at Brussels November 17, 1953.

Entered into force March 10, 1955.

6 UST 495; TIAS 3182; 251 UNTS 105.

Agreement concerning the participation of the Belgian forces in United Nations operations in Korea.

Signed at Washington July 15, 1955.

Entered into force July 15, 1955.

6 UST 2829; TIAS 3325; 223 UNTS 3.

Agreement relating to a weapons production program.

Exchange of notes at Brussels April 6 and 22, 1960.

Entered into force April 22, 1960.

11 UST 1368; TIAS 4472; 372 UNTS 277.

Arrangement pursuant to the mutual defense assistance agreement of January 27, 1950 relating to the disposition of equipment and materials furnished under the mutual defense assistance program.

Exchange of notes at Brussels July 7, 1961.

Entered into force July 7, 1961.

12 UST 1174; TIAS 4830; 416 UNTS 301.

Agreement concerning certain communications facilities.

Signed at Brussels April 19, 1963.

Entered into force April 19, 1963.

14 UST 414; TIAS 5334; 476 UNTS 29.

Memorandum of understanding concerning the principles governing mutual cooperation in the research, development, production, procurement and logistic support of defense equipment.

Signed at Brussels December 12, 1979.

Entered into force December 12, 1979.

TIAS

Agreement concerning provision of mutual logistic support, with annexes.

Signed at Brussels and Stuttgart May 6 and 11, 1982.

Entered into force May 11, 1982.

TIAS 12275.

Amendments

July 1 and 10, 1991 (TIAS 12275).

May 1 and 22, 1992 (TIAS 12275).

October 27 and 30, 1997.

Memorandum of understanding on the exchange of officers between the United States and Belgian air forces.

Signed at Brussels and Washington September 22 and November 2, 1983.

Entered into force November 2, 1983.

35 UST 2417; TIAS 10804.

Agreement concerning the status of a U.S. ground launched cruise missile (GLCM) unit to be located in Belgium.

Exchange of notes at Brussels February 13, 1984.

Entered into force February 13, 1984.

35 UST 4407; TIAS 10943.

Implementing arrangement concerning mutual logistic support, with annexes.

Signed at Evere, Belgium and Patch Barracks, Germany October 27 and 30, 1997.

Entered into force October 30, 1997.

TIAS

ECONOMIC AND TECHNICAL COOPERATION

Economic cooperation agreement.

Signed at Brussels July 2, 1948.

Entered into force July 29, 1948.

62 Stat. 2173; TIAS 1781; 5 Bevans 678; 19 UNTS 127.

Amendments

November 22 and 29, 1948 (62 Stat. 3776; TIAS 1906; 5 Bevans 703; 31 UNTS 485).

June 29, 1950 (1 UST 510; TIAS 2093; 76 UNTS 250).

September 10, 1951 (2 UST 2057; TIAS 2334; 140 UNTS 428).

December 11, 1952 and March 5, 1953 (4 UST 435; TIAS 2790; 207 UNTS 316).

EDUCATION

Agreement for the financing of certain academic and cultural exchanges and programs in the field of education.

Signed at Brussels December 12, 1968.

Entered into force May 13, 1971.

22 UST 1538; TIAS 7175; 806 UNTS 231.

EMPLOYMENT

Agreement on the gainful occupation of certain dependents of diplomatic and consular personnel.

Exchange of notes at Brussels February 19 and March 18, 2004.

Entered into force June 1, 2006.

TIAS

EXTRADITION

Extradition treaty.

Signed at Brussels April 27, 1987.

Entered into force September 1, 1997.

TIAS; 2093 UNTS 263.

FINANCE

Debt funding agreement.

Signed at Washington August 18, 1925; operative June 15, 1925.

Treasury Department print; 5 Bevans 531.

Agreement modifying the debt funding agreement of August 18, 1925.

Signed at Washington June 10, 1932; operative July 1, 1931.

Treasury Department print; 5 Bevans 561.

Agreement relating to guaranties authorized by Section 111(b)(3) of the Economic Cooperation Act of 1948, as amended.

Exchange of notes at Washington May 7 and 12, 1952.

Entered into force May 12, 1952.

3 UST 4285; TIAS 2575; 179 UNTS 15.

JUDICIAL ASSISTANCE

Procedures for mutual assistance in the administration of justice in connection with the Lockheed Aircraft Corporation matter.

Signed at Washington May 21, 1976.

Entered into force May 21, 1976.

27 UST 1966; TIAS 8292.

Treaty on mutual legal assistance in criminal matters, with attachment.

Signed at Washington January 28, 1988.

Entered into force January 1, 2000.

TIAS; 2096 UNTS 3.

LEND-LEASE

Preliminary agreement regarding principles applying to mutual aid in the prosecution of the war against aggression.

Signed at Washington June 16, 1942.

Entered into force June 16, 1942.

56 Stat. 1504; EAS 254; 5 Bevans 571; 105 UNTS 159.

Agreement relating to principles applying to the provision of aid to the armed forces of the United States.

Exchange of notes at Washington April 17 and 19, 1945; operative June 16, 1942.

59 Stat. 1642; EAS 481; 5 Bevans 606; 139 UNTS 279.

Agreement relating to supplies and services, with memorandum of interpretation and exchanges of notes.

Signed at Washington April 17 and 19 and May 19, 1945.

Entered into force April 17, 1945.

59 Stat. 1642; EAS 481; 5 Bevans 594; 139 UNTS 279.

LEND-LEASE SETTLEMENT

Memorandum of understanding regarding settlement for lend-lease, reciprocal aid, Plan A, surplus property and claims. Agreement relating to the transfer of United States surplus property in Belgium.

Memorandum of agreement regarding the purchase of Belgian francs for use by United States armed forces.

Signed at Washington September 24, 1946. Exchanges of letters signed at Washington September 24, 1946. Exchanges of memorandums signed at Washington July 23 and September 24, 1946.

Entered into force September 24, 1946.

62 Stat. 3984; TIAS 2064; 5 Bevans 631; 132 UNTS 80.

Amendments

May 12, 1949 (63 Stat. 2837; TIAS 2070; 5 Bevans 708; 132 UNTS 126).

January 20 and April 2, 1954 (5 UST 647; TIAS 2953; 229 UNTS 304).

MAPPING

Basic exchange and cooperative agreement concerning mapping, charting and geodesy cooperation.

Signed at Fairfax March 1, 1994.

Entered into force March 1, 1994.

NP

MILITARY CEMETERIES AND MONUMENTS

Agreement concerning American military cemeteries, and related note of December 24, 1959.

Signed at Brussels November 27, 1959.

Entered into force November 27, 1959.

10 UST 2124; TIAS 4383; 366 UNTS 331.

Amendment

January 8, 1962 and October 24, 1963 (14 UST 1542; TIAS 5455; 489 UNTS 393).

MUTUAL SECURITY

Agreement relating to the assurances required under the Mutual Security Act of 1951.

Exchange of notes at Brussels January 7, 1952.

Entered into force January 7, 1952.

3 UST 4529; TIAS 2601; 179 UNTS 81.

NARCOTIC DRUGS

Arrangement for the direct exchange of certain information regarding the traffic in narcotic drugs.

Exchange of notes at Brussels February 6 and June 13, 1928.

Entered into force June 13, 1928.

5 Bevans 545.

PACIFIC SETTLEMENT OF DISPUTES

Treaty of arbitration.

Signed at Washington March 20, 1929.

Entered into force August 25, 1930.

46 Stat. 2790; TS 823; 5 Bevans 547; 109 LNTS 267.

Treaty of conciliation.

Signed at Washington March 20, 1929.

Entered into force August 25, 1930.

46 Stat. 2794; TS 824; 5 Bevans 549; 109 LNTS 261.

PATENTS

Agreement to facilitate the interchange of patent rights and technical information for defense purposes.

Signed at Brussels October 12, 1954.

Entered into force October 12, 1954.

5 UST 2318; TIAS 3093; 202 UNTS 289.

Agreement approving the procedures for reciprocal filing of classified patent applications.

Exchange of notes at Brussels May 6 and 18, 1960.

Entered into force May 18, 1960.

11 UST 1464; TIAS 4488.

POSTAL MATTERS

Agreement concerning the exchange of parcel post, and regulations of execution.

Signed at Washington January 5, 1939.

Entered into force May 1, 1939.

53 Stat. 2100; Post Office Department print; 199 LNTS 321.

Memorandum of understanding relating to the initiation of express mail/datapost service.

Signed at Washington and Brussels March 6 and 28, 1975.

Entered into force March 28, 1975; effective April 1, 1975.

29 UST 95; TIAS 8796.

SCIENTIFIC COOPERATION

Memorandum of understanding concerning the furnishing of balloon launching and associated services.

Signed at Washington June 8 and 15, 1983.

Entered into force June 15, 1983.

35 UST 1653; TIAS 10754; 2011 UNTS 87.

SEABEDS

Agreement relating to the agreement of August 14, 1987 on the resolution of practical problems with respect to deep seabed mining areas.[1]

Exchange of notes at Brussels August 14, 1987.

Entered into force August 14, 1987.

TIAS 11438.

NOTE

1 Parties to the multilateral agreement of August 14, 1987 are Belgium, Canada, Italy, Netherlands and Union of Soviet Socialist Republics.

SHIPPING

Agreement relating to jurisdiction over vessels utilizing the Louisiana Offshore Oil Port.

Exchange of notes at Washington December 1 and 9, 1983.

Entered into force December 9, 1983.

35 UST 3244; TIAS 10853; 2015 UNTS 19.

SMUGGLING

Convention for the prevention of smuggling of alcoholic beverages into the United States.

Signed at Washington December 9, 1925.

Entered into force January 11, 1928.

45 Stat. 2456; TS 759; 5 Bevans 539; 72 LNTS 171.

SOCIAL SECURITY

Agreement on social security, with final protocol.

Signed at Washington February 19, 1982.

Entered into force July 1, 1984.

TIAS 11175; 2129 UNTS 495.

Additional protocol and administrative agreement for the implementation of the agreement on social security of February 19, 1982.

Signed at Brussels November 23, 1982.

Entered into force July 1, 1984.

TIAS 11175; 2131 UNTS 238.

TAXATION

Agreement relating to relief from taxation of United States expenditures in Belgium for common defense.

Exchange of notes at Brussels March 18 and April 7, 1952.

Entered into force April 7, 1952.

3 UST 5245; TIAS 2719; 205 UNTS 3.

Convention for the avoidance of double taxation and the prevention of fiscal evasion with respect to taxes on income.

Signed at Brussels July 9, 1970.

Entered into force October 13, 1972.

23 UST 2687; TIAS 7463.

Supplementary protocol modifying and supplementing the convention of July 9, 1970 for the avoidance of double taxation and the prevention of fiscal evasion with respect to taxes on income, with exchange of notes.

Signed at Washington December 31, 1987.

Entered into force August 3, 1989.

TIAS 11254; 2177 UNTS 99.

Agreement concerning relief from double taxation on income derived from the operation of ships and aircraft.

Exchange of notes at Washington October 14, 1987 and March 21, 1988.

Entered into force March 21, 1988.

TIAS 11571; 2185 UNTS 267.

TELECOMMUNICATION

Agreement relating to the reciprocal granting of authorizations to permit licensed amateur radio operators of either country to operate their stations in the other country.

Exchange of notes at Brussels June 15 and 18, 1965.

Entered into force June 18, 1965.

16 UST 869; TIAS 5824; 549 UNTS 95.

TRADE

See COMMERCE; BENELUX

VISAS

Agreement relating to the reciprocal waiver of visas and visa fees.

Exchange of notes at Brussels May 3 and 23, 1962.

Entered into force May 23, 1962; operative June 22, 1962.

13 UST 1246; TIAS 5071; 434 UNTS 133.

Amendment

March 9 and April 20, 1971 (22 UST 678; TIAS 7124; 778 UNTS 227).

BENELUX (BELGIUM, NETHERLANDS, LUXEMBOURG)

TRADE

Agreement providing trade concessions on certain items under the general agreement on tariffs and trade.

Signed at Geneva June 8, 1955.

Entered into force July 24, 1955.

6 UST 6229; TIAS 3473.

Agreement supplementary to the general agreement on tariffs and trade, with exchanges of notes.

Signed at Washington June 27, 1957.

Entered into force June 27, 1957.

8 UST 933; TIAS 3854; 284 UNTS 139.

Agreement providing compensatory concessions under the general agreement on tariffs and trade for certain tariff actions taken by the United States.

Exchange of notes at Geneva January 29 and February 1, 1962.

Entered into force February 1, 1962.

13 UST 928; TIAS 5032.

BELIZE

On September 21, 1981 Belize became an independent state. In a letter dated September 29, 1982 to the Secretary General of the United Nations, the Prime Minister and Minister of Foreign Affairs of Belize made a statement reading in part as follows:

"I have the honour to inform you that the Government of Belize has decided to continue to apply provisionally and on the basis of reciprocity, all treaties to which the Government of the United Kingdom of Great Britain and Northern Ireland was a party, the application of which was extended either expressly or by necessary implication to the then dependent territory of Belize.

Such provisional application would subsist until Belize otherwise notifies Your Excellency, the depository (in the case of a multilateral treaty), or the state party (in the case of a bilateral treaty.)"

AGRICULTURE

Agreement confirming the cooperative agreement for the prevention of foot-and-mouth disease and rinderpest in British Honduras.

Signed at Belize September 6 and 12, 1972.

Entered into force September 12, 1972.

23 UST 2592; TIAS 7447.

Memorandum of understanding relating to cooperative efforts to protect crops from plant pest damage and plant diseases.

Signed at Washington December 8, 1976.

Entered into force December 8, 1976.

28 UST 8703; TIAS 8767.

AVIATION

Agreement between the United States and the United Kingdom concerning air services, with annexes and exchange of letters.

Signed at Bermuda July 23, 1977.

Entered into force July 23, 1977.

28 UST 5367; TIAS 8641.

Amendments

April 25, 1978 (29 UST 2680; TIAS 8965).

December 27, 1979 (32 UST 524; TIAS 9722).

December 4, 1980 (33 UST 655; TIAS 10059).

CONSULS

Consular convention between the United States and the United Kingdom.

Signed at Washington June 6, 1951.

Entered into force September 7, 1952.

3 UST 3426; TIAS 2494; 165 UNTS 121.

DEFENSE

Agreement concerning the provision of training related to defense articles under the United States International Military Education and Training (IMET) Program.

Exchange of notes at Belize and Belmopan December 8, 1981 and January 15, 1982.

Entered into force January 15, 1982.

34 UST 23; TIAS 10334.

Agreement concerning grants of defense articles and services to Belize from U.S. military stocks.

Exchange of notes at Belize and Belmopan August 6 and 23, 1990.

Entered into force August 23, 1990.

TIAS 11743; 2202 UNTS 141.

Agreement regarding the status of members of the armed forces of the United States and civilian personnel of the United States Department of Defense temporarily present in Belize in connection with military exercises and training, counter-drug related activities, United States security assistance programs, or other agreed purposes.

Exchange of notes at Belize City September 4, 2001 and April 24, 2002.

Entered into force April 24, 2002.

TIAS

Agreement regarding the cooperating nation information exchange system.

Exchange of notes at Belize June 20 and 21, 2005.

Entered into force June 21, 2005.

TIAS

ECONOMIC AND TECHNICAL COOPERATION

Agreement relating to economic and technical cooperation.

Signed at Belmopan March 8, 1983.

Entered into force March 8, 1983.

TIAS 10670; 2001 UNTS 39.

EXTRADITION

Extradition treaty, with schedule.

Signed at Belize March 30, 2000.

Entered into force March 27, 2001.

TIAS

FINANCE

Agreement relating to investment guaranties.

Signed at Belize February 8, 1966.

Entered into force February 8, 1966.

17 UST 347; TIAS 5983; 685 UNTS 47.

Agreement regarding a debt-for-nature swap to prepay and cancel certain debt owed by the Government of Belize to the Government of the United States of America and its agencies, with attachments.

Signed at Washington August 2, 2001.

Entered into force August 22, 2001.

NP

INTERNATIONAL CRIMINAL COURT

Agreement regarding the surrender of persons to the International Criminal Court.

Exchange of notes at Washington December 8, 2003.

Entered into force December 8, 2003.

TIAS

JUDICIAL ASSISTANCE

Treaty on mutual legal assistance in criminal matters, with exchange of notes.

Signed at Belize September 19, 2000.

Entered into force July 2, 2003.

TIAS

NARCOTIC DRUGS

Mutual cooperation for reducing demand, preventing illicit use and combatting illicit production and traffic of drugs.

Signed at Belmopan February 9, 1989.

Entered into force February 9, 1989.

TIAS 11600; 2190 UNTS 355.

Agreement concerning maritime counter-drug operations.

Signed at Belmopan December 23, 1992.

Entered into force December 23, 1992.

TIAS 11914.

PEACE CORPS

Agreement relating to the establishment of a Peace Corps program in British Honduras.

Exchange of notes at Belize July 26 and August 15, 1962.

Entered into force August 15, 1962.

13 UST 1868; TIAS 5137; 580 UNTS 189.

POSTAL MATTERS

Money order agreement.

Signed at Washington August 1 and at Belize August 17, 1906; operative October 1, 1906.

NP

Parcel post agreement, with details of implementation.

Signed at Belize City and Washington September 14 and 28, 1982.

Entered into force January 1, 1983.

TIAS 10512; 1777 UNTS 373.

International express mail agreement, with detailed regulations.

Signed at Belize and Washington October 28 and November 13, 1992.

Entered into force December 14, 1992.

TIAS 11906.

PROPERTY

Convention between the United States and the United Kingdom relating to the tenure and disposition of real and personal property.

Signed at Washington March 2, 1899; applicable to Belize February 9, 1901.

31 Stat. 1939; TS 146; 12 Bevans 246.

Supplementary convention relating to the tenure and disposition of real and personal property of March 2, 1899.

Signed at Washington May 27, 1936.

Entered into force March 10, 1941.

55 Stat. 1101; TS 964; 5 Bevans 140; 203 LNTS 367.

STOLEN PROPERTY

Treaty for the return of stolen vehicles, with annexes and protocol.

Signed at Belmopan October 3, 1996.

Entered into force August 16, 2002.

TIAS

TELECOMMUNICATION

Agreement between the United States and the United Kingdom relating to the reciprocal granting of authorizations to permit licensed amateur radio operators of either country to operate their stations in the other country.

Exchange of notes at London November 26, 1965; applicable to Belize December 11, 1969.

16 UST 2047; TIAS 5941; 561 UNTS 193.

Agreement between the United States and the United Kingdom extending to certain territories the application of the agreement of November 26, 1965 relating to the reciprocal granting of authorizations to permit licensed amateur radio operators of either country to operate their stations in the other country.

Exchange of notes at London December 11, 1969.

Entered into force December 11, 1969.

20 UST 4089; TIAS 6800; 732 UNTS 334.

Arrangement relating to radio communications between amateur stations on behalf of third parties.

Exchange of notes at Belmopan and Belize May 3 and 23, 1984.

Entered into force June 22, 1984.

TIAS 11198.

Agreement concerning establishment of a radio relay station of the United States Information Agency (VOA) in Belize, with annexes.

Signed at Belize September 20, 1984.

Entered into force September 20, 1984.

TIAS 11199.

Amendment

October 5, 1995.

TRADE-MARKS

Declaration by the United States and the United Kingdom affording reciprocal protection to trade-marks.

Signed at London October 24, 1877.

Entered into force October 24, 1877.

20 Stat. 703; TS 138; 12 Bevans 198.

WEAPONS

Agreement concerning cooperation to suppress the proliferation of weapons of mass destruction, their delivery systems, and related materials by sea.

Signed at Washington August 4, 2005.

Entered into force October 19, 2005.

TIAS

WEATHER STATIONS

Agreement relating to the establishment, operation and maintenance of an upper air (rawinsonde) observation station at Belize International Airport, with memorandum of arrangement.

Exchange of letters at Belize and Belmopan August 26, 1981.

Entered into force August 26, 1981.

33 UST 3709; TIAS 10253; 1541 UNTS 71.

BENIN

DEFENSE

Agreement relating to the furnishing of military equipment, materials and services to Dahomey (Benin) to help assure its security and independence.

Exchange of notes at Cotonou June 5 and 13, 1962.

Entered into force June 13, 1962.

13 UST 1285; TIAS 5078; 458 UNTS 219.

Agreement concerning the provision of training related to defense articles under the United States International Military Education and Training (IMET) Program.

Exchange of notes at Cotonou May 15 and October 15, 1984.

Entered into force October 15, 1984.

TIAS 10988; 2021 UNTS 345.

Agreement regarding military assistance under the Foreign Assistance Act of 1961, as amended, and the furnishing of defense articles, related training and other defense services from the United States to Benin.

Exchange of notes at Cotonou September 26 and October 3, 1994.

Entered into force October 3, 1994.

TIAS 12276.

Agreement on the establishment of a joint commission for military cooperation.

Signed at Cotonou January 19, 1996.

Entered into force January 19, 1996.

TIAS 12720.

Agreement regarding the provision of commodities, services and related training to assist the Republic of Benin's forces participating in the African Crisis Response Initiative.

Exchange of notes at Cotonou June 24 and July 23, 1998.

Entered into force July 23, 1998.

TIAS

Agreement regarding the status of U.S. military personnel and civilian employees of the U.S. Department of Defense temporarily present in Benin in connection with the African Crisis Response Initiative and other activities.

Exchange of notes at Cotonou June 24 and July 29, 1998.

Entered into force July 29, 1998.

TIAS

ECONOMIC AND TECHNICAL COOPERATION

Agreement relating to economic, technical and related assistance.

Exchange of notes at Cotonou May 27, 1961.

Entered into force May 27, 1961.

13 UST 347; TIAS 4989; 455 UNTS 23.

Millennium challenge compact, with annexes.

Signed at Washington February 22, 2006.

Entered into force October 6, 2006.

TIAS

EMPLOYMENT

Agreement relating to the employment of dependents of official government employees.

Exchange of notes at Washington September 22 and December 3, 1998.

Entered into force December 3, 1998.

TIAS

ENVIRONMENTAL COOPERATION

Agreement regarding the Global Learning and Observations to Benefit the Environment (GLOBE) Program, with appendices.

Signed at Cotonou April 28, 1995.

Entered into force April 28, 1995.

TIAS 12639.

FINANCE

Agreement regarding the consolidation and rescheduling of certain debts owed to, guaranteed by, or insured by the United States Government and its agency, with annexes.

Signed at Cotonou November 20, 1989.

Entered into force December 28, 1989.

NP

Investment incentive agreement.

Signed at Washington November 30, 1998.

Entered into force November 30, 1998.

TIAS

INTERNATIONAL CRIMINAL COURT

Agreement regarding the surrender of persons to international tribunals.

Signed at Cotonou July 25, 2005.

Entered into force August 25, 2005.

TIAS

PEACE CORPS

Agreement relating to the establishment of a Peace Corps program.

Exchange of notes at Cotonou June 30 and July 3, 1967.

Entered into force July 3, 1967.

18 UST 1606; TIAS 6302; 692 UNTS 323.

POSTAL MATTERS

International express mail agreement, with detailed regulations.

Signed at Cotonou and Washington July 6 and 26, 1988.

Entered into force September 15, 1988.

TIAS 11590.

BHUTAN

EMPLOYMENT

Agreement relating to the employment of dependents of official government employees.

Exchange of notes at New York September 22, 2004.

Entered into force September 22, 2004.

TIAS

INTERNATIONAL CRIMINAL COURT

Agreement regarding the surrender of persons to the International Criminal Court.

Signed at Washington May 2, 2003.

Entered into force August 16, 2004.

TIAS

POSTAL MATTERS

International express mail agreement.

Signed at Thimphu and Washington June 3 and July 6, 1993.

Entered into force August 1, 1993.

NP

BOLIVIA

AGRICULTURAL COMMODITIES

Agricultural commodities agreement.

Signed at La Paz June 7, 1957.

Entered into force June 7, 1957.

8 UST 821; TIAS 3841; 291 UNTS 77.

Amendments

June 17 and 21, 1957 (8 UST 866; TIAS 3847; 291 UNTS 86).

August 30, 1957 (8 UST 1427; TIAS 3897; 291 UNTS 89).

Agricultural commodities agreement, with exchange of notes.

Signed at La Paz November 15, 1961.

Entered into force November 15, 1961.

13 UST 1197; TIAS 5064; 456 UNTS 191.

Agricultural commodities agreement, with exchange of notes.

Signed at La Paz February 12, 1962.

Entered into force February 12, 1962.

13 UST 1042; TIAS 5047; 451 UNTS 281.

Amendments

March 27, 1962 (13 UST 1042; TIAS 5047; 451 UNTS 281).

July 14, 1962 (13 UST 1773; TIAS 5121; 458 UNTS 368).

December 6, 1962 (13 UST 2631; TIAS 5233; 462 UNTS 370).

March 29, 1963 (14 UST 349; TIAS 5320; 474 UNTS 367).

Agricultural commodities agreement with exchange of notes.

Signed at La Paz December 17, 1962.

Entered into force December 17, 1962.

13 UST 3844; TIAS 5259; 469 UNTS 121.

Amendment

June 24, 1963 (14 UST 1727; TIAS 5478; 494 UNTS 341).

Agricultural commodities agreement.

Signed at La Paz February 4, 1963.

Entered into force February 4, 1963.

14 UST 172; TIAS 5292; 473 UNTS 65.

Amendments

March 29, 1963 (14 UST 361; TIAS 5323; 473 UNTS 74).

June 24, 1963 (14 UST 1730; TIAS 5479; 494 UNTS 346).

November 20, 1963 (14 UST 1730; TIAS 5479; 494 UNTS 349).

April 27, 1964 (15 UST 392; TIAS 5569; 526 UNTS 343).

Agricultural commodities agreement with exchange of notes.

Signed at La Paz March 25, 1964.

Entered into force March 25, 1964.

15 UST 2258; TIAS 5716; 532 UNTS 3.

Agricultural commodities agreement with exchange of notes.

Signed at La Paz May 12, 1965.

Entered into force May 12, 1965.

16 UST 1191; TIAS 5866; 564 UNTS 143.

Agricultural commodities agreement, with exchange of notes.

Signed at La Paz August 17, 1965.

Entered into force August 17, 1965.

16 UST 1218; TIAS 5871; 587 UNTS 289.

Amendment

November 30, 1966 (17 UST 2252; TIAS 6164; 681 UNTS 380).

Agricultural commodities agreement with exchange of notes.

Signed at La Paz April 22, 1966.

Entered into force April 22, 1966.

17 UST 645; TIAS 6013; 578 UNTS 73.

Agricultural commodities agreement with annex.

Signed at La Paz January 16, 1968.

Entered into force January 16, 1968.

19 UST 6153; TIAS 6571; 701 UNTS 285.

Amendment

February 12 and April 16, 1971 (22 UST 568; TIAS 7101; 792 UNTS 388).

Related agreements

January 16, 1968 (19 UST 6199; TIAS 6573; 701 UNTS 323).

March 7, 1969 (20 UST 481; TIAS 6652; 707 UNTS 167).

March 7, 1969 (20 UST 486; TIAS 6653; 707 UNTS 181).

March 24, 1971 and April 20, 1972 (23 UST 3192; TIAS 7497; 898 UNTS 327).

Agricultural commodities agreement with annex and memorandum of understanding.

Signed at La Paz April 29, 1971.

Entered into force April 29, 1971.

22 UST 1861; TIAS 7231, 837 UNTS 3.

Amendments

December 30, 1971 (22 UST 2122; TIAS 7257).

June 5 and 7, 1972 (23 UST 3221; TIAS 7500; 898 UNTS 344).

Related agreements

December 20, 1972 (25 UST 156; TIAS 7777).

November 9, 1973 (25 UST 164; TIAS 7777).

December 28, 1973 (25 UST 166; TIAS 7777).

September 22 and October 18, 1976 (28 UST 8180; TIAS 8753).

Agricultural commodities agreement, with memorandum of understanding.

Signed at La Paz February 4, 1985.

Entered into force February 4, 1985.

NP

Amendment

August 20, 1985 (NP).

Agricultural commodities agreement with annexes.

Signed at La Paz April 9, 1986.

Entered into force April 9, 1986.

NP

Amendments

April 22, 1987 (NP).

June 8 and 10, 1988 (NP).

February 15, 1989 (NP).

Agricultural commodities agreement.

Signed at Washington May 9, 1990.

Entered into force May 9, 1990.

NP

AVIATION

Agreement relating to the sending of a technical mission to Bolivia to assist in the development of Bolivian civil aviation.

Exchange of notes at La Paz August 26 and November 3, 1947.

Entered into force November 3, 1947.

61 Stat. 3863; TIAS 1739; 5 Bevans 778; 51 UNTS 33.

Air transport agreement.

Signed at La Paz September 29, 1948.

Entered into force November 4, 1948.

14 UST 2209; TIAS 5507; 505 UNTS 139.

Amendments

May 4 and 17, 1967 (18 UST 2362; TIAS 6340).

June 28 and August 23, 1988 (TIAS 11642; 2204 UNTS 252).

Memorandum of agreement concerning assistance in developing and modernizing Bolivia's civil aviation system, with annex.

Signed at Washington and La Paz March 1 and June 8, 1988.

Entered into force June 8, 1988.

TIAS 11587; 2192 UNTS 35.

COMMERCE

Treaty of peace, friendship, commerce and navigation.[1]

Signed at La Paz May 13, 1858.

Entered into force November 9, 1862.

12 Stat. 1003; TS 32; 5 Bevans 721.

NOTE

1 Article 34 terminated by the United States, effective July 1, 1916, in accordance with the Seamen's Act (38 Stat. 1164).

CONSULS

See COMMERCE

CULTURAL PROPERTY

Memorandum of understanding concerning the imposition of import restrictions on archaeological material from the Pre-Columbian cultures and certain ethnological material from the Colonial and Republican periods of Bolivia.

Signed at Washington December 4, 2001.

Entered into force December 4, 2001.

TIAS

DEFENSE

Military assistance agreement.

Exchange of notes at La Paz March 21 and April 22, 1958.

Entered into force April 22, 1958.

9 UST 953; TIAS 4061; 317 UNTS 209.

Agreement relating to the furnishing of defense articles and services to Bolivia.

Exchange of notes at La Paz April 26, 1962.

Entered into force April 26, 1962.

13 UST 2294; TIAS 5197; 461 UNTS 105.

Agreement relating to the deposit by Bolivia of ten percent of the value of grant military assistance and excess defense articles furnished by the United States.

Exchange of notes at La Paz March 27 and May 2, 1972.

Entered into force May 2, 1972; effective February 7, 1972.

23 UST 892; TIAS 7352.

Agreement concerning payment to the United States of net proceeds from the sale of defense articles furnished under the military assistance program.

Exchange of notes at La Paz May 31 and June 28, 1974.

Entered into force July 1, 1974.

25 UST 1557; TIAS 7893.

Amendment

March 15 and October 3, 2005.

Agreement concerning security assistance matters and the provision of articles, services and associated military education and training by the United States Government for anti-narcotics purposes.

Exchange of notes at La Paz October 27 and November 5, 1998.

Entered into force November 5, 1998.

TIAS

Agreement amending the letter of agreement of September 10, 2003.

Signed at La Paz March 18, 2004.

Entered into force March 18, 2004.

TIAS

Agreement concerning United States Armed Forces technical personnel deployments to Bolivia.

Exchange of notes at La Paz December 1 and 28, 2004.

Entered into force December 28, 2004.

TIAS

ECONOMIC AND TECHNICAL COOPERATION

General agreement for technical cooperation.

Signed at La Paz March 14, 1951.

Entered into force March 14, 1951.

2 UST 671; TIAS 2221; 132 UNTS 319.

Amendments

December 14, 1951 and January 2, 7 and 8, 1952 (3 UST 4686; TIAS 2625; 180 UNTS 346).

August 27, 1953 and January 15, 1954 (5 UST 518; TIAS 2944; 229 UNTS 213).

Agreement providing economic assistance to Bolivia.

Signed at La Paz November 6, 1953.

Entered into force November 6, 1953.

4 UST 2297; TIAS 2883; 222 UNTS 41.

Amendment

August 24 and November 11, 1959 (10 UST 3023; TIAS 4395; 367 UNTS 319).

Agency for International Development

December 29, 1975 (28 UST 437; TIAS 8475; 1071 UNTS 201).

March 24, 1976 (28 UST 1315; TIAS 8514; 1071 UNTS 279).

September 20, 1976 (28 UST 7529; TIAS 8714).

September 22 and October 18, 1976 (28 UST 8180; TIAS 8753).

August 30, 1977 (29 UST 2975; TIAS 8994).

November 24, 1977 (29 UST 3891; TIAS 9043).

January 9, 1978 (30 UST 1675; TIAS 9276; 1152 UNTS 69).

July 5, 1991 (NP).

August 21, 1992 (NP).

May 13, 1997 (NP).

July 27, 1998 (NP).

July 28, 1998 (NP).

August 27, 1998 (NP).

August 27, 1998 (NP).

August 27, 1998 (NP).

September 23, 1999 (NP).

August 18, 2000 (NP).

September 29, 2000 (NP).

December 19, 2000 (NP).

March 14, 2001 (NP).

August 7, 2001 (NP).

July 17, 2002 (NP).

June 10, 2003 (NP).

July 9, 2003 (NP).

July 16, 2003 (NP).

July 23, 2003 (NP).

September 15, 2003 (NP).

September 3, 2004 (NP).

August 2, 2006 (NP).

EMPLOYMENT

Agreement relating to the employment of dependents of official government employees.

Exchange of notes at La Paz May 9 and 30, 2005.

Entered into force May 30, 2005.

TIAS

ENVIRONMENTAL COOPERATION

Agreement concerning the establishment of an Enterprise for the Americas Environmental Account at the National Fund for the Environment.

Signed at Washington November 26, 1991.

Entered into force November 26, 1991.

TIAS 11849.

Agreement concerning cooperation in the Global Learning and Observations to Benefit the Environment (GLOBE) Program, with appendices.

Signed at La Paz April 22, 1995.

Entered into force April 22, 1995.

TIAS 12636.

EXTRADITION

Treaty on extradition.

Signed at La Paz June 27, 1995.

Entered into force November 21, 1996.

TIAS

FINANCE

Agreement relating to investment guaranties under section 413 (b)(4) of the Mutual Security Act of 1954, as amended.

Exchange of notes at La Paz September 23, 1955.

Entered into force September 23, 1955.

6 UST 3948; TIAS 3404; 256 UNTS 275.

Amendment

March 4, 1964 (15 UST 260; TIAS 5548; 524 UNTS 312).

Related agreements

December 19, 1985 (TIAS 12042).

May 20, 1992 (TIAS 12042).

Agreement regarding the consolidation and rescheduling of certain debts owed to, guaranteed by or insured by the United States Government and its agencies, with annexes.

Signed at La Paz March 27, 1987.

Entered into force May 6, 1987.

NP

Agreement regarding the consolidation and rescheduling of certain debts owed to, guaranteed by, or insured by the United States Government and its agencies, with annexes.

Signed at La Paz May 15, 1989.

Entered into force June 23, 1989.

NP

Swap agreement between the United States Treasury and the Central Bank of Bolivia/Government of Bolivia, with related letter.

Signed at La Paz and Washington July 11, 1989.

Entered into force July 11, 1989.

TIAS

Swap agreement between the United States Treasury and the Central Bank of Bolivia/Government of Bolivia, with related letter.

Signed at La Paz and Washington September 14 and 15, 1989.

Entered into force September 15, 1989.

TIAS

Extension

December 15, 1989.

Swap agreement between the United States Treasury and the Central Bank of Bolivia/Government of Bolivia, with related letter.

Signed at Washington and La Paz December 27, 1989.

Entered into force December 27, 1989.

TIAS

Agreement regarding the consolidation and rescheduling of certain debts owed to, guaranteed by, or insured by the United States Government and its agencies, with annexes.

Signed at La Paz November 27, 1990.

Entered into force February 6, 1991.

NP

Agreement regarding the discharge of certain debts owed to the United States, with annex.

Signed at Washington August 22, 1991.

Entered into force August 22, 1991.

NP

Agreement regarding the consolidation and rescheduling or refinancing of certain debts owed to, guaranteed by, or insured by the United States Government and its agencies, with annexes.

Signed at La Paz October 13, 1992.

Entered into force December 3, 1992.

NP

Amendments

March 2 and April 13, 1994 (NP).

August 9 and October 21, 1994 (NP).

Agreement regarding the consolidation and rescheduling of certain debts owed to, guaranteed by, or insured by the United States Government and its agencies, with annexes.

Signed at La Paz January 23, 1996.

Entered into force March 7, 1996.

NP

Agreement regarding the reduction and reorganization of certain debts owed to, guaranteed by, or insured by the United States Government and its agencies.

Signed at La Paz November 27, 1996.

Entered into force April 7, 1997.

NP

Agreement regarding the reduction and reorganization of certain debts owed to, guaranteed by, or insured by the United States Government and its agencies, with annexes.

Signed at Santa Cruz December 2, 1999.

Entered into force February 23, 2000.

NP

Agreement regarding the consolidation of debt owed to, guaranteed by, or insured by the United States Government and its agencies, with annexes.

Signed at La Paz November 27, 2002.

Entered into force January 6, 2003.

NP

INFORMATIONAL MEDIA GUARANTIES

Agreement providing for an informational media guaranty program.

Exchange of notes at La Paz February 27 and March 10, 1956.

Entered into force March 10, 1956.

7 UST 440; TIAS 3528; 270 UNTS 199.

INVESTMENT

Treaty concerning the encouragement and reciprocal protection of investment, with annex and protocol.

Signed at Santiago April 17, 1998.

Entered into force June 6, 2001.

TIAS

MAPPING

Cooperative arrangement for the production of topographic maps of Bolivia, with annexes.

Signed at Washington and La Paz April 21 and 30, 1986.

Entered into force April 30, 1986.

TIAS 11375.

MISSIONS, MILITARY

Agreement for establishment of an Air Force Mission to Bolivia.

Signed at La Paz June 30, 1956.

Entered into force June 30, 1956.

7 UST 2017; TIAS 3604; 271 UNTS 243.

Amendment

April 2 and 3, 1959 (10 UST 742; TIAS 4209; 342 UNTS 356).

Agreement for the establishment of an Army Mission to Bolivia.

Signed at La Paz June 30, 1956.

Entered into force June 30, 1956.

7 UST 2033; TIAS 3605; 271 UNTS 269.

Amendment

April 2 and 3, 1959 (10 UST 742; TIAS 4209; 342 UNTS 356).

NARCOTIC DRUGS

Agreement concerning cooperation to combat narcotics trafficking, with annexes and related letter.

Signed at La Paz February 24, 1987.

Entered into force August 13, 1987.

TIAS 12053.

Amendment

May 9, 1990.

Agreement regarding narcotics control, field support, reduction and control of coca.

Signed at La Paz July 15, 1999.

Entered into force July 15, 1999.

TIAS

Agreement regarding narcotics control, field support, reduction and control of coca.

Signed at La Paz August 24, 2000.

Entered into force August 24, 2000.

TIAS

Amendment to the counter-narcotics special objective sector grant agreement.

Signed at La Paz August 31, 2000.

Entered into force August 31, 2000.

TIAS

Agreement regarding narcotics control, field support, reduction and control of coca.

Signed at La Paz December 21, 2000.

Entered into force December 21, 2000.

TIAS

Agreement regarding narcotics control, field support, reduction and control of coca.

Signed at La Paz September 26 and 30, 2002.

Entered into force September 30, 2002.

TIAS

Amendment to the project agreement of August 11, 1983, as amended, regarding narcotics control, field support, reduction and control of cocoa production.

Signed at La Paz September 26 and 30, 2002.

Entered into force September 30, 2002.

TIAS

Letter of agreement regarding illicit narcotics trafficking.

Signed at La Paz September 11 and 17, 2003.

Entered into force September 17, 2003.

TIAS

Letter of agreement on narcotics control and law enforcement during 2004-2005, with attachment.

Signed at La Paz September 2, 2004.

Entered into force September 2, 2004.

TIAS

Letter of agreement on narcotics control and law enforcement during 2006-2007, with annex and attachment.

Signed at La Paz December 20, 2006.

Entered into force December 20, 2006.

TIAS

PACIFIC SETTLEMENT OF DISPUTES

Treaty looking to the advancement of the cause of general peace.

Signed at Washington January 22, 1914.

Entered into force January 8, 1915.

38 Stat. 1868; TS 606; 5 Bevans 740.

POSTAL MATTERS

International express mail agreement, with detailed regulations.

Signed at La Paz and Washington August 10 and November 21, 1988.

Entered into force December 15, 1988.

TIAS 11635.

Postal money order agreement.

Signed at La Paz and Washington February 26 and March 11, 1993.

Entered into force June 1, 1993.

NP

PRISONER TRANSFER

Treaty on the execution of penal sentences.

Signed at La Paz February 10, 1978.

Entered into force August 17, 1978.

30 UST 796; TIAS 9219; 1150 UNTS 11.

PUBLICATIONS

Agreement relating to the exchange of official publications.

Exchange of notes at La Paz January 26 and 31, 1942.

Entered into force January 31, 1942.

56 Stat. 1436; EAS 242; 5 Bevans 753; 101 UNTS 138.

RELIEF SUPPLIES AND PACKAGES

Agreement providing for payment by the United States of ocean freight costs on relief shipments to Bolivia, and duty and tax-free entry and payment of inland transportation to point of distribution by Bolivia.

Exchange of notes at La Paz June 3 and 16, 1954.

Entered into force June 16, 1954.

5 UST 1547; TIAS 3033; 234 UNTS 35.

Amendment

December 14 and 30, 1970 (22 UST 211; TIAS 7051; 781 UNTS 312).

SCIENTIFIC AND TECHNICAL COOPERATION

Memorandum of understanding for scientific and technical cooperation in the earth sciences.

Signed at La Paz and Reston April 24 and May 29, 1985.

Entered into force May 29, 1985.

TIAS 11214.

Amendment and extension

November 20, 1991 (TIAS 11828).

SEISMIC OBSERVATIONS

Memorandum of understanding concerning the installation and operation of a real-time seismic station.

Signed at La Paz and Reston September 7, 1983 and June 14, 1984.

Entered into force June 14, 1984.

TIAS 11250.

TAXATION

Agreement concerning reciprocal exemption from income tax of income derived from the international operation of ships and aircraft.

Exchange of notes at Washington July 21 and November 23, 1987.

Entered into force November 23, 1987.

TIAS 11542; 2191 UNTS 217.

TELECOMMUNICATION

Agreement relating to radio communications between amateur stations on behalf of third parties.

Exchange of notes at La Paz October 23, 1961.

Entered into force November 22, 1961.

12 UST 1695; TIAS 4888; 424 UNTS 93.

Agreement relating to the reciprocal granting of authorization to permit licensed amateur radio operators of either country to operate their stations in the other country.

Exchange of notes at La Paz March 16, 1965.

Entered into force April 15, 1965.

16 UST 165; TIAS 5777; 542 UNTS 209.

BOSNIA–HERZEGOVINA

For agreements prior to the independence of Bosnia-Herzegovina, see YUGOSLAVIA.

AVIATION

Air transport agreement, with annexes.

Signed at Washington November 22, 2005.

Entered into force November 22, 2005.

TIAS

DEFENSE

Agreement related to the provision of defense articles, related training or other defense services from the United States to Bosnia, with related exchange of notes.

Exchange of notes at Sarajevo January 6 and 7, 1996.

Entered into force January 7, 1996.

TIAS 12716.

Amendment

March 15 and November 28, 2006.

Acquisition and cross-servicing agreement.

Signed at Sarajevo June 11, 2004.

Entered into force June 11, 2004.

TIAS

Agreement on status protections and access to and use of facilities and areas in Bosnia and Herzegovina.

Signed at Washington November 22, 2005.

Entered into force November 20, 2006.

TIAS

ECONOMIC AND TECHNICAL COOPERATION

Agreement concerning economic, technical and related assistance for Bosnia and Herzegovina, with related letters.

Signed at Sarajevo May 3, 1996.

Entered into force May 3, 1996.

TIAS 12749.

EMPLOYMENT

Agreement relating to the employment of dependents of official government employees.

Exchange of notes at Washington March 7 and 15, 1995.

Entered into force March 15, 1995.

TIAS 12614.

FINANCE

Investment incentive agreement.

Signed at Sarajevo July 12, 1996.

Entered into force December 10, 1996.

TIAS 12780.

Agreement regarding the consolidation, reduction and rescheduling of certain debts owed to, guaranteed by, or insured by the United States Government and its agencies, with annexes.

Signed at Sarajevo August 19, 1999.

Entered into force October 21, 1999.

NP

INTERNATIONAL CRIMINAL COURT

Agreement regarding the surrender of persons to the International Criminal Court.

Signed at Sarajevo May 16, 2003.

Entered into force July 7, 2003.

TIAS

POSTAL MATTERS

Express mail service agreement, with detailed regulations.

Signed at Sarajevo and Washington March 29, 2000 and January 4, 2001.

Entered into force February 1, 2001.

NP

TELECOMMUNICATION

Agreement relating to radio communications between amateur stations on behalf of third parties.

Exchange of notes at New York September 24 and October 14, 1993.

Entered into force October 14, 1993.

TIAS 12511.

WEAPONS

Agreement concerning cooperation in the area of the prevention of proliferation of weapons of mass destruction and the promotion of defense and military relations.

Signed at Washington November 22, 2005.

Entered into force November 22, 2005.

TIAS

BOTSWANA

On September 30, 1966, Bechuanaland Protectorate became the independent state of Botswana.

In a note dated October 6, 1966 to the Secretary-General of the United Nations the President of Botswana made a statement reading in part as follows: "As regards bilateral treaties validly concluded by the Government of the United Kingdom on behalf of the former Bechuanaland Protectorate, or validly applied or extended by the said Government to the territory of the former Bechuanaland Protectorate, the Government of Botswana is willing to continue to apply within its territory, on a basis of reciprocity, the terms of all such treaties for a period of twenty-four months from the date of independence (i.e., until October 1, 1968) unless abrogated or modified earlier by mutual consent. At the expiry of that period, the Government of Botswana will regard such of these treaties which could not by the application of the rules of customary international law be regarded as otherwise surviving, as having terminated.

It is the earnest hope of the Government of Botswana that during the aforementioned period of twenty-four months, the normal processes of diplomatic negotiations will enable it to reach satisfactory accord with the States concerned upon the possibility of the continuance or modification of such treaties.

The Government of Botswana is conscious that the above declaration applicable to bilateral treaties cannot with equal facility be applied to multilateral treaties. As regards these, therefore, the Government of Botswana proposes to review each of them individually and to indicate to the depositary in each case what steps it wishes to take in relation to each such instrument whether by way of confirmation of termination, confirmation of succession or accession. During such interim period of review any party to a multilateral treaty which has, prior to independence, been applied or extended to the former Bechuanaland Protectorate, may, on a basis of reciprocity, rely as against Botswana on the terms of such treaty."

DEFENSE

Agreement concerning the provision of training related to defense articles under the United States International Military Education and Training (IMET) Program.

Exchange of notes at Gaborone February 26 and March 21, 1980.

Entered into force March 21, 1980.

32 UST 957; TIAS 9742; 1221 UNTS 217.

Agreement regarding grants under the Foreign Assistance Act of 1961, as amended, and the furnishing of defense articles, related training and other defense services from the United States to Botswana.

Exchange of notes at Gaborone May 21 and June 17, 1992.

Entered into force June 17, 1992.

TIAS 12277.

Agreement regarding matters related to U.S. military and civilian personnel of the U.S. Department of Defense temporarily present in Botswana for the purpose of carrying out exercises, training, humanitarian assistance, or other activities.

Exchange of notes at Gaborone January 22 and February 13, 2001.

Entered into force February 13, 2001.

NP

Acquisition and cross-servicing agreement, with annexes.

Signed at Gaborone and Stuttgart June 20 and 27, 2003.

Entered into force June 27, 2003.

TIAS

ECONOMIC AND TECHNICAL COOPERATION

Regional assistance program framework agreement.

Signed at Gaborone September 27, 1995.

Entered into force September 27, 1995.

TIAS

Agency for International Development

September 19, 1975 (28 UST 791; TIAS 8481).

May 13, 1986 (NP).

EMPLOYMENT

Agreement relating to the employment of dependents of official government employees.

Signed at Gaborone June 15, 1984.

Entered into force June 15, 1984.

TIAS 11134.

Amendment

August 16, 1999 and December 1, 2000.

Agreement concerning interpretation of the agreement of June 15, 1984, relating to the employment of dependents of official government employees.

Exchange of notes at New York March 14 and April 27, 1989.

Entered into force April 27, 1989.

TIAS

FINANCE

Investment incentive agreement.

Signed at Gaborone December 12, 1997.

Entered into force March 12, 1998.

TIAS

Agreement regarding the reduction of certain debts owed to the Government of the United States and its agencies, with attachment.

Signed at Gaborone October 5, 2006.

Entered into force November 19, 2006.

TIAS

Agreement concerning the establishment of a tropical forest conservation fund and a tropical forest conservation board, with attachments.

Signed at Gaborone October 5, 2006.

Entered into force November 19, 2006.

TIAS

INTERNATIONAL CRIMINAL COURT

Agreement regarding the surrender of persons to international tribunals.

Signed at Gaborone June 30, 2003.

Entered into force September 28, 2003.

TIAS

JUDICIAL ASSISTANCE

Agreement concerning an International Law Enforcement Academy.

Signed at Gaborone July 24, 2000.

Entered into force July 24, 2000.

TIAS

PEACE CORPS

Agreement relating to the establishment of a Peace Corps Program in Botswana.

Exchange of notes at Gaborone May 14, 1971.

Entered into force May 14, 1971.

22 UST 1025; TIAS 7145; 797 UNTS 13.

POSTAL MATTERS

International express mail agreement, with detailed regulations.

Signed at Gaborone and Washington October 24 and December 29, 1988.

Entered into force January 16, 1989.

TIAS 11624.

SEISMIC OBSERVATIONS

Memorandum of understanding concerning the development, installation and operation of a seismic data acquisition system.

Signed at Reston and Gaborone June 16 and August 13, 1986.

Entered into force August 13, 1986.

TIAS 11361.

Agreement concerning the operation of a seismic monitoring station in Botswana.

Signed at Washington and Lobatse October 14, 1999 and February 16, 2000.

Entered into force February 16, 2000.

TIAS

TELECOMMUNICATION

Agreement relating to the reciprocal granting of authorizations to permit licensed amateur radio operators of either country to operate their stations in the other country.

Exchange of notes at Gaborone November 7, 1978 and September 26, 1979.

Entered into force September 26, 1979.

32 UST 1357; TIAS 9776; 1221 UNTS 211.

Agreement concerning the construction, operation and maintenance of a Voice of America radio relay facility in Botswana, with appendix.

Signed at Gaborone September 5, 1985.

Entered into force September 5, 1985.

TIAS 11126.

BRAZIL

AGRICULTURAL COMMODITIES

Agricultural commodities agreement, agreed official minutes and related notes.

Signed at Washington December 31, 1956.

Entered into force December 31, 1956.

7 UST 3475; TIAS 3725; 266 UNTS 151.

Amendments

July 25, 1957 (8 UST 993; TIAS 3864; 290 UNTS 345).

June 30, 1958 (9 UST 1015; TIAS 4074; 321 UNTS 288).

December 12, 1958 (9 UST 1474; TIAS 4144; 337 UNTS 422).

March 2, 1959 (10 UST 200; TIAS 4183; 341 UNTS 405).

May 29, 1959 (10 UST 1033; TIAS 4239; 346 UNTS 339).

September 2, 1959 (10 UST 1638; TIAS 4311; 358 UNTS 320).

December 9, 1960 (11 UST 2532; TIAS 4639; 401 UNTS 284).

December 29, 1960 (11 UST 2559; TIAS 4644; 401 UNTS 288).

January 4 and April 18, 1961 (12 UST 728; TIAS 4775; 409 UNTS 316).

February 26, 1962 (13 UST 478; TIAS 5011; 435 UNTS 352).

October 5, 1967 (18 UST 2815; TIAS 6367; 701 UNTS 360).

Agricultural commodities agreement, with exchange of notes.

Signed at Rio de Janeiro May 4, 1961.

Entered into force May 4, 1961.

12 UST 3151; TIAS 4918; 433 UNTS 91.

Related agreement

October 5, 1967 (18 UST 2818; TIAS 6368; 701 UNTS 370).

Agricultural commodities agreement, with exchanges of notes.

Signed at Brasilia March 15, 1962.

Entered into force March 15, 1962.

13 UST 1167; TIAS 5061; 456 UNTS 209.

Amendments

October 4, 1962 (14 UST 405; TIAS 5333; 479 UNTS 402).

August 22, 1963 (14 UST 1248; TIAS 5425; 488 UNTS 310).

Related agreement

October 5, 1967 (18 UST 2821; TIAS 6369; 701 UNTS 382).

Agricultural commodities agreement, with exchanges of notes.

Signed at Rio de Janeiro September 11, 1963.

Entered into force September 11, 1963.

14 UST 1669; TIAS 5471; 493 UNTS 267.

Amendment

May 15, 1964 (15 UST 650; TIAS 5585; 526 UNTS 354).

Agricultural commodities agreement with exchange of notes.

Signed at Rio de Janeiro April 23, 1966.

Entered into force April 23, 1966.

17 UST 1622; TIAS 6118; 607 UNTS 117.

Agricultural commodities agreement with annex.

Signed at Rio de Janeiro October 5, 1967.

Entered into force October 5, 1967.

22 UST 2125; TIAS 7258.

Related agreements

May 14, 1968 (22 UST 2146; TIAS 7259).

August 28, 1969 (22 UST 2150; TIAS 7260).

Agricultural commodities agreement with annex.

Signed at Brasilia October 21, 1970.

Entered into force October 21, 1970.

22 UST 2155; TIAS 7261.

Amendments

December 30, 1970 (22 UST 2155; TIAS 7261).

April 28, 1971 (22 UST 2155; TIAS 7261).

AMITY

Treaty of peace, friendship, commerce and navigation.[1]

Signed at Rio de Janeiro December 12, 1828.

Entered into force March 18, 1829; operative December 12, 1828.

8 Stat. 390; TS 34; 5 Bevans 792.

NOTE

1 All articles terminated December 12, 1841 except those relating to peace and friendship.

ATOMIC ENERGY

Agreement providing for a grant to assist in the acquisition of a subcritical assembly for the Aeronautical Institute of Technology.

Exchange of notes at Rio de Janeiro October 20, 1959 and February 27, 1960.

Entered into force February 27, 1960.

11 UST 1977; TIAS 4547; 384 UNTS 131.

Agreement providing for a grant to assist in the acquisition of certain nuclear research and training equipment and materials.

Exchange of notes at Rio de Janeiro October 10, 1960 and March 17, 1961.

Entered into force March 17, 1961.

12 UST 381; TIAS 4727; 406 UNTS 241.

Agreement providing for a grant for assistance in obtaining materials and equipment for use in developing the Instituto de Biofisica da Universidade de Brasil radio-biological and research program.

Exchange of notes at Rio de Janeiro October 10, 1962 and March 29, 1963.

Entered into force March 29, 1963.

14 UST 424; TIAS 5337; 476 UNTS 67.

Agreement for cooperation concerning peaceful uses of nuclear energy, with annex and agreed minute.

Signed at Brasilia October 14, 1997.

Entered into force September 15, 1999.

TIAS

Arrangement for the exchange of technical information and cooperation in regulatory and safety research matters, with addenda.

Signed at Vienna September 30, 1999.

Entered into force September 30, 1999.

TIAS

Arrangement for the exchange of technical information and cooperation in regulatory and safety research matters, with addenda.

Signed at Vienna September 21, 2004.

Entered into force September 21, 2004.

TIAS

AVIATION

Agreement relating to reciprocal acceptance of airworthiness certifications.

Exchange of notes at Brasilia June 16, 1976.

Entered into force June 16, 1976.

27 UST 3700; TIAS 8384; 1054 UNTS 181.

Agreement on air transport, with annexes.

Signed at Brasilia March 21, 1989.

Entered into force January 13, 1992.

TIAS 11780; 1668 UNTS 59.

Agreement replacing annexes I and II to the air transport agreement of March 21, 1989, as amended.

Exchange of notes at Brasilia September 2, 1997.

Entered into force September 2, 1997; effective April 1, 1996.

TIAS

Memorandum of cooperation for mutual cooperation in the promotion and development of civil aviation, with letter of understanding.

Signed at Washington and Brasilia January 18 and February 9, 2000.

Entered into force February 9, 2000.

TIAS

Agreement for promotion of aviation safety.

Signed at Brasilia March 22, 2004.

Entered into force February 26, 2006.

TIAS

COMMERCE

See AMITY

COPYRIGHT

Agreement providing for reciprocal copyright protection of literary, artistic and scientific works.

Exchange of notes at Washington April 2, 1957.

Entered into force April 2, 1957.

8 UST 418; TIAS 3793; 290 UNTS 119.

CUSTOMS

Agreement granting reciprocal customs privileges for Foreign Service personnel.

Exchange of notes at Rio de Janeiro October 11, 1940.

Entered into force October 11, 1940.

54 Stat. 2419; EAS 185; 5 Bevans 897; 203 LNTS 261.

Agreement regarding mutual assistance between their Customs Administrations.

Signed at Brasilia June 20, 2002.

Entered into force February 1, 2005.

TIAS

DEFENSE

Agreement relating to the presence of military personnel of the United States in Brazil and the presence of military personnel of Brazil in the United States.

Exchange of notes at Rio de Janeiro December 15, 1947 and February 2, 1948.

Entered into force February 2, 1948.

62 Stat. 1957; TIAS 1759; 5 Bevans 1045; 67 UNTS 109.

Agreement for the establishment of the Joint Group on Emergency Supply Problems.

Exchange of notes at Rio de Janeiro July 24, 1951.

Entered into force July 24, 1951.

2 UST 1594; TIAS 2301; 134 UNTS 195.

Military assistance agreement.[1]

Signed at Rio de Janeiro March 15, 1952.

Entered into force May 19, 1953.

4 UST 170; TIAS 2776; 199 UNTS 221.

Understanding relating to military assistance.

Exchange of notes at Rio de Janeiro January 30, 1964.

Entered into force January 30, 1964.

15 UST 163; TIAS 5534; 511 UNTS 77.

Agreement relating to the deposit by Brazil of ten percent of the value of grant military assistance furnished by the United States.

Exchange of notes at Brasilia February 28 and June 27, 1972.

Entered into force June 27, 1972; effective February 7, 1972.

23 UST 1222; TIAS 7390.

Memorandum of understanding relating to the acquisition of military aircraft

Signed September 24, 1973.

Entered into force September 24, 1973.

27 UST 2810; TIAS 8350; 1066 UNTS 119.

Agreement relating to industrial and military cooperation, with memorandum of understanding.

Exchange of notes at Brasilia February 6, 1984.

Entered into force February 6, 1984.

TIAS 12278.

Master data exchange arrangement for the mutual development of military equipment.

Signed at Washington November 14, 1984.

Entered into force November 14, 1984.

TIAS 11164; 2126 UNTS 285.

Agreement concerning the provision of training related to defense articles under the United States International Military Education and Training (IMET) Program.

Exchange of notes at Brasilia April 19, 1988 and March 27, 1989.

Entered into force March 27, 1989.

NP

Agreement regarding grants under the Foreign Assistance Act of 1961, as amended, and the furnishing of defense articles from the United States of America to the Government of the Federative Republic of Brazil.

Exchange of notes at Washington June 2, 2000.

Entered into force October 19, 2000.

TIAS

NOTE

1 Terminated March 11, 1977 except that the safeguard clauses to which articles I and III refer remain in force.

ECONOMIC AND TECHNICAL COOPERATION

Agreement relating to the mobilization of productive resources of Brazil.

Exchange of notes at Washington March 3, 1942.

Entered into force March 3, 1942.

57 Stat. 1314; EAS 370; 5 Bevans 913; 105 UNTS 99.

Agreement relating to technical cooperation.

Exchange of notes at Rio de Janeiro December 19, 1950.

Entered into force December 19, 1950.

2 UST 845; TIAS 2239; 141 UNTS 3.

Amendment

January 8, 1952 (3 UST 4693; TIAS 2626; 200 UNTS 306).

Special services program agreement.

Signed at Rio de Janeiro May 30, 1953.

Entered into force provisionally May 30, 1953; definitively November 3, 1959.

13 UST 1061; TIAS 5049; 460 UNTS 89.

Extension

December 27 and 30, 1963 (15 UST 99; TIAS 5520; 511 UNTS 308).

Agreement on the cooperation for the promotion of economic and social development in the Brazilian Northeast, with exchange of letters.

Signed at Washington April 13, 1962.

Entered into force April 13, 1962.

13 UST 356; TIAS 4990; 445 UNTS 227.

EDUCATION

Agreement for financing certain educational exchange programs.

Exchange of notes at Rio de Janeiro October 5 and 19, 1966.

Entered into force October 19, 1966.

17 UST 2241; TIAS 6163; 680 UNTS 261.

EMPLOYMENT

Agreement relating to the employment of dependents of official government employees, with exchange of letters.

Exchange of notes at Brasilia July 8, 1987.

Entered into force July 8, 1987.

TIAS 11529.

Extension

July 6 and 8, 2005.

ENERGY

Implementing arrangement for cooperation in the area of energy technology, with annexes.

Signed at Brasilia October 14, 1997.

Entered into force October 14, 1997.

TIAS

EXTRADITION

Treaty of extradition.

Signed at Rio de Janeiro January 13, 1961.

Entered into force December 17, 1964.

15 UST 2093; TIAS 5691; 532 UNTS 177.

Additional protocol to the treaty of extradition.

Signed at Rio de Janeiro June 18, 1962.

Entered into force December 17, 1964.

15 UST 2112; TIAS 5691; 532 UNTS 198.

FINANCE

Agreement relating to investment guaranties.

Signed at Washington February 6, 1965.

Entered into force September 17, 1965.

18 UST 1807; TIAS 6327; 719 UNTS 3.

Agreement regarding the consolidation and rescheduling of certain debts owed to, guaranteed by or insured by the United States Government and its agencies, with annexes.

Signed at Brasilia April 15, 1985.

Entered into force May 28, 1985.

NP

Swap agreement between the United States Treasury and the Central Bank of Brazil/Government of Brazil, with memorandum of understanding.

Signed at Washington and Rio de Janeiro July 15, 1988.

Entered into force July 15, 1988.

TIAS

Agreement regarding the consolidation and rescheduling of certain debts owed to, guaranteed by, or insured by the United States Government and its agencies, with annexes.

Signed at Brasilia March 14, 1990.

Entered into force April 19, 1990.

NP

Agreement regarding the consolidation and rescheduling of certain debts owed to, guaranteed by or insured by the United States Government and its agencies, with annexes.

Signed at Brasilia December 20, 1991.

Entered into force March 9, 1992.

NP

Agreement regarding the consolidation and rescheduling or refinancing of certain debts owed to, guaranteed by, or insured by the United States Government and its agencies, with annexes.

Signed at Washington September 23, 1992.

Entered into force November 9, 1992.

NP

INDUSTRIAL AND MILITARY COOPERATION

See under DEFENSE

JUDICIAL ASSISTANCE

Treaty on mutual legal assistance in criminal matters.

Signed at Brasilia October 14, 1997.

Entered into force February 21, 2001.

TIAS

LEND-LEASE

Agreement on the disposition of lend-lease supplies in inventory or procurement in the United States.

Signed at Washington June 28, 1946.

Entered into force June 28, 1946.

60 Stat. 1797; TIAS 1537; 5 Bevans 1019; 6 UNTS 327.

MARITIME MATTERS

See also SHIPPING

Agreement relating to the transfer to Brazil of certain United States naval vessels.

Exchange of notes at Washington January 4, 1951 with memorandum of understanding dated January 9, 1951.

Entered into force January 4, 1951.

3 UST 2738; TIAS 2443; 165 UNTS 97.

NARCOTIC DRUGS

Agreement on cooperation in the field of control of illicit traffic of drugs, with annex.

Exchange of notes at Brasilia July 19, 1983.

Entered into force July 19, 1983.

35 UST 1663; TIAS 10756.

Amendments and extension

October 4 and December 3, 1984 (TIAS 11056).

June 2 and 19, 1986 (TIAS 12388).

Mutual cooperation agreement for reducing demand, preventing illicit use and combatting illicit production and trafficking of drugs.

Signed at Brasilia April 12, 1995.

Entered into force April 24, 1997.

TIAS; 1990 UNTS 27.

PACIFIC SETTLEMENT OF DISPUTES

Arbitration convention.

Signed at Washington January 23, 1909.

Entered into force July 26, 1911.

37 Stat. 1535; TS 562; 5 Bevans 818.

Treaty looking to the advancement of the cause of general peace.

Signed at Washington July 24, 1914.

Entered into force October 28, 1916.

39 Stat. 1698; TS 627; 5 Bevans 820.

PEACE CORPS

Agreement relating to the establishment of a Peace Corps program in Brazil.

Exchange of notes at Brasilia June 18, 1973.

Entered into force June 18, 1973.

24 UST 1650; TIAS 7669.

POSTAL MATTERS

Memorandum of understanding concerning the operation of the INTELPOST field trial, with attachment and details of implementation.

Signed at Brasilia and Washington December 18 and 28, 1984.

Entered into force January 7, 1985.

TIAS 11004; 2022 UNTS 209.

International express mail agreement, with detailed regulations.

Signed at Brasilia and Washington April 7 and May 11, 1988.

Entered into force May 11, 1988.

TIAS 11654.

PUBLICATIONS

Agreement relating to the exchange of official publications.

Exchange of notes at Washington June 15 and 24, 1940.

Entered into force June 24, 1940.

54 Stat. 2329; EAS 176; 5 Bevans 883; 203 LNTS 227.

Amendment

May 16 and 23, 1950 (3 UST 387; TIAS 2402; 151 UNTS 141).

RELATIONS

Memorandum of understanding concerning consultations on matters of mutual interest.

Signed at Brasilia February 21, 1976.

Entered into force February 21, 1976.

27 UST 1034; TIAS 8240.

SATELLITES

Agreement relating to a program of joint participation in intercontinental testing in connection with experimental communications satellites.

Exchange of notes at Rio de Janeiro October 27, 1961.

Entered into force October 27, 1961.

12 UST 3145; TIAS 4917; 433 UNTS 113.

SCIENTIFIC COOPERATION

Agreement relating to cooperation in science and technology.

Signed at Brasilia February 6, 1984.

Entered into force May 15, 1986.

TIAS 10990.

Amendment and extension

March 21, 1994 (TIAS 12537).

Memorandum of understanding concerning scientific and technical cooperation in the earth sciences.

Signed at Reston January 17 and 31, 1997.

Entered into force January 31, 1997.

TIAS 12829.

Implementing arrangement for the biological control of the Aedes Aegypti mosquito.

Signed at Washington February 29, 2000.

Entered into force February 29, 2000.

TIAS

SEISMIC OBSERVATIONS

Memorandum of understanding concerning the development, installation and operation of a seismic data acquisition system.

Signed at Reston and Brasilia April 8 and May 5, 1986.

Entered into force May 5, 1986.

TIAS 11360.

SHIPPING

Agreement relating to establishment of a mechanism for consultation on maritime transportation problems.

Exchange of notes at Rio de Janeiro September 18 and 20, 1968.

Entered into force September 20, 1968.

19 UST 6017; TIAS 6559; 702 UNTS 227.

SPACE COOPERATION

Memorandum of understanding for the smoke/sulfate, clouds and radiation experiment – Brazil, with exchange of letters.

Signed at Washington May 19, 1995.

Entered into force May 19, 1995.

TIAS 12213.

Framework agreement on cooperation in the peaceful uses of outer space, with annex.

Signed at Brasilia March 1, 1996.

Entered into force July 9, 1997.

TIAS

Memorandum of understanding for flight of the Humidity Sounder for Brazil (HSB) instrument on NASA's Earth Observing System PM–1 spacecraft.

Signed at Washington December 5, 1996.

Entered into force December 5, 1996.

TIAS 12820.

Implementing arrangement for the design, development, operation and use of flight equipment and payloads for the International Space Station Program.

Signed at Brasilia October 14, 1997.

Entered into force October 14, 1997.

TIAS

TELECOMMUNICATION

Agreement relating to radio communications between amateur stations on behalf of third parties.

Exchange of notes at Washington June 1, 1965.

Entered into force June 1, 1965.

16 UST 821; TIAS 5816; 546 UNTS 195.

Agreement relating to the reciprocal granting of authorizations to permit licensed amateur radio operators of either country to operate their stations in the other country.

Exchange of notes at Rio de Janeiro January 26 and Brasilia June 19, 1970.

Entered into force June 19, 1970.

21 UST 1960; TIAS 6936; 756 UNTS 109.

TRADE AND COMMERCE

Joint communique relating to trade, investment and financial matters. Issued at Brasilia May 11, 1976.

Entered into force May 11, 1976.

27 UST 4121; TIAS 8435; 1066 UNTS 131.

Agreement relating to the establishment of a United States Trade Center in Sao Paulo, with note of guarantee.

Exchange of notes at Brasilia June 22 and October 20, 1976.

Entered into force October 20, 1976.

28 UST 8146; TIAS 8748.

Agreement relating to trade in cotton, wool and man-made fiber textiles and textile products, with annexes.

Exchange of notes at Washington September 15 and 19, 1988.

Entered into force September 19, 1988; effective April 1, 1988.

NP

Amendments and extension

October 12 and November 25, 1988 (NP).

April 16 and 23, 1992 (NP).

May 4 and June 27, 1994 (NP).

Agreement on steel trade liberalization, with appendices and related letter.

Exchange of letters at Washington February 26 and March 5, 1990.

Entered into force March 5, 1990.

TIAS

Agreement regarding cooperation between their competition authorities in the enforcement of their competition laws.

Signed at Washington October 26, 1999.

Entered into force March 25, 2003.

TIAS

TRADE-MARKS

Agreement for the protection of the marks of manufacture and trade.

Signed at Rio de Janeiro September 24, 1878.

21 Stat. 659; TS 36; 5 Bevans 807.

VISAS

Agreement relating to the waiver of nonimmigrant passport visa fees.

Exchange of notes at Rio de Janeiro December 16 and 17, 1937; operative January 1, 1938.

5 Bevans 874; 186 LNTS 413.

Agreement relating to the reciprocal issuance of nonimmigrant visas free of charge to diplomatic, consular, and administrative officers and employees serving in diplomatic missions, and career consular officers, as well as officers and employees of governmental agencies of both countries.

Exchange of notes at Rio de Janeiro May 26, 1965.

Entered into force July 25, 1965.

16 UST 1006; TIAS 5843; 549 UNTS 125.

BRUNEI

On January 1, 1984, the former British protected state of Brunei gained full independence. In a letter dated January 1, 1984 to the Secretary General of the United Nations, the Sultan made a statement reading in part as follows:

"The Government of Brunei Darussalam recognises that it is desirable to maintain to the fullest extent compatible with the resumption by Brunei Darussalam of its status and emergence on 1st January 1984 as a fully independent and sovereign nation, legal continuity in treaty relations between Brunei Darussalam and other states. Accordingly, the Government of Brunei Darussalam makes the following declaration:

1] As regards bilateral treaties validly concluded by the United Kingdom on behalf of Brunei Darussalam or validly applied or extended by the former to the latter, the Government of Brunei Darussalam is willing to accept, on a basis of reciprocity, the rights and obligations under the terms of all such treaties for a period of five years from 1st January 1984 until 31st December 1988 unless abrogated or modified earlier by mutual consent. At the expiry of that period, the Government of Brunei Darussalam will regard such of those treaties which could not by the application of the rules of customary international law be regarded as otherwise surviving, as having terminated.

2] The Government of Brunei Darussalam acknowledges that the above declaration applicable to bilateral treaties cannot with equal facility be applied to multilateral treaties. As regards these, therefore, the Government of Brunei Darussalam proposes to examine each of them individually and to indicate to the depositary in each case what steps it wishes to take in relation to each such instrument — whether by confirmation of termination, confirmation of succession or accession. During the period of examination the Government of Brunei Darussalam will on a basis of reciprocity accept all treaty rights and obligations accruing and arising under all multilateral treaties which were prior to independence validly applied or extended to Brunei Darussalam."

AVIATION

Air transport agreement, with annexes.

Signed at Washington June 20, 1997.

Entered into force June 20, 1997.

TIAS

COMMERCE

Treaty of peace, friendship, commerce and navigation.

Signed at Brunei June 23, 1850.

Entered into force July 11, 1853.

10 Stat. 909; TS 33; 5 Bevans 1080.

CONSULS

Consular convention between the United States and the United Kingdom.

Signed at Washington June 6, 1951.

Entered into force September 7, 1952.

3 UST 3426; TIAS 2494; 165 UNTS 121.

ECONOMIC AND TECHNICAL COOPERATION

Economic cooperation agreement between the United States and the United Kingdom.

Signed at London July 6, 1948; applicable to Brunei October 26, 1949.

62 Stat. 2596; TIAS 1795; 12 Bevans 874; 22 UNTS 263.

Amendments

January 3, 1950 (1 UST 184; TIAS 2036; 86 UNTS 304).

May 25, 1951 (2 UST 1292; TIAS 2277; 99 UNTS 308).

February 25, 1953 (4 UST 1528; TIAS 2815; 172 UNTS 332).

INTERNATIONAL CRIMINAL COURT

Agreement regarding the surrender of persons to international tribunals.

Exchange of notes at Bandar Seri Begawan February 3 and March 3, 2004.

Entered into force March 3, 2004.

TIAS

POSTAL MATTERS

International express mail agreement, with detailed regulations.

Signed at Bandar Seri Begawan and Washington December 15, 1990 and January 8, 1991.

Entered into force February 18, 1991.

TIAS 11785.

TRADE-MARKS

Declaration by the United States and the United Kingdom affording reciprocal protection to trade-marks.

Signed at London October 24, 1877.

Entered into force October 24, 1877.

20 Stat. 703; TS 138; 12 Bevans 198.

BULGARIA

ATOMIC ENERGY

Agreement for cooperation in the field of peaceful uses of nuclear energy, with annex and agreed minute.

Signed at Sofia June 21, 1994.

Entered into force March 29, 1996.

TIAS 12549.

Agreement on cooperative thermal-hydraulic code applications and maintenance research and severe accident research, with addendum.

Signed at Rockville and Sofia August 6 and 17, 2004.

Entered into force August 17, 2004.

TIAS

AVIATION

Civil aviation security agreement.

Signed at Sofia April 24, 1991.

Entered into force April 24, 1991.

TIAS 11984.

CONSULS

Consular convention, with agreed memorandum and exchange of letters.

Signed at Sofia April 15, 1974.

Entered into force May 29, 1975.

26 UST 687; TIAS 8067.

CUSTOMS

Agreement regarding mutual assistance between customs administrations.

Signed at Sofia November 6, 2000.

Entered into force April 1, 2004.

TIAS

DEFENSE

Agreement concerning the provision of training related to defense articles under the United States International Military Education and Training (IMET) Program.

Exchange of notes at Sofia February 11 and April 7, 1992.

Entered into force April 7, 1992.

NP

Agreement regarding grants under the Foreign Assistance Act of 1961, as amended, and the furnishing of defense articles, related training and other defense services from the United States to Bulgaria.

Exchange of notes at Sofia May 4 and December 5, 1994.

Entered into force December 5, 1994.

TIAS 12279.

Agreement concerning the protection of classified military information.

Signed at Sofia February 1, 1995.

Entered into force February 1, 1995.

TIAS 12280.

Acquisition and cross-servicing agreement, with annexes.

Signed at Sofia February 21, 2001.

Entered into force February 21, 2001.

TIAS

Agreement concerning overflight, and transit through, and presence in the territory of the Republic of Bulgaria of U.S. forces, personnel and contractors in support of Operation Enduring Freedom.

Exchange of notes at Sofia November 12, 2001.

Entered into force November 16, 2001.

TIAS

Agreement on defense cooperation, with annexes.

Signed at Sofia April 28, 2006.

Entered into force June 12, 2006.

TIAS

ECONOMIC AND TECHNICAL COOPERATION

Agreement concerning economic, technical and related assistance.

Signed at Sofia July 27, 1998.

Entered into force February 1, 1999.

TIAS

EDUCATION

Agreement concerning the Bulgarian-American Commission for Educational Exchange.

Signed at Sofia December 3, 2003.

Entered into force July 1, 2004.

TIAS

EMPLOYMENT

Agreement relating to the employment of dependents of official government employees.

Exchange of notes at Sofia October 8 and 29, 1991.

Entered into force October 29, 1991.

TIAS 11983.

ENVIRONMENTAL COOPERATION

Agreement for cooperation in the Global Learning and Observations to Benefit the Environment (GLOBE) Program, with appendices.

Signed at Sofia September 8, 1998.

Entered into force September 8, 1998.

TIAS

EXTRADITION

Extradition treaty.

Signed at Sofia March 19, 1924.

Entered into force June 24, 1924.

43 Stat. 1886; TS 687; 5 Bevans 1086; 26 LNTS 27.

Supplementary extradition treaty.

Signed at Washington June 8, 1934.

Entered into force August 15, 1935.

49 Stat. 3250; TS 894; 5 Bevans 1103; 161 LNTS 409.

FINANCE

Investment incentive agreement.

Signed at Sofia June 7, 1991.

Entered into force September 30, 1991.

TIAS 11500.

INVESTMENT

Treaty concerning the encouragement and reciprocal protection of investment, with annex, protocol and exchange of letters.

Signed at Washington September 23, 1992.

Entered into force June 2, 1994.

TIAS

MAPPING

Basic exchange and cooperative agreement for topographic mapping, nautical and aeronautical charting, safety to flight and sea navigation information, geodesy and gravimetrics, digital data, and related global geospatial information and services.

Signed at Washington May 13, 1998.

Entered into force May 13, 1998.

NP

NATIONALITY

Naturalization treaty.

Signed at Sofia November 23, 1923.

Entered into force April 5, 1924.

43 Stat. 1759; TS 684; 5 Bevans 1083; 25 LNTS 238.

PACIFIC SETTLEMENT OF DISPUTES

Treaty of arbitration.

Signed at Washington January 21, 1929.

Entered into force July 22, 1929.

46 Stat. 2332; TS 792; 5 Bevans 1094; 93 LNTS 337.

Treaty of conciliation.

Signed at Washington January 21, 1929.

Entered into force July 22, 1929.

46 Stat. 2334; TS 793; 5 Bevans 1097; 93 LNTS 331.

PEACE CORPS

Agreement concerning the establishment of a Peace Corps program in Bulgaria.

Signed at Washington September 27, 1990.

Entered into force September 27, 1990.

TIAS 11498.

POSTAL MATTERS

Parcel post convention.

Signed at Sofia August 2, 1922, and at Washington August 26, 1922; operative November 11, 1919.

42 Stat. 2205; Post Office Department print.

Memorandum of understanding concerning the operation of the INTELPOST service, with details of implementation.

Signed at Sofia and Washington April 20 and June 13, 1990.

Entered into force June 25, 1990.

TIAS 11763.

International express mail agreement, with detailed regulations.

Signed at Sofia and Washington April 5 and May 20, 1991.

Entered into force June 17, 1991.

TIAS 11811.

SCIENTIFIC COOPERATION

Agreement on scientific and technological cooperation, with annexes.

Signed at Washington February 9, 1978.

Entered into force February 9, 1978.

TIAS

TRADE AND COMMERCE

Agreement for the reciprocal waiving of legalization on certificates of origin accompanying merchandise.

Exchange of notes at Sofia January 5, 1938.

Entered into force January 5, 1938.

52 Stat. 1509; EAS 124; 5 Bevans 1105; 191 LNTS 207.

Agreement on trade relations, with exchanges of letters.

Signed at Washington April 22, 1991.

Entered into force November 22, 1991.

TIAS

BURKINA FASO

AVIATION

Air transport agreement, with annexes.

Signed at Washington July 27, 2000.

Entered into force July 27, 2000.

TIAS

DEFENSE

Agreement concerning the provision of training related to defense articles under the United States International Military Education and Training (IMET) Program.

Exchange of notes at Ouagadougou February 20 and August 26, 1986.

Entered into force August 26, 1986.

TIAS 11282.

Agreement concerning the provision of training related to defense articles under the United States International Military Education and Training (IMET) Program.

Exchange of notes at Ouagadougou August 11 and 29, 2006.

Entered into force August 29, 2006.

NP

ECONOMIC AND TECHNICAL COOPERATION

Agreement providing for the furnishing of economic, technical and related assistance.

Exchange of notes at Ouagadougou June 1, 1961.

Entered into force June 1, 1961.

12 UST 867; TIAS 4787; 410 UNTS 223.

Agency for International Development

June 30 and July 1, 1977 (29 UST 5363; TIAS 9117).

September 9, 1977 (29 UST 5279; TIAS 9105).

June 8, 1978 (30 UST 3185; TIAS 9388).

FINANCE

Agreement relating to investment guaranties.

Exchange of notes at Ouagadougou June 18, 1965.

Entered into force June 18, 1965.

16 UST 1068; TIAS 5847; 549 UNTS 133.

GEODETIC SURVEY

Arrangement relating to a geodetic survey along the 12th parallel arc.

Exchange of notes at Ouagadougou June 28 and August 21, 1967.

Entered into force August 21, 1967.

18 UST 2848; TIAS 6374; 700 UNTS 297.

INTERNATIONAL CRIMINAL COURT

Agreement regarding the surrender of persons to the International Criminal Court.

Signed at Ouagadougou October 2 and 5, 2003.

Entered into force October 14, 2003.

TIAS

PEACE CORPS

Agreement on general conditions for the employment of Peace Corps volunteers.

Signed at Ouagadougou February 6, 1975.

Entered into force February 6, 1975.

26 UST 2681; TIAS 8183; 1052 UNTS 221.

POSTAL MATTERS

International express mail agreement, with detailed regulations.

Signed at Ouagadougou and Washington October 12 and November 5, 1987.

Entered into force December 5, 1987.

TIAS 11567.

BURMA

On January 4, 1948 Burma became a fully independent sovereign state. The treaty between the Government of the United Kingdom and the Provisional Government of Burma, signed at London October 17, 1947, provides in article 2 that "All obligations and responsibilities heretofore devolving on the Government of the United Kingdom which arise from any valid international instrument shall henceforth, insofar as such instrument may be held to have application to Burma, devolve upon the Provisional Government of Burma. The rights and benefits heretofore enjoyed by the Government of the United Kingdom in virtue of the application of any such international instrument to Burma shall henceforth be enjoyed by the Provisional Government of Burma."

AGRICULTURAL COMMODITIES

Agricultural commodities agreement with exchange of notes.

Signed at Rangoon November 9, 1962.

Entered into force November 9, 1962.

13 UST 2299; TIAS 5198; 461 UNTS 113.

AVIATION

Air transport agreement.

Signed at Rangoon September 28, 1949.

Entered into force September 28, 1949.

63 Stat. 2716; TIAS 1983; 5 Bevans 1121; 55 UNTS 3.

CONSULS

Convention to regulate commerce (article IV) between the United States and the United Kingdom.

Signed at London July 3, 1815.

Entered into force July 3, 1815.

8 Stat. 228; TS 110; 12 Bevans 49.

DEFENSE

Agreement concerning the provision of training related to defense articles under the United States International Military Education and Training (IMET) Program.

Exchange of notes at Rangoon April 8 and May 27, 1980.

Entered into force May 27, 1980.

32 UST 968; TIAS 9745; 1222 UNTS 337.

ECONOMIC AND TECHNICAL COOPERATION

Economic cooperation agreement.

Signed at Rangoon March 21, 1957.

Entered into force October 9, 1957.

8 UST 1862; TIAS 3931; 300 UNTS 11.

Amendments

September 12, 1959 (10 UST 1733; TIAS 4326; 358 UNTS 352).

June 29, 1960 (11 UST 2249; TIAS 4601; 394 UNTS 284).

Agreement providing special assistance to Burma on a grant basis to finance preliminary engineering and architectural surveys for two proposed construction projects.

Exchange of notes at Rangoon June 24, 1959.

Entered into force June 24, 1959.

10 UST 1730; TIAS 4325; 358 UNTS 91.

EDUCATION

Agreement providing for the United States Educational Foundation.

Signed at Rangoon December 22, 1947.

Entered into force December 22, 1947.

62 Stat. 1814; TIAS 1685; 5 Bevans 1108; 25 UNTS 27.

Amendments

December 18, 1948 and May 12, 1949 (63 Stat. 2704; TIAS 1976; 5 Bevans 1119; 80 UNTS 312).

August 29, 1961 (12 UST 1195; TIAS 4834; 418 UNTS 326).

EXTRADITION

Extradition treaty between the United States and the United Kingdom.

Signed at London December 22, 1931; applicable to Burma from November 1, 1941.

47 Stat. 2122; TS 849; 12 Bevans 482; 163 LNTS 59.

FINANCE

Agreement on the use of kyats accrued under Title I of the Agricultural Trade Development and Assistance Act of 1954, as amended.

Signed at Rangoon June 1, 1966.

Entered into force June 1, 1966.

17 UST 788; TIAS 6034; 580 UNTS 253.

INFORMATIONAL MEDIA GUARANTIES

Agreement relating to an informational media guaranty program in Burma.

Exchange of notes at Rangoon October 8 and 23, 1956.

Entered into force October 23, 1956.

7 UST 3165; TIAS 3695; 282 UNTS 37.

NARCOTIC DRUGS

Agreement relating to the provision of helicopters and related assistance by the United States to help Burma in suppressing illegal narcotic drug production and traffic.

Exchange of notes at Rangoon June 29, 1974.

Entered into force June 29, 1974.

25 UST 1518; TIAS 7887.

PROPERTY

Convention between the United States and the United Kingdom relating to tenure and disposition of real and personal property.

Signed at Washington March 2, 1899.[1]

31 Stat. 1939; TS 146; 12 Bevans 246.

Supplementary convention between the United States and the United Kingdom extending the time within which notifications may be given of the accession of British colonies or foreign possessions to the convention of March 2, 1899.

Signed at Washington January 13, 1902.[1]

32 Stat. 1914; TS 402; 12 Bevans 261.

NOTE

1 Convention considered to remain applicable to Burma after separation from India on April 1, 1937.

PUBLICATIONS

Agreement for the exchange of official publications.

Exchange of notes at Rangoon January 26 and April 5, 1948.

Entered into force April 5, 1948.

62 Stat. 1892; TIAS 1744; 5 Bevans 1116; 73 UNTS 73.

TRADE-MARKS

Declaration by the United States and the United Kingdom affording reciprocal protection to trade-marks.

Signed at London October 24, 1877.

Entered into force October 24, 1877.

20 Stat. 703; TS 138; 12 Bevans 198.

BURUNDI

DEFENSE

Agreement concerning the provision of training related to defense articles under the United States International Military Education and Training (IMET) Program.

Exchange of notes at Bujumbura September 21 and October 8, 1982.

Entered into force October 8, 1982.

TIAS 10577; 1871 UNTS 315.

ECONOMIC AND TECHNICAL COOPERATION

General agreement for special development assistance.

Exchange of notes at Bujumbura February 13 and 18, 1970.

Entered into force February 18, 1970.

21 UST 589; TIAS 6843; 740 UNTS 233.

FINANCE

Agreement relating to investment guaranties.

Exchange of notes at Bujumbura May 6, 1969.

Entered into force May 6, 1969.

21 UST 829; TIAS 6852; 753 UNTS 35.

INTERNATIONAL CRIMINAL COURT

Agreement regarding the surrender of persons to international tribunals.

Signed at Bujumbura July 5, 2003.

Entered into force July 24, 2003.

TIAS

PEACE CORPS

Agreement relating to the establishment of a Peace Corps program in Burundi.

Exchange of notes at Bujumbura August 31, 1982.

Entered into force August 31, 1982.

34 UST 1845; TIAS 10465; 1751 UNTS 105.

POSTAL MATTERS

International express mail agreement, with detailed regulations.

Signed at Bujumbura and Washington November 10 and December 13, 1989.

Entered into force January 15, 1990.

TIAS 11895.

C

CAMBODIA

AGRICULTURAL COMMODITIES

Agricultural commodities agreement with annex.

Signed at Phnom Penh March 2, 1971.

Entered into force March 2, 1971.

22 UST 441; TIAS 7079; 792 UNTS 123.

Amendments

September 7, 1971 (22 UST 1583; TIAS 7184; 807 UNTS 364).

November 4, 1971 (22 UST 1755; TIAS 7209).

December 21, 1971 (22 UST 2058; TIAS 7241).

Related agreements

January 13, 1972 (23 UST 14; TIAS 7269).

June 23, 1972 (23 UST 1238; TIAS 7394).

October 2, 1972 (23 UST 3128; TIAS 7487).

October 20, 1972 (23 UST 3131; TIAS 7487).

November 24, 1972 (23 UST 3693; TIAS 7515).

February 2, 1973 (24 UST 445; TIAS 7560).

July 25, 1973 (24 UST 1947; TIAS 7703).

August 2, 1973 (24 UST 1950; TIAS 7703).

August 9, 1973 (24 UST 1952; TIAS 7703).

August 13, 1973 (24 UST 1954; TIAS 7703).

October 8, 1973 (24 UST 2518; TIAS 7767).

October 18, 1973 (24 UST 2521; TIAS 7767).

November 10, 1973 (24 UST 2522; TIAS 7767).

November 15, 1973 (24 UST 2524; TIAS 7767).

December 14, 1973 (24 UST 2526; TIAS 7767).

April 8, 1974 (25 UST 1773; TIAS 7909).

May 16, 1974 (25 UST 1777; TIAS 7909).

May 24, 1974 (25 UST 1778; TIAS 7909).

Agricultural commodities agreement.

Signed at Phnom Penh August 10, 1974.

Entered into force August 10, 1974.

26 UST 45; TIAS 8008; 991 UNTS 330.

Amendments

September 17, 1974 (26 UST 66; TIAS 8008; 991 UNTS 342).

October 25, 1974 (26 UST 69; TIAS 8008; 991 UNTS 344).

January 14, 1975 (26 UST 72; TIAS 8008; 991 UNTS 346).

AVIATION

Memorandum of understanding for airfield upgrading at Ream, Pochentong and Battambang.

Signed at Phnom Penh August 12, 1972.

Entered into force August 12, 1972.

23 UST 3144; TIAS 7491; 898 UNTS 161.

CLAIMS

Agreement concerning the settlement of certain property claims.

Signed at Washington October 6, 1994.

Entered into force October 6, 1994.

TIAS 12193.

CULTURAL PROPERTY

Memorandum of understanding concerning the imposition of import restrictions on Khmer archaeological material.

Signed at Phnom Penh September 19, 2003.

Entered into force September 19, 2003.

TIAS

DEFENSE

Agreement relating to the provision of defense articles to Cambodia.

Exchange of notes at Phnom Penh August 20, 1970.

Entered into force August 20, 1970.

21 UST 2178; TIAS 6965; 764 UNTS 233.

Agreement concerning payment to the United States of net proceeds from the sale of defense articles furnished under the military assistance program.

Exchange of notes at Phnom Penh May 14 and June 19, 1974.

Entered into force July 1, 1974.

25 UST 1668; TIAS 7902.

Agreement regarding the status of United States military personnel and civilian employees of the Department of Defense who may be temporarily present in Cambodia in connection with military assistance activities and other official duties.

Exchange of notes at Phnom Penh October 12, 1995 and January 22, 1996.

Entered into force January 22, 1996.

NP

Agreement regarding grants under the Foreign Assistance Act of 1961, as amended, or successor legislation, and the furnishing of defense articles, defense services and related training, including pursuant to the United States International Military and Education Training Program (IMET), from the United States of America to the Kingdom of Cambodia.

Exchange of notes at Phnom Penh May 18 and July 14, 2006.

Entered into force July 14, 2006.

TIAS

ECONOMIC AND TECHNICAL COOPERATION

Economic, technical and related assistance agreement.

Signed at Phnom Penh October 25, 1994.

Entered into force October 25, 1994.

TIAS 12573.

Agency for International Development

September 18, 2006 (NP).

FINANCE

Investment incentive agreement.

Signed at Phnom Penh August 4, 1995.

Entered into force March 25, 1996.

TIAS

INTERNATIONAL CRIMINAL COURT

Agreement regarding the non-surrender of persons to the International Criminal Court.

Signed at Phnomh Penh June 27, 2003.

Entered into force June 29, 2005.

TIAS

MAPPING

Agreement relating to mutual mapping assistance between the Khmer Geographic Service and the American Mapping Service.

Signed at Phnom Penh October 17, 1957.

Entered into force October 17, 1957.

8 UST 1761; TIAS 3929; 299 UNTS 203.

PEACE CORPS

Agreement concerning the program of the Peace Corps in Cambodia.

Signed at Washington October 3, 1994.

Entered into force October 3, 1994.

TIAS 12569.

POSTAL MATTERS

International express mail agreement, with detailed regulations.

Signed at Phnom Penh and Washington April 27 and October 28, 1994.

Entered into force January 1, 1995.

NP

PUBLICATIONS

Agreement relating to the exchange of official publications.

Exchange of notes at Phnom Penh July 15, 1960.

Entered into force July 15, 1960.

11 UST 1923; TIAS 4540; 380 UNTS 129.

TRADE

Agreement on trade relations and intellectual property rights protection, with exchanges of notes.

Signed at Washington October 4, 1996.

Entered into force October 25, 1996.

TIAS

CAMEROON

DEFENSE

Agreement concerning the provision of training related to defense articles under the United States International Military Education and Training (IMET) Program.

Exchange of notes at Yaounde March 3 and June 19, 1980.

Entered into force June 19, 1980.

32 UST 2606; TIAS 9862; 1274 UNTS 103.

ECONOMIC AND TECHNICAL COOPERATION

Agreement providing for the furnishing of economic, technical and related assistance.

Exchange of notes at Yaounde May 26, 1961.

Entered into force May 26, 1961.

12 UST 967; TIAS 4801; 413 UNTS 195.

Amendment

December 8, 1961 (13 UST 282; TIAS 4973; 445 UNTS 367).

Agency for International Development

May 18, 1978 (30 UST 4547; TIAS 9477).

August 30, 1978 (30 UST 5031; TIAS 9497).

EMPLOYMENT

Agreement relating to the employment of dependents of official government employees.

Exchange of notes at Washington May 7, 1992 and January 15, 1993.

Entered into force January 15, 1993.

TIAS 11916.

ENVIRONMENTAL COOPERATION

Agreement for cooperation in the Global Learning and Observations to Benefit the Environment (GLOBE) Program, with appendices.

Signed at Yaounde November 6, 1998.

Entered into force November 6, 1998.

TIAS

FINANCE

Agreement relating to investment guaranties.

Exchange of notes at Washington March 7, 1967.

Entered into force March 7, 1967.

18 UST 292; TIAS 6231; 688 UNTS 315.

Agreement regarding the consolidation and rescheduling of certain debts owed to, guaranteed by, or insured by the United States Government and its agencies, with annexes.

Signed at Yaounde January 3, 1990.

Entered into force February 12, 1990.

NP

Agreement regarding the phased discharge of certain debts owed to the Government of the United States, with annexes.

Signed at Yaounde January 3, 1990.

Entered into force January 3, 1990.

NP

Agreement regarding the consolidation and rescheduling or refinancing of certain debts owed to, guaranteed by or insured by the United States Government and its agencies, with annexes.

Signed at Yaounde August 19, 1992.

Entered into force October 12, 1992.

NP

Agreement regarding the consolidation and rescheduling or refinancing of certain debts owed to, guaranteed by or insured by the United States Government and its agencies, with annexes.

Signed at Yaounde September 12, 1994.

Entered into force December 5, 1994.

NP

Agreement regarding the consolidation and rescheduling of certain debts owed to, guaranteed by, or insured by the United States Government and its agencies, with annexes.

Signed at Yaounde May 6, 1996.

Entered into force July 31, 1996.

NP

Agreement regarding the consolidation, reduction and rescheduling of certain debts owed to, guaranteed by, or insured by the United States Government and its agencies, with annexes.

Signed at Yaounde July 29, 1998.

Entered into force September 10, 1998.

NP

Agreement regarding the consolidation, reduction, and rescheduling of certain debts owed to, guaranteed by, or insured by the United States Government and its agencies, with annexes.

Signed at Yaounde February 5, 2002.

Entered into force March 21, 2002.

NP

Amendment

February 22 and March 31, 2006.

INTERNATIONAL CRIMINAL COURT

Agreement regarding the surrender of persons to international tribunals.

Signed at Yaounde December 1, 2003.

Entered into force December 1, 2003.

TIAS

INVESTMENT

Treaty concerning the reciprocal encouragement and protection of investment.

Signed at Washington February 26, 1986.

Entered into force April 6, 1989.

TIAS

PEACE CORPS

Agreement relating to the establishment of a Peace Corps program in Cameroon.

Exchange of notes at Yaounde July 23 and September 10, 1962.

Entered into force September 10, 1962.

13 UST 2114; TIAS 5171; 461 UNTS 177.

POSTAL MATTERS

International express mail agreement, with detailed regulations.

Signed at Yaounde and Washington April 25 and June 22, 1990.

Entered into force August 1, 1990.

TIAS 11762.

SCIENTIFIC COOPERATION

Memorandum of understanding concerning scientific and technical cooperation in the earth sciences, with annexes.

Signed at Reston and Yaounde July 11 and September 10, 2001.

Entered into force September 10, 2001.

TIAS

CANADA

AMITY

Treaty of amity, commerce and navigation between the United States and Great Britain (Jay Treaty).[1]

Signed at London November 19, 1794.

Entered into force October 28, 1795.

8 Stat. 116; TS 105; 12 Bevans 13.

Explanatory article to article 3 of the November 19, 1794 treaty of amity, commerce and navigation between the United States and Great Britain.[1]

Signed at Philadelphia May 4, 1796.

Entered into force October 6, 1796.

8 Stat. 130; TS 106; 12 Bevans 34.

Treaty of peace and amity between the United States and Great Britain.

Signed at Ghent December 24, 1814.

Entered into force February 17, 1815.

8 Stat. 218; TS 109; 12 Bevans 41.

Treaty for an amicable settlement of all causes of differences between the United States and Great Britain (Treaty of Washington).[2] Washington May 8, 1871.

Entered into force June 17, 1871.

17 Stat. 863; TS 133; 12 Bevans 170.

NOTES

1 Only article 3 so far as it relates to the right of Indians to pass across the border, and articles 9 and 10 appear to remain in force. But see <i>Akins v. U.S.,</i> 551 F.2d 1222 (1977).

2 Articles I-XVII and XXXIV-XLII have been executed; articles XVIII-XXV, XXX, and XXXII terminated July 1, 1885; articles XXVIII and XXIX not considered in force.

ARCTIC

Agreement on Arctic cooperation.

Signed at Ottawa January 11, 1988.

Entered into force January 11, 1988.

TIAS 11565.

ATOMIC ENERGY

Agreement for cooperation on civil uses of atomic energy.

Signed at Washington June 15, 1955.

Entered into force July 21, 1955.

6 UST 2595; TIAS 3304; 235 UNTS 175.

Extension and amendments[1]

June 26, 1956 (8 UST 275; TIAS 3771; 279 UNTS 318).

June 11, 1960 (11 UST 1780; TIAS 4518; 377 UNTS 412).

May 25, 1962 (13 UST 1400; TIAS 5102; 453 UNTS 362).

June 23, 1999.

Agreement for cooperation regarding atomic information for mutual defense purposes.

Signed at Washington June 15, 1955.

Entered into force July 22, 1955.

6 UST 2607; TIAS 3305; 235 UNTS 201.

Agreement for cooperation on uses of atomic energy for mutual defense purposes.

Signed at Washington May 22, 1959.

Entered into force July 27, 1959.

10 UST 1293; TIAS 4271; 354 UNTS 63.

Agreement regarding participation in the international piping integrity research group.

Signed at Ottawa and Bethesda April 28 and May 20, 1987.

Entered into force May 20, 1987.

TIAS 12227.

Agreement concerning cooperation on the application of non-proliferation assurances to Canadian uranium to be transferred from Canada to the U.S. for enrichment and fabrication into fuel and retransferred to Taiwan for use in nuclear reactors, with annex.

Exchange of letters at Washington February 24 and March 5, 1993.

Entered into force March 5, 1993.

TIAS 12490; 1914 UNTS 209.

Administrative arrangement for cooperation and the exchange of information in nuclear regulatory matters, with appendices and addenda.

Signed at Washington May 29, 2002.

Entered into force May 29, 2002.

TIAS

Agreement relating to participation in the USNRC program of severe accident research.

Signed at Rockville and Ontario October 27 and December 20, 2004.

Entered into force December 20, 2004.

TIAS

NOTE

1 See also agreement of May 22, 1959 for cooperation on uses of atomic energy for mutual defense purposes (10 UST 1293; TIAS 4271).

AVIATION

Arrangement relating to the issuance of certificates of competency or licenses for the piloting of civil aircraft.

Exchange of notes at Washington July 28, 1938.

Entered into force August 1, 1938.

53 Stat. 1937; EAS 130; 6 Bevans 108; 192 LNTS 115.

Agreement relating to cooperation between the United States and Canada in air search and rescue operations along the common boundary.

Exchange of notes at Washington January 24 and 31, 1949.

Entered into force January 31, 1949.

63 Stat. 2328; TIAS 1882; 6 Bevans 478; 43 UNTS 119.

Agreement relating to the use by civil aircraft of Stephenville and Argentia military air bases in Newfoundland.

Exchange of notes at Ottawa June 4, 1949.

Entered into force June 4, 1949.

63 Stat. 2486; TIAS 1933; 6 Bevans 488; 200 UNTS 201.

Agreement concerning air traffic control.

Exchange of notes at Ottawa December 20 and 27, 1963.

Entered into force December 27, 1963.

14 UST 1737; TIAS 5480; 494 UNTS 21.

Memorandum of agreement relating to the provision of flight inspection services.

Signed at Washington and Koblenz March 10 and April 1, 1978.

Entered into force April 1, 1978.

30 UST 278; TIAS 9198.

Amendment

February 4 and 24, 1982 (TIAS 10565; 1871 UNTS 516).

Agreement concerning the airworthiness and environmental certification of imported civil aeronautical products.

Exchange of letters at Ottawa August 31, 1984.

Entered into force August 31, 1984.

TIAS 11023; 1469 UNTS 339.

Air transport agreement, with annexes.

Signed at Ottawa February 24, 1995.

Entered into force February 24, 1995.

TIAS

Related agreement

January 20 and June 12, 2000.

Memorandum of cooperation for mutual cooperation in the area of civil aviation research, engineering and development, with annex.

Signed at Washington and Ottawa May 6 and July 9, 1996.

Entered into force July 9, 1996.

TIAS

Agreement for promotion of aviation safety.

Signed at Toronto June 12, 2000.

Entered into force June 12, 2000.

TIAS

Agreement on air transport preclearance, with annexes and agreed minute.

Signed at Toronto January 18, 2001.

Entered into force May 2, 2003.

TIAS

BOUNDARIES

See also AMITY

Convention respecting fisheries, boundary and the restoration of slaves.

Signed at London October 20, 1818.

Entered into force January 30, 1819.

8 Stat. 248; TS 112; 12 Bevans 57.

Treaty to settle and define the boundaries between the territories of the United States and the possessions of Her Britannic Majesty in North America; for the final suppression of the African slave trade, and for the giving up of criminals, fugitive from justice, in certain cases (Webster-Ashburton Treaty).[1] Washington August 9, 1842.

Entered into force October 13, 1842.

8 Stat. 572; TS 119; 12 Bevans 82.

Treaty establishing the boundary in the territory on the northwest coast of America lying westward of the Rocky Mountains (Oregon Treaty).

Signed at Washington June 15, 1846.

Entered into force July 17, 1846.

9 Stat. 869; TS 120; 12 Bevans 95.

Declaration adopting maps of boundary prepared by the Joint Commission of the Northwest Boundary for surveying and marking the boundaries between the United States and British possessions on the forty-ninth parallel of north latitude, under the first article of the treaty of June 15, 1846 between the United States and the United Kingdom.

Signed at Washington February 24, 1870.

Entered into force February 24, 1870.

TS 129; 12 Bevans 157.

Protocol of a conference respecting the northwest water boundary.

Signed at Washington March 10, 1873.

Entered into force March 10, 1873.

18 Stat. 369; TS 135; 12 Bevans 190.

Convention providing for the settlement of questions between the United States and the United Kingdom with respect to the boundary line between the territory of Alaska and the British possessions in North America.[2]

Signed at Washington January 24, 1903.

Entered into force March 3, 1903.

32 Stat. 1961; TS 419; 12 Bevans 263.

Acceptance of the report of the commissioners to complete the award under the convention of January 24, 1903 respecting the boundary line between Alaska and the British North American possessions.

Exchange of notes at Washington March 25, 1905.

Entered into force March 25, 1905.

TS 476; 12 Bevans 269.

Convention providing for the surveying and marking out upon the ground of the 141st degree of west longitude where said meridian forms the boundary line between Alaska and the British possessions in North America.[3]

Signed at Washington April 21, 1906.

Entered into force August 16, 1906.

34 Stat. 2948; TS 452; 12 Bevans 276.

Treaty concerning the Canadian international boundary.

Signed at Washington April 11, 1908.

Entered into force June 4, 1908.

35 Stat. 2003; TS 497; 12 Bevans 297.

Treaty concerning the boundary line in Passamaquoddy Bay.

Signed at Washington May 21, 1910.

Entered into force August 20, 1910.

36 Stat. 2477; TS 551; 12 Bevans 341.

Treaty in regard to the boundary between the United States and Canada.

Signed at Washington February 24, 1925.

Entered into force July 17, 1925.

44 Stat. 2102; TS 720; 6 Bevans 7; 43 LNTS 239.

Treaty to submit to binding dispute settlement the delimitation of the maritime boundary in the Gulf of Maine Area, with annexed agreements, as amended.

Signed at Washington March 29, 1979.

Entered into force November 20, 1981.[4]

33 UST 2797; TIAS 10204; 1288 UNTS 27.

NOTES

1 Article 10 supplemented by convention of July 12, 1889 (See under CANADA — EXTRADITION).

2 Obsolete except for first paragraph of article VI.

3 Obsolete except for article II.

4 For the subsequent judgment of the International Court of Justice of October 12, 1984, see Case concerning Delimitation of the Maritime Boundary in the Gulf of Maine Area. 1984 I.C.J. Reports 246. With the implementation of the special agreement to submit the dispute to a chamber of the I.C.J., the agreement for possible submission to a court of arbitration never entered into force.

BOUNDARY WATERS

See also AMITY, BOUNDARIES, MARITIME MATTERS and POLLUTION

Treaty relating to the boundary waters and questions arising along the boundary between the United States and Canada.[1]

Signed at Washington January 11, 1909.

Entered into force May 5, 1910.

36 Stat. 2448; TS 548; 12 Bevans 319.

Convention to regulate the level of the Lake of the Woods, with an accompanying protocol and an agreement.

Signed at Washington February 24, 1925.

Entered into force July 17, 1925.

44 Stat. 2108; TS 721; 6 Bevans 14; 43 LNTS 251.

Amendment

February 21 and June 19, 1979 (30 UST 5998; TIAS 9534; 1180 UNTS 77).

Arrangement relating to the level of Lake Memphremagog.

Exchange of notes at Ottawa September 20 and November 6, 1935.

Entered into force November 6, 1935.

Foreign Relations, 1935, Vol. II, p. 53; 6 Bevans 71.

Convention providing for emergency regulation of the level of Rainy Lake and of certain other boundary waters.

Signed at Ottawa September 15, 1938.

Entered into force October 3, 1940.

54 Stat. 1800; TS 961; 6 Bevans 115; 203 LNTS 207.

Arrangement relating to the early development of certain portions of the Great Lakes-St. Lawrence Basin project (Long Lac-Ogoki Works).

Exchange of notes at Washington October 14 and 31 and November 7, 1940.

Entered into force November 7, 1940.

54 Stat. 2426; EAS 187; 6 Bevans 199; 203 LNTS 267.

Agreement relating to the temporary raising of level of Lake St. Francis during low-water periods.

Exchange of notes at Washington November 10, 1941.

Entered into force November 10, 1941.

56 Stat. 1832; EAS 291; 6 Bevans 236; 23 UNTS 280.

Extension

August 31 and September 7, 1944 (58 Stat. 1437; EAS 424; 105 UNTS 310).

Agreement relating to the Upper Columbia River Basin.

Exchange of notes at Ottawa February 25 and March 3, 1944.

Entered into force March 3, 1944.

58 Stat. 1236; EAS 399; 6 Bevans 342; 109 UNTS 191.

Treaty relating to uses of waters of the Niagara River.

Signed at Washington February 27, 1950.

Entered into force October 10, 1950.

1 UST 694; TIAS 2130; 132 UNTS 223.

Related agreements

September 13, 1954 (5 UST 1979; TIAS 3064; 236 UNTS 382).

April 17, 1973 (24 UST 895; TIAS 7599).

Agreement relating to the St. Lawrence seaway project for the construction of certain navigation facilities.

Exchange of notes at Washington June 30, 1952.

Entered into force June 30, 1952.

5 UST 1788; TIAS 3053; 234 UNTS 199.

Agreement establishing the St. Lawrence River Joint Board of Engineers.

Exchange of notes at Washington November 12, 1953.

Entered into force November 12, 1953.

5 UST 2538; TIAS 3116; 234 UNTS 97.

Agreement relating to the St. Lawrence seaway project for the construction of certain navigation facilities.

Exchange of notes at Ottawa August 17, 1954.

Entered into force August 17, 1954.

5 UST 1784; TIAS 3053; 234 UNTS 210.

Related agreements

October 24, 1956 (7 UST 2865; TIAS 3668; 281 UNTS 281).

November 7 and December 4, 1956 (7 UST 3271; TIAS 3708).

July 23 and October 26, 1956 and February 26, 1957 (8 UST 279; TIAS 3772; 279 UNTS 179).

November 30, 1956 and April 8 and 9, 1957 (8 UST 637; TIAS 3814; 283 UNTS 217).

May 19, 1955 and February 27, 1959 (10 UST 383; TIAS 4199; 341 UNTS 3).

October 17, 1961 (12 UST 1284; TIAS 4851; 426 UNTS 201).

June 8, 1959 and October 17, 1961 (12 UST 1669; TIAS 4883; 424 UNTS 101).

Agreement governing tolls on the St. Lawrence Seaway.

Exchange of notes at Ottawa March 9, 1959.

Entered into force March 9, 1959.

10 UST 323; TIAS 4192; 340 UNTS 295.

Amendments

March 20, 1978 (29 UST 3165; TIAS 9003).

November 13 and 16, 1984 (TIAS 11061; 1884 UNTS 457).

May 3, 1985 (TIAS 11309; 1466 UNTS 436).

March 30 and August 1, 1989 (TIAS 11966).

April 26 and May 1, 1991 (TIAS 11885).

December 12 and 20, 1991 (TIAS 11866).

June 15 and 30, 1992 (TIAS 11866).

June 10 and July 12, 1994 (TIAS 12697; 2030 UNTS 41).

August 9 and October 18, 1995 (TIAS 12697; 2030 UNTS 30).

Treaty relating to cooperative development of the water resources of the Columbia River Basin.

Signed at Washington January 17, 1961.

Entered into force September 16, 1964, with related agreements effected by exchanges of notes at Washington January 22, 1964, and at Ottawa September 16, 1964.

15 UST 1555; TIAS 5638; 542 UNTS 244.

Related agreement

October 4, 1965 (16 UST 1263; TIAS 5877; 592 UNTS 272).

Agreement governing the operation of pilotage on the Great Lakes.

Exchange of notes at Ottawa August 23, 1978 and March 29, 1979.

Entered into force March 29, 1979; effective January 18, 1977.

30 UST 4027; TIAS 9445; 1171 UNTS 45.

Amendments

February 12, 1991 (TIAS 11813; 1853 UNTS 431).

October 15, 1992 and June 17, 1993 (TIAS 12154).

Treaty relating to the Skagit River and Ross Lake, and the Seven Mile Reservoir on the Pend d'Oreille River, with annex.

Signed at Washington April 2, 1984.

Entered into force December 14, 1984.

TIAS 11088; 1469 UNTS 309.

Agreement concerning cooperation in flood control, with construction plan.

Exchange of notes at Ottawa and Washington August 29 and 30, 1988.

Entered into force August 30, 1988.

TIAS 11641.

Agreement for water supply and flood control in the Souris River Basin, with annexes.

Signed at Washington October 26, 1989.

Entered into force October 26, 1989.

TIAS 11731.

Amendments

December 20 and 22, 2000.

January 14 and June 9, 2005.

Agreement for the sale of Canada's entitlement to downstream power benefits within the United States, with attachment.

Exchange of notes at Washington March 31, 1999.

Entered into force March 31, 1999.

TIAS

NOTE

1 Paragraphs 3, 4, and 5 of article V terminated October 10, 1950 upon the entry into force of the treaty relating to uses of waters of the Niagara River, signed February 27, 1950 (1 UST 694; TIAS 2130; 132 UNTS 223).

CAMPOBELLO

Agreement relating to the establishment of the Roosevelt Campobello International Park.

Signed at Washington January 22, 1964.

Entered into force August 14, 1964.

15 UST 1504; TIAS 5631; 530 UNTS 89.

CIVIL DEFENSE

Agreement on cooperation in comprehensive civil emergency planning and management, with annex.

Signed at Ottawa April 28, 1986.

Entered into force April 28, 1986.

TIAS

Amendment

December 19, 1997, March 17 and December 2, 1998.

CLAIMS

Convention for the establishment of a tribunal to decide questions of indemnity arising from the operation of the smelter at Trail, British Columbia.

Signed at Ottawa April 15, 1935.

Entered into force August 3, 1935.

49 Stat. 3245; TS 893; 6 Bevans 60; 162 LNTS 73.

Agreement supplementary to the convention signed April 15, 1935 for the establishment of a tribunal to decide questions of indemnity and future regime arising from the operation of the smelter at Trail, British Columbia.

Exchange of notes at Washington November 17, 1949 and January 24, 1950.

Entered into force January 24, 1950.

3 UST 539; TIAS 2412; 151 UNTS 171.

Agreement relating to claims arising out of traffic accidents involving vehicles of the armed forces of the United States and Canada.

Exchange of notes at Ottawa March 1 and 23, 1944.

Entered into force March 23, 1944.

60 Stat. 1948; TIAS 1581; 6 Bevans 345; 125 UNTS 345.

Agreement relating to waiver of certain claims involving government vessels.

Exchange of notes at Washington September 28 and November 13 and 15, 1946.

Entered into force November 15, 1946.

61 Stat. 2520; TIAS 1582; 6 Bevans 422; 7 UNTS 141.

Agreement relating to the settlement of certain war accounts and claims.

Exchange of notes at Washington March 14, 1949.

Entered into force March 14, 1949.

63 Stat. 2432; TIAS 1925; 6 Bevans 482; 82 UNTS 3.

COMMERCE

See AMITY

CONSERVATION

Convention for the protection of migratory birds in the United States and Canada.

Signed at Washington August 16, 1916.

Entered into force December 7, 1916.

39 Stat. 1702; TS 628; 12 Bevans 375.

Amendment

December 14, 1995 (TIAS 12721).

Arrangement prohibiting the importation of raccoon dogs.

Exchange of letters at Ottawa and Washington September 1 and 4, 1981.

Entered into force September 4, 1981.

33 UST 3764; TIAS 10259; 1541 UNTS 129.

Agreement on the conservation of the Porcupine Caribou Herd, with annex.

Signed at Ottawa July 17, 1987.

Entered into force July 17, 1987.

TIAS 11259; 2174 UNTS 267.

CONSULS

Convention to regulate commerce (article IV) between the United States and the United Kingdom.

Signed at London July 3, 1815; effective July 3, 1815.

8 Stat. 228; TS 110; 12 Bevans 49.

Arrangement relating to visits of consular officers to citizens of their own country serving sentences in penal institutions.

Exchange of notes at Ottawa July 29 and September 19, 1935.

Entered into force September 19, 1935.

Foreign Relations, 1935, Vol. II, p. 57; 6 Bevans 65.

CUSTOMS

Agreement relating to importation privileges for government officials and employees.

Exchanges of notes at Ottawa July 21, October 29 and November 9, 1942.

Entered into force November 9, 1942.

57 Stat. 1379; EAS 383; 6 Bevans 289; 101 UNTS 233.

Agreement regarding mutual assistance and cooperation between customs administrations.

Signed at Quebec June 20, 1984.

Entered into force January 8, 1985.

TIAS 11253; 1469 UNTS 319.

DEFENSE

Declaration by the Prime Minister of Canada and the President of the United States of America regarding the establishing of a Permanent Joint Board on Defense. Made at Ogdensburg, New York, August 18, 1940.

Department of State Bulletin, Vol. III, No. 61, August 24, 1940, p. 154; 6 Bevans 189; Canada Treaty Series, 1940, No. 14.

Arrangement relating to naval and air bases.

Exchange of notes at Washington September 2, 1940.

Entered into force September 2, 1940.

54 Stat. 2405; EAS 181; 12 Bevans 551; 203 LNTS 201.

Agreement regarding leased naval and air bases, and exchanges of notes.

Signed at London March 27, 1941.

Entered into force March 27, 1941.

55 Stat. 1560; EAS 235; 12 Bevans 560; 204 LNTS 15.

Amendment

May 22, 1985.

Protocol concerning the defense of Newfoundland.

Signed at London March 27, 1941.

Entered into force March 27, 1941.

55 Stat. 1599; EAS 235; 12 Bevans 560; 204 LNTS 70.

Hyde Park agreement. Announcement made at Hyde Park April 20, 1941 by the President of the United States of America and the Prime Minister of Canada.

Department of State Bulletin, Vol. IV, No. 96, April 26, 1941, p. 494; 6 Bevans 216.

Arrangement relating to visits in uniform by members of defense forces.

Exchange of notes at Ottawa August 28 and September 4, 1941.

Entered into force September 11, 1941.

55 Stat. 1551; EAS 233; 6 Bevans 231; 119 UNTS 285.

Agreement relating to payment for certain defense installations in Canada and at Goose Bay, Labrador.

Exchange of notes at Washington June 23 and 27, 1944.

Entered into force June 27, 1944.

58 Stat. 1290; EAS 405; 6 Bevans 360; 101 UNTS 273.

Agreement relating to reconversion of industry.

Exchange of notes at Ottawa May 7 and 15, 1945.

Entered into force May 15, 1945.

61 Stat. 3958; TIAS 1752; 6 Bevans 397; 125 UNTS 353.

United States-Canadian Permanent Joint Board on Defense to continue collaboration for security purposes. Announced in Ottawa and in Washington February 12, 1947.

Department of State Bulletin, Vol. XVI, No. 399, February 23, 1947, p. 361; 6 Bevans 430; Canada Treaty Series, 1947, No. 43.

Agreement relating to the leased naval base at Argentia, Newfoundland.

Exchange of notes at London August 13 and October 23, 1947.

Entered into force October 23, 1947.

61 Stat. 4065; TIAS 1809; 12 Bevans 827; 66 UNTS 277.

Amendment

May 22, 1985.

Agreement establishing a Joint Industrial Mobilization Committee.

Exchange of notes at Ottawa April 12, 1949.

Entered into force April 12, 1949.

63 Stat. 2331; TIAS 1889; 6 Bevans 486; 206 UNTS 241.

Agreement relating to a final settlement for all war surplus property disposed of pursuant to the agreements effected by exchanges of notes of November 22 and December 20, 1944; March 30, 1946; and July 11 and 15, 1946.

Exchange of notes at Ottawa June 17 and 18, 1949.

Entered into force June 18, 1949.

2 UST 2272; TIAS 2352; 200 UNTS 258.

Agreement relating to economic cooperation for defense.

Exchange of notes at Washington October 26, 1950.

Entered into force October 26, 1950.

1 UST 716; TIAS 2136; 132 UNTS 247.

Agreement relating to the extension and coordination of the continental radar defense system.[1]

Exchange of notes at Washington August 1, 1951.

Entered into force August 1, 1951.

5 UST 1721; TIAS 3049; 233 UNTS 109.

Related agreements

May 25, 1964 (15 UST 665; TIAS 5587; 526 UNTS 251).

September 30, 1966 (17 UST 1416; TIAS 6102; 616 UNTS 193).

June 30, 1971 (22 UST 1449; TIAS 7154; 797 UNTS 303).

March 22, 1974 (25 UST 283; TIAS 7799; 944 UNTS 173).

Agreement modifying the leased bases agreement of March 27, 1941 with the United Kingdom concerning bases in Canada.

Exchange of notes at Washington February 13 and March 19, 1952.

Entered into force March 19, 1952.

3 UST 4271; TIAS 2572; 174 UNTS 267.

Agreement relating to the application of the NATO status of forces agreement to U.S. forces in Canada, including those at the leased bases in Newfoundland and Goose Bay, Labrador except for certain arrangements under the leased bases agreement.

Exchange of notes at Washington April 28 and 30, 1952.

Entered into force September 27, 1953.

5 UST 2139; TIAS 3074; 235 UNTS 269.

Agreement on the establishment and operation of a distant early warning system between the United States and Canada.

Exchange of notes, with annex, at Washington May 5, 1955.

Entered into force May 5, 1955.[2]

6 UST 763; TIAS 3218; 241 UNTS 179.

Agreement relating to the establishment and operation of certain radar stations in the Newfoundland-Labrador area.

Exchange of notes at Ottawa June 13, 1955.

Entered into force June 13, 1955.

6 UST 6045; TIAS 3452; 268 UNTS 87.

Agreement relating to the construction and operation of certain radar stations in British Columbia, Ontario, and Nova Scotia.[1]

Exchange of notes at Ottawa June 15, 1955.

Entered into force June 15, 1955.

6 UST 6051; TIAS 3453; 268 UNTS 101.

Agreement relating to the construction of a petroleum products pipeline between the United States Air Force dock at St. John's, Newfoundland, and Pepperrell Air Force Base, Newfoundland, with annex.

Exchange of notes at Ottawa September 22, 1955.

Entered into force September 22, 1955.

6 UST 3899; TIAS 3392; 256 UNTS 227.

Agreement providing for the establishment of a Canada-United States Committee on Joint Defense.

Exchange of notes at Ottawa August 29 and September 2, 1958.

Entered into force September 2, 1958.

9 UST 1159; TIAS 4098; 335 UNTS 249.

Agreement relating to communications facilities at Cape Dyer, Baffin Island to support the Greenland extension of the distant early warning system.

Exchange of notes at Ottawa April 13, 1959.

Entered into force April 13, 1959, operative January 15, 1959.

10 UST 739; TIAS 4208; 342 UNTS 43.

Agreement relating to the establishment, maintenance and operation of short range tactical air navigation (TACAN) facilities in Canada, with annex.

Exchange of notes at Ottawa May 1, 1959.

Entered into force May 1, 1959.

10 UST 790; TIAS 4218; 343 UNTS 27.

Amendment

September 19 and 23, 1961 (12 UST 1357; TIAS 4856; 421 UNTS 79).

Agreement relating to the establishment of a ballistic missile early warning system.

Exchange of notes at Ottawa July 13, 1959.

Entered into force July 13, 1959.

10 UST 1260; TIAS 4264; 353 UNTS 237.

Agreement relating to the extension and strengthening of the continental air defense system (CADIN).

Exchange of notes at Ottawa September 27, 1961.

Entered into force September 27, 1961.

12 UST 1375; TIAS 4859; 421 UNTS 85.

Amendments

May 6, 1964 (15 UST 427; TIAS 5574; 524 UNTS 324).

November 24, 1965 (16 UST 1768; TIAS 5907; 573 UNTS 330).

Agreement concerning the establishment, operation and maintenance of certain ground-to-air communications facilities in northern Canada, with annex.

Exchange of notes at Ottawa December 1, 1965.

Entered into force December 1, 1965.

16 UST 1789; TIAS 5911; 574 UNTS 37.

Agreement relating to the establishment of a ferry service between North Sydney, Nova Scotia and Argentia, Newfoundland, with annex.

Exchange of notes at Washington June 6 and 10, 1966.

Entered into force June 10, 1966.

17 UST 792; TIAS 6035; 639 UNTS 13.

Agreement relating to the winter maintenance of the Haines Road.

Exchange of notes at Ottawa May 10 and June 23, 1967.

Entered into force June 23, 1967.

18 UST 1244; TIAS 6274; 685 UNTS 410.

Agreement relating to the use of certain facilities at the United States Air Force Pinetree radar site at Hopedale, Labrador.

Exchange of notes at Ottawa June 11, September 19, 1969 and February 24, 1970.

Entered into force February 24, 1970.

21 UST 596; TIAS 6844; 740 UNTS 241.

Agreement relating to the transfer of the Redcliff site to Canada.

Exchange of notes at Ottawa May 10, 1971.

Entered into force May 10, 1971.

22 UST 1778; TIAS 7217.

Agreement relating to new financial arrangements to govern the operation and maintenance of Pinetree radar stations in Canada with annex.

Exchange of notes at Ottawa August 16, 1971.

Entered into force August 16, 1971; operative August 1, 1971.

22 UST 1529; TIAS 7173; 807 UNTS 19.

Lease of three radar sets (AN/PPS-15) to Canada, with general provisions.

Signed at Washington November 18, 1975.

Entered into force November 18, 1975.

27 UST 2375; TIAS 8317; 1054 UNTS 319.

Agreement relating to the installation, operation, and maintenance of a circuit for narrative record traffic between the defense agencies.

Signed at Ottawa and at Washington January 7 and 19, 1976.

Entered into force January 19, 1976.

27 UST 1971; TIAS 8293.

Agreement relating to the continued operation and maintenance of the torpedo test range in the Strait of Georgia and the installation and utilization of an advanced underwater acoustic measurement system at Jervis Inlet, with annex.

Exchange of notes at Ottawa January 13 and April 14, 1976.

Entered into force April 14, 1976.

27 UST 3723; TIAS 8386.

Extension

June 3 and 17, 1986 (TIAS 11368; 2194 UNTS 298).

Agreement relating to the purchase by Canada of eighteen Lockheed P-3 long-range patrol aircraft, with related notes.

Exchange of letters at Washington July 6 and 7, 1976.

Entered into force July 7, 1976.

27 UST 3732; TIAS 8388.

Agreement relating to the continued use of facilities at Goose Bay airport by the United States, with annex.

Exchange of notes at Ottawa November 10 and 24, 1976.

Entered into force November 24, 1976; effective October 1, 1976.

27 UST 4322; TIAS 8454.

Memorandum of understanding concerning region operations control center.

Signed at Ottawa and Washington March 5 and April 11, 1977.

Entered into force April 11, 1977.

29 UST 1075; TIAS 8869.

Agreement relating to performance evaluation of a variable depth sonar system in conjunction with a high speed surface vessel, with annexes (Project Hytow).

Signed at Washington and Ottawa September 12 and October 12, 1977.

Entered into force October 12, 1977.

29 UST 5561; TIAS 9129.

Undertaking relating to the examination and audit of certain subcontracts awarded to Pratt and Whitney of Canada, with memorandum of understanding.

Exchange of notes at Washington October 13 and 28, 1977.

Entered into force October 28, 1977.

29 UST 2852; TIAS 8980.

Memorandum of understanding concerning NAVSTAR global positioning system, with annex.

Signed at Washington and Ottawa August 7 and October 5, 1978.

Entered into force October 5, 1978.

31 UST 5857; TIAS 9689; 1221 UNTS 23.

Memorandum of understanding pertaining to coordination of cooperative research and development

Signed February 1, 1979.

Entered into force February 1, 1979.

30 UST 3595; TIAS 9414; 1230 UNTS 349.

Letter of agreement concerning narrative record telecommunication interface arrangements, with appendices.

Signed at Ottawa and Washington September 15 and October 22, 1981.

Entered into force October 22, 1981.

33 UST 3852; TIAS 10265; 1543 UNTS 125.

Agreement concerning the test and evaluation of United States defense weapons systems in Canada.

Exchange of notes at Washington February 10, 1983.

Entered into force February 10, 1983.

TIAS 10659; 1469 UNTS 275.

Mutual logistical support agreement, with annexes.

Signed at Stuttgart February 11, 1983.

Entered into force February 11, 1983.

TIAS 10658; 2001 UNTS 17.

Master data exchange arrangement.

Signed at Brussels April 10, 1984.

Entered into force April 10, 1984.

TIAS

Memorandum of understanding on the exchange of service personnel between the United States Marine Corps and Canadian Forces.

Signed at Washington September 19, 1984.

Entered into force September 19, 1984.

TIAS 11135; 2126 UNTS 143.

Agreement regarding modernization of the North American Air Defense System, with memorandum of understanding.

Exchange of notes at Quebec March 18, 1985.

Entered into force March 18, 1985.

TIAS 12260.

Memorandum of understanding on reciprocal training of reserve officers between the Canadian Land Forces Command and Staff College and the U.S. Marine Corps Command and Staff College

Signed November 4, 1985.

Entered into force November 4, 1985.

TIAS 11321.

Memorandum of understanding on aviation cooperation.

Signed at Washington and Ottawa March 20 and April 9, 1987.

Entered into force April 9, 1987.

TIAS 11294.

Memorandum of understanding concerning the personnel exchange program between the United States Navy and the Canadian Forces, with appendix.

Signed at Washington May 27 and June 9, 1988.

Entered into force June 9, 1988.

NP

Memorandum of understanding concerning the exchange of defense professional personnel, with annexes.

Signed at Ottawa and Alexandria September 13 and October 2, 1991.

Entered into force October 2, 1991.

TIAS

Amendment

September 24 and October 1, 2004.

Agreement concerning cooperative testing and evaluation of defense systems.

Exchange of notes at Washington February 10, 1993.

Entered into force February 10, 1993.

TIAS 12262; 1914 UNTS 193.

Memorandum of understanding concerning defense communications service, with annex and appendices.

Signed at Ottawa and Arlington September 9 and October 13, 1993.

Entered into force October 13, 1993.

TIAS 12263.

Agreement concerning the establishment of certain mutual defense commitments.

Exchange of notes at Washington and Ottawa March 4 and August 19, 1994.

Entered into force August 19, 1994.

TIAS 12526; 2028 UNTS 97.

Memorandum of understanding concerning the measures to be taken for the transfer, security and safeguarding of technical information and equipment to the Department of National Defence for use in the Canadian arctic subsurface surveillance system.

Signed at Washington and Ottawa May 31 and September 23, 1994.

Entered into force September 23, 1994.

TIAS 12264.

Memorandum of understanding concerning counterterrorism research and development, with annex.

Signed at Washington and Ottawa June 12 and 23, 1995.

Entered into force June 23, 1995.

TIAS

Amendment

May 27 and June 23, 2004.

Agreement regarding the organization and operations of the North American Aerospace Defense Command (NORAD).

Exchange of notes at Washington March 28, 1996.

Entered into force March 28, 1996; effective May 12, 1996.

TIAS 12740; 2030 UNTS 111.

Amendment and extension

June 16, 2000 (TIAS 12740).

August 5, 2004.

Memorandum of understanding for technology research and development projects, with annex.

Signed at Washington and Ottawa July 18 and August 29, 1996.

Entered into force August 29, 1996.

TIAS 12797.

Agreement on a full and final settlement of all claims for costs of environmental clean-up at former U.S. military installations in Canada.

Exchange of notes at Washington October 7 and 9, 1996.

Entered into force October 9, 1996.

TIAS 12806; 2025 UNTS 341.

Memorandum of understanding concerning mutual support, with annex.

Signed at Norfolk and Ottawa October 21, 1999.

Entered into force October 21, 1999.

TIAS

Memorandum of understanding concerning development, documentation, production and initial fielding of military satellite communications.

Signed at Brussels November 16, 1999.

Entered into force November 16, 1999.

TIAS

Agreement for the loan of light armoured vehicles (LAV IIIs) for concept evaluation.

Signed at Washington and Ottawa February 15 and 17, 2000.

Entered into force February 17, 2000.

TIAS

Amendments

January 28 and 30, 2002.

August 27 and 31, 2004.

March 31 and April 11, 2005.

October 26 and November 4, 2005.

Agreement concerning the cooperative framework for system development and demonstration of the joint strike fighter.

Signed at Washington February 7, 2002.

Entered into force February 7, 2002.

TIAS

Memorandum of understanding for Test and Evaluation Program (TEP) cooperation.

Signed at Las Vegas September 10, 2002.

Entered into force September 10, 2002.

TIAS

Agreement regarding cooperation in broadening bi-national defense arrangements for North American security.

Exchange of notes at Ottawa and Washington December 5, 2002.

Entered into force December 5, 2002.

TIAS

Extension

July 28 and November 29, 2004.

Project arrangement concerning improved ballistic protection.

Signed at Arlington and Ottawa December 20, 2002 and January 9, 2003.

Entered into force January 9, 2003.

TIAS

Memorandum of understanding regarding the assignment of a Canadian forces officer as a visiting faculty instructor at the United States Army War College, with appendix.

Signed at Washington June 11 and 20, 2003.

Entered into force June 20, 2003.

TIAS

Agreement on the North American Aerospace Defense Command.

Signed at Ottawa April 28, 2006.

Entered into force May 12, 2006.

TIAS

NOTES

1 Provisions are terminated to the extent that they are inconsistent with the agreement of August 16, 1971 (TIAS 7173). See also agreements of June 13, 1955 (TIAS 3452), June 15, 1955 (TIAS 3453) and September 27, 1961 (TIAS 4859).

2 See also agreements of April 13, 1959 (TIAS 4208) and July 13, 1959 (TIAS 4264).

ECONOMIC AND TECHNICAL COOPERATION

Agreement relating to post-war economic settlements.

Exchange of notes at Washington November 30, 1942.

Entered into force November 30, 1942.

56 Stat. 1815; EAS 287; 6 Bevans 292; 119 UNTS 305.

EDUCATION

Agreement for the establishment of a binational educational exchange foundation.

Signed at Washington November 15, 1999.

Entered into force November 15, 1999.

TIAS

Amendment

July 29, 2003.

EMBASSY SITES

Agreement concerning construction of new chanceries in Washington and Ottawa.

Exchange of notes at Washington May 13 and October 2, 1985.

Entered into force October 2, 1985.

TIAS 11328.

EMPLOYMENT

See also LABOR; SOCIAL SECURITY

Arrangement relating to the employment of dependents of government employees.

Exchange of notes at Washington June 4 and 12, 1980.

Entered into force June 12, 1980.

TIAS 10693; 2005 UNTS 95.

Amendment

October 3 and November 13, 1997.

EXTRADITION

Treaty on extradition, as amended by exchange of notes of June 28 and July 9, 1974.[1]

Signed at Washington December 3, 1971.

Entered into force March 22, 1976.

27 UST 983; TIAS 8237.

Amendments

January 11, 1988 (1853 UNTS 407).

January 12, 2001.

NOTE

1 Applicable to all territories.

FINANCE

Agreement relating to exemptions from exchange control measures.

Exchange of notes at Ottawa June 18, 1940.

Entered into force June 18, 1940.

54 Stat. 2317; EAS 174; 6 Bevans 182; 203 LNTS 41.

FIRE PROTECTION

Agreement relating to the participation of the Provinces of New Brunswick and Quebec in the northeastern interstate forest fire protection compact.

Exchange of notes at Washington January 29, 1970.

Entered into force January 29, 1970.

21 UST 415; TIAS 6825; 753 UNTS 43.

Agreement concerning cooperation in the detection and suppression of forest fires along the boundary between the Yukon Territory and Alaska with memorandum of agreement.

Exchange of notes at Washington June 1, 1971.

Entered into force June 1, 1971.

22 UST 721; TIAS 7132; 793 UNTS 77.

Arrangement on mutual assistance in fighting forest fires.

Exchange of notes at Ottawa May 4 and 7, 1982.

Entered into force May 7, 1982.

34 UST 1557; TIAS 10436.

FISHERIES

Agreement adopting, with certain modifications, the rules and method of procedure recommended in the award of September 7, 1910, of the North Atlantic Coast Fisheries Arbitration.

Signed at Washington July 20, 1912.

Entered into force November 15, 1912.

37 Stat. 1634; TS 572; 12 Bevans 357.

Convention for the extension to halibut fishing vessels of port privileges on the Pacific Coasts of the United States of America and Canada.

Signed at Ottawa March 24, 1950.

Entered into force July 13, 1950.

1 UST 536; TIAS 2096; 200 UNTS 211.

Convention for the preservation of the halibut fishery of the Northern Pacific Ocean and Bering Sea.

Signed at Ottawa March 2, 1953.

Entered into force October 28, 1953.

5 UST 5; TIAS 2900; 222 UNTS 77.

Amendment

March 29, 1979 (32 UST 2483; TIAS 9855).

Convention on Great Lakes fisheries.

Signed at Washington September 10, 1954.

Entered into force October 11, 1955.

6 UST 2836; TIAS 3326; 238 UNTS 97.

Amendment

April 5, 1966 and May 19, 1967 (18 UST 1402; TIAS 6297).

Treaty on Pacific Coast albacore tuna vessels and port privileges, with annexes.

Signed at Washington May 26, 1981.

Entered into force July 29, 1981.

33 UST 615; TIAS 10057; 1274 UNTS 247.

Amendments

October 3 and 9, 1997.

August 21 and September 10, 2002.

Treaty concerning Pacific salmon, with annexes and memorandum of understanding.

Signed at Ottawa January 28, 1985.

Entered into force March 18, 1985.

TIAS 11091; 1469 UNTS 357.

Amendments

July 24 and August 12, 1998.

June 30, 1999.

December 4, 2002.

April 26 and June 17, 2005.

June 16, 2006.

Agreement on fisheries enforcement.

Signed at Ottawa September 26, 1990.

Entered into force December 16, 1991.

TIAS 11753.

Agreement on the establishment of a mediation procedure regarding the Pacific Salmon Treaty.

Signed at Montreal Sepember 11, 1995.

Entered into force September 11, 1995.

TIAS 12689; 2029 UNTS 307.

HEALTH AND SANITATION

Arrangement concerning quarantine inspection of vessels entering Puget Sound and waters adjacent thereto or the Great Lakes via the St. Lawrence River.

Exchange of notes at Ottawa October 10 and 23, 1929.

Entered into force October 23, 1929.

47 Stat. 2573; EAS 1; 6 Bevans 35; 96 LNTS 167.

Memorandum of understanding on the monitoring of food, beverage and sanitary services provided on common carriers operating between the United States and Canada.

Signed at Ottawa and at Washington August 20 and September 8, 1975.

Entered into force September 8, 1975.

28 UST 884; TIAS 8485.

HIGHWAYS

Agreement providing for the construction of a military highway to Alaska.

Exchange of notes at Ottawa March 17 and 18, 1942.

Entered into force March 18, 1942.

56 Stat. 1458; EAS 246; 6 Bevans 261; 101 UNTS 205.

Agreement relating to the southern terminus of the Alaska Highway.

Exchange of notes at Ottawa May 4 and 9, 1942.

Entered into force May 9, 1942.

57 Stat. 1373; EAS 380; 6 Bevans 274; 101 UNTS 215.

Agreement relating to the construction of flight strips along the Alaska Highway.

Exchange of notes at Ottawa August 26 and September 10, 1942.

Entered into force September 10, 1942.

57 Stat. 1375; EAS 381; 6 Bevans 282; 101 UNTS 221.

Agreement relating to the construction of the Haines-Champagne section of the Alaska Highway.

Exchange of notes at Ottawa November 28 and December 7, 1942.

Entered into force December 7, 1942.

57 Stat. 1377; EAS 382; 6 Bevans 295; 101 UNTS 227.

Agreement relating to access to the Alaska Highway.

Exchange of notes at Ottawa April 10, 1943.

Entered into force April 10, 1943.

57 Stat. 1274; EAS 362; 6 Bevans 319; 21 UNTS 237.

Agreement relating to the designation of the highway from Dawson Creek, British Columbia, to Fairbanks, Alaska, as the "Alaska Highway".

Exchange of notes at Washington July 19, 1943.

Entered into force July 19, 1943.

57 Stat. 1023; EAS 331; 6 Bevans 324; 29 UNTS 289.

Agreement relating to cooperation in reconstruction of Canadian portions of the Alaska Highway.

Exchange of notes at Ottawa January 11 and February 11, 1977.

Entered into force February 11, 1977.

28 UST 5303; TIAS 8631; 1087 UNTS 3.

HOUSING

Memorandum of understanding on cooperation in the field of housing and urban affairs.

Signed at Ottawa June 28, 1977.

Entered into force June 28, 1977.

29 UST 2363; TIAS 8942.

JUDICIAL PROCEDURE

Arrangement relating to the admission to practice before patent offices.

Exchange of notes at Washington December 3 and 28, 1937, and January 24, 1938; operative January 1, 1938.

52 Stat. 1475; EAS 118; 6 Bevans 97; 187 LNTS 27.

Procedures for mutual assistance in the administration of justice in connection with the Boeing Company matter.

Signed at Washington March 15, 1977.

Entered into force March 15, 1977.

28 UST 2463; TIAS 8567.

Treaty on mutual legal assistance in criminal matters, with annex.

Signed at Quebec March 18, 1985.

Entered into force January 24, 1990.

TIAS

Agreement regarding the sharing of forfeited assets and equivalent funds.

Signed at Ottawa March 22, 1995.

Entered into force March 22, 1995.

TIAS 12618; 2028 UNTS 335.

LABOR

Agreement relating to unemployment insurance benefits.

Exchange of notes at Ottawa March 6 and 12, 1942.

Entered into force April 12, 1942.

56 Stat. 1451; EAS 244; 6 Bevans 257; 119 UNTS 295.

Amendments

July 31 and September 11, 1951
(3 UST 2812; TIAS 2452; 206 UNTS 311).

October 29, 1984 and June 21, 1985
(TIAS 11334).

Agreement relating to workmen's compensation and unemployment insurance in connection with construction projects in Canada.

Exchange of notes at Ottawa November 2 and 4, 1942.

Entered into force November 4, 1942.

56 Stat. 1770; EAS 279; 6 Bevans 284; 24 UNTS 217.

Agreement relating to the extension of the Canadian Unemployment Insurance Act to Canadian employees of the United States Armed Services in Canada.

Exchange of notes at Washington December 20, 1955 and April 23, 1956.

Entered into force April 23, 1956.

8 UST 1879; TIAS 3933; 300 UNTS 29.

MAPPING

Memorandum of understanding concerning global geospatial information and services cooperation.

Signed at Ottawa and Bethesda January 11 and 19, 2000.

Entered into force January 19, 2000.

NP

MARITIME MATTERS

See also NAVAL VESSELS

Treaty providing for reciprocal rights for United States and Canada in matters of conveyance of prisoners and wrecking and salvage.

Signed at Washington May 18, 1908.

Entered into force June 30, 1908.

35 Stat. 2035; TS 502; 12 Bevans 314.

Load line convention.

Signed at Washington December 9, 1933.

Entered into force July 26, 1934.

49 Stat. 2685; TS 869; 6 Bevans 54; 152 LNTS 39.

Agreement relating to reciprocal recognition of load line regulations for vessels engaged in international voyages on the Great Lakes.

Exchanges of notes at Ottawa April 29, August 24, and October 22, 1938, September 2 and October 18, 1939, and January 10 and March 4, 1940.

Entered into force March 4, 1940.

54 Stat. 2300; EAS 172; 6 Bevans 171; 202 LNTS 429.

Search and rescue agreement, with attachment.

Signed at Ottawa and Washington September 12 and October 25, 1974.

Entered into force October 25, 1974.

TIAS 11963.

Memorandum of understanding concerning reciprocal recognition of Great Lakes load lines.

Signed at Ottawa November 21, 1977.

Entered into force November 21, 1977.

29 UST 4948; TIAS 9088; 1230 UNTS 345.

Agreement for a cooperative vessel traffic management system for the Juan de Fuca region, with annex.

Exchange of notes at Ottawa December 19, 1979.

Entered into force December 19, 1979.

32 UST 377; TIAS 9706; 1221 UNTS 67.

Memorandum of understanding concerning cooperation in marine transportation technology and systems research and development.

Signed at Ottawa June 18, 1981.

Entered into force June 18, 1981.

33 UST 2082; TIAS 10172; 1529 UNTS 483.

METEOROLOGICAL RESEARCH

Agreement relating to the establishment of a cooperative meteorological rocket project at Cold Lake, Alberta.

Exchange of notes at Ottawa September 29 and October 6, 1966.

Entered into force October 6, 1966.

17 UST 1832; TIAS 6128; 675 UNTS 63.

Amendment

February 13 and April 24, 1969
(20 UST 720; TIAS 6682; 714 UNTS 326).

NAVAL VESSELS

See also MARITIME MATTERS

Agreement relating to naval forces on the American Lakes (Rush-Bagot Agreement).

Exchange of notes at Washington April 28 and 29, 1817.

Entered into force April 29, 1817.

8 Stat. 231; TS 110 1/2; 12 Bevans 54.

Agreement relating to the construction of naval vessels on the Great Lakes (interpretation of the Rush-Bagot Agreement).

Exchange of notes at Ottawa June 9 and 10, 1939.

Entered into force June 10, 1939.

61 Stat. 4069; TIAS 1836; 6 Bevans 149; 149 UNTS 332.

Agreement relating to the armament of naval vessels to be incapable of immediate use (interpretation of the Rush-Bagot Agreement).

Exchange of notes at Ottawa October 30 and November 2, 1940.

Entered into force November 2, 1940.

61 Stat. 4077; TIAS 1836; 6 Bevans 196; 149 UNTS 350.

Agreement relating to naval vessels for training naval reserve personnel (interpretation of the Rush-Bagot Agreement).

Exchange of notes at Washington November 18 and December 6, 1946.

Entered into force December 6, 1946.

61 Stat. 4082; TIAS 1836; 6 Bevans 426; 149 UNTS 3.

NAVIGATION

Agreement relating to the transfer to Canada of Loran stations at Port aux Basques, Battle Harbour, and Bonavista.

Exchange of notes at Ottawa June 26 and 30, 1953.

Entered into force June 30, 1953.

4 UST 2174; TIAS 2865; 215 UNTS 103.

Agreement relating to the construction and operation of a Loran station at Cape Christian, Baffin Island.

Exchange of notes at Ottawa May 1 and 3, 1954.

Entered into force May 3, 1954.

5 UST 1459; TIAS 3019; 221 UNTS 339.

Agreement relating to the loan of certain equipment for use in Canadian Loran-A stations.

Exchange of notes at Ottawa June 7 and 8, 1965.

Entered into force June 8, 1965.

16 UST 824; TIAS 5817; 546 UNTS 201.

Amendments

April 19 and July 28, 1966 (17 UST 1140; TIAS 6072; 601 UNTS 366).

July 27 and October 25, 1967 (18 UST 2933; TIAS 6386; 701 UNTS 117).

Agreement relating to the establishment of a Loran-A station at Gray Point, British Columbia.

Exchange of notes at Ottawa April 8, 1971.

Entered into force April 8, 1971.

22 UST 531; TIAS 7095; 792 UNTS 315.

Agreement relating to the construction, operation and maintenance of a Loran-C station in the vicinity of Williams Lake, British Columbia, with annex.

Exchange of notes at Ottawa May 28 and June 3, 1976.

Entered into force June 3, 1976.

27 UST 2611; TIAS 8331; 1054 UNTS 327.

Amendment

May 3 and 8, 1991 (TIAS 11836; 1853 UNTS 417).

Agreement relating to the establishment of an experimental Loran-C power chain, with annex.

Exchange of notes at Washington March 29, 1977.

Entered into force March 29, 1977; effective August 1, 1975.

28 UST 2431; TIAS 8560.

Extension

October 23 and December 5, 1980 (32 UST 4229; TIAS 9944; 1265 UNTS 386).

Agreement concerning four OMEGA navigation system monitoring stations in Canada.

Exchange of notes at Ottawa July 26 and December 20, 1978.

Entered into force December 20, 1978.

30 UST 2840; TIAS 9365; 1180 UNTS 69.

Agreement relating to the construction, operation and maintenance of a Loran-C station in British Columbia.

Exchange of notes at Ottawa March 19 and 29, 1979.

Entered into force March 29, 1979.

30 UST 4049; TIAS 9446; 1171 UNTS 35.

Agreement relating to coordination between the United States and Canadian Coast Guards of icebreaking operations in the Great Lakes and St. Lawrence Seaway system.

Exchange of notes at Ottawa October 28 and December 5, 1980.

Entered into force December 5, 1980.

32 UST 4334; TIAS 9950; 1266 UNTS 87.

Extension

December 5, 2005.

Agreement for the establishment, operation and maintenance of two Loran-C chains for the Canadian east coast and the Labrador sea, with annex.

Exchange of notes at Ottawa March 30 and May 3, 1984.

Entered into force May 3, 1984.

TIAS 11146; 1469 UNTS 291.

PACIFIC SETTLEMENT OF DISPUTES

See also BOUNDARIES

Treaty amending in their application to Canada certain provisions of the treaty for the advancement of peace between the United States and the United Kingdom signed at Washington September 15, 1914.

Signed at Washington September 6, 1940.

Entered into force August 13, 1941.

55 Stat. 1214; TS 975; 6 Bevans 190.

PATENTS

Agreement relating to the mutual interchange of patent rights in connection with RDX and other explosives.

Exchange of notes at Washington September 3 and 27, 1946.

Entered into force September 27, 1946.

61 Stat. 2949; TIAS 1628; 6 Bevans 419; 21 UNTS 3.

PIPELINES

Agreement concerning transit pipelines.

Signed at Washington January 28, 1977.

Entered into force October 1, 1977.

28 UST 7449; TIAS 8720.

Agreement on principles applicable to a northern natural gas pipeline, with annexes.

Signed at Ottawa September 20, 1977.

Entered into force September 20, 1977 with respect to certain provisions; July 24, 1978 with respect to remaining provisions.

29 UST 3581; TIAS 9030; 1230 UNTS 311.

Amendment

June 6, 1978 (29 UST 3621; TIAS 9030; 1230 UNTS 340).

POLLUTION

Agreement relating to the establishment of a Canada-United States committee on water quality in the St. John River and its tributary rivers and streams which cross the Canada-United States boundary, with annex.

Exchange of notes at Ottawa September 21, 1972.

Entered into force September 21, 1972.

23 UST 2813; TIAS 7470.

Amendment

February 22, 1984 (35 UST 4426; TIAS 10947).

Agreement relating to the establishment of joint pollution contingency plans for spills of oil and other noxious substances.

Exchange of notes at Ottawa June 19, 1974.

Entered into force June 19, 1974.

25 UST 1280; TIAS 7861.

Agreement on Great Lakes water quality, 1978, with annexes and terms of reference.

Signed at Ottawa November 22, 1978.

Entered into force November 22, 1978.

30 UST 1383; TIAS 9257; 1153 UNTS 187.

Amendments

October 16, 1983 (35 UST 2370; TIAS 10798).

November 18, 1987 (TIAS 11551; 2185 UNTS 504).

Memorandum of intent concerning transboundary air pollution, with annex.

Signed at Washington August 5, 1980.

Entered into force August 5, 1980.

32 UST 2521; TIAS 9856; 1274 UNTS 235.

Memorandum of understanding regarding accidental and unauthorized discharges of pollutants along the inland boundary, with appendix.

Signed at Ottawa October 17, 1985.

Entered into force October 17, 1985.

TIAS 11170; 2126 UNTS 161.

Agreement concerning the transboundary movement of hazardous waste.

Signed at Ottawa October 28, 1986.

Entered into force November 8, 1986.

TIAS 11099; 2120 UNTS 97.

Amendment

November 4 and 25, 1992.

Agreement on air quality, with annexes.

Signed at Ottawa March 13, 1991.

Entered into force March 13, 1991.

TIAS

Amendment

December 7, 2000.

POSTAL MATTERS

Money order agreement.

Signed at Washington September 30 and at Ottawa October 3, 1901; operative July 1, 1901.

NP

International express mail agreement, with detailed regulations.

Signed at Ottawa and Washington July 18, 23 and August 14, 1979.

Entered into force August 14, 1979; effective August 1, 1979.

31 UST 5745; TIAS 9684; 1221 UNTS 43.

Postal convention, with detailed regulations.

Signed at Ottawa and Washington September 10 and 14, 1981.

Entered into force January 1, 1982.

33 UST 3810; TIAS 10263; 1541 UNTS 135.

PRISONER TRANSFER

See also under MARITIME MATTERS

Treaty on the execution of penal sentences.

Signed at Washington March 2, 1977.

Entered into force July 19, 1978.

30 UST 6263; TIAS 9552.

PRIVILEGES AND IMMUNITIES

Agreement concerning the privileges and immunities of members of the administrative and technical staffs of the Embassy of Canada in the United States and the Embassy of the United States in Canada.

Exchange of notes at Ottawa August 26 and September 2, 1993.

Entered into force September 21, 1993.

TIAS 12506.

PROPERTY

See also SURPLUS PROPERTY

Convention between the United States and the United Kingdom relating to tenure and disposition of real and personal property.

Signed at Washington March 2, 1899; applicable to Canada June 17, 1922.

31 Stat. 1939; TS 146; 12 Bevans 246.

Supplementary convention providing for the accession of the Dominion of Canada to the real and personal property convention of March 2, 1899.

Signed at Washington October 21, 1921.

Entered into force June 17, 1922.

42 Stat. 2147; TS 663; 12 Bevans 390; 12 LNTS 425.

REFUGEES

Agreement for cooperation in the examination of refugee status claims from nationals of third countries.

Signed at Washington December 5, 2002.

Entered into force December 29, 2004.

TIAS

REMOTE SENSING

Agreement on cooperation in the Boreal Ecosystem-Atmosphere Study (BOREAS).

Signed at Washington April 18, 1994.

Entered into force April 18, 1994.

TIAS 12538; 2026 UNTS 371.

Agreement concerning the operation of commercial remote sensing satellite systems, with annexes.

Signed at Washington June 16, 2000.

Entered into force June 16, 2000.

TIAS

SANCTIONS

Agreement confirming acceptance by Canada of the terms of the memorandum of understanding of August 1, 1994, for a multinational observer group to monitor and advise on Haiti.

Exchange of notes at Washington August 29, 1994.

Entered into force August 29, 1994.

TIAS

SATELLITES

Agreement on cooperation in inter-continental testing in connection with experimental communications satellites.

Exchange of notes at Washington August 13 and 23, 1963.

Entered into force August 23, 1963.

14 UST 1701; TIAS 5474; 494 UNTS 13.

Agreement regarding an experimental communications technology satellite project with memorandum of understanding.

Exchange of notes at Washington April 21 and 27, 1971.

Entered into force April 27, 1971.

22 UST 713; TIAS 7131.

Agreement concerning cooperation on the RADARSAT Project.

Exchange of notes at Washington November 12, 1991.

Entered into force November 12, 1991.

TIAS 12206; 1883 UNTS 467.

Amendment

October 24, 2000.

Agreement for cooperation in the CloudSat mission

Signed September 14, 2005.

Entered into force September 14, 2005.

TIAS

SCIENTIFIC COOPERATION

Memorandum of understanding concerning the furnishing of balloon launching and associated services.

Signed at Washington and Ottawa August 26 and September 12, 1983.

Entered into force September 12, 1983.

35 UST 2392; TIAS 10800.

Agreement regarding allocation of intellectual property rights, interests and royalties for intellectual property created or furnished under certain scientific and technological cooperative research activities, with attachment.

Exchange of notes at Ottawa February 4, 1997.

Entered into force February 4, 1997.

TIAS 12830.

Agreement for cooperation in science and technology for critical infrastructure protection and border security.

Signed at Washington June 1, 2004.

Entered into force June 1, 2004.

TIAS

SEABEDS

Agreement relating to the agreement of August 14, 1987 on the resolution of practical problems with respect to deep seabed mining areas.[1]

Exchange of notes at Ottawa August 14, 1987.

Entered into force August 14, 1987.

TIAS 11438.

NOTE

1 Parties to the multilateral agreement of August 14, 1987 are Belgium, Canada, Italy, Netherlands and Union of Soviet Socialist Republics.

SEWAGE DISPOSAL SYSTEM

Agreement relating to the construction of a sewage line from Dunseith, North Dakota to Boissevain, Manitoba.

Exchange of notes at Ottawa January 13, April 22 and June 9, 1966.

Entered into force June 9, 1966.

17 UST 810; TIAS 6037; 580 UNTS 263.

SHELLFISH

Agreement providing for cooperative efforts to be directed toward sanitary control of the shellfish industry.

Exchange of notes at Washington March 4 and April 30, 1948.

Entered into force April 30, 1948.

62 Stat. 1898; TIAS 1747; 6 Bevans 472; 77 UNTS 191.

SMUGGLING

Convention to suppress smuggling.

Signed at Washington June 6, 1924.

Entered into force July 27, 1925.

44 Stat. 2097; TS 718; 6 Bevans 1; 43 LNTS 225.

SOCIAL SECURITY

Agreement relating to Canada Pension Plan.

Signed at Ottawa May 5, 1967.

Entered into force May 5, 1967; effective January 1, 1967.

18 UST 486; TIAS 6254; 685 UNTS 245.

Amendment

October 12 and December 19, 1983 (35 UST 3521; TIAS 10864).

Agreement with respect to social security.[1]

Signed at Ottawa March 11, 1981.

Entered into force August 1, 1984.

35 UST 3403; TIAS 10863; 1469 UNTS 249.

Administrative arrangement for the implementation of the agreement of March 11, 1981 with respect to social security.

Signed at Washington May 22, 1981.

Entered into force August 1, 1984.

35 UST 3403; TIAS 10863.

Supplementary agreement amending the agreement of March 11, 1981 and the administrative arrangement of May 22, 1981 with respect to social security.

Signed at Ottawa May 10, 1983.

Entered into force August 1, 1984.

35 UST 3403; TIAS 10863; 1469 UNTS 271.

Second supplementary agreement amending the agreement of March 11, 1981, as amended, with respect to social security.

Signed at Ottawa May 28, 1996.

Entered into force October 1, 1997.

TIAS 12759; 2030 UNTS 283.

NOTE

1 See also understanding and administrative arrangement of March 30, 1983, with the Government of Quebec (TIAS 10863).

SPACE COOPERATION

Agreement relating to a cooperative program concerning the development and procurement of a space shuttle attached remote manipulator system.

Exchange of notes at Washington June 23, 1976.

Entered into force June 23, 1976.

27 UST 3801; TIAS 8400; 1059 UNTS 81.

Memorandum of understanding for a cooperative program concerning design (Phase B) of a permanently manned space station.

Signed at Ottawa April 16, 1985.

Entered into force April 16, 1985.

TIAS 11180; 2130 UNTS 217.

Memorandum of understanding concerning cooperation in the flight of the Canadian measurements of pollution in the troposphere (MOPITT) instrument on the NASA polar orbiting platform and related support for an international earth observing system, with appendix.

Signed at Washington November 15, 1994.

Entered into force November 15, 1994.

TIAS

Memorandum of understanding on the Orbiter Space Vision System.

Signed at Washington and St. Hubert November 9, 1995 and February 23, 1996.

Entered into force February 23, 1996.

TIAS 12726.

Agreement concerning the training of mission specialists for space shuttle flights, with implementing agreement.

Exchange of notes at Ottawa August 31, 1995 and May 17, 1996.

Entered into force May 17, 1996.

TIAS 12756; 2028 UNTS 133.

Agreement concerning cooperation on the Canadian Microgravity Isolation Mount, with attachment.

Exchange of notes at Ottawa July 31, 1997.

Entered into force July 31, 1997.

TIAS

Agreement concerning cooperation between the National Aeronautics and Space Administration of the United States of America and the Canadian Space Agency on the SciSat-1 Atmospheric Chemistry Experiment Mission, with memorandum of understanding.

Exchange of notes at Washington July 18, 2003.

Entered into force July 18, 2003.

TIAS

SURPLUS PROPERTY

Agreement relating to the disposal of government-owned surplus property.

Exchange of notes at Ottawa January 9, 1947.

Entered into force January 9, 1947.

61 Stat. 2738; TIAS 1603; 6 Bevans 428; 11 UNTS 341.

Agreement relating to the disposal of surplus United States property in Canada.

Exchange of notes at Ottawa August 28 and September 1, 1961.

Entered into force September 1, 1961.

12 UST 1228; TIAS 4841; 421 UNTS 199.

Amendment

December 21, 1983 and March 14, 1984 (TIAS 11063; 1466 UNTS 443).

TAXATION

Agreement relating to provincial and municipal taxation of United States defense projects in Canada.

Exchange of notes at Ottawa August 6 and 9, 1943.

Entered into force August 9, 1943.

57 Stat. 1065; EAS 339; 6 Bevans 326; 29 UNTS 295.

Agreement concerning the administration of income tax in Canada affecting employees within Canada of the United States Government who are subject to such tax.

Exchange of notes at Ottawa August 1 and September 17, 1973.

Entered into force September 17, 1973.

28 UST 1134; TIAS 8499.

Convention with respect to taxes on income and capital, with exchange of notes.

Signed at Washington September 26, 1980.

Entered into force August 16, 1984.[1]

TIAS 11087; 1469 UNTS 189.

Protocol amending the convention of September 26, 1980, with respect to taxes on income and on capital, with exchange of letters.

Signed at Ottawa June 14, 1983.

Entered into force August 16, 1984.

TIAS 11087; 2121 UNTS 364.

Second protocol amending the convention of September 26, 1980, with respect to taxes on income and on capital, as amended by the protocol of June 14, 1983.

Signed at Washington March 28, 1984.

Entered into force August 16, 1984.

TIAS 11087; 2121 UNTS 387.

Protocol amending the convention with respect to taxes on income and on capital of September 26, 1980, as amended by protocols of June 14, 1983 and March 28, 1984.

Signed at Washington March 17, 1995.

Entered into force November 9, 1995.

TIAS ; 2030 UNTS 236.

Protocol amending the convention with respect to taxes on income and on capital of September 26, 1980, as amended.

Signed at Ottawa July 29, 1997.

Entered into force December 16, 1997.

TIAS ; 2030 UNTS 276.

NOTE

1 With respect to estates of persons deceased prior to January 1, 1985, the convention of February 17, 1961 for the avoidance of double taxation and the prevention of fiscal evasion with respect to taxes on estates of deceased persons (13 UST 382; TIAS 4995; 445 UNTS 143) shall continue to have effect.

See also Article XXX of the 1980 convention for the continued effect of the convention and protocol of March 4, 1942 for the avoidance of double taxation and prevention of fiscal evasion in the case of income taxes (56 Stat. 1399; TS 983; 6 Bevans 244; 124 UNTS 271).

TELECOMMUNICATION

Arrangement governing radio communications between private experimental stations.

Exchanges of notes at Washington October 2 and December 29, 1928 and January 12, 1929; operative January 1, 1929.

TS 767-A; 6 Bevans 26; 102 LNTS 143.

Extension

April 23 and May 2 and 4, 1934 (48 Stat. 1876; EAS 62; 147 LNTS 338).

Agreement providing for the allocation of channels in the radio frequency band 88 to 108 megacycles for frequency modulation broadcasting.

Exchange of notes at Washington January 8 and October 15, 1947.

Entered into force October 15, 1947.

61 Stat. 3800; TIAS 1726; 6 Bevans 447; 82 UNTS 53.

Convention relating to the operation by citizens of either country of certain radio equipment or stations in the other country.

Signed at Ottawa February 8, 1951.

Entered into force May 15, 1952.

3 UST 3787; TIAS 2508; 207 UNTS 17.

Agreement concerning the coordination and use of radio frequencies above thirty megacycles per second, with annex.

Exchange of notes at Ottawa October 24, 1962.

Entered into force October 24, 1962.

13 UST 2418; TIAS 5205; 462 UNTS 68.

Amendments

June 16 and 24, 1965 (16 UST 923; TIAS 5833; 549 UNTS 300).

February 26 and April 7, 1982 (TIAS 10646).

November 2, 1993 and January 4, 1994 (TIAS 12529).

June 15 and 20, 2005.

Agreement for promotion of safety on the Great Lakes by means of radio, with technical regulations and exchange of notes of May 6, 1974.

Signed at Ottawa February 26, 1973.

Entered into force May 6, 1975.

25 UST 935; TIAS 7837.

Amendments

December 29, 1978 (30 UST 2523; TIAS 9352; 1170 UNTS 339).

December 22, 1987, August 10 and October 24, 1988.

Agreement relating to the AM broadcasting service in the medium frequency band, with annexes.

Signed at Ottawa January 17, 1984.

Entered into force January 17, 1984.

TIAS 11263.

TELEVISION

Agreement concerning the allotment and assignment of television broadcasting channels in areas adjacent to the border of the United States and Canada, with working arrangement.

Exchange of notes at Washington November 3, 1993 and January 5, 1994.

Entered into force January 5, 1994.

TIAS 12530.

TERRITORIAL ACQUISITION

Protocol of the cession of Horseshoe Reef.

Signed at London December 9, 1850.

Entered into force December 9, 1850.

18 Stat. 325; 12 Bevans 109.

TRADE AND COMMERCE

See also AMITY

Agreement supplementary to the general agreement on tariffs and trade, with exchange of notes.[1]

Signed at Geneva October 30, 1947.

Entered into force October 30, 1947; operative January 1, 1948.

61 Stat. 3695; TIAS 1702; 6 Bevans 451; 27 UNTS 19.

Agreement relating to the establishment of a Joint United States-Canadian Committee on Trade and Economic Affairs.

Exchange of notes at Washington November 12, 1953.

Entered into force November 12, 1953.

5 UST 314; TIAS 2922; 223 UNTS 139.

Amendments

October 2, 1961 (14 UST 1496; TIAS 5448; 470 UNTS 394).

September 17, 1963 (14 UST 1496; TIAS 5448).

Agreement relating to tariff duty on certain fish and fish products.

Signed at Geneva June 8, 1955.

Entered into force July 24, 1955.

6 UST 6231; TIAS 3474; 247 UNTS 163.

Agreement concerning automotive products.

Signed at Johnson City, Texas January 16, 1965.

Entered into force provisionally January 16, 1965 and definitively September 16, 1966.

17 UST 1372; TIAS 6093.

Interim agreement relating to the renegotiation of schedule XX (United States) to the general agreement on tariffs and trade.

Signed at Washington December 17, 1965.

Entered into force December 17, 1965.

16 UST 1789; TIAS 5912; 574 UNTS 49.

Amendment

June 30, 1967 (18 UST 1749; TIAS 6316; 693 UNTS 362).

Arrangement regarding levels of Canadian oil exports and the proposed looping of the Interprovincial Pipeline via Chicago.

Exchange of notes at Washington September 25, 1967.

Entered into force September 25, 1967.

20 UST 4108; TIAS 6806; 730 UNTS 317.

Agreement within the context of the multilateral trade negotiations relating to provincial liquor marketing practices and related letters of February 4 and March 20, 1980.

Exchange of letters at Geneva April 12, 1979.

Entered into force September 1, 1981.

TIAS

Arrangement within the context of the multilateral trade negotiations concerning cheeses and related letters of February 4 and March 20, 1980.

Signed at Geneva June 15, 1979.

Entered into force January 1, 1980.

32 UST 5292; TIAS 9980; 1266 UNTS 59.

Agreement within the context of the multilateral trade negotiations concerning canned turkey and related letters of February 4 and March 20, 1980.

Signed at Geneva July 10, 1979.

Entered into force September 1, 1981.

TIAS

Memorandum of understanding within the context of the multilateral trade negotiations regarding the staging of certain tariff reductions.

Signed at Washington September 17 and 21, 1979.

Entered into force September 21, 1979.

32 UST 5273; TIAS 9978; 1266 UNTS 69.

Amendment

October 9, 1979 (32 UST 5273; TIAS 9978; 1266 UNTS 77).

Understanding on safeguards relating to procedures under Article XIX of the general agreement on tariffs and trade, with related letter.

Exchange of letters at Washington and Ottawa February 17, 1984.

Entered into force February 17, 1984.

35 UST 4575; TIAS 10958; 2018 UNTS 593.

Memorandum of understanding on the exchange of import data, with annexes.

Signed at Montreal July 29, 1987.

Entered into force July 29, 1987.

TIAS

Free-trade agreement, with exchanges of letters.[2]

Signed at Ottawa, Washington and Palm Springs December 22 and 23, 1987 and January 2, 1988.

Entered into force January 1, 1989.

TIAS

Agreement regarding the application of their competition and deceptive marketing practices laws.

Signed at Washington and Ottawa August 1 and 3, 1995.

Entered into force August 3, 1995.

TIAS ; 2028 UNTS 135.

Agreement on the application of positive comity principles to the enforcement of their competition laws.

Signed at Washington October 5, 2004.

Entered into force October 5, 2004.

TIAS

NOTES

1 This agreement rendered inoperative, for such time as the United States and Canada are both contracting parties to the general agreement on tariffs and trade, the trade agreement of November 17, 1938 (53 Stat. 2348; EAS 149; 6 Bevans 117; 199 LNTS 91) and related agreement of March 18, 1947 (61 Stat. 3054; TIAS 1638; 6 Bevans 439; 117 UNTS 79).

2 This agreement is suspended, subject to certain transition arrangements with respect to dispute settlement proceedings under Chapters 18 and 19, for such time as the United States and Canada are parties to the North American Free Trade Agreement signed at Washington, Ottawa, and Mexico City December 8, 11, 14, and 17, 1992.

WEATHER MODIFICATION

Agreement relating to the exchange of information on weather modification activities.

Signed at Washington March 26, 1975.

Entered into force March 26, 1975.

26 UST 540; TIAS 8056.

CAPE VERDE

AVIATION

Agreement relating to the provision of site test, commissioning and/or periodic flight checks of air navigation aids by the Federal Aviation Administration.

Signed at Washington and Praia October 13 and November 19, 1976.

Entered into force November 19, 1976.

28 UST 8086; TIAS 8742; 1087 UNTS 111.

Extensions and amendments

August 17 and October 18, 1977 (29 UST 5893; TIAS 9158).

March 10 and April 4, 1978 (29 UST 5895; TIAS 9158).

Civil aviation security agreement.

Signed at Washington October 11, 1989.

Entered into force October 11, 1989.

TIAS 11705; 2208 UNTS 213.

Memorandum of agreement for the provision of technical assistance in developing and modernizing the civil aviation infrastructure of Cape Verde.

Signed at Washington and Praia November 20 and December 18, 2001.

Entered into force December 18, 2001.

TIAS

Amendment

December 9, 2002 and June 14, 2004.

Air transport agreement, with annexes.

Signed at Praia January 14, 2003.

Entered into force January 14, 2003.

TIAS

DEFENSE

Agreement concerning the provision of training related to defense articles under the United States International Military Education and Training (IMET) Program.

Exchange of notes at Praia December 9 and 16, 1987.

Entered into force December 16, 1987.

NP

Acquisition and cross-servicing agreement, with annexes.

Signed at Praia June 18, 2003.

Entered into force June 18, 2003.

TIAS

ECONOMIC AND TECHNICAL COOPERATION

Millennium challenge compact, with attachments and annexes.

Signed at Praia July 4, 2005.

Entered into force October 17, 2005.

TIAS

Agency for International Development

June 30, 1975 (28 UST 959; TIAS 8487).

June 30, 1975 (28 UST 2903; TIAS 8573).

November 3, 1975 (28 UST 970; TIAS 8487).

March 3 and 23, 1976 (28 UST 2921; TIAS 8573).

May 21, 1977 (29 UST 335; TIAS 8819).

May 22, 1978 (30 UST 3128; TIAS 9382; 1178 UNTS 289).

EMPLOYMENT

Agreement relating to the employment of dependents of official government employees.

Exchange of notes at Praia February 15 and 18, 2005.

Entered into force June 14, 2005.

TIAS

ENVIRONMENTAL COOPERATION

Agreement for cooperation in the Global Learning and Observations to Benefit the Environment (GLOBE) Program, with appendices.

Signed at Praia August 9, 2000.

Entered into force August 9, 2000.

TIAS

INTERNATIONAL CRIMINAL COURT

Agreement regarding the surrender of persons to international tribunals.

Signed at Washington April 16, 2004.

Entered into force November 19, 2004.

TIAS

POSTAL MATTERS

Postal money order agreement.

Signed at Washington and Praia April 17 and June 17, 1991.

Entered into force August 26, 1991.

TIAS 11818.

International express mail agreement, with detailed regulations.

Signed at Praia and Washington December 27, 1991 and February 25, 1992.

Entered into force March 7, 1992.

TIAS 11855.

TAXATION

Agreement for reciprocal exemption of taxes on income from the international operation of a ship or ships or aircraft.

Signed at Praia March 16, 2005.

Entered into force June 21, 2005.

TIAS

CARIBBEAN COMMUNITY SECRETARIAT

ECONOMIC AND TECHNICAL COOPERATION

Agency for International Development

August 30, 1978 (30 UST 5054; TIAS 9498; 1234 UNTS 29).

CENTRAL AFRICAN REPUBLIC

DEFENSE

Agreement concerning the provision of training related to the defense articles under the United States International Military Education and Training (IMET) Program.

Exchange of notes at Bangui August 31 and September 7, 1982.

Entered into force September 7, 1982.

TIAS 10709; 1607 UNTS 107.

ECONOMIC AND TECHNICAL COOPERATION

Agreement relating to economic, technical and related assistance.

Exchange of notes at Bangui February 10, 1963.

Entered into force February 10, 1963.

14 UST 185; TIAS 5294; 473 UNTS 83.

FINANCE

Agreement relating to investment guaranties.

Exchange of notes at Bangui December 31, 1964.

Entered into force January 1, 1965.

15 UST 2556; TIAS 5747; 542 UNTS 29.

Agreement regarding the consolidation and rescheduling of certain debts owed to, or guaranteed by the United States Government through the Export-Import Bank, with annexes.

Signed at Washington April 29, 1983.

Entered into force June 13, 1983.

TIAS 10721; 1578 UNTS 55.

Agreement regarding the consolidation and rescheduling of certain debts owed to, or guaranteed by the United States Government through the Export-Import Bank, with annexes.

Signed at Bangui February 16, 1984.

Entered into force April 16, 1984.

35 UST 4813; TIAS 10967.

Agreement regarding the consolidation and rescheduling of certain debts owed to or guaranteed by the United States Government through the Export-Import Bank of the United States.

Signed at Washington May 23, 1986.

Entered into force August 1, 1986.

NP

Agreement regarding the consolidation and rescheduling of certain debts owed to, guaranteed by or insured by the United States Government and its agencies, with annexes.

Signed at Bangui March 22, 1990.

Entered into force May 3, 1990.

NP

Agreement regarding the consolidation, reduction and rescheduling of certain debts owed to, guaranteed by or insured by the United States Government and its agencies, with annexes.

Signed at Bangui September 6, 1994.

Entered into force October 11, 1994.

NP

Agreement regarding the consolidation, reduction and rescheduling of certain debts owed to, guaranteed by, or insured by the United States Government and its Agency, with annexes.

Signed at Bangui September 1, 1999.

Entered into force December 15, 1999.

NP

INTERNATIONAL CRIMINAL COURT

Agreement regarding the surrender of persons to the International Criminal Court.

Signed at Washington and Bangui January 13 and 19, 2004.

Entered into force January 19, 2004.

TIAS

PEACE CORPS

Agreement relating to the establishment of a Peace Corps program in the Central African Republic.

Exchange of notes at Bangui September 9 and November 24, 1966.

Entered into force November 24, 1966.

17 UST 2205; TIAS 6157; 681 UNTS 21.

POSTAL MATTERS

International express mail agreement, with detailed regulations.

Signed at Bangui and Washington June 22 and September 21, 1988.

Entered into force November 1, 1988.

TIAS 11636.

CENTRAL AMERICAN BANK FOR ECONOMIC INTEGRATION

ECONOMIC AND TECHNICAL COOPERATION

Agency for International Development

February 2, 1977 (29 UST 921; TIAS 8855).

CHAD

DEFENSE

Agreement concerning the provision of training related to defense articles under the United States International Military Education and Training (IMET) Program.

Exchange of notes at N'Djamena February 22 and April 22, 1983.

Entered into force April 22, 1983.

35 UST 2840; TIAS 10822; 2014 UNTS 533.

Mutual defense assistance agreement.

Exchange of notes at N'Djamena July 19 and 20, 1983.

Entered into force July 20, 1983.

35 UST 1581; TIAS 10748; 2011 UNTS 97.

Agreement concerning the status of U.S. military personnel in Chad.

Exchange of notes at N'Djamena September 22 and 23, 1987.

Entered into force September 23, 1987.

NP

Agreement regarding the status of United States military personnel and civilian employees of the United States Department of Defense who may be temporarily present in Chad in connection with their official duties relating to humanitarian demining activities.

Exchange of notes at N'Djamena January 27 and February 23, 1998.

Entered into force February 23, 1998.

TIAS

Agreement regarding the status of personnel of the United States in Chad.

Signed at N'Djamena July 5, 2005.

Entered into force July 5, 2005.

TIAS

Aviation leadership program agreement.

Signed at Washington and N'Djamena July 1 and August 16, 2005.

Entered into force August 16, 2005.

TIAS

ECONOMIC AND TECHNICAL COOPERATION

Agreement on economic, technical and related assistance.

Signed at N'Djamena September 22, 1986.

Entered into force September 22, 1986.

TIAS

Agency for International Development

August 30, 1976 (29 UST 1139; TIAS 8871).

January 25, 1977 (29 UST 2581; TIAS 8959).

June 10, 1977 (29 UST 5741; TIAS 9146).

August 30, 1977 (29 UST 2596; TIAS 8959).

September 28, 1977 (29 UST 2613; TIAS 8959).

February 28, 1978 (30 UST 7393; TIAS 9594).

June 2, 1978 (30 UST 3132; TIAS 9383).

EMPLOYMENT

Agreement relating to the employment of dependents of official government employees.

Exchange of notes at N'Djamena April 19, 1991 and June 23, 1992.

Entered into force June 23, 1992.

TIAS

ENVIRONMENTAL COOPERATION

Agreement for cooperation in the Global Learning and Observations to Benefit the Environment (GLOBE) Program, with appendices.

Signed at N'Djamena and Washington September 27 and November 28, 1995.

Entered into force November 28, 1995.

TIAS

FINANCE

Agreement relating to investment guaranties.

Exchange of notes at Fort Lamy May 12, 1965.

Entered into force May 12, 1965.

16 UST 789; TIAS 5812; 546 UNTS 183.

INTERNATIONAL CRIMINAL COURT

Agreement regarding the surrender of persons to the International Criminal Court.

Exchange of notes at N'Djamena March 26 and June 30, 2003.

Entered into force June 30, 2003.

TIAS

PEACE CORPS

Agreement for the establishment of a Peace Corps program in Chad.

Exchange of notes at Fort Lamy August 31, 1966.

Entered into force August 31, 1966.

17 UST 1384; TIAS 6094.

POSTAL MATTERS

International express mail agreement, with detailed regulations.

Signed at N'Djamena and Washington July 19 and 23 and August 6, 1987.

Entered into force August 17, 1987.

TIAS 11553.

CHILE

AGRICULTURAL COMMODITIES

Agricultural commodities agreement.

Signed at Santiago November 8, 1960.

Entered into force November 8, 1960.

11 UST 2668; TIAS 4663; 405 UNTS 85.

Agricultural commodities agreement with exchanges of notes.

Signed at Santiago August 7, 1962.

Entered into force August 7, 1962.

13 UST 2269; TIAS 5195; 461 UNTS 61.

Amendments

August 29 and September 10, 1962 (13 UST 2269; TIAS 5195; 461 UNTS 70).

November 29, 1962 (13 UST 2878; TIAS 5252; 469 UNTS 440).

February 14, 1963 (14 UST 245; TIAS 5304; 474 UNTS 376).

June 30, 1964 (15 UST 1428; TIAS 5616; 530 UNTS 374).

November 17, 1964 (15 UST 2176; TIAS 5702; 531 UNTS 392).

Agreement setting forth certain understandings concerning the agricultural commodities agreement of August 7, 1962, as amended.

Exchange of notes at Santiago October 3 and 4, 1962.

Entered into force October 4, 1962.

13 UST 2269; TIAS 5195; 461 UNTS 74.

Amendment

March 1 and 27, 1963 (14 UST 468; TIAS 5342; 476 UNTS 354).

Agricultural commodities agreement with exchange of notes.

Signed at Santiago July 27, 1965.

Entered into force September 23, 1965.

16 UST 1725; TIAS 5898; 574 UNTS 83.

Amendment

February 8, 1966 (17 UST 251; TIAS 5974; 579 UNTS 349).

Agricultural commodities agreement with agreement and annex.

Exchange of notes at Santiago December 29, 1967.

Entered into force December 29, 1967.

18 UST 3106; TIAS 6403; 697 UNTS 63.

Amendment

December 17, 1968 (20 UST 388; TIAS 6641; 715 UNTS 382).

Related agreement

April 29, 1969 (20 UST 704; TIAS 6679; 715 UNTS 3).

Agricultural commodities agreement, with related notes.

Signed at Santiago October 25, 1974.

Entered into force October 25, 1974.

25 UST 3395; TIAS 7993.

Amendments

November 22, 1974 (25 UST 3427; TIAS 7993).

April 1, 1975 (26 UST 259; TIAS 8030; 992 UNTS 409).

May 22, 1975 (26 UST 962; TIAS 8083).

Related agreements

July 31, 1975 (26 UST 2718; TIAS 8188).

April 19, 1976 (27 UST 1551; TIAS 8262; 1052 UNTS 283).

October 29, 1976 (27 UST 3871; TIAS 8405; 1059 UNTS 169).

AGRICULTURE

Memorandum of understanding for scientific and technical cooperation in agricultural research and development.

Signed at Santiago August 28, 1981.

Entered into force August 28, 1981.

33 UST 3742; TIAS 10256; 1541 UNTS 113.

AMITY

Treaty of peace, amity, commerce, and navigation, with additional and explanatory convention signed at Santiago September 1, 1833.[1]

Signed at Santiago May 16, 1832.

Entered into force April 29, 1834.

8 Stat. 434; TS 40; 6 Bevans 518.

NOTE

1 Articles relating to commerce and navigation terminated January 20, 1850.

ATOMIC ENERGY

Agreement providing for a grant for the acquisition of certain nuclear research and training equipment and materials.

Exchange of notes at Santiago July 23, 1959 and February 19, 1960.

Entered into force February 19, 1960.

11 UST 395; TIAS 4457; 371 UNTS 255.

AVIATION

Air transport agreement with exchanges of notes.

Signed at Santiago May 10, 1947.

Entered into force December 30, 1948.

62 Stat. 3755; TIAS 1905; 6 Bevans 626; 55 UNTS 21.

Memorandum of cooperation in the promotion and development of civil aviation, with annex.

Signed at Washington and Santiago July 11, 1997.

Entered into force July 11, 1997.

TIAS

COMMERCE

Provisional commercial agreement.

Exchange of notes at Santiago January 6 and February 1, 1938.

Entered into force January 5, 1940.

52 Stat. 1479; EAS 119; 6 Bevans 584; 190 LNTS 9.

CUSTOMS

Reciprocal agreement relating to free importation privileges for consular officers.

Exchange of notes at Washington March 12, April 16, and May 12, 1952.

Entered into force May 12, 1952.

3 UST 4293; TIAS 2577; 177 UNTS 103.

DEFENSE

Military assistance agreement.

Signed at Santiago April 9, 1952.

Entered into force July 11, 1952.

3 UST 5123; TIAS 2703; 186 UNTS 53.

Agreement for disposition of equipment and materials furnished by the United States under the military assistance agreement of April 9, 1952, and no longer required by Chile.

Exchange of notes at Santiago November 30 and December 28, 1956.

Entered into force December 28, 1956.

8 UST 13; TIAS 3730; 266 UNTS 421.

Agreement relating to the deposit by Chile of ten percent of the value of grant military assistance and excess defense articles.

Exchange of notes at Santiago March 28 and April 11, 1972.

Entered into force April 11, 1972; effective February 7, 1972.

23 UST 930; TIAS 7361.

Memorandum of understanding on the exchange of officers between the U.S. Marine Corps and the Chilean Navy's Marine Corps.

Signed at Washington October 30, 1989.

Entered into force October 30, 1989.

NP

Memorandum of understanding on the exchange of staff noncommissioned officers between the U.S. Marine Corps and the Chilean Navy's Marine Corps.

Signed at Washington and Santiago February 7 and 26, 1992.

Entered into force February 26, 1992.

NP

Agreement governing the protection of classified military information or material.

Exchange of notes at Santiago August 13 and September 1, 1992.

Entered into force September 1, 1992.

TIAS 12281.

Fuel exchange agreement, with appendix.

Signed at Valparaiso and Washington August 1 and October 25, 1997.

Entered into force October 25, 1997.

TIAS

Amendments

April 2 and July 18, 2002.

July 18 and September 8, 2003.

August 26 and September 8, 2003.

Acquisition and cross-servicing agreement, with annexes.

Signed at Manaus October 17, 2000.

Entered into force October 17, 2000.

TIAS

Agreement concerning the exchange and reimbursement of marine aviation and propulsion fuels, with annexes.

Signed at Fort Belvoir and Valparaiso June 28 and July 13, 2005.

Entered into force July 13, 2005.

TIAS

Agreement regarding the exchange of military personnel, with annexes.

Signed at Santiago December 2, 2005.

Entered into force December 2, 2005.

TIAS

Agreement regarding the exchange of administrative and professional personnel in financial management headquarters organizations, with annexes and appendices.

Signed at Valparaiso December 31, 2005.

Entered into force December 31, 2005.

TIAS

Agreement regarding grants under the Foreign Assistance Act of 1961, as amended, and the furnishing of defense articles, defense services, and related training, including pursuant to the United States International Military Education and Training Program (IMET), from the United States to the Government of Chile.

Exchange of notes at Santiago December 5, 2005 and July 5, 2006.

Entered into force July 5, 2006.

NP

Memorandum of understanding concerning the inter-American naval telecommunications network.

Signed October 18 and November 14, 2006.

Entered into force November 14, 2006.

TIAS

ECONOMIC AND TECHNICAL COOPERATION

Basic agreement for technical cooperation.

Signed at Santiago January 16, 1951.

Entered into force July 27, 1951.

3 UST 390; TIAS 2403; 151 UNTS 147.

Amendments

January 8, 1952 (3 UST 4697; TIAS 2627; 179 UNTS 265).

October 17, 1952 (3 UST 5136; TIAS 2704; 184 UNTS 376).

Agreement providing for a loan to Chile for reconstruction and rehabilitation as a consequence of the May 1960 earthquakes.

Exchange of notes at Santiago August 3, 1961.

Entered into force August 3, 1961.

12 UST 1390; TIAS 4862; 433 UNTS 21.

Agreement concerning the establishment of an Americas Fund and Administering Board.

Signed at Santiago June 30, 1993.

Entered into force June 30, 1993.

TIAS 12504.

Agency for International Development

January 26, 1976 (28 UST 5038; TIAS 8611).

EDUCATION

Agreement for educational cooperation.

Signed at Washington February 26, 1997.

Entered into force November 9, 1998.

TIAS

ENVIRONMENTAL COOPERATION

Agreement for cooperation in the Global Learning and Observations to Benefit the Environment (GLOBE) Program, with appendices.

Signed at Santiago April 16, 1998.

Entered into force April 16, 1998.

TIAS

Agreement on environmental cooperation.

Signed at Santiago June 17, 2003.

Entered into force April 30, 2004.

TIAS

EXTRADITION

Treaty providing for the extradition of fugitives from justice.

Signed at Santiago April 17, 1900.

Entered into force June 26, 1902.

32 Stat. 1850; TS 407; 6 Bevans 543.

FINANCE

Agreement regarding the consolidation and rescheduling of certain debts owed to, guaranteed or insured by the United States Government and its agencies, with annexes.

Signed at Washington February 6, 1974.

Entered into force February 6, 1974.

25 UST 1712; TIAS 7908.

Memorandum of understanding regarding the consolidation and rescheduling of certain Chilean debts owed to, guaranteed or insured by the United States Government and its agencies.

Signed at Washington June 17, 1974.

Entered into force June 17, 1974; effective May 15, 1974.

25 UST 2683; TIAS 7940.

Agreement regarding the consolidation and rescheduling of certain debts owed to the Agency for International Development pursuant to certain loan agreements, with schedules.

Signed at Washington July 1, 1974.

Entered into force July 1, 1974.

25 UST 2691; TIAS 7940.

Agreement regarding the consolidation and rescheduling of payments under PL-480 Title I agricultural commodity agreements, with annexes.

Signed at Washington October 22, 1974.

Entered into force October 22, 1974.

25 UST 2704; TIAS 7940.

Agreement regarding the consolidation and rescheduling of certain debts owed to, guaranteed or insured by the United States Government and its agencies, with annexes and statement.

Signed at Washington July 3, 1975.

Entered into force September 8, 1975.

28 UST 5587; TIAS 8649.

Agreement regarding the consolidation and rescheduling of payments under PL 480 Title I agricultural commodity agreements.

Signed at Washington April 5, 1976.

Entered into force April 5, 1976.

28 UST 5587; TIAS 8649.

Agreement regarding the consolidation and rescheduling of certain debts owed to the Agency for International Development pursuant to certain loan agreements, with schedules.

Signed at Washington May 26, 1976.

Entered into force May 26, 1976.

28 UST 5609; TIAS 8649.

Investment incentive agreement.

Exchange of notes at Santiago September 22, 1983.

Entered into force February 14, 1984.

35 UST 2958; TIAS 10832; 2014 UNTS 537.

Agreement regarding the consolidation and rescheduling of certain debts owed to, guaranteed by or insured by the United States Government and its agencies, with annexes.

Signed at Washington February 6, 1986.

Entered into force March 17, 1986.

NP

Agreement regarding the consolidation and rescheduling or refinancing of certain debts owed to, guaranteed by or insured by the United States Government and its agencies, with annexes.

Signed at Washington August 13, 1987.

Entered into force September 21, 1987.

NP

Agreement regarding the reduction of certain debts owed to the United States Government and its agencies, with appendices.

Signed at Washington June 27, 1991.

Entered into force August 8, 1991.

NP

Agreement regarding the reduction of certain debts related to foreign assistance owed to the Government of the United States and its agencies, with appendices.

Signed at Washington and Santiago December 11 and 15, 1992.

Entered into force January 14, 1993.

NP

INFORMATIONAL MEDIA GUARANTIES

Agreement relating to an informational media guaranty program in Chile.

Exchange of notes at Santiago January 14, 1955.

Entered into force January 14, 1955.

6 UST 41; TIAS 3166; 238 UNTS 191.

MARITIME MATTERS

Agreement relating to the transfer to Chile of certain United States naval vessels.

Exchange of notes at Washington January 4, 1951, with memorandum of understanding dated January 9, 1951.

Entered into force January 4, 1951.

3 UST 2741; TIAS 2444; 165 UNTS 105.

Agreement for the loan of a submarine to Chile.

Exchange of notes at Santiago June 28 and July 16, 1960.

Entered into force July 16, 1960.

11 UST 2197; TIAS 4589; 393 UNTS 271.

Extension and amendment

December 2 and 7, 1960 (11 UST 2527; TIAS 4638; 401 UNTS 364).

May 13 and 17, 1968 (19 UST 5368; TIAS 6519; 706 UNTS 317).

NARCOTIC DRUGS

Agreement concerning cooperation to suppress the processing, trafficking, consumption and export of narcotic drugs.

Signed at Santiago August 5, 1994.

Entered into force August 5, 1994.

TIAS 12561.

NAVIGATION

Agreement for the establishment and operation of an OMEGA navigation system signal monitor.

Signed at Washington and Santiago August 23 and September 5, 1984.

Entered into force September 5, 1984.

TIAS 11201; 2130 UNTS 199.

PACIFIC SETTLEMENT OF DISPUTES

Treaty for the settlement of disputes that may occur between the United States of America and Chile.

Signed at Washington July 24, 1914.

Entered into force January 19, 1916.

39 Stat. 1645; TS 621; 6 Bevans 550.

POSTAL MATTERS

International express mail agreement with detailed regulations.

Signed at Montevideo September 8, 1986.

Entered into force September 26, 1986.

TIAS 11392.

PUBLICATIONS

Agreement relating to the exchange of official publications.

Exchange of notes at Santiago October 22 and 27, 1937.

Entered into force October 27, 1937.

51 Stat. 331; EAS 112; 6 Bevans 566.

RELIEF SUPPLIES AND PACKAGES

Agreement granting duty-free entry, exemption from internal taxation, and free transportation within Chile to ultimate beneficiary for certain relief supplies and equipment for U.S. rehabilitation and relief agencies.

Exchange of notes at Santiago April 5, 1955.

Entered into force April 5, 1955.

6 UST 717; TIAS 3210; 250 UNTS 253.

SCIENTIFIC COOPERATION

Memorandum of understanding for scientific cooperation in the earth sciences.

Signed at Reston and Santiago August 2 and 26, 1982.

Entered into force August 26, 1982.

34 UST 1791; TIAS 10457; 1751 UNTS 47.

Amendment and extension

April 30 and August 27, 1993 (TIAS 12161).

Agreement regarding the marine scientific research activities of the research vessel Hero.

Signed at Santiago June 1, 1983.

Entered into force June 1, 1983.

35 UST 2892; TIAS 10825; 2014 UNTS 535.

Basic agreement relating to scientific and technological cooperation, with annexes.

Signed at Washington May 14, 1992.

Entered into force January 19, 1994.

TIAS 12453; 1792 UNTS 321.

Extension

June 27 and 28, 2006.

Memorandum of understanding concerning scientific and technical cooperation in the earth sciences, with annexes.

Signed at Reston and Santiago September 30 and November 17, 1994.

Entered into force November 17, 1994.

TIAS

Memorandum of understanding concerning scientific and technical cooperation in the earth sciences.

Signed at Washington January 16 and 20, 2004.

Entered into force January 20, 2004.

TIAS

SMUGGLING

Convention for the prevention of smuggling of alcoholic beverages.

Signed at Washington May 27, 1930.

Entered into force November 25, 1930.

46 Stat. 2852; TS 829; 6 Bevans 558; 133 LNTS 141.

SPACE COOPERATION

Agreement concerning the use of Mataveri Airport, Isla de Pascua, as a space shuttle emergency landing and rescue site.

Signed at Santiago August 2, 1985.

Entered into force November 6, 1985.

TIAS 11248.

TAXATION

Agreement concerning the reciprocal exemption from income tax of income derived from the international operation of aircraft.

Exchange of notes at Washington and Santiago August 6 and December 4, 1990.

Entered into force December 4, 1990.

TIAS 11764; 2202 UNTS 297.

TELECOMMUNICATION

Agreement relating to radio communications between amateur stations on behalf of third parties.

Exchange of notes at Santiago August 2 and 17, 1934.

Entered into force August 17, 1934.

49 Stat. 3667; EAS 72; 6 Bevans 564; 157 LNTS 15.

Agreement relating to the reciprocal granting of authorizations to permit licensed amateur radio operators of either country to operate their stations in the other country.

Exchange of notes at Washington November 30, 1967.

Entered into force December 30, 1967.

18 UST 2882; TIAS 6380; 701 UNTS 175.

TRACKING STATIONS

Agreement concerning a cooperative program for tracking and receiving radio signals from earth satellites and space vehicles.

Exchange of notes at Santiago February 16 and 19, 1959.

Entered into force February 19, 1959; operative from December 31, 1958.

10 UST 783; TIAS 4216; 343 UNTS 17.

TRADE

United States–Chile free trade agreement, with annexes and related exchanges of letters.

Signed at Miami June 6, 2003.

Entered into force January 1, 2004.

TIAS

VISAS

Agreement relating to passport visas for nonimmigrants.

Exchange of notes at Santiago August 29, 1950; effective September 1, 1950.

1 UST 719; TIAS 2137; 122 UNTS 43.

WEATHER STATIONS

Agreement relating to a cooperative meteorological observation program in Chile.

Exchange of notes at Santiago February 23, June 2 and September 7, 1977.

Entered into force February 15, 1978; effective January 1, 1977.

29 UST 1969; TIAS 8912.

CHINA [1]

NOTE

1 See also note under CHINA (TAIWAN) at the end of Section 1.

In connection with Hong Kong, the People's Republic of China submitted to the Secretary General of the United Nations a note, dated June 20, 1997, which reads in pertinent part as follows:

"In accordance with the Joint Declaration of the Government of the United Kingdom of Great Britain and North Ireland and the Government of the People's Republic of China on the Question of Hong Kong signed on 19 December 1984 (hereinafter referred to as the Joint Declaration), the People's Republic of China will resume the exercise of sovereignty over Hong Kong with effect from 1 July 1997. Hong Kong will, with effect from that date, become a Special Administrative Region of the People's Republic of China.

It is provided in Section I of Annex I to the Joint Declaration, "Elaboration by the Government of the People's Republic of China of its Basic Policies Regarding Hong Kong", and in Articles 12, 13 and 14 of the Basic Law of the Hong Kong Special Administrative Region of the People's Republic of China, which was adopted on 4 April 1990 by the National People's Congress of the People's Republic of China (hereinafter referred to as the Basic law), that the Hong Kong Special Administrative Region will enjoy a high degree of autonomy, except in foreign and defence affairs which are the responsibility of the Central People's Government of the People's Republic of China. Furthermore, it is provided both in Section XI of Annex I to the Joint Declaration and Article 153 of the Basic Law that international agreements to which the People's Republic of China is not a party but which are implemented in Hong Kong may continue to be implemented in the Hong Kong Special Administrative Region.

In this connection, on behalf of the Government of the People's Republic of China, I would like to inform Your Excellency as follows:

I. The treaties listed in Annex I [not printed herein] to this Note, to which the People's Republic of China is a party, will be applied to the Hong Kong Special Administrative Region with effect from 1 July 1997 as they:

(i) are applied to Hong Kong before 1 July 1997; or

(ii) fall within the category of foreign affairs or defence or, owing to their nature and provisions, must apply to the entire territory of a State; or

(iii) are not applied to Hong Kong before 1 July 1997 but with respect to which it has been decided to apply them to the Hong Kong Special Administrative Region with effect from that date (denoted by an asterisk in Annex I.)

II. The treaties listed in Annex II [not printed herein] to this Note, to which the People's Republic of China is not yet a party and which apply to Hong Kong before 1 July 1997, will continue to apply to the Hong Kong Special Administrative Region with effect from 1 July 1997.

The provisions of the International Covenant on Civil and Political Rights and the International Covenant on Economic, Social and Cultural Rights as applied to Hong Kong shall remain in force beginning from 1 July 1997. . . .

III. The Government of the People's Republic of China has already carried out separately the formalities required for the application of the treaties listed in the aforesaid Annexes, including all the related amendments, protocols, reservations and declarations, to the Hong Kong Special Administrative Region with effect from 1 July 1997.

IV. With respect to any other treaty not listed in the Annexes to this Note, to which the People's Republic of China is or will become a party, in the event that it is decided to apply such treaty to the Hong Kong Special Administrative Region, the Government of the People's Republic of China will carry out separately the formalities for such application. For the avoidance of doubt, no separate formalities will need to be carried out by the Government of the People's Republic of China with respect to treaties which fall within the category of foreign affairs or defence or which, owing to their nature and provisions, must apply to the entire territory of a State."

In connection with Macao, the People's Republic of China submitted to the Secretary General of the United Nations a note, dated December 13, 1999, which reads in pertinent part as follows:

"In accordance with the Joint Declaration of the Government of the People's Republic of China and the Government of the Republic of Portugal on the Question of Macao signed on 13 April 1987 (hereinafter referred to as the Joint Declaration), the Government of the People's Republic of China will resume the exercise of sovereignty over Macao with effect from 20 December 1999. Macao will, from that date, become a Special Administrative Region of the People's Republic of China.

It is provided in Section I of Elaboration by the Government of the People's Republic of China of its Basic Policies Regarding Macao, which is Annex I to the Joint Declaration, and in Article 12, 13 and 14 of the Basic Law of the Macao Special Administrative Region of the People's Republic of China (hereinafter referred to as the Basic Law), which was adopted by the National People's Congress of the People's Republic of China on 31 March 1993, that the Macao Special Administrative Region will enjoy a high degree of autonomy, except in foreign and defence affairs which are the responsibilities of the Central People's Government of the People's Republic of China. Furthermore, it is provided both in Section VIII of Annex I to the Joint Declaration and Article 138 of the Basic Law that international agreements to which the People's Republic of China is not yet a party but which are implemented in Macao may continue to be implemented in the Macao Special Administrative Region.

In this connection, on behalf of the Government of the People's Republic of China, I have the honour to inform your Excellency that:

I. The Treaties listed in Annex I [not printed herein] to this Note, to which the People's Republic of China is a Party, will be applied to the Macao Special Administrative Region with effect from 20 December 1999 so long as they are one of the following categories:

(i) Treaties that apply to Macao before 20 December 1999;

(ii) Treaties that must apply to the entire territory of a state as they concern foreign affairs or defence or their nature or provisions so require.

II. The Treaties listed in Annex II [not printed herein] to this Note, to which the People's Republic of China is not yet a Party and which apply to Macao before 20 December 1999, will continue to apply to the Macao Special Administrative Region with effect from 20 December 1999.

III. The Government of the People's Republic of China has notified the treaty depositories concerned of the application of the treaties including their amendments and protocols as listed in the aforesaid Annexes as well as reservations and declarations made thereto by the Chinese Government to the Macao Special Administrative Region with effect from 20 December 1999.

IV. With respect to other treaties that are not listed in the Annexes to this Note, to which the People's Republic of China is or will become a Party, the Government of the People's Republic of China will go through separately the necessary formalities for their application to the Macao Special Administrative Region if it is so decided."

Listings and annotations in "Section 2: Multilateral Treaties and Other Agreements", to the effect that Hong Kong and Macao are parties to treaties or other agreements, are based on the above notes, annexes and notifications from depositaries.

ATOMIC ENERGY

Agreement for cooperation concerning peaceful uses of nuclear energy, with annexes and agreed minute.

Signed at Washington July 23, 1985.

Entered into force December 30, 1985.

TIAS 12027.

Agreement on cooperation concerning peaceful uses of nuclear technologies, with annex.

Signed at Beijing June 29, 1998.

Entered into force June 29, 1998.

TIAS

Protocol on cooperation in nuclear safety matters.

Signed at Beijing April 23, 2004.

Entered into force April 23, 2004.

TIAS

AVIATION

Agreement relating to civil air transport, with annexes and exchanges of letters.

Signed at Washington September 17, 1980.

Entered into force September 17, 1980.

33 UST 4559; TIAS 10326.

Amendments

February 10, 1992 (TIAS 12448).

February 16 and March 27, 1996.

April 8, 1999.

July 24, 2004.

Agreement concerning the airworthiness certification of imported civil aeronautical products.

Exchange of notes at Beijing October 8 and 14, 1991.

Entered into force October 14, 1991.

TIAS 12437.

Agreement for promotion of aviation safety.

Signed at Washington October 20, 2005.

Entered into force October 20, 2005.

TIAS

CLAIMS

Agreement concerning the settlement of claims.

Signed at Beijing May 11, 1979.

Entered into force May 11, 1979.

30 UST 1957; TIAS 9306; 1153 UNTS 289.

Amendment

September 28, 1979 (31 UST 5596; TIAS 9675).

Memorandum of understanding concerning settlement of claims relating to deaths, injuries or losses suffered by Chinese personnel as a result of the U.S. bombing of the Chinese Embassy in the Federal Republic of Yugoslavia, with annex.

Signed at Beijing July 30, 1999.

Entered into force July 30, 1999.

TIAS

CONSULS

Agreement on the mutual establishment of consular relations and the opening of consulates general, with annex.

Signed at Washington January 31, 1979.

Entered into force January 31, 1979.

30 UST 17; TIAS 9177.

Consular convention, with exchange of notes.

Signed at Washington September 17, 1980.

Entered into force February 19, 1982.

33 UST 2973; TIAS 10209; 1529 UNTS 199.

Agreement modifying the consular convention of September 17, 1980.

Exchange of notes at Beijing January 17, 1981.

Entered into force February 19, 1982.

33 UST 3048; TIAS 10209.

Agreement concerning the establishment of additional consulates general.

Exchange of notes at Washington September 17, 1980.

Entered into force September 17, 1980.

TIAS 12007.

Agreement concerning the establishment of additional consulates general, with annex and related letter.

Exchange of notes at Beijing June 16, 1981.

Entered into force June 16, 1981.

TIAS 12007.

Agreement concerning the enlargement of existing consular districts.

Exchange of notes at June 16, 1981.

Entered into force June 16, 1981.

TIAS

Agreement regarding the maintenance of the U.S. consulate general in the Hong Kong Special Administrative Region.

Signed at Beijing March 25, 1997.

Entered into force July 1, 1997.

TIAS

CUSTOMS

Agreement regarding mutual assistance in customs matters.

Signed at Washington April 9, 1999.

Entered into force April 10, 2003.

TIAS

EDUCATION

Agreement for cooperation in educational exchanges.

Signed at Washington April 20, 2006.

Entered into force April 20, 2006.

TIAS

EMBASSY SITES

Agreement concerning the mutual provision of properties for use of the two countries, with appendices.

Signed at Beijing March 23, 1991.

Entered into force April 22, 1991.

TIAS

Memorandum of understanding concerning the provision of properties in Washington, D.C., Beijing, and Guangzhou.

Signed at Beijing November 1, 2000.

Entered into force November 1, 2000.

TIAS

ENVIRONMENTAL COOPERATION

Agreement for cooperation in the Global Learning and Observations to Benefit the Environment (GLOBE) Program, with appendices.

Signed at Beijing October 18, 1995.

Entered into force October 18, 1995.

TIAS 12698.

FINANCE

Agreement relating to investment guaranties, with related notes and statement.

Exchange of notes at Beijing October 30, 1980.

Entered into force October 30, 1980.

32 UST 4010; TIAS 9924; 1267 UNTS 315.

FISHERIES

Agreement concerning fisheries off the coasts of the United States, with annexes and agreed minutes.

Signed at Washington July 23, 1985.

Entered into force November 19, 1985.

TIAS 12002; 1443 UNTS 151.

Amendments and extensions

March 14 and 22, 1990 (TIAS 11893).

May 12 and July 6, 1992 (TIAS 11907).

Memorandum of understanding on effective cooperation and implementation of United Nations General Assembly Resolution 46/215 of December 20, 1991.

Signed at Washington December 3, 1993.

Entered into force December 3, 1993.

TIAS

Extension

August 30 and December 31, 2001.

INDUSTRIAL AND TECHNOLOGICAL COOPERATION

Accord on industrial and technological cooperation.

Signed at Washington January 12, 1984.

Entered into force January 12, 1984.

35 UST 4233; TIAS 10920.

INTELLECTUAL PROPERTY

Memorandum of understanding on the protection of intellectual property.

Signed at Washington January 17, 1992.

Entered into force January 17, 1992.

TIAS 12036.

JUDICIAL ASSISTANCE

Agreement on mutual legal assistance in criminal matters.

Signed at Beijing June 19, 2000.

Entered into force March 8, 2001.

TIAS

LABOR

Memorandum of understanding on prohibiting import and export trade in prison labor products.

Signed at Washington August 7, 1992.

Entered into force August 7, 1992.

TIAS

Statement of cooperation on the implementation of the memorandum of understanding on prohibiting import and export trade in prison labor products.

Signed at Beijing March 14, 1994.

Entered into force March 14, 1994.

TIAS

MARITIME MATTERS

Agreement concerning maritime search and rescue cooperation.

Signed at Washington January 20, 1987.

Entered into force January 20, 1987.

TIAS 12013; 2244 UNTS 71.

Agreement on establishing a consultation mechanism to strengthen military maritime safety.

Signed at Beijing January 19, 1998.

Entered into force January 19, 1998.

TIAS

PEACE CORPS

Agreement concerning the United States volunteer program in China.

Signed at Beijing June 29, 1998.

Entered into force June 29, 1998.

TIAS

POSTAL MATTERS

Memorandum of understanding concerning the operation of the INTELPOST field trial, with details of implementation.

Signed at Beijing and Washington January 17 and February 5, 1987.

Entered into force March 1, 1987.

NP

PRIVILEGES AND IMMUNITIES

Agreement relating to privileges and immunities for the respective diplomatic missions in Washington and Beijing.

Exchange of notes at Washington January 5, 1981.

Entered into force January 5, 1981.

TIAS

REMOTE SENSING

Memorandum of understanding relating to establishment and operation of a Landsat system, with annex.

Signed at Washington and Beijing July 2 and 8, 1985.

Entered into force July 8, 1985.

TIAS 11128; 2120 UNTS 81.

SATELLITES

Memorandum of agreement on liability for satellite launches.

Signed at Washington December 17, 1988.

Entered into force March 16, 1989.

TIAS

SCIENTIFIC COOPERATION

Agreement on cooperation in science and technology, with exchange of letters.

Signed at Washington January 31, 1979.

Entered into force January 31, 1979.

30 UST 35; TIAS 9179; 1150 UNTS 349.

Amendment and extensions

May 22, 1991.

April 24 and 25, 2001.

April 18, 2006.

Memorandum of understanding covering ceramicware intended for use in the preparation, serving or storage of food or drink and offered for export to the United States, with attachments.

Signed at Washington May 20, 1999.

Entered into force May 20, 1999.

TIAS

Protocol on cooperation in agriculture science and technology.

Signed at Washington December 10, 2002.

Entered into force December 10, 2002.

TIAS

Memorandum of understanding on cooperative construction of the Chinese Garden.

Signed at Washington October 8, 2004.

Entered into force October 8, 2004.

TIAS

Protocol concerning scientific and technical cooperation in the mineral and earth sciences.

Signed at Reston and Beijing July 27, 2006.

Entered into force July 27, 2006.

TIAS

TAXATION

Agreement with respect to mutual exemption from taxation of transportation income of shipping and air transport enterprises.

Signed at Beijing March 5, 1982.

Entered into force September 23, 1983; effective January 1, 1981.

35 UST 3819; TIAS 10884; 2014 UNTS 419.

Agreement for the avoidance of double taxation and the prevention of tax evasion with respect to taxes on income, with protocol and exchange of notes.

Signed at Beijing April 30, 1984.

Entered into force November 21, 1986.

TIAS 12065.

Protocol concerning the interpretation of paragraph 7 of the protocol to the agreement for the avoidance of double taxation and the prevention of tax evasion with respect to taxes on income of April 30, 1984.

Signed at Beijing May 10, 1986.

Entered into force November 21, 1986.

TIAS 12065.

TECHNOLOGY TRANSFER

Memorandum of agreement on satellite technology safeguards.

Signed at Beijing February 11, 1993.

Entered into force February 11, 1993.

TIAS 12486.

TELECOMMUNICATION

Agreement on the establishment of the direct secure telephone link.

Signed at Beijing April 29, 1998.

Entered into force April 29, 1998.

TIAS

TOURISM

Memorandum of understanding on the development of bilateral tourism relations.

Signed at Beijing August 5, 1982.

Entered into force August 5, 1982.

34 UST 1418; TIAS 10426.

TRADE AND COMMERCE

Agreement on trade exhibitions.

Signed at Beijing May 10, 1979.

Entered into force May 10, 1979.

30 UST 4472; TIAS 9470; 1171 UNTS 305.

Agreement on trade relations.

Signed at Beijing July 7, 1979.

Entered into force February 1, 1980.

31 UST 4651; TIAS 9630; 1202 UNTS 179.

Arrangement relating to a visa system for exports to the United States of cotton, wool and manmade fiber textiles and textile products.

Exchange of letters at Washington February 16, 1984.

Entered into force February 16, 1984.

35 UST 4417; TIAS 10945.

Agreement for orderly trade in ammonium paratungstate and tungstic acid, with annexes.

Signed at Washington September 28, 1987.

Entered into force September 28, 1987; effective October 1, 1987.

TIAS

Agreement concerning trade in textiles and textile products, with annexes.

Exchange of letters at Beijing February 2, 1988.

Entered into force February 2, 1988; effective January 1, 1988.

NP

Amendments and extension

May 24 and 26, 1988 (NP).

August 26 and September 7, 1988 (NP).

November 7, 1988 and January 24, 1989 (NP).

April 28 and May 1, 1989 (NP).

April 23 and 24, 1991 (NP).

Memorandum of agreement regarding international trade in commercial launch services, with annexes.

Signed at Beijing March 13, 1995.

Entered into force March 13, 1995; effective January 1, 1995.

TIAS

Amendment

October 27, 1997.

Agreement concerning trade in textile and apparel products, with annexes.

Exchange of notes at Beijing March 29 and June 8, 1995.

Entered into force June 8, 1995; effective January 1, 1994.

NP

Agreement on agricultural cooperation, with addenda.

Signed at Washington April 10, 1999.

Entered into force April 10, 1999.

TIAS

Memorandum of understanding concerning trade in textile and apparel products, with annexes.

Signed at London November 8, 2005.

Entered into force January 1, 2006.

TIAS

VISAS

Agreement relating to the reciprocal issuance of visas to crew members of aircraft and vessels.

Exchange of notes at Beijing January 7, 1981.

Entered into force January 7, 1981.

32 UST 4533; TIAS 9965; 1267 UNTS 335.

Agreement relating to reciprocal facilitation of visa issuance.

Exchange of notes at Beijing December 2, 1985.

Entered into force January 2, 1986.

TIAS

Agreement relating to the reciprocal facilitation of visa issuance.

Exchange of notes at Beijing April 14, 1993.

Entered into force May 14, 1993.

TIAS 12495.

CHINA (HONG KONG)

AVIATION

Agreement concerning air services, with annex.

Signed at Hong Kong April 7, 1997.

Entered into force April 7, 1997.

TIAS ; 1981 UNTS 231.

EXTRADITION

Agreement for the surrender of fugitive offenders.

Signed at Hong Kong December 20, 1996.

Entered into force January 21, 1998.

TIAS

JUDICIAL ASSISTANCE

Agreement on mutual legal assistance in criminal matters, with annex.

Signed at Hong Kong April 15, 1997.

Entered into force January 21, 2000.

TIAS

POSTAL MATTERS

Parcel post agreement and regulations of execution.

Signed at Hong Kong January 18 and at Washington February 2, 1961.

Entered into force July 1, 1961.

12 UST 328; TIAS 4721.

International express mail agreement, with detailed regulations.

Signed at Hong Kong and Washington January 2 and February 6, 1979.

Entered into force March 15, 1979; effective February 1, 1979.

30 UST 3427; TIAS 9398; 1180 UNTS 25.

PRISONER TRANSFER

Agreement for the transfer of sentenced persons.

Signed at Hong Kong April 15, 1997.

Entered into force April 18, 1999.

TIAS

TAXATION

Agreement for the reciprocal exemption with respect to taxes on income from the international operation of ships.

Exchange of notes at Hong Kong August 1, 1989.

Entered into force August 1, 1989.

TIAS 11892; 1549 UNTS 91.

TRADE AND COMMERCE

Agreement relating to trade in certain textiles and textile products, with annexes.

Exchange of letters at Hong Kong August 4, 1986.

Entered into force August 4, 1986; effective January 1, 1986.

NP

Amendments

August 5 and 12, 1987 (NP).

August 5 and 12, 1987 (NP).

March 2 and 7, 1988 (NP).

July 15 and 20, 1988 (NP).

November 4 and 7, 1988 (NP).

December 20 and 21, 1989 and January 5, 1990 (NP).

Agreement concerning trade in textiles and textile products, with annexes.

Exchange of notes at Hong Kong October 9, 1991.

Entered into force October 9, 1991; effective January 1, 1992.

NP

Amendments

March 2 and 11, 1993 (NP).

February 3 and April 27, 1993 (NP).

Memorandum of understanding concerning cooperation in trade in textile and apparel goods.

Signed at Washington and Hong Kong August 1, 2005.

Entered into force August 1, 2005.

TIAS

CHINA (MACAO)

AVIATION

Air transport agreement, with annexes.

Signed at Macao July 3, 1996.

Entered into force July 3, 1996.

TIAS 12777.

POSTAL MATTERS

Parcel post agreement with detailed regulations for execution.

Signed at Macao February 23 and at Washington June 8, 1973.

Entered into force August 1, 1974.

25 UST 2982; TIAS 7961.

International express mail agreement, with detailed regulations.

Signed at Macao and Washington May 3 and June 14, 1983.

Entered into force October 1, 1983.

35 UST 1403; TIAS 10736; 2006 UNTS 333.

Memorandum of understanding concerning the operation of the INTELPOST field trial, with details of implementation.

Signed at Macao and Washington April 29 and May 21, 1985.

Entered into force May 21, 1985.

TIAS 11246.

TRADE AND COMMERCE

Administrative arrangement relating to a visa system.

Exchange of letters at Washington and Macao August 21, 1981.

Entered into force August 21, 1981.

TIAS

Amendment

November 2 and December 12, 1988.

Agreement relating to trade in cotton, wool, and man-made fiber textiles and textile products, with annexes.

Exchange of letters at Hong Kong and Macao December 28, 1983 and January 9, 1984.

Entered into force January 9, 1984; effective January 1, 1984.

35 UST 4188; TIAS 10917; 2015 UNTS 83.

Amendments and extension

February 26 and 28, 1986 (NP).

November 10 and 27, 1986 (NP).

April 14 and 28, 1987 (NP).

January 8 and 12, 1988 (NP).

November 7 and December 30, 1988 (NP).

February 10 and March 3, 1989 (NP).

November 1, 1991, January 21 and 27, 1992 (NP).

Agreement relating to trade in textiles and textile products, with annexes.

Exchange of notes at Hong Kong and Macao March 29 and May 21, 1994.

Entered into force May 21, 1994; effective January 1, 1991.

NP

COLOMBIA

AGRICULTURAL COMMODITIES

Agricultural commodities agreement with memorandum of understanding.

Exchange of notes at Bogota October 6, 1959.

Entered into force October 6, 1959.

10 UST 1799; TIAS 4337; 358 UNTS 145.

Amendments

April 26, 1961 (12 UST 516; TIAS 4747; 407 UNTS 285).

September 6 and 8, 1961 (13 UST 204; TIAS 4962; 442 UNTS 334).

November 9 and 20, 1961 (12 UST 3124; TIAS 4911; 433 UNTS 377).

January 31 and February 14, 1962 (13 UST 262; TIAS 4970; 445 UNTS 362).

June 20, 1962 (13 UST 1323; TIAS 5088; 458 UNTS 344).

Agricultural commodities agreement with exchange of notes of March 29 and April 15, 1963.

Signed at Bogota March 27, 1963.

Entered into force March 27, 1963.

14 UST 1502; TIAS 5450; 489 UNTS 289.

Amendment

October 11 and 25, 1963 (15 UST 146; TIAS 5531; 511 UNTS 313).

Agricultural commodities agreement with exchange of notes of October 8, 1964 and February 11, 1965.

Signed at Bogota October 8, 1964.

Entered into force October 8, 1964.

TIAS 5797; 16 UST 683; 579 UNTS 3.

Agricultural commodities agreement with exchange of notes.

Signed at Bogota March 10, 1966.

Entered into force March 10, 1966.

17 UST 1965; TIAS 6138; 674 UNTS 139.

Agricultural commodities agreement with annex.

Signed at Bogota May 31, 1968.

Entered into force May 31, 1968.

19 UST 6031; TIAS 6563; 702 UNTS 3.

Agricultural commodities agreement with annex.

Signed at Bogota March 4, 1970.

Entered into force March 4, 1970.

22 UST 1618; TIAS 7189; 806 UNTS 255.

Amendment

April 19, May 4 and 12, 1971 (24 UST 412; TIAS 7553; 898 UNTS 335).

Related agreements

April 24, 1973 (24 UST 1056; TIAS 7623).

May 11, 1973 (24 UST 1633; TIAS 7667).

December 11, 1973 (25 UST 180; TIAS 7781).

April 22, 1974 (25 UST 627; TIAS 7812).

Agricultural commodities agreement with annex.

Signed at Bogota June 26, 1972.

Entered into force June 26, 1972.

24 UST 751; TIAS 7580.

Amendments

June 26 and 28, 1972 (24 UST 761; TIAS 7580).

August 16 and September 1, 1972 (24 UST 764; TIAS 7580).

AGRICULTURE

Agreement for the eradication of foot-and-mouth disease in the areas adjacent to the Colombian-Panamanian border, with annex.

Signed at Bogota August 8, 1979.

Entered into force October 10, 1979.

33 UST 1643; TIAS 10138.

AMITY

See also COMMERCE

Treaty for the settlement of differences arising out of the events which took place on the Isthmus of Panama in November 1903.

Signed at Bogota April 6, 1914.

Entered into force March 1, 1922.

42 Stat. 2122; TS 661; 6 Bevans 900; 9 LNTS 301.

ATOMIC ENERGY

Agreement providing for a grant for the acquisition of nuclear training and research equipment and materials.

Exchange of notes at Bogota July 31, 1959 and January 11, 1960.

Entered into force January 11, 1960.

11 UST 138; TIAS 4421; 371 UNTS 37.

Agreement for cooperation concerning civil uses of nuclear energy, with annex and exchange of notes.

Signed at Bogota January 8, 1981.

Entered into force September 7, 1983.

TIAS 10722; 1607 UNTS 33.

AVIATION

Air transport agreement and exchanges of notes.

Signed at Bogota October 24, 1956.

Entered into force provisionally January 1, 1957.

14 UST 429; TIAS 5338; 476 UNTS 77.

Amendments and extension

October 23, 1968 (19 UST 7501; TIAS 6593; 701 UNTS 386).

October 16 and 22, 1981 and April 21, 1982 (34 UST 1152; TIAS 10404).

August 11, October 11 and November 22, 2000.

March 20 and April 13, 2002.

December 23 and 28, 2005.

March 23 and 31, 2006.

October 3, 2006.

Agreement relating to the sale of six C-47 aircraft to Colombia for civilian cargo and passenger service.

Signed at Bogota April 21, 1976.

Entered into force April 21, 1976.

27 UST 4317; TIAS 8453; 1071 UNTS 73.

Memorandum of agreement to furnish on a reimbursable basis to foreign governments technical cooperation and certain services to encourage and foster the development of civil aeronautics and air commerce

Signed August 2 and 4, 1994.

Entered into force August 4, 1994.

TIAS

COMMERCE

Treaty of peace, amity, navigation, and commerce, with additional article.[1]

Signed at Bogota December 12, 1846.

Entered into force June 10, 1848.

9 Stat. 881; TS 54; 6 Bevans 868.

NOTE

1 Article 33 terminated by the United States effective July 1, 1916, in accordance with the Seamen's Act (38 Stat. 1164).

CONSULS

See also COMMERCE

Consular convention.[1]

Signed at Washington May 4, 1850.

Entered into force October 30, 1851.

10 Stat. 900; TS 55; 6 Bevans 882.

NOTE

1 Article III, paragraphs 8 and 11, terminated by the United States as of July 1, 1916 in accordance with the Seamen's Act (38 Stat. 1164).

CULTURAL PROPERTY

Memorandum of understanding concerning the imposition restrictions on archaeological material from the Pre-Columbian cultures and certain ecclesiastical ethnological material from the colonial period in Colombia.

Signed at Bogota March 15, 2006.

Entered into force March 15, 2006.

TIAS

CUSTOMS

Agreement relating to reciprocal customs privileges for consular officers.

Exchange of notes at Washington May 9 and 10, 1968.

Entered into force May 10, 1968.

19 UST 4864; TIAS 6491; 698 UNTS 237.

Agreement regarding mutual assistance.

Signed at Miami September 21, 1999.

Entered into force September 21, 1999.

TIAS

DEFENSE

Agreement relating to the procurement of strategic materials.

Exchange of notes at Bogota March 29, 1943.

Entered into force March 29, 1943.

58 Stat. 1546; EAS 442; 6 Bevans 954; 124 UNTS 139.

Military assistance agreement.

Exchange of notes at Bogota April 17, 1952.

Entered into force April 17, 1952.

3 UST 3690; TIAS 2496; 174 UNTS 15.

Agreement for performance by members of Army, Navy, and Air Force missions of duties of military assistance advisory group specified in article V of military assistance agreement of April 17, 1952.

Exchange of notes at Bogota July 13 and September 16, 1955.

Entered into force September 20, 1955.

6 UST 3904; TIAS 3393; 256 UNTS 221.

Agreement providing for disposition of equipment and materials furnished by the United States under the military assistance agreement of April 17, 1952.

Exchange of notes at Bogota February 22 and March 14, 1956.

Entered into force March 14, 1956.

7 UST 475; TIAS 3531; 270 UNTS 392.

Agreement relating to the furnishing of military equipment, materials, and services.

Exchange of notes at Bogota April 3, 1961.

Entered into force April 3, 1961.

12 UST 492; TIAS 4740; 407 UNTS 3.

Agreement relating to the deposit of ten percent of the grants of military assistance and excess defense articles given by the United States with related aide memoire.

Exchange of notes at Bogota August 25, 1972.

Entered into force August 25, 1972; effective February 7, 1972.

23 UST 3149; TIAS 7492; 898 UNTS 171.

Agreement concerning general security of military information.

Exchange of notes at Bogota December 16, 1981.

Entered into force December 16, 1981.

33 UST 4444; TIAS 10315.

Memorandum of agreement on the exchange of naval personnel.

Signed at Bogota and Washington March 8 and April 30, 1985.

Entered into force April 30, 1985.

TIAS 11255.

Memorandum of understanding concerning Colombian integration into the Caribbean Basin Radar Network (CBRN).

Signed at Bogota February 22, 1989.

Entered into force February 22, 1989.

TIAS 12282.

Acquisition and cross-servicing agreement, with annexes.

Signed at Miami and Bogota May 23 and June 27, 2002.

Entered into force June 27, 2002.

TIAS

Aviation leadership program agreement.

Signed at Washington and Bogota August 4, 2004 and February 2, 2005.

Entered into force February 2, 2005.

TIAS

Agreement amending the agreement of August 10 and September 25, 1992 relating to payment to the United States of the net proceeds from the sale of defense articles furnished on a grant basis.

Exchange of notes at Bogota July 21, 2004 and April 20, 2005.

Entered into force April 20, 2005.

TIAS

Agreement regarding the assignment of liaison officers, with annex.

Signed at Washington and Bogota July 15 and October 22, 2005.

Entered into force October 22, 2005.

TIAS

ECONOMIC AND TECHNICAL COOPERATION

Agreement for a cooperative program of agriculture and natural resources in Colombia.

Exchange of notes at Bogota May 25 and June 9, 1953.

Entered into force June 9, 1953.

4 UST 1601; TIAS 2827; 213 UNTS 3.

Agreement for interchange of technical knowledge and skills and related activities for development of Cauca Valley region.

Exchange of notes at Bogota July 29 and November 15 and 28, 1955.

Entered into force November 28, 1955.

6 UST 6035; TIAS 3451; 241 UNTS 39.

General agreement for economic, technical and related assistance.

Signed at Bogota July 23, 1962.

Entered into force July 23, 1962.

13 UST 1778; TIAS 5123; 458 UNTS 123.

Related agreement

August 30, 2004.

Agreement concerning the establishment of an Americas Account and Administering Council.

Signed at Bogota June 18, 1993.

Entered into force June 18, 1993.

TIAS 12502.

Amendment

March 27, 2000.

Agency for International Development

December 24, 1975 (28 UST 179; TIAS 8467; 1071 UNTS 31).

March 12, 1976 (28 UST 1419; TIAS 8515).

April 22, 1976 (28 UST 1438; TIAS 8516; 1071 UNTS 79).

June 14, 1976 (28 UST 1515; TIAS 8519; 1071 UNTS 155).

October 19, 1976 (28 UST 8273; TIAS 8760).

October 19, 1976 (28 UST 8291; TIAS 8761).

November 29, 1976 (28 UST 8709; TIAS 8768).

November 29, 1976 (28 UST 8748; TIAS 8769; 1095 UNTS 3).

September 27, 2000 (NP).

September 27, 2000 (NP).

July 9, 2004 (NP).

June 30, 2005 (NP).

June 30, 2005 (NP).

June 30, 2005 (NP).

July 19, 2006 (NP).

July 19, 2006 (NP).

EDUCATION

Agreement for financing certain educational exchange programs.

Exchange of notes at Bogota June 12, 1967 and March 8, 1971.

Entered into force March 11, 1971.

22 UST 1705; TIAS 7198; 808 UNTS 368.

EMPLOYMENT

Agreement relating to the employment of dependents of official government employees.

Exchange of notes at Bogota March 30 and May 25, 1982.

Entered into force May 25, 1982.

35 UST 1301; TIAS 10729; 1607 UNTS 95.

ENVIRONMENTAL COOPERATION

Agreement for cooperation in the Global Learning and Observations to Benefit the Environment (GLOBE) Program, with appendices.

Signed at Washington October 28, 1998.

Entered into force October 28, 1998.

TIAS

EXTRADITION

Extradition treaty, with annex.

Signed at Washington September 14, 1979.

Entered into force March 4, 1982.

TIAS

FINANCE

Agreement relating to investment guaranties.

Exchange of letters at Bogota October 5, 1962.

Entered into force October 5, 1962.

13 UST 2465; TIAS 5210; 459 UNTS 191.

Investment incentive agreement.

Exchange of notes at Washington April 3, 1985.

Entered into force April 3, 1985.

TIAS 12043.

Amendment

July 18 and August 19, 1985 (TIAS 12043).

Agreement regarding the reduction of certain debts related to foreign assistance owed to the Government of the United States and its agencies, with appendices.

Signed at Washington December 15, 1992.

Entered into force January 14, 1993.

NP

Amendments

June 1 and 30, 1993 (NP).

July 2 and 19, 1993 (NP).

Agreement regarding a debt-for-nature swap to prepay and cancel certain debt owed by the Government of the Republic of Colombia to the Government of the United States of America, with attachments.

Signed at Bogota March 30, 2004.

Entered into force April 29, 2004.

TIAS

FISHERIES

Agreement on certain fishing rights in implementation of the treaty and exchange of notes of September 8, 1972 (TIAS 10120).

Exchange of notes at Bogota October 24 and December 6, 1983.

Entered into force December 6, 1983; effective March 1, 1984.

35 UST 3105; TIAS 10842; 2015 UNTS 3.

HIGHWAYS

Agreement for cooperation in the construction of the Colombia segment of the Darien Gap Highway.

Signed at Washington May 6, 1971.

Entered into force May 6, 1971.

22 UST 617; TIAS 7112; 793 UNTS 3.

INTERNATIONAL CRIMINAL COURT

Agreement regarding the surrender of persons of the United States of America to the International Criminal Court.

Signed at Bogota September 17, 2003.

Entered into force September 17, 2003.

TIAS

JUDICIAL ASSISTANCE

Procedures for mutual assistance in the administration of justice in connection with the Lockheed Aircraft Corporation matter.

Signed at Washington April 22, 1976.

Entered into force April 22, 1976.

27 UST 1059; TIAS 8244.

Related agreements

July 7 and 15, 1980 (32 UST 1921; TIAS 9809; 1234 UNTS 423).

August 28 and September 10, 1980 (32 UST 2599; TIAS 9860; 1274 UNTS 261).

MAPPING

Arrangement covering the accomplishment of aerial photographic coverage of Colombia with annexes.

Signed at Bogota July 4, 1975.

Entered into force July 4, 1975.

28 UST 1063; TIAS 8493.

Cooperative arrangement for the production of topographic maps of Colombia, with annexes.

Signed at Washington and Bogota April 21 and 28, 1986.

Entered into force April 28, 1986.

NP

Basic exchange and cooperative agreement concerning geospatial information and services cooperation, with annexes.

Signed at Bogota and Washington April 11 and 23, 2002.

Entered into force April 23, 2002.

NP

MISSIONS, MILITARY

Agreement concerning an army mission, a naval mission, and an air force mission of the United States armed forces in Colombia.

Signed at Bogota October 7, 1974.

Entered into force April 16, 1975.

29 UST 2901; TIAS 8986; 1148 UNTS 75.

NARCOTIC DRUGS

Agreement relating to cooperation to curb the illegal traffic in narcotics.

Exchange of notes at Bogota July 21 and August 6, 1980.

Entered into force August 6, 1980.

32 UST 2301; TIAS 9838; 1274 UNTS 255.

Memorandum of understanding concerning cooperation in the seizure and forfeiture of property and proceeds of illicit trafficking in narcotic drugs.

Signed at Bogota July 24, 1990.

Entered into force July 24, 1990.

TIAS 12417.

Mutual cooperation agreement to combat, prevent and control money laundering arising from illicit activities.

Signed at San Antonio February 27, 1992.

Entered into force February 27, 1992.

TIAS 12450.

Agreement to suppress illicit traffic by sea.

Signed at Bogota February 20, 1997.

Entered into force February 20, 1997.

TIAS

Supplemental memorandum through which mechanisms are established for implementing the July 24, 1990 memorandum of understanding concerning the transfer of forfeited assets.

Signed at Washington October 28, 1998.

Entered into force October 28, 1998.

TIAS

Agreement regarding the provision of articles, services and associated training by the Government of the United States for counter-narcotics purposes.

Exchange of notes at Bogota February 28 and 29, 2000.

Entered into force February 29, 2000.

TIAS

Agreement concerning the program for the suppression of illicit aerial traffic in narcotic drugs and psychotropic substances (Air Bridge Denial), with annexes.

Signed at Bogota April 28, 2003.

Entered into force April 28, 2003.

TIAS

PEACE CORPS

Agreement for using volunteers to carry out social and economic development projects in Colombia.

Signed at Bogota April 2, 1963.

Entered into force July 12, 1963.

26 UST 1764; TIAS 8134; 1006 UNTS 7.

POSTAL MATTERS

Parcel post agreement.

Signed at Bogota January 31 and at Washington February 7, 1939; operative April 1, 1939.

53 Stat. 2136; Post Office Department print; 196 LNTS 53.

International express mail agreement, with detailed regulations.

Signed at Washington and Bogota June 13 and July 7, 1983.

Entered into force September 3, 1983.

35 UST 1459; TIAS 10738; 2006 UNTS 361.

PUBLICATIONS

Agreement relating to the exchange of official publications.

Exchange of notes at Washington July 15 and 26, 1949.

Entered into force July 26, 1949.

63 Stat. 2799; TIAS 2048; 6 Bevans 998; 73 UNTS 105.

TAXATION

Agreement for relief from double taxation on earnings from operations of ships and aircraft.

Exchange of notes at Washington August 1, 1961.

Entered into force December 11, 1961.

12 UST 3141; TIAS 4916; 433 UNTS 123.

Amendment

October 16, 1987 (TIAS 11563; 2185 UNTS 464).

TELECOMMUNICATION

Agreement relating to radio communications between amateur stations on behalf of third parties.

Exchange of notes at Bogota November 16 and 29, 1963.

Entered into force December 29, 1963.

14 UST 1754; TIAS 5483; 494 UNTS 49.

Agreement relating to the reciprocal granting of authorizations to permit licensed amateur radio operators of either country to operate their stations in the other country.

Exchange of notes at Bogota October 19 and 28, 1965.

Entered into force November 28, 1965.

16 UST 1742; TIAS 5899; 574 UNTS 109.

TERRITORIAL STATUS

See also FISHERIES

Treaty concerning the status of Quita Sueno, Roncador and Serrana, with exchange of notes.

Signed at Bogota September 8, 1972.

Entered into force September 17, 1981.[1]

33 UST 1405; TIAS 10120; 1307 UNTS 379.

NOTE

1 With understanding.

TRADE

See also COMMERCE

Memorandum of understanding setting forth mutual trade concessions and contributions to the multilateral trade negotiations, and related letters of January 28 and June 30, 1980.

Signed at Bogota April 23, 1979.

Entered into force October 3, 1981.

33 UST 4459; TIAS 10316.

Agreement relating to trade in cotton textiles.

Signed at Washington April 3, 1992.

Entered into force April 3, 1992; effective January 1, 1992.

NP

Agreement regarding sanitary and phytosanitary measures and technical barriers to trade.

Exchange of letters at Bogota and Washington February 26, 2006.

Entered into force February 26, 2006.

TIAS

VISAS

Agreement relating to the extension of the validity of nonimmigrant visas.

Exchange of notes at Bogota June 13 and 26, 1956 and May 22, 1957.

Entered into force June 21, 1957.

10 UST 1250; TIAS 4263; 354 UNTS 21.

Amendment

June 5 and 11, 1957 (10 UST 1250; TIAS 4263; 354 UNTS 29).

WEATHER STATIONS

Agreement relating to the re-establishment, operation, and maintenance of the rawinsonde observation stations at Bogota and on San Andres Island, with memorandum of arrangement.

Exchange of letters at Bogota April 28 and September 8, 1981.

Entered into force September 8, 1981.

TIAS 12377.

COMMISSION OF THE CARTAGENA AGREEMENT (ANDEAN GROUP) [1]

NOTE

1 Representatives of Bolivia, Colombia, Ecuador, Peru, and Venezuela signed for the Commission.

ECONOMIC AND TECHNICAL COOPERATION

Memorandum of understanding concerning trade, financing, science and technology, development of industry, agriculture and infrastructure.

Signed at Washington November 21, 1979.

Entered into force November 21, 1979.

32 UST 4399; TIAS 9953; 1266 UNTS 293.

SCIENTIFIC COOPERATION

Memorandum of understanding on science and technology cooperation.

Signed at Washington November 21, 1979.

Entered into force November 21, 1979.

32 UST 4327; TIAS 9949; 1266 UNTS 285.

TRADE

Agreement within the context of the multilateral trade negotiations and related note of April 14, 1980.

Signed at Lima December 14, 1979.

Entered into force January 1, 1980.

32 UST 5283; TIAS 9979; 1266 UNTS 301.

COMOROS

DEFENSE

Agreement concerning the provision of training related to defense articles under the United States International Military Education and Training (IMET) Program.

Exchange of notes at Moroni August 5, 1986 and September 22, 1987.

Entered into force September 22, 1987.

TIAS 11403.

INTERNATIONAL CRIMINAL COURT

Agreement regarding the surrender of persons to the International Criminal Court.

Signed at Moroni June 30, 2004.

Entered into force June 30, 2004.

TIAS

PEACE CORPS

Agreement relating to the establishment of a Peace Corps program in the Comoros.

Exchange of notes at Moroni December 22, 1987.

Entered into force December 22, 1987.

TIAS 12070.

TELECOMMUNICATION

Agreement relating to radio communications between amateur stations on behalf of third parties.

Exchange of notes at Moroni March 8 and September 8, 1989.

Entered into force October 8, 1989.

TIAS 11699.

CONGO

AGRICULTURAL COMMODITIES

Agricultural commodities agreement.

Signed at Brazzaville August 16, 1982.

Entered into force August 16, 1982.

TIAS 11055; 2034 UNTS 191.

Agricultural commodities agreement.

Signed at Washington February 14, 1990.

Entered into force February 14, 1990.

NP

AVIATION

Air transport services agreement between the United States and France.

Signed at Paris March 27, 1946.

Entered into force March 27, 1946.

61 Stat. 3445; TIAS 1679; 7 Bevans 1109; 139 UNTS 114.

Extensions and amendments

June 23 and July 11, 1950 (1 UST 593; TIAS 2106; 139 UNTS 142).

March 19, 1951 (2 UST 1033; TIAS 2257; 139 UNTS 151).

March 19, 1951 (2 UST 1037; TIAS 2258; 139 UNTS 146).

August 27, 1959 (10 UST 1791; TIAS 4336; 358 UNTS 277).

EMPLOYMENT

Agreement relating to the employment of dependents of official government employees.

Exchange of notes at Washington April 11 and May 23, 1997.

Entered into force May 23, 1997.

TIAS

ENVIRONMENTAL COOPERATION

Agreement for cooperation in the Global Learning and Observations to Benefit the Environment (GLOBE) Program.

Signed at Brazzaville June 28, 2005.

Entered into force June 28, 2005.

TIAS

EXTRADITION

Extradition convention between the United States and France.

Signed at Paris January 6, 1909.

Entered into force July 27, 1911.

37 Stat. 1526; TS 561; 7 Bevans 872.

Supplementary extradition convention between the United States and France.

Signed at Paris January 15, 1929.

Entered into force May 19, 1929.

46 Stat. 2276; TS 787; 7 Bevans 972; 92 LNTS 259.

Supplementary extradition convention between the United States and France.

Signed at Paris April 23, 1936.

Entered into force September 24, 1936.

50 Stat. 1117; TS 909; 7 Bevans 995; 172 LNTS 197.

FINANCE

Agreement regarding the consolidation and rescheduling of certain debts owed to, guaranteed by or insured by the United States Government and its agencies, with annexes.

Signed at Brazzaville June 26, 1987.

Entered into force August 7, 1987.

NP

Agreement regarding the consolidation and rescheduling or refinancing of certain debts owed to, guaranteed by, or insured by the United States Government and its agency, with annexes.

Signed at Brazzaville May 6, 1994.

Entered into force June 30, 1994.

NP

Agreement regarding the consolidation and rescheduling or refinancing of certain debts owed to, guaranteed by or insured by the United States Government and its agency, with annexes.

Signed at Brazzaville November 21, 1994.

Entered into force January 19, 1995.

NP

Investment incentive agreement.

Signed at Washington September 12, 2002.

Entered into force September 12, 2002.

TIAS

Agreement regarding the consolidation and rescheduling of certain debts owed to, guaranteed by, or insured by the United States Government and its agencies.

Signed at Brazzaville May 6, 2005.

Entered into force June 13, 2005.

NP

Agreement regarding the consolidation and rescheduling of certain debts owed to, guaranteed by, or insured by the United States Government and its agencies, with annexes.

Signed at Brazzaville July 8, 2005.

Entered into force August 22, 2005.

NP

INTERNATIONAL CRIMINAL COURT

Agreement regarding the surrender of persons to the International Criminal Court.

Signed at Brazzaville June 2, 2004.

Entered into force June 2, 2004.

TIAS

INVESTMENT

Treaty concerning the reciprocal encouragement and protection of investment, with annex.

Signed at Washington February 12, 1990.

Entered into force August 13, 1994.

TIAS

PEACE CORPS

Agreement concerning the establishment of a Peace Corps program in the Congo.

Exchange of notes at Brazzaville April 21, 1990.

Entered into force April 21, 1990.

TIAS

POSTAL MATTERS

International express mail agreement, with detailed regulations.

Signed at Brazzaville and Washington July 15 and August 12, 1988.

Entered into force September 15, 1988.

TIAS 11659.

Memorandum of understanding concerning the operation of the INTELPOST service, with details of implementation.

Signed at Brazzaville and Washington March 20, 1990 and May 13, 1991.

Entered into force May 28, 1991.

TIAS 11835.

TREATY OBLIGATIONS

Treaty obligations assumed by the Congo upon its independence.

Exchange of notes at Brazzaville May 12 and August 5, 1961.

Entered into force August 5, 1961.

13 UST 2065; TIAS 5161; 603 UNTS 19.

VISAS

Reciprocal agreement between the United States and France relating to visa fees for nonimmigrants.

Exchanges of notes at Washington August 19 and September 4, 5, and 16, 1947.

Entered into force September 16, 1947; operative October 1, 1947.

61 Stat. 3776; TIAS 1721; 7 Bevans 1210; 84 UNTS 19.

CONGO, DEMOCRATIC REPUBLIC OF THE

AGRICULTURAL COMMODITIES

Agricultural commodities agreement, with exchange of letters.

Signed at Leopoldville November 18, 1961.

Entered into force November 18, 1961.

12 UST 3202; TIAS 4925; 433 UNTS 207.

Amendments

May 4 and 11, 1962 (13 UST 1241; TIAS 5069; 456 UNTS 514).

May 23 and June 8, 1962 (13 UST 2019; TIAS 5159; 460 UNTS 330).

July 27, 1962 (13 UST 2079; TIAS 5164; 462 UNTS 366).

August 31, 1962 (13 UST 2181; TIAS 5182; 460 UNTS 333).

November 2, 1962 (13 UST 2559; TIAS 5221; 460 UNTS 337).

August 28 and September 4, 1964 (15 UST 1803; TIAS 5653; 531 UNTS 378).

Agricultural commodities agreement, with exchange of notes and aide-memoire.

Signed at Leopoldville February 23, 1963.

Entered into force February 23, 1963.

14 UST 1562; TIAS 5460; 493 UNTS 3.

Amendment

August 28 and September 4, 1964 (15 UST 1803; TIAS 5653; 531 UNTS 378).

Agricultural commodities agreement, with exchange of notes and aide-memoire.

Signed at Leopoldville February 23, 1963.

Entered into force February 23, 1963.

14 UST 1573; TIAS 5461; 493 UNTS 17.

Amendments

December 18 and 19, 1963 (14 UST 1758; TIAS 5484; 505 UNTS 339).

August 28 and September 4, 1964 (15 UST 1803; TIAS 5653; 531 UNTS 378).

December 9, 1964 (15 UST 2235; TIAS 5711; 531 UNTS 413).

Agricultural commodities agreement with exchange of notes.

Signed at Leopoldville April 28, 1964.

Entered into force April 28, 1964.

15 UST 358; TIAS 5565; 526 UNTS 55.

Amendments

August 25, 1964 (15 UST 1884; TIAS 5662; 531 UNTS 426).

December 9, 1964 (15 UST 2235; TIAS 5711; 531 UNTS 413).

April 29, 1965 (16 UST 667; TIAS 5794; 546 UNTS 393).

September 21 and 28, 1965 (16 UST 1268; TIAS 5878; 579 UNTS 282).

Agricultural commodities agreement with exchange of notes.

Signed at Leopoldville December 9, 1964.

Entered into force December 9, 1964.

15 UST 2214; TIAS 5708; 531 UNTS 249.

Agricultural commodities agreement, with exchange of notes.

Signed at Leopoldville July 19, 1965.

Entered into force July 19, 1965.

16 UST 2001; TIAS 5935; 593 UNTS 215.

Amendment

April 22 and 25, 1966 (17 UST 835; TIAS 6042; 593 UNTS 233).

Agricultural commodities agreement with exchange of notes.

Signed at Kinshasa October 3, 1966.

Entered into force October 3, 1966.

17 UST 2258; TIAS 6166; 680 UNTS 241.

Agricultural commodities agreement with annex.

Signed at Kinshasa and Lubumbashi March 15, 1967.

Entered into force March 15, 1967.

18 UST 1826; TIAS 6329; 692 UNTS 120.

Amendments

April 6, 1967 (18 UST 1826; TIAS 6329; 692 UNTS 144).

June 16 and 26, 1967 (18 UST 1826; TIAS 6329; 692 UNTS 148).

December 15 and 21, 1967 (18 UST 3138; TIAS 6404; 692 UNTS 151).

Related agreements

December 11, 1967 (18 UST 3065; TIAS 6396; 701 UNTS 183).

August 12, 1968 (19 UST 5911; TIAS 6545; 707 UNTS 137).

May 14, 1969 (20 UST 762; TIAS 6687; 715 UNTS 23).

October 21, 1969 (20 UST 2401; TIAS 6712; 726 UNTS 223).

March 24 and July 7, 1970 (21 UST 1577; TIAS 6921).

October 7, 1971 (22 UST 1784; TIAS 7219).

Agricultural commodities agreement.

Signed at Kinshasa March 25, 1976.

Entered into force March 25, 1976.

27 UST 3841; TIAS 8403; 1059 UNTS 35.

Amendments

April 28, 1976 (27 UST 3863; TIAS 8403; 1059 UNTS 55).

August 23 and December 7, 1976 (28 UST 1269; TIAS 8507).

Related agreements

May 24, 1977 (29 UST 287; TIAS 8813).

August 15 and 19, 1977 (29 UST 292; TIAS 8813).

September 19 and 20, 1977 (29 UST 294; TIAS 8813).

July 7, 1978 (30 UST 1535; TIAS 9262; 1148 UNTS 445).

August 25, 1978 (30 UST 1521; TIAS 9261; 1150 UNTS 194).

December 27, 1978 and January 3, 1979 (30 UST 1532; TIAS 9261; 1150 UNTS 209).

July 27, 1979 (NP).

August 29 and 30, 1979 (NP).

Agricultural commodities agreement, with memorandum of understanding.

Signed at Kinshasa May 30, 1980.

Entered into force May 30, 1980.

NP

Amendment

October 10 and 31, 1980 (NP).

Related agreements

May 7, 1981 (NP).

April 3, 1982 (NP).

June 21 and July 7, 1982 (NP).

November 27, 1982 (NP).

December 10, 1983 (NP).

August 20 and 28, 1984 (NP).

December 22, 1984 (NP).

July 1 and 3, 1985 (NP).

August 6 and 19, 1985 (NP).

Agricultural commodities agreement.

Signed at Kinshasa November 27, 1985.

Entered into force November 27, 1985.

NP

Amendment

January 22, 1987 (NP).

July 2, 1987 (NP).

Agricultural commodities agreement.

Signed at Kinshasa February 24, 1988.

Entered into force February 24, 1988.

NP

Amendments

August 13, 1988 (NP).

October 4 and 5, 1988 (NP).

Related agreements

May 2, 1989 (NP).

July 29, 1989 (NP).

November 2 and 21, 1989 (NP).

Agricultural commodities agreement.

Signed at Kinshasa February 7, 1990.

Entered into force February 7, 1990.

NP

Amendment

August 3 and 15, 1990 (NP).

AVIATION

Air transport agreement.

Signed at New York August 14, 1970.

Entered into force August 14, 1970.

21 UST 1932; TIAS 6935; 763 UNTS 71.

DEFENSE

Agreement relating to military assistance and provision for a military mission to Congo (Leopoldville).

Exchange of notes at Leopoldville June 24 and July 19, 1963.

Entered into force July 19, 1963.

15 UST 142; TIAS 5530; 511 UNTS 47.

Agreement relating to the deposit by Zaire of ten percent of the value of grant military assistance and excess defense articles furnished by the United States.

Exchange of notes at Kinshasa April 18 and May 16, 1972.

Entered into force May 16, 1972; effective February 7, 1972.

23 UST 1442; TIAS 7422.

Agreement concerning the provision of training related to defense articles under the United States International Military Education and Training (IMET) Program.

Exchange of notes at Kinshasa December 22, 1983 and June 16, 1984.

Entered into force June 16, 1984.

TIAS 10985; 2022 UNTS 119.

Agreement regarding the status of U.S. military personnel and civilian employees of the Department of Defense who may be present in Zaire in connection with humanitarian efforts.

Exchange of notes at Kinshasa July 21 and 22, 1994.

Entered into force July 22, 1994.

Agreement regarding grants under the Foreign Assistance Act of 1961, as amended, or successor legislation, and the furnishing of defense articles, defense services and related training, including pursuant to the United States International Military and Education Training Program (IMET).

Exchange of notes at Kinshasa June 5 and October 11, 2006.

Entered into force October 11, 2006.

NP

Acquisition and cross-servicing agreement, with annexes.

Signed at Stuttgart and Kinshasa July 14 and September 29, 2006.

Entered into force September 29, 2006.

TIAS

ECONOMIC AND TECHNICAL COOPERATION

Economic cooperation agreement between the United States and Belgium.[1]

Signed at Brussels July 2, 1948.

Entered into force July 29, 1948.

62 Stat. 2173; TIAS 1781; 5 Bevans 678; 19 UNTS 127.

Agency for International Development

June 29, 1976 (28 UST 4501; TIAS 8604).

NOTE

1 Only article III is applicable to Congo (Leopoldville).

EMPLOYMENT

Agreement concerning the employment of dependents of official government employees, with attachment.

Exchange of notes at Kinshasa January 12, 2002 and October 8, 2003.

Entered into force October 8, 2003.

TIAS

FINANCE

Agreement regarding the consolidation and rescheduling of certain debts owed to, guaranteed or insured by the United States government and its agencies.

Signed at Washington June 17, 1977.

Entered into force August 30, 1977.

28 UST 7593; TIAS 8731.

Agreement regarding the consolidation and rescheduling of payments due under PL 480 Title I agricultural commodity agreements, with annexes.

Signed at Washington July 19, 1978.

Entered into force July 19, 1978.

30 UST 3511; TIAS 9405; 1179 UNTS 37.

Agreement regarding the consolidation and rescheduling of certain debts owed to, guaranteed or insured by the United States Government and its agencies, with annexes.

Signed at Washington February 7, 1979.

Entered into force April 4, 1979.

30 UST 3601; TIAS 9416; 1171 UNTS 135.

Agreement regarding the consolidation and rescheduling of payments due under PL 480 Title I agricultural commodities agreements, with annexes.

Signed at Washington August 1, 1979.

Entered into force August 1, 1979.

30 UST 6279; TIAS 9553; 1179 UNTS 49.

Agreement regarding the consolidation and rescheduling of certain debts owed to, guaranteed or insured by the United States Government and its agencies, with annexes.

Signed at Kinshasa July 28, 1980.

Entered into force October 20, 1980.

32 UST 3631; TIAS 9907.

Agreement regarding the consolidation and rescheduling of payments due under PL 480 Title I agricultural commodity agreements, with annexes.

Signed at Kinshasa March 10, 1981.

Entered into force March 10, 1981.

33 UST 1249; TIAS 10108; 1285 UNTS 3.

Implementation agreement regarding the consolidation and rescheduling of repayments due under Agency for International Development loans.

Signed at Kinshasa April 8, 1981.

Entered into force April 8, 1981.

33 UST 1725; TIAS 10141.

Agreement regarding the consolidation and rescheduling of certain debts owed to, guaranteed or insured by the United States Government and its agencies, with annexes.

Signed at Kinshasa July 23, 1982.

Entered into force August 30, 1982.

NP

Agreement regarding the consolidation and rescheduling of certain debts owed to, guaranteed or insured by the United States Government and its agencies, with annexes.

Signed at Kinshasa May 3, 1984.

Entered into force June 11, 1984.

NP

Agreement regarding the consolidation and rescheduling of certain debts owed to, guaranteed by or insured by the United States Government and its agencies, with annexes.

Signed at Kinshasa December 3, 1985.

Entered into force January 9, 1986.

NP

Agreement regarding the consolidation and rescheduling of certain debts owed to, guaranteed by or insured by the United States Government and its agencies, with annexes.

Signed at Kinshasa April 9, 1987.

Entered into force May 18, 1987.

NP

Agreement regarding the consolidation and rescheduling of certain debts owed to, guaranteed by or insured by the United States Government and its agencies, with annexes.

Signed at Kinshasa February 20, 1988.

Entered into force April 18, 1988.

NP

Agreement regarding the consolidation and rescheduling of certain debts owed to, guaranteed by, or insured by the United States Government and its agencies, with annexes.

Signed at Kinshasa December 23, 1989.

Entered into force February 5, 1990.

NP

Agreement regarding the reduction and consolidation of debts owed to, guaranteed by, or insured by the United States Government and its agencies, with annexes.

Signed at Kinshasa April 10, 2003.

Entered into force June 5, 2003.

NP

Agreement regarding the reduction and consolidation of debts owed to, guaranteed by, or insured by the United States Government and its agencies, with annexes.

Signed at Kinshasa September 14, 2005.

Entered into force October 20, 2005.

NP

Investment incentive agreement.

Signed at Kinshasa December 23, 2005.

Entered into force December 23, 2005.

TIAS

INTERNATIONAL CRIMINAL COURT

Agreement regarding the surrender of persons to the International Criminal Court.

Signed at Washington March 19, 2003.

Entered into force July 22, 2003.

TIAS

INVESTMENT

Treaty concerning the reciprocal encouragement and protection of investment, with protocol.

Signed at Washington August 3, 1984.

Entered into force July 28, 1989.

TIAS

PEACE CORPS

Agreement relating to the establishment of a Peace Corps program in the Democratic Republic of the Congo.

Exchange of notes at Kinshasa May 8 and October 12, 1970.

Entered into force October 12, 1970.

23 UST 268; TIAS 7304.

POSTAL MATTERS

International express mail agreement, with detailed regulations.

Signed at Kinshasa and Washington June 29 and July 20, 1990.

Entered into force August 30, 1990.

TIAS 11736.

COOK ISLANDS

BOUNDARIES

Treaty on friendship and delimitation of the maritime boundary between the United States and the Cook Islands.

Signed at Rarotonga June 11, 1980.

Entered into force September 8, 1983.

35 UST 2061; TIAS 10774; 1676 UNTS 223.

FINANCE

Investment incentive agreement.

Exchange of notes at Wellington and Rarotonga September 2 and October 10, 1983.

Entered into force April 16, 1984.

35 UST 3116; TIAS 10843; 1676 UNTS 235.

PEACE CORPS

Agreement relating to the establishment of a Peace Corps program in the Cook Islands.

Exchange of notes at Wellington and Rarotonga April 28, 1981.

Entered into force April 28, 1981.

33 UST 1080; TIAS-10093; 1285 UNTS 113.

COSTA RICA

AGRICULTURAL COMMODITIES

Agricultural commodities agreement, with memorandum of understanding.

Signed at San Jose March 25, 1982.

Entered into force April 28, 1982.

TIAS 11035; 2023 UNTS 467.

Related agreements

October 30, 1982 (TIAS 11035; 2021 UNTS 349).

April 26, 1983 (TIAS 11035).

Agricultural commodities agreement, with memorandum of understanding.

Signed at San Jose November 22, 1983.

Entered into force January 19, 1984.

TIAS 11036; 2021 UNTS 351.

Amendment

July 3 and 27, 1984 (TIAS 11036).

Agricultural commodities agreement.

Signed at San Jose November 19, 1984.

Entered into force January 2, 1985.

TIAS 11037.

Agricultural commodities agreement.

Signed at San Jose November 29, 1985.

Entered into force January 2, 1986.

NP

Agricultural commodities agreement.

Signed at San Jose January 14, 1987.

Entered into force April 29, 1987.

NP

Amendment

July 2 and 7, 1987 (NP).

Agricultural commodities agreement.

Signed at San Jose March 3, 1988.

Entered into force September 20, 1988.

NP

Amendment

October 17, 1988 (NP).

AGRICULTURE

Agreement relating to cooperative rubber investigations in Costa Rica.

Exchange of notes at San Jose April 19 and June 16, 1941.

Entered into force June 16, 1941.

55 Stat. 1368; EAS 222; 6 Bevans 1056; 103 LNTS 173.

Extensions and amendments

April 3, 1943 (57 Stat. 944; EAS 318; 6 Bevans 1074; 13 UNTS 463).

June 21 and July 1, 1943 (57 Stat. 1048; EAS 335).

Agreement confirming the cooperative agreement for the prevention of foot-and-mouth disease and rinderpest in Costa Rica.

Exchange of notes at San Jose April 5 and June 6, 1972.

Entered into force June 6, 1972.

23 UST 1122; TIAS 7372.

AVIATION

Agreement relating to the free movement of the military aircraft of each country into and through the airspace of the other.

Exchange of notes at San Jose February 19 and 25, 1952.

Entered into force February 25, 1952.

3 UST 3882; TIAS 2518; 174 UNTS 233.

Air transport agreement, with annexes.

Signed at San Jose May 8, 1997.

Entered into force October 15, 1999.

TIAS

COMMERCE

Treaty of friendship, commerce and navigation.

Signed at Washington July 10, 1851.

Entered into force May 26, 1852.

10 Stat. 916; TS 62; 6 Bevans 1013.

CONSULS

See also COMMERCE

Consular convention.[1]

Signed at San Jose January 12, 1948.

Entered into force March 19, 1950.

1 UST 247; TIAS 2045; 70 UNTS 27.

NOTE

1 Applicable to all areas of land and water subject to the sovereignty or authority of either state.

DEFENSE

Agreement relating to the furnishing of defense articles and services to Costa Rica for the purpose of contributing to its internal security.

Exchange of notes at San Jose May 21 and June 18, 1962.

Entered into force June 18, 1962.

13 UST 2094; TIAS 5167; 461 UNTS 155.

Agreement relating to privileges and immunities for United States personnel providing assistance to the drought stricken provinces in northern Costa Rica.

Exchange of notes at San Jose March 30, 1983.

Entered into force March 30, 1983.

NP

Memorandum of understanding establishing a Caribbean Basin Radar Network (CBRN) in Costa Rica.

Signed at San Jose August 17, 1990.

Entered into force August 17, 1990.

TIAS 12283.

Agreement concerning a Medical Readiness Training Exercise (MD 50701), with annexes.

Exchange of notes at San Jose December 21, 1994 and January 3, 1995.

Entered into force January 3, 1995.

NP

ECONOMIC AND TECHNICAL COOPERATION

General agreement for economic, technical and related assistance.

Signed at San Jose December 22, 1961.

Entered into force September 7, 1962.

13 UST 1978; TIAS 5155; 460 UNTS 277.

Agency for International Development

April 26, 1976 (28 UST 8929; TIAS 8777).

August 30, 1978 (30 UST 4993; TIAS 9496; 1179 UNTS 207).

EMPLOYMENT

Agreement relating to the employment of dependents of official government employees.

Exchange of notes at San Jose June 8, 1992.

Entered into force June 8, 1992.

TIAS 12455.

ENVIRONMENTAL COOPERATION

Agreement for cooperation in the Global Learning and Observations to Benefit the Environment (GLOBE) Program, with appendices.

Signed at San Jose April 22, 1996.

Entered into force April 22, 1996.

TIAS 12743.

EXTRADITION

Extradition treaty, with exchange of notes.

Signed at San Jose December 4, 1982.

Entered into force October 11, 1991.

TIAS

FINANCE

Agreement relating to investment guaranties.

Signed at San Jose November 22, 1968.

Entered into force October 24, 1969.

20 UST 3001; TIAS 6776; 726 UNTS 157.

Agreement regarding the consolidation and rescheduling of certain debts owed to, guaranteed or insured by the United States Government and its agencies, with annexes.

Signed at Washington May 18, 1984.

Entered into force June 22, 1984.

NP

Agreement regarding the consolidation and rescheduling of certain debts owed to, guaranteed by or insured by the United States Government and its agencies, with annexes.

Signed at San Jose December 16, 1985.

Entered into force January 29, 1986.

NP

Agreement regarding the consolidation and rescheduling of certain debts owed to, guaranteed by or insured by the United States Government and its agencies.

Signed at San Jose February 22, 1990.

Entered into force April 9, 1990.

NP

Swap agreement among the United States Treasury and the Central Bank of Costa Rica/Government of Costa Rica.

Signed at Washington and San Jose May 18, 1990.

Entered into force May 18, 1990.

TIAS

Agreement regarding the consolidation and rescheduling or refinancing of certain debts owed to, guaranteed by, or insured by the United States Government and its agencies, with annexes.

Signed at San Jose February 19, 1992.

Entered into force April 20, 1992.

NP

Agreement regarding the consolidation and rescheduling or refinancing of certain debts owed to, guaranteed by or insured by the United States Government and its agencies, with annexes.

Signed at San Jose November 22, 1993.

Entered into force August 10, 1994.

NP

HIGHWAYS

Agreement relating to the construction of the inter-American highway within the borders of Costa Rica.

Exchange of notes at Washington January 16, 1942.

Entered into force January 16, 1942.

56 Stat. 1840; EAS 293; 6 Bevans 1068; 23 UNTS 285.

Amendment

January 13 and 17, 1951 (2 UST 1844; TIAS 2319; 134 UNTS 215).

MAPPING

Agreement relating to photomapping project.

Exchange of notes at San Jose August 6 and October 2, 1946.

Entered into force October 2, 1946.

NP

Amendment

December 3 and 7, 1953 (NP).

Cooperative arrangement for the production of topographic maps of Costa Rica, with annexes.

Signed at San Jose and Washington June 4 and 18, 1986.

Entered into force June 18, 1986.

TIAS 11373.

Basic exchange and cooperative agreement for topographic mapping, nautical and aeronautical charting and information, geodesy and geophysics, digital data and related mapping, charting and geodesy materials, with glossary.

Signed at San Jose and Fairfax June 14 and July 2, 1996.

Entered into force July 2, 1996.

NP

NARCOTIC DRUGS

Agreement relating to the provision of assistance to curb the production and traffic in illegal narcotics.

Exchange of notes at San Jose May 29 and June 2, 1975.

Entered into force June 2, 1975.

26 UST 3868; TIAS 8220; 1045 UNTS 17.

Agreement relating to the provision of additional assistance to support cooperative efforts to curb illegal narcotics production and traffic.

Exchange of notes at San Jose June 21 and 24, 1976.

Entered into force June 24, 1976.

28 UST 2924; TIAS 8574; 1068 UNTS 189.

Agreement concerning cooperation to suppress illicit traffic.

Signed at San Jose December 1, 1998.

Entered into force November 19, 1999.

TIAS

Amendment

July 2, 1999.

PEACE CORPS

Agreement relating to the establishment of a Peace Corps program in Costa Rica.

Exchange of notes at San Jose November 21 and 23, 1962.

Entered into force August 11, 1964.

15 UST 2317; TIAS 5719; 541 UNTS 67.

POSTAL MATTERS

International express mail agreement, with detailed regulations.

Signed at San Jose and Washington August 19 and September 14, 1989.

Entered into force September 15, 1989.

TIAS 11690.

PUBLICATIONS

Agreement relating to the exchange of official publications.

Exchange of notes at San Jose November 30 and December 2, 1950.

Entered into force December 2, 1950.

2 UST 405; TIAS 2180; 133 UNTS 61.

TAXATION

Agreement for the exchange of information with respect to taxes, with exchange of notes.

Signed at San Jose March 15, 1989.

Entered into force February 12, 1991.

TIAS 12059.

TELECOMMUNICATION

Agreement relating to radio communications between amateur stations on behalf of third parties.

Exchange of notes at Washington August 13 and October 19, 1956.

Entered into force October 19, 1956.

7 UST 2839; TIAS 3665; 278 UNTS 65.

Agreement relating to the reciprocal granting of authorizations to permit licensed amateur radio operators of either country to operate their stations in the other country.

Exchange of notes at San Jose August 17 and 24, 1964.

Entered into force August 24, 1964.

15 UST 1787; TIAS 5649; 531 UNTS 107.

Agreement concerning the establishment and operation of a Voice of America radio broadcast station in Costa Rica.

Exchange of notes at San Jose July 17 and August 7, 1984.

Entered into force August 7, 1984.

TIAS 11236; 2143 UNTS 437.

TRADE

See also COMMERCE

Convention concerning commercial travelers and protocol.

Signed at San Jose March 31, 1924.

Entered into force June 24, 1924.

43 Stat. 1765; TS 688; 6 Bevans 1041.

Agreement on a consultative mechanism relating to trade in cotton, wool, and man-made fiber textiles and textile products, with annex.

Exchange of notes at San Jose February 7, 1984.

Entered into force February 7, 1984; effective January 1, 1984.

35 UST 4545; TIAS 10956.

Agreement relating to trade in cotton, wool and man-made fiber textiles and textile products, with annexes.

Signed at Washington March 20, 1992.

Entered into force March 20, 1992; effective January 1, 1992.

NP

Amendment and extension

May 5 and October 20, 1994 (NP).

VISAS

Agreement for the waiver of passport visa fees for nonimmigrants.

Exchange of notes at San Jose June 29, 1925; operative July 25, 1925.

6 Bevans 1046.

WEATHER STATIONS

Agreement relating to the operation and maintenance of a rawinsonde observation station at San Jose, with memorandum of arrangement.

Exchange of notes at San Jose April 29 and June 8, 1976.

Entered into force June 8, 1976; effective January 1, 1976.

28 UST 6075; TIAS 8669.

COTE D'IVOIRE

AGRICULTURAL COMMODITIES

Agricultural commodities agreement with exchange of notes.

Signed at Abidjan March 10, 1964.

Entered into force March 10, 1964.

15 UST 273; TIAS 5552; 526 UNTS 285.

Agricultural commodities agreement, with exchange of notes.

Signed at Abidjan April 5, 1965.

Entered into force April 5, 1965.

16 UST 624; TIAS 5784; 546 UNTS 143.

Amendment

June 1, 1966 (17 UST 768; TIAS 6030; 580 UNTS 318).

Agricultural commodities agreement.

Signed at Abidjan June 21, 1989.

Entered into force June 21, 1989.

NP

Agricultural commodities agreement.

Signed at Abidjan May 16, 1990.

Entered into force May 16, 1990.

NP

AVIATION

Air transport agreement, with memorandum of understanding and exchange of notes.

Signed at Abidjan February 24, 1978.

Entered into force provisionally February 24, 1978; definitively June 3, 1980.

32 UST 1165; TIAS 9766; 1220 UNTS 243.

DEFENSE

Agreement concerning the provision of training related to defense articles under the United States International Military Education and Training (IMET) Program.

Exchange of notes at Abidjan March 21 and April 21, 1983.

Entered into force April 21, 1983.

TIAS 10700; 2005 UNTS 153.

ECONOMIC AND TECHNICAL COOPERATION

Agreement providing for economic, technical and related assistance.

Exchange of notes at Abidjan May 17, 1961.

Entered into force May 17, 1961.

12 UST 652; TIAS 4765; 409 UNTS 241.

FINANCE

Agreement relating to investment guaranties.

Exchange of notes at Abidjan December 1, 1961.

Entered into force December 1, 1961.

13 UST 2711; TIAS 5242; 462 UNTS 221.

Agreement regarding the consolidation and rescheduling of certain debts owed to, guaranteed by or insured by the United States Government and its agencies, with annexes.

Signed at Abidjan February 27, 1985.

Entered into force April 10, 1985.

NP

Agreement regarding the consolidation and rescheduling of certain debts owed to, guaranteed by or insured by the United States Government and its agencies, with annexes.

Signed at Abidjan January 31, 1986.

Entered into force March 10, 1986.

NP

Agreement regarding the consolidation and rescheduling of certain debts owed to, guaranteed by or insured by the United States Government and its agencies, with annexes.

Signed at Abidjan March 31, 1987.

Entered into force May 21, 1987.

NP

Agreement regarding the consolidation and rescheduling of certain debts owed to, guaranteed by or insured by the United States Government and its agencies, with annexes.

Signed at Abidjan July 14, 1988.

Entered into force August 26, 1988.

NP

Agreement regarding the consolidation and rescheduling of certain debts owed to, guaranteed by or insured by the United States Government and its agencies, with annexes.

Signed at Abidjan September 29, 1990.

Entered into force November 16, 1990.

NP

Agreement regarding the consolidation and rescheduling or refinancing of certain debts owed to, guaranteed by, or insured by the United States Government and its agencies, with annexes.

Signed at Abidjan May 29, 1992.

Entered into force July 20, 1992.

NP

Agreement regarding the consolidation and rescheduling or refinancing of certain debts owed to, guaranteed by or insured by the United States Government and its agencies, with annexes.

Signed at Abidjan August 26, 1994.

Entered into force October 7, 1994.

NP

Agreement regarding the consolidation, reduction and rescheduling of certain debts owed to, guaranteed by, or insured by the United States Government and its Agencies, with annexes.

Signed at Washington July 29, 1998.

Entered into force September 10, 1998.

NP

Agreement regarding the reduction, consolidation and rescheduling of certain debts owed to, guaranteed by, or insured by the United States Government and its agencies, with annexes.

Signed at Washington July 29, 2002.

Entered into force October 8, 2002.

NP

INTERNATIONAL CRIMINAL COURT

Agreement regarding the surrender of persons to the International Criminal Court.

Signed at Abidjan June 30, 2003.

Entered into force October 16, 2003.

TIAS

PEACE CORPS

Agreement relating to the establishment of a Peace Corps program in Ivory Coast.

Exchange of notes at Abidjan April 5 and 21, 1962.

Entered into force April 21, 1962.

15 UST 345; TIAS 5561; 526 UNTS 39.

POSTAL MATTERS

International express mail agreement, with detailed regulations.

Signed at Abidjan and Washington May 5 and 27, 1987.

Entered into force June 15, 1987.

NP

CROATIA

For agreements prior to the independence of Croatia, see YUGOSLAVIA.

ATOMIC ENERGY

Agreement on thermal-hydraulic code applications and maintenance.

Signed at Rockville and Zagreb September 11 and October 17, 2002.

Entered into force October 17, 2002.

TIAS

DEFENSE

Acquisition and cross-servicing agreement, with annexes.

Signed at Zagreb and Stuttgart July 29 and August 2, 2002.

Entered into force August 2, 2002.

TIAS

Memorandum of understanding concerning the use of airspace, ranges, airports, seaports, and training facilities by the United States forces in Europe.

Signed at Ramstein July 15, 2004.

Entered into force January 11, 2006.

TIAS

ECONOMIC AND TECHNICAL COOPERATION

Agreement concerning economic, technical and related assistance.

Signed at Zagreb May 6, 1994.

Entered into force May 1, 1995.

TIAS

EDUCATION

Agreement on the status of the American International School of Zagreb.

Signed at Zagreb June 27, 2001.

Entered into force November 14, 2002.

TIAS

EMPLOYMENT

Agreement relating to the employment of dependents of official government employees.

Exchange of notes at Washington May 24 and June 20, 1995.

Entered into force June 20, 1995.

TIAS 12669.

ENVIRONMENTAL COOPERATION

Agreement for cooperation in the Global Learning and Observations to Benefit the Environment (GLOBE) Program, with appendices.

Signed at Zagreb April 12, 1995.

Entered into force April 12, 1995.

TIAS 12628.

FINANCE

Investment incentive agreement.

Signed at Washington January 15, 1993.

Entered into force January 15, 1993.

TIAS 12141.

Agreement regarding the consolidation and rescheduling of certain debts owed to, guaranteed by or insured by the United States Government and its agencies, with annexes.

Signed at Zagreb February 1, 1996.

Entered into force July 23, 1996.

NP

INVESTMENT

Treaty concerning the encouragement and reciprocal protection of investment, with annex and protocol.

Done at Zagreb July 13, 1996.

Entered into force June 20, 2001.

TIAS

MAPPING

Basic exchange and cooperative agreement concerning geospatial information and services cooperation, with annex.

Signed at Washington and Zagreb May 31 and June 15, 2001.

Entered into force June 15, 2001.

NP

POSTAL MATTERS

International express mail agreement.

Signed at Zagreb and Washington September 14 and 30, 1992.

Entered into force December 14, 1992.

TIAS 11908.

SCIENTIFIC COOPERATION

Agreement for scientific and technological cooperation, with annexes.

Signed at Washington March 18, 1994.

Entered into force May 18, 2000.

TIAS

WEAPONS

Agreement concerning cooperation in the area of the prevention of proliferation of weapons of mass destruction, and the promotion of defense and military relations.

Signed at Zagreb February 4, 2003.

Entered into force October 15, 2003.

TIAS

CUBA

AVIATION

Agreement to facilitate notification of private flights between Cuba and the United States.

Exchange of notes at Habana January 19 and February 26, 1953.

Entered into force February 26, 1953.

4 UST 210; TIAS 2779; 205 UNTS 213.

Air transport agreement.

Signed at Habana May 26, 1953.

Entered into force June 30, 1953.

4 UST 2837; TIAS 2892; 224 UNTS 75.

Amendment

May 21 and July 30, 1957 (8 UST 1407; TIAS 3891; 289 UNTS 322).

BOUNDARIES

Maritime boundary agreement.

Signed at Washington December 16, 1977.

Entered into force provisionally January 1, 1978.

TIAS

Agreement extending the provisional application of the maritime boundary agreement of December 16, 1977.

Exchange of notes at Washington and Havana December 16 and 30, 2003.

Entered into force December 30, 2003.

TIAS

CONSULS

Consular convention.

Signed at Habana April 22, 1926.

Entered into force December 1, 1926.

44 Stat. 2471; TS 75; 6 Bevans 1149; 60 LNTS 371.

CUSTOMS

Agreement relating to free-entry privileges for noncommissioned personnel.

Exchange of notes at Habana March 23 and May 16, 1932.

Entered into force May 16, 1932.

5 UST 1638; TIAS 3040; 234 UNTS 283.

DEFENSE

Agreement for the lease to the United States of lands in Cuba for coaling and naval stations.

Signed at Habana February 16, 1903, and at Washington February 23, 1903.

Entered into force February 23, 1903.

TS 418; 6 Bevans 1113.

Agreement providing conditions for the lease of coaling or naval stations.

Signed at Habana July 2, 1903.

Entered into force October 6, 1903.

TS 426; 6 Bevans 1120.

Agreement relating to the control of electromagnetic radiations in the event of attack.

Exchange of notes at Habana December 10 and 18, 1951.

Entered into force December 18, 1951.

3 UST 2860; TIAS 2459; 165 UNTS 3.

Military assistance agreement.

Signed at Habana March 7, 1952.

Entered into force March 7, 1952.

3 UST 2901; TIAS 2467; 165 UNTS 11.

Agreement providing for disposition of equipment and materials furnished by the United States under the agreement of March 7, 1952.

Exchange of notes at Habana March 18 and May 3, 1955.

Entered into force May 3, 1955.

6 UST 2059; TIAS 3272; 258 UNTS 408.

Agreement providing for performance by members of Army, Navy, and Air Force missions of duties of military assistance advisory group specified in article V of the military assistance agreement of March 7, 1952.

Exchange of notes at Habana June 24 and August 3, 1955.

Entered into force August 10, 1955.

6 UST 2955; TIAS 3343; 265 UNTS 41.

ECONOMIC AND TECHNICAL COOPERATION

General agreement for technical cooperation.

Signed at Habana June 20, 1951.

Entered into force June 20, 1951.

2 UST 1231; TIAS 2272; 148 UNTS 3.

Amendment

January 7 and 8, 1952 (3 UST 4704; TIAS 2629; 179 UNTS 254).

EXTRADITION

Treaty providing for the mutual extradition of fugitives from justice.

Signed at Washington April 6, 1904.

Entered into force March 2, 1905.[1]

33 Stat. 2265; TS 440; 6 Bevans 1128.

Additional extradition treaty.

Signed at Habana January 14, 1926.

Entered into force June 18, 1926.

44 Stat. 2392; TS 737; 6 Bevans 1136; 61 LNTS 363.

NOTE

1 For amendment to the Spanish text, see 33 Stat. 2273; TS 441; 6 Bevans 1134.

FINANCE

Agreement relating to investment guaranties under section 413 (b)(4) of the Mutual Security Act of 1954 as amended.

Exchange of notes at Habana February 4, 1957.

Entered into force November 29, 1957.

8 UST 2375; TIAS 3953; 302 UNTS 273.

GENERAL RELATIONS

Treaty for the adjustment of title to the ownership of the Isle of Pines.

Signed at Washington March 2, 1904.

Entered into force March 23, 1925.

44 Stat. 1997; TS 709; 6 Bevans 1124; 127 LNTS 143.

Treaty of relations.

Signed at Washington May 29, 1934.

Entered into force June 9, 1934.

48 Stat. 1682; TS 866; 6 Bevans 1161.

INTERESTS SECTIONS

Agreement relating to the establishment of interests sections of the United States and Cuba in the Embassy of Switzerland in Havana and the Embassy of Czechoslovakia in Washington, respectively.

Exchange of notes at New York May 30, 1977.

Entered into force May 30, 1977.

30 UST 2101; TIAS 9313.

Amendment

February 15 and 25, 1991.

MARITIME MATTERS

Agreement providing for the informal visits of warships.

Exchange of notes at Habana February 11 and 21, 1949.

Entered into force March 4, 1949.

5 UST 762; TIAS 2965; 231 UNTS 108.

Extension and amendments

February 13 and 28 and March 3, 1950 (5 UST 762; TIAS 2965; 231 UNTS 113).

November 23, 1953 and January 20, 1954 (5 UST 778; TIAS 2965; 231 UNTS 127).

Arrangement relating to the reciprocal exemption of the pleasure yachts of the two countries from navigation dues and from usual requirements of entry and clearance.

Exchange of notes at Washington December 12 and 17, 1951.

Entered into force December 17, 1951.

3 UST 52; TIAS 2391; 152 UNTS 87.

Agreement concerning financial arrangements for the furnishing of certain supplies and services to naval vessels of both countries.

Signed at Habana January 10, 1956.

Entered into force April 9, 1956.

7 UST 63; TIAS 3479; 240 UNTS 101.

MIGRATION

Joint communique on immigration matters, with minute on implementation.

Signed at New York December 14, 1984.

Entered into force December 14, 1984.

TIAS 11057; 2034 UNTS 193.

Joint communique concerning normalizing migration procedures.

Signed at New York September 9, 1994.

Entered into force September 9, 1994.

TIAS

Joint statement further normalizing migration procedures.

Signed at Washington May 2, 1995.

Entered into force May 2, 1995.

TIAS

MISSIONS, MILITARY

Agreement providing for the services of a United States Air Force mission to Cuba.

Signed at Washington December 22, 1950.

Entered into force December 22, 1950.

1 UST 887; TIAS 2166; 122 UNTS 97.

Extension

May 3 and 17, 1955 (6 UST 2266; TIAS 3295; 264 UNTS 351).

Agreement providing for the services of a United States Army mission to Cuba.

Signed at Washington August 28, 1951.

Entered into force August 28, 1951.

2 UST 1677; TIAS 2309; 134 UNTS 225.

Extension

May 3 and 17, 1955 (6 UST 2263; TIAS 3294; 264 UNTS 355).

Agreement providing for the services of a United States Naval mission to Cuba.

Signed at Washington August 28, 1951.

Entered into force August 28, 1951.

2 UST 1689; TIAS 2310; 140 UNTS 239.

Extension

May 3 and 17, 1955 (6 UST 784; TIAS 3222; 253 UNTS 360).

NARCOTIC DRUGS

See also SMUGGLING

Arrangement for the direct exchange of certain information regarding the traffic in narcotic drugs.

Exchange of notes at Habana February 12 and March 7, 1930.

Entered into force March 7, 1930.

6 Bevans 1157.

POSTAL MATTERS

Parcel post convention.

Signed at Washington July 24, 1930.

Entered into force September 1, 1930.

46 Stat. 2844; Post Office Department print.

PUBLICATIONS

Agreement for the exchange of official publications.

Exchange of notes at Habana May 4 and 12, 1938.

Entered into force May 12, 1938.

52 Stat. 1497; EAS 123; 6 Bevans 1173; 191 LNTS 19.

REFUGEES

Memorandum of understanding between the Embassy of Switzerland in Habana representing the interests of the United States in Cuba and the Foreign Ministry of the Government of Cuba concerning the movement to the United States of Cubans wishing to live in the United States, with related notes.

Exchange of notes at Habana November 6, 1965.

Entered into force November 6, 1965.

17 UST 1045; TIAS 6063; 601 UNTS 81.

SMUGGLING

See also NARCOTIC DRUGS

Convention between the United States of America and the Republic of Cuba for the suppression of smuggling operations between their respective territories.

Signed at Habana March 11, 1926.

Entered into force June 28, 1926.

44 Stat. 2402; TS 739; 6 Bevans 1144; 61 LNTS 383.

TELECOMMUNICATION

Agreement relating to the exchange of third-party messages between radio amateurs.

Exchange of notes at Habana September 17, 1951 and February 27, 1952.

Entered into force February 27, 1952.

3 UST 3892; TIAS 2520; 168 UNTS 3.

TRADE AND COMMERCE

Exclusive agreement supplementary to the general agreement on tariffs and trade, exchanges of notes and memoranda, and supplementary exchange of notes signed at Washington December 19 and 22, 1947.

Signed at Geneva October 30, 1947.

Entered into force October 30, 1947; operative January 1, 1948.

61 Stat. 3699; TIAS 1703; 6 Bevans 1229; 119 UNTS 163.

CUSTOMS COOPERATION COUNCIL

TAXATION

Tax reimbursement agreement, with annex.

Signed at Brussels January 26, 1990.

Entered into force January 26, 1990.

TIAS 11711; 2208 UNTS 3.

CYPRUS

A treaty concerning the establishment of the Republic of Cyprus was signed August 16, 1960 by the Governments of the United Kingdom, Greece, Turkey and Cyprus (British Treaty Series No. 4 (1691)). Article 8 of the treaty provides that the Republic of Cyprus assumes, from August 16, 1960, all international obligations and responsibilities of the United Kingdom in so far as they may be held to have application to the Republic of Cyprus. Also, the international rights and benefits enjoyed by the Government of the United Kingdom by virtue of their application to the territory of the Republic of Cyprus are from August 16, 1960 enjoyed by the Government of the Republic of Cyprus.

AGRICULTURAL COMMODITIES

Memorandum of understanding regarding the grant, delivery and free distribution of 12,000 metric tons of wheat and 10,000 metric tons of barley.

Signed at Nicosia December 8, 1960.

Entered into force December 8, 1960.

11 UST 2687; TIAS 4666; 405 UNTS 145.

Memorandum of understanding regarding the grant, sale and use of proceeds from the sale of 28,000 metric tons of wheat.

Signed at Nicosia December 8, 1960.

Entered into force December 8, 1960.

11 UST 2693; TIAS 4667; 405 UNTS 158.

Memorandum of understanding regarding the grant, sale and use of proceeds from the sale of 40,000 metric tons of wheat.

Signed at Nicosia January 15, 1962.

Entered into force January 15, 1962.

13 UST 113; TIAS 4945; 435 UNTS 15.

Memorandum of understanding regarding the grant to Cyprus of agricultural commodities for an expanded school lunch program.

Signed at Nicosia March 2, 1962.

Entered into force March 2, 1962.

13 UST 291; TIAS 4975; 445 UNTS 189.

Agricultural commodities agreement with exchange of notes.

Signed at Nicosia June 18, 1963.

Entered into force June 18, 1963.

14 UST 936; TIAS 5382; 479 UNTS 191.

AVIATION

Arrangement between the United States and the United Kingdom relating to pilot licenses to operate civil aircraft.

Exchange of notes at Washington March 28 and April 5, 1935.

Entered into force May 5, 1935.

49 Stat. 3731; EAS 77; 12 Bevans 501; 162 LNTS 59.

Agreement between the United States and the United Kingdom relating to air services.

Signed at Bermuda February 11, 1946.

Entered into force February 11, 1946.

60 Stat. 1499; TIAS 1507; 12 Bevans 726; 3 UNTS 253.

CONSULS

Consular convention between the United States and the United Kingdom.

Signed at Washington June 6, 1951.

Entered into force September 7, 1952.

3 UST 3426; TIAS 2494; 165 UNTS 121.

CULTURAL PROPERTY

Memorandum of understanding concerning the imposition of import restrictions on Pre-Classical and Classical archaeological objects.

Signed at Washington July 16, 2002.

Entered into force July 16, 2002.

TIAS

Amendment

August 17, 2006.

CUSTOMS

Agreement regarding mutual assistance between customs services.

Signed at Washington June 2, 1987.

Entered into force August 21, 1987.

TIAS 12113.

ECONOMIC AND TECHNICAL COOPERATION

Economic cooperation agreement between the United States and the United Kingdom.

Signed at London July 6, 1948; applicable to Cyprus July 6, 1948.

62 Stat. 2596; TIAS 1795; 12 Bevans 874; 22 UNTS 263.

Amendments

January 3, 1950 (1 UST 184; TIAS 2036; 86 UNTS 304).

May 25, 1951 (2 UST 1292; TIAS 2277; 99 UNTS 308).

February 25, 1953 (4 UST 1528; TIAS 2815; 172 UNTS 332).

General agreement for technical cooperation.

Signed at Nicosia June 29, 1961.

Entered into force June 29, 1961.

12 UST 890; TIAS 4792; 411 UNTS 55.

EDUCATION

Agreement for financing certain educational exchange programs.

Signed at Nicosia January 18, 1962.

Entered into force January 18, 1962.

13 UST 92; TIAS 4943; 435 UNTS 3.

Amendment

August 12 and September 7, 1968 (19 UST 6292; TIAS 6579; 701 UNTS 376).

ENVIRONMENTAL COOPERATION

Agreement for cooperation in the Global Learning and Observations to Benefit the Environment (GLOBE) Program, with appendices.

Signed at Nicosia November 24, 1998.

Entered into force November 24, 1998.

TIAS

EXTRADITION

Extradition treaty.

Signed at Washington June 17, 1996.

Entered into force September 14, 1999.

TIAS

FINANCE

Agreement relating to investment guaranties.

Exchange of notes at Nicosia May 29, 1963.

Entered into force May 29, 1963.

14 UST 843; TIAS 5364; 487 UNTS 283.

JUDICIAL ASSISTANCE

Treaty on mutual legal assistance in criminal matters.

Signed at Nicosia December 20, 1999.

Entered into force September 18, 2002.

TIAS

MUTUAL SECURITY

Agreement between the United States and the United Kingdom relating to the assurances required under the Mutual Security Act of 1951.

Exchange of notes at London January 8, 1952; applicable to Cyprus January 8, 1952.

3 UST 4665; TIAS 2622; 126 UNTS 307.

PEACE CORPS

Agreement relating to the establishment of a Peace Corps program in Cyprus.

Exchange of notes at Nicosia August 23, 1962.

Entered into force August 23, 1962.

13 UST 2089; TIAS 5166; 461 UNTS 147.

POSTAL MATTERS

Parcel post agreement with detailed regulations for execution.

Signed at Nicosia May 7 and at Washington June 8, 1973.

Entered into force September 1, 1974.

25 UST 3015; TIAS 7962.

International express mail/datapost special express memorandum of understanding, with detailed regulations.

Signed at Nicosia and Washington September 13 and October 18, 1985.

Entered into force November 1, 1985.

TIAS 11159; 2126 UNTS 281.

Memorandum of understanding concerning the operation of the INTELPOST service, with details of implementation.

Signed at Nicosia and Washington March 12 and April 3, 1987.

Entered into force May 6, 1987.

TIAS 11298.

PROPERTY

Convention between the United States and the United Kingdom relating to the tenure and disposition of real and personal property.

Signed at Washington March 2, 1899; applicable to Cyprus February 9, 1901.

31 Stat. 1939; TS 146; 12 Bevans 246.

SHIPPING

Agreement relating to jurisdiction over vessels utilizing the Louisiana Offshore Oil Port.

Exchange of notes at Nicosia August 3 and September 7, 1983.

Entered into force September 7, 1983.

35 UST 2170; TIAS 10782; 2011 UNTS 121.

TAXATION

Convention for the avoidance of double taxation and the prevention of fiscal evasion with respect to taxes on income, with related notes.

Signed at Nicosia March 19, 1984.

Entered into force December 31, 1985.

35 UST 4737; TIAS 10965; 2019 UNTS 79.

Agreement concerning reciprocal exemption from income tax of income derived from the international operation of ships and aircraft.

Exchange of notes at Nicosia June 21 and July 8, 1988.

Entered into force July 8, 1988.

TIAS 11595; 2192 UNTS 167.

TELECOMMUNICATION

Agreement relating to the reciprocal granting of authorizations to permit licensed amateur radio operators of either country to operate their stations in the other country.

Exchange of notes at Nicosia March 4 and 10, 1987.

Entered into force March 10, 1987.

TIAS 11521.

TRADE-MARKS

Declaration by the United States and the United Kingdom relating to reciprocal protection to trade-marks.

Signed at London October 24, 1877.

Entered into force October 24, 1877.

20 Stat. 703; TS 138; 12 Bevans 198.

VISAS

Agreement relating to the reciprocal waiver of fingerprinting requirements for nonimmigrants.

Exchange of notes at Nicosia July 11, 1962 and January 11, 1963.

Entered into force January 11, 1963.

14 UST 6; TIAS 5271; 471 UNTS 127.

WEAPONS

Agreement concerning cooperation to suppress the proliferation of weapons of mass destruction, their delivery systems, and related materials by sea, with appendix.

Signed at Washington July 25, 2005.

Entered into force January 12, 2006.

TIAS

CZECH REPUBLIC

For agreements prior to the independence of the Czech Republic, see CZECHOSLOVAKIA.

ATOMIC ENERGY

Arrangement for the exchange of technical information and cooperation in nuclear safety matters, with addenda.

Signed at Vienna September 22, 2005.

Entered into force September 22, 2005.

TIAS

Agreement regarding the transfer of fresh and spent nuclear fuel from the research reactor in the Nuclear Research Institute at Rez to the Russian Federation for management and storage.

Exchange of notes at Prague December 8 and 15, 2006.

Entered into force December 15, 2006.

TIAS

AVIATION

Air transport agreement, with annexes.

Signed at Prague September 10, 1996.

Entered into force September 10, 1996.

TIAS 12799.

Amendment

June 4, 2001 and February 14, 2002.

DEFENSE

Security agreement concerning security measures for the protection of classified military information.

Signed at Prague September 19, 1995.

Entered into force September 19, 1995.

TIAS 12245.

Agreement concerning exchange of scientific and technical information, with appendix.

Signed at Washington March 1, 1996.

Entered into force March 1, 1996.

TIAS 12731.

Acquisition and cross-servicing agreement, with annex and implementing arrangement.

Signed at Prague November 19, 1996.

Entered into force November 19, 1996.

TIAS 12815.

EMPLOYMENT

Agreement relating to the employment of dependents of official government employees.

Exchange of notes at Prague February 18 and October 1, 1993.

Entered into force October 1, 1993.

TIAS

ENVIRONMENTAL COOPERATION

Agreement for cooperation in the Global Learning and Observations to Benefit the Environment (GLOBE) Program, with appendices.

Signed at Prague April 20, 1995.

Entered into force April 20, 1995.

TIAS 12632.

JUDICIAL ASSISTANCE

Treaty on mutual legal assistance in criminal matters.

Signed at Washington February 4, 1998.

Entered into force May 7, 2000.

TIAS

MAPPING

Agreement concerning exchange and cooperation in the field of geospatial information and services.

Signed at Dobruska September 16, 2002.

Entered into force September 16, 2002.

NP

POSTAL MATTERS

International express mail agreement, with detailed regulations.

Signed at Prague and Washington June 29 and September 1, 1993.

Entered into force September 1, 1993.

NP

SCIENTIFIC COOPERATION

Memorandum of understanding on science and engineering cooperation, with annexes.

Signed at Prague July 13, 1994.

Entered into force July 13, 1994.

TIAS 12556.

Agreement for scientific and technological cooperation, with annexes.

Signed at Prague June 11, 1998.

Entered into force September 30, 1998.

TIAS

Memorandum of understanding concerning scientific and technical cooperation in the earth sciences.

Signed at Reston and Prague April 10 and June 15, 2000.

Entered into force June 15, 2000.

TIAS

TAXATION

Convention for the avoidance of double taxation and the prevention of fiscal evasion with respect to taxes on income and capital.

Signed at Prague September 16, 1993.

Entered into force December 23, 1993.

TIAS

TRADE

Agreement amending and extending the agreement of June 25, July 3 and 22, 1986, as amended and extended (U.S.–Czechoslovakia), concerning trade in textiles and textile products.

Exchange of notes at Prague August 11, 1993 and April 11, 1994.

Entered into force April 11, 1994.

NP

CZECHOSLOVAKIA

On December 31, 1992, at midnight, Czechoslovakia ceased to exist and was succeeded by two separate and independent states, the Czech Republic and the Slovak Republic.

The status of the agreements listed below is under review.

ARMS LIMITATION

Agreement regarding inspections on the territory of the Czechoslovak Socialist Republic provided for by the U.S.-U.S.S.R. treaty of December 8, 1987 on the elimination of their intermediate-range and shorter-range missiles.

Exchange of notes at Prague December 18, 1987 and January 4, 1988.

Entered into force June 1, 1988.

TIAS

ATOMIC ENERGY

Arrangement concerning the exchange of technical information and cooperation in nuclear safety matters, with addenda and exchange of letters.

Signed at Rockville April 14, 1989.

Entered into force April 14, 1989.

TIAS

Agreement on cooperation in peaceful uses of nuclear energy, with annex and agreed minute.

Signed at Vienna June 13, 1991.

Entered into force February 13, 1992.

TIAS

AVIATION

Agreement for the reciprocal acceptance of certificates of airworthiness for imported aircraft.

Exchange of notes at Prague October 1 and 21, 1970.

Entered into force October 21, 1970.

21 UST 2468; TIAS 6987; 776 UNTS 67.

Air transport agreement, with schedule and annex.

Signed at Prague June 29, 1987.

Entered into force June 29, 1987.

TIAS 11162.

Amendments and extension

March 21 and May 27, 1991 (TIAS 11838).

December 31, 1992 (TIAS 11915).

CLAIMS

Agreement regarding settlement for certain war accounts and claims incident to the operations of the United States Army in Europe, and accompanying notes.

Signed at Praha July 25, 1947.

Entered into force July 25, 1947.

61 Stat. 3410; TIAS 1675; 6 Bevans 1320; 90 UNTS 19.

Agreement on the settlement of certain outstanding claims and financial issues, with annexes and related exchange of letters.

Signed at Prague January 29, 1982.

Entered into force February 2, 1982.

TIAS 11264.

Amendments

February 2, 1982 (TIAS 11264; 2177 UNTS 417).

February 12, 1982 (TIAS 11264; 2177 UNTS 433).

COMMERCE

Agreement relating to commercial policy.

Exchange of notes at Washington November 14, 1946.

Entered into force November 14, 1946.

61 Stat. 2431; TIAS 1569; 6 Bevans 1314; 7 UNTS 119.

Agreement relating to the establishment of a New York branch of the commercial section of the Czechoslovak Embassy.

Exchange of notes at Washington August 8 and 28, 1967.

Entered into force August 28, 1967.

20 UST 2979; TIAS 6771; 726 UNTS 139.

CONSULS

Consular convention, with agreed memorandum and related notes.

Signed at Prague July 9, 1973.

Entered into force November 6, 1987.

TIAS 11083.

CULTURAL PROPERTY

Agreement for the protection and preservation of cultural properties, with annex.

Signed at Washington March 17, 1992.

Entered into force March 17, 1992.

TIAS 11399; 2190 UNTS 209.

CULTURAL RELATIONS

Agreement on cooperation in culture, education, science, technology and other fields, with annex.

Signed at Prague April 15, 1986.

Entered into force April 15, 1986.

TIAS

CUSTOMS

Agreement regarding mutual assistance between customs services.

Signed at Prague May 7, 1991.

Entered into force February 21, 1997.

TIAS

EXTRADITION

Treaty concerning the mutual extradition of fugitive criminals.

Signed at Prague July 2, 1925.

Entered into force March 29, 1926.

44 Stat. 2367; TS 734; 6 Bevans 1247; 50 LNTS 143.

Supplementary extradition treaty.

Signed at Washington April 29, 1935.

Entered into force August 28, 1935.

49 Stat. 3253; TS 895; 6 Bevans 1283; 162 LNTS 83.

FINANCE

Agreement relating to the funding of the indebtedness of Czechoslovakia to the United States.

Signed at Washington October 13, 1925; operative June 15, 1925.

Treasury Department print; 6 Bevans 1253.

Agreement modifying the debt funding agreement of October 13, 1925.

Signed at Washington June 10, 1932; operative July 1, 1931.

Treasury Department print; 6 Bevans 1277.

Investment incentive agreement.

Signed at Prague October 18, 1990.

Entered into force October 18, 1990.

TIAS

INVESTMENT

Treaty concerning the reciprocal encouragement and protection of investment, with annex, protocol and exchanges of letters.

Signed at Washington October 22, 1991.

Entered into force December 19, 1992.

TIAS

LEND-LEASE

Preliminary agreement regarding principles applying to mutual aid in the prosecution of the war against aggression.

Signed at Washington July 11, 1942.

Entered into force July 11, 1942.

56 Stat. 1562; EAS 261; 6 Bevans 1300; 90 UNTS 257.

Agreement on settlement for lend-lease and certain claims.

Signed at Praha September 16, 1948.

Entered into force September 16, 1948.

62 Stat. 2850; TIAS 1818; 6 Bevans 1326; 90 UNTS 35.

MAPPING

Basic exchange and cooperative agreement for topographic mapping, nautical and aeronautical charting, geodesy and geophysics, digital data and related MC & G materials.

Signed at Prague December 10, 1991.

Entered into force December 10, 1991.

NP

NARCOTIC DRUGS

Arrangement for the direct exchange of certain information regarding the traffic in narcotic drugs.

Exchange of notes at Prague February 9 and June 15, 1928.

Entered into force June 15, 1928.

6 Bevans 1263.

PACIFIC SETTLEMENT OF DISPUTES

Treaty of arbitration.

Signed at Washington August 16, 1928.

Entered into force April 11, 1929.

46 Stat. 2254; TS 781; 6 Bevans 1268; 89 LNTS 225.

Treaty of conciliation.

Signed at Washington August 16, 1928.

Entered into force April 11, 1929.

46 Stat. 2257; TS 782; 6 Bevans 1271; 89 LNTS 219.

PEACE CORPS

Agreement on the program of the United States Peace Corps in Czechoslovakia.

Signed at Prague June 25, 1990.

Entered into force June 25, 1990.

TIAS 12076.

POSTAL MATTERS

Agreement concerning exchange of parcel post, and regulations of execution.

Signed at Washington September 15, and at Praha September 29, 1950.

Entered into force October 1, 1950.

8 UST 997; TIAS 3865; 290 UNTS 3.

International express mail agreement, with detailed regulations.

Signed at Prague and Washington July 25 and August 17, 1988.

Entered into force September 30, 1988.

TIAS 11645.

SCIENTIFIC COOPERATION

Agreement for scientific and technological cooperation, with annexes.

Signed at Washington October 22, 1991.

Entered into force June 3, 1992.

TIAS 11971.

TRADE

See also COMMERCE

Agreement providing for consultations should textile or apparel exports from Czechoslovakia cause market disruptions in the United States.

Exchange of notes at Prague March 22 and 28, 1977.

Entered into force March 28, 1977.

28 UST 5463; TIAS 8645; 1087 UNTS 283.

Agreement concerning exports of certain textile products to the United States.

Exchange of notes at Prague June 25, July 3 and 22, 1986.

Entered into force July 22, 1986; effective June 1, 1986.

NP

Amendments and extensions

December 21, 1987, April 15 and May 4, 1988 (NP).

June 12 and August 10, 1989 (NP).

VISAS

Agreement relating to multiple entry visas for diplomatic personnel.

Exchange of notes at Prague December 18 and 21, 1962.

Entered into force December 21, 1962.

13 UST 3842; TIAS 5258; 469 UNTS 115.

Agreement relating to issuance of nonimmigrant visas on a facilitated basis to certain holders of diplomatic or official passports.

Exchange of notes at Prague June 20, 1978.

Entered into force June 20, 1978; effective July 1, 1978.

30 UST 1593; TIAS 9266; 1150 UNTS 107.

D

DENMARK

AUTOMOTIVE TRAFFIC

Agreement relating to reciprocal treatment of passenger motor vehicles.

Exchange of notes at Bar Harbor, Maine, September 4, 1928, and at Washington October 27, 1928, and February 2, 1929.

Entered into force February 2, 1929; operative February 1, 1929.

48 Stat. 1871; EAS 61; 7 Bevans 83.

AVIATION

Arrangement relating to pilot licenses to operate civil aircraft.

Exchange of notes at Copenhagen March 14 and 24, 1934.

Entered into force April 16, 1934.

48 Stat. 1865; EAS 59; 7 Bevans 99; 149 LNTS 485.

Agreement relating to air transport services.

Exchange of notes at Washington December 16, 1944.

Entered into force provisionally January 1, 1945; definitively September 29, 1945.

58 Stat. 1458; EAS 430; 7 Bevans 114; 10 UNTS 213.

Amendments

August 6, 1954 (5 UST 1422; TIAS 3014; 222 UNTS 366).

June 16, 1995 (TIAS 12663).

Air service agreement relating to facilities at Kastrup Airport in Denmark.

Exchange of notes at Copenhagen September 26 and October 1, 1946.

Entered into force October 1, 1946.

61 Stat. 3851; TIAS 1734; 7 Bevans 125; 42 UNTS 219.

Agreement concerning establishment and operation of certain aeronautical facilities and services in Greenland and Appendix.

Signed at Copenhagen July 7, 1960.

Entered into force July 7, 1960.

11 UST 1861; TIAS 4531; 380 UNTS 39.

Amendment

March 26 and September 6, 1976 (28 UST 3654; TIAS 8593).

Agreement relating to the reciprocal acceptance of airworthiness certifications.

Exchange of notes at Washington January 6, 1982.

Entered into force January 6, 1982.

34 UST 27; TIAS 10335.

Agreement for promotion of aviation safety.

Signed at Copenhagen November 6, 1998.

Entered into force November 6, 1998.

TIAS

COMMERCE

General convention of friendship, commerce, and navigation.[1]

Signed at Washington April 26, 1826.

Entered into force August 10, 1826; operative April 26, 1826.

8 Stat. 340; TS 65; 7 Bevans 1.

Treaty of friendship, commerce and navigation, with protocol and minutes of interpretation.[2]

Signed at Copenhagen October 1, 1951.

Entered into force July 30, 1961.

12 UST 908; TIAS 4797; 421 UNTS 105.

NOTES

1 Does not apply to Greenland and Iceland (article 6). This convention was abrogated April 15, 1856 and renewed, with the exception of article 5, by the convention of April 11, 1857 (TS 67), and terminated, with the exception of articles 8, 9 and 10 relating to consular matters, by the treaty of October 1, 1951 (TIAS 4797).

2 Applicable to all Danish territories except Greenland, and to all territories over which the United States has jurisdiction or international responsibility except the Trust Territory of the Pacific Islands.

CONSULS

See COMMERCE

DEFENSE

See also MUTUAL SECURITY

Mutual defense assistance agreement.

Signed at Washington January 27, 1950.

Entered into force January 27, 1950.

1 UST 19; TIAS 2011; 48 UNTS 115.

Agreement concerning the defense of Greenland.

Signed at Copenhagen April 27, 1951.

Entered into force June 8, 1951.

2 UST 1485; TIAS 2292; 94 UNTS 35.

Related agreements:

December 2, 1960 (11 UST 2642; TIAS 4657; 402 UNTS 245).

September 30, 1986 (TIAS 12284).

August 6, 2004.

Agreement relating to the disposition of equipment and material no longer required by Denmark in the furtherance of its mutual defense assistance program.

Exchange of notes at Copenhagen November 16, 1951 and April 28, 1952.

Entered into force April 28, 1952.

3 UST 5278; TIAS 2726; 180 UNTS 275.

Amendment

September 12, 1960 (11 UST 2116; TIAS 4570; 388 UNTS 356).

Agreement relating to the offshore procurement program in Denmark with model contract attached.

Exchange of notes at Copenhagen June 8, 1954.

Entered into force June 8, 1954.

9 UST 141; TIAS 3987; 307 UNTS 133.

Agreement relating to the status of the personnel of the U.S. Military Assistance Advisory Group and of the personnel of the offshore procurement program.

Exchange of notes at Copenhagen December 12, 1956.

Entered into force December 12, 1956.

9 UST 271; TIAS 4002; 304 UNTS 311.

Agreement relating to a weapons production program.

Exchange of notes at Copenhagen April 12, 1960.

Entered into force April 12, 1960.[1]

11 UST 1440; TIAS 4484.

Memorandum of understanding concerning the principles governing mutual cooperation in the research, development, production, procurement and logistic support of defense equipment.

Signed at Copenhagen and Washington January 2 and 30, 1980.

Entered into force January 30, 1980.

33 UST 3128; TIAS 10216.

Agreement on general security of military information.

Exchange of notes at Copenhagen January 23 and February 27, 1981.

Entered into force February 27, 1981.

33 UST 1264; TIAS 10109; 1264 UNTS 475.

Mutual logistical support agreement, with annex.

Signed at Vedbaek and Stuttgart-Vaihingen June 1 and 14, 1982.

Entered into force June 14, 1982.

34 UST 1235; TIAS 10411.

Memorandum of understanding concerning use of Sondrestrom Aviation Facility, Kulusuk Airfield and other matters related to U.S. military activities in Greenland.

Signed at Copenhagen March 13, 1991.

Entered into force March 13, 1991.

TIAS 12285; 1653 UNTS 389.

Acquisition and cross-servicing agreement, with annexes.

Signed at Vedbaek, Denmark and Patch Barracks, Germany January 5 and 8, 1998.

Entered into force January 8, 1998.

TIAS

Agreement regarding the exchange of administrative and professional personnel, with annexes.

Signed at Washington July 7, 1998.

Entered into force July 7, 1998.

NP

Memorandum of understanding concerning the Dundas area, with related exchange of notes.

Signed at Nuuk February 20, 2003.

Entered into force February 20, 2003.

TIAS

Agreement concerning ballistic missile defense technology.

Signed at Washington October 25, 2005.

Entered into force October 25, 2005.

TIAS

Memorandum of understanding regarding assignment of liaison officers, with annex.

Signed at Norfolk February 7, 2006.

Entered into force February 7, 2006.

TIAS

Memorandum of understanding regarding the assignment of a foreign liaison officer to the headquarters, United States Strategic Command, with annex.

Signed at Omaha and Vedbaek May 21 and June 2, 2006.

Entered into force June 2, 2006.

TIAS

NOTE

1 For amendment of paragraph 4.a.(4) of the agreement, see exchange of letters of May 11 and 18, 1960 (11 UST 1447; TIAS 4484).

ECONOMIC AND TECHNICAL COOPERATION

Economic cooperation agreement.[1]

Signed at Copenhagen June 29, 1948.

Entered into force July 2, 1948.

62 Stat. 2199; TIAS 1782; 7 Bevans 141; 22 UNTS 217.

Amendments

November 4 and 18, 1948 (62 Stat. 3753; TIAS 1904; 7 Bevans 157; 55 UNTS 322).

February 7, 1950 (1 UST 148; TIAS 2022; 79 UNTS 294).

February 2 and 9, 1951 (2 UST 647; TIAS 2218; 132 UNTS 380).

November 24, 1952 (3 UST 5181; TIAS 2713; 184 UNTS 327).

NOTE

1 Applicable to Greenland.

EDUCATION

Agreement for financing certain educational exchange programs.

Exchange of notes at Copenhagen May 28, 1962.

Entered into force May 28, 1962.

13 UST 1154; TIAS 5060; 450 UNTS 215.

Amendments

February 18 and 25, 1965 (16 UST 154; TIAS 5775; 542 UNTS 386).

November 2, 1971 and April 27, 1972 (23 UST 2683; TIAS 7462).

EMPLOYMENT

Agreement relating to the employment of dependents of official government employees, with addendum.

Exchange of notes at Washington May 16 and 20, 1983.

Entered into force May 20, 1983.

TIAS 10694; 2005 UNTS 187.

EXTRADITION

Treaty on extradition.[1]

Signed at Copenhagen June 22, 1972.

Entered into force July 31, 1974.

25 UST 1293; TIAS 7864.

NOTE

1 Applicable to all territories.

FINANCE

Agreement relating to guaranties authorized under Section 111(b)(3) of the Economic Cooperation Act of 1948, as amended.

Exchange of notes at Washington July 30 and August 8, 1952.

Entered into force August 9, 1952.

3 UST 5056; TIAS 2689; 181 UNTS 249.

INDUSTRIAL PROPERTY

See also TRADE-MARKS

Agreement with respect to the protection of industrial designs or models.

Exchange of notes at Washington and Bar Harbor, Maine, June 22 and 26, 1906.

Entered into force June 26, 1906.

TS 483; 7 Bevans 45.

MAPPING

Basic exchange and cooperative agreement concerning mapping, charting and geodesy cooperation, with glossary.

Signed at Fairfax and Vedbaek December 20, 1995 and February 7, 1996.

Entered into force February 7, 1996.

NP

MARITIME MATTERS

Agreement for mutual exemption of vessels from readmeasurement in the ports of their respective countries.

Signed at Washington February 26, 1886.

Entered into force April 1, 1886.

TS 70; 7 Bevans 27.

Amendment

October 2 and 28, 1895 (7 Bevans 32).

Agreement relating to a shipbuilding program in Denmark.

Exchange of notes at Copenhagen May 8, 1959.

Entered into force May 8, 1959.

10 UST 939; TIAS 4226; 344 UNTS 185.

Amendment

May 17, 1961 (12 UST 625; TIAS 4761; 410 UNTS 348).

MUTUAL SECURITY

Agreement relating to the assurances required by the Mutual Security Act of 1951.

Exchange of notes at Copenhagen January 8, 1952.

Entered into force January 8, 1952.

3 UST 4554; TIAS 2605; 179 UNTS 65.

NARCOTIC DRUGS

Arrangement for the direct exchange of certain information regarding the traffic in narcotic drugs.

Exchange of notes at Copenhagen February 3 and April 23, 1928.

Entered into force April 23, 1928.

7 Bevans 78.

NAVIGATION

Agreement concerning the closure of the long-range radio aid to navigation transmitting station at Angissoq, Greenland, with annex.

Signed at Copenhagen December 12, 1994.

Entered into force December 12, 1994.

TIAS

Agreement for the transfer of ownership of long-range radio aid to navigation transmitting station at Ejde, Faroe Islands, Denmark, with annex.

Signed at Copenhagen December 12, 1994.

Entered into force December 12, 1994.

TIAS

PACIFIC SETTLEMENT OF DISPUTES

Treaty for the advancement of peace.

Signed at Washington April 17, 1914.

Entered into force January 19, 1915.

38 Stat. 1883; TS 608; 7 Bevans 53.

Arbitration treaty.

Signed at Washington June 14, 1928.

Entered into force April 17, 1929.

46 Stat. 2265; TS 784; 7 Bevans 80; 88 LNTS 173.

PATENTS

Agreement to facilitate the interchange of patent rights and technical information for defense purposes.

Signed at Copenhagen February 19, 1960.

Entered into force February 19, 1960.

11 UST 148; TIAS 4423; 354 UNTS 151.

Agreement approving the procedures for the reciprocal filing of classified patent applications in the United States and Denmark.

Exchange of notes at Copenhagen June 13 and 20, 1960.

Entered into force June 20, 1960.

11 UST 1788; TIAS 4521; 378 UNTS 400.

POSTAL MATTERS

Agreement concerning the exchange of parcel post, and detailed regulations of execution.[1]

Signed at Copenhagen December 9 and at Washington December 28, 1932.

Entered into force provisionally July 1, 1932 and definitively August 18, 1933.

47 Stat. 2402; Post Office Department print; 140 LNTS 453.

Agreement for collect-on-delivery service.[1]

Signed at Copenhagen October 13, and at Washington November 11, 1933; operative November 1, 1933.

48 Stat. 1671; Post Office Department print; 145 LNTS 113.

International express mail agreement, with detailed regulations.

Signed at Copenhagen and Washington October 19 and November 19, 1984.

Entered into force January 2, 1985.

TIAS 11011; 2021 UNTS 353.

NOTE

1 Applicable to Puerto Rico, the Virgin Islands, Guam, Samoa, Faroe Islands and Greenland.

PUBLICATIONS

Agreement for the exchange of official publications.

Exchange of notes at Copenhagen July 27 and August 1, 1949.

Entered into force August 1, 1949.

63 Stat. 2680; TIAS 1971; 7 Bevans 159; 79 UNTS 147.

SCIENTIFIC COOPERATION

Memorandum of understanding concerning the furnishing of balloon launching and associated services.

Signed at Copenhagen and Washington September 14 and 20, 1983.

Entered into force September 20, 1983.

35 UST 2399; TIAS 10801.

Memorandum of understanding concerning scientific and technical cooperation in the earth sciences as related to Greenland, with annexes.

Signed at Copenhagen May 31, 2006.

Entered into force May 31, 2006.

TIAS

SHIPPING

Agreement relating to jurisdiction over vessels utilizing the Louisiana Offshore Oil Port.

Exchange of notes at Washington August 17 and 22, 1978.

Entered into force August 22, 1978.

30 UST 1702; TIAS 9278; 1153 UNTS 139.

SMUGGLING

Convention for prevention of smuggling of intoxicating liquors.

Signed at Washington May 29, 1924.

Entered into force July 25, 1924.

43 Stat. 1809; TS 693; 7 Bevans 72; 27 LNTS 361.

TAXATION

Agreement relating to relief from double income tax on shipping profits.

Exchanges of notes at Washington May 22, August 9 and 18, October 24, 25, and 28, and December 5 and 6, 1922.

Entered into force December 6, 1922; operative January 1, 1921.

47 Stat. 2612; EAS 14; 7 Bevans 65; 113 LNTS 381.

Amendment

July 6, 1987 (TIAS 11278).

Agreement relating to relief from taxation of United States expenditures in Denmark for common defense.

Exchange of notes at Copenhagen April 7 and 9, 1952.

Entered into force April 9, 1952; operative April 7, 1952.

3 UST 4041; TIAS 2546; 177 UNTS 257.

Convention for the avoidance of double taxation and the prevention of fiscal evasion with respect to taxes on estates.

Signed at Washington April 27, 1983.

Entered into force November 7, 1984.

TIAS 11089; 2120 UNTS 247.

Convention for the avoidance of double taxation and the prevention of fiscal evasion with respect to taxes on income, with protocol.

Signed at Washington August 19, 1999.

Entered into force March 31, 2000.

TIAS

TECHNOLOGICAL COOPERATION

Agreement concerning a Danish-American Fund for the exchange of technology, with appendix.

Signed at Copenhagen March 25, 1985.

Entered into force March 25, 1985.

TIAS 11179.

Amendment

May 2, 1988 (TIAS 11580).

TELECOMMUNICATION

Agreement relating to the registration with the International Telecommunication Union of frequencies used by United States authorities in Greenland.

Exchange of notes at Washington March 25 and April 4, 1952.

Entered into force April 4, 1952.

3 UST 4047; TIAS 2548; 177 UNTS 13.

Agreement relating to the reciprocal granting of authorizations to permit licensed amateur radio operators of either country to operate their stations in the other country.

Exchange of notes at Copenhagen October 11, 1973.

Entered into force October 11, 1973.

24 UST 2156; TIAS 7730; 938 UNTS 327.

TERRITORIAL ACQUISITION

Convention for the cession to the United States of the Danish West Indies, and declaration by the United States.

Signed at New York August 4, 1916.

Entered into force January 17, 1917.

39 Stat. 1706; TS 629; 7 Bevans 56.

TRADE

See also COMMERCE

Convention for discontinuance of the sound dues.

Signed at Washington April 11, 1857.

Entered into force January 12, 1858.

11 Stat. 719; TS 67; 7 Bevans 11.

Agreement providing compensatory concessions under the general agreement on tariffs and trade for certain tariff actions taken by the United States.

Exchange of notes at Geneva January 26 and February 12, 1962.

Entered into force February 12, 1962.

13 UST 936; TIAS 5032.

TRADE-MARKS

Convention for the reciprocal protection of trade-marks and trade labels.

Signed at Copenhagen June 15, 1892.

Entered into force September 28, 1892.

27 Stat. 963; TS 72; 7 Bevans 30.

Understanding granting persons domiciled in the United States engaged in gainful occupation the access by registration to the exclusive right of utilization of trade-marks in Denmark.

Exchange of notes at Washington June 26 and October 15, 1953.

Entered into force October 15, 1953.

4 UST 2040; TIAS 2860; 215 UNTS 111.

VISAS

Arrangement relating to the waiver of passport visa fees for nonimmigrants.

Exchange of notes at Copenhagen July 2 and September 29, 1925; operative August 6, 1925.

7 Bevans 76.

Agreement for the waiver of visa requirements for American citizens entering Denmark for a temporary period, and the granting of gratis visas valid for twenty-four months to Danish subjects coming to the United States for temporary visits.

Exchanges of notes at Copenhagen June 9 and 21 and July 7 and 8, 1947.

Entered into force July 8, 1947.

62 Stat. 4068; TIAS 2110; 7 Bevans 128; 132 UNTS 145.

Amendment

April 30 and May 1, 1958.

DJIBOUTI

AVIATION

Memorandum of agreement for the provision of assistance in developing and modernizing the civil aviation infrastructure in Djibouti

Signed February 3 and 14, 2005.

Entered into force February 14, 2005.

TIAS

DEFENSE

Agreement concerning the provision of training related to defense articles under the United States International Military Education and Training (IMET) Program.

Exchange of notes at Djibouti October 9, 1983 and June 3, 1984.

Entered into force June 3, 1984.

TIAS 10983.

Agreement regarding grants under the Foreign Assistance Act of 1961, as amended, and the furnishing of defense articles, related training and other defense services from the United States to Djibouti.

Exchange of notes at Djibouti June 3 and 13, 1992.

Entered into force June 13, 1992.

TIAS 12286.

Status of forces agreement, with related note.

Signed at Washington December 20, 2001.

Entered into force December 20, 2001.

TIAS

Acquisition and cross-servicing agreement.

Signed at MacDill Air Force Base and Djibouti January 18 and February 13, 2002.

Entered into force February 13, 2002.

TIAS

Agreement on access to and use of facilities in the Republic of Djibouti, with annex.

Signed at Djibouti February 19, 2003.

Entered into force February 19, 2003.

TIAS

ECONOMIC AND TECHNICAL COOPERATION

Agency for International Development

January 9, 1978 (29 UST 5764; TIAS 9150).

EMPLOYMENT

Agreement relating to the employment of dependents of official government employees.

Exchange of notes at Djibouti November 21 and December 24, 1991.

Entered into force December 24, 1991.

TIAS 11843.

FINANCE

Investment incentive agreement.

Exchange of notes at Djibouti May 11, 1983.

Entered into force May 11, 1983.

TIAS

INTERNATIONAL CRIMINAL COURT

Agreement regarding the surrender of persons to the International Criminal Court.

Signed at Washington January 24, 2003.

Entered into force July 2, 2003.

TIAS

POSTAL MATTERS

International express mail agreement, with detailed regulations.

Signed at Djibouti and Washington June 25, July 28 and August 11, 1987.

Entered into force August 17, 1987.

TIAS 11554.

SCIENTIFIC COOPERATION

Memorandum of understanding concerning scientific and technical cooperation in the earth and mapping sciences, with annexes.

Signed at Reston and Djibouti March 9 and 21, 2001.

Entered into force March 21, 2001.

TIAS

TELECOMMUNICATIONS

Agreement for the establishment of U.S. radio transmitting facilities in Djibouti, with annex.

Signed at Djibouti June 18, 2002.

Entered into force June 18, 2002.

TIAS

DOMINICA

On November 8, 1978 Dominica became an independent state. In a note dated December 23, 1982 to the Secretary-General of the United Nations, the Prime Minister made a statement reading in part as follows:

"The Government of the Commonwealth of Dominica hereby declares that, with regard to multilateral treaties applied or extended to the former British associated state of Dominica, it will continue to apply the terms of each such treaty provisionally and on the basis of reciprocity until such time as it notifies the depository authority of its decision in respect thereof.

As regards bilateral treaties applied or extended to, or entered into on behalf of the former British associated state of Dominica, the Government of the Commonwealth of Dominica declares that it will examine each such treaty and communicate its views to the other state party concerned. In the mean-time, the Government of the Commonwealth of Dominica will continue to observe the terms of each such treaty, which validly so applies and is not inconsistent with its independent sovereign status, provisionally and on the basis of reciprocity."

AVIATION

Agreement between the United States and the United Kingdom concerning air services, with annexes and exchange of letters.

Signed at Bermuda July 23, 1977.

Entered into force July 23, 1977.

28 UST 5367; TIAS 8641.

Amendment

April 25, 1978 (29 UST 2680; TIAS 8965).

CONSULS

Consular convention between the United States and the United Kingdom.

Signed at Washington June 6, 1951.

Entered into force September 7, 1952.

3 UST 3426; TIAS 2494; 165 UNTS 121.

DEFENSE

Agreement concerning the provision of training related to defense articles under the United States International Military Education and Training (IMET) Program.

Exchange of notes at Bridgetown and Roseau December 11, 1980 and February 4, 1981.

Entered into force February 4, 1981.

33 UST 856; TIAS 10069; 1267 UNTS 95.

ECONOMIC AND TECHNICAL COOPERATION

General agreement for economic, technical, and related assistance.

Signed at Dominica September 16, 1983.

Entered into force September 16, 1983.

35 UST 2948; TIAS 10830; 2014 UNTS 587.

EXTRADITION

Treaty on extradition.

Signed at Roseau October 10, 1996.

Entered into force May 25, 2000.

TIAS

FINANCE

Agreement relating to investment guaranties.

Signed at Roseau October 11, 1968.

Entered into force October 11, 1968.

19 UST 6063; TIAS 6568; 702 UNTS 263.

INTERNATIONAL CRIMINAL COURT

Agreement regarding the surrender of persons to the International Criminal Court.

Exchange of notes at Washington and Roseau May 10, 2004.

Entered into force May 10, 2004.

TIAS

JUDICIAL ASSISTANCE

Treaty on mutual legal assistance in criminal matters.

Signed at Roseau October 10, 1996.

Entered into force May 25, 2000.

TIAS

NARCOTIC DRUGS

Agreement concerning maritime counter-drug operations.

Signed at Roseau April 19, 1995.

Entered into force April 19, 1995.

TIAS 12630.

Agreement regarding the provision of articles, services and associated training by the Government of the United States for anti-narcotics purposes.

Exchange of notes at Bridgetown and Roseau November 13 and 30, 1998.

Entered into force November 30, 1998.

TIAS

PEACE CORPS

Agreement relating to the establishment of a Peace Corps program in Dominica.

Exchange of letters at Bridgetown and Roseau May 15 and 22, 1980.

Entered into force May 22, 1980.

32 UST 5811; TIAS 10016; 1267 UNTS 87.

PEACEKEEPING

Agreement for the furnishing of commodities and services in connection with the peacekeeping force for Grenada.

Exchange of notes at Bridgetown and Roseau November 25, 1983 and January 13, 1984.

Entered into force January 13, 1984.

35 UST 4249; TIAS 10923; 2014 UNTS 595.

POSTAL MATTERS

Postal money order agreement.

Signed at Washington July 24, 1989.

Entered into force [1]

NP

International express mail agreement.

Signed at Roseau and Washington September 24, 1997 and December 30, 1999.

Entered into force February 15, 2000.

NP

NOTE

1 The Department of State Treaty Office is pursuing obtaining information from the United States Postal Service about the date that this agreement entered into force, or became operative.

PRIVILEGES AND IMMUNITIES

Agreement relating to privileges and immunities for Department of Defense engineering personnel temporarily in Dominica for the purpose of emergency repairs.

Exchange of letters at Bridgetown and Roseau September 17, 1979.

Entered into force September 17, 1979.

31 UST 5056; TIAS 9655.

REFUGEES

Memorandum of understanding for the establishment within the territory of Dominica of facilities to provide temporary protection under the auspices of the United Nations High Commissioner for Refugees for nationals of Haiti fleeing their country, with related letter.

Signed at Dominica July 10, 1994.

Entered into force July 10, 1994.

TIAS

TAXATION

Agreement for the exchange of information with respect to taxes.

Signed at Washington October 1, 1987.

Entered into force May 9, 1988.

TIAS 11543; 2191 UNTS 203.

TELECOMMUNICATION

Agreement between the United States and the United Kingdom relating to the reciprocal granting of authorizations to permit licensed amateur radio operators of either country to operate their stations in the other country.

Exchange of notes at London November 26, 1965; applicable to Dominica December 11, 1969.

16 UST 2047; TIAS 5941; 561 UNTS 193.

Agreement between the United States and the United Kingdom extending to certain territories the application of the agreement of November 26, 1965 relating to the reciprocal granting of authorizations to permit licensed amateur radio operators of either country to operate their stations in the other country.

Exchange of notes at London December 11, 1969.

Entered into force December 11, 1969.

20 UST 4089; TIAS 6800; 732 UNTS 334.

Agreement relating to radio communications between amateur stations on behalf of third parties.

Exchange of telexes at Bridgetown and Roseau December 8, 1983 and February 9, 1984.

Entered into force March 10, 1984.

TIAS 11145; 2126 UNTS 183.

TRADE-MARKS

Declaration by the United States and the United Kingdom affording reciprocal protection to trade-marks.

Signed at London October 24, 1877.

Entered into force October 24, 1877.

20 Stat. 703; TS 138; 12 Bevans 198.

DOMINICAN REPUBLIC

AGRICULTURAL COMMODITIES

Agricultural commodities agreement with exchange of notes.

Signed at Santo Domingo November 30, 1962.

Entered into force November 30, 1962.

13 UST 3863; TIAS 5261; 471 UNTS 25.

Amendment

September 14, 1963 (14 UST 1531; TIAS 5453; 505 UNTS 332).

Agricultural commodity agreement.

Signed at Washington August 13, 1963.

Entered into force August 13, 1963.

14 UST 1027; TIAS 5398; 492 UNTS 327.

Agricultural commodities agreement, with exchange of notes.

Signed at Santo Domingo March 18, 1965.

Entered into force March 18, 1965.

16 UST 168; TIAS 5778; 542 UNTS 215.

Agricultural commodities agreement with annex.

Signed at Santo Domingo April 1, 1968.

Entered into force April 1, 1968.

20 UST 817; TIAS 6696; 713 UNTS 241.

Amendment

May 9 and 10, 1968 (20 UST 837; TIAS 6696; 713 UNTS 266).

Related agreements

May 10, 1968 (20 UST 2739; TIAS 6739; 719 UNTS 87).

June 11, 1968 (20 UST 839; TIAS 6697; 713 UNTS 285).

Agricultural commodities agreement with annex.

Signed at Santo Domingo March 28, 1969.

Entered into force March 28, 1969.

20 UST 735; TIAS 6685; 713 UNTS 295.

Amendments

April 15, 1969 (20 UST 756; TIAS 6685; 713 UNTS 295).

June 23, 1969 and June 24, 1970 (21 UST 1738; TIAS 6929; 756 UNTS 330).

Agricultural commodities agreement with annex.

Signed at Santo Domingo March 31, 1970.

Entered into force March 31, 1970.

21 UST 1069; TIAS 6863; 741 UNTS 15.

Amendment

May 14 and June 24, 1970 (21 UST 1741; TIAS 6930).

Related agreements

April 1, 1971 (22 UST 562; TIAS 7100; 792 UNTS 273).

February 14, 1972 (23 UST 149; TIAS 7285; 829 UNTS 259).

March 30 and April 14, 1972 (23 UST 603; TIAS 7320).

May 4 and 17, 1972 (23 UST 779; TIAS 7340).

June 12, 1973 (26 UST 3839; TIAS 8215).

Agricultural commodities agreement.

Signed at Santo Domingo September 28, 1977.

Entered into force September 28, 1977.

29 UST 2377; TIAS 8944.

Amendment

December 13 and 20, 1977 (29 UST 2416; TIAS 8944).

Related agreements

January 11, 1979 (30 UST 6567; TIAS 9568; 1182 UNTS 121).

January 3, 1980 (32 UST 792; TIAS 9730; 1222 UNTS 95).

April 9 and 11, 1980 (32 UST 1029; TIAS 9753; 1222 UNTS 107).

June 13 and July 22, 1980 (TIAS 10494).

February 20, 1981 (33 UST 1707; TIAS 10139).

May 21, 1982 (34 UST 1047; TIAS 10391).

August 2 and 26, 1982 (34 UST 2281; TIAS 10487).

December 11, 1982 (TIAS 10629).

August 22, 1983 (35 UST 1917; TIAS 10769; 2012 UNTS 386).

January 13, 1984 (NP).

May 21, 1984 (NP).

August 30, 1984 (NP).

October 23 and 30, 1984 (NP).

Agricultural commodities agreement.

Signed at Santo Domingo May 15, 1985.

Entered into force July 3, 1985.

NP

Amendments

August 1, 1985 (NP).

August 19, 1985 (NP).

August 18, 1986 (NP).

Agricultural commodities agreement, with memorandum of understanding.

Signed at Santo Domingo June 30, 1987.

Entered into force June 1, 1988.

NP

Amendment

April 29, 1988 (NP).

Related agreements

August 24, 1989 (NP).

September 27, 1989 (NP).

AVIATION

Air transport agreement and exchange of notes.

Signed at Ciudad Trujillo July 19, 1949.

Entered into force July 19, 1949.

63 Stat. 2615; TIAS 1955; 7 Bevans 289; 51 UNTS 145.

Amendment

October 19, 1971 (22 UST 1732; TIAS 7202).

Agreement relating to the transit of military aircraft.

Exchange of notes at Ciudad Trujillo August 11, 1950.

Entered into force August 11, 1950.

1 UST 747; TIAS 2143; 92 UNTS 329.

Memorandum of agreement relating to the provision of flight inspection services.

Signed at Washington and Santo Domingo August 16, 1978 and June 22, 1979.

Entered into force June 22, 1979; effective October 1, 1978.

TIAS

Amendment

May 19 and July 13, 1998.

Memorandum of agreement concerning assistance in developing and modernizing the Dominican Republic's civil aviation system, with annex.

Signed at Santo Domingo March 11 and 17, 1988.

Entered into force March 17, 1988.

TIAS 11777; 2202 UNTS 335.

CUSTOMS

Agreement providing free entry upon arrival for Embassy employees, and certain duty-free importations, including new and used automobiles, for six months thereafter.

Exchange of notes at Washington January 12 and 23, 1950.

Entered into force January 23, 1950.

5 UST 1064; TIAS 2989; 236 UNTS 3.

Agreement regarding mutual assistance between their customs administrations.

Signed at Santo Domingo October 31, 2005.

Entered into force October 31, 2005.

TIAS

DEFENSE

Military assistance agreement.[1]

Signed at Washington March 6, 1953.

Entered into force June 10, 1953.

4 UST 184; TIAS 2777; 199 UNTS 267.

Agreement providing for disposition of equipment and materials furnished by the United States under the military assistance agreement of March 6, 1953.

Exchange of notes at Ciudad Trujillo March 23 and April 22, 1955.

Entered into force April 22, 1955.

6 UST 1185; TIAS 3263; 239 UNTS 325.

Military assistance agreement.

Signed at Santo Domingo March 8, 1962.

Entered into force June 10, 1964.

15 UST 699; TIAS 5590; 527 UNTS 29.

Agreement relating to the deposit by the Dominican Republic of ten percent of the value of military grant assistance and excess defense articles furnished by the United States.

Exchange of notes at Santo Domingo March 23 and April 17, 1972.

Entered into force April 17, 1972; effective February 7, 1972.

23 UST 1094; TIAS 7366; 852 UNTS 235.

Agreement concerning payment to the United States of net proceeds from the sale of defense articles furnished under the military assistance program.

Exchange of notes at Santo Domingo May 30 and August 8, 1974.

Entered into force August 8, 1974; effective July 1, 1974.

25 UST 2433; TIAS 7924.

Amendment

February 10 and October 21, 2005.

Agreement concerning the status of United States Government personnel temporarily present in the Dominican Republic in connection with their official duties.

Exchange of notes at Santo Domingo July 20 and August 4, 1988.

Entered into force August 4, 1988.

NP

Acquisition and cross-servicing agreement, with annexes.

Signed at Santo Domingo and Miami May 16 and June 10, 2003.

Entered into force June 10, 2003.

TIAS

Memorandum of understanding concerning the inter-American naval telecommunications network.

Signed August 7, 2006.

Entered into force August 7, 2006.

TIAS

NOTE

1 Terminated June 20, 1961 except that the provisions of paragraphs 2, 3, 4, 5 and 6 of article 1 continue in force.

ECONOMIC AND TECHNICAL COOPERATION

General agreement for economic, technical and related assistance.

Signed at Santo Domingo January 11, 1962.

Entered into force January 11, 1962.

13 UST 60; TIAS 4936; 433 UNTS 133.

Agency for International Development

October 16, 1974 (27 UST 2835; TIAS 8353; 1068 UNTS 49).

October 1, 1975 (27 UST 2387; TIAS 8319; 1054 UNTS 235).

February 25, 1976 (28 UST 2125; TIAS 8537; 1068 UNTS 74).

September 30, 1976 (28 UST 3007; TIAS 8579).

April 7, 1977 (29 UST 1683; TIAS 8901).

EVACUATION

Convention entered into in accordance with the "modus operandi" of evacuation, signed June 30, 1922, for the purpose of rectifying certain orders, resolutions, and contracts.

Signed at Santo Domingo June 12, 1924.

Entered into force December 4, 1925.

44 Stat. 2193; TS 729; 7 Bevans 206; 48 LNTS 91.

EXTRADITION

Convention for the mutual extradition of fugitives from justice.

Signed at Santo Domingo June 19, 1909.

Entered into force August 2, 1910.

36 Stat. 2468; TS 550; 7 Bevans 200.

FINANCE

Agreement relating to investment guaranties.

Signed at Washington May 2, 1962.

Entered into force May 2, 1962.

13 UST 440; TIAS 5005; 442 UNTS 99.

Agreement regarding the consolidation and rescheduling of certain debts owed to, guaranteed by or insured by the United States Government and its agencies, with annexes.

Signed at Santo Domingo March 6, 1986.

Entered into force September 9, 1986.

NP

Agreement regarding the consolidation and rescheduling or refinancing of certain debts owed to, guaranteed by, or insured by the United States Government and its agencies, with annexes.

Signed at Santo Domingo October 30, 1992.

Entered into force November 9, 1993.

NP

Agreement regarding the consolidation and rescheduling of certain debts owed to, guaranteed by, or insured by the United States Government and its agencies, with annexes.

Signed at Santo Domingo September 9, 2005.

Entered into force April 28, 2006.

NP

Agreement regarding the consolidation and rescheduling of certain debts owed to, guaranteed by, or insured by the United States Government or its agencies, with annexes.

Signed at Santo Domingo August 29, 2006.

Entered into force November 22, 2006.

NP

INTERNATIONAL CRIMINAL COURT

Agreement regarding the surrender of persons to the International Criminal Court.

Signed at Santo Domingo September 13, 2002.

Entered into force August 12, 2004.

TIAS

LABOR

Agreement relating to workmen's compensation in connection with certain projects under construction or operation in the Dominican Republic.

Exchange of notes at Ciudad Trujillo October 14 and 19, 1943.

Entered into force October 19, 1943.

57 Stat. 1180; EAS 353; 7 Bevans 268; 21 UNTS 295.

MAPPING

Basic exchange and cooperative agreement for topographic mapping, nautical and aeronautical charting and information, geodesy and geophysics, digital data and related mapping, charting and geodesy materials, with glossary.

Signed at Santo Domingo and Fairfax September 18 and 25, 1995.

Entered into force September 25, 1995.

NP

MARITIME MATTERS

Search and rescue agreement.

Signed at Washington May 21, 2003.

Entered into force May 21, 2003.

TIAS

MIGRATION

Agreement concerning cooperation in maritime migration law enforcement.

Signed at Washington May 20, 2003.

Entered into force May 20, 2003.

TIAS

NARCOTIC DRUGS

Agreement on international narcotics control cooperation.

Signed at Santo Domingo November 18, 1985.

Entered into force November 18, 1985.

TIAS 11350; 2192 UNTS 329.

Agreement concerning maritime counter-drug operations.

Signed at Santo Domingo March 23, 1995.

Entered into force March 23, 1995.

TIAS 12620.

Protocol to the agreement of March 23, 1995 concerning maritime counter-drug operations.

Signed at Washington May 20, 2003.

Entered into force May 20, 2003.

TIAS

PEACE CORPS

Agreement relating to the establishment of a Peace Corps program in the Dominican Republic.

Signed at Washington May 2, 1962.

Entered into force May 2, 1962.

13 UST 447; TIAS 5007; 442 UNTS 107.

POSTAL MATTERS

International express mail agreement, with detailed regulations.

Signed at Santo Domingo and Washington December 3, 1990 and January 8, 1991.

Entered into force February 18, 1991.

TIAS 11782.

Postal money order agreement.

Signed at Washington and Santo Domingo August 6 and 14, 1995.

Entered into force September 1, 1995.

NP

PUBLICATIONS

Agreement relating to the exchange of official publications.

Exchange of notes at Ciudad Trujillo December 9 and 10, 1942.

Entered into force December 10, 1942.

56 Stat. 1851; EAS 297; 7 Bevans 248; 24 UNTS 257.

SANCTIONS

Memorandum of understanding for a multinational observer group to monitor and advise on Haiti sanctions enforcement.

Signed at Santo Domingo August 1, 1994.

Entered into force August 1, 1994.

TIAS

STOLEN PROPERTY

Treaty for the return of stolen or embezzled vehicles, with annexes.

Done at Santo Domingo April 30, 1996.

Entered into force August 3, 2001.

TIAS

TAXATION

Agreement for the exchange of information with respect to taxes.

Signed at Santo Domingo August 7, 1989.

Entered into force October 12, 1989.

TIAS 11694; 2190 UNTS 247.

TELECOMMUNICATION

Agreement relating to radio communications between amateur stations on behalf of third parties.

Exchange of notes at Santo Domingo April 18 and 22, 1963.

Entered into force May 22, 1963.

14 UST 817; TIAS 5360; 487 UNTS 169.

Agreement relating to the reciprocal granting of authorizations to permit licensed amateur radio operators of either country to operate their stations in the other country.

Exchange of notes at Santo Domingo January 28 and February 2, 1965.

Entered into force February 2, 1965.

16 UST 93; TIAS 5766; 542 UNTS 117.

TRADE AND COMMERCE

Agreement relating to the multilateral trade negotiations.

Exchange of letters at Santo Domingo December 21, 1979 and January 2, 1980.

Entered into force January 2, 1980.

32 UST 5301; TIAS 9981; 1266 UNTS 311.

Agreement relating to trade in cotton, wool and man-made fiber textiles and textile products, with annexes.

Exchange of notes at Santo Domingo June 11 and September 23, 1992.

Entered into force September 23, 1992; effective June 1, 1991.

NP

Amendments and extension

February 16 and March 12, 1993 (NP).

April 13 and August 11, 1994 (NP).

Agreement on trade in textile and apparel goods.

Exchange of letters at Santo Domingo and Washington October 19 and 24, 2006.

Entered into force October 24, 2006.

NP

VISAS

Agreement concerning period of validity of and fees for nonimmigrant visas.

Exchange of notes at Ciudad Trujillo December 14 and 16, 1955.

Entered into force February 1, 1956.

7 UST 135; TIAS 3484; 241 UNTS 101.

WEATHER STATIONS

Agreement for the continuation of a cooperative program for meteorological observations.

Exchange of notes at Santo Domingo April 7 and 11, 1969.

Entered into force April 11, 1969; effective July 1, 1968.

20 UST 647; TIAS 6670; 707 UNTS 243.

E

EAST AFRICAN COMMON SERVICES ORGANIZATION

AGRICULTURAL COMMODITIES

Agricultural commodities agreement between the United States, and Kenya, Tanzania, Uganda, and the East African Common Services Organization with memorandum of understanding.

Signed at Dar-es-Salaam February 18, 1966, and at Nairobi February 19 and 22 and March 4, 1966.

Entered into force March 4, 1966.

17 UST 628; TIAS 6010; 578 UNTS 57.

EAST TIMOR

DEFENSE

Agreement regarding grants under the Foreign Assistance Act of 1961, as amended, and the furnishing of defense articles, related training to include training related to defense articles under the International Military and Education Training program, and other defense services from the United States of America to the Government of the Democratic Republic of East Timor.

Exchange of notes at Dili July 8 and 10, 2002.

Entered into force July 10, 2002.

TIAS

Status of forces agreement.

Signed at Washington October 1, 2002.

Entered into force October 1, 2002.

TIAS

ECONOMIC AND TECHNICAL COOPERATION

Agreement for economic and technical cooperation.

Signed at Dili June 6, 2003.

Entered into force April 25, 2005; effective January 1, 2003.

TIAS

EMPLOYMENT

Agreement relating to the employment of dependents of official government employees.

Exchange of notes at Dili July 31 and August 8, 2002.

Entered into force August 8, 2002.

TIAS

FINANCE

Investment incentive agreement.

Signed at Washington July 25, 2002.

Entered into force July 25, 2002.

TIAS

INTERNATIONAL CRIMINAL COURT

Agreement regarding the surrender of persons to the International Criminal Court.

Signed at Dili August 23, 2002.

Entered into force October 30, 2003.

TIAS

PEACE CORPS

Agreement concerning the program of the Peace Corps in the Democratic Republic of East Timor.

Signed at Dili May 24, 2002.

Entered into force May 24, 2002.

TIAS

ECONOMIC COMMUNITY OF WEST AFRICAN STATES (ECOWAS)

DEFENSE

Agreement regarding grants under the Foreign Assistance Act of 1961, as amended, and the furnishing of defense articles, related training and other defense services from the United States of America to ECOWAS in support of the ECOFORCE peacekeeping operation in Cote d'Ivoire.

Exchange of notes at Abuja January 24 and February 14, 2003.

Entered into force February 14, 2003.

TIAS

ECUADOR

AGRICULTURAL COMMODITIES

Agricultural commodities agreement with memorandum of understanding and exchange of notes.

Signed at Quito September 27, 1960.

Entered into force September 27, 1960.

11 UST 2427; TIAS 4626; 401 UNTS 115.

Agricultural commodities agreement with exchanges of notes.

Signed at Quito April 3, 1961.

Entered into force April 3, 1961.

12 UST 671; TIAS 4768; 409 UNTS 139.

Agricultural commodities agreement with exchange of notes.

Signed at Quito April 5, 1963.

Entered into force April 5, 1963.

14 UST 775; TIAS 5356; 477 UNTS 135.

Amendment

October 6, 1964 (15 UST 1967; TIAS 5673; 531 UNTS 400).

Agricultural commodities agreement, with exchange of notes.

Signed at Quito June 25, 1965.

Entered into force June 25, 1965.

16 UST 960; TIAS 5835; 549 UNTS 23.

Amendment

October 24, 1966 (17 UST 2275; TIAS 6168; 680 UNTS 400).

Agricultural commodities agreement.

Signed at Quito June 30, 1969.

Entered into force June 30, 1969.

21 UST 1107; TIAS 6867; 745 UNTS 90.

Amendments

September 29 and October 1, 1969 (21 UST 1134; TIAS 6867; 745 UNTS 116).

March 4 and April 6, 1970 (21 UST 1137; TIAS 6867; 745 UNTS 120).

May 18 and June 23, 1972 (23 UST 1216; TIAS 7388; 852 UNTS 307).

Related agreements

June 30, 1971 (22 UST 1561; TIAS 7179; 806 UNTS 355).

October 7 and November 4, 1971 (22 UST 1757; TIAS 7210).

December 20 and 22, 1971 (22 UST 2071; TIAS 7247).

May 18 and June 23, 1972 (23 UST 1216; TIAS 7388; 852 UNTS 307).

July 31, 1972 (23 UST 2449; TIAS 7436).

January 19, 1973 (24 UST 442; TIAS 7559).

Agricultural commodities agreement.

Signed at Quito May 17, 1985.

Entered into force May 17, 1985.

NP

Amendment

June 20, 1986 (NP).

AMITY

Treaty of peace, friendship, navigation and commerce.[1]

Signed at Quito June 13, 1839.

Entered into force April 9, 1842.

8 Stat. 534; TS 76; 7 Bevans 296.

NOTE

1 Articles with respect to commerce and navigation terminated August 25, 1892.

AVIATION

Agreement relating to transit and technical stop rights for U.S. military planes in Ecuador.

Exchange of notes at Quito June 7 and 11, 1946.

Entered into force June 11, 1946.

3 UST 536; TIAS 2411; 167 UNTS 135.

Commercial air transport services agreement.

Signed at Quito January 8, 1947.

Entered into force April 24, 1947.

61 Stat. 2773; TIAS 1606; 7 Bevans 409; 22 UNTS 119.

Amendment

January 3 and 10, 1951 (2 UST 482; TIAS 2196; 133 UNTS 312).

Agreement relating to a civil aviation mission to Ecuador.

Exchange of notes at Quito October 24 and 27, 1947.

Entered into force October 27, 1947.

61 Stat. 4013; TIAS 1774; 7 Bevans 422; 44 UNTS 45.

Amendment

June 30 and October 13, 1949 (7 Bevans 460).

Memorandum of agreement concerning assistance in developing and modernizing Ecuador's civil aviation system.

Signed at Washington and Quito October 9 and November 6, 1985.

Entered into force November 6, 1985.

TIAS 11313; 2174 UNTS 357.

Agreement relating to Annex I of the air transport agreement of September 26, 1986.[1]

Exchange of notes at Quito October 23 and December 19, 1995.

Entered into force December 19, 1995; effective July 1, 1994.

TIAS

Memorandum of agreement concerning assistance in developing and modernizing Ecuador's civil aviation infrastructure.

Signed at Washington and Quito March 5 and 23, 1998.

Entered into force March 23, 1998.

NP

Agreement continuing air transport services in accordance with the terms of the agreement of September 26, 1986,[1] as modified.

Exchange of notes at Quito June 21 and July 9, 2004.

Entered into force July 9, 2004.

TIAS

NOTE

1 Not yet in force.

COMMERCE

See AMITY

CULTURAL PROPERTY

Agreement for the recovery and return of stolen archaeological, historical and cultural properties.

Signed at Washington November 17, 1983.

Entered into force January 14, 1987.

TIAS 11075; 2039 UNTS 253.

CUSTOMS

Agreement providing for certain customs courtesies and free entry privileges for consular officers and administrative personnel on a reciprocal basis.

Exchange of notes at Quito October 22 and November 6, 1957, and related note of November 11, 1957.

Entered into force November 6, 1957.

8 UST 2469; TIAS 3967; 307 UNTS 49.

Agreement regarding mutual assistance between customs administrations.

Signed at Quito November 6, 2002.

Entered into force November 6, 2002.

TIAS

DEFENSE

Agreement for the return of equipment and materials furnished Ecuador under the military assistance agreement.

Exchange of notes at Quito June 20 and July 19, 1956.

Entered into force July 19, 1956.

11 UST 246; TIAS 4439; 372 UNTS 149.

Agreement relating to eligibility for United States military assistance and training pursuant to the International Security Assistance and Arms Export Control Act of 1976.

Exchange of notes at Quito August 17 and September 3, 1976.

Entered into force September 3, 1976.

27 UST 4009; TIAS 8420; 1059 UNTS 143.

General security of military information agreement.

Exchange of notes at Quito July 12, 1985.

Entered into force July 12, 1985.

TIAS 11257; 2174 UNTS 281.

Agreement regarding the furnishing of defense articles and services on a grant basis to Ecuador from the United States.

Exchange of notes at Quito January 30 and March 4, 1992.

Entered into force March 4, 1992.

TIAS

Acquisition and cross-servicing agreement, with annexes.

Signed at Manaus October 18, 2000.

Entered into force October 18, 2000.

TIAS

Agreement concerning joint military training exercises.

Exchange of notes at Quito September 20, 2005 and June 1, 2006.

Entered into force June 1, 2006, effective October 1, 2005.

TIAS

Memorandum of understanding concerning the inter-American naval telecommunications network.

Signed September 25 and November 8, 2006.

Entered into force November 8, 2006.

TIAS

ECONOMIC AND TECHNICAL COOPERATION

General agreement for economic, technical and related assistance.

Signed at Quito April 17, 1962.

Entered into force April 17, 1962.

13 UST 425; TIAS 5003; 442 UNTS 69.

EDUCATION

Agreement for financing certain educational exchange programs.

Signed at Quito September 20, 1963.

Entered into force September 20, 1963.

14 UST 1418; TIAS 5439; 488 UNTS 147.

ENVIRONMENTAL COOPERATION

Agreement for cooperation in the Global Learning and Observations to Benefit the Environment (GLOBE) Program, with appendices.

Signed at Quito April 22, 1996.

Entered into force April 22, 1996.

TIAS 12744.

EXTRADITION

Extradition treaty.

Signed at Quito June 28, 1872.

Entered into force November 12, 1873.

18 Stat. 199; TS 79; 7 Bevans 321.

Supplementary extradition treaty.

Signed at Quito September 22, 1939.

Entered into force May 29, 1941.

55 Stat. 1196; TS 972; 7 Bevans 346.

FINANCE

Agreement relating to investment guaranties under section 413(b)(4) of the Mutual Security Act of 1954.

Exchange of notes at Washington March 28 and 29, 1955.

Entered into force March 29, 1955.

6 UST 843; TIAS 3230; 261 UNTS 343.

Amendments

September 4, 1963 (14 UST 1251; TIAS 5426; 488 UNTS 262).

July 9, 1993 (TIAS 12156).

Related agreement

November 28, 1984 (TIAS 11001; 2024 UNTS 11).

Agreement regarding the consolidation and rescheduling of debts owed to, guaranteed by or insured by the United States Government and its agencies, with annexes.

Signed at Quito March 19, 1984.

Entered into force May 4, 1984.

35 UST 4793; TIAS 10966.

Agreement regarding the consolidation and rescheduling of certain debts owed to, guaranteed by or insured by the United States Government and its agencies, with annexes.

Signed at Washington January 14, 1986.

Entered into force March 10, 1986.

NP

Swap agreement between the United States Treasury and the Central Bank of Ecuador/Republic of Ecuador, with related letter.

Signed at Washington and Quito December 3, 1987.

Entered into force December 3, 1987.

TIAS

Agreement regarding the consolidation and rescheduling of certain debts owed to, guaranteed by or insured by the United States Government and its agencies, with annexes.

Signed at Quito July 8, 1988.

Entered into force August 22, 1988.

NP

Agreement regarding the consolidation and rescheduling or refinancing of certain debts owed to, guaranteed by or insured by the United States Government and its agencies, with annexes.

Signed at Washington July 30, 1990.

Entered into force September 12, 1990.

NP

Agreement regarding the consolidation and rescheduling or refinancing of certain debts owed to, guaranteed by, or insured by the United States Government and its agencies, with annexes.

Signed at Quito July 30, 1992.

Entered into force September 11, 1992.

NP

Agreement regarding the consolidation and rescheduling or refinancing of certain debts owed to, guaranteed by or insured by the United States Government and its agencies, with annexes.

Signed at Washington January 19, 1995.

Entered into force March 1, 1995.

NP

Agreement regarding the consolidation and rescheduling of certain debts owed to, guaranteed by, or insured by the United States Government and its agencies, with annexes.

Signed at Washington February 7, 2002.

Entered into force March 28, 2002.

NP

Agreement regarding the reduction of certain debts owed to, guaranteed by, or insured by the United States Government, with annexes.

Signed at Quito April 7, 2005.

Entered into force May 31, 2005.

NP

INTELLECTUAL PROPERTY

Agreement concerning the protection and enforcement of intellectual property rights.

Signed at Washington October 15, 1993.

Entered into force October 15, 1993.

TIAS 12679.

Amendment

July 28, 1995 (TIAS 12679).

INVESTMENT

Treaty concerning the encouragement and reciprocal protection of investment, with protocol.

Signed at Washington August 27, 1993.

Entered into force May 11, 1997.

TIAS

MAPPING

Agreement on mapping, charting and geodesy.

Signed at Quito February 29, 1976.

Entered into force February 29, 1976.

27 UST 1943; TIAS 8290.

Cooperative arrangement for the production of topographic maps of Ecuador, with annexes.

Signed at Washington and Quito April 21 and June 12, 1986.

Entered into force June 12, 1986.

TIAS 11374.

MARITIME MATTERS

Agreement concerning financial arrangements for the furnishing of certain supplies and services to naval vessels of both countries.

Signed at Quito July 8, 1955.

Entered into force October 6, 1955.

6 UST 2959; TIAS 3344; 265 UNTS 49.

NARCOTIC DRUGS

Agreement concerning cooperation in the control of the illicit traffic in narcotic drugs.

Exchange of notes at Quito November 5 and 20, 1971.

Entered into force November 10, 1971.

22 UST 2109; TIAS 7255.

Memorandum of understanding on measures to prevent the diversion of chemical substances.

Signed at Quito June 17, 1991.

Entered into force June 17, 1991.

TIAS 12129.

Agreement for the prevention and control of narcotic related money laundering.

Signed at Quito August 7, 1992.

Entered into force February 4, 1993.

TIAS 12471.

Agreement to implement the United Nations convention against illicit trafficking in narcotic drugs and psychotropic substances of December 20, 1988, as it relates to the transfer of confiscated property, securities and instrumentalities.

Signed at Quito June 27, 1994.

Entered into force July 15, 1994.

TIAS

Agreement of cooperation concerning United States access to and use of installations at the Ecuadorian Air Force Base in Manta for aerial counter-narcotics activities, with implementing arrangement.

Signed at Quito November 12, 1999.

Entered into force November 17, 1999.

TIAS

PACIFIC SETTLEMENT OF DISPUTES

Arbitration convention.

Signed at Washington January 7, 1909.

Entered into force June 22, 1910.

36 Stat. 2456; TS 549; 7 Bevans 328.

Treaty for the advancement of peace.

Signed at Washington October 13, 1914.

Entered into force January 22, 1916.

39 Stat. 1650; TS 622; 7 Bevans 330.

PEACE CORPS

Agreement relating to the establishment of a Peace Corps program in Ecuador.

Exchange of notes at Quito August 3, 1962.

Entered into force August 3, 1962.

13 UST 1903; TIAS 5145; 460 UNTS 133.

POSTAL MATTERS

Agreement for the exchange of registered and insured parcel post packages.

Signed at Quito July 11 and at Washington August 6, 1929; operative July 1, 1929.

46 Stat. 2378; Post Office Department print.

International express mail agreement, with detailed regulations.

Signed at Quito and Washington March 20 and April 11, 1990.

Entered into force March 30, 1990.

TIAS 11900.

Postal money order agreement.

Signed at Quito and Washington August 1 and 8, 1990.

Entered into force October 15, 1990.

TIAS 11741.

PRIVILEGES AND IMMUNITIES

Agreement on immunities and privileges for the United States Inter-American Geodetic Survey mission.

Signed at Quito November 23, 1973.

Entered into force November 23, 1973.

24 UST 2304; TIAS 7755; 938 UNTS 403.

PUBLICATIONS

Agreement relating to the exchange of official publications.

Exchange of notes at Quito October 21 and 29, 1947.

Entered into force October 29, 1947.

61 Stat. 3322; TIAS 1668; 7 Bevans 427; 21 UNTS 21.

RELIEF SUPPLIES AND PACKAGES

Agreement granting duty-free entry, exemption from internal taxation, and free transportation within Ecuador to ultimate beneficiary for certain relief supplies and equipment for American voluntary relief and rehabilitation agencies.

Exchange of notes at Quito September 6, 1955.

Entered into force September 6, 1955.

6 UST 3871; TIAS 3388; 256 UNTS 185.

Amendment

August 3, 1970 (21 UST 2502; TIAS 6992; 772 UNTS 450).

TELECOMMUNICATION

Agreement relating to radio communications between amateur stations on behalf of third parties.

Exchange of notes at Quito March 16 and 17, 1950.

Entered into force March 17, 1950.

3 UST 2672; TIAS 2433; 177 UNTS 115.

Agreement relating to the reciprocal granting of authorizations to permit licensed amateur radio operators of either country to operate their stations in the other country.

Exchange of notes at Quito March 26, 1965.

Entered into force March 26, 1965.

16 UST 181; TIAS 5779; 542 UNTS 237.

VISAS

Agreement relating to the reciprocal issuance of nonimmigrant visas.

Exchange of notes at Quito December 11, 1962 and January 7, 1963.

Entered into force January 7, 1963; operative February 7, 1963.

14 UST 757; TIAS 5354; 477 UNTS 101.

EGYPT

AGRICULTURAL COMMODITIES

Agricultural commodities agreement with exchanges of notes.

Signed at Cairo September 2, 1961.

Entered into force September 2, 1961.

12 UST 1240; TIAS 4844; 421 UNTS 251.

Amendments

October 7, 1961 (12 UST 1434; TIAS 4868; 433 UNTS 406).

November 11, 1961 (12 UST 1661; TIAS 4881; 424 UNTS 394).

March 28, 1962 (13 UST 318; TIAS 4982; 445 UNTS 374).

Agricultural commodities agreement with exchange of notes.

Signed at Cairo February 10, 1962.

Entered into force February 10, 1962.

13 UST 121; TIAS 4947; 435 UNTS 107.

Amendments

April 23, 1962 (13 UST 369; TIAS 4991; 445 UNTS 394).

May 21, 1962 (13 UST 1244; TIAS 5070; 459 UNTS 324).

September 1, 1962 (13 UST 1921; TIAS 5149; 460 UNTS 340).

Agricultural commodities agreement with exchange of notes.

Signed at Washington October 8, 1962.

Entered into force October 8, 1962.

13 UST 2166; TIAS 5179; 462 UNTS 39.

Amendments

June 15, 1963 (14 UST 1426; TIAS 5440; 488 UNTS 322).

October 7, 1963 (14 UST 1426; TIAS 5440; 488 UNTS 326).

April 20, 1964 (15 UST 527; TIAS 5579; 524 UNTS 330).

June 30, 1964 (15 UST 1437; TIAS 5617; 530 UNTS 386).

July 20, 1964 (15 UST 1676; TIAS 5640; 531 UNTS 396).

Agricultural commodities agreement with exchange of notes.

Signed at Cairo January 3, 1966.

Entered into force January 3, 1966.

17 UST 17; TIAS 5951; 579 UNTS 83.

Agricultural commodities agreement with exchange of notes.

Signed at Cairo January 3, 1966.

Entered into force January 3, 1966.

17 UST 6; TIAS 5950; 579 UNTS 63.

Agricultural commodities agreement.

Signed at Cairo June 7, 1974.

Entered into force June 7, 1974.

25 UST 1245; TIAS 7855.

Amendments

September 11 and 12, 1974 (25 UST 2482; TIAS 7930).

November 10, 1974 (26 UST 863; TIAS 8070).

April 1, 1975 (26 UST 865; TIAS 8070).

May 2 and 6, 1975 (26 UST 867; TIAS 8070).

June 30, 1975 (26 UST 1915; TIAS 8147; 1021 UNTS 470).

December 30, 1986 (NP).

August 26 and 27, 1987 (NP).

Related agreements

October 28, 1975 (26 UST 2928; TIAS 8201).

March 6, 1976 (27 UST 1505; TIAS 8259; 1049 UNTS 369).

May 4, 1976 (27 UST 1509; TIAS 8259; 1049 UNTS 371).

June 14, 1976 (27 UST 1512; TIAS 8259; 1049 UNTS 373).

September 28 and 29, 1976 (28 UST 5693; TIAS 8654).

October 26, 1976 (27 UST 3877; TIAS 8406; 1059 UNTS 161).

February 14, 1977 (28 UST 2449; TIAS 8564).

April 18, 1977 (29 UST 332; TIAS 8818).

August 4, 1977 (29 UST 496; TIAS 8828).

December 7, 1977 (29 UST 3856; TIAS 9040; 1124 UNTS 77).

April 20, 1978 (29 UST 3870; TIAS 9040; 1124 UNTS 85).

August 3, 1978 (29 UST 3872; TIAS 9040; 1124 UNTS 85).

November 8, 1978 (30 UST 966; TIAS 9230; 1150 UNTS 337).

March 20, 1979 (30 UST 3974; TIAS 9437; 1171 UNTS 380).

July 10, 1979 (30 UST 3976; TIAS 9437; 1171 UNTS 380).

October 4, 1979 (32 UST 1664; TIAS 9793).

May 22, 1980 (32 UST 1644; TIAS 9793).

June 30, 1980 (33 UST 1033; TIAS 10089; 1279 UNTS 332).

July 31, 1980 (32 UST 1664; TIAS 9793).

August 27, 1980 (32 UST 2347; TIAS 9843).

December 14, 1980 (33 UST 695; TIAS 10060).

April 21, 1981 (33 UST 995; TIAS 10083).

December 21, 1981 (33 UST 4658; TIAS 10328).

February 5, 1982 (33 UST 4658; TIAS 10328).

August 11, 1982 (34 UST 1091; TIAS 10393).

November 23, 1982 (TIAS 10613; 2000 UNTS 447).

August 18, 1983 (35 UST 1729; TIAS 10762; 2012 UNTS 401).

January 23, 1984 (TIAS 11044; 2022 UNTS 3).

April 19 and May 3, 1984 (TIAS 11044).

August 2, 1984 (TIAS 11044).

December 16, 1984 (TIAS 11047; 2022 UNTS 5).

November 12, 1985 (NP).

September 21, 1986 (NP).

December 30, 1986 (NP).

March 21, 1988 (NP).

October 13, 1988 (NP).

Agricultural commodities agreement, with annexes.

Signed at Cairo March 20, 1979.

Entered into force March 20, 1979.

31 UST 5714; TIAS 9683; 1221 UNTS 121.

Amendments

June 30, 1980 (33 UST 1033; TIAS 10089).

June 28, 1981 (33 UST 1033; TIAS 10089).

May 24, 1982 (34 UST 1425; TIAS 10427; 1736 UNTS 392).

August 17 and 18, 1983 (35 UST 1734; TIAS 10763; 2012 UNTS 350).

Agricultural commodities agreement.

Signed at Cairo March 20, 1989.

Entered into force March 20, 1989.

NP

Amendment

July 26, 1989 (NP).

Related agreements

January 28, 1990 (NP).

August 26, 1990 (NP).

ATOMIC ENERGY

Agreement for cooperation concerning peaceful uses of nuclear energy, with annex and agreed minute.

Signed at Washington June 29, 1981.

Entered into force December 29, 1981.

33 UST 2915; TIAS 10208; 1529 UNTS 143.

AVIATION

Agreement relating to the use of Payne Field for international civil air traffic.

Exchange of notes at Cairo June 15, 1946.

Entered into force June 15, 1946.

3 UST 363; TIAS 2397; 151 UNTS 135.

Air transport agreement.

Signed at Cairo May 5, 1964.

Entered into force provisionally May 5, 1964; definitively April 7, 1965.

15 UST 2202; TIAS 5706; 531 UNTS 229.

Memorandum of agreement concerning assistance in evaluating Egypt's civil aviation infrastructure.

Signed at Cairo July 24, 1995.

Entered into force July 24, 1995.

TIAS

Memorandum of agreement concerning the provision of civil aviation assistance.

Signed at Washington and Cairo September 12 and 14, 1997.

Entered into force September 14, 1997.

TIAS

CANALS

Arrangement relating to assistance by the United States in the salvage and/or removal from the Suez Canal of sunken vessels and certain other hazards to navigation, with annex.

Exchange of notes at Cairo June 11, 1974.

Entered into force June 11, 1974.

25 UST 1273; TIAS 7859.

CLAIMS

Agreement concerning claims of nationals of the United States, with agreed minute and related notes.

Signed at Cairo May 1, 1976.

Entered into force October 27, 1976.

27 UST 4214; TIAS 8446.

Agreement concerning United States Government and other claims, with exchange of notes.

Signed at Cairo May 19, 1979.

Entered into force November 5, 1979.

30 UST 7303; TIAS 9589; 1182 UNTS 51.

CULTURAL RELATIONS

Cultural agreement.

Signed at Cairo May 21, 1962.

Entered into force May 21, 1962.

13 UST 1253; TIAS 5072; 458 UNTS 197.

CUSTOMS

Arrangement providing for reciprocal privileges for consular officers to import articles for their personal use free of duty.

Exchange of notes at Washington March 16 and April 7, 1932.

Entered into force April 7, 1932.

11 Bevans 1337.

DEFENSE

Agreement relating to mutual defense assistance.

Exchange of notes at Cairo April 29, 1952.

Entered into force April 29, 1952.

7 UST 841; TIAS 3564; 241 UNTS 3.

Amendment

December 9 and 10, 1952 (7 UST 844; TIAS 3565; 241 UNTS 8).

Agreement concerning privileges and immunities of United States military and related personnel in Egypt, with related letter and agreed minute.

Exchange of notes at Cairo July 26, 1981.

Entered into force December 5, 1981.

33 UST 3353; TIAS 10238.

General security of military information agreement.

Signed at Cairo February 10, 1982.

Entered into force February 10, 1982.

34 UST 203; TIAS 10349.

Memorandum of understanding concerning the principles governing scientist and engineer exchange and mutual cooperation in research and development, procurement and logistic support of defense equipment, with annex.

Signed at Washington March 23, 1988.

Entered into force March 23, 1988.

TIAS 11572; 2185 UNTS 277.

Memorandum of understanding relating to the coproduction of the M1A1 tank in Egypt, with annexes.

Signed at Cairo November 1, 1988.

Entered into force November 1, 1988.

TIAS 12287.

Amendment

April 11 and August 7, 1989.

Memorandum of understanding concerning a cooperative project for the development of a display subprogram for the E-2C L-304 mission computer.

Signed at Washington and Cairo May 6 and 15, 1991.

Entered into force May 15, 1991.

TIAS 11837.

Agreement for technology research and development projects.

Signed at Cairo and Washington February 24 and 27, 1998.

Entered into force February 27, 1998.

TIAS

ECONOMIC AND TECHNICAL COOPERATION

Economic, technical, and related assistance agreement, with exchanges of notes.

Signed at Cairo August 16, 1978.

Entered into force October 15, 1978.

30 UST 4609; TIAS 9481; 1169 UNTS 271.

Statement relating to greater support to economic progress in Egypt. Released at Washington February 4, 1982.

Entered into force February 4, 1982.

34 UST 165; TIAS 10346; 1556 UNTS 327.

Agency for International Development

February 13, 1975 (26 UST 371; TIAS 8039; 992 UNTS 181).

December 18, 1975 (27 UST 4081; TIAS 8427).

May 22, 1976 (28 UST 2956; TIAS 8577).

May 30, 1976 (27 UST 2636; TIAS 8335; 1055 UNTS 57).

May 30, 1976 (27 UST 2649; TIAS 8336; 1055 UNTS 79).

June 30, 1976 (28 UST 1441; TIAS 8517).

July 22, 1976 (28 UST 2969; TIAS 8577).

July 29, 1976 (28 UST 2231; TIAS 8541).

July 29, 1976 (28 UST 2349; TIAS 8548).

July 29, 1976 (28 UST 6971; TIAS 8699).

July 31, 1976 (28 UST 2930; TIAS 8575).

July 31, 1976 (28 UST 6989; TIAS 8700).

July 31, 1976 (28 UST 7017; TIAS 8702).

September 4, 1976 (28 UST 2971; TIAS 8578).

September 30, 1976 (28 UST 2932; TIAS 8575).

September 30, 1976 (28 UST 6197; TIAS 8679).

September 30, 1976 (28 UST 8419; TIAS 8764).

September 30, 1976 (28 UST 8877; TIAS 8775).

September 30, 1976 (28 UST 8064; TIAS 8741).

January 22, 1977 (29 UST 1039; TIAS 8866).

March 6, 1977 (29 UST 304; TIAS 8815).

March 29, 1977 (29 UST 501; TIAS 8830).

June 2, 1977 (30 UST 6551; TIAS 9567).

July 10, 1977 (30 UST 6565; TIAS 9567).

August 11, 1977 (30 UST 2282; TIAS 9336; 1169 UNTS 11).

August 31, 1977 (30 UST 2288; TIAS 9336; 1169 UNTS 18).

September 20, 1977 (30 UST 2226; TIAS 9330; 1171 UNTS 352).

September 27, 1977 (30 UST 4265; TIAS 9458; 1169 UNTS 31).

September 27, 1977 (30 UST 4462; TIAS 9469; 1169 UNTS 61).

September 28, 1977 (30 UST 2230; TIAS 9331; 1169 UNTS 111).

September 28, 1977 (30 UST 4388; TIAS 9464; 1169 UNTS 93).

September 29, 1977 (30 UST 2258; TIAS 9334; 1169 UNTS 165).

September 29, 1977 (30 UST 2271; TIAS 9335; 1169 UNTS 147).

September 29, 1977 (30 UST 4401; TIAS 9465; 1169 UNTS 185).

September 29, 1977 (30 UST 4424; TIAS 9466; 1169 UNTS 205).

September 29, 1977 (30 UST 4699; TIAS 9486; 1169 UNTS 127).

September 30, 1977 (29 UST 5628; TIAS 9136; 1152 UNTS 453).

September 30, 1977 (29 UST 5631; TIAS 9137; 1152 UNTS 439).

September 30, 1977 (30 UST 2240; TIAS 9332; 1169 UNTS 223).

September 30, 1977 (30 UST 4491; TIAS 9473; 1178 UNTS 75).

December 29, 1977 (29 UST 5621; TIAS 9134).

December 29, 1977 (29 UST 5624; TIAS 9135; 1152 UNTS 443).

February 27, 1978 (30 UST 4577; TIAS 9479; 1169 UNTS 247).

March 7, 1978 (30 UST 4711; TIAS 9486; 1169 UNTS 136).

March 29, 1978 (30 UST 4515; TIAS 9473; 1178 UNTS 84).

March 29, 1978 (30 UST 4569; TIAS 9478).

May 18, 1978 (30 UST 2289; TIAS 9336; 1169 UNTS 19).

June 1, 1978 (30 UST 2891; TIAS 9370; 1177 UNTS 401).

August 15, 1978 (30 UST 2290; TIAS 9336; 1169 UNTS 20).

August 17, 1978 (30 UST 4626; TIAS 9483).

August 28, 1978 (30 UST 6661; TIAS 9575; 1181 UNTS 279).

August 31, 1978 (30 UST 2269; TIAS 9334; 1169 UNTS 174).

August 31, 1978 (30 UST 6059; TIAS 9538).

September 28, 1978 (30 UST 6225; TIAS 9550; 1178 UNTS 157).

September 30, 1978 (30 UST 6338; TIAS 9558; 1178 UNTS 177).

September 30, 1978 (30 UST 6579; TIAS 9569; 1182 UNTS 3).

August 29, 1979 (31 UST 872; TIAS 9624; 1202 UNTS 233).

September 22, 1979 (32 UST 42; TIAS 9699).

October 19, 1979 (32 UST 426; TIAS 9709).

June 30, 1980 (32 UST 1834; TIAS 9802).

June 30, 1980 (32 UST 1857; TIAS 9803).

June 30, 1980 (32 UST 1889; TIAS 9806; 1274 UNTS 131).

September 28, 1980 (32 UST 2696; TIAS 9872; 1274 UNTS 420).

June 28, 1981 (33 UST 2463; TIAS 10191; 1529 UNTS 103).

June 28, 1981 (33 UST 2487; TIAS 10192; 1529 UNTS 123).

August 27, 1981 (33 UST 3718; TIAS 10254).
August 29, 1981 (33 UST 3664; TIAS 10247; 1541 UNTS 438).
September 22, 1981 (33 UST 3981; TIAS 10277).
September 27, 1981 (33 UST 4010; TIAS 10279).
September 27, 1981 (33 UST 4028; TIAS 10280).
September 27, 1981 (33 UST 4052; TIAS 10281).
February 5, 1982 (34 UST 171; TIAS 10347; 1556 UNTS 333).
April 12, 1982 (34 UST 582; TIAS 10377).
August 16, 1982 (34 UST 1937; TIAS 10471).
August 31, 1982 (34 UST 1967; TIAS 10473; 1751 UNTS 524).
June 30, 1983 (35 UST 1295; TIAS 10728; 2006 UNTS 557).
July 25, 1983 (35 UST 1744; TIAS 10764; 2011 UNTS 101).
July 25, 1983 (35 UST 2434; TIAS 10806; 2012 UNTS 351).
August 9, 1983 (35 UST 1924; TIAS 10770).
September 12, 1983.
September 28, 1983.
November 10, 1983 (35 UST 3940; TIAS 10895; 2016 UNTS 123).
November 10, 1983.
May 14, 1984 (TIAS 11065).
May 14, 1984 (NP).
July 31, 1984 (NP).
August 8, 1984 (NP).
September 26, 1984 (NP).
March 12, 1985 (NP).
March 12, 1985 (NP).
March 13, 1985 (NP).
March 31, 1985 (NP).
May 13, 1985 (NP).
August 15, 1985 (NP).
September 12, 1985 (NP).
September 12, 1985 (NP).
September 24, 1985 (NP).
September 26, 1985 (NP).
December 31, 1985 (NP).
December 31,1985 (NP).
December 31,1985 (NP).
March 31, 1986 (NP).
June 19, 1986 (NP).
August 21, 1986 (NP).
August 21, 1986 (NP).
August 27, 1986 (NP).
August 28, 1986 (NP).
September 29, 1986 (NP).
September 30, 1986 (NP).
March 8, 1987 (NP).
May 18, 1987 (NP).
June 25, 1987 (NP).
June 25, 1987 (NP).
July 30, 1987 (NP).
September 21, 1987 (NP).
September 21, 1987 (NP).
September 24, 1987 (NP).
February 9, 1988 (NP).
June 22, 1988 (NP).
June 23, 1988 (NP).
September 27, 1988 (NP).
September 30, 1988 (NP).
June 14, 1989 (NP).
June 21, 1989 (NP).
August 17, 1989 (NP).
September 27, 1989 (NP).
July 9, 1990 (NP).
August 21, 1990 (NP).
August 21, 1990 (NP).
August 21, 1990 (NP).
August 31, 1990 (NP).
September 30, 1990 (NP).
September 30, 1990 (NP).
May 30, 1991 (NP).
September 9, 1991 (NP).
September 9, 1991 (NP).
February 12, 1992 (NP).
August 24, 1992 (NP).
September 14, 1992 (NP).
September 13, 1993 (NP).
September 23, 1993 (NP).
September 29, 1994 (NP).
May 18, 1995 (NP).
August 12, 1995 (NP).
September 30, 1995 (NP).
August 25, 1997 (NP).
September 28, 1997 (NP).
September 28, 1997 (NP).
September 29, 1997 (NP).
September 29, 1997 (NP).
September 29, 1997 (NP).
September 29, 1997 (NP).
August 31, 1998 (NP).
August 31, 1998 (NP).
August 31, 1998 (NP).
August 31, 1998 (NP).
September 3, 1998 (NP).
September 3, 1998 (NP).
September 6, 1998 (NP).
September 17, 1998 (NP).
September 17, 1998 (NP).
September 17, 1998 (NP).
September 23, 1998 (NP).
September 23, 1998 (NP).
September 23, 1998 (NP).
September 29, 1998 (NP).
September 29, 1998 (NP).
September 29, 1998 (NP).
September 30, 1998 (NP).
September 30, 1998 (NP).
June 17, 1999 (NP).
June 23, 1999 (NP).
July 1, 1999 (NP).
September 20, 1999 (NP).
September 22, 1999 (NP).
September 23, 1999 (NP).
September 23, 1999 (NP).
April 5, 2000 (NP).
June 4, 2000 (NP).
June 28, 2000 (NP).
June 28, 2000 (NP).
September 30, 2000 (NP).
September 27, 2001 (NP).
September 30, 2001 (NP).
December 13, 2001 (NP).
March 28, 2002 (NP).
June 12, 2002 (NP).
September 30, 2002 (NP).
September 30, 2002 (NP).
September 30, 2002 (NP).
September 30, 2002 (NP).
September 30, 2002 (NP).
September 30, 2002 (NP).
September 30, 2002 (NP).
June 22, 2003 (NP).
September 30, 2003 (NP).
September 30, 2003 (NP).
September 30, 2003 (NP).
September 30, 2003 (NP).
September 30, 2003 (NP).
June 3, 2004 (NP).
September 28, 2004 (NP).
September 30, 2004 (NP).
March 20, 2005 (NP).

EDUCATION

Agreement for financing certain educational exchange programs.

Exchange of notes at Cairo January 5 and February 21, 1967.

Entered into force February 21, 1967.

TIAS 6234; 18 UST 307; 688 UNTS 229.

ENVIRONMENTAL COOPERATION

Agreement for cooperation in the Global Learning and Observations to Benefit the Environment (GLOBE) Program, with appendices.

Signed at Cairo March 20, 1995.

Entered into force March 20, 1995.

TIAS 12616.

EXTRADITION

Convention between the United States and the Ottoman Empire relating to extradition.

Signed at Constantinople August 11, 1874.

Entered into force April 22, 1875.

19 Stat. 572; TS 270; 10 Bevans 642.

FINANCE

Agreement regarding the consolidation and rescheduling of past due debts owed to United States Government agencies with annexes.

Signed at Cairo December 6, 1971.

Entered into force August 28, 1972.

23 UST 1457; TIAS 7424; 852 UNTS 3.

Agreement regarding the consolidation and rescheduling of certain debts owed to, guaranteed by, or insured by the United States Government and its agencies, with annexes and related letter.

Signed at Cairo November 14, 1987.

Entered into force February 22, 1988.

NP

Agreement regarding the reorganization of certain debts owed to, guaranteed by, or insured by the United States Government and its agencies, with annexes.

Signed at Washington July 18, 1991.

Entered into force September 3, 1991.

NP

Investment incentive agreement.

Signed at Washington July 1, 1999.

Entered into force July 1, 1999.

TIAS

GENERAL RELATIONS

Agreement concerning principles of relations and cooperation.

Signed at Cairo June 14, 1974.

Entered into force June 14, 1974.

25 UST 2359; TIAS 7913.

INFORMATIONAL MEDIA GUARANTIES

Agreement relating to an informational media guaranty program.

Exchange of notes at Washington March 3 and 7, 1955.

Entered into force March 7, 1955.

6 UST 691; TIAS 3206; 252 UNTS 159.

INTERNATIONAL CRIMINAL COURT

Agreement regarding the surrender of persons to the International Criminal Court.

Exchange of notes at Cairo February 26 and March 5, 2003.

Entered into force March 5, 2003.

TIAS

Extension

March 1 and 2, 2005.

INVESTMENT

Treaty concerning the reciprocal encouragement and protection of investments, with annex and protocol.

Signed at Washington September 29, 1982.

Entered into force June 27, 1992.

TIAS

Related agreements

March 11, 1985.

March 11, 1986.

JUDICIAL ASSISTANCE

Agreement on procedures for mutual assistance in connection with matters relating to the Westinghouse Electric Corporation.

Signed at Washington November 29, 1978.

Entered into force November 29, 1978.

30 UST 3996; TIAS 9441; 1169 UNTS 328.

Related agreements

December 21, 1978 and January 3, 1979 (30 UST 4005; TIAS 9442; 1169 UNTS 335).

March 19 and April 17, 1979 (30 UST 4007; TIAS 9443; 1169 UNTS 337).

Agreement on procedures for mutual assistance in connection with matters relating to the General Electric Company.

Signed at Washington September 17, 1993.

Entered into force September 17, 1993.

NP

Amendment

November 18, 1994 (NP).

Treaty on mutual legal assistance in criminal matters.

Signed at Cairo May 3, 1998.

Entered into force November 29, 2001.

TIAS

MAPPING

Mapping, charting and geodesy cooperative and exchange agreement, with annexes.

Signed at Washington June 25, 1981.

Entered into force June 25, 1981.

NP

NARCOTIC DRUGS

Arrangement for the direct exchange of certain information regarding the traffic in narcotic drugs.

Exchange of notes at Alexandria June 20, 1930 and Cairo August 26, 1930.

Entered into force August 26, 1930.

11 Bevans 1331.

Agreement regarding the transfer of forfeited assets.

Signed at Cairo May 20, 1993.

Entered into force May 20, 1993.

TIAS 12499.

NAVIGATION

Agreement for the establishment and operation of an OMEGA navigation system monitoring station.

Signed at Alexandria June 14, 1980.

Entered into force June 14, 1980.

TIAS 12375.

PACIFIC SETTLEMENT OF DISPUTES

Treaty of arbitration.

Signed at Washington August 27, 1929.

Entered into force August 24, 1932.

47 Stat. 2130; TS 850; 11 Bevans 1325; 142 LNTS 323.

Treaty of conciliation.

Signed at Washington August 27, 1929.

Entered into force August 24, 1932.

47 Stat. 2132; TS 851; 11 Bevans 1327; 142 LNTS 317.

PEACEKEEPING

Agreement relating to implementation of the Egyptian-Israeli peace treaty of March 26, 1979.[1]

Letter signed at Washington March 26, 1979.

Entered into force March 26, 1979.

32 UST 2148; TIAS 9827.

Agreement to transfer title of the United States Field Mission base camp at Umm Khusheib from the United States Sinai Support Mission to the Government of the Arab Republic of Egypt.

Signed at Umm Khusheib April 22, 1982.

Entered into force April 22, 1982.

34 UST 1229; TIAS 10410.

NOTE

1 See also MULTINATIONAL FORCE AND OBSERVERS in bilateral section and PEACEKEEPING in multilateral section.

POSTAL MATTERS

Agreement concerning the exchange of parcel post and regulations of execution.

Signed at Cairo December 30, 1958 and at Washington January 13, 1959.

Entered into force October 1, 1959.

10 UST 1664; TIAS 4315; 358 UNTS 3.

International express mail agreement with detailed regulations.

Signed at Cairo and Washington December 3 and 22, 1983.

Entered into force February 1, 1984.

35 UST 3249; TIAS 10854; 2015 UNTS 69.

Memorandum of understanding concerning the operation of the INTELPOST field trial, with details of implementation.

Signed at Cairo and Washington August 18 and September 13, 1985.

Entered into force September 13, 1985.

TIAS 11157.

RELIEF SUPPLIES AND PACKAGES

Agreement relating to duty-free entry and defrayment of inland transportation charges on relief supplies and packages.

Exchange of notes at Cairo October 30, 1954.

Entered into force October 30, 1954.

5 UST 2551; TIAS 3119; 234 UNTS 139.

SCIENTIFIC COOPERATION

Agreement on science and technology cooperation, with annexes.

Signed at Cairo January 29, 2001.

Entered into force December 31, 2001.

TIAS

Extension

May 5 and August 27, 2006.

TAXATION

Convention for the avoidance of double taxation and the prevention of fiscal evasion with respect to taxes on income.[1]

Signed at Cairo August 24, 1980.

Entered into force December 31, 1981.

33 UST 1809; TIAS 10149; 1529 UNTS 41.

NOTE

1 With an understanding and a reservation.

TOURISM

Agreement on the development and facilitation of tourism.

Signed at Cairo February 21, 1983.

Entered into force August 16, 1983.

TIAS 10680; 2005 UNTS 119.

TRADE AND COMMERCE

Provisional commercial agreement relating to most-favored-nation treatment in customs matters.

Exchange of notes at Cairo May 24, 1930.

Entered into force May 24, 1930.

47 Stat. 2582; EAS 5; 11 Bevans 1329; 117 LNTS 419.

Agreement relating to trade in textiles and textile products.

Exchange of notes at Cairo December 7 and 28, 1977.

Entered into force December 28, 1977; effective January 1, 1978.

29 UST 2774; TIAS 8973.

Amendments and extension

June 21 and 25, 1984 (NP).

March 7 and 14, 1988 (NP).

January 16 and February 26, 1990 (NP).

March 15 and June 9, 1992 (NP).

VISAS

Agreement providing for the abolition of nonimmigrant visa fees.

Exchange of notes at Cairo June 3 and August 1, 1963.

Entered into force August 1, 1963; operative September 1, 1963.

14 UST 1191; TIAS 5416; 488 UNTS 189.

EL SALVADOR

AGRICULTURAL COMMODITIES

Agricultural commodities agreement, with exchange of notes.

Signed at San Salvador August 21, 1961.

Entered into force August 21, 1961.

12 UST 1210; TIAS 4838; 418 UNTS 35.

Agricultural commodity agreement.

Signed at Washington May 7, 1963.

Entered into force May 7, 1963.

14 UST 418; TIAS 5335; 476 UNTS 35.

Amendments

June 16, 1981 (TIAS 11050).

June 19, 1981 (TIAS 11050).

August 31 and September 2, 1981 (TIAS 11050).

Related agreements

September 1, 1982 (TIAS 11051).

May 18, 1983 (TIAS 11052).

August 6, 1983 (TIAS 11052).

July 13, 1984 (TIAS 11053).

August 20, 1984 (TIAS 11053).

January 29, 1985 (NP).

August 8, 1985 (NP).

Amendment

June 27, 1986 (NP).

Amendment

September 29, 1987 (NP).

Agricultural commodities agreement.

Signed at San Salvador March 10, 1988.

Entered into force September 11, 1988.

NP

Amendments

July 20, 1988 (NP).

September 7, 1988 (NP).

Related agreements

July 20, 1989 (NP).

Agricultural commodities agreement.

Signed at San Salvador January 19, 1990.

Entered into force March 6, 1990.

NP

Amendment

August 2, 1990 (NP).

Agricultural commodities agreement.

Signed at San Salvador December 12, 1990.

Entered into force May 24, 1991.

NP

AGRICULTURE

Agreement confirming the cooperative agreement for the prevention of foot-and-mouth disease and rinderpest in El Salvador.

Exchange of notes at San Salvador February 28 and March 2, 1973.

Entered into force March 2, 1973.

24 UST 1931; TIAS 7701.

AVIATION

Air transport agreement, with annexes.

Signed at San Jose May 8, 1997.

Entered into force January 3, 2000.

TIAS

CULTURAL PROPERTY

Memorandum of understanding concerning the imposition of import restrictions on certain categories of archaeological material from the prehispanic cultures of the Republic of El Salvador, with appendix.

Signed at Washington March 8, 1995.

Entered into force March 8, 1995.

TIAS 12609.

Amendment and extension

March 7, 2000.

CUSTOMS

Agreement granting reciprocal customs privileges for Foreign Service personnel.

Exchange of notes at Washington March 18 and May 9, 1958.

Entered into force May 9, 1958.

9 UST 617; TIAS 4043; 316 UNTS 29.

DEFENSE

Agreement relating to the furnishing of defense articles and services to El Salvador for the purpose of contributing to its internal security.

Exchange of notes at San Salvador April 10 and 13, 1962.

Entered into force April 13, 1962.

13 UST 985; TIAS 5040; 451 UNTS 307.

Agreement relating to the deposit by El Salvador of ten percent of the value of grant military assistance and excess defense articles furnished by the United States.

Exchange of notes at San Salvador April 25 and June 15, 1972.

Entered into force June 15, 1972; effective February 1, 1972.

23 UST 1331; TIAS 7416.

Agreement concerning payment to the United States of net proceeds from the sale of defense articles furnished under the military assistance program.

Exchange of notes at San Salvador October 24 and December 6, 1974.

Entered into force December 6, 1974; effective July 1, 1974.

25 UST 3155; TIAS 7979.

Acquisition and cross-servicing agreement, with annexes.

Signed at San Salvador June 26, 2002.

Entered into force June 26, 2002.

TIAS

ECONOMIC AND TECHNICAL COOPERATION

General agreement for economic, technical and related assistance.

Signed at San Salvador December 19, 1961.

Entered into force January 16, 1962.

13 UST 266; TIAS 4971; 445 UNTS 175.

Agreement concerning the establishment of an Americas Fund and Administering Commission.

Signed at Washington June 18, 1993.

Entered into force July 5, 1994.

TIAS

Agency for International Development

August 28, 1987 (NP).

February 1, 1988 (NP).

June 30, 1988 (NP).

June 7, 2002 (NP).

EMPLOYMENT

Agreement relating to employment of dependents of official government employees.

Exchange of notes at San Salvador January 19 and March 11, 1983.

Entered into force March 11, 1983.

TIAS 12380.

EXTRADITION

Treaty of extradition.

Signed at San Salvador April 18, 1911.

Entered into force July 10, 1911.

37 Stat. 1516; TS 560; 7 Bevans 507.

FINANCE

Agreement relating to the guaranty of private investments.

Signed at San Salvador January 29, 1960.

Entered into force April 8, 1960.

11 UST 405; TIAS 4459; 372 UNTS 3.

Agreement regarding the consolidation and rescheduling or refinancing of certain debts owed to, guaranteed by, or insured by the United States Government and its agencies, with annexes.

Signed at Washington November 13, 1990.

Entered into force January 4, 1991.

NP

Agreement regarding the reduction of certain debts related to agriculture owed to the Government of the United States and its agencies, with appendices.

Signed at San Salvador December 15, 1992.

Entered into force January 14, 1993.

NP

Agreement regarding the reduction of certain debts related to foreign assistance owed to the Government of the United States and its agencies, with appendices.

Signed at San Salvador December 15, 1992.

Entered into force January 14, 1993.

NP

Agreement regarding the reduction of a certain debt related to agricultural trade owed to the Government of the United States and its agencies, with appendix.

Signed at San Salvador July 12, 2001.

Entered into force July 12, 2001.

NP

HIGHWAYS

Agreement relating to the construction of the inter-American highway.

Exchange of notes at Washington January 30 and February 13, 1942.

Entered into force February 13, 1942.

56 Stat. 1842; EAS 294; 7 Bevans 558; 23 UNTS 293.

Amendment

February 19 and March 19, 1951 (2 UST 1840; TIAS 2318; 134 UNTS 245).

JUDICIAL ASSISTANCE

Agreement concerning the establishment of an International Law Enforcement Academy (ILEA).

Signed at San Salvador September 20, 2005.

Entered into force March 1, 2006.

TIAS

LABOR

Arrangement relating to workmen's compensation and unemployment insurance for American citizens employed on projects in El Salvador.

Exchange of notes at San Salvador September 24, 28, and 29, 1943.

Entered into force September 29, 1943.

7 Bevans 586.

MAPPING

Basic exchange and cooperative agreement for topographic mapping, nautical and aeronautical charting and information, geodesy and geophysics, digital data and related mapping, charting and geodesy materials, with glossary.

Signed at Delgado (San Salvador) and Fairfax May 10 and 22, 1996.

Entered into force May 22, 1996.

NP

MISSIONS, MILITARY

Agreement providing for a United States Army mission to El Salvador.

Signed at San Salvador September 23, 1954.

Entered into force November 17, 1954.

5 UST 2870; TIAS 3144; 237 UNTS 91.

Extensions and amendments

March 16 and 31, 1959 (10 UST 730; TIAS 4206; 342 UNTS 351).

March 27 and May 3, 1963 (14 UST 484; TIAS 5345; 476 UNTS 333).

Air Force mission agreement.

Signed at San Salvador November 21, 1957.

Entered into force November 21, 1957.

8 UST 2356; TIAS 3951; 303 UNTS 19.

Extension and amendments

March 16 and 31, 1959 (10 UST 730; TIAS 4206; 342 UNTS 361).

January 15 and 22, 1960 (11 UST 76; TIAS 4410; 371 UNTS 324).

NARCOTIC DRUGS

Agreement of cooperation concerning United States access to and use of facilities at the International Airport of El Salvador for aerial counter-narcotics activities.

Signed at San Salvador March 31, 2000.

Entered into force August 23, 2000.

TIAS

Agreement regarding the Cooperating Nation Information Exchange System.

Exchange of notes at San Salvador November 29 and December 17, 2004.

Entered into force December 17, 2004.

TIAS

PEACE CORPS

Agreement relating to the establishment of a Peace Corps program in El Salvador.

Exchange of notes at San Salvador August 11, November 13 and 20, 1961.

Entered into force November 13, 1961.

12 UST 2983; TIAS 4899; 433 UNTS 221.

POSTAL MATTERS

International express mail agreement, with detailed regulations.

Signed at San Salvador and Washington August 29 and October 6, 1989.

Entered into force October 30, 1989.

TIAS 11689.

Postal money order agreement.

Signed at Mexico August 16, 1991.

Entered into force October 1, 1991.

TIAS 11800.

PUBLICATIONS

Agreement relating to the exchange of official publications.

Exchange of notes at San Salvador November 21 and 27, 1941.

Entered into force November 27, 1941.

55 Stat. 1478; EAS 230; 7 Bevans 551; 120 UNTS 161.

TAXATION

Agreement concerning relief from double taxation on income derived from operation of aircraft.

Exchange of notes at San Salvador December 17, 1987.

Entered into force December 17, 1987.

TIAS 11557; 2185 UNTS 343.

TELECOMMUNICATION

Arrangement relating to radio communications between amateur stations on behalf of third parties.

Exchange of notes at San Salvador April 5, 1962.

Entered into force May 5, 1962.

13 UST 411; TIAS 5001; 442 UNTS 41.

Agreement relating to the granting of authorizations to permit licensed amateur radio operators of either country to operate their stations in the other country.

Exchange of notes at San Salvador May 24 and June 5, 1967.

Entered into force June 5, 1967.

18 UST 1661; TIAS 6309; 692 UNTS 221.

TRADE AND COMMERCE

Convention facilitating the work of traveling salesmen.

Signed at Washington January 28, 1919.

Entered into force January 18, 1921.

41 Stat. 1725; TS 651; 7 Bevans 514.

Trade agreement.

Signed at San Salvador February 19, 1937.

Entered into force May 31, 1937.

50 Stat. 1564; EAS 101; 7 Bevans 536; 179 LNTS 219.

Agreement terminating certain provisions of the reciprocal trade agreement of February 19, 1937.

Exchange of notes at San Salvador June 29, 1962.

Entered into force June 29, 1962.

13 UST 1358; TIAS 5095.

Agreement relating to trade in cotton textiles.

Exchange of notes at San Salvador March 2 and April 30, 1987.

Entered into force April 30, 1987.

NP

Amendments and extension

November 23, 1988 and April 26, 1989 (NP).

December 18 and 27, 1989 (NP).

Agreement regarding the treatment of certain textile and apparel goods under the Dominican Republic-Central America-United States free trade agreement.

Exchange of letters at Washington and San Salvador January 27, 2006.

Entered into force January 27, 2006.

TIAS

VISAS

Agreement providing for the reciprocal abolishment of certain visa fees and tourist and immigration charges.

Exchange of notes at San Salvador December 7 and 15, 1953.

Entered into force January 14, 1954.

5 UST 859; TIAS 2977; 236 UNTS 25.

EQUATORIAL GUINEA

DEFENSE

Agreement concerning the provision of training related to defense articles under the United States International Military Education and Training (IMET) Program.

Exchange of notes at Malabo March 9 and 30, 1983.

Entered into force March 30, 1983.

35 UST 3889; TIAS 10891.

FINANCE

Investment incentive agreement.

Signed at Washington June 11, 1998.

Entered into force June 11, 1998.

TIAS

INTERNATIONAL CRIMINAL COURT

Agreement regarding the surrender of persons to the International Criminal Court.

Signed at New York September 25, 2003.

Entered into force May 6, 2004.

TIAS

PEACE CORPS

Agreement relating to the establishment of a Peace Corps program in Equatorial Guinea.

Exchange of notes at Malabo November 18, 1987.

Entered into force November 18, 1987.

TIAS

POSTAL MATTERS

International express mail agreement, with detailed regulations.

Signed at Malabo and Washington April 9 and May 21, 1991.

Entered into force July 1, 1991.

TIAS 11810.

ERITREA

For agreements prior to the independence of Eritrea, see ETHIOPIA.

DEFENSE

Agreement concerning the provision of training under the United States International Military Education and Training (IMET) Program.

Exchange of notes at Asmara December 28 and 31, 1993.

Entered into force December 31, 1993.

NP

Agreement regarding grants under the Foreign Assistance Act of 1961, as amended, and the furnishing of defense articles, related training and other services from the United States to Eritrea.

Exchange of notes at Asmara August 31 and September 30, 1995.

Entered into force September 30, 1995.

TIAS

FINANCE

Investment incentive agreement.

Signed at Washington May 4, 1994.

Entered into force July 7, 1994.

TIAS 12179.

INTERNATIONAL CRIMINAL COURT

Agreement regarding the surrender of persons to the International Criminal Court.

Signed at Washington July 8, 2004.

Entered into force July 8, 2004.

TIAS

PEACE CORPS

Agreement relating to the establishment of a Peace Corps Program in Eritrea.

Exchange of notes at Asmara May 20, 1994.

Entered into force May 20, 1994.

TIAS 12103.

POSTAL MATTERS

International express mail agreement, with detailed regulations.

Signed at Asmara and Washington July 4 and 18, 1994.

Entered into force November 1, 1994.

NP

ESTONIA

COMMERCE

Treaty of friendship, commerce, and consular rights, and protocol.

Signed at Washington December 23, 1925.

Entered into force May 22, 1926.

44 Stat. 2379; TS 736; 7 Bevans 620; 50 LNTS 13.

CONSULS

See COMMERCE

CULTURAL PROPERTY

Agreement on the protection and preservation of certain cultural properties.

Signed at Tallinn January 16, 2003.

Entered into force July 22, 2003.

TIAS

DEFENSE

Agreement concerning the provision of training related to defense articles under the United States International Military, Education and Training (IMET) Program.

Exchange of notes at Tallinn May 18 and 25, 1992.

Entered into force May 25, 1992.

NP

Agreement regarding grants under the Foreign Assistance Act of 1961, as amended, and the furnishing of defense articles, related training or other defense services from the United States to the Republic of Estonia.

Exchange of notes at Tallinn February 11 and 12, 1993.

Entered into force February 12, 1993.

TIAS 12288.

Acquisition and cross-servicing agreement, with annex.

Signed at Tallinn and Stuttgart September 9 and October 21, 1998.

Entered into force October 21, 1998.

TIAS

Agreement concerning security measures for the protection of classified military information.

Signed at Tallinn February 23, 2000.

Entered into force February 23, 2000.

TIAS; 2109 UNTS 3.

DIPLOMATIC RELATIONS

Memorandum of understanding concerning diplomatic relations.

Signed at Tallinn September 4, 1991.

Entered into force September 4, 1991.

TIAS 12131; 1939 UNTS 93.

EMPLOYMENT

Agreement concerning the employment on a reciprocal basis of dependents of official government employees.

Exchange of notes at Tallinn September 25 and October 20, 2000.

Entered into force November 22, 2000.

TIAS

EXTRADITION

Treaty for extradition of fugitives from justice.

Signed at Tallinn November 8, 1923.

Entered into force November 15, 1924.

43 Stat. 1849; TS 703; 7 Bevans 602; 43 LNTS 277.

Supplementary extradition treaty.

Signed at Washington October 10, 1934.

Entered into force May 7, 1935.

49 Stat. 3190; TS 888; 7 Bevans 645; 159 LNTS 149.

FINANCE

Debt funding agreement.

Signed at Washington October 28, 1925; operative December 15, 1922.

Treasury Department print; 7 Bevans 613.

Agreement modifying the debt funding agreement of October 28, 1925.

Signed at Washington June 11, 1932; operative July 1, 1931.

Treasury Department print; 7 Bevans 642.

Investment incentive agreement.

Signed at Indianapolis October 28, 1991.

Entered into force October 28, 1991.

TIAS 12099; 1939 UNTS 101.

INVESTMENT

Treaty for the encouragement and reciprocal protection of investment, with annex.

Signed at Washington April 19, 1994.

Entered into force February 16, 1997.

TIAS; 1987 UNTS 131.

Protocol to the treaty for the encouragement and reciprocal protection of investment.

Signed at Brussels October 24, 2003.

Entered into force August 10, 2004.

TIAS

JUDICIAL ASSISTANCE

Treaty on mutual legal assistance in criminal matters.

Signed at Washington April 2, 1998.

Entered into force October 20, 2000.

TIAS

MAPPING

Basic exchange and cooperative agreement for topographic mapping, nautical and aeronautical charting, geodesy and geophysics, digital data and related mapping, charting and geodesy materials.

Signed at Tallinn December 7, 1993.

Entered into force December 7, 1993.

NP

MARITIME MATTERS

Agreement relating to mutual recognition of ship measurement certificates.

Exchange of notes at Washington August 21, 1926 and at New York November 30, 1926.

Entered into force November 30, 1926.

47 Stat. 2597; EAS 9; 7 Bevans 635; 62 LNTS 313.

NORTH ATLANTIC TREATY

Agreement to treat the agreement of June 19, 1995, among the States Parties to the North Atlantic Treaty and other States participating in the Partnership for Peace regarding the status of their forces as binding between the United States and Estonia.

Exchange of notes at Tallinn July 14 and 18, 1995.

Entered into force July 18, 1995.

TIAS

PACIFIC SETTLEMENT OF DISPUTES

Treaty of arbitration.

Signed at Tallinn August 27, 1929.

Entered into force June 18, 1930.

46 Stat. 2757; TS 816; 7 Bevans 637; 102 LNTS 233.

Treaty of conciliation.

Signed at Tallinn August 27, 1929.

Entered into force June 18, 1930.

46 Stat. 2760; TS 817; 7 Bevans 639; 102 LNTS 239.

PEACE CORPS

Agreement concerning the program of the Peace Corps of the United States in Estonia.

Signed at Tallinn February 6, 1992.

Entered into force February 6, 1992.

TIAS; 1939 UNTS 113.

POSTAL MATTERS

International express mail agreement, with detailed regulations.

Signed at Tallinn and Washington December 31, 1991 and February 10, 1992.

Entered into force March 7, 1992.

TIAS 11852.

PUBLICATIONS

Agreement relating to the exchange of official publications.

Exchange of notes at Tallinn December 6, 1938.

Entered into force July 15, 1939.

53 Stat. 2059; EAS 138; 7 Bevans 647.

TAXATION

Convention for the avoidance of double taxation and the prevention of fiscal evasion with respect to taxes on income.

Signed at Washington January 25, 1998.

Entered into force December 30, 1999.

TIAS

TRADE

See also COMMERCE

Agreement according mutual unconditional most-favored-nation treatment in customs matters.

Exchange of notes at Washington March 2, 1925.

Entered into force August 1, 1925.

TS 722; 7 Bevans 608; 43 LNTS 289.

WEAPONS

Agreement concerning cooperation in the area of the prevention of proliferation of weapons of mass destruction and the promotion of defense and military relations.

Signed at Tallinn October 11, 2002.

Entered into force December 4, 2002.

TIAS; 2211 UNTS 121.

ETHIOPIA

Eritrea announced its independence from Ethiopia April 27, 1993.

The status of the agreements listed below is under review.

AGRICULTURAL COMMODITIES

Agricultural commodities agreement, with exchange of notes.

Signed at Addis Ababa August 13, 1962.

Entered into force August 13, 1962.

13 UST 1833; TIAS 5132; 459 UNTS 31.

Agricultural commodities agreement, with exchange of notes.

Signed at Addis Ababa June 11, 1963.

Entered into force June 11, 1963.

14 UST 836; TIAS 5363; 487 UNTS 269.

Agricultural commodities agreement, with exchange of notes.

Signed at Addis Ababa August 17, 1965.

Entered into force August 17, 1965.

16 UST 1119; TIAS 5854; 564 UNTS 119.

Agricultural commodities agreement with exchange of notes.

Signed at Addis Ababa December 14, 1965.

Entered into force December 14, 1965.

16 UST 2019; TIAS 5937; 574 UNTS 115.

Agricultural commodities agreement.

Signed at Addis Ababa June 15, 1976.

Entered into force June 15, 1976.

28 UST 7344; TIAS 8715.

AVIATION

Agreement on civil aviation safety and security.

Exchange of notes at Addis Ababa May 29 and June 2, 1998.

Entered into force June 2, 1998.

TIAS

Memorandum of agreement for the provision of assistance in developing and modernizing the civil aviation infrastructure of Ethiopia

Signed September 21 and November 24, 2005.

Entered into force November 24, 2005.

NP

Air transport agreement, with annexes.

Signed at Washington May 17, 2005.

Entered into force July 21, 2006.

TIAS

CLAIMS

Compensation agreement, with agreed minutes.

Signed at Addis Ababa December 19, 1985.

Entered into force December 19, 1985.

TIAS 11193.

COMMERCE

Treaty of amity and economic relations, and related notes.

Signed at Addis Ababa September 7, 1951.

Entered into force October 8, 1953.

4 UST 2134; TIAS 2864; 206 UNTS 41.

Agreement amending the treaty of amity and economic relations of September 7, 1951, to terminate notes concerning administration of justice.

Exchange of notes at Addis Ababa September 16, 1965 and October 20, 1972.

Entered into force May 3, 1973.

24 UST 2136; TIAS 7726.

CONSULS

See COMMERCE

DEFENSE

Agreement relating to mutual defense assistance.

Exchange of notes at Addis Ababa June 12 and 13, 1952.

Entered into force June 13, 1952.

3 UST 5498; TIAS 2751; 205 UNTS 17.

Agreement relating to a special program of facilities assistance.

Exchange of notes at Addis Ababa December 26, 1957.

Entered into force December 26, 1957.

8 UST 2483; TIAS 3969; 307 UNTS 71.

Agreement relating to the disposition of equipment and materials no longer needed in the furtherance of the mutual defense assistance program.

Exchange of notes at Addis Ababa January 2 and 6, 1958.

Entered into force January 6, 1958.

9 UST 339; TIAS 4013; 303 UNTS 342.

Agreement concerning payment to the United States of net proceeds from the sale of defense articles furnished under the military assistance program.

Exchange of notes at Addis Ababa May 13 and June 26, 1974.

Entered into force July 1, 1974.

25 UST 1437; TIAS 7872.

Agreement regarding the status of U.S. military personnel and civilian employees of the Department of Defense present in Ethiopia.

Exchange of notes at Addis Ababa May 27 and 31, 1994.

Entered into force May 31, 1994.

NP

Agreement regarding the furnishing of commodities, services and related training to assist Ethiopia's forces participating in the African Crisis Response Initiative, with attachment.

Exchange of notes at Addis Ababa February 2 and 6, 1998.

Entered into force February 6, 1998.

TIAS

Agreement relating to United States military and civilian personnel of the United States Department of Defense who may be temporarily present in Ethiopia in connection with humanitarian relief, joint exercises and training, and other agreed activities.

Exchange of notes at Addis Ababa February 21 and 27, 2002.

Entered into force February 27, 2002.

NP

Acquisition and cross-servicing agreement, with annexes.

Signed at Tampa and Addis Ababa July 8 and 17, 2002.

Entered into force July 17, 2002.

TIAS

ECONOMIC AND TECHNICAL COOPERATION

Agreement for economic and technical cooperation.

Signed at Addis Ababa November 15, 1993.

Entered into force November 15, 1993.

TIAS 12167.

Agency for International Development

September 10, 2004 (NP).

August 8, 2006 (NP).

EDUCATION

Agreement for financing certain educational programs, with exchange of notes.

Signed at Addis Ababa December 6, 1961.

Entered into force December 6, 1961.

TIAS 4905; 12 UST 3057; 433 UNTS 231.

EMPLOYMENT

Agreement relating to the employment of dependents of official government employees.

Exchange of notes at Addis Ababa August 31 and September 2, 1999.

Entered into force September 2, 1999.

TIAS

ENVIRONMENTAL COOPERATION

Agreement for cooperation in the Global Learning and Observations to Benefit the Environment (GLOBE) Program.

Signed at Addis Ababa August 24, 2005.

Entered into force August 24, 2005.

TIAS

FINANCE

Agreement relating to investment guaranties.

Exchange of notes at Addis Ababa August 3, 1962.

Entered into force August 3, 1962.

13 UST 1856; TIAS 5134; 459 UNTS 79.

Amendment

March 17, 1967 and March 8, 1968
(19 UST 4725; TIAS 6469; 697 UNTS 280).

Agreement regarding the consolidation and rescheduling or refinancing of certain debts owed to, guaranteed by or insured by the United States Government and its agencies, with annexes.

Signed at Washington May 3, 1993.

Entered into force June 18, 1993.

NP

Agreement regarding the consolidation and rescheduling of certain debts owed to the United States Government and its Agency, with annexes.

Signed at Addis Ababa October 9, 1997.

Entered into force December 3, 1997.

NP

Agreement regarding the consolidation and rescheduling of certain debts owed to the United States Government, with annexes.

Signed at Addis Ababa December 17, 2001.

Entered into force January 22, 2002.

NP

Agreement regarding the consolidation and reduction of certain debts owed to the United States Government, with annexes.

Signed at Addis Ababa January 28, 2003.

Entered into force March 12, 2003.

NP

Agreement regarding the cancellation of certain debts owed to, guaranteed by, or insured by the United States Government, with annexes.

Signed at Addis Ababa December 30, 2004.

Entered into force March 4, 2005.

NP

LEND-LEASE

Agreement on the principles applying to mutual aid in the prosecution of the war against aggression, and exchange of notes.

Signed at Washington August 9, 1943.

Entered into force August 9, 1943.

57 Stat. 1043; EAS 334; 7 Bevans 668; 29 UNTS 303.

Agreement on lend-lease settlement.

Signed at Addis Ababa May 20, 1949.

Entered into force May 20, 1949.

63 Stat. 2446; TIAS 1931; 7 Bevans 678; 89 UNTS 99.

PACIFIC SETTLEMENT OF DISPUTES

Treaty of arbitration.

Signed at Addis Ababa January 26, 1929.

Entered into force August 5, 1929.

46 Stat. 2357; TS 799; 7 Bevans 662; 101 LNTS 517.

Treaty of conciliation.

Signed at Addis Ababa January 26, 1929.

Entered into force August 5, 1929.

46 Stat. 2368; TS 800; 7 Bevans 665; 101 LNTS 529.

PEACE CORPS

Agreement relating to the establishment of a Peace Corps program in Ethiopia.

Exchange of notes at Addis Ababa May 23, 1962.

Entered into force May 23, 1962.

13 UST 1227; TIAS 5067; 456 UNTS 293.

POSTAL MATTERS

Parcel post agreement, with regulations of execution.

Signed at Addis Ababa and Washington June 3 and 15, 1967.

Entered into force September 1, 1967.

18 UST 1622; TIAS 6305; 692 UNTS 263.

International express mail agreement, with detailed regulations.

Signed at Addis Ababa and Washington August 3 and September 1, 1989.

Entered into force September 15, 1989.

TIAS 11954.

Memorandum of understanding concerning the operation of the INTELPOST service, with details of implementation.

Signed at Addis Ababa and Washington March 26 and July 16, 1990.

Entered into force August 15, 1990.

TIAS 11955.

PUBLICATIONS

Agreement relating to the exchange of official publications.

Exchange of notes at Addis Ababa November 25, 1964.

Entered into force November 25, 1964.

15 UST 2150; TIAS 5698; 532 UNTS 125.

SCIENTIFIC COOPERATION

Memorandum of understanding concerning scientific and technical cooperation in the earth sciences, with annexes.

Signed at Reston and Addis Ababa December 9, 2002 and August 28, 2003.

Entered into force August 28, 2003.

TIAS

TAXATION

Agreement to exempt from income tax, on a reciprocal basis, income derived from the international operation of aircraft and ships.

Exchange of notes at Addis Ababa October 30 and November 12, 1998.

Entered into force November 12, 1998; effective January 1, 1998.

TIAS

EUROPEAN ATOMIC ENERGY COMMUNITY (EURATOM)

ATOMIC ENERGY

Agreement in the field of nuclear material safeguards research and development, with annexes.

Signed at Brussels and Washington January 6, 1995.

Entered into force January 6, 1995.

TIAS 12596.

Agreement for cooperation in the peaceful uses of nuclear energy, with annexes, agreed minute and declaration.

Signed at Brussels November 7, 1995 and March 29, 1996.

Entered into force April 12, 1996.

TIAS

Technical exchange and cooperation arrangement in the field of nuclear safety research, with annexes.

Signed at Rockville October 29, 1999.

Entered into force October 29, 1999.

TIAS

Agreement for cooperation in the field of fusion energy research and development, with annex.

Signed at Brussels May 14, 2001.

Entered into force May 14, 2001.

TIAS

EUROPEAN COMMUNITY

CUSTOMS

Agreement on customs cooperation and mutual assistance in customs matters.

Done at The Hague May 28, 1997.

Entered into force August 1, 1997.

TIAS

EDUCATION

Agreement renewing a programme of cooperation in higher education and vocational education and training, with annex.

Signed at Washington December 18, 2000.

Entered into force March 1, 2001.

TIAS

ENERGY

Agreement on the coordination of energy–efficient labeling programs for office equipment, with annexes.

Signed at Washington December 19, 2000.

Entered into force June 7, 2001.

TIAS

JUDICIAL ASSISTANCE

Agreement on the processing and transfer of PNR data by air carriers to the United States Department of Homeland Security, Bureau of Customs and Border Protection.

Signed at Washington May 28, 2004.

Entered into force May 28, 2004.

TIAS

LIQUOR

Agreement on the mutual recognition of certain distilled spirits/spirit drinks, with related exchange of letters.

Exchange of letters at Brussels and Washington March 15 and 25, 1994.

Entered into force March 25, 1994.

TIAS

METROLOGY

Implementing arrangement for cooperation in the fields of metrology and measurement standards.

Signed at Brussels October 5, 1999.

Entered into force October 5, 1999.

TIAS

NARCOTIC DRUGS

Agreement on precursors and chemical substances frequently used in the illicit manufacture of narcotic drugs or psychotropic substances, with annexes and exchange of letters.

Signed at The Hague May 28, 1997.

Entered into force July 1, 1997.

TIAS

SCIENTIFIC COOPERATION

Agreement for scientific and technological cooperation, with annex.

Signed at Washington December 5, 1997.

Entered into force October 14, 1998.

TIAS

Amendment

October 8, 2004.

TRADE AND COMMERCE

Joint declaration on commercial relations.

Signed at Geneva March 7, 1962.

Entered into force March 7, 1962.

13 UST 958; TIAS 5033; 445 UNTS 195.

Agreement suspending the agreements of March 7, 1962 (TIAS 5034 and 5035), relating to quality wheat and other grains.

Exchange of notes at Geneva June 30, 1967.

Entered into force January 5, 1968; effective July 1, 1967.

20 UST 2864; TIAS 6761; 723 UNTS 411.

Agreement regulating certain trade in cheese.

Exchange of letters at Brussels December 20, 1974 and January 14, 1975.

Entered into force January 14, 1975.

26 UST 1773; TIAS 8135; 1006 UNTS 85.

Agreement within the context of the multilateral trade negotiations regarding trade in certain agricultural products, and related letter of October 28, 1980.

Done at Geneva April 12, 1979.

Entered into force January 1, 1980.

32 UST 5309; TIAS 9982; 1265 UNTS 249.

Agreement within the context of the multilateral trade negotiations concerning tariff concessions for table grapes, and related letter of October 28, 1980.

Letter signed at Brussels July 27, 1979.

Entered into force January 1, 1980.

32 UST 5322; TIAS 9983; 1265 UNTS 281.

Agreement within the context of the multilateral trade negotiations concerning beer containers and beer, and related letter of October 28, 1980

Signed October 31, 1979.

Entered into force January 1, 1980.

32 UST 5328; TIAS 9984; 1265 UNTS 265.

Agreement relating to certain chemicals in United States schedule XX to the general agreement on tariffs and trade

Signed December 21, 1979.

Entered into force December 21, 1979.

32 UST 5332; TIAS 9985; 1265 UNTS 269.

Agreement relating to staging of a chemical concession in United States schedule XX to the general agreement on tariffs and trade.

Signed at Brussels December 27, 1979.

Entered into force December 27, 1979.

32 UST 5335; TIAS 9986; 1265 UNTS 273.

Agreement relating to modification of United States schedule XX to the general agreement on tariffs and trade, pursuant to article XXVIII

Signed January 2, 1980.

Entered into force January 2, 1980.

32 UST 5337; TIAS 9987; 1265 UNTS 277.

Agreement for the conclusion of negotiations under GATT article XXIV:6, with annexes and related letter.

Signed at Washington and Brussels January 30, 1987.

Entered into force January 30, 1987.

NP

Agreement concerning exports of pasta, with settlement, annex and related letter.

Exchange of letters at Brussels and Washington August 12 and September 15, 1987.

Entered into force September 15, 1987.

TIAS

Agreement on steel trade liberalization, with appendices.

Exchange of letters at Washington and Brussels November 20, 1989.

Entered into force November 20, 1989.

TIAS

Agreement regarding the application of competition laws.

Signed at Washington September 23, 1991.

Entered into force September 23, 1991.

TIAS

Agreement for the conclusion of negotiations between the European Community and the United States under Article XXIV:6, with annexes and exchanges of letters.

Signed at Geneva July 22, 1996.

Entered into force July 22, 1996; effective December 30, 1995.

NP

Agreement on mutual recognition, with annexes.

Signed at London May 18, 1998.

Entered into force December 1, 1998.

TIAS

Agreement on the application of positive comity principles in the enforcement of their competition laws.

Signed at Brussels and Washington June 3 and 4, 1998.

Entered into force June 4, 1998.

TIAS

Agreement on sanitary measures to protect public and animal health in trade in live animals and animal products.

Signed at Brussels July 20, 1999.

Entered into force August 1, 1999.

TIAS

Proces-verbal amending the proces-verbal of July 15, 1997, on rules of origin for certain textile products.

Signed at Geneva August 16, 1999.

Entered into force August 16, 1999.

NP

Agreement on the mutual recognition of certificates of conformity for marine equipment.

Signed at Washington February 27, 2004.

Entered into force July 1, 2004.

TIAS

Agreement relating to the method of calculation of applied duties for husked rice.

Exchange of letters at Brussels and Washington June 27 and 30, 2005.

Entered into force June 30, 2005; effective March 1, 2005.

TIAS

Agreement on matters related to trade in wine.

Exchange of letters at Brussels November 23, 2005.

Entered into force November 23, 2005.

TIAS

Agreement on trade in wine, with annexes.

Signed at London March 10, 2006.

Entered into force March 10, 2006.

TIAS

EUROPEAN ORGANIZATION FOR THE EXPLOITATION OF METEOROLOGICAL SATELLITES (EUMETSAT)

SATELLITES

Agreement on an initial joint polar-orbiting operational satellite system, with annex.

Signed at Washington November 19, 1998.

Entered into force November 19, 1998.

TIAS

Agreement on access to images and meteorological data distribution material from the EUMETSAT geostationary meteorological satellites.

Signed at Darmstadt July 19, 2000.

Entered into force July 19, 2000.

TIAS

Agreement on access to images and meteorological data distribution material from the EUMETSAT geostationary Meteosat Second Generation satellites.

Signed at Darmstadt June 24, 2003.

Entered into force June 24, 2003.

TIAS

Agreement on joint transition activities regarding polar-orbiting operational environmental satellite systems, with annex.

Signed at Darmstadt June 24, 2003.

Entered into force June 24, 2003.

TIAS

EUROPEAN ORGANIZATION FOR NUCLEAR RESEARCH (CERN)

ATOMIC ENERGY

Agreement concerning scientific and technical cooperation on Large Hadron Collider activities.

Signed at Washington December 8, 1997.

Entered into force December 8, 1997.

TIAS

Experiments Protocol relating to the agreement of December 8, 1997, concerning scientific and technical cooperation on Large Hadron Collider activities.

Signed at Geneva December 19, 1997.

Entered into force December 19, 1997.

TIAS

Accelerator Protocol relating to the agreement of December 8, 1997, concerning scientific and technical cooperation on Large Hadron Collider activities.

Signed at Geneva December 19, 1997.

Entered into force December 19, 1997.

TIAS

EUROPEAN POLICE OFFICE

JUDICIAL ASSISTANCE

Agreement to enhance cooperation in preventing, detecting, suppressing, and investigating serious forms of international crime, with annex.

Signed at Brussels December 6, 2001.

Entered into force December 7, 2001.

TIAS

Supplemental agreement on the exchange of personal data and related information, with exchange of letters.

Signed at Copenhagen December 20, 2002.

Entered into force December 21, 2002.

TIAS

EUROPEAN SOUTHERN OBSERVATORY

SPACE

Agreement concerning the joint construction and operation of the Atacama Large Millimeter Array (ALMA), with annexes.

Signed at Arlington February 7 and 25, 2003.

Entered into force February 25, 2003.

TIAS

EUROPEAN SPACE AGENCY

SPACE COOPERATION

Memorandum of understanding concerning European Space Agency participation in the Hubble Space Telescope Program.

Signed October 7, 1977.

Entered into force October 7, 1977.

TIAS

Amendments and extension

April 20 and 23, 2001.

October 19 and 23, 2001.

April 20 and 24, 2006.

Memorandum of understanding for a cooperative program concerning design (Phase B) of a permanently manned space station.

Signed at Paris June 3, 1985.

Entered into force June 3, 1985.

TIAS 11351.

Memorandum of understanding concerning the Solar Terrestrial Science Program, with related exchange of letters.

Signed at Washington November 30, 1989.

Entered into force November 30, 1989.

TIAS 12216.

Memorandum of understanding concerning space shuttle flight activities in the launch and retrieval of the European Retrieval Carrier Spacecraft.

Signed at Paris October 3, 1991.

Entered into force October 3, 1991.

TIAS 12217.

Memorandum of understanding enabling early utilization opportunities of the international space station.

Signed at Washington and Paris March 11 and 18, 1997.

Entered into force March 18, 1997.

TIAS

Agreement for reciprocal tracking support.

Exchange of letters at Washington and Paris June 18 and 20, 2003.

Entered into force June 20, 2003.

TIAS

F

FIJI

On October 10, 1970 Fiji became an independent state. In a note dated October 10, 1970 to the Secretary-General of the United Nations, the Prime Minister of Fiji made a statement reading in part as follows: "[M]any treaty rights and obligations of the Government of the United Kingdom in respect to Fiji were succeeded to by Fiji upon independence by virtue of customary international law.... It is desired that it be presumed that each treaty has been legally succeeded to by Fiji and that action be based on this presumption until a decision is reached that it should be regarded as having lapsed. Should the Government of Fiji be of the opinion that it has legally succeeded to a treaty, and wishes to terminate the operation of the treaty, it will in due course give notice of termination in the terms thereof."

AVIATION

Air transport agreement.

Signed at Suva October 1, 1979.

Entered into force provisionally October 1, 1979; definitively October 11, 1979.

32 UST 3747; TIAS 9917.

Amendment

July 10 and August 19, 1996 (TIAS 12792).

CONSULS

Consular convention between the United States and the United Kingdom.

Signed at Washington June 6, 1951.

Entered into force September 7, 1952.

3 UST 3426; TIAS 2494; 165 UNTS 121.

Agreement continuing in force between the United States and Fiji the consular convention of June 6, 1951 (3 UST 3426) between the United States and the United Kingdom.

Exchange of notes at Suva and Washington October 16 and December 12, 1972.

Entered into force December 12, 1972.

23 UST 3770; TIAS 7525.

DEFENSE

Agreement concerning the provision of training related to defense articles under the United States International Military Education and Training (IMET) Program.

Exchange of notes at Suva November 18, 1985 and February 14, 1986.

Entered into force February 14, 1986.

TIAS 11105.

Acquisition and cross-servicing agreement, with annexes.

Signed at Suva April 14, 1998.

Entered into force April 14, 1998.

TIAS

EMPLOYMENT

Agreement concerning the employment of dependents of official government employees.

Exchange of notes at Suva June 20 and November 25, 2003.

Entered into force November 25, 2003.

TIAS

ENVIRONMENTAL COOPERATION

Agreement for cooperation in the Global Learning and Observations to Benefit the Environment (GLOBE) Program, with appendices.

Signed at Suva January 28, 1997.

Entered into force January 28, 1997.

TIAS 12827.

EXTRADITION

Extradition treaty between the United States and the United Kingdom.

Signed at London December 22, 1931.

Entered into force June 24, 1935.

47 Stat. 2122; TS 849; 12 Bevans 482; 163 LNTS 59.

Agreement continuing in force between the United States and Fiji the extradition treaty of December 22, 1931 (47 Stat. 2122) between the United States and the United Kingdom.

Exchange of notes at Suva and Washington July 14, 1972 and August 17, 1973.

Entered into force August 17, 1973.

24 UST 1965; TIAS 7707.

FINANCE

Agreement relating to investment guaranties.

Exchange of notes at Suva December 30, 1975 and January 9, 1976.

Entered into force January 9, 1976.

27 UST 1826; TIAS 8281.

INTERNATIONAL CRIMINAL COURT

Agreement regarding the surrender of persons to the International Criminal Court.

Signed at Suva December 17, 2003.

Entered into force December 17, 2003.

TIAS

PEACE CORPS

Agreement relating to the establishment of a Peace Corps program in Fiji.

Exchange of notes at Suva June 25, 1968.

Entered into force June 25, 1968.

19 UST 5208; TIAS 6515; 648 UNTS 65.

Agreement continuing in force the agreement of June 25, 1968 relating to the establishment of a Peace Corps program in Fiji.

Exchange of notes at Suva and Washington April 25 and June 27, 1972.

Entered into force June 27, 1972.

23 UST 1156; TIAS 7377.

POSTAL MATTERS

Parcel post agreement, with detailed regulations of execution.

Signed at Washington November 15, 1938, and at Suva January 10, 1939; operative January 2, 1939.

53 Stat. 2031; Post Office Department print; 196 LNTS 185.

Agreement providing for parcel post insurance.

Signed at Suva April 12 and at Washington April 22, 1965.

Entered into force July 1, 1965.

16 UST 850; TIAS 5822; 685 UNTS 23.

Express mail service agreement, with detailed regulations.

Signed at Suva and Arlington August 3 and December 21, 2001.

Entered into force March 1, 2002.

NP

PROPERTY

Convention between the United States and the United Kingdom relating to tenure and disposition of real and personal property.

Signed at Washington March 2, 1899.

Entered into force August 7, 1900; applicable to Fiji February 9, 1901.

31 Stat. 1939; TS 146; 12 Bevans 246.

Supplementary convention relating to the tenure and disposition of real and personal property of March 2, 1899.

Signed at Washington May 27, 1936.

Entered into force March 10, 1941.

55 Stat. 1101; TS 964; 5 Bevans 140; 203 LNTS 367.

Agreement continuing in force between the United States and Fiji the conventions of March 2, 1899 and May 27, 1936 between the United States and the United Kingdom relating to tenure and disposition of real and personal property.

Exchange of notes at Suva and at Washington November 2 and December 9, 1971.

Entered into force December 9, 1971.

22 UST 1806; TIAS 7222.

TAXATION

Agreement for the reciprocal exemption with respect to taxes on income from the international operation of ships and aircraft.

Exchange of notes at Suva June 19 and August 12, 1996.

Entered into force August 12, 1996; effective January 1, 1996.

TIAS

TELECOMMUNICATION

Agreement relating to the reciprocal granting of authorizations to permit licensed amateur radio operators of either country to operate their stations in the other country.

Exchange of notes at London November 26, 1965.

Entered into force November 26, 1965; applicable to Fiji December 11, 1969.

16 UST 2047; TIAS 5941; 561 UNTS 193.

Agreement extending to certain territories the application of the agreement of November 26, 1965 relating to the reciprocal granting of authorizations to permit licensed amateur radio operators of either country to operate their stations in the other country.

Exchange of notes at London December 11, 1969.

Entered into force December 11, 1969.

20 UST 4089; TIAS 6800; 732 UNTS 334.

Agreement continuing in force between the United States and Fiji the agreement of November 25, 1965 between the United States and the United Kingdom relating to the reciprocal granting of authorizations to permit licensed amateur radio operators of either country to operate their stations in the other country.

Exchange of notes at Suva and Washington July 10 and August 14, 1972.

Entered into force August 14, 1972.

23 UST 1334; TIAS 7417.

TRADE AND COMMERCE

Agreement concerning trade in cotton and man-made fiber textiles and textile products, with annexes.

Exchange of notes at Suva May 24 and August 20, 1991.

Entered into force August 20, 1991; effective January 1, 1990.

NP

Agreement concerning trade in textiles and textile products, with annexes.

Exchange of notes at Suva August 27, 1993 and February 18, 1994.

Entered into force February 18, 1994; effective January 1, 1993.

NP

Amendments and extensions

October 11 and November 10, 1994 (NP).

October 26 and December 29, 1995 (NP).

TRADE-MARKS

Declaration affording reciprocal protection to trade-marks.

Signed at London October 24, 1877.

Entered into force October 24, 1877.

20 Stat. 703; TS 138; 12 Bevans 198.

Agreement continuing in force between the United States and Fiji the declaration affording reciprocal protection to trademarks of October 24, 1877 (20 Stat. 703) by the United States and the United Kingdom.

Exchange of notes at Suva and at Washington August 30 and November 4, 1971.

Entered into force November 4, 1971.

22 UST 1891; TIAS 7232.

FINLAND

ATOMIC ENERGY

Agreement for cooperation concerning peaceful uses of nuclear energy, with annexes and agreed minute.

Signed at Washington May 2, 1985.

Entered into force March 27, 1992.

TIAS 12384; 1678 UNTS 127.

Agreement relating to participation in the USNRC Program of severe accident research, with addendum.

Signed at Rockville and Espoo October 29 and November 12, 1998.

Entered into force November 12, 1998.

TIAS

Arrangement for the exchange of technical information and cooperation in nuclear safety matters, with addenda.

Signed at Rockville and Helsinki November 19 and December 31, 2001.

Entered into force December 31, 2001.

TIAS

Agreement relating to participation in the U.S. Nuclear Regulatory Commission program of severe accident research, with addendum and appendices.

Signed at Rockville and Espoo April 12 and June 2, 2004.

Entered into force June 2, 2004; with effect from January 1, 2004.

TIAS

Arrangement for the exchange of technical information and cooperation in nuclear safety matters, with addenda.

Signed at Vienna September 20, 2006.

Entered into force September 20, 2006.

TIAS

AVIATION

Air transport agreement.

Signed at Helsinki March 29, 1949.

Entered into force April 28, 1949.

63 Stat. 2550; TIAS 1945; 7 Bevans 752; 55 UNTS 59.

Amendment

June 9, 1995 (TIAS 12657; 2142 UNTS 23).

Related agreement

May 12, 1980 (32 UST 2368; TIAS 9845).

Agreement relating to the reciprocal acceptance of certificates of airworthiness for imported civil glider aircraft and civil aircraft appliances.

Exchange of notes at Washington March 7, 1974.

Entered into force March 7, 1974.

25 UST 262; TIAS 7795; 944 UNTS 165.

Agreement for promotion of air safety.

Signed at Helsinki November 2, 2000.

Entered into force July 8, 2001.

TIAS; 2160 UNTS 195.

COMMERCE

Treaty of friendship, commerce, and consular rights, and protocol.

Signed at Washington February 13, 1934.

Entered into force August 10, 1934.

49 Stat. 2659; TS 868; 7 Bevans 718; 152 LNTS 45.

Protocol modifying article IV of the treaty of friendship, commerce, and consular rights of February 13, 1934.

Signed at Washington December 4, 1952.

Entered into force September 24, 1953.

4 UST 2047; TIAS 2861; 205 UNTS 149.

Protocol to the treaty of friendship, commerce and consular rights of February 13, 1934, as modified.

Signed at Washington July 1, 1991.

Entered into force December 1, 1992.

TIAS

CONSULS

See COMMERCE

CUSTOMS

Agreement regarding mutual assistance in customs matters.

Signed at Washington January 5, 1988.

Entered into force July 13, 1989.

TIAS 12116; 1557 UNTS 155.

DEFENSE

General security of military information agreement, with exchange of letters.

Exchange of notes at Helsinki October 11, 1991.

Entered into force October 11, 1991.

TIAS 12238; 1676 UNTS 193.

Agreement concerning exchange of research and development information, with appendix.

Signed at Washington and Helsinki September 11 and October 5, 1995.

Entered into force October 5, 1995.

TIAS 12289.

Acquisition and cross-servicing agreement, with annex.

Signed at Helsinki and Stuttgart June 25 and July 25, 1998.

Entered into force July 25, 1998.

TIAS

Memorandum of agreement regarding foreign liaison officers.

Signed at Helsinki and Norfolk February 8 and 13, 2004.

Entered into force February 13, 2004.

NP

Memorandum of understanding concerning air force exercises and activities in Finland

Signed March 31 and April 21, 2005.

Entered into force April 21, 2005.

TIAS

Memorandum of agreement regarding reciprocal exchange of military personnel, with annexes.

Signed at Helsinki July 13, 2005.

Entered into force July 13, 2005.

TIAS

Master information exchange agreement annex concerning defense environmental cooperation.

Signed at Washington October 5, 2005.

Entered into force October 5, 2005.

TIAS

EDUCATION

Agreement for financing certain educational exchange programs.

Signed at Helsinki July 2, 1952.

Entered into force July 2, 1952.

3 UST 4126; TIAS 2555; 165 UNTS 203.

Amendments

November 30, 1956 (7 UST 3255; TIAS 3704; 263 UNTS 418).

May 30, 1959 (10 UST 1043; TIAS 4241; 346 UNTS 334).

November 14, 1960 (11 UST 2351; TIAS 4614; 400 UNTS 382).

October 29, 1975 (26 UST 2898; TIAS 8196).

EMPLOYMENT

Agreement relating to the employment of dependents of official government employees.

Exchange of notes at Helsinki March 1 and 12, 1996.

Entered into force April 11, 1996.

TIAS 12734; 1927 UNTS 77.

ENVIRONMENTAL COOPERATION

Agreement for cooperation in the Global Learning and Observations to Benefit the Environment (GLOBE) Program, with appendices.

Signed at Helsinki March 23, 1995.

Entered into force March 23, 1995.

TIAS 12621.

EXTRADITION

Extradition treaty.

Signed at Helsinki June 11, 1976.

Entered into force May 11, 1980.

31 UST 944; TIAS 9626; 1203 UNTS 165.

FINANCE

Debt funding agreement.

Signed at Washington May 1, 1923; operative December 15, 1922.

Treasury Department print; 7 Bevans 689.

Agreement modifying the debt funding agreement of May 1, 1923.

Signed at Washington May 23, 1932; operative July 1, 1931.

Treasury Department print; 7 Bevans 716.

Agreement relating to investment guaranties under section 413(b)(4) of the Mutual Security Act of 1954, as amended.

Exchange of notes at Helsinki July 22, 1959.

Entered into force July 22, 1959.

10 UST 1317; TIAS 4275; 354 UNTS 39.

MAPPING

Basic exchange and cooperative agreement concerning geospatial information and services cooperation.

Signed at Helsinki August 30, 2000.

Entered into force August 30, 2000.

NP

NATIONALITY

Convention regulating military obligations of persons having dual nationality.

Signed at Helsinki January 27, 1939.

Entered into force October 3, 1939.

54 Stat. 1712; TS 953; 7 Bevans 747; 201 LNTS 197.

PACIFIC SETTLEMENT OF DISPUTES

Treaty of arbitration.

Signed at Washington June 7, 1928.

Entered into force January 14, 1929.

45 Stat. 2724; TS 768; 7 Bevans 711; 87 LNTS 9.

Treaty of conciliation.

Signed at Washington June 7, 1928.

Entered into force January 14, 1929.

45 Stat. 2726; TS 769; 7 Bevans 713; 87 LNTS 15.

POSTAL MATTERS

Parcel post convention.

Signed at Helsingfors September 1 and at Washington September 23, 1932; operative August 1, 1932.

47 Stat. 2169; Post Office Department print.

International express mail agreement, with detailed regulations.

Signed at Washington November 19, 1984.

Entered into force February 7, 1985.

TIAS 11010; 2022 UNTS 9.

Memorandum of understanding concerning the operation of the INTELPOST field trial, with details of implementation.

Signed at Helsinki and Washington August 23 and September 23, 1985.

Entered into force September 23, 1985.

TIAS 11158.

PUBLICATIONS

Agreement relating to the exchange of official publications.

Exchange of notes at Washington December 28 and 30, 1938.

Entered into force December 30, 1938; operative January 1, 1939.

53 Stat. 2071; EAS 139; 7 Bevans 744; 195 LNTS 419.

SCIENTIFIC COOPERATION

Memorandum of understanding concerning scientific and technical cooperation in the earth sciences.

Signed at Reston and Espoo March 30 and May 3, 2000.

Entered into force May 3, 2000.

TIAS

SHIPPING

Agreement relating to jurisdiction over vessels utilizing the Louisiana Offshore Oil Port.

Exchange of notes at Washington December 1, 1982.

Entered into force December 1, 1982.

TIAS 10615; 2000 UNTS 451.

SOCIAL SECURITY

Agreement on social security, with administrative arrangement.

Signed at Helsinki June 3, 1991.

Entered into force November 1, 1992.

TIAS 12105; 1705 UNTS 153.

TAXATION

Convention for the avoidance of double taxation and the prevention of fiscal evasion with respect to taxes on estates and inheritances.

Signed at Washington March 3, 1952.

Entered into force December 18, 1952.

3 UST 4464; TIAS 2595; 177 UNTS 141.

Agreement for relief from double taxation on earnings from operation of ships and aircraft.

Exchange of notes at Helsinki April 8 and 22, 1988.

Entered into force April 22, 1988.

TIAS 11576.

Convention for the avoidance of double taxation and the prevention of fiscal evasion with respect to taxes on income and on capital.[1]

Signed at Helsinki September 21, 1989.

Entered into force December 30, 1990.

TIAS 12101.

NOTE

1 With an understanding.

TELECOMMUNICATION

Agreement relating to the reciprocal granting of authorizations to permit licensed amateur radio operators of either country to operate their stations in the other country.

Exchange of notes at Helsinki December 15 and 27, 1967.

Entered into force December 27, 1967.

18 UST 3153; TIAS 6406; 697 UNTS 55.

TRADE

See also COMMERCE

Letter and arrangement within the context of the multilateral trade negotiations concerning cheeses, and related letter of January 30, 1980.

Done at Geneva April 12, 1979.

Entered into force January 1, 1980.

32 UST 5340; TIAS 9988; 1267 UNTS 3.

Agreement relating to article XII of the general agreement on tariffs and trade, and related letter of January 30, 1980. Letter signed at Geneva April 12, 1979.

Entered into force March 13, 1980.

32 UST 5348; TIAS 9989; 1267 UNTS 19.

Agreement within the context of the multilateral trade negotiations regarding alcoholic beverages, and related letter of January 30, 1980. Letters signed at Geneva and Washington April 12 and December 4, 1979.

Entered into force March 13, 1980.

32 UST 5351; TIAS 9990; 1267 UNTS 13.

Agreement on removal of trade distorting practices in steel, with appendix and related exchange of letters.

Exchange of letters at Washington and Helsinki February 28 and March 23, 1990.

Entered into force March 23, 1990.

TIAS; 1591 UNTS 427.

TRANSPORTATION

Memorandum of understanding concerning cooperation in the field of transportation.

Signed at Washington July 23, 1981.

Entered into force July 23, 1981.

33 UST 3258; TIAS 10222.

Project agreement for cooperation in the field of icebreaking technology.

Signed at Washington July 23, 1981.

Entered into force July 23, 1981.

33 UST 3261; TIAS 10223.

Extension

May 9 and June 13, 1983 (35 UST 1320; TIAS 10731; 1607 UNTS 540).

Memorandum of understanding on highway transportation technology exchange.

Signed at Madrid May 19, 1993.

Entered into force May 19, 1993.

TIAS 12498.

VISAS

Agreement relating to the maximum validity of visas for four years and the abolition of visa fees for certain classes of nonimmigrant visas.

Exchange of notes at Helsinki July 7, August 26 and December 14, 1955.

Entered into force December 14, 1955; operative January 1, 1956.

9 UST 1175; TIAS 4102; 335 UNTS 263.

Amendment

February 15 and 20, 1956 (9 UST 1179; TIAS 4102; 335 UNTS 272).

Agreement relating to the waiver of visa requirements for nonimmigrants.

Exchange of notes at Washington August 15, 1958.

Entered into force August 15, 1958, operative September 15, 1958.

9 UST 1183; TIAS 4103; 314 UNTS 43.

FOOD AND AGRICULTURE ORGANIZATION

ECONOMIC AND TECHNICAL COOPERATION

Agreement relating to a Fund-in-Trust grant to the FAO to supplement activities under the Off-Shore Fishery Development Project for Viet-Nam.

Exchange of notes at Washington and Rome May 26, 1967.

Entered into force May 26, 1967.

18 UST 1618; TIAS 6304.

PEACE CORPS

Agreement concerning the Peace Corps.

Exchange of notes at Rome March 23 and 29, 1962.

Entered into force March 29, 1962.

13 UST 1391; TIAS 5101; 454 UNTS 13.

FRANCE

ATOMIC ENERGY

Agreement for cooperation on uses of atomic energy for mutual defense purposes.

Signed at Washington May 7, 1959.

Entered into force July 20, 1959.

10 UST 1279; TIAS 4268; 354 UNTS 83.

Agreement for cooperation in the operation of atomic weapons systems for mutual defense purposes.

Signed at Paris July 27, 1961.

Entered into force October 9, 1961.

12 UST 1423; TIAS 4867; 433 UNTS 29.

Amendment

July 22, 1985 (TIAS 11208; 2145 UNTS 20).

Agreement concerning the retransfer of nuclear power light water reactor technology, with annexes and exchange of notes.

Signed at Washington January 22, 1981.

Entered into force March 13, 1981.

33 UST 968; TIAS 10080.

Agreement regarding participation in the USNRC international piping integrity research group, with appendices.

Signed at Fontenay-aux-Roses and Bethesda February 20 and March 5, 1987.

Entered into force March 5, 1987.

TIAS 12220.

Agreement concerning cooperation on the application of non-proliferation assurances to material, nuclear material, equipment and facilities transferred from France to Taiwan for use in Taiwan's nuclear research and light water nuclear power reactor programs, with annex and related exchanges of notes.

Exchange of notes at Washington January 19, 1993.

Entered into force January 19, 1993.

TIAS

Agreement for cooperation in the advanced nuclear reactor science and technology, with annex.

Signed at Vienna September 18, 2000.

Entered into force September 18, 2000.

TIAS

Amendment:

January 24, 2006.

Arrangement for the exchange of technical information and cooperation in the regulation of nuclear safety, with annex.

Signed at Rockville April 17, 2003.

Entered into force April 17, 2003.

TIAS

Agreement extending the agreement of August 9, 1994, for cooperation in research, development and application of high energy lasers and high energy laser-matter interaction physics.

Signed at Washington and Paris April 24 and May 5, 2006.

Entered into force May 5, 2006; effective August 10, 2004.

TIAS

Agreement regarding the technical exchange and cooperation arrangement in the field of nuclear safety research.

Signed at Rockville July 26 and August 4, 2006.

Entered into force August 4, 2006.

TIAS

Implementing agreement regarding the IRSN-USNRC PHEBUS source term separate effects test program, with appendices.

Signed at Rockville and Paris August 24 and 31, 2006.

Entered into force August 31, 2006.

TIAS

AVIATION

Agreement relating to air service facilities in French territory.

Exchange of notes at Paris June 18, 1946.

Entered into force June 18, 1946.

61 Stat. 4088; TIAS 1852; 7 Bevans 1172; 42 UNTS 183.

Amendment

May 8 and 17, 1947 (61 Stat. 4095; TIAS 1853; 7 Bevans 1208; 42 UNTS 194).

Agreement relating to the reciprocal acceptance of airworthiness certifications.

Exchange of notes at Paris August 29 and September 26, 1973.

Entered into force September 26, 1973.

24 UST 2142; TIAS 7728.

Agreement relating to cooperation with respect to research and development activities in the field of civil aviation.

Signed at Washington and Paris July 10, 1980.

Entered into force July 10, 1980.

32 UST 2873; TIAS 9881; 1274 UNTS 201.

Agreement for promotion of aviation safety.

Signed at Paris May 14, 1996.

Entered into force May 14, 1996.

TIAS 12754.

Air transport agreement, with annexes.

Signed at Washington June 18, 1998.

Entered into force June 18, 1998.

TIAS

Amendments

October 10, 2000 (2155 UNTS 233).

January 22, 2002.

CLAIMS

See also LEND-LEASE

Agreement relating to the procedure for the settlement of claims of French nationals who were prisoners of war of United States forces during World War II.

Exchange of notes at Paris June 4, October 15 and December 6, 1951; and January 17 and February 2, 1952.

Entered into force February 2, 1952.

5 UST 622; TIAS 2951; 247 UNTS 223.

Agreement concerning payments for certain losses suffered during World War II, with annexes.

Signed at Washington January 18, 2001.

Entered into force February 5, 2001.

TIAS; 2156 UNTS 281.

Amendments

May 30 and 31, 2002.

February 21, 2006.

COMMERCE

Convention of navigation and commerce, with separate article.[1]

Signed at Washington June 24, 1822.

Entered into force February 12, 1823; operative October 1, 1822.

8 Stat. 278; TS 87; 7 Bevans 822.

Agreement modifying the provisions of article VII of the convention of navigation and commerce of June 24, 1822.

Signed at Washington July 17, 1919.

Entered into force January 10, 1921.

41 Stat. 1723; TS 650; 7 Bevans 899.

Convention of establishment, protocol, and declaration.[2]

Signed at Paris November 25, 1959.

Entered into force December 21, 1960.

11 UST 2398; TIAS 4625; 401 UNTS 75.

NOTES

1 Article VI terminated by the United States July 1, 1916 in accordance with the Seamen's Act (38 Stat. 1164).

2 Applicable to Martinique, Guadeloupe, French Guiana and Reunion.

CONSULS

Consular convention, with protocol and exchange of notes.

Signed at Paris July 18, 1966.

Entered into force January 7, 1968.

18 UST 2939; TIAS 6389; 700 UNTS 257.

CUSTOMS

Agreement for cooperation with respect to the operation of distribution license systems.

Exchange of notes at Paris September 5, 1986.

Entered into force September 5, 1986.

TIAS 12389.

Convention regarding mutual administration assistance in customs matters.

Signed at Paris December 3, 1993.

Entered into force July 1, 1994.

TIAS; 2084 UNTS 13.

DEFENSE

See also MUTUAL SECURITY

Mutual defense assistance agreement.

Signed at Washington January 27, 1950.

Entered into force January 27, 1950.

1 UST 34; TIAS 2012; 80 UNTS 171.

Agreement regarding the establishment of an air depot at Deols-La Martinerie.

Signed at Paris February 27, 1951.

Entered into force February 27, 1951.

17 UST 1865; TIAS 6130; 674 UNTS 55.

Agreement regarding certain air bases and facilities in Metropolitan France placed at the disposition of the United States Air Force.

Signed at Paris October 4, 1952.

Entered into force October 4, 1952.

17 UST 1873; TIAS 6131; 674 UNTS 65.

Agreement relating to the transfer to Paris of the headquarters of the Deputy Commander of the Allied Forces in Europe.

Exchange of notes at Paris June 17, 1953.

Entered into force June 17, 1953.

17 UST 1906; TIAS 6134; 674 UNTS 83.

Agreement relating to the disposition of equipment and material no longer required in the furtherance of the mutual defense assistance program, and related notes.

Exchange of notes at Paris September 23, 1955.

Entered into force September 23, 1955.

6 UST 5971; TIAS 3440; 270 UNTS 341.

Memorandum of understanding relating to sales to France of military equipment, materials, and services under the mutual defense assistance agreement of January 27, 1950, and exchange of letters.

Signed at Washington January 30, 1958.

Entered into force January 30, 1958.

9 UST 71; TIAS 3980; 304 UNTS 349.

Agreement for the transfer of special tools to France under the mutual defense assistance agreement of January 27, 1950.

Exchange of notes at Paris October 28, 1958.

Entered into force October 28, 1958.

9 UST 1450; TIAS 4140; 337 UNTS 397.

Agreement concerning system of communications and depots.

Signed at Paris December 8, 1958.

Entered into force December 8, 1958.

17 UST 1890; TIAS 6132; 674 UNTS 99.

Agreement relating to a weapons production program.

Exchange of notes at Paris September 19, 1960.

Entered into force September 19, 1960.

11 UST 2333; TIAS 4611; 400 UNTS 21.

Memorandum of understanding relating to military procurement, with an exchange of letters.

Signed at Washington December 20, 1961.

Entered into force December 20, 1961.

12 UST 3132; TIAS 4914; 433 UNTS 340.

Agreement regarding the operation, maintenance and security of the Donges-Metz pipeline system, with protocol and exchange of letters.

Signed at Paris March 24, 1967.

Entered into force April 1, 1967.

18 UST 352; TIAS 6242; 688 UNTS 357.

Memorandum of understanding relating to a cooperative research project in titanium alloys, with annex.

Signed at Washington and Paris June 23 and August 26, 1977.

Entered into force August 26, 1977.

TIAS 12290.

General security of information agreement.

Signed at Paris September 7, 1977.

Entered into force September 7, 1977.

29 UST 1985; TIAS 8914.

Memorandum of agreement concerning the use of Diane Range, Solenzara, Corsica.

Signed at Paris March 27, 1986.

Entered into force March 27, 1986.

TIAS 11402; 2190 UNTS 279.

Agreement on mutual logistic support, with annexes.

Signed at Casteau February 23, 1987.

Entered into force February 23, 1987.

TIAS 12293.

Amendments

October 15, 1987 (TIAS 12293).

August 19 and September 11, 1991 (TIAS 12293).

Memorandum of understanding for a cooperative deep submergence rescue system program, with annexes.

Signed at Washington and Paris January 27 and February 21, 1989.

Entered into force February 21, 1989.

TIAS 12291.

Memorandum of agreement concerning a cooperative program of information exchange and development of cooperative research projects on free electron laser technology.

Signed at Paris January 31, 1990.

Entered into force January 31, 1990.

TIAS 12292.

Agreement concerning air defense simulation.

Signed at Washington and Paris January 13 and July 19, 1993.

Entered into force July 19, 1993.

TIAS 12294.

Agreement concerning technology research and development projects, with annex.

Signed at Paris and Washington December 9, 1993 and January 10, 1994.

Entered into force January 10, 1994.

TIAS 12295.

Agreement regarding the exchange of scientists and engineers, with annexes.

Signed at Washington and Paris January 14 and 28, 1994.

Entered into force January 28, 1994.

NP

Agreement regarding the continuous processing of composite propellants, with annexes.

Signed at Paris and Washington April 5 and May 16, 1994.

Entered into force May 16, 1994.

TIAS 12316.

Agreement for cooperative research in the field of helicopter aeromechanics, with annex.

Signed at Paris October 27, 1994.

Entered into force October 27, 1994.

TIAS 12528.

Amendment and extension

October 20 and 27, 2003.

Agreement concerning cooperation on the image/information reformatter for reconnaissance system interoperability, with annex.

Signed at Paris and Washington January 18 and 30, 1995.

Entered into force January 30, 1995.

TIAS 12318.

Agreement for the adaptation and testing of a dry/low emissions upgrade for the intercooled recuperated (ICR) gas turbine engine, with annexes.

Signed at Washington and Paris June 13 and August 30, 1995.

Entered into force August 30, 1995.

TIAS 12687.

Amendment

July 11 and September 22, 2000.

Agreement concerning the application of Article VIII of the agreement between the parties to the North Atlantic Treaty regarding the status of their forces of June 19, 1951.

Exchange of notes at Paris April 15 and May 2, 2002.

Entered into force May 2, 2002.

TIAS; 2212 UNTS 383.

Agreement for Test and Evaluation Program (TEP) Cooperation, with annexes.

Signed at Paris January 22 and 23, 2003.

Entered into force January 23, 2003.

TIAS

Agreement concerning spartan scout advanced concept technology demonstration, with annexes.

Signed at Washington and Paris January 23 and 29, 2004.

Entered into force January 29, 2004.

TIAS

Agreement concerning common operational picture interoperability for coalition warfare, with annexes.

Signed at Washington and Paris June 15 and July 22, 2004.

Entered into force July 22, 2004.

TIAS

Technical arrangement regarding the exchange of military personnel, with annexes.

Signed at Washington July 22, 2004.

Entered into force July 22, 2004.

TIAS

Agreement concerning the exchange and reimbursement of marine aviation and propulsion fuels, with annexes.

Signed at Paris and Ft. Belvoir March 6 and May 2, 2006.

Entered into force May 2, 2006.

TIAS

Agreement concerning geospatial-intelligence exchange and cooperation, with annexes and appendices.

Signed at Bethesda December 18 and 19, 2006.

Entered into force December 19, 2006.

TIAS

ECONOMIC AND TECHNICAL COOPERATION

See also INDUSTRIAL COOPERATION

Economic cooperation agreement.[1]

Signed at Paris June 28, 1948.

Entered into force July 10, 1948.

62 Stat. 2223; TIAS 1783; 7 Bevans 1257; 19 UNTS 9.

Amendments

September 21 and October 8, 1948 (62 Stat. 3720; TIAS 1897; 7 Bevans 1278; 34 UNTS 418).

November 17 and 20, 1948 (62 Stat. 3720; TIAS 1897; 7 Bevans 1288; 34 UNTS 421).

January 9, 1950 (1 UST 151; TIAS 2023; 79 UNTS 270).

May 22, 1951 (2 UST 1173; TIAS 2264; 141 UNTS 358).

September 25 and 27, 1951 (2 UST 2376; TIAS 2359; 174 UNTS 284).

September 11, 1953 (4 UST 2036; TIAS 2859; 214 UNTS 350).

NOTE

1 Applicable to Reunion, New Caledonia, Tuamotu Archipelago, including Society Islands, Austral Islands, Marquesas Archipelago, St. Pierre and Miquelon, Martinique, Guadeloupe, French Guiana.

EDUCATION

Agreement relating to certain academic and cultural exchanges and programs in the field of education.

Signed at Paris May 7, 1965.

Entered into force May 28, 1965.

16 UST 1659; TIAS 5889; 573 UNTS 183.

EXTRADITION

Extradition treaty, with agreed minute.

Signed at Paris April 23, 1996.

Entered into force February 1, 2002.

TIAS; 2179 UNTS 341.

FINANCE

Debt funding agreement.

Signed at Washington April 29, 1926; operative June 15, 1925.

100 LNTS 27; Treasury Department print; 7 Bevans 949.

Agreement modifying the debt funding agreement of April 29, 1926.

Signed at Washington June 10, 1932; operative July 1, 1931.

Treasury Department print; 7 Bevans 987.

Agreement relating to the allocation of the proceeds of German assets to be received from Sweden as a result of Swedish-Allied negotiations of July 18, 1946.

Exchange of notes at Washington July 18, 1946.

Entered into force July 18, 1946.

61 Stat. 3840; TIAS 1731; 7 Bevans 1176; 125 UNTS 165.

Agreement relating to guaranties authorized by Section 111(b)(3) of the Economic Cooperation Act of 1948, as amended.

Exchange of notes at Washington July 9 and 22, 1952.

Entered into force July 24, 1952.

3 UST 5048; TIAS 2687; 181 UNTS 319.

FISHERIES

Agreement on matters relating to fishing in the economic zones of the French overseas territories of New Caledonia and Wallis and Futuna Islands.

Signed at Washington March 1, 1991.

Entered into force November 1, 1991.

TIAS 11781; 2202 UNTS 277.

INDUSTRIAL PROPERTY

Agreement relating to industrial property rights affected by World War II.

Signed at Washington April 4, 1947.

Entered into force November 10, 1947.

61 Stat. 3316; TIAS 1667; 7 Bevans 1202; 24 UNTS 133.

Amendment

October 28, 1947 (62 Stat. 1876; TIAS 1725; 7 Bevans 1222; 77 UNTS 348).

JUDICIAL ASSISTANCE

Treaty on mutual legal assistance in criminal matters.

Signed at Paris December 10, 1998.

Entered into force December 1, 2001.

TIAS; 2172 UNTS 69.

LEND-LEASE

Agreement relating to principles applying to mutual aid in the prosecution of the war against aggression.

Signed at Washington February 28, 1945.

Entered into force February 28, 1945.

59 Stat. 1304; EAS 455; 7 Bevans 1075; 76 UNTS 193.

Agreement relating to supplies and services.

Signed at Washington February 28, 1945.

Entered into force February 28, 1945.

59 Stat. 1307; EAS 455; 7 Bevans 1081; 76 UNTS 223.

Agreement, with accompanying memorandum and exchanges of letters, relating to principles applying to the provision of aid to the armed forces of the United States.

Exchange of notes at Washington February 28, 1945.

Entered into force February 28, 1945; operative June 6, 1944.

59 Stat. 1313; EAS 455; 7 Bevans 1078; 76 UNTS 213.

Understanding relating to article VII of the lend-lease agreement signed February 28, 1945.

Exchange of notes at Washington November 8, 1945.

Entered into force November 8, 1945.

7 Bevans 1098; 76 UNTS 151.

LEND-LEASE SETTLEMENT

Memorandum of understanding regarding settlement for lend-lease, reciprocal aid, surplus war property, and claims, with related documents.

Signed at Washington May 28, 1946.

Entered into force May 28, 1946.

61 Stat. 4175; TIAS 1928; 7 Bevans 1126; 84 UNTS 59.

Agreement relating to the transfer of surplus United States property and installations in France and certain French overseas territories, with related documents.

Signed at Washington May 28, 1946.

Entered into force May 28, 1946.

61 Stat. 4179; TIAS 1928; 7 Bevans 1130; 84 UNTS 80.

Memorandum of agreement regarding expenditures of the United States armed forces in France and French overseas territories, with related documents.

Signed at Washington May 28, 1946.

Entered into force May 28, 1946.

61 Stat. 4206; TIAS 1928; 7 Bevans 1155; 84 UNTS 141.

Agreement relating to expenditures of the United States armed forces in France and French overseas territories, implementing the agreement of May 28, 1946.

Exchange of notes at Washington February 27, 1948.

Entered into force February 27, 1948.

62 Stat. 3826; TIAS 1930; 7 Bevans 1245; 84 UNTS 207.

Agreement respecting maritime claims and litigation.

Signed at Washington March 14, 1949.

Entered into force March 14, 1949.

63 Stat. 2499; TIAS 1935; 7 Bevans 1300; 84 UNTS 225.

Agreement regarding settlement of certain residual financial claims and accounts.

Signed at Washington March 14, 1949.

Entered into force March 14, 1949.

63 Stat. 2507; TIAS 1936; 7 Bevans 1304; 84 UNTS 237.

Agreement on postponement of installations pursuant to paragraph 3 of the lend-lease agreement of May 28, 1946, and paragraph 2 of the surplus property agreement of December 6, 1947.

Signed at Washington January 30, 1958.

Entered into force January 30, 1958.

9 UST 67; TIAS 3979; 304 UNTS 9.

LIQUOR

Agreement providing for the recognition and protection by France of the appellation of origin of bourbon whiskey and continued protection by the United States of appellations of origin of the French brandies, cognac, armagnac and calvados.

Exchange of notes at Paris December 2, 1970 and January 18, 1971.

Entered into force March 20, 1971.

22 UST 36; TIAS 7041; 777 UNTS 77.

MAPPING

Agreement for the mapping of certain French territories in the Pacific.

Exchange of notes at Paris November 27, 1948.

Entered into force November 27, 1948.

3 UST 491; TIAS 2407; 168 UNTS 119.

Agreement concerning mapping, charting and geodesy cooperation, with annex.

Signed at Paris January 20, 1993.

Entered into force January 20, 1993.

NP

MARITIME MATTERS

Agreement concerning the wreck of the CSS *Alabama*.

Signed at Paris October 3, 1989.

Entered into force October 3, 1989.

TIAS 11687.

Agreement regarding the wreck of La Belle.

Signed at Washington March 31, 2003.

Entered into force March 31, 2003.

TIAS

MILITARY CEMETERIES AND MONUMENTS

Agreement concerning the interment in France and in territories of the French Union, or removal to the United States, of the bodies of American soldiers killed in the war of 1939-1945.

Signed at Paris October 1, 1947.

Entered into force October 1, 1947.

61 Stat. 3767; TIAS 1720; 7 Bevans 1215; 148 UNTS 303.

Agreement regarding the transport, burial, and embalming of bodies of members of United States forces dying in France.

Signed at Paris July 1, 1955.

Entered into force July 1, 1955.

6 UST 3787; TIAS 3380; 270 UNTS 19.

Agreement relating to the grant of plots of land located in France for the creation of permanent military cemeteries or the construction of war memorials, with annexes.

Signed at Paris March 19, 1956.

Entered into force March 19, 1956.

7 UST 561; TIAS 3537; 275 UNTS 37.

MUTUAL SECURITY

Agreement relating to the assurances required by the Mutual Security Act of 1951.

Exchange of notes at Paris January 5, 1952.

Entered into force January 5, 1952.

3 UST 4559; TIAS 2606; 181 UNTS 177.

NARCOTIC DRUGS

Arrangement for the direct exchange of certain information regarding the traffic in narcotic drugs.

Exchange of notes at Paris December 27, 1927, and January 30, 1928.

Entered into force January 30, 1928.

7 Bevans 966.

Agreement for the co-ordination of preventive and repressive action against the illicit narcotic and dangerous drug traffic.

Signed at Paris February 26, 1971.

Entered into force February 26, 1971.

28 UST 8045; TIAS 8739.

Extension and amendment

September 11, 1974 (28 UST 8056; TIAS 8739).

January 28, 1981 (TIAS 10538).

NATIONALITY

Agreement relating to the fulfillment of military obligations during the wars of 1914-1918 and 1939-1945 by persons with dual nationality.

Exchange of notes at Paris December 22, 1948.

Entered into force December 22, 1948.

62 Stat. 3621; TIAS 1876; 7 Bevans 1294; 67 UNTS 38.

Extension

November 18 and December 31, 1952 (3 UST 5345; TIAS 2741; 185 UNTS 396).

NAVIGATION

Memorandum of understanding concerning the operation and maintenance of OMEGA station Le Reunion, with appendices.

Signed at Washington June 24, 1981.

Entered into force June 24, 1981.

33 UST 2109; TIAS 10176; 1530 UNTS 13.

OCEANOGRAPHY

Memorandum of understanding on the participation of France in the ocean drilling program, with annex.

Signed at Paris October 23, 1984.

Entered into force October 23, 1984.

TIAS 11219.

Memorandum of understanding on the participation of France in the ocean drilling program as a regular member, with annexes.

Signed at Washington and Paris July 22 and August 2, 1993.

Entered into force August 2, 1993; effective October 1, 1993.

TIAS

PACIFIC SETTLEMENT OF DISPUTES

Treaty to facilitate the settlement of disputes.

Signed at Washington September 15, 1914.

Entered into force January 22, 1915.

38 Stat. 1887; TS 609; 7 Bevans 883.

Treaty of arbitration and exchange of notes dated March 1 and 5, 1928.

Signed at Washington February 6, 1928.

Entered into force April 22, 1929.

46 Stat. 2269; TS 785; 7 Bevans 968; 91 LNTS 323.

PATENTS

Agreement to facilitate interchange of patent rights and technical information for defense purposes.

Signed at Paris March 12, 1957.

Entered into force March 12, 1957.

8 UST 353; TIAS 3782; 279 UNTS 275.

Agreement approving the procedures for reciprocal filing of classified patent application in the United States and France.

Exchange of notes at Paris May 28 and July 10, 1959.

Entered into force July 10, 1959.

10 UST 2151; TIAS 4386; 367 UNTS 336.

POSTAL MATTERS

Convention relative to the exchange of parcel post.

Signed at Paris December 7 and at Washington December 30, 1935; operative August 1, 1935.

49 Stat. 3322; Post Office Department print; 171 LNTS 117.

International express mail agreement, with detailed regulations.

Signed at Washington and Paris March 17 and April 13, 1981.

Entered into force May 18, 1981.

33 UST 1305; TIAS 10113; 1285 UNTS 75.

PRISONER TRANSFER

Convention on the transfer of sentenced persons.

Signed at Washington January 25, 1983.

Entered into force February 1, 1985.

35 UST 2847; TIAS 10823.

PUBLICATIONS

Agreement relating to exchange of official publications.

Exchange of notes at Paris August 14, 1945.

Entered into force January 1, 1946.

60 Stat. 1944; TIAS 1579; 7 Bevans 1095; 73 UNTS 237.

RELIEF SUPPLIES AND PACKAGES

Agreement for free entry and free inland transportation of relief supplies and packages.

Signed at Paris December 23, 1948.

Entered into force Decmeber 23, 1948.

62 Stat. 3587; TIAS 1873; 7 Bevans 1296; 67 UNTS 171.

Amendments

January 31, 1950 (1 UST 224; TIAS 2043; 67 UNTS 171).

August 3, 1950 (1 UST 597; TIAS 2107; 93 UNTS 367).

July 2 and August 5, 1952 (3 UST 5039; TIAS 2684; 181 UNTS 345).

SATELLITES

Agreement on cooperation in intercontinental testing in connection with experimental communications satellites.

Exchange of notes at Paris March 31, 1961.

Entered into force March 31, 1961.

12 UST 483; TIAS 4738; 409 UNTS 135.

Agreement concerning development of satellite and balloon techniques and instrumentation for the study of meteorological phenomena (Project EOLE).

Exchange of notes at Washington June 16 and 17, 1966.

Entered into force June 17, 1966.

17 UST 1123; TIAS 6069; 601 UNTS 113.

Memorandum of understanding for joint development of the TOPEX/POSEIDON (oceanographic satellite) project.

Signed at Washington March 23, 1987.

Entered into force March 23, 1987.

TIAS 12207.

SCIENTIFIC COOPERATION

Memorandum of understanding concerning the furnishing of balloon launching and associated services.

Signed at Washington and Paris August 26 and November 11, 1983.

Entered into force November 11, 1983.

35 UST 2410; TIAS 10803.

Agreement incorporating an intellectual property annex into cooperative agreements between scientific and technical agencies of the United States and France.

Exchange of notes at Paris July 27, 1994 and June 6, 1997.

Entered into force June 6, 1997.

TIAS

SHIPPING

Agreement relating to jurisdiction over vessels utilizing the Louisiana Offshore Oil Port, with annex.

Exchange of notes at Washington March 24 and April 6, 1983.

Entered into force April 6, 1983.

TIAS 10682.

SMUGGLING

Convention for prevention of smuggling of intoxicating liquors.

Signed at Washington June 30, 1924.

Entered into force March 12, 1927.

45 Stat. 2403; TS 755; 7 Bevans 938; 61 LNTS 415.

SOCIAL SECURITY

Agreement on social security.

Signed at Paris March 2, 1987.

Entered into force July 1, 1988.

TIAS 12106.

Administrative arrangement concerning the application of the agreement on social security of March 2, 1987.

Signed at Washington October 21, 1987.

Entered into force July 1, 1988.

TIAS 12106.

SPACE COOPERATION

Memorandum of understanding for cooperation in the Jason program.

Signed at Washington and Paris December 14 and 20, 1996.

Entered into force December 20, 1996.

TIAS 12823.

Memorandum of understanding for cooperation in the CALIPSO Mission.

Signed at Paris June 18, 2003.

Entered into force June 18, 2003.

TIAS

Agreement concerning the use of Istres Le Tube 125 Air Base as a transoceanic abort landing site.

Signed at Washington June 7, 2005.

Entered into force June 7, 2005.

TIAS

TAXATION

Agreement relating to relief from taxation of United States Government expenditures in France in the interests of common defense.

Exchange of notes at Paris June 13, 1952.

Entered into force June 13, 1952.

3 UST 4828; TIAS 2655; 181 UNTS 3.

Amendment

November 27, 1956 (7 UST 3405; TIAS 3712; 265 UNTS 356).

Agreement relating to the payment by the United States of taxes on electricity provided the surplus commodity housing units in France.

Exchange of notes at Paris August 1, 1963.

Entered into force August 1, 1963.

15 UST 727; TIAS 5595; 527 UNTS 89.

Convention for the avoidance of double taxation and the prevention of fiscal evasion with respect to taxes on estates, inheritances and gifts.

Signed at Washington November 24, 1978.

Entered into force October 1, 1980.

32 UST 1935; TIAS 9812; 1234 UNTS 187.

Convention for the avoidance of double taxation and the prevention of fiscal evasion with respect to taxes on income and capital, with exchanges of notes.

Signed at Paris August 31, 1994.

Entered into force December 30, 1995.

TIAS; 1963 UNTS 67.

TELECOMMUNICATION

Agreement relating to the reciprocal granting of authorizations to permit licensed amateur radio operators of either country to operate their stations in the other country.[1]

Exchange of notes at Paris May 5, 1966.

Entered into force July 1, 1966.

17 UST 719; TIAS 6022; 593 UNTS 279.

Amendment

October 3, 1969 (20 UST 2398; TIAS 6711).

NOTE

1 Applicable to all territories.

TERRITORIAL ACQUISITION

Treaty for the cession of Louisiana.

Signed at Paris April 30, 1803.

Entered into force October 21, 1803.

8 Stat. 200; TS 86; 7 Bevans 812.

TRADE AND COMMERCE
See COMMERCE

VISAS

Reciprocal agreement relating to visa fees for nonimmigrants.[1]

Exchanges of notes at Washington August 19 and September 4, 5, and 16, 1947.

Entered into force September 16, 1947; operative October 1, 1947.

61 Stat. 3776; TIAS 1721; 7 Bevans 1210; 84 UNTS 19.

Arrangement for the waiver by France of visa requirements for United States citizens visiting Metropolitan France and certain French territories, and for the granting by the United States of gratis passport visas to French citizens as nonimmigrants.

Exchange of notes at Paris March 16 and 31, 1949.

Entered into force March 31, 1949.

63 Stat. 2737; TIAS 1987; 7 Bevans 1311; 84 UNTS 283.

Agreement relating to the reciprocal issuance of nonimmigrant visas for treaty traders and treaty investors.

Exchange of notes at Paris September 1 and 21, 1961.

Entered into force September 21, 1961; operative October 21, 1961.

12 UST 3197; TIAS 4924; 433 UNTS 243.

NOTE

1 Applicable to all territories.

FRANCE (FRENCH GUIANA)

POSTAL MATTERS

Parcel post convention.

Signed at Washington August 21, 1914; operative November 1, 1914.

38 Stat. 1829; Post Office Department print.

FRANCE (FRENCH POLYNESIA)

POSTAL MATTERS

International express mail agreement, with detailed regulations.

Signed at Papeete and Washington November 30, 1995 and April 5, 1996.

Entered into force June 15, 1996.

NP

FRANCE (GUADELOUPE)

POSTAL MATTERS

Parcel post convention.

Signed at Washington February 20, 1913; operative April 1, 1913.

38 Stat. 1633; Post Office Department print.

FRANCE (MARTINIQUE)

POSTAL MATTERS

Money order agreement.

Signed at Washington November 16, 1911; operative January 1, 1912.

NP

Parcel post convention.

Signed at Washington February 20, 1913; operative April 1, 1913.

38 Stat. 1623; Post Office Department print.

FRANCE (SOCIETY ISLANDS)

POSTAL MATTERS

Parcel post convention.

Signed at Washington April 30, 1918; operative June 1, 1918.

41 Stat. 1645; Post Office Department print.

G

GABON

AVIATION

Air transport agreement, with annexes.

Signed at Washington May 26, 2004.

Entered into force May 26, 2004.

TIAS

DEFENSE

Agreement concerning the provision of training related to defense articles under the United States International Military Education and Training (IMET) Program.

Exchange of notes at Libreville March 21, 1983 and July 5, 1984.

Entered into force July 5, 1984.

TIAS 10986; 2022 UNTS 169.

Agreement regarding the status of United States military and civilian personnel of the U.S. Department of Defense temporarily present in Gabon in connection with "Gabon 2000" and other activities.

Exchange of notes at Libreville November 26 and December 1, 1999.

Entered into force December 1, 1999.

NP

Acquisition and cross service agreement, with annexes.

Signed at Libreville July 19, 2006.

Entered into force July 19, 2006.

TIAS

ECONOMIC AND TECHNICAL COOPERATION

Agency for International Development

February 21, 1976 (28 UST 5041; TIAS 8612).

ENVIRONMENTAL COOPERATION

Agreement for cooperation in the Global Learning and Observations to Benefit the Environment (GLOBE) program.

Signed at Libreville August 11, 2003.

Entered into force August 11, 2003.

TIAS

FINANCE

Agreement relating to investment guaranties.

Exchange of notes at Libreville April 10, 1963.

Entered into force April 10, 1963.

14 UST 380; TIAS 5328; 474 UNTS 113.

Agreement regarding the consolidation and rescheduling of certain debts owed to, guaranteed by or insured by the United States Government and its agencies, with annexes.

Signed at Libreville February 11, 1988.

Entered into force March 21, 1988.

NP

Agreement regarding the consolidation and rescheduling of certain debts owed to, guaranteed by or insured by the United States Government and its agencies, with annexes.

Signed at Libreville February 16, 1989.

Entered into force March 30, 1989.

NP

Agreement regarding the consolidation and rescheduling or refinancing of certain debts owed to, guaranteed by or insured by the United States Government and its agencies, with annexes.

Signed at Libreville March 5, 1990.

Entered into force April 9, 1990.

NP

Agreement regarding the consolidation and rescheduling or refinancing of certain debts owed to, guaranteed by or insured by the United States Government and its agencies, with annexes.

Signed at Libreville September 2, 1994.

Entered into force November 28, 1994.

NP

Agreement regarding the consolidation and rescheduling of certain debts owed to, guaranteed by or insured by the United States Government and its agencies, with annexes.

Signed at Libreville June 17, 1996.

Entered into force August 12, 1996.

NP

Agreement regarding the consolidation and rescheduling of certain debts owed to, guaranteed by, or insured by the United States Government and its agencies, with annexes.

Signed at Libreville November 9, 2001.

Entered into force December 26, 2001.

NP

Agreement regarding the consolidation and rescheduling of certain debts owed to, guaranteed by, or insured by the United States government and its agencies, with annexes.

Signed at Libreville May 13, 2005.

Entered into force June 20, 2005.

NP

INTERNATIONAL CRIMINAL COURT

Agreement regarding the surrender of persons to the International Criminal Court.

Exchange of notes at Libreville February 26 and April 15, 2003.

Entered into force April 15, 2003.

TIAS

POSTAL MATTERS

International express mail agreement, with detailed regulations.

Signed at Libreville and Washington January 23 and March 8, 1989.

Entered into force April 17, 1989.

TIAS 11616.

SCIENTIFIC COOPERATION

Agreement concerning scientific and technical cooperation in the earth sciences, with annexes.

Signed at Reston and Libreville September 26, 2001 and April 22 and 23, 2003.

Entered into force April 23, 2003.

TIAS

SHIPPING

Agreement relating to jurisdiction over vessels utilizing the Louisiana Offshore Oil Port.

Exchange of notes at Libreville July 25 and August 2, 1984.

Entered into force August 2, 1984.

TIAS 11215.

SOCIAL SECURITY

Agreement to provide certain social security benefits for certain employees of the United States in Gabon.

Signed at Libreville August 25, 1970.

Entered into force August 25, 1970; effective January 1, 1968.

21 UST 2570; TIAS 6999; 175 UNTS 205.

THE GAMBIA

On February 18, 1965 The Gambia became an independent state. By an exchange of letters on June 20, 1966 between the High Commissioner for the United Kingdom in The Gambia and the Prime Minister of The Gambia, the Government of The Gambia agreed "that all obligations and responsibilities of the Government of the United Kingdom which arose from any valid international instrument applying to The Gambia immediately before the 18th of February, 1965 continued to apply to The Gambia and were assumed by the Government of The Gambia as from that date; and (ii) that the rights and benefits enjoyed by the

Government of the United Kingdom by virtue of the application of any such international instrument to The Gambia continued to be enjoyed by the Government of The Gambia."

AVIATION

Arrangement between the United States and the United Kingdom relating to pilot licenses to operate civil aircraft.

Exchange of notes at Washington March 28 and April 5, 1935.

Entered into force May 5, 1935.

49 Stat. 3731; EAS 77; 12 Bevans 513; 162 UNTS 59.

Agreement between the United States and the United Kingdom relating to air services.

Signed at Bermuda February 11, 1946.

Entered into force February 11, 1946.

60 Stat. 1499; TIAS 1507; 12 Bevans 726; 3 UNTS 253.

Amendment

May 27, 1966 (17 UST 683; TIAS 6019; 573 UNTS 274).

Air transport agreement, with annexes.

Signed at Washington May 2, 2000.

Entered into force January 18, 2001.

TIAS

Agreement concerning the provision of assistance in developing and modernizing the civil aviation infrastructure of The Gambia

Signed May 20 and 30, 2004.

Entered into force May 30, 2004.

TIAS

Amendment

January 31 and February 2, 2005.

CONSULS

Consular convention between the United States and the United Kingdom.

Signed at Washington June 6, 1951.

Entered into force September 7, 1952.

3 UST 3426; TIAS 2494; 165 UNTS 121.

DEFENSE

Agreement concerning the provision of training related to defense articles under the United States International Military Education and Training (IMET) Program.

Exchange of notes at Banjul December 27, 1983 and January 5, 1984.

Entered into force January 5, 1984.

35 UST 4183; TIAS 10916; 2015 UNTS 81.

Agreement regarding grants under the Foreign Assistance Act of 1961, as amended, and the furnishing of defense articles, related training and other defense services from the United States to The Gambia.

Exchange of notes at Banjul August 14 and 18, 2003.

Entered into force August 18, 2003.

TIAS

ECONOMIC AND TECHNICAL COOPERATION

Economic cooperation agreement between the United States and the United Kingdom.

Signed at London July 6, 1948; applicable to The Gambia July 6, 1948.

62 Stat. 2596; TIAS 1795; 12 Bevans 874; 22 UNTS 263.

Amendments

January 3, 1950 (1 UST 184; TIAS 2036; 86 UNTS 304).

May 25, 1951 (2 UST 1292; TIAS 2277; 99 UNTS 308).

February 25, 1953 (4 UST 1528; TIAS 2815; 172 UNTS 332).

June 26 and August 20, 1959 (11 UST 2680; TIAS 4664; 405 UNTS 288).

Agency for International Development

October 26 and 28, 1977 (29 UST 5753; TIAS 9148).

January 12 and February 20, 1978 (29 UST 5772; TIAS 9152).

EMPLOYMENT

Agreement relating to the employment of dependents of official government employees.

Exchange of notes at Banjul June 7 and August 13, 2002.

Entered into force August 13, 2002.

TIAS

EXTRADITION

Extradition treaty between the United States and the United Kingdom.

Signed at London December 22, 1931.

Entered into force June 24, 1935.

47 Stat. 2122; TS 849; 12 Bevans 482; 163 LNTS 59.

FINANCE

Agreement relating to investment guaranties.

Exchange of notes at Bathurst July 24 and November 4, 1967.

Entered into force November 4, 1967.

18 UST 2997; TIAS 6392; 701 UNTS 139.

INTERNATIONAL CRIMINAL COURT

Agreement regarding the surrender of persons to the International Criminal Court.

Signed at Banjul October 5, 2002.

Entered into force June 27, 2003.

TIAS

MUTUAL SECURITY

Agreement between the United States and the United Kingdom relating to the assurances required under the Mutual Security Act of 1951.

Exchange of notes at London January 8, 1952.

Entered into force January 8, 1952.

3 UST 4665; TIAS 2622; 126 UNTS 307.

PEACE CORPS

Agreement relating to the establishment of a Peace Corps program in The Gambia.

Exchange of notes at Bathurst November 26 and December 5, 1966.

Entered into force December 5, 1966.

17 UST 2346; TIAS 6181; 681 UNTS 49.

PROPERTY

Convention between the United States and the United Kingdom relating to the tenure and disposition of real and personal property.

Signed at Washington March 2, 1899; applicable to The Gambia February 9, 1901.

31 Stat. 1939; TS 146; 12 Bevans 246.

Supplementary convention relating to the tenure and disposition of real and personal property.

Signed at Washington May 27, 1936.

Entered into force March 10, 1941.

55 Stat. 1101; TS 964; 5 Bevans 140; 203 LNTS 367.

SPACE COOPERATION

Agreement concerning the use of Banjul International Airport as a space shuttle emergency landing site.

Signed at Banjul March 7, 1988.

Entered into force March 7, 1988.

TIAS 12148.

TELECOMMUNICATION

Agreement relating to radio communications between amateur stations on behalf of third parties.

Exchange of notes at Banjul March 17, 1981.

Entered into force April 16, 1981.

33 UST 1401; TIAS 10119.

TRADE-MARKS

Declaration by the United States and the United Kingdom affording reciprocal protection to trade-marks.

Signed at London October 24, 1877.

Entered into force October 24, 1877.

20 Stat. 703; TS 138; 12 Bevans 198.

GEORGIA

For agreements prior to December 31, 1991, see UNION OF SOVIET SOCIALIST REPUBLICS.

DEFENSE

Agreement concerning the provision of training under the United States International Military Education and Training (IMET) Program.

Exchange of notes at Tbilisi December 30, 1993.

Entered into force December 30, 1993.

NP

Agreement regarding grants under the Foreign Assistance Act of 1961, as amended, and the furnishing of defense articles, related training, and other defense services from the United States of America to the Government of Georgia.

Exchange of notes at Tbilisi June 4 and July 15, 1999.

Entered into force July 15, 1999.

TIAS

Agreement on defense cooperation, with annex.

Signed at Tbilisi November 10, 2002.

Entered into force March 25, 2003.

TIAS

ECONOMIC AND TECHNICAL COOPERATION

Agreement regarding cooperation to facilitate humanitarian and technical economic assistance.

Signed at Tbilisi July 31, 1992.

Entered into force July 31, 1992.

TIAS 12468.

Millennium challenge compact, with annexes.

Signed at New York September 12, 2005.

Entered into force April 7, 2006.

TIAS

EMPLOYMENT

Agreement relating to the employment of dependents of official government employees.

Exchange of notes at Washington December 5, 1994 and June 20, 1995.

Entered into force June 20, 1995.

TIAS 12667.

ENVIRONMENTAL COOPERATION

Agreement concerning the Regional Environmental Centre for the Caucasus

Signed November 8, 2000.

Entered into force November 8, 2000.

TIAS

FINANCE

Investment incentive agreement.

Signed at Tbilisi June 27, 1992.

Entered into force June 27, 1992.

TIAS 12463.

Agreement regarding the consolidation and rescheduling of certain debts owed to the United States Government, with annexes.

Signed at Tbilisi March 6, 2002.

Entered into force January 28, 2003.

NP

Agreement regarding the rescheduling of certain debts owed to, guaranteed by, or insured by the United States Government, with annexes.

Signed at Tbilisi November 18, 2005.

Entered into force June 2, 2006.

NP

INTERNATIONAL CRIMINAL COURT

Agreement regarding the surrender of persons to the International Criminal Court.

Signed at Tbilisi February 10, 2003.

Entered into force June 26, 2003.

TIAS

INVESTMENT

Treaty concerning the encouragement and reciprocal protection of investment, with annex.

Signed at Washington March 7, 1994.

Entered into force August 17, 1997.

TIAS

JUDICIAL ASSISTANCE

Agreement on co–operation in the field of law enforcement, with annex.

Signed at Tbilisi June 18, 2001.

Entered into force June 18, 2001.

TIAS

MAPPING

Agreement concerning geospatial-intelligence exchange and cooperation, with annex.

Signed at Bethesda and Tbilisi July 5 and 17, 2006.

Entered into force July 17, 2006.

NP

PEACE CORPS

Agreement on the Peace Corps program.

Signed at Tbilisi April 24, 2001.

Entered into force August 14, 2003.

TIAS

POSTAL MATTERS

Express mail agreement, with detailed regulations.

Signed at Tbilisi and Washington August 16 and September 3, 1996.

Entered into force November 1, 1996.

NP

SCIENTIFIC COOPERATION

Memorandum of understanding concerning scientific and technical cooperation in the earth sciences.

Signed at Reston July 21 and August 9, 2006.

Entered into force August 9, 2006.

TIAS

TRADE

Agreement on trade relations, with exchanges of letters.

Signed at Tbilisi March 1, 1993.

Entered into force August 13, 1993.

TIAS 12489.

WEAPONS

Agreement concerning cooperation in the area of the prevention of proliferation of weapons of mass destruction and the promotion of defense and military relations.

Signed at Washington July 17, 1997.

Entered into force November 10, 1997.

TIAS

Extension

May 16 and 17, 2002.

Agreement extending the agreement of January 26 and 30, 1998 concerning the provision of assistance to Georgia related to the establishment of export control systems to prevent the proliferation of weapons of mass destruction.

Exchange of notes at Tbilisi February 23 and July 13, 2001.

Entered into force July 13, 2001; effective February 27, 2001.

TIAS

Agreement concerning cooperation in the area of prevention of proliferation of technology, pathogens and expertise related to the development of biological weapons.

Signed at Washington December 30, 2002.

Entered into force June 3, 2003.

TIAS

Amendments

March 19 and 23, 2004.

August 30, 2004.

October 25 and November 3, 2005.

June 21 and 23, 2006.

GERMANY, FEDERAL REPUBLIC OF

The Federal Republic of Germany provided a note to the Department dated October 15, 1990, which reads in pertinent part as follows:

"The Embassy of the Federal Republic of Germany presents its compliments to the Department of State and has the honor to inform the Department that, with regard to the continued application of treaties of the Federal Republic of Germany and the treatment of treaties of the German Democratic Republic following its accession to the Federal Republic of Germany with effect from 3 October 1990, the Treaty of 31 August 1990 between the Federal Republic of Germany and the German Democratic Republic on the Establishment of German Unity (Unification Treaty) contains the following relevant provisions.

1. Article 11

Treaties of the Federal Republic of Germany

The Contracting Parties proceed on the understanding that international treaties and agreements to which the Federal Republic of Germany is a Contracting Party, including treaties establishing its membership of international organizations or institutions, shall retain their validity and that the rights and obligations arising therefrom, with the exception of the treaties named in Annex I (not included herein), shall also relate to the territory specified in Article 3. Where adjustments become necessary in individual cases, the all-German Government shall consult with the respective Contracting Parties.

...

2. Article 12

Treaties of the German Democratic Republic

(1) The Contracting Parties are agreed that, in connection with the establishment of German unity, international treaties of the German Democratic Republic shall be discussed with the Contracting Parties concerned with a view to regulating or confirming their continued application, adjustment or expiry, taking into account protection of confidence, the interests of the states concerned, the treaty obligations of the Federal Republic of Germany as well as the principles of a free, democratic basic order governed by the rule of law, and respecting the competence of the European Communities.

(2) The United Germany shall determine its position with regard to the adoption of international treaties of the German Democratic Republic following consultations with the respective Contracting Parties and with the European Communities where the latter's competence is affected.

...

The Federal Republic of Germany will proceed in accordance with these provisions."

AGRICULTURAL COMMODITIES

Agreement for the sale of feed grain and the purchase of building materials for United States defense purposes.

Signed at Washington February 18, 1955.

Entered into force February 18, 1955.

6 UST 655; TIAS 3199; 247 UNTS 257.

AGRICULTURE

Agreement on cooperation in the field of agricultural science and technology.

Signed at Bonn June 1, 1981.

Entered into force June 1, 1981.

34 UST 958; TIAS 10381; 1560 UNTS 423.

ARMS LIMITATION

Agreement regarding inspections on the territory of the German Democratic Republic provided for by the U.S.-U.S.S.R. treaty of December 8, 1987 on the elimination of their intermediate-range and shorter-range missiles.

Exchange of notes at Berlin December 23, 1987.

Entered into force June 1, 1988.[1]

TIAS

NOTE

1 Agreement concluded with the German Democratic Republic.

ATOMIC ENERGY

Agreement for cooperation on uses of atomic energy for mutual defense purposes.

Signed at Bonn May 5, 1959.

Entered into force July 27, 1959.

10 UST 1322; TIAS 4276; 355 UNTS 307.

Agreement for cooperation in the field of nuclear materials safeguards and physical security research and development, with annex.

Exchange of notes at Bonn and Washington September 29, 1977.

Entered into force September 29, 1977.

29 UST 4709; TIAS 9076.

Extension

April 23 and July 22, 1985 (TIAS 12386).

Agreement for the exchange of classified information, with related exchange of letters.

Signed at Washington July 6, 1981.

Entered into force July 6, 1981.

35 UST 3615; TIAS 10872.

Agreement concerning the listing of reactors supplied from the Federal Republic of Germany to the Taiwan Power Company on the inventory of the IAEA safeguards agreement of December 6, 1971 (TIAS 7228).

Exchange of letters at Washington November 5, 1981.

Entered into force November 5, 1981.

33 UST 4505; TIAS 10321.

Arrangement for the exchange of information and cooperation in nuclear safety matters, with annexes.

Signed at Berlin October 19, 1995.

Entered into force October 19, 1995.

TIAS 12699.

Extension

January 24, 2002.

AVIATION

Air transport agreement and exchanges of notes.

Signed at Washington July 7, 1955.

Entered into force April 16, 1956.

7 UST 527; TIAS 3536; 275 UNTS 3.

Amendments

November 1, 1978 (30 UST 7323; TIAS 9591; 1203 UNTS 280).

April 25, 1989 (TIAS 11942).

Agreement relating to the reciprocal acceptance of airworthiness certifications.

Exchange of notes at Bonn-Bad Godesberg and Bonn March 12 and May 31, 1974.

Entered into force May 31, 1974.

25 UST 3056; TIAS 7965.

Agreement for application to Land Berlin of agreement of March 12 and May 31, 1974 relating to the reciprocal acceptance of airworthiness certifications.

Exchange of notes at Bonn and Bonn-Bad Godesberg November 3, 1976 and March 18, 1980.

Entered into force March 18, 1980.

32 UST 538; TIAS 9724; 1220 UNTS 353.

Memorandum of understanding relating to cooperation in the development of national airspace systems, with annex.

Signed at Washington and Bonn October 3 and November 6, 1984.

Entered into force November 6, 1984.

TIAS 11025; 2022 UNTS 97.

Memorandum of understanding concerning air navigation services in Berlin, with related exchange of letters.

Signed at Bonn October 23, 1990.

Entered into force October 23, 1990.

TIAS 11746; 2202 UNTS 73.

Agreement for promotion of aviation safety.

Signed at Milwaukee May 23, 1996.

Entered into force July 18, 1997.

TIAS 12758.

CLAIMS

Agreement regarding the settlement of the claim of the United States for postwar economic assistance (other than surplus property) to Germany.

Signed at London February 27, 1953.

Entered into force September 16, 1953.

4 UST 893; TIAS 2795; 224 UNTS 13.

Agreement relating to the indebtedness of Germany for awards made by the Mixed Claims Commission, United States and Germany.

Signed at London February 27, 1953.

Entered into force September 16, 1953.

4 UST 908; TIAS 2796; 224 UNTS 31.

Agreement concerning the settlement of claims against United States forces and authorities which arose during the period of August 1, 1945 to June 30, 1947.

Exchange of letters at Bonn March 24 and 30, 1953.

Entered into force March 30, 1953.

5 UST 2149; TIAS 3076; 235 UNTS 285.

Agreement relating to an advance payment by Germany on its indebtedness to the United States for postwar economic assistance.

Exchange of notes at Bonn March 20, 1959.

Entered into force March 20, 1959.

10 UST 401; TIAS 4200; 341 UNTS 15.

Agreement relating to partial settlement of German postwar debt to the United States resulting from postwar economic assistance (other than surplus property).

Exchange of notes at Bonn April 25, 1961.

Entered into force April 25, 1961.

12 UST 477; TIAS 4737; 410 UNTS 340.

Agreement concerning the settlement of claims which have arisen through the non-duty use of private motor vehicles of members of the United States Forces insured by the Brandaris insurance company.[1]

Exchange of letters at Bonn February 28 and March 14, 1963.

Entered into force March 14, 1963.

14 UST 342; TIAS 5318; 474 UNTS 71.

Agreement relating to prepayment of the remaining German debt to the United States resulting from postwar economic assistance (excluding surplus property).

Exchange of notes at Bonn December 29, 1966.

Entered into force December 29, 1966.

18 UST 101; TIAS 6204; 688 UNTS 63.

Agreement concerning the settlement of certain property claims, with annex.

Signed at Bonn May 13, 1992.

Entered into force December 28, 1992.

TIAS 11959; 1911 UNTS 27.

Agreement concerning final benefits to certain United States nationals who were victims of National Socialist measures of persecution, with exchange of notes.

Signed at Bonn September 19, 1995.

Entered into force September 19, 1995.

TIAS

Supplementary agreement to the agreement of September 19, 1995 concerning final benefits to certain United States nationals who were victims of National Socialist measures of persecution.

Exchange of notes at Bonn January 25, 1999.

Entered into force January 25, 1999.

TIAS

Agreement concerning the Foundation "Remembrance, Responsibility and the Future", with annexes.

Signed at Berlin July 17, 2000.

Entered into force October 19, 2000.

TIAS; 2130 UNTS 249.

NOTE

1 Applicable also in respect of incidents which occurred in West Berlin.

COMMERCE

Treaty of friendship, commerce, and consular rights.[1]

Signed at Washington December 8, 1923.

Entered into force October 14, 1925.

44 Stat. 2132; TS 725; 8 Bevans 153; 52 LNTS 133.

Agreement concerning the treaty of friendship, commerce, and consular rights of December 8, 1923, as amended.[1]

Signed at Bonn June 3, 1953.

Entered into force October 22, 1954.

5 UST 1939; TIAS 3062; 253 UNTS 89.

Treaty of friendship, commerce and navigation with protocol and exchanges of notes.

Signed at Washington October 29, 1954.

Entered into force July 14, 1956.

7 UST 1839; TIAS 3593; 273 UNTS 3.

NOTE

1 Articles I-V, VII-XVI, and XXIX-XXXII of the 1923 treaty as amended and as applied by the agreement of June 3, 1953 (TIAS 3062) were replaced and terminated by the treaty of October 29, 1954 (TIAS 3593). Article VI of the 1923 treaty terminated June 2, 1954 (see 5 UST 827; TIAS 2972).

CONSULS

See COMMERCE

COPYRIGHT

Copyright agreement.

Signed at Washington January 15, 1892.

Entered into force May 6, 1892.

TS 100; 8 Bevans 129.

Agreement relating to the extension of time for fulfilling the conditions and formalities of the copyright laws of the United States.

Exchange of notes at Washington November 20, 1964 and July 12, 1967.

Entered into force July 12, 1967.

18 UST 2366; TIAS 6341; 692 UNTS 331.

CULTURAL RELATIONS

Agreement concerning cultural relations.

Exchange of notes at Washington April 9, 1953.

Entered into force April 9, 1953.

4 UST 939; TIAS 2798; 204 UNTS 79.

Agreement with respect to the transfer of certain works of art seized in Germany by the United States Army at the end of World War II, with annex.

Exchange of notes at Washington January 28, 1986.

Entered into force January 28, 1986.

TIAS 11977; 2244 UNTS 101.

CUSTOMS

Agreement regarding mutual assistance between the customs services of the United States and the Federal Republic of Germany.

Signed at Washington August 23, 1973.

Entered into force June 13, 1975.

26 UST 1092; TIAS 8098.

DEFENSE

See also MUTUAL SECURITY

Agreement relating to the purchase by the Federal Republic of Germany from the United States of certain equipment for police use.

Exchange of notes at Washington November 23, 1953.

Entered into force November 23, 1953.

5 UST 170; TIAS 2911; 224 UNTS 107.

Agreement relating to offshore procurement.

Signed at Bonn April 4, 1955.

Entered into force February 7, 1957.

8 UST 157; TIAS 3755; 279 UNTS 73.

Agreement on the model contract containing standard contract clauses referred to in article 16 of the agreement of April 4, 1955 relating to offshore procurement.

Exchange of notes at Bonn April 4, 1955.

Entered into force February 7, 1957.

8 UST 497; TIAS 3804; 289 UNTS 326.

Mutual defense assistance agreement.

Signed at Bonn June 30, 1955.

Entered into force December 27, 1955.

6 UST 5999; TIAS 3443; 240 UNTS 47.

Agreement for the return of equipment pursuant to the mutual defense assistance agreement.

Exchange of notes at Bonn June 30, 1955.

Entered into force December 27, 1955.

6 UST 6005; TIAS 3444; 240 UNTS 69.

Amendment

March 9, 1961 (12 UST 243; TIAS 4703; 405 UNTS 323).

Agreement relating to the sale to the Federal Republic of certain military equipment, materials, and services pursuant to sec. 106 of the Mutual Security Act of 1954, as amended.

Exchange of notes at Washington October 8, 1956.

Entered into force October 8, 1956.

7 UST 2787; TIAS 3660; 278 UNTS 9.

Extensions and amendments

June 15 and October 24, 1960 (11 UST 2242; TIAS 4599; 393 UNTS 332).

November 24, 1961 (12 UST 3045; TIAS 4903; 434 UNTS 328).

Agreement relating to the training of German army personnel pursuant to the mutual defense assistance agreement.

Exchange of notes at Bonn December 12, 1956.

Entered into force December 12, 1956.

8 UST 149; TIAS 3753; 280 UNTS 63.

Agreement relating to the training of German navy personnel pursuant to the mutual defense assistance agreement.

Exchange of notes at Bonn December 12, 1956.

Entered into force December 12, 1956.

8 UST 153; TIAS 3754; 280 UNTS 71.

Agreement relating to the disbandment of the German element of the Civilian Service Organization maintained by American Forces in Germany under the Forces Convention.

Exchange of notes at Bonn April 11, 1957.

Entered into force April 11, 1957.

8 UST 645; TIAS 3815; 283 UNTS 233.

Amendment

April 11, 1957 (8 UST 645; TIAS 3815; 283 UNTS 237).

Agreement relating to the training of German air force and the transfer to the Federal Republic of the air bases at Landsberg, Kaufbeuren and Fuerstenfeldbruck and the air depot at Erding.

Exchange of notes at Bonn December 10, 1957.

Entered into force December 10, 1957.

8 UST 2475; TIAS 3968; 307 UNTS 59.

Agreements implementing the NATO status of forces agreement of August 3, 1959 (TIAS 5351).

Signed at Bonn August 3, 1959.

Entered into force July 1, 1963.

14 UST 689; TIAS 5352; 490 UNTS 30.

Agreement relating to the use of the International Airport Frankfurt/Main and related papers.

Exchange of letters at Bonn November 10 and 18, 1959.

Entered into force November 18, 1959; effective April 1, 1959.

TIAS

Agreement relating to a weapons production program.

Exchange of notes at Bonn May 27, 1960.

Entered into force May 27, 1960.

11 UST 1606; TIAS 4504; 377 UNTS 45.

Agreement relating to the disposition of equipment and materials furnished to the Federal Republic on a grant basis under the mutual defense assistance agreement of June 30, 1955.

Exchange of notes at Bonn May 25, 1962.

Entered into force May 25, 1962.

13 UST 1341; TIAS 5092; 458 UNTS 259.

Agreement to support personnel from the Federal Republic of Germany stationed in the United States during emergencies.

Signed at Bonn October 21, and at Washington December 18, 1965.

Entered into force December 18, 1965.

16 UST 1912; TIAS 5922; 579 UNTS 193.

Agreement relating to the AIM-9L Sidewinder air-to-air missile.

Signed at Washington February 14, 1975.

Entered into force February 14, 1975.

29 UST 2924; TIAS 8987; 1120 UNTS 23.

Memorandum of understanding relating to cooperative tests for the ROLAND 2 all weather short range air defense system, with annexes.

Signed at Bonn and Washington February 18 and 28, 1975.

Entered into force February 28, 1975.

31 UST 4754; TIAS 9636.

Agreement concerning the transfer of the U.S. bridge and ferry equipment to the Federal Republic of Germany, with annex.

Signed at Heidelberg and Bonn May 26 and June 1, 1976.

Entered into force June 1, 1976.

29 UST 1497; TIAS 8893; 1115 UNTS 45.

Memorandum of understanding concerning cooperative development of an advanced surface-to-air missile system.

Signed at Washington and Bonn July 16 and 22, 1976.

Entered into force July 22, 1976.

28 UST 5771; TIAS 8658.

Agreement on the release and testing of strebo submunitions and on the exchange of information.

Signed at Washington and Bonn August 4 and November 4, 1976.

Entered into force November 4, 1976.

TIAS 12298.

Agreement relating to the security of information on the JT-10D aircraft engine.

Exchange of notes at Washington February 24 and March 18, 1977.

Entered into force March 18, 1977.

28 UST 7146; TIAS 8708.

Agreement on the provision of United States Army training to the German Air Force in the United States, with annexes.

Signed at Bonn and Washington May 24 and July 6, 1977.

Entered into force July 6, 1977.

29 UST 4859; TIAS 9081; 1148 UNTS 107.

Agreement on the stationing of training components of the Federal Minister of Defense in the United States, with annexes.

Signed at Bonn and Washington May 24 and July 6, 1977.

Entered into force July 6, 1977.

30 UST 2671; TIAS 9358.

Memorandum of understanding for coproduction and sale of the sidewinder AIM-9L missile system.

Signed at Washington October 7, 1977.

Entered into force October 14, 1977.

30 UST 298; TIAS 9202; 1148 UNTS 117.

Amendment

March 17 and April 21, 1978 (30 UST 315; TIAS 9202; 1148 UNTS 125).

Memorandum of understanding for coproduction and sale of modular thermal imaging systems (MOD FLIR) and their components, with annexes.[1]

Signed at Washington and Bonn February 27 and March 3, 1978.

Entered into force April 20, 1978.

35 UST 3651; TIAS 10876; 2014 UNTS 359.

Related agreement and amendment

March 26, 1979 (35 UST 3651; TIAS 10876; 2016 UNTS 311).

May 9 and June 24, 1997.

Administrative agreement relating to addition of an educational program under paragraph 4, article 71 of the supplementary agreement of August 3, 1959 (TIAS 5351).

Exchange of notes at Bonn November 23 and December 28, 1979.

Entered into force January 1, 1980.

32 UST 783; TIAS 9729; 1220 UNTS 307.

Memorandum of understanding for cooperation within the area of army tactical data systems for the purpose of standardization and interoperability.

Signed at Washington and Bonn January 6 and April 14, 1980.

Entered into force April 14, 1980.

32 UST 1003; TIAS 9751; 1221 UNTS 3.

Agreement concerning the support of USAFE A-10 aircraft at forward operating locations (FOLS) in the territory of the Federal Republic of Germany, with related letter.

Signed at Bonn and Ramstein November 5 and 9, 1981.

Entered into force November 9, 1981; effective October 1, 1979.

33 UST 4170; TIAS 10293.

Agreement concerning host nation support during crisis or war, with annexes.

Signed at Bonn April 15, 1982.

Entered into force April 15, 1982.

34 UST 557; TIAS 10376.

Agreement concerning mutual support in Europe and adjacent waters, with annex.

Signed at Bonn January 21, 1983.

Entered into force January 21, 1983.

TIAS 12299.

Amendments

December 21, 1987 (TIAS 12299).

January 21 and 26, 1994 (TIAS 12299).

December 7, 2001.

Memorandum of understanding for the dual production and sale of the stinger weapon system, with agreed minute and annexes.

Signed at Washington April 27, 1983.

Entered into force April 27, 1983.

TIAS 12795.

Amendments

March 20 and 26, 1986 (TIAS 12795).

March 23 and April 24, 1995 (TIAS 12795).

April 24 and May 14, 1996 (TIAS 12795).

July 10 and August 22, 1996 (TIAS 12795).

Memorandum of understanding concerning a cooperative project of research in the field of powder metallurgy of titanium alloys.

Signed at Washington January 8, 1985.

Entered into force January 8, 1985.

TIAS 11140; 2126 UNTS 283.

Memorandum of understanding concerning the exchange of Air Force officers.

Signed at Bonn and Washington January 15 and February 20, 1986.

Entered into force February 20, 1986.

NP

Memorandum of understanding for a cooperative software development and implementation for the EIFEL system, with annex.

Signed at Bonn and Washington March 10 and June 13, 1986.

Entered into force June 13, 1986.

TIAS

Memorandum of understanding concerning cooperative production of the EX-31 guided missile weapon system, with annexes.

Signed at Washington August 3, 1987.

Entered into force September 17, 1987.

TIAS 12300.

Amendment

December 27, 1999 and March 1, 2000.

Memorandum of understanding concerning a cooperative program for harmonization, development, production and support of a maritime patrol aircraft, with annexes.

Signed at Bonn and Washington February 17 and April 5, 1989.

Entered into force April 5, 1989.

TIAS 12302.

Memorandum of understanding for cooperative projects of research and development in the field of high energy laser technology, with annex.

Signed at Bonn April 14, 1989.

Entered into force April 14, 1989.

TIAS 12303.

Amendment and extension

April 7 and May 26, 1994 (TIAS 12303).

Memorandum of agreement concerning a cooperative program for extended air defense, with attachment and annex.

Signed at Washington and Bonn April 28 and May 17, 1989.

Entered into force May 17, 1989.

TIAS 11702; 2207 UNTS 425.

Memorandum of understanding concerning the joint research, development and demonstration of advanced armor protection systems (AAPS), with annexes.

Signed at Washington and Bonn January 4 and 11, 1990.

Entered into force January 11, 1990.

TIAS 12304.

Memorandum of understanding on the mutual exchange of documents.

Signed at Bonn and Washington January 18, 1989 and February 9, 1990.

Entered into force February 9, 1990.

TIAS 12305.

Memorandum of understanding concerning the SAXON-FPN synthetic aperture radar experiment, with annexes.

Signed at Washington and Bonn May 25 and June 1, 1990.

Entered into force June 1, 1990.

TIAS 12306.

Memorandum of understanding for cooperative projects of research and development in the field of modular avionics, with supplement.

Signed at Bonn and Washington June 26 and July 3, 1990.

Entered into force July 3, 1990.

TIAS 12307.

Memorandum of understanding for cooperation within the area of short range air defense (SHORAD) command and control systems for the purpose of standardization and interoperability.

Signed at Alexandria and Bonn June 14 and December 20, 1991.

Entered into force December 20, 1991.

TIAS 12308.

Memorandum of agreement concerning a joint enhanced maneuverable fighter aircraft research, development and flight test program, with annexes.

Signed at Arlington and Bonn March 25 and June 11, 1992.

Entered into force June 11, 1992.

TIAS 12309.

Memorandum of understanding concerning a cooperative program on biological effects of ionizing radiation.

Signed at Bonn and Washington August 2 and 23, 1993.

Entered into force August 23, 1993.

TIAS 12310.

Memorandum of understanding for cooperative research in the field of helicopter aeromechanics, with annex.

Signed at Alexandria and Bonn September 2 and 16, 1994.

Entered into force September 16, 1994.

TIAS 12311.

Amendment and extension

August 13 and September 15, 2003.

Memorandum of agreement concerning German participation in the George C. Marshall European Center for Security Studies at Garmisch-Partenkirchen, with annexes.

Signed at Stuttgart December 2, 1994.

Entered into force December 2, 1994.

TIAS 12312.

Memorandum of understanding for research and technology projects, with annex.

Signed at Bonn and Washington March 9 and 17, 1995.

Entered into force March 17, 1995.

TIAS 12313.

Extension

September 9 and 19, 2003.

Memorandum of agreement for the acquisition and co-production of air-to-air STINGER (ATAS) subsystem components, with annex.

Signed at Bonn and Washington January 24 and March 27, 1995.

Entered into force March 27, 1995.

TIAS 12314.

Amendment

August 20 and November 23, 1999.

Agreement concerning collaborative logistics support measures for the Nuclear, Biological, Chemical Reconnaissance System (NBCRS).

Signed at Alexandria and Bonn March 30 and April 18, 1995.

Entered into force April 18, 1995.

TIAS 12629.

Amendment and extension

October 3 and 26, 2005.

Agreement concerning cooperative engineering and manufacturing development of the RAM Block I Upgrade to the MK–31 Guided Missile Weapon System (GMWS), with annexes.

Signed at Bonn and Washington March 14 and 27, 1996.

Entered into force March 27, 1996.

TIAS 12738.

Amendment

October 9 and 21, 1998.

Agreement amending the memorandum of understanding of June 10, 1991 for the coproduction and sale of modular thermal imaging (MOD FLIR) common modules

Signed May 9 and June 24, 1997.

Entered into force June 24, 1997.

TIAS

Arrangement relating to the status of troop care enterprises and their employees under Article 72, paragraph 4 of the Supplementary Agreement of August 3, 1959 to the NATO Status of Forces Agreement, with related letters.

Exchange of notes at Bonn March 27, 1998.

Entered into force March 27, 1998.

TIAS

Arrangement regarding the application of Article 73 of the Supplementary Agreement of August 3, 1959 to the NATO Status of Forces Agreement.

Exchange of notes at Bonn March 27, 1998.

Entered into force March 27, 1998.

TIAS

Agreement regarding the exchange of engineers and scientists, with annexes

Signed on November 6, 1998.

Entered into force November 6, 1998.

TIAS

Agreement for participation in the German Geoscience Space Mission CHAMP.

Signed at Washington and Bonn January 28 and February 12, 1999.

Entered into force February 12, 1999.

TIAS

Memorandum of agreement for the Vectoring Extremely Short Take Off and Landing (ESTOL) Control Tailless Operation Research (VECTOR) technology demonstration project, with annex.

Signed at Bonn and Washington April 6 and 15, 1999.

Entered into force April 15, 1999.

TIAS

Amendment

August 31 and September 12, 2002.

Agreement regarding the exchange of military personnel, with annexes.

Signed at Bonn March 15, 2000.

Entered into force March 15, 2000.

NP

Agreement concerning in-service support of the rolling airframe missile MK-31 guided missile weapon system

Signed January 16 and February 9, 2001.

Entered into force February 9, 2001.

TIAS

Memorandum of understanding for the production of the rolling airframe missile Block 1 and Block 1 helicopter aircraft surface upgrade system.

Signed at Koblenz and Washington November 14 and December 18, 2001.

Entered into force December 18, 2001.

TIAS

Agreement for the simulation and command and control information system connectivity experimentation project.

Signed at Rosslyn and Koblenz September 24 and November 25, 2002.

Entered into force November 25, 2002.

TIAS

Agreement for the loan of residual Precision Navigation Upgrade (PNU) assets.

Signed at Washington and Koblenz December 16, 2004 and January 4, 2005.

Entered into force January 4, 2005.

TIAS

Agreement on the reception and use of meteorological data and products which are distributed via the satellite broadcast system DWDSAT in cooperation with EUMETSAT/EUMETCast.

Signed at Offenbach and Ramstein May 11, 2005 and June 12, 2006.

Entered into force June 12, 2006.

TIAS

NOTE

1 Articles IE, VIIIA, and XII superseded by agreement of February 12, May 21, and December 22, 1981; see NORTH ATLANTIC TREATY ORGANIZATION — COOPERATIVE AGREEMENTS in multilateral section.

ECONOMIC AND TECHNICAL COOPERATION

Economic cooperation agreement.

Signed at Bonn December 15, 1949.

Entered into force provisionally December 29, 1949; definitively February 6, 1950.

64 Stat. (3) B81; TIAS 2024; 8 Bevans 268; 92 UNTS 269.

Amendments

February 27 and March 28, 1951 (2 UST 1295; TIAS 2278; 141 UNTS 390).

November 14 and December 30, 1952 (3 UST 5323; TIAS 2736; 212 UNTS 329).

EDUCATION

Agreement for conducting certain educational exchange programs.

Signed at Bonn November 20, 1962.

Entered into force January 24, 1964.

15 UST 78; TIAS 5518; 505 UNTS 263.

Amendment

January 11, 1974 (25 UST 169; TIAS 7778).

ENERGY

Agreement on cooperation in energy research, science and technology, and development.

Signed at Washington February 20, 1998.

Entered into force February 20, 1998.

TIAS

ENVIRONMENTAL COOPERATION

Agreement on cooperation in environmental affairs.

Signed at Bonn May 9, 1974.

Entered into force March 26, 1975.

26 UST 840; TIAS 8069.

Amendment and extension

March 22, 1985 (TIAS 11251; 2177 UNTS 184).

EXTRADITION

Extradition treaty, with protocol.

Signed at Bonn June 20, 1978.

Entered into force August 29, 1980.

32 UST 1485; TIAS 9785; 1220 UNTS 269.

Supplementary treaty to the treaty concerning extradition of June 20, 1978.

Signed at Washington October 21, 1986.

Entered into force March 11, 1993.

TIAS; 1909 UNTS 441.

FINANCE

Agreement regarding the validation of dollar bonds of German issue.

Signed at Bonn February 27, 1953.

Entered into force February 27, 1953.

4 UST 797; TIAS 2793; 223 UNTS 167.

Agreement regarding certain matters arising from the validation of German dollar bonds.

Signed at Bonn April 1, 1953.

Entered into force September 16, 1953.

4 UST 885; TIAS 2794; 224 UNTS 3.

Confirmation of effectiveness in Berlin of agreements relating to the validation of certain German dollar bonds (TIAS 2793 and 2794).

Exchange of notes at Washington February 25 and April 9, 1954.

5 UST 1; 223 UNTS 167.

Second agreement regarding certain matters arising from the validation of German dollar bonds.

Signed at Bonn August 16, 1960.

Entered into force June 30, 1961.

12 UST 943; TIAS 4798; 418 UNTS 235.

Investment incentive agreement.

Signed at Berlin September 14, 1990.

Entered into force August 9, 1991.

TIAS 12130; 2049 UNTS 291.

Agreement relating to and bringing into force the investment incentive agreement of September 14, 1990.

Exchange of notes at Washington August 9, 1991.

Entered into force August 9, 1991.

TIAS 12130; 2052 UNTS 195.

GENERAL RELATIONS

Treaty establishing friendly relations.

Signed at Berlin August 25, 1921.

Entered into force November 11, 1921.

42 Stat. 1939; TS 658; 8 Bevans 145; 12 LNTS 192.

HEALTH

Agreement on cooperation in the field of bio-medical research and technology.

Signed at Bonn September 22, 1976.

Entered into force September 22, 1976.

27 UST 4358; TIAS 8457; 1066 UNTS 223.

Extension

October 23 and December 10, 1986.

JUDICIAL ASSISTANCE

Agreement relating to the taking of evidence.

Exchange of notes at Bad Godesberg and Bonn February 11, 1955, January 13 and October 8, 1956.

Entered into force October 8, 1956.

32 UST 4181; TIAS 9938; 1265 UNTS 41.

Agreement relating to reciprocal legal assistance in penal matters and information from penal register.

Exchange of notes at Bonn November 7 and December 28, 1960, and January 3, 1961.

Entered into force January 3, 1961.

12 UST 1156; TIAS 4826; 416 UNTS 93.

Agreement concerning mutual assistance in the administration of justice in connection with the Lockheed Aircraft Corporation matter, with agreed minutes.

Signed at Washington September 24, 1976.

Entered into force September 24, 1976.

27 UST 3429; TIAS 8373.

Related agreement

January 10 and February 1, 1979 (30 UST 3533; TIAS 9407; 1169 UNTS 3).

Agreement relating to the taking of evidence.

Exchange of notes at Bonn October 17, 1979 and February 1, 1980.

Entered into force February 1, 1980.

32 UST 4189; TIAS 9938; 1265 UNTS 46.

MAPPING

Basic exchange and cooperative agreement concerning global geospatial information and services cooperation.

Signed at Euskirchen January 25, 2002.

Entered into force January 25, 2002.

NP

MARITIME MATTERS

Agreement relating to the return to the Federal Republic of Germany of Tripartite Naval Commission vessels.

Signed at Bonn August 20, 1953.

Entered into force August 20, 1953.

4 UST 2815; TIAS 2891; 224 UNTS 49.

Agreement relating to the transfer of title of the United States destroyer, *U.S.S. Charles Ausburne,* to the Federal Republic.

Exchange of notes at Bonn February 27, 1968.

Entered into force February 27, 1968.

19 UST 5015; TIAS 6502; 706 UNTS 251.

MUTUAL SECURITY

Agreement relating to the assurances required under the Mutual Security Act of 1951.

Exchange of letters at Bonn December 19 and 28, 1951.

Entered into force December 28, 1951.

3 UST 4564; TIAS 2607; 181 UNTS 45.

NARCOTIC DRUGS

Arrangement concerning the exchange of information relating to the illicit traffic in narcotics.

Exchange of notes at Washington January 17 and August 24, 1955, and March 7, 1956.

Entered into force March 7, 1956.

7 UST 371; TIAS 3514; 271 UNTS 361.

Agreement concerning cooperation in the field of control of drug and narcotics abuse.

Exchange of notes at Bonn and Bonn-Bad Godesberg June 9, 1978.

Entered into force June 9, 1978.

30 UST 4434; TIAS 9467; 1177 UNTS 317.

OCEANOGRAPHY

Memorandum of understanding on the participation of the Federal Republic of Germany in the ocean drilling program as a regular member, with annex.

Signed at Washington and Bonn March 5 and 31, 1993.

Entered into force March 31, 1993; effective October 1, 1993.

TIAS

PACIFIC SETTLEMENT OF DISPUTES

Treaty of arbitration.

Signed at Washington May 5, 1928.

Entered into force February 25, 1929.

45 Stat. 2744; TS 774; 8 Bevans 192; 90 LNTS 177.

Treaty of conciliation.

Signed at Washington May 5, 1928.

Entered into force February 25, 1929.

45 Stat. 2748; TS 775; 8 Bevans 194; 90 LNTS 171.

PATENTS

Patent agreement.

Signed at Washington February 23, 1909.

Entered into force August 1, 1909.

36 Stat. 2178; TS 531; 8 Bevans 143.

Agreement to facilitate interchange of patent rights and technical information for defense purposes, and exchange of notes.

Signed at Bonn January 4, 1956.

Entered into force January 4, 1956.

7 UST 45; TIAS 3478; 268 UNTS 143.

Agreement approving the procedures for reciprocal filing of classified patent applications in the United States and the Federal Republic of Germany.

Exchange of notes at Bonn March 9 and May 23, 1959, and related note of July 31, 1959.

Entered into force May 26, 1959.

10 UST 2001; TIAS 4369; 361 UNTS 337.

Amendment

January 14 and May 28, 1964 (15 UST 765; TIAS 5601; 529 UNTS 350).

POSTAL MATTERS

Agreement concerning the exchange of parcel post together with regulations of execution.

Signed at Berlin February 6 and at Washington March 16, 1939.

Entered into force March 16, 1939; operative from January 2, 1939.

53 Stat. 2183; Post Office Department print; 198 LNTS 237.

International express mail/datapost agreement, with detailed regulation.

Signed at Bonn and Washington December 15, 1978 and January 22, 1979.

Entered into force August 8, 1979; effective February 1, 1979.

30 UST 3789; TIAS 9426.

PROPERTY TRANSFER

Agreement concerning the transfer of the Berlin Document Center to the Federal Republic of Germany, with exchanges of notes.

Signed at Berlin October 18, 1993.

Entered into force October 18, 1993.

TIAS; 2033 UNTS 387.

Agreement concerning real property exchange, with attachments.

Signed at Bonn September 23, 1994.

Entered into force September 23, 1994.

TIAS

PUBLICATIONS

Agreement relating to the exchange of official publications.

Exchange of notes at Washington October 27, 1954.

Entered into force October 27, 1954.

5 UST 2563; TIAS 3121; 234 UNTS 131.

RELIEF SUPPLIES AND PACKAGES

Agreement relating to duty-free entry into the Federal Republic of Germany of relief shipments and the defrayment of transportation costs of such shipments, with memorandum attached.

Exchange of notes at Bonn April 10, May 25, and June 7, 1951.

Entered into force May 29, 1951; operative December 29, 1949.

5 UST 2820; TIAS 3135; 238 UNTS 161.

Extension and amendment

July 8 and September 6, 1952 (5 UST 2835; TIAS 3137; 238 UNTS 167).

SATELLITES

Agreement on cooperation in intercontinental testing in connection with experimental communications satellites.

Exchange of notes at Bonn September 5 and 29, 1961.

Entered into force September 29, 1961.

12 UST 1682; TIAS 4885; 424 UNTS 113.

Memorandum of understanding on the Roentgensatellit program.

Signed at Vienna August 8, 1982.

Entered into force August 8, 1982.

TIAS 10669; 2000 UNTS 445.

SCIENTIFIC COOPERATION

Agreement incorporating an intellectual property annex into cooperative agreements between US-FRG scientific and technical agencies.

Exchange of notes at Washington March 4 and 7, 1994.

Entered into force March 7, 1994.

TIAS 12176.

Agreement on cooperation in research in the geosciences, with annex.

Signed at Bonn March 7, 1994.

Entered into force March 7, 1994.

TIAS 12535.

SHIPPING

Agreement relating to jurisdiction over vessels utilizing the Louisiana Offshore Oil Port.

Exchange of notes at Washington July 2, September 4 and 15, 1981.

Entered into force September 15, 1981.

33 UST 3278; TIAS 10225.

SOCIAL SECURITY

Agreement on the pension insurance of certain employees of the United States Army.

Signed at Bonn September 11, 1970.

Entered into force June 1, 1972; effective November 1, 1950.

23 UST 638; TIAS 7326.

Agreement on social security, with final protocol.

Signed at Washington January 7, 1976.

Entered into force December 1, 1979.

30 UST 6099; TIAS 9542; 1177 UNTS 257.

Administrative agreement for the implementation of the agreement on social security of January 7, 1976.

Signed at Washington June 21, 1978.

Entered into force October 30, 1979; effective December 1, 1979.

30 UST 6150; TIAS 9542; 1177 UNTS 270.

Amendments

October 2, 1986 (TIAS 12115).

March 6, 1995.

SPACE COOPERATION

Memorandum of understanding on the project of active magnetospheric particle tracer explorers.

Signed at Washington October 15, 1981.

Entered into force October 15, 1981.

33 UST 4088; TIAS 10286; 1549 UNTS 339.

Memorandum of understanding for cooperative flights of spaceborne imaging radar.

Signed at Bonn October 6, 1987.

Entered into force October 6, 1987.

TIAS

Amendments

February 18 and March 25, 1994.

September 26 and 30, 1997.

Memorandum of understanding for the Stratospheric Observatory for Infrared Astronomy Program.

Signed at Washington and Bonn December 16 and 20, 1996.

Entered into force December 20, 1996.

TIAS

Memorandum of understanding for participation in the German Geoscience Challenging Mini-Satellite Payload for Geoscientific Research and Applications (CHAMP) program.

Signed at Washington July 31, 1997.

Entered into force July 31, 1997.

TIAS

SURPLUS PROPERTY

Agreement regarding the settlement of the obligations of the Federal Republic of Germany to the United States for surplus property furnished Germany.

Signed at London February 27, 1953.

Entered into force September 16, 1953.

4 UST 923; TIAS 2797; 205 UNTS 103.

Agreement relating to the deduction of $2,350,000 from the indebtedness of the Federal Republic to the United States for certain claims pursuant to articles I and VII of the surplus property payments agreement of February 27, 1953.

Exchange of notes at Washington May 17 and August 17, 1954.

Entered into force August 18, 1954.

5 UST 1476; TIAS 3021; 233 UNTS 31.

Agreement for the final disposition of certain claims to be paid from the amount deducted from the indebtedness of the Federal Republic pursuant to article I of the surplus property payments agreement of February 27, 1953.

Exchange of notes at Washington March 11 and April 14, 1955.

Entered into force April 19, 1955.

6 UST 1065; TIAS 3245; 263 UNTS 351.

TAXATION

Agreement concerning tax relief to be accorded by the Federal Republic of Germany to United States expenditures in interest of the common defense, with annex and exchange of letters.

Signed at Bonn October 15, 1954.

Entered into force November 8, 1955.

6 UST 3081; TIAS 3360; 239 UNTS 135.

Convention for the avoidance of double taxation with respect to taxes on estates.

Signed at Bonn December 3, 1980.

Entered into force June 27, 1986.

TIAS 11082; 2120 UNTS 283.

Convention for the avoidance of double taxation and the prevention of fiscal evasion with respect to taxes on income and capital and to certain other taxes, with a related protocol, exchanges of notes and memorandum of understanding.[1]

Signed at Bonn August 29, 1989.

Entered into force August 21, 1991.

TIAS; 1708 UNTS 3.

Protocol amending the convention of December 3, 1980 for the avoidance of double taxation with respect to taxes on estates, inheritances and gifts.

Signed at Washington December 14, 1998.

Entered into force December 14, 2000.

TIAS

NOTE

1 With an understanding.

TELECOMMUNICATION

Agreement regarding the operation of certain radio installations from within the Federal Republic.

Signed at Bonn June 11, 1952.

Entered into force May 5, 1955.

7 UST 789; TIAS 3559; 273 UNTS 105.

Agreement relating to the return of the Emden-Cherbourg-Horta submarine telegraph cable to German ownership.[1]

Exchange of notes at Washington November 4, 1959 and March 16, 1960.

Entered into force March 16, 1960.

11 UST 254; TIAS 4441; 371 UNTS 101.

Agreement relating to the reciprocal granting of authorizations to permit licensed amateur radio operators of either country to operate their station in the other country.

Exchange of notes at Bonn June 23 and 30, 1966.

Entered into force June 30, 1966.

17 UST 1120; TIAS 6068; 601 UNTS 107.

Agreement regarding operation of the radio installation at Erching.

Signed at Bonn January 22 and 26, 1979.

Entered into force January 26, 1979.

30 UST 3540; TIAS 9408.

NOTE

1 The U.S. signed in its own behalf and in behalf of the United Kingdom and France.

TRADE

See also COMMERCE

Agreement regarding the importation of foreign films into and the screen time quota for exhibition in the Federal Republic of Germany.

Signed at Bonn April 26, 1956.

Entered into force August 17, 1957.

8 UST 735; TIAS 3829; 283 UNTS 267.

Agreement providing compensatory concessions under the general agreement on tariffs and trade for certain tariff actions taken by the United States.

Exchange of notes at Geneva January 29, 1962.

Entered into force January 29, 1962.

13 UST 939; TIAS 5032.

Agreement relating to mutual cooperation regarding restrictive business practices.

Signed at Bonn June 23, 1976.

Entered into force September 11, 1976.

27 UST 1956; TIAS 8291.

TRANSPORTATION

Memorandum of understanding regarding cooperation on the development of advanced ground transportation.

Signed at Bonn June 12, 1973.

Entered into force June 12, 1973.

27 UST 3831; TIAS 8402; 1059 UNTS 3.

Extension and amendments

March 23 and June 9 and 15, 1976 (27 UST 3836; TIAS 8402; 1059 UNTS 8).

July 12 and August 30, 1978 (30 UST 4100; TIAS 9449; 1228 UNTS 472).

Memorandum of understanding concerning cooperation in the field of transportation.

Signed at Washington September 3, 1975.

Entered into force September 3, 1975.

28 UST 8024; TIAS 8736.

GHANA

On March 6, 1957 Ghana became an independent state. In an exchange of letters dated November 25, 1957 between the Government of the United Kingdom and the Government of Ghana it was agreed that all obligations and responsibilities of the Government of the United Kingdom which arise from any valid international instrument shall henceforth in so far as such instrument may be held to have application to Ghana be assumed by the Government of Ghana. The rights and benefits heretofore enjoyed by the Government of the United Kingdom by virtue of the application of any such international instrument to the Gold Coast shall as from March 6, 1957 be enjoyed by the Government of Ghana.

AGRICULTURAL COMMODITIES

Agricultural commodities agreement with exchange of notes.

Signed at Accra April 1, 1966.

Entered into force April 1, 1966.

17 UST 484; TIAS 5991; 579 UNTS 157.

Agricultural commodities agreement with annex.

Signed at Accra March 3, 1967.

Entered into force March 3, 1967.

18 UST 369; TIAS 6245; 688 UNTS 283.

Amendments

April 6, 1967 (18 UST 369; TIAS 6245; 688 UNTS 310).

December 18, 1967 (18 UST 3071; TIAS 6397; 702 UNTS 404).

Related agreements

October 27, 1967 (18 UST 2824; TIAS 6370).

January 3, 1968 (19 UST 4645; TIAS 6453; 697 UNTS 3).

February 9 and 21, 1968 (19 UST 4653; TIAS 6454).

July 16 and 18, 1968 (19 UST 5906; TIAS 6544; 706 UNTS 330).

August 2 and 8, 1968 (19 UST 5906; TIAS 6544; 706 UNTS 334).

December 10, 1968 (19 UST 7848; TIAS 6621; 714 UNTS 3).

June 9, 1969 (20 UST 813; TIAS 6695; 714 UNTS 13).

June 22, 1970 (21 UST 1352; TIAS 6891; 752 UNTS 67).

November 12, 1971 (22 UST 1760; TIAS 7211).

August 2 and December 12, 1971 (23 UST 68; TIAS 7272).

Agricultural commodities agreement, with agreed minutes.

Signed at Accra February 9, 1979.

Entered into force February 9, 1979.

30 UST 3555; TIAS 9411; 1171 UNTS 147.

Agricultural commodities agreement, with related letter and agreed minutes.

Signed at Accra April 14, 1980.

Entered into force April 14, 1980.

32 UST 909; TIAS 9738; 1222 UNTS 247.

Related agreements

March 31, 1981 (33 UST 1521; TIAS 10127).

August 19, 1982 (TIAS 10496; 1750 UNTS 521).

Agricultural commodities agreement.

Signed at Accra July 31, 1985.

Entered into force July 31, 1985.

NP

Agricultural commodities agreement.

Signed at Accra July 14, 1986.

Entered into force July 14, 1986.

NP

Agricultural commodities agreement.

Signed at Accra June 15, 1987.

Entered into force June 15, 1987.

NP

Related agreements

September 23, 1988 (NP).

March 28 and 31, 1989 (NP).

Agricultural commodities agreement.

Signed at Accra February 8, 1990.

Entered into force February 8, 1990.

NP

AVIATION

Arrangement between the United States and the United Kingdom relating to pilot licenses to operate civil aircraft.

Exchange of notes at Washington March 28 and April 5, 1935.

Entered into force May 5, 1935.

49 Stat. 3731; EAS 77; 12 Bevans 513; 162 LNTS 59.

Air transport agreement, with annexes.

Signed at Washington October 11, 2000.

Entered into force August 17, 2001.

TIAS

CONSULS

Consular convention and protocol of signature between the United States and the United Kingdom.[1]

Signed at Washington June 6, 1951.

Entered into force September 7, 1952.

3 UST 3426; TIAS 2494; 165 UNTS 121.

NOTE

1 Paragraph 1 of article 7 not in force for Ghana.

DEFENSE

Mutual defense assistance agreement between the United States and the United Kingdom.

Signed at Washington January 27, 1950; made applicable to the Gold Coast July 19, 1952.[1]

1 UST 126; TIAS 2017; 80 UNTS 261.

Agreement relating to the deposit by Ghana of ten percent of the value of grant military assistance furnished by the United States.

Exchange of notes at Accra April 13 and May 29, 1972.

Entered into force May 29, 1972; effective February 7, 1972.

23 UST 1310; TIAS 7410.

Agreement concerning the provision of training related to defense articles under the United States International Military Education and Training (IMET) Program.

Exchange of notes at Accra December 4, 1985 and February 28, 1986.

Entered into force February 28, 1986.

TIAS 11102.

Agreement concerning assistance under the Foreign Assistance Act of 1961, as amended, and the furnishing of defense articles, related training and other defense services from the United States to Ghana.

Exchange of notes at Accra March 2 and 7, 1995.

Entered into force March 7, 1995.

TIAS

Agreement regarding the provision of commodities, services and associated military education and training to Ghanaian forces participating in ECOMOG peacekeeping operations.

Exchange of notes at Accra October 28 and November 19, 1996.

Entered into force November 19, 1996.

TIAS 12817.

Agreement regarding the provision of commodities, services and related training to assist the Republic of Ghana's forces participating in the African Crisis Response Initiative.

Exchange of notes at Accra November 24, 1997 and January 8, 1998.

Entered into force January 8, 1998.

NP

Agreement regarding the status of U.S. military personnel and civilian employees of the U.S. Department of Defense temporarily present in Ghana in connection with the African Crisis Response Initiative and other activities.

Exchange of notes at Accra November 24, 1997 and February 24, 1998.

Entered into force February 24, 1998.

TIAS

Agreement regarding the status of U.S. military and civilian personnel of the U.S. Department of Defense temporarily present in Ghana in connection with humanitarian relief operations in Southern Africa.

Exchange of notes at Accra March 22 and April 7, 2000.

Entered into force April 7, 2000.

NP

Acquisition and cross-servicing agreement, with annexes.

Signed at Accra and Stuttgart September 3, 2004 and January 11, 2005.

Entered into force January 11, 2005.

TIAS

Technical arrangement for the establishment and use of U.S. military support capabilities in the Republic of Ghana, with addendum.

Signed at Accra and Stuttgart September 3, 2004 and May 19, 2005.

Entered into force May 19, 2005.

TIAS

NOTE

1 Only article IV is applicable to Ghana.

ECONOMIC AND TECHNICAL COOPERATION

Economic cooperation agreement between the United States and the United Kingdom.

Signed at London July 6, 1948; applicable to the Gold Coast July 6, 1948.

62 Stat. 2596; TIAS 1795; 12 Bevans 874; 22 UNTS 263.

Amendments

January 3, 1950 (1 UST 184; TIAS 2036; 86 UNTS 304).

May 25, 1951 (2 UST 1292; TIAS 2277; 99 UNTS 308).

February 25, 1953 (4 UST 1528; TIAS 2815; 172 UNTS 332).

General agreement for technical cooperation.

Signed at Accra June 3, 1957.

Entered into force June 3, 1957.

8 UST 793; TIAS 3838; 284 UNTS 63.

Agency for International Development

September 29, 1976 (29 UST 173; TIAS 8804).

May 24, 1977 (29 UST 342; TIAS 8820).

March 31, 1978 (30 UST 4534; TIAS 9476).

EDUCATION

Agreement for financing certain educational exchange programs.

Signed at Accra January 24, 1962.

Entered into force January 24, 1962.

TIAS 4942; 13 UST 87; 435 UNTS 23.

EMPLOYMENT

Agreement relating to the employment of dependents of official government employees.

Exchange of notes at Accra July 28, 1989 and April 17, 1991.

Entered into force April 17, 1991.

TIAS

ENVIRONMENTAL COOPERATION

Agreement for cooperation in the Global Learning and Observations to Benefit the Environment (GLOBE) Program, with appendices.

Signed at Accra March 20, 1998.

Entered into force March 20, 1998.

TIAS

EXTRADITION

Extradition treaty between the United States and the United Kingdom.

Signed at London December 22, 1931; applicable to the Gold Coast June 24, 1935.

47 Stat. 2122; TS 849; 12 Bevans 482; 163 LNTS 59.

FINANCE

Agreement relating to investment guaranties under section 413(b)(4) of the Mutual Security Act of 1954, as amended.

Exchange of notes at Accra September 30, 1958.

Entered into force September 30, 1958.

9 UST 1321; TIAS 4121; 336 UNTS 169.

Amendment

March 3, 1967 (18 UST 231; TIAS 6222; 688 UNTS 376).

Investment incentive agreement.

Signed at Washington February 26, 1999.

Entered into force November 24, 2004.

TIAS

Agreement regarding the consolidation and rescheduling of certain debts owed to, guaranteed by, or insured by the United States Government, with annexes.

Signed at Accra March 28, 2002.

Entered into force May 10, 2002.

NP

Agreement regarding the reduction of certain debts owed to, guaranteed by, or insured by the United States Government, with annexes.

Signed at Accra March 31, 2005.

Entered into force May 16, 2005.

NP

INTERNATIONAL CRIMINAL COURT

Agreement regarding the surrender of persons to the International Criminal Court.

Signed at Accra April 17, 2003.

Entered into force October 31, 2003.

TIAS

PEACE CORPS

Agreement relating to the establishment and operation of a Peace Corps program in Ghana.

Exchange of notes at Accra July 19, 1961.

Entered into force July 19, 1961.

12 UST 1066; TIAS 4811; 416 UNTS 167.

POSTAL MATTERS

Parcel post agreement and detailed regulations.

Signed at Accra June 3 and at Washington June 14, 1951.

Entered into force August 1, 1951.

2 UST 1859; TIAS 2322; 137 UNTS 81.

International express mail agreement, with detailed regulations.

Signed at Accra and Washington February 9 and March 1, 1990.

Entered into force April 16, 1990.

TIAS 11714.

PROPERTY

Convention between the United States and the United Kingdom relating to tenure and disposition of real and personal property.

Signed at Washington March 2, 1899; applicable to the Gold Coast July 6, 1901.

31 Stat. 1939; TS 146; 12 Bevans 246.

RELIEF SUPPLIES AND PACKAGES

Agreement providing for duty-free entry into Ghana and exemption from internal taxation of relief supplies and packages.

Exchange of notes at Accra April 9, 1959.

Entered into force April 9, 1959.

10 UST 720; TIAS 4203; 342 UNTS 21.

Amendment

April 8 and May 3, 1971 (22 UST 575; TIAS 7104; 791 UNTS 376).

SOCIAL SECURITY

Agreement concerning United States participation on a voluntary, limited basis in the Ghanaian social security system.

Exchange of notes at Accra May 16, September 10 and October 30, 1973.

Entered into force October 30, 1973.

24 UST 2202; TIAS 7734; 938 UNTS 353.

TAXATION

Agreement to exempt from income tax, on a reciprocal basis, certain income derived from the international operation of a ship or ships and aircraft.

Exchange of notes at Accra April 24 and November 12, 2001.

Entered into force November 12, 2001.

TIAS

TELECOMMUNICATION

Agreement relating to radio communications between amateur stations on behalf of third parties.

Exchange of notes at Accra October 13 and 27, 1977.

Entered into force November 26, 1977.

29 UST 2787; TIAS 8975.

TRADE-MARKS

Declaration by the United States and the United Kingdom relating to reciprocal protection to trade-marks.

Signed at London October 24, 1877.

Entered into force October 24, 1877.

20 Stat. 703; TS 138; 12 Bevans 198.

TREATY OBLIGATIONS

Agreement relating to treaty rights and obligations assumed by Ghana upon its independence.

Exchange of notes at Accra September 4 and December 21, 1957, and February 12, 1958.

Entered into force February 12, 1958.

13 UST 240; TIAS 4966; 442 UNTS 175.

GREECE

ATOMIC ENERGY

Agreement for cooperation on the uses of atomic energy for mutual defense purposes.

Exchange of notes at Athens May 6, 1959.

Entered into force August 11, 1959.

10 UST 1429; TIAS 4292; 357 UNTS 163.

Arrangement for the exchange of technical information and cooperation in nuclear safety matters, with addenda.

Signed at Vienna September 16, 2003.

Entered into force September 16, 2003.

TIAS

AVIATION

Air service agreement.

Exchange of notes at Athens March 11 and June 16 and 25, 1952.

Entered into force June 25, 1952.

3 UST 4856; TIAS 2658; 181 UNTS 53.

Air transport agreement, with annex.

Signed at Athens July 31, 1991.

Entered into force May 15, 1992.

TIAS

Extension

July 19 and 25, 2005.

June 22 and 28, 2006.

COMMERCE

Agreement regarding commercial relations.

Exchange of notes at Washington January 2 and 11, 1946.

Entered into force January 11, 1946.

60 Stat. 1483; TIAS 1505; 8 Bevans 396; 3 UNTS 203.

Treaty of friendship, commerce, and navigation.

Signed at Athens August 3, 1951.

Entered into force October 13, 1954.

5 UST 1829; TIAS 3057; 224 UNTS 279.

CONSULS

Convention concerning the rights and privileges of consuls, [1] and protocol of amendment signed March 5 and 18, 1903.

Signed at Athens November 19 and December 2, 1902.

Entered into force July 9, 1903.

33 Stat. 2122; TS 424; 8 Bevans 313.

NOTE

1 Notice of termination was given by the United States of articles XII and XIII, effective July 1, 1916, in accordance with the Seamen's Act (38 Stat. 1164). The notice was accepted by the Greek Government with the understanding that only such provisions of these articles as were in conflict with the Act should be abrogated, and all other provisions, especially those concerning the arrest, detention, and imprisonment of deserters from war vessels, should continue in force.

CUSTOMS

Agreement regarding reciprocal free entry privileges of consular officers and clerks.

Exchange of notes at Athens October 10, 1940.

Entered into force October 10, 1940.

8 Bevans 373.

Agreement relating to the importation of goods by American personnel in Greece under the military facilities agreement.

Exchange of notes at Athens June 27, 1955.

Entered into force June 27, 1955.

6 UST 3711; TIAS 3368.

Agreement regarding mutual assistance between customs administrations.

Signed at Athens July 31, 1991.

Entered into force January 17, 1993.

TIAS 12078.

DEFENSE

See also MUTUAL SECURITY

Agreement relating to the use of certain Greek Islands for training exercises by Marine units of the United States fleet in the Mediterranean.

Exchange of notes at Athens February 11 and 21, 1949.

Entered into force February 21, 1949.

63 Stat. 2683; TIAS 1972; 8 Bevans 455; 88 UNTS 29.

Agreement relating to the disposition of equipment and material furnished by the United States under the Act to Provide Assistance to Greece and Turkey, as amended, found surplus to the needs of the armed forces of Greece.

Exchange of notes at Athens December 21, 1951, and January 7, 1952.

Entered into force January 7, 1952.

3 UST 3997; TIAS 2537; 177 UNTS 249.

Amendment

April 17 and 18, 1961 (12 UST 496; TIAS 4741; 407 UNTS 238).

Agreement concerning the inspection and acceptance testing, security, and storage of military items produced by Greek industries under the offshore procurement program, with memoranda of understanding.

Exchange of notes at Athens December 17 and 24, 1952.

Entered into force December 24, 1952.

3 UST 5330; TIAS 2738; 185 UNTS 193.

Agreement concerning military facilities.[1]

Signed at Athens October 12, 1953.

Entered into force October 12, 1953.

4 UST 2189; TIAS 2868; 191 UNTS 319.

Agreement concerning the status of United States forces in Greece.

Signed at Athens September 7, 1956.

Entered into force September 7, 1956.

7 UST 2555; TIAS 3649; 278 UNTS 141.

Agreement relating to the deposit by Greece of ten percent of the value of grant military assistance and excess defense articles furnished by the United States.

Exchange of notes at Athens January 11 and 12, 1973.

Entered into force January 12, 1973; effective February 7, 1972.

24 UST 225; TIAS 7543; 938 UNTS 155.

Agreement relating to payment to the United States of net proceeds from the sale of defense articles and eligibility for United States military assistance and training under the military assistance program.

Exchange of notes at Athens August 31, 1976.

Entered into force August 31, 1976.

27 UST 3999; TIAS 8418; 1059 UNTS 137.

Amendment

December 27, 2005 and April 13, 2006.

Agreement concerning the grant of defense articles and services under the military assistance program.

Exchange of notes at Athens August 30, 1979.

Entered into force August 30, 1979.

30 UST 7267; TIAS 9583; 1182 UNTS 147.

Amendment

August 13 and 26, 1982 (34 UST 1841; TIAS 10464; 1751 UNTS 498).

Agreement on defense and economic cooperation, with annex.

Signed at Athens September 8, 1983.

Entered into force December 20, 1983.

35 UST 2641; TIAS 10814; 1590 UNTS 117.

Amendment

February 27, 1990.

General security of military information agreement, with annex on industrial security procedures.

Exchange of notes at Athens January 7, 1986.

Entered into force January 7, 1986.

TIAS 11980.

Defense industrial cooperation agreement, with annexes and exchange of letters.

Signed at Athens November 10, 1986.

Entered into force November 10, 1986.

TIAS 12320.

Amendment

March 17 and April 4, 1997.

Mutual defense cooperation agreement, with annex.

Signed at Athens July 8, 1990.

Entered into force November 6, 1990.

TIAS 12321.

Extension

April 25 and May 5, 2006.

Memorandum of understanding concerning the joint use of Hellenic Air Force bases by United States Air Force operational units, with annex.

Signed at Athens and Ramstein AB May 6 and June 8, 1992.

Entered into force June 8, 1992.

TIAS 12322.

Memorandum of agreement concerning the exchange of engineers and scientists, with annexes.

Signed at Athens October 12, 1992.

Entered into force October 12, 1992.

NP

Agreement concerning the transfer of U.S. Government-origin defense articles or related training or other defense services to the Government of the Hellenic Republic.

Exchange of notes at Athens January 22 and 27, 1993.

Entered into force January 27, 1993.

TIAS 12323.

Agreement concerning mutual logistic support, with annexes.

Signed at Papagos Camp (Greece) and Patch Barracks (Germany) June 28 and August 5, 1996.

Entered into force August 5, 1996.

TIAS

Amendment and extension

December 10, 1999 and January 31, 2000.

Comprehensive technical agreement.

Signed at Brussels June 13, 2001.

Entered into force April 8, 2003.

TIAS

Agreement regarding grants under the Foreign Assistance Act of 1961, as amended, and the furnishing of defense articles, related training and other defense services from the United States to Greece.

Exchange of notes at Athens August 9 and September 11, 2002.

Entered into force September 11, 2002.

TIAS

NOTE

1 Article III, Paragraph 1, abrogated by agreement of September 7, 1956 (TIAS 3649), except for reference to memorandum of understanding of Feb. 4, 1953 (TIAS 2775) which continues in effect.

ECONOMIC AND TECHNICAL COOPERATION

Agreement on aid to Greece, and exchanges of notes of May 26 and June 15 and 18, 1947.

Signed at Athens June 20, 1947.

Entered into force June 20, 1947.

61 Stat. 2907; TIAS 1625; 8 Bevans 403; 7 UNTS 267.

Economic cooperation agreement.

Signed at Athens July 2, 1948.

Entered into force July 3, 1948.

62 Stat. 2293; TIAS 1786; 8 Bevans 431; 23 UNTS 43.

Amendments

December 15 and 24, 1949 (64 Stat. B104; TIAS 2025; 8 Bevans 459; 79 UNTS 298).

March 6 and 30, 1951 (2 UST 843; TIAS 2238; 132 UNTS 384).

October 14, 1952 and December 2, 1953 (5 UST 2844; TIAS 3139; 225 UNTS 250).

April 19, 1963 (14 UST 397; TIAS 5331; 476 UNTS 250).

Agreement for cooperation in the economic, scientific, technological, and educational and cultural fields.

Signed at Athens April 22, 1980.

Entered into force April 22, 1980.

32 UST 1034; TIAS 9754; 1234 UNTS 327.

EDUCATION

Agreement for financing educational exchange programs.

Signed at Athens December 13, 1963.

Entered into force December 13, 1963.

14 UST 1770; TIAS 5486; 494 UNTS 55.

EMPLOYMENT

Agreement relating to employment of dependents of official government employees.

Exchange of notes at Athens January 30 and February 17, 1995.

Entered into force July 7, 1995.

TIAS 12605.

ENVIRONMENTAL COOPERATION

Agreement for cooperation in the Global Learning and Observations to Benefit the Environment (GLOBE) Program, with appendices.

Signed at Athens December 12, 1995.

Entered into force December 12, 1995.

TIAS 12709.

EXTRADITION

Treaty of extradition, and exchange of notes.

Signed at Athens May 6, 1931.

Entered into force November 1, 1932.

47 Stat. 2185; TS 855; 8 Bevans 353; 138 LNTS 293.

Protocol interpreting article I of the treaty of extradition signed at Athens May 6, 1931.

Signed at Athens September 2, 1937.

Entered into force September 2, 1937.

51 Stat. 357; EAS 114; 8 Bevans 366; 185 LNTS 408.

FINANCE

Debt funding agreement.

Signed at Washington May 10, 1929; operative January 1, 1928.

Treasury Department print; 8 Bevans 333.

Agreement modifying the debt funding agreement of May 10, 1929.

Signed at Washington May 24, 1932; operative July 1, 1931.

Treasury Department print; 8 Bevans 361.

Agreement relating to guaranties authorized by Section 111(b)(3) of the Economic Cooperation Act of 1948, as amended.

Exchange of notes at Washington April 21 and 23, 1952.

Entered into force April 29, 1952.

3 UST 4250; TIAS 2568; 177 UNTS 283.

Amendment

April 19, 1963 (14 UST 397; TIAS 5331; 476 UNTS 250).

Agreement concerning the uses of the drachmae deposited under the agricultural commodities agreement of January 7, 1960.

Exchange of notes at Athens April 20 and 29, 1961.

Entered into force April 29, 1961.

12 UST 499; TIAS 4742; 407 UNTS 290.

Agreement providing for the refunding of certain indebtedness due from Greece to the United States and amortization schedule.

Signed at Athens May 28, 1964.

Entered into force November 5, 1966.

17 UST 2331; TIAS 6178; 680 UNTS 143.

INDUSTRIAL COOPERATION

See under DEFENSE

JUDICIAL ASSISTANCE

Procedures for mutual assistance in the administration of justice in connection with the Lockheed Aircraft Corporation matter.

Signed at Washington May 20, 1976.

Entered into force May 20, 1976.

27 UST 2006; TIAS 8300; 1052 UNTS 349.

Treaty on mutual legal assistance in criminal matters.

Signed at Washington May 26, 1999.

Entered into force November 20, 2001.

TIAS

LEND-LEASE

Preliminary agreement regarding principles applying to mutual aid in the prosecution of the war against aggression.

Signed at Washington July 10, 1942.

Entered into force July 10, 1942.

56 Stat. 1559; EAS 260; 8 Bevans 381; 103 UNTS 289.

MAPPING

Basic exchange and cooperative agreement for topographic mapping, nautical and aeronautical charting, digital data, goedesy and geophysics and related materials.

Signed at Athens May 25, 1993.

Entered into force May 25, 1993.

NP

MUTUAL SECURITY

Agreement relating to the assurances required under the Mutual Security Act of 1951.

Exchange of notes at Athens December 21, 1951, and January 7, 1952.

Entered into force January 7, 1952.

3 UST 4569; TIAS 2608; 180 UNTS 171.

NARCOTIC DRUGS

Arrangement for the direct exchange of certain information regarding the traffic in narcotic drugs.

Exchange of notes at Athens February 7 and October 15, 1928.

Entered into force October 15, 1928.

8 Bevans 331.

PACIFIC SETTLEMENT OF DISPUTES

Treaty of arbitration.

Signed at Washington June 19, 1930.

Entered into force September 23, 1932.

47 Stat. 2161; TS 853; 8 Bevans 349; 136 LNTS 393.

Treaty of conciliation.
Signed at Washington June 19, 1930.
Entered into force September 23, 1932.
47 Stat. 2165; TS 854; 8 Bevans 351; 136 LNTS 399.

PATENTS

Agreement to facilitate interchange of patent rights and technical information for defense purposes.
Signed at Athens June 16, 1955.
Entered into force June 16, 1955.
6 UST 2173; TIAS 3286; 262 UNTS 137.

Agreement approving the procedures for the reciprocal filing of classified patent applications.
Exchange of notes at Athens April 26, 1960.
Entered into force April 26, 1960.
11 UST 1389; TIAS 4476; 372 UNTS 299.

POSTAL MATTERS

Agreement concerning the exchange of parcel post, and regulations of execution.
Signed at Athens July 14 and at Washington August 1, 1933; operative June 1, 1933.
48 Stat. 1594; Post Office Department print.

International express mail agreement, with detailed regulations.
Signed at Athens and Washington June 5 and 21, 1985.
Entered into force July 1, 1985.
TIAS 11152.

Memorandum of understanding concerning the operation of the INTELPOST field trial, with details of implementation.
Signed at Athens and Washington July 25 and August 15, 1985.
Entered into force August 19, 1985.
TIAS 11247.

PUBLICATIONS

Agreement relating to the exchange of official publications.
Exchange of notes at Athens September 26 and October 24, 1950.
Entered into force October 24, 1950.
2 UST 473; TIAS 2193; 133 UNTS 41.

RELIEF SUPPLIES AND PACKAGES

Agreement relating to duty-free entry and free inland transportation of relief supplies and packages.
Signed at Athens February 9, 1949.
Entered into force February 9, 1949.
63 Stat. 2359; TIAS 1898; 8 Bevans 450; 79 UNTS 95.

Amendments
December 19, 1951 and May 7, 1952 (3 UST 4282; TIAS 2574; 179 UNTS 216).
July 18 and December 22, 1952 (3 UST 5327; TIAS 2737; 185 UNTS 400).

SHIPPING

Agreement relating to jurisdiction over vessels utilizing the Louisiana Offshore Oil Port.
Exchange of notes at Athens May 7 and 12, 1982.
Entered into force May 12, 1982.
34 UST 1747; TIAS 10453; 1750 UNTS 417.

SMUGGLING

Convention for prevention of smuggling of alcoholic beverages.
Signed at Washington April 25, 1928.
Entered into force February 18, 1929.
45 Stat. 2736; TS 772; 8 Bevans 327; 91 LNTS 231.

SOCIAL SECURITY

Agreement on social security, with administrative arrangement.
Signed at Athens June 22, 1993.
Entered into force September 1, 1994.
TIAS

TAXATION

Convention and protocol for the avoidance of double taxation and the prevention of fiscal evasion with respect to taxes on the estates of deceased persons.[1]
Signed at Athens February 20, 1950; protocol signed at Athens July 18, 1953.
Entered into force December 30, 1953.
5 UST 12; TIAS 2901; 196 UNTS 269.

Protocol modifying and supplementing the convention of February 20, 1950, for the avoidance of double taxation and the prevention of fiscal evasion with respect to taxes on the estates of deceased persons.
Signed at Athens February 12, 1964.
Entered into force October 27, 1967.
18 UST 2853; TIAS 6375; 632 UNTS 315.

Convention and protocol for the avoidance of double taxation and prevention of fiscal evasion with respect to taxes on income.[2]
Signed at Athens February 20, 1950; protocol signed at Athens April 20, 1953.
Entered into force December 30, 1953.
5 UST 47; TIAS 2902; 196 UNTS 291.

Agreement regarding privileges, immunities, and exemptions from taxes or other levies and charges accorded by Greece in implementation of the common defense program and any and all foreign aid programs of the United States.
Exchange of notes at Athens February 4, 1953.
Entered into force February 4, 1953.
4 UST 166; TIAS 2775; 189 UNTS 3.

Agreement concerning relief from double taxation on earnings derived from the operation of ships and aircraft.
Exchange of notes at Washington June 10, 1988.
Entered into force June 10, 1988.
TIAS 11585; 2191 UNTS 249.

NOTES
1 For understanding regarding certain errors in the English text, see exchange of notes of August 3 and 19, 1954 (5 UST 1543; TIAS 3032; 222 UNTS 423).
2 For understanding regarding certain errors in the Greek text, see exchange of notes of November 29 and December 19, 1961 (13 UST 151; TIAS 4951; 435 UNTS 334).

TELECOMMUNICATION

Agreement concerning the transfer of community radios to the Government of Greece, with three schedules attached.
Signed at Athens August 18, 1954.
Entered into force August 18, 1954.
5 UST 1725; TIAS 3050; 234 UNTS 161.

Agreement relating to the reciprocal granting of authorizations to permit licensed amateur radio operators of either country to operate their stations in the other country.
Exchanges of notes at Athens June 20 and July 5, 1978.
Entered into force July 5, 1978.
30 UST 1648; TIAS 9272; 1153 UNTS 81.

Agreement for the operation of [Voice of America] re-broadcasting stations in Greece, with annexes.
Signed at Washington May 20, 1996.
Entered into force March 17, 1997.
TIAS 12757.

TERMINATION

Agreement concerning termination of certain bilateral agreements.
Exchange of notes at Athens January 17 and February 22, 1995.
Entered into force February 22, 1995.
TIAS 12606.

TRADE

See also COMMERCE

Protocol relating to compensatory tariff concessions made by Greece to the United States under the general agreement on tariffs and trade with exchange of letters.

Signed at Athens May 31, 1971.

Entered into force May 31, 1971.

22 UST 787; TIAS 7138; 797 UNTS 241.

Agreement providing for consultations should cotton textile or cotton textile product exports from Greece cause market disruption in the United States.

Exchange of notes at Athens December 29, 1975 and January 5, 1976.

Entered into force January 5, 1976.

27 UST 1632; TIAS 8273.

VISAS

Arrangement for the reciprocal reduction of nonimmigrant passport visa fees.

Exchange of notes at Athens January 7 and 29, 1949.

Entered into force January 29, 1949.

63 Stat. 2905; TIAS 2144; 8 Bevans 447; 88 UNTS 35.

Agreement concerning the reciprocal waiver of visas for non-immigrants.

Exchange of notes at Athens December 28, 1999 and January 24, 2000.

Entered into force January 24, 2000.

TIAS

GRENADA

On February 7, 1974 Grenada became an independent state. In a note dated August 19, 1974 to the Secretary-General of the United Nations, the Prime Minister made a statement reading in part as follows:

"I have the honour to inform you that the Government of Grenada, having attained Independence on the 7th February, 1974, and being conscious of the desirability of continuing and maintaining existing International Agreements which applied before Independence and being willing to accept its obligations under International Law to honour its treaty commitments, acknowledges that the many treaty rights and obligations entered into by the Government of the United Kingdom in respect of the Government of Grenada, were succeeded to by the Government of Grenada upon the attainment of Independence and in accordance with customary International Law and Practice.

2. It is desirous, therefore, that it be accepted that each treaty has been legally succeeded to by the Government of Grenada and that actions relating to all treaties be based on this succession until a decision is otherwise taken and due notification communicated to the United Nations and to the states signatories thereto in respect of any such particular treaty.

3. The Government of Grenada reserves the right to terminate the operation of any such treaty succeeded to if it is desirable to do so. In such circumstances due notice will be given of any such termination and in the terms thereof."

AVIATION

Agreement between the United States and the United Kingdom relating to air services.

Signed at Bermuda February 11, 1946.

Entered into force February 11, 1946.

60 Stat. 1499; TIAS 1507; 3 UNTS 253.

Amendment

May 27, 1966 (17 UST 683; TIAS 6019; 573 UNTS 274).

Agreement modifying the agreement of February 11, 1946, as amended, as applied to air services between the United States and Grenada.

Exchange of notes at St. George's March 19 and May 11, 1987.

Entered into force May 11, 1987.

TIAS 11279.

CONSULS

Consular convention between the United States and the United Kingdom.

Signed at Washington June 6, 1951.

Entered into force September 7, 1972.

3 UST 3426; TIAS 2494; 165 UNTS 121.

DEFENSE

Agreement concerning the status of United States forces in Grenada.

Exchange of notes at St. George's March 12 and 13, 1984.

Entered into force March 13, 1984.

TIAS

Agreement concerning the provision of training related to defense articles under the United States International Military Education and Training (IMET) Program.

Exchange of notes at St. George's May 18 and 24, 1984.

Entered into force May 24, 1984.

NP

Agreement concerning the status of United States Armed Forces personnel in Grenada.

Exchange of notes at St. George's December 7, 1992 and October 11, 1993.

Entered into force October 11, 1993.

NP

ECONOMIC AND TECHNICAL COOPERATION

General agreement for economic, technical and related assistance.

Signed at Grenada May 7, 1984.

Entered into force May 7, 1984.

TIAS 11132; 2120 UNTS 123.

EMPLOYMENT

Agreement relating to employment of dependents of official government employees, with addendum.

Exchange of notes at St. George's September 14 and 15, 1987.

Entered into force September 15, 1987.

TIAS 11539.

EXTRADITION

Extradition treaty.

Done at St. George's May 30, 1996.

Entered into force September 14, 1999.

TIAS

FINANCE

Agreement relating to investment guaranties.

Signed at St. Georges June 27, 1968.

Entered into force June 27, 1968.

19 UST 5211; TIAS 6516; 730 UNTS 217.

INTERNATIONAL CRIMINAL COURT

Agreement regarding the surrender of persons to the International Criminal Court.

Exchange of notes at Washington and New York March 11, 2004.

Entered into force March 11, 2004.

TIAS

INVESTMENT

Treaty concerning the reciprocal encouragement and protection of investment.

Signed at Washington May 2, 1986.

Entered into force March 3, 1989.

TIAS

JUDICIAL ASSISTANCE

Treaty on mutual legal assistance in criminal matters, with forms.

Done at St. George's May 30, 1996.

Entered into force September 14, 1999.

TIAS

NARCOTIC DRUGS

Agreement concerning maritime counter-drug operations.

Signed at St. George's May 16, 1995.

Entered into force May 16, 1995.

TIAS 12648.

Agreement regarding the provision of articles, services and associated military education and training by the United States Government for anti-narcotics purposes.

Exchange of notes at St. George's December 23, 1996 and March 14, 1997.

Entered into force March 14, 1997.

TIAS

Agreement regarding the provision of articles, services and associated training by the Government of the United States for anti-narcotics purposes.

Exchange of notes at St. George's November 18 and December 3, 1998.

Entered into force December 3, 1998.

TIAS

PEACE CORPS

Agreement relating to the establishment of a Peace Corps program in Grenada.

Exchange of notes at Bridgetown and Grenada December 19, 1966 and December 16, 1967.

Entered into force December 16, 1967.

18 UST 3073; TIAS 6398; 701 UNTS 277.

POSTAL MATTERS

Money order agreement.

Signed at Washington July 29 and at Grenada August 29, 1904; operative October 1, 1904.

NP

Agreement for the direct exchange of parcels by parcel post.

Signed at Grenada May 20 and at Washington June 21, 1935; operative July 1, 1935.

49 Stat. 3229; Post Office Department print; 162 LNTS 157.

International express mail agreement.

Signed at St. George's and Washington January 4 and April 4, 1995.

Entered into force May 1, 1995.

NP

PROPERTY

Convention between the United States and the United Kingdom relating to tenure and disposition of real and personal property.

Signed at Washington March 2, 1899; applicable to Grenada February 9, 1901.

31 Stat. 1939; TS 146; 12 Bevans 246.

Supplementary convention relating to the tenure and disposition of real and personal property.

Signed at Washington May 27, 1936.

Entered into force March 10, 1941.

55 Stat. 1101; TS 964; 203 LNTS 367.

SCIENTIFIC COOPERATION

Memorandum of understanding concerning scientific and technical cooperation in earth sciences, with annexes.

Signed at Reston and St. George's December 9, 2005.

Entered into force December 9, 2005.

TIAS

TAXATION

Agreement for the exchange of information with respect to taxes.

Signed at Washington December 18, 1986.

Entered into force July 13, 1987.

TIAS 11410; 2191 UNTS 43.

TELECOMMUNICATION

Agreement relating to the reciprocal granting of authorizations to permit licensed amateur radio operators of either country to operate their stations in the other country.

Exchange of notes at London November 26, 1965; applicable to Grenada December 11, 1979.

16 UST 2047; TIAS 5941; 561 UNTS 193.

Agreement between the United States and the United Kingdom extending to certain territories the application of the agreement of November 26, 1965 relating to the reciprocal granting of authorizations to permit licensed amateur radio operators of either country to operate their stations in the other country.

Exchange of notes at London December 11, 1969.

Entered into force December 11, 1969.

20 UST 4089; TIAS 6800; 732 UNTS 334.

Arrangement relating to radio communications between amateur stations on behalf of third parties.

Exchange of notes at St. George's December 5 and 8, 1983.

Entered into force December 8, 1983.

35 UST 3275; TIAS 10855; 2015 UNTS 17.

Agreement concerning establishment of a radio relay station of the United States Information Agency (VOA) on the Island of Grenada.

Signed at St. George's September 29, 1987.

Entered into force March 23, 1988.

TIAS 12394.

TRADE-MARKS

Declaration by the United States and the United Kingdom affording reciprocal protection to trade-marks.

Signed at London October 24, 1877.

Entered into force October 24, 1877.

20 Stat. 703; TS 138; 12 Bevans 198.

GUATEMALA

AGRICULTURAL COMMODITIES

Agricultural commodities agreement, with memorandum of understanding.

Signed at Guatemala August 1, 1984.

Entered into force September 28, 1984.

TIAS 11043; 2022 UNTS 11.

Agricultural commodities agreement, with memorandum of understanding.

Signed at Guatemala June 6, 1985.

Entered into force August 7, 1985.

NP

Amendments

August 9, 1985 (NP).

July 2, 1986 (NP).

August 29, 1986 (NP).

Agricultural commodities agreement.

Signed at Guatemala May 26, 1987.

Entered into force November 5, 1987.

NP

Amendment

September 22, 1987 (NP).

Agricultural commodities agreement.

Signed at Guatemala June 16, 1988.

Entered into force June 26, 1989.

NP

Agricultural commodities agreement.

Signed at Guatemala October 28, 1988.

Entered into force June 27, 1989.

NP

AGRICULTURE

Memorandum of understanding relating to cooperative efforts to protect crops from pest damage and diseases.

Signed at Guatemala February 21, 1977.

Entered into force February 21, 1977.

29 UST 228; TIAS 8807.

Agreement relating to a cooperative program for the prevention of foot-and-mouth disease, rinderpest, and other exotic diseases in Guatemala.

Signed at Guatemala March 3, 1977.

Entered into force March 3, 1977.

29 UST 242; TIAS 8808.

Cooperative agreement to assist the Government of Guatemala in execution of an eradication program of the Mediterranean fruit fly (MEDFLY).

Signed at Guatemala October 22, 1981.

Entered into force October 22, 1981.

33 UST 4123; TIAS 10288; 1549 UNTS 361.

Extension

September 17, 1985 (TIAS 11930).

AMITY

Treaty of peace, amity, commerce, and navigation.[1]

Signed at Guatemala March 3, 1849.

Entered into force May 13, 1852.

10 Stat. 875; TS 149; 8 Bevans 461.

NOTE

1 Articles relating to commerce and navigation terminated November 4, 1874.

ATOMIC ENERGY

Agreement providing for a grant to assist in the acquisition of certain nuclear research and training equipment and materials.

Exchange of notes at Guatemala April 7 and 23, 1960.

Entered into force April 23, 1960.

11 UST 1449; TIAS 4485.

AVIATION

Military air transit agreement.

Exchange of notes at Guatemala December 20, 1949.

Entered into force December 20, 1949.

64 Stat. B122; TIAS 2042; 8 Bevans 610; 70 UNTS 71.

Memorandum of cooperation for mutual cooperation in the promotion and development of civil aviation.

Signed at Washington and Guatemala May 26 and June 11, 1999.

Entered into force June 11, 1999.

TIAS

Air transport agreement, with annexes.

Signed at San Jose May 8, 1997.

Entered into force September 3, 2001.

TIAS

COMMERCE

See also AMITY

Convention for the development of commerce and to increase the exchange of commodities by facilitating the work of traveling salesmen.

Signed at Washington December 3, 1918.

Entered into force August 25, 1919.

41 Stat. 1669; TS 642; 8 Bevans 498.

CULTURAL PROPERTY

Agreement for the recovery and return of stolen archaeological, historical and cultural properties.

Signed at Washington May 21, 1984.

Entered into force August 22, 1984.

TIAS 11077; 2039 UNTS 241.

DEFENSE

Agreement providing for the transfer of equipment and material to the Government of Guatemala subject to certain understandings.

Exchange of notes at Guatemala July 27 and 30, 1954.

Entered into force July 30, 1954.

5 UST 1926; TIAS 3059; 234 UNTS 235.

Military assistance agreement.

Signed at Guatemala June 18, 1955.

Entered into force June 18, 1955.

6 UST 2107; TIAS 3283; 262 UNTS 105.

Agreement relating to the disposition of equipment and materials no longer required in furtherance of the mutual defense assistance program.

Exchange of notes at Guatemala December 16, 1957.

Entered into force December 16, 1957.

8 UST 2463; TIAS 3966; 307 UNTS 306.

Agreement relating to the furnishing of defense articles and services to Guatemala for the purpose of contributing to its internal security.

Exchange of notes at Guatemala May 25 and August 2, 1962.

Entered into force August 2, 1962.

13 UST 2128; TIAS 5173; 461 UNTS 199.

Agreement concerning payment to the United States of net proceeds from the sale of defense articles furnished under the military assistance program.

Exchange of notes at Guatemala September 20 and 27, 1974.

Entered into force September 27, 1974; effective July 1, 1974.

25 UST 2489; TIAS 7932.

Amendment

January 20 and April 20, 2005.

Agreement concerning security assistance matters and the provision of articles, services and associated military education and training by the United States Government for anti-narcotics purposes.

Exchange of notes at Guatemala January 12 and February 1, 1999.

Entered into force February 1, 1999.

TIAS

Agreement regarding the status of United States personnel who may be temporarily present in Guatemala.

Exchange of notes at Guatemala September 8 and 19, 2005.

Entered into force November 2, 2005.

TIAS

Agreement regarding the furnishing of articles and services from the United States of America to the Government of the Republic of Guatemala pursuant to the global peacekeeping operations initiative.

Exchange of notes at Guatemala December 1, 2005 and January 3, 2006.

Entered into force March 14, 2006.

TIAS

ECONOMIC AND TECHNICAL COOPERATION

General agreement for technical cooperation.

Signed at Guatemala September 1, 1954.

Entered into force September 1, 1954.

5 UST 2010; TIAS 3068; 199 UNTS 51.

Development assistance agreement.

Signed at Washington December 13, 1954.

Entered into force December 13, 1954.

5 UST 2972; TIAS 3155; 237 UNTS 169.

Agency for International Development

November 3, 1975 (27 UST 4267; TIAS 8450).

April 8, 1976 (28 UST 1581; TIAS 8521).

September 20, 1976 (28 UST 7213; TIAS 8713).

September 14, 1977 (29 UST 3337; TIAS 9015; 1123 UNTS 191).

May 18, 1978 (30 UST 2699; TIAS 9360; 1231 UNTS 329).

April 13, 1987 (NP).

September 24, 1987 (NP).

June 27, 1988 (NP).

July 7, 1989 (NP).

January 13, 1997 (NP).

July 24, 1997 (NP).

September 16, 1997 (NP).

April 21, 1998 (NP).

June 3, 1998 (NP).

EMPLOYMENT

Agreement relating to the employment of dependents of official government employees, with agreement and addendum.

Exchange of notes at Washington March 22 and 23, 1990.

Entered into force March 23, 1990.

TIAS

ENVIRONMENTAL COOPERATION

Agreement for cooperation in the Global Learning and Observations to Benefit the Environment (GLOBE) Program, with appendices.

Signed at Guatemala December 5, 1997.

Entered into force December 5, 1997.

TIAS

EXTRADITION

Treaty for the mutual extradition of fugitives from justice.

Signed at Washington February 27, 1903.

Entered into force August 15, 1903.

33 Stat. 2147; TS 425; 8 Bevans 482.

Supplementary extradition convention.

Signed at Guatemala February 20, 1940.

Entered into force March 13, 1941.

55 Stat. 1097; TS 963; 8 Bevans 528.

FINANCE

Agreement relating to investment guaranties.[1]

Exchange of notes at Guatemala August 9, 1960.

Entered into force August 29, 1962.

13 UST 2008; TIAS 5158; 461 UNTS 15.

NOTE

1 For corrections in the Spanish text, see exchange of notes of August 23 and 27, 1962 (13 UST 2008; TIAS 5158; 461 UNTS 15).

Agreement regarding a debt-for-nature swap to prepay and cancel certain debt owed.

Signed at Guatemala September 8, 2006.

Entered into force September 8, 2006.

TIAS

HIGHWAYS

Agreement relating to the construction of the inter-American highway.

Exchange of notes at Guatemala May 19, 1943.

Entered into force May 19, 1943.

57 Stat. 1111; EAS 345; 8 Bevans 545; 28 UNTS 377.

Amendments

May 18, 1948 (62 Stat. 3923; TIAS 2001; 8 Bevans 596; 67 UNTS 161).

July 28 and August 28, 1954 (5 UST 2244; TIAS 3084; 237 UNTS 294).

Agreement providing for cooperation in the construction of the inter-American Highway in Guatemala.

Exchange of notes at Guatemala September 25 and October 3, 1963.

Entered into force October 3, 1963.

14 UST 1591; TIAS 5463; 493 UNTS 45.

MAPPING

Agreement governing cooperation in mapping, charting and geodesy.

Signed at Washington and Guatemala February 14 and 27, 1986.

Entered into force February 27, 1986.

TIAS 11211.

Basic exchange and cooperative agreement for topographic mapping, nautical and aeronautical charting and information, geodesy and geophysics, digital data and related mapping, charting and geodesy materials, with glossary.

Signed at Guatemala and Fairfax June 7 and July 2, 1996.

Entered into force July 2, 1996.

NP

MISSIONS, MILITARY

Agreement relating to the status of the Army and Air Force missions to Guatemala.

Exchange of notes at Guatemala April 29 and May 4, 1965.

Entered into force May 4, 1965.

16 UST 742; TIAS 5802; 545 UNTS 163.

NARCOTIC DRUGS

Agreement concerning cooperation to suppress illicit traffic in narcotic drugs and psychotropic substances by sea and air.

Signed at Guatemala June 19, 2003.

Entered into force October 10, 2003.

TIAS

Agreement regarding the Cooperating Nation Information Exchange System.

Exchange of notes at Guatemala November 30, 2004.

Entered into force November 30, 2004.

TIAS

PATENTS

Convention for the reciprocal protection of patents.

Signed at Guatemala November 10, 1906.

Entered into force July 9, 1907.

35 Stat. 1878; TS 463; 8 Bevans 489.

PEACE CORPS

Agreement relating to the establishment of a Peace Corps program in Guatemala.

Exchange of notes at Guatemala City December 28 and 29, 1962.

Entered into force December 29, 1962.

14 UST 280; TIAS 5307; 474 UNTS 31.

POSTAL MATTERS

Parcel post agreement.

Signed at Guatemala October 25, and at Washington November 30, 1945; operative August 1, 1945.

59 Stat. 1827; EAS 499; 139 UNTS 45.

International express mail agreement, with detailed regulations.

Signed at Guatemala and Washington November 7 and December 19, 1989.

Entered into force February 15, 1990.

TIAS 11717.

PROPERTY

Convention relating to tenure and disposition of real and personal property.

Signed at Guatemala August 27, 1901.

Entered into force September 26, 1902.

32 Stat. 1944; TS 412; 8 Bevans 480.

PUBLICATIONS

Agreement relating to the exchange of official publications.

Exchange of notes at Guatemala March 23 and April 13, 1944.

Entered into force March 23, 1944.

58 Stat. 1362; EAS 412; 8 Bevans 555; 106 UNTS 213.

SCIENTIFIC COOPERATION

Memorandum of cooperation on research collaboration in the area of human infectious diseases, with annex.

Signed at Barcenas May 13, 1999.

Entered into force September 7, 2000.

TIAS

TELECOMMUNICATION

Agreement relating to the reciprocal granting of authorizations to permit licensed amateur radio operators of either country to operate their stations in the other country.

Exchange of notes at Guatemala November 30 and December 11, 1967.

Entered into force October 2, 1969.

20 UST 2883; TIAS 6766; 726 UNTS 147.

Arrangement relating to radio communications between amateur stations on behalf of third parties.

Exchange of notes at Guatemala October 21 and November 19, 1971.

Entered into force May 26, 1973.

24 UST 1120; TIAS 7636.

TRADE

Agreement on trade in textile and apparel goods.

Exchange of letters at Guatemala and Washington June 23, 2006.

Entered into force June 23, 2006.

NP

TRADE-MARKS

Convention for the reciprocal protection of trade-marks and trade labels.

Signed at Guatemala April 15, 1901.

Entered into force April 7, 1902.

32 Stat. 1866; TS 404; 8 Bevans 478.

VISAS

Agreement providing reciprocally for gratis nonimmigrant visas valid for multiple entries.

Exchange of notes at Guatemala May 30, 1956.

Entered into force May 30, 1956.

7 UST 1075; TIAS 3589; 275 UNTS 271.

GUINEA

AGRICULTURAL COMMODITIES

Agricultural commodities agreement, with exchanges of notes.

Signed at Conakry February 2, 1962.

Entered into force February 2, 1962.

13 UST 131; TIAS 4948; 435 UNTS 35.

Amendments

May 3, 1962 (13 UST 1114; TIAS 5057; 451 UNTS 341).

June 29, 1962 (13 UST 1800; TIAS 5126; 458 UNTS 364).

Agricultural commodities agreement with exchange of notes.

Signed at Conakry May 22, 1963.

Entered into force May 22, 1963.

14 UST 1003; TIAS 5394; 487 UNTS 251.

Amendments

November 2, 1963 (14 UST 1784; TIAS 5487; 494 UNTS 362).

July 1 and 11, 1964 (15 UST 2169; TIAS 5700; 531 UNTS 408).

September 18, 1965 (16 UST 1671; TIAS 5890; 574 UNTS 256).

Agricultural commodities agreement with exchange of notes.

Signed at Conakry June 13, 1964.

Entered into force June 13, 1964.

15 UST 1926; TIAS 5668; 531 UNTS 263.

Amendments

October 7, 1964 (15 UST 2172; TIAS 5701; 531 UNTS 280).

December 21, 1964 (15 UST 2238; TIAS 5712; 531 UNTS 284).

Agricultural commodities agreement, with exchange of notes.

Signed at Conakry February 4, 1966.

Entered into force February 4, 1966.

17 UST 109; TIAS 5966; 579 UNTS 213.

Agricultural commodities agreement, with annex.

Signed at Conakry October 18, 1967.

Entered into force October 18, 1967.

18 UST 2887; TIAS 6381; 701 UNTS 65.

Related agreements

February 3, 1969 (20 UST 380; TIAS 6640; 714 UNTS 157).

October 23 and 28, 1969 (20 UST 3045; TIAS 6782; 727 UNTS 436).

August 8, 1970 (21 UST 2208; TIAS 6971; 764 UNTS 211).

March 12, 1971 (22 UST 1035; TIAS 7147; 796 UNTS 317).

June 17, 1971 (22 UST 1574; TIAS 7182; 806 UNTS 347).

May 15 and 23, 1972 (23 UST 1296; TIAS 7406).

March 15, 1973 (25 UST 2729; TIAS 7942; 1279 UNTS 271).

March 30 and April 11, 1973 (25 UST 2747; TIAS 7942; 1279 UNTS 283).

May 8, 1974 (25 UST 917; TIAS 7835).

May 24, 1974 (25 UST 924; TIAS 7835).

June 13 and 14, 1974 (25 UST 1277; TIAS 7860).

Agricultural commodities agreement.

Signed at Conakry May 8, 1975.

Entered into force May 8, 1975.

27 UST 1474; TIAS 8258; 1049 UNTS 87.

Agricultural commodities agreement.

Signed at Conakry April 21, 1976.

Entered into force April 21, 1976.

27 UST 3467; TIAS 8378.

Related agreements

September 22, 1976 (28 UST 3269; TIAS 8585; 1087 UNTS 27).

June 13 and 15, 1977 (29 UST 1028; TIAS 8864; 1115 UNTS 363).

December 10, 1977 (TIAS 10726; 2006 UNTS 289).

May 29, 1979 (34 UST 529; TIAS 10375).

May 22, 1980 (32 UST 1375; TIAS 9779; 1274 UNTS 51).

May 9, 1981 (TIAS 10726; 2006 UNTS 291).

June 7, 1982 (TIAS 10726; 2006 UNTS 293).

June 4, 1983 (TIAS 10726; 2006 UNTS 295).

June 11, 1984 (TIAS 11039).

Agricultural commodities agreement.

Signed at Conakry June 14, 1985.

Entered into force June 14, 1985.

NP

Agricultural commodities agreement.

Signed at Conakry January 3, 1986.

Entered into force January 3, 1986.

NP

Related agreement

May 18, 1987 (NP).

Agricultural commodities agreement under food for progress, with attachments.

Signed at Conakry September 15, 1986.

Entered into force September 15, 1986.

NP

CULTURAL RELATIONS

Cultural relations agreement.

Exchange of notes at Washington October 28, 1959.

Entered into force October 28, 1959.

10 UST 1829; TIAS 4342; 358 UNTS 169.

DEFENSE

Agreement relating to military assistance.

Exchange of notes at Conakry June 29, 1965.

Entered into force June 29, 1965.

16 UST 1073; TIAS 5848; 549 UNTS 139.

Agreement concerning the provision of training related to defense articles under the United States International Military Education and Training (IMET) Program.

Exchange of notes at Conakry March 29, 1983 and February 13, 1984.

Entered into force February 13, 1984.

35 UST 4412; TIAS 10944.

Agreement regarding grants under the Foreign Assistance Act of 1961, as amended, and the furnishing of defense articles, related training, and other defense services from the United States of America to the Government of the Republic of Guinea.

Exchange of notes at Conakry July 13 and December 22, 2000.

Entered into force December 22, 2000.

NP

Agreement concerning the status of United States military and civilian personnel of the United States Department of Defense who may be temporarily present in the Republic of Guinea in connection with training exercises, humanitarian relief operations, and other activities as may be agreed upon by the two governments.

Exchange of notes at Conakry September 4, 2001 and May 10, 2002.

Entered into force May 10, 2002.

NP

ECONOMIC AND TECHNICAL COOPERATION

Agreement providing for the furnishing of economic, technical and related assistance.

Exchange of notes at Conakry September 30, 1960.

Entered into force September 30, 1960.

11 UST 2258; TIAS 4603; 394 UNTS 103.

Agency for International Development

September 27, 1977 (29 UST 5043; TIAS 9091).

March 31, 1978 (29 UST 5098; TIAS 9091).

April 14 and June 5, 1978 (29 UST 5756; TIAS 9149).

ENVIRONMENTAL COOPERATION

Agreement for cooperation in the Global Learning and Observations to Benefit the Environment (GLOBE) Program, with Appendices.

Signed at Conakry May 14, 1998.

Entered into force May 14, 1998.

TIAS

FINANCE

Agreement relating to investment guaranties.

Exchange of notes at Washington May 9, 1962.

Entered into force May 9, 1962.

13 UST 1091; TIAS 5052; 451 UNTS 197.

Agreement regarding the consolidation and rescheduling of certain debts owed to or guaranteed by the United States Government and its agencies, with annexes.

Signed at Conakry February 27, 1987.

Entered into force April 8, 1987.

NP

Agreement regarding the consolidation and rescheduling of certain debts owed to, guaranteed by or insured by the United States Government and its agencies, with annexes.

Signed at Conakry November 22, 1989.

Entered into force January 22, 1990.

NP

Agreement regarding the consolidation and rescheduling or refinancing of certain debts owed to, guaranteed by or insured by the United States Government and its agencies, with annexes.

Signed at Conakry June 24, 1993.

Entered into force September 13, 1993.

NP

Agreement regarding the consolidation, reduction and rescheduling of certain debts owed to, guaranteed by, or insured by the United States Government and its agencies.

Signed at Conakry November 18, 1996.

Entered into force April 9, 1997.

NP

Agreement regarding the consolidation, reduction and rescheduling of certain debts owed to, guaranteed by, or insured by the United States Government and its agencies, with annexes.

Signed at Conakry October 29, 1997.

Entered into force December 17, 1997.

NP

Agreement regarding the consolidation and reduction of certain debts owed to, guaranteed by, or insured by the United States Government and its agencies, with annexes.

Signed at Conakry April 8, 2002.

Entered into force May 22, 2002.

NP

INFORMATIONAL MEDIA GUARANTIES

Agreement relating to an informational media guaranty program in Guinea.

Exchange of notes at Conakry October 31 and November 3, 1962.

Entered into force November 3, 1962.

13 UST 2508; TIAS 5217; 459 UNTS 259.

INTERNATIONAL CRIMINAL COURT

Agreement regarding the surrender of persons to the International Criminal Court.

Signed at Conakry August 23, 2003.

Entered into force March 25, 2004.

TIAS

PEACE CORPS

Agreement relating to the establishment of a Peace Corps program in Guinea.

Exchange of notes at Conakry December 11 and 14, 1962.

Entered into force December 14, 1962.

13 UST 2729; TIAS 5246; 462 UNTS 247.

POSTAL MATTERS

International express mail agreement, with detailed regulations.

Signed at Conakry and Washington December 31, 1987 and February 2, 1988.

Entered into force March 15, 1988.

TIAS 11562.

Postal money order agreement.

Signed at Washington February 23, 1999.

Entered into force February 23, 1999.

NP

TELECOMMUNICATION

Agreement relating to radio communication facilities at or near Embassy sites for transmission of official messages.

Exchange of notes at Conakry February 19 and April 23, 1963.

Entered into force April 23, 1963.

14 UST 847; TIAS 5365; 487 UNTS 291.

GUINEA-BISSAU

DEFENSE

Agreement concerning the provision of training related to defense articles under the United States International Military Education and Training (IMET) Program.

Exchange of notes at Bissau September 10 and October 16, 1986.

Entered into force October 16, 1986.

TIAS 11378.

ECONOMIC AND TECHNICAL COOPERATION

Agency for International Development

November 10, 1977 (29 UST 5289; TIAS 9107).

January 8, 1978 (29 UST 5768; TIAS 9151).

EMPLOYMENT

Agreement relating to the employment of dependents of official government employees.

Exchange of notes at Bissau July 23, 1997 and February 16, 1998.

Entered into force February 16, 1998.

TIAS

FINANCE

Investment incentive agreement.

Exchange of notes at Bissau August 14 and 15, 1985.

Entered into force August 20, 1986.

TIAS 12088.

INTERNATIONAL CRIMINAL COURT

Agreement regarding the surrender of persons to international tribunals.

Exchange of notes at Dakar and Bissau January 28 and February 2, 2005.

Entered into force February 8, 2005.

TIAS

PEACE CORPS

Agreement relating to the establishment of a Peace Corps program in Guinea-Bissau.

Exchange of notes at Bissau January 12 and 15, 1988.

Entered into force January 15, 1988.

TIAS 12104.

POSTAL MATTERS

International express mail agreement, with detailed regulations.

Signed at Bissau and Washington July 17 and August 28, 1991.

Entered into force September 30, 1991.

TIAS 11797.

GUYANA

On May 26, 1966, Guyana (former British Guiana) became an independent state. In a letter dated June 30, 1966 to the Secretary General of the United Nations, the Prime Minister of Guyana made a statement reading in part as follows:

"I have the honour to inform you that the Government of Guyana, conscious of the desirability of maintaining existing legal relationships, and conscious of its obligations under international law to honour its treaty commitments, acknowledges that many treaty rights and obligations of the Government of the United Kingdom in respect to British Guiana were succeeded to by Guyana upon independence by virtue of customary international law.

2. Since, however, it is likely that by virtue of customary international law certain treaties may have lapsed at the date of independence of Guyana, it seems essential that each treaty should be subjected to legal examination. It is proposed after this examination has been completed, to indicate which, if any, of the treaties which may have lapsed by customary international law the Government of Guyana wishes to treat as having lapsed.

3. As a result, the manner in which British Guiana was acquired by the British Crown, and its to be given to the question which, if any, treaties contracted previous to 1804 remain in force by virtue of customary international law.

4. It is desired that it be presumed that each treaty has been legally succeeded to by Guyana and that action be based on this presumption until a decision is reached that it should be regarded as having lapsed. Should the Government of Guyana be of the opinion that it has legally succeeded to a treaty and wishes to terminate the operation of the treaty, it will in due course give notice of termination in the terms thereof."

AGRICULTURAL COMMODITIES

Agricultural commodities agreement with annex.

Signed at Georgetown September 17, 1968.

Entered into force September 17, 1968.

19 UST 6692; TIAS 6585; 702 UNTS 183.

Related agreements

October 14, 1970 (21 UST 2201; TIAS 6969; 776 UNTS 57).

June 8, 1972 (23 UST 922; TIAS 7359).

Agricultural commodities agreement.

Signed at Georgetown January 27, 1978.

Entered into force January 27, 1978.

29 UST 5725; TIAS 9145.

Amendment

May 16 and 29, 1978 (29 UST 5739; TIAS 9145).

Related agreements

June 1, 1979 (30 UST 5936; TIAS 9527; 1180 UNTS 407).

April 23, 1980 (32 UST 1046; TIAS 9755; 1222 UNTS 287).

July 12 and 14, 1980 (32 UST 2063; TIAS 9818).

Agricultural commodities agreement.

Signed at Georgetown August 7, 1986.

Entered into force August 7, 1986.

NP

Amendment

September 25 and 30, 1986 (NP).

Agricultural commodities agreement.

Signed at Georgetown May 2, 1987.

Entered into force May 2, 1987.

NP

Amendment

August 18, 1987 (NP).

Related agreements

November 25, 1987 (NP).

July 28, 1988 (NP).

February 22, 1989 (NP).

July 31, 1989 (NP).

January 9, 1990 (NP).

July 19 and 23, 1990 (NP).

October 3 and 23, 1990 (NP).

November 9, 1990 (NP).

AVIATION

Arrangement between the United States and the United Kingdom relating to pilot licenses to operate civil aircraft.

Exchange of notes at Washington March 28, and April 5, 1935.

Entered into force May 5, 1935.

49 Stat. 3731; EAS 77; 12 Bevans 513; 162 LNTS 59.

Agreement between the United States and the United Kingdom relating to air services.

Signed at Bermuda February 11, 1946.

Entered into force February 11, 1946.

60 Stat. 1499; TIAS 1507; 12 Bevans 726; 3 UNTS 253.

CONSULS

Consular convention between the United States and the United Kingdom.

Signed at Washington June 6, 1951.

Entered into force September 7, 1952.

3 UST 3426; TIAS 2494; 165 UNTS 121.

DEFENSE

See also MUTUAL SECURITY

Agreement concerning the provision of training related to defense articles under the United States International Military Education and Training (IMET) Program.

Exchange of notes at Georgetown January 13 and 22, 1981.

Entered into force January 22, 1981.

33 UST 850; TIAS 10068.

Agreement regarding grants under the Foreign Assistance Act of 1961, as amended, and the furnishing of defense articles, related training and other defense services from the United States to Guyana.

Exchange of notes at Georgetown March 31 and June 8, 1994.

Entered into force June 8, 1994.

TIAS 12253.

Agreement regarding the status of military and civilian personnel of the United States Department of Defense temporarily present in Guyana in connection with military exercises and training, counter-drug related activities, United States security assistance programs, or other agreed purposes.

Exchange of notes at Georgetown December 28 and 29, 2000.

Entered into force December 29, 2000.

NP

Amendment

April 4 and May 10, 2006.

ECONOMIC AND TECHNICAL COOPERATION

General agreement for economic, technical and related assistance.

Signed at Georgetown November 8, 1979.

Entered into force November 8, 1979.

31 UST 4826; TIAS 9644.

Agency for International Development

November 9, 1971 (28 UST 1019; TIAS 8491).

September 14, 1972 (28 UST 1043; TIAS 8492).

November 6, 1975 (28 UST 1038; TIAS 8491).

November 6, 1975 (28 UST 1060; TIAS 8492).

June 6 and July 6, 1977 (29 UST 4881; TIAS 9083; 1134 UNTS 217).

July 13, 1977 (29 UST 2623; TIAS 8962; 1123 UNTS 111).

EMPLOYMENT

Agreement concerning the employment on a reciprocal basis of dependents of official employees.

Exchange of notes at Georgetown August 16 and 21, 2001.

Entered into force August 21, 2001.

TIAS

EXTRADITION

Extradition treaty between the United States and the United Kingdom.

Signed at London December 22, 1931.

Entered into force June 24, 1935.

47 Stat. 2122; TS 849; 12 Bevans 482; 163 LNTS 59.

FINANCE

Agreement relating to investment guaranties.

Signed at Georgetown May 29, 1965.

Entered into force August 18, 1965.

16 UST 2050; TIAS 5942; 605 UNTS 87.

Agreement regarding the consolidation and rescheduling or refinancing of certain debts owed to, guaranteed by, or insured by the United States Government and its agencies, with annexes.

Signed at Georgetown September 8, 1989.

Entered into force October 13, 1989.

NP

Swap agreement among the United States Treasury and the Bank of Guyana/Republic of Guyana, with memorandum of understanding.

Signed at Georgetown and Washington June 19 and 20, 1990.

Entered into force June 20, 1990.

TIAS

Agreement regarding the consolidation and rescheduling of certain debts owed to, guaranteed by, or insured by the United States Government and its agencies, with annexes.

Signed at Georgetown March 28, 1991.

Entered into force May 13, 1991.

NP

Agreement regarding the discharge of certain debts owed to the Government of the United States, with annex.

Signed at Georgetown September 30, 1991.

Entered into force September 30, 1991.

NP

Agreement regarding the consolidation and rescheduling or refinancing of certain debts owed to, guaranteed by or insured by the United States Government and its agencies, with annexes.

Signed at Washington April 5, 1994.

Entered into force May 23, 1994.

NP

Agreement regarding the reduction and reorganization of certain debts owed to, guaranteed by, or insured by the United States Government and its agencies, with annexes.

Signed at Georgetown March 27, 1997.

Entered into force June 6, 1997.

NP

Agreement regarding the reduction and reorganization of certain debts owed to, guaranteed by, or insured by the United States Government and its agencies, with annexes and side letter.

Signed at Georgetown December 20, 2000.

Entered into force March 1, 2001.

NP

Agreement regarding the cancellation of debt owed to, guaranteed by, or insured by the United States Government.

Signed at Georgetown June 24, 2004.

Entered into force September 2, 2004.

NP

INTERNATIONAL CRIMINAL COURT

Agreement regarding the surrender of persons to the International Criminal Court.

Signed at Georgetown December 11, 2003.

Entered into force May 18, 2004.

TIAS

PEACE CORPS

Agreement relating to the establishment of a Peace Corps program in Guyana.

Exchange of notes at Georgetown May 31 and June 7, 1967.

Entered into force June 7, 1967.

18 UST 1259; TIAS 6277; 686 UNTS 25.

POSTAL MATTERS

Parcel post agreement with detailed regulations of execution.

Signed at Georgetown August 13 and at Washington September 6, 1938.

Entered into force October 1, 1938.

53 Stat. 1989; Post Office Department print; 193 LNTS 117.

International express mail agreement with detailed regulations.

Signed at Georgetown and Washington February 25 and March 31, 1986.

Entered into force July 1, 1986.

TIAS 11406.

Postal money order agreement.

Signed at Georgetown and Washington September 23 and October 10, 1991.

Entered into force November 15, 1991.

TIAS 11792.

International express mail agreement, with detailed regulations.

Signed at Georgetown and Washington June 22 and July 16, 1994.

Entered into force November 1, 1994.

NP

PROPERTY

Convention between the United States and the United Kingdom relating to the tenure and disposition of real and personal property.

Signed at Washington March 2, 1899; applicable to British Guiana June 17, 1901.

31 Stat. 1939; TS 146; 12 Bevans 246.

Supplementary convention relating to the tenure and disposition of real and personal property of March 2, 1899.

Signed at Washington May 27, 1936.

Entered into force March 10, 1941.

55 Stat. 1101; TS 964; 5 Bevans 140; 203 UNTS 367.

SCIENTIFIC COOPERATION

Memorandum of understanding concerning scientific and technical cooperation in the earth and mapping sciences, with annexes.

Signed at Georgetown July 21, 1993.

Entered into force July 21, 1993.

TIAS 12158.

TAXATION

Agreement for the exchange of information with respect to taxes.

Signed at Georgetown July 22, 1992.

Entered into force August 27, 1992.

TIAS 12137.

TELECOMMUNICATION

Agreement relating to the reciprocal granting of authorizations to permit licensed amateur radio operators of either country to operate their stations in the other country.

Exchange of notes at Georgetown May 6 and 13, 1968.

Entered into force May 13, 1968.

19 UST 4892; TIAS 6494; 698 UNTS 243.

Arrangement relating to radio communications between the amateur stations on behalf of third parties.

Exchange of notes at Georgetown May 30 and June 6, 1972.

Entered into force July 6, 1972.

23 UST 906; TIAS 7355.

TRADE-MARKS

Declaration by the United States and the United Kingdom affording reciprocal protection to trade-marks.

Signed at London October 24, 1877.

Entered into force October 24, 1877.

20 Stat. 703; TS 138; 12 Bevans 198.

VISAS

Agreement relating to extended validity of passports issued by Guyana.

Exchange of notes at Georgetown May 20 and July 18, 1970.

Entered into force January 18, 1971.

22 UST 233; TIAS 7056; 781 UNTS 159.

H

HAGUE CONFERENCE ON PRIVATE INTERNATIONAL LAW

TAXATION

Tax reimbursement agreement, with annex.

Signed at The Hague January 27, 1993.

Entered into force January 27, 1993.

TIAS 12142.

HAITI

AGRICULTURAL COMMODITIES

Agricultural commodities agreement.

Signed at Port-au-Prince March 20, 1975.

Entered into force March 20, 1975.

28 UST 4462; TIAS 8600.

Related agreements

March 22, 1976 (28 UST 4483; TIAS 8601).

May 14 and 17, 1976 (28 UST 4490; TIAS 8601).

November 30, 1976 (NP).

April 13, 1977 (NP).

June 23, 1978 (NP).

Agricultural commodities agreement, with memorandum of understanding.

Signed at Port-au-Prince June 8, 1979.

Entered into force June 8, 1979.

NP

Related agreements

June 24, 1980 (NP).

May 25, 1981 (NP).

May 28, 1982 (NP).

August 17 and 18, 1982 (NP).

June 8, 1983 (NP).

June 12, 1984 (NP).

Agricultural commodities agreement, with annexes and memorandum of understanding.

Signed at Port-au-Prince May 30, 1985.

Entered into force May 30, 1985.

NP

Amendments

June 2 and 5, 1986 (NP).

June 19, 1987 (NP).

AVIATION

Memorandum of agreement [NAT–I–3448] concerning the provision of civil aviation assistance.

Signed at Washington and Port Au Prince August 27 and September 3, 1997.

Entered into force September 3, 1997.

TIAS

CUSTOMS

Agreement relating to reciprocal customs privileges for consular officers and clerks.

Exchange of notes at Port-au-Prince August 14 and 24, 1945.

Entered into force August 24, 1945.

59 Stat. 1868; EAS 503; 8 Bevans 791; 139 UNTS 311.

DEFENSE

Military assistance agreement.

Signed at Washington January 28, 1955.

Entered into force September 12, 1955.

6 UST 3847; TIAS 3386; 270 UNTS 83.

Agreement for disposition of equipment and materials furnished by the United States under the military assistance agreement of January 28, 1955 and no longer required by Haiti.

Exchange of notes at Port-au-Prince March 21 and April 5, 1955.

Entered into force April 5, 1955.

6 UST 3867; TIAS 3387; 270 UNTS 97.

Agreement relating to the transfer of military equipment, materials and services to Haiti.

Exchange of notes at Port-au-Prince September 1, 1960.

Entered into force September 1, 1960.

11 UST 2097; TIAS 4567; 388 UNTS 249.

Agreement between the governments participating in the multinational force (MNF) authorized pursuant to security council resolution 940 and the Republic of Haiti on the status of MNF forces in Haiti, with related letter.

Signed at Miami and Washington December 8 and 22, 1994.

Entered into force December 22, 1994.

NP

Agreement regarding the status of U.S. military personnel and civilian employees of the Department of Defense temporarily in Haiti in connection with their official duties.

Exchange of notes at Port-au-Prince May 10 and 11, 1995.

Entered into force May 11, 1995.

NP

ECONOMIC AND TECHNICAL COOPERATION

General agreement for technical cooperation.

Exchange of notes at Port-au-Prince May 2, 1951.

Entered into force May 2, 1951.

3 UST 545; TIAS 2414; 151 UNTS 191.

Amendment

December 15, 1951 and January 8, 1952 (3 UST 4731; TIAS 2635; 180 UNTS 372).

Agreement providing for emergency assistance to Haiti in connection with hurricane disaster.

Exchange of notes at Port-au-Prince March 22 and April 1, 1955.

Entered into force April 1, 1955; operative October 15, 1954.

6 UST 855; TIAS 3232; 261 UNTS 361.

Agency for International Development

June 29, 1976 (29 UST 1525; TIAS 8897; 1115 UNTS 183).

September 28 and 30, 1976 (29 UST 67; TIAS 8790; 1115 UNTS 219).

April 27, 1977 (29 UST 1249; TIAS 8877; 1115 UNTS 233).

August 30, 1977 (29 UST 5159; TIAS 9094).

EXTRADITION

Treaty for the mutual extradition of fugitives from justice.

Signed at Washington August 9, 1904.

Entered into force June 28, 1905.

TS 447; 34 Stat. 2858; 8 Bevans 653.

FINANCE

Agreement relating to guaranties authorized by Section 111(b)(3) of the Economic Cooperation Act of 1948, as amended.

Exchange of notes at Washington March 13 and April 2, 1953.

Entered into force April 2, 1953.

4 UST 1546; TIAS 2818; 212 UNTS 143.

Amendments

November 25 and December 1, 1970 (21 UST 2651; TIAS 7006; 776 UNTS 331).

October 7 and 14, 1975 (29 UST 3387; TIAS 9018).

Agreement regarding the consolidation, reduction and rescheduling of certain debts owed to, guaranteed by or insured by the United States Government and its agencies, with annexes.

Signed at Port au Prince August 7, 1995.

Entered into force September 7, 1995.

NP

Investment incentive agreement.

Signed at Port au Prince June 29, 1998.

Entered into force June 29, 1998.

TIAS

INTERNATIONAL CRIMINAL COURT

Agreement regarding the surrender of persons to the International Criminal Court.

Signed at Monterrey January 12, 2004.

Entered into force January 12, 2004.

TIAS

JUDICIAL ASSISTANCE

Agreement on procedures for mutual assistance in law enforcement matters.

Signed at Port-au-Prince August 15, 1986.

Entered into force August 15, 1986.

TIAS 11389; 2191 UNTS 265.

MARITIME MATTERS

Agreement for the loan of a US Navy net tender to Haiti.

Exchange of notes at Port-au-Prince July 8, 1960.

Entered into force July 8, 1960.

11 UST 1881; TIAS 4534; 380 UNTS 135.

NARCOTIC DRUGS

Memorandum of understanding for the interdiction of narcotics trafficking.

Signed at Port–au–Prince August 31, 1988.

Entered into force August 31, 1988.

TIAS

Agreement concerning cooperation to suppress illicit maritime drug traffic.

Signed at Port au Prince October 17, 1997.

Entered into force September 5, 2002.

TIAS

PACIFIC SETTLEMENT OF DISPUTES

Arbitration convention.

Signed at Washington January 7, 1909.

Entered into force November 15, 1909.

36 Stat. 2193; TS 535; 8 Bevans 658.

PEACE CORPS

Agreement relating to the establishment of a Peace Corps program in Haiti.

Exchange of notes at Port-au-Prince August 12 and 13, 1982.

Entered into force August 13, 1982.

34 UST 1694; TIAS 10445.

POSTAL MATTERS

International express mail agreement, with detailed regulations.

Signed at Port au Prince and Washington January 22 and and March 13, 1997.

Entered into force July 1, 1997.

NP

PROPERTY

Agreement relating to exchange of lands in Haiti.

Signed at Port-au-Prince October 19, 1942.

Entered into force October 19, 1942.

56 Stat. 1784; EAS 283; 8 Bevans 764; 120 LNTS 171.

PUBLICATIONS

Agreement relating to the exchange of official publications.

Exchange of notes at Port-au-Prince May 29, and June 5, 1941.

Entered into force May 29, 1941.

55 Stat. 1278; EAS 210; 8 Bevans 734; 101 LNTS 125.

RELIEF SUPPLIES AND PACKAGES

Agreement providing for duty-free entry into Haiti and exemption from internal taxation of relief supplies and packages.

Exchange of notes at Port-au-Prince September 8 and 9, 1958.

Entered into force September 9, 1958.

9 UST 1170; TIAS 4101; 335 UNTS 257.

TECHNICAL ASSISTANCE

Agreement for the furnishing of commodities to Haiti on a reimbursable basis, with annex.

Signed at Washington September 28, 1993.

Entered into force September 28, 1993.

TIAS

Amendment and extension

October 7, 1994.

TELECOMMUNICATION

Agreement for the exchange of third party messages between radio amateurs of the United States and Haiti.

Exchange of notes at Port-au-Prince January 4 and 6, 1960.

Entered into force February 5, 1960.

11 UST 1; TIAS 4399; 367 UNTS 75.

Agreement relating to the reciprocal granting of authorizations to permit licensed amateur radio operators of either country to operate their stations in the other country.

Exchange of notes at Port-au-Prince April 17 and May 17, 1979.

Entered into force May 17, 1979.

30 UST 4245; TIAS 9456.

Agreement regarding terms of reference for the operation of the Radio Democracy project.

Exchange of letters at Washington July 1 and 7, 1994.

Entered into force July 7, 1994.

TIAS 12555.

TRADE AND COMMERCE

Agreement relating to trade in cotton, wool and man-made fiber textiles and textile products, with annexes.

Exchange of letters at Port-au-Prince September 26 and 30, 1986.

Entered into force September 30, 1986; effective January 1, 1987.

NP

Amendments and extension

June 9 and 23, 1987 (NP).

July 18, November 19 and 28, 1990 (NP).

HONDURAS

AGRICULTURAL COMMODITIES

Agricultural commodities agreement.

Signed at Tegucigalpa March 5, 1975.

Entered into force March 5, 1975.

26 UST 318; TIAS 8037.

Amendment

April 18, 1975 (26 UST 1068; TIAS 8094).

Related agreement

June 9, 1976 (27 UST 2353; TIAS 8313; 1055 UNTS 93).

Agricultural commodities agreement, with annexes and minutes.

Signed at Tegucigalpa February 27, 1979.

Entered into force February 27, 1979.

30 UST 5695; TIAS 9521; 1178 UNTS 29.

Amendments

July 18, 1980 (32 UST 3256; TIAS 9894).

May 22, 1981 (33 UST 1965; TIAS 10160).

Agricultural commodities agreement, with annexes.

Signed at Tegucigalpa June 11, 1982.

Entered into force June 11, 1982.

NP

Amendments

August 30, 1982 (NP).

December 3, 1982 (NP).

Related agreements

June 27, 1983 (NP).

June 21, 1985 (NP).

Agreement for sales of agricultural commodities.

Signed at Tegucigalpa December 16, 1983.

Entered into force December 16, 1983.

NP

Amendments

February 24, 1984 (NP).

June 19, 1984 (NP).

July 26, 1984 (NP).

Related agreements

March 11, 1985 (NP).

June 21, 1985 (NP).

Agricultural commodities agreement.

Signed at Tegucigalpa March 15, 1986.

Entered into force March 15, 1986.

NP

Agricultural commodities agreement.

Signed at Tegucigalpa March 11, 1987.

Entered into force March 11, 1987.

NP

Related agreements

March 7, 1988 (NP).

February 9, 1989 (NP).

July 24, 1989 (NP).

March 29, 1990 (NP).

AGRICULTURE

Agreement continuing in force the agreement of February 28, 1941 relating to plantation rubber investigations in Honduras.

Exchange of notes at Tegucigalpa June 18 and 28, 1943.

Entered into force July 1, 1943.

57 Stat. 1220; EAS 358; 8 Bevans 948; 117 UNTS 220.

Agreement confirming the cooperative agreement for the prevention of foot-and-mouth disease and rinderpest in Honduras.

Exchange of notes at Tegucigalpa November 17 and December 20, 1972.

Entered into force December 20, 1972.

24 UST 942; TIAS 7604; 938 UNTS 139.

Memorandum of understanding relating to cooperative efforts to protect crops from plant pest damage and plant diseases.

Signed at Washington and Tegucigalpa March 4 and April 18, 1977.

Entered into force April 18, 1977.

29 UST 319; TIAS 8816.

AVIATION

Military air transit agreement.

Exchange of notes at Tegucigalpa January 22, March 20, and April 23, 1952.

Entered into force April 23, 1952.

3 UST 3734; TIAS 2502; 198 UNTS 251.

Civil aviation security agreement.

Signed at Tegucigalpa August 5, 1991.

Entered into force August 5, 1991.

TIAS 11804; 2207 UNTS 381.

Memorandum of agreement concerning assistance in developing and modernizing Honduras' civil aviation infrastructure.

Signed at Washington and Tegucigalpa July 24 and August 23, 1996.

Entered into force August 23, 1996.

TIAS 12796.

COMMERCE

Treaty of friendship, commerce and consular rights.[1]

Signed at Tegucigalpa December 7, 1927.

Entered into force July 19, 1928.

45 Stat. 2618; TS 764; 8 Bevans 905; 87 LNTS 421.

NOTE

1 Provisions which are inconsistent with the trade agreement of December 18, 1935 (49 Stat. 3851; EAS 86) are replaced by that agreement.

CONSULS

See COMMERCE

CULTURAL PROPERTY

Memorandum of understanding concerning the imposition of import restrictions on archaeological material from the Pre-Columbian cultures of Honduras.

Signed at Tegucigalpa March 12, 2004.

Entered into force March 12, 2004.

TIAS

DEFENSE

Military assistance agreement.

Signed at Tegucigalpa May 20, 1954.

Entered into force May 20, 1954.[1]

5 UST 843; TIAS 2975; 222 UNTS 87.

Agreement for performance by members of Army and Air Force missions of duties of military assistance advisory group specified in article V of military assistance agreement.

Exchange of notes at Tegucigalpa April 17 and 25, 1956.

Entered into force April 26, 1956.

7 UST 929; TIAS 3576; 269 UNTS 25.

Agreement relating to the disposition of equipment and materials furnished by the United States under the military assistance agreement of May 20, 1954.

Exchange of notes at Tegucigalpa May 20 and 24, 1954.

Entered into force May 24, 1954.

13 UST 78; TIAS 4940; 433 UNTS 155.

Agreement relating to military assistance.

Exchange of notes at Tegucigalpa October 24, 1962.

Entered into force October 24, 1962.

13 UST 2474; TIAS 5213; 459 UNTS 211.

Agreement relating to the deposit by Honduras of ten percent of the value of grant military assistance and excess defense articles furnished by the United States.

Exchange of notes at Tegucigalpa April 4 and June 26, 1972.

Entered into force June 26, 1972; effective February 7, 1972.

23 UST 1235; TIAS 7393.

Agreement relating to the military assistance agreement of May 20, 1954, concerning the use of certain facilities in Honduras by the United States, with annex.

Exchange of notes at Tegucigalpa May 6 and 7, 1982.

Entered into force May 7, 1982.

TIAS 10578; 1871 UNTS 456.

Agreement relating to privileges and immunities for U.S. armed forces personnel participating in combined military exercises in Honduras.

Exchange of notes at Tegucigalpa December 8, 1982.

Entered into force December 8, 1982.

35 UST 3884; TIAS 10890; 2014 UNTS 459.

Protocol I to the military assistance agreement of May 20, 1954 concerning the exercise of criminal jurisdiction over United States personnel present in Honduras, with annex.

Signed at Washington May 20, 1985.

Entered into force April 9, 1987.

TIAS 11256; 2177 UNTS 50.

Protocol II to the military assistance agreement of May 20, 1954, concerning the conduct of combined military exercises and maneuvers, with annex.

Signed at Tegucigalpa November 14, 1988.

Entered into force May 10, 1989.

TIAS 12254.

Agreement concerning security assistance matters and the provision of articles, services and associated military education and training by the United States Government for anti-narcotics purposes.

Exchange of notes at Tegucigalpa October 16 and 22, 1998.

Entered into force October 22, 1998.

TIAS

Acquisition and cross-servicing agreement, with annexes.

Signed at Tegucigalpa and Miami April 7 and 21, 2003.

Entered into force April 21, 2003.

TIAS

Agreement regarding grants under the Foreign Assistance Act of 1961, as amended, and the furnishing of defense articles, defense services, and related training, including pursuant to the United States International Military and Education Training Program (IMET), from the United States to the Government of the Republic of Honduras.

Exchange of notes at Tegucigalpa January 13 and March 28, 2006.

Entered into force March 28, 2006.

NP

Memorandum of understanding concerning the inter-American naval telecommunications network.

Signed July 28, 2006.

Entered into force July 28, 2006.

TIAS

NOTE

1 See also agreements of May 6 and 7, 1982 and May 20, 1985 (TIAS 11202).

ECONOMIC AND TECHNICAL COOPERATION

General agreement for economic and technical cooperation.

Signed at Tegucigalpa April 12, 1961.

Entered into force May 27, 1961.

12 UST 959; TIAS 4800; 413 UNTS 181.

Millennium challenge compact, with annexes.

Signed at Washington June 13, 2005.

Entered into force September 29, 2005.

TIAS

Agency for International Development

February 19, 1975 (27 UST 3311; TIAS 8366; 1068 UNTS 221).

November 28, 1977 (30 UST 90; TIAS 9181).

September 24, 1982 (TIAS 10505; 1777 UNTS 357).

March 25, 1985 (NP).

May 21, 1985 (NP).

July 25, 1985 (NP).

June 19, 1986 (NP).

June 19, 1987 (NP).

August 28, 1987 (NP).

August 20, 1988 (NP).

March 29, 1990 (NP).

June 5, 1991 (NP).

September 10, 1992 (NP).

June 9, 1999 (NP).

July 30, 1999 (NP).

August 16, 1999 (NP).

August 31, 1999 (NP).

August 31, 1999 (NP).

August 31, 1999 (NP).

March 14, 2000 (NP).

March 14, 2000 (NP).

EMPLOYMENT

Agreement relating to the employment of dependents of official government employees.

Exchange of notes at Tegucigalpa June 11 and November 27, 1985.

Entered into force November 27, 1985.

TIAS 11340

ENVIRONMENTAL COOPERATION

Agreement for cooperation in the Global Learning and Observations to Benefit the Environment (GLOBE) Program, with appendices.

Signed at Tegucigalpa November 13, 1997.

Entered into force November 13, 1997.

TIAS

EXTRADITION

Treaty for the extradition of fugitives from justice.

Signed at Washington January 15, 1909.

Entered into force July 10, 1912.

37 Stat. 1616; TS 569; 8 Bevans 892.

Supplementary extradition convention.

Signed at Tegucigalpa February 21, 1927.

Entered into force June 5, 1928.

45 Stat. 2489; TS 761; 8 Bevans 903; 85 LNTS 491.

FINANCE

Agreement relating to investment guaranties under section 413(b)(4) of the Mutual Security Act of 1954.

Exchange of notes at Tegucigalpa April 22 and June 10, 1955.

Entered into force June 10, 1955.

6 UST 2049; TIAS 3270; 258 UNTS 51.

Swap agreement among the United States Treasury and the Central Bank of Honduras/Government of Honduras, with memorandum of understanding.

Signed at Tegucigalpa and Washington June 27 and 28, 1990.

Entered into force June 28, 1990.

TIAS

Amendment and extension

November 30 and December 13, 1990.

Agreement regarding the consolidation and rescheduling or refinancing of certain debts owed to, guaranteed by, or insured by the United States Government and its agencies, with annexes.

Signed at Tegucigalpa December 20, 1990.

Entered into force February 1, 1991.

NP

Amendment

February 25 and 28, 1992 (NP).

Agreement regarding the discharge of certain debts owed to the Government of the United States, with annex.

Signed at Washington September 26, 1991.

Entered into force September 26, 1991.

NP

Agreement regarding the consolidation and rescheduling or refinancing of certain debts owed to, guaranteed by or insured by the United States Government and its agencies, with annexes.

Signed at Tegucigalpa February 2, 1993.

Entered into force March 29, 1993.

NP

Agreement regarding the consolidation, reduction and rescheduling of certain debts owed to, guaranteed by, or insured by the United States Government and its agencies.

Signed at Tegucigalpa December 4, 1996.

Entered into force April 10, 1997.

NP

Agreement regarding the reduction, consolidation, and rescheduling of certain debts owed to, guaranteed by, or insured by the United States Government and its agencies, with annexes.

Signed at Tegucigalpa August 23, 1999.

Entered into force September 27, 1999.

NP

Agreement regarding the reduction of certain debts owed to, guaranteed by, or insured by the United States Government, with annexes.

Signed at Tegucigalpa June 1, 2004.

Entered into force July 8, 2004.

NP

Investment incentive agreement.

Signed at Tegucigalpa July 21, 2004.

Entered into force July 21, 2004.

TIAS

Agreement regarding the reduction of certain debts owed to, guaranteed by, or insured by the United States Government and its agencies, with annexes.

Signed at Tegucigalpa October 7, 2005.

Entered into force November 28, 2005.

NP

HIGHWAYS

Agreement relating to the inter-American highway.

Exchange of notes at Washington September 9 and October 26, 1942.

Entered into force October 26, 1942.

56 Stat. 1848; EAS 296; 8 Bevans 945; 24 UNTS 209.

Amendment

May 10 and 12, 1955 (6 UST 3763; TIAS 3376; 270 UNTS 3).

INTERNATIONAL CRIMINAL COURT

Agreement regarding the surrender of persons to the International Criminal Court.

Signed at New York September 19, 2002.

Entered into force June 30, 2003.

TIAS

INVESTMENT

Treaty concerning the encouragement and reciprocal protection of investment, with annex and protocol.

Signed at Denver July 1, 1995.

Entered into force July 11, 2001.

TIAS

MAPPING

Arrangement for hydrographic and nautical cartography.

Signed at Tegucigalpa August 30, 1976.

Entered into force August 30, 1976.

30 UST 3453; TIAS 9399; 1178 UNTS 5.

Basic exchange and cooperative agreement for topographic mapping, nautical and aeronautical charting and information, geodesy and geophysics, digital data and related mapping, charting and geodesy materials, with glossary.

Signed at Comayaguela and Fairfax August 24 and September 5, 1995.

Entered into force September 5, 1995.

NP

MISSIONS, MILITARY

Agreement establishing a United States Air Force mission to the Republic of Honduras.

Signed at Washington March 6, 1950.

Entered into force March 6, 1950.

1 UST 199; TIAS 2040; 80 UNTS 51.

Extension and amendment

April 22 and May 20, 1960 (11 UST 1507; TIAS 4494; 376 UNTS 408).

Agreement establishing a United States Army mission to the Republic of Honduras.

Signed at Washington March 6, 1950.

Entered into force March 6, 1950.

1 UST 212; TIAS 2041; 80 UNTS 71.

Extension and amendment

April 22 and May 20, 1960 (11 UST 1507; TIAS 4494; 376 UNTS 408).

NARCOTIC DRUGS

Agreement on mutual cooperation to combat the production of and illicit trafficking in drugs.

Signed at Tegucigalpa November 14, 1988.

Entered into force May 15, 1989.

TIAS 11632; 2191 UNTS 133.

Agreement concerning cooperation for the suppression of illicit maritime traffic in narcotic drugs and psychotropic substances, with implementing agreement.

Signed at Tegucigalpa March 29, 2000.

Entered into force January 30, 2001.

TIAS

Agreement regarding the Cooperating Nation Information Exchange System.

Exchange of notes at Tegucigalpa October 19 and November 30, 2004.

Entered into force November 30, 2004.

TIAS

PEACE CORPS

Agreement relating to the establishment of a Peace Corps program in Honduras.

Exchange of notes at Tegucigalpa July 16 and 20, 1962.

Entered into force July 20, 1962.

13 UST 1892; TIAS 5142; 460 UNTS 125.

POSTAL MATTERS

Money order convention.

Signed at Washington June 25 and at Tegucigalpa July 16, 1896; operative October 1, 1896.

30 Stat. 1607.

International express mail agreement, with detailed regulations.

Signed at Buenos Aires September 11, 1990.

Entered into force November 15, 1990.

TIAS 11748.

Postal money order agreement.

Signed at Montevideo March 14, 1991.

Entered into force May 1, 1991.

TIAS 11926.

PUBLICATIONS

Agreement relating to the exchange of official publications.

Exchange of notes at Tegucigalpa March 1 and 24, 1950.

Entered into force March 24, 1950.

1 UST 391; TIAS 2057; 93 UNTS 11.

RELIEF SUPPLIES AND PACKAGES

Agreement providing duty-free entry into Honduras, exemption from internal taxation and transportation within Honduras to ultimate beneficiary, for certain relief supplies and equipment.

Exchange of notes at Tegucigalpa March 21, 1955.

Entered into force March 21, 1955.

6 UST 795; TIAS 3225; 253 UNTS 3.

SCIENTIFIC COOPERATION

Memorandum of understanding concerning scientific, technical and policy cooperation in the earth and mapping sciences, with annexes.

Signed at Tegucigalpa June 10, 1991.

Entered into force June 10, 1991.

TIAS 12432.

TAXATION

Agreement for the exchange of information with respect to taxes.

Signed at Washington September 27, 1990.

Entered into force October 11, 1991.

TIAS 11745; 2202 UNTS 47.

TELECOMMUNICATION

Agreement relating to radio communications between amateur radio stations on behalf of third parties.

Exchange of notes at Tegucigalpa October 26, 1959, and February 17, 1960, and related note of February 19, 1960.

Entered into force March 17, 1960.

11 UST 257; TIAS 4442; 371 UNTS 109.

Agreement relating to the reciprocal granting of authorizations to permit licensed amateur radio operators of either country to operate their stations in the other country.

Exchange of notes at Tegucigalpa December 29, 1966, January 24 and April 17, 1967.

Entered into force April 17, 1967.

18 UST 525; TIAS 6259; 685 UNTS 165.

TERRITORIAL SOVEREIGNTY

Treaty on the Swan Islands with related notes.

Signed at San Pedro Sula November 22, 1971.

Entered into force September 1, 1972.

23 UST 2630; TIAS 7453.

TRADE

See also COMMERCE

Trade agreement.[1]

Signed at Tegucigalpa December 18, 1935.

Entered into force March 2, 1936.

49 Stat. 3851; EAS 86; 8 Bevans 919; 167 LNTS 313.

Agreement on trade in textile and apparel goods under the Dominican Republic-Central America-United States Free Trade Agreement.

Exchange of letters at Tegucigalpa and Washington March 7, 2006.

Entered into force March 7, 2006.

NP

NOTES

1 The schedules, articles I, II, IV and V, together with references to article V contained in article XVI, terminated February 28, 1961 (12 UST 84; TIAS 4677; 402 UNTS 169).

HUNGARY

ATOMIC ENERGY

Agreement for cooperation concerning peaceful uses of nuclear energy, with annex and agreed minute.

Signed at Vienna June 10, 1991.

Entered into force February 13, 1992.

TIAS 12433.

Agreement relating to participation in the U.S. Nuclear Regulatory Commission program of severe accident research, with addendum.

Signed at Rockville and Budapest January 27 and February 2, 1999.

Entered into force February 2, 1999; effective January 1, 1998.

TIAS

Agreement in the area of probabilistic risk assessment research, with appendices and addendum.

Signed at Rockville and Budapest May 12 and 28, 2004.

Entered into force May 28, 2004.

TIAS

AVIATION

Air transport agreement, with annex and memorandum of understanding.

Signed at Budapest July 12, 1989.

Entered into force definitively February 8, 1990.

TIAS 11260; 2174 UNTS 297.

Extension

July 11 and 20, 2006.

CLAIMS

Agreement regarding the settlement of claims, with exchanges of letters and negotiating records.

Signed at Washington March 6, 1973.

Entered into force March 6, 1973.

24 UST 522; TIAS 7569; 938 UNTS 167.

CONSULS

Consular convention.

Signed at Budapest July 7, 1972.

Entered into force July 6, 1973.

24 UST 1141; TIAS 7641.

COPYRIGHT

Copyright convention.

Signed at Budapest January 30, 1912.

Entered into force October 16, 1912.

37 Stat. 1631; TS 571; 5 Bevans 444.

CULTURAL PROPERTY

Agreement on the protection and preservation of certain cultural properties.

Signed at Budapest April 15, 2004.

Entered into force June 30, 2004.

TIAS

CULTURAL RELATIONS

Agreement on cooperation in culture, education, science and technology.

Signed at Budapest April 6, 1977.

Entered into force May 21, 1979.

30 UST 1502; TIAS 9259.

DEFENSE

Agreement regarding grants under the Foreign Assistance Act of 1961, as amended, or successor legislation, and the furnishing of defense articles, related training, or other defense services from the United States to Hungary.

Exchange of notes at Budapest February 12 and August 31, 1993.

Entered into force August 31, 1993.

TIAS

Agreement concerning exchange of scientific and technical information, with attachment (Master Data Exchange Agreement).

Signed at Washington May 16, 1995.

Entered into force May 16, 1995.

TIAS 12319.

Agreement concerning security measures for the protection of classified military information.

Signed at Washington May 16, 1995.

Entered into force June 4, 1996.

TIAS 12649; 2044 UNTS 67.

Mutual logistic support agreement, with annex and implementing arrangement.

Signed at Budapest December 9, 1996.

Entered into force December 9, 1996.

TIAS 12822.

Agreement concerning the activities of United States Forces in the territory of the Republic of Hungary.

Signed at Budapest May 14, 1997.

Entered into force June 23, 1997.

TIAS

Memorandum of understanding regarding assignment of liaison officers, with annex.

Signed at Budapest and Norfolk September 22 and October 23, 2006.

Entered into force October 23, 2006.

TIAS

ECONOMIC AND TECHNICAL COOPERATION

Agreement concerning economic, technical and related assistance, with related letter.

Signed at Budapest December 22, 1995.

Entered into force December 22, 1995.

TIAS; 2044 UNTS 31.

EDUCATION

Agreement regarding the status of the American International School of Budapest.

Exchange of notes at Budapest November 30, 1998.

Entered into force November 30, 1998.

TIAS

EMBASSY SITES

Agreement regarding new chancery facilities in Budapest, with associated agreement on purchase of lots.

Signed at Budapest September 29, 1989.

Entered into force September 29, 1989.

TIAS

EMPLOYMENT

Agreement relating to employment of dependents of official government employees.

Exchange of notes at Budapest November 18, 1991 and January 16, 1992.

Entered into force January 16, 1992.

TIAS 11841.

ENVIRONMENTAL COOPERATION

Agreement for cooperation in the Global Learning and Observations to Benefit the Environment (GLOBE) Program, with appendices.

Signed at Washington March 10, 1999.

Entered into force March 10, 1999.

TIAS

EXTRADITION

Treaty on extradition.

Signed at Budapest December 1, 1994.

Entered into force March 18, 1997.

TIAS

FINANCE

Debt funding agreement.

Signed at Washington April 25, 1924; operative December 15, 1923.

Treasury Department print; 8 Bevans 1108.

Agreement modifying the debt funding agreement of April 25, 1924.

Signed at Washington May 27, 1932; operative July 1, 1931.

Treasury Department print; 8 Bevans 1140.

Investment guaranty agreement.

Signed at Budapest October 9, 1989.

Entered into force December 27, 1989.

TIAS 12040.

Swap agreement among the United States Treasury and the National Bank of Hungary/Government of Hungary, with memorandum of understanding.

Signed at Washington and Budapest June 19, 1990.

Entered into force June 19, 1990.

TIAS

GENERAL RELATIONS

Treaty establishing friendly relations.

Signed at Budapest August 29, 1921.

Entered into force December 17, 1921.

42 Stat. 1951; TS 660; 8 Bevans 982; 48 LNTS 191.

INTELLECTUAL PROPERTY

Agreement on intellectual property, with protocol and exchanges of letters.

Signed at Washington September 24, 1993.

Entered into force November 9, 1994.

TIAS 12138.

JUDICIAL ASSISTANCE

Agreement on establishing an International Law Enforcement Academy, with implementing agreement.

Signed at Budapest April 24, 1995.

Entered into force November 3, 1995.

TIAS 12637.

Treaty on mutual legal assistance in criminal matters, with attachments.

Signed at Budapest December 1, 1994.

Entered into force March 18, 1997.

TIAS; 2181 UNTS 271.

MAPPING

Exchange and cooperative agreement for military, topographic mapping, aeronautical charting, digital data and related MC & G materials.

Signed at Budapest December 9, 1991.

Entered into force December 9, 1991.

NP

MILITARY CEMETERIES AND MONUMENTS

Agreement relating to interment of American military personnel in Hungary.

Exchange of notes at Budapest June 18, July 15, and August 9, 1946.

Entered into force August 9, 1946.

61 Stat. 3898; TIAS 1748; 8 Bevans 1145; 148 UNTS 313.

NORTH ATLANTIC TREATY

Agreement to treat the agreement of June 19, 1995, among the States Parties to the North Atlantic Treaty and other States participating in the Partnership for Peace regarding the status of their forces as legally binding between the United States and Hungary.

Exchange of notes at Budapest July 6, 1995.

Entered into force July 6, 1995.

TIAS

PACIFIC SETTLEMENT OF DISPUTES

Arbitration treaty.

Signed at Washington January 26, 1929.

Entered into force July 24, 1929.

46 Stat. 2349; TS 797; 8 Bevans 1134; 96 LNTS 173.

Conciliation treaty.

Signed at Washington January 26, 1929.

Entered into force July 24, 1929.

46 Stat. 2353; TS 798; 8 Bevans 1137; 96 LNTS 207.

PEACE CORPS

Agreement concerning the operation of the United States Peace Corps in Hungary.

Signed at Budapest February 14, 1990.

Entered into force July 12, 1990.

TIAS 12072.

POSTAL MATTERS

Agreement for collect-on-delivery service.

Signed at Budapest December 15, 1930 and at Washington January 15, 1931; operative February 1, 1931.

46 Stat. 2894; Post Office Department print.

Parcel post agreement, with detailed regulations.

Signed at Washington May 11, 1979.

Entered into force provisionally May 11, 1979; definitively August 8, 1979.

32 UST 1695; TIAS 9797; 1734 UNTS 165.

International express mail agreement, with detailed regulations.

Signed at Budapest and Washington June 24 and July 10, 1987.

Entered into force September 1, 1987.

TIAS 11306.

SCIENTIFIC COOPERATION

Agreement for scientific and technological cooperation, with annexes.

Signed at Washington March 15, 2000.

Entered into force May 11, 2000.

TIAS

Memorandum of understanding concerning scientific and technical cooperation in the earth sciences.

Signed at Budapest and Reston November 22, 2000.

Entered into force November 22, 2000.

TIAS

SPACE COOPERATION

Agreement on cooperation in the exploration and use of outer space for peaceful purposes.

Signed at Budapest May 14, 2001.

Entered into force May 14, 2001.

TIAS

TAXATION

Convention for the avoidance of double taxation and the prevention of fiscal evasion with respect to taxes on income, with exchange of notes.

Signed at Washington February 12, 1979.

Entered into force September 18, 1979.

30 UST 6357; TIAS 9560; 1180 UNTS 205.

TRADE AND COMMERCE

Agreement relating to the establishment in New York of a branch office of the commercial section of the Hungarian Embassy.

Exchange of notes at Washington September 19, 1969.

Entered into force September 19, 1969.

20 UST 2982; TIAS 6772; 726 UNTS 177.

Agreement providing for consultations should exports of cotton, wool, and man-made fiber textiles and apparel products from Hungary cause market disruption in the United States.

Exchange of notes at Budapest February 12 and 18, 1976.

Entered into force February 18, 1976.

27 UST 1619; TIAS 8270.

Agreement on trade relations.

Signed at Budapest March 17, 1978.

Entered into force July 7, 1978.

29 UST 2711; TIAS 8967.

Agreement within the context of the multilateral trade negotiations on nontariff matters, and related letters of May 30, 1980. Letters done at Geneva August 31 and December 27, 1978 and January 10, 1979.

Entered into force January 1, 1980.

32 UST 5357; TIAS 9991.

Agreement within the context of the multilateral trade negotiations on tariff matters, with annexes and exchange of letters.

Signed at Budapest November 18, 1978.

Entered into force January 1, 1980.

32 UST 5371; TIAS 9992; 1265 UNTS 86.

Amendments

June 13, 1979 and May 30, 1980 (32 UST 5371; TIAS 9992; 1265 UNTS 115).

September 4 and 18, 1980 (32 UST 5371; TIAS 9992; 1265 UNTS 117).

Arrangement relating to a visa system for exports to the United States of wool textiles and textile products.

Exchange of letters at Washington February 2 and 3, 1984.

Entered into force February 3, 1984.

35 UST 4357; TIAS 10937; 2015 UNTS 53.

Amendment

October 27 and 31, 1988 (NP).

Agreed minutes on a comprehensive trade package, with annex and related letters.

Signed at Budapest January 30, 2002.

Entered into force March 26, 2002.

TIAS

TRANSPORTATION

Understanding concerning research cooperation in the field of transportation.

Signed at Budapest October 11, 1978.

Entered into force October 11, 1978.

30 UST 743; TIAS 9216.

VISAS

Agreement relating to issuance of nonimmigrant visas on a facilitated basis to certain holders of diplomatic or official passports.

Exchange of notes at Budapest March 29 and April 7, 1976.

Entered into force April 7, 1976.

28 UST 1311; TIAS 8513.

Agreement relating to reciprocal facilitation of visas for diplomatic and official passport holders.

Exchange of notes at Budapest February 10, 1978.

Entered into force February 10, 1978.

30 UST 248; TIAS 9193.

Agreement relating to reciprocal facilitation of transit or temporary duty visas for diplomatic and official passport holders.

Exchange of notes at Budapest February 10, 1978.

Entered into force April 11, 1978.

30 UST 255; TIAS 9194.

I

ICELAND

AVIATION

Air transport agreement, with annexes.
Signed at Washington June 14, 1995.
Entered into force October 12, 1995.
TIAS 12661.
Amendment
March 1, 2002.

Memorandum of agreement relating to the loan of aviation-related equipment to the Civil Aviation Administration of Iceland.
Signed at Washington December 8, 1997.
Entered into force December 8, 1997.
TIAS

DEFENSE

See also MUTUAL SECURITY

Defense agreement pursuant to the North Atlantic Treaty.
Signed at Reykjavik May 5, 1951.
Entered into force May 5, 1951.
2 UST 1195; TIAS 2266; 205 UNTS 173.

Annex on the status of United States personnel and property.
Signed at Reykjavik May 8, 1951.
Entered into force May 8, 1951.
2 UST 1533; TIAS 2295; 205 UNTS 180.

Agreement concerning the sale to Iceland of certain military equipment, materials, and services.
Exchange of notes at Reykjavik October 4 and December 10, 1954.
Entered into force December 10, 1954.
5 UST 2991; TIAS 3157; 237 UNTS 191.

Agreement relating to the presence of defense forces in Iceland, discontinuing the discussions for revision of the 1951 defense agreement and setting up an Iceland Defense Standing Group.
Exchanges of notes at Reykjavik December 6, 1956.
Entered into force December 6, 1956.
7 UST 3437; TIAS 3716; 265 UNTS 261.

Agreement relating to the continuation of the defense agreement of May 5, 1951, with memorandum of understanding and agreed minute.
Exchange of notes at Reykjavik October 22, 1974.
Entered into force October 22, 1974.
25 UST 3079; TIAS 7969.

Agreement concerning the provision of training related to defense articles under the United States International Military Education and Training (IMET) Program.
Exchange of notes at Reykjavik January 7 and February 12, 1986.
Entered into force February 12, 1986.
TIAS 11107.

Treaty to facilitate defense relationship, with related memorandum of understandings.
Signed at New York September 24, 1986.
Entered into force October 31, 1986.
TIAS 11098; 2120 UNTS 109.

Memorandum of understanding regarding the resolution of certain groundwater contamination.
Signed at Reykjavik July 17, 1989.
Entered into force July 17, 1989.
TIAS 12315.

Implementing arrangement in connection with the return of the Lower Nikel Agreed Area site, with attachment.
Signed at Keflavik July 3, 2002.
Entered into force July 3, 2002.
TIAS

Agreement regarding the withdrawal of United States forces from and the return to Iceland of certain agreed areas and facilities in Iceland, with attachments.
Signed at Washington September 27 and 29, 2006.
Entered into force September 29, 2006.
TIAS

ECONOMIC AND TECHNICAL COOPERATION

Economic cooperation agreement.
Signed at Reykjavik July 3, 1948.
Entered into force July 3, 1948.
62 Stat. 2363; TIAS 1787; 8 Bevans 1193; 20 UNTS 141.
Amendments
February 7, 1950 (1 UST 154; TIAS 2026; 79 UNTS 280).
February 23, 1951 (2 UST 1317; TIAS 2284; 148 UNTS 398).
October 9, 1952 and October 1, 1953 (5 UST 166; TIAS 2910; 223 UNTS 316).

Agreement concerning special economic assistance to Iceland on a loan basis.
Exchange of notes at Reykjavik June 23, 1959.
Entered into force June 23, 1959.
10 UST 1237; TIAS 4260; 354 UNTS 3.

Agreement providing for an assistance grant in support of Iceland's economic stabilization program.
Exchange of notes at Washington December 30, 1960.
Entered into force December 30, 1960.
11 UST 2574; TIAS 4647; 401 UNTS 43.

EDUCATION

Agreement for financing certain educational exchange programs.
Signed at Reykjavik February 13, 1964.
Entered into force February 13, 1964.
15 UST 226; TIAS 5542; 524 UNTS 235.

EXTRADITION

Conventions between the United States and Denmark applicable to Iceland:

Treaty for the extradition of fugitives from justice.
Signed at Washington January 6, 1902; effective May 16, 1902.
TS 405; 32 Stat. 1096; 7 Bevans 38.

Supplementary treaty for the extradition of criminals.
Signed at Washington November 6, 1905.
Entered into force February 19, 1906.
TS 449; 34 Stat. 2887; 7 Bevans 43.

LEND-LEASE

Agreement relating to aid for defense, with note.
Signed at Washington November 21, 1941.
Entered into force November 21, 1941.
58 Stat. 1455; EAS 429; 8 Bevans 1163; 124 UNTS 179.

MAPPING

Basic exchange and cooperative agreement concerning global geospatial information and services cooperation, with annexes.
Signed at Bethesda and Reykjavik June 7 and July 1, 1999.
Entered into force July 1, 1999.
NP

MUTUAL SECURITY

Agreement relating to the assurances required under the Mutual Security Act of 1951.
Exchange of notes at Reykjavik January 7 and 8, 1952.
Entered into force January 8, 1952.
3 UST 4577; TIAS 2609; 180 UNTS 183.

PACIFIC SETTLEMENT OF DISPUTES

Treaty between the United States and Denmark looking to the advancement of the cause of general peace.

Signed at Washington April 17, 1914.

Entered into force January 19, 1915.

38 Stat. 1883; TS 608; 7 Bevans 53.

Treaty of arbitration.

Signed at Washington May 15, 1930.

Entered into force October 2, 1930.

46 Stat. 2841; TS 828; 8 Bevans 1154; 108 LNTS 109.

POSTAL MATTERS

Agreement concerning the exchange of parcel post and detailed regulations of execution.

Signed at Reykjavik October 11 and at Washington October 31, 1938; operative September 1, 1938.

53 Stat. 2006; Post Office Department print.

International express mail agreement, with detailed regulations.

Signed at Reykjavik and Washington July 10 and August 8, 1985.

Entered into force November 7, 1985.

TIAS 11155; 2126 UNTS 265.

Memorandum of understanding concerning the operation of the INTELPOST service, with details of implementation.

Signed at Reykjavik and Washington March 5 and April 3, 1987.

Entered into force May 6, 1987.

TIAS 11299.

PUBLICATIONS

Agreement relating to the exchange of official publications.

Exchange of notes at Reykjavik August 17, 1942.

Entered into force August 17, 1942.

56 Stat. 1600; EAS 269; 8 Bevans 1166; 24 UNTS 163.

SCIENTIFIC COOPERATION

Memorandum of understanding for scientific and technical cooperation in earth sciences.

Signed at Reykjavik and Reston January 28 and April 9, 1982.

Entered into force April 9, 1982.

34 UST 1223; TIAS 10409.

Amendments and extensions

March 5 and August 9, 1991 (TIAS 11801).

June 9 and July 8, 1999.

Memorandum of understanding on cooperation in science and engineering research, with annexes.

Signed at Reykjavik September 30, 2000.

Entered into force September 30, 2000.

TIAS

SHELLFISH

Memorandum of understanding concerning cooperation to assure the sanitary quality of bivalve mollusca exported to the United States.

Signed at Reykjavik and Washington October 25 and December 28, 1978.

Entered into force December 28, 1978.

30 UST 2873; TIAS 9368; 1180 UNTS 89.

TAXATION

Agreement relating to relief from taxation of United States expenditures in Iceland for common defense.

Exchange of notes at Reykjavik March 5 and 18, 1952.

Entered into force March 18, 1952.

3 UST 4150; TIAS 2557; 177 UNTS 263.

Convention for the avoidance of double taxation and the prevention of fiscal evasion with respect to taxes on income and capital.

Signed at Reykjavik May 7, 1975.

Entered into force December 26, 1975.

26 UST 2004; TIAS 8151.

TELECOMMUNICATION

Agreement relating to the registration with the International Frequency Registration Board of radio frequencies for the use of the Iceland defense force.

Exchange of notes at Reykjavik July 11 and 20, 1955.

Entered into force July 20, 1955.

6 UST 3910; TIAS 3395; 256 UNTS 245.

Agreement relating to the reciprocal granting of authorizations to permit licensed amateur radio operators of either country to operate their stations in the other country.

Exchange of notes at Reykjavik April 26, 1978.

Entered into force April 26, 1978.

30 UST 1516; TIAS 9260; 1150 UNTS 41.

TRADE AND COMMERCE

Agreement within the context of the multilateral trade negotiations concerning cheese and other agricultural products, and related letter of January 30, 1980.

Exchanges of letters at Washington May 16 and 25, June 12, [undated], September 18 and October 15, 1979.

Entered into force January 1, 1980.

32 UST 5428; TIAS 9993; 1267 UNTS 37.

VISAS

Arrangement relating to the waiver of passport visa fees for nonimmigrants.

Exchange of notes at Copenhagen November 3 and December 21, 1925; and June 11, 19, and 21, 1926.

Entered into force June 21, 1926; operative August 6, 1925.

8 Bevans 1150.

Agreement relating to the reciprocal extension of the validity period of visas for certain nonimmigrants.

Exchange of notes at Reykjavik June 4, 1956.

Entered into force June 4, 1956; operative August 1, 1956.

7 UST 1017; TIAS 3584; 275 UNTS 189.

WHALING

Agreement concerning Icelandic whaling for scientific purposes, with summary of discussions.

Exchange of letters at Washington September 14 and 15, 1987.

Entered into force September 15, 1987.

TIAS 11541; 2192 UNTS 19.

INDIA

The Schedule to the Indian Independence (International Arrangements) Order, 1947, provides that (1) membership of all international organizations together with the rights and obligations attached to such membership devolves solely upon India; (2) rights and obligations under all international agreements to which India is a party immediately before the appointed day [August 15, 1947] devolve upon India and Pakistan and will, if necessary, be apportioned between them, except that rights and obligations under international agreements having an exclusive application to an area comprised in the Dominion of India devolve upon it.

The Dominion of India, which came into being August 15, 1947, became the Republic of India on January 26, 1950, but remains a member of the British Commonwealth of Nations. This change is understood not to have affected any agreements listed below in their application between the United States and India.

AGRICULTURAL COMMODITIES

Agricultural commodities agreement with exchange of notes.

Signed at Washington May 4, 1960.

Entered into force May 4, 1960.

11 UST 1544; TIAS 4499; 376 UNTS 279.

Amendments

July 29, 1960 (11 UST 1941; TIAS 4543; 384 UNTS 386).

September 23, 1960 (11 UST 2132; TIAS 4574; 389 UNTS 336).

March 9, 1961 (12 UST 177; TIAS 4691; 406 UNTS 346).

Agricultural commodities agreement with exchange of notes.

Signed at New Delhi May 1, 1962.

Entered into force May 1, 1962.

13 UST 1080; TIAS 5051; 451 UNTS 179.

Amendment

May 17, 1962 (13 UST 1080; TIAS 5051; 451 UNTS 179).

Agricultural commodities agreement, with exchange of notes.

Signed at New Delhi November 26, 1962.

Entered into force November 26, 1962.

13 UST 2589; TIAS 5225; 460 UNTS 203.

Amendments

April 1, 1963 (14 UST 340; TIAS 5317; 474 UNTS 372).

September 4, 1963 (14 UST 1246; TIAS 5424; 488 UNTS 314).

April 17, 1964 (15 UST 349; TIAS 5562; 526 UNTS 326).

Agricultural commodities agreement with exchange of notes.

Signed at Washington November 30, 1962.

Entered into force November 30, 1962.

13 UST 2492; TIAS 5215; 459 UNTS 231.

Agricultural commodity agreement.

Signed at Washington May 9, 1963.

Entered into force May 9, 1963.

14 UST 422; TIAS 5336; 476 UNTS 43.

Agricultural commodities agreement.

Signed at Washington June 27, 1963.

Entered into force June 27, 1963.

14 UST 950; TIAS 5384; 479 UNTS 215.

Amendment

December 9 and 20, 1963 (14 UST 1787; TIAS 5488; 494 UNTS 358).

Agricultural commodities agreement with exchange of notes.

Signed at New Delhi September 30, 1964.

Entered into force September 30, 1964.

15 UST 1941; TIAS 5669; 532 UNTS 321.

Amendments

December 31, 1964 (15 UST 2393; TIAS 5729; 532 UNTS 340).

April 21, 1965 (16 UST 664; TIAS 5793; 546 UNTS 412).

July 26, 1965 (16 UST 1064; TIAS 5846; 579 UNTS 324).

September 29, 1965 (16 UST 1257; TIAS 5875; 579 UNTS 330).

November 4, 1965 (16 UST 1707; TIAS 5895; 574 UNTS 280).

December 10, 1965 (16 UST 1833; TIAS 5913; 574 UNTS 284).

February 5, 1966 (17 UST 106; TIAS 5965; 579 UNTS 334).

May 27, 1966 (17 UST 778; TIAS 6032; 593 UNTS 324).

October 14, 1966 (17 UST 1564; TIAS 6113; 607 UNTS 348).

November 21, 1966 (17 UST 2057; TIAS 6146; 676 UNTS 380).

December 23, 1966 (18 UST 73; TIAS 6198; 680 UNTS 378).

Agricultural commodities agreement with annex.

Signed at New Delhi February 20, 1967.

Entered into force February 20, 1967.

18 UST 217; TIAS 6221; 688 UNTS 197.

Related agreements

June 24, 1967 (18 UST 2351; TIAS 6338; 692 UNTS 309).

September 12, 1967 (18 UST 2372; TIAS 6342; 693 UNTS 77).

December 30, 1967 (18 UST 3182; TIAS 6414; 697 UNTS 107).

December 23, 1968 (20 UST 394; TIAS 6642; 714 UNTS 69).

April 25, 1969 (20 UST 758; TIAS 6686; 714 UNTS 117).

May 29, 1969 (20 UST 776; TIAS 6691; 714 UNTS 78).

October 13, 1969 (20 UST 3038; TIAS 6781; 726 UNTS 211).

March 17, 1970 (21 UST 851; TIAS 6855).

June 26, 1970 (21 UST 1519; TIAS 6914; 753 UNTS 424).

April 1, 1971 (22 UST 638; TIAS 7115; 792 UNTS 283).

May 7, 1971 (22 UST 644; TIAS 7115; 792 UNTS 296).

May 20, 1971 (22 UST 646; TIAS 7115; 792 UNTS 300).

Agricultural commodities agreement.

Signed at Washington March 20, 1975.

Entered into force March 20, 1975.

26 UST 195; TIAS 8026; 992 UNTS 117.

Agricultural commodities agreement, with agreed minutes.

Signed at New Delhi May 3, 1976.

Entered into force May 3, 1976.

27 UST 2331; TIAS 8312; 1055 UNTS 21.

Agricultural commodities agreement, with agreed minutes.

Signed at New Delhi February 3, 1977.

Entered into force February 3, 1977.

28 UST 6027; TIAS 8668; 1087 UNTS 159.

Agricultural commodities agreement with agreed minutes.

Signed at New Delhi January 27, 1978.

Entered into force January 27, 1978.

29 UST 5663; TIAS 9142.

ATOMIC ENERGY

Agreement providing for a grant of nuclear research equipment in the field of agriculture.

Exchange of notes at New Delhi April 22 and June 13, 1960.

Entered into force June 13, 1960.

11 UST 1619; TIAS 4505; 377 UNTS 37.

Agreement providing for a grant for assistance in obtaining materials and equipment for establishing a Radiation Medicine Centre at Tata Memorial Hospital, Bombay.

Exchange of notes at New Delhi January 4 and February 1, 1963.

Entered into force February 1, 1963.

14 UST 156; TIAS 5288; 473 UNTS 37.

AVIATION

Agreement relating to transit privileges for military aircraft.

Exchange of notes at New Delhi July 2 and 4, 1949.

Entered into force July 5, 1949.

3 UST 575; TIAS 2417; 200 UNTS 181.

Amendments

June 9 and 15, 1955 (14 UST 1449; TIAS 5442; 488 UNTS 242).

March 5 and July 22, 1963 (14 UST 1449; TIAS 5442; 488 UNTS 246).

March 5 and August 29, 1963 (14 UST 1449; TIAS 5442; 488 UNTS 250).

Agreement amending and implementing the air transport agreement of February 3, 1956, and replacing the notes relating thereto exchanged the same date.

Exchange of notes at New Delhi October 26, 1964.

Entered into force October 26, 1964.

15 UST 2031; TIAS 5682; 533 UNTS 334.

Memorandum of cooperation for the promotion and development of technical cooperation in civil aviation

Signed December 7, 1993 and January 3, 1994.

Entered into force January 3, 1994.

TIAS

Air transport agreement, with annexes.

Signed at New Delhi April 14, 2005.

Entered into force June 21, 2005.

TIAS

COMMERCE

Convention to regulate commerce (article III) between the United States and the United Kingdom.

Signed at London July 3, 1815.

Entered into force July 3, 1815.

8 Stat. 228; TS 110; 12 Bevans 49.

CONSULS

Convention to regulate commerce (article IV) between the United States and the United Kingdom.

Signed at London July 3, 1815; effective July 3, 1815.

8 Stat. 228; TS 110; 12 Bevans 49.

COPYRIGHT

Agreement relating to copyright relations.

Exchange of notes at Washington October 21, 1954.

Entered into force October 21, 1954; operative August 15, 1947.

5 UST 2525; TIAS 3114; 234 UNTS 119.

DEFENSE

Agreement relating to the transfer by the Government of the United States to the Government of India of certain military supplies and equipment (military sales agreement).

Exchange of notes at Washington March 7 and 16, 1951.

Entered into force March 16, 1951.

2 UST 872; TIAS 2241; 14 UNTS 47.

Understanding that the assurances contained in the agreement of March 7 and 16, 1951 are applicable to equipment, materials, information, and services furnished under the Mutual Security Act of 1954, as amended, and such other applicable U.S. laws as may come into effect.

Exchange of notes at New Delhi April 16 and December 17, 1958.

Entered into force December 17, 1958.

10 UST 1713; TIAS 4322; 358 UNTS 77.

Agreement supplementing the 1951 military sales agreement.

Exchange of notes at Washington November 14, 1962.

Entered into force November 14, 1962.

13 UST 2449; TIAS 5206; 461 UNTS 224.

Agreement relating to military assistance.

Exchange of notes at New Delhi January 13, 1965.

Entered into force January 13, 1965.

16 UST 33; TIAS 5753; 541 UNTS 107.

Agreement concerning security measures for the protection of classified military information.

Signed at Washington January 17, 2002.

Entered into force January 17, 2002.

TIAS

Aviation leadership program agreement.

Signed at Washington and New Delhi July 5 and 29, 2004.

Entered into force July 29, 2004.

TIAS

Memorandum of agreement for research, development, testing and evaluation projects, with annexes.

Signed at Washington and New Delhi December 6, 2005 and January 9, 2006.

Entered into force January 9, 2006.

TIAS

ECONOMIC AND TECHNICAL COOPERATION

General agreement for technical cooperation.

Signed at New Delhi December 28, 1950.

Entered into force December 28, 1950.

2 UST 425; TIAS 2185; 99 UNTS 39.

Agreement relating to the technical cooperation program.

Signed at New Delhi January 5, 1952.

Entered into force January 5, 1952.

3 UST 2921; TIAS 2470; 157 UNTS 39.

Extension

June 29, 1957 (8 UST 732; TIAS 3828; 288 UNTS 368).

Agreement to establish a Joint Commission on Economic, Commercial, Scientific, Technological, Educational and Cultural Cooperation.

Signed at New Delhi October 28, 1974.

Entered into force October 28, 1974.

25 UST 2807; TIAS 7947.

Agreed minutes of the second session of the United States-India Joint Commission on Economic, Commercial, Scientific, Technological, Educational and Cultural Cooperation.

Signed at Washington October 7, 1975.

Entered into force October 7, 1975.

26 UST 2590; TIAS 8176; 1028 UNTS 23.

Agency for International Development

August 26, 1978 (30 UST 4749; TIAS 9488; 1170 UNTS 231).

August 26, 1978 (30 UST 4789; TIAS 9489; 1233 UNTS 269).

May 27, 1980 (32 UST 5941; TIAS 10022).

June 30, 1980 (32 UST 5969; TIAS 10023).

December 15, 1980 (32 UST 5941; TIAS 10022).

December 15, 1980 (32 UST 5969; TIAS 10023).

July 30, 1983 (35 UST 1767; TIAS 10765).

July 30, 1983 (35 UST 1787; TIAS 10766).

March 9, 1984 (35 UST 1767; TIAS 10765).

July 31, 1984 (NP).

July 31, 1984 (NP).

September 29, 1984 (NP).

June 26, 1985 (NP).

August 19, 1998 (NP).

August 24, 1998 (NP).

September 25, 1998 (NP).

September 24, 2001 (NP).

September 24, 2001 (NP).

September 26, 2001 (NP).

EDUCATION

Agreement for financing certain educational exchange programs.

Signed at New Delhi June 19, 1963.

Entered into force June 19, 1963.

TIAS 5379; 14 UST 918; 479 UNTS 175.

EMPLOYMENT

Arrangement on employment for family members of a diplomatic mission or consular post.

Signed at New Delhi April 10, 2000.

Entered into force April 10, 2000.

TIAS

ENVIRONMENTAL COOPERATION

Agreement for cooperation in the Global Learning and Observations to Benefit the Environment (GLOBE) Program, with appendices.

Signed at New Delhi August 25, 2000.

Entered into force August 25, 2000.

TIAS

EXTRADITION

Extradition treaty, with exchange of letters.

Signed at Washington June 25, 1997.

Entered into force July 21, 1999.

TIAS

FINANCE

Agreement regarding the consolidation and rescheduling of certain debts owed to the United States Government and its agencies, with annexes.

Signed at Washington March 30, 1973.

Entered into force March 30, 1973.

24 UST 907; TIAS 7601.

Agreement on Public Law 480 and other funds, with annexes.

Signed at New Delhi February 18, 1974.

Entered into force February 18, 1974.

25 UST 866; TIAS 7831.

Agreements regarding the consolidation and rescheduling of certain debts owed to the United States Government and its agencies, with annexes.

Signed at Washington June 7, 1974.

Entered into force June 7, 1974.

25 UST 1547; TIAS 7890.

Agreement regarding the consolidation and rescheduling of certain debts owed to the United States Government and its agencies, with annexes.

Signed at Washington May 2, 1975.

Entered into force June 13, 1975.

26 UST 951; TIAS 8082.

Investment incentive agreement.

Signed at New Delhi November 19, 1997.

Entered into force April 16, 1998.

TIAS

INTERNATIONAL CRIMINAL COURT

Agreement regarding the surrender of persons to international tribunals.

Signed at New Delhi December 26, 2002.

Entered into force December 3, 2003.

TIAS

JUDICIAL ASSISTANCE

Agreement on procedures for mutual assistance in connection with matters relating to the Boeing Company.

Signed at Washington August 19, 1977.

Entered into force August 19, 1977.

28 UST 7497; TIAS 8726; 1087 UNTS 209.

Related agreements

March 28 and April 17, 1979 (35 UST 3721; TIAS 10878; 2016 UNTS 58).

November 18 and December 10, 1981 (35 UST 3721; TIAS 10878; 2016 UNTS 62).

Treaty on mutual legal assistance in criminal matters.

Signed at New Delhi October 17, 2001.

Entered into force October 3, 2005.

TIAS

LEND-LEASE

Agreement on settlement for lend-lease, reciprocal aid, surplus war property, and claims.

Signed at Washington May 16, 1946.

Entered into force May 16, 1946.

60 Stat. 1753; TIAS 1532; 8 Bevans 1226; 4 UNTS 183.

Amendment

June 24 and 26, 1946 (8 Bevans 1233).

METEOROLOGY

Agreement on cooperation in the conduct of the monsoon experiment (MONEX-79), with annexes.

Signed at New Delhi May 24, 1979.

Entered into force May 24, 1979.

30 UST 5877; TIAS 9524; 1180 UNTS 355.

NARCOTIC DRUGS

Mutual cooperation agreement for reducing demand, preventing illicit use of and traffic in drugs, and for matters relating to licit trade in opiates.

Signed at New Delhi March 29, 1990.

Entered into force March 29, 1990.

TIAS 12412.

PEACE CORPS

Agreement relating to the establishment of a Peace Corps program in India.

Exchange of notes at New Delhi November 13 and 21, 1962.

Entered into force November 21, 1962; operative December 20, 1961.

13 UST 2735; TIAS 5247; 462 UNTS 255.

POSTAL MATTERS

Parcel post agreement with detailed regulations.

Signed at New Delhi July 29 and at Washington September 17, 1954.

Entered into force January 1, 1955.

6 UST 819; TIAS 3229; 239 UNTS 69.

International express mail agreement, with detailed regulations.

Signed at New Delhi and Washington November 20 and December 11, 1986.

Entered into force January 17, 1987.

TIAS 11415.

PROPERTY

Convention between the United States and the United Kingdom applicable to India from June 30, 1902:

PUBLICATIONS

Agreement for the exchange of official publications.

Exchange of notes at New Delhi November 8, 1950 and January 11, 1951.

Entered into force January 11, 1951.

2 UST 1563; TIAS 2297; 148 UNTS 49.

RELIEF SUPPLIES AND PACKAGES

Agreement for duty-free entry and defrayment of inland transportation charges of voluntary agency supplies and equipment.

Signed at New Delhi December 5, 1968.

Entered into force December 5, 1968.

19 UST 7836; TIAS 6617; 713 UNTS 351.

SCIENTIFIC COOPERATION

Agreement on the Indo-U.S. Science and Technology Forum.

Signed at New Delhi March 21, 2000.

Entered into force March 21, 2000.

TIAS

Agreement on science and technology cooperation, with annexes.

Signed at Washington October 17, 2005.

Entered into force March 14, 2006.

TIAS

SPACE COOPERATION

Memorandum of understanding on cooperation concerning NASA's miniature synthetic aperture radar instrument on ISRO's Chandrayaan-1 Mission.

Signed at Bangalore May 9, 2006.

Entered into force May 9, 2006.

TIAS

Memorandum of understanding on cooperation concerning NASA's moon mineralogy mapper (M3) instrument on ISRO's Chandrayaan-1 Mission.

Signed at Bangalore May 9, 2006.

Entered into force May 9, 2006.

TIAS

SURPLUS PROPERTY

Agreement concerning fulfillment of India's obligations under the agreement of May 16, 1946, as amended, on settlement for lend-lease, reciprocal aid, surplus war property, and claims.

Exchange of letters at New Delhi January 24, 1975.

Entered into force January 24, 1975.

26 UST 305; TIAS 8035; 992 UNTS 111.

TAXATION

Agreement concerning the reciprocal exemption from income tax of income derived from the international operation of ships and aircraft.

Exchange of notes at New Delhi April 12, 1989.

Entered into force April 12, 1989.

TIAS 11771; 2204 UNTS 529.

Convention for the avoidance of double taxation and the prevention of fiscal evasion with respect to taxes on income.

Signed at New Delhi September 12, 1989.

Entered into force December 18, 1990.

TIAS

TELECOMMUNICATION

Agreement relating to the reciprocal granting of authorizations to permit licensed amateur radio operators of either country to operate their stations in the other country.

Exchange of notes at New Delhi May 16 and 25, 1966.

Entered into force May 25, 1966.

17 UST 813; TIAS 6038; 593 UNTS 157.

TRADE

See also COMMERCE

Memorandum of understanding setting forth mutual trade concessions and contributions to the multilateral trade negotiations, and related letters of September 4 and October 30, 1980.

Signed at Geneva March 24, 1979.

Entered into force April 24, 1980.

32 UST 5436; TIAS 9994; 1265 UNTS 197.

Agreement relating to trade in textiles and textile products, with annexes.

Exchange of notes at Washington February 6, 1987.

Entered into force February 6, 1987; effective January 1, 1987.

NP

Amendments

March 4 and 10, 1987 (NP).

September 15 and October 2 and 16, 1987 (NP).

April 21 and May 30, 1988 (NP).

May 24, June 23, August 26 and September 12, 1988 (NP).

December 6 and 21, 1989 (NP).

TRADE-MARKS

Declaration by the United States and the United Kingdom affording reciprocal protection to trade-marks.

Signed at London October 24, 1877.

Entered into force October 24, 1877.

20 Stat. 703; TS 138; 12 Bevans 198.

VISAS

Arrangement for the continuance, on a reciprocal basis, of the existing practice of levying a fee of $2.00 for a nonimmigrant visa.

Exchange of notes at New Delhi July 19 and August 11, 1948.

Entered into force August 11, 1948.

5 UST 193; TIAS 2913; 224 UNTS 115.

INDONESIA

Sovereignty over Indonesia was transferred on December 27, 1949, by the Kingdom of the Netherlands to the Republic of Indonesia in accordance with the Charter of the Transfer of Sovereignty signed on that date.

The Agreement on Transitional Measures adopted by the Round Table Conference at The Hague on November 2, 1949, provides that the treaty obligations of the Republic of Indonesia arising out of treaties and other international agreements concluded by the Netherlands are considered "as the rights and obligations of the Republic of the United States of Indonesia only where and inasmuch as such treaties and agreements are applicable to the jurisdiction of the Republic of the United States of Indonesia and with the exception of rights and duties arising out of treaties and agreements to which the Republic of the United States of Indonesia cannot become a party on the ground of the provisions of such treaties and agreements."

AGRICULTURAL COMMODITIES

Agricultural commodities agreement with exchange of notes.

Signed at Djakarta October 26, 1961.

Entered into force October 26, 1961.

12 UST 2955; TIAS 4897; 433 UNTS 249.

Amendment

November 17, 1961 (12 UST 2955; TIAS 4897; 433 UNTS 249).

Agricultural commodities agreement, with exchange of notes.

Signed at Djakarta February 19, 1962.

Entered into force February 19, 1962.

13 UST 154; TIAS 4952; 435 UNTS 137.

Amendments

May 15, 1962 (13 UST 1100; TIAS 5054; 451 UNTS 346).

July 11, 1962 (13 UST 1765; TIAS 5118; 460 UNTS 344).

December 10, 1962 (13 UST 3824; TIAS 5254; 469 UNTS 436).

June 28, 1963 (14 UST 929; TIAS 5381; 479 UNTS 394).

August 13, 1964 (15 UST 1508; TIAS 5632; 530 UNTS 370).

Agricultural commodities agreement with exchange of notes.

Signed at Djakarta April 18, 1966.

Entered into force April 18, 1966.

17 UST 669; TIAS 6016; 578 UNTS 107.

Amendment

June 6, 1966 (17 UST 786; TIAS 6033; 593 UNTS 339).

Agricultural commodities agreement with exchange of notes.

Signed at Washington June 28, 1966.

Entered into force June 28, 1966.

17 UST 841; TIAS 6044; 593 UNTS 201.

Agricultural commodities agreement with exchange of notes.

Signed at Washington September 30, 1966.

Entered into force September 30, 1966.

17 UST 1515; TIAS 6107; 616 UNTS 199.

Agricultural commodities agreement with annex.

Signed at Djakarta September 15, 1967.

Entered into force September 15, 1967.

18 UST 2393; TIAS 6346; 693 UNTS 87.

Amendment

November 6, 1967 (18 UST 3100; TIAS 6401).

Related agreements

November 1, 1967 (18 UST 2921; TIAS 6382; 701 UNTS 133).

November 22, 1967 (18 UST 3156; TIAS 6407; 697 UNTS 19).

February 15, 1968 (19 UST 4757; TIAS 6473; 697 UNTS 27).

August 5, 1968 (19 UST 5987; TIAS 6551; 702 UNTS 125).

August 16, 1968 (19 UST 6006; TIAS 6556; 702 UNTS 135).

September 5, 1968 (19 UST 6009; TIAS 6557; 702 UNTS 143).

April 23, 1969 (20 UST 2698; TIAS 6731; 720 UNTS 334).

November 17, 1969 (20 UST 4084; TIAS 6799; 726 UNTS 249).

April 10, 1970 (21 UST 1509; TIAS 6911; 753 UNTS 251).

June 17, 1970 (21 UST 2638; TIAS 7003; 775 UNTS 89).

October 2, 1970 (21 UST 2641; TIAS 7004; 772 UNTS 157).

December 17, 1970 (22 UST 369; TIAS 7067; 792 UNTS 416).

December 23, 1970 (22 UST 10; TIAS 7036; 775 UNTS 99).

March 17, 1971 (22 UST 477; TIAS 7085; 792 UNTS 187).

August 7, 1971 (22 UST 1571; TIAS 7181; 807 UNTS 9).

November 10, 1971 (22 UST 1831; TIAS 7225).

November 18, 1971 (22 UST 1833; TIAS 7226).

December 21, 1971 (22 UST 2100; TIAS 7251).

December 23, 1971 (22 UST 2102; TIAS 7252).

December 30, 1971 (22 UST 2104; TIAS 7253).

January 5, 1972 (23 UST 4; TIAS 7266).

May 26, 1972 (23 UST 919; TIAS 7358).

August 28, 1972 (23 UST 2624; TIAS 7451).

October 27, 1972 (23 UST 3225; TIAS 7501).

November 3, 1972 (23 UST 3724; TIAS 7520).

November 13, 1972 (23 UST 3724; TIAS 7520).

November 13, 1972 (23 UST 3724; TIAS 7520).

December 11, 1972 (23 UST 4317; TIAS 7538).

December 12, 1972 (23 UST 4317; TIAS 7538).

December 13, 1972 (23 UST 4317; TIAS 7538).

January 22, 1973 (24 UST 452; TIAS 7562).

February 14, 1973 (24 UST 858; TIAS 7589).

December 31, 1973 (24 UST 2516; TIAS 7766).

Agricultural commodities agreement, with agreed minutes.

Signed at Jakarta May 30, 1975.

Entered into force May 30, 1975.

26 UST 1748; TIAS 8133; 1006 UNTS 211.

Agricultural commodities agreement.

Signed at Jakarta April 19, 1976.

Entered into force April 19, 1976.

27 UST 2279; TIAS 8308; 1052 UNTS 233.

Amendments

May 26 and 28, 1976 (27 UST 2296; TIAS 8308; 1052 UNTS 245).

June 14 and 15, 1976 (27 UST 2298; TIAS 8308; 1052 UNTS 247).

September 8 and 11, 1976 (27 UST 3534; TIAS 8379; 1059 UNTS 466).

October 15, 1976 (27 UST 3866; TIAS 8404; 1059 UNTS 468).

October 18 and 19, 1976 (27 UST 3869; TIAS 8404; 1059 UNTS 470).

November 15 and 17, 1976 (27 UST 4095; TIAS 8428).

Agricultural commodities agreement, with agreed minutes.

Signed at Jakarta May 17, 1977.

Entered into force May 17, 1977.

28 UST 6172; TIAS 8677.

Amendments

September 9, 1977 (29 UST 1982; TIAS 8913; 1115 UNTS 361).

December 16, 1977 (29 UST 2877; TIAS 8984; 1115 UNTS 361).

February 23, 1978 (29 UST 6059; TIAS 9169).

July 13, 1978 (29 UST 6065; TIAS 9169).

December 6, 1978 (29 UST 6070; TIAS 9169).

July 19, 1979 (30 UST 5941; TIAS 9528; 1177 UNTS 395).

October 2, 1979 (31 UST 5506; TIAS 9665; 1221 UNTS 355).

Agricultural commodities agreement, with agreed minutes.

Signed at Jakarta March 6, 1980.

Entered into force March 6, 1980.

32 UST 851; TIAS 9734; 1221 UNTS 247.

Agricultural commodities agreement, with agreed minutes.

Signed at Jakarta December 2, 1980.

Entered into force December 2, 1980.

33 UST 805; TIAS 10063; 1268 UNTS 3.

Amendment

June 2, 1986 (NP).

Related agreements

March 20, 1982 (34 UST 153; TIAS 10345; 1557 UNTS 31).

April 16, 1983 (TIAS 10716; 1578 UNTS 39).

August 12, 1983 (TIAS 10716; 1578 UNTS 46).

December 9, 1983 (NP).

March 22, 1984 (NP).

August 31, 1984 (NP).

February 13, 1985 (NP).

June 2, 1986 (NP).

September 18 and 22, 1986 (NP).

Agricultural commodities agreement.

Signed at Jakarta June 16, 1987.

Entered into force June 16, 1987.

NP

Amendment

September 2 and 3, 1987 (NP).

Agricultural commodities agreement.

Signed at Jakarta June 3, 1988.

Entered into force June 3, 1988.

NP

Amendment

July 28, 1988 (NP).

Related agreements

October 22, 1988 (NP).

February 11 and 13, 1989 (NP).

ATOMIC ENERGY

Agreement for cooperation concerning peaceful uses of atomic energy, with annex and agreed minute.

Signed at Washington June 30, 1980.

Entered into force December 30, 1981.

33 UST 3194; TIAS 10219.

Amendment and extension

February 20, 2004.

Arrangement for the exchange of technical information and cooperation in nuclear safety matters, with addenda.

Signed at Vienna September 17, 2003.

Entered into force September 17, 2003.

TIAS

AVIATION

Air transport agreement with schedule.

Signed at Djakarta January 15, 1968.

Entered into force January 15, 1968.

19 UST 4496; TIAS 6441; 697 UNTS 209.

Amendments

May 2, 1986 (TIAS 11371; 2194 UNTS 181).

April 12 and June 19, 1990 (TIAS 11760).

Agreement concerning the airworthiness and environmental certification of imported civil aeronautical products.

Exchange of notes at Jakarta January 23, 1987.

Entered into force January 23, 1987.

TIAS 11320.

Memorandum of agreement concerning assistance in developing and modernizing the Indonesian civil aviation infrastructure, with annexes.

Signed at Washington and Jakarta August 23 and October 19, 1990.

Entered into force October 19, 1990.

TIAS 11749; 2202 UNTS 149.

Memorandum of agreement concerning assistance in the development of Indonesia's civil aeronautics and air commerce, with annex.

Signed at Washington and Jakarta April 3 and May 3, 1996.

Entered into force May 3, 1996.

TIAS 12748.

COPYRIGHT

Agreement on copyright protection.

Signed at Washington March 22, 1989.

Entered into force August 1, 1989.

TIAS 11608; 2192 UNTS 101.

CUSTOMS

Agreement granting reciprocal customs privileges to diplomatic and consular officers and personnel.

Exchange of notes at Washington March 23 and 31, 1961.

Entered into force March 31, 1961.

12 UST 251; TIAS 4706; 405 UNTS 119.

Memorandum of understanding regarding mutual assistance between customs administrations.

Signed at Jakarta November 17, 2006.

Entered into force November 17, 2006.

TIAS

DEFENSE

Agreement for a program of military assistance in the form of constabulary equipment to be supplied by the United States to the Republic of Indonesia.

Exchange of notes at Djakarta August 15, 1950.

Entered into force August 15, 1950.

2 UST 1619; TIAS 2306; 134 UNTS 255.

Agreement for the transfer from a grant to an aid on a reimbursable basis of the undelivered balance of constabulary equipment authorized under the agreement of August 15, 1950.

Exchange of notes at Washington January 5, and at Djakarta January 12, 1953.

Entered into force January 12, 1953.

4 UST 113; TIAS 2768; 198 UNTS 400.

Agreement relating to the sale to Indonesia of military equipment, materials, and services.

Exchange of notes at Djakarta August 13, 1958.

Entered into force August 13, 1958.

9 UST 1149; TIAS 4095; 335 UNTS 187.

Agreement relating to the furnishing of military equipment, materials, and services for a program of civic action.

Exchange of notes at Djakarta April 14, 1967.

Entered into force April 14, 1967.

18 UST 384; TIAS 6247; 689 UNTS 3.

Agreement relating to the provision by the United States of basic pilot training aircraft.

Exchange of notes at Djakarta April 9 and 17, 1969.

Entered into force April 17, 1969.

20 UST 702; TIAS 6678; 719 UNTS 121.

Agreement relating to the furnishing of combat equipment to Indonesia as additional military assistance.

Exchange of notes at Djakarta August 18 and 19, 1970.

Entered into force August 19, 1970.

21 UST 2140; TIAS 6959; 764 UNTS 219.

Agreement concerning payment to the United States of net proceeds from the sale of defense articles furnished under the military assistance program.

Exchange of notes at Jakarta June 12 and 29, 1974.

Entered into force July 1, 1974.

25 UST 2609; TIAS 7938.

Agreement relating to eligibility for United States military assistance and training pursuant to the International Security Assistance and Arms Export Control Act of 1976.

Exchange of notes at Jakarta August 3 and 24, 1976.

Entered into force August 24, 1976.

27 UST 4006; TIAS 8419; 1059 UNTS 131.

Agreement relating to payment to the United States of the net proceeds from the sale of defense articles by Indonesia.

Exchange of notes at Jakarta June 29 and September 6, 2006.

Entered into force September 6, 2006.

TIAS

ECONOMIC AND TECHNICAL COOPERATION

Economic cooperation agreement.

Signed at Djakarta October 16, 1950.

Entered into force provisionally October 16, 1950 (recognized by the Republic of Indonesia as a binding obligation pending Parliamentary action).

7 UST 2241; TIAS 3624; 281 UNTS 105.

Agreement relating to continuation of economic and technical cooperation under the agreement of October 16, 1950.

Exchange of notes at Washington January 5 and at Djakarta January 12, 1953.

Entered into force Janury 12, 1953.

4 UST 18, TIAS 2762; 215 UNTS 121.

Agreement relating to the assumption by Indonesia of all responsibilities and obligations of the Netherlands incurred under the economic cooperation agreements of July 2, 1948, as amended, and April 26, 1949, as amended, and the loan agreements of October 28, 1948 and December 22, 1949; and memorandum of understanding.

Signed at Washington February 11, 1952 by the United States, Indonesia, and the Netherlands.

Entered into force February 11, 1952.

3 UST 2989; TIAS 2484; 165 UNTS 77.

Agency for International Development

June 30, 1975 (28 UST 3227; TIAS 8584).
July 28, 1976 (29 UST 5107; TIAS 9092).
October 28, 1976 (28 UST 3265; TIAS 8584).
October 28, 1976 (28 UST 8201; TIAS 8755; 1095 UNTS 33).
October 28, 1976 (28 UST 8245; TIAS 8759).
October 28, 1976 (28 UST 8389; TIAS 8763; 1095 UNTS 63).
January 24, 1977 (29 UST 685; TIAS 8848).
January 24, 1977 (29 UST 711; TIAS 8849).
July 27, 1977 (29 UST 5124; TIAS 9092).
January 3, 1978 (29 UST 2156; TIAS 8931).
March 30, 1978 (30 UST 1831; TIAS 9294).
April 12, 1978 (29 UST 5126; TIAS 9092).
April 12, 1978 (30 UST 1988; TIAS 9308; 1152 UNTS 333).
April 12, 1978 (30 UST 2030; TIAS 9310).
April 12, 1978 (30 UST 2123; TIAS 9317).
April 12, 1978 (30 UST 2354; TIAS 9342).
April 12, 1978 (30 UST 2379; TIAS 9343).
May 6, 1978 (30 UST 2643; TIAS 9357).
July 13, 1978 (30 UST 3339; TIAS 9394).
August 31, 1978 (30 UST 5509; TIAS 9514).
August 31, 1987 (NP).
August 31, 1988 (NP).
March 21, 1990 (NP).
September 28, 1992 (NP).
August 31, 1993 (NP).
March 3, 1994 (NP).
March 21, 1995 (NP).
June 11, 1996 (NP).
August 6, 1996 (NP).
August 30, 1996 (NP).
May 7, 1997 (NP).
August 1, 1997 (NP).
August 12, 1998 (NP).
September 17, 1998 (NP).
June 22, 1999 (NP).
June 30, 1999 (NP).
August 6, 1999 (NP).
August 13, 1999 (NP).
May 31, 2000 (NP).
June 6, 2000 (NP).

August 31, 2000 (NP).
September 28, 2000 (NP).
July 31, 2001 (NP).
September 21, 2001 (NP).
September 28, 2001 (NP).
July 10, 2002 (NP).
August 26, 2002 (NP).
August 30, 2004 (NP).
August 30, 2004 (NP).
July 7, 2005 (NP).
July 8, 2005 (NP).
July 8, 2005 (NP).
July 11, 2005 (NP).
November 16, 2005 (NP).
August 15, 2006 (NP).
August 29, 2006 (NP).
August 29, 2006 (NP).

EDUCATION

Educational and cultural agreement.
Signed at Jakarta July 15, 1992.
Entered into force July 15, 1992.
TIAS 12466.

FINANCE

Agreement relating to investment guaranties.
Exchange of notes at Djakarta January 7, 1967.
Entered into force August 22, 1967.
18 UST 1850; TIAS 6330; 692 UNTS 109.

Memorandum of agreement regarding debt rescheduling under the agricultural commodities agreement of June 28, 1966, with annexes.
Signed at Djakarta December 30, 1967.
Entered into force December 30, 1967.
20 UST 501; TIAS 6656; 724 UNTS 364.

Memorandum of agreement regarding debt rescheduling under the agricultural commodities agreement of April 18, 1966, as amended, with annexes.
Signed at Djakarta December 30, 1967.
Entered into force December 30, 1967.
20 UST 494; TIAS 6655; 724 UNTS 350.

Memorandum of agreement regarding debt rescheduling under the agricultural commodities agreement of April 18, 1966, as amended, with annexes.
Signed at Djakarta December 20, 1968.
Entered into force December 20, 1968.
20 UST 494; TIAS 6655; 724 UNTS 356.

Memorandum of agreement regarding debt rescheduling under the agricultural commodities agreement of June 28, 1966, with annexes.
Signed at Djakarta December 20, 1968.
Entered into force December 20, 1968.
20 UST 501; TIAS 6656; 724 UNTS 370.

Memorandum of agreement regarding debt rescheduling under the agricultural commodities agreement of April 18, 1966, as amended, with annexes.
Signed at Djakarta February 6, 1970.
Entered into force February 6, 1970.
21 UST 437; TIAS 6830; 740 UNTS 424.

Memorandum of agreement regarding debt rescheduling under the agricultural commodities agreement of June 28, 1966, with annexes.
Signed at Djakarta February 6, 1970.
Entered into force February 6, 1970.
21 UST 442; TIAS 6831; 740 UNTS 442.

Memorandum of agreement regarding the rescheduling of payments under the agricultural commodities agreements of April 18, 1966, as amended, and June 28, 1966, as amended; the surplus property agreement of May 28, 1947, as amended and certain loan and credit agreements.
Signed at Djakarta March 16, 1971.
Entered into force March 16, 1971.
22 UST 514; TIAS 7092; 792 UNTS 170.

Agreement regarding the consolidation and rescheduling of certain debts owed to, guaranteed by, or insured by the United States Government and its agencies, with annexes.
Signed at Washington September 1, 1999.
Entered into force October 22, 1999.
NP

Agreement regarding the consolidation and rescheduling of certain debts owed to, guaranteed by, or insured by the United States Government and its agencies, with annexes.
Signed at Jakarta December 8, 2000.
Entered into force January 16, 2001.
NP

Agreement regarding the consolidation and rescheduling of certain debts owed to, guaranteed by, or insured by the United States Government and its agencies, with annexes.
Signed at Jakarta October 1, 2002.
Entered into force November 12, 2002.
NP

Agreement regarding the consolidation and rescheduling of certain debts owed to, guaranteed by, or insured by the United States Government or its agencies, with annexes.
Signed at Jakarta June 14, 2005.
Entered into force July 19, 2005.
NP

HEALTH

Agreement concerning the establishment of a United States naval medical research unit in Indonesia.
Signed at Djakarta January 16, 1970.
Entered into force January 16, 1970.
21 UST 1; TIAS 6813; 240 UNTS 143.

INFORMATIONAL MEDIA GUARANTIES

Agreement relating to an informational media guaranty program pursuant to Section 1011 of the U.S. Information and Educational Exchange Act of 1948, as amended.
Exchange of notes at Djakarta September 15, 1955.
Entered into force September 15, 1955.
6 UST 3957; TIAS 3406; 256 UNTS 293.

MAPPING

Memorandum of understanding concerning mapping, charting, and geodesy cooperation.
Signed at Jakarta October 21, 1977.
Entered into force October 21, 1977.
29 UST 4810; TIAS 9079; 1134 UNTS 339.

MARITIME MATTERS

Agreement on maritime search and rescue.
Signed at Jakarta July 5, 1988.
Entered into force July 5, 1988.
TIAS 11655; 2202 UNTS 23.

NARCOTIC DRUGS

Understandings concerning the assignment of a Drug Enforcement Administration representative to the American Embassy in Jakarta to advance the U.S.-Indonesian common interest in preventing illegal traffic in narcotic drugs, with annex.
Exchange of letters at Jakarta April 1, 1975.
Entered into force April 1, 1975.
27 UST 2001; TIAS 8299; 1052 UNTS 227.

PEACE CORPS

Agreement relating to the establishment of a Peace Corps program in Indonesia.

Exchange of notes at Djakarta March 8 and 14, 1963.

Entered into force March 14, 1963.

14 UST 1789; TIAS 5489; 505 UNTS 79.

POSTAL MATTERS

Agreement concerning the exchange of parcel post, and detailed regulations of execution.

Signed at Bandoeng June 14 and at Washington October 4, 1934; operative October 4, 1933.

49 Stat. 2967; Post Office Department print; 158 LNTS 395.

International express mail agreement, with detailed regulations.

Signed at Jakarta and Washington January 23 and February 26, 1987.

Entered into force April 1, 1987.

TIAS 11300.

PUBLICATIONS

Agreement relating to the exchange of official publications.

Exchange of notes at Djakarta May 17 and June 7, 1950.

Entered into force June 7, 1950.

1 UST 649; TIAS 2122; 98 UNTS 167.

SATELLITES

Agreement concerning the furnishing of launching and associated services by the National Aeronautics and Space Administration for Indonesian satellites, with annexes.

Exchange of notes at Washington March 26, 1975.

Entered into force March 26, 1975.

26 UST 524; TIAS 8054; 992 UNTS 308.

Agreement concerning the furnishing of launching and associated services for Palapa-B spacecraft.

Exchange of notes at Washington April 11, 1979.

Entered into force April 11, 1979.

30 UST 4253; TIAS 9457; 1171 UNTS 255.

SCIENTIFIC COOPERATION

Memorandum of understanding on general cooperation in science and technology for natural hazard assessment, analysis, warning, preparedness and mitigation, with annexes.

Signed at Jakarta November 20, 2006.

Entered into force November 20, 2006.

TIAS

SURPLUS PROPERTY

Agreement regarding a line of credit for the purchase of United States surplus property. (Part of U.S.-Netherlands lend-lease settlement).

Signed at Washington May 28, 1947 by the United States, Netherlands Indies, and the Netherlands.

Entered into force May 28, 1947.

61 Stat. 3947; TIAS 1750; 8 Bevans 1250; 17 UNTS 29.

Agreement relating to the release of the Netherlands from its obligations as guarantor for Indonesia under the surplus property agreement of May 28, 1947.

Exchange of notes at The Hague September 17, 1952, at Djakarta October 15, 1952, and at Washington April 8, 1953.

Entered into force April 8, 1953.

4 UST 1557; TIAS 2820; 205 UNTS 324.

Memorandum of agreement regarding the rescheduling of payments under the surplus property agreement of May 28, 1947.

Signed at Djkarta December 30, 1967.

Entered into force December 30, 1967.

18 UST 3261; TIAS 6419; 697 UNTS 119.

Memorandum of agreement regarding the second rescheduling of payments under the surplus property agreement of May 28, 1947, with annexes.

Signed at Djakarta December 20, 1968.

Entered into force December 20, 1968.

19 UST 7838; TIAS 6618; 723 UNTS 432.

Memorandum of agreement regarding the third rescheduling of payments under the surplus property agreement of May 28, 1947, with annexes.

Signed at Djakarta February 6, 1970.

Entered into force February 6, 1970.

21 UST 447; TIAS 6832; 740 UNTS 464.

TAXATION

Convention for the avoidance of double taxation and the prevention of fiscal evasion with respect to taxes on income, with protocol and exchange of notes.

Signed at Jakarta July 11, 1988.

Entered into force December 30, 1990.

TIAS 11593; 2190 UNTS 287.

Protocol amending the convention of July 11, 1988, for the avoidance of double taxation and the prevention of fiscal evasion with respect to taxes on income.

Signed at Jakarta July 24, 1996.

Entered into force December 23, 1996.

TIAS

TELECOMMUNICATION

Agreement relating to the reciprocal granting of authorizations to permit licensed amateur radio operators of either country to operate their stations in the other country.

Exchange of notes at Djakarta December 10, 1968.

Entered into force December 10, 1968.

20 UST 490; TIAS 6654; 707 UNTS 149.

TRADE AND COMMERCE

Memorandum of understanding setting forth mutual trade concessions and contributions to the multilateral trade negotiations, with exchange of letters, and related letter of February 21, 1980.

Signed at Jakarta November 29, December 20 and 27, 1979.

Entered into force January 1, 1980.

TIAS 10569.

Arrangement relating to a visa system for exports of apparel and non apparel of cotton, wool and man-made fiber manufactured in Indonesia.

Exchange of notes at Jakarta June 1 and 14, 1984.

Entered into force June 14, 1984.

NP

Agreement relating to subsidization of exports in the context of the agreement on interpretation and application of articles VI, XVI and XXIII (subsidies code) of the General Agreement on Tariffs and Trade (TIAS 9619).

Exchange of letters at Washington February 28, 1985.

Entered into force February 28, 1985.

TIAS 11325.

Amendment

April 10, 1986.

Administrative arrangement relating to visa and certification procedures for exports of textiles and textile products from Indonesia.

Exchange of letters at Washington March 25, 1987.

Entered into force March 25, 1987; effective July 1, 1987.

NP

Amendment

December 1 and 3, 1988 (NP).

Agreement concerning trade in textiles and textile products, with annexes.

Signed at Jakarta May 8, 1992.

Entered into force May 8, 1992; effective July 1, 1992.

NP

Amendment

June 16 and July 21, 1993 (NP).

INTER–AMERICAN DEVELOPMENT BANK

FINANCE

Social progress trust fund agreement with exchange of letters.

Signed at Washington June 19, 1961.

Entered into force June 19, 1961.

12 UST 632; TIAS 4763; 410 UNTS 33.

Related agreements

February 17, 1964 (15 UST 104; TIAS 5522; 511 UNTS 296).

September 7, 1966 (17 UST 1200; TIAS 6081).

April 28, 1972 (23 UST 1497; TIAS 7430).

October 3, 1975 (27 UST 2627; TIAS 8333; 1054 UNTS 338).

INTER–AMERICAN INSTITUTE FOR COOPERATION ON AGRICULTURE

TAXATION

Tax reimbursement agreement.

Signed at Washington December 30, 1994.

Entered into force December 30, 1994.

TIAS 12594.

INTERNATIONAL ATOMIC ENERGY AGENCY

ATOMIC ENERGY [1]

Agreement for cooperation in the civil uses of atomic energy.

Signed at Vienna May 11, 1959.

Entered into force August 7, 1959.

10 UST 1424; TIAS 4291; 339 UNTS 359.

Extension and amendments

February 12, 1974 (25 UST 1199; TIAS 7852).

January 14, 1980 (32 UST 1143; TIAS 9762; 1220 UNTS 316).

Agreement for the application of safeguards in the United States, with protocol.

Done at Vienna November 18, 1977.

Entered into force December 9, 1980.

32 UST 3059; TIAS 9889.

Agreement relating to provision by the United States Nuclear Regulatory Commission to the International Atomic Energy Agency of experts in the various fields of the peaceful applications of atomic energy.

Signed at Vienna and Bethesda May 29 and September 16, 1981.

Entered into force September 16, 1981.

33 UST 3849; TIAS 10264; 1543 UNTS 111.

Agreement for the application of safeguards in connection with the treaty of February 14, 1967, for the prohibition of nuclear weapons in Latin America, with protocol.

Signed at Vienna February 17, 1989.

Entered into force April 6, 1989.

TIAS 12398.

NOTE

1 For agreements between the IAEA, the United States, and other countries, see under ATOMIC ENERGY in multilateral section.

NUCLEAR MATERIAL

Memorandum of understanding concerning supply of feed material FP-33 for separation of high-purity plutonium-244, with annex.

Signed at Washington and Vienna April 15 and 21, 2005.

Entered into force April 21, 2005.

TIAS

TAXATION

Tax reimbursement agreement, with annex.

Signed at Vienna April 5, 1989.

Entered into force April 5, 1989.

TIAS 11774.

INTERNATIONAL CENTRE FOR THE STUDY OF THE PRESERVATION AND THE RESTORATION OF CULTURAL PROPERTY (ICCROM)

TAXATION

Agreement relating to a procedure for United States income tax reimbursement.

Exchange of letters at Rome April 1 and May 4, 1981.

Entered into force May 4, 1981; effective January 1981.

33 UST 1922; TIAS 10155.

INTERNATIONAL CIVIL AVIATION ORGANIZATION

AVIATION

Memorandum of agreement regarding the detail of Federal Aviation Administration personnel to the International Civil Aviation Organization

Signed February 19, 1999.

Entered into force February 19, 1999.

TIAS

Agreement amending the memorandum of cooperation of September 7 and 18, 1989 for the provision of technical expertise in the field of aviation security.

Signed at Washington and Montreal August 8 and 29, 2000.

Entered into force August 29, 2000.

TIAS

Memorandum of understanding

Signed September 23, 2003.

Entered into force September 23, 2003.

TIAS

Memorandum of understanding

Signed September 29, 2004.

Entered into force September 29, 2004.

TIAS

TAXATION

Tax reimbursement agreement, with annex.
Signed at Montreal July 14, 1992.
Entered into force July 14, 1992.
TIAS 12465.

INTERNATIONAL COTTON ADVISORY COMMITTEE

TAXATION

Agreement relating to a procedure for United States income tax reimbursement.
Exchange of notes at Washington November 17 and 19, 1981.
Entered into force January 1, 1982.
33 UST 4242; TIAS 10299.

INTERNATIONAL HYDROGRAPHIC BUREAU

TAXATION

Agreement relating to a procedure for United States income tax reimbursement.
Exchange of letters at Marseilles December 7 and 13, 1982.
Entered into force January 1, 1983.
TIAS 12058.

INTERNATIONAL LABOR ORGANIZATION

PEACE CORPS

Agreement concerning the Peace Corps program.
Exchange of notes at Geneva February 21 and 22, 1963.
Entered into force February 22, 1963.
14 UST 1554; TIAS 5458; 489 UNTS 347.

TAXATION

Agreement relating to a procedure for United States income tax reimbursement, with annex.
Signed at Washington May 18, 1984.
Entered into force May 18, 1984, effective January 1, 1984.
TIAS 11076; 2039 UNTS 267.

INTERNATIONAL MARITIME ORGANIZATION

TAXATION

Tax reimbursement agreement, with annex.
Signed at London January 12, 1995.
Entered into force January 12, 1995.
TIAS 12597.

INTERNATIONAL MONETARY FUND

FINANCE

Agreement relating to provision of financing by the United States in connection with the establishment of the Supplementary Financing Facility.
Exchange of letters at Washington January 5 and 12, 1979.
Entered into force January 16, 1979.
30 UST 3526; TIAS 9406; 1180 UNTS 131.

INTERNATIONAL NATURAL RUBBER ORGANIZATION

TAXATION

Tax reimbursement agreement, with annex.
Signed at Kuala Lumpur October 5, 1988.
Entered into force October 5, 1988.
TIAS 11627; 2191 UNTS 169.

INTERNATIONAL ORGANIZATION FOR MIGRATION

TAXATION

Tax reimbursement agreement, with annex.
Signed at Washington September 17, 1997.
Entered into force September 17, 1997.
TIAS

INTERNATIONAL TELECOMMUNICATION UNION

TAXATION

Tax reimbursement agreement, with annex.
Signed at Geneva January 19, 1990.
Entered into force January 19, 1990.
TIAS 11710; 2207 UNTS 371.

TELECOMMUNICATION

Special arrangement permitting third party exchanges between the International Telecommunications Union amateur radio station and amateur radio stations under United States jurisdiction.
Exchange of letters at Geneva and Washington April 28 and June 7, 1976.
Entered into force June 7, 1976.
28 UST 5019; TIAS 8608.

INTERNATIONAL TELECOMMUNICATIONS SATELLITE ORGANIZATION

HEADQUARTERS

Headquarters agreement.
Signed at Washington November 22 and 24, 1976.
Entered into force November 24, 1976.
28 UST 2248; TIAS 8542.

SATELLITES

Memorandum of agreement with respect to the Pan American Satellite Corporation consultation, with related letter.
Signed at Washington November 10, 1986.
Entered into force November 10, 1986.
TIAS 12390.

INTERNATIONAL TRIBUNAL FOR THE PROSECUTION OF PERSONS RESPONSIBLE FOR GENOCIDE AND OTHER SERIOUS VIOLATIONS OF INTERNATIONAL HUMANITARIAN LAW COMMITTED IN THE TERRITORY OF RWANDA

WAR CRIMES

Agreement on surrender of persons, with statement of understanding.

Signed at The Hague January 24, 1995.

Entered into force February 14, 1996.

TIAS 12601.

INTERNATIONAL TRIBUNAL FOR THE PROSECUTION OF PERSONS RESPONSIBLE FOR SERIOUS VIOLATIONS OF INTERNATIONAL HUMANITARIAN LAW IN THE TERRITORY OF THE FORMER YUGOSLAVIA

WAR CRIMES

Agreement on surrender of persons.

Signed at The Hague October 5, 1994.

Entered into force February 14, 1996.

TIAS 12570; 1911 UNTS 223.

INTERNATIONAL TROPICAL TIMBER ORGANIZATION

TAXATION

Tax reimbursement agreement, with annex.

Signed at Tokyo December 27, 1988.

Entered into force December 27, 1988.

TIAS 11629; 2191 UNTS 189.

IRAN

AGRICULTURAL COMMODITIES

Agricultural commodities agreement with exchanges of notes of July 26 and 28, 1960.

Signed at Tehran July 26, 1960.

Entered into force July 26, 1960.

11 UST 1944; TIAS 4544; 384 UNTS 141.

Amendments

September 26, 1960 (11 UST 2208; TIAS 4592; 394 UNTS 318).

October 20, 1960 (11 UST 2239; TIAS 4598; 394 UNTS 324).

April 10 and 17, 1961 (12 UST 321; TIAS 4719; 405 UNTS 370).

May 18 and June 1, 1961 (12 UST 855; TIAS 4785; 410 UNTS 355).

Agreement concerning the closeout of the collection account of the agricultural commodities agreement of February 20, 1956.

Exchange of notes at Tehran March 29 and July 2, 1961.

Entered into force July 2, 1961.

12 UST 3221; TIAS 4928; 434 UNTS 321.

Agricultural commodities agreement, with exchange of notes of January 29 and February 8, 1962.

Signed at Tehran January 29, 1962.

Entered into force January 29, 1962.

13 UST 174; TIAS 4956; 435 UNTS 53.

Amendments

February 17 and 20, 1962 (13 UST 174; TIAS 4956; 435 UNTS 53).

February 10 and September 1, 1964 (15 UST 1955; TIAS 5671; 531 UNTS 382).

Agricultural commodities agreement with exchanges of notes of October 15 and December 30, 1962 and February 3, 1963.

Signed at Tehran October 15, 1962.

Entered into force October 15, 1962.

14 UST 215; TIAS 5300; 473 UNTS 291.

Agricultural commodities agreement, with exchange of notes of November 18, 1963 and June 11, 1964.

Signed at Tehran November 17, 1963.

Entered into force November 17, 1963.

15 UST 755; TIAS 5600; 530 UNTS 41.

Agricultural commodities agreement, with exchange of notes.

Signed at Tehran September 29, 1964.

Entered into force September 29, 1964.

15 UST 1958; TIAS 5672; 531 UNTS 163.

Agricultural commodities agreement with exchange of notes.

Signed at Tehran November 16, 1964.

Entered into force November 16, 1964.

15 UST 2140; TIAS 5696; 532 UNTS 213.

Amendments

December 15, 1964 (15 UST 2327; TIAS 5721; 532 UNTS 213).

April 28, 1965 (16 UST 662; TIAS 5792; 546 UNTS 408).

October 13, 1965 (16 UST 1870; TIAS 5918; 574 UNTS 276).

Agricultural commodities agreement with exchange of notes.

Signed at Tehran December 20, 1966.

Entered into force December 20, 1966.

17 UST 2372; TIAS 6183; 681 UNTS 101.

AVIATION

Air transport agreement, with exchange of notes.

Signed at Tehran February 1, 1973.

Entered into force January 9, 1974.

26 UST 1929; TIAS 8149; 1027 UNTS 129.

Memorandum of agreement relating to the provision of technical assistance to the Iranian Civil Aviation Organization, with annex.

Signed at Washington and Tehran May 12 and June 9, 1977.

Entered into force June 9, 1977.

29 UST 5319; TIAS 9111.

CLAIMS

Declarations of the Government of the Democratic and Popular Republic of Algeria concerning commitments and settlement of claims by the United States and Iran with respect to resolution of the crisis arising out of the detention of 52 United States nationals in Iran, with Undertakings and Escrow Agreement.[1]

Initialed at Algiers January 19, 1981.

Entered into force January 19, 1981.

TIAS

Settlement agreement regarding certain claims before the Iran-U.S. Claims Tribunal, with annex.

Signed at The Hague February 9, 1996.

Entered into force February 9, 1996.

TIAS

Settlement agreement on the case concerning the aerial incident of July 3, 1988 before the International Court of Justice, with annexes.

Signed at The Hague February 9, 1996.

Entered into force February 9, 1996.

TIAS

General agreement on the settlement of certain I.C.J. and Tribunal cases, with related statement.

Signed at The Hague February 9, 1996.

Entered into force February 9, 1996.

TIAS

NOTE

1 For technical agreements concerning the security account, see NETHERLANDS — CLAIMS.

COMMERCE

Treaty of amity, economic relations, and consular rights.

Signed at Tehran August 15, 1955.

Entered into force June 16, 1957.

8 UST 899; TIAS 3853; 284 UNTS 93.

CONSULS

See COMMERCE

DEFENSE

Mutual defense assistance agreement.

Exchange of notes at Washington May 23, 1950.

Entered into force May 23, 1950.

1 UST 420; TIAS 2071; 81 UNTS 3.

Agreement relating to the continuation of military assistance to Iran.

Exchange of notes at Tehran April 24, 1952.

Entered into force April 24, 1952.

5 UST 788; TIAS 2967.

Agreement relating to the disposition of equipment and materials no longer required in the furtherance of the mutual defense assistance program.

Exchange of notes at Tehran July 12 and October 31, 1957.

Entered into force October 31, 1957.

8 UST 2369; TIAS 3952; 303 UNTS 320.

Agreement relating to the safeguarding of classified information, with annex.

Exchange of notes at Tehran May 28 and June 6, 1974.

Entered into force June 6, 1974.

25 UST 1266; TIAS 7857.

Agreement relating to the furnishing of certain federal catalog data and cataloging services to Iran.

Signed at Washington December 5, 1974 and at Tehran January 25, 1975.

Entered into force January 25, 1975.

26 UST 302; TIAS 8034; 991 UNTS 401.

Agreement concerning management, disposal, and utilization of funds derived from the sale of military assistance program property.

Signed at Tehran October 6, 1975.

Entered into force October 6, 1975.

TIAS

Agreement concerning management, disposal, and utilization of funds derived from sale of military assistance program property.

Signed at Tehran October 19, 1976.

Entered into force October 19, 1976.

TIAS

Memorandum of understanding concerning revisions of Foreign Military Sales letters of offer and acceptance in force between the United States and Iran.

Signed at Tehran February 3, 1979.

Entered into force February 3, 1979.

30 UST 3597; TIAS 9415.

DISASTER ASSISTANCE

Memorandum of understanding relating to the provision of advisory technical assistance to Iran in organizing its civil emergency preparedness capability

Signed January 26, 1977.

Entered into force January 26, 1977.

30 UST 4354; TIAS 9461.

ECONOMIC AND TECHNICAL COOPERATION

General agreement for economic cooperation.

Signed at Tehran December 21, 1961.

Entered into force December 21, 1961.

12 UST 3229; TIAS 4930; 433 UNTS 269.

Joint communique concerning United States-Iran relations and establishment of a Joint Commission for cooperation in various fields.

Issued at Tehran November 2, 1974.

Entered into force November 2, 1974.

25 UST 3073; TIAS 7967.

Agreed minutes of the Joint Commission:

March 4, 1975 (26 UST 420; TIAS 8042).

August 7, 1976 (27 UST 4329; TIAS 8455).

February 28, 1978 (30 UST 1027; TIAS 9238; 1152 UNTS 103).

EDUCATION

Agreement for financing certain educational exchange programs.

Signed at Tehran October 24, 1963.

Entered into force October 24, 1963.

14 UST 1510; TIAS 5451; 489 UNTS 303.

FINANCE

Agreement relating to investment guaranties under section 413(b)(4) of the Mutual Security Act of 1954, as amended.

Exchange of notes at Tehran September 17 and 21, 1957.

Entered into force September 24, 1957.

8 UST 1599; TIAS 3913; 293 UNTS 287.

Agreement supplementing the agreement of September 17 and 21, 1957 relating to investment guaranties.

Exchange of notes at Tehran March 12, 1970.

Entered into force March 12, 1970.

22 UST 1030; TIAS 7146; 797 UNTS 396.

HOSTAGES

See CLAIMS

JUDICIAL ASSISTANCE

Agreement on procedures for mutual assistance in connection with matters relating to the Lockheed Aircraft Corporation, Grumman Corporation and Northrop Corporation.

Signed at Washington June 14, 1977.

Entered into force June 14, 1977.

28 UST 5205; TIAS 8621.

METEOROLOGY

Agreement relating to a cooperative program to improve and modernize the Iranian meteorological services, with annexes.

Signed at Tehran November 26, 1977.

Entered into force November 26, 1977.

29 UST 5546; TIAS 9127; 1134 UNTS 359.

MISSIONS, MILITARY

Agreement relating to the privileges and immunities granted American military and non-military technicians assisting in the modernization program of the Imperial Iranian Armed Forces.

Exchange of notes at Tehran May 24 and 30, 1973.

Entered into force May 30, 1973.

25 UST 3048; TIAS 7963.

PEACE CORPS

Agreement relating to the establishment of a Peace Corps program in Iran.

Exchange of notes at Tehran September 5 and 16, 1962.

Entered into force September 16, 1962.

22 UST 434; TIAS 7078; 791 UNTS 19.

POSTAL MATTERS

Parcel post agreement with detailed regulations for execution.

Signed at Tehran July 15 and at Washington August 28, 1969.

Entered into force January 1, 1971.

21 UST 2605; TIAS 7002; 775 UNTS 17.

PUBLICATIONS

Agreement relating to the exchange of official publications.

Exchange of notes at Tehran August 21, 1943.

Entered into force August 21, 1943.

57 Stat. 1133; EAS 349; 8 Bevans 1280; 101 UNTS 189.

RELIEF SUPPLIES AND PACKAGES

Agreement relating to duty-free entry and defrayment of inland transportation charges for relief supplies to Iran.

Exchange of notes at Tehran September 22 and October 5 and 13, 1953.

Entered into force October 13, 1953.

4 UST 2809; TIAS 2890; 222 UNTS 67.

TRADE

See also COMMERCE

Agreement terminating the reciprocal trade agreement of April 8, 1943, as amended.

Exchange of notes at Tehran July 27, 1960.

Entered into force July 27, 1960.

11 UST 2163; TIAS 4581; 393 UNTS 338.

VISAS

Agreement relating to the reciprocal waiver of passport visa fees for nonimmigrants.

Exchange of notes at Tehran March 27 and April 20 and 21, 1926.

Entered into force April 21, 1926; operative May 15, 1926.

8 Bevans 1260.

Agreement relating to the reciprocal issuance of multiple-entry nonimmigrant visas.

Exchange of letters at Tehran December 13 and 16, 1976.

Entered into force December 16, 1976; effective January 1, 1977.

28 UST 8161; TIAS 8751.

IRAQ

CLAIMS

Agreement concerning claims resulting from attack on the U.S.S. *Stark*.

Exchange of notes at Baghdad March 27 and 28, 1989.

Entered into force March 28, 1989.

TIAS 12030.

COMMERCE

See also ECONOMIC AND TECHNICAL COOPERATION

Treaty of commerce and navigation.

Signed at Baghdad December 3, 1938.

Entered into force June 19, 1940.

54 Stat. 1790; TS 960; 9 Bevans 7; 203 LNTS 107.

CULTURAL RELATIONS

Cultural agreement.

Signed at Baghdad January 23, 1961.

Entered into force August 13, 1963.

14 UST 1168; TIAS 5411; 488 UNTS 163.

CUSTOMS

Agreement relating to the privilege, on a reciprocal basis, of free entry to all articles imported for the personal use of consular officers.

Exchange of notes at Washington March 14, May 15, June 19, and August 8, 1951.

Entered into force August 8, 1951.

5 UST 657; TIAS 2956; 229 UNTS 185.

DEFENSE

Agreement confirming understanding of Iraq that paragraphs 1 and 4 of the military assistance agreement of April 21, 1954 apply to equipment or materials transferred by the United States to Iraq on a reimbursable basis.

Exchange of notes at Baghdad December 3, 1955.

Entered into force December 3, 1955.

6 UST 6014; TIAS 3447; 241 UNTS 19.

Agreement terminating the military assistance agreement of April 21, 1954 (TIAS 3108), the agreement of July 25, 1955 relating to the disposition of military equipment and materials (TIAS 3289), and the economic assistance agreement of May 18 and 22, 1957 (TIAS 3835).

Exchange of notes at Baghdad May 30 and July 7, 1959.

Entered into force July 21, 1959.

10 UST 1415; TIAS 4289; 357 UNTS 153.

Agreement regarding grants under the Foreign Assistance Act of 1961, as amended, or successor legislation, and such items as the Government of the United States of America may otherwise furnish, or authorize under the furnishing of, from time to time, under other authority, to the Government of Iraq.

Exchange of notes at Baghdad July 24 and August 14, 2004.

Entered into force August 14, 2004.

TIAS

Agreement regarding bilateral end use, retransfer and security assurances.

Exchange of notes at Baghdad July 28 and August 14, 2004.

Entered into force August 14, 2004.

TIAS

ECONOMIC AND TECHNICAL COOPERATION

General agreement for technical cooperation.

Signed at Baghdad April 10, 1951.

Entered into force June 2, 1951.

3 UST 541; TIAS 2413; 151 UNTS 179.

Amendment

December 18, 1951 and February 21, 1952 (3 UST 4748; TIAS 2638; 198 UNTS 225).

Commercial, economic and technical cooperation agreement.

Signed at Washington August 26, 1987.

Entered into force October 27, 1987.

TIAS 12020.

EDUCATION

Agreement providing for the United States education foundation in Iraq.

Signed at Baghdad August 16, 1951.

Entered into force August 16, 1951.

2 UST 1908; TIAS 2327; 147 UNTS 65.

EMBASSY SITES

Agreement on diplomatic and consular property, with notes.

Signed at Baghdad October 31, 2004.

Entered into force October 31, 2004.

TIAS

EXTRADITION

Extradition treaty.

Signed at Baghdad June 7, 1934.

Entered into force April 23, 1936.

49 Stat. 3380; TS 907; 9 Bevans 1; 170 LNTS 267.

FINANCE

Agreement regarding the cancellation of certain debts owed to, guaranteed by, or insured by the United States Government, with annex.

Signed at Washington December 17, 2004.

Entered into force March 7, 2005.

TIAS

LEND-LEASE

Agreement on the principles applying to aid for defense, and exchange of notes.

Signed at Washington July 31, 1945.

Entered into force July 31, 1945.

59 Stat. 1535; EAS 470; 9 Bevans 22; 121 UNTS 239.

POSTAL MATTERS

International express mail agreement, with detailed regulations.

Signed at Baghdad and Washington April 6 and May 5, 1989.

Entered into force June 15, 1989.

TIAS 11609.

PUBLICATIONS

Agreement relating to the exchange of official publications.

Exchange of notes at Baghdad February 16, 1944.

Entered into force February 16, 1944.

58 Stat. 1253; EAS 403; 9 Bevans 14; 109 UNTS 223.

IRELAND

ATOMIC ENERGY

Agreement providing for a grant to assist in the acquisition of certain nuclear research and training equipment and materials.

Exchange of notes at Dublin March 24, 1960.

Entered into force April 7, 1960.

11 UST 376; TIAS 4453; 371 UNTS 237.

AVIATION

Arrangement relating to air navigation.

Exchange of notes at Dublin September 29 and November 4, 1937.

Entered into force November 4, 1937; operative December 4, 1937.

51 Stat. 319; EAS 110; 9 Bevans 36; 185 LNTS 71.

Agreement relating to air transport services.

Exchange of notes at Washington February 3, 1945.

Entered into force February 3, 1945; operative February 15, 1945.

59 Stat. 1402; EAS 460; 9 Bevans 43; 122 UNTS 305.

Amendments

January 25, 1988 and September 29, 1989 (TIAS 11692).

July 25 and September 6, 1990 (TIAS 11739).

Memorandum of agreement relating to flight inspection services.

Signed at Washington and Dublin March 10 and August 4, 1978.

Entered into force August 4, 1978; effective September 1, 1978.

30 UST 230; TIAS 9190; 1150 UNTS 141.

Agreement on preinspection of aircraft passengers and crew at Shannon airport.

Signed at Dublin June 25, 1986.

Entered into force June 25, 1986.

TIAS 11379.

Related agreement

March 31, 1988 (TIAS 11379; 2194 UNTS 391).

Agreement for promotion of aviation safety.

Signed at Dublin February 5, 1997.

Entered into force February 5, 1997.

TIAS; 2141 UNTS 293.

Agreement on technical cooperation in civil aviation matters.

Signed at Dublin June 11, 1999.

Entered into force June 11, 1999.

TIAS

COMMERCE

Treaty of friendship, commerce and navigation, with protocol.

Signed at Dublin January 21, 1950.

Entered into force September 14, 1950.

1 UST 785; TIAS 2155; 206 UNTS 269.

Protocol to the treaty of friendship, commerce and navigation of January 21, 1950.

Signed at Washington June 24, 1992.

Entered into force November 18, 1992.

TIAS

CONSULS

Consular convention.[1]

Signed at Dublin May 1, 1950.

Entered into force June 12, 1954.

5 UST 949; TIAS 2984; 222 UNTS 107.

Amendment

June 16, 1998.

Supplementary protocol to the consular convention of May 1, 1950.

Signed at Dublin March 3, 1952.

Entered into force June 12, 1954.

5 UST 949; TIAS 2984; 222 UNTS 107.

NOTE

1 Applicable to all territories.

CUSTOMS

Agreement regarding mutual assistance between their customs administrations.

Signed at Dublin September 16, 1996.

Entered into force May 21, 1998.

TIAS 12800; 2141 UNTS 51.

DEFENSE

Agreement concerning security measures for the protection of classified military information.

Signed at Dublin January 31, 2003.

Entered into force January 31, 2003.

TIAS

Acquisition and cross-servicing agreement, with annexes.

Signed at Stuttgart-Vaihingen and Dublin February 26 and 27, 2004.

Entered into force February 27, 2004.

TIAS

EDUCATION

Agreement for a program of educational exchange.

Signed at Dublin October 27, 1988.

Entered into force February 3, 1992.

TIAS; 1732 UNTS 141.

EMPLOYMENT

Agreement relating to the employment of dependents of official government employees.

Exchange of notes at Washington September 17, 1996 and August 1, 1997.

Entered into force August 1, 1997.

TIAS ; 2080 UNTS 83.

ENVIRONMENTAL COOPERATION

Agreement for cooperation in the Global Learning and Observations to Benefit the Environment (GLOBE) Program, with appendices.

Signed at Dublin June 12, 1995.

Entered into force June 12, 1995.

TIAS 12659.

EXTRADITION

Treaty on extradition.

Signed at Washington July 13, 1983.

Entered into force December 15, 1984.

TIAS 10813.

FINANCE [1]

NOTE:

1 For international fund for Ireland, see under FINANCE in multilateral section.

Agreement relating to investment guaranties under section 413(b)(4) of the Mutual Security Act of 1954, as amended.

Exchange of notes at Dublin October 5, 1955.

Entered into force October 5, 1955.

6 UST 3953; TIAS 3405; 256 UNTS 285.

POSTAL MATTERS

Parcel post convention.

Signed at Dublin April 23 and at Washington May 6, 1926; operative May 1, 1926.

44 Stat. 2412; Post Office Department print; 56 LNTS 433.

International express mail agreement with detailed regulations.

Signed at Dublin and Washington February 29 and March 20, 1984.

Entered into force May 19, 1984.

35 UST 4856; TIAS 10971; 1566 UNTS 169.

PROPERTY

Convention between the United States and the United Kingdom relating to tenure and disposition of real and personal property.[1]

Signed at Washington March 2, 1899.

Entered into force August 7, 1900.

31 Stat. 1939; TS 146; 12 Bevans 246.

NOTE

1 Only article III is in force for Ireland.

SOCIAL SECURITY

Agreement on social security, with administrative arrangement.

Signed at Washington April 14, 1992.

Entered into force September 1, 1993.

TIAS 12117.

TAXATION

Convention for the avoidance of double taxation and the prevention of fiscal evasion with respect to taxes on the estates of deceased persons.

Signed at Dublin September 13, 1949.

Entered into force December 20, 1951.

2 UST 2294; TIAS 2355; 127 UNTS 119.

Convention for the avoidance of double taxation and the prevention of fiscal evasion with respect to taxes on income and capital gains, with protocol and related agreement.[1]

Signed at Dublin July 28, 1997.

Entered into force December 17, 1997.

TIAS; 2141 UNTS 167.

Amendment

September 24, 1999 (2142 UNTS 330).

NOTE

1 With understanding.

TELECOMMUNICATION

Agreement relating to the reciprocal granting of authorizations to permit licensed amateur radio operators of either country to operate their stations in the other country.

Exchange of notes at Dublin October 10, 1968.

Entered into force October 10, 1968.

19 UST 6057; TIAS 6566; 694 UNTS 103.

VISAS

Agreement relating to the relaxation of visa requirements for American citizens entering Ireland and the granting of gratis nonimmigrant passport visas to Irish citizens entering the United States.

Exchange of notes at Dublin August 1, 1949.

Entered into force August 1, 1949.

63 Stat. 2807; TIAS 2050; 9 Bevans 66; 82 UNTS 37.

ISRAEL

AGRICULTURAL COMMODITIES

Agricultural commodities agreement, with memorandum of understanding.

Signed at Washington May 3, 1962.

Entered into force May 3, 1962.

13 UST 432; TIAS 5004; 442 UNTS 83.

Amendments

October 12 and 16, 1962 (13 UST 2176; TIAS 5180; 460 UNTS 348).

January 26 and February 1, 1963 (14 UST 200; TIAS 5296; 473 UNTS 368).

Agreement relating to the closeout of the collection accounts of the agricultural commodities agreements of April 29, 1955, November 10, 1955, September 11, 1956, and November 7, 1957.

Exchange of notes at Tel Aviv June 14 and Jerusalem August 28, 1962.

Entered into force August 28, 1962.

13 UST 2068; TIAS 5162; 448 UNTS 317.

Agricultural commodities agreement, with memorandum of understanding.

Signed at Washington December 6, 1962.

Entered into force December 6, 1962.

13 UST 2550; TIAS 5220; 460 UNTS 151.

Amendments

December 24 and 30, 1963 (14 UST 1794; TIAS 5490; 494 UNTS 334).

April 27, 1964 (15 UST 314; TIAS 5557; 515 UNTS 310).

June 23, 1964 (15 UST 730; TIAS 5596; 515 UNTS 314).

July 6, 1964 (15 UST 1396; TIAS 5610; 515 UNTS 318).

May 26 and 27, 1965 (16 UST 770; TIAS 5808; 545 UNTS 352).

June 22, 1965 (16 UST 770; TIAS 5808; 545 UNTS 356).

Agreement providing agricultural commodities for the improvement and expansion of the school feeding program in Israel, with annex.

Exchange of notes at Tel Aviv and Jerusalem February 28 and March 21, 1963.

Entered into force March 21, 1963.

14 UST 471; TIAS 5344; 476 UNTS 131.

Agricultural commodities agreement, with exchange of notes.

Signed at Washington December 22, 1964.

Entered into force December 22, 1964.

15 UST 2329; TIAS 5722; 532 UNTS 231.

Agricultural commodities agreement with exchange of notes.

Signed at Washington June 6, 1966.

Entered into force June 6, 1966.

17 UST 727; TIAS 6023; 578 UNTS 143.

Agricultural commodities agreement with exchange of notes.

Signed at Washington June 6, 1966.

Entered into force June 6, 1966.

17 UST 817; TIAS 6039; 593 UNTS 165.

Agricultural commodities agreement with annexes.

Signed at Washington August 4, 1967.

Entered into force August 4, 1967.

18 UST 1684; TIAS 6314; 653 UNTS 81.

Related agreements

March 29, 1968 (19 UST 4716; TIAS 6466; 653 UNTS 113).

August 19, 1968 (19 UST 5924; TIAS 6547; 653 UNTS 121).

January 17, 1969 (20 UST 1; TIAS 6625; 714 UNTS 129).

May 7, 1970 (21 UST 1115; TIAS 6871; 745 UNTS 209).

August 27, 1970 (21 UST 1965; TIAS 6938).

October 5, 1970 (21 UST 2152; TIAS 6962).

February 9, 1971 (22 UST 216; TIAS 7052; 792 UNTS 99).

June 4, 1971 (22 UST 676; TIAS 7123; 792 UNTS 108).

August 4, 1971 (22 UST 1471; TIAS 7161; 792 UNTS 112).

January 13, 1972 (23 UST 11; TIAS 7268; 829 UNTS 203).

July 18, 1972 (23 UST 1241; TIAS 7395).

October 13, 1972 (23 UST 2823; TIAS 7472).

November 19, 1973 (24 UST 2255; TIAS 7745).

Agricultural commodities agreement.

Signed at Washington December 16, 1974.

Entered into force December 16, 1974.

25 UST 3140; TIAS 7978; 991 UNTS 413.

Amendment

October 17, 1975 (26 UST 2926; TIAS 8200; 1021 UNTS 479).

Related agreements

September 30, 1976 (27 UST 3543; TIAS 8382).

October 12, 1976 (27 UST 3545; TIAS 8382).

December 10, 1976 (27 UST 4173; TIAS 8443).

December 21, 1977 (29 UST 3281; TIAS 9012; 1124 UNTS 69).

January 16, 1979 (30 UST 2896; TIAS 9371; 1179 UNTS 377).

July 23, 1980 (32 UST 2571; TIAS 9858; 1274 UNTS 217).

ATOMIC ENERGY

Agreement providing for a grant to assist in the acquisition of certain nuclear research and training equipment and materials.

Exchange of notes at Tel Aviv October 19 and at Jerusalem December 19, 1960.

Entered into force December 19, 1960.

11 UST 2631; TIAS 4655; 401 UNTS 195.

Agreement continuing in effect safeguards and guarantee provisions of the agreement of July 12, 1955 (6 UST 2641; TIAS 3311), as amended, for cooperation concerning civil uses of atomic energy.

Exchange of notes at Washington April 7 and 8, 1977.

Entered into force April 8, 1977.

28 UST 2407; TIAS 8557.

Arrangement for the exchange of technical information and cooperation in nuclear safety and research matters, with addenda.

Signed at Rockville April 7, 2005.

Entered into force April 7, 2005.

TIAS

AVIATION

Air transport agreement.

Signed at Tel Aviv June 13, 1950.

Entered into force June 13, 1950.[1]

3 UST 4582; TIAS 2610; 212 UNTS 93.

Amendments

August 16, 1978 (29 UST 3144; TIAS 9002; 1123 UNTS 321).

December 16, 1986 and January 5, 1987 (TIAS 11524).

July 11, 2001.

March 24 and 30, 2004.

March 29 and 31, 2005.

April 4 and May 9, 2006.

Agreement relating to the reciprocal acceptance of certificates of airworthiness for imported aircraft.

Exchange of notes at Washington July 23, 1968.

Entered into force July 23, 1968.

19 UST 5459; TIAS 6530; 653 UNTS 159.

Amendment

September 4, 1974 (25 UST 2445; TIAS 7926).

Memorandum of agreement relating to technical assistance in developing and improving air traffic operation in the Ben Gurion Airport.

Signed at Washington January 27, 1983.

Entered into force January 27, 1983.

35 UST 3061; TIAS 10838; 1590 UNTS 73.

Memorandum of cooperation concerning technical cooperation in civil aviation security with annex.

Signed at Washington and Tel Aviv July 6 and September 30, 1990.

Entered into force September 30, 1990.

TIAS 11970; 2244 UNTS 283.

Agreement for promotion of aviation safety

Signed December 19, 2000.

Entered into force December 19, 2000.

TIAS

NOTE

1 For correction of Hebrew text, see exchange of notes of February 21, 1951 (3 UST 4610; TIAS 2610).

CLAIMS

Agreement concerning claims arising from damage to the United States ship "Liberty".

Exchange of notes at Washington December 15 and 17, 1980.

Entered into force December 17, 1980.

32 UST 4434; TIAS 9957; 1268 UNTS 33.

COMMERCE

Treaty of friendship, commerce, and navigation, with protocol and exchange of notes.

Signed at Washington August 23, 1951.

Entered into force April 3, 1954.

5 UST 550; TIAS 2948; 219 UNTS 237.

COPYRIGHT

Agreement relating to reciprocal copyright relations.

Exchange of notes at Washington May 4, 1950.

Entered into force May 4, 1950; operative May 15, 1948.

1 UST 645; TIAS 2121; 132 UNTS 189.

CUSTOMS

Agreement regarding mutual assistance in customs matters.

Signed at Washington May 16, 1996.

Entered into force September 24, 1997.

TIAS 12755; 2017 UNTS 213.

DEFENSE

See also MUTUAL SECURITY

Agreement relating to mutual defense assistance.

Exchange of notes at Tel Aviv July 1 and 23, 1952.

Entered into force July 23, 1952.

3 UST 4985; TIAS 2675; 179 UNTS 139.

Agreement relating to general procurement arrangements for goods and services.

Exchange of notes at Washington July 15 and 20, 1965.

Entered into force July 20, 1965.

16 UST 983; TIAS 5839; 549 UNTS 55.

Agreement relating to the purchase of various goods from Israel for sale in United States Navy ships stores overseas.

Exchange of notes at Washington July 20 and 26, 1965.

Entered into force July 26, 1965.

16 UST 981; TIAS 5838; 549 UNTS 49.

Agreement regarding payment for tooling costs of accelerated production of M-60A1 tanks.

Signed at Washington and New York August 22 and October 23, 1975.

Entered into force October 23, 1975.

TIAS 12324.

Agreement concerning construction of airbase facilities.

Signed at Tel Aviv April 6, 1979.

Entered into force April 6, 1979.

30 UST 4107; TIAS 9450; 1171 UNTS 233.

Agreement concerning funding of airbase construction.

Signed at Tel Aviv April 6, 1979.

Entered into force April 6, 1979.

30 UST 4134; TIAS 9451; 1171 UNTS 251.

General security of information agreement.

Exchange of notes at Tel Aviv and Jerusalem July 30 and December 10, 1982.

Entered into force December 10, 1982.

TIAS 10617; 2001 UNTS 3.

Memorandum of agreement concerning the principles governing mutual cooperation in research and development, scientist and engineer exchange, and procurement and logistic support of defense equipment, with annexes and attachment.

Signed at Washington December 14, 1987.

Entered into force December 14, 1987.

TIAS

Amendment

December 19, 1997 and January 8, 1998.

Agreement on the status of United States personnel, with annexes and related letter.

Signed at Jerusalem January 22, 1991.

Entered into force January 12, 1994.

TIAS

Agreement on the status of Israeli personnel.

Signed at Jerusalem January 22, 1991.

Entered into force January 12, 1994.

TIAS

Memorandum of agreement for a cooperative project of research in the field of rotorcraft aeromechanics and man-machine integration technology, with annex.

Signed at Alexandria December 2, 1992.

Entered into force December 2, 1992.

TIAS

Amendment

June 23 and August 28, 2003.

Agreement for technology research and development projects, with annex.

Signed at Washington and Tel Aviv August 22 and September 3, 1996.

Entered into force September 3, 1996.

TIAS 12798.

Acquisition and cross-servicing agreement, with annexes.

Signed at Washington and Stuttgart February 9 and 10, 1998.

Entered into force February 10, 1998.

TIAS

Agreement amending and extending the memorandum of agreement of March 30, 1989, as amended and extended, concerning cooperative research on development and implementation of a theater ballistic missile defense test bed.

Signed at Washington and New York March 29, 1999.

Entered into force March 29, 1999.

TIAS

Memorandum of agreement concerning combating terrorism research and development, with annex.

Signed at Washington and Tel Aviv February 7 and March 24, 2005.

Entered into force March 24, 2005.

TIAS

Memorandum of agreement regarding the assignment of individuals at government facilities to serve as liaison officers.

Signed at Washington September 6 and 7, 2005.

Entered into force September 7, 2005.

TIAS

Annex to the master defense development data exchange agreement of December 22, 1970 on chemical and biological warfare defense modeling and simulation.

Signed at Fort Belvoir February 7, 2006.

Entered into force February 7, 2006.

TIAS

Memorandum of agreement regarding the assignment of liaison officers, with annex.

Signed at Tel Aviv June 11, 2006.

Entered into force June 11, 2006.

NP

ECONOMIC AND TECHNICAL COOPERATION

General agreement for technical cooperation.

Signed at Tel Aviv February 26, 1951.

Entered into force February 26, 1951.

3 UST 379; TIAS 2401; 137 UNTS 57.

Amendment

June 21, 1954 (5 UST 1401; TIAS 3010; 219 UNTS 348).

Agreement relating to emergency economic assistance.

Exchange of notes at Washington May 1, 1952.

Entered into force May 1, 1952.

3 UST 4266; TIAS 2571; 177 UNTS 89.

Agreement relating to economic assistance.

Signed at Tel Aviv May 9, 1952.

Entered into force May 9, 1952.

3 UST 4174; TIAS 2561; 177 UNTS 269.

Agreement relating to special economic assistance.

Exchange of notes at Tel Aviv and Jerusalem November 25, 1953.

Entered into force November 25, 1953.

4 UST 2308; TIAS 2884; 219 UNTS 205.

Amendment

January 31, 1955 (6 UST 561; TIAS 3189; 241 UNTS 520).

Joint statement of the U.S.-Israel Joint Committee for Investment and Trade relating to expansion of economic cooperation.

Signed at Washington May 13, 1975.

Entered into force May 13, 1975.

26 UST 1674; TIAS 8127; 1006 UNTS 153.

Agreement establishing the Israel-United States Binational Industrial Research and Development Foundation, with annexes.

Signed at Jerusalem March 3, 1976.

Entered into force May 18, 1977.

28 UST 5129; TIAS 8615.

Agency for International Development

June 27, 1975 (26 UST 1873; TIAS 8144).

September 22, 1976 (28 UST 3179; TIAS 8581).

November 23, 1976 (28 UST 5813; TIAS 8660).

December 5, 1977 (29 UST 3559; TIAS 9028; 1124 UNTS 49).

December 5, 1977 (29 UST 5213; TIAS 9097).

December 5, 1977 (29 UST 5231; TIAS 9098).

November 15, 1979 (31 UST 4794; TIAS 9639).

December 12, 1979 (31 UST 5545; TIAS 9670).

December 3, 1980 (32 UST 4204; TIAS 9941; 1268 UNTS 27).

March 27, 1981 (33 UST 1952; TIAS 10158).

July 1, 1981 (33 UST 1956; TIAS 10158).

December 31, 1981 (33 UST 4064; TIAS 10283).

March 31, 1982 (34 UST 1096; TIAS 10394).

May 18, 1982 (34 UST 1100; TIAS 10394).

December 16, 1982 (TIAS 10630; 1935 UNTS 311).

December 30, 1982 (TIAS 10630).

March 31, 1983 (TIAS 10685; 2005 UNTS 542).

December 29, 1983 (35 UST 4143; TIAS 10912; 2015 UNTS 73).

October 31, 1984 (NP).

September 11, 1985 (NP).

October 30, 1985 (NP).

May 15, 1986 (NP).

September 29, 1986 (NP).

November 17, 1986 (NP).

December 31, 2001 (NP).

December 19, 2002 (NP).

February 19, 2004 (NP).

December 14, 2005 (NP).

EDUCATION

Agreement for financing certain educational exchange programs, with memorandum of understanding.

Exchange of notes at Tel Aviv and Jerusalem June 18 and 22, 1962.

Entered into force June 22, 1962.

TIAS 5097; 13 UST 1364; 448 UNTS 273

Amendments

March 21 and 23, 1967 (TIAS 6240; 18 UST 346; 630 UNTS 404).

January 10 and 30, 1985 (TIAS 11223).

EMBASSY SITES

Land lease and purchase agreement for construction of diplomatic facilities, with annexes.

Signed at Jerusalem January 18, 1989.

Entered into force January 18, 1989.

TIAS

Amendments

March 21 and April 10, 1989.

July 14 and 23, 1989.

January 22 and 30, 1990.

January 21 and March 8, 1992 (TIAS 11858).

February 9 and December 13, 2000.

December 3, 2001 and January 15, 2002.

January 2 and 14, 2003.

EMPLOYMENT

Agreement relating to the employment of dependents of official government employees.

Exchange of notes at Tel Aviv and Jerusalem September 23 and October 3, 1985.

Entered into force October 3, 1985.

TIAS 11171; 2126 UNTS 227.

ENERGY

Memorandum of agreement concerning an oil supply arrangement, with related understanding.

Signed at Washington June 22, 1979.

Entered into force November 25, 1979.

30 UST 5994; TIAS 9533; 1234 UNTS 224.

Amendment and extensions

October 19 and November 13, 1994 (TIAS 12580).

November 23, 2004.

Contingency implementing arrangements for the memorandum of agreement of June 22, 1979, concerning an oil supply arrangement, with related letter.

Signed at Washington October 17, 1980.

Entered into force October 17, 1980.

32 UST 3667; TIAS 9908; 1266 UNTS 370.

Amendment

June 21 and 27, 1995 (TIAS 12670).

ENVIRONMENTAL COOPERATION

Memorandum of understanding concerning cooperation in the field of environmental protection, with annexes.

Signed at Jerusalem February 20, 1991.

Entered into force February 20, 1991.

TIAS 11832.

Agreement for cooperation in the Global Learning and Observations to Benefit the Environment (GLOBE) Program, with appendices.

Signed at Jerusalem March 24, 1995.

Entered into force March 24, 1995.

TIAS 12622.

EXTRADITION

Convention relating to extradition.

Signed at Washington December 10, 1962.

Entered into force December 5, 1963.[1]

14 UST 1707; TIAS 5476; 484 UNTS 283.

NOTE

1 For understanding regarding certain errors in the translation of the Hebrew text, see exchange of notes of April 4 and 11, 1967 (18 UST 382; TIAS 6246).

FINANCE

Agreement relating to the industrial investment guaranty program pursuant to Section 111(b)(3) of the Economic Cooperation Act of 1948, as amended.

Exchange of notes at Tel Aviv August 7 and 8, 1952.

Entered into force August 8, 1952.

3 UST 5045; TIAS 2686; 181 UNTS 37.

Amendments

July 31 and August 11, 1957 (8 UST 1410; TIAS 3892; 289 UNTS 318).

February 5 and 20, 1963 (14 UST 337; TIAS 5316; 474 UNTS 332).

Agreement on encouragement of investment.

Signed at Washington September 12, 1994.

Entered into force September 12, 1994.

TIAS 12190.

INFORMATIONAL MEDIA GUARANTIES

Agreement relating to the informational media guaranty program pursuant to Section 111(b)(3) of the Economic Cooperation Act of 1948, as amended.

Exchange of notes at Tel Aviv June 9, 1952.

Entered into force June 9, 1952.

3 UST 4398; TIAS 2588; 178 UNTS 297.

INTERNATIONAL CRIMINAL COURT

Agreement regarding the surrender of persons to the International Criminal Court.

Signed at Jerusalem August 4, 2002.

Entered into force November 27, 2003.

TIAS

JUDICIAL ASSISTANCE

Treaty on mutual legal assistance in criminal matters, with related exchange of notes.

Signed at Jerusalem January 26, 1998.

Entered into force May 25, 1999.

TIAS; 2094 UNTS 17.

MUTUAL SECURITY

Agreement relating to assurances and economic assistance as authorized in the Mutual Security Act of 1951.

Exchange of notes at Washington December 7, 1951.

Entered into force December 7, 1951.

3 UST 2874; TIAS 2462; 157 UNTS 53.

PEACEKEEPING

Memorandum of agreement concerning assurances, consultations, and United States policy on matters related to Middle East peace.

Initialed at Jerusalem September 1, 1975; signed at Washington and Jerusalem February 27, 1976.

Entered into force February 27, 1976.[1]

32 UST 2150; TIAS 9828.

Memorandum of agreement concerning the United States role at any future Geneva peace conference.

Initialed at Jerusalem September 1, 1975; signed at Washington and Jerusalem February 27, 1976.

Entered into force February 27, 1976.[1]

32 UST 2160; TIAS 9829.

Memorandum of agreement relating to assurances concerning Middle East peace.

Signed at Washington March 26, 1979.

Entered into force March 26, 1979.

32 UST 2141; TIAS 9825; 1252 UNTS 77.

Agreement relating to implementation of the Egyptian-Israeli peace treaty of March 26, 1979.[2]

Letter signed at Washington March 26, 1979.

Entered into force March 26, 1979.

32 UST 2146; TIAS 9826.

Agreement relating to privileges and immunities for United States military members and civilian observers of the Multinational Force and Observers on leave in Israel.

Exchange of notes at Jerusalem and Tel Aviv September 28 and October 1, 1982.

Entered into force October 1, 1982.

TIAS 10558; 1871 UNTS 323.

Memorandum of agreement concerning ballistic missile threats.

Signed at Washington and Jerusalem October 31, 1998.

Entered into force October 31, 1998.

TIAS

NOTES

1 Some provisions are no longer in force.

2 See also MULTINATIONAL FORCE AND OBSERVERS in bilateral section and PEACEKEEPING in multilateral section.

POSTAL MATTERS

International express mail agreement, with detailed regulations.

Signed at Washington and Jerusalem September 8 and October 24, 1982.

Entered into force January 24, 1983.

TIAS 10548; 1777 UNTS 397.

Memorandum of understanding concerning the operation of the INTELPOST service, with details of implementation.

Signed at Jerusalem and Washington July 20 and November 5, 1987.

Entered into force November 5, 1987; effective September 1, 1987.

TIAS 11568.

PUBLICATIONS

Agreement relating to the exchange of official publications.

Exchange of notes at Tel Aviv February 13 and 19, 1950.

Entered into force February 19, 1950.

1 UST 912; TIAS 2169; 122 UNTS 117.

RELATIONS

Memorandum of agreement regarding joint political, security and economic cooperation.

Signed at Washington and Jerusalem April 21 and 28, 1988.

Entered into force April 21, 1988.

TIAS 11578.

SCIENTIFIC COOPERATION

Agreement on the United States-Israel binational science foundation with exchange of letters.

Signed at New York September 27, 1972.

Entered into force September 27, 1972.

23 UST 2669; TIAS 7460.

SEISMIC OBSERVATIONS

Memorandum of understanding concerning the installation, operation and maintenance of a seismic station.

Signed at Tel Aviv May 1, 1985.

Entered into force May 1, 1985.

TIAS 11176; 2130 UNTS 3.

SPACE COOPERATION

Agreement for cooperation in the peaceful use of space.

Signed at Washington October 2, 1996.

Entered into force October 2, 1996.

TIAS

TAXATION

Convention with respect to taxes on income.[1]

Signed at Washington November 20, 1975.

Entered into force December 30, 1994.

TIAS

Amendments

May 30, 1980.[1]

January 26, 1993.[2]

NOTES

1 With understanding.

2 With understanding and declaration.

TELECOMMUNICATION

Agreement relating to radio communication facilities at or near Embassy sites for transmission of official messages.

Exchange of notes at Tel Aviv and Jerusalem May 10 and 21, 1963.

Entered into force May 21, 1963.

14 UST 866; TIAS 5367; 487 UNTS 319.

Agreement relating to radio communications between amateur stations on behalf of third parties.

Exchange of notes at Washington July 7, 1965.

Entered into force August 6, 1965.

16 UST 883; TIAS 5827; 549 UNTS 281.

Agreement relating to the reciprocal granting of authorizations to permit licensed amateur radio operators of either country to operate their stations in the other country.

Exchange of notes at Washington June 15, 1966.

Entered into force June 15, 1966.

17 UST 760; TIAS 6028; 578 UNTS 159.

Agreement terminating the agreement of June 18, 1987, for the establishment and operation of a radio relay station in Israel.

Exchange of notes at Tel Aviv and Jerusalem November 3, 1994.

Entered into force November 3, 1994.

TIAS

TERRORISM

Counterterrorism cooperation accord.

Signed at Washington April 30, 1996.

Entered into force July 29, 1996.

TIAS 12747; 1966 UNTS 3.

TRADE

See also COMMERCE

Agreement on the establishment of a free trade area, with annexes, exchange of letters and related letter.

Signed at Washington April 22, 1985.

Entered into force August 19, 1985.

TIAS

Agreement regarding the application of their competition laws.

Signed at Washington March 15, 1999.

Entered into force November 7, 2000.

TIAS

Agreement concerning certain aspects of trade in agricultural products, with attachment and annexes.

Exchange of letters at Washington and Jerusalem July 27, 2004.

Entered into force September 10, 2004; effective January 1, 2004.

TIAS

Agreement concerning certain aspects of trade in agricultural products, with attachment and annexes.

Exchange of letters at Washington and Jerusalem July 27, 2004.

Entered into force September 11, 2004.

TIAS

VISAS

Agreement relating to the issue of visas to authorized crew members of aircraft operated by air carriers designated by Israel and the United States.

Exchange of notes at Tel Aviv March 27 and June 1, 1951.

Entered into force June 1, 1951.

3 UST 4796; TIAS 2650; 212 UNTS 129.

Agreement providing for the reciprocal waiver of nonimmigrant passport visa fees.

Exchanges of notes at Jerusalem and Tel Aviv February 14 and 28 and March 2, 1955.

Entered into force March 2, 1955.

7 UST 2125; TIAS 3614; 220 UNTS 113.

WEATHER STATIONS

Agreement relating to a cooperative meteorological program in support of the rawinsonde observation station at Bet Dagan.

Exchange of notes at Tel Aviv and Jerusalem April 29 and May 22, 1968.

Entered into force May 22, 1968; effective January 1, 1968.

19 UST 5180; TIAS 6510; 653 UNTS 143.

ITALY

AGRICULTURAL COMMODITIES

Agreement relating to the use of lira equivalent for the purchase of agricultural commodities allocated to Italy pursuant to the Mutual Security Act of 1951, as amended.

Exchange of letters at Rome May 19, 1955.

Entered into force May 19, 1955.

6 UST 3718; TIAS 3369; 269 UNTS 83.

ATOMIC ENERGY

Agreement for cooperation on uses of atomic energy for mutual defense purposes.

Signed at Rome December 3, 1960.

Entered into force May 24, 1961.

12 UST 641; TIAS 4764; 410 UNTS 3.

Arrangement for the exchange of technical information and cooperation in nuclear safety matters, with addenda.

Signed at Vienna September 26, 2005.

Entered into force September 26, 2005.

TIAS

AVIATION

Air navigation arrangement.[1]

Exchange of notes at Washington October 13 and 14, 1931.

Entered into force October 31, 1931.

47 Stat. 2668; EAS 24; 9 Bevans 167; 137 LNTS 209.

Agreement relating to air service facilities in Italy with annex.

Exchange of notes at Rome June 9, 1947.

Entered into force June 9, 1947.

62 Stat. 4074; TIAS 2127; 9 Bevans 200; 104 UNTS 157.

Air transport agreement with memorandum and exchange of notes.

Signed at Rome June 22, 1970.

Entered into force provisionally June 22, 1970; definitively August 9, 1973.

21 UST 2096; TIAS 6957; 764 UNTS 161.

Amendments

October 25, 1988 (TIAS 11634; 2204 UNTS 508).

December 30, 1998 and February 2, 1999.

Memorandum of understanding relating to the air transport services agreement of June 22, 1970, as amended, with related exchange of letters.

Signed at Rome September 27, 1990.

Entered into force September 27, 1990.[2]

TIAS 11767.

Agreement amending and supplementing the air transport services agreement of June 22, 1970, as amended, and amending the memorandum of understanding of September 27, 1990, with memorandum of understanding.

Exchange of notes at Rome November 22 and December 23, 1991.

Entered into force December 23, 1991.

TIAS 11845.

Agreement amending and supplementing the air transport agreement of June 22, 1970, as amended, and amending the memorandum of understanding of September 27, 1990, as amended.

Exchange of notes at Rome May 30 and October 21, 1997.

Entered into force October 21, 1997.

TIAS

Agreement relating to reciprocal acceptance of airworthiness certifications.

Exchange of notes at Rome June 30 and August 3, 1973.

Entered into force August 3, 1973.

25 UST 1565; TIAS 7895.

Agreement for promotion of aviation safety.

Signed at Rome October 27, 1999.

Entered into force October 27, 1999.

TIAS

NOTES

1 Article 9 terminated January 26, 1955 (see 6 UST 25; TIAS 3164).

2 Amendment to Article 10 not yet in force.

CLAIMS

Memorandum of understanding regarding settlement of certain wartime claims and related matters; memorandum of understanding regarding Italian assets in the United States and certain claims of United States nationals, and supplementary exchanges of notes.

Signed at Washington August 14, 1947.

Entered into force August 14, 1947.[1]

61 Stat. 3962; TIAS 1757; 9 Bevans 215; 36 UNTS 53.

Agreement relating to procedure for final settlement of claims of Italian prisoners of war.

Exchange of letters at Rome February 14, 1948.

Entered into force February 14, 1948.

62 Stat. 3853; TIAS 1948; 9 Bevans 299; 67 UNTS 115.

Amendment

January 14, 1949 (63 Stat. 2602; TIAS 1950; 9 Bevans 338; 67 UNTS 115).

Memorandum of understanding regarding war damage claims.

Signed at Rome March 29, 1957.

Entered into force October 22, 1957.

8 UST 1725; TIAS 3924; 299 UNTS 157.

Agreement supplementing the memorandum of understanding of March 29, 1957 regarding war damage claims.

Exchange of notes at Rome July 12, 1960.

Entered into force June 15, 1961.

12 UST 904; TIAS 4796; 411 UNTS 312.

NOTE

1 For agreed interpretation of the agreement signed August 14, 1947, see exchange of notes verbales of February 24, 1949 (63 Stat. 2415; TIAS 1919; 9 Bevans 342; 80 UNTS 319).

COMMERCE

Agreement relating to the resumption of normal commercial relations.

Exchange of notes at Washington December 6, 1945.

Entered into force December 6, 1945.

59 Stat. 1731; EAS 492; 9 Bevans 190; 3 UNTS 131.

Treaty of friendship, commerce, and navigation, protocol, additional protocol, and exchange of notes.

Signed at Rome February 2, 1948.

Entered into force July 26, 1949.

63 Stat. 2255; TIAS 1965; 9 Bevans 261; 79 UNTS 171.

Agreement supplementing the treaty of friendship, commerce and navigation of February 2, 1948.

Signed at Washington September 26, 1951.

Entered into force March 2, 1961.

12 UST 131; TIAS 4685; 404 UNTS 326.

CONSULS

Consular convention.[1]

Signed at Washington May 8, 1878.

Entered into force September 18, 1878.

20 Stat. 725; TS 178; 9 Bevans 91.

NOTE

1 Article XI replaced by convention of February 24, 1881 (22 Stat. 831; TS 179); articles XI and XIII abrogated by the United States, effective July 1, 1916, in accordance with the Seamen's Act (38 Stat. 1164).

COPYRIGHT

Reciprocal copyright arrangement.

Exchange of notes at Washington October 28, 1892.

Entered into force October 28, 1892.

9 Bevans 104.

Reciprocal copyright arrangement.

Exchanges of notes at Manchester, Massachusetts, September 2, 1914; and at Washington February 12 and March 4 and 11, 1915.

Entered into force March 11, 1915; operative May 1, 1915.

9 Bevans 129.

CULTURAL PROPERTY

Memorandum of understanding concerning the imposition of import restrictions on categories of archaeological material representing the Pre-Classical, Classical and Imperial Roman periods of Italy.

Signed at Washington January 19, 2001.

Entered into force January 19, 2001.

TIAS

DEFENSE

See also MUTUAL SECURITY

Mutual defense assistance agreement.

Exchange of notes at Washington January 27, 1950.

Entered into force January 27, 1950.

1 UST 50; TIAS 2013; 80 UNTS 145.

Agreement relating to the disposition of equipment and material furnished Italy and no longer required in the furtherance of its mutual defense assistance program.

Exchange of notes at Rome November 20 and December 14, 1951.

Entered into force December 14, 1951.

5 UST 2829; TIAS 3136; 238 UNTS 310.

Amendment

September 7, 1960 (11 UST 2129; TIAS 4573; 389 UNTS 307).

Agreement relating to offshore procurement program with memorandum of understanding and model contract attached.

Exchange of notes at Rome March 31, 1954.

Entered into force March 31, 1954.

5 UST 2185; TIAS 3083; 235 UNTS 293.

Agreement concerning facilities for overhaul and repair of jet engines in Torino, Italy.

Signed at Rome July 8, 1955.

Entered into force July 8, 1955.

6 UST 3797; TIAS 3381; 270 UNTS 29.

Agreement relating to a weapons production program.

Exchange of notes at Rome July 7, 1960.

Entered into force July 7, 1960.

11 UST 1912; TIAS 4538; 380 UNTS 143.

Agreement relating to the safeguarding of classified information with annex.

Exchange of notes at Washington August 4, 1964.

Entered into force August 4, 1964.

15 UST 1494; TIAS 5629; 529 UNTS 205.

Amendment

April 15 and September 2, 1982 (TIAS 10632; 1935 UNTS 420).

Mutual logistical support agreement, with annexes.

Signed at Stuttgart February 23, 1983.

Entered into force February 23, 1983.

TIAS 11165; 2126 UNTS 201.

Memorandum of understanding on the exchange of officers between the United States Air Force and the Italian Air Force.

Signed at Rome and Washington May 30 and August 12, 1988.

Entered into force August 12, 1988.

NP

Technical arrangement concerning the installation and maintenance of a U.S. interface with the Italian MRCS-403 radar at Capo Frasca, Sardinia.

Signed at Rome and Ramstein AB August 1 and 23, 1988.

Entered into force August 23, 1988.

TIAS 12343.

Memorandum of agreement on the exchange of officers between the United States Marine Corps and the Italian Navy.

Signed at Rome and Washington June 7 and July 26, 1993.

Entered into force July 26, 1993.

NP

Memorandum of understanding concerning use of installations/infrastructure by U.S. forces in Italy, with annexes.

Signed at Rome February 2, 1995.

Entered into force February 2, 1995.

TIAS 12317.

Memorandum of understanding for Project Ulysses, with annexes.

Signed at Washington April 23 and August 1, 1997.

Entered into force August 1, 1997.

TIAS

Acquisition and cross-servicing agreement, with annexes.

Signed at Rome and Stuttgart April 4 and 15, 2001.

Entered into force April 15, 2001.

TIAS

Agreement regarding the cooperative framework for system development and demonstration of the joint strike fighter.

Signed at Washington June 24, 2002.

Entered into force July 17, 2002.

TIAS

Agreement for the six degree of freedom reynolds averaged navier stokes project.

Signed at Washington and Rome July 25 and October 8, 2002.

Entered into force October 8, 2002.

TIAS

Agreement for the development of the High Speed Anti-Radiation Missile (HARM) upgrade, known as the AGM-88E Advanced Anti-Radiation Guided Missile (AARGM).

Signed at Rome and Washington October 24 and November 15, 2005.

Entered into force November 15, 2005.

TIAS

Agreement regarding the participation of Italy and other member nations of the South Eastern European Brigade in peacekeeping operations and the furnishing of articles and services from the United States of America to the Government of Italy pursuant to the Global Peace Operations Initiative.

Exchange of notes at Rome April 6 and 12, 2006.

Entered into force April 12, 2006.

TIAS

Agreement concerning the exchange and reimbursement of aviation and ground fuels, with annexes and attachments.

Signed at Ft. Belvoir and Rome June 2 and July 10, 2006.

Entered into force July 10, 2006.

TIAS

Memorandum of agreement for research, development, test and evaluation projects, with annex and appendix.

Signed at Washington and Rome September 15 and 26, 2006.

Entered into force September 26, 2006.

TIAS

Memorandum of understanding concerning the mutual exchange of military satellite communications services and support, with annex.

Signed at Offutt AFB and Rome July 20 and November 6, 2006.

Entered into force November 6, 2006.

TIAS

DISASTER ASSISTANCE

Agreement relating to the provision of assistance to earthquake victims of Italy.

Exchange of notes at Rome June 9, 1976.

Entered into force June 9, 1976.

27 UST 3988; TIAS 8416; 1059 UNTS 73.

ECONOMIC AND TECHNICAL COOPERATION

Economic cooperation agreement.

Signed at Rome June 28, 1948.

Entered into force June 28, 1948.

62 Stat. 2421; TIAS 1789; 9 Bevans 306; 20 UNTS 43.

Amendments

September 28 and October 2, 1948 (62 Stat. 3815; TIAS 1917; 9 Bevans 326; 55 UNTS 318).

February 7, 1950 (1 UST 160; TIAS 2028; 79 UNTS 274).

May 21, 1951 (2 UST 1169; TIAS 2263; 141 UNTS 362).

January 13, 1953 (4 UST 116; TIAS 2769; 200 UNTS 264).

Agreement relating to the use of counterpart funds derived from United States economic aid to Trieste.

Exchange of notes at Rome February 11, 1955.

Entered into force February 11, 1955.

6 UST 593; TIAS 3195; 241 UNTS 91.

EDUCATION

Agreement for exchanges in the fields of education and culture.

Signed at Rome December 15, 1975.

Entered into force July 28, 1980.

32 UST 1981; TIAS 9813; 1228 UNTS 145.

Memorandum of understanding relating to exchanges and cooperation in the field of education, with annex.

Signed at Rome May 4, 1978.

Entered into force May 4, 1978.

30 UST 116; TIAS 9182; 1150 UNTS 67.

EMPLOYMENT

Agreement relating to the employment of dependents of diplomatic agents, consular personnel and administrative and technical staff.

Exchange of notes at Rome June 9, 1997.

Entered into force April 30, 1999.

TIAS

ENVIRONMENTAL COOPERATION

Memorandum of understanding concerning cooperation in the field of environmental protection.

Signed at Rome March 3, 1987.

Entered into force March 3, 1987.

TIAS 11283.

EXTRADITION

Extradition treaty.

Signed at Rome October 13, 1983.

Entered into force September 24, 1984.

35 UST 3023; TIAS 10837; 1590 UNTS 161.

FINANCE

Agreement relating to the funding of the indebtedness of Italy to the United States.

Signed at Washington November 14, 1925; operative June 15, 1925.

Treasury Department print; 9 Bevans 145.

Agreement modifying the agreement of November 14, 1925.

Signed at Washington June 3, 1932; operative July 1, 1931.

Treasury Department print; 9 Bevans 176.

Agreement relating to the disposal of currencies, securities and articles of value taken in Italy from the German forces.

Exchange of notes at Rome May 16, 1951.

Entered into force May 16, 1951.

3 UST 2950; TIAS 2476; 206 UNTS 325.

Agreement relating to guaranties authorized by Section 111(b)(3) of the Economic Cooperation Act of 1948, as amended.

Exchange of notes at Rome December 28, 1951.

Entered into force December 28, 1951.

3 UST 2877; TIAS 2463; 157 UNTS 63.

Amendment

October 18, 1957 (8 UST 1881; TIAS 3934; 291 UNTS 309).

Agreement relating to the establishment of a revolving industrial loan fund for Southern Italy.

Exchange of notes at Rome June 16, 1954.

Entered into force June 16, 1954.

5 UST 2116; TIAS 3073; 236 UNTS 149.

FISHERIES

Agreement concerning large-scale driftnet fishing on the high seas.

Exchange of notes at Washington July 22 and 26, 1996.

Entered into force July 26, 1996.

TIAS 12787.

HEALTH

Memorandum of understanding for cooperation in the field of health and medicine, with annex.

Signed at Rome November 21, 1977.

Entered into force November 21, 1977.

29 UST 5897; TIAS 9159.

JUDICIAL ASSISTANCE

Procedures for mutual assistance in the administration of justice in connection with the Lockheed Aircraft Corporation matter.

Signed at Washington March 29, 1976.

Entered into force April 12, 1976.

27 UST 3437; TIAS 8374.

Treaty on mutual assistance in criminal matters, with memorandum of understanding.

Signed at Rome November 9, 1982.

Entered into force November 13, 1985.[1]

TIAS

NOTE

1 Except for the application of Article 18, paragraph 2.

MAPPING

Basic exchange and cooperative agreement concerning global geospatial information and services cooperation, with annexes.

Signed at Rome October 28, 2002.

Entered into force October 28, 2002.

NP

MARRIAGE

Agreement relating to documentary requirements for marriage of American citizens in Italy.

Exchange of notes at Rome July 29 and August 18, 1964.

Entered into force March 26, 1966.

18 UST 342; TIAS 6239; 688 UNTS 37.

MILITARY CEMETERIES AND MONUMENTS

Agreement relating to interment of American military personnel in Italy.

Exchange of notes verbales at Rome September 13 and 24, 1946.

Entered into force September 24, 1946.

61 Stat. 3750; TIAS 1713; 9 Bevans 194; 148 UNTS 323.

Amendment

December 18, 1947, January 21, March 24, and April 19, 1948 (62 Stat. 1889; TIAS 1743; 9 Bevans 258, 304; 148 UNTS 332).

MUTUAL SECURITY

Agreement relating to the assurances required by the Mutual Security Act of 1951.

Exchange of notes at Rome January 7, 1952.

Entered into force January 7, 1952.

3 UST 4613; TIAS 2611; 179 UNTS 165.

NARCOTIC DRUGS

Arrangement for the direct exchange of certain information regarding the traffic in narcotic drugs.

Exchange of notes at Rome January 5 and April 27, 1928.

Entered into force April 27, 1928.

9 Bevans 156.

NAVIGATION

Memorandum of understanding concerning the installation and management of U.S. navigational aids.

Signed at Rome and Ramstein October 8 and 11, 1985.

Entered into force October 11, 1985.

TIAS 11191; 2129 UNTS 431.

Agreement for the transfer of ownership of the long-range radio aid to navigation transmitting and monitoring stations at Lampedusa, Sellia Marina and Crotone, Italy.

Signed at Rome November 17, 1994.

Entered into force February 4, 1997.

TIAS

PACIFIC SETTLEMENT OF DISPUTES

Treaty for the advancement of peace.

Signed at Washington May 5, 1914.

Entered into force March 19, 1915.

39 Stat. 1618; TS 615; 9 Bevans 126.

Treaty modifying the terms of article II of the treaty for the advancement of peace.

Signed at Washington September 23, 1931.

Entered into force July 30, 1932.

47 Stat. 2102; TS 848; 9 Bevans 164; 134 LNTS 191.

Treaty of arbitration.

Signed at Washington April 19, 1928.

Entered into force January 20, 1931.

46 Stat. 2890; TS 831; 9 Bevans 153; 113 LNTS 183.

PATENTS

Agreement on arrangements respecting patents and technical information in defense programs.

Signed at Rome October 3, 1952.

Entered into force provisionally October 3, 1952; definitively December 16, 1960.

12 UST 189; TIAS 4693.

Agreement approving the procedures for reciprocal filing of classified patent applications in the United States and Italy.

Exchange of notes at Rome March 9 and October 27, 1959.

Entered into force provisionally October 27, 1959; definitively December 16, 1960.

12 UST 189; TIAS 4693.

Amendment

April 29 and August 2, 1960 (12 UST 208; TIAS 4693).

PEACE TREATIES

Agreement concerning the designation of a permanent third member of the United States-Italian Conciliation Commission established pursuant to article 83 of the treaty of peace with Italy (TIAS 1648; 4 Bevans 311; 49 and 50 UNTS).

Exchange of notes at Rome February 12 and 13, 1951.

Entered into force February 13, 1951.

2 UST 807; TIAS 2232; 148 UNTS 57.

Agreement regarding the release of Italy from certain of its obligations to the United States under the treaty of peace with Italy (TIAS 1648; 4 Bevans 311; 49 and 50 UNTS).

Exchange of notes at Washington December 8 and 21, 1951.

Entered into force December 21, 1951.

3 UST 2869; TIAS 2461; 167 UNTS 163.

POSTAL MATTERS

Parcel post convention.

Signed at Washington October 11, 1929.

Entered into force December 1, 1929.

46 Stat. 2397; Post Office Department print.

International express mail agreement with detailed regulations.

Signed at Rome and Washington November 21 and December 9, 1983.

Entered into force February 18, 1984.

35 UST 3167; TIAS 10848; 2014 UNTS 603.

RELIEF SUPPLIES AND PACKAGES

Agreement providing for duty-free entry of relief supplies and packages and for the payment of transportation charges.

Exchange of notes at Rome November 26, 1948.

Entered into force November 26, 1948.

62 Stat. 3809; TIAS 1914; 9 Bevans 328; 79 UNTS 71.

Amendments

November 26, 1948 (62 Stat. 3809; TIAS 1914; 9 Bevans 331; 79 UNTS 71).

July 19, 1952 (3 UST 5078; TIAS 2694; 181 UNTS 353).

SATELLITES

Agreement concerning cooperation in a scientific experiment for the purpose of launching a scientific satellite into an equatorial orbit.

Exchange of notes at Rome September 5, 1962.

Entered into force September 5, 1962.

13 UST 2120; TIAS 5172; 461 UNTS 185.

Agreement confirming a memorandum of understanding regarding the launching of NASA satellites from the San Marco Range.

Exchange of notes at Rome April 30 and June 12, 1969.

Entered into force June 12, 1969.

20 UST 4119; TIAS 6809; 732 UNTS 3.

Extension

November 25 and 26, 1974 (25 UST 3110; TIAS 7972).

Agreement confirming a memorandum of understanding concerning the furnishing of certain services by NASA for Italian satellites.

Exchange of notes at Rome June 15 and 20, 1970.

Entered into force June 20, 1970.

21 UST 1465; TIAS 6903; 753 UNTS 259.

Memorandum of understanding concerning furnishing of launch and associated services for ITALSAT program.

Signed at Washington and Rome September 29 and October 10, 1983.

Entered into force March 5, 1984.

35 UST 3076; TIAS 10840; 2014 UNTS 599.

Agreement concerning development of the Tethered Satellite System (TSS), with memorandum of understanding.

Exchange of notes at Rome June 6 and 27, 1984.

Entered into force June 6, 1986.

TIAS 12205.

Amendment

February 9 and 12, 1996.

Agreement concerning development and launch of the Laser Geodynamics Satellite-2 (Lageos-2), with memorandum of understanding.

Exchange of notes at Rome April 22 and July 30, 1985.

Entered into force February 13, 1989.

TIAS

SCIENTIFIC COOPERATION

Memorandum of understanding concerning the furnishing of balloon launching and associated services.

Signed at Washington and Rome September 2 and 30, 1983.

Entered into force September 30, 1983.

35 UST 2335; TIAS 10794; 2011 UNTS 179.

Agreement for scientific and technological cooperation.

Signed at Rome April 1, 1988.

Entered into force April 1, 1988.

TIAS 11574; 2185 UNTS 305.

Amendment and extension

October 4, 1993 (TIAS 12165).

Memorandum of understanding for scientific and technical cooperation in the earth sciences.

Signed at Rome April 14, 2000.

Entered into force April 14, 2000.

TIAS

Memorandum of understanding concerning scientific and technical cooperation in the earth sciences.

Signed at Reston and Rome February 7 and July 11, 2002.

Entered into force July 11, 2002.

TIAS

SEABEDS

Agreement relating to the agreement of August 14, 1987 on the resolution of practical problems with respect to deep seabed mining areas.[1]

Exchange of notes at Rome August 14, 1987.

Entered into force August 14, 1987.

TIAS 11438.

NOTE

1 Parties to the multilateral agreement of August 14, 1987 are Belgium, Canada, Italy, Netherlands and Union of Soviet Socialist Republics.

SHIPPING

Agreement relating to jurisdiction over vessels utilizing the Louisiana Offshore Oil Port.

Exchange of notes at Washington January 12 and 19, 1982.

Entered into force January 19, 1982.

TIAS 10598; 1871 UNTS 195.

SOCIAL SECURITY

Agreement on social security, with administrative protocol.

Signed at Washington May 23, 1973.

Entered into force November 1, 1978.

29 UST 4263; TIAS 9058; 1228 UNTS 81.

Supplemental agreement to the agreement of May 23, 1973 on the matter of social security.

Signed at Rome April 17, 1984.

Entered into force January 1, 1986.

TIAS 11173.

SPACE COOPERATION

Agreement for the design, development, operation and utilization of two mini pressurized logistics modules and a mini laboratory for Space Station Freedom, with memorandum of understanding.

Exchange of notes at Rome January 29 and June 1, 1992.

Entered into force June 1, 1992.

TIAS

Agreement for the design, development, operation and utilization of three mini pressurized logistics modules for the International Space Station.

Exchange of notes at Rome April 18, 2001 and January 11, 2005.

Entered into force January 11, 2005.

TIAS

SURPLUS PROPERTY

Agreement for the sale in Italy of waste material and scrap and of usable property in excess of the requirements of the United States military authorities.

Signed at Rome June 22, 1957.

Entered into force June 22, 1957.

8 UST 881; TIAS 3850; 284 UNTS 51.

TAXATION

Agreement relating to relief from taxation of United States expenditures in Italy for the common defense.

Exchange of notes at Rome March 5, 1952.

Entered into force March 5, 1952.

3 UST 4234; TIAS 2566; 179 UNTS 3.

Convention for the avoidance of double taxation and the prevention of fiscal evasion with respect to taxes on estates and inheritances.

Signed at Washington March 30, 1955.

Entered into force October 26, 1956.

7 UST 2977; TIAS 3678; 257 UNTS 199.

Agreement concerning taxation of income of some U.S. Navy employees in Italy.

Exchange of notes at Rome July 24, 1982.

Entered into force September 28, 1984; effective January 1, 1982.

TIAS 11499.

Convention with protocol for the avoidance of double taxation with respect to taxes on income and the prevention of fraud or fiscal evasion, with exchange of notes.[1]

Signed at Rome April 17, 1984.

Entered into force December 30, 1985; effective with respect to certain provisions February 1, 1986, with respect to others January 1, 1985.

TIAS 11064.

NOTE

1 With understanding.

TELECOMMUNICATION

Agreement relating to the reciprocal granting of authorizations to permit licensed amateur radio operators of either country to operate their stations in the other country.

Exchange of notes at Rome July 28 and August 28, 1981.

Entered into force August 28, 1981.

33 UST 4393; TIAS 10308; 1549 UNTS 309.

TRADE

See also COMMERCE

Agreement providing compensatory concessions under the general agreement on tariffs and trade for certain tariff actions taken by the United States.

Exchange of notes at Geneva December 8 and 9, 1961, and March 7, 1962.

Entered into force March 7, 1962.

13 UST 942; TIAS 5032.

TRADE-MARKS

Declaration for the reciprocal protection of marks of manufacture and trade.

Signed at Washington June 1, 1882.

Entered into force June 1, 1882.

23 Stat. 726; TS 180; 9 Bevans 101.

VISAS

Agreement relating to the waiver of passport visa fees for nonimmigrants.

Exchange of notes at Rome February 11, 21, and 26, 1929; operative March 1, 1929.

9 Bevans 158.

Arrangement relating to the waiver of passport visas and passport visa fees. Exchange of notes verbales dated at Rome September 28 and 29, 1948.

Entered into force September 29, 1948; operative November 1, 1948.

62 Stat. 3480; TIAS 1867; 9 Bevans 323; 84 UNTS 43.

J

JAMAICA

On August 6, 1962 Jamaica attained fully responsible status within the British Commonwealth. By an exchange of notes on August 7, 1962 between the High Commissioner for the United Kingdom in Jamaica and the Prime Minister and Minister of External Affairs and Defense of Jamaica, the Government of Jamaica agreed to assume, from August 6, 1962, all obligations and responsibilities of the United Kingdom which arise from any valid instrument (including any instrument made by the Government of the Federation of The West Indies by virtue of the authority entrusted by the Government of the United Kingdom). The rights and benefits heretofore enjoyed by the Government of the United Kingdom by virtue of application of any such international instrument to Jamaica are from August 6, 1962 enjoyed by the Government of Jamaica.

AGRICULTURAL COMMODITIES

Agricultural commodities agreement with annex.

Signed at Kingston October 11, 1973.

Entered into force October 11, 1973.

24 UST 2211; TIAS 7737.

Agricultural commodities agreement with annex.

Signed at Kingston April 16, 1975.

Entered into force April 16, 1975.

26 UST 1705; TIAS 8130.

Amendments

June 9, 1975 (26 UST 1722; TIAS 8130).

December 3 and 15, 1976 (28 UST 2388; TIAS 8551).

Related agreement

September 30, 1976 (28 UST 2385; TIAS 8550).

Agricultural commodities agreement.

Signed at Kingston August 8 1977.

Entered into force August 8, 1977.

29 UST 373; TIAS 8824.

Amendment

December 2 and 21, 1977 (29 UST 373; TIAS 8824).

Related agreements

August 2, 1978 (30 UST 213; TIAS 9188; 1148 UNTS 328).

September 5, 1978 (30 UST 217; TIAS 9188; 1148 UNTS 333).

October 13 and 25, 1978 (30 UST 221; TIAS 9188; 1148 UNTS 336).

March 7 and 29, 1979 (30 UST 3979; TIAS 9438).

May 2, 1979 (30 UST 3983; TIAS 9438).

July 5, 1979 (30 UST 3987; TIAS 9438).

February 8, 1980 (32 UST 1819; TIAS 9799).

February 6, 1981 (33 UST 1497; TIAS 10124; 1284 UNTS 275).

August 5, 1981 (33 UST 1501; TIAS 10124; 1284 UNTS 279).

Agricultural commodities agreement, with memorandum of understanding.

Signed at Kingston April 30, 1982.

Entered into force April 30, 1982.

TIAS 10495; 1750 UNTS 375.

Related agreements

February 24, 1983 (TIAS 10665; 1750 UNTS 405).

May 30, 1984 (NP).

December 17, 1984 (NP).

March 19 and 28, 1985 (NP).

July 25 and 30, 1985 (NP).

Agricultural commodities agreement.

Signed at Kingston January 15, 1986.

Entered into force January 15, 1986.

NP

Amendments

May 29 and June 4, 1986 (NP).

August 18 and 27, 1986 (NP).

September 24 and October 8, 1986 (NP).

October 30 and 31, 1986 (NP).

Agricultural commodities agreement, with agreed minutes.

Signed at Kingston January 15, 1987.

Entered into force January 15, 1987.

NP

Amendments

June 25 and July 1, 1987 (NP).

September 29 and October 2, 1987 (NP).

November 9, 1987 (NP).

January 5 and 6, 1988 (NP).

April 29 and May 2, 1988 (NP).

June 27 and 28, 1988 (NP).

August 10, 1988 (NP).

September 8 and 27, 1988 (NP).

Related agreements

September 22, 1988 (NP).

February 21, 1989 (NP).

August 18 and September 12, 1989 (NP).

November 24, 1989 (NP).

February 14 and March 1, 1990 (NP).

June 6, 1990 (NP).

July 20 and 23, 1990 (NP).

October 12, 1990 (NP).

March 8 and 14, 1991 (NP).

AVIATION

Arrangement between the United States and the United Kingdom relating to pilot licenses to operate civil aircraft.

Exchange of notes at Washington March 28 and April 5, 1935.

Entered into force May 5, 1935.

49 Stat. 3731; EAS 77; 12 Bevans 513; 162 UNTS 59.

Air transport agreement with exchange of notes.

Signed at Kingston October 2, 1969.

Entered into force October 2, 1969.

20 UST 2962; TIAS 6770; 726 UNTS 183.

Amendments

April 4, 1979 (31 UST 308; TIAS 9613; 1220 UNTS 333).

June 6 and December 13, 1994 (TIAS 12586).

Agreement concerning conversion and remittance of Jamaica dollar earnings by U.S. airlines.

Exchange of notes at Kingston March 22 and 30, 1984.

Entered into force March 30, 1984.

35 UST 4896; TIAS 10975; 1658 UNTS 309.

CONSULS

Consular convention between the United States and the United Kingdom.

Signed at Washington June 6, 1951.

Entered into force September 7, 1952.

3 UST 3426; TIAS 2494; 165 UNTS 121.

DEFENSE

Agreement relating to the furnishing of defense articles and services to Jamaica.

Exchange of notes at Kingston June 6, 1963.

Entered into force June 6, 1963.

14 UST 821; TIAS 5361; 477 UNTS 29.

Agreement concerning the provision of training related to defense articles under the United States International Military Education and Training (IMET) Program.

Exchange of notes at Kingston November 13, 1980 and February 17, 1981.

Entered into force February 17, 1981.

TIAS 10536; 1777 UNTS 319.

Agreement concerning multi-national military training exercises.

Exchange of notes at Kingston April 28, 2003.

Entered into force April 28, 2003; effective April 1, 2003.

TIAS

ECONOMIC AND TECHNICAL COOPERATION

General agreement for economic, technical and related assistance.

Signed at Kingston October 24, 1963.

Entered into force October 24, 1963.

14 UST 1550; TIAS 5457; 489 UNTS 337.

Agency for International Development

November 13, 1975 (29 UST 5905; TIAS 9160; 1148 UNTS 275).

November 25, 1977 (29 UST 5932; TIAS 9160; 1148 UNTS 294).

December 15, 1977 (29 UST 4049; TIAS 9048; 1135 UNTS 43).

March 23, 1978 (30 UST 4518; TIAS 9474; 1170 UNTS 49).

January 19, 1981 (33 UST 1560; TIAS 10133; 1529 UNTS 347).

December 29, 1981 (33 UST 4071; TIAS 10284).

December 17, 1982 (TIAS 10644; 1647 UNTS 51).

EMPLOYMENT

Agreement relating to the employment of dependents of official government employees.

Exchange of notes at Kingston May 3 and October 11, 1982.

Entered into force October 11, 1982.

TIAS 10886; 35 UST 3834; 1577 UNTS 417.

ENVIRONMENTAL COOPERATION

Agreement concerning the establishment of an Enterprise for the Americas Environmental Foundation.

Signed at Washington November 26, 1991.

Entered into force November 26, 1991.

TIAS 11848.

EXTRADITION

Extradition treaty.

Signed at Kingston June 14, 1983.

Entered into force July 7, 1991.

TIAS

FINANCE

Agreement relating to investment guaranties.

Exchange of notes at Kingston December 11, 1962 and January 4, 1963.

Entered into force January 4, 1963.

14 UST 1; TIAS 5270; 471 UNTS 119.

Agreement regarding the consolidation and rescheduling of certain debts owed to, guaranteed or insured by the United States Government and its agencies, with annexes.

Signed at Washington November 8, 1984.

Entered into force December 13, 1984.

TIAS 10999; 2022 UNTS 83.

Agreement regarding the consolidation and rescheduling of certain debts owed to, guaranteed by or insured by the United States Government and its agencies, with annexes.

Signed at Washington September 26, 1985.

Entered into force November 18, 1985.

NP

Agreement regarding the consolidation and rescheduling of certain debts owed to, guaranteed by, or insured by the United States Government and its agencies, with annexes.

Signed at Kingston November 12, 1987.

Entered into force January 7, 1988.

NP

Amendment

February 2 and March 15, 1989 (NP).

Agreement regarding the consolidation and rescheduling of certain debts owed to, guaranteed by, or insured by the United States Government and its agencies, with annexes.

Signed at Kingston July 6, 1989.

Entered into force August 24, 1989.

NP

Amendment

November 27, 1989 and January 18, 1990 (NP).

Agreement regarding the consolidation and rescheduling or refinancing of certain debts owed to, guaranteed by, or insured by the United States Government and its agencies, with annexes.

Signed at Kingston December 20, 1990.

Entered into force February 8, 1991.

NP

Agreement regarding the consolidation and rescheduling or refinancing of certain debts owed to, guaranteed by, or insured by the United States Government and its agencies, with annexes.

Signed at Kingston January 14, 1992.

Entered into force March 2, 1992.

NP

Amendment

August 28 and September 11, 1992 (NP).

Agreement regarding the reduction of certain debts related to foreign assistance owed to the Government of the United States and its agencies, with appendices.

Signed at Washington and Kingston January 13 and 15, 1993.

Entered into force February 14, 1993.

NP

Agreement regarding the consolidation and rescheduling or refinancing of certain debts owed to, guaranteed by or insured by the United States Government and its agencies, with annexes.

Signed at Kingston October 22, 1993.

Entered into force January 3, 1994.

NP

Agreement regarding a debt-for-nature swap to prepay and cancel certain debt owed by the Government of Jamaica to the Government of the United States of America, with attachments.

Signed at Kingston September 21, 2004.

Entered into force September 21, 2004.

TIAS

INVESTMENT

Treaty concerning the reciprocal encouragement and protection of investment, with annex and protocol.

Signed at Washington February 4, 1994.

Entered into force March 7, 1997.

TIAS

JUDICIAL ASSISTANCE

Procedures for mutual assistance in connection with matters relating to the Jamaica Nutrition Holdings Ltd., its holding company, State Trading Corporation and its associated companies.

Signed at Washington March 30, 1979.

Entered into force March 30, 1979.

30 UST 3868; TIAS 9430; 1170 UNTS 59.

Treaty on mutual legal assistance in criminal matters, with attachments.

Signed at Kingston July 7, 1989.

Entered into force July 25, 1995.

TIAS

NARCOTIC DRUGS

Agreement relating to the provision of helicopters and related assistance to Jamaica in connection with a program to interdict the illicit narcotics traffic between Jamaica and the United States (Operation Buccaneer).

Exchange of notes at Kingston August 9 and 21 and September 23, 1974.

Entered into force September 23, 1974.

25 UST 3068; TIAS 7966.

Agreement concerning cooperation in suppressing illicit maritime drug trafficking.

Signed at Kingston May 6, 1997.

Entered into force March 10, 1998.

TIAS

Agreement regarding the sharing of forfeited assets or the proceeds of disposition of such assets, with exchange of letters.

Signed at Kingston August 22, 2001.

Entered into force August 22, 2001.

TIAS

Protocol to the agreement of May 6, 1997 concerning cooperation in suppressing illicit maritime drug trafficking.

Signed at Kingston February 6, 2004.

Entered into force February 6, 2004.

TIAS

Agreement regarding the cooperating nation information exchange system.

Exchange of notes at Kingston August 26 and September 23, 2005.

Entered into force September 23, 2005.

TIAS

PEACE CORPS

Agreement relating to the establishment of a Peace Corps program in Jamaica.

Exchange of notes at Kingston February 15 and 22, 1962.

Entered into force February 22, 1962.

13 UST 166; TIAS 4954; 435 UNTS 127.

PEACEKEEPING

Agreement for the furnishing of commodities and services in connection with the peacekeeping force for Grenada.

Exchange of notes at Kingston November 29 and December 6, 1983.

Entered into force December 6, 1983.

35 UST 3192; TIAS 10849; 2015 UNTS 15.

Agreement concerning the disposition of commodities and services furnished in connection with peacekeeping operations for Grenada.

Exchange of notes at Kingston February 2 and April 21, 1987.

Entered into force April 21, 1987.

TIAS 11270.

POSTAL MATTERS

Postal convention.

Signed at Washington July 22 and at Kingston September 3, 1887; operative October 1, 1887.

25 Stat. 1393.

Money order agreement.

Signed at Washington September 20 and at Kingston October 6, 1922; operative November 1, 1922.

International express mail agreement, with detailed regulations.

Signed at Kingston and Washington January 9 and February 11, 1991.

Entered into force March 18, 1991.

TIAS 11812.

PROPERTY

Convention between the United States and the United Kingdom relating to the tenure and disposition of real and personal property.

Signed at Washington March 2, 1899; applicable to Jamaica February 9, 1901.

31 Stat. 1939; TS 146; 12 Bevans 246.

Supplementary convention relating to the tenure and disposition of real and personal property.

Signed at Washington May 27, 1936; applicable to Jamaica March 10, 1941.

55 Stat. 1101; TS 964; 5 Bevans 140; 203 LNTS 367.

PUBLICATIONS

Agreement for the exchange of official publications.

Exchange of notes at Kingston December 20, 1966.

Entered into force December 20, 1966.

17 UST 2409; TIAS 6187; 681 UNTS 115.

TAXATION

Convention for the avoidance of double taxation and the prevention of fiscal evasion with respect to taxes on income, with exchange of notes.[1]

Signed at Kingston May 21, 1980.

Entered into force December 29, 1981.

33 UST 2865; TIAS 10206.

Protocol amending the convention for the avoidance of double taxation and the prevention of fiscal evasion with respect to taxes on income, with exchange of notes.[1]

Signed at Kingston July 17, 1981.

Entered into force December 29, 1981.

33 UST 2903; TIAS 10207.

Agreement concerning administration of income tax affecting Jamaican citizens employed by the U.S. Government.

Exchange of notes at Kingston April 3 and May 1, 1986.

Entered into force May 1, 1986.

TIAS 11362.

Agreement for the exchange of information with respect to taxes.

Signed at Washington December 18, 1986.

Entered into force December 18, 1986.

TIAS 11411; 2191 UNTS 79.

NOTE

1 With reservation and understanding.

TELECOMMUNICATION

Agreement relating to the reciprocal granting of authorizations to permit licensed amateur radio operators of either country to operate their stations in the other country.

Exchange of notes at Kingston March 4 and April 28, 1971.

Entered into force April 28, 1971.

22 UST 694; TIAS 7127; 792 UNTS 337.

Agreement relating to radio communications between amateur stations on behalf of third parties.

Exchange of notes at Kingston February 24 and May 12, 1977.

Entered into force June 11, 1977.

29 UST 1888; TIAS 8908.

TRADE AND COMMERCE

Agreement relating to trade in textiles, with annexes.

Exchange of letters at Washington August 27, 1986.

Entered into force August 27, 1986; effective September 1, 1986.

NP

Amendments and extension

January 29 and February 4, 1987 (NP).

March 3 and 30 and April 7, 1987 (NP).

August 7, 10 and 18, 1987 (NP).

September 2 and October 1 and 20, 1987 (NP).

December 17, 1987 and February 1, 1988 (NP).

April 5 and 14, 1988 (NP).

October 26 and November 1, 1988 (NP).

November 9 and 30, 1988 (NP).

September 14 and December 19, 1988 (NP).

October 29 and 31, 1990 (NP).

November 27 and December 10, 1992 (NP).

May 10 and June 22, 1993 (NP).

Administrative arrangement relating to visa and certification procedures for exports of textile products from Jamaica.

Exchange of letters at Washington August 27, 1986.

Entered into force August 27, 1986; effective September 1, 1986.

NP

Amendments

March 3 and 30 and April 7, 1987 (NP).

September 14 and December 19, 1988 (NP).

May 10 and June 22, 1993 (NP).

TRADE-MARKS

Declaration by the United States and the United Kingdom affording reciprocal protection to trade-marks.

Signed at London October 24, 1877.

Entered into force October 24, 1877.

20 Stat. 703; TS 138; 12 Bevans 198.

WEATHER STATIONS

Agreement for a cooperative meteorological program in Jamaica, with memorandum of arrangement.

Exchange of notes at Kingston August 27 and 29, 1985.

Entered into force August 29, 1985.

TIAS 11324.

JAPAN

AMAMI ISLANDS

Agreement concerning the Amami Islands, and exchange of notes.

Signed at Tokyo December 24, 1953.

Entered into force December 25, 1953.

4 UST 2912; TIAS 2895; 222 UNTS 193.

ATOMIC ENERGY

Agreement on cooperation in fast-reactor safety research.

Signed at Washington and Tokyo August 22 and September 20, 1983.

Entered into force September 20, 1983.

TIAS

Agreement concerning severe nuclear accident research.

Signed at Tokyo and Washington September 27 and October 1, 1984.

Entered into force October 1, 1984.

TIAS

Agreement for cooperation concerning peaceful uses of nuclear energy, with annexes, agreed minutes, implementing agreement and exchanges of notes.

Signed at Tokyo November 4, 1987.

Entered into force July 17, 1988.

TIAS; 1574 UNTS 287.

Agreement for cooperation in the field of nuclear regulation matters and nuclear safety research and development.

Exchange of notes at Washington October 15, 1997.

Entered into force October 15, 1997.

TIAS

Agreement extending the implementing arrangement of October 23, 1997 for cooperation in the field of nuclear regulatory matters and nuclear safety research and development.

Signed at Rockville and Tokyo March 3 and 7, 2003.

Entered into force March 7, 2003; effective October 23, 2002.

TIAS

Agreement extending the implementing arrangement of October 23, 1997 for cooperation in the field of nuclear regulatory matters and nuclear safety research and development.

Signed at Rockville and Tokyo March 3 and 11, 2003.

Entered into force March 11, 2003; effective October 23, 2002.

TIAS

Implementing agreement in the field of nuclear reactor safety research, with appendices.

Signed at Rockville and Chiba August 12 and September 3, 2003.

Entered into force September 3, 2003.

TIAS

Agreement in the field of research and development of innovative nuclear energy technologies.

Exchange of notes at Washington April 21, 2004.

Entered into force April 21, 2004.

TIAS

AVIATION

Civil air transport agreement and exchange of notes relating to provisional application.

Signed at Tokyo August 11, 1952.

Entered into force provisionally August 11, 1952; definitively September 15, 1953.

4 UST 1948; TIAS 2854; 212 UNTS 27.

Amendments

May 9, 1972 (23 UST 677; TIAS 7333).

July 26, 1977 (29 UST 1375; TIAS 8882).

August 21, 1996 (TIAS 12793).

April 20, 1998.

Agreement relating to acceptance of air-worthiness certification.

Exchange of notes at Washington November 29, 1977.

Entered into force November 29, 1977.

29 UST 2167; TIAS 8934.

Interim agreement relating to the civil air transport agreement of August 11, 1952, as amended (TIAS 2854, 7333, 8882), with record of consultations, memorandum of understanding and exchange of letters.

Exchange of letters at Washington September 7, 1982.

Entered into force September 7, 1982.[1]

34 UST 1541; TIAS 10434; 1736 UNTS 284.

Interim agreement relating to the civil air transport agreement of August 11, 1952, as amended, with memorandum of understanding, exchange of letters and related letter.

Exchange of notes at Bonn May 1, 1985.

Entered into force May 1, 1985.

TIAS 11999.

Interim agreement relating to the civil air transport agreement of August 11, 1952, as amended, with memorandum of understanding.

Exchange of notes at Washington December 27, 1989.

Entered into force December 27, 1989.

TIAS 12406.

Interim arrangement relating to the civil air transport agreement of August 11, 1952, as amended, with attachment.

Exchange of notes at Washington February 26, 1996.

Entered into force February 26, 1996.

TIAS 12728.

Agreement annexing the memorandum of cooperation for mutual cooperation in the promotion and development of civil aviation.

Signed October 13 and 24, 2006.

Entered into force October 24, 2006.

TIAS

NOTE

1 Provisions relating to Guam, Saipan and Micronesia have been superseded by the 1985 memorandum of understanding.

BONIN ISLANDS

Agreement concerning Nanpo Shoto and other islands with exchange of notes.

Signed at Tokyo April 5, 1968.

Entered into force June 26, 1968.

19 UST 4895; TIAS 6495; 683 UNTS 285.

CANALS

Agreement concerning Japanese participation in the commission for the study of alternatives to the Panama Canal, with attachments.

Exchange of notes at New York September 26, 1985.

Entered into force September 26, 1985.[1]

TIAS

Extension

September 25, 1990.

NOTE

1 Similar notes were exchanged on the same date between Japan and Panama.

CLAIMS

Agreement for settlement for the AWA MARU claim.

Signed at Tokyo April 14, 1949.

Entered into force April 14, 1949.

63 Stat. 2397; TIAS 1911; 9 Bevans 467; 89 UNTS 141.

Agreement relating to compensation for personal and property damage as a result of nuclear tests in the Marshall (Bikini) Islands.

Exchange of notes at Tokyo January 4, 1955.

Entered into force January 4, 1955.

6 UST 1; TIAS 3160; 237 UNTS 197.

Agreement relating to settlement of claims of Japanese nationals formerly resident in certain Japanese Islands arising from measures taken by the United States in connection with the exercise of its rights under article 3 of the peace treaty.

Exchange of notes at Tokyo June 8, 1961.

Entered into force June 8, 1961.

12 UST 830; TIAS 4781; 410 UNTS 183.

COMMERCE

Treaty of friendship, commerce, and navigation, protocol, and exchange of notes of August 29, 1953.[1]

Signed at Tokyo April 2, 1953.

Entered into force October 30, 1953.

4 UST 2063; TIAS 2863; 206 UNTS 143.

NOTE

1 Applicable to Bonin Islands and Ryukyu Islands.

CONSERVATION

Convention for the protection of migratory birds and birds in danger of extinction, and their environment, with annex.

Signed at Tokyo March 4, 1972.

Entered into force September 19, 1974.

25 UST 3329; TIAS 7990.

Amendment

September 19, 1974 (25 UST 3329; TIAS 7990).

CONSULS

Consular convention and protocol.

Signed at Tokyo March 22, 1963.

Entered into force August 1, 1964.

15 UST 768; TIAS 5602; 518 UNTS 179.

CULTURAL AND EDUCATIONAL RELATIONS

Agreement establishing the Joint Committee on United States-Japan Cultural and Educational Cooperation.

Exchange of notes at Tokyo November 8, 1968.

Entered into force November 8, 1968.

19 UST 7549; TIAS 6597; 702 UNTS 277.

Amendment

February 25, 1977 (28 UST 5326; TIAS 8635).

Agreement on educational exchange programs.

Signed at Tokyo February 15, 1979.

Entered into force December 24, 1979.

31 UST 381; TIAS 9615; 1202 UNTS 149.

Agreement concerning the Mike Mansfield Fellowship Program.

Exchange of notes at Tokyo August 21, 1996.

Entered into force August 21, 1996.

TIAS 12794.

CUSTOMS

Agreement regarding mutual assistance between customs administrations, with exchange of notes.

Signed at Washington June 17, 1997.

Entered into force June 17, 1997.

TIAS

DEFENSE

Mutual defense assistance agreement, with annexes.[1]

Signed at Tokyo March 8, 1954.

Entered into force May 1, 1954.

5 UST 661; TIAS 2957; 232 UNTS 169.

Amendments

April 18, 2006.

June 23, 2006.

Agreement for return of equipment under article I of the mutual defense assistance agreement.

Signed at Tokyo March 8, 1954.

Entered into force May 1, 1954.

5 UST 708; TIAS 2958; 232 UNTS 215.

Agreement relating to the transfer of military equipment and supplies to Japan.

Exchange of notes at Tokyo November 19, 1954.

Entered into force November 19, 1954.

5 UST 2404; TIAS 3101; 238 UNTS 207.

Arrangement relating to the furnishing of military equipment pursuant to article I of the mutual defense assistance agreement.[2]

Exchange of notes at Tokyo January 7, 1955.

Entered into force January 7, 1955.

6 UST 9; TIAS 3161; 251 UNTS 404.

Agreement relating to a program of aircraft assembly or manufacture in Japan.

Exchange of notes at Tokyo June 3, 1955.

Entered into force June 3, 1955.

6 UST 3817; TIAS 3383; 270 UNTS 51.

Agreement setting forth understandings with respect to the program of aircraft assembly or manufacture in Japan pursuant to the agreement of June 3, 1955.

Exchange of notes at Tokyo April 13, 1956.

Entered into force April 13, 1956.

7 UST 649; TIAS 3547; 273 UNTS 223.

Agreement relating to a cost-sharing program for the production and development in Japan of P2V anti-submarine and sea patrol aircraft.

Exchange of notes at Tokyo January 25, 1958.

Entered into force January 25, 1958.

9 UST 124; TIAS 3984; 304 UNTS 81.

Treaty of mutual cooperation and security, with agreed minute and exchanges of notes.

Signed at Washington January 19, 1960.

Entered into force June 23, 1960.

11 UST 1632; TIAS 4509; 373 UNTS 186.

Amendment

December 26, 1990 (TIAS 12335).

Agreement under article VI of the treaty of mutual cooperation and security regarding facilities and areas and the status of United States armed forces in Japan, with agreed minutes and exchange of notes.[3]

Signed at Washington January 19, 1960.

Entered into force June 23, 1960.

11 UST 1652; TIAS 4510; 373 UNTS 248.

Understanding revising references to the mutual security treaty (TIAS 4509) and the administrative agreement in the mutual defense assistance agreement of March 8, 1954 (TIAS 2957).

Exchange of notes at Washington January 19, 1960.

Entered into force June 23, 1960.

11 UST 1758; TIAS 4511.

Agreement relating to a program for the assembly and manufacture in Japan of F-104 type aircraft by Japanese industry.

Exchange of notes at Tokyo April 15, 1960.

Entered into force April 15, 1960.

11 UST 1361; TIAS 4471; 372 UNTS 267.

Agreement relating to cost-sharing of United States furnished equipment for one NIKE and two HAWK surface-to-air missile battalions with annex.

Exchange of notes at Tokyo April 26, 1963.

Entered into force April 26, 1963.

14 UST 490; TIAS 5347; 477 UNTS 37.

Agreement relating to a joint cost-sharing program for the production of equipment and the providing of technical assistance for the base air defense ground environment (BADGE) system.

Exchange of notes at Tokyo December 4, 1964.

Entered into force December 4, 1964.

15 UST 2339; TIAS 5724; 532 UNTS 249.

Related agreement

June 18, 1965 (16 UST 861; TIAS 5823; 550 UNTS 415).

Agreement relating to a production program in Japan of the Hawk and Nike Hercules missile system.

Exchange of notes at Tokyo October 13, 1967.

Entered into force October 13, 1967.

18 UST 2804; TIAS 6365; 701 UNTS 33.

Related agreements

December 22, 1972 (24 UST 434; TIAS 7558).

July 12, 1977 (29 UST 1892; TIAS 8909).

Agreement relating to a program for the acquisition and production in Japan of the F-4EJ aircraft and related equipment and material.

Exchange of notes at Tokyo April 4, 1969.

Entered into force April 4, 1969.

20 UST 545; TIAS 6664; 707 UNTS 207.

Related agreements

November 21, 1972 (23 UST 3794; TIAS 7529).

July 12, 1977 (29 UST 1901; TIAS 8910).

Agreement relating to the change in designation of organization of its personnel from Military Assistance Advisory Group to the Mutual Defense Assistance Office pursuant to the mutual defense assistance agreement of March 8, 1954 (TIAS 2957).

Exchange of notes at Tokyo July 4, 1969.

Entered into force July 4, 1969.

20 UST 2525; TIAS 6715; 719 UNTS 294.

Agreement relating to the production and acquisition in Japan of the Sparrow missile for ship-to-air application.

Exchange of notes at Tokyo July 12, 1977.

Entered into force October 7, 1977.

29 UST 1513; TIAS 8896.

Agreement relating to acquisition and production in Japan of F-15 aircraft and related equipment and materials.

Exchange of notes at Tokyo June 20, 1978.

Entered into force June 20, 1978.

30 UST 1599; TIAS 9267.

Related agreements

December 28, 1984 (TIAS 11978).

February 14, 1989 (TIAS 12331).

March 31, 1992 (TIAS 12331).

Agreement relating to acquisition and production in Japan of P-3C aircraft and related equipment and materials.

Exchange of notes at Tokyo June 20, 1978.

Entered into force June 20, 1978.

30 UST 1608; TIAS 9268; 1150 UNTS 123.

Related agreements

September 10, 1985 (TIAS 12017).

March 24, 1989 (TIAS 12017).

March 24, 1995 (TIAS 12341).

Agreement for the transfer of defense-related technologies, with annex.

Exchange of notes at Tokyo November 8, 1983.

Entered into force November 8, 1983.

35 UST 2981; TIAS 10835; 2014 UNTS 563.

Amendments

January 8, 1988 (TIAS 12329).

December 22, 1994 (TIAS 12329).

February 6, 1998.

Agreement relating to the acquisition and production in Japan of the patriot weapon system.

Exchange of notes at Tokyo October 4, 1985.

Entered into force October 4, 1985.

TIAS 11979.

Agreement relating to the furnishing of assistance in the field of training for defense services personnel and defense-related civilian personnel.

Exchange of notes at Tokyo January 21, 1986.

Entered into force January 21, 1986.

TIAS 12005.

Agreement relating to a program for the development of the XSH-60J weapon system.

Exchange of notes at Tokyo January 20, 1987.

Entered into force January 20, 1987.

TIAS 12014; 2244 UNTS 91.

Agreement concerning Japanese participation in research in the strategic defense initiative.

Signed at Washington July 21, 1987.

Entered into force July 21, 1987.

TIAS

Agreement concerning the acquisition and production of the EP-3 aircraft in Japan.

Exchange of notes at Tokyo March 29, 1988.

Entered into force March 29, 1988.

TIAS

Amendments

March 31, 1992.

March 26, 1993.

March 29, 1994.

March 31, 1995.

March 29, 1996.

March 28, 1997.

March 27, 1998.

Agreement concerning the acquisition and production in Japan of the HYDRA 70 Rocket System.

Exchange of notes at Tokyo March 31, 1989.

Entered into force March 31, 1989.

TIAS 12332.

Agreement concerning the acquisition and production in Japan of the SH-60J and UH-60J aircraft.

Exchange of notes at Tokyo March 31, 1989.

Entered into force March 31, 1989.

TIAS

Amendments

March 30, 1990.

March 29, 1991.

March 31, 1992.

January 8, 1993.

March 22, 1994.

March 10, 1995.

March 29, 1996.

March 28, 1997.

March 27, 1998.

March 23, 1999.

Agreement concerning the acquisition and production in Japan of the Sparrow Missile System (AIM-7M).

Exchange of notes at Tokyo March 27, 1990.

Entered into force March 27, 1990.

TIAS 12333.

Amendment

March 29, 1991 (TIAS 12333).

Agreement concerning new special measures relating to Article XXIV of the agreement of January 19, 1960, under Article VI of the treaty of mutual cooperation and security regarding facilities and areas and the status of United States armed forces in Japan, with agreed minutes and exchange of notes.

Signed at Washington January 14, 1991.

Entered into force April 17, 1991.

TIAS; 1853 UNTS 87.

Agreement amending the agreement of December 17, 1982, as amended, for the acquisition and production in Japan of the AH-1S helicopter system.

Exchange of notes at Tokyo March 31, 1992.

Entered into force March 31, 1992.

TIAS

Agreement for the assembly and repair in Japan of the AN/ALQ-131 System (Electronic Countermeasures Pod) and related equipment and materials, with exchange of letters.

Exchange of notes at Tokyo March 12, 1993.

Entered into force March 12, 1993.

TIAS 12338.

Agreement concerning new special measures relating to Article XXIV of the agreement of January 19, 1960, under Article VI of the treaty of mutual cooperation and security regarding facilities and areas and the status of United States armed forces in Japan, with agreed minutes and exchange of notes.

Signed at New York September 27, 1995.

Entered into force April 1, 1996.

TIAS 12693.

Agreement concerning cooperative research of fighting vehicle propulsion technology using ceramic materials.

Exchange of notes at Tokyo October 31, 1995.

Entered into force October 31, 1995.

TIAS 12701.

Agreement concerning cooperative research of advanced steel technology.

Exchange of notes at Tokyo October 31, 1995.

Entered into force October 31, 1995.

TIAS 12344.

Agreement concerning the furnishing of information from the Government of the United States to the Government of Japan which will be necessary for the effective conduct of the studies on ballistic missile defense by the Government of Japan.

Exchange of notes at Tokyo February 23, 1996.

Entered into force February 23, 1996.

TIAS 12727.

Agreement concerning reciprocal provision of logistic support, supplies and services between the Armed Forces of the United States of America and the Self-Defense Forces of Japan, with annex.

Signed at Tokyo April 15, 1996.

Entered into force October 22, 1996.

TIAS 12742.

Amendments

April 28, 1998.

February 27, 2004.

Agreement relating to the production of the Support Fighter (F-2) Weapon system.

Exchange of notes at Tokyo July 30, 1996.

Entered into force July 30, 1996.

TIAS 12788.

Agreement concerning a program for the cooperative research of eyesafe laser radar.

Exchange of notes at Washington September 20, 1996.

Entered into force September 20, 1996.

TIAS 12802.

Agreement concerning a cooperative modification program for the ACES II Ejection Seat.

Exchange of notes at Tokyo March 27, 1998.

Entered into force March 27, 1998.

TIAS

Agreement concerning a program for the cooperative research of Advanced Hybrid Propulsion Technologies.

Exchange of notes at Tokyo May 26, 1998.

Entered into force May 26, 1998.

TIAS

Agreement concerning a program for the cooperative research of Shallow Water Acoustic Technology (SWAT).

Exchange of notes at Tokyo June 18, 1999.

Entered into force June 18, 1999.

TIAS

Agreement concerning a program for the cooperative research on ballistic missile defense technologies.

Exchange of notes at Tokyo August 16, 1999.

Entered into force August 16, 1999.

TIAS

Agreement concerning the acquisition and production in Japan of the UH-60J and UH-60JA aircraft and related equipment and material.

Exchange of notes at Tokyo March 10, 2000.

Entered into force March 10, 2000.

TIAS

Agreement concerning a program for the cooperative research of Low Vulnerability Gun Propellant for Artillery.

Exchange of notes at Tokyo March 24, 2000.

Entered into force March 24, 2000.

TIAS

Agreement concerning new special measures relating to Article XXIV of the agreement under Article VI of the treaty of mutual cooperation and security between the United States and Japan regarding facilities and areas and the status of United States armed forces in Japan, with agreed minutes and exchange of notes.

Signed at New York September 11, 2000.

Entered into force April 1, 2001.

TIAS

Agreement concerning the acquisition and production in Japan of the UH-60J and UH-60JA aircraft and related equipment and materials.

Exchange of notes at Tokyo March 23, 2001.

Entered into force March 23, 2001.

TIAS

Agreement concerning the acquisition and production in Japan of the UP-3C aircraft and related equipment and materials.

Exchange of notes at Tokyo March 23, 2001.

Entered into force March 23, 2001.

TIAS

Agreement concerning logistic support, supplies and services contributed by Japan to the armed forces or other similar entities of the United States of America.

Exchange of notes at Tokyo November 16, 2001.

Entered into force November 16, 2001.

TIAS

Agreement concerning the acquisition and production in Japan of the Multiple Launch Rocket Systems and related equipment and materials.

Exchange of notes at Tokyo March 26, 2002.

Entered into force March 26, 2002.

TIAS

Agreement concerning the acquisition and production in Japan of the OP-3C Aircraft and related equipment and materials.

Exchange of notes at Tokyo March 26, 2002.

Entered into force March 26, 2002.

TIAS

Agreement concerning the acquisition and production in Japan of the SH-60J/UH-60J/UH-60JA Aircraft and related equipment and materials and the SH-60JMOD Aircraft.

Exchange of notes at Tokyo March 26, 2002.

Entered into force March 26, 2002.

TIAS

Agreement concerning a program for the cooperative research of Software Radio.

Exchange of notes at Tokyo March 26, 2002.

Entered into force March 26, 2002.

TIAS

Agreement concerning a program for the Cooperative Avionics and Missions Systems Study for Maritime Patrol Aircraft of Japan and Multi-Mission Maritime Aircraft of the United States of America.

Exchange of notes at Tokyo March 26, 2002.

Entered into force March 26, 2002.

TIAS

Agreement concerning the program for the acquisition and production in Japan of the SH-60J/UH-60J/UH-60JA/SH-60JMOD Aircraft, and related equipment and materials.

Exchange of notes at Tokyo March 18, 2003.

Entered into force March 18, 2003.

TIAS

Agreement concerning the program for the acquisition and production in Japan of the AH-64 Helicopter System and related equipment and materials.

Exchange of notes at Tokyo March 18, 2003.

Entered into force March 18, 2003.

TIAS

Agreement concerning an engineers and scientists exchange program arising from implementation of the mutual defense assistance agreement of March 8, 1954.

Exchange of notes at Tokyo May 9, 2003.

Entered into force May 9, 2003.

TIAS

Agreement concerning a cash contribution by Japan for administrative and related expenses arising from implementation of the mutual defense assistance agreement of March 8, 1954.

Exchange of notes at Tokyo November 25, 2003.

Entered into force November 25, 2003.

TIAS

Agreement concerning the acquisition and production in Japan of the EP-3, UP-3C, UP-3D and OP-3C aircraft and related equipment and materials.

Exchange of notes at Tokyo March 30, 2004.

Entered into force March 30, 2004.

TIAS

Procedural agreement pursuant to the agreement of April 15, 1996, as amended, concerning reciprocal provision of logistic support, supplies and services.

Signed at Tokyo July 14, 2004.

Entered into force July 29, 2004.

TIAS

Memorandum of understanding concerning Naha air base, Japan, with attachment.

Signed at Okinawa October 18, 2004.

Entered into force October 18, 2004.

TIAS

Memorandum of understanding defining responsibilities for the training of civil aviation bureau, Japan air traffic controllers in Okinawa approach control.

Signed at Okinawa November 30 and December 5, 2004.

Entered into force December 5, 2004.

TIAS

Agreement concerning a cash contribution by Japan for administrative and related expenses arising from implementation of the mutual defense assistance agreement of March 8, 1954.

Exchange of notes at Tokyo December 14, 2004.

Entered into force December 14, 2004.

TIAS

Arrangement concerning cooperation on ballistic missile defense.

Exchange of notes at Tokyo December 14, 2004.

Entered into force December 14, 2004.

TIAS

Memorandum of understanding concerning ballistic missile defense.

Signed at Washington and Tokyo December 14 and 17, 2004.

Entered into force December 17, 2004.

TIAS

Memorandum of agreement regarding assignment of liaison officers, with annex.

Signed at Norfolk and Japan March 11 and 16, 2005.

Entered into force March 16, 2005.

TIAS

Agreement concerning the Advance Hull Materials & Structures Technology (AHM&ST) cooperative research project.

Exchange of notes at Tokyo April 14, 2005.

Entered into force April 14, 2005.

TIAS

Agreement concerning a cash contribution by Japan for administrative and related expenses arising from implementation of the mutual defense assistance agreement of March 8, 1954.

Exchange of notes at Tokyo October 21, 2005.

Entered into force October 21, 2005.

TIAS

Agreement concerning new special measures relating to Article XXIV of the agreement under Article VI of the treaty of mutual cooperation and security between the United States and Japan regarding facilities and areas and the status of United States armed forces in Japan, with agreed minute.

Signed at Tokyo January 23, 2006.

Entered into force April 1, 2006.

TIAS

Memorandum of understanding international defining responsibilities for the Government of Japan's use of the Kadena munitions storage area, with enclosures.

Signed at Okinawa February 10, 2006.

Entered into force February 10, 2006.

TIAS

Annex to the agreement of December 14, 2004 concerning cooperation on Ballistic Missile Defense Open Architecture Research (BMDOAR Project).

Signed at Tokyo and Washington April 5, 2006.

Entered into force April 5, 2006.

TIAS

Annex to the agreement of December 2004 concerning cooperation on Ballistic Missile Defense Radar Research Project.

Signed at Tokyo and Washington April 5, 2006.

Entered into force April 5, 2006.

TIAS

Agreement concerning the cooperation on information assurance and computer network defense, with exchange of notes.

Signed at Tokyo and Washington April 18 and 24, 2006.

Entered into force April 24, 2006.

TIAS

Agreement for cooperation on ballistic missile defense.

Exchange of notes at Tokyo June 23, 2006.

Entered into force June 23, 2006.

TIAS

Agreement concerning a cash contribution by Japan for administrative and related expenses arising from implementation of the mutual defense assistance agreement of March 8, 1954.

Exchange of notes at Tokyo October 13, 2006.

Entered into force October 13, 2006.

TIAS

NOTES

1 For the revision of references in the agreement consequent to the mutual security treaty (TIAS 4509), see exchange of notes of January 19, 1960 (11 UST 1758; TIAS 4511). See also agreement of July 4, 1969 (TIAS 6715).

2 For agreement on the clarification of terms, see exchange of notes of November 25, 1957 (8 UST 2413; TIAS 3958; 303 UNTS 348).

3 For the understanding concerning the application of the agreement to small maritime claims, see exchange of notes of August 22, 1960 (11 UST 2160; TIAS 4580; 394 UNTS 310). For special measures under Article XXIV, see agreement of January 30, 1987.

ECONOMIC AND TECHNICAL COOPERATION

Productivity agreement.

Signed at Tokyo April 7, 1955.

Entered into force April 7, 1955.

6 UST 1007; TIAS 3241; 263 UNTS 285.

Agreement providing for a third-country technical assistance training program in Japan.

Exchange of notes at Tokyo March 23, 1960.

Entered into force March 23, 1960.

11 UST 1382; TIAS 4475; 372 UNTS 289.

EDUCATION

See CULTURAL AND EDUCATIONAL RELATIONS

ENERGY

Agreement on cooperation in research and development in energy and related fields, with exchange of notes.

Signed at Washington May 2, 1979.

Entered into force May 2, 1979.

30 UST 4365; TIAS 9463; 1171 UNTS 283.

Related agreement

January 24, 1983 (TIAS 10656; 1647 UNTS 67).

Amendment and extensions

February 1, 1990 (TIAS 12599).

January 13, 1995 (TIAS 12599).

January 28, 2000.

April 18, 2000.

April 28, 2005.

ENVIRONMENTAL COOPERATION

Agreement on cooperation in the field of environmental protection, with agreed minutes.

Signed at Washington August 5, 1975.

Entered into force August 5, 1975.

26 UST 2534; TIAS 8172; 1027 UNTS 371.

Extensions and amendment

August 5, 1980 (32 UST 2468; TIAS 9853; 1274 UNTS 336).

July 31, 1985 (TIAS 12387).

Agreement concerning cooperation in the Global Learning and Observations to Benefit the Environment (GLOBE) Program.

Exchange of notes at Washington August 29, 1995.

Entered into force August 29, 1995.

TIAS 12686.

EXTRADITION

Treaty on extradition, with exchange of notes.

Signed at Tokyo March 3, 1978.

Entered into force March 26, 1980.

31 UST 892; TIAS 9625; 1203 UNTS 225.

FINANCE

Agreement regarding guaranty of investments in Japan, with a related exchange of notes.

Signed at Tokyo March 8, 1954.

Entered into force May 1, 1954.

5 UST 791; TIAS 2968; 232 UNTS 251.

Agreement concerning payments from Japanese utility companies for uranium enrichment services.

Exchange of notes at Washington September 1, 1978.

Entered into force September 1, 1978.

30 UST 1850; TIAS 9295; 1153 UNTS 151.

HEALTH

Agreement relating to the establishment of the Radiation Effects Research Foundation.

Exchange of notes at Tokyo December 27, 1974.

Entered into force December 27, 1974.

26 UST 7; TIAS 8001.

JUDICIAL ASSISTANCE

Procedures for mutual assistance in the administration of justice in connection with the Lockheed Aircraft Corporation matter.

Signed at Washington March 23, 1976.

Entered into force March 23, 1976.

27 UST 946; TIAS 8233.

Related agreement

January 20 and 22, 1979 (30 UST 3473; TIAS 9400; 1180 UNTS 157).

MAPPING

Agreement concerning cooperation in the field of geospatial information.

Exchange of notes at Tokyo December 22, 2006.

Entered into force December 22, 2006.

NP

MARITIME MATTERS

Agreement on maritime search and rescue.

Signed at Tokyo December 12, 1986.

Entered into force December 12, 1986.

TIAS 11413; 2191 UNTS 57.

Amendment

September 30, 1998.

METROLOGY

Implementing arrangement for cooperation in the fields of metrology and measurement standards.

Signed at Tokyo November 2, 1999.

Entered into force November 2, 1999.

TIAS

MISSIONS, TECHNICAL

Agreement relating to the sending of technical missions by Japan to the United States to study the production of defense equipment and supplies.

Exchange of notes at Washington January 21, 1954.

Entered into force January 21, 1954.

5 UST 317; TIAS 2923; 223 UNTS 145.

NARCOTIC DRUGS

Arrangement for the direct exchange of certain information regarding the traffic in narcotic drugs.

Exchange of notes at Tokyo February 16 and July 6, 1928.

Entered into force July 6, 1928.

9 Bevans 452.

Arrangement for the exchange of information relating to the seizure of illicit narcotic drugs and to persons engaged in the illicit traffic.

Exchange of notes at Tokyo April 23 and September 6, 1929.

Entered into force September 6, 1929.

9 Bevans 455.

NAVIGATION

Agreement relating to the establishment, operation, and maintenance of an OMEGA navigational aid station in Japan.

Exchange of notes at Tokyo August 15, 1972.

Entered into force August 15, 1972.

23 UST 1480; TIAS 7428; 898 UNTS 55.

NUCLEAR MATERIAL

Agreement for cooperation in research and development concerning nuclear material control and accounting measures for safeguards and non-proliferation, with annex.

Signed at Washington July 21, 2006.

Entered into force July 21, 2006.

TIAS

OCEANOGRAPHY

Memorandum of understanding on the participation of Japan in the ocean drilling program as a regular member, with annex.

Signed at Washington and Tokyo September 21, 1993.

Entered into force September 21, 1993; effective October 1, 1993.

TIAS

PATENTS

Agreement to facilitate the interchange of patent rights and technical information for purposes of defense, and protocol.

Signed at Tokyo March 22, 1956.

Entered into force June 6, 1956.

7 UST 1021; TIAS 3585; 275 UNTS 195.

Agreement implementing the agreement of March 22, 1956, to facilitate interchange of patent rights and technical information for purposes of defense, with memorandum of understanding, procedures, related notes and letters.

Exchange of notes at Tokyo April 12, 1988.

Entered into force April 12, 1988.

TIAS

POSTAL MATTERS

Memorandum of understanding relating to the initiation of accelerated mail service.

Signed at Tokyo and Washington May 8 and 27, 1975.

Entered into force May 27, 1975; effective June 16, 1975.

29 UST 90; TIAS 8794.

Memorandum of understanding relating to the exchange of postal money orders.

Signed at Tokyo and Washington August 31 and December 24, 1984; effective January 1, 1985.

NP

Amendment

June 21 and July 12, 1985.

PROPERTY

Arrangement relating to perpetual leaseholds.

Exchange of notes at Tokyo March 25, 1937.

Entered into force March 25, 1937.

50 Stat. 1611; EAS 104; 9 Bevans 464; 181 LNTS 217.

Agreement relating to the payment of damages caused by United States aircraft to property of Japanese nationals.

Exchange of notes at Tokyo August 24, 1955.

Entered into force August 24, 1955.

6 UST 4064; TIAS 3418; 257 UNTS 297.

PUBLICATIONS

Agreement relating to the exchange of official publications.

Exchange of notes at Tokyo September 5, 1956.

Entered into force September 5, 1956.

7 UST 2497; TIAS 3638; 277 UNTS 267.

REMOTE SENSING

Memorandum of understanding relating to the operation of the Landsat system, with annex.

Signed at Washington and Tokyo July 5 and August 11, 1983.

Entered into force August 11, 1983.

35 UST 2177; TIAS 10784; 1581 UNTS 143.

Agreement concerning the acquisition by the Government of Japan of remote sensing parts and components and related information for the indigenous development of an Information Gathering Satellite System.

Exchange of notes at Tokyo September 29, 1999.

Entered into force September 29, 1999.

TIAS

RYUKYU ISLANDS

Agreement concerning the Ryukyu Islands and the Daito Islands with related arrangements.

Signed at Washington and Tokyo June 17, 1971.

Entered into force May 15, 1972.

23 UST 446; TIAS 7314.

SATELLITES

Agreement providing for a program of cooperation in the testing of experimental communications satellites.

Exchange of notes at Tokyo November 6, 1962.

Entered into force November 6, 1962.

13 UST 2470; TIAS 5212; 459 UNTS 203.

Agreement concerning the furnishing of launching and associated services by NASA for Japanese satellites, with memorandum of understanding.

Exchange of notes at Washington May 23, 1975.

Entered into force May 23, 1975.

26 UST 1029; TIAS 8090.

Agreement concerning cooperation regarding the Geotail Scientific Satellite Program.

Exchange of notes at Tokyo September 25, 1989.

Entered into force September 25, 1989.

TIAS 12203.

Memorandum of understanding for cooperation in the Advanced Earth Observing Satellite Program, with appendix and exchange of notes.

Signed at Washington and Tokyo October 14 and 25, 1994.

Entered into force October 25, 1994.

TIAS 12202.

Amendment

June 4 and 10, 1996 (TIAS 12765).

Agreement concerning cooperation on the Advanced Earth Observation Satellite–II (ADEOS–II) Program, with memorandum of understanding.

Exchange of notes at Washington March 14, 1997.

Entered into force March 14, 1997.

TIAS

Amendment

March 13, 2003.

Agreement concerning cooperation to maintain meteorological satellite observation over the Western Pacific region through the back-up of Geostationary Meteorological Satellite-5, with implementing arrangement.

Exchange of notes at Washington May 10, 2002.

Entered into force May 10, 2002.

TIAS

Memorandum of understanding for the x-ray astronomy satellite (ASTRO-EII) project.

Signed at Washington and Tokyo June 21 and 23, 2005.

Entered into force June 23, 2005.

TIAS

Memorandum of understanding concerning activities related to the solar physics satellite (Solar B) project.

Signed at Washington and Tokyo June 21 and 23, 2005.

Entered into force June 23, 2005.

TIAS

Memorandum of understanding for cooperation on the formulation activity of the global precipitation measurement program.

Signed at Washington and Tokyo June 21 and 27, 2005.

Entered into force June 23, 2005.

TIAS

SCIENTIFIC COOPERATION

Agreement on cooperation in research and development in science and technology, with annexes and exchanges of letters.

Signed at Toronto June 20, 1988.

Entered into force June 20, 1988.

TIAS 12025.

Amendment and extension

July 16, 1999.

July 19, 2004.

Agreement concerning cooperation in joint scientific balloon launchings, with memorandum of understanding.

Exchange of notes at Washington June 2, 1993.

Entered into force June 2, 1993.

TIAS

SHELLFISH

Agreement providing for cooperative efforts to be directed toward sanitary control of the shellfish industry.

Exchange of notes at Washington October 24, 1962.

Entered into force October 24, 1962.

13 UST 2452; TIAS 5207; 462 UNTS 119.

SMUGGLING

Convention for prevention of smuggling of intoxicating liquors.

Signed at Washington May 31, 1928.

Entered into force January 16, 1930.

46 Stat. 2446; TS 807; 9 Bevans 446; 101 LNTS 63.

SOCIAL SECURITY

Agreement concerning enrollment of Japanese employees of the Okinawa office of the Voice of America in the employment insurance scheme of Japan.

Exchange of notes at Tokyo September 30 and October 15, 1976.

Entered into force October 15, 1976; effective April 1, 1976.

27 UST 4312; TIAS 8452; 1066 UNTS 291.

SPACE COOPERATION

Agreement concerning cooperation in space activities for peaceful purposes.

Exchange of notes at Tokyo July 31, 1969.

Entered into force July 31, 1969.

20 UST 2720; TIAS 6735; 720 UNTS 79.

Agreement relating to space launch assistance, with exchange of letters.

Exchange of notes at Washington December 3, 1980.

Entered into force December 3, 1980.

32 UST 4197; TIAS 9940; 1266 UNTS 143.

Agreement relating to space shuttle contingency landing sites.

Exchange of notes at Tokyo January 24, 1985.

Entered into force January 24, 1985.

TIAS 12382.

Agreement concerning the furnishing of launch and associated services for the Spacelab mission, with memorandum of understanding.

Exchange of notes at Washington March 29, 1985.

Entered into force March 29, 1985.

TIAS 11938.

Memorandum of understanding for a cooperative program concerning design (Phase B) of a permanently manned space station.

Signed at Tokyo May 9, 1985.

Entered into force May 9, 1985.

TIAS 11327.

Agreement concerning collaboration in the Space Flyer Unit (SFU) program.

Exchange of notes at Washington February 4, 1994.

Entered into force February 4, 1994.

TIAS

Agreement concerning cross-waiver of liability for cooperation in the exploration and use of space for peaceful purposes, with annex and exchanges of notes.

Signed at Washington April 24, 1995.

Entered into force July 20, 1995.

TIAS 12638.

Agreement concerning cooperation on the Advanced Spaceborne Thermal Emission and Reflection Radiometer Program, with memorandum of understanding.

Exchange of notes at Washington October 24, 1996.

Entered into force October 24, 1996.

TIAS 12809.

Agreement concerning cooperation on the Tropical Rainfall Measuring Mission Program, with amendment of the Memorandum of Understanding of October 20, 1995.

Exchange of notes at Washington May 30, 1997.

Entered into force May 30, 1997.

TIAS

Extension

May 28, 2002.

Agreement concerning cooperation on the Mars Exploration PLANET-B Program, with memorandum of understanding.

Exchange of notes at Washington June 29, 1998.

Entered into force June 29, 1998.

TIAS

Extension

June 27, 2003.

Agreement concerning cooperation on the Advanced Microwave Scanning Radiometer-E (AMSR-E) Program.

Exchange of notes at Washington November 30, 1998.

Entered into force November 30, 1998.

TIAS

Agreement concerning cooperation on the X-ray Astronomy Satellite (ASTRO-E) Program.

Exchange of notes at Washington November 30, 1998.

Entered into force November 30, 1998.

TIAS

Agreement concerning cooperation on the Imager for Magnetopause-to-Aurora Global Exploration (IMAGE) Mission.

Exchange of notes at Washington November 30, 1998.

Entered into force November 30, 1998.

TIAS

Agreement extending the agreement of December 12, 1994, as amended and extended, on the Astronaut Training Program, with attachment.

Exchange of notes at Washington December 8, 2000.

Entered into force December 12, 2000.

TIAS

Agreement concerning cooperation on the Second Balloon-Borne Superconducting Magnet Spectrometer Program, with memorandum of understanding.

Exchange of notes at Washington July 12, 2002.

Entered into force July 12, 2002.

TIAS

TAXATION

Agreement relating to tax relief for expenditures made by the United States in Japan under mutual security programs.

Exchange of notes at Tokyo July 14 and 25, 1952.

Entered into force July 25, 1952.

3 UST 2955; TIAS 2477; 198 UNTS 281.

Convention for the avoidance of double taxation and the prevention of fiscal evasion with respect to taxes on estates, inheritances, and gifts.

Signed at Washington April 16, 1954.

Entered into force April 1, 1955.

6 UST 113; TIAS 3175; 238 UNTS 3.

Convention for the avoidance of double taxation and prevention of fiscal evasion with respect to taxes on income with related notes.

Signed at Tokyo March 8, 1971.

Entered into force July 9, 1972.

23 UST 967; TIAS 7365.

Agreement concerning reciprocal exemption from taxation of income accruing from the business of shipping.

Exchange of notes at Washington August 29, 1989.

Entered into force August 29, 1989.

TIAS 11697; 2207 UNTS 401.

Convention for the avoidance of double taxation and the prevention of fiscal evasion with respect to taxes on income, with protocol and related exchange of notes.

Signed at Washington November 6, 2003.

Entered into force March 30, 2004.

TIAS

TELECOMMUNICATION

Agreement relating to the reciprocal granting of authorizations to permit licensed amateur radio operators of either country to operate their stations in the other country.

Exchange of notes at Tokyo August 8, 1985.

Entered into force September 7, 1985.

TIAS 12004.

TRACKING STATIONS

Agreement relating to the establishment by Japan of a satellite tracking station in Okinawa.

Exchange of notes at Tokyo September 2, 1968.

Entered into force September 2, 1968.

19 UST 6011; TIAS 6558; 702 UNTS 151.

Amendment

September 25, 1969 (20 UST 3017; TIAS 6778; 727 UNTS 429).

TRADE

See also COMMERCE

Agreement for the establishment of a Joint United States-Japan Committee on Trade and Economic Affairs.

Exchange of notes at Washington June 22, 1961.

Entered into force June 22, 1961.

12 UST 731; TIAS 4776; 410 UNTS 53.

Agreement providing compensatory concessions under the general agreement on tariffs and trade for certain tariff actions taken by the United States.

Exchange of notes at Geneva February 9, 1962.

Entered into force February 9, 1962.

13 UST 948; TIAS 5032.

Agreement supplementary to the general agreement on tariffs and trade to provide compensatory concessions for increases in certain import duties.

Signed at Geneva December 31, 1962.

Entered into force December 31, 1962.

13 UST 3906; TIAS 5267; 471 UNTS 83.

Interim agreement relating to the renegotiation of Schedule XX (United States) to the general agreement on tariffs and trade.

Signed at Geneva September 6, 1966.

Entered into force September 6, 1966.

17 UST 1485; TIAS 6106; 616 UNTS 215.

Amendment

June 30, 1967 (18 UST 1751; TIAS 6317; 693 UNTS 376).

Agreement within the context of the multilateral trade negotiations concerning Japanese importation of peas and beans.

Exchange of letters at Geneva July 11, 1979.

Entered into force April 25, 1980.

32 UST 5450; TIAS 9995; 1266 UNTS 95.

Agreement within the context of the multilateral trade negotiations relating to agricultural and wood products, with annex.

Exchange of letters at Geneva July 11, 1979.

Entered into force April 25, 1980.

32 UST 5453; TIAS 9996; 1266 UNTS 101.

Agreement to accelerate tariff reductions.

Exchange of letters at Washington September 30, 1981.

Entered into force September 30, 1981.

33 UST 4490; TIAS 10318.

Agreement continuing in effect agreement of December 19, 1980 (TIAS 9961) relating to government procurement in the field of telecommunications, with related letters.

Exchange of letters at Washington January 30, 1984.

Entered into force January 30, 1984; effective January 1, 1984.

35 UST 4338; TIAS 10935; 2016 UNTS 89.

Extension

December 23, 1986.

Agreement concerning trade in certain steel products, with arrangement, agreed minutes and related letter.

Exchange of letters at Washington May 14, 1985.

Entered into force May 14, 1985; effective October 1, 1984.

TIAS

Agreement concerning trade in cotton, wool and man-made fiber textiles with visa arrangement and related exchanges of notes with record of understanding.

Exchange of notes at Washington February 6, 1987.

Entered into force February 6, 1987.

NP

Amendment

July 20, 1989 (NP).

Agreement concerning market access for beef, fresh oranges, orange juice and other products, with annex.

Exchange of letters at Washington July 5, 1988.

Entered into force July 5, 1988.

TIAS

Agreement concerning market access for various agricultural products, with annexes.

Exchange of letters at Washington August 2, 1988.

Entered into force August 2, 1988.

Framework on steel trade liberalization, with appendix.

Signed at Washington February 14, 1990.

Entered into force February 14, 1990.

TIAS

Agreement concerning trade in semiconductor products, with arrangement.

Exchange of letters at Washington June 11, 1991.

Entered into force June 11, 1991; effective August 1, 1991.

TIAS

Agreement concerning trade in certain machine tools, with arrangement, agreed minutes, exchanges of notes and related letters.

Exchange of letters at Washington June 30, 1992.

Entered into force June 30, 1992.

TIAS

Agreement concerning cooperation on anticompetitive activities.

Signed at Washington October 7, 1999.

Entered into force October 7, 1999.

TIAS

TRUST TERRITORY OF THE PACIFIC ISLANDS

Agreement concerning the trust territory of the Pacific Islands with exchanges of notes.

Signed at Tokyo April 18, 1969.

Entered into force July 7, 1969.

20 UST 2654; TIAS 6724; 719 UNTS 127.

Agreement implementing the agreement of April 18, 1969 concerning the trust territory of the Pacific Islands.

Exchange of notes at Washington March 13, 1973.

Entered into force March 13, 1973.

24 UST 767; TIAS 7581.

Agreement relating to the use of interest accrued in connection with payments made under the agreement of April 18, 1969 concerning the trust territory of the Pacific Islands.

Exchange of notes at Tokyo April 18, 1975.

Entered into force April 18, 1975.

26 UST 671; TIAS 8064; 992 UNTS 340.

Agreement extending the period for provision of products and services by Japan under the agreement of April 18, 1969 concerning the trust territory of the Pacific Islands.

Exchange of notes at Tokyo April 18, 1975.

Entered into force April 18, 1975.

26 UST 666; TIAS 8063; 992 UNTS 336.

VISAS

Agreement relating to the reciprocal waiver of nonimmigrant visa fees.

Exchange of notes at Tokyo May 21, August 12 and 26, and September 18, 1952.

Entered into force September 18, 1952; operative October 1, 1952.

5 UST 363; TIAS 2930; 227 UNTS 85.

Agreement relating to the reciprocal issuance of nonimmigrant visas.

Exchange of notes at Tokyo August 9 and 23, 1966.

Entered into force September 22, 1966.

17 UST 1228; TIAS 6087.

WHALING

Agreement concerning commercial sperm whaling in the western division stock of the North Pacific, with summary of discussions.

Exchange of letters at Washington November 13, 1984.

Entered into force November 13, 1984.

TIAS 11070; 2039 UNTS 213.

JORDAN

AGRICULTURAL COMMODITIES

Agricultural commodities agreement with exchange of notes.

Signed at Amman April 5, 1966.

Entered into force April 5, 1966.

17 UST 361; TIAS 5985; 593 UNTS 239.

Amendment

August 25, 1966 (17 UST 361; TIAS 5985; 593 UNTS 254).

Agricultural commodities agreement with exchange of notes.

Signed at Amman August 25, 1966.

Entered into force August 25, 1966.

17 UST 1215; TIAS 6085.

Agricultural commodities agreement with annex.

Signed at Amman April 4, 1968.

Entered into force April 4, 1968.

19 UST 4764; TIAS 6475; 698 UNTS 177.

Related agreements

April 21, 1969 (20 UST 694; TIAS 6675; 707 UNTS 253).

August 20, 1970 (21 UST 2051; TIAS 6949; 763 UNTS 95).

February 17, 1972 (23 UST 87; TIAS 7276;).

May 20, 1973 (24 UST 2019; TIAS 7716; 938 UNTS 206).

July 25, 1973 (24 UST 2031; TIAS 7716; 938 UNTS 218).

August 2, 1973 (24 UST 2033; TIAS 7716; 938 UNTS 220).

September 25 and 29, 1973 (24 UST 2363; TIAS 7760; 938 UNTS 222).

March 12, 1974 (25 UST 280; TIAS 7798; 944 UNTS 396).

Agricultural commodities agreement.

Signed at Amman November 27, 1974.

Entered into force November 27, 1974.

25 UST 3438; TIAS 7995.

Amendment

March 20, 1975 (26 UST 481; TIAS 8050; 992 UNTS 410).

Related agreements

October 14, 1975 (26 UST 2905; TIAS 8197).

March 4, 1976 (27 UST 1465; TIAS 8257; 1049 UNTS 381).

April 27, 1976 (27 UST 1471; TIAS 8257; 1049 UNTS 384).

June 23, 1976 (27 UST 2362; TIAS 8314; 1054 UNTS 372).

November 29, 1976 (28 UST 1292; TIAS 8511).

August 10, 1977 (29 UST 365; TIAS 8822).

January 10, 1978 (29 UST 4243; TIAS 9057; 1134 UNTS 41).

April 15, 1978 (29 UST 4260; TIAS 9057; 1134 UNTS 49).

January 17, 1979 (30 UST 2913; TIAS 9373; 1180 UNTS 141).

June 29, 1980 (32 UST 2258; TIAS 9834).

AVIATION

Agreement relating to the provision of technical assistance and services to the Civil Aviation Department of Jordan.

Signed at Amman and Washington April 1 and May 3, 1980.

Entered into force June 1, 1980.

32 UST 1360; TIAS 9777; 1267 UNTS 77.

Extension

May 31 and June 25, 1990 (TIAS 11738; 2204 UNTS 565).

Air transport agreement, with annexes.

Signed at Amman November 10, 1996.

Entered into force November 10, 1996.

TIAS 12813.

Memorandum of agreement for the provision of technical assistance in developing, modernizing, operating or maintaining the civil aviation infrastructure in Jordan

Signed May 24 and June 20, 2005.

Entered into force June 20, 2005.

TIAS

CUSTOMS

Agreement regarding mutual assistance between their customs administrations.

Signed at Amman December 8, 2004.

Entered into force December 8, 2004.

TIAS

DEFENSE

Agreement concerning payment to the United States of net proceeds from the sale of defense articles furnished under the military assistance program.

Exchange of letters at Amman May 20 and August 24, 1974.

Entered into force August 24, 1974; effective July 1, 1974.

25 UST 2422; TIAS 7921.

Amendment

November 10, 2004 and February 7, 2005.

Agreement relating to the furnishing of defense articles and services to Jordan.

Exchange of notes at Amman October 20, 1976 and February 23, 1977.

Entered into force February 23, 1977.

28 UST 4494; TIAS 8602.

Agreement concerning the grant of defense articles and services under the military assistance program.

Exchange of notes at Amman August 27, 1979.

Entered into force August 28, 1979.

30 UST 7537; TIAS 9597; 1205 UNTS 9.

Amendment

August 18 and September 20, 1982 (TIAS 10501).

Agreement concerning the grant of defense articles and services under the military assistance program.

Exchange of notes at Amman August 14 and 30, 1980.

Entered into force August 30, 1980; effective August 28, 1980.

32 UST 2412; TIAS 9850.

Amendment

August 18 and September 20, 1982 (TIAS 10501).

Mutual support agreement with annexes.

Signed at Amman October 30, 1988.

Entered into force October 30, 1988.

TIAS 12345.

Amendment

February 16 and 29, 2000.

Agreement concerning the transfer of United States Government granted or sold defense articles or related training or other defense services to the Government of Jordan.

Exchange of notes at Amman August 13 and 27, 2000.

Entered into force August 27, 2000.

TIAS

Aviation leadership program agreement.

Signed at Washington and Amman April 21 and 29, 2004.

Entered into force April 29, 2004.

TIAS

Acquisition and cross servicing agreement, with annexes.

Signed at Tampa and Amman March 21 and 29, 2006.

Entered into force March 29, 2006.

TIAS

Memorandum of arrangement regarding the assignment of liaison officers, with annex.

Signed at Norfolk and Washington July 12, 2006.

Entered into force July 12, 2006.

TIAS

ECONOMIC AND TECHNICAL COOPERATION

Agreement relating to economic assistance.

Exchange of notes at Amman June 29, 1957.

Entered into force June 29, 1957.

8 UST 1069; TIAS 3869; 288 UNTS 263.

General agreement providing for economic, technical, and related assistance to Jordan.

Exchange of notes at Amman June 25 and 27, 1957.

Entered into force July 1, 1957.

8 UST 1073; TIAS 3870; 288 UNTS 269.

Agency for International Development

June 9, 1977 (29 UST 4922; TIAS 9085; 1134 UNTS 19).
September 1, 1993 (NP).
June 26, 1997 (NP).
August 26, 1997 (NP).
August 26, 1997 (NP).
February 5, 1998 (NP).
June 9, 1998 (NP).
August 10, 1998 (NP).
August 10, 1998 (NP).
June 30, 1999 (NP).
June 30, 1999 (NP).
June 30, 1999 (NP).
August 30, 1999 (NP).
April 27, 2000 (NP).
May 7, 2000 (NP).
August 23, 2000 (NP).
April 19, 2001 (NP).
April 29, 2001 (NP).
September 30, 2002 (NP).
September 30, 2002 (NP).
September 30, 2002 (NP).
November 7, 2002 (NP).
January 26, 2003 (NP).
January 26, 2003 (NP).
May 13, 2003 (NP).
June 10, 2003 (NP).
June 10, 2003 (NP).
June 10, 2003 (NP).
February 23, 2004 (NP).
March 23, 2004 (NP).
June 2, 2004 (NP).
June 2, 2004 (NP).
June 22, 2004 (NP).
June 22, 2004 (NP).
July 20, 2005 (NP).
July 20, 2005 (NP).
July 20, 2005 (NP).
July 20, 2005 (NP).
August 10, 2006 (NP).
August 10, 2006 (NP).
August 10, 2006 (NP).
August 10, 2006 (NP).

EDUCATION

Agreement for the establishment of the American-Jordanian Commission for Educational Exchange, with attachment.

Signed at Amman May 12, 1993.

Entered into force May 12, 1993.

TIAS 12497

ENVIRONMENTAL COOPERATION

Agreement for cooperation in the Global Learning and Observations to Benefit the Environment (GLOBE) Program, with appendices.

Signed at Amman October 31, 1996.

Entered into force October 31, 1996.

TIAS 12812.

EXTRADITION

Extradition treaty.

Signed at Washington March 28, 1995.

Entered into force July 29, 1995.

TIAS

FINANCE

Agreement relating to investment guaranties under section 413(b)(4) of the Mutual Security Act of 1954.

Exchange of notes at Amman July 10 and September 24, 1956.

Entered into force September 24, 1956.

7 UST 2829; TIAS 3663; 278 UNTS 51.

Amendments

November 20, 1957 and February 22, 1958 (9 UST 335; TIAS 4012; 303 UNTS 377).

June 25, 1963 (14 UST 1017; TIAS 5395; 487 UNTS 356).

Agreement regarding the consolidation and rescheduling or refinancing of certain debts owed to, guaranteed by, or insured by the United States Government and its agencies, with annexes.

Signed at Amman October 31, 1989.

Entered into force December 6, 1989.

NP

Agreement regarding the consolidation and rescheduling or refinancing of certain debts owed to, guaranteed by, or insured by the United States Government and its agencies, with annexes.

Signed at Amman May 10, 1992.

Entered into force June 22, 1992.

NP

Amendment

October 7 and November 1, 1993 (NP).

Agreement regarding the consolidation and rescheduling or refinancing of certain debts owed to, guaranteed by or insured by the United States Government and its agencies, with annexes.

Signed at Amman August 18, 1994.

Entered into force September 19, 1994.

NP

Agreement regarding the reduction of certain debts related to foreign assistance owed to the Government of the United States, with annexes.

Signed at Amman September 29, 1994.

Entered into force September 29, 1994.

NP

Agreement regarding the reduction of certain debts owed to, guaranteed by or insured by the Government of the United States and its agencies, with annexes.

Signed at Amman September 25, 1995.

Entered into force September 30, 1995.

NP

Agreement regarding the consolidation and rescheduling of certain debts owed to, guaranteed by, or insured by the United States Government and its agencies, with annexes.

Signed at Amman August 25, 1997.

Entered into force September 25, 1997.

NP

Agreement regarding the reduction of certain debts owed to the Government of the United States, with annex.

Signed at Amman September 25, 1997.

Entered into force September 25, 1997.

NP

Agreement regarding the consolidation and rescheduling of certain debts owed to, guaranteed by, or insured by the United States Government and its agencies, with annexes.

Signed at Amman October 17, 1999.

Entered into force December 13, 1999.

NP

Agreement regarding the consolidation of certain debts owed to, guaranteed or insured by the United States Government and its agencies, with annexes.

Signed at Amman March 23, 2003.

Entered into force April 28, 2003.

NP

INVESTMENT

Treaty concerning the encouragement and reciprocal protection of investment, with annex and protocol.

Signed at Amman July 2, 1997.

Entered into force June 12, 2003.

TIAS

JUDICIAL ASSISTANCE

Agreement concerning the training of Iraqi police in Jordan.

Signed at Amman and Washington September 24, 2004.

Entered into force September 6, 2005.

TIAS

MAPPING

Arrangement concerning cooperation in mapping, charting and geodesy, with annexes.

Signed at Amman December 1, 1986.

Entered into force December 1, 1986.

NP

PEACE CORPS

Agreement concerning the program of the Peace Corps in Jordan.

Signed at Amman October 28, 1996.

Entered into force October 28, 1996.

TIAS 12810.

POSTAL MATTERS

International express mail agreement, with detailed regulations.

Signed at Amman and Washington December 31, 1986 and January 30, 1987.

Entered into force March 27, 1987.

TIAS 11308.

RELATIONS

Joint statement on United States-Jordan relations.

Issued at Amman June 18, 1974.

Entered into force June 18, 1974.

25 UST 1510; TIAS 7885.

RELIEF SUPPLIES AND PACKAGES

Agreement relating to duty-free entry and defrayment of inland transportation charges for relief supplies of United States voluntary agencies.

Exchange of notes at Amman May 1 and June 29, 1954.

Entered into force June 29, 1954.

5 UST 2896; TIAS 3145; 237 UNTS 111.

Amendment

July 6, September 28, and October 15, 1955 (8 UST 369; TIAS 3784; 279 UNTS 324).

SCIENTIFIC COOPERATION

Memorandum of understanding concerning scientific and technical cooperation in the earth sciences, with annexes.

Signed at Reston and Amman December 9, 2002 and August 26, 2003.

Entered into force August 26, 2003.

TIAS

TAXATION

Agreement concerning the reciprocal exemption from income tax of income derived from the international operation of ships and aircraft.

Exchange of notes at Amman April 7, 1988.

Entered into force April 7, 1988.

TIAS 11888.

TELECOMMUNICATION

Agreement relating to radio communications between amateur stations on behalf of third parties.

Exchange of notes at Washington November 13 and 30, 1972.

Entered into force December 30, 1972.

23 UST 3492; TIAS 7508.

Agreement relating to the reciprocal granting of authorizations to permit licensed amateur radio operators of either country to operate their stations in the other country.

Exchange of letters at Amman February 6 and March 11, 1979.

Entered into force March 11, 1979.

30 UST 3783; TIAS 9425; 1170 UNTS 9.

TRADE AND COMMERCE

Agreement on the establishment of a free trade area, with annexes, schedules, memoranda of understanding, joint statements and exchanges of letters.

Signed at Washington October 24, 2000.

Entered into force December 17, 2001.

TIAS

K

KAZAKHSTAN

For agreements prior to December 31, 1991, see UNION OF SOVIET SOCIALIST REPUBLICS.

ATOMIC ENERGY

Agreement for cooperation concerning peaceful uses of nuclear energy, with annex and agreed minute.

Signed at Washington November 18, 1997.

Entered into force November 5, 1999.

TIAS

Implementing arrangement concerning the decommissioning of the BN-350 Reactor.

Signed at Washington December 19, 1999.

Entered into force December 19, 1999.

TIAS

Arrangement for the exchange of technical information and cooperation in nuclear safety matters, with addendum.

Signed at Vienna September 22, 2004.

Entered into force September 22, 2004.

TIAS

DEFENSE

Agreement concerning the conversion of military technologies and capabilities into civilian activities.

Signed at Almaty March 19, 1994.

Entered into force March 19, 1994.

TIAS

Extension

July 20, 1998.

Agreement concerning the establishment and operation of nuclear test seismic monitoring stations in Kazakhstan.

Signed at Washington November 18, 1997.

Entered into force November 18, 1997.

TIAS

Agreement regarding grants under the Foreign Assistance Act of 1961, as amended, and the furnishing of defense articles, related training, and other defense services from the United States to Kazakhstan.

Exchange of notes at Almaty and Astana April 15, 1999 and April 4, 2000.

Entered into force April 4, 2000.

TIAS

Memorandum of mutual understanding on overflight of United States military aircraft supporting Operation Enduring Freedom.

Signed at Astana December 15, 2001.

Entered into force December 15, 2001.

TIAS

Acquisition and cross-servicing agreement, with annexes.

Signed at Tampa July 9 and 10, 2003.

Entered into force July 10, 2003.

TIAS

Acquisition and cross-servicing agreement, with annexes.

Signed at Tampa July 9 and 10, 2003.

Entered into force July 10, 2003.

TIAS

ECONOMIC AND TECHNICAL COOPERATION

Agreement regarding cooperation to facilitate the provision of assistance.

Signed at Washington May 20, 1992.

Entered into force May 20, 1992.

TIAS 11474.

Agency for International Development

July 28 and August 5, 1997 (NP).

EMPLOYMENT

Agreement relating to the employment of dependents of official government employees.

Exchange of notes at Washington May 23 and June 3, 1996.

Entered into force June 3, 1996.

TIAS 11496.

ENVIRONMENTAL COOPERATION

Agreement on cooperation in the fields of protection of the environment and natural resources, with annex.

Signed at Washington March 27, 1995.

Entered into force March 27, 1995.

TIAS 12623.

Agreement for cooperation in the Global Learning and Observations to Benefit the Environment (GLOBE) Program, with appendices.

Signed at Washington March 27, 1995.

Entered into force March 27, 1995.

TIAS 12624.

Memorandum of understanding concerning the Regional Environmental Center for Central Asia.

Signed at Almaty March 1, 2002.

Entered into force March 1, 2002.

TIAS

FINANCE

Investment incentive agreement.

Signed at Washington May 19, 1992.

Entered into force May 19, 1992.

TIAS

INTERNATIONAL CRIMINAL COURT

Agreement regarding the surrender of persons to the International Criminal Court.

Signed at New York September 22, 2003.

Entered into force October 10, 2004.

TIAS

INVESTMENT

Treaty concerning the reciprocal encouragement and protection of investment, with annex.

Signed at Washington May 19, 1992.

Entered into force January 12, 1994.

TIAS

NARCOTIC DRUGS

Agreement concerning the elimination of the illicit production, processing, trafficking and consumption of narcotics within Kazakhstan, with annex.

Signed at Almaty May 6, 1997.

Entered into force May 6, 1997.

TIAS

NORTH ATLANTIC TREATY

Agreement to treat the agreement of June 19, 1995, among the States Parties to the North Atlantic Treaty and other States participating in the Partnership for Peace regarding the status of their forces as binding between the United States and Kazakhstan.

Exchange of notes at Almaty March 21 and 28, 1997.

Entered into force March 28, 1997.

TIAS

NUCLEAR MATERIAL

Agreement concerning control, accounting and physical protection of nuclear material to promote the prevention of nuclear weapons proliferation.

Signed at Almaty December 13, 1993.

Entered into force December 13, 1993.

TIAS

Amendments

June 30, 1995.

November 17, 1997.

November 17 and 26, 2003.

Implementing arrangements concerning long-term disposition of BN–350 nuclear material.

Signed at Washington November 18, 1997.

Entered into force November 18, 1997.

TIAS

PEACE CORPS

Agreement concerning the activity of the Peace Corps of the United States in the Republic of Kazakhstan.

Signed at Washington December 22, 1992.

Entered into force December 22, 1992.

TIAS 12084.

SEISMIC OBSERVATIONS

Agreement concerning the establishment and operation of nuclear test seismic monitoring stations in Kazakhstan.

Signed at Washington November 18, 1997.

Entered into force November 18, 1997.

TIAS

TAXATION

Convention for the avoidance of double taxation and the prevention of fiscal evasion with respect to taxes on income and capital, with protocol.

Signed at Almaty October 24, 1993.

Entered into force December 30, 1996.

TIAS

Agreement concerning the relationship between the taxation convention of October 24, 1993 and the General Agreement on Trade in Services with regard to the consultation, most-favored-nation and national treatment provisions.

Exchange of notes at Washington July 10, 1995.

Entered into force December 30, 1996.

TIAS

TELECOMMUNICATION

Agreement for the establishment of a government-to-government communications link, with annexes.

Signed at Almaty December 13, 1993.

Entered into force December 13, 1993.

TIAS

Amendment

June 30, 1995.

TRADE AND COMMERCE

Agreement on trade relations, with related exchanges of letters.

Signed at Washington May 19, 1992.

Entered into force February 18, 1993.

TIAS

WEAPONS

Agreement concerning the provision of assistance to the Republic of Kazakhstan related to the establishment of export control systems to prevent the proliferation of weapons of mass destruction.

Signed at Almaty December 13, 1993.

Entered into force December 13, 1993.

TIAS

Amendment

June 30, 1995.

Agreement concerning the destruction of silo launchers of intercontinental ballistic missiles, emergency response and the prevention of proliferation of nuclear weapons.

Signed at Almaty December 13, 1993.

Entered into force December 13, 1993.

TIAS

Extension

December 1 and 5, 2000.

Agreement concerning the provision of material, services and related training to Kazakhstan in connection with the destruction of silo launchers of intercontinental ballistic missiles and associated equipment and components.

Signed at Almaty December 13, 1993.

Entered into force December 13, 1993.

TIAS

Amendment

July 1, 1995.

Agreement concerning the elimination of nuclear weapons infrastructure.

Signed at Almaty September 22 and October 3, 1995.

Entered into force October 3, 1995.

TIAS

Amendments and extensions

June 10, 1996.

September 9, 1998.

December 17, 1999.

July 29, 2000.

May 13 and 31, 2002.

March 11 and April 2, 2003.

June 25 and 28, 2004.

November 29 and December 7, 2004.

August 15 and 23, 2005

April 28 and May 2, 2006.

Agreement concerning cooperation in the area of the prevention of proliferation of weapons of mass destruction.

Signed at Washington November 18, 1997.

Entered into force November 18, 1997.

TIAS

Extension

March 10 and April 9, 2004.

Implementing arrangement for cooperation in the prevention of illicit trafficking in nuclear material.

Signed at Astana May 5, 2006.

Entered into force May 5, 2006.

TIAS

KENYA

AGRICULTURAL COMMODITIES

Agricultural commodities agreement with exchange of notes.

Signed at Nairobi December 7, 1964.

Entered into force December 7, 1964.

15 UST 2348; TIAS 5725; 532 UNTS 263.

Amendments

February 15, 1965 (16 UST 122; TIAS 5769; 542 UNTS 398).

September 1, 1965 (16 UST 1216; TIAS 5870; 579 UNTS 318).

December 1, 1965 (16 UST 1873; TIAS 5919).

February 28, 1966 (17 UST 81; TIAS 5963).

March 14 and April 25, 1967 (18 UST 397; TIAS 6249; 688 UNTS 422).

Agricultural commodities agreement, with minutes of negotiation.

Signed at Nairobi March 6, 1980.

Entered into force March 6, 1980.

32 UST 869; TIAS 9735; 1222 UNTS 127.

Amendment

May 15, 1980 (32 UST 2027; TIAS 9815).

Agricultural commodities agreement.

Signed at Nairobi December 31, 1980 and January 7, 1981.

Entered into force December 31, 1980.

32 UST 4555; TIAS 9969; 1268 UNTS 47.

Amendment

May 4 and 22, 1981 (33 UST 3136; TIAS 10217).

Related agreements

June 3, 1982 (34 UST 1870; TIAS 10468; 1750 UNTS 423).

October 29, 1982 (TIAS 10554; 1871 UNTS 391).

August 24, 1984 (TIAS 11045; 2022 UNTS 47).

Agricultural commodities agreement.

Signed at Nairobi July 16, 1985.

Entered into force July 16, 1985.

NP

Agricultural commodities agreement.

Signed at Nairobi July 16, 1986.

Entered into force July 16, 1986.

NP

Agricultural commodities agreement.
Signed at Nairobi June 29, 1987.
Entered into force June 29, 1987.
NP

Agricultural commodities agreement.
Signed at Nairobi February 26, 1988.
Entered into force February 26, 1988.
NP

Amendment
July 15 and 20, 1988 (NP).

Agricultural commodities agreement.
Signed at Nairobi October 17, 1988.
Entered into force October 17, 1988.
NP

AVIATION

Memorandum of agreement for the provision of technical assistance in developing and modernizing the civil aviation infrastructure of Kenya.
Signed at Washington and Nairobi November 2, 2001.
Entered into force November 2, 2001.
TIAS

Amendment
March 15 and 19, 2004.

DEFENSE

Agreement relating to eligibility for United States military assistance and training pursuant to the International Security Assistance and Arms Export Control Act of 1976.
Exchange of notes at Nairobi August 10 and 24, 1976.
Entered into force August 24, 1976.
28 UST 2468; TIAS 8568.

Agreement regarding Kenya's participation in the African Crisis Response Initiative and the furnishing of commodities, services, and related training by the Government of the United States of America for peacekeeping and humanitarian response purposes.
Exchange of notes at Nairobi March 10 and August 23, 2000.
Entered into force August 23, 2000.
TIAS

Agreement regarding grants under the Foreign Assistance Act of 1961, as amended, and the furnishing of defense articles, related training, and other defense services from the United States of America to the Government of Kenya.
Exchange of notes at Nairobi July 28 and August 23, 2000.
Entered into force August 23, 2000.
TIAS

ECONOMIC AND TECHNICAL COOPERATION

Economic cooperation agreement between the United States and the United Kingdom.
Signed at London July 6, 1948; applicable to Kenya July 6, 1948.
62 Stat. 2596; TIAS 1795; 22 UNTS 263.

Amendments
January 3, 1950 (1 UST 184; TIAS 2036; 86 UNTS 304).
May 25, 1951 (2 UST 1292; TIAS 2277; 99 UNTS 308).
February 25, 1953 (4 UST 1528; TIAS 2815; 172 UNTS 332).

Agreement between the United States and the United Kingdom for technical cooperation in respect of the territories for the international relations of which the Government of the United Kingdom are responsible.
Signed at London July 13, 1951; applicable to Kenya July 14, 1961.
2 UST 1307; TIAS 2281; 105 UNTS 71.

Agency for International Development
September 11, 1974 (28 UST 5617; TIAS 8650).
November 10, 1975 (28 UST 265; TIAS 8470).
June 30, 1976 (28 UST 1562; TIAS 8520).
July 1, 1977 (29 UST 2509; TIAS 8954).
July 20, 1977 (28 UST 5661; TIAS 8650).

ENVIRONMENTAL COOPERATION

Agreement for cooperation in the Global Learning and Observations to Benefit the Environment (GLOBE) Program.
Signed at Nairobi June 9, 1997.
Entered into force June 9, 1997.
TIAS

EXTRADITION

Extradition treaty between the United States and the United Kingdom.
Signed at London December 22, 1931; applicable to Kenya June 24, 1935.
47 Stat. 2122; TS 849; 12 Bevans 482; 163 LNTS 59.

Agreement to continue in force between the United States and Kenya the extradition treaty of December 22, 1931 between the United States and the United Kingdom.
Exchange of notes at Nairobi May 14 and August 19, 1965.
Entered into force August 19, 1965.
16 UST 1866; TIAS 5916; 574 UNTS 153.

FINANCE

Agreement regarding the consolidation and rescheduling of certain debts owed to, guaranteed by or insured by the United States Government and its agency, with annexes.
Signed at Nairobi July 1, 1994.
Entered into force August 26, 1994.
NP

Investment incentive agreement.
Signed at Nairobi December 3, 1998.
Entered into force December 3, 1998.
TIAS

Agreement regarding the consolidation and rescheduling of certain debts owed to, guaranteed by, or insured by the United States Government and its agencies, with annexes.
Signed at Nairobi February 24, 2001.
Entered into force March 30, 2001.
NP

Agreement regarding the consolidation and rescheduling of certain debts owed to, guaranteed by, or insured by the United States Government and its agencies, with annexes.
Signed at Nairobi May 11, 2004.
Entered into force June 21, 2004.
NP

PEACE CORPS

Agreement relating to the establishment of a peace corps program in Kenya.
Exchange of notes at Nairobi August 26, 1964.
Entered into force August 26, 1964.
15 UST 1906; TIAS 5666; 531 UNTS 51.

POSTAL MATTERS

International express mail agreement.
Signed at Washington December 11, 1989.
Entered into force January 30, 1990.
NP

SOCIAL SECURITY

Agreement concerning United States participation on a limited voluntary basis in the National Social Security Fund of Kenya.
Exchange of notes at Nairobi January 31 and March 21, 1977.
Entered into force March 25, 1977.
29 UST 678; TIAS 8847.

TRADE AND COMMERCE

Agreement concerning trade in textiles and textile products, with attachment.

Exchange of notes at Nairobi August 26 and October 25, 1994.

Entered into force October 25, 1994; effective January 1, 1994.

NP

KIRIBATI

On July 12, 1979, the Gilbert Islands became the independent state of Kiribati. Referring to the status of conventions, treaties and other international instruments applied to, or entered into on behalf of the Gilbert Islands by the United Kingdom prior to independence, the Beretitenti (President) of Kiribati, in a note dated September 11, 1979, to the Secretary-General of the United Nations, made a statement reading in part as follows:

"The Government of the Republic of Kiribati desires that questions of succession to such conventions, treaties and other international instruments be governed by accepted rules of international law and by the relevant principles contained in the Convention on Succession of States in respect of Treaties, done at Vienna on 23 August 1978. Accordingly, the Government of the Republic of Kiribati declares that, with regard to multilateral treaties applied or extended to the former Gilbert Islands it will continue to apply the terms of each such treaty provisionally and on the basis of reciprocity until such time as it notifies the depositary authority of its decision with respect thereto. With regard to bilateral treaties applied or extended to, or entered into on behalf of, the former Gilbert Islands, the Government of the Republic of Kiribati declares that it will examine each such treaty and communicate its views to the other State Party concerned. In the meantime the Government of the Republic of Kiribati will continue to observe the terms of each such treaty, which validly so applies and is not inconsistent with its advent to independence, provisionally and on a basis of reciprocity."

AVIATION

Agreement between the United States and the United Kingdom concerning air services, with annexes and exchange of letters.

Signed at Bermuda July 23, 1977.

Entered into force July 23, 1977.

28 UST 5367; TIAS 8641.

Amendment

April 25, 1978 (29 UST 2680; TIAS 8965).

CONSULS

Consular convention between the United States and the United Kingdom.

Signed at Washington June 6, 1951.

Entered into force September 7, 1952.

3 UST 3426; TIAS 2494; 165 UNTS 121.

EXTRADITION

Extradition treaty between the United States and the United Kingdom with protocol of signature and exchange of notes.

Signed at London June 8, 1972.

Entered into force January 21, 1977.

28 UST 227; TIAS 8468.

FINANCE

Investment incentive agreement.

Exchange of notes at Suva and Tarawa January 22, 1990.

Entered into force January 22, 1990.

TIAS 12095.

FRIENDSHIP

Treaty of friendship, with agreed minute.

Signed at Tarawa September 20, 1979.

Entered into force September 23, 1983.

35 UST 2095; TIAS 10777.

INTERNATIONAL CRIMINAL COURT

Agreement regarding the surrender of persons to the International Criminal Court.

Signed at Tarawa March 4, 2004.

Entered into force March 4, 2004.

TIAS

PEACE CORPS

Agreement relating to the establishment of a Peace Corps program in the Gilbert and Ellice Islands.

Exchange of notes at Suva and Tarawa November 12 and 20, 1974.

Entered into force November 20, 1974.

25 UST 3383; TIAS 7991.

SCIENTIFIC COOPERATION

Memorandum of understanding concerning scientific and technical cooperation in the earth sciences on global seismic data acquisition, with annexes.

Signed at Suva February 23, 2006.

Entered into force February 23, 2006.

TIAS

TELECOMMUNICATION

Agreement between the United States and the United Kingdom relating to the reciprocal granting of authorizations to permit licensed amateur radio operators of either country to operate their stations in the other country.

Exchange of notes at London November 26, 1965; applicable to Kiribati December 11, 1969.

16 UST 2047; TIAS 5941; 561 UNTS 193.

Agreement between the United States and the United Kingdom extending to certain territories the application of the agreement of November 26, 1965 relating to the reciprocal granting of authorizations to permit licensed amateur radio operators of either country to operate their stations in the other country.

Exchange of notes at London December 11, 1969.

Entered into force December 11, 1969.

20 UST 4089; TIAS 6800; 732 UNTS 334.

TERRITORIAL SOVEREIGNTY

See FRIENDSHIP

TRADE-MARKS

Declaration by the United States and the United Kingdom affording reciprocal protection to trade-marks.

Signed at London October 24, 1877.

Entered into force October 24, 1877.

20 Stat. 703; TS 138; 12 Bevans 198.

KOREA

AGRICULTURAL COMMODITIES

Agricultural commodities agreement, with exchange of notes.

Signed at Seoul March 2, 1962.

Entered into force March 2, 1962.

13 UST 254; TIAS 4969; 442 UNTS 185.

Amendment

June 12, 1962 (13 UST 1297; TIAS 5082; 459 UNTS 342).

Agricultural commodities agreement with exchange of notes.

Signed at Seoul November 7, 1962.

Entered into force November 7, 1962.

13 UST 2455; TIAS 5208; 462 UNTS 129.

Amendments

June 17, 1963 (14 UST 903; TIAS 5375; 479 UNTS 416).

July 5, 1963 (14 UST 983; TIAS 5388; 479 UNTS 420).

August 16, 1963 (14 UST 1050; TIAS 5403; 487 UNTS 386).

Agricultural commodities agreement with exchanges of notes.

Signed at Seoul March 18, 1964.

Entered into force March 18, 1964.

15 UST 250; TIAS 5547; 524 UNTS 263.

Amendment

June 15, 1964 (15 UST 732; TIAS 5597; 526 UNTS 372).

Agricultural commodities agreement with exchange of notes.

Signed at Seoul December 31, 1964.

Entered into force December 31, 1964.

15 UST 2396; TIAS 5730; 535 UNTS 315.

Agricultural commodities agreement with exchange of notes.

Signed at Seoul March 7, 1966.

Entered into force March 7, 1966.

17 UST 239; TIAS 5973; 579 UNTS 137.

Amendment

December 5, 1966 (18 UST 98; TIAS 6203; 688 UNTS 438).

Agricultural commodities agreement with annex.

Signed at Seoul March 25, 1967.

Entered into force March 25, 1967.

18 UST 1228; TIAS 6272; 685 UNTS 101.

Amendment

February 24, 1968 (19 UST 4656; TIAS 6455; 697 UNTS 344).

Related agreements

May 10, 1968 (19 UST 5495; TIAS 6536; 707 UNTS 21).

October 23, 1968 (19 UST 7541; TIAS 6595; 707 UNTS 31).

February 26, 1969 (20 UST 522; TIAS 6661; 707 UNTS 41).

April 8, 1969 (20 UST 644; TIAS 6669; 707 UNTS 53).

March 7, 1970 (21 UST 600; TIAS 6845).

March 20, 1970 (21 UST 1057; TIAS 6859; 741 UNTS 3).

January 27, 1971 (22 UST 236; TIAS 7057).

January 28, 1971 (22 UST 238; TIAS 7058; 781 UNTS 350).

January 29, 1971 (22 UST 241; TIAS 7059; 781 UNTS 187).

April 12, 1971 (22 UST 1685; TIAS 7193; 806 UNTS 287).

April 12, 1971 (22 UST 1689; TIAS 7194; 806 UNTS 297).

May 6, 1971 (22 UST 632; TIAS 7113; 792 UNTS 394).

December 17, 1971 (22 UST 2069; TIAS 7246).

February 14, 1972 (23 UST 70; TIAS 7273).

May 19, 1972 (23 UST 782; TIAS 7341).

October 20, 1972 (23 UST 3138; TIAS 7489).

November 17, 1972 (23 UST 3806; TIAS 7531).

November 24, 1972 (23 UST 3806; TIAS 7531).

December 7, 1972 (23 UST 3806; TIAS 7531).

February 21, 1973 (24 UST 735; TIAS 7578).

April 12, 1973 (24 UST 987; TIAS 7610).

May 29, 1973 (24 UST 1129; TIAS 7638).

December 7, 1974 (25 UST 3128; TIAS 7976).

February 26, 1975 (26 UST 177; TIAS 8023; 992 UNTS 361).

March 13, 1975 (26 UST 182; TIAS 8023; 992 UNTS 363).

May 27, 1975 (26 UST 1857; TIAS 8142; 1021 UNTS 449).

July 1, 1975 (26 UST 1861; TIAS 8142; 1021 UNTS 451).

Agricultural commodities agreement.

Signed at Seoul February 18, 1976.

Entered into force February 18, 1976.

27 UST 1527; TIAS 8261; 1049 UNTS 109).

Amendments

April 9, 1976 (27 UST 1527; TIAS 8261; 1049 UNTS 118).

August 9, 1976 (27 UST 3536; TIAS 8380).

December 22, 1976 (28 UST 1272; TIAS 8508).

December 7, 1977 (29 UST 2768; TIAS 8971).

Agricultural commodities agreement.

Signed at Seoul July 21, 1977.

Entered into force July 21, 1977.

29 UST 345; TIAS 8821.

Amendment

July 18, 1978 (30 UST 193; TIAS 9186; 1148 UNTS 441).

Agricultural commodities agreement.

Signed at Seoul June 7, 1979.

Entered into force June 7, 1979.

30 UST 6471; TIAS 9562.

Amendment

January 25, 1980 (32 UST 845; TIAS 9733).

Related agreement

May 18, 1981 (33 UST 1894; TIAS 10151; 1529 UNTS 365).

ATOMIC ENERGY

Agreement providing for a grant to the Government of Korea to assist in the acquisition of certain nuclear research and training equipment and materials.

Exchange of notes at Seoul October 14 and November 18, 1960.

Entered into force November 18, 1960.

11 UST 2364; TIAS 4617; 400 UNTS 49.

Agreement for cooperation concerning civil uses of atomic energy with appendix.

Signed at Washington November 24, 1972.

Entered into force March 19, 1973.

24 UST 775; TIAS 7583.

Extension and amendment

NOTE

1 Applicable to all areas of land and water subject to the sovereignty or authority of either state.

CULTURAL RELATIONS

Agreement establishing the Korean-American Cultural Exchange Committee.

Exchange of notes at Seoul April 17, 1981.

Entered into force April 17, 1981.

33 UST 1773; TIAS 10145; 1529 UNTS 359.

CUSTOMS

Agreement on mutual customs service assistance.

Signed at Washington November 3, 1986.

Entered into force March 10, 1987.

TIAS 12010.

DEFENSE

See also MUTUAL SECURITY

Arrangement relating to the transfer of authority to the Government of the Republic of Korea and the withdrawal of United States occupation forces.

Exchange of letters at Seoul August 9 and 11, 1948.

Entered into force August 11, 1948.

Agreement concerning interim military and security matters during the transitional period.

Signed at Seoul August 24, 1948.

Entered into force August 24, 1948.

62 Stat. 3817; TIAS 1918; 9 Bevans 477; 79 UNTS 57.

Mutual defense assistance agreement.

Signed at Seoul January 26, 1950.

Entered into force January 26, 1950.

1 UST 137; TIAS 2019; 80 UNTS 205.

Mutual defense treaty.

Signed at Washington October 1, 1953.

Entered into force November 17, 1954.

5 UST 2368; TIAS 3097; 238 UNTS 199.

Agreed minute relating to continued cooperation in economic and military matters.

Initialed at Seoul November 17, 1954.

Entered into force November 17, 1954.

6 UST 3913; TIAS 3396; 256 UNTS 251.

Amendment

January 30, 1962 (13 UST 244; TIAS 4967; 442 UNTS 323).

Agreement relating to the establishment of minimum facilities for an arsenal and the reworking of ammunition.

Exchange of notes at Seoul May 29, 1955.

Entered into force May 29, 1955.

6 UST 3919; TIAS 3397; 256 UNTS 263.

Agreement providing for the disposition of equipment and materials furnished to Korea under the mutual defense assistance agreement.

Exchange of notes at Seoul May 28 and July 2, 1956.

Entered into force July 2, 1956.

7 UST 2174; TIAS 3616; 281 UNTS 41.

Agreement under article IV of the mutual defense treaty of October 1, 1953, regarding facilities and areas and the status of United States armed forces in Korea, with agreed minutes and exchange of notes.

Signed at Seoul July 9, 1966.

Entered into force February 9, 1967.

17 UST 1677; TIAS 6127; 674 UNTS 163.

Amendments

January 18, 2001.

January 18, 2001.

Agreement regarding the status of the Korean Service Corps with agreed understandings.

Signed at Seoul February 23, 1967.

Entered into force March 10, 1967.

18 UST 249; TIAS 6226; 688 UNTS 245.

Memorandum of understanding relating to the establishment of an M-16 rifle production program in Korea, with annexes.

Signed at Seoul and Washington March 31 and April 22, 1971.

Entered into force April 22, 1971.

29 UST 3537; TIAS 9026.

Amendments

July 30, 1976 (29 UST 3547; TIAS 9026).

October 14, 1977 (29 UST 3550; TIAS 9026).

Agreement concerning payment to the United States of net proceeds from the sale of defense articles furnished under the military assistance program.

Exchange of notes at Seoul June 25 and 27, 1974.

Entered into force July 1, 1974.

25 UST 1434; TIAS 7871.

Memorandum of agreement concerning conventional ammunition logistics, with protocol.

Signed at Seoul November 25, 1974.

Entered into force November 25, 1974.

27 UST 2817; TIAS 8351.

Agreement relating to eligibility for United States military assistance and training pursuant to the International Security Assistance and Arms Export Control Act of 1976.

Exchange of notes at Seoul February 14 and 25, 1977.

Entered into force February 25, 1977.

TIAS 10559; 1577 UNTS 289.

Memorandum of agreement regarding the construction of facilities at 2nd ID USA to improve combined defense capabilities.

Signed at Seoul February 2, 1982.

Entered into force February 2, 1982.

34 UST 125; TIAS 10343.

Memorandum of understanding for fuel exchange between the United States Navy and the Korean Air Force, with appendix.

Signed at Seoul October 31, 1986.

Entered into force October 31, 1986.

TIAS

Mutual logistics support agreement, with annexes.

Signed at Seoul June 8, 1988.

Entered into force June 8, 1988.

TIAS 12024.

Amendments

February 5, 1991.

February 23, 2004.

Memorandum of understanding on defense technological and industrial cooperation.

Signed at Seoul June 8, 1988.

Entered into force June 8, 1988.

TIAS

Memorandum of understanding on royalty fees for U.S. origin defense articles.

Signed at Washington July 18, 1989.

Entered into force July 18, 1989.

TIAS 12032.

Amendment

August 2, 1993 (TIAS 12505).

Agreement for the establishment of the Joint United States Military Affairs Group to the Republic of Korea.

Signed at Seoul January 25, 1991.

Entered into force February 27, 1991.

TIAS 12035.

Agreement terminating the agreed understandings and exchange of letters related to the agreement of July 9, 1966 under Article IV of the mutual defense treaty regarding facilities and areas and the status of United States Armed Forces in Korea.

Exchange of letters at Seoul February 1, 1991.

Entered into force February 1, 1991.

TIAS

Agreement concerning wartime host nation support, with annexes and agreed minute.

Signed at Seoul November 21, 1991.

Entered into force December 23, 1992.

TIAS; 1738 UNTS 265.

Memorandum of understanding concerning technology research and development projects, with annex.

Signed at Washington and Seoul May 29, 1996.

Entered into force May 29, 1996.

TIAS 12761.

Memorandum of understanding concerning combat cross-servicing of U.S. Air Force and Republic of Korea Air Force aircraft

Signed June 6, 1998.

Entered into force June 6, 1998.

TIAS

Memorandum of agreement concerning construction, operation and maintenance of a munitions demilitarization facility (DEFAC) in the Republic of Korea.

Signed at Seoul April 21, 1999.

Entered into force April 21, 1999.

TIAS

Agreement regarding the exchange of engineers and scientists, with annexes.

Signed at Washington June 30, 2000.

Entered into force June 30, 2000.

NP

Understandings to the agreement under Article IV of the mutual defense treaty regarding facilities and areas and the status of United States armed forces in the Republic of Korea and related agreed minutes, as amended.

Signed at Seoul January 18, 2001.

Entered into force April 2, 2001.

TIAS

Memorandum of understanding on preferential hiring of Korean employees and employment of family members.

Signed at Seoul January 18, 2001.

Entered into force April 2, 2001.

TIAS

Agreement for the land partnership plan, with appendices, annexes, and agreed recommendation.

Signed at Seoul March 29, 2002.

Entered into force March 29, 2002.

TIAS

Amendment

October 26, 2004.

Memorandum of agreement regarding liaison officers, with annex.

Signed at Arlington September 5, 2002.

Entered into force September 5, 2002.

TIAS

Agreement concerning mutual airlift support utilizing aircraft operated by/for the military forces of the parties in case of military hostilities in the Republic of Korea, with annexes.

Signed at Daejeon and Belleville June 25 and July 6, 2004.

Entered into force August 18, 2004.

TIAS

Memorandum of agreement for mutual aid in fire protection, with attachments.

Signed at Daegu September 21 and October 5, 2004.

Entered into force October 5, 2004.

TIAS

Agreement on the relocation of United States forces from the Seoul metropolitan area.

Signed at Seoul October 26, 2004.

Entered into force December 13, 2004.

TIAS

Memorandum of agreement regarding the agreed recommendation for implementation of the agreement on the relocation of United States forces from the Seoul metropolitan area, with annex.

Signed at Seoul October 26, 2004.

Entered into force December 13, 2004.

TIAS

Memorandum of understanding concerning liquid oxygen support.

Signed at Seoul November 12 and December 6, 2004.

Entered into force December 6, 2004.

TIAS

Agreement concerning special measures relating to Article V of the agreement under Article IV of the mutual defense treaty regarding facilities and areas and the status of United States armed forces in the Republic of Korea.

Signed at Seoul June 9, 2005.

Entered into force July 6, 2005.

TIAS

Memorandum of understanding international concerning reduced vertical separation minimum in the Republic of Korea.

Signed at Osan September 29, 2005.

Entered into force September 29, 2005.

TIAS

Memorandum of understanding regarding assignment of liaison officers, with annex.

Signed at Seoul and Norfolk August 29 and November 21, 2005.

Entered into force November 21, 2005.

TIAS

Memorandum of understanding regarding reciprocal exchange of military personnel, with annexes.

Signed at Seoul and Norfolk November 2 and 30, 2005.

Entered into force November 30, 2005.

TIAS

Annex to the data exchange agreement of May 15, 1963 on rocket motor defect assessment.

Signed at Arlington and Seoul May 4 and 22, 2006.

Entered into force May 22, 2006.

TIAS

Memorandum of understanding international concerning combined disaster management, with annexes.

Signed June 7, 2006.

Entered into force June 7, 2006.

TIAS

ECONOMIC AND TECHNICAL COOPERATION

Agreement on economic coordination between the Republic of Korea and the United States acting as the Unified Command, with exchange of notes and minutes.[1]

Signed at Pusan May 24, 1952.

Entered into force May 24, 1952.

3 UST 4420; TIAS 2593; 179 UNTS 23.

Agreement providing for economic, technical and related assistance, with agreed minute and related exchange of notes.

Exchange of notes at Seoul February 8, 1961.

Entered into force February 28, 1961.

12 UST 268; TIAS 4710; 405 UNTS 37.

Agreements relating to exemptions from Korean income and social security taxes in connection with economic and technical programs in Korea.

Exchanges of notes at Seoul February 8, 1961.

Entered into force February 8, 1961.

12 UST 976; TIAS 4802; 413 UNTS 392.

Agreement concerning supplemental economic assistance.

Letter of October 16, 1971.

Entered into force October 16, 1971.

28 UST 7591; TIAS 8730.

Agency for International Development

September 11, 1974 (28 UST 555; TIAS 8476).

April 30, 1975 (28 UST 569; TIAS 8476).

September 13, 1975 (28 UST 572; TIAS 8476).

September 13, 1975 (28 UST 860; TIAS 8484).

September 13, 1975 (28 UST 311; TIAS 8471).

September 19, 1975 (28 UST 827; TIAS 8483).

July 1, 1976 (28 UST 2382; TIAS 8549).

July 26, 1976 (28 UST 2325; TIAS 8546).

January 19, 1977 (29 UST 2017; TIAS 8921).

NOTE

1 Superseded February 28, 1961 with exception of paragraph 13, article III, by agreement of February 8, 1961 (TIAS 4710).

EDUCATION

Agreement for financing certain educational exchange programs.

Signed at Seoul June 18, 1963.

Entered into force June 18, 1963.

14 UST 850; TIAS 5366; 487 UNTS 297.

Amendments

June 10 and November 2, 1965 (17 UST 71; TIAS 5960; 586 UNTS 282).

September 24 and November 26, 1971 (22 UST 2056; TIAS 7240).

June 1 and July 10, 1972 (23 UST 1328; TIAS 7415; 852 UNTS 282).

Memorandum of understanding on education, with annex.

Signed at Seoul October 28, 1981.

Entered into force October 28, 1981.

33 UST 1993; TIAS 10163.

ENVIRONMENTAL COOPERATION

Agreement for cooperation in the Global Learning and Observations to Benefit the Environment (GLOBE) Program, with appendices.

Signed at Seoul April 21, 1995.

Entered into force April 21, 1995.

TIAS 12635.

EXTRADITION

Extradition treaty.

Signed at Washington June 9, 1998.

Entered into force December 20, 1999.

TIAS

FINANCE

Initial financial and property settlement.[1]

Signed at Seoul September 11, 1948.

Entered into force September 20, 1948.

62 Stat. 3422; TIAS 1851; 9 Bevans 481; 89 UNTS 155.

Amendment

September 11, 1948 (62 Stat. 3443; TIAS 1851; 9 Bevans 489; 89 UNTS 186).

Electric power agreement.

Signed at Seoul June 13, 1949.

Entered into force December 28, 1949.

9 UST 509; TIAS 4026; 316 UNTS 278.

Agreement regarding expenditures by forces under command of the Commanding General of the Armed Forces of Member States of the United Nations, and exchange of notes of September 5 and 6, 1950.

Signed at Taegu July 28, 1950.

Entered into force July 28, 1950.

1 UST 705; TIAS 2135; 140 UNTS 57.

Agreement relating to investment guaranties under section 413(b)(4) of the Mutual Security Act of 1954, as amended.

Exchange of notes at Seoul February 19, 1960.

Entered into force February 19, 1960.

11 UST 202; TIAS 4431; 372 UNTS 109.

Amendment

April 16, 1965 (16 UST 655; TIAS 5790; 546 UNTS 372).

Investment incentive agreement.

Signed at Washington July 30, 1998.

Entered into force July 30, 1998.

TIAS

NOTE

1 Article VII superseded by electric power agreement of June 13, 1949 (9 UST 509; TIAS 4026; 316 UNTS 278). Agreement superseded in part by article II of agreement on facilities and areas and the status of United States armed forces in Korea of July 9, 1966 (17 UST 1677; TIAS 6127).

FISHERIES

Agreement regarding the collection and exchange of data on fisheries harvests in the international waters of the Bering Sea.

Exchange of notes at Washington April 25 and July 14, 1988.

Entered into force July 14, 1988.

TIAS 11596; 2190 UNTS 239.

HEALTH

Agreement relating to the provision of medical treatment to Korean veterans of the Korean and Vietnam conflicts in Veterans Administration hospitals in the United States.

Exchange of notes at Seoul February 3, 1978.

Entered into force February 3, 1978.

30 UST 4479; TIAS 9471; 1170 UNTS 17.

INFORMATIONAL MEDIA GUARANTIES

Agreement for an informational media guaranty program.

Exchange of notes at Seoul April 4, 1958 and September 25, 1959.

Entered into force September 25, 1959.

10 UST 1826; TIAS 4341; 358 UNTS 163.

INTELLECTUAL PROPERTY

Record of understanding on intellectual property rights, with related letter.

Signed at Washington August 28, 1986.

Entered into force August 28, 1986.

TIAS 11948.

JUDICIAL ASSISTANCE

Treaty on mutual legal assistance in criminal matters, with annex and exchange of notes.

Signed at Washington November 23, 1993.

Entered into force May 23, 1997.

TIAS

MAPPING

Basic exchange and cooperative agreement concerning geospatial information and services cooperation, with annexes.

Signed at Seoul September 26, 2002.

Entered into force September 26, 2002.

NP

METEOROLOGY

Protocol on cooperation in the field of atmospheric science and technology.

Signed at Washington November 22, 2005.

Entered into force November 22, 2005.

TIAS

METROLOGY

Memorandum of understanding for cooperation relating to standardization, conformity assessment and legal metrology.

Signed at Washington May 9, 2000.

Entered into force May 9, 2000.

TIAS

MISSIONS, MILITARY

Agreement for the establishment of the United States military advisory group to the Republic of Korea.

Signed at Seoul January 26, 1950.

Entered into force January 26, 1950; operative July 1, 1949.

3 UST 2696; TIAS 2436; 178 UNTS 97.

Amendment

October 21, 1960 (11 UST 2348; TIAS 4613; 400 UNTS 386).

MUTUAL SECURITY

Agreement relating to the assurances required by the Mutual Security Act of 1951.

Exchange of notes at Pusan January 4 and 7, 1952.

Entered into force January 7, 1952.

3 UST 4619; TIAS 2612; 179 UNTS 105.

PATENTS

Agreement relating to the reciprocal granting and protection of the right of priority on patents.

Exchange of notes at Seoul October 30, 1978.

Entered into force October 30, 1978.

30 UST 2183; TIAS 9324; 1170 UNTS 23.

Agreement for the safeguarding of secrecy of inventions relating to defense and for which applications for patents have been made.

Signed at Seoul January 6, 1992.

Entered into force July 29, 1993.

TIAS 12445; 1751 UNTS 153.

PETROLEUM

Petroleum agreement of 1964, with agreed minutes.

Signed at Seoul May 12, 1964.

Entered into force September 3, 1964.

15 UST 1412; TIAS 5614; 529 UNTS 299.

POSTAL MATTERS

Parcel post agreement and detailed regulations.

Signed at Seoul February 17, 1949.

Entered into force December 1, 1949.

64 Stat. (3) B46; TIAS 2002; 9 Bevans 500; 74 UNTS 167.

Insured parcel post agreement.

Signed at Seoul July 15 and at Washington August 17, 1960.

Entered into force January 1, 1961.

11 UST 2456; TIAS 4630; 400 UNTS 339.

International express mail agreement, with detailed regulations.

Signed at Seoul and Washington December 27, 1979 and January 14, 1980.

Entered into force March 1, 1980.

32 UST 4343; TIAS 9951; 1274 UNTS 3.

Memorandum of understanding concerning the operation of the INTELPOST field trial, with details of implementation.

Signed at Seoul and Washington February 19 and March 4, 1985.

Entered into force March 4, 1985.

TIAS 11244.

PRISONER TRANSFER

Memorandum of agreement on the transfer of prisoners of war/civilian internees.

Signed at Seoul February 12, 1982.

Entered into force February 12, 1982.

34 UST 1173; TIAS 10406; 1734 UNTS 295.

PUBLICATIONS

Agreement for the exchange of official publications.

Exchange of notes at Seoul April 18 and September 24, 1966.

Entered into force September 24, 1966.

17 UST 1552; TIAS 6110; 607 UNTS 157.

RELIEF SUPPLIES AND PACKAGES

Agreement relating to duty-free entry and defrayment of inland transportation charges on relief supplies and packages, with memorandum of interpretation.

Exchange of notes at Seoul April 22 and May 2, 1955.

Entered into force May 2, 1955.

6 UST 1189; TIAS 3264; 258 UNTS 3.

Amendments

November 9 and December 28, 1962 (13 UST 3838; TIAS 5257; 469 UNTS 428).

May 19, 1971 (22 UST 698; TIAS 7128; 791 UNTS 360).

SCIENTIFIC COOPERATION

Memorandum of understanding concerning technical cooperation in chemistry, physics and engineering measurement sciences.

Signed at Gaithersburg September 12, 1994.

Entered into force September 12, 1994.

TIAS 12563.

Amendment and extension

March 22 and April 1, 2000.

Agreement relating to scientific and technical cooperation, with annexes.

Signed at Washintgon July 2, 1999.

Entered into force July 2, 1999; effective April 29, 1999.

TIAS

Extension

June 24 and 25, 2004.

Memorandum of understanding concerning cooperation in science and technology.

Signed at Arlington September 21, 2000.

Entered into force September 21, 2000.

TIAS

Memorandum of understanding concerning scientific and technical cooperation in the earth sciences.

Signed at Seoul and Reston February 14 and March 5, 2002.

Entered into force March 5, 2002.

TIAS

Amendment and extension

May 15 and 19, 2006.

Memorandum of understanding concerning scientific and technical cooperation in the earth and marine sciences.

Signed at Ansan and Reston November 4, 2005 and January 5, 2006.

Entered into force January 5, 2006.

TIAS

SEISMIC OBSERVATIONS

Agreement concerning the Korean seismic research station Wonju, Republic of Korea, with appendices.

Signed at Seoul December 22, 2006.

Entered into force December 27, 2006.

TIAS

SHELLFISH

Agreement concerning the improvement and standardization of shellfish sanitation practices and exchanges of information on sanitary controls applied to the production and handling of fresh or frozen oysters, clams and mussels, with related notes.

Exchange of notes at Washington November 24, 1972.

Entered into force November 24, 1972.

23 UST 3696; TIAS 7516; 898 UNTS 91.

SOCIAL SECURITY

Agreement on social security, with administrative arrangement.

Signed at Washington March 13, 2000.

Entered into force April 1, 2001.

TIAS

SURPLUS PROPERTY

Agreement on disposal of United States excess property located in Korea, with memorandum of interpretation.[1]

Signed at Seoul October 1, 1959.

Entered into force October 1, 1959.

10 UST 1747; TIAS 4328; 358 UNTS 115.

NOTE

1 For waiver of restriction in paragraph 4 of the memorandum, see exchange of notes of February 1, 1963 (14 UST 212; TIAS 5299; 473 UNTS 354).

TAXATION

Convention for the avoidance of double taxation and the prevention of fiscal evasion with respect to taxes on income and the encouragement of international trade and investment, with related notes.

Signed at Seoul June 4, 1976.

Entered into force October 20, 1979.

30 UST 5253; TIAS 9506; 1178 UNTS 3.

TRADE

See also COMMERCE

Agreement on tariff and non-tariff measures within the context of the multilateral trade negotiations with related letters of May 30 and June 12, 1980.

Exchange of letters at Seoul December 27, 1979.

Entered into force January 6, 1981.

TIAS

Agreement on access of United States firms to Korea's insurance markets.

Exchange of letters at Washington August 28, 1986.

Entered into force August 28, 1986.

TIAS

Related agreement

September 10, 1987.

Agreement concerning trade in certain textiles and textile products, with annexes.

Exchange of letters at Washington November 21 and December 4, 1986.

Entered into force December 4, 1986; effective January 1, 1986.

NP

Amendments

December 18 and 23, 1986 (NP).

January 20 and February 11, 1987 (NP).

February 2 and 11, 1987 (NP).

March 4 and 20, 1987 (NP).

September 14, 1990 (NP).

September 14, 1990 (NP).

November 30 and December 3, 1990 (NP).

Agreement relating to limitation of imports of specialty steel from Korea, with annexes and agreed minutes.

Exchange of letters at Washington October 20, 1987.

Entered into force October 20, 1987.

TIAS

Record of understanding concerning market access for cigarettes.

Signed at Washington May 27, 1988.

Entered into force May 27, 1988.

TIAS

Agreement concerning market access for wine and wine products in Korea, with annexes.

Exchange of letters at Washington January 18, 1989.

Entered into force January 18, 1989.

TIAS

Arrangement concerning trade in certain steel products, with appendices.

Exchange of letters at Washington April 20, 1990.

Entered into force April 20, 1990; effective October 1, 1989.

TIAS

Framework agreement for agreements on steel trade liberalization, with appendices and exchange of letters.

Signed at Washington April 20, 1990.

Entered into force April 20, 1990.

TIAS

Agreement relating to trade in textiles and textile products, with attachment.

Exchange of notes at Washington September 14, 1990.

Entered into force September 14, 1990; effective January 1, 1990.

NP; 1882 UNTS 129.

Amendments and extension

January 24 and February 1, 1991 (NP).

November 8 and 30, 1993 (NP; 1929 UNTS 461).

April 2 and 8, 1997 (NP).

Visa arrangement concerning trade in textiles and textile products, with annexes.

Exchange of letters at Washington April 8 and 10, 1991.

Entered into force April 10, 1991.

NP

VISAS

Agreement relating to the issuance of nonimmigrant visas and the reciprocal waiver of fees.

Exchange of notes at Seoul March 28, 1968.

Entered into force April 27, 1968.

19 UST 4789; TIAS 6479; 693 UNTS 199.

KUWAIT

AVIATION

Agreement on aviation security.

Exchange of notes at Kuwait November 22, 1987 and January 11, 1988.

Entered into force July 5, 1988.

TIAS 12023.

CONSULS

Consular convention between the United States and the United Kingdom.

Signed at Washington June 6, 1951.

Entered into force September 7, 1952.

3 UST 3426; TIAS 2494; 165 UNTS 121.

DEFENSE

Agreement concerning the procurement of defense articles and defense services by Kuwait and the establishment of a U.S. Liaison Office in Kuwait.

Exchange of notes at Kuwait February 24 and April 15, 1975.

Entered into force April 15, 1975.

26 UST 682; TIAS 8066; 992 UNTS 199.

Technical security arrangement.

Signed at Kuwait January 18, 1976.

Entered into force January 18, 1976.

27 UST 4177; TIAS 8444; 1071 UNTS 377.

Amendment

June 26, 1977 (29 UST 1874; TIAS 8905).

FINANCE

Agreement on investment guaranties.

Signed at Kuwait April 24, 1989.

Entered into force October 24, 1989.

TIAS 12071.

JUDICIAL ASSISTANCE

Agreement on procedures for mutual assistance in connection with matters relating to the Boeing Company.

Signed at Washington October 6, 1978.

Entered into force October 6, 1978.

NP

Related agreement

December 21, 1978 and January 2, 1979 (NP).

MAPPING

Basic exchange and cooperative agreement for geospatial information and services.

Signed at Washington and Kuwait August 7, 1998.

Entered into force August 7, 1998.

NP

POSTAL MATTERS

Agreement concerning the exchange of parcel post and regulations of execution.

Signed at Kuwait October 9, 1963 and at Washington October 21, 1963.

Entered into force September 16, 1964.

15 UST 1841; TIAS 5658; 530 UNTS 281.

International express mail agreement with detailed regulations.

Signed at Kuwait and Washington February 28 and March 11, 1981.

Entered into force April 1, 1981.

33 UST 1353; TIAS 10114; 1285 UNTS 29.

TELECOMMUNICATION

Agreement relating to the reciprocal granting of authorizations to permit licensed amateur radio operators of either country to operate their stations in the other country.

Exchange of notes at Kuwait July 19 and 24, 1966.

Entered into force July 19, 1966.

17 UST 1039; TIAS 6061; 593 UNTS 289.

Agreement for the establishment and operation of a United States radio relay station in the State of Kuwait.

Signed at Kuwait August 2, 1992.

Entered into force August 29, 1992.

TIAS 12469.

VISAS

Agreement relating to the reciprocal granting of nonimmigrant passport visas.

Exchange of notes at Kuwait December 11 and 27, 1960.

Entered into force December 27, 1960; operative January 26, 1961.

11 UST 2650; TIAS 4659; 401 UNTS 185.

KYRGYZ REPUBLIC

For agreements prior to December 31, 1991, see UNION OF SOVIET SOCIALIST REPUBLICS.

DEFENSE

Agreement concerning the provision of training related to defense articles under the United States International Military Education and Training (IMET) Program.

Exchange of notes at Bishkek February 7 and 25, 1994.

Entered into force February 25, 1994.

NP

Agreement concerning the status of United States military and civilian personnel of the United States Department of Defense who may be present in Kyrgyzstan in connection with cooperative efforts in response to terrorism, humanitarian assistance and other agreed activities.

Exchange of notes at Bishkek December 4 and 5, 2001.

Entered into force December 15, 2001.

TIAS

ECONOMIC AND TECHNICAL COOPERATION

Agreement regarding cooperation to facilitate the provision of assistance.

Signed at Washington May 19, 1993.

Entered into force May 19, 1993.

TIAS 12152.

EMPLOYMENT

Agreement relating to the employment of dependents of official government employees.

Exchange of notes at Washington December 6 and 22, 1993.

Entered into force December 22, 1993.

TIAS 12170.

ENVIRONMENTAL COOPERATION

Agreement for cooperation in the Global Learning and Observations to Benefit the Environment (GLOBE) Program, with appendices.

Signed at Washington June 9, 1995.

Entered into force June 9, 1995.

TIAS 12658.

FINANCE

Investment incentive agreement.

Signed at Washington May 8, 1992.

Entered into force May 8, 1992.

TIAS 12452.

INVESTMENT

Treaty concerning the encouragement and reciprocal protection of investment, with annex.

Signed at Washington January 19, 1993.

Entered into force January 12, 1994.

TIAS

PEACE CORPS

Agreement concerning the activity of the Peace Corps in Kyrgyzstan.

Signed at Washington November 5, 1992.

Entered into force November 5, 1992.

TIAS 11502.

TRADE AND COMMERCE

Agreement on trade relations, with related exchanges of letters.

Signed at Washington May 8, 1992.

Entered into force August 21, 1992.

TIAS

L

LAKE CHAD BASIN COMMISSION

ECONOMIC AND TECHNICAL COOPERATION

Agency for International Development
June 25, 1976 (28 UST 6098; TIAS 8671).

LAOS

DEFENSE

Memorandum of understanding concerning payment to the United States of the net proceeds from the sale of defense articles furnished under the military assistance program.
Signed at Vientiane May 31, 1974.
Entered into force May 31, 1974; effective July 1, 1974.
27 UST 2989; TIAS 8357; 1066 UNTS 115.

Agreement regarding the furnishing of defense articles, related training and other defense services from the United States to Laos.
Exchange of notes at Vientiane December 7, 1992 and September 29, 1993.
Entered into force September 29, 1993.
TIAS 12346.

ECONOMIC AND TECHNICAL COOPERATION

Economic cooperation agreement, with annex and exchange of notes.
Signed at Vientiane September 9, 1951.
Entered into force September 9, 1951.
2 UST 2177; TIAS 2344; 174 UNTS 141.

Agreement providing for additional direct economic assistance.
Exchange of notes at Vientiane July 6 and 8, 1955.
Entered into force July 8, 1955; operative from January 1, 1955.
7 UST 2833; TIAS 3664; 278 UNTS 59.

FINANCE

Investment incentive agreement.
Signed at Washington March 8, 1996.
Entered into force March 26, 1996.
TIAS 12733.

INTERNATIONAL CRIMINAL COURT

Agreement regarding the surrender of persons to international tribunals.
Signed at Vientiane December 24, 2003.
Entered into force December 24, 2003.
TIAS

MUTUAL SECURITY

Agreement relating to the assurances required by the Mutual Security Act of 1951.
Exchange of notes at Vientiane December 18 and 31, 1951.
Entered into force December 31, 1951.
3 UST 4622; TIAS 2613; 198 UNTS 243.

NARCOTIC DRUGS

Memorandum of understanding concerning cooperation on narcotics issues.
Signed at Vientiane January 9, 1990.
Entered into force January 9, 1990.
TIAS 12407.

POSTAL MATTERS

International express mail agreement.
Signed at Vientiane and Washington September 10 and October 16, 1991.
Entered into force November 16, 1991.
NP

TECHNICAL ASSISTANCE

Memorandum of understanding concerning prosthetics and rehabilitation assistance.
Signed at Vientiane May 15, 1990.
Entered into force May 15, 1990.
TIAS 11721; 2207 UNTS 291.

TRADE

Agreement relating to trade in textiles and textile products, with annexes.
Signed at Washington September 15, 1994.
Entered into force September 15, 1994.
NP

Amendment and extension
June 23 and August 4, 2000.

LATVIA

ATOMIC ENERGY

Agreement concerning cooperation in the area of countering the proliferation of nuclear materials and technologies.
Signed at Washington April 25, 2005.
Entered into force April 25, 2005.
TIAS

COMMERCE

Provisional commercial agreement according mutual unconditional most-favored-nation treatment in customs matters.
Signed at Riga February 1, 1926.
Entered into force April 30, 1926.
TS 740; 9 Bevans 528; 55 LNTS 33.

Treaty of friendship, commerce, and consular rights.
Signed at Riga April 20, 1928.
Entered into force July 25, 1928.
45 Stat. 2641; TS 765; 9 Bevans 531; 80 LNTS 35.

CONSULS

See COMMERCE

CULTURAL PROPERTY

Agreement on the protection and preservation of certain cultural properties.
Signed at Riga October 7, 2002.
Entered into force November 12, 2004.
TIAS

CUSTOMS

Agreement regarding mutual assistance between their customs administrations.
Signed at Washington April 17, 1998.
Entered into force July 23, 1999.
TIAS

DEFENSE

Agreement concerning the provision of training related to defense articles under the United States International Military Education and Training (IMET) Program.
Exchange of notes at Riga February 21 and March 4, 1992.
Entered into force March 4, 1992.
NP

Agreement concerning security measures for the protection of classified military information.
Signed at Washington January 15, 1998.
Entered into force January 15, 1998.
TIAS

Acquisition and cross-servicing agreement, with annexes.
Signed at Riga and Patch Barracks March 28 and 30, 1998.
Entered into force March 30, 1998.
TIAS

Agreement regarding U.S. government equipment and provision of logistic support services to Polish-led multinational division and its members in support of Peacekeeping Operations (PKO) in Iraq.

Exchange of notes at Riga August 22 and September 18, 2003.

Entered into force September 18, 2003.

TIAS

DIPLOMATIC RELATIONS

Memorandum of understanding concerning diplomatic relations.

Signed at Riga September 5, 1991.

Entered into force September 5, 1991.

TIAS 12132.

ECONOMIC AND TECHNICAL ASSISTANCE

Agreement concerning economic, technical and related assistance.

Signed at Riga December 20, 1995.

Entered into force February 7, 1996.

TIAS; 2060 UNTS 103.

EDUCATION

Agreement concerning the status of private educational institution "The International School of Latvia".

Signed at Riga March 12, 2003.

Entered into force August 29, 2006.

TIAS

EMPLOYMENT

Agreement relating to the employment of dependents of official government employees.

Exchange of notes at Riga April 24 and July 16, 1996.

Entered into force July 16, 1996.

TIAS 12781.

ENVIRONMENTAL COOPERATION

Agreement for cooperation in the Global Learning and Observations to Benefit the Environment (GLOBE) Program, with appendices.

Signed at Riga January 27, 1999.

Entered into force January 27, 1999.

TIAS

EXTRADITION

Treaty of extradition.

Signed at Riga October 16, 1923.

Entered into force March 1, 1924.

43 Stat. 1738; TS 677; 9 Bevans 515; 27 LNTS 371.

Supplementary extradition treaty.

Signed at Washington October 10, 1934.

Entered into force March 29, 1935.

49 Stat. 3131; TS 884; 9 Bevans 554; 158 LNTS 263.

FINANCE

Agreement relating to the funding of the indebtedness of Latvia to the United States.

Signed at Washington September 24, 1925; operative December 15, 1922.

Treasury Department print; 9 Bevans 521.

Agreement modifying the debt funding agreement of September 24, 1925.

Signed at Washington June 11, 1932; operative July 1, 1931.

Treasury Department print; 9 Bevans 551.

Investment incentive agreement.

Signed at Indianapolis October 28, 1991.

Entered into force October 28, 1991.

TIAS 12440.

INVESTMENT

Treaty concerning the encouragement and reciprocal protection of investment, with annex and protocol.

Signed at Washington January 13, 1995.

Entered into force December 26, 1996.

TIAS

JUDICIAL ASSISTANCE

Memorandum of understanding concerning cooperation in the pursuit of Nazi war criminals.

Signed at Riga September 11, 1992.

Entered into force September 11, 1992.

TIAS 12477.

Treaty on mutual legal assistance in criminal matters, with exchange of notes.

Signed at Washington June 13, 1997.

Entered into force September 17, 1999.

TIAS

MAPPING

Basic exchange and cooperative agreement for topographic mapping, nautical and aeronautical charting, geodesy and geophysics, digital data and related mapping, charting and geodesy materials, with attachment.

Signed at Riga August 24, 1993.

Entered into force August 24, 1993.

NP

Basic exchange and cooperative agreement concerning global geospatial information and services cooperation, with annexes.

Signed at Riga May 18, 2004.

Entered into force May 18, 2004.

NP

PACIFIC SETTLEMENT OF DISPUTES

Treaty of arbitration.

Signed at Riga January 14, 1930.

Entered into force July 10, 1930.

46 Stat. 2763; TS 818; 9 Bevans 546; 105 LNTS 307.

Treaty of conciliation.

Signed at Riga January 14, 1930.

Entered into force July 10, 1930.

46 Stat. 2766; TS 819; 9 Bevans 548; 105 LNTS 301.

PEACE CORPS

Agreement concerning the program of the Peace Corps of the United States in Latvia.

Signed at Riga February 6, 1992.

Entered into force February 6, 1992.

TIAS 12081.

POSTAL MATTERS

International express mail agreement, with detailed regulations.

Signed at Washington April 17, 1992.

Entered into force April 17, 1992.

TIAS 11860.

SCIENTIFIC COOPERATION

Agreement on science and technology cooperation, with annex.

Signed at Riga July 6, 1994.

Entered into force July 6, 1994.

TIAS 12187.

Extension

May 24 and September 7, 2000.

TAXATION

Convention for the avoidance of double taxation and the prevention of fiscal evasion with respect to taxes on income.

Signed at Washington January 15, 1998.

Entered into force December 30, 1999.

TIAS

TRADE

Agreement on trade relations and intellectual property rights protection.

Signed at Riga July 6, 1994.

Entered into force January 20, 1995.

TIAS

VISAS

Agreement for the reciprocal waiver of passport visa fees for nonimmigrants.

Exchange of notes at Riga February 18 and March 27, 1935.

Entered into force March 27, 1935; operative April 1, 1935.

9 Bevans 556.

WEAPONS

Agreement concerning technical assistance related to the elimination of conventional weapons systems and facilities formerly controlled by the Russian Federation Armed Forces stationed in the territory of the Republic of Latvia.

Signed at Riga August 12, 1994.

Entered into force August 12, 1994.

TIAS

Agreement concerning the provision of assistance related to the dismantlement of the unfinished Skrunda LPAR Facility formerly controlled by the Russian Federation Armed Forces stationed in the territory of the Republic of Latvia.

Signed at Riga August 12, 1994.

Entered into force August 12, 1994.

TIAS

Agreement concerning cooperation in the area of the prevention of proliferation of weapons of mass destruction.

Signed at Washington December 11, 2001.

Entered into force May 5, 2003.

TIAS

LEBANON

AGRICULTURAL COMMODITIES

Agricultural commodities agreement with annex.

Signed at Beirut June 11, 1970.

Entered into force June 11, 1970.

21 UST 2039; TIAS 6948; 763 UNTS 15.

Related agreements

August 31, 1971 (22 UST 1568; TIAS 7180; 807 UNTS 41).

October 7 and 25, 1971 (22 UST 1764; TIAS 7212).

April 28 and May 4, 1972 (23 UST 668; TIAS 7331).

Agricultural commodities agreement.

Signed at Beirut April 25, 1977.

Entered into force June 21, 1977.

28 UST 6153; TIAS 8676.

Related agreements

March 23, 1978 (30 UST 1934; TIAS 9303; 1152 UNTS 176).

May 17 and June 23, 1978 (30 UST 1941; TIAS 9304; 1152 UNTS 182).

September 26 and October 6, 1978 (30 UST 1948; TIAS 9304; 1152 UNTS 186).

November 24, 1978 (30 UST 1950; TIAS 9304; 1152 UNTS 188).

ATOMIC ENERGY

Agreement providing for a grant to the Government of Lebanon to assist in the acquisition of nuclear research and training equipment and supplies.

Exchange of notes at Beirut September 16, 1959.

Entered into force September 16, 1959.

10 UST 1834; TIAS 4343; 358 UNTS 175.

AVIATION

Air transport agreement with exchange of notes.

Signed at Beirut September 1, 1972.

Entered into force provisionally September 1, 1972; definitively June 5, 1974.

24 UST 245; TIAS 7546.

Agreement relating to air transport route rights.

Exchange of notes at Beirut September 24 and October 13, 1977.

Entered into force October 13, 1977.

28 UST 7479; TIAS 8722; 1087 UNTS 313.

Agreement relating to air transport route rights.

Exchange of notes at Washington December 22, 1982.

Entered into force December 22, 1982.

34 UST 2358; TIAS 10489; 1751 UNTS 17.

Amendment

April 29, 1983 (TIAS 10701; 2005 UNTS 536).

CUSTOMS

Agreement between the United States and France relating to customs privileges for educational, religious, and philanthropic institutions in Syria and Lebanon.

Exchange of notes at Paris February 18, 1937.

Entered into force February 18, 1937.

51 Stat. 279; EAS 107; 7 Bevans 1017; 184 LNTS 479.

DEFENSE

Agreement relating to reimbursable military aid.

Exchange of notes at Beirut March 6 and 23, 1953.

Entered into force March 23, 1953.

5 UST 2908; TIAS 3147; 239 UNTS 45.

Military assistance agreement.

Exchange of notes at Beirut June 3 and 6, 1957.

Entered into force June 6, 1957.

8 UST 943; TIAS 3855; 284 UNTS 155.

Amendment

June 9 and 12, 1958 (9 UST 927; TIAS 4055; 317 UNTS 350).

Agreement relating to the deposit by Lebanon of ten percent of the value of grant military assistance furnished by the United States.

Exchange of notes at Beirut April 12 and May 8, 1972.

Entered into force May 8, 1972; effective February 7, 1972.

23 UST 687; TIAS 7334.

Agreement regarding grants under the Foreign Assistance Act of 1961, as amended, and the furnishing of defense articles, related training and other defense services from the United States to Lebanon.

Exchange of notes at Beirut June 21 and July 18, 1994.

Entered into force July 18, 1994.

TIAS 12347.

Acquisition and cross-servicing agreement.

Signed at Beirut May 3 and 20, 2006.

Entered into force September 30, 2006.

TIAS

ECONOMIC AND TECHNICAL COOPERATION

General agreement for technical cooperation.

Signed at Beirut May 29, 1951.

Entered into force December 13, 1951.

3 UST 2843; TIAS 2457; 160 UNTS 49.

Agreement relating to the assurances required under section 511(b) of the Mutual Security Act of 1951.

Exchange of notes at Beirut December 26, 1951 and January 5, 1952.

Entered into force January 5, 1952.

3 UST 4751; TIAS 2639; 180 UNTS 199.

Technical cooperation program agreement.

Signed at Beirut June 26, 1952.

Entered into force June 26, 1952.

3 UST 4860; TIAS 2659; 181 UNTS 187.

Amendments

April 14, 1953 (4 UST 1563; TIAS 2821; 212 UNTS 360).

April 30, 1954 (5 UST 1078; TIAS 2991; 247 UNTS 442).

Agreement relating to special economic assistance.

Exchange of notes at Beirut June 11 and 18, 1954.

Entered into force June 18, 1954.

5 UST 1392; TIAS 3009; 233 UNTS 177.

Agreement granting special assistance to Lebanon for budgetary support.

Exchange of notes at Beirut September 2 and 3, 1958.

Entered into force September 3, 1958.

9 UST 1260; TIAS 4113; 336 UNTS 91.

Agency for International Development

March 21, 1978 (30 UST 1710; TIAS 9280; 1152 UNTS 163).

ENVIRONMENTAL COOPERATION

Agreement for cooperation in the Global Learning and Observations to Benefit the Environment (GLOBE) Program, with appendices.

Signed at Antelias December 23, 1998.

Entered into force December 23, 1998.

TIAS

FINANCE

Investment incentive agreement.

Exchange of notes at Beirut September 17, 1980 and February 10, 1981.

Entered into force April 30, 1981.

33 UST 861; TIAS 10070; 1280 UNTS 471.

GENERAL RELATIONS

Convention between the United States and France relating to rights in Syria and Lebanon.

Signed at Paris April 4, 1924.

Entered into force July 13, 1924.

43 Stat. 1821; TS 695; 7 Bevans 925.

Agreement relating to rights of American nationals.

Exchange of notes at Beirut September 7 and 8, 1944.

Entered into force September 8, 1944.

58 Stat. 1493; EAS 435; 9 Bevans 562; 124 UNTS 187.

NARCOTIC DRUGS

Grant agreement for a cooperative program to curtail illicit traffic in narcotics and dangerous drugs.

Signed at Beirut June 29, 1973.

Entered into force June 29, 1973.

24 UST 1672; TIAS 7673.

PEACEKEEPING

Agreement on United States participation in a multinational force in Beirut.

Exchange of notes at Beirut August 18 and 20, 1982.

Entered into force August 20, 1982.

34 UST 1833; TIAS 10463; 1751 UNTS 3.

Agreement on United States participation in a multinational force in Beirut.

Exchange of notes at Beirut September 25, 1982.

Entered into force September 25, 1982.

TIAS 10509; 1777 UNTS 363.

LESOTHO

In a note dated September 7, 1971 to the Secretary General of the United Nations, the Minister of Foreign Affairs of Lesotho made a Declaration reading in part as follows:

"Reference is made to the Declarations of the Government of the Kingdom of Lesotho in relation to its treaty relationships dated 22 March 1967 and 5 March 1969.

As regards bilateral treaties validly concluded by the Government of the United Kingdom on behalf of the country formerly known as Basutoland, or validly applied or extended by the said Government to the country known as Basutoland, the Government of the Kingdom of Lesotho, it will be recalled, willingly undertook to apply within its territory, on a basis of reciprocity, the terms of all such treaties from the date of Independence until October 4, 1970, unless abrogated or modified earlier by mutual consent. That time has now expired before it has been possible to evaluate all the treaties.

The Government of the Kingdom of Lesotho, mindful of the desirability of the continuity of treaty relationships consistent with its independent status, and desirous of continuing negotiations with the various States concerned in relation to the possible continuation, modification or termination of such treaties, has decided that the period during which it will apply, on a basis of reciprocity, the terms of such bilateral treaties shall be extended without limit of time, pending the reaching of a satisfactory accord with each State concerned.

Nothing in this Declaration shall, however, be held to constitute a succession to treaties which are not consistent with the accession to full sovereign status by the Kingdom of Lesotho, nor shall it be held to constitute an extension or renewal of treaties which, by virtue of their termination clauses, have already expired or have been terminated before the date of this Declaration.

Under the terms of the Declaration of the Government of the Kingdom of Lesotho of 22 March 1967 it is not necessary to extend the period in relation to multilateral treaties. As represented in that Declaration, the Government of the Kingdom of Lesotho will review each of the multilateral treaties which has been applied or extended to the country formerly known as Basutoland and indicate to the depositary concerned what steps it desires to take in relation to such instrument.

During this period of review, as stated in the Declaration of 22 March 1967, any party to a multilateral treaty which has, prior to independence, been applied or extended to the country known as Basutoland, may, on a basis of reciprocity, rely as against Lesotho on the terms of such treaty, the Government of the Kingdom of Lesotho wishes it to be understood, as stated in its Declaration of 5 March 1969, that this is merely a transitional arrangement. Under no circumstances should it be implied that by these Declarations of Lesotho has either acceded to any particular treaty or indicated continuity of any particular treaty by way of succession."

ECONOMIC AND TECHNICAL COOPERATION

Agreement for economic, technical and related assistance.

Signed at Maseru October 17, 1984.

Entered into force October 17, 1984.

TIAS 11167; 2126 UNTS 145.

EXTRADITION

Extradition treaty between the United States and the United Kingdom.

Signed at London December 22, 1931.

Entered into force June 24, 1935.

47 Stat. 2122; TS 849; 12 Bevans 482; 163 LNTS 59.

FINANCE

Agreement relating to investment guaranties.

Signed at Maseru February 24, 1967.

Entered into force March 7, 1967.

18 UST 273; TIAS 6227; 688 UNTS 275.

INTERNATIONAL CRIMINAL COURT

Agreement regarding the surrender of persons to the international criminal court.

Signed at Maseru June 21, 2006.

Entered into force June 21, 2006.

TIAS

PEACE CORPS

Agreement relating to the establishment of a Peace Corps program in Lesotho.

Exchange of notes at Washington September 22, 1967.

Entered into force September 22, 1967.

18 UST 2357; TIAS 6339; 693 UNTS 141.

POSTAL MATTERS

International express mail agreement, with detailed regulations.

Signed at Maseru and Washington June 19 and July 20, 1990.

Entered into force August 30, 1990.

TIAS 11737.

PROPERTY

Convention between the United States and the United Kingdom relating to the tenure and disposition of real and personal property.

Signed at Washington March 2, 1899; applicable to Basutoland July 24, 1902.

31 Stat. 1939; TS 146; 12 Bevans 246.

Supplementary convention relating to the tenure and disposition of real and personal property of March 2, 1899.

Signed at Washington May 27, 1936.

Entered into force March 10, 1941.

55 Stat. 1101; TS 964; 5 Bevans 140; 203 LNTS 367.

TRADE

Agreement concerning trade in textiles and textile products, with annexes.

Exchange of notes at Maseru March 2 and May 25, 1994.

Entered into force May 25, 1994; effective December 1, 1992.

NP

TRADE-MARKS

Declaration by the United States and the United Kingdom affording reciprocal protection to trade-marks.

Signed at London October 24, 1877.

Entered into force October 24, 1877.

20 Stat. 703; TS 138; 12 Bevans 198.

LIBERIA

AGRICULTURAL COMMODITIES

Agricultural commodities agreement with exchange of notes.

Signed at Monrovia April 12, 1962.

Entered into force April 12, 1962.

13 UST 391; TIAS 4996; 445 UNTS 213.

Agricultural commodities agreement with exchange of notes.

Signed at Monrovia January 6, 1966.

Entered into force January 6, 1966.

17 UST 543; TIAS 6001; 592 UNTS 101.

Agricultural commodities agreement, with annex.

Signed at Monrovia October 23, 1967.

Entered into force October 23, 1967.

18 UST 2777; TIAS 6363; 701 UNTS 91.

Related agreements

June 24, 1970 (21 UST 1967; TIAS 6939; 763 UNTS 43).

April 26, 1972 (23 UST 1275; TIAS 7401).

Agricultural commodities agreement.

Signed at Monrovia August 13, 1980.

Entered into force August 13, 1980.

32 UST 2319; TIAS 9841.

Related agreements

January 8, 1981 (TIAS 10618; 2000 UNTS 443).

June 12 and July 3, 1981 (35 UST 2472; TIAS 10810; 2012 UNTS 400).

August 25 and 28, 1981 (35 UST 2472; TIAS 10810; 2012 UNTS 400).

April 6, 1982 (TIAS 10820; 2014 UNTS 429).

November 19 and December 8, 1982 (35 UST 2802; TIAS 10820; 2016 UNTS 321).

December 17, 1982 (35 UST 4131; TIAS 10911; 2014 UNTS 431).

December 15, 1983 (35 UST 4131; TIAS 10911; 2014 UNTS 433).

Agricultural commodities agreement.

Signed at Monrovia July 22, 1985.

Entered into force July 22, 1985.

NP

Related agreement

April 28, 1986 (NP).

Agricultural commodities agreement.

Signed at Monrovia June 22, 1987.

Entered into force June 22, 1987.

NP

AVIATION

Air navigation agreement.

Exchange of notes at Monrovia June 14, 1939.

Entered into force June 15, 1939.

54 Stat. 2018; EAS 166; 9 Bevans 615; 202 LNTS 93.

Air transport agreement, with memorandum of understanding.

Signed at Monrovia March 30, 1978.

Entered into force March 30, 1978.

29 UST 3063; TIAS 8997; 1124 UNTS 193.

COMMERCE

Treaty of friendship, commerce and navigation.

Signed at Monrovia August 8, 1938.

Entered into force November 21, 1939.

54 Stat. 1739; TS 956; 9 Bevans 595; 201 LNTS 163.

CONSULS

Consular convention.

Signed at Monrovia October 7, 1938.

Entered into force December 21, 1939.

54 Stat. 1751; TS 957; 9 Bevans 607; 201 LNTS 183.

CUSTOMS

Agreement relating to privileges, on a reciprocal basis, of free entry to all articles imported for the personal use of diplomatic and consular personnel.

Exchange of notes at Washington May 2 and July 22, 1949.

Entered into force July 22, 1949.

5 UST 734; TIAS 2961; 232 UNTS 283.

DEFENSE

Agreement relating to mutual defense assistance.

Exchange of notes at Washington November 16 and 19, 1951.

Entered into force November 19, 1951.

3 UST 2805; TIAS 2450; 167 UNTS 141.

Understanding that the assurances contained in the agreement of November 16 and 19, 1951 are applicable to equipment, materials, information, and services furnished under the Mutual Security Act of 1954, as amended, and such other applicable U.S. laws as may come into effect.

Exchange of notes at Monrovia April 10 and July 19, 1958.

Entered into force July 19, 1958.

10 UST 1995; TIAS 4367; 361 UNTS 316.

Agreement relating to the transfer to Liberia of certain property located at Roberts Field, Liberia.

Exchange of notes at Washington April 19, 1955, and August 21 and September 22, 1956.

Entered into force January 4, 1957.

8 UST 141; TIAS 3751; 278 UNTS 109.

Agreement of cooperation.

Signed at Washington July 8, 1959.

Entered into force July 8, 1959.

10 UST 1598; TIAS 4303; 357 UNTS 93.

Agreement concerning the furnishing of military equipment and materials to Liberia.

Exchange of notes at Monrovia May 23 and June 17, 1961.

Entered into force June 17, 1961.

12 UST 876; TIAS 4788; 410 UNTS 233.

Amendment

January 18 and 23, 1962 (13 UST 58; TIAS 4935; 433 UNTS 390).

Agreement relating to the transfer of the Port of Monrovia to Liberia.

Exchange of notes at Monrovia April 13 and 14, 1964.

Entered into force April 14, 1964.

15 UST 641; TIAS 5583; 526 UNTS 221.

Agreement relating to the deposit by Liberia of ten percent of the value of grant military assistance and excess defense articles furnished by the United States.

Exchange of notes at Monrovia April 27 and May 10, 1972.

Entered into force May 10, 1972; effective February 7, 1972.

23 UST 886; TIAS 7350.

Agreement on construction of additional facilities at Roberts International Airport.

Signed at Monrovia February 3, 1983.

Entered into force February 3, 1983.

TIAS 10677.

Amendment

March 25 and April 4, 1983 (TIAS 10677).

Agreement concerning the provision of training related to defense articles under the United States International Military Education and Training (IMET) Program.

Exchange of notes at Monrovia February 23 and September 7, 1983.

Entered into force September 7, 1983.

35 UST 2173; TIAS 10783.

Agreement regarding the status of United States personnel who may be temporarily present in Liberia.

Exchange of notes at Monrovia April 15 and 20, 2005.

Entered into force April 20, 2005.

TIAS

ECONOMIC AND TECHNICAL COOPERATION

Memorandum of understanding on the Joint Liberian-United States Commission for Economic Development.

Signed at Monrovia October 6, 1955.

Entered into force October 6, 1955; operative February 3, 1956.

7 UST 600; TIAS 3541; 275 UNTS 87.

General agreement for technical assistance and cooperation.

Signed at Monrovia October 6, 1955.

Entered into force February 3, 1956.

7 UST 603; TIAS 3542; 275 UNTS 93.

Agency for International Development

August 12, 1977 (29 UST 978; TIAS 8857).

August 12, 1977 (29 UST 2663; TIAS 8963).

EDUCATION

Agreement for financing certain educational exchange programs.

Signed at Monrovia May 8, 1964.

Entered into force May 8, 1964.

15 UST 660; TIAS 5586; 526 UNTS 239.

EMPLOYMENT

Agreement relating to the employment of dependents of official government employees.

Exchange of notes at Washington October 2 and 16, 1984.

Entered into force October 16, 1984.

TIAS

EXTRADITION

Treaty of extradition.

Signed at Monrovia November 1, 1937.

Entered into force November 21, 1939.

54 Stat. 1733; TS 955; 9 Bevans 589; 201 LNTS 151.

FINANCE

Agreement relating to investment guaranties under section 413(b)(4) of the Mutual Security Act of 1954, as amended.[1]

Exchange of notes at Monrovia September 6 and 12, 1960.

Entered into force September 12, 1960.

11 UST 2119; TIAS 4571; 389 UNTS 245.

Amendment

September 26 and 29, 1964 (15 UST 2064; TIAS 5686; 533 UNTS 348).

December 15, 2006.

Agreement regarding the consolidation and rescheduling of certain debts owed to, or guaranteed by the United States Government and its agencies, with annexes.

Signed at Monrovia May 7, 1981.

Entered into force June 29, 1981.

33 UST 1929; TIAS 10156.

Agreement regarding the consolidation and rescheduling of payments due under P. L. 480 Title I agricultural commodity agreement, with annexes.

Signed at Monrovia October 15, 1981.

Entered into force October 15, 1981.

33 UST 1945; TIAS 10157.

Agreements regarding the consolidation and rescheduling of certain debts owed to, or guaranteed by the United States Government and its agencies, with annexes.

Signed at Monrovia October 19 and November 1, 1982.

Entered into force December 22, 1982.

TIAS 10528; 1777 UNTS 393.

Agreement regarding the consolidation and rescheduling of certain debts owed to or guaranteed by the United States Government and its agencies, with annexes and implementing agreement regarding payments due under P. L. 480 agricultural commodity agreements, with annexes.

Signed at Monrovia June 22, 1984.

Entered into force July 27, 1984.

TIAS 10995; 2022 UNTS 85.

Agreement regarding the consolidation and rescheduling of certain debts owed to, guaranteed by or insured by the United States Government and its agencies, with annexes and implementing agreement regarding payments due under P.L. 480 agricultural commodity agreements.

Signed at Monrovia May 3, 1985.

Entered into force June 24, 1985.

NP

NOTE

1 Subparagraphs (d) and (e) of paragraph 3 terminated September 29, 1964.

INTERNATIONAL CRIMINAL COURT

Agreement regarding the surrender of persons to the International Criminal Court.

Signed at Washington October 8, 2003.

Entered into force November 3, 2003.

TIAS

LEND-LEASE

Preliminary agreement regarding principles applying to mutual aid for defense and exchange of notes.

Signed at New York June 8, 1943.

Entered into force June 8, 1943.

57 Stat. 978; EAS 324; 9 Bevans 630; 117 UNTS 241.

PACIFIC SETTLEMENT OF DISPUTES

Arbitration convention with exchange of notes.

Signed at Monrovia February 10, 1926.

Entered into force September 27, 1926.

44 Stat. 2438; TS 747; 9 Bevans 585; 88 LNTS 346.

Treaty of conciliation.

Signed at Monrovia August 21, 1939.

Entered into force March 13, 1941.

55 Stat. 1137; TS 968; 9 Bevans 618; 204 LNTS 165.

PEACE CORPS

Agreement relating to the establishment of a Peace Corps program in Liberia.

Exchange of notes at Monrovia March 5 and 8, 1962.

Entered into force March 12, 1962.

13 UST 308; TIAS 4980; 445 UNTS 41.

POSTAL MATTERS

Agreement concerning the exchange of parcel post, and regulations of execution.

Signed at Monrovia March 16, and at Washington May 9, 1957.

Entered into force August 1, 1957.

8 UST 1035; TIAS 3866; 290 UNTS 59.

International express mail agreement, with detailed regulations.

Signed at Monrovia and Washington November 15, 1988 and January 6, 1989.

Entered into force January 30, 1989.

TIAS 11620.

PUBLICATIONS

Agreement relating to the exchange of official publications.

Exchange of notes at Monrovia January 15, 1942.

Entered into force January 15, 1942.

56 Stat. 1419; EAS 239; 9 Bevans 621; 117 UNTS 227.

SHIPPING

Agreement relating to jurisdiction over vessels utilizing the Louisiana Offshore Oil Port.

Exchange of notes at Washington October 27, 1978 and January 15, 1979.

Entered into force January 15, 1979.

30 UST 1706; TIAS 9279; 1153 UNTS 283.

TAXATION

Agreement for reciprocal relief from double taxation on earnings from operation of ships and aircraft.

Exchange of notes at Monrovia July 1 and August 11, 1982.

Entered into force August 11, 1982.

34 UST 1553; TIAS 10435.

Amendment

October 7 and 23, 1987 (TIAS 11921).

TELECOMMUNICATION

Agreement relating to radio communications between amateur stations on behalf of third parties.

Exchange of notes at Monrovia November 9, 1950 and January 8, 9, and 10, 1951.

Entered into force January 11, 1951.

2 UST 683; TIAS 2223; 132 UNTS 255.

Agreement providing for radio relay facilities to be used by the Voice of America.

Signed at Monrovia August 13, 1959.

Entered into force August 13, 1959.

10 UST 1444; TIAS 4293; 357 UNTS 181.

Agreement supplementing articles III and VII of the agreement of August 13, 1959 relating to radio relay facilities in Liberia.

Exchange of notes at Monrovia August 8 and 15, 1960.

Entered into force August 15, 1960.

12 UST 1367; TIAS 4858; 421 UNTS 332.

Amendment

July 11 and 24, 1961 (12 UST 1367; TIAS 4858; 421 UNTS 340).

Agreement relating to the reciprocal granting of authorizations to permit licensed amateur radio operators of either country to operate their stations in the other country.

Exchange of notes at Monrovia March 20, 1974 and July 22, 1977.

Entered into force July 22, 1977.

29 UST 1494; TIAS 8892.

VISAS

Agreement relating to the waiver of passport visa fees for nonimmigrants.

Signed at Monrovia August 31, 1925.

Entered into force August 31, 1925; operative September 1, 1925.

9 Bevans 584.

Arrangement relating to the period of validity of temporary visitors' visas.

Exchange of notes at Monrovia October 27 and 28, 1947.

Entered into force October 28, 1947; operative December 1, 1947.

62 Stat. 3930; TIAS 2021; 9 Bevans 641; 82 UNTS 23.

WEAPONS

Agreement concerning cooperation to suppress the proliferation of weapons of mass destruction, their delivery systems, and related materials by sea.

Signed at Washington February 11, 2004.

Entered into force December 8, 2004.

TIAS

LIBYA

DEFENSE

Military assistance agreement.[1]

Signed at Tripoli June 30, 1957.

Entered into force June 30, 1957.

8 UST 957; TIAS 3857; 284 UNTS 177.

Arrangement for return of equipment and material no longer needed in the furtherance of the mutual defense assistance program.

Signed at Tripoli June 30, 1957.

Entered into force June 30, 1957.

8 UST 963; TIAS 3858; 284 UNTS 188.

Agreement relating to the termination of outstanding agreements with Libya.

Exchange of notes at Tripoli February 5, 1972.

Entered into force February 5, 1972.

23 UST 82; TIAS 7275.

NOTE

1 Terminated February 5, 1972 except that article I paragraphs 2 and 4, arrangements under article I, paragraphs 3, 5, and 7, and under article II remain in force.

LIECHTENSTEIN

EMPLOYMENT

Agreement relating to employment of dependents of official government employees.

Exchange of notes at Bern and Vaduz September 18 and November 14, 1997.

Entered into force November 14, 1997.

TIAS

ENVIRONMENTAL COOPERATION

Agreement for cooperation in the Global Learning and Observations to Benefit the Environment (GLOBE) Program.

Signed at Vaduz March 26, 2003.

Entered into force March 26, 2003.

TIAS

EXTRADITION

Extradition treaty.

Signed at Bern May 20, 1936.

Entered into force June 28, 1937.

50 Stat. 1337; TS 915; 9 Bevans 648; 183 LNTS 181.

JUDICIAL ASSISTANCE

Treaty on mutual legal assistance in criminal matters, with exchange of notes.

Signed at Vaduz July 8, 2002.

Entered into force August 1, 2003.

TIAS

SOCIAL SECURITY

Agreement concerning reciprocity of payment of certain social security benefits.

Exchange of notes at Bern April 13, 1972.

Entered into force April 13, 1972; effective July 1, 1968.

23 UST 2896; TIAS 7476.

VISAS

Arrangement for the waiver of passport visa fees for nonimmigrants.

Exchange of notes at Bern April 22 and June 18 and 30, 1926.

Entered into force June 30, 1926; operative June 1, 1925.

9 Bevans 644.

Arrangement relating to the waiver of passport visa fees for nonimmigrants.

Exchanges of notes at Washington October 22 and 31 and November 4 and 13, 1947.

Entered into force November 13, 1947.

6 UST 93; TIAS 3172; 251 UNTS 79.

LITHUANIA

ATOMIC ENERGY

Arrangement for the exchange of technical information and cooperation in nuclear safety matters, with addenda.

Signed at Vienna September 28, 2005.

Entered into force September 28, 2005.

TIAS

CULTURAL PROPERTY

Agreement on the protection and preservation of certain cultural properties.

Signed at Vilnius October 15, 2002.

Entered into force August 4, 2006.

TIAS

CUSTOMS

Arrangement regarding reciprocal privileges for consular officers to import articles free of duty for their personal use.

Exchanges of notes at Washington July 28, September 17 and 19, and October 4, 1934.

Entered into force October 4, 1934; operative October 15, 1934.

9 Bevans 685.

DEFENSE

Agreement concerning the provision of training related to defense articles under the United States International Military Education and Training (IMET) Program.

Exchange of notes at Vilnius March 31 and June 10, 1992.

Entered into force June 10, 1992.

NP

Agreement regarding grants under the Foreign Assistance Act of 1961, as amended, and the furnishing of defense articles, related training or other defense services from the United States to Lithuania.

Exchange of notes at Vilnius February 11 and March 26, 1993.

Entered into force March 26, 1993.

TIAS 12348.

Security agreement concerning security measures for the protection of classified military information.

Signed at Vilnius November 21, 1995.

Entered into force November 21, 1995.

TIAS 12243.

Acquisition and cross-servicing agreement, with annexes.

Signed at Vilnius and Patch Barracks (Germany) March 29 and April 30, 1996.

Entered into force April 30, 1996.

TIAS 12746.

Agreement concerning exchange of research and development information, with appendix.

Signed at Washington October 16, 1997.

Entered into force October 16, 1997.

TIAS

Agreement regarding logistic support, supplies and services, with annexes.

Signed at Stuttgart and Vilnius May 22 and 31, 2006.

Entered into force May 31, 2006.

TIAS

DIPLOMATIC RELATIONS

Memorandum of understanding concerning diplomatic relations.

Signed at Vilnius September 6, 1991.

Entered into force September 6, 1991.

TIAS 12133.

EMPLOYMENT

Agreement relating to the employment of dependents of official government employees.

Exchange of notes at Washington November 21 and December 8, 1994.

Entered into force December 8, 1994.

TIAS 12197.

ENVIRONMENTAL COOPERATION

Agreement for cooperation in the Global Learning and Observations to Benefit the Environment (GLOBE) Program, with appendices.

Signed at Vilnius October 3, 2002.

Entered into force October 3, 2002.

TIAS

EXTRADITION

Extradition treaty.

Signed at Vilnius October 23, 2001.

Entered into force March 31, 2003.

TIAS

FINANCE

Agreement for the funding of the debt of Lithuania to the United States.

Signed at Washington September 22, 1924; operative June 15, 1924.

Treasury Department print; 9 Bevans 661.

Amendment

June 9, 1932 (Treasury Department print; 9 Bevans 681).

Investment incentive agreement.

Signed at Indianapolis October 28, 1991.

Entered into force February 7, 1992.

TIAS 12640; 1775 UNTS 291.

INVESTMENT

Treaty for the encouragement and reciprocal protection of investment, with annex and protocol.

Signed at Washington January 14, 1998.

Entered into force November 22, 2001.

TIAS

Additional protocol to the treaty for the encouragement and reciprocal protection of investment of January 14, 1998.

Signed at Brussels September 22, 2003.

Entered into force July 13, 2004.

TIAS

JUDICIAL ASSISTANCE

Memorandum of understanding concerning cooperation in the pursuit of war criminals, with related note.

Signed at Vilnius August 3, 1992.

Entered into force August 3, 1992.

TIAS 12470.

Treaty on mutual legal assistance in criminal matters.

Signed at Washington January 16, 1998.

Entered into force August 26, 1999.

TIAS

MAPPING

Basic exchange and cooperative agreement for topographic mapping, nautical and aeronautical charting, geodesy and geophysics, digital data and related mapping, charting and geodesy materials.

Signed at Vilnius January 21, 1994.

Entered into force February 15, 1994.

NP

Basic exchange and cooperative agreement concerning global geospatial information and services cooperation, with annexes.

Signed at Vilnius June 11, 1999.

Entered into force June 11, 1999.

NP

PACIFIC SETTLEMENT OF DISPUTES

Arbitration treaty.

Signed at Washington November 14, 1928.

Entered into force January 20, 1930.

46 Stat. 2457; TS 809; 9 Bevans 671; 100 LNTS 111.

Treaty of conciliation.

Signed at Washington November 14, 1928.

Entered into force January 20, 1930.

46 Stat. 2459; TS 810; 9 Bevans 673; 100 LNTS 117.

PEACE CORPS

Agreement concerning the program of the Peace Corps of the United States in Lithuania.

Signed at Vilnius February 7, 1992.

Entered into force February 7, 1992.

TIAS 12447.

POSTAL MATTERS

Parcel post agreement.

Signed at Kaunas December 4 and at Washington December 28, 1939; operative February 1, 1940.

54 Stat. 2021; Post Office Department print; 202 LNTS 381.

International express mail agreement, with detailed regulations.

Signed at Vilnius and Washington September 21 and October 29, 1992.

Entered into force December 14, 1992.

TIAS 11905.

TAXATION

Convention for the avoidance of double taxation and the prevention of fiscal evasion with respect to taxes on income.

Signed at Washington January 15, 1998.

Entered into force December 30, 1999.

TIAS

TRADE AND COMMERCE

Agreement according mutual unconditional most-favored-nation treatment in customs matters.

Exchange of notes at Washington December 23, 1925.

Entered into force July 10, 1926.

TS 742; 9 Bevans 668; 54 LNTS 377.

TRADE-MARKS

Agreement relating to the registration of trade-marks.

Exchange of notes at Riga September 14, 1929 and at Kaunas October 11, 1929.

Entered into force October 11, 1929.

9 Bevans 675.

VISAS

Arrangement for the reciprocal waiver of passport visa fees for nonimmigrants.

Exchange of notes at Washington April 17, 1937.

Entered into force April 17, 1937; operative May 1, 1937.

9 Bevans 688.

WEAPONS

Agreement concerning cooperation in the area of the prevention of proliferation of weapons of mass destruction and the promotion of defense and military relations.

Signed at Vilnius October 10, 2002.

Entered into force April 24, 2003.

TIAS

LUXEMBOURG

AVIATION

Air transport agreement, with annex.

Signed at Luxembourg August 19, 1986.

Entered into force August 3, 1988.

TIAS 11249; 2174 UNTS 239.

Amendment

June 6, 1995 (TIAS 12656).

CLAIMS

Memorandum of understanding regarding claims between the two Governments arising out of the conduct of the war.

Signed at Luxembourg September 12, 1946.

Entered into force September 12, 1946.

62 Stat. 4006; TIAS 2067; 9 Bevans 721; 149 UNTS 19.

Agreement relating to war damage to private property.

Exchange of notes at Luxembourg June 15, 1955.

Entered into force June 15, 1955.

6 UST 2577; TIAS 3302; 264 UNTS 279.

COMMERCE

Treaty of friendship, establishment and navigation, and protocol.

Signed at Luxembourg February 23, 1962.

Entered into force March 28, 1963.

14 UST 251; TIAS 5306; 474 UNTS 3.

DEFENSE

See also MUTUAL SECURITY

Mutual defense assistance agreement.

Signed at Washington January 27, 1950.

Entered into force March 28, 1950.

1 UST 69; TIAS 2014; 80 UNTS 187.

Agreement relating to the offshore procurement program.

Signed at Luxembourg April 17, 1954.

Entered into force September 30, 1955.

6 UST 3989; TIAS 3415; 257 UNTS 255.

Agreement approving the offshore procurement contract with Luxembourg.

Exchange of notes at Luxembourg April 17, 1954.

Entered into force September 30, 1955.

6 UST 4009; TIAS 3416; 257 UNTS 270.

Amendment

May 10 and July 16, 1954 (6 UST 4009; TIAS 3416; 257 UNTS 292).

Memorandum of understanding relating to the disposal of redistributable and excess property furnished in connection with the mutual defense assistance program, with related notes.

Signed at Luxembourg July 7, 1954.

Entered into force July 7, 1954.

5 UST 1524; TIAS 3029; 233 UNTS 23.

Amendment

March 4 and June 10, 1960 (11 UST 2169; TIAS 4583; 393 UNTS 328).

Agreement concerning general security of military information.

Signed at Luxembourg September 17, 1981.

Entered into force September 17, 1981.

33 UST 3922; TIAS 10270; 1543 UNTS 117.

Memorandum of understanding on reciprocal defense procurement, with annex.

Signed at Luxembourg December 2, 1982.

Entered into force December 2, 1982.

TIAS

Mutual logistics support agreement, with annexes.

Signed at Luxembourg December 15, 1983.

Entered into force December 15, 1983.

35 UST 3313; TIAS 10859; 2015 UNTS 55.

Amendment

July 21, 1992 (TIAS 12524).

Agreement concerning NATO civil air augmentation.

Signed at Scott AFB and Luxembourg March 11 and May 17, 1985.

Entered into force May 17, 1985.

TIAS 11108; 2120 UNTS 345.

Agreement amending the agreement of December 21, 1978 on the establishment and operation of storage sites for the U.S. Army in Luxembourg.

Exchange of notes at Luxembourg March 23 and July 21, 2006.

Entered into force July 21, 2006.

TIAS

ECONOMIC AND TECHNICAL COOPERATION

Economic cooperation agreement.

Signed at Luxembourg July 3, 1948.

Entered into force July 3, 1948.

62 Stat. 2451; TIAS 1790; 9 Bevans 722; 24 UNTS 35.

Amendments

November 17 and December 22, 1948 (62 Stat. 3750; TIAS 1903; 9 Bevans 740; 55 UNTS 324).

January 17 and 19, 1950 (1 UST 163; TIAS 2030; 79 UNTS 306).

August 30 and October 17, 1951 (2 UST 2149; TIAS 2342; 137 UNTS 280).

December 31, 1952 and February 26, 1953 (4 UST 226; TIAS 2780; 212 UNTS 286).

EDUCATION

Agreement for the financing of certain academic and cultural exchanges and programs in the field of education.

Signed at Brussels December 12, 1968.

Entered into force May 13, 1971.

22 UST 1538; TIAS 7175; 806 UNTS 231.

ENVIRONMENTAL COOPERATION

Agreement concerning cooperation in the Global Learning and Observations to Benefit the Environment (GLOBE) Program, with appendices.

Signed at Luxembourg October 10, 1996.

Entered into force October 10, 1996.

TIAS 12807.

EXTRADITION

Extradition treaty.

Signed at Washington October 1, 1996.

Entered into force February 1, 2002.

TIAS 12804.

FINANCE

Agreement relating to investment guaranties under section 413(b)(4) of the Mutual Security Act of 1954, as amended.

Exchange of notes at Luxembourg November 26 and December 7, 1956.

Entered into force December 7, 1956.

7 UST 3432; TIAS 3715; 265 UNTS 255.

JUDICIAL ASSISTANCE

Treaty on mutual legal assistance in criminal matters, with exchange of notes.

Signed at Luxembourg March 13, 1997.

Entered into force February 1, 2001.

TIAS; 2147 UNTS 391.

LEND-LEASE

Mutual aid settlement.

Exchange of memorandums at Luxembourg August 29, 1946.

Entered into force August 29, 1946.

62 Stat. 4003; TIAS 2065; 9 Bevans 718; 140 UNTS 101.

MILITARY CEMETERIES AND MONUMENTS

Agreement concerning the establishment of a permanent World War II cemetery in Luxembourg with exchange of notes.

Signed at Luxembourg March 20, 1951.

Entered into force June 11, 1952.

3 UST 2745; TIAS 2445; 180 UNTS 283.

Agreement concerning concessions granted to United States in establishing a permanent World War II cemetery in Luxembourg.

Exchange of notes at Luxembourg March 20, 1951.

Entered into force March 20, 1951.

3 UST 2750; TIAS 2446; 180 UNTS 289.

MUTUAL SECURITY

Agreement relating to the assurances required under the Mutual Security Act of 1951.

Exchange of notes at Luxembourg January 8, 1952.

Entered into force January 8, 1952.

3 UST 4627; TIAS 2614; 180 UNTS 191.

PACIFIC SETTLEMENT OF DISPUTES

Treaty of arbitration.

Signed at Luxembourg April 6, 1929.

Entered into force September 2, 1930.

46 Stat. 2809; TS 825; 9 Bevans 701; 106 LNTS 475.

Treaty of conciliation.

Signed at Luxembourg April 6, 1929.

Entered into force September 2, 1930.

46 Stat. 2813; TS 826; 9 Bevans 704; 106 LNTS 469.

POSTAL MATTERS

International express mail agreement, with detailed regulations.

Signed at Luxembourg and Washington April 21 and June 14, 1983.

Entered into force October 1, 1983.

35 UST 1431; TIAS 10737; 2006 UNTS 331.

Memorandum of understanding concerning the operation of the INTELPOST field trial, with details of implementation.

Signed at Luxembourg and Washington April 29 and May 28, 1985.

Entered into force June 3, 1985.

TIAS 11245.

SOCIAL SECURITY

Agreement on social security, with administrative arrangement.

Signed at Luxembourg February 12, 1992.

Entered into force November 1, 1993.

TIAS 12119.

TAXATION

Agreement relating to relief from taxation of United States expenditures in Luxembourg for common defense.

Exchange of notes at Luxembourg March 10 and 13, 1952.

Entered into force March 13, 1952.

3 UST 4001; TIAS 2538; 168 UNTS 57.

Agreement concerning the reciprocal exemption from income tax of income derived from the international operation of ships and aircraft.

Exchange of notes at Luxembourg April 11 and June 22, 1989.

Entered into force January 8, 1993.

TIAS 12056.

Convention for the avoidance of double taxation and the prevention of fiscal evasion with respect to taxes on income and capital, with related exchange of notes.

Signed at Luxembourg April 3, 1996.

Entered into force December 20, 2000.

TIAS; 2148 UNTS 81..

TELECOMMUNICATION

Agreement relating to the establishment of a radio range station in Luxembourg.

Exchange of notes at Luxembourg July 22 and August 17, 1953.

Entered into force August 17, 1953.

5 UST 1823; TIAS 3056; 234 UNTS 219.

Agreement relating to reciprocal granting of authorizations to permit licensed amateur radio operators of either country to operate their stations in the other country.

Exchange of notes at Luxembourg July 7 and 29, 1965.

Entered into force July 29, 1965.

16 UST 1746; TIAS 5900; 573 UNTS 197.

TRADE AND COMMERCE

See COMMERCE. See also BENELUX

VISAS

Agreement relating to the waiver of visas and visa fees for nonimmigrants.

Exchange of notes at Luxembourg April 25 and May 22 and 26, 1936.

Entered into force May 26, 1936; operative June 15, 1936.

9 Bevans 710.

M

MACEDONIA

For agreements prior to the independence of Macedonia, see YUGOSLAVIA.

DEFENSE

Agreement regarding grants under the Foreign Assistance Act of 1961, as amended, or successor legislation, and the furnishing of defense articles, related training, and other defense services from the United States of America to the Former Yugoslav Republic of Macedonia.

Exchange of notes at Skopje June 5, 1997.

Entered into force June 5, 1997.

TIAS

Acquisition and cross-servicing agreement, with attachment.

Exchange of notes at Skopje July 27 and September 23, 1998.

Entered into force September 23, 1998.

TIAS

ECONOMIC AND TECHNICAL COOPERATION

Agreement concerning economic, technical and related assistance, with attachment.

Exchange of letters at Skopje September 9, 2001.

Entered into force September 9, 2001.

TIAS

EMPLOYMENT

Agreement concerning the reciprocal employment of dependents of official government employees, with attachment.

Exchange of notes at Washington December 10, 1998.

Entered into force December 10, 1998.

TIAS

FINANCE

Investment incentive agreement, with attachment.

Exchange of notes at Skopje April 5, 1996.

Entered into force April 5, 1996.

TIAS

Agreement on the consolidation of the debt of the borrower, with attachment.

Exchange of letters at Skopje September 17, 1997.

Entered into force December 3, 1997.

NP

Agreement regarding the reorganization of certain debts owed to the United States Government and its agencies, with attachment.

Exchange of notes at Skopje January 15 and 30, 2003.

Entered into force March 17, 2003.

NP

INTERNATIONAL CRIMINAL COURT

Agreement regarding the surrender of persons to the International Criminal Court.

Signed at Skopje June 30, 2003.

Entered into force November 12, 2003.

TIAS

NORTH ATLANTIC TREATY

Agreement to treat as binding the agreement of June 19, 1995, among the States Parties to the North Atlantic Treaty and the other States participating in the Partnership for Peace regarding the status of their forces between the United States and Macedonia.

Exchange of notes at Skopje June 3, 1996.

Entered into force June 3, 1996.

TIAS 12762.

TRADE

Bilateral textile agreement.

Signed at Skopje November 7, 1997.

Entered into force November 7, 1997.

NP

Amendments

September 17, 1999.

June 2, 2000.

WEAPONS

Agreement concerning cooperation in the area of the prevention of proliferation of weapons of mass destruction, and the promotion of defense and military relations.

Signed at Skopje October 11, 2004.

Entered into force October 11, 2004.

TIAS

MADAGASCAR

By a note dated December 4, 1962, the Minister of Foreign Affairs of the Malagasy Republic informed the American Ambassador of the following (translation): "No official act specifies, in the agreements with the French Republic, the juridical position of the Malagasy Republic with regard to the rights and obligations contracted for Madagascar in the treaties, agreements, and conventions signed by France prior to Madagascar's accession to international sovereignty. In accordance with usage, the Malagasy Republic considers itself implicitly bound by such texts unless it explicitly denounces them. The Ministry of Foreign Affairs informs the Embassy of the United States of America that, in order to avoid any ambiguity, the Malagasy Republic transmits, as soon as it is in a position to reach an affirmative decision on each of the texts in question, a formal declaration in which it declares itself bound by the Treaty, the Agreement or the Convention under consideration."

AGRICULTURAL COMMODITIES

Agricultural commodities agreement, with minutes of negotiation.

Signed at Antananarivo August 19, 1981.

Entered into force August 19, 1981.

33 UST 3139; TIAS 10218.

Related agreements

August 12, 1982 (34 UST 2052; TIAS 10479; 1750 UNTS 509).

December 28, 1982 (TIAS 10627; 1581 UNTS 97).

July 13, 1983 (35 UST 1550; TIAS 10744; 2006 UNTS 553).

March 7, 1984 (TIAS 11046).

December 12, 1984 (TIAS 11046).

Agricultural commodities agreement.

Signed at Antananarivo September 27, 1985.

Entered into force September 27, 1985.

NP

Amendments

October 28 and November 7, 1985 (NP).

July 2 and August 8, 1986 (NP).

Related agreements

June 10, 1987 (NP).

October 23 and 30, 1987 (NP).

Agricultural commodities agreement under food for progress, with attachments.

Signed at Antananarivo August 13, 1986.

Entered into force August 13, 1986.

NP

AVIATION

Air transport services agreement between the United States and France.

Signed at Paris March 27, 1946.

Entered into force March 27, 1946.

61 Stat. 3445; TIAS 1679; 7 Bevans 1109; 139 UNTS 114.

Extensions and amendments

June 23 and July 11, 1950 (1 UST 593; TIAS 2106; 139 UNTS 142).

March 19, 1951 (2 UST 1033; TIAS 2257; 139 UNTS 151).

March 19, 1951 (2 UST 1037; TIAS 2258; 139 UNTS 146).

August 27, 1959 (10 UST 1791; TIAS 4336; 358 UNTS 277).

COMMERCE

Convention of navigation and commerce between the United States and France, with separate article.[1]

Signed at Washington June 24, 1822; extended to Madagascar in 1896.

8 Stat. 278; TS 87; 7 Bevans 822.

Agreement modifying the provisions of article VII of the convention of navigation and commerce of June 24, 1822.

Signed at Washington July 17, 1919.

Entered into force January 10, 1921.

41 Stat. 1723; TS 650; 7 Bevans 899.

NOTE

1 Article VI abrogated by the United States July 1, 1916 in accordance with the Seamen's Act (38 Stat. 1164).

DEFENSE

Agreement concerning the provision of training related to defense articles under the United States International Military Education and Training (IMET) Program.

Exchange of notes at Antananarivo February 25, 1983 and May 3, 1984.

Entered into force May 3, 1984.

TIAS 10982.

Agreement relating to the status of United States military and civilian personnel of the United States Department of Defense temporarily present in Madagascar in connection with humanitarian relief operations.

Exchange of notes at Antananarivo March 11 and 13, 2000.

Entered into force March 13, 2000.

NP

ECONOMIC AND TECHNICAL COOPERATION

Agreement providing for the furnishing of economic, technical and related assistance.

Exchange of notes at Tananarive June 22, 1961.

Entered into force June 22, 1961.

12 UST 1049; TIAS 4808; 413 UNTS 219.

Millennium challenge compact, with annexes.

Signed at Washington April 18, 2005.

Entered into force July 27, 2005.

TIAS

Agency for International Development

July 25, 1973 (24 UST 2159; TIAS 7731; 938 UNTS 257).

EMPLOYMENT

Agreement relating to the employment of dependents of official government employees.

Exchange of notes at Antananarivo April 12, 2001 and September 3, 2004.

Entered into force September 3, 2004.

TIAS

FINANCE

Agreement regarding the consolidation and rescheduling of certain debts owed to, guaranteed by or insured by the United States Government, with annexes.

Signed at Washington September 28, 1984.

Entered into force November 19, 1984.

TIAS 10998; 2022 UNTS 79.

Agreement regarding the consolidation and rescheduling of certain debts owed to, guaranteed by or insured by the United States Government and its agencies, with annex.

Signed at Antananarivo October 8, 1985.

Entered into force November 12, 1985.

NP

Agreement regarding the consolidation and rescheduling of certain debts owed to, guaranteed by or insured by the United States Government and its agencies, with annexes.

Signed at Antananarivo May 7, 1987.

Entered into force June 15, 1987.

NP

Agreement regarding the consolidation and rescheduling of certain debts owed to, guaranteed by, or insured by the United States Government and its agencies, with annexes.

Signed at Antananarivo August 9, 1989.

Entered into force September 14, 1989.

NP

Amendment

March 23 and May 2, 1990 (NP).

Agreement regarding the consolidation and rescheduling of certain debts owed to, guaranteed by, or insured by the United States Government and its agencies, with annexes.

Signed at Antananarivo June 19, 1991.

Entered into force August 9, 1991.

NP

Agreement regarding the consolidation, reduction and rescheduling of certain debts owed to, guaranteed by, or insured by the United States Government and its Agency, with annexes.

Signed at Washington December 16, 1997.

Entered into force March 4, 1998.

NP

Amendment

February 14 and May 20, 2003.

Investment incentive agreement.

Signed at Washington March 31, 1998.

Entered into force February 7, 2000.

TIAS

Agreement regarding the reduction of certain debts owed to, guaranteed by, or insured by the United States Government and its agency.

Signed at Antananarivo January 7, 2004.

Entered into force March 10, 2004.

NP

Agreement regarding the reduction of certain debts owed to, guaranteed by, or insured by the United States Government, with annexes.

Signed at Antananarivo March 18, 2005.

Entered into force May 19, 2005.

NP

INTERNATIONAL CRIMINAL COURT

Agreement regarding the surrender of persons to the International Criminal Court.

Signed at Antananarivo April 23, 2003.

Entered into force August 4, 2003.

TIAS

PEACE CORPS

Agreement relating to the establishment of a Peace Corps program in Madagascar.

Exchange of notes at Antananarivo June 11, 1992.

Entered into force June 11, 1992.

TIAS 12107.

POSTAL MATTERS

International express mail agreement, with detailed regulations.

Signed at Antananarivo and Washington April 28 and May 26, 1988.

Entered into force July 15, 1988.

TIAS 11597.

VISAS

Reciprocal agreement between the United States and France relating to visa fees for nonimmigrants.

Exchanges of notes at Washington August 19 and September 4, 5, and 16, 1947.

Entered into force September 16, 1947; operative October 1, 1947.

61 Stat. 3776; TIAS 1721; 7 Bevans 1210; 84 UNTS 19.

MALAWI

AGRICULTURAL COMMODITIES

Agricultural commodities agreement, with agreed minutes.

Signed at Blantyre December 30, 1980.

Entered into force December 30, 1980.

33 UST 1571; TIAS 10134; 1529 UNTS 317.

Amendment

May 22, 1981 (33 UST 1599; TIAS 10134; 1529 UNTS 331).

DEFENSE

Agreement concerning the provision of training related to defense articles under the United States International Military Education and Training (IMET) Program.

Exchange of notes at Lilongwe March 20 and May 1, 1980.

Entered into force May 1, 1980.

32 UST 965; TIAS 9744; 1222 UNTS 331.

Agreement regarding grants under the Foreign Assistance Act of 1961, as amended, and the furnishing of defense articles, related training and other defense services from the United States to Malawi.

Exchange of notes at Lilongwe May 28 and July 24, 1992.

Entered into force July 24, 1992.

TIAS 12525.

Agreement regarding the provision of commodities, services and associated military education and training to assist the Republic of Malawi's forces participating in the African Crisis Response Initiative.

Exchange of notes at Lilongwe July 28 and August 27, 1997.

Entered into force August 27, 1997.

TIAS

ECONOMIC AND TECHNICAL COOPERATION

Agency for International Development

April 29, 1976 (29 UST 5245; TIAS 9099).

EMPLOYMENT

Agreement concerning the employment of dependents of official government employees.

Exchange of notes at Washington October 29, 1998 and April 16, 1999.

Entered into force April 16, 1999.

TIAS

EXTRADITION

Extradition treaty between the United States and the United Kingdom.

Signed at London December 22, 1931; applicable to Nyasaland June 24, 1935.

47 Stat. 2122; TS 849; 12 Bevans 482; 163 LNTS 59.

Agreement continuing in force between the United States and Malawi the extradition treaty and the double taxation convention [1] between the United States and the United Kingdom.

Exchange of notes at Zomba and Blantyre December 17, 1966, January 6 and April 4, 1967.

Entered into force April 4, 1967.

18 UST 1822; TIAS 6328; 692 UNTS 191.

NOTE

1 Notification of termination of the 1945 taxation convention as applicable to Malawi given by the United States June 28, 1983, effective January 1, 1984.

FINANCE

Agreement relating to investment guaranties.

Exchange of notes at Blantyre May 1 and July 21, 1967.

Entered into force July 21, 1967.

18 UST 2335; TIAS 6334; 693 UNTS 3.

Agreement regarding the consolidation and rescheduling of certain debts owed to, guaranteed or insured by the United States Government and its agencies, with annexes.

Signed at Lilongwe March 10, 1983.

Entered into force May 16, 1983.

TIAS 10684; 2005 UNTS 133.

Agreement regarding the consolidation and rescheduling of certain debts owed to, guaranteed or insured by the United States Government and its agencies with annexes and implementing agreement regarding repayments due under A.I.D. loans, with annexes.

Signed at Lilongwe April 30, 1984.

Entered into force June 11, 1984.

TIAS 10993; 2022 UNTS 81.

Agreement regarding the consolidation and rescheduling of certain debts owed to, guaranteed by or insured by the United States Government and its agencies, with annexes.

Signed at Lilongwe February 21, 1989.

Entered into force April 6, 1989.

NP

INTERNATIONAL CRIMINAL COURT

Agreement regarding the surrender of persons to the International Criminal Court.

Signed at Lilongwe September 23, 2003.

Entered into force September 23, 2003.

TIAS

PEACE CORPS

Agreement relating to the establishment of a Peace Corps program in Malawi.

Exchange of notes at Blantyre and Zomba September 14, 1971.

Entered into force September 14, 1971.

22 UST 1633; TIAS 7191.

POSTAL MATTERS

International express mail agreement, with detailed regulations.

Signed at Lilongwe and Washington April 26 and June 21, 1988.

Entered into force July 15, 1988.

TIAS 11582.

MALAYSIA

On August 31, 1957 the Federation of Malaya attained fully responsible status within the British Commonwealth (Federation of Malaya Independence Act, 1957). By an exchange of notes dated September 12, 1957 between the United Kingdom and the Federation of Malaya there were formally transferred to the Federation, as of August 31, 1957, the rights and obligations of treaties and agreements entered into between the United Kingdom and any other government in so far as such instruments may be held to have application to or in respect of the Federation of Malaya. The British Colonies of North Borneo and Sarawak and the State of Singapore were federated with the existing States of the Federation of Malaya under the provisions of a general agreement between them and the United Kingdom, signed at London July 9, 1963. On September 16, 1963 the Federation of Malaya changed its name to Malaysia. The Constitution of the Federation of Malaya was amended by the Malaysia Act of 1963 to provide for the Government of Malaysia's assumption of rights and obligations of treaties and agreements entered into between the United Kingdom and any other government on behalf of the Borneo States and Singapore. On August 9, 1965 Singapore became an independent and sovereign state.

AVIATION

Arrangement between the United States and the United Kingdom relating to pilot licenses to operate civil aircraft.

Exchange of notes at Washington March 28 and April 5, 1935.

Entered into force May 5, 1935.

49 Stat. 3731; EAS 77; 12 Bevans 513; 162 LNTS 59.

Agreement concerning assistance in developing and modernizing Malaysia's civil aviation infrastructure.

Signed at Washington and Kuala Lumpur July 22 and August 6, 1994.

Entered into force August 6, 1994.

TIAS

Agreement for promotion of aviation safety.

Signed at Kuala Lumpur May 28, 1996.

Entered into force May 28, 1996.

TIAS 12760.

Air transport agreement, with annexes.

Signed at San Francisco June 21, 1997.

Entered into force June 21, 1997.

TIAS

Amendment

August 7 and October 20, 2006.

CONSULS

Consular convention and protocol of signature between the United States and the United Kingdom.

Signed at Washington June 6, 1951.

Entered into force September 7, 1952.

3 UST 3426; TIAS 2494; 165 UNTS 121.

DEFENSE

Agreement relating to the purchase by Malaya of military equipment, materials, and services from the United States.

Exchange of notes at Washington June 30 and July 9, 1958.

Entered into force July 9, 1958.

9 UST 1235; TIAS 4108; 336 UNTS 79.

Agreement relating to the deposit by Malaysia of ten percent of the value of grant military assistance furnished by the United States.

Exchange of notes at Kuala Lumpur March 8 and April 4, 1972.

Entered into force April 4, 1972; effective February 7, 1972.

23 UST 294; TIAS 7309.

Agreement relating to eligibility for United States military assistance and training pursuant to the International Security Assistance and Arms Export Control Act of 1976.

Exchange of notes at Kuala Lumpur February 11 and March 14, 1977.

Entered into force March 14, 1977.

29 UST 663; TIAS 8845.

Agreement concerning a military education exchange program.

Exchange of letters at Washington and Kuala Lumpur May 16 and 29, 1991.

Entered into force May 29, 1991.

NP

Acquisition and cross-servicing agreement, with annexes

Signed May 9, 2005.

Entered into force May 9, 2005.

TIAS

Agreement regarding grants under the Foreign Assistance Act of 1961, as amended, or successor legislation, and the furnishing of defense articles, defense services and related training, including pursuant to the United States International Military and Education Training Program (IMET).

Exchange of notes at Kuala Lumpur March 3 and September 18, 2006.

Entered into force September 18, 2006.

TIAS

ECONOMIC AND TECHNICAL COOPERATION

Economic cooperation agreement between the United States and the United Kingdom.

Signed at London July 6, 1948; applicable to the Federation of Malaya July 20, 1948.

62 Stat. 2596; TIAS 1795; 12 Bevans 874; 22 UNTS 263.

Amendments

January 3, 1950 (1 UST 184; TIAS 2036; 86 UNTS 304).

May 25, 1951 (2 UST 1292; TIAS 2277; 99 UNTS 308).

February 25, 1953 (4 UST 1528; TIAS 2815; 172 UNTS 332).

EDUCATION

Agreement concerning the establishment of the Malaysian-American Commission on Educational Exchange.

Signed at Kuala Lumpur August 3, 1995.

Entered into force August 3, 1995.

TIAS 12681.

EXTRADITION

Extradition treaty, with exchange of notes.

Signed at Kuala Lumpur August 3, 1995.

Entered into force June 2, 1997.

TIAS

FINANCE

Agreement relating to investment guaranties under section 413(b)(4) of the Mutual Security Act of 1954, as amended.

Exchange of notes at Kuala Lumpur April 21, 1959.

Entered into force April 21, 1959.

10 UST 776; TIAS 4214; 343 UNTS 3.

Amendment

June 24, 1965 (16 UST 1086; TIAS 5850; 564 UNTS 230).

NARCOTIC DRUGS

Agreement relating to a cooperative program to combat the spread of heroin addiction and other forms of drug abuse in Malaysia.

Exchange of notes at Kuala Lumpur November 16 and December 8, 1978.

Entered into force December 8, 1978.

30 UST 7183; TIAS 9577; 1182 UNTS 101.

Amendment

April 9 and May 18, 1979 (30 UST 7192; TIAS 9577; 1182 UNTS 105).

Memorandum of understanding for reducing demand, preventing illicit use and combatting illicit production and traffic of drugs, including precursor chemicals.

Signed at Kuala Lumpur April 20, 1989.

Entered into force April 20, 1989.

TIAS 12399.

PEACE CORPS

Agreement relating to the establishment of a Peace Corps program in the Federation of Malaya.

Exchange of notes at Kuala Lumpur September 4, 1961.

Entered into force September 4, 1961.

12 UST 1236; TIAS 4843; 421 UNTS 215.

Agreement between the United States and the United Kingdom relating to the establishment of a Peace Corps program in North Borneo.

Exchange of notes at London October 25, 1962.

Entered into force October 25, 1962.

13 UST 2389; TIAS 5201; 457 UNTS 137.

Agreement between the United States and the United Kingdom relating to the establishment of a Peace Corps program in Sarawak.

Exchange of notes at London October 25, 1962.

Entered into force October 25, 1962.

13 UST 2394; TIAS 5202; 457 UNTS 129.

POLLUTION

Agreement concerning the transboundary movement of hazardous wastes from Malaysia to the United States.

Signed at Kuala Lumpur March 10, 1995.

Entered into force March 10, 1995.

TIAS 12612.

POSTAL MATTERS

Parcel post convention.

Signed at Kuala Lumpur January 21 and at Washington March 22, 1935.

Entered into force April 1, 1935.

49 Stat. 3133; Post Office Department print; 161 LNTS 41.

International express mail agreement, with detailed regulations.

Signed at Washington and Kuala Lumpur February 14 and March 14, 1983.

Entered into force June 1, 1983.

TIAS 10671; 2001 UNTS 47.

PROPERTY

Convention between the United States and the United Kingdom relating to tenure and disposition of real and personal property.[1]

Signed at Washington March 2, 1899.

Entered into force August 7, 1900.

31 Stat. 1939; TS 146; 12 Bevans 246.

NOTE

1 Notification given on February 9, 1901 of application to the Straits Settlements.

TAXATION

Agreement concerning reciprocal exemption with respect to taxes on income of shipping and air transport enterprises.

Signed at Kuala Lumpur April 18, 1989.

Entered into force March 12, 1990.

TIAS 11618; 2191 UNTS 143.

TRADE AND COMMERCE

Agreement relating to trade in cotton, wool and man-made fiber textiles and textile products, with annexes.

Exchange of notes at Kuala Lumpur July 1 and 11, 1985.

Entered into force July 11, 1985.

NP

Amendments and extension

September 9 and 15, 1987 (NP).

March 29 and April 19, 1988 (NP).

November 10 and 21, 1988 (NP).

February 6 and May 20, 1992 (NP).

TRADE-MARKS

Declaration by the United States and the United Kingdom relating to reciprocal protection to trade-marks.

Signed at London October 24, 1877.

Entered into force October 24, 1877.

20 Stat. 703; TS 138; 12 Bevans 198.

VISAS

Agreement between the United States and the United Kingdom relating to visas.

Exchange of notes at London October 15 and 22, 1954.

Agreement continuing in force the 1954 agreement with respect to the Federation of Malaya.

Exchange of letters at Kuala Lumpur March 5 and 12, 1958.

MALDIVES

AGRICULTURAL COMMODITIES

Agricultural commodities agreement.

Signed at Colombo July 13, 1985.

Entered into force July 13, 1985.

NP

Amendment

August 25, 1986 (NP).

Agricultural commodities agreement.

Signed at Male August 18, 1987.

Entered into force August 18, 1987.

NP

AVIATION

Memorandum of agreement concerning assistance in developing and modernizing Maldives's civil aviation infrastructure, with annex.

Signed at Washington and Male February 12 and 17, 1997.

Entered into force February 17, 1997.

TIAS

Air transport agreement, with annexes.

Signed at Washington May 5, 2005.

Entered into force May 5, 2005.

TIAS

CUSTOMS

Agreement regarding mutual assistance between their customs administrations.

Signed at Brussels June 25, 2005.

Entered into force June 25, 2005.

TIAS

DEFENSE

Agreement concerning the provision of training related to defense articles under the United States International Military Education and Training (IMET) Program.

Exchange of notes and telex at Colombo and Male March 4 and April 9, 1983.

Entered into force April 9, 1983.

35 UST 3236; TIAS 10851; 2014 UNTS 531.

Agreement regarding military and Department of Defense civilian personnel.

Exchange of notes at Colombo December 31, 2004.

Entered into force December 31, 2004.

TIAS

ENVIRONMENTAL COOPERATION

Agreement for cooperation in the Global Learning and Observations to Benefit the Environment (GLOBE) Program.

Signed at Male December 8, 2003.

Entered into force December 8, 2003.

TIAS

INTERNATIONAL CRIMINAL COURT

Agreement regarding the surrender of persons to international tribunals.

Signed at Male and Colombo April 8 and 10, 2003.

Entered into force July 8, 2003.

TIAS

POSTAL MATTERS

International express mail agreement, with detailed regulations.

Signed at Male and Washington October 20 and November 8, 1990.

Entered into force December 5, 1990.

TIAS 11766.

TRADE AND COMMERCE

Arrangement relating to a visa system for exports of cotton, wool and man-made fiber apparel products from the Republic of Maldives.

Exchange of letters at Colombo and Male December 29, 1981 and March 22, 1982.

Entered into force March 22, 1982; effective October 1, 1982.

34 UST 1616; TIAS 10442.

Agreement relating to trade in wool sweaters, with annex.

Exchange of notes at Colombo and Male September 7 and 19, 1984.

Entered into force September 19, 1984; effective September 29, 1982.

NP

Amendments and extension

January 6 and 14, 1986 (NP).

July 16 and October 13, 1986 (NP).

December 18, 1987 and February 17, 1988 (NP).

MALI

AGRICULTURAL COMMODITIES

Agricultural commodities agreement, with exchange of notes.

Signed at Washington July 14, 1965.

Entered into force July 14, 1965.

16 UST 1099; TIAS 5852; 564 UNTS 101.

Amendment

December 8 and 15, 1965 (16 UST 1765; TIAS 5906).

AVIATION

Civil aviation security agreement.

Signed at Bamako June 25, 1993.

Entered into force June 25, 1993.

TIAS 12155.

Air transport agreement, with annexes.

Signed at Washington October 17, 2005.

Entered into force October 17, 2005.

TIAS

DEFENSE

Military assistance agreement.

Exchange of notes at Bamako May 20, 1961.

Entered into force May 20, 1961.

12 UST 1030; TIAS 4805; 413 UNTS 205.

Understanding regarding delivery of two C-47 aircraft and related articles and services.

Exchange of notes at Bamako January 5, 1967.

Entered into force January 5, 1967.

18 UST 338; TIAS 6238.

Agreement relating to the deposit by Mali of ten percent of the value of grant military assistance and excess defense articles furnished by the United States.

Exchange of notes at Bamako April 18 and June 6, 1972.

Entered into force June 6, 1972; effective February 7, 1972.

23 UST 1106; TIAS 7368.

Agreement concerning the provision of training related to defense articles under the United States International Military Education and Training (IMET) Program.

Exchange of notes at Bamako November 4, 1983 and March 23, 1984.

Entered into force March 23, 1984.

NP

Agreement regarding the status of U.S. military personnel and civilian employees of the Department of Defense who may be temporarily present in Mali in connection with the African Crisis Response Initiative.

Exchange of notes at Bamako July 30 and September 30, 1997.

Entered into force September 30, 1997.

NP

Agreement regarding grants under the Foreign Assistance Act of 1961, as amended, and the furnishing of defense articles, related training, and other defense services from the United States of America to the Government of Mali for purposes of participation in peacekeeping operations (PKO) in Liberia under Economic Community of West African States (ECOWAS) or other ECOWAS PKO.

Exchange of notes at Bamako August 18 and 22, 2003.

Entered into force August 22, 2003.

TIAS

Acquisition and cross-servicing agreement, with annexes.

Signed at Bamako September 20, 2006.

Entered into force September 20, 2006.

TIAS

ECONOMIC AND TECHNICAL COOPERATION

Agreement providing for the furnishing of economic, technical and related assistance.

Exchange of notes at Bamako January 4, 1961.

Entered into force January 4, 1961.

12 UST 1; TIAS 4668; 405 UNTS 165.

Agency for International Development

January 28, 1974 (28 UST 1; TIAS 8461; 1066 UNTS 172).

January 28, 1975 (28 UST 17; TIAS 8461; 1066 UNTS 181).

November 6, 1974 and May 7, 1975 (29 UST 5746; TIAS 9147).

May 29, 1975 (29 UST 5749; TIAS 9147).

June 30, 1975 (28 UST 19; TIAS 8461; 1066 UNTS 182).

August 22, 1975 (28 UST 21; TIAS 8461; 1066 UNTS 183).

January 11 and February 2, 1977 (29 UST 5751; TIAS 9147).

May 13, 1977 (29 UST 2305; TIAS 8940).

May 13, 1977 (29 UST 5129; TIAS 9093).

EMPLOYMENT

Agreement relating to the employment of dependents of official government employees.

Exchange of notes at Washington March 6 and June 20, 1995.

Entered into force June 20, 1995.

TIAS 12668.

ENVIRONMENTAL COOPERATION

Agreement for cooperation in the Global Learning and Observations to Benefit the Environment (GLOBE) Program, with appendices.

Signed at Washington November 19, 1997.

Entered into force November 19, 1997.

TIAS

FINANCE

Agreement relating to investment guaranties.

Exchange of notes at Bamako June 4 and 9, 1964.

Entered into force June 9, 1964.

15 UST 1533; TIAS 5636; 530 UNTS 133.

Agreement regarding the consolidation and rescheduling of certain debts owed to, guaranteed by, or insured by the United States Government and its agencies, with annexes.

Signed at Bamako June 3, 1989.

Entered into force July 21, 1989.

NP

Agreement regarding the consolidation of debt owed to, guaranteed by, or insured by the United States Government, with annexes.

Signed at Bamako September 10 and October 29, 2004.

Entered into force January 18, 2005.

NP

GEODETIC SURVEY

Geodetic survey agreement.

Signed at Bamako January 17, 1968.

Entered into force January 17, 1968.

19 UST 4568; TIAS 6446; 697 UNTS 231.

PEACE CORPS

Agreement relating to the establishment of a Peace Corps program in Mali.

Exchange of notes at Bamako December 23, 1969 and April 17, 1971.

Entered into force April 17, 1971.

26 UST 2611; TIAS 8178; 1027 UNTS 121.

POSTAL MATTERS

International express mail agreement, with detailed regulations.

Signed at Bamako and Washington April 2 and 16, 1987.

Entered into force June 1, 1987.

TIAS 11304.

Postal money order agreement.

Signed at Bamako and Washington February 10 and April 7, 1994.

Entered into force May 1, 1994.

NP

SOCIAL SECURITY

Agreement to provide social security benefits for certain employees of the United States in Mali.

Signed at Bamako December 2, 1969.

Entered into force January 1, 1970.

21 UST 2145; TIAS 6961; 764 UNTS 151.

MALTA

On September 21, 1964 Malta attained fully responsible status within the British Commonwealth (Malta Independence Act, 1964). By an exchange of letters dated December 31, 1964 between the Government of the United Kingdom and the Government of Malta, it was agreed that all obligations and responsibilities of the Government of the United Kingdom which arise from any valid international instrument shall, as from September 21, 1964, be assumed by the Government of Malta insofar as such instruments may be held to have application to Malta. Also, rights and benefits heretofore enjoyed by the Government of the United Kingdom in virtue of the application of any such international instrument to Malta shall, as from September 21, 1964, be enjoyed by the Government of Malta.

AVIATION

Arrangement between the United States and the United Kingdom relating to pilot licenses to operate civil aircraft.

Exchange of notes at Washington March 28 and April 5, 1935; applicable to Malta May 5, 1935.

49 Stat. 3731; EAS 77; 12 Bevans 513; 162 LNTS 59.

Air transport agreement, with annexes.

Signed at Washington October 12, 2000.

Entered into force October 12, 2000.

TIAS

COMMERCE

Convention to regulate the commerce between the United States and the United Kingdom.[1]

Signed at London July 3, 1815.

Entered into force July 3, 1815.

8 Stat. 228; TS 110; 12 Bevans 49.

Convention continuing in force indefinitely the convention of July 3, 1815 between the United States and the United Kingdom.

Signed at London August 6, 1827.

Entered into force April 2, 1828.

8 Stat. 361; TS 117; 12 Bevans 76.

NOTE

1 Article IV superseded from September 7, 1952 by consular convention of June 6, 1951 (3 UST 3426; TIAS 2494).

CONSULS

Consular convention between the United States and the United Kingdom.

Signed at Washington June 6, 1951.

Entered into force September 7, 1952.

3 UST 3426; TIAS 2494; 165 UNTS 121.

CUSTOMS

Agreement regarding mutual assistance between Customs Administrations.

Signed at Valletta March 6, 2001.

Entered into force March 6, 2001.

TIAS

DEFENSE

Agreement concerning the provision of training related to defense articles under the United States International Military Education and Training (IMET) Program.

Exchange of notes at Floriana February 6 and 13, 1989.

Entered into force February 13, 1989.

NP

ECONOMIC AND TECHNICAL COOPERATION

Economic cooperation agreement between the United States and the United Kingdom.

Signed at London July 6, 1948; applicable to Malta July 6, 1948.

62 Stat. 2596; TIAS 1795; 12 Bevans 874; 22 UNTS 263.

Amendments

January 3, 1950 (1 UST 184; TIAS 2036; 86 UNTS 304).

May 25, 1951 (2 UST 1292; TIAS 2277; 99 UNTS 308).

February 25, 1953 (4 UST 1528; TIAS 2815; 172 UNTS 332).

Agency for International Development

June 15, 1973 (24 UST 1914; TIAS 7699).

EMPLOYMENT

Agreement relating to employment of dependents of official government employees.

Exchange of notes at Floriana September 25 and October 3, 1991.

Entered into force October 3, 1991.

TIAS 11795.

EXTRADITION

Extradition treaty between the United States and the United Kingdom.

Signed at London December 22, 1931; applicable to Malta June 24, 1935.

47 Stat. 2122; TS 849; 12 Bevans 482; 163 UNTS 59.

FINANCE

Agreement relating to investment guaranties.

Signed at Washington November 16, 1966.

Entered into force January 26, 1967.

18 UST 106; TIAS 6205; 688 UNTS 45.

PEACE CORPS

Agreement relating to the establishment of a Peace Corps program in Malta.

Exchange of notes at Valletta April 29 and June 24, 1970.

Entered into force June 24, 1970.

21 UST 1486; TIAS 6907; 753 UNTS 281.

POSTAL MATTERS

International express mail agreement.

Signed at Valletta August 20 and October 29, 1991.

Entered into force December 2, 1991.

TIAS 11789.

PROPERTY

Convention between the United States and the United Kingdom relating to the tenure and disposition of real and personal property.

Signed at Washington March 2, 1899; applicable to Malta May 29, 1947.

31 Stat. 1939; TS 146; 12 Bevans 246.

Supplementary convention between the United States and the United Kingdom relating to the tenure and disposition of real and personal property.

Signed at Washington May 27, 1936; applicable to Malta May 29, 1947.

55 Stat. 1101; TS 964; 5 Bevans 140; 203 LNTS 367.

TAXATION

Agreement on reciprocal exemption from taxes on earnings derived from the operation of ships and aircraft.

Exchange of notes at Washington December 26, 1996 and March 11, 1997.

Entered into force March 11, 1997.

TIAS

TRADE

See also COMMERCE

Agreement providing for consultations on problems of market disruption caused by cotton textile or cotton textile product exports from Malta.

Exchange of notes at Floriana and Valletta September 17 and 22, 1975.

Entered into force September 22, 1975.

26 UST 2747; TIAS 8192; 1045 UNTS 107.

TRADE-MARKS

Declaration by the United States and the United Kingdom affording reciprocal protection to trade-marks.

Signed at London October 24, 1877.

Entered into force October 24, 1877.

20 Stat. 703; TS 138; 12 Bevans 198.

VISAS

Arrangement between the United States and the United Kingdom providing for waiver of the visa requirement for United States citizens visiting Malta and for waiver of visa fees for British subjects residents of Malta visiting the United States.

Exchange of notes at Washington October 31 and December 12, 1949.

Entered into force December 12, 1949; operative December 1, 1949.

64 Stat. B137; TIAS 2069; 12 Bevans 950; 92 UNTS 191.

MARSHALL ISLANDS

AVIATION

Memorandum of agreement concerning assistance in developing and modernizing the Marshall Island's civil aviation system.

Signed at Washington and Majuro May 23 and June 15, 1989.

Entered into force June 15, 1989.

TIAS 11665.

COMPACT OF FREE ASSOCIATION

Agreement for the implementation of the Compact of Free Association between the Government of the United States and the Government of the Republic of the Marshall Islands (Title II, PL 99-239), with related agreements.

Signed at Majuro October 10, 1986.

Entered into force October 15, 1986; effective October 21, 1986.

TIAS

Amendments

October 20, 1986.

March 18, 1988 (TIAS 11661).

Agreement amending the agreement of June 25, 1983 concerning the Compact of Free Association, as amended.

Signed at Majuro April 30, 2003.

Entered into force May 1, 2004.

TIAS

Agreement regarding protections for citizens of the Republic of the Marshall Islands seeking to engage in employment in the United States pursuant to recruitment or other placement services.

Signed at Majuro April 30, 2003.

Entered into force May 1, 2004.

TIAS

Agreement on extradition, mutual assistance in law enforcement matters and penal sanctions, with agreed minute.

Signed at Majuro April 30, 2003.

Entered into force May 1, 2004; effective October 21, 1986.

TIAS

Agreement regarding the military use and operating rights of the Government of the United States in the Republic of the Marshall Islands, with agreed minutes and annexes.

Signed at Majuro April 30, 2003.

Entered into force May 1, 2004.

TIAS

Related agreement

March 23, 2004.

Status of forces agreement, with agreed minutes.

Signed at Majuro April 30, 2003.

Entered into force May 1, 2004.

TIAS

Agreement implementing section 216 and section 217 of the Compact, as amended, regarding a trust fund.

Signed at Majuro April 30, 2003.

Entered into force May 1, 2004.

TIAS

Federal programs and services agreement, with annex and agreed minute.

Signed at Majuro March 23, 2004.

Entered into force May 1, 2004.

TIAS

Agreement concerning procedures for the implementation of United States economic assistance provided in the Compact, as amended, of Free Association.

Signed at Majuro March 23, 2004.

Entered into force May 1, 2004.

TIAS

DEFENSE

Agreement regarding the provision of services of a military civic action team to the Marshall Islands.

Signed at Honolulu July 26, 1988.

Entered into force October 24, 1988.

TIAS 11657.

EDUCATION

Agreement regarding augmentation of educational assistance.

Signed at Washington September 7, 1988.

Entered into force September 7, 1988.

TIAS 11639.

ENVIRONMENTAL COOPERATION

Agreement for cooperation in the Global Learning and Observations to Benefit the Environment (GLOBE) Program, with appendices.

Signed at Majuro October 17, 1996.

Entered into force October 17, 1996.

TIAS 12808.

FINANCE

Investment incentive agreement.

Exchange of notes at Majuro January 20, 1988 and January 25, 1989.

Entered into force January 25, 1989.

TIAS 12092.

INTERNATIONAL CRIMINAL COURT

Agreement regarding the surrender of persons to the International Criminal Court.

Signed at Majuro September 10, 2002.

Entered into force June 26, 2003.

TIAS

RELATIONS

Agreement relating to diplomatic relations, with related notes.

Exchange of notes at Washington August 23 and September 6, 1989.

Entered into force September 6, 1989.

TIAS 11890.

TAXATION

Agreement concerning the reciprocal exemption from income tax of income derived from the international operation of ships and aircraft.

Exchange of notes at Majuro December 5, 1989.

Entered into force December 5, 1989.

TIAS 11728.

Agreement for the exchange of information with respect to taxes, with attachment and exchange of notes.

Signed at Majuro March 14, 1991.

Entered into force March 14, 1991.

TIAS 11830; 2211 UNTS 401.

TELECOMMUNICATION

Agreement relating to radio communications between amateur radio stations on behalf of third parties.

Exchange of notes at Majuro October 8 and 15, 1991.

Entered into force November 14, 1991.

TIAS 12439.

Agreement relating to the reciprocal granting of authorizations to permit licensed amateur radio operators of either country to operate their stations in the other country.

Exchange of notes at Majuro October 15 and 18, 1993.

Entered into force October 18, 1993.

TIAS 12512.

WEAPONS

Agreement concerning cooperation to suppress the proliferation of weapons of mass destruction, their delivery systems, and related materials by sea.

Signed at Honolulu August 13, 2004.

Entered into force November 24, 2004.

TIAS

MAURITANIA

AGRICULTURAL COMMODITIES

Agreement relating to the transfer of agricultural commodities to Mauritania to assist in alleviating the shortage caused by prolonged drought.

Signed at Nouakchott May 28, 1976.

Entered into force May 28, 1976.

29 UST 5775; TIAS 9153; 1146 UNTS 227

Agreement for the transfer of food grain (sorghum).

Signed at Nouakchott April 18, 1978.

Entered into force April 18, 1978.

30 UST 3067; TIAS 9379; 1178 UNTS 269.

Amendment

April 18, 1978 (30 UST 3073; TIAS 9379; 1178 UNTS 273).

DEFENSE

Agreement concerning the provision of training related to defense articles under the United States International Military Education and Training (IMET) Program.

Exchange of notes at Nouakchott May 21, 1982 and August 26, 1984.

Entered into force August 26, 1984.

TIAS 10987; 2022 UNTS 117.

Agreement of cooperation regarding the Pan-Sahel initiative project.

Signed at Nouakchott June 3, 2005.

Entered into force June 3, 2005.

TIAS

Acquisition and cross-servicing agreement, with annexes.

Signed at Nouakchott June 22, 2005.

Entered into force June 22, 2005.

TIAS

ECONOMIC AND TECHNICAL COOPERATION

General agreement for special development assistance.

Signed at Nouakchott March 23, 1971.

Entered into force March 23, 1971.

22 UST 667; TIAS 7121; 792 UNTS 205.

Agency for International Development

February 26, 1974 (26 UST 3894; TIAS 8224; 1045 UNTS 3).

FINANCE

Agreement relating to investment guaranties.

Exchange of Notes at Nouakchott May 4 and July 3, 1964.

Entered into force July 3, 1964.

15 UST 2385; TIAS 5727; 532 UNTS 307.

Agreement regarding the consolidation and rescheduling of certain debts owed to, guaranteed by or insured by the United States Government and its agencies, with annex.

Signed at Washington August 14, 1985.

Entered into force September 23, 1985.

NP

Agreement regarding the consolidation and rescheduling of certain debts owed to, guaranteed by, or insured by the United States Government and its agency, with annexes.

Signed at Nouakchott February 4, 1990.

Entered into force March 12, 1990.

NP

Agreement regarding the consolidation and rescheduling of certain debts owed to, guaranteed by or insured by the United States Government and its agencies, with annexes.

Signed at Washington July 29, 1993.

Entered into force September 13, 1993.

NP

Agreement regarding the consolidation and reduction of certain debts owed to, guaranteed by, or insured by the United States Government and its agency, with annexes.

Signed at Nouakchott November 9, 2000.

Entered into force February 15, 2001.

NP

Agreement regarding the consolidation of debt owed to, guaranteed by, or insured by the United States Government, with annexes.

Signed at Nouakchott April 1, 2003.

Entered into force June 30, 2003.

NP

INTERNATIONAL CRIMINAL COURT

Agreement regarding the surrender of persons to the International Criminal Court.

Signed at New York September 17, 2002.

Entered into force July 6, 2003.

TIAS

PEACE CORPS

Agreement relating to the establishment of a Peace Corps program in Mauritania.

Exchange of notes at Nouakchott September 19 and October 17, 1966.

Entered into force October 17, 1966.

17 UST 2046; TIAS 6143; 676 UNTS 3.

POSTAL MATTERS

International express mail agreement, with detailed regulations.

Signed at Nouakchott and Washington June 28 and July 17, 1992.

Entered into force September 21, 1992.

TIAS 11872.

MAURITIUS

On March 12, 1968 Mauritius became an independent state. In a note dated March 12, 1968 to the Secretary-General of the United Nations, the Prime Minister and Minister of External Affairs made a statement reading in part as follows:

"I have the honour to inform you that the Government of Mauritius, conscious of the desirability of maintaining existing legal relationships, and conscious of its obligation under international law to honour its treaty commitments, acknowledges that many treaty rights and obligations of the Government of the United Kingdom in respect of Mauritius were succeeded to by Mauritius upon independence by virtue of customary international law.

Since, however, it is likely that by virtue of customary international law certain treaties may have lapsed at the date of independence of Mauritius, it seems essential that each treaty should be subjected to legal examination. It is proposed after this examination has been completed, to indicate which, if any, of the treaties which may have lapsed by customary international law the Government of Mauritius wish to treat as having lapsed.

It is desired that it be presumed that each treaty has been legally succeeded to by Mauritius and that action be based upon this presumption until a decision is reached that it should be regarded as having lapsed. Should the Government of Mauritius be of the opinion that they have legally succeeded to a treaty but subsequently wish to terminate its operation, they will in due course give notice of termination in the terms thereof."

AGRICULTURAL COMMODITIES

Agricultural commodities agreement, with agreed minutes.

Signed at Port Louis June 29, 1979.

Entered into force June 29, 1979.

30 UST 6079; TIAS 9541; 1180 UNTS 421.

Related agreements

July 11, 1980 (32 UST 1927; TIAS 9811; 1234 UNTS 411).

May 27, 1981 (33 UST 3249; TIAS 10221).

June 25, 1981 (34 UST 2035; TIAS 10477).

April 8, 1982 (34 UST 471; TIAS 10372).

December 30, 1982 (TIAS 10628; 1581 UNTS 109).

March 29 and July 4, 1984 (TIAS 11041).

AVIATION

Agreement between the United States and the United Kingdom relating to air services.

Signed at Bermuda February 11, 1946.

Entered into force February 11, 1946.

60 Stat. 1499; TIAS 1507; 12 Bevans 726; 3 UNTS 253.

Amendment

May 27, 1966 (17 UST 683; TIAS 6019).

Agreement relating to the installation, operation and use of distance measuring equipment at Plaisance Airfield.

Exchange of notes at Port Louis November 4 and December 29, 1969.

Entered into force December 29, 1969.

21 UST 434; TIAS 6829; 740 UNTS 135.

CONSULS

Consular convention between the United States and the United Kingdom.

Signed at Washington June 6, 1951.

Entered into force September 7, 1952.

3 UST 3426; TIAS 2494; 165 UNTS 121.

ECONOMIC AND TECHNICAL COOPERATION

Economic cooperation agreement between the United States and the United Kingdom.

Signed at London July 6, 1948; applicable to Mauritius July 6, 1948.

62 Stat. 2596; TIAS 1795; 12 Bevans 874; 22 UNTS 263.

Amendments

January 3, 1950 (1 UST 184; TIAS 2036; 86 UNTS 304).

May 25, 1951 (2 UST 1292; TIAS 2277; 99 UNTS 308).

February 25, 1953 (4 UST 1528; TIAS 2815; 172 UNTS 332).

EMPLOYMENT

Agreement relating to the employment of dependents of official government employees.

Exchange of notes at Port Louis March 17 and June 13, 1997.

Entered into force June 13, 1997.

TIAS

EXTRADITION

Extradition treaty between the United States and the United Kingdom.

Signed at London December 22, 1931.

Entered into force June 24, 1935.

47 Stat. 2122; TS 849; 12 Bevans 482; 163 LNTS 59.

FINANCE

Investment incentive agreement.

Signed at Port Louis December 15, 1997.

Entered into force May 26, 1998.

TIAS

INTERNATIONAL CRIMINAL COURT

Agreement regarding the surrender of persons to the International Criminal Court.

Signed at Washington June 25, 2003.

Entered into force June 30, 2003.

TIAS

PEACE CORPS

Agreement relating to the establishment of a Peace Corps program in Mauritius.

Exchange of notes at Port Louis March 18, 1971.

Entered into force March 18, 1971.

22 UST 453; TIAS 7080; 792 UNTS 197.

POSTAL MATTERS

International express mail agreement.

Signed at Port Louis and Washington September 9 and October 2, 1992.

Entered into force December 14, 1992.

TIAS 11909.

PROPERTY

Convention between the United States and the United Kingdom relating to the tenure and disposition of real and personal property.

Signed at Washington March 2, 1899; applicable to Mauritius June 10, 1901.

31 Stat. 1939; TS 146; 12 Bevans 246.

Supplementary convention relating to the tenure and disposition of real and personal property of March 2, 1899.

Signed at Washington May 27, 1936.

Entered into force March 10, 1941.

55 Stat. 1101; TS 964; 5 Bevans 140; 203 LNTS 367.

TRADE-MARKS

Declaration by the United States and the United Kingdom relating to reciprocal protection to trade-marks.

Signed at London October 24, 1877.

Entered into force October 24, 1877.

20 Stat. 703; TS 138; 12 Bevans 198.

MEXICO

AGRICULTURAL COMMODITIES

Agreement concerning the closeout of the collection accounts of the agricultural commodities agreement of October 23, 1957, as amended (TIAS 3935, 4070, 4129, and 4178).

Exchange of notes at Mexico July 6, 1961 and August 9, 1962.

Entered into force August 9, 1962.

13 UST 1953; TIAS 5153; 461 UNTS 325.

AGRICULTURE

Convention safeguarding livestock interests through the prevention of infectious and contagious diseases.

Signed at Washington March 16, 1928.

Entered into force January 18, 1930.

46 Stat. 2451; TS 808; 9 Bevans 959; 106 LNTS 481.

Agreement relating to plantation rubber investigations.

Exchange of notes at Mexico July 10 and September 20, 1943.

Entered into force July 1, 1943.

57 Stat. 1278; EAS 364; 117 UNTS 323.

Agreement relating to the establishment of an agricultural commission.

Exchange of notes at Mexico January 6 and 27, 1944.

Entered into force January 27, 1944.

58 Stat. 1425; EAS 421; 9 Bevans 1162; 106 UNTS 275.

Agreement establishing the Mexican-United States Commission for the Prevention of Foot-and-Mouth Disease.

Exchange of notes at Washington August 26, 1952.

Entered into force August 26, 1952.

6 UST 2543; TIAS 3300; 264 UNTS 269.

Amendment

December 12, 1953 and July 30, 1954 (7 UST 937; TIAS 3578).

Agreement confirming an agreement to eradicate screw-worms.

Exchange of notes at Mexico August 28, 1972.

Entered into force August 28, 1972.

23 UST 2465; TIAS 7438.

Amendment

October 19 and December 7, 1990 (TIAS 12427).

Memorandum of understanding concerning cooperative efforts to protect crops from plant pest damage and diseases.

Signed at Mexico February 8, 1973.

Entered into force February 8, 1973.

28 UST 7004; TIAS 8701.

Amendments

September 10 and October 9, 1973 (28 UST 7013; TIAS 8701).

July 15 and 24, 1976 (28 UST 7015; TIAS 8701).

Cooperative agreement relating to provision of services to assist in eradication of the Mediterranean fruit fly (MEDFLY).

Signed at Guatemala October 22, 1981.

Entered into force October 22, 1981.

34 UST 481; TIAS 10373; 1561 UNTS 33.

Extension

September 30, 1985 (TIAS 11934).

Memorandum of understanding regarding mutual cooperation in the regulation of raw agricultural products involved in commerce between Mexico and the United States, with annex.

Signed at Mexico November 28, 1988.

Entered into force November 28, 1988.

TIAS

ATOMIC ENERGY

Arrangement for the exchange of technical information and cooperation in nuclear safety and research matters.

Signed at Mexico March 5, 1997.

Entered into force March 5, 1997.

TIAS

Amendment and extension

November 12, 2002.

AVIATION

Agreement to facilitate the reciprocal transit of military aircraft.

Signed at Washington April 1, 1941.

Entered into force April 25, 1941.

55 Stat. 1191; TS 971; 9 Bevans 1049.

Agreement to facilitate flight notifications on non-scheduled, private, commercial or industrial flights between Mexico and the United States in both directions across the border.

Exchange of notes at Washington July 15, 1952.

Entered into force August 1, 1952.

3 UST 4943; TIAS 2667; 181 UNTS 263.

Air transport agreement.

Signed at Mexico August 15, 1960.

Entered into force provisionally August 15, 1960 and definitively January 17, 1961.

12 UST 60; TIAS 4675; 402 UNTS 177.

Extensions and amendments

July 31, 1970 (22 UST 1492; TIAS 7167; 800 UNTS 356).

September 23, 1988.

November 21, 1991 (TIAS 11950).

September 25 and December 4, 1997.

February 15, 1999.

December 12, 2005.

Agreement for acceptance by the United States of certificates of airworthiness for aircraft manufactured by Lockheed Azcarate, S.A.

Exchange of notes at Washington June 26 and July 19, 1961.

Entered into force July 19, 1961.

12 UST 1384; TIAS 4861; 433 UNTS 43.

Amendment

January 19 and 30, 1962 (13 UST 199; TIAS 4961; 442 UNTS 343).

Memorandum of agreement relating to technical assistance in reviewing air traffic operations in Mexico City terminal area.

Signed at Washington February 19, 1981.

Entered into force February 19, 1981.

35 UST 3599; TIAS 10870; 1577 UNTS 345.

Agreement on reduced air fares.

Exchange of letters at Mexico September 23, 1988.

Entered into force September 23, 1988.

TIAS

Memorandum of understanding on additional services (double designation), with annex.

Signed at Mexico September 23, 1988.

Entered into force September 23, 1988.

TIAS

Agreement concerning assistance in developing and modernizing Mexico's civil aviation infrastructure in the managerial, operational and technical areas, with annex.

Signed at Washington and Mexico June 4 and July 4, 1991.

Entered into force July 4, 1991.

TIAS

Memorandum of cooperation for Research and Development of the Global Navigation Satellite System (GNSS).

Signed at Mexico July 11, 1996.

Entered into force July 11, 1996.

TIAS

Memorandum of cooperation in the promotion and development of civil aviation, with letter of understanding.

Signed at Washington and Mexico September 17, October 14 and 16, 1997.

Entered into force October 16, 1997.

TIAS

Memorandum of agreement for the provision of assistance in developing and modernizing Mexico's civil aviation infrastructure.

Signed at Mexico City and Washington October 14 and 20, 1997.

Entered into force October 20, 1997.

TIAS

BOUNDARIES

Treaty relating to the boundary line, transit of persons, etc., across the Isthmus of Tehuantepec (Gadsden Treaty).[1]

Signed at Mexico December 30, 1853.

Entered into force June 30, 1854.

10 Stat. 1031; TS 208; 9 Bevans 812.

Treaty terminating article VIII of the boundary treaty of December 30, 1853.

Signed at Washington April 13, 1937.

Entered into force December 21, 1937.

52 Stat. 1457; TS 932; 9 Bevans 1023.

Convention for the solution of the problem of the Chamizal.

Signed at Mexico August 29, 1963.

Entered into force January 14, 1964.

15 UST 21; TIAS 5515; 505 UNTS 185.

Act approving minute no. 228 of the International Boundary and Water Commission concerning demarcation of new international boundary between the United States and Mexico.

Signed at Washington October 27, 1967.

Entered into force October 28, 1967.

18 UST 2836; TIAS 6372; 724 UNTS 308.

Treaty to resolve pending boundary differences and maintain the Rio Grande and Colorado River as the international boundary between the United States and Mexico, with maps.

Signed at Mexico November 23, 1970.

Entered into force April 18, 1972.

23 UST 371; TIAS 7313.

Act approving Minute 257 of the International Boundary and Water Commission confirming relocation of the channel of the Rio Grande.

Signed at Washington May 26, 1977.

Entered into force May 26, 1977.

28 UST 5256; TIAS 8625.

Treaty on maritime boundaries.

Signed at Mexico City May 4, 1978.

Entered into force November 13, 1997.

TIAS; 2143 UNTS 405.

Treaty on the delimitation of the continental shelf in the western Gulf of Mexico beyond 200 nautical miles, with annexes.

Signed at Washington June 9, 2000.

Entered into force January 17, 2001.

TIAS; 2143 UNTS 417.

NOTE

1 Article VIII terminated December 21, 1937.

BOUNDARY WATERS

Convention to avoid the difficulties occasioned by reason of the changes which take place in the beds of the Rio Grande and Colorado River.[1]

Signed at Washington March 1, 1889.

Entered into force December 24, 1890.

26 Stat. 1512; TS 232; 9 Bevans 877.

Convention providing for the equitable distribution of the waters of the Rio Grande for irrigation purposes.

Signed at Washington May 21, 1906.

Entered into force January 16, 1907.

34 Stat. 2953; TS 455; 9 Bevans 924.

Convention for the rectification of the Rio Grande (Rio Bravo del Norte) in the El Paso-Juarez Valley, and exchanges of notes of February 1 and September 8, 1933.

Signed at Mexico February 1, 1933.

Entered into force November 10, 1933.

48 Stat. 1621; TS 864; 9 Bevans 976.

Treaty relating to the utilization of waters of the Colorado and Tijuana Rivers and of the Rio Grande, and supplementary protocol signed November 14, 1944.

Signed at Washington February 3, 1944.

Entered into force November 8, 1945.

59 Stat. 1219; TS 994; 9 Bevans 1166; 3 UNTS 313.

Agreement to proceed with the construction of Amistad Dam on the Rio Grande to form part of the system of international storage dams provided for by the water treaty of February 3, 1944.

Signed at Ciudad Acuna October 24, 1960.

Entered into force October 24, 1960.

11 UST 2396; TIAS 4624; 401 UNTS 137.

Minute 234 of the International Boundary and Water Commission: Waters of the Rio Grande allotted to the United States from the Conchos, San Diego, San Rodrigo, Escondido and Salado Rivers and the Las Vacas Arroyo.

Signed at Ciudad Juarez December 2, 1969.

Entered into force December 19, 1969.

TIAS

Agreement approving Minute 242 of the International Boundary and Water Commission setting forth a permanent and definitive solution to the international problem of the salinity of the Colorado River.

Exchange of notes at Mexico August 30, 1973.

Entered into force August 30, 1973.

24 UST 1968; TIAS 7708.

Minute 261 of the International Boundary and Water Commission concerning recommendations for the solution to the border sanitation problems.

Signed at El Paso September 24, 1979.

Entered into force October 2, 1979.

31 UST 5099; TIAS 9658; 1221 UNTS 189.

Minute 264 of the International Boundary and Water Commission: Recommendations for solution of the New River border sanitation problem at Calexico, California Mexicali, Baja California Norte.

Signed at Ciudad Juarez August 26, 1980.

Entered into force December 4, 1980.

32 UST 3764; TIAS 9918; 1267 UNTS 163.

Minute 270 of the International Boundary and Water Commission: Recommendations concerning border sanitation problem at San Diego, California-Tijuana, Baja California.

Signed at Ciudad Juarez April 30, 1985.

Entered into force July 16, 1985.

TIAS 11267.

Minute 273 of the International Boundary and Water Commission: Recommendations for the solution of the border sanitation problem at Naco, Arizona-Naco, Sonora.

Signed at El Paso March 19, 1987.

Entered into force April 15, 1987.

TIAS 11292.

Amendment

September 19, 1996.

Minute 274 of the International Boundary and Water Commission: Joint project for improvement of the quality of waters of the New River at Calexico, California-Mexicali, Baja California, with joint report.

Signed at Ciudad Juarez April 15, 1987.

Entered into force May 13, 1987.

TIAS 11316.

Agreement concerning rediversion of Rio Grande waters allocated to Mexico under the convention of 1906.

Exchange of notes at Mexico June 24 and November 10, 1987.

Entered into force November 10, 1987.

TIAS 11549.

Minute 276 of the International Boundary and Water Commission: Conveyance, treatment and disposal of sewage from Nogales, Arizona and Nogales, Sonora exceeding the capacities allocated to the United States and Mexico at the Nogales international sewage treatment plant under Minute 227, with joint report.

Signed at Ciudad Juarez July 26, 1988.

Entered into force August 19, 1988.

TIAS 12396.

Minute 279 of the International Boundary and Water Commission: Joint measures to improve the quality of the waters of the Rio Grande at Laredo, Texas/Nuevo Laredo, Tamaulipas, with joint report.

Signed at Laredo and Nuevo Laredo August 28, 1989.

Entered into force August 28, 1989.

TIAS 11701.

Minute 283 of the International Boundary and Water Commission: Conceptual plan for the international solution to the border sanitation problem in San Diego, California/Tijuana, Baja California.

Signed at El Paso July 2, 1990.

Entered into force August 8, 1990.

TIAS 11735.

Minute 290 of the International Boundary and Water Commission: Replacement of the International Cordova-Bridge of the Americas over the Rio Grande at El Paso, Texas-Ciudad Juarez, Chihuahua, Mexico.

Signed at Ciudad Juarez September 21, 1993.

Entered into force September 24, 1993.

TIAS

Minute 291 of the International Boundary and Water Commission: Improvements to the conveying capacity of the international boundary segment of the Colorado River.

Signed at San Diego July 16, 1994.

Entered into force August 16, 1994.

TIAS

Minute 298 of the International Boundary and Water Commission: Recommendations for construction of works parallel to the city of Tijuana, B.C. wastewater pumping and disposal system and rehabilitation of the San Antonio de los Buenos treatment plant.

Signed at El Paso December 2, 1997.

Entered into force January 23, 1998.

TIAS

Minute 306 of the International Boundary and Water Commission: Conceptual framework for United States-Mexico studies for future recommendations concerning the riparian and estuarine ecology of the limitrophe section of the Colorado River and its associated delta.

Signed at El Paso December 12, 2000.

Entered into force December 13, 2000.

TIAS

Minute 307 of the International Boundary and Water Commission: Partial coverage of allocation of the Rio Grande Treaty tributary water deficit from Fort Quitman to Falcon Dam.

Signed at Washington March 16, 2001.

Entered into force March 16, 2001.

TIAS

Minute 308 of the International Boundary and Water Commission: United States allocation of Rio Grande waters during the last year of the current cycle.

Signed at Ciudad Juarez June 28, 2002.

Entered into force June 28, 2002.

TIAS

Minute 309 of the International Boundary and Water Commission: Volumes of water saved with the modernization and improved technology projects for the irrigation districts in the Rio Conchos Basin and measures for their conveyance to the Rio Grande.

Signed at El Paso July 3, 2003.

Entered into force July 7, 2003.

TIAS

Minute 310 of the International Boundary and Water Commission: Emergency delivery of Colorado River water for use in Tijuana, Baja California.

Signed at Ciudad Juarez July 28, 2003.

Entered into force October 1, 2003.

TIAS

Minute 311 of the International Boundary and Water Commission: Recommendations for secondary treatment in Mexico of the sewage emanating from the Tijuana River area in Baja California, Mexico.

Signed at El Paso February 20, 2004.

Entered into force March 5, 2004.

TIAS

NOTE

1 Extended indefinitely by article 2 of treaty signed February 3, 1944 (59 Stat. 1219; TS 994). This convention established the International Boundary Commission, subsequently the International Boundary and Water Commission.

CHAMIZAL

See BOUNDARIES

CLAIMS

Convention for the adjustment and settlement of certain outstanding claims.

Signed at Washington November 19, 1941.

Entered into force April 2, 1942.

56 Stat. 1347; TS 980; 9 Bevans 1059; 125 UNTS 287.

CONSERVATION

Convention for the protection of migratory birds and game mammals.

Signed at Mexico February 7, 1936.

Entered into force March 15, 1937.

50 Stat. 1311; TS 912; 9 Bevans 1017; 178 LNTS 309.

Amendment

May 5, 1997.

Agreement supplementing the convention of February 7, 1936 for the protection of migratory birds and game mammals.

Exchange of notes at Mexico and Tlatelolco March 10, 1972.

Entered into force March 10, 1972.

23 UST 260; TIAS 7302.

Memorandum of understanding on cooperation in management and protection of national parks and other protected natural and cultural heritage sites, with annex.

Signed at Mexico and Washington November 30, 1988 and January 24, 1989.

Entered into force January 24, 1989.

TIAS 11599.

Extension

March 16, 1994.

CONSULS

Consular convention.

Signed at Mexico August 12, 1942.

Entered into force July 1, 1943. Exchanges of notes dated August 12 and December 11 and 12, 1942.

57 Stat. 800; TS 985; 9 Bevans 1076; 125 UNTS 301.

CULTURAL PROPERTY

Treaty of cooperation providing for the recovery and return of stolen archaeological, historical and cultural properties.

Signed at Mexico July 17, 1970.

Entered into force March 24, 1971.

22 UST 494; TIAS 7088; 791 UNTS 313.

CULTURAL RELATIONS

Agreement establishing a United States-Mexican Commission on Cultural Cooperation.

Exchange of notes at Mexico December 28, 1948 and August 30, 1949.

Entered into force August 30, 1949.

63 Stat. 2842; TIAS 2086; 9 Bevans 1264; 98 UNTS 183.

Amendments

June 15, 1972 (23 UST 925; TIAS 7360).

October 30, 1978 and January 23, 1979 (30 UST 2932; TIAS 9374; 1177 UNTS 338).

CUSTOMS

Agreement relating to the opening of a border inspection station for the international traffic of persons and goods between the United States and Mexico.

Exchange of notes at Washington July 31 and August 5, 1959.

Entered into force August 5, 1959.

10 UST 1398; TIAS 4285; 356 UNTS 3.

Agreement regarding mutual assistance between their customs administrations.

Signed at Washington June 20, 2000.

Entered into force June 20, 2000.

TIAS

DEFENSE

Agreement relating to the deposit by Mexico of ten percent of the value of military training scholarships provided by the United States.

Exchange of notes at Mexico April 4 and July 12, 1972.

Entered into force July 12, 1972; effective February 7, 1972.

23 UST 2809; TIAS 7469.

Agreement concerning the provision of training related to defense articles under the United States International Military Education and Training (IMET) Program.

Exchange of notes at Mexico August 21 and September 24, 1987.

Entered into force September 24, 1987.

NP

Agreement concerning health care for military members and their dependents.

Signed at Washington May 23, 2003.

Entered into force August 23, 2003.

TIAS

Agreement regarding the exchange of naval personnel.

Signed at Washington January 26, 2004.

Entered into force January 26, 2004.

NP

Agreement regarding the assignment of a liaison officer, with annex.

Signed at Washington and Mexico August 17 and September 11, 2004.

Entered into force September 11, 2004.

TIAS

DISASTER ASSISTANCE

Agreement on cooperation in cases of natural disasters.

Signed at Mexico January 15, 1980.

Entered into force provisionally January 15, 1980; definitively March 18, 1981.

32 UST 5714; TIAS 10013; 1241 UNTS 207.

DRIVER'S LICENSES

Memorandum of understanding relating to the recognition and validity of commercial driver's licenses and licencias federales de conductor, with annex.

Signed at Washington November 21, 1991.

Entered into force November 21, 1991.

TIAS 12442.

ECONOMIC AND TECHNICAL COOPERATION

General agreement for technical cooperation.

Exchange of notes at Mexico June 27, 1951.

Entered into force June 27, 1951.

2 UST 1243; TIAS 2273; 141 UNTS 211.

Amendments

January 21 and 22, 1952 (3 UST 4781; TIAS 2646; 200 UNTS 312).

April 13, 1954 (5 UST 1373; TIAS 3006; 233 UNTS 306).

Agreement relating to a program of industrial productivity in Mexico.

Exchange of notes at Mexico February 21 and November 15, 1961.

Entered into force November 15, 1961.

13 UST 1882; TIAS 5140; 460 UNTS 113.

Agreement providing for the designation of officials to maintain contact between Mexico and the United States in matters relating to economic and social development of the border area.

Exchange of notes at Mexico June 23, 1970.

Entered into force June 23, 1970.

21 UST 1475; TIAS 6905; 753 UNTS 275.

EDUCATION

Agreement relating to creation of a joint commission to review operation of the Abraham Lincoln and Benito Juarez scholarship funds.

Exchange of notes at Mexico September 30 and October 25, 1966.

Entered into force October 25, 1966.

17 UST 2023; TIAS 6140; 676 UNTS 11.

Agreement for the establishment of the U.S.-Mexico commission for educational and cultural exchange, with memorandum of understanding.

Signed at Monterrey November 27, 1990.

Entered into force November 27, 1990.

TIAS 11769; 2001 UNTS 143.

Amendments and extension

March 30 and May 10, 1995.

May 5, 1997 (2001 UNTS 143).

May 18, 2000.

ENERGY

Agreement on natural gas.
Announced September 21, 1979.
Entered into force September 21, 1979.
31 UST 5097; TIAS 9657; 1221 UNTS 185.

ENVIRONMENTAL COOPERATION

See also BOUNDARY WATERS; POLLUTION

Agreement on cooperation for the protection and improvement of the environment in the border area.
Signed at La Paz August 14, 1983.
Entered into force February 16, 1984.
35 UST 2916; TIAS 10827; 1352 UNTS 67.

Annexes

Agreement of cooperation for solution of the border sanitation problem at San Diego, California-Tijuana, Baja California. Signed at San Diego July 18, 1985; entered into force July 18, 1985.
TIAS 11269.

Agreement of cooperation regarding pollution of the environment along the inland international boundary by discharges of hazardous substances, with appendices. Signed at San Diego July 18, 1985; entered into force November 29, 1985.
TIAS 11269.

Agreement of cooperation regarding the transboundary shipments of hazardous wastes and hazardous substances. Signed at Washington November 12, 1986; entered into force January 29, 1987.
TIAS 11269.

Agreement of cooperation regarding transboundary air pollution caused by copper smelters along their common border. Signed at Washington January 29, 1987; entered into force January 29, 1987.
TIAS 11269.

Agreement of cooperation regarding international transport of urban air pollution, with appendix. Signed at Washington October 3, 1989, entered into force August 22, 1990.
TIAS 11269.

Amendments

May 7, 1996.
June 4, 1999.

Agreement on cooperation for the protection and improvement of the environment in the metropolitan area of Mexico City.
Signed at Washington October 3, 1989.
Entered into force August 22, 1990.
TIAS 11688; 2191 UNTS 269.

Agreement concerning the establishment of a border environment cooperation commission and a North American development bank, with annex.
Signed at Washington and Mexico November 16 and 18, 1993.
Entered into force January 1, 1994.
TIAS 12516.

Agreement for cooperation in the Global Learning and Observations to Benefit the Environment (GLOBE) Program, with appendices.
Signed at Mexico November 15, 1996.
Entered into force November 15, 1996.
TIAS 12814.

Agreement on cooperation in the management and protection of national parks and other protected natural areas.
Signed at Washington March 23, 2006.
Entered into force March 23, 2006.
TIAS

EXTRADITION

Extradition treaty, with appendix.
Signed at Mexico May 4, 1978.
Entered into force January 25, 1980.
31 UST 5059; TIAS 9656.

Protocol to the extradition treaty of May 4, 1978.
Signed at Washington November 13, 1997.
Entered into force May 21, 2001.
TIAS

FINANCE

Agreement regarding the consolidation and rescheduling of certain debts owed to, guaranteed or insured by the United States through the Export-Import Bank of the United States.
Signed at Mexico March 7, 1984.
Entered into force May 2, 1984.
35 UST 4609; TIAS 10961.

Agreement regarding the consolidation and rescheduling of certain debts owed to, guaranteed by, or insured by the United States Government and its agencies, with annexes.
Signed at Washington April 9, 1987.
Entered into force May 21, 1987.
NP

Swap agreement between the United States Treasury and the Banco de Mexico/Government of Mexico, with memorandum of understanding.
Signed at Washington and Mexico September 14, 1989.
Entered into force September 14, 1989.
TIAS

Agreement regarding the consolidation and rescheduling or refinancing of certain debts owed to, guaranteed by, or insured by the United States Government and its agencies, with annexes.
Signed at Mexico March 14, 1990.
Entered into force April 23, 1990.
NP

Swap agreement among the United States Treasury and the Banco de Mexico/Government of Mexico, with memorandum of understanding.
Signed at Washington and Mexico March 23, 1990.
Entered into force March 23, 1990.
TIAS

Exchange stabilization agreement between the United States Treasury and the Banco de Mexico/Government of Mexico.
Signed at Washington and Mexico April 26, 1994.
Entered into force April 26, 1994.
TIAS

Investment incentive agreement.
Signed at San Francisco June 9, 2003.
Entered into force June 14, 2004.
TIAS

FIRE PROTECTION

Wildfire protection agreement for the common border.
Signed at Mexico City June 4, 1999.
Entered into force June 4, 1999.
TIAS

Amendment

November 12, 2003.

HEALTH

Memorandum of understanding concerning exchange of information on, and control of, products involved in commerce between the United States and Mexico which are regulated on behalf of the United States by the Food and Drug Administration.
Signed at Mazatlan August 13, 1974.
Entered into force August 13, 1974.
28 UST 1622; TIAS 8522.

Agreement to establish a United States-Mexico Border Health Commission.

Signed at Washington and Mexico July 14 and 24, 2000.

Entered into force November 24, 2000.

TIAS

HOUSING

Agreement for cooperation in the field of housing and urban development.

Signed at Mexico February 16, 1979.

Entered into force February 16, 1979.

30 UST 5865; TIAS 9523; 1180 UNTS 255.

JUDICIAL ASSISTANCE

Procedures for mutual assistance in the administration of justice in connection with the General Tire and Rubber Company and the Firestone Tire and Rubber Company matters.

Signed at Washington June 23, 1976.

Entered into force June 23, 1976.

28 UST 2083; TIAS 8533.

Related agreements

February 23 and March 6, 1978 (29 UST 2153; TIAS 8930).

May 31 and June 1, 1978 (29 UST 3200; TIAS 9005; 1124 UNTS 433).

November 17 and December 5, 1978 (30 UST 2177; TIAS 9322).

August 25 and November 9, 1981 (33 UST 4353; TIAS 10305).

November 10 and 25, 1981 (33 UST 4353; TIAS 10305).

Treaty on cooperation for mutual legal assistance.

Signed at Mexico December 9, 1987.

Entered into force May 3, 1991.

TIAS

Mutual cooperation agreement for the exchange of information in respect to transactions in currency through financial institutions in order to combat illicit activities.

Signed at Washington October 28, 1994.

Entered into force February 3, 1995.

TIAS; 1901 UNTS 3.

Amendment

May 5, 1997.

Agreement regarding the sharing of forfeited assets.

Signed at Washington September 4, 2001.

Entered into force September 4, 2001.

TIAS

MAPPING

Memorandum concerning cooperation and mutual assistance in mapping, charting and geodesy.

Signed at Mexico July 25, 1975.

Entered into force July 25, 1975.

27 UST 1083; TIAS 8248.

MARITIME MATTERS

Treaty for the sending of vessels for purposes of assistance and salvage.

Signed at Mexico June 13, 1935.

Entered into force March 7, 1936.

49 Stat. 3359; TS 905; 9 Bevans 1015; 168 LNTS 135.

Agreement on maritime search and rescue.

Signed at Mexico August 7, 1989.

Entered into force June 25, 1990.

TIAS 11700; 1580 UNTS 385.

MIGRATORY WORKERS

Joint statement relating to the problem of illegal entry into the United States by Mexican migratory workers, with annexes.

Signed at Washington July 18, 1973.

Entered into force July 18, 1973.

26 UST 1724; TIAS 8131; 1006 UNTS 25.

NARCOTIC DRUGS

Arrangement for the direct exchange of certain information regarding the traffic in narcotic drugs.

Exchange of notes at Mexico August 5 and October 2, 1930.

Entered into force October 2, 1930.

9 Bevans 967.

Agreement concerning a grant to Mexico of reference books in the field of narcotics abuse.

Exchange of letters at Mexico June 26 and 27, 1973.

Entered into force June 27, 1973.

24 UST 1805; TIAS 7694.

Agreement relating to the provision by the United States of communications equipment to combat contraband and especially the illegal flow of narcotics across the border.

Exchange of notes at Mexico and Tlatelolco August 31, 1973.

Entered into force August 31, 1973.

24 UST 1978; TIAS 7709.

Agreement relating to the provision by the United States of technical assistance in an epidemiological study of drug abuse in Mexico.

Exchange of notes at Mexico October 26 and November 7, 1973.

Entered into force November 7, 1973.

24 UST 2245; TIAS 7742; 938 UNTS 367.

Agreement concerning the provision of four helicopters and related assistance by the United States to help Mexico in curbing traffic in illegal narcotics.

Exchange of letters at Mexico December 3, 1973.

Entered into force December 3, 1973.

25 UST 1694; TIAS 7906.

Amendments

December 21, 1973 (25 UST 1698; TIAS 7906).

June 24, 1974 (25 UST 1700; TIAS 7906).

Agreement providing additional helicopters and related assistance to Mexico in support of its efforts to curb production and traffic in illegal narcotics.

Exchange of letters at Mexico February 1, 1974.

Entered into force February 1, 1974.

25 UST 1704; TIAS 7907.

Amendments

June 24, 1974 (25 UST 1708; TIAS 7907).

December 4, 1974 (25 UST 3172; TIAS 7983).

Agreement relating to the provision of support by the United States for a multi-spectral aerial photographic system capable of detecting opium poppy cultivation, with annexes.

Exchange of letters at Mexico June 10 and 24, 1974.

Entered into force June 24, 1974.

25 UST 1286; TIAS 7863.

Amendment

September 19, 1974 (25 UST 2963; TIAS 7956).

Agreement providing additional helicopters and related assistance to Mexico in support of its efforts to curb illegal production and traffic in narcotics.

Exchange of letters at Mexico November 1, 1974.

Entered into force November 1, 1974.

25 UST 2956; TIAS 7955.

Agreement relating to a training program for Mexican helicopter pilots and mechanics as part of U.S.-Mexican cooperative efforts to reduce traffic in illegal narcotics.

Exchange of letters at Mexico September 30, 1974.

Entered into force September 30, 1974.

25 UST 3166; TIAS 7982; 991 UNTS 367.

Agreement relating to the provision of assistance to Mexico in narcotics enforcement training activities.

Exchange of letters at Mexico December 4, 1974.

Entered into force December 4, 1974.

25 UST 3176; TIAS 7984; 991 UNTS 373.

Agreement relating to cooperative arrangements to support Mexican efforts to curb the illegal traffic in narcotics.

Exchange of letters at Mexico December 11, 1974.

Entered into force December 11, 1974.

26 UST 1274; TIAS 8108.

Amendments

February 24, 1975 (26 UST 1285; TIAS 8108).

March 20, 1975 (26 UST 1289; TIAS 8108).

May 18, 1976 (27 UST 1977; TIAS 8295).

Agreement concerning the provision by the United States of four mobile interdiction systems for use in curbing the illicit flow of narcotic substances through Mexico.

Exchange of letters at Mexico February 24, 1975.

Entered into force February 24, 1975.

26 UST 414; TIAS 8041; 991 UNTS 379.

Agreement relating to the provision of equipment and training by the United States to support U.S.-Mexican efforts to curb illegal narcotics traffic.

Exchange of letters at Mexico May 29, 1975.

Entered into force May 29, 1975.

26 UST 1633; TIAS 8123; 1006 UNTS 37.

Agreement relating to the provision of equipment and training by the United States to support U.S.-Mexican efforts to curb illegal narcotics traffic.

Exchange of letters at Mexico June 25, 1975.

Entered into force June 25, 1975.

26 UST 1659; TIAS 8125; 1006 UNTS 43.

Agreement to indemnify and safeguard the United States Government, its personnel and contractors for liability arising out of aircraft operations training in support of the cooperative program to curb illegal narcotics traffic.

Exchange of letters at Mexico September 12, 1975.

Entered into force September 12, 1975.

27 UST 1985; TIAS 8296.

Amendment

August 13, 1976 (28 UST 8241; TIAS 8758).

Agreement relating to the provision of two helicopters by the United States to support U.S.-Mexican efforts to curb the production and traffic in illegal narcotics.

Exchange of letters at Mexico October 24 and 29, 1975.

Entered into force October 29, 1975.

27 UST 1996; TIAS 8298.

Agreement relating to the provision of aircraft by the United States to support U.S.-Mexican efforts to curb the illegal production and traffic in narcotics.

Exchange of letters at Mexico January 29, 1976.

Entered into force January 29, 1976.

27 UST 4261; TIAS 8449.

Agreement relating to the provision of supplies, equipment, and services by the United States to support U.S.-Mexican efforts to curb the illegal production and traffic in narcotics.

Exchange of letters at Mexico February 4, 1976.

Entered into force February 4, 1976.

27 UST 1973; TIAS 8294.

Amendment

May 18, 1976 (27 UST 1977; TIAS 8295).

Agreement relating to additional cooperative arrangements to curb illegal traffic in narcotics.

Exchange of letters at Mexico June 30, 1976.

Entered into force June 30, 1976.

27 UST 1990; TIAS 8297.

Agreement relating to the provision of additional equipment, material and technical support by the United States to curb illegal traffic in narcotics.

Exchange of letters at Mexico August 9, 1976.

Entered into force August 9, 1976.

27 UST 3937; TIAS 8411; 1059 UNTS 123.

Agreement relating to the provision of additional assistance by the United States to curb illegal traffic in narcotics and amending the agreements of August 9, 1976 and May 18, 1976.

Exchange of letters at Mexico September 30, 1976.

Entered into force September 30, 1976.

27 UST 4306; TIAS 8451.

Agreement relating to additional cooperative arrangements to curb the illegal production and traffic in narcotics.

Exchange of letters at Mexico February 16, 1977.

Entered into force February 16, 1977.

29 UST 5334; TIAS 9113; 1148 UNTS 2.

Extension and amendments

July 28, 1977 (29 UST 5334; TIAS 9113; 1148 UNTS 8).

December 19, 1977 (29 UST 5347; TIAS 9114; 1148 UNTS 11).

January 3, 1978 (29 UST 5352; TIAS 9115; 1148 UNTS 14).

Agreement relating to additional cooperative arrangements to curb the illegal traffic in narcotics.

Exchange of letters at Mexico March 8, 1977.

Entered into force March 8, 1977.

29 UST 268; TIAS 8810.

Agreement relating to additional cooperative arrangements to curb the illegal traffic in narcotics, with annexes.

Exchange of notes at Mexico June 2, 1977.

Entered into force June 2, 1977.

29 UST 2483; TIAS 8952.

Amendments

September 28, 1977 (29 UST 2496; TIAS 8952).

July 20 and 26, 1978 (30 UST 1285; TIAS 9251; 1153 UNTS 454).

August 24, 1978 (30 UST 1289; TIAS 9251; 1153 UNTS 457).

January 15, 1979 (30 UST 1294; TIAS 9251; 1153 UNTS 460).

September 27 and 28, 1979 (31 UST 4760; TIAS 9637; 1202 UNTS 416).

December 5, 1979 (31 UST 5913; TIAS 9695; 1221 UNTS 376).

April 11, 1980 (32 UST 992; TIAS 9749; 1221 UNTS 379).

November 6, 1980 (32 UST 4157; TIAS 9933; 1266 UNTS 326).

January 2, 1981 (32 UST 4525; TIAS 9963; 1266 UNTS 329).

August 19, 1981 (33 UST 3683; TIAS 10249; 1541 UNTS 433).

October 14, 1981 (33 UST 4081; TIAS 10285; 1549 UNTS 463).

December 4, 1981 (33 UST 4406; TIAS 10310; 1549 UNTS 466).

January 6 and 8, 1982 (34 UST 35; TIAS 10336).

March 15 and 17, 1982 (34 UST 350; TIAS 10360; 1556 UNTS 386).

August 6, 1982 (34 UST 1449; TIAS 10430; 1736 UNTS 365).

November 8, 1982 (TIAS 10582; 1871 UNTS 502).

February 9, 1983 (TIAS 10657; 2001 UNTS 417).

May 12 and 27, 1983 (TIAS 10657; 2001 UNTS 422).

November 10, 1983 (35 UST 4104; TIAS 10907; 2016 UNTS 67).

January 4, 1984 (TIAS 11124).

May 29, 1984 (TIAS 11124).

October 29, 1984 (TIAS 11124).

February 4, 1985.

April 3, 1985.

September 13 and 25, 1985.

November 13 and 29, 1985.

November 29 and December 2, 1985.

January 13 and March 12, 1986 (TIAS 11517).

March 13 and April 7, 1986 (TIAS 11517).

June 3 and July 1, 1986 (TIAS 11517).

November 3 and December 18, 1986 (TIAS 11517).

July 14 and 28, 1987 (TIAS 11561).

August 7 and 28, 1987 (TIAS 11561).

August 10 and 28, 1987 (TIAS 11561).

December 22, 1987 and February 11, 1988 (TIAS 11652; 2204 UNTS 535).

Agreement relating to additional cooperative arrangements to curb the illegal traffic in narcotics.

Exchange of letters at Mexico July 29, 1977.

Entered into force July 29, 1977.

29 UST 1509; TIAS 8895.

Agreement relating to additional cooperative arrangements to curb the illegal traffic in narcotics.

Exchange of letters at Mexico August 5, 1977.

Entered into force August 5, 1977.

29 UST 2500; TIAS 8953.

Amendment

September 29, 1977 (29 UST 2505; TIAS 8953).

Agreement relating to computerization of information in support of programs against illegal narcotics production and traffic.

Exchange of letters at Mexico September 6, 1977.

Entered into force September 6, 1977.

29 UST 2551; TIAS 8955.

Agreement relating to the development of telecommunications capability to support the narcotics control effort.

Exchange of letters at Mexico September 7, 1977.

Entered into force September 7, 1977.

29 UST 1994; TIAS 8915.

Agreement concerning training for helicopter pilots as part of the cooperative effort to reduce illegal narcotics traffic.

Exchange of letters at Mexico April 3, 1978.

Entered into force April 3, 1978.

30 UST 1007; TIAS 9234; 1152 UNTS 235.

Agreement relating to additional cooperative arrangements to curb the illegal production and traffic in narcotics.

Exchange of letters at Mexico May 15, 1978.

Entered into force May 15, 1978.

30 UST 1270; TIAS 9250; 1152 UNTS 241.

Amendments

January 5, 1979 (30 UST 1276; TIAS 9250; 1152 UNTS 245).

February 7, 1979 (30 UST 1280; TIAS 9250; 1152 UNTS 248).

July 23, 1979 (30 UST 6186; TIAS 9544; 1179 UNTS 414).

Agreement relating to additional cooperative arrangements to curb the illegal traffic in narcotics.

Exchange of letters at Mexico May 16, 1978.

Entered into force May 16, 1978.

30 UST 1299; TIAS 9252; 1152 UNTS 257.

Amendments

January 8, 1979 (30 UST 1305; TIAS 9252; 1152 UNTS 261).

July 24, 1979 (30 UST 6197; TIAS 9546; 1179 UNTS 419).

Agreement concerning an illicit crop detection system to be used in curbing the illegal traffic in narcotics.

Exchange of letters at Mexico May 22, 1978.

Entered into force May 22, 1978.

30 UST 1237; TIAS 9248; 1152 UNTS 269.

Amendments

September 26, 1978 (30 UST 1247; TIAS 9248; 1152 UNTS 275).

January 12, 1979 (30 UST 1251; TIAS 9248; 1152 UNTS 278).

December 6, 1979 (31 UST 5904; TIAS 9693; 1221 UNTS 449).

January 27, 1981 (33 UST 990; TIAS 10082; 1274 UNTS 411).

Agreement relating to additional cooperative arrangements to curb the illegal traffic in narcotics.

Exchange of letters at Mexico May 23, 1978.

Entered into force May 23, 1978.

30 UST 1255; TIAS 9249; 1152 UNTS 289.

Amendments

July 11 and 13, 1978 (30 UST 1262; TIAS 9249; 1152 UNTS 293).

January 11, 1979 (30 UST 1266; TIAS 9249; 1152 UNTS 296).

Agreement relating to additional cooperative arrangements to curb the illegal traffic in narcotics.

Exchange of letters at Mexico May 24, 1978.

Entered into force May 24, 1978.

30 UST 1488; TIAS 9258; 1148 UNTS 26.

Amendments

January 9, 1979 (30 UST 1494; TIAS 9258; 1148 UNTS 31).

April 20, 1979 (30 UST 1498; TIAS 9258; 1148 UNTS 34).

Agreement relating to the provision and utilization of aircraft to curb the illegal traffic in narcotics.

Exchange of letters at Mexico August 23, 1978.

Entered into force August 23, 1978.

30 UST 1319; TIAS 9254; 1152 UNTS 305.

Amendment

July 26, 1979 (30 UST 6191; TIAS 9545; 1179 UNTS 424).

Agreement relating to computerization of information in support of programs against illegal narcotics production and traffic.

Exchange of letters at Mexico August 25, 1978.

Entered into force August 25, 1978.

30 UST 1309; TIAS 9253; 1152 UNTS 311.

Amendment

January 10, 1979 (30 UST 1315; TIAS 9253; 1152 UNTS 315).

Agreement concerning the provision of additional technical assistance to curb the illegal traffic in narcotics.

Exchange of letters at Mexico September 28, 1978.

Entered into force September 28, 1978.

30 UST 1729; TIAS 9282; 1152 UNTS 323.

Agreement relating to salary supplements to personnel dedicated to opium poppy eradication and narcotics interdiction.

Exchange of letters at Mexico December 3, 1979.

Entered into force December 3, 1979.

31 UST 5918; TIAS 9696; 1221 UNTS 199.

Amendments

April 25, 1980 (32 UST 1324; TIAS 9772; 1221 UNTS 203).

October 10, 1980 (32 UST 2901; TIAS 9884; 1274 UNTS 436).

December 29, 1981 (33 UST 4679; TIAS 10329).

Agreement relating to additional cooperative arrangements to curb the illegal traffic in narcotics.

Exchange of letters at Mexico April 7, 1980.

Entered into force April 7, 1980.

32 UST 997; TIAS 9750.

Agreement relating to additional cooperative arrangements to curb the illegal traffic in narcotics.

Exchange of letters at Mexico July 25, 1980.

Entered into force July 25, 1980.

32 UST 2105; TIAS 9822.

Amendments

December 2, 1980 (33 UST 1217; TIAS 10106; 1285 UNTS 347).

March 31, 1981 (33 UST 1535; TIAS 10129).

April 2, 1982 (TIAS 10519).

May 17, 1984 (TIAS 11122).

September 25 and October 10, 1984 (TIAS 11122).

April 2, 1985 (TIAS 11346; 2194 UNTS 483).

July 24 and August 20, 1985 (TIAS 11347; 2194 UNTS 490).

Agreement relating to additional cooperative arrangements to curb the illegal traffic in narcotics.

Exchange of letters at Mexico January 3, 1981.

Entered into force January 3, 1981.

33 UST 823; TIAS 10064; 1267 UNTS 181.

Agreement relating to additional cooperative arrangements to curb the illegal traffic in narcotics.

Exchange of letters at Mexico April 8, 1981.

Entered into force April 8, 1981.

33 UST 1757; TIAS 10142.

Agreement relating to additional cooperative arrangements to curb the illegal traffic in narcotics.

Exchange of letters at Mexico March 29, 1983.

Entered into force March 29, 1983.

TIAS 10675; 2005 UNTS 155.

Amendments

April 25, 1985 (TIAS 11348).

November 25 and 29, 1985 (TIAS 11349).

January 29 and March 12, 1986 (TIAS 11348).

August 25 and September 29, 1986 (TIAS 11349).

September 27 and 30, 1986 (TIAS 12090).

March 16 and April 14, 1987 (TIAS 11548).

Agreement relating to additional cooperative arrangements to curb the illegal traffic in narcotics.

Exchange of letters at Mexico November 5, 1984.

Entered into force November 5, 1984.

TIAS 11125.

Agreement on cooperation in combatting narcotics trafficking and drug dependency.

Signed at Mexico February 23, 1989.

Entered into force July 30, 1990.

TIAS 11604; 2192 UNTS 107.

PEACE CORPS

Agreement to establish a Program of the Peace Corps in Mexico.

Signed at Washington November 12, 2003.

Entered into force November 12, 2003.

TIAS

Agreement to establish a program of the Peace Corps in Mexico in the areas of environment and natural resources.

Signed at Mexico City June 13, 2006.

Entered into force June 13, 2006.

TIAS

PEACE TREATIES

Treaty of peace, friendship, limits, and settlement.[1]

Signed at Guadalupe Hidalgo February 2, 1848.

Entered into force May 30, 1848.

9 Stat. 922; TS 207; 9 Bevans 791.

NOTE

1 Articles V, VI and VII were amended and article XI was abrogated by the Gadsden treaty, signed December 30, 1853 (10 Stat. 1031; TS 208). Articles II-IV, XII-XV, and XVII-XX have been executed.

POLICE EQUIPMENT

Agreement relating to the transfer of equipment for the use of the national police force of Mexico.

Exchange of notes at Washington June 26, 1961.

Entered into force June 26, 1961.

12 UST 1063; TIAS 4810; 413 UNTS 229.

POLLUTION

See also BOUNDARY WATERS; ENVIRONMENTAL COOPERATION

Agreement of cooperation regarding pollution of the marine environment by discharges of hydrocarbons and other hazardous substances, with annexes.

Signed at Mexico July 24, 1980.

Entered into force provisionally July 24, 1980; definitively March 30, 1981.

32 UST 5899; TIAS 10021; 1241 UNTS 225.

POSTAL MATTERS

International express mail agreement, with detailed regulations, as amended by declaration of July 28, 1987.

Signed at Mexico February 13, 1981.

Entered into force September 1, 1987.

TIAS 11005; 2023 UNTS 321.

Postal money order agreement.

Signed at Mexico and Washington May 31 and June 17, 1988.

Entered into force August 1, 1988.

TIAS 11584.

PRISONER TRANSFER

Treaty on the execution of penal sentences.

Signed at Mexico November 25, 1976.

Entered into force November 30, 1977.

28 UST 7399; TIAS 8718.

PUBLICATIONS

Agreement relating to the exchange of official journals and parliamentary papers.

Exchange of notes at Mexico September 9 and 24, 1937.

Entered into force September 24, 1937.

51 Stat. 311; EAS 108; 9 Bevans 1025; 185 LNTS 23.

Agreement relating to the exchange of official publications.

Exchange of notes at Washington June 3 and August 29, 1938.

Entered into force September 1, 1938.

53 Stat. 1977; EAS 134; 9 Bevans 1028; 195 LNTS 359.

SATELLITES

Agreement concerning the transmission and reception of signals from satellites for the provision of satellite services to users in the United States and Mexico.

Signed at Mexico April 28, 1996.

Entered into force November 6, 1996.

TIAS

Protocol concerning the transmission and reception of signals from satellites for the provision of direct-to-home satellite services in the United States and Mexico, with exchange of letters.

Signed at Washington November 8, 1996.

Entered into force November 11, 1996.

TIAS

Protocol concerning the transmission and reception of signals from satellites for the provision of mobile-satellite services and associated feeder links in the United States of America and the United Mexican States, with appendix.

Signed at Mexico City December 21, 1998.

Entered into force December 21, 1998.

TIAS

SCIENTIFIC COOPERATION

Agreement for scientific and technical cooperation.

Exchange of notes at Washington June 15, 1972.

Entered into force June 15, 1972.

23 UST 934; TIAS 7362.

Amendment

August 10 and September 22, 1994 (TIAS 12566).

Memorandum of understanding on scientific and technical cooperation in the mapping and earth sciences, with annex.

Signed at Washington August 12, 1992.

Entered into force August 12, 1992.

TIAS 11961.

Memorandum of understanding concerning scientific and technical cooperation in the earth and mapping sciences, with annexes.

Signed at Mexico May 9, 1994.

Entered into force May 9, 1994.

TIAS 12180.

Memorandum of understanding concerning scientific and technical cooperation in the earth and mapping sciences.

Signed at Mexico November 29, 1994.

Entered into force November 29, 1994.

TIAS 12583.

Memorandum of understanding concerning scientific and technical cooperation on biological data and information, with annex.

Signed at Washington May 16, 1995.

Entered into force May 16, 1995.

TIAS 12650.

Memorandum of understanding concerning scientific and technical cooperation in the earth and mapping sciences, with annex.

Signed at Mexico May 7, 1996.

Entered into force May 7, 1996.

TIAS 12751.

Memorandum of cooperation in epidemiology.

Signed at Mexico City June 4, 1999.

Entered into force June 4, 1999.

TIAS

SOCIAL SECURITY

Agreement relating to the payment of social security benefits.

Exchange of notes at Mexico and Tlatelolco March 27, 1968.

Entered into force March 27, 1968.

24 UST 1045; TIAS 7620.

SPACE COOPERATION

Agreement for participation by Mexican scientists in certain programs of space research by the National Aeronautics and Space Administration.

Exchange of notes at Mexico February 27, 1965.

Entered into force February 27, 1965.

16 UST 620; TIAS 5783; 546 UNTS 135.

STOLEN PROPERTY

See also CULTURAL PROPERTY

Convention for the recovery and return of stolen or embezzled vehicles and aircraft.

Signed at Washington January 15, 1981.

Entered into force June 28, 1983.

TIAS 10653.

TAXATION

Agreement for the exchange of information with respect to taxes.

Signed at Washington November 9, 1989.

Entered into force January 18, 1990.

TIAS 12404.

Convention for the avoidance of double taxation and the prevention of fiscal evasion with respect to taxes on income, with protocol.[1]

Signed at Washington September 18, 1992.

Entered into force December 28, 1993.

TIAS

Additional protocol that modifies the convention of September 18, 1992, for the avoidance of double taxation and the prevention of fiscal evasion with respect to taxes on income.

Signed at Mexico September 8, 1994.

Entered into force October 26, 1995.

TIAS

Protocol that modifies the agreement of November 9, 1989, for the exchange of information with respect to taxes.

Signed at Mexico September 8, 1994.

Entered into force October 26, 1995.

TIAS 12404.

Second additional protocol that modifies the convention of September 18, 1992, as amended, for the avoidance of double taxation and the prevention of fiscal evasion with respect to taxes on income.

Signed at Mexico City November 26, 2002.

Entered into force July 3, 2003.

TIAS

NOTE

1 With understandings.

TELECOMMUNICATION

Arrangement for radio communications between amateur stations on behalf of third parties.

Exchange of notes at Mexico July 31, 1959.

Entered into force August 30, 1959.

10 UST 1449; TIAS 4295; 357 UNTS 187.

Agreement relating to the assignment and use of television channels along the United States-Mexican border.

Exchange of notes at Mexico April 18, 1962.

Entered into force April 18, 1962.

13 UST 997; TIAS 5043; 452 UNTS 3.

Amendments

August 20, 1975 (26 UST 2700; TIAS 8185; 1052 UNTS 374).

August 23 and September 4, 1979 (31 UST 4810; TIAS 9641).

January 22 and April 7, 1980 (32 UST 975; TIAS 9746; 1220 UNTS 327).

December 22, 1981 and August 17, 1982 (34 UST 1708; TIAS 10447; 1736 UNTS 316).

October 12, November 13, 1984, April 8 and 25, 1985.

September 14 and 26, 1988 (1540 UNTS 404).

Agreement concerning frequency modulation broadcasting in the 88 to 108 MHz band with annexes and related notes.

Signed at Washington November 9, 1972.

Entered into force August 9, 1973.

24 UST 1815; TIAS 7697.

Amendments

March 20 and November 9, 1978 (30 UST 3927; TIAS 9436; 1169 UNTS 368).

February 2 and April 24, 1979 (30 UST 3967; TIAS 9436; 1169 UNTS 382).

June 4 and August 1, 1979 (31 UST 4841; TIAS 9647).

October 2 and 11, 1979 (31 UST 4841; TIAS 9647).

September 5, 1979 and January 23, 1980 (31 UST 4841; TIAS 9647).

February 18 and May 20, 1981 (33 UST 1959; TIAS 10159).

March 3 and May 21, 1981 (33 UST 3330; TIAS 10234).

May 22 and August 4, 1981 (33 UST 3333; TIAS 10234).

August 19 and October 26, 1981 (33 UST 3336; TIAS 10234).

October 7 and December 9, 1981 (33 UST 3339; TIAS 10234).

March 18 and July 2, 1982 (34 UST 1857; TIAS 10466; 1751 UNTS 428).

August 11 and September 8, 1982 (34 UST 1857; TIAS 10466; 1751 UNTS 433).

February 14 and April 8, 1983 (TIAS 10688; 2005 UNTS 453).

October 13, 1982 and June 7, 1983.

February 25 and June 7, 1983.

July 21 and September 22, 1983 (35 UST 2323; TIAS 10792; 2011 UNTS 210).

June 24, 1983, January 10, February 6, February 27, April 11, and June 12, 1984.

July 6 and September 10, 1984 (TIAS 11231).

November 6 and December 7, 1984 (TIAS 11231).

December 21, 1984 and March 18, 1985 (TIAS 11268).

September 7, 1984, February 28, March 21 and May 14, 1985 (TIAS 11344).

Agreement relating to assignments and usage of television broadcasting channels in the frequency range 470-806 MHz (channels 14-69) along the United States-Mexico border.

Signed at Mexico June 18, 1982.

Entered into force January 17, 1983.

TIAS 10535.

Amendments

October 31, 1984 and April 8, 1985 (TIAS 11237).

June 22 and October 19, 1988 (TIAS 12426).

Agreement relating to the AM broadcasting service in the medium frequency band, with annexes.

Signed at Mexico August 28, 1986.

Entered into force April 27, 1987.

TIAS

Agreement regarding an earth station coordination procedure, with annex.

Signed at Chestertown July 2, 1991.

Entered into force February 25, 1993.

TIAS 12434; 1733 UNTS 215.

Administrative arrangement concerning frequencies used by the International Boundary and Water Commission, with annex.

Signed at Queretaro August 11, 1992.

Entered into force August 11, 1992.

TIAS 12472.

Agreement relating to the FM broadcasting service in the band 88–108 MHz, with annexes.

Signed at Queretaro August 11, 1992.

Entered into force June 2, 1995.

TIAS 12474.

Agreement for the use of the band 1605 to 1705 KHz in the AM broadcasting service, with annexes.

Signed at Queretaro August 11, 1992.

Entered into force May 30, 1995.

TIAS 12473.

Agreement on the use of the 17.7–17.8 GHz band.

Signed at Washington June 21, 1993.

Entered into force March 8, 1994.

TIAS; 1792 UNTS 303.

Agreement concerning the allocation and use of frequency bands by terrestrial non-broadcasting radiocommunication services along the common border, with annexes.

Signed at Williamsburg June 16, 1994.

Entered into force June 2, 1995.

TIAS 12548.

Protocol concerning the allocation and use of the bands 901–902 MHz, 930–931 MHz and 940–941 MHz bands for personal communications services along the common border, with appendices.

Signed at Washington May 16, 1995.

Entered into force May 16, 1995.

TIAS 12651.

Protocol concerning the use of the band 1850–1990 MHz for personal communications services along the common border.

Signed at Washington May 16, 1995.

Entered into force May 16, 1995.

TIAS 12652.

Protocol concerning the use of bands allocated to the aeronautical radionavigation and aeronautical communications services along the common border, with appendices.

Signed at Morelia, Michoacan April 26, 1996.

Entered into force April 26, 1996.

TIAS 12745.

Protocol concerning use of the 929–930 MHz and 931–932 MHz bands for paging services along the common border, with appendices and letter of understanding.

Signed at Washington February 27, 1997.

Entered into force February 27, 1997.

TIAS

Memorandum of understanding for the use of radio frequencies, coordination and cooperation for emergency purposes, with annexes.

Signed at Washington and Mexico City December 9, 1998.

Entered into force December 9, 1998.

TIAS

Agreement concerning the use of the 2310-2360 MHz band, with appendices.

Signed at Mexico City July 24, 2000.

Entered into force January 25, 2001.

TIAS

Protocol concerning the allotment and use of the 380-399.9 MHz band for fixed and mobile terrestrial non-broadcasting services along the common border, with appendices.

Signed at Mexico City July 27, 2005.

Entered into force July 27, 2005.

TIAS

Amendment

July 17, 2006.

Protocol concerning the allotment and use of the 406.1-420 MHz band for fixed and mobile services along the common border, with appendices.

Signed at Mexico City July 27, 2005.

Entered into force July 27, 2005.

TIAS

Protocol concerning the allotment and use of the 138-144 MHz band for terrestrial non-broadcasting radio communication services along the common border, with appendices.

Signed at Washington July 17, 2006.

Entered into force July 17, 2006.

TIAS

Protocol concerning the allotment and use of the 698-806 MHz band for terrestrial non-broadcasting radiocommunication services along the common border, with appendices.

Signed at Mexico and Antalya November 1 and 8, 2006.

Entered into force November 8, 2006.

TIAS

TOURISM

Agreement on the development and facilitation of tourism.

Signed at Washington October 3, 1989.

Entered into force August 22, 1990.

TIAS 12403.

TRADE AND COMMERCE

Agreement relating to tariff concessions on certain lead products.

Exchange of letters at Mexico October 31 and November 8, 1979.

Entered into force November 8, 1979; effective January 1, 1980.

TIAS 10568; 1871 UNTS 61.

Related agreement

August 5, 1980 (TIAS 10568; 1871 UNTS 61).

Understanding regarding subsidies and countervailing duties.

Signed at Washington April 23, 1985.

Entered into force April 23, 1985.

TIAS

Understanding concerning a framework of principles and procedures for consultations regarding trade and investment relations, with agenda.

Signed at Mexico November 6, 1987.

Entered into force November 6, 1987.

TIAS 12395.

Agreement concerning trade in cotton, wool, and man-made fiber textiles and textile products, with annexes.

Signed at Mazatlan February 13, 1988.

Entered into force February 13, 1988; effective January 1, 1988.

NP

Amendments and extension

August 26 and September 7, 1988 (NP).

October 25 and November 17, 1988 (NP).

November 17 and 23, 1988 (NP).

November 7, 1988 and January 3, 1989 (NP).

October 2 and November 1, 1989 (NP).

April 20, July 25 and August 1, 1990 (NP).

July 19 and August 3, 1990 (NP).

October 31 and November 13, 19 and 21, 1991 (NP).

Agreement on steel trade liberalization, with appendices.

Signed at Washington October 3, 1989.

Entered into force October 3, 1989.

TIAS

Agreement regarding the application of their competition laws.

Signed at Mexico July 11, 2000.

Entered into force July 11, 2000.

TIAS

Memorandum of understanding regarding areas of food and agricultural trade, with annex.

Signed at Washington and Mexico March 28 and April 1 and 3, 2002.

Entered into force April 3, 2002.

TIAS

Agreement on the application by Mexico of a North American Free Trade Agreement safeguard measure on certain poultry products.

Exchange of letters at Mexico City and Washington July 24 and 25, 2003.

Entered into force July 25, 2003.

TIAS

Agreement on trade on tequila, with annex.

Signed at Washington January 17, 2006.

Entered into force January 17, 2006.

TIAS

TRANSPORTATION

Memorandum of understanding concerning research cooperation in the field of transportation.

Signed at Merida November 16, 1972.

Entered into force November 16, 1972.

30 UST 823; TIAS 9221.

VISAS

Agreement on documentation for nonimmigrants traveling between the United States and Mexico.

Exchange of notes at Mexico October 28 and November 10 and 12, 1953.

Entered into force November 12, 1953.

5 UST 174; TIAS 2912; 224 UNTS 187.

Amendment

May 29, 1974 (25 UST 1172; TIAS 7847).

WEATHER STATIONS

Agreement for a cooperative meteorological observation program in Mexico, with memorandum of understanding.

Exchange of notes at Mexico and Tlatelolco July 31, 1970.

Entered into force August 1, 1970.

21 UST 1978; TIAS 6941; 756 UNTS 117.

Amendment and extension

December 10, 2001 and February 27, 2002.

MICRONESIA

A letter of November 2, 1995, from the Government of the Federated States of Micronesia to the Secretary-General of the United Nations refers to a letter of May 22, 1992, "... containing a declaration setting out the position of the Government of the Federated States of Micronesia (FSM) with regard to international agreements entered into by the United States of America and made applicable to the FSM pursuant to the United Nations Trusteeship Agreement for the former Japanese Mandated Islands."

"The Declaration stated that as to bilateral treaties validly concluded by the United States on behalf of the FSM, or validly applied or extended by the former to the latter before 3 November 1986, the Government of the FSM would examine each such treaty and communicate its views to the other State Party concerned. The Declaration also stated that the Government of the FSM would continue to observe the terms of each treaty which validly so applied and was not inconsistent with the letter or the spirit of the Constitution of the FSM, provisionally and on a basis of reciprocity. The period of examination was to extend until 3 November 1995, except in the case of any treaty in respect of which an earlier statement of views was or had been made. At the expiration of this period, the Government of the FSM would consider such of these treaties that could not by the application of the rules of customary international law be regarded as otherwise surviving, as having terminated."

The letter of November 2, 1995, extends "... the period of examination of the bilateral treaties indicated above for two additional years, or until 3 November 1997."

"With regard to multilateral treaties previously applied, the Declaration of 22 May 1992 stated that the Government of the FSM intends to review each of them individually and to communicate to the depositary in each case what steps it would take, whether by way of confirmation of termination or confirmation of succession or accession. During such period of review, any party to a multilateral treaty that had been validly applied or extended to the Federated States of Micronesia prior to 3 November 1986, and was not inconsistent with the letter or spirit of the Constitution of the FSM, may, on the basis of reciprocity, rely as against the FSM on the terms of such treaty."

AGRICULTURE

Agreement concerning technical assistance in soil and water conservation.

Signed at Palikir April 20, 1990.

Entered into force April 20, 1990.

TIAS 12221.

AVIATION

Memorandum of agreement concerning assistance in developing and modernizing Micronesia's civil aviation infrastructure.

Signed at Washington and Kolonia October 30, 1989 and January 10, 1990.

Entered into force January 10, 1990.

TIAS 12408.

COMPACT OF FREE ASSOCIATION

Agreement for the implementation of the Compact of Free Association between the Government of the United States and the Government of the Federated States of Micronesia (Title II, PL 99-239), with related agreements.

Signed at Washington October 24, 1986.

Entered into force October 24, 1986; effective November 3, 1986.

TIAS

Amendment

March 9, 1988 (TIAS 11660).

Agreement amending the Compact of Free Association of October 1, 1982, as amended.

Signed at Palikir May 14, 2003.

Entered into force June 25, 2004.

TIAS

Federal programs and services agreement, with annex.

Signed at Palikir May 14, 2003.

Entered into force June 25, 2004.

TIAS

Agreement concerning procedures for the implementation of United States economic assistance provided in the Compact of Free Association, as amended, with annex.

Signed at Palikir May 14, 2003.

Entered into force June 25, 2004.

TIAS

Agreement regarding protections for citizens of the Republic of the Federated States of Micronesia seeking to engage in employment in the United States pursuant to recruitment or other placement services.

Signed at Palikir May 14, 2003.

Entered into force June 25, 2004.

TIAS

Agreement on extradition, mutual assistance in law enforcement matters and penal sanctions, with agreed minute.

Signed at Palikir May 14, 2003.

Entered into force June 25, 2004; effective November 3, 1986.

TIAS

Agreement regarding the military use and operating rights of the Government of the United States in the Federated States of Micronesia, with annex.

Signed at Palikir May 14, 2003.

Entered into force June 25, 2004.

TIAS

Status of forces agreement, with agreed minutes.

Signed at Palikir May 14, 2003.

Entered into force June 25, 2004.

TIAS

Agreement implementing section 215 and section 216 of the Compact, as amended, regarding a trust fund.

Signed at Palikir May 14, 2003.

Entered into force June 25, 2004.

TIAS

DEFENSE

Agreement regarding grants under the Foreign Assistance Act of 1961, as amended, and the furnishing of defense articles, related training, and other defense services from the United States of America to the Government of the Federated States of Micronesia.

Exchange of notes at Kolonia and Pohnpei November 6, 2001 and March 14, 2002.

Entered into force March 14, 2002.

TIAS

EDUCATION

Agreement regarding augmentation of educational assistance.

Signed at Washington August 19, 1987.

Entered into force August 19, 1987.

TIAS 11277.

ENVIRONMENTAL COOPERATION

Agreement for cooperation in the Global Learning and Observations to Benefit the Environment (GLOBE) Program, with appendices.

Signed at Kolonia November 7, 1997.

Entered into force November 7, 1997.

TIAS

FINANCE

Agreement relating to investment guaranties.

Exchange of notes at Kolonia February 13 and March 3, 1988.

Entered into force March 3, 1988.

TIAS 12047.

INTERNATIONAL CRIMINAL COURT

Agreement regarding the surrender of persons to the International Criminal Court.

Signed at Washington September 24, 2002.

Entered into force June 30, 2003.

TIAS

MARITIME MATTERS

Maritime search and rescue agreement.

Signed at Honolulu June 10, 1988.

Entered into force June 10, 1988.

TIAS 11586; 2192 UNTS 195.

RELATIONS

Agreement relating to diplomatic relations, with related notes.

Exchange of notes at Washington August 23 and 24, 1989.

Entered into force August 24, 1989.

TIAS 11891.

TELECOMMUNICATION

Agreement relating to radio communications between amateur stations on behalf of third parties.

Exchange of notes at Kolonia April 4 and September 12, 1989.

Entered into force October 12, 1989.

TIAS 12401.

Agreement terminating the agreement of June 25, 1983, regarding the provision of telecommunication services.

Exchange of notes at Kolonia and Palikir May 28 and June 7, 1993.

Entered into force June 7, 1993.

TIAS 12501.

MOLDOVA

For agreements prior to December 31, 1991, see UNION OF SOVIET SOCIALIST REPUBLICS.

DEFENSE

Agreement regarding grants under the Foreign Assistance Act of 1961, as amended, and the furnishing of defense articles, related training and other defense services from the United States to Moldova.

Exchange of notes at Chisinau October 9 and 10, 1997.

Entered into force October 10, 1997.

TIAS

Acquisition and cross-servicing agreement, with annexes.

Signed at Chisinau and Stuttgart-Vaihingen July 8 and 19, 2003.

Entered into force November 6, 2003.

TIAS

ECONOMIC AND TECHNICAL COOPERATION

Agreement regarding cooperation to facilitate the provision of assistance.

Signed at Chisinau March 21, 1994.

Entered into force March 21, 1994.

TIAS

EMPLOYMENT

Agreement relating to the employment of dependents of official government employees, with attachment.

Exchange of notes at Chisinau September 8 and 13, 1994.

Entered into force September 13, 1994.

TIAS 12191.

ENVIRONMENTAL COOPERATION

Agreement for cooperation in the Global Learning and Observations to Benefit the Environment (GLOBE) Program, with appendices.

Signed at Washington January 30, 1995.

Entered into force January 30, 1995.

TIAS 12603.

FINANCE

Investment incentive agreement.

Signed at Washington June 19, 1992.

Entered into force December 2, 1992.

TIAS 12459.

INVESTMENT

Treaty concerning the encouragement and reciprocal protection of investment, with annex, protocol and exchange of letters.

Signed at Washington April 21, 1993.

Entered into force November 25, 1994.

TIAS

MAPPING

Basic exchange and cooperative agreement concerning global geospatial information and services cooperation, with annexes.

Signed at Brussels June 24, 2002.

Entered into force February 3, 2003.

NP

NORTH ATLANTIC TREATY

Agreement to treat the agreement of June 19, 1995, among the States Parties to the North Atlantic Treaty and the other States participating in the Partnership for Peace regarding the status of their forces as binding between the United States and Moldova.

Exchange of notes at Chisinau August 1, 1996.

Entered into force August 1, 1996.

TIAS

PEACE CORPS

Agreement concerning the program of the Peace Corps of the United States in the Republic of Moldova.

Signed at Chisinau February 2, 1993.

Entered into force February 2, 1993.

TIAS 12485.

TRADE

Agreement on trade relations, with exchanges of letters.

Signed at Washington June 19, 1992.

Entered into force July 2, 1992.

TIAS

WEAPONS

Agreement concerning cooperation in the area of the prevention of proliferation of weapons of mass destruction and the promotion of defense and military relations.

Signed at Chisinau June 23, 1997.

Entered into force June 23, 1997.

Extension

April 14 and May 14, 2003.

MONACO

COPYRIGHT

Agreement relating to reciprocal copyright relations.

Exchange of notes at Monaco and Nice September 24, 1952.

Entered into force September 24, 1952; operative October 15, 1952.

3 UST 5112; TIAS 2702; 186 UNTS 43.

EXTRADITION

Extradition treaty.

Signed at Monaco February 15, 1939.

Entered into force March 28, 1940.

54 Stat. 1780; TS 959; 9 Bevans 1272; 202 LNTS 61.

TELECOMMUNICATION

Agreement relating to the reciprocal granting of authorizations to permit licensed amateur radio operators of either country to operate their stations in the other country.

Exchange of notes at Monaco March 29 and at Paris October 16, 1968.

Entered into force December 1, 1968.

19 UST 7852; TIAS 6622; 719 UNTS 115.

VISAS

Agreement relating to the reciprocal waiver of passport visa fees for nonimmigrants.

Exchange of notes at Monaco and Nice March 31, 1952.

Entered into force March 31, 1952; operative May 1, 1952.

3 UST 3942; TIAS 2528; 177 UNTS 195.

MONGOLIA

AGRICULTURAL COMMODITIES

Agreement for the donation of agricultural commodities.

Signed at Ulaanbaatar February 26 and March 12, 1999.

Entered into force March 12, 1999.

TIAS

CUSTOMS

Agreement regarding cooperation and mutual assistance in customs matters.

Signed at Hong Kong June 19, 1996.

Entered into force June 19, 1996.

TIAS 12769.

DEFENSE

Acquisition and cross-servicing agreement, with annexes.

Signed at Honolulu May 1, 2003.

Entered into force May 1, 2003.

TIAS

Agreement concerning the provision of equipment, training and related services under the United States International Military Education and Training (IMET) Program.

Exchange of notes at Ulaanbaatar August 11, 2003 and July 27, 2005.

Entered into force July 27, 2005.

NP

ECONOMIC AND TECHNICAL COOPERATION

Agreement concerning economic, technical and related assistance with protocol and memorandum of understanding.

Signed at Ulaanbaatar September 8, 1992.

Entered into force September 8, 1992.

TIAS 12476.

Agency for International Development

November 3, 1994 (NP).

September 19, 1995 (NP).

August 7, 1996 (NP).

May 22, 1997 (NP).

May 29, 1998 (NP).

July 28, 1998 (NP).
September 28, 1998 (NP).
September 28, 1998 (NP).
May 25, 1999 (NP).
August 27, 1999 (NP).
May 3, 2000 (NP).
May 3, 2000 (NP).
May 2, 2001 (NP).
June 28, 2002 (NP).

EDUCATION

Agreement concerning the international school of Ulaanbaatar.
Signed at Ulaanbaatar May 26, 2004.
Entered into force November 19, 2005.
TIAS

EMBASSY SITES

Memorandum of understanding concerning facilitation of the work of diplomatic missions, with attachments.
Signed at Washington March 27, 1992.
Entered into force March 27, 1992.
TIAS

EMPLOYMENT

Agreement concerning the employment of dependents of official government employees.
Exchange of notes at Ulaanbaatar March 24 and April 5, 1999.
Entered into force April 5, 1999.
TIAS

ENVIRONMENTAL COOPERATION

Agreement for cooperation in the Global Learning and Observations to Benefit the Environment (GLOBE) Program, with appendices.
Signed at Ulaanbaatar May 6, 1997.
Entered into force May 6, 1997.
TIAS

FINANCE

Investment incentive agreement.
Signed at New York September 29, 1990.
Entered into force January 4, 1991.
TIAS 11501.

INTERNATIONAL CRIMINAL COURT

Agreement regarding the surrender of U.S. persons to third parties.
Exchange of notes at Washington June 6, 2003.
Entered into force June 27, 2003.
TIAS

INVESTMENT

Treaty concerning the encouragement and reciprocal protection of investment, with annex and protocol.
Signed at Washington October 6, 1994.
Entered into force January 1, 1997.
TIAS

MAPPING

Basic exchange and cooperative agreement concerning geospatial information and services cooperation, with annexes.
Signed at Bethesda March 22, 2004.
Entered into force March 22, 2004.
NP

PEACE CORPS

Agreement on cooperation through the United States Peace Corps in Mongolia.
Signed at Ulaanbaatar August 2, 1990.
Entered into force August 2, 1990.
TIAS 11505.

POSTAL MATTERS

Express mail agreement, with detailed regulations.
Signed at Ulaanbaatar and Washington June 5 and July 1, 1996.
Entered into force September 1, 1996.
NP

RELATIONS

Memorandum of understanding concerning facilitation of the work of diplomatic missions.
Signed at Washington January 27, 1987.
Entered into force January 27, 1987.
TIAS 11457.

SCIENTIFIC COOPERATION

Agreement relating to scientific and technical cooperation, with annex.
Signed at Washington January 23, 1991.
Entered into force January 23, 1991.
TIAS 11495.

Extension
February 20 and April 3, 2001.

Memorandum of understanding concerning scientific and technical cooperation in the earth sciences.
Signed at Reston November 16, 1999 and January 25, 2000.
Entered into force January 25, 2000.
TIAS

Memorandum of understanding concerning scientific and technical cooperation in the earth sciences, with annexes.
Signed at Reston and Ulaanbaatar April 2 and June 26, 2003.
Entered into force June 26, 2003.
TIAS

TRADE AND COMMERCE

Agreement on trade relations, with exchange of letters.
Signed at Washington January 23, 1991.
Entered into force November 27, 1991.
TIAS

VISAS

Agreement concerning the reciprocal issuance of visas to government officials.
Exchange of notes at Ulaanbaatar August 2, 1990.
Entered into force August 2, 1990.
TIAS 12418.

MONTENEGRO

For agreements prior to June 3, 2006, see SERBIA AND MONTENEGRO and YUGOSLAVIA.

FINANCE

Investment incentive agreement.
Signed at Washington and Brussels March 23 and 29, 2000.
Entered into force March 29, 2000.
TIAS

MOROCCO

The independence of Morocco was recognized in a joint declaration signed March 2, 1956 on behalf of the Government of France and the Sultan of Morocco.

A diplomatic agreement on general relations between France and Morocco signed at Paris May 28, 1956, provided *inter alia* (1) that none of the provisions of that agreement must be interpreted as affecting the obligations which result either from the Charter of the United Nations or from agreements, treaties, or conventions in force between one of the High Contracting Parties and third powers (article 6), and (2) that Morocco assumes the obligations resulting from international treaties passed by France in the name of Morocco as well as those resulting from international acts relating to Morocco which have not been subject to observations on its part (article 11).

AGRICULTURAL COMMODITIES

Agricultural commodities agreement with exchange of notes.

Exchange of notes at Rabat February 9, 1962.

Entered into force February 9, 1962.

13 UST 210; TIAS 4964; 442 UNTS 135.

Agricultural commodities agreement with exchange of notes.

Exchange of notes at Rabat September 11, 1962.

Entered into force September 11, 1962.

13 UST 2698; TIAS 5241; 462 UNTS 207.

Agricultural commodities agreement with related notes.

Exchange of notes at Rabat December 29, 1964.

Entered into force December 29, 1964.

17 UST 847; TIAS 6045; 593 UNTS 185.

Agricultural commodities agreement, with related notes.

Exchange of notes at Rabat April 23, 1965.

Entered into force April 23, 1965.

17 UST 873; TIAS 6049; 594 UNTS 4.

Amendments

October 8, 1965 (17 UST 873; TIAS 6049; 594 UNTS 20).

April 21, 1966 (17 UST 873; TIAS 6049; 594 UNTS 24).

August 12, 1966 (17 UST 1644; TIAS 6122; 676 UNTS 388).

October 25, 1966 (17 UST 2026; TIAS 6141; 676 UNTS 392).

Agricultural commodities agreement with related notes.

Exchange of notes at Rabat April 21, 1966.

Entered into force April 21, 1966.

17 UST 2288; TIAS 6172; 680 UNTS 201.

Agricultural commodities agreement with exchange of notes.

Signed at Rabat August 12, 1966.

Entered into force August 12, 1966.

17 UST 2029; TIAS 6142; 675 UNTS 293.

Amendment

October 25, 1966 (17 UST 2029; TIAS 6142; 675 UNTS 308).

Agricultural commodities agreement with annexes.

Signed at Rabat April 20, 1967.

Entered into force April 20, 1967.

18 UST 496; TIAS 6256; 685 UNTS 177.

Related agreements

October 27, 1967 (18 UST 2925; TIAS 6384; 701 UNTS 123).

May 2, 1968 (19 UST 4845; TIAS 6488; 698 UNTS 209).

February 25, 1969 (20 UST 464; TIAS 6648; 714 UNTS 193).

September 13, 1969 (20 UST 4060; TIAS 6793; 727 UNTS 440).

September 4, 1970 (21 UST 2142; TIAS 6960; 764 UNTS 239).

January 21, 1971 (22 UST 220; TIAS 7053; 792 UNTS 75).

April 21 and May 4, 1971 (22 UST 651; TIAS 7117; 792 UNTS 82).

August 18, 1971 (22 UST 1552; TIAS 7176; 807 UNTS 31).

March 2, 1972 (23 UST 163; TIAS 7288).

April 19, 1973 (24 UST 2274; TIAS 7749; 938 UNTS 195).

May 11, 1973 (24 UST 2277; TIAS 7749; 938 UNTS 202).

Agricultural commodities agreement.

Signed at Rabat May 17, 1976.

Entered into force May 17, 1976.

27 UST 2301; TIAS 8309; 1052 UNTS 329.

Related agreements

July 26, 1977 (29 UST 5867; TIAS 9156).

February 3, 1978 (29 UST 5954; TIAS 9162).

August 28, 1979 (31 UST 1009; TIAS 9628; 1202 UNTS 203).

May 21, 1980 (33 UST 1093; TIAS 10094; 1284 UNTS 247).

July 3, 1981 (33 UST 2688; TIAS 10197).

August 18 and 19, 1981 (33 UST 2693; TIAS 10197).

January 19, 1982 (34 UST 356; TIAS 10361).

August 13 and 18, 1982 (35 UST 1615; TIAS 10750).

July 15, 1983 (35 UST 1907; TIAS 10768; 2011 UNTS 95).

August 26, 1983 (35 UST 1907; TIAS 10768; 2011 UNTS 95).

February 2, 1984 (TIAS 11042; 2022 UNTS 49).

July 5, 1984 (TIAS 11042).

Agricultural commodities agreement.

Signed at Rabat February 19, 1985.

Entered into force February 19, 1985.

NP

Amendment

May 27, 1986 (NP).

Related agreements

February 19, 1985 (NP).

April 26, 1985 (NP).

July 24, 1985 (NP).

May 27, 1986 (NP).

July 24, 1986 (NP).

January 22, 1987 (NP).

Agricultural commodities agreement with memorandum of understanding.

Signed at Rabat June 25, 1987.

Entered into force June 25, 1987.

NP

Amendments

March 25, 1988 (NP).

August 31 and September 2, 1988 (NP).

Related agreements

October 20, 1988 (NP).

April 24, 1990 (NP).

ATOMIC ENERGY

Agreement for cooperation concerning peaceful uses of nuclear energy, with annex and agreed minute.

Signed at Washington May 30, 1980.

Entered into force May 16, 1981.

32 UST 5823; TIAS 10018; 1267 UNTS 101.

Amendment

September 20, 2001.

AVIATION

Memorandum of agreement on technical assistance with the Federal Aviation Administration, with annex.

Signed at Rabat April 18, 1983.

Entered into force April 18, 1983.

TIAS 10702; 2005 UNTS 175.

Air transport agreement, with annexes.

Signed at Rabat October 10, 2001.

Entered into force August 19, 2002.

TIAS

COMMERCE

See PEACE TREATIES

CONSULS

See PEACE TREATIES

CULTURAL RELATIONS

Cultural agreement.

Signed at Washington February 10, 1967.

Entered into force February 10, 1967.

18 UST 174; TIAS 6215; 688 UNTS 149.

DEFENSE

Agreement concerning the use of certain facilities in Morocco by the United States.

Exchange of notes at Washington May 27, 1982.

Entered into force May 27, 1982.

34 UST 1127; TIAS 10399; 1566 UNTS 139.

Memorandum of arrangement regarding the assignment of liaison officers, with annexes.

Signed at Norfolk March 10, 2006.

Entered into force March 10, 2006.

TIAS

Agreement regarding the furnishing of defense articles, related training and other defense services, including pursuant to the United States International Military and Education Training Program (IMET).

Exchange of notes at Rabat July 21 and November 24, 2006.

Entered into force November 24, 2006.

NP

ECONOMIC AND TECHNICAL COOPERATION

Agreement providing for economic, technical, and related assistance.

Exchange of notes at Rabat April 2, 1957.

Entered into force April 2, 1957.

8 UST 459; TIAS 3799; 288 UNTS 157.

Amendment

May 19, 1958 (9 UST 923; TIAS 4054; 317 UNTS 354).

Agency for International Development

November 7, 1975 (28 UST 57; TIAS 8464)

June 14, 1976 (28 UST 1479; TIAS 8518).

EDUCATION

Agreement establishing a Binational Commission for Educational and Cultural Exchange.

Signed at Marrakech February 12, 1982.

Entered into force May 20, 1982.

TIAS 10407; 34 UST 1180.

EMPLOYMENT

Agreement relating to the employment of dependents of official government employees.

Exchange of notes at Rabat February 27 and April 2, 1992.

Entered into force April 2, 1992.

TIAS

ENERGY

Agreement concerning cooperation in energy efficiency and renewable energy

Signed October 16, 2000.

Entered into force October 16, 2000.

TIAS

ENVIRONMENTAL COOPERATION

Agreement for cooperation in the Global Learning and Observations to Benefit the Environment (GLOBE) Program, with appendices.

Signed at Rabat March 27, 1996.

Entered into force March 27, 1996.

TIAS 12739.

FINANCE

Agreement regarding the consolidation and rescheduling of certain debts owed to, guaranteed by or insured by the United States Government and its agencies, with annexes.

Signed at Rabat December 30, 1983.

Entered into force February 10, 1984.

TIAS 11015; 2022 UNTS 73.

Agreement regarding the consolidation and rescheduling of certain debts owed to, guaranteed by or insured by the United States Government and its agencies, with annexes.

Signed at Rabat December 23, 1985 and February 13, 1986.

Entered into force January 21, 1986.

NP

Agreement regarding the consolidation and rescheduling of certain debts owed to, guaranteed by, or insured by the United States Government and its agencies, with annexes.

Signed at Rabat March 1, 1988.

Entered into force April 11, 1988.

NP

Agreement regarding the consolidation and rescheduling of certain debts owed to, guaranteed by, or insured by the United States Government and its agencies, with annexes.

Signed at Rabat August 21, 1989.

Entered into force September 25, 1989.

NP

Agreement regarding the consolidation and rescheduling or refinancing of certain debts owed to, guaranteed by, or insured by the United States Government and its agencies, with annexes.

Signed at Rabat February 14, 1991.

Entered into force March 29, 1991.

NP

Agreement regarding the consolidation and rescheduling or refinancing of certain debts owed to, guaranteed by, or insured by the United States Government and its agencies, with annexes.

Signed at Rabat August 24, 1992.

Entered into force October 12, 1992.

NP

Investment incentive agreement.

Signed at Washington March 15, 1995.

Entered into force September 22, 1999.

TIAS

INTERNATIONAL CRIMINAL COURT

Agreement regarding the surrender of persons to the International Criminal Court.

Signed at New York September 24, 2003.

Entered into force November 19, 2003.

TIAS

INVESTMENT

Treaty concerning the encouragement and reciprocal protection of investments, with protocol.

Signed at Washington July 22, 1985.

Entered into force May 29, 1991.

TIAS

JUDICIAL ASSISTANCE

Convention on mutual assistance in criminal matters.

Signed at Rabat October 17, 1983.

Entered into force June 23, 1993.

TIAS

MAPPING

Agreement concerning mapping, charting and geodesy cooperation.

Signed at Rabat April 29, 1982.

Entered into force April 29, 1982.

34 UST 987; TIAS 10386.

Memorandum of agreement concerning hydrographic surveys and nautical charting.

Signed at Rabat November 20, 1985.

Entered into force November 20, 1985.

TIAS 11210.

NARCOTIC DRUGS

Agreement regarding joint cooperation in fighting against international terrorism, organized crime, and the illicit production, trafficking and abuse of narcotics.

Signed at Rabat February 10, 1989.

Entered into force February 10, 1989.

TIAS 12029.

PEACE CORPS

Agreement relating to the establishment of a Peace Corps program in Morocco.

Exchange of notes at Rabat February 8 and 9, 1963.

Entered into force February 9, 1963.

23 UST 209; TIAS 7297.

Amendment

March 10, 1972 (23 UST 209; TIAS 7297).

PEACE TREATIES

Treaty of peace.[1]

Signed at Meccanez September 16, 1836.

Entered into force January 28, 1837.

8 Stat. 484; TS 244-2; 9 Bevans 1286.

NOTE

1 Extraterritorial jurisdiction in Morocco relinquished by the United States October 6, 1956.

POSTAL MATTERS

International express mail agreement, with detailed regulations.

Signed at Rabat and Washington March 18 and May 11, 1988.

Entered into force June 1, 1988.

TIAS 11588.

SCIENTIFIC COOPERATION

Memorandum of understanding concerning scientific and technical cooperation in the earth sciences, with annexes.

Signed at Reston and Rabat January 13 and March 9, 2000.

Entered into force March 9, 2000.

TIAS

SPACE COOPERATION

Agreement concerning the use of Ben Guerir Air Base as a space shuttle emergency landing site.

Signed at Rabat and Washington January 21 and 28, 1987.

Entered into force January 28, 1987.

TIAS 12209.

TAXATION

Convention for the avoidance of double taxation and the prevention of fiscal evasion with respect to taxes on income, with related notes.[1]

Signed at Rabat August 1, 1977.

Entered into force December 30, 1981.

33 UST 2545; TIAS 10194.

Agreement interpreting certain articles of the convention of August 1, 1977 (TIAS 10194).

Signed at Washington and Rabat October 25, 1979 and at Rabat April 17, 1981.

Entered into force December 30, 1981.

33 UST 2672; TIAS 10195.

NOTE

1 With reservation and understanding.

TOURISM

Agreement on the development and facilitation of tourism.

Signed at Washington July 22, 1985.

Entered into force July 22, 1985.

TIAS 12001.

TRADE

The United States-Morocco free trade agreement, with annexes.

Signed at Washington June 15, 2004.

Entered into force January 1, 2006.

TIAS

VISAS

Arrangement between the United States and France for the waiver by France of visa requirements for United States citizens visiting Metropolitan France and certain French territories, and for the granting by the United States of gratis passport visas to French citizens resident in those territories who enter the United States as nonimmigrants.

Exchange of notes at Paris March 16 and 31, 1949.

Entered into force March 31, 1949.

63 Stat. 2737; TIAS 1987; 7 Bevans 1311; 84 UNTS 283.

MOZAMBIQUE

AGRICULTURAL COMMODITIES

Agricultural commodities agreement, with agreed minutes.

Signed at Maputo June 28, 1979.

Entered into force June 28, 1979.

31 UST 4711; TIAS 9635.

Related agreements

June 23, 1980 (32 UST 2548; TIAS 9857; 1274 UNTS 109).

July 24, 1980 (32 UST 2548; TIAS 9857; 1274 UNTS 119).

February 23, 1981 (33 UST 1143; TIAS 10100; 1281 UNTS 25).

Agricultural commodities agreement.

Signed at Maputo January 11, 1985.

Entered into force January 11, 1985.

NP

Amendments

January 17 and 18, 1985 (NP).

May 23, 1985 (NP).

Related agreements

April 11, 1986 (NP).

July 9, 1986 (NP).

August 22, 1986 (NP).

DEFENSE

Agreement concerning the provision of training related to defense articles under the United States International Military Education and Training (IMET) Program.

Exchange of notes at Maputo November 7, 1984 and April 12, 1985.

Entered into force April 12, 1985.

TIAS 11338.

Agreement regarding grants under the Foreign Assistance Act of 1961, as amended, and the furnishing of defense articles, related training and other defense services from the United States to Mozambique.

Exchange of notes at Maputo March 30 and May 13, 1994.

Entered into force May 13, 1994.

TIAS

Amendment

June 23 and August 23, 2004.

Agreement concerning the status of United States military and civilian personnel of the U.S. Department of Defense temporarily present in Mozambique in connection with humanitarian relief operations.

Exchange of notes at Maputo March 3 and 7, 2000.

Entered into force March 7, 2000.

NP

DIPLOMATIC PROPERTIES

Agreement concerning reciprocal and property ownership rights for the diplomatic and consular missions of the United States and the Republic of Mozambique.

Exchange of notes at Maputo September 21 and October 7, 2005.

Entered into force October 7, 2005.

TIAS

ECONOMIC AND TECHNICAL COOPERATION

Agency for International Development

September 14, 1976 (28 UST 7165; TIAS 8711; 1087 UNTS 19).

December 2, 1977 (29 UST 5294; TIAS 9108; 1134 UNTS 375).

EMPLOYMENT

Agreement relating to the employment of dependents of official government employees.

Exchange of notes at Washington June 29 and July 14, 1998.

Entered into force July 14, 1998.

TIAS

FINANCE

Agreement regarding the consolidation and rescheduling of certain debts owed to, guaranteed by or insured by the United States Government and its agencies, with annex.

Signed at Maputo February 12, 1987.

Entered into force March 27, 1987.

NP

Agreement regarding the consolidation and rescheduling of certain debts owed to, guaranteed by, or insured by the United States Government and its agencies, with annexes.

Signed at Maputo March 6, 1990.

Entered into force April 23, 1990.

NP

Agreement regarding the consolidation and rescheduling of certain debts owed to, guaranteed by, or insured by the United States Government and its agencies, with annexes.

Signed at Maputo August 27, 1991.

Entered into force September 30, 1991.

NP

Agreement regarding the consolidation and rescheduling of certain debts owed to, guaranteed by or insured by the United States Government and its agency, with annexes.

Signed at Maputo August 13, 1993.

Entered into force September 27, 1993.

NP

Amendment

July 13 and August 31, 1995 (NP).

Agreement regarding the consolidation, reduction and rescheduling of certain debts owed to, guaranteed by, or insured by the United States Government and its agency, with annexes.

Signed at Maputo August 13, 1997.

Entered into force September 29, 1997.

NP

Amendment

September 30 and October 27, 1998.

Investment incentive agreement.

Signed at Maputo September 23, 1999.

Entered into force September 23, 1999.

TIAS

Agreement regarding the consolidation and reduction of debt owed to, guaranteed by, or insured by the United States Government and its agency, with annexes.

Signed at Maputo May 28, 2002.

Entered into force July 11, 2002.

NP

INTERNATIONAL CRIMINAL COURT

Agreement regarding the surrender of persons to international tribunals.

Signed at Maputo June 24, 2003.

Entered into force March 2, 2004.

TIAS

INVESTMENT

Treaty concerning the encouragement and reciprocal protection of investment, with annex, protocol and exchange of letters.

Signed at Washington December 1, 1998.

Entered into force March 3, 2005.

TIAS

PEACE CORPS

Agreement concerning the program of the Peace Corps in Mozambique.

Signed at Maputo December 27, 1991.

Entered into force December 27, 1991.

TIAS

POSTAL MATTERS

International express mail agreement, with detailed regulations.

Signed at Maputo and Washington July 9 and 23, 1990.

Entered into force August 30, 1990.

TIAS 11758.

MULTINATIONAL FORCE AND OBSERVERS

CLAIMS

Agreement concerning the settlement of claims by the United States against the Multinational Force and Observers (MFO).

Exchange of notes at Rome May 3, 1990.

Entered into force May 3, 1990.

TIAS 11899.

PEACEKEEPING

Agreement relating to participation of United States military and civilian personnel in the Multinational Force and Observers established by Egypt and Israel, with annexes and agreed minute, and related exchange of letters.[1]

Exchange of letters at Washington March 26, 1982.

Entered into force March 26, 1982.

TIAS 10557.

NOTE

1 See also PEACEKEEPING in multilateral section and in bilateral section under EGYPT and ISRAEL.

MUTUAL AID AND LOAN GUARANTY FUND OF THE COUNCIL OF THE ENTENTE STATES

ECONOMIC AND TECHNICAL COOPERATION

Agency for International Development

August 31, 1976 (28 UST 8807; TIAS 8773).

August 31 and September 29, 1976 (28 UST 8637; TIAS 8766).

N

NAMIBIA

DEFENSE

Agreement regarding grants under the Foreign Assistance Act of 1961, as amended, and the furnishing of defense articles, related training and other defense services from the United States Government to the Republic of Namibia.

Exchange of notes at Windhoek May 21, 1992 and February 19, 1998.

Entered into force February 19, 1998.

NP

ECONOMIC AND TECHNICAL COOPERATION

General agreement for special development assistance.

Signed at New York September 28, 1990.

Entered into force September 28, 1990.

TIAS 11901.

Agreement for special development assistance.

Signed at Windhoek May 27, 1992.

Entered into force May 27, 1992.

TIAS 11863.

EMPLOYMENT

Agreement relating to the employment of dependents of official government employees.

Exchange of notes at Windhoek January 24 and June 8, 1994.

Entered into force June 8, 1994.

TIAS 12184.

ENVIRONMENTAL COOPERATION

Agreement for cooperation in the Global Learning and Observations to Benefit the Environment (GLOBE) Program, with appendices.

Signed at Windhoek October 8, 1997.

Entered into force October 8, 1997.

TIAS

FINANCE

Investment incentive agreement.

Signed at Washington June 20, 1990.

Entered into force June 5, 1991.

TIAS 12096.

POSTAL MATTERS

International express mail agreement, with detailed regulations.

Signed at Windhoek and Washington September 30 and October 24, 1994.

Entered into force December 1, 1994.

NP

NAURU

On January 31, 1968 Nauru became an independent state. In a note dated May 28, 1968 to the Secretary-General of the United Nations, the Chief Secretary made a statement reading in part as follows:

"Prior to Nauru attaining independence on 31st January, 1968, treaty relationships were entered into, on its behalf, by the Government of the Commonwealth of Australia. The Government of Nauru now wishes to make clear its position in regard to obligations arising from those treaties entered into prior to 31st January, 1968 by the Government of the Commonwealth of Australia, and accordingly makes the following declarations.

In respect of all bilateral treaties validly concluded by Australia on behalf of Nauru, or validly applied or extended by Australia to Nauru, before 31st January, 1968, the Government of Nauru will continue, on a basis of reciprocity, to apply the terms of such treaties for a period of twenty-four months unless such treaties are abrogated or modified earlier by agreement with the other contracting parties. At the expiration of this period the Government of Nauru will regard each such treaty as having terminated unless it has earlier agreed with the other contracting party to continue that treaty in existence.

It is the earnest hope of the Government of Nauru that during the aforementioned period of twenty-four months, the normal processes of diplomatic negotiations will enable it to reach satisfactory accord with the States concerned upon the possibility of the continuance or modification or termination of such treaties. In respect of multilateral treaties, the Government of Nauru intends to review each of them individually and to indicate to the depositary in each case what steps it wishes to take, whether by way of confirmation of succession, confirmation of termination or accession, in relation to each such instrument. During such period of review, any party to a multilateral treaty which was, prior to independence, validly applied or extended to Nauru may, on a basis of reciprocity, rely as against Nauru on the terms of the treaty." In subsequent notes to the Secretary-General of the United Nations this period of review has been extended indefinitely.

EXTRADITION

Extradition treaty between the United States and the United Kingdom, signed at London December 22, 1931; applicable to Australia (including Papua, Norfolk Island, and the mandated territories of New Guinea and Nauru), in accordance with article 14, from August 30, 1935.

47 Stat. 2122; TS 849; 12 Bevans 482; 163 LNTS 59.

INTERNATIONAL CRIMINAL COURT

Agreement regarding the surrender of persons to the International Criminal Court.

Signed at Washington February 26, 2003.

Entered into force December 4, 2003.

TIAS

POSTAL MATTERS

International express mail agreement, with detailed regulations.

Signed at Washington and Nauru October 8, 1993 and January 17, 1994.

Entered into force April 4, 1994.

NP

WEATHER STATIONS

Agreement providing for the construction and operation of a weather station on Nauru Island.

Exchange of notes at Canberra February 19 and 25, 1958.

Entered into force February 25, 1958.

9 UST 266; TIAS 4001; 317 UNTS 153.

NEPAL

COMMERCE

Agreement relating to friendship and commerce.

Exchange of notes at Kathmandu April 25, 1947.

Entered into force April 25, 1947.

61 Stat. 2566; TIAS 1585; 10 Bevans 1; 16 UNTS 97.

CONSULS

See COMMERCE

DEFENSE

Agreement regarding military assistance under the Foreign Assistance Act of 1961, as amended, and the furnishing of defense articles, related training and other defense services from the United States to Nepal.

Exchange of notes at Kathmandu September 19, 1994 and January 25, 1995.

Entered into force January 25, 1995.

TIAS 12350.

Agreement concerning the status of United States military and civilian personnel of the U.S. Department of Defense temporarily present in the Kingdom of Nepal in connection with the Multi-Platoon Training Event.

Exchange of notes at Kathmandu January 12 and 13, 2000.

Entered into force January 13, 2000.

NP

ECONOMIC AND TECHNICAL COOPERATION

General agreement for technical cooperation.

Signed at New Delhi January 23, 1951.

Entered into force January 23, 1951.

2 UST 489; TIAS 2198; 184 UNTS 65.

Amendment

January 2 and 8, 1952 (3 UST 4760; TIAS 2642; 184 UNTS 74).

Agency for International Development

June 5, 1975 (29 UST 137; TIAS 8801).

July 21, 1975 (29 UST 2473; TIAS 8949).

January 13, 1976 (28 UST 1950; TIAS 8531; 1071 UNTS 353).

February 4, 1976 (28 UST 2934; TIAS 8576).

June 30, 1976 (29 UST 114; TIAS 8799).

September 21, 1976 (29 UST 137; TIAS 8801).

August 4, 1977 (29 UST 561; TIAS 8832).

August 4, 1977 (29 UST 2458; TIAS 8948).

EDUCATION

Agreement for financing certain educational exchange programs.

Signed at Kathmandu June 9, 1961.

Entered into force June 9, 1961.

TIAS 4845; 12 UST 1253; 421 UNTS 223.

Amendment

July 10 and December 13, 1974 and May 18, 1975 (TIAS 8352; 27 UST 2831).

EMPLOYMENT

Agreement relating to the employment of dependents of official government employees.

Exchange of notes at Washington December 19, 1996 and May 13, 1997.

Entered into force May 13, 1997.

TIAS

ENVIRONMENTAL COOPERATION

Agreement for cooperation in the Global Learning and Observations to Benefit the Environment (GLOBE) Program, with appendices.

Signed at Kathmandu March 3, 2000.

Entered into force March 3, 2000.

TIAS

FINANCE

Agreement relating to investment guaranties authorized by section 413 (b)(4) of the Mutual Security Act of 1954, as amended.

Exchange of notes at Washington May 17, 1960.

Entered into force May 17, 1960.

11 UST 1396; TIAS 4477; 372 UNTS 313.

Amendment

June 4, 1963 (14 UST 994; TIAS 5391; 487 UNTS 376).

INTERNATIONAL CRIMINAL COURT

Agreement regarding the surrender of persons to the International Criminal Court.

Signed at Kathmandu December 31, 2002.

Entered into force July 22, 2003.

TIAS

JUDICIAL ASSISTANCE

Procedures for mutual assistance in connection with matters relating to the Boeing Company.

Signed at Washington January 5, 1979.

Entered into force January 5, 1979.

30 UST 2495; TIAS 9347; 1171 UNTS 111.

PEACE CORPS

Agreement relating to the establishment of a Peace Corps program in Nepal.

Exchange of notes at Kathmandu August 24, 1962.

Entered into force August 24, 1962.

13 UST 1909; TIAS 5146; 460 UNTS 143.

POSTAL MATTERS

Express mail agreement, with detailed regulations.

Signed at Nepal and Washington July 9 and October 25, 1996.

Entered into force January 1, 1997.

NP

TRADE

See also COMMERCE

Agreement relating to trade in cotton textiles, with annexes.

Exchange of notes at Kathmandu May 30 and June 1, 1986.

Entered into force June 1, 1986.

NP

Amendments and extensions

November 17 and December 4, 1988 (NP).

December 21, 1989 and January 10, 1990 (NP).

November 19 and 28, 1990 (NP).

December 2, 1993 and July 22, 1994 (NP).

April 18 and 30, 1996 (NP).

June 20, 1997.

July 13, 2000.

Administrative arrangement relating to a visa system for exports of Nepalese textile products.

Exchange of notes at Kathmandu July 28 and August 18, 1986.

Entered into force August 18, 1986; effective October 1, 1986.

NP

Amendment

November 19 and 28, 1990 (NP).

NETHERLANDS

ATOMIC ENERGY

Agreement for cooperation on uses of atomic energy for mutual defense purposes.

Signed at The Hague May 6, 1959.

Entered into force July 27, 1959.

10 UST 1334; TIAS 4277; 355 UNTS 327.

Arrangement for the exchange of technical information and cooperation in regulatory and safety research matters, with addendum.

Signed at Vienna September 17, 2003.

Entered into force September 17, 2003.

TIAS

AVIATION

Agreement providing for nonassertion of sovereign immunity from suit of air transport enterprises.[1]

Exchange of notes at Washington June 19, 1953.

Entered into force June 19, 1953.

4 UST 1610; TIAS 2828; 212 UNTS 249.

Air transport agreement.[1]

Signed at Washington April 3, 1957.

Entered into force provisionally April 3, 1957; definitively May 31, 1957.

12 UST 837; TIAS 4782; 410 UNTS 193.

Amendments

March 31, 1978 (29 UST 3088; TIAS 8998; 1123 UNTS 345).[2]

June 11, 1986 (TIAS 11365; 2194 UNTS 122).

October 13 and December 22, 1987 (TIAS 11927).

January 29 and March 13, 1992 (TIAS 11929).

October 14, 1992 (TIAS 11976).

Memorandum of agreement relating to the provision of flight inspection services.

Signed at Washington and The Hague March 10 and June 15, 1978.

Entered into force June 15, 1978; effective April 1, 1978.

30 UST 283; TIAS 9199.

Amendment

February 19 and May 4, 1982 (TIAS 10546).

TIAS

Agreement for the promotion of aviation safety.

Signed at The Hague September 13, 1995.

Entered into force December 1, 1996.

TIAS 12691; 1999 UNTS 31.

Memorandum of agreement for the provision of technical assistance in developing and modernizing the civil aviation infrastructure of Aruba.

Signed at Washington and Oranjestad May 9 and 17, 1996.

Entered into force May 17, 1996.

TIAS

Agreement relating to air transportation between the United States and Aruba, with annexes.

Signed at Washington September 18, 1997.

Entered into force June 11, 1998.

TIAS; 2032 UNTS 359.

NOTES

1 Applicable to all territories, except Aruba.

2 Articles 3, 4, 6 and 9 have been superseded by subsequent amendments.

CLAIMS

Memorandum of understanding regarding claims by the Netherlands to looted securities, with annex and related note.

Signed at Washington January 19, 1951.

Entered into force January 19, 1951.

2 UST 1262; TIAS 2275; 141 UNTS 221.

Agreement relating to selection of De Nederlandsche Bank of Amsterdam by the United States, Iran, and Algeria as the mutually agreeable central bank to manage the depositary of funds in the security account established by the January 19, 1981 Declaration of the Government of the Democratic and Popular Republic of Algeria, [1] with related technical agreements signed August 17, 1981.

Exchange of notes at The Hague July 10, 1981.

Entered into force July 10, 1981.

TIAS

NOTE

1 See IRAN — CLAIMS.

COMMERCE

Agreement relating to commercial policy.

Exchange of notes at Washington November 21, 1946.

Entered into force November 21, 1946.

61 Stat. 2424; TIAS 1564; 10 Bevans 181; 12 UNTS 173.

Treaty of friendship, commerce and navigation, with protocol and exchange of notes.[1]

Signed at The Hague March 27, 1956.

Entered into force December 5, 1957.

8 UST 2043; TIAS 3942; 285 UNTS 231.

NOTES

1 Applicable to Aruba and Netherlands Antilles, and to all territories over which the United States has jurisdiction or international responsibility except the Trust Territory of Pacific Islands.

CUSTOMS

Arrangement regarding reciprocal free entry privileges for consular officers.

Exchange of notes at The Hague and at Washington April 7, June 17, August 20, and September 19, 1930.

Entered into force September 19, 1930.

Foreign Relations, 1931, Vol. II, p. 771; 10 Bevans 105.

Amendment

February 1, 1947 and August 20, 1948.

Reciprocal arrangement providing that trade commissioners may import, free of duty, articles for their personal use during their official residence.

Exchange of notes at The Hague July 2 and November 10, 1936.

Entered into force November 10, 1936.

Agreement on mutual administrative assistance for the proper application of customs law and for the prevention, investigation and combating of customs offences, with annex.

Signed at Washington October 28, 1996.

Entered into force May 1, 1998.

TIAS 12811; 2015 UNTS 411.

DEFENSE

See also MUTUAL SECURITY

Mutual defense assistance agreement.

Signed at Washington January 27, 1950.

Entered into force January 27, 1950.

1 UST 88; TIAS 2015; 80 UNTS 219.

Agreement concerning the participation of the Netherlands forces in the United Nations operations in Korea.

Signed at Washington May 15, 1952.

Entered into force May 15, 1952.

3 UST 3987; TIAS 2534; 177 UNTS 233.

Agreement relating to the disposition of equipment and materials furnished by the United States under the mutual defense assistance agreement and no longer required for the purposes for which originally made available.

Exchange of notes at The Hague November 12 and 26, 1953.

Entered into force November 26, 1953.

11 UST 2017; TIAS 4556; 388 UNTS 303.

Amendment

August 10 and 13, 1960 (11 UST 2017; TIAS 4556; 388 UNTS 303).

Agreement relating to a memorandum of understanding and a model contract for the offshore procurement program.

Exchange of notes at The Hague April 15 and May 7, 1954.

Entered into force July 30, 1954.

5 UST 2027; TIAS 3069; 213 UNTS 325.

Agreement relating to the stationing of United States armed forces in the Netherlands, with annex.

Exchange of notes at The Hague August 13, 1954.

Entered into force November 16, 1954.

6 UST 103; TIAS 3174; 251 UNTS 91.

Agreement establishing an air defense technical center with cost reimbursement contract attached.

Exchange of notes at The Hague December 14, 1954.

Entered into force December 14, 1954.

6 UST 915; TIAS 3236; 262 UNTS 35.

Agreement relating to a weapons production program.

Exchange of notes at The Hague March 24, 1960.

Entered into force provisionally March 24, 1960; definitively January 2, 1962.

12 UST 180; TIAS 4692; 406 UNTS 165.

Agreement relating to the safeguarding of classified information.

Exchange of notes at Washington August 18, 1960.

Entered into force August 18, 1960.

TIAS

Amendment

March 4 and April 6, 1981.

Administrative arrangements pertaining to prefinanced NATO common infrastructure projects.

Exchange of letters at The Hague and Heidelberg May 30 and July 24, 1975.

Entered into force July 24, 1975.

30 UST 2885; TIAS 9369; 1177 UNTS 247.

General arrangement relating to the cooperative production of the M109 vehicle and its components.

Signed at The Hague May 3, 1966.

Entered into force May 3, 1966.

29 UST 5713; TIAS 9144.

Amendments

March 17, 1969 (29 UST 5721; TIAS 9144).

December 30, 1974 and June 5, 1975 (29 UST 5722; TIAS 9144).

March 2 and April 14, 1979 (TIAS 10641).

January 31, 1983 (TIAS 10641).

Memorandum of understanding concerning principles governing mutual cooperation in research and development, production and procurement of conventional defense equipment.

Signed at Washington and The Hague July 25 and August 24, 1978.

Entered into force August 24, 1978.

33 UST 3105; TIAS 10214.

Agreement relating to storage of prepositioned war readiness materials by United States forces.

Exchange of notes at The Hague January 15, 1981.

Entered into force August 20, 1981.

33 UST 891; TIAS 10073; 1268 UNTS 77.

Agreement establishing a television transmitter at Soesterberg Airfield.

Exchange of notes at The Hague December 7, 1981 and March 4, 1982.

Entered into force July 19, 1983.

35 UST 3814; TIAS 10883; 1359 UNTS 249.

Mutual logistical support agreement, with annexes.

Signed at Stuttgart February 22, 1983.

Entered into force February 22, 1983.

TIAS 10663; 1359 UNTS 257.

Amendment

February 27 and March 20, 1992 (TIAS 12353).

Memorandum of understanding regarding the exchange of Air Force officers.

Signed at The Hague and Washington May 22, 1984 and May 7, 1985.

Entered into force May 7, 1985.

TIAS 11233.

Agreement on termination of agreement of November 4, 1985 concerning the stationing, support and operation of the Ground Launched Cruise Missile (GLCM) system in the territory of the Netherlands.

Exchange of notes at The Hague December 18, 1987.

Entered into force June 1, 1988.

TIAS

Memorandum of understanding between the United States Air Forces in Europe and the Royal Netherlands Air Force concerning the logistical support/services for the Soviet inspection(s) under the INF Treaty at Woensdrecht AB, Netherlands, with annexes.

Signed at Royal Netherlands Air Force Headquarters and Ramstein Air Base, Germany, July 13 and August 10, 1989.

Entered into force August 10, 1989.

TIAS 12351.

Memorandum of understanding regarding the joint training of Royal Netherlands Air Force and United States Air Force aircrews on the F-16 weapons system in the United States.

Signed at The Hague October 30, 1989.

Entered into force October 30, 1989.

NP

Memorandum of understanding concerning the residual value of the U.S. funded facilities for the Ground Launched Cruise Missile (GLCM) at Woensdrecht Air Base, the Netherlands, with annexes.

Signed at The Hague December 6, 1989.

Entered into force December 6, 1989.

TIAS 12352.

Memorandum of understanding concerning measures to be taken for the transfer, security and safeguarding of technical information, software and equipment to the Ministry of Defense to enable industry to establish North Sea ACMI range display and debriefing system facilities in the Netherlands.

Signed at Washington July 6, 1992.

Entered into force July 6, 1992.

TIAS 12354.

Memorandum of understanding for the dynamic behavior of composite ship structures (DYCOSS) project, with annexes.

Signed at The Hague and Washington July 18 and August 11, 1994.

Entered into force August 11, 1994.

TIAS 12355.

Memorandumm of understanding concerning technology research and development projects, with annex.

Signed at Washington May 14, 1998.

Entered into force May 14, 1998.

TIAS

Agreement concerning the cooperative framework for system development and demonstration of the joint strike fighter.

Signed at Soesterberg Airbase and Washington June 5 and 10, 2002.

Entered into force July 10, 2002.

TIAS

Memorandum of understanding for test and evaluation program cooperation, with annexes.

Signed at The Hague and Washington January 26 and February 12, 2004.

Entered into force February 12, 2004.

TIAS

Memorandum of agreement for information exchange and research, development, testing and evaluation projects.

Signed at The Hague May 25, 2004.

Entered into force May 25, 2004.

TIAS

Agreement regarding the status of military and civilian personnel of the United States armed forces who will be present in the Netherlands Antilles and Aruba for military training and exercises.

Exchange of notes at The Hague May 3, 2005.

Entered into force May 3, 2005.

TIAS

Amendment and extension

April 11, 2006.

Memorandum of understanding regarding the assignment of naval liaison officers, with annex.

Signed at Washington and The Hague September 21 and November 12, 2005.

Entered into force November 12, 2005.

TIAS

ECONOMIC AND TECHNICAL COOPERATION

Economic cooperation agreement.

Signed at The Hague July 2, 1948.

Entered into force July 2, 1948.

62 Stat. 2477; TIAS 1791; 10 Bevans 240; 20 UNTS 91.

Amendments

January 16 and February 2, 1950 (1 UST 665; TIAS 2126; 93 UNTS 361).

March 7 and April 3, 1951 (2 UST 1319; TIAS 2285; 141 UNTS 368).

November 28, 1952 (3 UST 5260; TIAS 2721; 173 UNTS 382).

Agreement relating to the assumption by Indonesia of all responsibilities and obligations of the Netherlands incurred under the economic cooperation agreements of July 2, 1948, as amended, and April 26, 1949, as amended, and the loan agreements of October 28, 1948, and December 22, 1949, and memorandum of understanding.

Signed at Washington February 11, 1952, by the United States, Indonesia, and the Netherlands.

Entered into force February 11, 1952.

3 UST 2989; TIAS 2484; 165 UNTS 77.

General agreement for technical cooperation for Suriname and Netherlands Antilles.[1]

Signed at The Hague January 22, 1954.

Entered into force April 21, 1954.

5 UST 919; TIAS 2982; 190 UNTS 207.

NOTE

1 Also applicable to Aruba.

EDUCATION

Agreement for the financing of certain education exchange programs.

Signed at The Hague October 16, 1972.

Entered into force August 8, 1973.

24 UST 1924; TIAS 7700.

EMPLOYMENT

Agreement relating to the employment of dependents of official government employees.

Exchange of notes at The Hague June 23, 1986.

Entered into force May 13, 1987.

TIAS 11359.

ENVIRONMENTAL COOPERATION

Memorandum of understanding concerning cooperation in the field of environmental protection.

Signed at Paris June 17, 1985.

Entered into force June 17, 1985.

TIAS 11161; 2126 UNTS 267.

Memorandum of understanding for cooperation in the GLOBE program.

Signed at Washington February 28, 1995.

Entered into force February 28, 1995.

TIAS 12607.

EXTRADITION

Extradition treaty, with appendix.[1]

Signed at The Hague June 24, 1980.

Entered into force September 15, 1983.

35 UST 1334; TIAS 10733.

NOTE

1 Applicable to Aruba and Netherlands Antilles.

FINANCE

Agreement relating to the guaranties authorized by Section 111 (b)(3) of the Economic Cooperation Act of 1948, as amended.

Exchange of notes at Washington September 24 and October 7, 1952.

Entered into force October 8, 1952.

3 UST 5060; TIAS 2690; 173 UNTS 378.

JUDICIAL ASSISTANCE

Procedures for mutual assistance in the administration of justice in connection with the Lockheed Aircraft Corporation matter.

Signed at Washington March 29, 1976.

Entered into force March 29, 1976.

27 UST 1064; TIAS 8245.

Related agreement

March 21, 1979 (30 UST 2500; TIAS 9348; 1171 UNTS 215).

Treaty on mutual assistance in criminal matters, with exchange of notes.[1]

Signed at The Hague June 12, 1981.

Entered into force September 15, 1983.

35 UST 1361; TIAS 10734; 1359 UNTS 209.

Agreement on mutual administrative assistance in the exchange of information in securities matters.

Signed at The Hague December 11, 1989.

Entered into force July 1, 1992.

TIAS 12405; 1921 UNTS 163.

Agreement regarding mutual cooperation in the tracing, freezing, seizure and forfeiture of proceeds and instrumentalities of crime and the sharing of forfeited assets.[2]

Signed at Washington November 20, 1992.

Entered into force August 4, 1994.

TIAS 12482; 2029 UNTS 189.

Agreement on mutual administrative assistance in the exchange of information in futures matters.

Signed at Washington April 29, 1993.

Entered into force February 1, 1994.

TIAS 12151.

NOTES

1 Not applicable to requests for assistance relating to fiscal offenses addressed to Aruba or the Netherlands Antilles.

2 Applicable to Aruba and the Netherlands Antilles.

LEND-LEASE

Preliminary agreement regarding principles applying to mutual aid in the prosecution of the war against aggression, and exchange of notes.

Signed at Washington July 8, 1942.

Entered into force July 8, 1942.

56 Stat. 1554; EAS 259; 10 Bevans 142; 103 UNTS 277.

Mutual aid agreement relating to supplies and services, with accompanying memorandum and exchange of notes.

Signed at Washington April 30, 1945.

Entered into force April 30, 1945.

59 Stat. 1627; EAS 480; 10 Bevans 158; 139 UNTS 341.

Agreement relating to principles applying to the provision of aid to the armed forces of the United States, and exchange of notes.

Exchange of notes at Washington April 30, 1945; operative from July 8, 1942.

59 Stat. 1635; EAS 480; 10 Bevans 167; 139 UNTS 319.

LEND-LEASE SETTLEMENT

Agreement regarding settlement for lend-lease, reciprocal aid, surplus property, military relief, and claims, and exchanges of notes with memorandum of arrangement between the United States, the United Kingdom, and the Netherlands.

Signed at Washington May 28, 1947.

Entered into force May 28, 1947.

61 Stat. 3924; TIAS 1750; 8 Bevans 1250; 10 Bevans 188 and 213; 17 UNTS 29.

Amendment

June 1 and 8, 1950 (1 UST 638; TIAS 2119; 81 UNTS 320).

MAINTENANCE

Agreement for the enforcement of maintenance (support) obligations.

Signed at Washington May 30, 2001.

Entered into force May 1, 2002.

TIAS

MAPPING

Basic exchange and cooperative agreement concerning mapping, charting and geodesy cooperation, with glossary.

Signed at Fairfax April 26, 1995.

Entered into force April 26, 1995.

NP

MILITARY CEMETERIES AND MONUMENTS

Agreement concerning American military cemeteries with annex.

Signed at The Hague May 4, 1970.

Entered into force November 18, 1970.

21 UST 2416; TIAS 6978; 775 UNTS 77.

MUTUAL SECURITY

Agreement relating to the assurances required by the Mutual Security Act of 1951.

Exchange of notes at The Hague January 8, 1952.

Entered into force January 8, 1952.

3 UST 4633; TIAS 2615; 173 UNTS 372.

NARCOTIC DRUGS

Agreement of cooperation concerning access to and use of the facilities in the Netherlands Antilles and Aruba for aerial counter-narcotics activities.

Signed at Oranjestad March 2, 2000.

Entered into force November 2, 2001.

TIAS

NAVIGATION

Arrangement concerning the installation and support of a USAFE Loran C/D transmitter site, with annex.

Signed at Ramstein and The Hague May 17 and July 12, 1982.

Entered into force July 12, 1982.

TIAS 12379.

PACIFIC SETTLEMENT OF DISPUTES

Treaty for the advancement of peace.

Signed at Washington December 18, 1913.

Entered into force March 10, 1928.
Declaration interpretative of article I, signed at Washington February 13, 1928, entered into force February 27, 1928.

45 Stat. 2462; TS 760; 10 Bevans 64.

Treaty of arbitration.

Signed at Washington January 13, 1930.

Entered into force July 17, 1930.

46 Stat. 2769; TS 820; 10 Bevans 100; 107 LNTS 69.

PATENTS

Agreement to facilitate the interchange of patent rights and technical information for defense purposes with exchange of notes.

Signed at The Hague April 29, 1955.

Entered into force provisionally April 29, 1955; definitively July 13, 1955.

6 UST 2187; TIAS 3287; 219 UNTS 105.

Agreement approving the procedures for reciprocal filing of classified patent applications in the United States and the Netherlands.

Exchange of notes at The Hague October 8, 1959.

Entered into force October 8, 1959.

10 UST 1774; TIAS 4332; 358 UNTS 286.

POSTAL MATTERS

Parcel post agreement and detailed regulations.

Signed at Washington September 5 and at The Hague September 20, 1937.

Entered into force November 1, 1937.

51 Stat. 295; Post Office Department print; 184 LNTS 319.

International express mail agreement, with detailed regulations.

Signed at The Hague and Washington May 19 and June 10, 1980.

Entered into force September 1, 1980.

32 UST 2033; TIAS 9816; 1252 UNTS 153.

International express mail agreement, with detailed regulations.

Signed at Oranjestad and Washington August 15 and September 14, 1989.

Entered into force October 16, 1989.

TIAS 11695.

RELIEF SUPPLIES AND PACKAGES

Agreement relating to duty-free entry of relief goods, relief packages, and standard packs and to the defrayment of transportation charges thereon.

Exchange of notes at The Hague January 17, 1949.

Entered into force January 17, 1949.

63 Stat. 2322; TIAS 1881; 10 Bevans 259; 32 UNTS 241.

SEABEDS

Agreement relating to the agreement of August 14, 1987 on the resolution of practical problems with respect to deep seabed mining areas.[1]

Exchange of notes at The Hague August 14, 1987.

Entered into force October 19, 1988.

TIAS 11438; 1649 UNTS 117.

<u>NOTE</u>

1 Parties to the multilateral agreement of August 14, 1987 are Belgium, Canada, Italy, Netherlands and Union of Soviet Socialist Republics.

SHIPPING

Agreement relating to jurisdiction over vessels utilizing the Louisiana Offshore Oil Port.

Exchange of notes at Washington March 9 and 16, 1981.

Entered into force November 2, 1981.

33 UST 1555; TIAS 10132; 1307 UNTS 409.

SMUGGLING

Convention for the prevention of smuggling of alcoholic liquors.

Signed at Washington August 21, 1924.

Entered into force April 8, 1925.

44 Stat. 2013; TS 712; 10 Bevans 76; 33 LNTS 434.

SOCIAL SECURITY

Agreement on social security, with administrative arrangement.

Signed at The Hague December 8, 1987.

Entered into force November 1, 1990.

TIAS

Protocol to the agreement on social security and administrative arrangement of December 8, 1987.

Signed at The Hague December 7, 1989.

Entered into force November 1, 1990.

TIAS

Second protocol to the agreement on social security of December 8, 1987.

Signed at The Hague August 30, 2001.

Entered into force May 1, 2003.

TIAS

SURPLUS PROPERTY

Agreement relating to the release of the Netherlands from its obligations as guarantor for Indonesia under the surplus property agreement of May 28, 1947.

Exchange of notes at The Hague September 17, 1952, at Djakarta October 15, 1952, and at Washington April 8, 1953.

Entered into force April 8, 1953.

4 UST 1557; TIAS 2820; 205 UNTS 324.

TAXATION

Convention with respect to taxes on income and certain other taxes.[1]

Signed at Washington April 29, 1948.

Entered into force December 1, 1948.

62 Stat. 1757; TIAS 1855; 10 Bevans 225; 32 UNTS 167.

Convention modifying and supplementing the convention of April 29, 1948, as amended, for avoidance of double taxation with respect to taxes on income and certain other taxes.

Signed at Washington December 30, 1965.

Entered into force July 8, 1966.

17 UST 896; TIAS 6051; 577 UNTS 295.

Agreement relating to relief from taxation on United States Government expenditures in the Netherlands for the common defense.

Exchange of notes, with memorandum attached, at The Hague March 7, 1952.

Entered into force March 7, 1952.

3 UST 4183; TIAS 2563; 135 UNTS 199.

Agreement concerning the tax relief techniques and procedures pursuant to the agreement of March 7, 1952.

Exchange of notes at The Hague May 29 and June 22, 1953.

Entered into force June 22, 1953.

5 UST 2556; TIAS 3120; 234 UNTS 320.

Convention for the avoidance of double taxation and the prevention of fiscal evasion with respect to taxes on estates and inheritances with protocol.

Signed at Washington July 15, 1969.

Entered into force February 3, 1971.

22 UST 247; TIAS 7061; 791 UNTS 201.

Convention for the avoidance of double taxation and the prevention of fiscal evasion with respect to taxes on income with understanding and exchange of notes.

Signed at Washington December 18, 1992.

Entered into force December 31, 1993.

TIAS

Protocol amending the convention of December 18, 1992, for the avoidance of double taxation and the prevention of fiscal evasion with respect to taxes on income, with exchange of notes.

Signed at Washington October 13, 1993.

Entered into force December 30, 1993.

TIAS

Protocol amending Article VIII of the convention of April 29, 1948, with respect to taxes on income and certain other taxes as applicable to the Netherlands Antilles.

Signed at Washington October 10, 1995.

Entered into force December 30, 1996.

TIAS

Agreement in respect of Aruba for the exchange of information with respect to taxes.

Signed at Washington November 21, 2003.

Entered into force September 13, 2004.

TIAS

Protocol amending the convention of December 18, 1992, as amended, for the avoidance of double taxation and the prevention of fiscal evasion with respect to taxes on income, with exchange of notes.

Signed at Washington March 8, 2004.

Entered into force December 28, 2004.

TIAS

NOTE

1 The convention was supplemented by a protocol, signed at Washington June 15, 1955, for the purpose of facilitating the extension of the convention to the Netherlands Antilles (6 UST 3696; TIAS 3366; 239 UNTS 342). This was effectuated in accordance with exchanges of notes at Washington June 24 and August 7, 1952 and September 15 and November 4 and 10, 1955 (6 UST 3703; TIAS 3367; 239 UNTS 346). A further protocol modifying and supplementing the extension of the convention to the Netherlands Antilles was signed at The Hague October 23, 1963 (15 UST 1900; TIAS 5665; 521 UNTS 377). The convention became applicable to Aruba as a separate entity as of January 1, 1986.

In accordance with notifications given by the United States on June 29 and July 10, 1987, the convention ceased to apply to Aruba and the Netherlands Antilles, as of January 1, 1988, with the exception of Article VIII of the convention and such ancillary provisions as apply to effectuate, modify, or limit that article.

TELECOMMUNICATION

Agreement relating to the reciprocal granting of authorizations to permit licensed amateur radio operators of either country to operate their stations in the other country.[1]

Exchange of notes at The Hague June 22, 1966.

Entered into force December 21, 1966.

17 UST 2426; TIAS 6189; 590 UNTS 109.

NOTE

1 Applicable to Aruba and Netherlands Antilles.

TRADE AND COMMERCE

See COMMERCE. See also BENELUX

TRANSPORTATION

Memorandum of understanding concerning cooperation in the field of transportation.

Signed at Washington and The Hague September 28 and October 6, 1977.

Entered into force October 6, 1977.

29 UST 3577; TIAS 9029; 1134 UNTS 327.

VISAS

Agreement relating to the reciprocal waiver of passport visa fees for nonimmigrants.[1]

Exchanges of notes at The Hague January 21, February 11, and March 5 and 13, 1946.

Entered into force April 15, 1946.

61 Stat. 3834; TIAS 1728; 10 Bevans 178; 84 UNTS 3.

Agreement relating to visa requirements.

Exchange of notes at The Hague July 30 and August 20, 1947.

Entered into force August 20, 1947.

61 Stat. 3838; TIAS 1729; 10 Bevans 220; 84 UNTS 11.

NOTE

1 Applicable to Aruba and Netherlands Antilles.

WEATHER STATIONS

Agreement providing for lending ultra high frequency radio equipment for installation on Netherlands ocean weather ships stationed along the North Atlantic route.

Exchange of notes at Washington March 16 and 21, 1955.

Entered into force March 21, 1955.

9 UST 1302; TIAS 4119; 289 UNTS 129.

Agreement relating to continuation of the cooperative meteorological observation program in the Netherlands Antilles.[1]

Exchange of notes at The Hague June 15, 1970.

Entered into force provisionally June 15, 1970; definitively December 11, 1970.

21 UST 2643; TIAS 7005; 772 UNTS 147.

Agreement relating to cooperation regarding a hurricane monitoring and forecasting program for the Caribbean, with memorandum of arrangement.

Exchange of notes at The Hague July 26, 1979.

Entered into force May 8, 1980.

32 UST 414; TIAS 9708; 1221 UNTS 175.

NOTE

1 Also applicable to Aruba.

NETHERLANDS (NETHERLANDS ANTILLES)

AVIATION

Memorandum of agreement concerning assistance in developing and modernizing the Netherlands Antilles civil aviation infrastructure.

Signed at Washington and Willemstad March 28 and August 6, 1991.

Entered into force August 6, 1991.

TIAS 11803.

Agreement relating to air transport between the Netherlands Antilles and the United States of America, with annexes.

Signed at Washington July 14, 1998.

Entered into force February 16, 1999.

TIAS; 2066 UNTS 437.

POSTAL MATTERS

Parcel post agreement and detailed regulations for execution.

Signed at Willemstad May 10 and at Washington May 17, 1951; operative February 1, 1951.

2 UST 1509; TIAS 2294.

International express mail agreement, with detailed regulations.

Signed at Willemstad and Washington June 10 and 22, 1987.

Entered into force August 3, 1987.

TIAS 11305.

NEW CALEDONIA

POSTAL MATTERS

International express mail agreement, with detailed regulations.

Signed at Noumea and Washington April 9 and May 28, 1991.

Entered into force July 1, 1991.

TIAS 11809.

NEW ZEALAND

AEROSPACE DISTURBANCES

Agreement concerning a program of research on aerospace disturbances, with memorandum of understanding.

Exchange of notes at Wellington May 15, 1963.

Entered into force May 15, 1963.

14 UST 524; TIAS 5350; 477 UNTS 55.

ANTARCTICA

Agreement relating to cooperation in scientific and logistical operations in Antarctica, with memorandum of understanding.

Exchange of notes at Wellington December 24, 1958.

Entered into force December 24, 1958.

9 UST 1502; TIAS 4151; 324 UNTS 111.

Extension

October 18, 1960 (11 UST 2205; TIAS 4591; 447 UNTS 356).

ATOMIC ENERGY

Agreement providing for a grant to assist in the acquisition of nuclear research and training equipment and materials.

Exchange of notes at Wellington March 23, 1960.

Entered into force March 23, 1960.

11 UST 277; TIAS 4445; 371 UNTS 147.

AVIATION

Air transport agreement, with annexes.

Signed at Washington June 18, 1997.

Entered into force June 18, 1997.

TIAS; 2049 UNTS 379.

BOUNDARIES

Treaty on the delimitation of the maritime boundary between Tokelau and the United States of America.

Signed at Atafu December 2, 1980.

Entered into force September 3, 1983.

35 UST 2073; TIAS 10775.

CONSULS

Convention to regulate commerce (article IV) between the United States and the United Kingdom.

Signed at London July 3, 1815.

Entered into force July 3, 1815.

8 Stat. 228; TS 110; 12 Bevans 49.

CUSTOMS

Agreement regarding mutual assistance between their customs services.

Signed at Hong Kong June 13, 1996.

Entered into force June 13, 1996.

TIAS 12767; 1950 UNTS 3.

DEFENSE

Agreement relating to mutual defense assistance.

Exchange of notes at Washington June 19, 1952.

Entered into force June 19, 1952.

3 UST 4408; TIAS 2590; 178 UNTS 315.

Understanding that the assurances contained in the mutual defense assistance agreement of June 19, 1952 are applicable to equipment, materials, information and services furnished under the Mutual Security Act of 1954, as amended, and such other applicable United States laws as may come into effect.

Exchange of notes at Wellington March 25, 1960.

Entered into force March 25, 1960.

11 UST 315; TIAS 4450; 380 UNTS 424.

Agreement relating to a reciprocal arrangement under which, in certain circumstances, either of the respective armed forces would advance funds to units or personnel of the other for their temporary support, with annex.

Exchange of notes at Wellington September 3, 1969.

Entered into force September 3, 1969.

20 UST 2839; TIAS 6755; 723 UNTS 233.

Agreement concerning defense communications services, with annexes.

Signed at Wellington and Arlington August 12 and November 18, 1992.

Entered into force November 18, 1992.

TIAS 12357; 1937 UNTS 283.

Memorandum of agreement concerning the Navstar Global Positioning System, with annex.

Signed at Washington September 2, 1994.

Entered into force September 2, 1994.

TIAS 12358; 1937 UNTS 367.

Agreement concerning certain mutual defense commitments.

Exchange of notes at Washington July 16, 1996.

Entered into force July 16, 1996.

TIAS 12782; 1950 UNTS 15.

Agreement concerning defense communications services, with annexes and appendices.

Signed at Wellington and Arlington December 13, 2005 and March 30, 2006.

Entered into force March 30, 2006.

TIAS

EDUCATION

Agreement for the financing of certain educational and cultural exchange programs.

Signed at Wellington February 3, 1970.

Entered into force March 3, 1970.

21 UST 421; TIAS 6827; 240 UNTS 217.

Amendment

June 21, 1995.

EMPLOYMENT

Agreement relating to the employment of dependents of official government employees.

Exchange of notes at Washington May 18 and 21, 1999.

Entered into force May 21, 1999.

TIAS

EXTRADITION

Treaty on extradition.[1]

Signed at Washington January 12, 1970.

Entered into force December 8, 1970.

22 UST 1; TIAS 7035; 791 UNTS 253.

NOTE

1 Applicable to all territories.

HEALTH

Memorandum of understanding relative to exporting dry milk products to the United States.

Signed at Wellington and at Washington October 23 and November 11, 1975.

Entered into force November 11, 1975.

28 UST 345; TIAS 8472.

LEND-LEASE

Agreement relating to the principles applying to the provision of aid in the prosecution of war.

Exchange of notes at Washington September 3, 1942.

Entered into force September 3, 1942.

56 Stat. 1611; EAS 272; 10 Bevans 285; 24 UNTS 185.

Agreement on settlement for lend-lease and reciprocal aid, surplus war property, and claims.

Signed at Washington July 10, 1946.

Entered into force July 10, 1946.

60 Stat. 1791; TIAS 1536; 10 Bevans 296; 6 UNTS 341.

MAPPING

Agreement relating to an aerial photographic survey of the New Zealand coastline.

Exchange of notes at Washington October 30, 1959.

Entered into force October 30, 1959.

10 UST 1983; TIAS 4364; 361 UNTS 21.

NAVIGATION

Agreement for the establishment and operation of an OMEGA navigation system monitoring facility.

Exchange of notes at Wellington March 3, 1983.

Entered into force March 3, 1983.

TIAS 10668; 1675 UNTS 265.

OCEANOGRAPHY

Agreement concerning the installation, operation and maintenance in New Zealand of Global Sea Level Data Collection (GSL) Stations, with arrangements.

Exchange of notes at Wellington November 18, 1992.

Entered into force November 18, 1992.

TIAS 11973; 1937 UNTS 271.

PACIFIC SETTLEMENT OF DISPUTES

Treaty amending in their application to New Zealand certain provisions of the treaty for the advancement of peace between the United States and the United Kingdom signed at Washington September 15, 1914.

Signed at Washington September 6, 1940.

Entered into force August 13, 1941.

55 Stat. 1217; TS 976; 10 Bevans 282.

POSTAL MATTERS

Agreement concerning the exchange of parcel post.

Signed at Wellington March 3 and at Washington April 24, 1933; operative October 1, 1932.

48 Stat. 1491; Post Office Department print.

Memorandum of understanding concerning international express mail service, with detailed regulations.

Signed at Wellington and Washington August 1 and 20, 1984.

Entered into force October 28, 1984.

TIAS 11003; 2022 UNTS 51.

Memorandum of understanding concerning the operation of the INTELPOST service, with details of implementation.

Signed at Berne April 28, 1989.

Entered into force May 1, 1989.

TIAS 11610.

PROPERTY

Convention between the United States and the United Kingdom relating to tenure and disposition of real and personal property.

Signed at Washington March 2, 1899.

Entered into force for New Zealand June 10, 1901.

31 Stat. 1939; TS 146; I Malloy 774.

Supplementary convention relating to the tenure and disposition of real and personal property.

Signed at Washington May 27, 1936, by the United States, United Kingdom, Australia, and New Zealand.

Entered into force March 10, 1941.

55 Stat. 1101; TS 964; 5 Bevans 140; 203 LNTS 367.

SCIENTIFIC COOPERATION

Agreement concerning the establishment of an astronomical observatory at Blackbirch Ridge, with memorandum of understandings and agreed minute.

Exchange of notes at Wellington November 11, 1982.

Entered into force November 11, 1982.

TIAS 10604; 1675 UNTS 247.

Agreement for scientific and technological cooperation, with annex and exchange of letters.

Signed at Washington May 21, 1991.

Entered into force May 21, 1991.

TIAS 11829; 1937 UNTS 235.

SHELLFISH

Memorandum of understanding concerning cooperation to assure the sanitary quality of bivalve mulluscs exported to the United States.

Signed at Washington and Wellington October 14 and 30, 1980.

Entered into force October 30, 1980.

32 UST 4545; TIAS 9968; 1266 UNTS 35.

TAXATION

Convention for the avoidance of double taxation and the prevention of fiscal evasion with respect to taxes on income, with protocol.[1]

Signed at Wellington July 23, 1982.

Entered into force November 2, 1983.

35 UST 1949; TIAS 10772.

NOTE

1 Does not include Tokelau or the Associated Self Governing States of the Cook Islands and Niue.

TELECOMMUNICATION

Agreement relating to the reciprocal granting of authorizations to permit licensed amateur radio operators of either country to operate their stations in the other country.

Exchange of notes at Wellington June 21, 1967.

Entered into force June 21, 1967.

18 UST 1272; TIAS 6281; 644 UNTS 77.

TRACKING STATIONS

Agreement for a space vehicle tracking program.

Exchange of notes at Wellington July 9, 1968.

Entered into force July 9, 1968.

19 UST 5836; TIAS 6539; 644 UNTS 99.

TRADE AND COMMERCE

Agreement relating to the multilateral trade negotiations, and related letter of February 4, 1980.

Signed at Geneva May 21, 1979.

Entered into force January 1, 1980.

32 UST 5868; TIAS 10019; 1266 UNTS 23.

VISAS

Agreement relating to the reciprocal reduction of nonimmigrant passport visa fees and the extension of validity of temporary visitors' visas.[1]

Exchange of notes at Wellington March 14, 1949.

Entered into force March 14, 1949; operative April 1, 1949.

63 Stat. 2538; TIAS 1940; 10 Bevans 331; 32 UNTS 369.

Agreement relating to the abolition of visa fees and the extension of the period of validity for certain types of nonimmigrant visas.

Exchange of notes at Wellington December 16, 1957, and May 2 and 5, 1958.

Entered into force May 5, 1958; operative June 1, 1958.

9 UST 913; TIAS 4053; 317 UNTS 59.

Amendment

May 13, 1958 (9 UST 919; TIAS 4053; 317 UNTS 70).

NOTE

1 Applicable to all territories.

NICARAGUA

AGRICULTURAL COMMODITIES

Agricultural commodities agreement.

Signed at Managua August 31, 1979.

Entered into force August 31, 1979.

32 UST 1615; TIAS 9790; 1234 UNTS 230.

Amendments

February 11 and 13, 1980 (32 UST 1628; TIAS 9790; 1234 UNTS 241).

March 20 and 25, 1980 (32 UST 1632; TIAS 9790; 1234 UNTS 244).

June 19, 1980 (32 UST 1814; TIAS 9798; 1234 UNTS 247).

AGRICULTURE

Agreement continuing in force an agreement of January 11, 1941, relating to plantation rubber investigations in Nicaragua.

Exchange of notes at Managua June 23 and 26, 1943.

Entered into force July 1, 1943.

57 Stat. 1212; EAS 357; 10 Bevans 436; 117 UNTS 253.

Agreement confirming the cooperative agreement for the prevention of foot-and-mouth disease and rinderpest in Nicaragua.

Exchange of notes at Managua March 24 and April 13, 1972.

Entered into force April 13, 1972.

23 UST 1228; TIAS 7392; 852 UNTS 201.

Cooperative agreement for the eradication of screwworms.

Signed at Washington November 26, 1991.

Entered into force January 11, 1993.

TIAS 12444.

AVIATION

Air transport agreement, with annexes.

Signed at San Jose May 8, 1997.

Entered into force December 5, 1997.

TIAS

Memorandum of agreement for the provision of assistance in developing and modernizing Nicaragua's civil aviation infrastructure.

Signed at Washington and Managua April 29 and August 30, 1999.

Entered into force August 30, 1999.

TIAS

CULTURAL PROPERTY

Agreement concerning the imposition of import restrictions on archaeological material from the pre-Hispanic cultures of the Republic of Nicaragua.

Signed at Managua June 16, 1999.

Entered into force October 20, 2000.

TIAS

CUSTOMS

Interim agreement relating to customs exemptions of diplomatic and consular officials.

Exchange of notes at Washington December 3, 1951, and October 9, 1952.

Entered into force October 9, 1952.

3 UST 5154; TIAS 2708; 184 UNTS 105.

DEFENSE

Military assistance agreement.

Signed at Managua April 23, 1954.

Entered into force April 23, 1954.

5 UST 453; TIAS 2940; 229 UNTS 37.

Agreement relating to the disposition of equipment and materials furnished by the United States under the military assistance agreement of April 23, 1954.

Exchange of notes at Managua April 23, 1954.

Entered into force April 23, 1954.

13 UST 116; TIAS 4946; 435 UNTS 340.

Agreement for performance by members of army and air force missions of duties of military assistance advisory group specified in article V of military assistance agreement.

Exchange of notes at Managua January 17 and February 9, 1957.

Entered into force February 9, 1957.

8 UST 285; TIAS 3773; 279 UNTS 191.

Agreement relating to deposit by Nicaragua of ten percent of the value of grant military assistance and excess defense articles furnished by the United States.

Exchange of notes at Managua March 6 and April 10, 1972.

Entered into force April 10, 1972; effective February 7, 1972.

23 UST 671; TIAS 7332.

Agreement concerning payment to the United States of net proceeds from the sale of defense articles furnished under the military assistance program.

Exchange of notes at Managua May 15 and June 28, 1974.

Entered into force July 1, 1974.

25 UST 1450; TIAS 7876.

Amendment

January 20 and February 3, 2005.

Agreement regarding the status of U.S. military and civilian personnel of the Department of Defense present in Nicaragua in connection with the disaster relief/assistance effort and mutually agreed follow-on activities.

Exchange of notes at Managua November 7 and 25, 1998.

Entered into force November 25, 1998.

NP

Agreement regarding loan of military equipment.

Exchange of notes at Managua August 26 and September 4, 2003.

Entered into force September 4, 2003.

TIAS

Agreement regarding grants under the Foreign Assistance Act of 1961, as amended, and the furnishing of defense articles, defense services, and related training, including pursuant to the United States International Military and Education Training Program (IMET), from the United States to the Government of the Republic of Nicaragua.

Exchange of notes at Managua December 5, 2005 and April 19, 2006.

Entered into force April 19, 2006.

NP

ECONOMIC AND TECHNICAL COOPERATION

General agreement for economic, technical and related assistance.

Exchange of notes at Managua March 30, 1962.

Entered into force May 14, 1962.

13 UST 1208; TIAS 5065; 456 UNTS 241.

Millennium challenge compact, with attachments and annexes.

Signed at Washington July 14, 2005.

Entered into force May 26, 2006.

TIAS

Agency for International Development

August 30, 1978 (30 UST 5157; TIAS 9502).

May 31, 1990 (NP).

September 26, 1990 (NP).

May 8, 1991 (NP).

December 5, 1992 (NP).

January 19, 1994 (NP).

EMPLOYMENT

Agreement relating to the employment of dependents of official government employees.

Exchange of notes at Managua January 26 and February 2, 1994.

Entered into force February 2, 1994.

TIAS 12173.

EXTRADITION

Treaty on extradition.

Signed at Washington March 1, 1905.

Entered into force July 14, 1907.

35 Stat. 1869; TS 462; 10 Bevans 356.

FINANCE

Agreement regarding the discharge of certain debts owed to the Government of the United States, with annex.

Signed at Managua September 25, 1991.

Entered into force September 25, 1991.

NP

Agreement regarding the consolidation and rescheduling or refinancing of certain debts owed to, guaranteed by, or insured by the United States Government and its agencies, with annexes.

Signed at Managua May 13, 1992.

Entered into force July 10, 1992.

NP

Amendment

July 21 and September 26, 1997 (NP).

Agreement among the United States and the Government of Nicaragua/Central American Business Administration Institute regarding the assumption, payment and discharge of certain debts.

Exchange of notes at Managua August 28, 1995.

Entered into force August 28, 1995.

NP

Agreement regarding the consolidation and rescheduling of certain debts owed to, guaranteed by or insured by the United States Government and its agencies, with annexes.

Signed at Managua August 28, 1995.

Entered into force November 1, 1995.

NP

Agreement regarding the consolidation, reduction and rescheduling of certain debts owed to, guaranteed by, or insured by the United States Government and its agencies, with annexes.

Signed at Managua October 20, 1998.

Entered into force December 21, 1998.

NP

Amendment

April 9 and May 19, 1999 (NP).

Agreement regarding the reduction of certain debts owed to, guaranteed by, or insured by the United States Government, with annexes.

Signed at Managua April 25, 2003.

Entered into force June 9, 2003.

NP

Investment incentive agreement.

Signed at Managua July 20, 2004.

Entered into force July 20, 2004.

TIAS

Agreement regarding the cancellation of certain debts owed to, guaranteed by, or insured by the United States Government, with annexes.

Signed at Managua August 17, 2004.

Entered into force December 27, 2004.

NP

HIGHWAYS

Agreement relating to the construction of the inter-American highway.

Exchange of notes at Washington April 8, 1942.

Entered into force April 8, 1942.

56 Stat. 1845; EAS 295; 10 Bevans 424; 24 UNTS 145.

Amendment

April 4 and 20, 1951 (2 UST 1848; TIAS 2320; 138 UNTS 57).

Agreement relating to the construction of the Rama Road.

Exchange of notes at Washington April 8 and 18, 1942.

Entered into force April 18, 1942.

2 UST 722; TIAS 2229; 132 UNTS 343.

Amendments

September 2, 1953 (4 UST 1944; TIAS 2853; 215 UNTS 69).

March 13 and August 2, 1956 (7 UST 2237; TIAS 3623; 281 UNTS 99).

INTERNATIONAL CRIMINAL COURT

Agreement regarding the surrender of persons to the International Criminal Court.

Signed at Managua June 4, 2003.

Entered into force September 12, 2003.

TIAS

MAPPING

Basic exchange and cooperative agreement for topographic mapping, nautical and aeronautical charting and information, geodesy and geophysics, digital data and related mapping, charting and geodesy materials.

Signed at Managua and Fairfax November 28 and December 1, 1994.

Entered into force December 1, 1994.

NP

MISSIONS, MILITARY[1]

1

Agreement relating to an air force mission to Nicaragua.

Signed at Managua November 19, 1952.

Entered into force November 19, 1952.

3 UST 5027; TIAS 2683; 186 UNTS 2.

Extensions and amendments

August 21 and 27, 1956 (7 UST 2465; TIAS 3634; 277 UNTS 352).

March 25 and May 22, 1959 (10 UST 1446; TIAS 4294; 357 UNTS 369).

1

Agreement providing for a United States Army mission to Nicaragua.

Signed at Managua November 19, 1953.

Entered into force November 19, 1953.

4 UST 2238; TIAS 2876; 206 UNTS 117.

Amendment

March 25 and May 22, 1959 (10 UST 1446; TIAS 4294; 357 UNTS 369).

NOTE

1 The Air Force and Army missions were consolidated September 10, 1965.

NARCOTIC DRUGS

Agreement concerning cooperation to suppress illicit traffic by sea and air.

Signed at Managua June 1, 2001.

Entered into force November 15, 2001.

TIAS

Agreement concerning Cooperating Nation Information Exchange System (CNIES).

Exchange of notes at Managua October 18 and November 23, 2004.

Entered into force November 23, 2004.

NP

PEACE CORPS

Agreement relating to the establishment of a Peace Corps program in Nicaragua.

Exchange of notes at Managua May 23 and 25, 1968.

Entered into force May 25, 1968.

19 UST 5073; TIAS 6507; 707 UNTS 61.

POSTAL MATTERS

Agreement for parcel post service.

Signed at Managua March 19 and at Washington April 4, 1956.

Entered into force July 1, 1956.

7 UST 1051; TIAS 3586; 275 UNTS 231.

International express mail agreement, with detailed regulations.

Signed at Managua and Washington July 24 and August 16, 1991.

Entered into force September 30, 1991.

TIAS 11798.

PUBLICATIONS

Agreement relating to the exchange of official publications.

Exchange of notes at Managua February 14 and 19, 1940.

Entered into force February 14, 1940.

54 Stat. 2294; EAS 171; 10 Bevans 411; 203 LNTS 47.

SCIENTIFIC COOPERATION

Memorandum of understanding concerning scientific cooperation in the earth and mapping sciences, with annexes.

Signed at Reston and Managua March 4 and 10, 1999.

Entered into force March 10, 1999.

TIAS

Amendment and extension

May 24 and June 25, 2004.

TELECOMMUNICATION

Agreement relating to radio communications between amateur stations on behalf of third parties.

Exchange of notes at Managua October 8 and 16, 1956.

Entered into force October 16, 1956.

7 UST 3159; TIAS 3694; 282 UNTS 29.

Agreement relating to the reciprocal granting of authorizations to permit licensed amateur radio operators of either country to operate their stations in the other country.

Exchange of notes at Managua September 3 and 20, 1966.

Entered into force September 20, 1966.

17 UST 1560; TIAS 6112; 607 UNTS 167.

TRADE

Agreement terminating the agreement of September 5, 1972 relating to trade in cotton textiles and providing for consultations on problems of market disruption as defined in the arrangement regarding international trade in textiles of December 20, 1973.

Exchange of notes at Managua December 26, 1974 and January 3, 1975.

Entered into force January 3, 1975.

26 UST 41; TIAS 8007.

Agreement on trade in textile and apparel goods under the Dominican Republic-Central America-United States Free Trade Agreement.

Exchange of letters at Managua and Washington March 24 and 27, 2006.

Entered into force March 27, 2006.

NP

VISAS

Agreement relating to the reciprocal granting of nonimmigrant visas, without fee, for maximum validity for four years.

Exchange of notes at Managua July 6, September 30 and October 22, 1955.

Entered into force October 22, 1955.

10 UST 1696; TIAS 4319; 358 UNTS 51.

NIGER

DEFENSE

Agreement relating to the furnishing of military equipment, materials and services to Niger to help assure its security and independence.

Exchange of notes at Niamey May 22 and June 14, 1962.

Entered into force June 14, 1962.

13 UST 1301; TIAS 5083; 458 UNTS 233.

Agreement concerning the provision of training related to defense articles under the United States International Military Education and Training (IMET) Program.

Exchange of notes at Niamey March 11 and June 9, 1980.

Entered into force June 9, 1980.

33 UST 576; TIAS 10049; 1267 UNTS 123.

Agreement regarding the terms and conditions relating to the furnishing of defense articles and services on a grant basis to the Government of Niger by the United States.

Exchange of notes at Niamey July 18 and September 24, 1992.

Entered into force September 24, 1992.

TIAS 12359.

Amendment

January 13 and February 18, 2005.

Agreement regarding grants under the Foreign Assistance Act of 1961, as amended, and the furnishing of defense articles, related training to include training related to defense articles under the United States International Military Education and Training (IMET) Program, and other defense services from the United States of America to the Government of Niger.

Exchange of notes at Niamey January 22 and March 12, 2004.

Entered into force March 12, 2004.

NP

ECONOMIC AND TECHNICAL COOPERATION

Agreement providing for the furnishing of economic, technical and related assistance.

Exchange of notes at Niamey May 26, 1961.

Entered into force May 26, 1961.

12 UST 858; TIAS 4786; 410 UNTS 213.

Agency for International Development

June 9, 1976 (29 UST 5708; TIAS 9143).

July 1, 1977 (29 UST 5711; TIAS 9143).

September 26, 1977 (29 UST 4737; TIAS 9078).

April 25, 1978 (30 UST 3077; TIAS 9380; 1178 UNTS 281).

June 10, 1987 (NP).

ENVIRONMENTAL COOPERATION

Agreement for cooperation in the GLOBE program.

Signed at Niamey August 11, 2005.

Entered into force August 11, 2005.

TIAS

FINANCE

Agreement relating to investment guaranties.

Exchange of notes at Niamey February 28 and April 26, 1962.

Entered into force April 26, 1962.

13 UST 2203; TIAS 5187; 459 UNTS 129.

Agreement regarding the consolidation and rescheduling of certain debts owed to, guaranteed by or insured by the United States Government and its agencies, with annexes.

Signed at Niamey June 11, 1984.

Entered into force July 24, 1984.

TIAS 10994; 2022 UNTS 77.

Agreement regarding the consolidation and rescheduling of certain debts owed to, guaranteed by or insured by the United States Government and its agencies, with annexes.

Signed at Niamey April 9, 1985.

Entered into force May 28, 1985.

NP

Agreement regarding the consolidation and rescheduling of certain debts owed to, guaranteed by, or insured by the United States Government and its agencies, with annexes.

Signed at Niamey April 11, 1986.

Entered into force May 19, 1986.

NP

Agreement regarding the consolidation and rescheduling of certain debts owed to, guaranteed by or insured by the United States Government and its agencies, with annexes.

Signed at Niamey February 10, 1988.

Entered into force March 17, 1988.

NP

Agreement regarding the consolidation and rescheduling of certain debts owed to, guaranteed by or insured by the United States Government and its agencies, with annexes.

Signed at Niamey February 21, 1989.

Entered into force March 30, 1989.

NP

Agreement regarding the consolidation and rescheduling of certain debts owed to, guaranteed by, or insured by the United States Government and its agencies, with annexes.

Signed at Washington June 29, 1989.

Entered into force August 24, 1989.

NP

Agreement regarding the consolidation and rescheduling of certain debts owed to, guaranteed by, or insured by the United States Government and its agencies, with annexes.

Signed at Washington February 12, 1991.

Entered into force March 28, 1991.

NP

Agreement regarding the consolidation, reduction and rescheduling of certain debts owed to, guaranteed by or insured by the United States Government and its agencies, with annexes.

Signed at Niamey July 29, 1994.

Entered into force August 29, 1994.

NP

Agreement regarding the consolidation, reduction and rescheduling of certain debts owed to, guaranteed by, or insured by the United States Government and its Agencies, with annexes.

Signed at Niamey January 14, 1998.

Entered into force March 27, 1998.

NP

Agreement regarding the consolidation, reduction, and rescheduling of certain debts owed to, guaranteed by, or insured by the United States Government and its agencies, with annexes.

Signed at Niamey August 1, 2001.

Entered into force September 4, 2001.

NP

Amendment

January 29 and 30, 2003.

Agreement regarding the reduction of certain debts owed to, guaranteed by, or insured by the United States Government, with annexes.

Signed at Niamey January 31, 2005.

Entered into force March 10, 2005.

NP

PEACE CORPS

Agreement relating to the establishment of a Peace Corps program in Niger.

Exchange of notes at Niamey July 23, 1962.

Entered into force July 23, 1962.

14 UST 868; TIAS 5368; 487 UNTS 325.

POSTAL MATTERS

International express mail agreement, with detailed regulations.

Signed at Niamey and Washington May 6 and 29, 1987.

Entered into force June 15, 1987.

TIAS 11302.

SOCIAL SECURITY

Agreement to provide certain social security benefits for certain employees of the United States in Niger.

Signed at Niamey July 21, 1975.

Entered into force July 21, 1975; effective January 1, 1974.

26 UST 2758; TIAS 8194; 1045 UNTS 65.

NIGERIA

On October 1, 1960 the territories formerly comprising the British Colony and Protectorate of Nigeria attained fully responsible status within the British Commonwealth under the name of the Federation of Nigeria (Federation of Nigeria Independence Act, 1960). By an exchange of notes, dated October 1, 1960, between the High

Commissioner for the United Kingdom in the Federation of Nigeria and the Prime Minister of the Federation of Nigeria, Nigeria agreed to assume, from October 1, 1960, all obligations and responsibilities of the United Kingdom which arise from any valid international instrument insofar as such instruments may be held to have application to or in respect of Nigeria are from October 1, 1960 enjoyed by the Federation of Nigeria.

AGRICULTURE

Agreement for the provision of technical services in the preparation of a comprehensive soil survey of Nigeria.

Signed at Lagos September 22, 1980.

Entered into force August 1, 1981.

33 UST 798; TIAS 10062; 1267 UNTS 225.

AVIATION

Arrangement between the United States and the United Kingdom relating to pilot licenses to operate civil aircraft.

Exchange of notes at Washington March 28 and April 5, 1935.

Entered into force May 5, 1935.

49 Stat. 3731; EAS 77; 12 Bevans 513; 162 LNTS 59.

Air transport agreement, with memorandum of understanding.

Signed at Lagos April 27, 1978.

Entered into force provisionally April 27, 1978; definitively June 16, 1978.

29 UST 3102; TIAS 8999; 1124 UNTS 255.

CONSULS

Consular convention between the United States and the United Kingdom.

Signed at Washington June 6, 1951.

Entered into force September 7, 1952.

3 UST 3426; TIAS 2494; 165 UNTS 121.

DEFENSE

See also MUTUAL SECURITY

Agreement relating to the deposit by Nigeria of ten percent of the value of grant military assistance furnished by the United States.

Exchange of notes at Lagos April 12 and 20, 1972.

Entered into force April 20, 1972; effective February 7, 1972.

23 UST 773; TIAS 7338.

Agreement concerning the provision of training related to defense articles under the United States International Military Education and Training (IMET) Program.

Exchange of notes at Lagos November 19, 1985 and February 26, 1986.

Entered into force February 26, 1986.

TIAS 11106.

Agreement regarding the provision of commodities and services to Nigerian forces participating in ECOMOG peacekeeping operations.

Exchange of notes at Abuja November 9, 1996.

Entered into force November 9, 1996.

TIAS 12778.

Agreement regarding grants under the Foreign Assistance Act of 1961, as amended, and the furnishing of defense articles, related training, and other defense services from the United States of America to the Government of the Federal Republic of Nigeria.

Exchange of notes at Abuja July 27 and August 17, 2000.

Entered into force August 17, 2000.

TIAS

Agreement concerning the status of United States military and civilian personnel of the U.S. Department of Defense temporarily present in Nigeria in connection with military training and other activities as may be agreed upon by the two governments.

Exchange of notes at Abuja August 24 and September 7, 2000.

Entered into force September 7, 2000.

NP

Agreement concerning end-use, retransfer and security assurances regarding AKM rifles and related equipment provided to the Government of Nigeria for use in connection with regional efforts concerning Sierra Leone and Operation Focus Relief and other purposes related to self-defense and regional security, with attachment.

Exchange of notes at Abuja January 29 and March 6, 2002.

Entered into force March 6, 2002.

TIAS

ECONOMIC AND TECHNICAL COOPERATION

Economic cooperation agreement between the United States and the United Kingdom.

Signed at London July 6, 1948; applicable to Nigeria July 6, 1948.

62 Stat. 2596; TIAS 1795; 12 Bevans 874; 22 UNTS 263.

Amendments

January 3, 1950 (1 UST 184; TIAS 2036; 86 UNTS 304).

May 25, 1951 (2 UST 1292; TIAS 2277; 99 UNTS 308).

February 25, 1953 (4 UST 1528; TIAS 2815; 172 UNTS 332).

Agency for International Development

June 30, 2004 (NP).

EDUCATION

Agreement on the training of Nigerian technical educators, with annexes.

Signed at Washington September 9, 1981.

Entered into force September 9, 1981.

TIAS 10261; 33 UST 3783; 1541 UNTS 181.

EMPLOYMENT

Bilateral employment agreement.

Signed at Abuja May 12, 2005.

Entered into force May 12, 2005.

TIAS

EXTRADITION

Extradition treaty between the United States and the United Kingdom.

Signed at London December 22, 1931; applicable to Nigeria June 24, 1935.

47 Stat. 2122; TS 849; 12 Bevans 482; 163 LNTS 59.

FINANCE

Agreement regarding the consolidation and rescheduling of certain debts owed to, guaranteed by or insured by the United States Government and its agencies, with annexes.

Signed at Lagos December 23, 1987.

Entered into force February 16, 1988.

NP

Agreement regarding the consolidation and rescheduling of certain debts owed to, guaranteed by, or insured by the United States Government and its agencies.

Signed at Lagos December 4, 1989.

Entered into force January 22, 1990.

NP

Agreement regarding the consolidation and rescheduling or refinancing of certain debts owed to, guaranteed by, or insured by the United States Government and its agencies, with annexes.

Signed at Lagos August 2, 1991.

Entered into force September 18, 1991.

NP

Investment incentive agreement.

Signed at Abuja December 6, 1999.

Entered into force January 20, 2003.

TIAS

Agreement regarding the reduction of certain debts owed to, guaranteed by, or insured by the United States Government and its agency, with annexes.

Signed at Abuja December 17, 2005.

Entered into force January 20, 2006.

NP

INTERNATIONAL CRIMINAL COURT

Agreement regarding the surrender of persons to the International Criminal Court.

Signed at Abuja June 30, 2003.

Entered into force October 6, 2003.

TIAS

JUDICIAL ASSISTANCE

Procedures for mutual assistance in the administration of justice in connection with the Lockheed Aircraft Corporation matter.

Signed at Washington April 20, 1976.

Entered into force April 20, 1976.

27 UST 1054; TIAS 8243.

Related agreement

March 8 and 26, 1979 (NP).

Agreement on procedures for mutual assistance in law enforcement matters.

Signed at Washington November 2, 1987.

Entered into force November 2, 1987.

TIAS 11540; 2192 UNTS 29.

Treaty on mutual legal assistance in criminal matters, with attachments.

Signed at Washington September 13, 1989.

Entered into force January 14, 2003.

TIAS

MUTUAL SECURITY

Agreement between the United States and the United Kingdom relating to the assurances required under the Mutual Security Act of 1951.

Exchange of notes at London January 8, 1952; applicable to Nigeria January 8, 1952.

3 UST 4665; TIAS 2622; 126 UNTS 307.

NARCOTIC DRUGS

Mutual cooperation agreement for reducing demand, preventing illicit use and combatting illicit production and trafficking in drugs.

Exchange of notes at Lagos January 13 and 24, 1989.

Entered into force January 24, 1989.

TIAS 11598; 2190 UNTS 333.

PEACE CORPS

Agreement establishing a Peace Corps program in Nigeria.

Exchange of notes at Lagos August 19 and 22, 1991.

Entered into force August 22, 1991.

TIAS 12108.

POSTAL MATTERS

International express mail agreement, with detailed regulations.

Signed at Lagos and Washington March 7 and April 21, 1986.

Entered into force July 1, 1986.

TIAS 11407.

Postal money order agreement, with attachments.

Signed at Lagos and Washington June 14 and 28, 1990.

Entered into force September 1, 1990.

TIAS 11759.

PROPERTY

Convention between the United States and the United Kingdom relating to the tenure and disposition of real and personal property.[1]

Signed at Washington March 2, 1899.

31 Stat. 1939; TS 146; 12 Bevans 246.

NOTE

1 Notification given on July 22, 1901 of application to Northern Nigeria, and on July 27, 1901 of application to Southern Nigeria.

TELECOMMUNICATION

Agreement relating to the installation and operation of a radio transmitter by the Embassy of Nigeria.

Exchange of notes at Washington November 19 and 22, 1974 and June 4, 1975.

Entered into force June 4, 1975.

27 UST 3297; TIAS 8364; 1068 UNTS 457.

TRADE

Agreement concerning trade in textiles and textile products, with annexes.

Signed at Lagos July 30, 1992.

Entered into force July 30, 1992; effective January 1, 1990.

NP

TRADE-MARKS

Declaration by the United States and the United Kingdom relating to reciprocal protection to trade-marks.

Signed at London October 24, 1877.

Entered into force October 24, 1877.

20 Stat. 703; TS 138; 12 Bevans 198.

NIUE

PEACE CORPS

Agreement concerning the program of the Peace Corps in Niue.

Signed at Alofi September 23, 1994.

Entered into force September 23, 1994.

TIAS 12109.

NORTH ATLANTIC TREATY ORGANIZATION (NATO)

DEFENSE

Agreement regarding U.S. approval for retransfer of U.S. defense articles and services to NATO for purposes of supporting the NATO–led Implementation Force (IFOR).

Exchange of letters at Brussels December 18, 1995.

Entered into force December 18, 1995.

TIAS

EMPLOYMENT

Arrangement concerning the employment by the North Atlantic Treaty Organization of United States nationals.

Signed at London September 29, 1951.

Entered into force September 29, 1951.

5 UST 1112; TIAS 2992.

Agreement concerning the employment by the International Military Headquarters of United States nationals.

Signed at Paris February 25, 1953.

Entered into force February 25, 1953.

5 UST 890; TIAS 2978.

Supplemental arrangement concerning the employment by NATO bodies of United States nationals.

Signed at Brussels June 3, 1983.

Entered into force June 3, 1983.

TIAS 10695; 2005 UNTS 189.

HEADQUARTERS

Agreement between the United States and the Headquarters of the Supreme Allied Commander Atlantic regarding the headquarters, with exchange of letters.

Signed at Washington October 22, 1954.

Entered into force October 22, 1954; operative April 10, 1954.

5 UST 2519; TIAS 3113; 249 UNTS 175.

PRIVILEGES AND IMMUNITIES

Agreement concerning the application of part IV of the agreement on the status of the North Atlantic Treaty Organization, national representatives and international staff, September 20, 1951 (TIAS 2992) to the officials of NATO civilian bodies located on the territory of the United States of America.

Signed at Brussels March 3, 1981.

Entered into force March 3, 1981.

33 UST 1272; TIAS 10110; 1307 UNTS 423.

SATELLITE COMMUNICATIONS

Agreement concerning the North Atlantic Treaty Organization satellite communications earth terminal in the United States.

Signed at Washington July 10 and at Mons, Belgium August 20, 1970.

Entered into force August 20, 1970.

21 UST 2089; TIAS 6955; 764 UNTS 225.

TAXATION

Tax reimbursement agreement, with annex.

Signed at Brussels July 18, 1990.

Entered into force July 18, 1990.

TIAS 11947.

TELECOMMUNICATION

Memorandum of understanding concerning the interconnection of the NICS TARE and the US AUTODIN network, with annex.

Signed at Brussels and Washington April 26 and May 31, 1991.

Entered into force May 31, 1991.

TIAS

Memorandum of agreement concerning the interconnection of the Initial Voice Switched Network (IVSN) of the NATO Integrated Communications System and the Defense Switched Network (DSN) of the U.S. Defense Information Infrastructure, with annex.

Signed at Brussels and Arlington February 16 and April 21, 1995.

Entered into force April 21, 1995.

TIAS 12633.

NORTH ATLANTIC TREATY ORGANIZATION AEW&C PROGRAMME MANAGEMENT ORGANIZATION (NAPMO)

DEFENSE

Memorandum of agreement concerning the cooperative production of radar system improvements for the E-3 aircraft.

Signed at Hanscom AFB and Washington August 3 and 11, 1995.

Entered into force August 11, 1995.

TIAS 12682.

Memorandum of agreement concerning cooperative projects for the E-3 aircraft, with annex.

Signed at Washington and Brunssum August 10 and 30, 1999.

Entered into force August 30, 1999.

TIAS

NORTH ATLANTIC TREATY ORGANIZATION CONSULTATION, COMMAND AND CONTROL ORGANIZATION

DEFENSE

Memorandum of agreement concerning air command, control, communications and intelligence capabilities.

Signed at Washington and Brussels April 23 and May 7, 2002.

Entered into force May 7, 2002.

TIAS

NORTH ATLANTIC TREATY ORGANIZATION HAWK PRODUCTION AND LOGISTICS ORGANIZATION

DEFENSE

Amendment one to the agreement for the fire direction operation center project.

Signed at Biloxi March 12, 2002.

Entered into force March 12, 2002.

TIAS

NORTH ATLANTIC TREATY ORGANIZATION MAINTENANCE AND SUPPLY ORGANIZATION (NAMSO)

SUPPLIES

Agreement for credit sales of military equipment, materials, and services.

Signed at Paris June 22, 1959.

Entered into force June 22, 1959.

10 UST 1156; TIAS 4252.

Basic agreement on mutual support, with annex.

Signed at Stuttgart-Vaihingen February 2, 1982.

Entered into force February 2, 1982.

34 UST 118; TIAS 10342; 1556 UNTS 315.

Amendment

April 30 and May 7, 1990 (TIAS 12414).

Agreement regarding consolidated procurement of munitions.

Signed at Washington and Capellen April 5 and 12, 1988.

Entered into force April 12, 1988.

TIAS

Agreement regarding the transfer of USG-origin spare parts and components maintained and serviced by NAMSO.

Exchange of notes at Brussels and Capellen November 16, 1992 and March 5, 1993.

Entered into force March 5, 1993.

TIAS

NORWAY

ATOMIC ENERGY

Revised agreement for cooperation concerning civil uses of atomic energy, with annex and agreed minute.

Signed at Oslo January 12, 1984.

Entered into force July 2, 1984.

TIAS 10979; 2019 UNTS 3.

AVIATION

Arrangement relating to pilot licenses to operate civil aircraft.

Exchange of notes at Washington October 16, 1933.

Entered into force November 15, 1933.

48 Stat. 1818; EAS 51; 10 Bevans 514; 145 LNTS 31.

Agreement relating to air transport services.

Exchange of notes at Washington October 6, 1945.

Entered into force October 6, 1945; operative October 15, 1945.

59 Stat. 1658; EAS 482; 10 Bevans 553; 122 UNTS 319.

Amendments

August 6, 1954 (5 UST 1433; TIAS 3015; 222 UNTS 269).

June 16, 1995 (TIAS 12664).

Agreement relating to air service facilities at Gardermoen Airfield.

Signed at Oslo November 12, 1946.

Entered into force November 12, 1946.

61 Stat. 3861; TIAS 1737; 10 Bevans 560; 42 UNTS 227.

Agreement relating to certificates of airworthiness for imported aircraft.

Exchange of notes at Oslo February 5, 1957.

Entered into force February 5, 1957.

8 UST 265; TIAS 3769; 279 UNTS 169.

Amendment

January 24, 1978 (29 UST 5660; TIAS 9141).

Agreement for promotion of aviation safety.

Signed at Oslo June 27, 2001.

Entered into force June 27, 2001.

TIAS

CLAIMS

Memorandum of understanding on conflicting claims to enemy property.

Signed at Washington June 21, 1952.

Entered into force April 27, 1954.

5 UST 907; TIAS 2980; 236 UNTS 9.

COMMERCE

Treaty of commerce and navigation, with separate article.[1]

Signed at Stockholm July 4, 1827.

Entered into force January 18, 1828.

8 Stat. 346; TS 348; 11 Bevans 876.

Treaty of friendship, commerce, and consular right with exchange of notes and additional article signed February 25, 1929.

Signed at Washington June 5, 1928.

Entered into force September 13, 1932.

47 Stat. 2135; TS 852; 10 Bevans 481; 134 LNTS 81.

NOTE

1 Articles 13 and 14 were abrogated effective July 1, 1916; the entire treaty, with the exception of that part of article 1 concerning entry and residence of nationals of one country in territories of the other for purposes of trade, was terminated September 13, 1932, by the treaty of friendship, commerce, and consular rights signed June 5, 1928, and the additional article thereto signed February 25, 1929 (TS 852).

CONSULS

See COMMERCE

CUSTOMS

Arrangement relating to customs treatment of importations for consular offices and officers.

Exchange of notes at Washington January 20, 1932.

Entered into force January 20, 1932; operative February 1, 1932.

47 Stat. 2698; EAS 32; 10 Bevans 505; 126 LNTS 393.

Agreement regarding mutual assistance between customs authorities.

Signed at Oslo May 17, 1989.

Entered into force August 30, 1989.

TIAS 12118.

DEFENSE

See also MUTUAL SECURITY

Mutual defense assistance agreement.

Signed at Washington January 27, 1950.

Entered into force February 24, 1950.

1 UST 106; TIAS 2016; 80 UNTS 241.

Agreement relating to the disposition of excess equipment and materials furnished by the United States under the mutual defense assistance agreement.

Exchange of notes at Oslo December 12 and 28, 1950.

Entered into force December 28, 1950.

6 UST 6151; TIAS 3467; 240 UNTS 391.

Agreement relating to the disposition of equipment and materials furnished by the United States under the mutual defense assistance agreement and found surplus to the needs of the armed forces of Norway.

Exchange of notes at Oslo May 15 and June 26, 1953.

Entered into force June 26, 1953.

6 UST 6153; TIAS 3468; 240 UNTS 396.

Amendment

September 1, 1960 and January 14, 1961 (12 UST 214; TIAS 4695; 406 UNTS 312).

Agreement concerning participation of a Norwegian mobile surgical hospital in the United Nations operations in Korea.

Signed at Washington September 17, 1951.

Entered into force September 17, 1951.

2 UST 1903; TIAS 2325; 140 UNTS 313.

Agreement concerning the status of military assistance advisory group under article I, paragraph 1(a) of the NATO status of forces agreement (TIAS 2846).

Exchange of notes at Oslo April 13, 1954.

Entered into force April 13, 1954.

5 UST 619; TIAS 2950; 229 UNTS 223.

Agreement relating to a weapons production program.

Exchange of notes at Oslo February 13, 1960.

Entered into force February 13, 1960.

11 UST 2105; TIAS 4569; 388 UNTS 255.

Amendment

April 26 and September 16, 1960 (11 UST 2105; TIAS 4569; 388 UNTS 255).

Agreement relating to a shipbuilding program for the Norwegian Navy.

Exchange of notes at Oslo July 6, 1960.

Entered into force July 6, 1960.

11 UST 1796; TIAS 4522; 378 UNTS 25.

Agreement relating to a shipbuilding program of the Norwegian Navy.

Exchange of notes at Oslo November 29, 1960.

Entered into force January 31, 1961.

12 UST 101; TIAS 4681; 404 UNTS 251.

Agreement relating to the safeguarding of classified information with annex.

Exchange of notes at Oslo February 26, 1970.

Entered into force February 26, 1970.

21 UST 462; TIAS 6836; 240 UNTS 251.

Amendment

September 27, 1984 (TIAS 11136).

Agreement relating to the coproduction of the M109G vehicles.

Signed at Oslo December 30, 1966.

Entered into force December 30, 1966.

TIAS 12360.

Amendment

February 6, 1976 (TIAS 12360).

Memorandum of understanding governing prestockage and reinforcement of Norway.

Signed at Washington January 16, 1981.

Entered into force January 16, 1981.

32 UST 4538; TIAS 9966; 1266 UNTS 17.

Mutual logistical support agreement, with annex.

Signed at Stuttgart-Vaihingen and Oslo January 29 and August 20, 1982.

Entered into force August 20, 1982.

34 UST 1721; TIAS 10449.

Amendment

November 14, 1992 and January 15, 1993 (TIAS 12361).

Memorandum of understanding on the exchange of officers between the United States and Royal Norwegian Air Forces.

Signed at Oslo and Washington November 14, 1983 and January 5, 1984.

Entered into force January 5, 1984.

35 UST 4173; TIAS 10915; 2014 UNTS 529.

Memorandum of understanding on the exchange of officers between the United States Marine Corps and the Norwegian Army.

Signed at Oslo and Washington May 21 and July 3, 1986.

Entered into force July 3, 1986.

NP

Memorandum of understanding concerning the provision of United States hospital prepositioned storage to support Allied Forces during operations in the Norwegian Sea and in Norway.

Signed at London and Oslo February 17 and April 10, 1987.

Entered into force April 10, 1987.

TIAS 11662.

Memorandum of agreement concerning the exchange of engineers and scientists, with annexes.

Signed at Washington and Oslo September 2 and 24, 1992.

Entered into force September 24, 1992.

NP

Agreement concerning the transfer of U.S. Government-origin defense articles or related training or other defense services to the Government of Norway.

Exchange of notes at Oslo September 18 and October 1, 1992.

Entered into force October 1, 1992.

TIAS 12362.

Agreement regarding cooperation on environmental protection in defense matters.

Signed at Baltimore May 19, 1994.

Entered into force May 19, 1994.

TIAS 12363.

Memorandum of understanding for the dynamic analysis support system project, with annexes.

Signed at Washington and Haakonsvern August 12 and November 14, 1994.

Entered into force November 14, 1994.

TIAS 12364.

Memorandum of understanding for the composite hull embedded sensor system (CHESS), with annex.

Signed at Washington and Kjeller June 6 and 24, 1996.

Entered into force June 24, 1996.

TIAS 12770.

Agreement regarding the exchange of engineers and scientists, with annexes.

Signed at Oslo and Washington January 11 and April 15, 1999.

Entered into force April 15, 1999.

NP

Agreement for technology demonstration and system prototype projects, with annexes.

Signed June 25 and July 18, 2001.

Entered into force July 18, 2001.

TIAS

Memorandum of understanding concerning the assignment of liaison army officers, with appendix

Signed December 5, 2005.

Entered into force December 5, 2005.

TIAS

ECONOMIC AND TECHNICAL COOPERATION

Economic cooperation agreement.

Signed at Oslo July 3, 1948.

Entered into force July 3, 1948.

62 Stat. 2514; TIAS 1792; 10 Bevans 580; 20 UNTS 185.

Amendments

January 17, 1950 (1 UST 166; TIAS 2032; 79 UNTS 284).

July 5, 1951 (2 UST 1289; TIAS 2276; 148 UNTS 402).

January 8, 1953 (4 UST 109; TIAS 2767; 198 UNTS 366).

EDUCATION

Agreement relating to the United States Educational Foundation in Norway, and exchange of notes.

Signed at Oslo May 25, 1949.

Entered into force May 25, 1949.

63 Stat. 2764; TIAS 2000; 10 Bevans 598; 32 UNTS 345.

Amendments

August 12 and October 30, 1954 (5 UST 2545; TIAS 3118; 234 UNTS 298).

June 15, 1955 (6 UST 2103; TIAS 3282; 261 UNTS 380).

June 21, 1960 (11 UST 1602; TIAS 4503; 377 UNTS 390).

March 16, 1964 (15 UST 241; TIAS 5545; 524 UNTS 294).

EMPLOYMENT

Agreement relating to the employment of dependents of official government employees.

Exchange of notes at Oslo April 15 and July 21, 1981.

Entered into force July 21, 1981.

35 UST 3810; TIAS 10882; 2015 UNTS 711.

ENVIRONMENTAL COOPERATION

Agreement for cooperation in the Global Learning and Observations to Benefit the Environment (GLOBE) Program.

Signed at Washington April 5, 1995.

Entered into force April 5, 1995.

TIAS 12627.

EXTRADITION

Extradition treaty.

Signed at Oslo June 9, 1977.

Entered into force March 7, 1980.

31 UST 5619; TIAS 9679; 1220 UNTS 221.

FINANCE

Agreement relating to guaranties authorized by Section 111 (b)(3) of the Economic Cooperation Act of 1948, as amended.

Exchange of notes at Washington March 28 and April 1, 1952.

Entered into force April 1, 1952.

3 UST 4246; TIAS 2567; 177 UNTS 291.

LEND-LEASE

Preliminary agreement regarding principles applying to mutual aid in the prosecution of the war against aggression, and exchange of notes.

Signed at Washington July 11, 1942.

Entered into force July 11, 1942.

56 Stat. 1565; EAS 262; 10 Bevans 531.

Agreement regarding settlement for lend-lease, military relief, and claims, and exchanges of notes.

Signed at Washington February 24, 1948.

Entered into force February 24, 1948.

62 Stat. 1848; TIAS 1716; 10 Bevans 566; 34 UNTS 155.

MAINTENANCE

Agreement for the enforcement of maintenance obligations.

Signed at Washington June 10, 2002.

Entered into force June 10, 2002.

TIAS

MAPPING

Basic exchange and cooperative agreement concerning geospatial information and services cooperation.

Signed at Oslo July 8, 1998.

Entered into force July 8, 1998.

NP

MUTUAL SECURITY

Agreement relating to the assurances required under the Mutual Security Act of 1951.

Exchange of notes at Oslo January 8, 1952.

Entered into force January 8, 1952.

3 UST 4639; TIAS 2616; 179 UNTS 185.

NATIONALITY

Treaty relating to exemption from military service or other act of allegiance of persons having dual nationality.

Signed at Oslo November 1, 1930.

Entered into force February 11, 1931.

46 Stat. 2904; TS 832; 10 Bevans 503; 112 LNTS 399.

NAVIGATION

Agreement for the transfer of ownership of the long-range radio aid to navigation transmitting stations at Bo and Jan Mayen Island, Norway, with annex.

Signed at Oslo December 15, 1994.

Entered into force December 15, 1994.

TIAS

PACIFIC SETTLEMENT OF DISPUTES

Treaty for the advancement of peace.

Signed at Washington June 24, 1914.

Entered into force October 21, 1914.

38 Stat. 1843; TS 599; 10 Bevans 456.

Treaty of arbitration.

Signed at Washington February 20, 1929.

Entered into force June 7, 1929.

46 Stat. 2278; TS 788; 10 Bevans 498; 91 LNTS 413.

PATENTS

Agreement to facilitate interchange of patent rights and technical information for defense purposes, with agreed minutes.

Signed at Oslo April 6, 1955.

Entered into force April 6, 1955.

6 UST 799; TIAS 3226; 269 UNTS 65.

Agreement approving procedures for reciprocal filing of classified patent applications in the United States and Norway.

Exchange of notes at Oslo December 5, 1958 and January 6 and 17, 1959.

Entered into force January 17, 1959.

10 UST 302; TIAS 4187; 341 UNTS 410.

Amendment

April 25 and August 12, 1960 (11 UST 2002; TIAS 4552; 388 UNTS 374).

POSTAL MATTERS

Parcel post convention.

Signed at Oslo October 6 and at Washington November 9, 1934; operative November 1, 1934.

49 Stat. 3042; Post Office Department print; 156 LNTS 33.

International express mail agreement, with detailed regulations.

Signed at Oslo and Washington July 5 and August 10, 1984.

Entered into force October 15, 1984.

TIAS 11007; 2022 UNTS 91.

Memorandum of understanding concerning the operation of the INTELPOST field trial, with details of implementation.

Signed at Oslo and Washington July 9 and 25, 1985.

Entered into force July 25, 1985.

TIAS 11154.

PUBLICATIONS

Agreement for the exchange of official publications.

Exchange of notes at Oslo June 20, 1947 and March 15, 1948.

Entered into force March 15, 1948.

62 Stat. 1954; TIAS 1758; 10 Bevans 577; 73 UNTS 81.

Amendment

August 10 and 11, 1964 (15 UST 1502; TIAS 5630; 530 UNTS 334).

RELIEF SUPPLIES AND PACKAGES

Agreement for free entry and free inland transportation of relief supplies and packages.

Exchange of notes at Oslo October 31, 1949.

Entered into force October 31, 1949.

64 Stat. (3) B71; TIAS 2006; 10 Bevans 607; 68 UNTS 3.

SCIENTIFIC COOPERATION

Memorandum of understanding concerning scientific and technical cooperation in the earth sciences, with annexes.

Signed at Reston November 25, 2003.

Entered into force November 25, 2003.

TIAS

SEISMOLOGICAL RESEARCH

Agreement relating to the installation, operation and management of a seismic array facility in Norway.

Exchange of notes at Oslo June 15, 1968.

Entered into force June 15, 1968.

19 UST 5439; TIAS 6526; 707 UNTS 79.

SHIPPING

Agreement relating to jurisdiction over vessels utilizing the Louisiana Offshore Oil Port.

Exchange of notes at Washington July 11, 1978.

Entered into force July 11, 1978.

30 UST 1671; TIAS 9275; 1153 UNTS 89.

SMUGGLING

Convention for prevention of smuggling of intoxicating liquors.

Signed at Washington May 24, 1924.

Entered into force July 2, 1924.

43 Stat. 1772; TS 689; 10 Bevans 473; 26 LNTS 44.

SOCIAL SECURITY

Agreement on social security, with administrative agreement.

Signed at Oslo November 30, 2001.

Entered into force September 1, 2003.

TIAS

SPACE COOPERATION

Agreement for cooperation in the civil uses of outer space, with annex

Signed October 20 and November 14, 2001.

Entered into force November 14, 2001.

TIAS

Extension

October 23, 2006.

TAXATION

Convention for the avoidance of double taxation and the prevention of fiscal evasion with respect to taxes on estates and inheritances.

Signed at Washington June 13, 1949.

Entered into force December 11, 1951.

2 UST 2353; TIAS 2358; 127 UNTS 163.

Agreement relating to relief from taxation of United States Government expenditures in Norway for common defense.

Exchange of notes at Oslo June 27, 1952.

Entered into force June 27, 1952.

3 UST 5253; TIAS 2720; 184 UNTS 271.

Convention for the avoidance of double taxation and the prevention of fiscal evasion with respect to taxes on income and property with related notes.

Signed at Oslo December 3, 1971.

Entered into force November 29, 1972.

23 UST 2832; TIAS 7474.

Protocol amending the convention of December 3, 1971 (TIAS 7474) for the avoidance of double taxation and the prevention of fiscal evasion with respect to taxes on income and property.[1]

Signed at Oslo September 19, 1980.

Entered into force December 15, 1981.

33 UST 2828; TIAS 10205.

Agreement concerning the reciprocal exemption from income tax of income derived from the international operation of ships and aircraft.

Exchange of notes at Washington May 24, 1990.

Entered into force May 24, 1990.

TIAS 11715; 2207 UNTS 205.

NOTE

1 With understanding.

TELECOMMUNICATION

Agreement relating to the reciprocal granting of authorizations to permit licensed amateur radio operators of either country to operate their stations in the other country.

Exchange of notes at Oslo May 27 and June 1, 1967.

Entered into force June 1, 1967.

18 UST 1241; TIAS 6273; 631 UNTS 119.

TRADE

See also COMMERCE

Arrangement within the context of the multilateral trade negotiations concerning cheeses, and related letter of January 30, 1980.

Signed at Geneva May 17, 1979.

Entered into force January 1, 1980.

32 UST 5460; TIAS 9997; 1266 UNTS 3.

Agreement within the context of the multilateral trade negotiations regarding turkey rolls, and related letter of January 30, 1980.

Letter done at Geneva June 28, 1979.

Entered into force January 1, 1980.

32 UST 5468; TIAS 9998; 1266 UNTS 11.

VISAS

Agreement for the waiver by Norway of visa requirements for United States citizens entering continental Norway and of the visa fee for United States citizens entering Norwegian territory outside continental Norway, and for the waiver by the United States of the visa fee for Norwegian citizens entering the United States and possessions as nonimmigrants.

Exchange of notes at Washington July 7 and 29, 1947.

Entered into force July 29, 1947; operative August 1, 1947.

61 Stat. 3101; TIAS 1644; 10 Bevans 563; 87 UNTS 343.

Amendment

April 25, 1958.

Agreement relating to the waiver of visas for American citizens proceeding to Svalbard (Spitzbergen) and the temporary suspension of visa requirements for American citizens proceeding to certain Norwegian possessions.

Exchange of notes at Washington September 10 and October 19, 1948.

Entered into force October 19, 1948.

62 Stat. 3649; TIAS 1884; 10 Bevans 596; 87 UNTS 348.

O

OMAN

AVIATION

Agreement on aviation security.

Exchange of notes at Muscat June 28 and 30, 1994.

Entered into force June 30, 1994.

TIAS 12554.

COMMERCE

Treaty of amity, economic relations and consular rights and protocol.

Signed at Salalah December 20, 1958.

Entered into force June 11, 1960.

11 UST 1835; TIAS 4530; 380 UNTS 181.

CONSULS

See COMMERCE

DEFENSE

Agreement concerning the provision of training related to defense articles under the United States International Military Education and Training (IMET) Program.

Exchange of notes at Muscat January 4 and April 28, 1986.

Entered into force April 28, 1986.

TIAS 11981.

Agreement regarding grants under the Foreign Assistance Act of 1961, as amended, and the furnishing of defense articles, related training and other defense services from the United States to Oman.

Exchange of notes at Muscat May 5 and June 1, 1992.

Entered into force June 1, 1992.

TIAS

ECONOMIC AND MILITARY COOPERATION

Agreement concerning the use of certain facilities in Oman by the United States.

Exchange of notes at Muscat June 4, 1980.

Entered into force June 4, 1980.

32 UST 1636; TIAS 9791; 1234 UNTS 353.

ECONOMIC AND TECHNICAL COOPERATION

Agreement to establish a joint commission on economic and technical cooperation.

Signed at Muscat August 19, 1980.

Entered into force August 19, 1980.

33 UST 2428; TIAS 10189; 1529 UNTS 13.

Amendment and extension

December 1, 1990.

Agreement on economic and technical cooperation.

Signed at Muscat December 1, 1990.

Entered into force December 1, 1990.

TIAS

FINANCE

Agreement relating to investment guaranties.

Exchange of notes at Muscat September 9, 1976.

Entered into force September 9, 1976.

28 UST 5670; TIAS 8651; 1087 UNTS 11.

INTERNATIONAL CRIMINAL COURT

Agreement regarding the surrender of persons to the International Criminal Court.

Exchange of notes at Muscat July 26 and August 1, 2004.

Entered into force August 1, 2004.

TIAS

PEACE CORPS

Agreement relating to the establishment of a Peace Corps program in Oman.

Exchange of notes at Muscat November 15 and 28, 1972.

Entered into force November 28, 1972.

24 UST 1013; TIAS 7614.

Amendment

May 4 and August 25, 1977 (29 UST 5358; TIAS 9116; 1148 UNTS 366).

POSTAL MATTERS

International express mail agreement.

Signed at Muscat and Washington February 12 and March 27, 1986.

Entered into force May 1, 1986.

NP

ORGANIZATION FOR THE DEVELOPMENT OF THE SENEGAL RIVER

ECONOMIC AND TECHNICAL COOPERATION

Agency for International Development

February 25, 1976 (28 UST 5081; TIAS 8613).

August 31, 1976 (28 UST 8985; TIAS 8779).

ORGANIZATION FOR ECONOMIC COOPERATION AND DEVELOPMENT (OECD)

ATOMIC ENERGY

Cooperative arrangement with the Nuclear Energy Agency of OECD in the field of nuclear data and computer programs.

Signed at Paris December 16, 1985.

Entered into force December 16, 1985.

TIAS

Agreement for cooperation in the field of nuclear data and computer programs.

Signed at Washington April 10, 2006.

Entered into force April 10, 2006.

TIAS

TAXATION

Tax reimbursement agreement, with annex.

Signed at Paris October 15, 1987.

Entered into force October 15, 1987.

TIAS

ORGANIZATION FOR THE PROHIBITION OF CHEMICAL WEAPONS

TAXATION

Tax reimbursement agreement, with annex.

Signed at The Hague February 25, 1999.

Entered into force February 25, 1999.

TIAS

ORGANIZATION OF AMERICAN STATES

ECONOMIC AND TECHNICAL COOPERATION

Understanding relating to the establishment and operation of training centers and other services under the program of technical cooperation of the Organization of American States.

Exchange of notes at Washington February 12 and March 3, 1952.

Entered into force March 3, 1952.

3 UST 2995; TIAS 2485; 165 UNTS 67.

Agreement between the United States and the Pan American Union (General Secretariat of the Organization of American States) concerning certain funds to be made available under the Alliance of Progress.

Signed at Washington November 29, 1961.

Entered into force November 29, 1961.

12 UST 1690; TIAS 4887; 424 UNTS 119.

Related agreement

February 17, 1964 (15 UST 105; TIAS 5523; 511 UNTS 298).

HEADQUARTERS

Headquarters agreement, with annexes.

Signed at Washington May 14, 1992.

Entered into force November 17, 1994.

TIAS

Amendments

May 24 and 29, 1996.

September 27, 2000 and March 19, 2001.

PRIVILEGES AND IMMUNITIES

Agreement relating to privileges and immunities.

Signed at Washington March 20, 1975.

Entered into force March 20, 1975.

26 UST 1025; TIAS 8089.

TAXATION

Agreement relating to a procedure for United States income tax reimbursement, with addenda.

Signed at Washington January 10, 1984.

Entered into force January 10, 1984; effective January 1, 1984.

35 UST 4224; TIAS 10919; 2015 UNTS 101.

P

PAKISTAN

The Schedule to the Independence (International Arrangements) Order, 1947, provides that rights and obligations under all international agreements to which India is a party immediately before the appointed day [August 15, 1947] devolve upon India and Pakistan and will, if necessary, be apportioned between them; except that (1) Pakistan will take such steps as may be necessary to apply for membership of such international organizations as it chooses to join, and (2) rights and obligations under international agreements having an exclusive application to an area comprised in the Dominion of Pakistan will devolve upon it.

AGRICULTURAL COMMODITIES

Agreement for additional emergency assistance in agricultural commodities.

Exchange of notes at Karachi January 18, 1955.

Entered into force January 18, 1955.

6 UST 557; TIAS 3188; 241 UNTS 53.

Agreement relating to the sale of certain surplus agricultural commodities and providing for the use of proceeds for urgent relief requirements of Pakistan.

Signed at Karachi September 29, 1955.

Entered into force September 29, 1955.

6 UST 6145; TIAS 3466; 268 UNTS 374.

Agricultural commodities agreement with exchange of notes.

Signed at Karachi October 14, 1961.

Entered into force October 14, 1961.

12 UST 1287; TIAS 4852; 426 UNTS 237.

Amendments

December 3, 1962 (13 UST 2613; TIAS 5228; 460 UNTS 326).

May 31, 1963 (14 UST 1187; TIAS 5415; 488 UNTS 304).

February 10, 1964 (15 UST 108; TIAS 5524; 511 UNTS 304).

November 28, 1964 (15 UST 2211; TIAS 5707; 531 UNTS 374).

March 30, 1966 (17 UST 642; TIAS 6012; 578 UNTS 281).

Agricultural commodities agreement with exchange of notes.

Signed at Karachi May 26, 1966.

Entered into force May 26, 1966.

17 UST 925; TIAS 6052; 594 UNTS 27.

Amendments

August 10, 1966 (17 UST 1167; TIAS 6074; 603 UNTS 348).

October 6, 1966 (17 UST 1654; TIAS 6125; 674 UNTS 394).

October 25, 1966 (17 UST 1654; TIAS 6125; 674 UNTS 398).

December 28, 1966 (18 UST 22; TIAS 6194; 681 UNTS 386).

June 28, 1967 (18 UST 1307; TIAS 6286).

Agricultural commodities agreement with annex.

Signed at Islamabad May 11, 1967.

Entered into force May 11, 1967.

18 UST 512; TIAS 6258; 685 UNTS 291.

Related agreements

August 3, 1967 (18 UST 1757; TIAS 6320; 693 UNTS 21).

December 26, 1967 (18 UST 3275; TIAS 6422; 697 UNTS 43).

May 16, 1968 (19 UST 4915; TIAS 6496; 697 UNTS 137).

May 16 and June 13, 1969 (20 UST 2696; TIAS 6730; 720 UNTS 330).

July 3, 1969 (20 UST 2878; TIAS 6765; 726 UNTS 167).

October 3, 1969 (20 UST 4111; TIAS 6807; 732 UNTS 47).

January 10, 1970 (21 UST 375; TIAS 6821; 732 UNTS 59).

November 25, 1970 (22 UST 484; TIAS 7087; 792 UNTS 3).

March 25, 1971 (22 UST 492; TIAS 7087; 792 UNTS 22).

July 27, 1971 (22 UST 1517; TIAS 7170; 792 UNTS 26).

August 6, 1971 (22 UST 1893; TIAS 7233).

March 9, 1972 (23 UST 257; TIAS 7301).

March 18, 1972 (23 UST 912; TIAS 7357).

April 6, 1972 (23 UST 912; TIAS 7357).

May 3, 1972 (23 UST 912; TIAS 7357).

May 11, 1972 (23 UST 776; TIAS 7339).

July 21, 1972 (23 UST 1474; TIAS 7426).

September 1, 1972 (23 UST 2658; TIAS 7457).

September 21, 1972 (23 UST 2802; TIAS 7466).

October 12, 1972 (23 UST 3142; TIAS 7490).

November 15, 1972 (23 UST 3730; TIAS 7521).

January 31, 1973 (24 UST 454; TIAS 7563).

March 19, 1973 (24 UST 882; TIAS 7595).

June 20, 1973 (24 UST 1655; TIAS 7670).

September 10, 1973 (24 UST 2009; TIAS 7714).

November 2, 1973 (24 UST 2242; TIAS 7741).

November 12, 1973 (24 UST 2249; TIAS 7743).

July 5, 1974 (25 UST 1444; TIAS 7874).

Agricultural commodities agreement.

Signed at Islamabad November 23, 1974.

Entered into force November 23, 1974.

25 UST 3090; TIAS 7971; 1052 UNTS 160.

Amendments

March 3, 1975 (26 UST 185; TIAS 8024; 1052 UNTS 173).

May 27, 1975 (26 UST 678; TIAS 8065; 1052 UNTS 176).

Related agreements

August 7, 1975 (26 UST 2725; TIAS 8189; 1052 UNTS 195).

February 5, 1976 (27 UST 1555; TIAS 8263; 1052 UNTS 203).

August 10, 1976 (27 UST 3820; TIAS 8401).

August 20, 1976 (27 UST 3826; TIAS 8401).

December 29, 1976 (28 UST 1277; TIAS 8509).

December 22, 1977 (29 UST 3654; TIAS 9035; 1124 UNTS 107).

April 10, 1978 (29 UST 3673; TIAS 9035; 1124 UNTS 117).

January 24, 1979 (30 UST 2903; TIAS 9372; 1180 UNTS 185).

Agricultural commodities agreement, with minutes.

Signed at Islamabad March 25, 1980.

Entered into force March 25, 1980.

32 UST 1434; TIAS 9782; 1222 UNTS 183.

Amendment

July 2, 1980 (32 UST 1885; TIAS 9805).

Related agreements

June 4, 1981 (33 UST 3937; TIAS 10273).

April 15, 1982 (34 UST 968; TIAS 10382).

May 15, 1983 (TIAS 10715; 1578 UNTS 79).

March 20, 1984 (35 UST 4849; TIAS 10970).

Agricultural commodities agreement.

Signed at Islamabad April 28, 1985.

Entered into force April 28, 1985.

NP

Related agreement

May 19, 1986 (NP).

Agricultural commodities agreement.

Signed at Islamabad June 25, 1987.

Entered into force June 25, 1987.

NP

Related agreements

March 24, 1988 (NP).

September 22, 1988 (NP).

March 15, 1990 (NP).

AVIATION

Understanding that the air services agreement between the United States and India, signed November 14, 1946 (61 Stat. 2573; TIAS 1586), is deemed to have been concluded between Pakistan and the United States, and that United States airlines may carry traffic between points in India and Pakistan subject to the terms of that agreement.

Exchange of notes at Karachi June 1 and 16, 1948.

5 UST 2164; TIAS 3078; 235 UNTS 29.

Agreement revising that route annex to the air transport agreement of November 14, 1946.

Exchange of notes at Karachi March 28 and April 18, 1961.

Entered into force April 18, 1961.

12 UST 846; TIAS 4783; 410 UNTS 300.

Air transport agreement, with annexes.

Signed at Rawalpindi April 10, 1997.

Entered into force April 10, 1997.

TIAS

Amendment

April 12 and 29, 1999.

COMMERCE

Treaty of friendship and commerce, and protocol.

Signed at Washington November 12, 1959.

Entered into force February 12, 1961.

12 UST 110; TIAS 4683; 404 UNTS 259.

CONSULS

Convention to regulate commerce (article IV) between the United States and the United Kingdom.

Signed at London July 3, 1815; effective July 3, 1815.

8 Stat. 228; TS 110; 12 Bevans 49.

CUSTOMS

Arrangement relating to reciprocal concessions and privileges accorded to diplomatic and consular officers.

Exchange of notes at Washington October 27, 1948, and February 4, 1949.

Entered into force February 4, 1949.

10 Bevans 646.

DEFENSE

Agreement relating to transfer of military supplies and equipment to Pakistan.

Exchange of notes at Washington November 29 and December 15, 1950.

Entered into force December 15, 1950.

1 UST 884; TIAS 2165; 122 UNTS 89.

Mutual defense assistance agreement.

Signed at Karachi May 19, 1954.

Entered into force May 19, 1954.

5 UST 852; TIAS 2976; 202 UNTS 301.

Defense support assistance agreement.

Signed at Karachi January 11, 1955.

Entered into force January 11, 1955.

6 UST 501; TIAS 3183; 251 UNTS 111.

Amendment

March 11, 1961 (12 UST 226; TIAS 4698; 406 UNTS 318).

Agreement providing for the disposition of equipment and materials furnished to Pakistan under the mutual defense assistance agreement of May 19, 1954.

Signed at Karachi March 15 and May 15, 1956.

Entered into force May 15, 1956.

7 UST 2389; TIAS 3627; 280 UNTS 368.

Construction agreement pursuant to article I, paragraph 1, of the mutual defense assistance agreement of May 19, 1954.

Signed at Karachi May 28, 1956.

Entered into force May 28, 1956.

7 UST 923; TIAS 3575.

Agreement of cooperation.

Signed at Ankara March 5, 1959.

Entered into force March 5, 1959.

10 UST 317; TIAS 4190; 327 UNTS 285.

Agreement concerning general security of military information.

Exchange of notes at Islamabad April 6, June 21 and 24, 1982.

Entered into force June 24, 1982.

34 UST 1765; TIAS 10455; 1750 UNTS 443.

Agreement concerning the provision of training related to defense articles under the United States International Military Education and Training (IMET) Program.

Exchange of notes at Islamabad December 10, 1985 and July 30, 1986.

Entered into force July 30, 1986.

NP

Memorandum of understanding on coassembly and coproduction of AN/UAS-12A night sight equipment, with appendix.

Signed at Rawalpindi January 27, 1990.

Entered into force January 27, 1990.

TIAS 12365.

Acquisition and cross-servicing agreement.

Signed at MacDill Air Force Base and Rawalpindi on February 9, 2002.

Entered into force February 9, 2002.

TIAS

Project agreement.

Signed at Islamabad May 23 and 28, 2002.

Entered into force May 28, 2002.

TIAS

Agreement regarding grants under the Foreign Assistance Act of 1961, as amended, and the furnishing of defense articles, related training and other defense services from the United States to Pakistan.

Exchange of notes at Islamabad June 27, 2003.

Entered into force June 27, 2003.

TIAS

ECONOMIC AND TECHNICAL COOPERATION

Agreement for technical cooperation.

Signed at Karachi February 9, 1951.

Entered into force February 9, 1951.

2 UST 1008; TIAS 2254; 100 UNTS 67.

Amendment

January 8, 1952 (3 UST 2616; TIAS 2427; 157 UNTS 370).

Supplementary agreement for technical cooperation.

Signed at Karachi February 2, 1952.

Entered into force February 2, 1952.

3 UST 3767; TIAS 2506; 131 UNTS 346.

Amendments

March 27, 1953 (4 UST 1478; TIAS 2811; 172 UNTS 350).

December 28, 1953 (4 UST 2805; TIAS 2889; 222 UNTS 410).

June 24, 1954 (5 UST 1361; TIAS 3004; 233 UNTS 302).

January 18, 1955 (6 UST 511; TIAS 3185; 239 UNTS 358).

Agreement relating to emergency flood assistance for East Pakistan.

Exchange of notes at Washington August 23, 1954.

Entered into force August 23, 1954.

5 UST 1779; TIAS 3052; 234 UNTS 243.

Amendment

November 29 and December 16, 1954 (5 UST 2182; TIAS 3082; 234 UNTS 250).

Agreement relating to the commitment of $500 million by the United States to the Pakistan second five-year plan.

Exchange of notes at Karachi July 25, 1962.

Entered into force July 25, 1962.

13 UST 1864; TIAS 5136; 459 UNTS 87.

Joint Commission on Economic, Commercial, Scientific, Technological, Educational, and Cultural Cooperation.

Signed at Washington December 6, 1982.

Entered into force December 6, 1982.

TIAS 10623; 2000 UNTS 457.

Agency for International Development

October 10, 1975 (28 UST 123; TIAS 8466).

March 9, 1976 (28 UST 2328; TIAS 8547).

April 8, 1976 (28 UST 3615; TIAS 8588).

September 9, 1976 (28 UST 7160; TIAS 8710).

September 22, 1976 (28 UST 7419; TIAS 8719).

October 27, 1976 (28 UST 8105; TIAS 8747).

January 18, 1977 (28 UST 2345; TIAS 8547).

April 1, 1977 (29 UST 1577; TIAS 8899; 1115 UNTS 103).

April 2, 1977 (29 UST 1623; TIAS 8900; 1115 UNTS 135).

January 12, 1978 (29 UST 2161; TIAS 8932).

November 8, 1978 (30 UST 7541; TIAS 9598; 1181 UNTS 364).

April 13, 1982 (34 UST 597; TIAS 10378).

May 23, 1983 (TIAS 10724).

July 25, 1983 (35 UST 3558; TIAS 10867; 2016 UNTS 124).

December 19, 1983 (NP).

June 25, 1985 (NP).

July 8, 1986 (NP).

July 15, 1986 (NP).

September 25, 1986 (NP).

July 31, 1987 (NP).

September 24, 1987 (NP).

September 29, 1987 (NP).

August 4, 1988 (NP).

August 4, 1988 (NP).

August 29, 1988 (NP).

August 29, 1988 (NP).

September 22, 1988 (NP).

September 29, 1988 (NP).

September 29, 1988 (NP).

September 27, 1989 (NP).

August 9, 1990 (NP).

November 15, 2001 (NP).

May 26, 2005 (NP).

May 26, 2005 (NP).

June 10, 2005 (NP).

January 21, 2006 (NP).

June 15, 2006 (NP).

July 1, 2006 (NP).

August 8, 2006 (NP).

EDUCATION

Agreement for financing certain educational exchange programs.

Signed at Islamabad October 18, 1972.

Entered into force October 18, 1972.

TIAS 7483; 23 UST 3115; 938 UNTS 11.

EMPLOYMENT

Agreement relating to the employment of dependents of official government employees.

Exchange of notes at Washington January 21 and February 13, 2004.

Entered into force February 13, 2004.

TIAS

ENVIRONMENTAL COOPERATION

Agreement for co-operation in the Global Learning and Observations to Benefit the Environment (GLOBE) Program, with appendices.

Signed at Islamabad November 18, 1997.

Entered into force November 18, 1997.

TIAS

EXTRADITION

Extradition treaty between the United States and the United Kingdom, signed at London December 22, 1931, made applicable to India, in accordance with the provisions of article 14, from March 9, 1942.

47 Stat. 2122; TS 849; 12 Bevans 482; 163 LNTS 59.

FINANCE

Agreements regarding the consolidation and rescheduling of certain debts owed to the United States Government and its agencies with annexes and related letter.

Signed at Washington September 20, 1972.

Entered into force September 20, 1972.

23 UST 2601; TIAS 7449.

Agreement regarding the consolidation and rescheduling of certain debts owed to the United States Government, with annexes.

Signed at Washington March 4, 1976.

Entered into force May 12, 1976.

27 UST 4231; TIAS 8447.

Amendment

April 13 and June 5, 1979 (30 UST 5985; TIAS 9532; 1177 UNTS 391).

Agreement regarding the consolidation and rescheduling of certain debts owed to the United States Government and the Agency for International Development, with annexes.

Signed at Islamabad May 10, 1981.

Entered into force July 13, 1981.

33 UST 3628; TIAS 10246; 1541 UNTS 3.

Implementing agreement regarding the consolidation and rescheduling of certain debts owed to the Agency for International Development.

Signed at Islamabad August 18, 1981.

Entered into force September 7, 1981.

33 UST 3628; TIAS 10246; 1541 UNTS 21.

Agreement regarding the consolidation and rescheduling of payments due under P.L. 480 Title I agricultural commodity agreements, with annexes.

Signed at Islamabad September 27, 1981.

Entered into force September 27, 1981.

33 UST 3628; TIAS 10246.

Investment incentive agreement.

Signed at Islamabad November 18, 1997.

Entered into force January 28, 1998.

TIAS

Agreement regarding the consolidation and rescheduling of certain debts owed to, guaranteed by, or insured by the United States Government and its agencies, with annexes.

Signed at Islamabad November 26, 1999.

Entered into force February 23, 2000.

NP

Agreement regarding the consolidation and rescheduling of certain debts owed to, guaranteed by, or insured by the United States Government and its agencies, with annexes.

Signed at Islamabad September 24, 2001.

Entered into force October 26, 2001.

NP

Agreement regarding the consolidation of debt owed to, guaranteed by, or insured by the United States Government and its agencies, with annexes.

Signed at Islamabad August 23, 2002.

Entered into force October 21, 2002.

NP

Agreement regarding the reduction of certain debts owed to, guaranteed or insured by the United States Government, with annexes.

Signed at Islamabad April 5, 2003.

Entered into force June 5, 2003.

NP

Agreement regarding the reduction of certain debts owed to, guaranteed or insured by the United States Government.

Signed at Islamabad July 16, 2004.

Entered into force September 2, 2004.

NP

INFORMATIONAL MEDIA GUARANTIES

Agreement relating to an informational media guaranty program pursuant to Section 111 (b)(3) of the Economic Cooperation Act of 1948, as amended.

Exchange of notes at Karachi February 12 and May 1, 1954.

Entered into force May 1, 1954.

5 UST 2272; TIAS 3088; 237 UNTS 231.

Amendments

January 1 and 8, 1957 (8 UST 1757; TIAS 3928; 299 UNTS 420).

August 10, 1962 and April 15, 1963 (15 UST 167; TIAS 5535; 510 UNTS 318).

INTERNATIONAL CRIMINAL COURT

Agreement regarding the surrender of persons to international tribunals.

Signed at Washington July 21, 2003.

Entered into force November 6, 2003.

TIAS

JUDICIAL ASSISTANCE

Agreement on procedures for mutual assistance in connection with matters relating to the Lockheed Aircraft Corporation and the Boeing Company.

Signed at Washington September 9, 1977.

Entered into force September 9, 1977.

28 UST 7488; TIAS 8724.

Related agreement

January 6 and 10, 1978 (29 UST 492; TIAS 8827; 1115 UNTS 177).

LEND-LEASE

In a note of June 12, 1948, to the American Ambassador at Karachi, the Minister of Foreign Affairs gave assurance that: "the terms of the United States Settlement Agreement with India of May 16, 1946 [60 Stat. 1753; TIAS 1532], would continue to devolve on the Government of Pakistan to the extent to which they are applicable and have to be fulfilled in Pakistan."

MARITIME MATTERS

Agreement concerning financial arrangements for the furnishing of certain supplies and services to naval vessels.

Signed at Karachi September 10, 1956.

Entered into force December 9, 1956.

7 UST 2493; TIAS 3637; 277 UNTS 259.

NARCOTIC DRUGS

Letters of agreement.

Signed at Islamabad May 23 and 28, 2002.

Entered into force May 28, 2002.

TIAS

PEACE CORPS

Agreement relating to the establishment of a Peace Corps program in Pakistan.

Exchange of notes at Karachi May 31, 1962.

Entered into force May 31, 1962; operative from October 28, 1961.

13 UST 1563; TIAS 5113; 460 UNTS 75.

POSTAL MATTERS

Agreement for the exchange of parcels by parcel post, and detailed regulations of execution.

Signed at Karachi July 20 and at Washington October 7, 1955.

Entered into force January 1, 1956.

7 UST 1; TIAS 3475; 241 UNTS 255.

International express mail agreement, with detailed regulations.

Signed at Islamabad and Washington March 11 and 30, 1987.

Entered into force May 1, 1987.

TIAS 11315.

INTELPOST memorandum of understanding, with detailed regulations.

Signed at Islamabad and Washington February 23 and March 11, 1993.

Entered into force March 15, 1993.

TIAS 11917.

PROPERTY

Convention between the United States and the United Kingdom applicable to Pakistan:

Convention relating to tenure and disposition of real and personal property.

Signed at Washington March 2, 1899.

TS 146; 31 Stat. 1939; 12 Bevans 246.

Supplementary convention extending the time within which notifications may be given of the accession of British colonies or foreign possessions to the convention of March 2, 1899.

Signed at Washington January 13, 1902.

TS 402; 32 Stat. 1914; 12 Bevans 261.

PUBLICATIONS

Agreement for the exchange of official publications.

Exchange of notes at Karachi April 25 and May 23, 1951.

Entered into force May 23, 1951.

2 UST 1701; TIAS 2311; 134 UNTS 265.

Amendment

April 22 and December 29, 1953 (5 UST 2850; TIAS 3141; 237 UNTS 312).

REFUGEE RELIEF

Agreement for assistance in the transport of relief commodities to Afghan refugee camps in Pakistan.

Signed at Islamabad September 30, 1981.

Entered into force September 30, 1981.

33 UST 3932; TIAS 10272.

RELIEF SUPPLIES AND PACKAGES

Agreement relating to duty-free entry and defrayment of inland transportation charges on relief supplies and packages for Pakistan.

Exchange of notes at Karachi June 18, 1953, and October 2, 1954.

Entered into force October 2, 1954.

5 UST 1983; TIAS 3065; 236 UNTS 187.

SCIENTIFIC COOPERATION

Agreement on science and technology cooperation, with annexes.

Signed at Washington June 25, 2003.

Entered into force October 16, 2003.

TIAS

TAXATION

Convention for the avoidance of double taxation and the prevention of fiscal evasion with respect to taxes on income.

Signed at Washington July 1, 1957.

Entered into force May 21, 1959.

10 UST 984; TIAS 4232; 344 UNTS 203.

Agreement for the reciprocal exemption with respect to taxes on income from the international operation of ships.

Exchange of notes at Islamabad July 26 and 27, 1989.

Entered into force July 27, 1989.

TIAS 11679; 2190 UNTS 411.

TRADE

See also COMMERCE

Memorandum of understanding relating to concessions and contributions to be made to the multilateral trade negotiations, with related letters, and related letter of January 28, 1980.

Done at Geneva April 2 and 11, and August 2 and 30, 1979.

Entered into force August 30, 1979.

32 UST 5471; TIAS 9999; 1265 UNTS 213.

Agreement concerning trade in textiles and textile products, with annexes and exchange of letters.

Exchange of notes at Washington May 20 and June 11, 1987.

Entered into force June 11, 1987.

NP

Amendments and extension

July 20 and 31, 1987 (NP).

April 24 and May 30, 1988 (NP).

October 14 and 17, 1988 (NP).

March 4 and 10, July 17, September 15 and November 13, 1988 (NP).

November 30 and December 20, 1990 (NP).

January 23 and March 12, 1992 (NP).

TRADE-MARKS

Declaration by the United States and the United Kingdom affording reciprocal protection to trade-marks.

Signed at London October 24, 1877.

Entered into force October 24, 1877.

20 Stat. 703; TS 138; I Malloy 737.

VISAS

Agreement relating to the reciprocal reduction of visa fees.

Exchange of notes at Karachi October 10 and 18, 1949.

Entered into force October 18, 1949; operative November 15, 1949.

3 UST 365; TIAS 2398; 141 UNTS 333.

Amendments

August 16, October 11, November 19, and December 16 and 29, 1952, and March 19 and April 8, 1953 (4 UST 11; TIAS 2761; 204 UNTS 378).

August 4, October 20, and November 25 and 29, 1955 (6 UST 6107; TIAS 3463; 240 UNTS 438).

Agreement relating to the reciprocal issuance of nonimmigrant visas, and related notes of July 28, 1959, September 6 and 29, 1961.

Exchange of notes at Karachi March 16 and June 27, 1959.

Entered into force June 27, 1959; operative August 1, 1959.

12 UST 1685; TIAS 4886; 360 UNTS 327.

PALAU

Agreement for the implementation of the Compact of Free Association between the Government of the United States and the Government of Palau.

Signed January 10, 1986.

Entered into force October 1, 1994.

AVIATION

Memorandum of agreement concerning assistance in developing and modernizing Palau's civil aviation infrastructure.

Signed at Washington and Koror December 11, 1995 and January 17 and February 8, 1996.

Entered into force February 8, 1996.

TIAS 12722.

ENVIRONMENTAL COOPERATION

Agreement concerning cooperation in the Global Learning and Observations to Benefit the Environment (GLOBE) Program, with appendices.

Signed at Koror January 30, 1997.

Entered into force January 30, 1997.

TIAS 12828.

FINANCE

Investment incentive agreement.

Signed at Washington March 15, 2002.

Entered into force March 15, 2002.

TIAS

INTERNATIONAL CRIMINAL COURT

Agreement regarding the surrender of persons to the International Criminal Court.

Signed at Koror September 13, 2002.

Entered into force July 7, 2003.

TIAS

PEACE CORPS

Agreement concerning the program of the Peace Corps in Palau.

Signed at Koror March 8, 1995.

Entered into force March 8, 1995.

TIAS 12610.

RELATIONS

Agreement concerning relations under the Vienna convention on diplomatic relations.

Signed at Washington December 14, 1994.

Entered into force March 2, 1995.

TIAS 12587.

PALESTINE LIBERATION ORGANIZATION

FINANCE

Agreement on encouragement of investment.

Signed at Gaza and Washington August 11 and September 12, 1994.

Entered into force September 12, 1994.

TIAS 12564.

PANAMA

AGRICULTURE

Agreement confirming the cooperative agreement for the prevention of foot-and-mouth disease and rinderpest in Panama.

Exchange of notes at Panama June 21 and October 5, 1972.

Entered into force October 5, 1972.

23 UST 3108; TIAS 7482.

Amendment

May 28 and June 12, 1974 (25 UST 1522; TIAS 7888).

Agreement on cooperation in agricultural products.

Signed at Washington and Panama City December 20, 2006.

Entered into force December 20, 2006.

TIAS

AVIATION

Agreement concerning the regulation of commercial aviation in the Republic of Panama.

Exchange of notes at Panama April 22, 1929.

Entered into force April 22, 1929.

Foreign Relations, 1929, Vol. III, p. 729; 10 Bevans 729.

Agreement relating to the establishment of headquarters in Panama for a civil aviation technical assistance group for the Latin American area.

Exchange of notes at Panama August 8, 1952.

Entered into force August 8, 1952.

3 UST 5064; TIAS 2691; 181 UNTS 257.

Agreement relating to the furnishing by the Federal Aviation Agency of certain services and materials for air navigation aids.

Exchange of notes at Panama December 5, 1967 and February 22, 1968.

Entered into force February 22, 1968.

19 UST 4731; TIAS 6471; 698 UNTS 79.

Memorandum of agreement relating to the provision of flight inspection services.

Signed at Washington and Panama August 16 and September 1, 1978.

Entered into force September 1, 1978; effective October 1, 1978.

30 UST 268; TIAS 9196; 1150 UNTS 231.

Memorandum of agreement concerning assistance in developing and modernizing Panama's civil aviation infrastructure, with annexes.

Signed at Panama and Washington January 24 and February 15, 1990.

Entered into force February 15, 1990.

TIAS 11707; 2208 UNTS 223.

Air transport agreement, with annexes.

Signed at Panama May 8, 1997.

Entered into force December 28, 1998.

TIAS

Amendments

May 27 and June 29, 1998.

August 7 and September 27, 2006.

Memorandum of cooperation for the promotion and development of civil aviation.

Signed at Washington and Panama February 17 and March 3, 1998.

Entered into force March 3, 1998.

TIAS

CANALS

Agreement for enlargement and use by Canal Zone of sewerage facilities in Colon Free Zone Area.

Exchange of notes at Panama March 8 and 25, 1954.

Entered into force March 25, 1954.

5 UST 782; TIAS 2966; 232 UNTS 289.

Treaty concerning the permanent neutrality and operation of the Panama Canal, with annexes and protocol.[1]

Signed at Washington September 7, 1977.

Entered into force October 1, 1979, subject to amendments, conditions, reservations, and understandings.

33 UST 1; TIAS 10029; 1161 UNTS 177.

NOTE

1 Parties to the Protocol:

Argentina
Barbados
Belize
Bolivia
Chile
Costa Rica
Denmark
Dominican Republic
Ecuador
Egypt
El Salvador
Equatorial Guinea
Finland
Germany, Federal Republic of
Guatemala
Honduras
Israel
Jamaica
Korea
Liberia
Malawi
Netherlands
Nicaragua
Norway
Philippines
Saudi Arabia
Spain
St. Vincent and the Grenadines
Sweden
Tunisia
Union of Soviet Socialist Republics
United Kingdom
Uruguay
Venezuela
Vietnam, Soc. Rep.
China (Taiwan)

Agreement concerning creation of a preparatory committee to study alternatives to the Panama Canal.

Exchange of notes at Washington September 30, 1982.

Entered into force September 30, 1982.

TIAS

Agreement concerning establishment of the commission for the study of alternatives to the Panama Canal, with annex and related notes.

Exchange of notes at New York September 26, 1985.

Entered into force September 26, 1985.[1]

TIAS 11935.

Extension

September 25, 1990.

Agreement concerning enforcement of alimony and child support obligations of Panama Canal Commission employees, with annexes.

Exchange of notes at Panama February 22, 1988.

Entered into force February 22, 1988.

TIAS

NOTE

1 See also exchanges of notes of the same date concerning Japanese participation.

CEMETERIES

Agreement authorizing the United States to construct a custodian's house in the Corozal Cemetery.

Exchange of notes at Panama September 29 and 30, 1982.

Entered into force September 29, 1982.

TIAS 10518; 1777 UNTS 343.

Agreement concerning the use of Corozal Cemetery.

Signed at Panama City June 11, 1999.

Entered into force June 27, 2000.

TIAS

CONSERVATION

Agreement pursuant to article VI of the convention on nature protection and wildlife preservation in the Western Hemisphere of October 12, 1940 (56 Stat. 1354; TS 981), with related notes.

Signed at Washington September 7, 1977.

Entered into force October 1, 1979.

33 UST 446; TIAS 10035; 1280 UNTS 311.

Agreement relating to custodianship of the Barro Colorado Nature Monument by the Smithsonian Tropical Research Institute.

Exchange of notes signed at Washington September 7, 1977.

Entered into force October 1, 1979.

33 UST 457; TIAS 10036; 1280 UNTS 319.

CUSTOMS

Declaration permitting consuls to take note in person, or by authorized representatives, of declarations of values of exports made by shippers before customs officers.

Exchange of notes at Washington April 17, 1913.

Entered into force June 1, 1913.

TS 578; 10 Bevans 699.

Agreement relating to customs privileges for consular officers.

Exchange of notes at Panama January 7 and 31, 1935.

Entered into force January 31, 1935.

5 UST 1520; TIAS 3028; 234 UNTS 277.

DEFENSE

Agreement relating to the sale of military equipment, materials, and services to Panama.

Exchange of notes at Panama May 20, 1959.

Entered into force May 20, 1959; operative from April 27, 1959.

10 UST 1000; TIAS 4234; 346 UNTS 235.

Agreement relating to the furnishing of defense articles and services to Panama for the purpose of contributing to its internal security.

Exchange of notes at Panama March 26 and May 23, 1962.

Entered into force May 23, 1962.

13 UST 1294; TIAS 5081; 458 UNTS 225.

Agreement relating to the deposit by Panama of ten percent of the value of grant military assistance and excess defense articles furnished by the United States.

Exchange of notes at Panama April 4 and May 9, 1972.

Entered into force May 9, 1972; effective February 7, 1972.

23 UST 897; TIAS 7353.

Agreement concerning payment to the United States of net proceeds from the sale of defense articles furnished under the military assistance program.

Exchange of notes at Panama May 20 and December 6, 1974.

Entered into force December 6, 1974; effective July 1, 1974.

25 UST 3135; TIAS 7977; 991 UNTS 317.

Agreement concerning general security of military information.

Signed at Panama August 17, 1984.

Entered into force August 17, 1984.

TIAS 11196; 2129 UNTS 265.

Agreement regarding the status of United States personnel who may be temporarily present in Panama.

Exchange of notes at Panama July 3 and 10, 2001.

Entered into force July 10, 2001.

TIAS

ECONOMIC AND TECHNICAL COOPERATION

General agreement for technical and economic cooperation.

Signed at Panama December 11, 1961.

Entered into force March 5, 1962.

13 UST 274; TIAS 4972; 445 UNTS 161.

Agency for International Development

May 6, 1969 (28 UST 5711; TIAS 8656).

September 30, 1971 (28 UST 5732; TIAS 8656).

September 10, 1975 (28 UST 353; TIAS 8473).

November 19, 1975 (28 UST 5471; TIAS 8647).

November 28, 1975 (29 UST 2037; TIAS 8925).

June 2, 1976 (28 UST 5739; TIAS 8656).

October 14, 1976 (28 UST 8295; TIAS 8762).

December 30, 1976 (28 UST 2258; TIAS 8543).

December 30, 1976 (28 UST 2276; TIAS 8544).

November 25, 1977 (29 UST 5781; TIAS 9154; 1231 UNTS 83).

December 21, 1977 (29 UST 5599; TIAS 9133; 1148 UNTS 414).

August 23, 1978 (30 UST 4827; TIAS 9490; 1233 UNTS 205).

December 24, 1984 (NP).

EMPLOYMENT

Agreements relating to the employment of dependents of official government employees.

Exchange of notes at Panama November 26, 1993.

Entered into force November 26, 1993.

TIAS 12517.

ENERGY

Agreement relating to electric power.

Exchange of notes at Panama October 1, 1979.

Entered into force October 1, 1979.

TIAS 10600; 1581 UNTS 3.

EXTRADITION

Treaty providing for the extradition of criminals.

Signed at Panama May 25, 1904.

Entered into force May 8, 1905.

34 Stat. 2851; TS 445; 10 Bevans 673.

FINANCE

Agreement relating to legal tender and fractional silver coinage by Panama.

Exchange of notes at Washington and New York June 20, 1904.

Entered into force June 20, 1904.

10 Bevans 681.

Amendments

March 26 and April 2, 1930 (10 Bevans 731).

May 28 and June 6, 1931 (10 Bevans 734).

March 2, 1936 (53 Stat. 1807; TS 945).

June 17, 1946 (10 Bevans 834).

May 9 and 24, 1950.

September 11 and October 22, 1953.

August 23 and October 25, 1961.

September 26 and October 23, 1962.

Agreement relating to payment to be made by Panama to the Panama Canal Company and the Canal Zone Government for goods and services, with agreed minute.

Exchange of notes at Panama March 25, 1980.

Entered into force March 25, 1980.

TIAS 10601; 1590 UNTS 3.

Agreement relating to payments to be made by the Panama Canal Commission to Panama pursuant to articles III(5) and XIII(4) of the Panama Canal Treaty, with agreed minute.

Exchange of notes at Panama March 25, 1980.

Entered into force March 25, 1980.

TIAS 10601; 1590 UNTS 17.

Understanding relating to Article X of the treaty concerning the treatment and protection of investments of October 27, 1982.

Exchange of notes at Panama July 1 and 12, 1985.

Entered into force May 30, 1991.

TIAS

Agreement regarding the consolidation and rescheduling of certain debts owed to, guaranteed by or insured by the United States Government and its agencies, with annexes.

Signed at Washington July 2, 1986.

Entered into force August 18, 1986.

NP

Agreement regarding the consolidation and rescheduling of certain debts owed to, guaranteed by, or insured by the United States Government and its agencies, with annexes.

Signed at Panama August 21, 1991.

Entered into force September 27, 1991.

NP

Swap agreement among the United States Treasury and the Government of Panama/Banco Nacional de Panama, with letter of understandings.

Signed at Washington and Panama January 29 and 30, 1992.

Entered into force January 30, 1992.

TIAS

Investment incentive agreement.

Signed at Panama City April 19, 2000.

Entered into force July 12, 2000.

TIAS

Agreement regarding a debt–for–nature swap, with attachments.

Signed at Panama City July 10, 2003.

Entered into force July 30, 2003.

TIAS

Agreement regarding a debt-for-nature swap, with attachments.

Signed at Panama August 19, 2004.

Entered into force August 19, 2004.

TIAS

HIGHWAYS

Agreement relating to the construction of the inter-American highway.

Exchange of notes at Panama May 15 and June 7, 1943.

Entered into force June 7, 1943.

57 Stat. 1298; EAS 365; 10 Bevans 826; 21 UNTS 269.

Amendment

January 16 and 26, 1951 (2 UST 1852; TIAS 2321; 137 UNTS 69).

Agreement for cooperation in the construction of the Panama segment of the Darien Gap highway.

Signed at Washington May 6, 1971.

Entered into force May 6, 1971.

22 UST 602; TIAS 7111; 793 UNTS 31.

Amendments

May 15, 1974 (33 UST 3622; TIAS 10245; 1540 UNTS 420).

September 13, 1979 (33 UST 3622; TIAS 10245; 1540 UNTS 421).

July 18, 1980 (33 UST 3622; TIAS 10245; 1540 UNTS 422).

HOUSING

Agreement regarding housing civilian and military personnel of U.S. Forces stationed in Panama.

Exchange of notes November 29, 1984; effective October 1, 1984.

TIAS

INTERNATIONAL CRIMINAL COURT

Agreement regarding the surrender of persons to the International Criminal Court.

Signed at Panama City June 23, 2003.

Entered into force November 6, 2003.

TIAS

INVESTMENT

Treaty concerning the treatment and protection of investments, with annex and agreed minutes.

Signed at Washington October 27, 1982.

Entered into force May 30, 1991.

TIAS

Amendment

June 1, 2000.

JUDICIAL ASSISTANCE

Informal arrangement relating to cooperation between the American Embassy, or Consulate, and Panamanian authorities when American merchant seamen or tourists are brought before a magistrate's court.

Exchange of notes at Panama September 18 and October 15, 1947; effective October 15, 1947.

10 Bevans 841.

Arrangement concerning assistance in the development of civilian law enforcement institutions.

Signed at Panama December 28, 1990.

Entered into force December 28, 1990.

TIAS 12425.

Treaty on mutual assistance in criminal matters, with annex and appendix.

Signed at Panama April 11, 1991.

Entered into force September 6, 1995.

TIAS

MAPPING

Cooperative arrangement for the production of topographic maps of Panama, with annexes.

Signed at Washington and Panama January 29, 1986.

Entered into force January 29, 1986.

TIAS 11212.

MARITIME MATTERS

Agreement relating to the mutual recognition of ship measurement certificates.

Exchange of notes at Washington August 17, 1937.

Entered into force August 17, 1937.

50 Stat. 1626; EAS 106; 10 Bevans 781; 182 LNTS 159.

METEOROLOGY

Agreement relating to the Port Meteorological Office.

Exchange of notes at Panama October 1, 1979.

Entered into force October 1, 1979.

TIAS 10599; 1871 UNTS 33.

MISSIONS, MILITARY

Agreement relating to the detail of a military officer to serve as adviser to the Minister of Foreign Affairs of Panama.

Signed at Washington July 7, 1942.

Entered into force July 7, 1942.

56 Stat. 1545; EAS 258; 10 Bevans 817; 9 UNTS 289.

Extension and amendments

February 17, March 23, September 22, and November 6, 1959 (12 UST 718; TIAS 4773; 409 UNTS 307).

March 26 and July 6, 1962 (13 UST 2598; TIAS 5226; 460 UNTS 360).

September 20 and October 8, 1962 (13 UST 2600; TIAS 5226; 460 UNTS 362).

NARCOTIC DRUGS

Mutual cooperation for reducing demand, preventing illicit use and combatting illicit production and traffic of drugs.

Signed at Panama January 10, 1990.

Entered into force January 10, 1990.

TIAS 12409.

Arrangement for support and assistance from the United States Coast Guard for the National Maritime Service of the Ministry of Government and Justice.

Signed at Panama March 18, 1991.

Entered into force March 18, 1991.

TIAS 11833; 2212 UNTS 7.

Memorandum of understanding concerning the provision of helicopters for the purpose of more effectively combatting the illicit production and trafficking of drugs and other international criminal activities, with general provisions.

Signed at Washington September 6, 1995.

Entered into force September 6, 1995.

TIAS 12688.

Supplementary arrangement to the arrangement of March 18, 1991 for support and assistance from the United States Coast Guard for the National Maritime Service of the Ministry of Government and Justice.

Signed at Panama February 5, 2002.

Entered into force February 5, 2002.

TIAS

Agreement regarding the Cooperating Nation Information Exchange System.

Exchange of notes at Panama February 2 and 10, 2005.

Entered into force February 10, 2005.

TIAS

PEACE CORPS

Agreement relating to the establishment of a Peace Corps program in Panama.

Exchange of notes at Washington May 1, 1990.

Entered into force November 23, 1990.

TIAS

POSTAL MATTERS

International express mail agreement, with detailed regulations.

Signed at Panama and Washington March 29 and May 21, 1985.

Entered into force July 1, 1985.

TIAS 11151; 2126 UNTS 179.

PRISONER TRANSFER

Treaty on the execution of penal sentences.

Signed at Panama January 11, 1979.

Entered into force June 27, 1980.

32 UST 1565; TIAS 9787; 1280 UNTS 363.

PROPERTY TRANSFER

Agreement relating to the status of the Cardenas (FAA housing) area under the agreement in implementation of Article III of the Panama Canal Treaty.

Signed at Panama August 29, 1980.

Entered into force August 29, 1980.

33 UST 570; TIAS 10048; 1280 UNTS 415.

Agreement concerning disposition of the Mount Hope warehouse and transportation areas.

Exchange of notes at Panama February 12 and May 7, 1982.

Entered into force May 7, 1982.

34 UST 1972; TIAS 10474; 1750 UNTS 287.

Agreement concerning transfer of the Ancon District Court (Building 310) from the United States to Panama.

Exchange of notes at Panama July 13, 1982.

Entered into force July 13, 1982.

TIAS 10544; 1777 UNTS 333.

Agreement concerning transfer of Mindi and Coco Solo housing units from the United States to Panama.

Exchange of notes at Panama August 9 and 11, 1982.

Entered into force August 11, 1982.

TIAS

PUBLICATIONS

Agreement relating to the exchange of official publications.

Exchange of notes at Panama November 27, 1941, and March 7, 1942.

Entered into force November 27, 1941.

56 Stat. 1444; EAS 243; 10 Bevans 805; 101 UNTS 157.

SCIENTIFIC COOPERATION

Agreement relating to the operation in Panama of the Smithsonian Tropical Research Institute, with annex.

Exchange of notes at Washington September 7, 1977.

Entered into force September 7, 1977; effective October 1, 1979.

33 UST 465; TIAS 10037; 1280 UNTS 327.

SHIPPING

Agreement relating to jurisdiction over vessels utilizing the Louisiana Offshore Oil Port.

Exchange of notes at Washington August 15 and October 10, 1980.

Entered into force October 10, 1980.

32 UST 2906; TIAS 9885; 1275 UNTS 97.

SMUGGLING

Convention for prevention of smuggling of intoxicating liquors.

Signed at Washington June 6, 1924.

Entered into force January 19, 1925.

43 Stat. 1875; TS 707; 10 Bevans 717; 138 LNTS 397.

SOCIAL SECURITY

Agreement concerning participation by members of the Panama Canal Commission and United States forces in the Panamanian social security system.

Exchange of notes at Panama March 9, 1982.

Entered into force March 9, 1982.

TIAS 10492; 1750 UNTS 273.

STOLEN PROPERTY

Treaty for the return of stolen, robbed, or converted vehicles and aircraft, with annexes.

Signed at Panama June 6, 2000.

Entered into force September 13, 2001.

TIAS

TAXATION

Arrangement providing for relief from double income tax on shipping profits.

Exchange of notes at Washington January 15, February 8, and March 28, 1941.

Entered into force March 28, 1941; operative January 1, 1936.

55 Stat. 1363; EAS 221; 10 Bevans 801; 103 UNTS 163.

Amendment

July 30 and December 30, 1987 (TIAS 11555; 2185 UNTS 333).

Agreement for withholding of Panamanian income tax from compensation paid to Panamanians employed within Canal Zone by the canal, railroad, or auxiliary works.

Exchange of notes at Panama August 12 and 30, 1963.

Entered into force August 30, 1963.

14 UST 1478; TIAS 5445; 488 UNTS 11.

Agreement relating to the withholding of contributions for educational insurance from salaries paid to certain Canal Zone employees.

Exchange of notes at Panama September 8 and October 13, 1972.

Entered into force October 13, 1972.

23 UST 3495; TIAS 7509; 898 UNTS 189.

Agreement relating to the agreements in implementation of articles III and IV of the Panama Canal Treaty with respect to tax on moveable property.

Exchange of notes at Panama October 1, 1979.

Entered into force October 1, 1979.

33 UST 565; TIAS 10047; 1280 UNTS 409.

Agreement concerning taxation of income of United States contractors and subcontractors of the Panama Canal Commission or United States Forces, with attachments and related note.

Exchange of notes at Panama September 11, 1986.

Entered into force September 11, 1986.

TIAS

TELECOMMUNICATION

Agreement for radio communications between amateur stations on behalf of third parties.

Exchange of notes at Panama July 19 and August 1, 1956.

Entered into force September 1, 1956.

7 UST 2179; TIAS 3617; 281 UNTS 49.

Agreement relating to the granting of reciprocal authorizations to permit licensed amateur radio operators of either country to operate their stations in the other country.

Exchange of notes at Panama November 16, 1966.

Entered into force November 16, 1966.

17 UST 2215; TIAS 6159; 680 UNTS 303.

TRADE AND COMMERCE

Convention facilitating the work of traveling salesmen.

Signed at Washington February 8, 1919.

Entered into force December 8, 1919.

41 Stat. 1696; TS 646; 10 Bevans 714.

Agreement relating to trade in cotton, wool and man-made fiber textiles and textile products, with annexes.

Exchange of notes at Panama November 22 and 29, 1991.

Entered into force November 29, 1991.

NP

Amendment

March 16 and April 10, 1992 (NP).

VISAS

Reciprocal agreement for gratis nonimmigrant visas.

Exchange of notes at Panama March 27 and May 22 and 25, 1956.

Entered into force June 1, 1956.

7 UST 905; TIAS 3573; 268 UNTS 333.

Agreement modifying the agreement of March 27 and May 22 and 25, 1956 for gratis nonimmigrant visas.

Exchange of notes at Panama June 14 and 17, 1971.

Entered into force June 17, 1971.

22 UST 815; TIAS 7142; 796 UNTS 353.

PAN AMERICAN UNION

(See ORGANIZATION OF AMERICAN STATES)

PAPUA NEW GUINEA

On September 16, 1975 Papua New Guinea became an independent state. In a note dated September 16, 1975 to the Secretary-General of the United Nations, the Governor-General made a statement reading in part as follows:

"1. The Government of Papua New Guinea will make an examination of all treaties applying to its territory before independence, both bilateral and multilateral, with a view to making a statement of intention in respect of each of them. The statement will declare the Government's view as to whether the treaty continues or should be continued in force (on the basis of either succession or mutual consent, and with or without modification), or should be treated as having lapsed, or should be terminated. The statement will be forwarded to the other party or parties or to the depository, as may be appropriate.

2. During the period of examination, the Government will, on a basis of reciprocity, accept all treaty rights and obligations accruing and arising under treaties previously applicable. The period of examination will extend for five years from the date of Independence, that is, until 15th September, 1980, except in the case of any treaty in respect of which an earlier statement of intention is made."

CONSULS

Convention to regulate commerce (article IV) between the United States and the United Kingdom.

Signed at London July 3, 1815.

Entered into force July 3, 1815.

8 Stat. 228; TS 110; 12 Bevans 49.

DEFENSE

Status of forces agreement.

Signed at Port Moresby February 28, 1989.

Entered into force February 28, 1989.

TIAS 11612.

Memorandum of understanding concerning an exchange of officers.

Signed at Port Moresby and Honolulu May 17 and June 13, 1989.

Entered into force June 13, 1989.

TIAS 11667.

Memorandum of understanding concerning joint and combined military activities by Papua New Guinea defense forces and United States military forces in independent Papua New Guinea, with appendices.

Signed at Port Moresby March 26, 1990.

Entered into force March 26, 1990.

TIAS 12366.

ECONOMIC AND TECHNICAL COOPERATION

Development cooperation agreement.

Signed at Port Moresby May 7, 1990.

Entered into force May 7, 1990.

TIAS 11722; 2207 UNTS 261.

EXTRADITION

Extradition treaty between the United States and the United Kingdom.

Signed at London December 22, 1931, applicable to Australia (including Papua, Norfolk Island, and the mandated territories of New Guinea and Nauru), in accordance with article 14, from August 30, 1935.

47 Stat. 2122; TS 849; 12 Bevans 482; 163 LNTS 59.

Agreement continuing in force between the United States and Papua New Guinea the extradition treaty of December 22, 1931, between the United States and the United Kingdom, with enclosures.

Exchange of notes at Port Moresby and Waigani February 2 and 23, 1988.

Entered into force February 23, 1988.

TIAS

FINANCE

Agreement relating to investment guaranties.

Exchange of notes at Port Moresby and Waigani November 28, 1977 and April 4, 1978.

Entered into force April 13, 1978.

29 UST 3190; TIAS 9004; 1124 UNTS 237.

FISHERIES

Agreement concerning fishing by United States vessels in Papua New Guinea's archipelagic waters pursuant to the treaty on fisheries between the United States and certain Pacific Island states.

Exchange of notes at Waigani and Port Moresby March 4, 5 and 25, 1987.

Entered into force March 25, 1987.

TIAS 11290.

INTERNATIONAL CRIMINAL COURT

Agreement regarding the surrender of persons to the International Criminal Court.

Signed at Washington September 30, 2004.

Entered into force September 30, 2004.

TIAS

PEACE CORPS

Agreement relating to the establishment of a Peace Corps program in Papua New Guinea, with related note.

Exchange of notes at Washington October 6, 1980.

Entered into force October 6, 1980.

32 UST 2984; TIAS 9882; 1275 UNTS 89.

POSTAL MATTERS

Agreement for exchange of postal parcels between the United States and the Territory of Papua and the Trust Territory of New Guinea, and detailed regulations of execution.

Signed at Canberra May 22 and at Washington June 20, 1958.

Entered into force October 1, 1958.

9 UST 1266; TIAS 4115; 336 UNTS 97.

Memorandum of understanding concerning the operation of the INTELPOST field trial, with details of implementation.

Signed at Boroko and Washington June 30 and November 23, 1987.

Entered into force January 1, 1988.

TIAS 11301.

International express mail agreement with detailed regulations.

Signed at Boroko and Washington August 4 and 19, 1988.

Entered into force September 30, 1988.

TIAS 11644.

TELECOMMUNICATION

Agreement relating to the reciprocal granting of authorizations to permit licensed amateur radio operators of either country to operate their stations in the other country.

Exchange of notes at Port Moresby and Waigani August 17, 1989 and April 26, 1990.

Entered into force April 26, 1990.

TIAS

PARAGUAY

AGRICULTURAL COMMODITIES

Agricultural commodities agreement with exchanges of notes.

Signed at Asuncion July 7, 1961.

Entered into force July 7, 1961.

12 UST 1397; TIAS 4864; 433 UNTS 53.

Agricultural commodities agreement with exchanges of notes.

Signed at Asuncion November 24, 1962.

Entered into force November 24, 1962.

13 UST 3874; TIAS 5263; 471 UNTS 49.

Agricultural commodities agreement with exchange of notes.

Signed at Asuncion September 16, 1963.

Entered into force September 16, 1963.

14 UST 1807; TIAS 5493; 494 UNTS 101.

Agricultural commodities agreement with exchange of notes.

Signed at Asuncion November 14, 1963.

Entered into force November 14, 1963.

14 UST 1818; TIAS 5494; 505 UNTS 87.

Agricultural commodities agreement with exchange of notes.

Signed at Asuncion September 5, 1964.

Entered into force September 5, 1964.

15 UST 1807; TIAS 5654; 530 UNTS 225.

Agricultural commodities agreement with exchange of notes.

Signed at Asuncion April 27, 1966.

Entered into force April 27, 1966.

17 UST 699; TIAS 6020; 578 UNTS 121.

Agricultural commodities agreement with annex.

Signed at Asuncion December 22, 1967.

Entered into force December 22, 1967.

20 UST 668; TIAS 6674; 706 UNTS 217.

Agricultural commodities agreement with annex.

Signed at Asuncion June 7, 1969.

Entered into force June 7, 1969.

20 UST 854; TIAS 6701; 719 UNTS 161.

Agricultural commodities agreement with annex.

Signed at Asuncion July 14, 1970.

Entered into force July 14, 1970.

21 UST 2226; TIAS 6974; 775 UNTS 155.

Agricultural commodities agreement with annex.

Signed at Asuncion March 22, 1971.

Entered into force March 22, 1971.

23 UST 97; TIAS 7279.

AVIATION

Air transport agreement.

Signed at Asuncion February 28, 1947.

Entered into force February 16, 1948.

62 Stat. 1940; TIAS 1753; 10 Bevans 948; 44 UNTS 25.

Agreement amending the air transport agreement of February 28, 1947, and relating to charter air services.

Exchange of notes at Asuncion March 8 and 9, 1978.

Entered into force March 9, 1978.

29 UST 2697; TIAS 8966.

Memorandum of agreement concerning assistance in developing and modernizing the Paraguay civil aviation infrastructure, with annex.

Signed at Washington May 27, 1992.

Entered into force May 27, 1992.

TIAS 11862.

Air Transport agreement, with annexes.

Signed at Asuncion May 2, 2005.

Entered into force August 1, 2006.

TIAS

COMMERCE

Treaty of friendship, commerce, and navigation.

Signed at Asuncion February 4, 1859.

Entered into force March 7, 1860.

12 Stat. 1091; TS 272; 10 Bevans 888.

CONSERVATION

Agreement concerning the establishment of a Tropical Forest Conservation Fund and a Tropical Forest Conservation Board.

Signed at Asuncion June 7, 2006.

Entered into force July 17, 2006.

TIAS

CONSULS

See COMMERCE

CUSTOMS

Agreement for reciprocal import privileges for non-diplomatic personnel.

Exchange of notes at Asuncion May 9 and 11, 1956.

Entered into force May 11, 1956.

7 UST 933; TIAS 3577.

Agreement regarding mutual assistance between their customs administrations.

Signed at Asuncion December 19, 2002.

Entered into force December 19, 2002.

TIAS

DEFENSE

Agreement concerning the furnishing of assistance to Paraguay for the purpose of increasing the air transport capability of the Paraguayan Air Force.

Exchange of notes at Asuncion August 25, 1962.

Entered into force August 25, 1962.

13 UST 2132; TIAS 5174; 461 UNTS 207.

Agreement providing for assistance to increase the road construction and maintenance capability of the Paraguayan Army.

Exchange of notes at Asuncion February 10, 1964.

Entered into force February 10, 1964.

15 UST 149; TIAS 5532; 511 UNTS 53.

Agreement relating to the furnishing of additional military assistance to Paraguay.

Exchange of notes at Asuncion April 11, 1966.

Entered into force April 11, 1966.

17 UST 661; TIAS 6014; 578 UNTS 99.

Agreement concerning payment to the United States of net proceeds from the sale of defense articles furnished under the military assistance program.

Exchange of notes at Asuncion June 27, 1974.

Entered into force July 1, 1974.

25 UST 1440; TIAS 7873.

Agreement concerning United States Armed Forces technical personnel deployments to Paraguay.

Exchange of notes at Asuncion February 28, 1995.

Entered into force February 28, 1995.

NP

Agreement regarding bilateral military exercises and exchanges in Paraguay.

Exchange of notes at Asuncion November 12 and 24, 2004.

Entered into force November 24, 2004.

TIAS

Agreement regarding the status of United States personnel who may be temporarily present in Paraguay.

Exchange of notes at Asuncion March 8 and 31, 2005.

Entered into force July 1, 2005.

TIAS

ECONOMIC AND TECHNICAL COOPERATION

General agreement for economic, technical and related assistance.

Signed at Asuncion September 26, 1961.

Entered into force September 26, 1961.

13 UST 2287; TIAS 5196; 461 UNTS 91.

Agency for International Development

June 30, 1975 (28 UST 5867; TIAS 8665).

December 7, 1976 (28 UST 5923; TIAS 8665).

August 15, 1977 (29 UST 2940; TIAS 8990; 1120 UNTS 31).

May 8, 2006 (NP).

EDUCATION

Agreement for financing certain educational exchange programs.

Signed at Asuncion August 20, 1963.

Entered into force October 1, 1964.

TIAS 5675; 15 UST 1982; 531 UNTS 197.

ENVIRONMENTAL COOPERATION

Agreement for cooperation in the Global Learning and Observations to Benefit the Environment Program, with appendices.

Signed at Asuncion October 27, 2000.

Entered into force October 27, 2000.

TIAS

EXTRADITION

Extradition treaty.

Signed at Washington November 9, 1998.

Entered into force March 9, 2001.

TIAS

FINANCE

Investment incentive agreement.

Signed at Asuncion September 24, 1992.

Entered into force May 19, 1993.

TIAS 12478.

Agreement regarding the reduction of certain debts owed to the Government of the United States and its agencies, with attachment.

Signed at Asuncion June 7, 2006.

Entered into force July 17, 2006.

NP

INTELLECTUAL PROPERTY

Memorandum of understanding on intellectual property rights, with annex.

Signed at Washington March 30, 2004.

Entered into force March 30, 2004.

TIAS

MAPPING

Cooperative mapping agreement.

Signed at Asuncion January 16, 1962.

Entered into force January 16, 1962.

13 UST 52; TIAS 4934; 433 UNTS 169.

NARCOTIC DRUGS

Agreement on the control of the unlawful use of and illicit trafficking in narcotics and other dangerous drugs.

Signed at Asuncion October 26, 1972.

Entered into force provisionally October 26, 1972; definitively January 11, 1973.

24 UST 1008; TIAS 7613.

Mutual cooperation agreement for reducing demand, illicit production and traffic of drugs.

Signed at Asuncion September 22, 1988.

Entered into force September 22, 1988.

TIAS 12397.

Agreement to cooperate in the prevention and control of money laundering arising from illegal trafficking in narcotics and psychotropic substances.

Signed at Asuncion November 30, 1993.

Entered into force August 17, 1994.

TIAS

PACIFIC SETTLEMENT OF DISPUTES

Treaty for the advancement of peace.

Signed at Asuncion August 29, 1914.

Entered into force March 9, 1915.

39 Stat. 1615; TS 614; 10 Bevans 902.

PEACE CORPS

Agreement relating to the establishment of a Peace Corps program in Paraguay.

Exchange of notes at Asuncion November 4, 1966.

Entered into force November 4, 1966.

17 UST 2050; TIAS 6144; 676 UNTS 17.

POSTAL MATTERS

International express mail agreement, with detailed regulations.

Signed at Asuncion and Washington July 13 and August 22, 1988.

Entered into force September 30, 1988.

TIAS 11643.

PUBLICATIONS

Agreement relating to the exchange of official publications.

Exchange of notes at Asuncion November 26 and 28, 1942.

Entered into force November 28, 1942; operative August 5, 1942.

56 Stat. 1868; EAS 301; 10 Bevans 916; 101 UNTS 173.

RELIEF SUPPLIES AND PACKAGES

Agreement providing for duty-free entry into Paraguay and exemption from internal taxation of relief supplies and packages.

Signed at Asuncion April 4, 1957.

Entered into force April 4, 1957.

8 UST 617; TIAS 3811; 283 UNTS 193.

Amendments

December 27, 1960 and March 7, 1961 (12 UST 240; TIAS 4702; 405 UNTS 328).

September 25 and October 26, 1970 (21 UST 2507; TIAS 6993; 772 UNTS 462).

SEISMIC OBSERVATIONS

Memorandum of understanding concerning the operation of a seismic monitoring station in Paraguay.

Signed at Asuncion September 13, 1999.

Entered into force September 13, 1999.

TIAS

TELECOMMUNICATION

Agreement relating to radio communications between amateur stations on behalf of third parties.

Exchange of notes at Asuncion August 31 and October 6, 1960.

Entered into force November 5, 1960.

11 UST 2229; TIAS 4596; 393 UNTS 281.

Agreement relating to the reciprocal granting of authorizations to permit licensed amateur radio operators of either country to operate their stations in the other country.

Exchange of notes at Asuncion March 18, 1966.

Entered into force March 18, 1966.

17 UST 328; TIAS 5978; 586 UNTS 189.

Agreement relating to establishing and maintaining monitoring premises and installations of the Foreign Broadcast Information Service (FBIS).

Exchange of notes at Asuncion May 24, 1973.

Entered into force May 24, 1973.

24 UST 1132; TIAS 7639.

TRADE

See also COMMERCE

Convention facilitating the work of traveling salesmen.

Signed at Washington October 20, 1919.

Entered into force March 22, 1922.

42 Stat. 2128; TS 662; 10 Bevans 906.

Reciprocal trade agreement and supplemental exchanges of notes.

Signed at Asuncion September 12, 1946.

Entered into force April 9, 1947.

61 Stat. 2688; TIAS 1601; 10 Bevans 933; 125 UNTS 179.

Related agreement

April 2, 1962 (13 UST 407; TIAS 5000; 442 UNTS 315).

Agreement terminating parts and amending and continuing parts of the agreement of September 12, 1946.

Exchange of notes at Asuncion June 26, 1963.

Entered into force June 26, 1963.

14 UST 1021; TIAS 5396; 487 UNTS 334.

PERU

AGRICULTURAL COMMODITIES

Agricultural commodities agreement for drought assistance.

Exchange of notes at Lima April 17 and May 4 and 8, 1956.

Entered into force May 8, 1956.

7 UST 2529; TIAS 3645; 278 UNTS 117.

Agricultural commodities agreement for drought assistance.

Exchange of notes at Washington July 16 and 19, 1957.

Entered into force July 19, 1957.

8 UST 970; TIAS 3860; 289 UNTS 271.

Agricultural commodities agreement with exchanges of notes.

Signed at Lima February 12, 1960.

Entered into force February 12, 1960.

11 UST 186; TIAS 4430; 372 UNTS 83.

Amendments

October 25 and November 24, 1960 (11 UST 2621; TIAS 4652; 402 UNTS 360).

October 4 and December 27, 1960 (12 UST 259; TIAS 4708; 405 UNTS 354).

April 25 and July 31, 1961 (12 UST 1178; TIAS 4831; 418 UNTS 412).

June 4 and 18, 1962 (13 UST 1346; TIAS 5093; 458 UNTS 349).

Agricultural commodities agreement with exchange of notes.

Signed at Lima March 20, 1962.

Entered into force March 20, 1962.

13 UST 326; TIAS 4984; 445 UNTS 61.

Agricultural commodity agreement.

Signed at Washington September 23, 1963.

Entered into force September 23, 1963.

14 UST 1260; TIAS 5428; 488 UNTS 91.

Agricultural commodities agreement with exchange of notes.

Signed at Lima February 13, 1964.

Entered into force February 13, 1964.

15 UST 187; TIAS 5539; 511 UNTS 119.

Agricultural commodities agreement.

Signed at Lima April 26, 1978.

Entered into force April 26, 1978.

30 UST 7662; TIAS 9604.

Amendments

October 27, 1978 (30 UST 7691; TIAS 9604).

February 7, 1979 (30 UST 7695; TIAS 9604).

June 22, 1979 (30 UST 7699; TIAS 9604).

Related agreements

February 14, 1980 (32 UST 2700; TIAS 9873).

February 5, 1981 (33 UST 4297; TIAS 10301).

April 5, 1982 (34 UST 1714; TIAS 10448).

March 29, 1983 (TIAS 10679).

July 18, 1983 (TIAS 10679).

Agricultural commodities agreement.

Signed at Lima May 11, 1984.

Entered into force May 11, 1984.

TIAS 11040; 2022 UNTS 95.

Agricultural commodities agreement, with memorandum of understanding.

Signed at Lima April 17, 1985.

Entered into force April 17, 1985.

NP

Related agreement

August 11, 1986 (NP).

Agricultural commodities agreement.

Signed at Lima July 10, 1987.

Entered into force July 10, 1987.

NP

Agricultural commodities agreement.

Signed at Lima June 28, 1988.

Entered into force June 28, 1988.

NP

Amendment

August 12, 1988 (NP).

Related agreements

May 3, 1989 (NP).

August 31, 1990 (NP).

AGRICULTURE

Memorandum of understanding relating to cooperative efforts to protect crops from plant pest damage and plant diseases.

Signed at Lima November 30, 1981.

Entered into force November 30, 1981.

33 UST 4360; TIAS 10306.

ATOMIC ENERGY

Agreement providing for a grant to the Government of Peru to assist in the acquisition of nuclear research and training equipment and materials.

Exchange of notes at Lima July 12 and August 22, 1959.

Entered into force August 22, 1959.

10 UST 1600; TIAS 4304; 357 UNTS 99.

Agreement for cooperation concerning peaceful uses of nuclear energy, with annex and agreed minute.

Signed at Washington June 26, 1980.

Entered into force April 15, 1982.

33 UST 4246; TIAS 10300.

AVIATION

Memorandum of agreement concerning the provision of assistance in developing and modernizing Peru's civil aviation infrastructure.

Signed at Washington and Lima August 17 and 23, 1995.

Entered into force August 23, 1995.

TIAS

Air transport agreement, with annexes.

Signed at Lima June 10, 1998.

Entered into force February 8, 1999.

TIAS

Memorandum of cooperation concerning mutual cooperation in the promotion and development of civil aviation.

Signed at Washington and Lima March 16 and 27, 2000.

Entered into force March 27, 2000.

TIAS

CULTURAL PROPERTY

Agreement for the recovery and return of stolen archaeological, historical and cultural properties.

Signed at Lima September 15, 1981.

Entered into force September 15, 1981.

33 UST 1607; TIAS 10136.

Memorandum of understanding concerning the imposition of import restrictions on archaeological material from the prehispanic cultures and certain ethnological material from the colonial period of Peru.

Signed at Washington June 9, 1997.

Entered into force June 9, 1997.

TIAS

Amendment and extension

March 22, 2002.

CUSTOMS

Agreement granting reciprocal customs privileges to diplomatic and consular officers and personnel.

Exchange of notes at Lima November 7 and December 28, 1960, and February 4 and 13, 1961.

Entered into force February 13, 1961.

12 UST 217; TIAS 4696; 406 UNTS 177.

Agreement regarding mutual assistance between their customs administrations.

Signed at Washington March 1, 2006.

Entered into force March 1, 2006.

TIAS

DEFENSE

Military assistance agreement.

Signed at Lima February 22, 1952.

Entered into force April 26, 1952.

3 UST 2890; TIAS 2466; 165 UNTS 31.

Agreement providing for disposition of equipment and materials furnished by the United States under the military assistance agreement of February 22, 1952.

Exchange of notes at Lima March 22 and April 30, 1955.

Entered into force April 30, 1955.

6 UST 2064; TIAS 3273; 258 UNTS 415.

Agreement for performance by members of Army, Navy, and military aviation missions of duties specified in article V of the military assistance agreement of February 22, 1952.

Exchanges of notes at Lima June 28, July 18, and October 20 and 28, 1955.

Entered into force October 26, 1955.

6 UST 3771; TIAS 3377; 239 UNTS 181.

Agreement relating to the furnishing of defense articles and services to Peru.

Exchange of notes at Lima December 17 and 20, 1962.

Entered into force December 20, 1962.

13 UST 3896; TIAS 5265; 471 UNTS 75.

Agreement relating to the deposit by Peru of ten percent of the value of grant military assistance furnished by the United States.

Exchange of notes at Lima May 3, 1972.

Entered into force May 3, 1972; effective February 7, 1972.

23 UST 877; TIAS 7348.

Memorandum of understanding on exchange of officers between United States and Peruvian Marine Corps.

Signed at Lima and Washington August 20 and September 22, 1986.

Entered into force September 22, 1986.

TIAS 11383.

Agreement concerning the status of certain United States military personnel who may serve for a period of less than ninety days at the ground-based radar site at Yurimaguas, and at other locations as agreed by the Peruvian Air Force.

Exchange of notes at Lima November 7, 1995.

Entered into force November 7, 1995.

NP

Agreement concerning security assistance matters and the provision of articles, services and associated military educational training by the United States Government for antinarcotics purposes.

Exchange of notes at Lima October 14, 1999 and January 14, 2000.

Entered into force January 14, 2000.

TIAS

Acquisition and cross-servicing agreement, with annexes.

Signed at Miami and Lima December 18, 2000 and February 1, 2001.

Entered into force February 1, 2001.

TIAS

ECONOMIC AND TECHNICAL COOPERATION

General agreement for technical cooperation.

Signed at Lima January 25, 1951.

Entered into force January 15, 1953.

4 UST 132; TIAS 2772.

Amendments

January 7, 1952 (4 UST 139; TIAS 2772).

February 21 and 28, 1952 (4 UST 143; TIAS 2772).

January 15, 1953 (4 UST 146; TIAS 2772).

Agreement concerning the establishment of an Americas Fund and Administering Board.

Signed at Lima December 24, 1997.

Entered into force December 24, 1997.

TIAS

Agency for International Development

September 29, 1976 (28 UST 6235; TIAS 8681).

September 29, 1976 (28 UST 6313; TIAS 8682).

May 31, 1978 (30 UST 2793; TIAS 9363; 1233 UNTS 37).

June 30, 1978 (30 UST 3303; TIAS 9393; 1233 UNTS 87).

July 19, 1978 (30 UST 3141; TIAS 9385; 1179 UNTS 21).

July 19, 1978 (30 UST 3147; TIAS 9385; 1179 UNTS 27).

July 20, 1983 (35 UST 4903; TIAS 10977).

September 30, 1983 (35 UST 4903; TIAS 10977).

October 17, 1983 (35 UST 4903; TIAS 10977).

March 30, 1984 (35 UST 4903; TIAS 10977).

May 11, 1984 (NP).

September 27, 1984 (NP).

September 25, 1987 (NP).

September 30, 1991 (NP).

May 12, 1995 (NP).

September 26, 1996 (NP).

August 18, 1997 (NP).

August 17, 1999 (NP).

September 12, 2002 (NP).

September 30, 2003 (NP).

February 9, 2004 (NP).

July 27, 2004 (NP).

July 19, 2005 (NP).

July 6, 2006. (NP).

July 24, 2006 (NP).

EDUCATION

Agreement for financing certain educational exchange programs.

Signed at Lima January 28, 1965.

Entered into force August 25, 1965.

TIAS 5858; 16 UST 1149; 587 UNTS 273.

Amendment

November 23, 1981 and January 19, 1982 (TIAS 10332; 34 UST 15).

EMPLOYMENT

Agreement relating to employment of dependents of official government employees.

Exchange of notes at Lima August 27, 1987 and February 17, 1988.

Entered into force February 17, 1988.

TIAS 11650.

ENVIRONMENTAL COOPERATION

Agreement for cooperation in the Global Learning and Observations to Benefit the Environment (GLOBE) Program, with appendices.

Signed at Lima July 10, 1997.

Entered into force July 10, 1997.

TIAS

EXTRADITION

Extradition treaty.

Signed at Lima July 26, 2001.

Entered into force August 25, 2003.

TIAS

FINANCE

Agreement relating to investment guaranties under section 413 (b)(4)(B)(i) of the Mutual Security Act of 1954.

Exchange of notes at Lima March 14 and 16, 1955.

Entered into force March 16, 1955.

6 UST 678; TIAS 3203; 252 UNTS 151.

Agreement regarding the consolidation and rescheduling of certain debts owed to, guaranteed or insured by the United States Government and its agencies, with annexes.

Signed at Lima July 5, 1979.

Entered into force August 22, 1979.

32 UST 1; TIAS 9698; 1221 UNTS 159.

Agreement regarding the consolidation and rescheduling of certain debts owed to, guaranteed by or insured by the United States Government and its agencies, with implementing agreement.

Signed at Lima November 29, 1983.

Entered into force March 9, 1984.

35 UST 4944; TIAS 10978.

Agreement regarding the consolidation and rescheduling or refinancing of certain debts owed to, guaranteed by, or insured by the United States Government and its agencies, with annexes.

Signed at Washington August 27, 1992.

Entered into force September 30, 1992.

NP

Investment incentive and financial agreement.

Signed at Washington December 16, 1992.

Entered into force December 16, 1992.

TIAS 12542.

SWAP agreement between the United States Treasury and the Government of Peru/Central Bank of Peru, with memorandum of understanding.

Signed at Washington March 9, 1993.

Entered into force March 9, 1993.

TIAS

Agreement regarding the consolidation and rescheduling or refinancing of certain debts owed to, guaranteed by or insured by the United States Government and its agencies, with annexes.

Signed at Washington August 30, 1993.

Entered into force September 30, 1993.

NP

Agreement supplementing the investment incentive and financial agreement of December 16, 1992, relating to the Export-Import Bank.

Signed at Washington May 20, 1994.

Entered into force May 20, 1994.

TIAS 12542.

Agreement regarding the rescheduling and reorganization of certain debts owed to or guaranteed by the United States Government and its agencies.

Signed at Lima December 31, 1996.

Entered into force February 18, 1997.

NP

Agreement regarding a debt-for-nature swap, with attachments.

Signed at Washington June 26, 2002.

Entered into force July 16, 2002.

TIAS

HEALTH

Agreement for the establishment and operation of the Naval Medical Research Institute (NAMRID) in Lima.

Signed at Lima October 21, 1983.

Entered into force October 21, 1983.

35 UST 3003; TIAS 10836; 2014 UNTS 617.

JUDICIAL ASSISTANCE

Procedures for mutual assistance in connection with matters relating to the Lockheed Aircraft Corporation.

Signed at Washington August 8, 1979.

Entered into force August 8, 1979.

NP

MAPPING

Agreement relating to the making of aeronautical charts for air navigation.

Exchange of notes at Lima March 7 and April 23, 1942.

Entered into force April 23, 1942.

10 Bevans 1138.

Agreement relating to a program of aerial and topographic cartography of Peru and exchanges of notes.

Signed at Lima February 5, 1948.

Entered into force February 5, 1948.

10 Bevans 1269.

Cooperative arrangement for the production of topographic maps of Peru.

Signed at Washington and Lima April 25 and May 22, 1986.

Entered into force May 22, 1986.

TIAS 11372.

MARITIME MATTERS

Agreement concerning financial arrangements for the furnishing of certain supplies and services to naval vessels of both countries.

Signed at Lima January 7, 1955.

Entered into force April 7, 1955.

6 UST 806; TIAS 3227; 261 UNTS 321.

Agreement relating to the loan of a floating dry dock to Peru.

Exchange of notes at Washington June 15, 1959.

Entered into force June 15, 1959.

10 UST 1053; TIAS 4244; 346 UNTS 279.

Memorandum of understanding on maritime trade.

Signed at Washington May 1, 1987.

Entered into force May 1, 1987.

TIAS 11273.

NARCOTICS

Agreement regarding cooperation in the prevention and control of money laundering arising from illicit trafficking in narcotic drugs and psychotropic substances, with attachment.

Signed at Lima October 14, 1991.

Entered into force October 14, 1991.

TIAS 12438.

Agreement regarding the cooperating nation information exchange system, with annex.

Exchange of notes at Lima August 16, 2005.

Entered into force October 6, 2005.

TIAS

PACIFIC SETTLEMENT OF DISPUTES

Arbitration convention.

Signed at Washington December 5, 1908.

Entered into force June 29, 1909.

36 Stat. 2169; TS 528; 10 Bevans 1081.

Treaty for the advancement of peace.

Signed at Lima July 14, 1914.

Entered into force March 4, 1915.

39 Stat. 1611; TS 613; 10 Bevans 1083.

PEACE CORPS

Agreement concerning the program of the Peace Corps in the Republic of Peru.

Signed at Lima March 23, 2002.

Entered into force March 23, 2002.

TIAS

POSTAL MATTERS

International express mail agreement, with detailed regulations.

Signed at Lima and Washington October 29 and November 30, 1990.

Entered into force January 14, 1991.

TIAS 11787.

Agreement for the transmission and payment of postal money orders.

Signed at Washington and Lima August 21 and September 8, 1995.

Entered into force December 1, 1995.

NP

PRISONER TRANSFER

Treaty on the execution of penal sentences.

Signed at Washington July 6, 1979.

Entered into force July 21, 1980.

32 UST 1471; TIAS 9784; 1233 UNTS 139.

PUBLICATIONS

Agreement relating to the exchange of official publications.

Exchange of notes at Lima October 16 and 20, 1936.

Entered into force October 20, 1936.

50 Stat. 1601; EAS 103; 10 Bevans 1106; 181 LNTS 161.

RELIEF SUPPLIES AND PACKAGES

Agreement granting duty-free entry, exemption from internal taxation, and free transportation within Peru for supplies for U.S. rehabilitation and relief agencies distributing surplus agricultural food products in Peru.

Exchange of notes at Lima October 21 and 25, 1954.

Entered into force October 29, 1954.

5 UST 2725; TIAS 3128; 238 UNTS 247.

Amendment

June 23 and August 3, 1955 (7 UST 781; TIAS 3557; 273 UNTS 295).

RULES OF WARFARE

Convention regarding the rights of neutrals at sea.

Signed at Lima July 22, 1856.

Entered into force October 31, 1857.

11 Stat. 695; TS 277; 10 Bevans 1019.

SCIENTIFIC COOPERATION

Agreement concerning scientific and technical cooperation in the earth and mapping sciences, with annexes.

Signed at Lima July 19, 1990.

Entered into force July 19, 1990.

TIAS 12416.

TAXATION

Agreement concerning the reciprocal exemption from income tax of income derived from the international operation of ships.

Exchange of notes at Lima December 15, 1988.

Entered into force December 15, 1988.

TIAS 11621.

Agreement for the exchange of tax information.

Signed at Cartagena February 15, 1990.

Entered into force March 31, 1993.

TIAS 12060.

TELECOMMUNICATION

Arrangement concerning radio communications between amateur stations on behalf of third parties.

Exchange of notes at Lima February 16 and May 23, 1934.

Entered into force May 23, 1934.

49 Stat. 3555; EAS 66; 10 Bevans 1103.

Agreement relating to the reciprocal granting of authorizations to permit licensed amateur radio operators of either country to operate their stations in the other country.

Exchange of notes at Lima June 28 and August 11, 1965.

Entered into force August 11, 1965.

16 UST 1160; TIAS 5860; 564 UNTS 135.

TRADE AND COMMERCE

Convention concerning commercial travelers, and protocol.

Signed at Lima January 19, 1923.

Entered into force July 8, 1924.

43 Stat. 1802; TS 692; 10 Bevans 1091.

Agreement terminating the agreement of November 23, 1971 relating to trade in cotton textiles and providing for consultation on problems of market disruption caused by exports of textiles or textile products from Peru.

Exchange of notes at Lima June 13 and September 10, 1975.

Entered into force September 10, 1975.

26 UST 2125; TIAS 8153.

Memorandum of understanding within the context of the multilateral trade negotiations concerning concessions and contributions, with related letters of January 24 and 29, 1980.

Signed at Geneva and Lima March 8 and June 28, 1979.

Entered into force February 8, 1980.

35 UST 1322; TIAS 10732.

Agreement relating to trade in cotton, wool and man-made fiber textiles and textile products, with annexes.

Exchange of notes at Lima January 3, 1985.

Entered into force January 3, 1985.

NP

Extensions and amendments

July 17 and September 26, 1985 (NP).

October 24, 1985 and January 23, 1986 (NP).

March 19 and April 8, 1987 (NP).

November 27, 1987 and January 6, February 3, March 18 and June 2 and 10, 1988 (NP).

July 26, 1989 (NP).

July 11 and October 4, 1990 (NP).

Visa arrangement regarding trade in textiles, with annex.

Exchange of letters at Washington July 17 and August 22, 1985.

Entered into force August 22, 1985; effective September 1, 1985.

NP

Amendment

February 19 and 28, 1991 (NP).

Agreement regarding sanitary and phytosanitary measures and technical barriers to trade, with annexes.

Exchange of letters at Washington January 5, 2006.

Entered into force January 5, 2006.

TIAS

Agreement additional to the agreement of January 5, 2006 regarding sanitary and phytosanitary measures and technical barriers to trade, with annex.

Exchange of letters at Lima and Washington April 10, 2006.

Entered into force April 10, 2006.

TIAS

Agreement on beef SPS issues for United States-Peru trade promotion, with annex.

Exchange of letters at Lima and Washington October 6 and 25, 2006.

Entered into force October 25, 2006.

NP

VISAS

Agreement relating to the waiver of nonimmigrant passport visas and visa fees.

Exchange of notes at Lima April 6 and September 26, and related note of October 9, 1956.

Entered into force September 26, 1956; operative January 1, 1957.

8 UST 468; TIAS 3800; 288 UNTS 165.

Amendment

January 4 and 7, 1957 (8 UST 468; TIAS 3800; 288 UNTS 170).

Agreement relating to the reciprocal liberalization of nonimmigrant visa regulations.

Exchange of notes at Lima March 18 and April 23, 1970.

Entered into force April 23, 1970.

21 UST 1317; TIAS 6885; 751 UNTS 355.

WEATHER STATIONS

Agreement for the continuation of the cooperative meteorological program in Peru.

Exchange of notes at Lima July 7, 1964.

Entered into force July 7, 1964; operative January 1, 1963.

15 UST 1523; TIAS 5634; 530 UNTS 113.

PHILIPPINES

AGRICULTURAL COMMODITIES

Agricultural commodities agreement with exchanges of notes.

Signed at Manila November 24, 1961.

Entered into force November 24, 1961.

12 UST 3036; TIAS 4902; 433 UNTS 315.

Agreement relating to the deposit rate for pesos under the agricultural commodities agreement of November 24, 1961.

Exchange of notes at Manila August 14 and September 5, 1962.

Entered into force September 5, 1962.

14 UST 128; TIAS 5281; 473 UNTS 364.

Agricultural commodities agreement with exchange of notes.

Signed at Manila May 14, 1964.

Entered into force May 14, 1964.

15 UST 531; TIAS 5580; 526 UNTS 113.

Agricultural commodities agreement, with exchange of notes.

Signed at Manila April 23, 1965.

Entered into force April 23, 1965.

16 UST 632; TIAS 5785; 546 UNTS 157.

Agricultural commodities agreement with exchange of notes.

Signed at Manila December 22, 1966.

Entered into force December 22, 1966.

18 UST 89; TIAS 6202; 591 UNTS 219.

Agricultural commodities agreement with annex.

Signed at Manila March 24, 1970.

Entered into force March 24, 1970.

21 UST 1046; TIAS 6858; 745 UNTS 151.

Amendment

May 21 and 28, 1970 (21 UST 1315; TIAS 6884; 752 UNTS 415).

Related agreements

April 16, 1971 (22 UST 544; TIAS 7097; 792 UNTS 321).

November 22, 1971 (22 UST 1835; TIAS 7227).

May 4, 1972 (23 UST 627; TIAS 7324).

August 16, 1972 (23 UST 1499; TIAS 7431).

October 27 and 31, 1972 (23 UST 3487; TIAS 7506).

March 9, 1973 (24 UST 1089; TIAS 7629).

April 30, 1974 (25 UST 723; TIAS 7822).

Agricultural commodities agreement.

Signed at Manila May 12, 1977.

Entered into force May 12, 1977.

28 UST 6708; TIAS 8684.

Agricultural commodities agreement.

Signed at Manila August 24, 1978.

Entered into force August 24, 1978.

30 UST 198; TIAS 9187; 1150 UNTS 149.

Related agreement

Agricultural commodities agreement.

Signed at Manila July 8, 1985.

Entered into force July 8, 1985.

NP

Amendment

April 14, 1988 (NP).

Agricultural commodities agreement.

Signed at Manila June 20, 1986.

Entered into force June 20, 1986.

NP

Agricultural commodities agreement.

Signed at Manila April 19, 1988.

Entered into force April 19, 1988.

NP

Amendments

May 23, 1988 (NP).

July 31, 1990 (NP).

AVIATION

Agreement, with memorandum of consultation, concerning air transport services, with exchanges of letters.

Exchange of notes at Washington September 16, 1982.

Entered into force September 16, 1982.

34 UST 1623; TIAS 10443; 2126 UNTS 297.

Amendments

May 29, 1987 and January 13, 1988 (TIAS 11564; 2185 UNTS 595).

November 20, 1995 (TIAS 12702).

CLAIMS

Agreement relating to settlement of claims for damages arising from maneuvers at Laur Training Area.

Exchange of aide memoire at Manila February 6, 1957.

Entered into force February 6, 1957.

9 UST 313; TIAS 4009; 303 UNTS 237.

Agreement relating to settlement of claims for damages arising from SEATO maneuvers and ground field training exercises.

Exchange of aide memoire at Manila November 1, 1957.

Entered into force November 1, 1957.

8 UST 2456; TIAS 3965; 307 UNTS 39.

Agreement relating to settlement of claims for damages arising from maneuvers in Laur-Dingalan Bay area.

Exchange of aide memoire at Manila February 20, 1958.

Entered into force February 20, 1958.

9 UST 327; TIAS 4011; 303 UNTS 261.

Agreement relating to settlement of claims arising from maneuvers at Laur Training Area during January and February 1959.

Exchange of aide memoire at Manila January 21, 1959.

Entered into force January 21, 1959.

10 UST 204; TIAS 4184; 341 UNTS 255.

Agreement on the settlement of claims for pay and allowances of recognized Philippine guerillas not previously paid in full and for erroneous deductions of advanced salary from the backpay of eligible Philippine veterans.

Signed at Manila June 29, 1967.

Entered into force June 29, 1967.

18 UST 1392; TIAS 6295; 686 UNTS 71.

CONSERVATION

Agreement concerning the establishment of a Tropical Forest Conservation Fund and a Tropical Forest Conservation Board.

Signed at Manila September 19, 2002.

Entered into force November 1, 2002.

TIAS

CONSULS

See also GENERAL RELATIONS

Consular convention.

Signed at Manila March 14, 1947.

Entered into force November 18, 1948.

62 Stat. 1593; TIAS 1741; 11 Bevans 74; 45 UNTS 23.

COPYRIGHT

Arrangement relating to reciprocal copyright relations between the United States and the Philippines.

Exchange of notes at Washington October 21, 1948.

Entered into force October 21, 1948.

62 Stat. 2996; TIAS 1840; 11 Bevans 160; 77 UNTS 197.

CUSTOMS

Agreement relating to extension of free-entry privileges to dependents of United States Government employees newly assigned to South Viet-Nam who elect to reside in the Philippines.

Exchange of notes at Manila May 14 and 28, 1965.

Entered into force May 28, 1965.

19 UST 7807; TIAS 6612; 713 UNTS 235.

Agreement concerning matters of customs administration with annexes.

Signed at Washington January 4, 1967.

Entered into force January 4, 1967.

18 UST 148; TIAS 6212; 590 UNTS 51.

Agreement relating to customs regulations governing cargo consigned to United States military authorities or armed forces personnel, with annexes.

Exchange of notes at Manila April 24, 1969.

Entered into force May 4, 1969.

20 UST 2816; TIAS 6752; 723 UNTS 185.

DEFENSE

See also MUTUAL SECURITY

Mutual defense treaty.

Signed at Washington August 30, 1951.

Entered into force August 27, 1952.

3 UST 3947; TIAS 2529; 177 UNTS 133.

Agreement relating to military assistance.

Exchange of notes at Manila June 26, 1953.

Entered into force July 5, 1953.

4 UST 1682; TIAS 2834; 213 UNTS 77.

Agreement relating to military assistance.

Exchange of notes at Manila April 27, 1955.

Entered into force April 27, 1955.

6 UST 847; TIAS 3231; 261 UNTS 351.

Amendments

April 20, 1956 (7 UST 727; TIAS 3551; 273 UNTS 316).

June 14, 1957 (8 UST 859; TIAS 3845; 291 UNTS 342).

April 14, 1958 (9 UST 397; TIAS 4019; 308 UNTS 324).

Related agreements

August 23 and 30, 1979 (30 UST 7275; TIAS 9584; 1182 UNTS 153).

August 12 and 22, 1980 (32 UST 2393; TIAS 9847; 1274 UNTS 287).

August 19 and 30, 1981 (33 UST 3347; TIAS 10236).

August 16 and September 30, 1982 (TIAS 10504).

Agreement relating to the administration by the Philippine Department of Education of public schools within the United States Naval Reservation, Subic Bay.

Exchange of notes at Manila October 28, 1955.

Entered into force October 28, 1955; operative December 1, 1955.

6 UST 3109; TIAS 3361; 239 UNTS 165.

Agreement providing for disposition of equipment and material furnished by the United States.

Exchange of notes at Manila July 27, 1953 and March 3, 1956.

Entered into force March 3, 1956.

7 UST 425; TIAS 3523; 270 UNTS 400.

Interim arrangement to permit the exploitation of mineral resources located on specific sites within the U.S. Military Reservation, Fort Stotsenberg, Tarlac.

Exchange of notes at Manila April 8, 1957.

Entered into force April 8, 1957.

9 UST 309; TIAS 4008; 303 UNTS 227.

Agreement for the establishment of a Mutual Defense Board and the assignment of Philippine military liaison officers to United States military bases in the Philippines.

Exchange of notes at Manila May 15, 1958.

Entered into force May 15, 1958.

9 UST 547; TIAS 4033; 316 UNTS 163.

Agreement relating to the relocation of the Air Post Office from the Manila Air Station to the chancery grounds of the Embassy.

Exchange of notes at Manila March 27 and July 17, 1958.

Entered into force July 17, 1958.

9 UST 1073; TIAS 4082; 335 UNTS 199.

Agreement relating to the establishment of a United States communications facility at Mt. Cabuyao.

Exchange of notes at Manila March 16, 1965.

Entered into force March 16, 1965.

16 UST 158; TIAS 5776; 542 UNTS 199.

Agreement relating to the revision of Article XIII of the military base agreement of March 14, 1947, as amended, on criminal jurisdiction arrangements, with annex, agreed minutes and implementing arrangements.

Exchange of notes at Manila August 10, 1965.

Entered into force August 10, 1965.

16 UST 1090; TIAS 5851; 564 UNTS 208.

Agreement relating to the installation of a submarine cable with a terminal facility at San Miguel Communications Station.

Exchange of notes at Manila August 12, 1965.

Entered into force August 12, 1965.

16 UST 1127; TIAS 5855; 579 UNTS 47.

Agreement relating to the establishment of commercial banking facilities at the United States naval base at Subic Bay.

Exchange of notes at Manila November 3 and 15, 1965.

Entered into force November 15, 1965.

16 UST 1948; TIAS 5931; 574 UNTS 205.

Agreement relating to the installation and operation of a petroleum products pipeline from Subic Bay Naval Reservation through Basa Air Base to Clark Air Base.

Exchange of notes at Manila August 26, 1966.

Entered into force August 26, 1966.

17 UST 1206; TIAS 6083.

Agreement relating to the exploitation of natural resources within United States bases in the Philippines.

Exchange of notes at Manila August 24, 1967.

Entered into force August 24, 1967.

18 UST 2340; TIAS 6335; 693 UNTS 53.

Agreement relating to the expansion of banking facilities at Clark Air Base and Sangley Point Navy Base.

Exchange of notes at Manila January 17 and 23, 1968.

Entered into force January 23, 1968.

19 UST 4513; TIAS 6443; 698 UNTS 37.

Agreement relating to the employment of Philippine nationals in the United States military bases in the Philippines.

Signed at Manila May 27, 1968.

Entered into force May 27, 1968.

19 UST 5892; TIAS 6542; 658 UNTS 347.

Amendments

September 5, 1985.

July 19, 1989.

Agreement relating to the recruitment and employment of Filipino citizens by the United States military forces and contractors of military and civilian agencies of the United States in certain areas of the Pacific and Southeast Asia.

Signed at Manila December 28, 1968.

Entered into force December 28, 1968.

19 UST 7560; TIAS 6598; 658 UNTS 365.

Agreement relating to the installation of a submarine cable from Southern Taiwan to the United States Navy Communications Station, San Miguel, Zambales, Philippines.

Exchange of notes at Manila December 21, 1970 and January 6, 1971.

Entered into force January 6, 1971.

22 UST 363; TIAS 7065; 792 UNTS 37.

Agreement concerning payment to the United States of net proceeds from the sale of defense articles furnished under the military assistance program.

Exchange of notes at Manila May 16 and July 16, 1974.

Entered into force July 16, 1974; effective July 1, 1974.

25 UST 1447; TIAS 7875.

Amendment

March 8 and May 2, 2006.

Agreement amending the agreement of March 14, 1947, as amended, concerning military bases, with implementing arrangements, exchanges of notes, and related letters.[1]

Exchange of notes at Manila January 7, 1979.

Entered into force January 7, 1979.

30 UST 863; TIAS 9224.

Memorandum of understanding for the exchange of individual personnel between the United States Army Western Command and the Armed Forces of the Philippines.

Signed at Manila March 25, 1981.

Entered into force March 25, 1981.

35 UST 3606; TIAS 10871; 1577 UNTS 355.

Administrative arrangements, implementing the agreement of January 7, 1979 (TIAS 9224), for the performance of customs, immigration and quarantine functions at United States facilities at Clark Air Base and Subic Naval Base in the Republic of the Philippines, with annex and exchanges of notes.

Signed at Manila December 8, 1982.

Entered into force December 8, 1982.

TIAS 10585; 1871 UNTS 433.

Agreement regarding the relinquishment of certain areas at the San Miguel Naval Communications Station, Province of Zambales and the U.S. Navy transmitter site at Capas, Province of Tarlac, with maps.

Exchange of notes at Manila January 31 and May 13, 1991.

Entered into force May 13, 1991.

TIAS

Agreement regarding the relinquishment of the U.S. Facility at Wallace Air Station, the Crow Valley Weapons Range and the U.S. Air Force Transmitter site at O'Donnell.

Exchange of notes at Manila September 11 and 16, 1991.

Entered into force September 16, 1991.

TIAS

Agreement modifying the agreement of May 15, 1958, for the establishment of a Mutual Defense Board and the assignment of Philippine military liaison officers to U.S. military bases in the Philippines.

Exchange of notes at Manila April 2 and May 10, 1993.

Entered into force May 10, 1993.

TIAS 12496.

Agreement regarding the status of U.S. military and civilian personnel.

Exchange of notes at Manila April 2, June 11 and 21, 1993.

Entered into force June 21, 1993.

TIAS

Extensions

September 19, 1994.

April 28, 1995.

November 29, December 1 and 8, 1995.

Agreement regarding the treatment of United States armed forces visiting the Philippines.

Signed at Manila February 10, 1998.

Entered into force June 1, 1999.

TIAS

Amendment

April 11 and 12, 2006.

Agreement regarding the treatment of Republic of Philippines personnel visiting the United States of America.

Signed at Manila October 9, 1998.

Entered into force June 1, 1999.

TIAS

NOTE

1 See also administrative arrangement of December 8, 1982 (TIAS 10585).

ECONOMIC AND TECHNICAL COOPERATION

Economic and technical cooperation agreement.

Signed at Manila April 27, 1951.

Entered into force May 21, 1951.

3 UST 3707; TIAS 2498; 174 UNTS 251.

Agency for International Development

December 23, 1975 (28 UST 975; TIAS 8489).

March 11, 1976 (28 UST 2296; TIAS 8545).

April 28, 1976 (28 UST 5955; TIAS 8666).

August 6, 1976 (28 UST 7035; TIAS 8703; 1087 UNTS 349).
August 6, 1976 (28 UST 7073; TIAS 8704).
February 7, 1977 (28 UST 7070; TIAS 8703; 1087 UNTS 349).
June 27, 1977 (29 UST 1911; TIAS 8911).
August 31, 1977 (29 UST 5477; TIAS 9124).
January 13, 1978 (29 UST 4383; TIAS 9059).
January 13, 1978 (29 UST 4383; TIAS 9060; 1230 UNTS 3).
January 13, 1978 (29 UST 4415; TIAS 9061).
March 6, 1978 (29 UST 5534; TIAS 9125).
April 19, 1978 (30 UST 2403; TIAS 9344; 1230 UNTS 43).
May 3, 1978 (30 UST 2545; TIAS 9353; 1230 UNTS 93).
May 3, 1978 (30 UST 2577; TIAS 9354; 1230 UNTS 127).
May 3, 1978 (30 UST 2601; TIAS 9355; 1230 UNTS 159).
May 3, 1978 (30 UST 2622; TIAS 9356; 1230 UNTS 179).
May 19, 1978 (30 UST 2763; TIAS 9362, 1230 UNTS 199).
June 2, 1978 (30 UST 3153; TIAS 9387).
August 18, 1978 (30 UST 4645; TIAS 9484; 1230 UNTS 261).
May 28, 1987 (NP).
September 28, 1987 (NP).
September 28, 1988 (NP).
August 1, 1989 (NP).
August 28, 1989 (NP).
May 10, 1990 (NP).
September 28, 1990 (NP).
September 28, 1990 (NP).
September 28, 1990 (NP).
August 30, 1991 (NP).
September 30, 1996 (NP).
June 19, 1997 (NP).
June 23, 1997 (NP).
August 6, 1997 (NP).
August 29, 1997 (NP).
August 29, 1997 (NP).
August 29, 1997 (NP).
April 7, 1998 (NP).
May 4, 1998 (NP).
May 8, 1998 (NP).
June 11, 1998 (NP).
June 11, 1998 (NP).
July 2, 1998 (NP).
July 2, 1998 (NP).
September 30, 1998 (NP).
August 6, 1999 (NP).
September 28, 1999 (NP).
September 28, 1999 (NP).
July 13, 2000 (NP).
August 7, 2000 (NP).
August 31, 2000 (NP).
September 26, 2000 (NP).
September 26, 2000 (NP).
January 9, 2001 (NP).
August 30, 2001 (NP).
August 30, 2001 (NP).
August 30, 2001 (NP).

EDUCATION

Agreement for financing certain educational exchange programs.

Signed at Manila March 23, 1963.

Entered into force March 23, 1963.

14 UST 352; TIAS 5321; 474 UNTS 81.

Amendment

December 11, 1968, January 31 and March 19, 1969 (20 UST 508; TIAS 6657; 719 UNTS 354).

Agreement concerning the Special Fund for Education.

Exchange of notes at Manila April 26, 1966.

Entered into force April 26, 1966.[1]

19 UST 5079; TIAS 6508; 706 UNTS 110.

NOTE

1 For implementing agreements, see 19 UST 5082; TIAS 6508; 706 UNTS 57 (May 18, 1967, June 26, 1967, August 11, 1967 and June 11, 1968); 20 UST 2845; TIAS 6756; 723 UNTS 243 (September 5, 1969); 22 UST 501; TIAS 7089; 792 UNTS 261 (March 30, 1971); 23 UST 251; TIAS 7300 (March 21, 1972).

EMPLOYMENT

Agreement relating to the employment of dependents of official government employees.

Exchange of notes at Washington September 20 and October 20, 1983.

Entered into force October 20, 1983.

35 UST 2428; TIAS 10805.

ENVIRONMENTAL COOPERATION

Agreement for cooperation in the Global Learning and Observations to Benefit the Environment (GLOBE) Program, with appendices.

Signed at Manila January 14, 1999.

Entered into force January 14, 1999.

TIAS

EXTRADITION

Extradition treaty.

Signed at Manila November 13, 1994.

Entered into force November 22, 1996.

TIAS; 1994 UNTS 279.

FINANCE

Agreement establishing a joint American-Philippine financial commission.

Exchange of notes at Manila September 13 and 17, 1946.

Entered into force September 17, 1946.

61 Stat. 2840; TIAS 1612; 11 Bevans 34; 15 UNTS 249.

Agreement relating to the repayment of funds advanced to the National Defense Forces, Republic of the Philippines, by the United States Philippines-Ryukyus Command.

Signed at Washington November 6, 1950.

Entered into force November 6, 1950.

1 UST 765; TIAS 2151; 122 UNTS 63.

Agreement for adjustment of the amount and final settlement of obligations under the agreement of November 6, 1950 relating to the repayment of funds advanced to Philippine National Defense Forces.

Exchange of notes at Washington March 27, 1961.

Entered into force March 27, 1961.

12 UST 297; TIAS 4715; 405 UNTS 304.

Agreement regarding the consolidation and rescheduling of certain debts owed to, guaranteed by or insured by the United States Government and its agencies, with annexes.

Signed at Manila July 29, 1985.

Entered into force August 30, 1985.

NP

Agreement regarding the consolidation and rescheduling of certain debts owed to, guaranteed by, or insured by the United States Government and its agencies, with annexes.

Signed at Manila May 16, 1988.

Entered into force June 17, 1988.

NP

Amendment

April 25, 1989 (NP).

Agreement regarding the consolidation and rescheduling or refinancing of certain debts owed to, guaranteed by, or insured by the United States Government and its agencies, with annexes.

Signed at Manila November 3, 1989.

Entered into force December 13, 1989.

NP

Agreement regarding the consolidation and rescheduling or refinancing of certain debts owed to, guaranteed by, or insured by the United States Government and its agencies with annexes.

Signed at Washington December 11, 1991.

Entered into force March 2, 1992.

NP

Amendment

March 4 and 9, 1993 (NP).

Agreement relating to investments supported by the Overseas Private Investment Corporation.

Signed at Manila October 22, 1998.

Entered into force February 15, 2000.

TIAS

Agreement regarding the reduction of a certain debt owed to the Government of the United States and its agencies, with attachments.

Signed at Manila September 19, 2002.

Entered into force November 1, 2002.

NP

GENERAL RELATIONS

Provisional agreement concerning friendly relations and diplomatic and consular representation.

Signed at Manila July 4, 1946.

Entered into force July 4, 1946.

60 Stat. 1800; TIAS 1539; 11 Bevans 1; 6 UNTS 335.

Treaty of general relations, and protocol.

Signed at Manila July 4, 1946.

Entered into force October 22, 1946.

61 Stat. 1174; TIAS 1568; 11 Bevans 3; 7 UNTS 3.

HEALTH

Agreement permanently locating the United States Naval Medical Research Unit-Two (NAMRU-2) in the Philippines.

Exchange of notes at Manila February 26, 1979 and June 5, 1981.

Entered into force June 5, 1981.

33 UST 2093; TIAS 10174; 1529 UNTS 469.

Agreement on employees' compensation and medical care programs [for Philippine employees of U.S. Forces], with annex.

Signed at Manila March 10, 1982.

Entered into force March 10, 1982.

34 UST 312; TIAS 10358; 1557 UNTS 21.

Amendment

July 19, 1989.

Agreement continuing the operations of the United States Department of Veterans Affairs in the Philippines.

Signed at Manila May 3, 1990.

Entered into force May 3, 1990; effective October 1, 1989.

TIAS 11725; 2207 UNTS 281.

INFORMATIONAL MEDIA GUARANTIES

Agreement relating to an informational media guaranty program.

Exchange of notes at Manila October 14, 1954 and January 19, 1955.

Entered into force January 19, 1955.

6 UST 549; TIAS 3187; 241 UNTS 514.

Amendment

December 12, 1955 and February 10, 1958 (9 UST 274; TIAS 4003; 303 UNTS 336).

INTERNATIONAL CRIMINAL COURT

Agreement regarding the surrender of persons to international tribunals.

Exchange of notes at Manila May 9 and 13, 2003.

Entered into force May 13, 2003.

TIAS

JUDICIAL ASSISTANCE

Agreement concerning the provision of documents to Government of the Republic of the Philippines.

Exchange of notes at Washington March 15, 1986.

Entered into force March 15, 1986.

NP

Agreement on procedures for mutual legal assistance.

Signed at Manila March 31, 1987.

Entered into force March 31, 1987.

NP

Treaty on mutual legal assistance in criminal matters, with attachments.

Signed at Manila November 13, 1994.

Entered into force November 22, 1996.

TIAS; 1994 UNTS 309.

MAPPING

Agreement concerning mapping, charting and geodesy cooperation, with annexes.

Signed at Makati and Fairfax June 27 and September 9, 1991.

Entered into force September 9, 1991.

NP

MARITIME MATTERS

Agreement relating to naval charter for lease of vessels to the Philippines. Exchanges of notes at Manila September 26 and December 9, 1947, and May 6 and June 7, 1948.

Entered into force June 7, 1948.

62 Stat. 3870; TIAS 1954; 11 Bevans 137; 70 UNTS 280.

Agreement relating to the loan of a floating dry dock to the Republic of the Philippines.

Exchange of notes at Manila September 28 and October 4, 1961.

Entered into force October 4, 1961.

12 UST 1415; TIAS 4865; 433 UNTS 83.

Extension and amendment

November 4, 1966 (17 UST 1963; TIAS 6137; 674 UNTS 382).

MILITARY CEMETERIES AND MONUMENTS

Agreement relating to cooperation in consecrating Corregidor Island as a World War II memorial site, with annex.

Exchange of notes at Manila December 22, 1965.

Entered into force December 22, 1965.

16 UST 1925; TIAS 5925; 579 UNTS 203.

MUTUAL SECURITY

Agreement relating to the assurances required under the Mutual Security Act of 1951.

Exchange of notes at Manila January 4 and 7, 1952.

Entered into force January 7, 1952.

3 UST 4644; TIAS 2617; 179 UNTS 193.

PATENTS

Agreement relating to the reciprocal application of certain rights of priority in the filing of patent applications.

Exchange of notes at Washington February 12 and August 4 and 23, 1948.

Entered into force August 23, 1948.

62 Stat. 3461; TIAS 1861; 11 Bevans 149; 82 UNTS 11.

PEACE CORPS

Agreement relating to the establishment of a Peace Corps program in the Republic of the Philippines.

Exchange of notes at Manila October 11 and 31, 1961.

Entered into force October 31, 1961.

12 UST 1699; TIAS 4889; 424 UNTS 129.

POSTAL MATTERS

Parcel post convention.

Signed at Manila September 21 and at Washington November 12, 1964.

Entered into force November 1, 1965.

16 UST 1680; TIAS 5893; 574 UNTS 159.

International express mail agreement, with detailed regulations.

Signed at Manila and Washington April 21 and May 22, 1992.

Entered into force September 21, 1992.

TIAS 11861.

PUBLICATIONS

Agreement relating to the exchange of official publications.

Exchange of notes at Manila April 12 and June 7, 1948.

Entered into force June 7, 1948.

62 Stat. 2024; TIAS 1767; 11 Bevans 134; 73 UNTS 89.

Amendment

December 2 and 20, 1965 (16 UST 1909; TIAS 5921; 578 UNTS 196).

RELIEF SUPPLIES AND PACKAGES

Agreement providing for duty-free entry into the Philippines and exemption from internal taxation of relief supplies and packages.

Exchange of notes at Manila April 29, 1954 and October 18, 1956.

Entered into force October 18, 1956.

8 UST 144; TIAS 3752; 280 UNTS 55.

Amendment

August 6 and September 19, 1970 (21 UST 2510; TIAS 6994; 772 UNTS 458).

SCIENTIFIC COOPERATION

Agreement on cooperation in science and technology, with annex.

Signed at Washington May 20, 2003.

Entered into force November 25, 2003.

TIAS

SOCIAL SECURITY

Agreement providing for social security coverage for non-United States citizen employees of the United States armed forces in the Philippines.

Exchange of notes at Manila April 23, 1962 and August 30, 1963.

Entered into force August 30, 1963.

14 UST 1523; TIAS 5452; 489 UNTS 323.

Agreement providing for social security coverage for non-United States citizen employees of the United States Employees Association, JUSMAG Officers Club, JUSMAG NCO Club, and the AID Employees' Recreation Association in the Philippines.

Exchange of notes at Manila August 30 and October 8, 1963.

Entered into force October 8, 1963.

14 UST 1523; TIAS 5452; 489 UNTS 332.

Agreement providing for social security coverage for Philippine citizen civilian employees of the Agency for International Development Mission to the Philippines, with annex.

Exchange of notes at Manila November 12, 1964 and March 10, 1965.

Entered into force March 10, 1965.

20 UST 536; TIAS 6663; 706 UNTS 41.

Agreement providing for social security coverage for Philippine citizen civilian employees of the Peace Corps and United States Joint Military Advisory Group (JUSMAG), with annex.

Exchange of notes at Manila April 5 and July 15, 1965.

Entered into force July 15, 1965.

20 UST 540; TIAS 6663; 706 UNTS 49.

TAXATION

Convention with respect to taxes on income.[1]

Signed at Manila October 1, 1976.

Entered into force October 16, 1982.

34 UST 1277; TIAS 10417.

NOTE

1 With reservations and understandings.

TELECOMMUNICATION

Agreement regarding radio broadcasting facilities with protocol and exchange of notes.

Signed at Manila May 6, 1963.

Entered into force May 6, 1963.

14 UST 741; TIAS 5353; 477 UNTS 67.

Amendment

September 10, 1965 (16 UST 1186; TIAS 5865; 595 UNTS 368).

Agreement relating to the transfer to the Philippines of radio broadcasting facilities at Malolos, Bulacan Province pursuant to the agreement of May 6, 1963, as amended.

Exchange of notes at Manila July 13, 1966.

Entered into force July 13, 1966.

17 UST 1028; TIAS 6060; 595 UNTS 374.

Agreement relating to the reciprocal granting of authorizations to permit licensed amateur radio operators of either country to operate their stations in the other country.

Exchange of notes at Manila October 25, 1976.

Entered into force October 25, 1976.

27 UST 3985; TIAS 8415; 1059 UNTS 67.

Agreement relating to radio communications between amateur stations on behalf of third parties, with attachment.

Exchange of notes at Manila February 13 and June 4, 1991.

Entered into force June 4, 1991.

TIAS 12431.

TOURISM

Agreement on the development and facilitation of reciprocal tourism.

Signed at Washington September 17, 1982.

Entered into force September 17, 1982.

TIAS 10498.

TRADE AND COMMERCE

Agreement relating to entry of nationals of either country into the territories of the other for purposes of trade, investment, and related activities.

Exchange of notes at Washington September 6, 1955.

Entered into force September 6, 1955.

6 UST 3030; TIAS 3349; 238 UNTS 109.

Agreement on trade concessions and contributions within the framework of the multilateral trade negotiations, and related letters of January 28 and February 4, 1980.

Signed at Manila October 30, 1979.

Entered into force October 30, 1979.

33 UST 4468; TIAS 10317; 1156 UNTS 105.

Agreement relating to subsidization of exports in the context of the agreement on interpretation and application of articles VI, XVI and XXIII (subsidies code) of the General Agreement on Tariffs and Trade (TIAS 9619).

Exchange of letters at Manila and Washington March 14 and 15, 1985.

Entered into force March 15, 1985.

TIAS 11333.

Agreement relating to trade in textiles and textile products, with annexes.

Exchange of letters at Washington March 4, 1987.

Entered into force March 4, 1987.

NP

Amendments and extensions

December 28, 1990 and February 26, 1991 (NP).

July 12, 1991 (NP).

March 6, 1992 (NP).

July 7 and 29, 1994 (NP).

February 25, 1999.

Memorandum of understanding concerning cooperation in trade in textile and apparel goods.

Signed at Kuala Lumpur August 23, 2006.

Entered into force August 23, 2006.

NP

VISAS

Agreement relating to waiver of nonimmigrant passport visa fees.

Exchange of notes at Manila November 24, 1952.

Entered into force November 24, 1952; operative December 24, 1952.

3 UST 5196; TIAS 2715; 181 UNTS 155.

POLAND

AGRICULTURAL COMMODITIES

Agricultural commodities agreement with exchange of notes.

Signed at Washington June 7, 1957.

Entered into force June 7, 1957.

8 UST 799; TIAS 3839; 291 UNTS 41.

Amendments

August 14, 1957 (8 UST 1289; TIAS 3878; 291 UNTS 52).

January 8, 1958 (9 UST 1; TIAS 3973; 307 UNTS 330).

May 26 and 29, 1959 (10 UST 1049; TIAS 4243; 346 UNTS 350).

July 21, 1960 (11 UST 1871; TIAS 4532; 380 UNTS 464).

April 10 and 11, 1967 (19 UST 7788; TIAS 6610; 723 UNTS 296).

Agricultural commodities agreement and exchange of notes.

Signed at Washington February 15, 1958.

Entered into force February 15, 1958.

9 UST 199; TIAS 3991; 307 UNTS 217.

Amendments

June 6, 1958 (9 UST 707; TIAS 4046; 317 UNTS 376).

May 26 and 29, 1959 (10 UST 1049; TIAS 4243; 346 UNTS 350).

July 21, 1960 (11 UST 1871; TIAS 4532; 380 UNTS 469).

April 10 and 11, 1967 (19 UST 7788; TIAS 6610; 723 UNTS 296).

Agricultural commodities agreement with exchange of notes.

Signed at Washington June 10, 1959.

Entered into force June 10, 1959.

10 UST 1058; TIAS 4245; 347 UNTS 41.

Amendments

November 10, 1959 (10 UST 1410; TIAS 4288; 357 UNTS 396).

February 11, 1960 (11 UST 99; TIAS 4415; 371 UNTS 364).

July 21, 1960 (11 UST 1871; TIAS 4532; 380 UNTS 474).

April 10 and 11, 1967 (19 UST 7788; TIAS 6610; 723 UNTS 296).

Agricultural commodities agreement with exchanges of notes.

Signed at Washington July 21, 1960.

Entered into force July 21, 1960.

11 UST 1887; TIAS 4535; 380 UNTS 157.

Amendment

April 10 and 11, 1967 (19 UST 7788; TIAS 6610; 723 UNTS 296).

Agricultural commodities agreement with exchanges of notes.

Signed at Washington December 15, 1961.

Entered into force December 15, 1961.

12 UST 3065; TIAS 4907; 434 UNTS 3.

Amendments

April 19, 1962 (13 UST 401; TIAS 4998; 445 UNTS 383).

April 10 and 11, 1967 (19 UST 7788; TIAS 6610; 723 UNTS 296).

Agricultural commodities agreement with exchanges of notes.

Signed at Washington February 1, 1963.

Entered into force February 1, 1963.

14 UST 803; TIAS 5359; 487 UNTS 143.

Amendment

April 10 and 11, 1967 (19 UST 7788; TIAS 6610; 723 UNTS 296).

Agricultural commodities agreement with exchanges of notes.

Signed at Washington February 3, 1964.

Entered into force February 3, 1964.

15 UST 40; TIAS 5516; 505 UNTS 215.

Amendment

April 10 and 11, 1967 (19 UST 7788; TIAS 6610; 723 UNTS 296).

Agricultural commodities agreement with exchanges of notes.

Signed at Washington February 3, 1964.

Entered into force February 3, 1964.

15 UST 59; TIAS 5517; 505 UNTS 245.

Related agreements

April 10, 1967 (19 UST 7788; TIAS 6610; 724 UNTS 324).

April 10 and 11, 1967 (19 UST 7788; TIAS 6610; 723 UNTS 296).

Agricultural commodities agreement, with agreed minute.

Signed at Warsaw August 28, 1981.

Entered into force August 28, 1981.

34 UST 1134; TIAS 10400.

Agricultural commodities agreement.

Signed at Warsaw November 30, 1989.

Entered into force November 30, 1989.

NP

Amendment

March 16 and 28, 1990 (NP).

ATOMIC ENERGY

Agreement for cooperation concerning peaceful uses of nuclear energy, with annex and agreed minute.

Signed at Vienna September 18, 1991.

Entered into force September 3, 1992.

TIAS 12435.

AVIATION

Agreement relating to the acceptance of airworthiness certifications, with annex.

Exchange of notes at Washington November 8, 1976.

Entered into force November 8, 1976.

27 UST 3882; TIAS 8407; 1059 UNTS 179.

Amendments

January 28, 1980 (32 UST 529; TIAS 9723; 1221 UNTS 342).

September 5, 2003 and February 9, 2004.

Memorandum of agreement concerning assistance in developing and modernizing Poland's civil aviation infrastructure.

Signed at Washington and Warsaw January 5 and 14, 1998.

Entered into force January 14, 1998.

TIAS

Air transport agreement, with annexes.

Signed at Warsaw June 16, 2001.

Entered into force September 15, 2003.

TIAS

CLAIMS

Agreement relating to settlement of claims of nationals of the United States against Poland and exchange of notes.

Signed at Washington July 16, 1960.

Entered into force July 16, 1960.

11 UST 1953; TIAS 4545; 384 UNTS 169.

Protocol to the claims settlement agreement of July 16, 1960.

Signed at Warsaw November 29, 1960.

Entered into force November 29, 1960.

11 UST 2450; TIAS 4629; 401 UNTS 338.

CONSULS

Consular convention, with protocols and exchanges of notes.

Signed at Warsaw May 31, 1972.

Entered into force July 6, 1973.

24 UST 1231; TIAS 7642.

CUSTOMS

Agreement relating to reciprocal customs privileges for foreign service personnel.

Exchange of notes at Warsaw October 5 and 30, 1945.

Entered into force October 30, 1945.

61 Stat. 2297; TIAS 1544; 11 Bevans 283; 15 UNTS 225.

Agreement regarding cooperation and mutual assistance between customs services.

Signed at Warsaw August 8, 1990.

Entered into force May 15, 1991.

TIAS 12077.

DEFENSE

Agreement concerning provision of training related to defense articles under the United States International Military Education Training (IMET) Program.

Exchange of notes at Warsaw April 25 and June 6, 1991.

Entered into force June 6, 1991.

NP

Agreement regarding grants under the Foreign Assistance Act of 1961, as amended, or successor legislation, and the furnishing of defense articles, related training, or other defense services from the United States to Hungary.

Exchange of notes at Warsaw February 10 and October 13, 1993.

Entered into force October 13, 1993.

TIAS

Agreement concerning security measures for the protection of classified military information.

Signed at Washington February 17, 1995.

Entered into force February 17, 1995.

TIAS 12247.

Agreement concerning exchange of research and development information, with appendix (Master Information Exchange Agreement).

Signed at Warsaw June 9, 1995.

Entered into force June 9, 1995.

TIAS 12367.

Acquisition and cross-servicing agreement, with annexes.

Signed at Warsaw November 22, 1996.

Entered into force November 22, 1996.

TIAS 12816.

Amendment

July 8 and 11, 2003.

Agreement regarding the exchange of engineers and scientists.

Signed at Washington and Warsaw July 21 and 31, 2006.

Entered into force July 31, 2006.

TIAS

Memorandum of arrangement regarding assignment of liaison officers, with annex.

Signed September 22, 2006.

Entered into force September 22, 2006.

TIAS

EDUCATION

Agreement for the establishment of an office for U.S.-Polish educational exchanges.

Signed at Washington March 22, 1990.

Entered into force March 22, 1990.

TIAS

Agreement for the establishment of the U.S.-Polish Fulbright Commission.

Signed at Warsaw October 20, 1995.

Entered into force May 31, 1996.

TIAS

EMPLOYMENT

Agreement relating to the employment of dependents of official government employees, with annex.

Exchange of notes at Warsaw April 30 and May 16, 1991.

Entered into force May 16, 1991.

TIAS 12430.

ENERGY

Agreement for collaboration to demonstrate an emerging retrofit of clean coal technology at a powerplant in Cracow, Poland, with annexes.

Signed at Washington March 15, 1990.

Entered into force March 15, 1990.

TIAS

ENVIRONMENTAL COOPERATION

Memorandum of understanding concerning cooperation in the field of environmental protection.

Signed at Washington May 15, 1995.

Entered into force May 15, 1995.

TIAS 12646.

Agreement for cooperation in the Global Learning and Observations to Benefit the Environment (GLOBE) Program, with appendices.

Signed at Warsaw April 22, 1997.

Entered into force April 22, 1997.

TIAS

EXTRADITION

Extradition treaty.

Signed at Washington July 10, 1996.

Entered into force September 17, 1999.

TIAS

FINANCE

Agreement relating to the funding of the indebtedness of Poland to the United States.

Signed at Washington November 14, 1924; operative December 15, 1922.

Treasury Department print; 11 Bevans 195; 58 LNTS 97.

Agreement modifying the debt funding agreement of November 14, 1924.

Signed at Washington June 10, 1932; operative July 1, 1931.

Treasury Department print; 11 Bevans 260.

Agreement establishing a procedure for funding international travel and transportation and other travel-related expenses from U.S.-owned zlotys in Poland.

Exchange of notes at Washington October 7, 1972.

Entered into force October 7, 1972; effective January 1, 1973.

24 UST 426; TIAS 7557.

Agreement deferring purchase by the United States, scheduled for January 2, 1973, of dollar exchange for zlotys accrued under certain agricultural commodities agreements.

Exchange of notes at Washington December 29, 1972.

Entered into force December 29, 1972.

24 UST 424; TIAS 7557.

Agreement deferring purchase by the United States of dollar exchange for zlotys accrued under certain agricultural commodities agreements.

Exchange of notes at Washington February 5, 1973.

Entered into force February 5, 1973.

24 UST 431; TIAS 7557.

Agreement deferring purchase by the United States of dollar exchange for zlotys accrued under certain agricultural commodities agreements and terminating the agreement of August 6, 1968 (TIAS 7473) relating to United States Government pensions, with schedule.

Exchange of notes at Washington May 15, 1975.

Entered into force May 15, 1975.

26 UST 2398; TIAS 8164; 1027 UNTS 323.

Agreement regarding the consolidation and rescheduling of certain debts owed to, guaranteed by or assured by the United States Government and its agencies, with annexes.

Signed at Warsaw August 27, 1981.

Entered into force October 20, 1981.

33 UST 3727; TIAS 10255; 1541 UNTS 85.

Agreement regarding the consolidation and rescheduling of certain debts owed to, guaranteed by or insured by the United States Government and its agencies.

Signed at Warsaw July 29, 1986.

Entered into force September 8, 1986.

NP

Agreement regarding the consolidation and rescheduling of certain debts for 1985, owed to, guaranteed by, or insured by the United States Government and its agencies, with annexes.

Signed at Warsaw July 10, 1989.

Entered into force September 6, 1989.

NP

Agreement regarding the consolidation and rescheduling of certain debts for 1987, owed to, guaranteed by, or insured by the United States Government and its agencies, with annexes.

Signed at Warsaw July 10, 1989.

Entered into force September 6, 1989.

NP

Investment guaranty agreement.

Signed at Warsaw October 13, 1989.

Entered into force February 21, 1990.

TIAS 12039.

Swap agreement among the United States Treasury and the Narodowy Bank Polski/Government of Poland, with memorandum of understanding.

Signed at Washington and Poland December 22, 1989.

Entered into force December 22, 1989.

TIAS

Agreement between the United States and the Narodowy Bank Polski/Government of Poland concerning the contribution by the United States to the Polish Stabilization Fund, with memorandum of understanding.

Signed at Washington December 29, 1989.

Entered into force December 29, 1989.

TIAS

Amendment and extension

December 6 and 18, 1991.

Agreement regarding the consolidation and rescheduling of certain debts owed to, guaranteed by, or insured by the United States Government and its agencies, with annexes.

Signed at Warsaw August 24, 1990.

Entered into force October 22, 1990.

NP

Agreement regarding the reduction and reorganization of certain debts owed to, guaranteed by, or insured by the Government of the United States and its agencies, with annexes.

Signed at Warsaw July 17, 1991.

Entered into force September 3, 1991.

NP

Agreement between the United States and the Government of Poland/Narodowy Bank Polski concerning the Polish Bank Privatization Fund Account, with memorandum of understanding.

Signed at Washington December 28, 1992.

Entered into force December 28, 1992.

TIAS

HEALTH

Agreement on cooperation in the field of health.

Signed at Washington October 8, 1974.

Entered into force October 8, 1974.

25 UST 2750; TIAS 7943.

INFORMATIONAL MEDIA GUARANTIES

Agreement providing for an informational media guaranty program.

Exchange of notes at Warsaw February 12, 1958.

Entered into force February 12, 1958.

9 UST 253; TIAS 3999; 304 UNTS 287.

INVESTMENT

Treaty concerning business and economic relations, with annex, protocol and related exchanges of letters.

Signed at Washington March 21, 1990.

Entered into force August 6, 1994.

TIAS

Additional protocol to the treaty concerning business and economic relations done at Washington on March 21, 1990.

Signed at Brussels January 12, 2004.

Entered into force August 20, 2004.

TIAS

JUDICIAL ASSISTANCE

Treaty on mutual legal assistance in criminal matters, with forms.

Done at Washington July 10, 1996.

Entered into force September 17, 1999.

TIAS

LEND-LEASE

Preliminary agreement regarding principles applying to mutual aid in the prosecution of the war against aggression.

Signed at Washington July 1, 1942.

Entered into force July 1, 1942.

56 Stat. 1542; EAS 257; 11 Bevans 274; 103 UNTS 267.

Agreement on the settlement for lend-lease and certain claims.

Signed at Washington June 28, 1956.

Entered into force June 28, 1956.

7 UST 1930; TIAS 3594; 273 UNTS 79.

MAPPING

Basic exchange and cooperative agreement for military topographic mapping, nautical and aeronautical charting, geodesy and geophysics, digital data and related MC&G materials.

Signed at Washington November 10, 1992.

Entered into force November 10, 1992.

NP

MARITIME MATTERS

Agreement relating to the mutual recognition of ship measurement certificates.

Exchanges of notes at Washington January 17, March 14, and April 22, 1930, and October 5, 1934; operative April 22, 1930.

49 Stat. 3663; EAS 71; 11 Bevans 229; 156 LNTS 91.

NARCOTIC DRUGS

Arrangement for the direct exchange of certain information regarding the traffic in narcotic drugs.

Exchange of notes at Warsaw August 17 and September 17, 1931.

Entered into force September 17, 1931.

11 Bevans 257.

PACIFIC SETTLEMENT OF DISPUTES

Treaty of arbitration.

Signed at Washington August 16, 1928.

Entered into force February 3, 1930.

46 Stat. 2438; TS 805; 11 Bevans 218; 99 LNTS 409.

Treaty of conciliation.

Signed at Washington August 16, 1928.

Entered into force February 3, 1930.

46 Stat. 2442; TS 806; 11 Bevans 221; 99 LNTS 403.

PEACE CORPS

Agreement concerning the program of the United States Peace Corps in Poland.

Signed at Warsaw February 23, 1990.

Entered into force February 23, 1990.

TIAS 12073.

POSTAL MATTERS

Convention concerning the exchange of parcel post.

Signed at Warsaw February 19 and at Washington April 26, 1923.

Entered into force April 1, 1923.

43 Stat. 1640; Post Office Department print.

International express mail agreement, with detailed regulations.

Signed at Washington December 11, 1989.

Entered into force February 1, 1990.

TIAS 11720.

PUBLICATIONS

Agreement relating to the distribution in Poland of a Polish-language magazine on life in the United States.

Exchange of notes at Warsaw May 30, 1958.

Entered into force May 30, 1958.

9 UST 601; TIAS 4040; 315 UNTS 231.

SCIENTIFIC COOPERATION

Memorandum of understanding on science and engineering cooperation, with annex.

Signed at Washington October 26, 1994.

Entered into force October 26, 1994.

TIAS 12576.

Agreement for scientific and technical cooperation, with annexes.

Signed at Washington February 10, 2006.

Entered into force February 10, 2006.

TIAS

SHIPPING

Agreement relating to jurisdiction over vessels utilizing the Louisiana Offshore Oil Port.

Exchange of notes at Washington March 30 and April 10, 1984.

Entered into force April 10, 1984.

TIAS; 2174 UNTS 199.

SMUGGLING

Convention to aid in the prevention of smuggling of alcoholic beverages into the United States.

Signed at Washington June 19, 1930.

Entered into force August 2, 1930.

46 Stat. 2773; TS 821; 11 Bevans 233; 108 LNTS 323.

SOCIAL SECURITY

Agreement concerning the United States Government participation in the Polish social insurance system for Polish national employees of the United States Government in Poland.

Exchange of notes at Warsaw June 15 and September 30, 1971.

Entered into force September 30, 1971.

22 UST 1725; TIAS 7200.

SURPLUS PROPERTY

Credit arrangement for the purchase of American surplus property abroad.

Signed at Washington April 22, 1946.

Entered into force April 22, 1946.

12 UST 368; TIAS 4725; 406 UNTS 214.

Extensions and amendments

September 17, 1947 (12 UST 368; TIAS 4725; 406 UNTS 219).

December 10, 1947 (12 UST 368; TIAS 4725; 406 UNTS 221).

Agreement relating to the payment of arrearages on the surplus property agreement of April 22, 1946.

Exchange of notes at Warsaw March 20, 1961.

Entered into force March 20, 1961.

12 UST 368; TIAS 4725; 406 UNTS 222.

TAXATION

Convention for the avoidance of double taxation and the prevention of fiscal evasion with respect to taxes on income, with related notes.

Signed at Washington October 8, 1974.

Entered into force July 22, 1976.

28 UST 891; TIAS 8486.

TRADE AND COMMERCE

Agreement relating to economic and financial cooperation.

Exchange of notes at Washington April 24, 1946.

Entered into force April 24, 1946.

60 Stat. 1609; TIAS 1516; 11 Bevans 286; 4 UNTS 155.

Joint statement on the development of agricultural trade.

Signed at Washington October 8, 1974.

Entered into force October 8, 1974.

25 UST 2763; TIAS 7944.

Agreement relating to tariff and nontariff matters within the framework of the multilateral trade negotiations, and related letters of June 27 and October 20, 1980.

Exchange of letters at Geneva February 28, 1979.

Entered into force January 1, 1980.

32 UST 5498; TIAS 10001; 1265 UNTS 187.

Agreement concerning trade in textiles and textile products, with annexes.

Exchange of notes at Washington December 30 and 31, 1991.

Entered into force December 31, 1991; effective January 1, 1992.

NP

Amendment and extension

December 6 and 31, 1993 (NP).

TRANSPORTATION

Memorandum of understanding concerning research cooperation in the field of transportation.

Signed at Warsaw November 3, 1971.

Entered into force November 3, 1971.

29 UST 5642; TIAS 9139; 1152 UNTS 19.

Extension and amendments

October 16, 1978 (29 UST 5649; TIAS 9139; 1152 UNTS 22).

February 28 and June 22, 1979 (30 UST 7287; TIAS 9586; 1182 UNTS 401).

VISAS

Agreement relating to the reciprocal waiver of visa fees for performing artists.

Exchange of notes at Warsaw December 17, 1962 and January 21, 1963.

Entered into force January 21, 1963; operative February 1, 1963.

14 UST 118; TIAS 5279; 471 UNTS 151.

PORTUGAL

AVIATION

Memorandum of agreement concerning provision of site test and commissioning and/or periodic flight checks of Portuguese Civil Aviation Administration air navigation aids.

Signed at Washington and Lisbon March 10 and April 13, 1978.

Entered into force April 13, 1978; effective April 1, 1978.

30 UST 293; TIAS 9201.

Memorandum of agreement concerning the provision of assistance in developing and modernizing Portugal's civil aviation infrastructure.

Signed at Washington and Lisbon July 30, 1998.

Entered into force July 30, 1998.

NP

Air transport agreement, with annexes.

Signed at Lisbon May 30, 2000.

Entered into force May 9, 2002.

TIAS

CULTURAL RELATIONS

Protocol relating to exchanges in the field of physical education and sports.

Signed at Lisbon December 22, 1976.

Entered into force December 22, 1976.

28 UST 5342; TIAS 8637.

CUSTOMS

Agreement regarding mutual assistance between customs services.

Signed at Washington September 15, 1994.

Entered into force June 20, 1996.

TIAS 12565.

DEFENSE

See also MUTUAL SECURITY

Mutual defense assistance agreement.

Signed at Lisbon January 5, 1951.

Entered into force January 5, 1951.

2 UST 438; TIAS 2187; 133 UNTS 75.

Agreement relating to the disposition of equipment and material furnished by the United States under the mutual defense assistance agreement of January 5, 1951, found surplus to the needs of the armed forces of Portugal.

Exchange of notes at Lisbon June 16 and July 9, 1952.

Entered into force July 9, 1952.

3 UST 4979; TIAS 2674; 180 UNTS 251.

Amendment

September 15, 1960 (11 UST 2202; TIAS 4590; 393 UNTS 315).

Agreement relating to a weapons production program.

Exchange of notes at Lisbon September 26, 1960.

Entered into force September 26, 1960.

11 UST 2218; TIAS 4594; 393 UNTS 257.

Agreement relating to the deposit by Portugal of ten percent of the value of grant military assistance and excess defense articles furnished by the United States.

Exchange of notes at Lisbon March 16 and May 2, 1972.

Entered into force May 2, 1972; effective February 7, 1972.

23 UST 881; TIAS 7349.

Agreement relating to payment to the United States of net proceeds from the sale of defense articles furnished under the military assistance program.

Exchange of notes at Lisbon May 30, 1974 and June 30, 1975.

Entered into force June 30, 1975; effective July 1, 1974.

26 UST 1004; TIAS 8087.

Amendment

December 19, 2004 and January 19, 2005.

Memorandum of understanding concerning the principles governing mutual cooperation in the research, development, production, procurement and logistic support of defense equipment.

Signed at Lisbon and Washington December 18, 1978 and March 28, 1979.

Entered into force March 28, 1979.

30 UST 3892; TIAS 9433; 1171 UNTS 221.

Agreement concerning the grant of defense articles and services under the military assistance program.

Exchange of notes at Lisbon August 14 and 27, 1979.

Entered into force August 27, 1979.

30 UST 7555; TIAS 9599; 1205 UNTS 3.

Amendment

August 16 and September 29, 1982 (TIAS 10503).

Agreement concerning the grant of defense articles and services under the military assistance program.

Exchange of notes at Lisbon August 12 and 28, 1980.

Entered into force August 28, 1980.

32 UST 2388; TIAS 9846; 1275 UNTS 3.

Amendment

August 16 and September 29, 1982 (TIAS 10503).

Agreement concerning the grant of defense articles and services under the military assistance program.

Exchange of notes at Lisbon August 24 and 28, 1981.

Entered into force August 28, 1981.

33 UST 3702; TIAS 10252; 1541 UNTS 105.

Amendment

August 16 and September 29, 1982 (TIAS 10503).

Agreement concerning general security of military information.

Exchange of notes at Lisbon August 19 and September 10, 1982.

Entered into force September 10, 1982.

TIAS 11060; 2039 UNTS 199.

Agreement concerning the installation in Portugal of a ground-based electro-optical deep space surveillance (GEODSS) station.

Exchange of notes at Lisbon March 27, 1984.

Entered into force March 27, 1984.

35 UST 4885; TIAS 10973; 2019 UNTS 159.

Agreement on cooperation and defense, with supplemental technical and labor agreements and exchange of notes.

Signed at Lisbon June 1, 1995.

Entered into force November 21, 1995.

TIAS

Acquisition and cross-servicing agreement, with annexes.

Signed at Lisbon January 14, 1998.

Entered into force January 14, 1998.

TIAS

ECONOMIC AND TECHNICAL COOPERATION

Economic cooperation agreement.[1]

Signed at Lisbon September 28, 1948.

Entered into force September 28, 1948.

62 Stat. 2856; TIAS 1819; 11 Bevans 370; 29 UNTS 213.

Amendments

February 14, 1950 (1 UST 169; TIAS 2033; 79 UNTS 310).

May 17, 1951 (2 UST 1298; TIAS 2279; 134 UNTS 370).

March 9 and 18, 1953 (4 UST 1437; TIAS 2801; 207 UNTS 320).

Agreement relating to the provision of economic assistance to Portugal, with related letter.

Exchange of letters at Brussels December 9, 1971.

Entered into force December 9, 1971.

23 UST 264; TIAS 7303.

Agency for International Development

February 28, 1975 (26 UST 238; TIAS 8028; 992 UNTS 239).

February 28, 1975 (26 UST 348; TIAS 8038; 992 UNTS 251).

June 30, 1975 (26 UST 1072; TIAS 8095; 1006 UNTS 279).

November 3, 1975 (28 UST 1123; TIAS 8496).

August 13, 1976 (28 UST 5991; TIAS 8667).

August 13, 1976 (30 UST 647; TIAS 9209).

August 13, 1976 (32 UST 5991; TIAS 10025; 1274 UNTS 329).

March 4, 1977 (30 UST 757; TIAS 9218).

September 30, 1977 (29 UST 3927; TIAS 9044).

September 30, 1977 (32 UST 5991; TIAS 10025; 1274 UNTS 331).

September 30, 1977 (32 UST 6001; TIAS 10026).

September 30, 1977 (32 UST 6025; TIAS 10027).

September 30, 1977 (32 UST 6051; TIAS 10028).

March 1, 1978 (30 UST 1761; TIAS 9286; 1152 UNTS 149).

December 30, 1986 (NP).

NOTE

1 Applicable to all Portuguese territories.

EDUCATION

Agreement for financing certain educational exchange programs.

Signed at Lisbon March 19, 1960.

Entered into force March 19, 1960.

TIAS 4444; 11 UST 268; 371 UNTS131.

Amendments

June 3 and December 4, 1963 (TIAS 5536; 15 UST 171; 511 UNTS 288).

July 6, August 16 and September 3, 1982 (TIAS 10438; 34 UST 1585; 1736 UNTS 304).

EXTRADITION

Extradition convention and exchange of notes concerning the death penalty.[1]

Signed at Washington May 7, 1908.

Entered into force November 14, 1908.

35 Stat. 2071; TS 512; 11 Bevans 314.

NOTE

1 Applicable to all territories.

FINANCE

Agreement relating to guaranties authorized under Section 111 (b)(3) of the Economic Cooperation Act of 1948, as amended.

Exchange of notes at Washington May 22 and 25, 1953.

Entered into force May 26, 1953.

4 UST 1596; TIAS 2826; 212 UNTS 290.

Agreement relating to resumption of the investment guaranty program and interpretation of the agreement of May 22 and 25, 1953.

Exchange of notes at Lisbon October 31 and November 10, 1977.

Entered into force November 10, 1977.

29 UST 2792; TIAS 8977.

MAINTENANCE

Agreement for the recovery of maintenance.

Signed at Lisbon May 30, 2000.

Entered into force March 17, 2001.

TIAS

MAPPING

Basic exchange and cooperative agreement concerning mapping, charting and geodesy cooperation, with annexes.

Signed at Fairfax and Lisbon July 30, 1997.

Entered into force July 30, 1997.

NP

MUTUAL SECURITY

Agreement relating to the assurances required by the Mutual Security Act of 1951.

Exchange of notes at Lisbon January 8, 1952.

Entered into force January 8, 1952.

3 UST 4648; TIAS 2618; 207 UNTS 51.

NARCOTIC DRUGS

Arrangement for the direct exchange of certain information regarding the traffic in narcotic drugs.

Exchange of notes at Lisbon February 11, 1928, and February 22, 1929.

Entered into force February 22, 1929.

11 Bevans 341.

PACIFIC SETTLEMENT OF DISPUTES

Treaty for the advancement of peace.

Signed at Lisbon February 4, 1914.

Entered into force October 24, 1914.

38 Stat. 1847; TS 600; 11 Bevans 331.

Arbitration treaty.

Signed at Washington March 1, 1929.

Entered into force October 31, 1929.

46 Stat. 2421; TS 803; 11 Bevans 344; 99 LNTS 375.

PATENTS

Agreement to facilitate interchange of patent rights and technical information for defense purposes.

Signed at Lisbon October 31, 1960.

Entered into force October 31, 1960.

11 UST 2314; TIAS 4608; 394 UNTS 127.

POSTAL MATTERS

Parcel post agreement and regulations of execution.[1]

Signed at Lisbon January 12, 1959 and at Washington February 27, 1959.

Entered into force May 1, 1959.

10 UST 801; TIAS 4220; 343 UNTS 49.

International express mail agreement, with detailed regulations.

Signed at Washington and Lisbon November 20 and December 21, 1984.

Entered into force January 15, 1985.

TIAS 11013; 2022 UNTS 93.

Memorandum of understanding concerning the operation of the INTELPOST field trial, with details of implementation.

Signed at Lisbon and Washington April 15 and July 3, 1985.

Entered into force August 1, 1985.

TIAS 11243.

NOTE

1 Applicable to Puerto Rico, the Virgin Islands, Guam, Samoa, the Azores and Madeira Archipelagoes.

SHIPPING

Agreement relating to jurisdiction over vessels utilizing the Louisiana Offshore Oil Port.

Exchange of notes at Washington June 22 and July 11, 1979.

Entered into force July 11, 1979.

30 UST 5931; TIAS 9526; 1179 UNTS 125.

SOCIAL SECURITY

Agreement on social security, with administrative arrangement.

Signed at Lisbon March 30, 1988.

Entered into force August 1, 1989.

TIAS 12121.

TAXATION

Agreement relating to relief from taxation of United States expenditures in Portugal for the common defense.

Exchange of notes at Lisbon April 1, 1953.

Entered into force April 1, 1953.

4 UST 361; TIAS 2784; 205 UNTS 41.

Convention for the avoidance of double taxation and the prevention of fiscal evasion with respect to taxes on income, with protocol.

Signed at Washington September 6, 1994.

Entered into force December 18, 1995.

TIAS

TELECOMMUNICATION

Agreement relating to the reciprocal granting of authorizations to permit licensed amateur radio operators of either country to operate their stations in the other country.

Exchange of notes at Lisbon May 17 and 26, 1965.

Entered into force May 26, 1965.

16 UST 817; TIAS 5815; 546 UNTS 189.

Agreement relating to the continuation of international broadcast activities carried out in Portugal by RARET.

Exchange of notes at Lisbon February 15, 1977.

Entered into force February 15, 1977.

29 UST 660; TIAS 8844.

TRADE AND COMMERCE

Commercial arrangement.

Exchange of notes at Washington June 28, 1910.

Entered into force June 28, 1910.

TS 514 1/2; 11 Bevans 324.

Agreement terminating the agreement of November 17, 1970 (TIAS 6980), relating to trade in cotton textiles and providing for consultations on problems of market disruption from exports of cotton, wool and man-made fiber textiles and apparel products from Portugal.

Exchange of notes at Washington August 20, 1975.

Entered into force August 20, 1975.

26 UST 2713; TIAS 8187; 1052 UNTS 291.

Agreement relating to beef and cheese within the context of the multilateral trade negotiations, and related letters of February 4 and 12, 1980.

Exchanges of letters at Washington June 12 and 18 and November 5 and 7, 1979.

Entered into force January 1, 1980.

32 UST 5504; TIAS 10002; 1266 UNTS 213.

VISAS

Agreement relating to reciprocal facilitation of visa issuance.

Exchange of notes at Lisbon June 7, 1983.

Entered into force July 7, 1983.

TIAS 10723; 1607 UNTS 139.

PREPARATORY COMMISSION FOR THE COMPREHENSIVE NUCLEAR-TEST-BAN TREATY ORGANIZATION

TAXATION

Tax reimbursement agreement, with annex.

Signed at Washington October 21, 1998.

Entered into force October 21, 1998.

TIAS

Q

QATAR

AVIATION

Agreement on the security of civil aviation.

Signed at Doha June 27, 1994.

Entered into force June 30, 1994.

TIAS

FINANCE

Investment incentive agreement.

Exchange of notes at Doha March 28, 1987.

Entered into force April 1, 1987.

TIAS

POSTAL MATTERS

International express mail agreement, with detailed regulations.

Signed at Doha and Washington January 19 and February 14, 1983.

Entered into force June 1, 1983.

TIAS 10661; 2001 UNTS 33.

Memorandum of understanding concerning the operation of the INTELPOST field trial, with details of implementation.

Signed at Doha and Washington August 12 and September 13, 1985.

Entered into force September 13, 1985.

TIAS 11156.

TRADE

Agreement concerning trade in textiles and textile products, with annexes.

Exchange of notes at Doha February 11 and May 30, 1995.

Entered into force May 30, 1995; effective January 1, 1994.

NP

R

ROMANIA

AGRICULTURAL COMMODITIES

Agricultural commodities agreement.

Signed at Bucharest March 13, 1990.

Entered into force March 13, 1990.

NP

AGRICULTURE

Protocol on cooperation in agriculture.

Signed at Washington September 11, 1975.

Entered into force September 11, 1975.

26 UST 2486; TIAS 8166; 1028 UNTS 3.

ATOMIC ENERGY

Agreement clarifying certain understandings relating to the supply of enriched uranium to Romania for the TRIGA reactor.

Exchange of notes at Washington February 13, 1978.

Entered into force February 13, 1978.

29 UST 2961; TIAS 8992; 1120 UNTS 97.

Agreement for cooperation concerning peaceful uses of nuclear energy, with annex and agreed minute.

Signed at Washington July 15, 1998.

Entered into force August 25, 1999.

TIAS

AVIATION

Agreement relating to the reciprocal acceptance of airworthiness certifications.

Exchange of notes at Washington December 7, 1976.

Entered into force December 7, 1976.

27 UST 4138; TIAS 8440.

Air transport agreement, with annexes.

Signed at Washington July 15, 1998.

Entered into force August 19, 1999.

TIAS

Agreement for promotion of aviation safety.

Signed at Bucharest September 10, 2002.

Entered into force October 18, 2004.

TIAS

CONSULS

Consular convention with protocol.

Signed at Bucharest July 5, 1972.

Entered into force July 6, 1973.

24 UST 1317; TIAS 7643.

CULTURAL PROPERTY

Agreement for the protection and preservation of certain cultural properties.

Signed at Bucharest July 8, 1992.

Entered into force provisionally, July 8, 1992; definitively, July 29, 1993.

TIAS 12136.

CULTURAL RELATIONS

Understanding regarding the establishment and operation in the United States and Romania of an American and a Romanian library, respectively.

Signed at Bucharest August 3, 1969.

Entered into force August 3, 1969.

20 UST 2712; TIAS 6733; 720 UNTS 91.

Agreement on cooperation and exchanges in the cultural, educational, scientific and technological fields.

Signed at Bucharest December 13, 1974.

Entered into force January 1, 1975.

26 UST 31; TIAS 8006.

CUSTOMS

Agreement regarding mutual assistance between their customs administrations.

Signed at Washington July 16, 1998.

Entered into force June 1, 1999.

TIAS

DEFENSE

Agreement concerning the provision of training related to defense articles under the United States International Military Education and Training (IMET) program.

Exchange of notes at Bucharest November 23 and December 7, 1992.

Entered into force December 7, 1992.

NP

Agreement concerning military assistance under the United States Foreign Assistance Act of 1961, as amended, and the furnishing of defense articles, related training, and other defense services from the United States to Romania.

Exchange of notes at Bucharest October 3, 1994 and March 31, 1995.

Entered into force March 31, 1995.

TIAS

Agreement regarding the status of United States forces in Romania.

Signed at Washington October 30, 2001.

Entered into force June 10, 2002.

TIAS

Memorandum of understanding concerning training conducted in Romania by the United States Marine Corps.

Signed at Stuttgart June 12, 2002.

Entered into force June 12, 2002.

NP

Agreement regarding the activities of United States forces located on the territory of Romania, with annexes.

Signed at Bucharest December 6, 2005.

Entered into force July 21, 2006.

TIAS

Agreement regarding assignment of liaison officers.

Signed at Norfolk May 30, 2006.

Entered into force May 30, 2006.

TIAS

Amendment

September 14 and 15, 2006.

ECONOMIC AND TECHNICAL COOPERATION

Joint statement on economic, industrial and technological cooperation.

Issued at Washington December 5, 1973.

26 UST 2342; TIAS 8159.

Long term agreement on economic, industrial and technical cooperation, with annexes.

Signed at Bucharest November 21, 1976.

Entered into force May 5, 1977.

28 UST 5228; TIAS 8624; 1087 UNTS 119.

EMPLOYMENT

Agreement relating to the employment of dependents of official government employees.

Exchange of notes at Washington July 1 and 28, 1993.

Entered into force July 28, 1993.

TIAS 12159.

ENVIRONMENTAL COOPERATION

Agreement for cooperation in the Global Learning and Observations to Benefit the Environment (GLOBE) Program, with appendices.

Signed at Bucharest and Washington April 11 and May 22, 1995.

Entered into force May 22, 1995.

TIAS 12653.

EXTRADITION

Extradition treaty.

Signed at Bucharest July 23, 1924.

Entered into force April 7, 1925.

44 Stat. 2020; TS 713; 11 Bevans 391.

Supplementary extradition treaty.

Signed at Bucharest November 10, 1936.

Entered into force July 27, 1937.

50 Stat. 1349; TS 916; 11 Bevans 423; 181 LNTS 177.

FINANCE

Agreement relating to the funding of the debt of Romania to the United States.

Signed at Washington December 4, 1925; operative June 15, 1925.

Treasury Department print; 11 Bevans 398.

Agreement modifying the debt funding agreement of December 4, 1925.

Signed at Washington June 11, 1932; operative July 1, 1931.

Treasury Department print; 11 Bevans 420.

Agreement relating to investment guaranties.

Exchange of notes at Bucharest April 28, 1973.

Entered into force April 28, 1973.

24 UST 1073; TIAS 7627.

Agreement regarding the consolidation and rescheduling of certain debts owed to, guaranteed or insured by the United States Government and its agencies, with annexes.

Signed at Bucharest March 10, 1983.

Entered into force April 22, 1983.

TIAS 10683.

Agreement regarding the consolidation and rescheduling of certain debts owed to, guaranteed or insured by the United States Government and its agencies, with annexes.

Signed at Bucharest February 15, 1984.

Entered into force April 16, 1984.

35 UST 4563; TIAS 10957.

Swap agreement among the United States Treasury, the National Bank of Romania/Government of Romania, with memorandum of understanding.

Signed at Washington and Bucharest March 6, 1991.

Entered into force March 6, 1991.

TIAS

Investment incentive agreement.

Signed at Bucharest June 30, 1992.

Entered into force December 4, 1992.

TIAS 12464.

INVESTMENT

Treaty concerning the reciprocal encouragement and protection of investment, with annex, protocol and related letter.

Signed at Bucharest May 28, 1992.

Entered into force January 15, 1994.

TIAS

JUDICIAL ASSISTANCE

Treaty on mutual legal assistance in criminal matters.

Signed at Washington May 26, 1999.

Entered into force October 17, 2001.

TIAS

MILITARY CEMETERIES AND MONUMENTS

Agreement relating to war graves registration and associated matters.

Exchange of notes at Bucharest June 19 and 28, 1946.

Entered into force June 28, 1946.

61 Stat. 4042; TIAS 1796; 11 Bevans 428; 148 UNTS 355.

NARCOTIC DRUGS

Arrangement for the direct exchange of certain information regarding the traffic in narcotic drugs.

Exchange of notes at Bucharest February 4, 1928, and April 17, 1929.

Entered into force April 17, 1929.

11 Bevans 414.

PACIFIC SETTLEMENT OF DISPUTES

Treaty of arbitration.

Signed at Washington March 21, 1929.

Entered into force July 22, 1929.

46 Stat. 2336; TS 794; 11 Bevans 408; 105 LNTS 79.

Treaty of conciliation.

Signed at Washington March 21, 1929.

Entered into force July 22, 1929.

46 Stat. 2339; TS 795; 11 Bevans 411; 105 LNTS 85.

PEACE CORPS

Agreement concerning the program of the United States Peace Corps in Romania.

Signed at Washington January 24, 1992.

Entered into force January 24, 1992.

TIAS 12080.

POSTAL MATTERS

Agreement concerning the exchange of parcel post, and regulations of execution.

Signed at Washington August 10, 1937, and at Bucharest March 12, 1937.

Entered into force September 1, 1937.

50 Stat. 1630; Post Office Department print; 183 LNTS 7.

Parcel post agreement, with detailed regulations.

Signed at Washington June 19, 1981.

Entered into force July 19, 1981.

NP

International express mail agreement, with detailed regulations.

Signed at Washington December 14, 1989.

Entered into force February 15, 1990.

TIAS 11718.

RELATIONS

Joint statement concerning relations between the United States and Romania.

Signed at Washington December 5, 1973.

Entered into force December 5, 1973.

24 UST 2257; TIAS 7746; 938 UNTS 457.

SCIENTIFIC COOPERATION

Agreement on cooperation in science and technology, with annexes.

Signed at Washington July 15, 1998.

Entered into force April 5, 2000.

TIAS

TAXATION

Convention with respect to taxes on income.

Signed at Washington December 4, 1973.

Entered into force February 26, 1976; effective January 1, 1974.

27 UST 165; TIAS 8228.

TRADE AND COMMERCE

Agreement on trade relations.

Signed at Bucharest April 2, 1975.

Entered into force August 3, 1975.

26 UST 2305; TIAS 8159.

Agreement relating to tariff and nontariff matters within the framework of the multilateral trade negotiations, and related letters of September 30, 1980.

Letters done at Bucharest and Washington March 2 and November 8, 1979.

Entered into force January 1, 1980.

32 UST 5489; TIAS 10000; 1266 UNTS 253.

Agreement relating to trade in cotton textiles, with annex.

Exchange of notes at Bucharest January 28 and March 31, 1983.

Entered into force March 31, 1983; effective January 1, 1983.

NP

Amendments and extensions

December 5 and 12, 1984 (NP).

May 8 and June 15, 1985 (NP).

June 16 and 30, 1987 (NP).

December 30 and 31, 1987 (NP).

November 28, 1988 and January 12, 1989 (NP).

December 28, 1988 and May 27, 1989 (NP).

May 7, June 10 and August 15, 1991 (NP).

February 17 and 24, 1993 (NP).

December 9, 1993 and January 5, 1994 (NP).

Administrative arrangement concerning a visa system relating to trade in certain textile products.

Exchange of letters at Bucharest October 13, 1982 and August 25, 1983.

Entered into force August 25, 1983.

NP

Amendment

September 16, 1988 and January 18 and 31, 1989 (NP).

Agreement relating to trade in wool and man-made fiber textiles and textile products.

Exchange of notes at Bucharest November 7 and 16, 1984.

Entered into force November 16, 1984; effective January 1, 1985.

NP

Amendments and extensions

December 30 and 31, 1987 (NP).

November 28, 1988 and January 12, 1989 (NP).

December 28, 1988 and May 27, 1989 (NP).

March 18, 1988 and May 29, 1989 (NP).

February 26 and March 13, 1992 (NP).

December 9, 1993 and January 5, 1994 (NP).

June 6 and July 25, 1994 (NP).

Agreement suspending mutual application of most-favored-nation tariff treatment under the trade agreement of April 2, 1975.

Signed at Bucharest June 22, 1988.

Entered into force June 22, 1988; effective July 3, 1988.

TIAS

Agreement on trade relations, with related exchanges of letters.

Signed at Bucharest April 3, 1992.

Entered into force November 8, 1993.

TIAS

TRADE-MARKS

Convention for the reciprocal protection of trade-marks.

Signed at Bucharest March 18/31, 1906.

Entered into force June 25, 1906.

34 Stat. 2901; TS 451; 11 Bevans 389.

VISAS

Agreement relating to the issuance of visas to diplomatic and non-diplomatic personnel.

Exchange of notes at Bucharest April 20, May 14 and 26, 1962.

Entered into force May 26, 1962; operative June 1, 1962.

13 UST 1192; TIAS 5063; 456 UNTS 265.

Amendment

May 31 and June 17, 1967 (18 UST 1266; TIAS 6279; 685 UNTS 404).

Agreement relating to reciprocal simplification of procedures for issuance of diplomatic and official visas.

Exchange of notes at Bucharest September 12 and October 10, 1977.

Entered into force October 10, 1977.

29 UST 2765; TIAS 8970.

Agreement relating to reciprocal facilitation of visa issuance.

Exchange of notes at Bucharest September 1 and October 10, 1977.

Entered into force October 10, 1977.

29 UST 4705; TIAS 9075; 1134 UNTS 209.

WEAPONS

Agreement concerning cooperation in the area of counterproliferation of weapons of mass destruction, and the promotion of defense and military relations.

Signed at Washington March 30, 1998.

Entered into force July 8, 2003.

TIAS

Amendment

January 16 and June 14, 2004.

Agreement concerning cooperation in the area of countering the proliferation of nuclear materials and technologies.

Signed at New York July 19, 2004.

Entered into force July 19, 2004.

TIAS

RUSSIAN FEDERATION

For agreements prior to December 31, 1991, see UNION OF SOVIET SOCIALIST REPUBLICS.

ARMS LIMITATION

Treaty on strategic offensive reductions.

Signed at Moscow May 24, 2002.

Entered into force June 1, 2003.

TIAS

ATOMIC ENERGY

Agreement concerning the disposition of highly enriched uranium extracted from nuclear weapons.

Signed at Washington February 18, 1993.

Entered into force February 18, 1993.

TIAS

Memorandum of understanding relating to transparency and additional arrangements concerning the agreement of February 18, 1993 concerning the disposition of highly enriched uranium extracted from nuclear weapons.

Signed at Washington September 1, 1993.

Entered into force September 1, 1993.

TIAS

Agreement on cooperation in research on radiation effects for the purpose of minimizing the consequences of radioactive contamination on health and the environment, with annex.

Signed at Moscow January 14, 1994.

Entered into force January 14, 1994.

TIAS 11481.

Amendment and extension

March 10, 2000.

Protocol on highly enriched uranium (HEU) transparency arrangements in furtherance of the memorandum of understanding of September 1, 1993.

Signed at Washington March 18, 1994.

Entered into force March 18, 1994.

TIAS

Agreement for cooperation on enhancing the safety of Russian nuclear fuel cycle facilities and research reactors.

Signed at Moscow June 30, 1995.

Entered into force June 30, 1995.

TIAS 12672.

Extension

January 31 and February 26, 2002.

Agreement concerning cooperation regarding plutonium production reactors, with annexes.

Signed at Moscow September 23, 1997.

Entered into force September 23, 1997.

TIAS

Amendment

March 12, 2003.

Agreement concerning the modification of the operating Seversk (Tomsk Region) and Zheleznogorsk (Krasnoyarsk Region) plutonium production reactors, with related letter.

Signed at Moscow September 23, 1997.

Entered into force September 23, 1997.

TIAS

Amendments

June 10, 1998.

October 20, 1999 and January 21, 2000.

Memorandum of understanding concerning cooperation regarding plutonium production reactors.

Signed at Moscow September 23, 1997.

Entered into force September 23, 1997.

TIAS

Amendment

March 12, 2003.

Agreement regarding assurances concerning the source material transferred from the United States to the Russian Federation, with annex.

Exchange of notes at Washington March 24, 1999.

Entered into force March 24, 1999.

TIAS

Agreement concerning the transfer of source material to the Russian Federation, with annex and administrative arrangement.

Signed at Washinton March 24, 1999.

Entered into force March 24, 1999.

TIAS

Agreement concerning the cessation of plutonium production at the operating ADE–4 and ADE–5 reactors in Seversk (Tomsk Region) and the ADE–2 reactor in Zheleznogorsk (Krasnoyarsk Region).

Signed at Vienna March 12, 2003.

Entered into force March 12, 2003.

TIAS

Agreement concerning cooperation for the transfer of Russian-produced research reactor nuclear fuel to the Russian Federation.

Signed at Moscow May 27, 2004.

Entered into force May 27, 2004.

TIAS

AVIATION

Memorandum of understanding on air navigation, airspace use and air traffic control.

Signed at Washington June 17, 1992.

Entered into force June 17, 1992.

TIAS 11477.

Air transport agreement, with annexes.

Signed at Moscow January 14, 1994.

Entered into force January 14, 1994.

TIAS

Memorandum of understanding on technical cooperation towards a bilateral airworthiness agreement.

Signed at Moscow June 30, 1995.

Entered into force June 30, 1995.

TIAS 12673.

Agreement for promotion of aviation safety.

Signed at Moscow September 2, 1998.

Entered into force September 2, 1998.

TIAS

Memorandum of understanding on cooperation in the field of civil aircraft accident/incident investigation and prevention.

Signed at Moscow September 2, 1998.

Entered into force September 2, 1998.

TIAS

Memorandum of cooperation concerning cooperation in the promotion and development of civil aviation.

Signed at Washington and Moscow February 19 and March 22, 1999.

Entered into force March 22, 1999.

TIAS

CUSTOMS

Agreement on cooperation and mutual assistance in customs matters.

Signed at Washington September 28, 1994.

Entered into force December 15, 1994.

TIAS

Agreement concerning the procedure for the customs documentation and duty-free entry of goods transported within the framework of US-Russian cooperation in the exploration and use of space for peaceful purposes.

Signed at Moscow December 16, 1994.

Entered into force August 26, 1996.

TIAS 12588.

DEFENSE

Agreement concerning the provision of training related to defense articles under the United States International Military Education and Training (IMET) Program.

Exchange of notes at Moscow and Washington April 22 and June 17, 1992.

Entered into force June 17, 1992.

NP

Memorandum on cooperation in the field of defense conversion.

Signed at Moscow December 16, 1993.

Entered into force December 16, 1993.

TIAS

Protocol on cooperation in the implementation of certain defense conversion projects.

Signed at Moscow December 16, 1993.

Entered into force December 16, 1993.

TIAS

Amendment and extension

March 18, 1994.

January 21 and March 1, 2000.

Agreement for cooperation in installing and operating seismic stations for monitoring nuclear weapons tests.

Signed at Washington and Moscow October 15 and 19, 1996.

Entered into force October 19, 1996.

TIAS

ECONOMIC AND TECHNICAL COOPERATION

Agreement regarding cooperation to facilitate the provision of assistance.

Signed at Moscow April 4, 1992.

Entered into force April 4, 1992.

TIAS 11464.

Grant agreement for an energy efficiency and environment commodity import program.

Signed at Moscow December 16, 1993.

Entered into force December 16, 1993.

TIAS 11483.

Memorandum of understanding for the establishment of the Russian-American oil and gas technology center in Tyumen City, with annex.

Signed at Washington and Tyumen City June 23 and July 26, 1994.

Entered into force July 26, 1994.

TIAS 12558.

EMBASSY SITES

Memorandum of mutual understanding on settlement of the problem of the new embassy administrative buildings in Washington and Moscow.

Signed at Washington June 17, 1992.

Entered into force June 17, 1992.

TIAS

Amendment

December 15, 1992.

EMERGENCY PREPAREDNESS

Memorandum of understanding on cooperation in natural and man-made technological emergency prevention and response.

Signed at Moscow July 16, 1996.

Entered into force July 16, 1996.

TIAS 12783.

Extension

September 11, 2006.

ENVIRONMENTAL COOPERATION

Agreement on cooperation in the field of protection of the environment and natural resources, with annex.

Signed at Washington June 23, 1994.

Entered into force June 23, 1994.

TIAS 12550.

Agreement on cooperation in the prevention of pollution of the environment in the Arctic.

Signed at Moscow December 16, 1994.

Entered into force December 16, 1994.

TIAS 12589.

Agreement for cooperation in the Global Learning and Observations to Benefit the Environment (GLOBE) Program, with appendices.

Signed at Moscow December 16, 1994.

Entered into force December 16, 1994.

TIAS 12590.

FINANCE

Investment incentive agreement.

Signed at Washington April 3, 1992.

Entered into force June 17, 1992.

TIAS 11471.

Agreement regarding the consolidation and rescheduling of certain debts owed to or guaranteed by the United States Government, with annexes.

Signed at Washington September 30, 1993.

Entered into force November 4, 1993.

NP

Agreement regarding the consolidation and rescheduling of certain debts owed to or guaranteed by the United States Government, with annexes.

Signed at Moscow October 25, 1994.

Entered into force December 19, 1994.

NP

Agreement regarding the rescheduling of certain debts owed to or guaranteed by the United States Government, with annexes.

Signed at Washington October 9, 1995.

Entered into force November 29, 1995.

NP

Amendment

November 28 and December 1, 1995 (NP).

Agreement regarding the rescheduling of certain debts owed to or guaranteed by the United States Government, with annexes.

Signed at Washington February 6, 1997.

Entered into force May 7, 1997.

NP

Agreement regarding the rescheduling of certain debts owed to or guaranteed by the United States Government, with annexes.

Signed at Moscow May 26, 2000.

Entered into force June 29, 2000.

NP

FISHERIES

Agreement concerning Pacific salmon fishing within the respective 200-nautical mile zones of the United States and Russia.

Exchange of notes at Washington August 27 and September 3, 1992.

Entered into force September 3, 1992.

TIAS 11449.

Agreement on the conservation of straddling fish stocks in the central part of the Sea of Okhotsk.

Signed at Moscow June 13, 1996.

Entered into force June 13, 1996.

TIAS 12768.

FORESTRY

Memorandum of understanding on cooperation in the field of forestry, with annex.

Signed at Washington May 13, 1994.

Entered into force May 13, 1994.

TIAS 12541.

JUDICIAL ASSISTANCE

Treaty on mutual legal assistance in criminal matters, with related note.

Signed at Moscow June 17, 1999.

Entered into force January 31, 2002.

TIAS

MARITIME MATTERS

Agreement amending the agreement of May 25, 1972 on the prevention of incidents on and over the high seas.

Exchange of notes at Moscow October 12, 1997 and May 28, 1998.

Entered into force May 28, 1998.

TIAS

Agreement on maritime transport.

Signed at St. Petersburg June 20, 2001.

Entered into force June 20, 2001.

TIAS

METEOROLOGY

Memorandum of understanding for cooperation in the areas of meteorology, hydrology and oceanography, with annexes.

Signed at Geneva June 23, 2005.

Entered into force June 23, 2005.

TIAS

NUCLEAR MATERIAL

Agreement to cooperate on national protection, control and accounting of nuclear materials.

Signed at Moscow June 30, 1995.

Entered into force June 30, 1995.

TIAS

Amendment and extension

September 27, 2005.

NUCLEAR RISK REDUCTION

Memorandum of agreement on the establishment of a joint center for the exchange of data from early warning systems and notifications of missile launches, with appendices.

Signed at Moscow June 4, 2000.

Entered into force June 4, 2000.

TIAS

Memorandum of understanding on notifications of missile launches, with appendices and joint statement.

Signed at Brussels December 16, 2000.

Entered into force December 16, 2000.

TIAS

NUCLEAR WAR

Agreement concerning the future consultation procedure for implementation of the agreement of September 30, 1971 on measures to reduce the risk of outbreak of nuclear war between the United States and the Union of Soviet Socialist Republics.

Exchange of notes at Moscow May 13 and June 25, 2004.

Entered into force June 25, 2004.

TIAS

SCIENTIFIC COOPERATION

Agreement on science and technology cooperation, with annexes.

Signed at Moscow December 16, 1993.

Entered into force December 16, 1993.

TIAS 12527.

Extension

December 15 and 16, 2005.

Memorandum of understanding on cooperation in geoscience, with annexes.

Signed at Washington June 23, 1994.

Entered into force June 23, 1994.

TIAS 12552.

Memorandum of understanding on basic scientific research cooperation, with annexes.

Signed at Washington June 23, 1994.

Entered into force June 23, 1994.

TIAS 12551.

Memorandum of understanding on basic scientific research cooperation, with annexes.

Signed at Washington February 7, 1997.

Entered into force February 7, 1997.

TIAS

Memorandum of understanding on cooperation in seismology and geodynamics, with appendix.

Signed at Washington March 24, 1999.

Entered into force March 24, 1999.

TIAS

Memorandum of understanding concerning scientific and technical cooperation in the earth sciences, with annexes.

Signed at Reston November 14, 2003.

Entered into force November 14, 2003.

TIAS

Memorandum of understanding on cooperation in technology and innovation.

Signed at Washington April 19, 2004.

Entered into force April 19, 2004.

TIAS

SPACE COOPERATION

Agreement concerning cooperation in the exploration and use of outer space for peaceful purposes, with annex.

Signed at Washington June 17, 1992.

Entered into force June 17, 1992.

TIAS 12457.

Amendment and extension

July 3 and August 9, 2002.

Protocol to the implementing agreement of October 5, 1992 on human space flight cooperation.

Signed at Moscow December 16, 1993.

Entered into force December 16, 1993.

TIAS 12522.

Interim agreement for the conduct of activities leading to Russian partnership in the detailed design, development, operation and utilization of the permanently manned civil space station.

Signed at Washington June 23, 1994.

Entered into force June 30, 1995.

TIAS

Implementing agreement on the flight of a U.S. stratospheric aerosol and gas experiment (SAGE) III and a total ozone mapping spectrometer (TOMS) aboard Russian meteor–3M spacecraft, with annexes.

Signed at Moscow December 16, 1994.

Entered into force February 22, 1995.

TIAS 12592.

Protocol regarding the balance of their contributions and obligations to the International Space Station, with appendices.

Signed at Moscow June 11, 1996.

Entered into force June 11. 1996.

TIAS

Addendum to the protocol of June 11, 1996 regarding the balance of their contributions to the International Space Station.

Signed at Moscow September 9, 2004.

Entered into force January 26, 2005.

TIAS

Agreement extending agreement of April 6, 2001 on the flight of the Russian high energy neutron detector (HEND) instrument on the United States 2001 Mars Odyssey Orbiter Mission.

Signed at Washington September 12 and 18, 2006.

Entered into force September 18, 2006.

TIAS

TAXATION

Convention for the avoidance of double taxation and the prevention of fiscal evasion with respect to taxes on income and capital, with protocol.

Signed at Washington June 17, 1992.

Entered into force December 16, 1993.

TIAS

TRADE

Agreement on trade relations, with related exchanges of letters.

Signed at Washington June 1, 1990.

Entered into force June 17, 1992.

TIAS

Amendment

September 26 and October 31, 1990.

Agreement on the exports of firearms and ammunition from the Russian Federation to the United States, with annexes.

Signed at Washington April 3, 1996

Entered into force April 3, 1996.

TIAS

Amendment

June 25, 2003 and March 4, 2004.

Agreement on trade in certain types of poultry, beef and pork, with annex.

Signed at Washington June 15, 2005

Entered into force June 15, 2005.

NP

Agreement on importation of pork and pork-by-products into the Russian Federation.

Exchange of letters at Washington and Hanoi November 19, 2006.

Entered into force November 19, 2006.

NP

Agreement on tariff treatment of certain combine harvester-threshers and self-propelled forage harvesters.

Exchange of letters at Washington and Hanoi November 19, 2006.

Entered into force November 19, 2006.

NP

Agreement on tariff treatment of certain aircraft imported under operational lease.

Exchange of letters at Washington and Hanoi November 19, 2006.

Entered into force November 19, 2006.

NP

Agreement on agricultural biotechnology.

Exchange of letters at Washington and Hanoi November 19, 2006.

Entered into force November 19, 2006.

NP

Agreement on exporting pork and poultry to the Russian Federation.

Exchange of letters at Washington and Hanoi November 19, 2006.

Entered into force November 19, 2006.

NP

Agreement concerning inspection and certification of slaughter, processing and cold storage facilities.

Exchange of letters at Washington and Hanoi November 19, 2006.

Entered into force November 19, 2006.

NP

Agreement on market access for beef and beef by-products.

Exchange of letters at Washington and Hanoi November 19, 2006.

Entered into force November 19, 2006.

NP

Agreement on establishment of import licensing procedures for imports of goods containing encryption technology.

Exchange of letters at Washington and Hanoi November 19, 2006.

Entered into force November 19, 2006.

NP

Agreement on protection and enforcement of intellectual property rights.

Exchange of letters at Washington and Hanoi November 19, 2006.

Entered into force November 19, 2006.

NP

WEAPONS

Agreement concerning the safe and secure transportation, storage and destruction of weapons and the prevention of weapons proliferation, with implementing agreements.

Signed at Washington June 17, 1992.

Entered into force June 17, 1992.

TIAS

Agreement concerning the safe, secure and ecologically sound destruction of chemical weapons.

Signed at Washington July 30, 1992.

Entered into force July 30, 1992.

TIAS

Amendments

March 18, 1994.

May 28, 1996.

April 10, 1997.

December 29, 1997.

November 6, 1998 and January 14, 1999.

November 9 and 14, 2000.

July 21 and 28, 2004.

September 28 and October 6, 2005.

August 23 and September 8, 2006.

Agreement concerning the safe and secure transportation of nuclear weapons and nuclear weapons material through the provision of cargo and guard railcar conversion kits.

Signed at Moscow August 28, 1992.

Entered into force August 28, 1992.

TIAS

Amendment

March 23, 1994.

Agreement concerning technical assistance for design of a safe, secure and ecologically sound storage facility for fissile material derived from the destruction of nuclear weapons.

Signed at Washington October 6, 1992.

Entered into force October 6, 1992.

TIAS

Protocol to the agreement of June 17, 1992 concerning the safe and secure transportation and storage of nuclear weapons through the provision of emergency response equipment and related training.

Signed at Moscow March 26, 1993.

Entered into force March 26, 1993.

TIAS

Amendment and extensions

March 23, 1994.

May 25, 1994.

May 28, 1996.

February 6 and April 1, 1998.

Agreement concerning cooperation in the elimination of strategic offensive arms, with annexes.

Signed at Moscow August 26, 1993.

Entered into force August 26, 1993.

TIAS

Amendments and extension

April 3, 1995.

June 19, 1995.

May 27, 1996.

April 11, 1997.

February 11, 1998.

June 9, 1998.

August 9 and 16, 1999.

July 26 and August 8, 2000.

August 30, 2002.

May 29 and June 9, 2003.

January 14, 2005.

May 15 and 25, 2006.

August 12 and September 5, 2006.

Agreement concerning the provision of material, services and training relating to the construction of a safe, secure and ecologically sound storage facility for fissile material derived from the destruction of nuclear weapons.

Signed at Washington September 2, 1993.

Entered into force September 2, 1993.

TIAS

Amendments and extension

June 20, 1995.

September 5 and 6, 1996.

April 9, 1997.

January 27, 1999.

May 21 and 26, 1999.

August 9 and September 15, 1999.

August 8 and 21, 2000.

Agreement concerning control, accounting and physical protection of nuclear material.

Signed at Washington September 2, 1993.

Entered into force September 2, 1993.

TIAS

Amendment

January 20, 1995.

Agreement concerning cooperation in nuclear weapons storage security through provision of material, services and related training.

Signed at Moscow April 3, 1995.

Entered into force April 3, 1995.

TIAS

Amendments and extensions

June 21, 1995.

May 27, 1996.

April 8, 1997.

December 14, 1998 and January 14, 1999.

December 14, 1998 and January 14, 1999.

August 9 and November 1, 1999.

August 9, 1999 and January 25, 2000.

June 1 and 12, 2000.

September 16 and 19, 2002.

January 31 and February 21, 2003.

January 31 and February 21, 2003.

March 1 and 5, 2004.

July 7 and 12, 2004.

March 14 and 22, 2006.

June 17, 2006.

Agreement concerning cooperation in nuclear weapons transportation security through provision of material, services and related training.

Signed at Moscow April 3, 1995.

Entered into force April 3, 1995.

TIAS

Amendments and extension

June 21, 1995.

May 27, 1996.

December 14, 1998 and January 14, 1999.

August 9, 1999 and January 25, 2000.
June 1 and 12, 2000.
February 14 and 28, 2002.
September 16 and 19, 2002.
March 1 and 5, 2004.
July 7 and 12, 2004.
April 26 and May 5, 2005.
May 4 and 23, 2005.
August 15 and 26, 2005.
March 14 and 22, 2006.
June 17, 2006.

Agreement extending the agreement of June 17, 1992 concerning the safe and secure transportation and storage of nuclear weapons material through the provision of fissile material containers.
Signed at Moscow May 28, 1996.
Entered into force May 28, 1996.
TIAS

Arrangement for access to Russian Federation facilities by United States representatives to conduct work pursuant to the agreement concerning cooperation in the elimination of strategic offensive arms.
Signed at Moscow November 20, 2003.
Entered into force November 20, 2003; with effect from October 8, 2003.
TIAS

RWANDA

DEFENSE

Agreement concerning the provision of training related to defense articles under the United States International Military Education and Training (IMET) Program.
Exchange of notes at Kigali March 6 and 11, 1980.
Entered into force March 11, 1980.
33 UST 3064; TIAS 10211; 1529 UNTS 7.

Agreement regarding grants under the Foreign Assistance Act of 1961, as amended, and the furnishing of defense articles, related training and other defense services from the United States to Rwanda.
Exchange of notes at Kigali January 26 and February 6, 1998.
Entered into force February 6, 1998.
NP

Acquisition and cross-servicing agreement, with annexes.
Signed at Kigali July 13, 2004.
Entered into force July 13, 2004.
TIAS

Agreement regarding the status of United States military and civilian personnel of the United States Department of Defense who may be present in Rwanda in connection with the military airlift of Rwandan military forces in support of operations in Darfur and future mutually agreed activities.
Exchange of notes at Kigili July 5 and 11, 2005.
Entered into force July 11, 2005.
NP

ECONOMIC AND TECHNICAL COOPERATION

Economic and technical cooperation agreement.
Signed at Kigali June 7, 1989.
Entered into force January 17, 1992.
TIAS 12063.

Agency for International Development
April 26 and 29, 1977 (29 UST 5269; TIAS 9102; 1134 UNTS 157).

EMPLOYMENT

Agreement relating to the employment of dependents of official government employees, with related note.
Exchange of notes at Washington July 15 and October 22, 1992.
Entered into force October 22, 1992.
TIAS 11904.

ENVIRONMENTAL COOPERATION

Agreement for cooperation in the Global Learning and Observations to Benefit the Environment (GLOBE) Program.
Signed at Kigali August 21, 2003.
Entered into force August 21, 2003.
TIAS

FINANCE

Agreement relating to investment guaranties.
Exchange of notes at Kigali July 6 and August 9, 1965.
Entered into force April 27, 1967.
18 UST 2346; TIAS 6337; 692 UNTS 101.

Agreement regarding the consolidation, reduction, and rescheduling of certain debts owed to the United States Government and its Agency, with annexes.
Signed at Kigali October 26, 1999.
Entered into force December 13, 1999.
NP

Agreement regarding the reduction of certain debts owed to, guaranteed by, or insured by the United States Government, with annexes.
Signed at Kigali April 22, 2003.
Entered into force June 9, 2003.
NP

Agreement regarding the reduction of certain debts owed to, guaranteed by, or insured by the United States Government, or its agency, with annexes.
Signed at Kigali October 13, 2005.
Entered into force November 30, 2005.
NP

HEALTH

Memorandum of understanding for cooperation in preventing and controlling HIV/AIDS and other infectious diseases, with annexes.
Signed at Kigali October 3, 2002.
Entered into force October 3, 2002.
TIAS

INTERNATIONAL CRIMINAL COURT

Agreement regarding the surrender of persons to international tribunals.
Signed at Washington March 4, 2003.
Entered into force July 11, 2003.
TIAS

PEACE CORPS

Agreement relating to the establishment of a Peace Corps program in Rwanda.
Exchange of notes at Kigali December 20, 1974.
Entered into force December 20, 1974.
25 UST 3387; TIAS 7992.

POSTAL MATTERS

International express mail agreement with detailed regulations.
Signed at Kigali and Washington January 15 and February 8, 1988.
Entered into force March 15, 1988.
TIAS 11648.

S

SAINT KITTS AND NEVIS

On September 19, 1983 Saint Christopher and Nevis became an independent state. In a note dated November 2, 1983 to the Secretary-General of the United Nations, the Prime Minister and Minister of Foreign Affairs made a statement reading in part as follows:

"I have the honour to refer to the attainment of independence by the former British Associated State of St. Christopher and Nevis on 19th September, 1983, as Saint Christopher and Nevis or Saint Kitts and Nevis, and to the question of status of conventions, treaties and other international instruments applied to, or entered into on behalf of Saint Christopher and Nevis by the United Kingdom Government prior to independence.

The Government of Saint Christopher and Nevis considers that questions of succession to such conventions, treaties and other international instruments should be governed by the accepted rules of international law and by the relevant principles contained in the Convention on Succession of States in respect of Treaties done at Vienna on 23rd August, 1978.

The Government of Saint Christopher and Nevis hereby declares that, with regard to multilateral treaties applied or extended to the former British Associated State of Saint Christopher and Nevis, it will continue to apply the terms of each treaty provisionally and on the basis of reciprocity until such time as it notifies the depositary authority of its decision in respect thereof.

As regards bilateral treaties applied or extended to, or entered into on behalf of the former British Associated State of Saint Christopher and Nevis, the Government of Saint Christopher and Nevis declares that it will examine each such treaty and communicate its views to the other State Party concerned. In the meantime, the Government of Saint Christopher and Nevis will continue to observe the terms of each treaty, which validly so applies and is not inconsistent with its independent sovereign status, provisionally and on basis of reciprocity."

AVIATION

Agreement between the United States and the United Kingdom concerning air services, with annexes and exchange of letters.

Signed at Bermuda July 23, 1977.

Entered into force July 23, 1977.

28 UST 5367; TIAS 8641.

Amendments

April 25, 1978 (29 UST 2680; TIAS 8965).

December 29, 1979 (32 UST 524; TIAS 9722).

December 4, 1980 (33 UST 655; TIAS 10059).

August 11 and November 30, 1987 (TIAS 11545).

CONSULS

Consular convention between the United States and the United Kingdom.

Signed at Washington June 6, 1951.

Entered into force September 7, 1952.

3 UST 3426; TIAS 2494; 165 UNTS 121.

DEFENSE

Agreement concerning the provision of training related to defense articles under the United States International Military Education and Training (IMET) Program.

Exchange of notes at St. John's and Basseterre March 19 and 20, 1984.

Entered into force March 20, 1984.

35 UST 4881; TIAS 10972.

Agreement concerning the status of United States Armed Forces personnel present in St. Christopher and Nevis.

Exchange of notes at St. John's and Basseterre March 2 and June 9, 1987.

Entered into force June 9, 1987.

TIAS

ECONOMIC AND TECHNICAL COOPERATION

General agreement for economic, technical and related assistance.

Signed at Basseterre April 24, 1986.

Entered into force April 24, 1986.

TIAS 11514.

EMPLOYMENT

Agreement relating to the employment of dependents of official government employees.

Exchange of notes at Bridgetown and Basseterre February 26 and April 14, 2003.

Entered into force April 14, 2003.

TIAS

EXTRADITION

Extradition treaty.

Signed at Basseterre September 18, 1996.

Entered into force February 23, 2000.

TIAS 12805.

FINANCE

Agreement relating to investment guaranties.

Signed at Basseterre November 21, 1968.

Entered into force November 21, 1968.

19 UST 7546; TIAS 6596; 702 UNTS 311.

INTERNATIONAL CRIMINAL COURT

Agreement regarding the surrender of persons to the International Criminal Court.

Exchange of notes at Washington January 31, 2005.

Entered into force January 31, 2005.

TIAS

JUDICIAL ASSISTANCE

Treaty on mutual legal assistance in criminal matters, with related exchange of notes.

Signed at Basseterre September 18, 1997.

Entered into force February 23, 2000.

TIAS

NARCOTIC DRUGS

Agreement concerning maritime counter-drug operations.

Signed at Basseterre April 13, 1995.

Entered into force April 13, 1995.

TIAS 12775.

Amendment

June 27, 1996 (TIAS 12775).

Agreement regarding the provision of articles, services and associated training by the Government of the United States for anti-narcotics purposes.

Exchange of notes at Bridgetown and Basseterre November 13, 1998 and March 11, 1999.

Entered into force March 11, 1999.

TIAS

PEACE CORPS

Agreement relating to the establishment of a Peace Corps program in St. Kitts/Nevis.

Exchange of letters at Bridgetown and Basseterre May 15, 1980 and January 13, 1981.

Entered into force January 13, 1981.

33 UST 846; TIAS 10067; 1275 UNTS 131.

PEACEKEEPING

Agreement for the furnishing of commodities and services in connection with the peacekeeping force for Grenada.

Exchange of notes at St. John's and Basseterre January 19 and 20, 1984.

Entered into force January 20, 1984.

35 UST 4276; TIAS 10929; 2015 UNTS 123.

POSTAL MATTERS

Convention for the exchange of postal money orders with the British Colony of Saint Christopher, Nevis and Anguilla.

Signed at Basseterre, St. Kitts, June 27 and at Washington September 14, 1959.

Entered into force February 1, 1960.

11 UST 1433; TIAS 4483.

International express mail agreement, with detailed regulations.

Signed at St. Kitts and Washington June 16 and August 21, 1997.

Entered into force October 1, 1997.

NP

PROPERTY

Convention between the United States and the United Kingdom relating to tenure and disposition of real and personal property.

Signed at Washington March 2, 1899; applicable to St. Christopher-Nevis June 17, 1901.

31 Stat. 1939; TS 146; 12 Bevans 246.

Supplementary convention relating to the tenure and disposition of real and personal property.

Signed at Washington May 27, 1936.

Entered into force March 10, 1941.

55 Stat. 1101; TS 964; 5 Bevans 140; 203 LNTS 367.

TELECOMMUNICATION

Agreement relating to radio communications between amateur stations on behalf of third parties.

Exchange of notes at St. John's and St. Kitts July 6 and 9, 1984.

Entered into force August 8, 1984.

TIAS 11147; 2126 UNTS 185.

TRADE-MARKS

Declaration by the United States and the United Kingdom affording reciprocal protection to trade-marks.

Signed at London October 24, 1877.

Entered into force October 24, 1877.

20 Stat. 703; TS 138; 12 Bevans 198.

SAINT LUCIA

On February 22, 1979, Saint Lucia became an independent state. In a note dated March 14, 1979, to the Secretary-General of the United Nations, the Prime Minister made a statement reading in part as follows: "Saint Lucia … is now ready to participate with other nations in fulfilling obligations under international law with respect to treaties to which this Government succeeded upon Independence. However, it is necessary to examine in depth such treaties to ascertain whether or not under customary international law any may have lapsed. Until this has been done the Government of Saint Lucia wish:

You will be notified in due course of those treaties this Government regards as having lapsed and those treaties which this Government wishes to terminate."

AVIATION

Agreement between the United States and the United Kingdom concerning the opening of certain military air bases in the Caribbean area and Bermuda to use by civil aircraft and exchange of notes.

Signed at Washington February 24, 1948.

Entered into force February 24, 1948.

62 Stat. 1860; TIAS 1717; 12 Bevans 850; 73 UNTS 143.

Agreement between the United States and the United Kingdom relating to the future status and use of Beane Field, St. Lucia.

Exchange of notes at London August 20, 1964.

Entered into force August 20, 1964.

15 UST 1685; TIAS 5642; 531 UNTS 85.

Agreement between the United States and the United Kingdom concerning air services, with annexes and exchange of letters.

Signed at Bermuda July 23, 1977.

Entered into force July 23, 1977.

28 UST 5367; TIAS 8641.

Amendment

April 25, 1978 (29 UST 2680; TIAS 8965).

CONSULS

Consular convention between the United States and the United Kingdom.

Signed at Washington June 6, 1951.

Entered into force September 7, 1952.

3 UST 3426; TIAS 2494; 165 UNTS 121.

DEFENSE

Agreement concerning the provision of training related to defense articles under the United States International Military Education and Training (IMET) Program.

Exchange of notes at Bridgetown and Castries December 11, 1980 and January 27, 1981.

Entered into force January 27, 1981.

33 UST 983; TIAS 10081; 1275 UNTS 185.

Agreement regarding the status of members of the armed forces of the United States and civilian personnel of the United States Department of Defense present in St. Lucia in connection with military exercises and training, counter-drug related activities, United States security assistance programs, or other agreed peaceful purposes.

Exchange of notes at Bridgetown and Castries December 28 and 29, 2000.

Entered into force December 29, 2000.

NP

ECONOMIC AND TECHNICAL COOPERATION

General agreement for economic, technical and related assistance.

Signed at Castries October 20, 1983.

Entered into force October 20, 1983.

35 UST 2953; TIAS 10831; 2014 UNTS 607.

EXTRADITION

Extradition treaty.

Signed at Castries April 18, 1996.

Entered into force February 2, 2000.

TIAS

FINANCE

Agreement relating to investment guaranties.

Signed at Castries August 9, 1968.

Entered into force August 9, 1968.

19 UST 5921; TIAS 6546; 730 UNTS 225.

JUDICIAL ASSISTANCE

Treaty on mutual legal assistance in criminal matters, with forms.

Signed at Castries April 18, 1996.

Entered into force February 2, 2000.

TIAS

NARCOTIC DRUGS

Agreement concerning maritime counter-drug operations.

Signed at Castries April 20, 1995.

Entered into force April 20, 1995.

TIAS 12764.

Amendment

June 5, 1996 (TIAS 12764).

Agreement regarding the provision of articles, services and associated training by the Government of the United States for anti-narcotics purposes.

Exchange of notes at Bridgetown and Castries November 13, 1998 and April 8, 1999.

Entered into force April 8, 1999.

TIAS

PEACE CORPS

Agreement relating to the establishment of a Peace Corps program in St. Lucia.

Exchange of letters at Bridgetown and Castries May 15 and July 8, 1980.

Entered into force July 8, 1980.

32 UST 4408; TIAS 9954; 1267 UNTS 137.

PEACEKEEPING

Agreement for the furnishing of commodities and services in connection with the peacekeeping force for Grenada.

Exchange of notes at Bridgetown and Castries November 25, 1983 and January 13, 1984.

Entered into force January 13, 1984.

35 UST 4253; TIAS 10924; 2014 UNTS 615.

POSTAL MATTERS

Money order agreement.

Signed at Washington July 29 and at Grenada August 29, 1904; operative October 1, 1904.

NP

Agreement for the direct exchange of parcels by parcel post.

Signed at Grenada May 20 and at Washington June 21, 1935; operative July 1, 1935.

49 Stat. 3229; 162 LNTS 157.

International express mail agreement with detailed regulations.

Signed at Castries and Washington August 11 and September 14, 1989.

Entered into force September 15, 1989.

TIAS 11953.

INTELPOST memorandum of understanding, with detailed regulations.

Signed at Castries and Washington September 22 and October 29, 1992.

Entered into force November 23, 1992.

TIAS 11902.

PROPERTY

Convention between the United States and the United Kingdom relating to tenure and disposition of real and personal property.

Signed at Washington March 2, 1899; applicable to St. Lucia February 9, 1901.

31 Stat. 1939; TS 146; 12 Bevans 246.

Supplementary convention relating to the tenure and disposition of real and personal property.

Signed at Washington May 27, 1936.

Entered into force March 10, 1941.

55 Stat. 1101; TS 964; 5 Bevans 140; 203 LNTS 367.

REFUGEES

Memorandum of understanding for the establishment within the territory of St. Lucia of facilities to provide temporary protection under the auspices of the United Nations High Commissioner for Refugees for nationals of Haiti fleeing their country.

Signed at St. Lucia July 15, 1994.

Entered into force July 15, 1994.

TIAS

TAXATION

Agreement for the exchange of information with respect to taxes, with annex.

Signed at Washington January 30, 1987.

Entered into force April 22, 1991.

TIAS 12057.

TELECOMMUNICATIONS

Agreement between the United States and the United Kingdom relating to the reciprocal granting of authorizations to permit licensed amateur radio operators of either country to operate their stations in the other country.

Exchange of notes at London November 26, 1965; applicable to St. Lucia December 11, 1969.

16 UST 2047; TIAS 5941; 561 UNTS 193.

Agreement between the United States and the United Kingdom extending to certain territories the application of the agreement of November 26, 1965 relating to the reciprocal granting of authorizations to permit licensed amateur radio operators of either country to operate their stations in the other country.

Exchange of notes at London December 11, 1969.

Entered into force December 11, 1969.

20 UST 4089; TIAS 6800; 732 UNTS 334.

Arrangement relating to radio communications between amateur stations on behalf of third parties.

Exchange of notes at Bridgetown and Castries August 10, 1981 and February 17, 1982.

Entered into force March 19, 1982.

34 UST 287; TIAS 10354; 1557 UNTS 3.

TRADE-MARKS

Declaration by the United States and the United Kingdom affording reciprocal protection to trade-marks.

Signed at London October 24, 1877.

Entered into force October 24, 1877.

20 Stat. 703; TS 138; 12 Bevans 198.

SAINT VINCENT AND THE GRENADINES

On October 27, 1979 Saint Vincent and the Grenadines became an independent state. In a note dated September 30, 1983, to the Secretary-General of the United Nations, the Prime Minister and Minister of Finance made a statement reading in part as follows:

"I have the honour to refer to the attainment of independence by the former British Associated State of St. Vincent on 27th October, 1979, as the State of St. Vincent and the Grenadines, and to the question of status of convention, treaties and other international instruments applied to or entered into on behalf of St. Vincent by the United Kingdom Government prior to independence.

The Government of the State of St. Vincent and the Grenadines considers that questions of succession to such conventions, treaties and other international instruments should be governed by the accepted rules of international law and by the relevant principles contained in the Convention on Succession of States in respect of treaties done at Vienna on 23rd August, 1978.

The Government of the State of St. Vincent and the Grenadines hereby declares that, with regard to multilateral treaties applied or extended to the former British Associated State of St. Vincent, it will continue to apply the terms of each such treaty provisionally and on the basis of reciprocity until such time as it notifies the depository authority of its decision in respect thereof.

As regards bilateral treaties applied or extended to, or entered into on behalf of the former British Associated State of St. Vincent, the Government of the State of St. Vincent and the Grenadines declares that it will examine each such treaty and communicate its views to the other State Party concerned. In the meantime, the Government of the State of St. Vincent and the Grenadines will continue to observe the terms of each such treaty, which validly so applies and is not inconsistent with its independent sovereign status, provisionally and on basis of reciprocity."

AVIATION

Agreement between the United States and the United Kingdom concerning air services, with annexes and exchange of letters.

Signed at Bermuda July 23, 1977.

Entered into force July 23, 1977.

28 UST 5367; TIAS 8641.

Amendment

April 25, 1978 (29 UST 2680; TIAS 8965).

CONSULS

Consular convention between the United States and the United Kingdom.

Signed at Washington June 6, 1951.

Entered into force September 7, 1952.

3 UST 3426; TIAS 2494; 165 UNTS 121.

DEFENSE

Agreement concerning the provision of training related to defense articles under the United States International Military Education and Training (IMET) Program.

Exchange of notes at Bridgetown and Kingstown December 11, 1980 and January 20, 1981.

Entered into force January 20, 1981.

33 UST 912; TIAS 10076; 1275 UNTS 149.

ECONOMIC AND TECHNICAL COOPERATION

General agreement for economic, technical and related assistance.

Signed at Kingstown September 30, 1983.

Entered into force September 30, 1983.

35 UST 2970; TIAS 10833; 2014 UNTS 441.

EMPLOYMENT

Agreement relating to the employment of dependents of official government employees.

Exchange of notes at Bridgetown and Kingstown February 26 and June 16, 2003.

Entered into force June 16, 2003.

TIAS

EXTRADITION

Extradition treaty.

Signed at Kingstown August 15, 1996.

Entered into force September 8, 1999.

TIAS

FINANCE

Agreement relating to investment guaranties.

Exchange of notes at Bridgetown and St. Vincent May 15 and June 14, 1972.

Entered into force June 14, 1972.

23 UST 3802; TIAS 7530.

JUDICIAL ASSISTANCE

Treaty on mutual legal assistance in criminal matters, with a related protocol.

Signed at Kingstown January 8, 1998.

Entered into force September 8, 1999.

TIAS

NARCOTIC DRUGS

Agreement concerning maritime counter-drug operations.

Signed at Kingstown and Bridgetown June 29 and July 4, 1995.

Entered into force July 4, 1995.

TIAS 12676.

Agreement regarding the provision of articles, services and associated training by the Government of the United States for anti-narcotics purposes.

Exchange of notes at Bridgetown and Kingstown November 13 and 26, 1998.

Entered into force November 26, 1998.

TIAS

PEACE CORPS

Agreement relating to the establishment of a Peace Corps program in St. Vincent.

Exchange of letters at Bridgetown and St. Vincent May 15 and June 26, 1980.

Entered into force June 26, 1980.

32 UST 5815; TIAS 10017; 1267 UNTS 129.

PEACEKEEPING

Agreement for the furnishing of commodities and services in connection with the peacekeeping force for Grenada.

Exchange of notes at Bridgetown and St. Vincent November 25, 1983 and January 13, 1984.

Entered into force January 13, 1984.

35 UST 4257; TIAS 10925; 2014 UNTS 449.

POSTAL MATTERS

Money order agreement.

Signed at Washington July 29 and at Grenada August 29, 1904; operative October 1, 1904.

NP

Agreement for the direct exchange of parcels by parcel post.

Signed at Grenada May 20 and at Washington June 21, 1935; operative July 1, 1935.

49 Stat. 3229; Post Office Department print; 162 LNTS 157.

International express mail agreement, with detailed regulations.

Signed at Kingston and Washington January 27 and February 25, 1992.

Entered into force March 7, 1992.

TIAS 11854.

PROPERTY

Convention between the United States and the United Kingdom relating to tenure and disposition of real and personal property.

Signed at Washington March 2, 1899; applicable to St. Vincent February 9, 1901.

31 Stat. 1939; TS 146; 12 Bevans 246.

Supplementary convention relating to the tenure and disposition of real and personal property.

Signed at Washington May 27, 1936.

Entered into force March 10, 1941.

55 Stat. 1101; TS 964; 5 Bevans 140; 203 LNTS 367.

TAXATION

Agreement concerning reciprocal exemption from income tax of income derived from the international operation of ships and aircraft.

Exchange of notes at Bridgetown and Kingston October 11, 1988 and February 15, 1989.

Entered into force February 15, 1989.

TIAS 11601; 2191 UNTS 241.

TELECOMMUNICATION

Agreement between the United States and the United Kingdom relating to the reciprocal granting of authorizations to permit licensed amateur radio operators of either country to operate their stations in the other country.

Exchange of notes at London November 26, 1965; applicable to St. Vincent December 11, 1969.

16 UST 2047; TIAS 5941; 561 UNTS 193.

Agreement between the United States and the United Kingdom extending to certain territories the application of the agreement of November 26, 1965 relating to the reciprocal granting of authorizations to permit licensed amateur radio operators of either country to operate their stations in the other country.

Exchange of notes at London December 11, 1969.

Entered into force December 11, 1969.

20 UST 4089; TIAS 6800; 732 UNTS 334.

Agreement relating to radio communications between amateur stations on behalf of third parties.

Exchange of notes at Bridgetown and St. Vincent April 22 and September 27, 1982.

Entered into force September 27, 1982; effective October 27, 1982.

35 UST 3830; TIAS 10885; 2014 UNTS 439.

TRADE-MARKS

Declaration by the United States and the United Kingdom affording reciprocal protection to trade-marks.

Signed at London October 24, 1877.

Entered into force October 24, 1877.

20 Stat. 703; TS 138; 12 Bevans 198.

SAN MARINO

EXTRADITION

Treaty for the mutual extradition of fugitive criminals.

Signed at Rome January 10, 1906.

Entered into force July 8, 1908.

35 Stat. 1971; TS 495; 11 Bevans 440.

Supplementary extradition convention.

Signed at Washington October 10, 1934.

Entered into force June 28, 1935.

49 Stat. 3198; TS 891; 11 Bevans 446; 161 LNTS 149.

SAO TOME AND PRINCIPE

DEFENSE

Agreement concerning the provision of training related to defense articles under the United States International Military Education and Training (IMET) Program.

Exchange of notes at Libreville and Sao Tome April 2, 1985 and February 26, 1986.

Entered into force February 26, 1986.

NP

Agreement regarding grants under the Foreign Assistance Act of 1961, as amended, and the furnishing of defense articles, related training and other defense services from the United States to the Government of Sao Tome and Principe.

Exchange of notes at Libreville and Sao Tome March 14 and August 19, 2005.

Entered into force August 19, 2005.

TIAS

FINANCE

Investment incentive agreement.

Signed at Washington September 10, 1998.

Entered into force September 10, 1998.

TIAS

INTERNATIONAL CRIMINAL COURT

Agreement regarding the surrender of persons to the International Criminal Court.

Exchange of notes at Libreville and Sao Tome November 6 and 12, 2003.

Entered into force November 12, 2003.

TIAS

TELECOMMUNICATION

Agreement for the operation of radio transmission facilities.

Signed at Sao Tome May 22, 1992.

Entered into force June 21, 1992.

TIAS

SAUDI ARABIA

AVIATION

Memorandum of arrangement relating to technical assistance in developing and modernizing Saudi Arabia's civil aviation system, with annex.

Signed at Washington and Riyadh May 16 and August 3, 1985.

Entered into force August 3, 1985.

TIAS 11397.

Air transport agreement, with annexes.

Signed at Jeddah October 2, 1993.

Entered into force October 2, 1993.

TIAS 12508.

COMMERCE

Provisional agreement in regard to diplomatic and consular representation, juridical protection, commerce, and navigation.

Signed at London November 7, 1933.

Entered into force November 7, 1933.

48 Stat. 1826; EAS 53; 11 Bevans 456; 142 LNTS 329.

CONSULS

See COMMERCE

CULTURAL RELATIONS

Agreement for cultural exchange.

Signed at Jidda July 25, 1968.

Entered into force July 25, 1968.

20 UST 2804; TIAS 6749; 723 UNTS 141.

DEFENSE[1]

1

Agreement relating to the extending of procurement assistance to Saudi Arabia for the transfer of military supplies and equipment.

Exchange of notes at Jidda June 18, 1951.

Entered into force June 18, 1951.

2 UST 1460; TIAS 2289; 141 UNTS 67.

1

Agreement providing for a military assistance advisory group.[2]

Exchange of notes at Jidda June 27, 1953.

Entered into force June 27, 1953.

4 UST 1482; TIAS 2812; 212 UNTS 335.

1

Agreement for the loan of F-86 aircraft to Saudi Arabia.[3]

Exchange of notes at Jidda November 10 and 13, 1962.

Entered into force November 13, 1962.

14 UST 1181; TIAS 5414; 488 UNTS 175.

Amendment

May 1 and 22, 1963 (14 UST 1184; TIAS 5414; 488 UNTS 180).

1

Agreement relating to the transfer of F-86 aircraft to Saudi Arabia.

Exchange of notes at Jidda May 16 and November 11, 1965.

Entered into force November 11, 1965.

17 UST 1390; TIAS 6095.

1

Agreement on privileges and immunities for United States personnel engaged in the training program for the maintenance and operation of F-5 aircraft in Saudi Arabia.

Exchange of notes at Jidda April 4 and July 5, 1972.

Entered into force July 5, 1972.

23 UST 1469; TIAS 7425.

1

Agreement relating to the deposit by Saudi Arabia of ten percent of the value of grant military assistance provided by the United States.

Exchange of notes at Jidda April 11, 19 and May 15, 1972.

Entered into force May 15, 1972.

23 UST 2664; TIAS 7459.

1

Memorandum of understanding concerning the Saudi Arabian National Guard modernization program.

Signed at Jidda March 19, 1973.

Entered into force March 19, 1973.

24 UST 1106; TIAS 7634.

NOTES

1 See also agreement on cooperation in the field of economics, technology, industry and defense (TIAS 7974) under ECONOMIC AND TECHNICAL COOPERATION.

2 Terminated February 27, 1977, except that the provisions of paragraph 7 remain in force in respect of activities under the agreement of February 8 and 27, 1977 (28 UST 2409; TIAS 8558). See MISSIONS, MILITARY.

3 Paragraph 1, first sentence of paragraph 5 and paragraphs 7 and 8 terminated by agreement of May 16 and November 11, 1965 (17 UST 1390; TIAS 6095).

ECONOMIC AND TECHNICAL COOPERATION

Economic assistance agreement for the expansion of the Port of Damman.

Exchange of notes at Jidda March 1 and at Riyadh May 1, 1958.

Entered into force May 1, 1958.

9 UST 589; TIAS 4038; 315 UNTS 221.

Agreement on cooperation in the fields of economics, technology, industry and defense.

Signed at Washington June 8, 1974.

Entered into force June 8, 1974.

25 UST 3115; TIAS 7974.

Joint communique on the first session of the U.S.-Saudi Arabian Joint Commission on Economic Cooperation.

Done at Washington February 27, 1975.

Entered into force February 27, 1975.

26 UST 1689; TIAS 8128; 1006 UNTS 121.

Project agreement for technical cooperation in agriculture and water.

Signed at Riyadh November 23, 1975.

Entered into force January 27, 1976.

28 UST 1103; TIAS 8494.

Project agreement for technical cooperation in science and technology, with appendices.

Signed at Riyadh February 29, 1976.

Entered into force August 7, 1978.

29 UST 3393; TIAS 9019; 1123 UNTS 3.

Project agreement for technical cooperation in upgrading and improving the scientific and technical capability of the consumer protection department in the Saudi Arabian Ministry of Commerce.

Signed at Washington May 3, 1977.

Entered into force August 8, 1977.

29 UST 1240; TIAS 8876.

Project agreement for technical cooperation in establishing an information center.

Signed at Washington May 3, 1977.

Entered into force August 10, 1977.

29 UST 1232; TIAS 8875.

Agreement for technical cooperation in desalination, with appendices.

Signed at Washington May 3, 1977.

Entered into force August 30, 1977.

29 UST 1323; TIAS 8878.

Project agreement for technical cooperation in audit administration and training, with annexes.

Signed at Riyadh May 16, 1978.

Entered into force May 25, 1978.

30 UST 1205; TIAS 9246; 1152 UNTS 353.

Project agreement for technical cooperation in customs administration and training.

Signed at Riyadh and Washington June 11 and 22, 1978.

Entered into force August 10, 1978.

30 UST 2165; TIAS 9321; 1170 UNTS 121.

Project agreement for technical cooperation in supply management development, with attachments.

Signed at Riyadh July 13, 1978.

Entered into force August 10, 1978.

30 UST 1719; TIAS 9281; 1152 UNTS 409.

Project agreement for technical cooperation in executive management development.

Signed at Jeddah November 18, 1978.

Entered into force March 4, 1979.

30 UST 2161; TIAS 9320; 1170 UNTS 135.

ENVIRONMENTAL COOPERATION

Agreement for cooperation in the Global Learning and Observations to Benefit the Environment (GLOBE) Program, with appendices.

Signed at Washington September 30, 2002.

Entered into force September 30, 2002.

TIAS

FINANCE

Agreement on guaranteed private investment.

Signed at Washington February 27, 1975.

Entered into force April 26, 1975.

26 UST 459; TIAS 8045; 992 UNTS 231.

METEOROLOGY

Memorandum of understanding for technical cooperation in a meteorological and environmental program, with annex.

Signed at Washington and Jeddah December 7, 2000 and March 3, 2001.

Entered into force March 3, 2001.

TIAS

Amendments

March 15 and April 27, 2006.

August 31 and September 9, 2006.

MISSIONS, MILITARY

Agreement relating to a United States military training mission in Saudi Arabia.

Exchange of notes at Jidda February 8 and 27, 1977.

Entered into force February 27, 1977.

28 UST 2409; TIAS 8558.

POSTAL MATTERS

Memorandum of understanding for the exchange of international express mail, with details of implementation.

Signed at Washington November 2, 1984.

Entered into force February 1, 1985.

TIAS 11009; 2022 UNTS 137.

SHIPPING

Agreement relating to jurisdiction over vessels utilizing the Louisiana Offshore Oil Port.

Exchange of notes at Jidda March 1, 1981 and October 20, 1982.

Entered into force October 20, 1982.

TIAS 10552; 1871 UNTS 165.

TAXATION

Agreement for reciprocal exemption of taxes on income from the international operation of a ship or ships or aircraft.

Signed at Riyadh December 11, 1999.

Entered into force January 31, 2000.

TIAS

SENEGAL

AGRICULTURAL COMMODITIES

Agricultural commodities agreement with exchange of notes.

Signed at Dakar July 3, 1963.

Entered into force July 3, 1963.

15 UST 738; TIAS 5599; 527 UNTS 95.

Amendment

January 24, 1964 (15 UST 738; TIAS 5599; 527 UNTS 95).

Agricultural commodities agreement, with annexes and memorandum of understanding.

Signed at Dakar May 16, 1980.

Entered into force May 16, 1980.

33 UST 3385; TIAS 10239.

Amendments

December 23, 1980 (33 UST 3471; TIAS 10239).

July 14 and 16, 1982 (TIAS 10647; 1935 UNTS 447).

July 22 and 28, 1983 (35 UST 1623; TIAS 10752; 2012 UNTS 376).

March 22 and April 3, 1984 (35 UST 1623; TIAS 10752; 2012 UNTS 376).

Agricultural commodities agreement, with memorandum of understanding and related letter.

Signed at Dakar December 17, 1985.

Entered into force December 17, 1985.

NP

Amendment

July 3, 1986 (NP).

Agricultural commodities agreement.

Signed at Dakar June 1, 1987.

Entered into force June 1, 1987.

NP

Amendment
July 24, 1987 (NP).

Agricultural commodities agreement, with memorandum of understanding.
Signed at Dakar August 3, 1988.
Entered into force August 3, 1988.
NP

Agricultural commodities agreement.
Signed at Dakar April 11, 1989.
Entered into force April 11, 1989.
NP

Agricultural commodities agreement.
Signed at Dakar March 9, 1990.
Entered into force March 9, 1990.
NP

AVIATION

Air transport agreement, with annexes.
Signed at Washington January 11, 2001.
Entered into force August 11, 2003.
TIAS

Memorandum of agreement for the provision of assistance in developing and modernizing the civil aviation infrastructure of Senegal
Signed July 28, 2000.
Entered into force July 28, 2000.
TIAS

DEFENSE

Agreement relating to the furnishing of military equipment, materials and services to Senegal for the purpose of assuring its security and supporting its development.
Exchange of notes at Dakar July 20, 1962.
Entered into force July 20, 1962.
13 UST 1803; TIAS 5127; 458 UNTS 137.

Agreement concerning the provision of training related to defense articles under the United States International Military Education and Training (IMET) Program.
Exchange of notes at Dakar February 25 and July 15, 1983.
Entered into force July 15, 1983.
35 UST 3070; TIAS 10839; 2014 UNTS 555.

Agreement regarding the provision of commodities, services and associated military education and training to assist Senegalese forces participating in the African Crisis Response Initiative.
Exchange of notes at Dakar July 24 and August 29, 1997.
Entered into force August 29, 1997.
TIAS

Agreement regarding the status of United States military and civilian personnel of the United States Department of Defense temporarily present in Senegal in connection with training, humanitarian relief operations, exercises and other agreed activities.
Exchange of notes at Dakar December 21, 2000 and January 11, 2001.
Entered into force January 11, 2001.
NP

Agreement regarding grants under the Foreign Assistance Act of 1961, as amended, and the furnishing of defense articles, related training, and other defense services from the United States of America to the Government of Senegal.
Exchange of notes at Dakar November 22, 2000 and February 2, 2001.
Entered into force February 2, 2001.
TIAS

Acquisition and cross-servicing (mutual logistic support) agreement, with annexes.
Signed at Dakar and Patch Barracks May 8 and 14, 2001.
Entered into force May 14, 2001.
TIAS

ECONOMIC AND TECHNICAL COOPERATION

Agreement providing for economic, financial, technical and related assistance.
Signed at Washington May 13, 1961.
Entered into force May 13, 1961.
12 UST 566; TIAS 4754; 409 UNTS 231.

Agency for International Development
March 23, 1974 (27 UST 2672; TIAS 8339; 1066 UNTS 231).
November 6, 1974 and May 28, 1975 (29 UST 1006; TIAS 8862).
August 5 and 7, 1975 (27 UST 2688; TIAS 8339; 1066 UNTS 239).
March 2 and May 28, 1976 (29 UST 1009; TIAS 8862).
February 21, 1978 (30 UST 3052; TIAS 9377; 1178 UNTS 209).
March 29, 1978 (30 UST 3058; TIAS 9377; 1178 UNTS 213).

EMPLOYMENT

Agreement relating to employment of dependents of staff members of diplomatic and consular missions.
Signed at Dakar April 28, 1998.
Entered into force April 28, 1998.
TIAS

ENVIRONMENTAL COOPERATION

Agreement for cooperation in the Global Learning and Observations to Benefit the Environment (GLOBE) Program, with appendices.
Signed at Dakar March 17, 1995.
Entered into force March 17, 1995.
TIAS

FINANCE

Agreement relating to investment guaranties.
Signed at Dakar June 12, 1963.
Entered into force provisionally June 12, 1963; definitively March 27, 1970.
18 UST 3197; TIAS 6417.

Agreement regarding the consolidation and rescheduling of certain debts owed to or guaranteed by the United States Government and its agencies, with annexes.
Signed at Dakar August 26, 1982.
Entered into force October 25, 1982.
34 UST 1987; TIAS 10475; 1751 UNTS 55.

Agreement regarding the consolidation and rescheduling of certain debts owed to or guaranteed by the United States Government and its agencies, with annexes.
Signed at Washington August 11, 1983.
Entered into force September 13, 1983.
35 UST 2444; TIAS 10808; 2011 UNTS 105.

Agreement regarding the consolidation and rescheduling of certain debts owed to, guaranteed or insured by the United States Government and its agencies, with annexes.
Signed at Dakar August 22, 1984.
Entered into force September 24, 1984.
NP

Agreement regarding the consolidation and rescheduling of certain debts owed to, guaranteed by or insured by the United States Government and its agencies, with annexes.
Signed at Dakar June 5, 1985.
Entered into force July 15, 1985.
NP

Agreement regarding the consolidation and rescheduling of certain debts owed to, guaranteed by or insured by the United States Government and its agencies, with annexes.
Signed at Washington April 10, 1987.
Entered into force May 18, 1987.
NP

Agreement regarding the consolidation and rescheduling of certain debts owed to, guaranteed by or insured by the United States Government and its agencies, with annexes.

Signed at Dakar June 10, 1988.

Entered into force July 28, 1988.

NP

Agreement regarding the consolidation and rescheduling of certain debts owed to, guaranteed by, or insured by the United States Government and its agencies, with annexes.

Signed at Dakar July 14, 1989.

Entered into force August 24, 1989.

NP

Agreement regarding the consolidation and rescheduling of certain debts owed to, guaranteed by, or insured by the United States Government and its agencies, with annexes.

Signed at Dakar July 13, 1990.

Entered into force September 5, 1990.

NP

Agreement regarding the consolidation and rescheduling of certain debts owed to, guaranteed by, or insured by the United States Government and its agencies, with annexes.

Signed at Dakar November 26, 1991.

Entered into force February 10, 1992.

NP

Agreement regarding the consolidation, reduction and rescheduling of certain debts owed to, guaranteed by or insured by the United States Government and its agencies, with annexes.

Signed at Dakar July 28, 1994.

Entered into force August 29, 1994.

NP

Agreement regarding the consolidation, reduction and rescheduling of certain debts owed to, guaranteed by or insured by the United States Government and its agencies, with annexes.

Signed at Dakar August 28, 1995.

Entered into force November 1, 1995.

NP

Amendment

November 17, 1997 and May 28, 1998 (NP).

Agreement regarding the reduction and reorganization of certain debts owed to, guaranteed by, or insured by the United States Government and its agencies, with annexes.

Signed at Dakar December 17, 1998.

Entered into force March 17, 1999.

NP

Agreement regarding the consolidation and reduction of certain debts owed to, guaranteed by, or insured by the United States Government and its agencies, with annexes.

Signed at Dakar July 17, 2001.

Entered into force September 6, 2001.

NP

Amendments

November 26, 2002 and February 24, 2003.

March 18 and May 25, 2004.

Agreement regarding the reduction of certain debts owed to, guaranteed by, or insured by the United States Government, with annexes.

Signed at Dakar November 19, 2004.

Entered into force January 18, 2005.

NP

INTERNATIONAL CRIMINAL COURT

Agreement concerning the surrender of persons to the International Criminal Court.

Signed at Dakar June 19, 2003.

Entered into force June 27, 2003.

TIAS

INVESTMENT

Treaty concerning the reciprocal encouragement and protection of investment, with annex and protocol.

Signed at Washington December 6, 1983.

Entered into force October 25, 1990.

TIAS

PEACE CORPS

Agreement relating to the establishment of a Peace Corps program in Senegal.

Exchange of notes at Dakar January 10 and 17, 1963.

Entered into force January 17, 1963.

14 UST 1622; TIAS 5467.

POSTAL MATTERS

International express mail agreement, with detailed regulations.

Signed at Dakar and Washington June 5 and July 3, 1986.

Entered into force September 1, 1986.

TIAS 11519.

TRACKING STATIONS

Agreement regarding the establishment and operation of a space vehicle tracking and communication facility in connection with the space shuttle.

Exchange of notes at Dakar January 30 and February 5, 1981.

Entered into force February 5, 1981.

33 UST 1028; TIAS 10088; 1295 UNTS 161.

Amendments and extensions

November 30 and December 22, 1981 (33 UST 4550; TIAS 10325).

SERBIA

For agreements prior to June 3, 2006, see SERBIA AND MONTENEGRO and YUGOSLAVIA.

SERBIA AND MONTENEGRO

On June 3, 2006, the Republic of Montenegro declared its independence.

The U.S. is reviewing the continued applicability of the agreements listed below.

For agreements prior to the independence of Serbia and Montenegro, see YUGOSLAVIA.

ECONOMIC AND TECHNICAL COOPERATION

Agreement concerning economic, technical and related assistance.

Signed at Belgrade March 6, 2001.

Entered into force May 11, 2001.

TIAS

FINANCE

Investment incentive agreement.

Signed at Belgrade July 21, 2001.

Entered into force December 12, 2001.

TIAS

Agreement regarding the consolidation, reduction and rescheduling of certain debts owed to, guaranteed by, or insured by the United States Government and its agencies, with annexes.

Signed at Belgrade October 3, 2002.

Entered into force November 12, 2002.

NP

SEYCHELLES

On June 28, 1976 Seychelles became an independent state. By an exchange of notes dated June 29, 1976 between the Government of the United Kingdom and the Government of

Seychelles, it was agreed that all obligations and responsibilities of the Government of the United Kingdom which arise from any valid international instrument shall, as from the 29th of June 1976, be assumed by the Government of Seychelles insofar as such instruments may be held to have application to Seychelles. Also, rights and benefits heretofore enjoyed by the Government of the United Kingdom in virtue of the application of any such international instrument to Seychelles shall, as from the 29th of June 1976, be enjoyed by the Government of Seychelles.

CONSULS

Consular convention between the United States and the United Kingdom.

Signed at Washington June 6, 1951.

Entered into force September 7, 1952.

3 UST 3426; TIAS 2494; 165 UNTS 121.

DEFENSE

Agreement concerning the provision of training related to defense articles under the United States International Military Education and Training (IMET) Program.

Exchange of notes at Victoria November 14, 1985 and February 21, 1986.

Entered into force February 21, 1986.

TIAS 11104.

ECONOMIC AND TECHNICAL COOPERATION

Economic cooperation agreement between the United States and the United Kingdom.

Signed at London July 6, 1948; applicable to Seychelles July 6, 1948.

62 Stat. 2596; TIAS 1795; 12 Bevans 874; 22 UNTS 263.

Amendments

January 3, 1950 (1 UST 184; TIAS 2036; 86 UNTS 304).

May 25, 1951 (2 UST 1292; TIAS 2277; 99 UNTS 308).

February 25, 1953 (4 UST 1528; TIAS 2815; 172 UNTS 332).

EXTRADITION

Extradition treaty between the United States and the United Kingdom.

Signed at London December 22, 1931.

Entered into force June 24, 1935.

47 Stat. 2122; TS 849; 12 Bevans 482; 163 LNTS 59.

INTERNATIONAL CRIMINAL COURT

Agreement regarding the surrender of persons to the International Criminal Court.

Signed at Victoria June 4, 2003.

Entered into force July 17, 2003.

TIAS

MUTUAL SECURITY

Agreement between the United States and the United Kingdom relating to the assurances required under the Mutual Security Act of 1951.

Exchange of notes at London January 8, 1952.

Entered into force January 8, 1952.

3 UST 4665; TIAS 2622; 126 UNTS 307.

PEACE CORPS

Agreement relating to the establishment of a Peace Corps program in the Seychelles.

Exchange of notes at Victoria May 31 and June 9, 1978.

Entered into force June 9, 1978.

30 UST 1916; TIAS 9300; 1153 UNTS 41.

POSTAL MATTERS

International express mail agreement, with detailed regulations.

Signed at Victoria and Washington May 13 and June 15, 1992.

Entered into force September 21, 1992.

TIAS 11871.

TELECOMMUNICATION

Agreement between the United States and the United Kingdom relating to the reciprocal granting of authorizations to permit licensed amateur radio operators of either country to operate their stations in the other country.

Exchange of notes at London November 26, 1965; applicable to Seychelles December 11, 1969.

16 UST 2047; TIAS 5941; 561 UNTS 193.

Agreement between the United States and the United Kingdom extending to certain territories the application of the agreement of November 26, 1965 relating to the reciprocal granting of authorizations to permit licensed amateur radio operators of either country to operate their stations in the other country.

Exchange of notes at London December 11, 1969.

Entered into force December 11, 1969.

20 UST 4089; TIAS 6800; 732 UNTS 334.

TRADE-MARKS

Declaration by the United States and the United Kingdom affording reciprocal protection to trade-marks.

Signed at London October 24, 1877.

Entered into force October 24, 1877.

20 Stat. 703; TS 138; 12 Bevans 198.

SIERRA LEONE

On April 27, 1961 Sierra Leone attained fully responsible status within the British Commonwealth (Sierra Leone Independence Act, 1961). By an exchange of letters, dated May 5, 1961, between the High Commissioner for the United Kingdom in Sierra Leone and the Minister of External Affairs of Sierra Leone, the Government of Sierra Leone agreed to assume, from April 27, 1961, all obligations and responsibilities of the United Kingdom which arise from any valid international instrument insofar as such instrument may be held to have application to Sierra Leone. Also, rights and benefits enjoyed by the Government of the United Kingdom by virtue of the application of any such international instrument to Sierra Leone are from April 27, 1961 enjoyed by the Government of Sierra Leone.

AGRICULTURAL COMMODITIES

Agricultural commodities agreement with exchange of notes.

Signed at Freetown, January 29, 1965.

Entered into force January 29, 1965.

16 UST 71; TIAS 5762; 542 UNTS 87.

Amendments

May 5, 1965 (16 UST 908; TIAS 5831; 549 UNTS 346).

March 10, 1966 (17 UST 187; TIAS 5970; 579 UNTS 338).

June 2, 1966 (17 UST 833; TIAS 6041; 593 UNTS 334).

Agricultural commodities agreement with annex.

Signed at Freetown January 23, 1968.

Entered into force January 23, 1968.

19 UST 4516; TIAS 6444; 698 UNTS 43.

Related agreements

April 8, 1969 (20 UST 664; TIAS 6673; 707 UNTS 233).

April 30, 1971 (22 UST 599; TIAS 7110; 792 UNTS 351).

November 30, 1971 (22 UST 1781; TIAS 7218).

Agricultural commodities agreement.

Signed at Freetown August 18, 1977.

Entered into force August 18, 1977.

29 UST 1482; TIAS 8891.

Agricultural commodities agreement.
Signed at Freetown August 31, 1978.
Entered into force August 31, 1978.
30 UST 672; TIAS 9210; 1150 UNTS 211.

Related agreements
August 23, 1979 (31 UST 496; TIAS 9617).
September 5 and 6, 1979 (31 UST 503; TIAS 9617).
August 8, 1980 (32 UST 2310; TIAS 9840).
September 29, 1980 (32 UST 4194; TIAS 9939).
March 25, 1981 (33 UST 1505; TIAS 10125; 1307 UNTS 429).
August 17 and 18, 1981 (33 UST 1515; TIAS 10125; 1307 UNTS 437).
July 28, 1982 (TIAS 10516).
April 29, 1983 (35 UST 4835; TIAS 10968).
February 23, 1984 (35 UST 4835; TIAS 10968).

Agricultural commodities agreement.
Signed at Freetown May 9, 1985.
Entered into force May 9, 1985.
NP

Agricultural commodities agreement.
Signed at Freetown May 5, 1986.
Entered into force May 5, 1986.
NP

Amendment
August 1, 1986 (NP).

Agricultural commodities agreement.
Signed at Freetown June 10, 1987.
Entered into force June 10, 1987.
NP

Amendments
August 18, 1987 (NP).
June 16, 1988 (NP).
September 27, 1988 (NP).

Agricultural commodities agreement.
Signed at Freetown June 8, 1990.
Entered into force June 8, 1990.
NP

AVIATION

Arrangement between the United States and the United Kingdom relating to pilot licenses to operate civil aircraft.
Exchange of notes at Washington March 28 and April 5, 1935.
Entered into force May 5, 1935.
49 Stat. 3731; EAS 77; 12 Bevans 513; 162 LNTS 59.

Agreement between the United States and the United Kingdom relating to air services.
Signed at Bermuda February 11, 1946.
Entered into force February 11, 1946.
60 Stat. 1499; TIAS 1507; 12 Bevans 726; 3 UNTS 253.

CONSULS

Consular convention between the United States and the United Kingdom.
Signed at Washington June 6, 1951.
Entered into force September 7, 1952.
3 UST 3426; TIAS 2494; 165 UNTS 121.

DEFENSE

Agreement concerning the provision of training related to defense articles under the United States International Military Education and Training (IMET) Program.
Exchange of notes at Freetown April 1 and May 26, 1982.
Entered into force May 26, 1982.
34 UST 1115; TIAS 10397; 1566 UNTS 125.

Agreement regarding grants under the Foreign Assistance Act of 1961, as amended, and the furnishing of defense articles, related training and other defense services to the Government of Sierra Leone.
Exchange of notes at Freetown May 3 and 19, 1999.
Entered into force May 19, 1999.
TIAS

ECONOMIC AND TECHNICAL COOPERATION

General agreement for a program of economic, technical and related assistance.
Signed at Freetown May 5, 1961.
Entered into force May 5, 1961.
12 UST 547; TIAS 4752; 409 UNTS 193.

EMPLOYMENT

Agreement relating to the employment of dependents of official government employees.
Exchange of notes at Freetown January 17 and February 24, 1997.
Entered into force February 24, 1997.
TIAS

EXTRADITION

Extradition treaty between the United States and the United Kingdom.
Signed at London December 22, 1931.
Entered into force June 24, 1935.
47 Stat. 2122; TS 849; 12 Bevans 482; 163 LNTS 59.

FINANCE

Agreement relating to investment guaranties under section 413 (b)(4) of the Mutual Security Act of 1954, as amended.
Exchange of notes at Freetown May 16 and 19, 1961.
Entered into force May 19, 1961.
12 UST 619; TIAS 4759; 409 UNTS 251.

Amendment
December 28, 1962 and November 13, 1963 (14 UST 1667; TIAS 5470; 494 UNTS 324).

Agreement regarding the consolidation and rescheduling of certain debts owed to, guaranteed by or insured by the United States Government and its agencies, with annex.
Signed at Freetown August 28, 1985.
Entered into force October 23, 1985.
NP

Agreement regarding the consolidation and rescheduling of certain debts owed to, guaranteed by or insured by the United States Government and its agencies, with annexes.
Signed at Freetown August 21, 1987.
Entered into force November 5, 1987.
NP

Agreement regarding the consolidation and rescheduling or refinancing of certain debts owed to, guaranteed by, or insured by the United States Government and its agencies, with annexes.
Signed at Freetown April 19, 1993.
Entered into force June 18, 1993.
NP

Agreement regarding the consolidation and rescheduling of certain debts owed to, guaranteed by or insured by the United States Government, with annexes.
Signed at Freetown January 11, 1995.
Entered into force March 1, 1995.
NP

Agreement regarding the consolidation and rescheduling of certain debts owed to, guaranteed by or insured by the United States Government, with annexes.
Signed at Freetown August 7, 1996.
Entered into force October 16, 1996.
NP

Agreement regarding the consolidation and reduction of certain debts owed to, guaranteed by, or insured by the United States Government, with annexes.
Signed at Freetown April 25, 2003.
Entered into force June 9, 2003.
NP

INTERNATIONAL CRIMINAL COURT

Agreement regarding the surrender of persons to the International Criminal Court.

Signed at Freetown March 31, 2003.

Entered into force May 20, 2003.

TIAS

JUDICIAL PROCEDURE

Agreement to facilitate the conduct of litigation with international aspects in either country.

Exchange of notes at Freetown March 31 and May 6, 1966.

Entered into force May 6, 1966.

17 UST 944; TIAS 6056; 594 UNTS 47.

PEACE CORPS

Agreement relating to the establishment of a Peace Corps program in Sierra Leone.

Exchange of notes at Freetown December 29, 1961.

Entered into force December 29, 1961.

12 UST 3181; TIAS 4922; 434 UNTS 43.

POSTAL MATTERS

Parcel post convention.

Signed at Freetown February 27 and at Washington April 16, 1930; operative May 1, 1930.

46 Stat. 2736; Post Office Department print; 109 LNTS 9.

International express mail agreement, with detailed regulations.

Signed at Freetown and Washington May 31 and July 26, 1988.

Entered into force August 15, 1988.

TIAS 11591.

Postal money order agreement.

Signed at Freetown and Washington March 29 and July 18, 1989.

Entered into force September 18, 1989.

TIAS 11683.

INTELPOST memorandum of understanding, with detailed regulations.

Signed at Freetown and Washington June 5 and 19, 1995.

Entered into force August 1, 1995.

NP

PROPERTY

Convention between the United States and the United Kingdom relating to the tenure and disposition of real and personal property.

Signed at Washington March 2, 1899; applicable to Sierra Leone February 9, 1901.

31 Stat. 1939; TS 146; 12 Bevans 246.

TELECOMMUNICATION

Agreement relating to the reciprocal granting of authorizations to permit licensed amateur radio operators of either country to operate their stations in the other country.

Exchange of notes at Freetown August 14 and 16, 1965.

Entered into force August 16, 1965.

16 UST 1131; TIAS 5856; 579 UNTS 55.

Agreement relating to radio communications between amateur stations on behalf of third parties.

Exchange of notes at Freetown October 23, 1985 and June 18, 1986.

Entered into force July 18, 1986.

TIAS 11358.

TRADE-MARKS

Declaration by the United States and the United Kingdom relating to reciprocal protection to trade-marks.

Signed at London October 24, 1877.

Entered into force October 24, 1877.

20 Stat. 703; TS 138; 12 Bevans 198.

SINGAPORE

On August 9, 1965 Singapore became an independent and sovereign state. Article 13 of the Constitution and Malaysia (Singapore Amendment) Act, 1965 annexed to the Independence of Singapore agreement, 1965 reads in part as follows: "Any treaty, agreement or convention entered into before Singapore Day between the Yang di-Pertuan Agong or the Government of Malaysia and another country or countries, including those deemed to be so by Article 169 of the Constitution of Malaysia shall insofar as such instruments have application to Singapore, be deemed to be a treaty, agreement or convention between Singapore and that country or countries, and any decision taken by an international organization and accepted before Singapore Day by the Government of Malaysia shall insofar as that decision has application to Singapore be deemed to be a decision of an international organization of which Singapore is a member."

AVIATION

Arrangement between the United States and the United Kingdom relating to pilot licenses to operate civil aircraft.

Exchange of notes at Washington March 28, and April 5, 1935.

Entered into force May 5, 1935.

49 Stat. 3731; EAS 77; 12 Bevans 513; 162 LNTS 59.

Memorandum of agreement relating to the provision of flight inspection services.

Signed at Washington and Singapore August 16 and October 25, 1978.

Entered into force October 25, 1978; effective October 1, 1978.

30 UST 263; TIAS 9195; 1150 UNTS 263.

Air transport agreement, with annexes.

Signed at Singapore April 8, 1997.

Entered into force April 8, 1997.

TIAS

Agreement for the promotion of aviation safety.

Signed at Singapore February 24, 2004.

Entered into force February 24, 2004.

TIAS

CONSULS

Consular convention between the United States and the United Kingdom.

Signed at Washington June 6, 1951.

Entered into force September 7, 1952.

3 UST 3426; TIAS 2494; 165 UNTS 121.

COPYRIGHT

Agreement regarding the establishment of copyright relations, with enclosures.

Exchange of letters at Washington April 16 and 27, 1987.

Entered into force April 27, 1987; effective May 18, 1987.

TIAS 11928.

DEFENSE

Agreement relating to the purchase by Malaya of military equipment, materials, and services from the United States.

Exchange of notes at Washington June 30 and July 9, 1958.

Entered into force July 9, 1958.

9 UST 1235; TIAS 4108; 336 UNTS 79.

Agreement relating to the establishment of a United States Air Force management training assistance team in Singapore, with appendices.

Exchange of letters at Singapore February 23 and 24, 1977.

Entered into force February 24, 1977.

29 UST 1474; TIAS 8889.

Memorandum of understanding for the exchange of individual personnel between the United States Army Western Command and the Republic of Singapore Armed Forces.

Signed at Singapore January 5, 1981.

Entered into force January 5, 1981.

NP

Agreement concerning the provision of training related to defense articles under the United States International Military Education and Training (IMET) Program.

Exchange of notes at Singapore May 12 and June 23, 1981.

Entered into force June 23, 1981.

33 UST 2034; TIAS 10166; 1529 UNTS 491.

Memorandum of understanding concerning exchange of service personnel between the United States Navy and Republic of Singapore Air Force.

Signed at Singapore and Washington July 19 and September 1, 1982.

Entered into force September 1, 1982.

34 UST 2151; TIAS 10482; 1751 UNTS 115.

Agreement concerning general security of military information.

Exchange of notes at Singapore June 25, 1982 and March 9, 1983.

Entered into force March 9, 1983.

35 UST 2796; TIAS 10819; 1590 UNTS 85.

Memorandum of understanding concerning configuration management of tactical command, control and communications standards, with annexes.

Signed at Camp Smith, Hawaii February 22, 1991.

Entered into force February 22, 1991.

TIAS 12369.

Agreement on the status of Singapore personnel in the United States, with agreed minutes.

Signed at Singapore December 3, 1993.

Entered into force December 3, 1993.

TIAS 12519.

Agreement concerning exchange of research and development information, with appendix.

Signed at Washington December 4, 1995.

Entered into force December 4, 1995.

TIAS 12370.

Agreement concerning technology research and development projects, with annex.

Signed at Washington May 2, 1998.

Entered into force May 2, 1998.

TIAS

Memorandum of agreement for research, development, testing, and evaluation projects, with annex.

Signed at Honolulu February 21, 2003.

Entered into force February 21, 2003.

TIAS

Agreement regarding the exchange of engineers and scientists, with annexes.

Signed at Singapore and Washington March 8 and 22, 2004.

Entered into force March 22, 2004.

NP

Strategic framework agreement for a closer cooperation partnership in defense and security.

Signed at Washington July 12, 2005.

Entered into force July 12, 2005.

TIAS

Memorandum of arrangement regarding assignment of liaison officers, with annex.

Signed at Norfolk and Washington January 9 and 23, 2006.

Entered into force January 23, 2006.

TIAS

Information exchange annex to the agreement of December 4, 1995 regarding master information exchange.

Signed at Singapore March 21, 2006.

Entered into force March 21, 2006.

TIAS

Agreement regarding the assignment of liaison officers, with annex.

Signed at Arlington May 15, 2006.

Entered into force May 15, 2006.

TIAS

ECONOMIC AND TECHNICAL COOPERATION

Economic cooperation agreement between the United States and the United Kingdom.

Signed at London July 6, 1948; applicable to Singapore July 6, 1948.

62 Stat. 2596; TIAS 1795; 12 Bevans 874; 22 UNTS 263.

Amendments

January 3, 1950 (1 UST 184; TIAS 2036; 86 UNTS 304).

May 25, 1951 (2 UST 1292; TIAS 2277; 99 UNTS 308).

February 25, 1953 (4 UST 1528; TIAS 2815; 172 UNTS 332).

EXTRADITION

Extradition treaty between the United States and the United Kingdom.

Signed at London December 22, 1931.

Entered into force June 24, 1935.

47 Stat. 2122; TS 849; 12 Bevans 482; 163 LNTS 59.

Agreement confirming the continuance in force between the United States and Singapore of the December 22, 1931 extradition treaty between the United States and the United Kingdom.

Exchange of notes at Singapore April 23 and June 10, 1969.

Entered into force June 10, 1969.

20 UST 2764; TIAS 6744; 723 UNTS 201.

FINANCE

Agreement relating to investment guaranties.

Exchange of notes at Singapore March 25, 1966.

Entered into force March 25, 1966.

17 UST 534; TIAS 5999; 580 UNTS 221.

HEALTH

Agreement establishing the Regional Emergency Diseases Intervention (REDI) Center.

Signed at Singapore November 22, 2005.

Entered into force April 7, 2006.

TIAS

INTERNATIONAL CRIMINAL COURT

Agreement regarding the surrender of persons to international tribunals.

Exchange of notes at Singapore October 17, 2003.

Entered into force October 17, 2003.

TIAS

JUDICIAL ASSISTANCE

Agreement concerning the investigation of drug trafficking offences and the seizure and forfeiture of proceeds and instrumentalities of drug trafficking, with exchange of notes.

Signed at Singapore November 3, 2000.

Entered into force February 12, 2001.

TIAS

MAPPING

Basic exchange and cooperative agreement concerning geospatial information, with annexes and appendices.

Signed at Bethesda December 21, 2006.

Entered into force December 21, 2006.

NP

POSTAL MATTERS

Parcel post convention.

Signed at Kuala Lumpur January 21 and at Washington March 22, 1935.

Entered into force April 1, 1935.

49 Stat. 3133; Post Office Department print; 161 LNTS 41.

International express mail agreement, with detailed regulations.

Signed at Singapore and Washington January 5 and 10, 1979.

Entered into force February 9, 1979; effective January 1, 1979.

30 UST 3383; TIAS 9396; 1180 UNTS 109.

Memorandum of understanding concerning the operation of the INTELPOST field trial, with details of implementation.

Signed at Singapore and Washington November 26, 1986 and February 5, 1987.

Entered into force February 5, 1987; effective December 1, 1986.

TIAS 11307.

PROPERTY

Convention between the United States and the United Kingdom relating to tenure and disposition of real and personal property.[1]

Signed at Washington March 2, 1899.

Entered into force August 7, 1900.

31 Stat. 1939; TS 146; 12 Bevans 246.

NOTE

1 Notification given on February 9, 1901 of application to the Straits Settlements.

SHIPPING

Agreement relating to jurisdiction over vessels utilizing the Louisiana Offshore Oil Port.

Exchange of notes at Singapore September 1, 1983 and January 16, 1984.

Entered into force January 17, 1984.

35 UST 4262; TIAS 10926; 2015 UNTS 117.

SOCIAL SECURITY

Agreement concerning United States participation on a limited voluntary basis in the Central Provident Fund Act for certain employees of the United States Government in Singapore.

Exchange of notes at Singapore September 8 and 9, 1975.

Entered into force September 9, 1975.

26 UST 2734; TIAS 8190; 1052 UNTS 297.

TAXATION

Agreement concerning reciprocal exemption from income tax of income derived from the international operation of ships and aircraft.

Exchange of notes at Singapore July 5 and 28, 1988.

Entered into force July 28, 1988.

TIAS 11658; 2204 UNTS 699.

TRADE AND COMMERCE

Agreement relating to trade in cotton, wool and man-made fiber textiles and textile products, with annexes.

Exchange of notes at Singapore May 30 and June 5, 1986.

Entered into force June 5, 1986; effective January 1, 1986.

NP

Amendment and extension

March 6, April 1 and July 22, 1991 (NP).

United States–Singapore free trade agreement, with annexes and related exchanges of letters.

Signed at Washington May 6, 2003.

Entered into force January 1, 2004.

TIAS

TRADE-MARKS

Declaration by the United States and the United Kingdom relating to reciprocal protection to trade-marks.

Signed at London October 24, 1877.

Entered into force October 24, 1877.

20 Stat. 703; TS 138; 12 Bevans 198.

VISAS

Agreement relating to visas.

Exchange of notes at London October 15 and 22, 1954.

Agreement continuing in force the 1954 agreement with respect to the Federation of Malaya.

Exchange of letters at Kuala Lumpur March 5 and 12, 1958.

SLOVAK REPUBLIC

For agreements prior to the independence of the Slovak Republic, see CZECHOSLOVAKIA.

ATOMIC ENERGY

Renewal arrangement for the exchange of technical information and cooperation in nuclear safety matters, with addenda.

Signed at Vienna September 21, 2000.

Entered into force September 21, 2000.

TIAS

Extension

September 26, 2005.

AVIATION

Air transport agreement, with annexes.

Signed at Bratislava January 22, 2001.

Entered into force February 7, 2001.

TIAS

CULTURAL HERITAGE

Agreement on protection and preservation of certain cultural sites and monuments.

Signed at Washington March 9, 2001.

Entered into force March 9, 2001.

TIAS

DEFENSE

Agreement concerning security measures for the protection of classified military information.

Signed at Washington April 11, 1995.

Entered into force April 11, 1995.

TIAS 12246.

Acquisition and cross-servicing agreement, with annex.

Signed at Bratislava December 15, 1998.

Entered into force December 15, 1998.

TIAS

EDUCATION

Agreement concerning the J. William Fulbright Commission for Educational Exchange in the Slovak Republic.

Signed at Bratislava March 22, 2005.

Entered into force April 21, 2005; effective September 23, 2004.

TIAS

EMPLOYMENT

Agreement relating to the employment of dependents of official government employees.

Exchange of notes at Bratislava April 8, 1994, February 17 and July 12, 1995.

Entered into force July 12, 1995.

TIAS 12677.

INVESTMENT

Additional protocol to the treaty between the United States and the Czech and Slovak Federal Republic concerning the reciprocal encouragement and protection of investment of October 22, 1991.

Signed at Brussels September 22, 2003.

Entered into force July 13, 2004.

TIAS

NORTH ATLANTIC TREATY

Agreement to treat the agreement of June 19, 1995, among the States Parties to the North Atlantic Treaty and other States participating in the Partnership for Peace regarding the status of their forces as binding between the United States and Slovakia.

Exchange of notes at Bratislava August 2 and 4, 1995.

Entered into force August 4, 1995.

TIAS

POSTAL MATTERS

International express mail agreement, with detailed regulations.

Signed at Bratislava and Washington June 24 and 27, 1994.

Entered into force August 1, 1994.

NP

SCIENTIFIC COOPERATION

Memorandum of understanding on science and engineering cooperation, with annexes.

Signed at Bratislava July 14, 1994.

Entered into force July 14, 1994.

TIAS 12557.

Agreement on scientific and technological cooperation, with annexes.

Signed at Washington September 12, 2000.

Entered into force October 24, 2000.

TIAS

TAXATION

Convention for the avoidance of double taxation and the prevention of fiscal evasion with respect to taxes on income and capital.[1]

Signed at Bratislava October 8, 1993.

Entered into force December 30, 1993.

TIAS

NOTE

1 With understanding.

TRADE AND COMMERCE

Agreement relating to trade in textiles and textile products, with attachment.

Exchange of notes at Bratislava August 6 and October 6, 1993.

Entered into force October 6, 1993; effective June 1, 1993.

NP

Amendment

April 6 and 29, 1994 (NP).

SLOVENIA

For agreements prior to the independence of Slovenia, see YUGOSLAVIA.

CULTURAL PROPERTY

Agreement on the protection and preservation of certain cultural properties.

Signed at Washington May 8, 1996.

Entered into force June 23, 1997.

TIAS 12752.

DEFENSE

Agreement concerning the provision of training related to defense articles under the United States International Military Education and Training (IMET) Program.

Exchange of notes at Ljubljana July 29 and August 6, 1993.

Entered into force August 6, 1993.

NP

Security agreement concerning security measures for the protection of classified military information.

Signed at Washington May 8, 1996.

Entered into force June 27, 1997.

TIAS 12753.

Agreement concerning the overflight and transit through the territory and airspace of Slovenia by U.S. aircraft, vehicles and personnel for purposes of supporting security, transition and reconstruction operations in Iraq.

Exchange of notes at Ljubljana June 9 and 11, 2003.

Entered into force September 2, 2003.

TIAS

Acquisition and cross servicing agreement, with annexes and attachment.

Signed at Ljubljana December 23, 2003.

Entered into force July 6, 2005.

TIAS

EDUCATION

Memorandum of understanding concerning the exchange of graduate students, post-doctoral researchers and lecturers under the auspices of the Fulbright Program.

Signed at Ljubljana December 8, 1993.

Entered into force January 20, 1999.

TIAS

EMPLOYMENT

Agreement relating to the employment of dependents of official government employees.

Exchange of notes at Ljubljana April 30 and May 8, 1998.

Entered into force June 10, 1998.

TIAS

FINANCE

Investment incentive agreement.

Signed at Washington April 26, 1994.

Entered into force September 8, 1994.

TIAS 12178.

NUCLEAR MATERIAL

Agreement for cooperation in the prevention of illicit trafficking in nuclear and other radioactive materials.

Signed at Ljubljana April 4, 2005.

Entered into force May 23, 2005.

TIAS

POSTAL MATTERS

International express mail agreement, with detailed regulations.

Signed at Ljubljana and Washington January 27 and March 22, 1993.

Entered into force May 1, 1993.

TIAS 11918.

SCIENTIFIC COOPERATION

Agreement for scientific and technological cooperation, with annexes.

Signed at Ljubljana June 21, 1999.

Entered into force December 17, 1999.

TIAS

TAXATION

Convention for the avoidance of double taxation and the prevention of fiscal evasion with respect to taxes on income and capital.

Signed at Ljubljana June 21, 1999.

Entered into force June 22, 2001.

TIAS

WEAPONS

Agreement concerning cooperation in the prevention of the proliferation of weapons of mass destruction.

Signed at Ljubljana June 21, 1999.

Entered into force June 26, 2000.

TIAS

Amendment

February 27 and April 5, 2004.

SOLOMON ISLANDS

On July 7, 1978, Solomon Islands became an independent state. In a note dated July 7, 1978 to the Secretary General of the United Nations, the Prime Minister made a statement reading in part as follows:

"I have the honour to inform you that Solomon Islands is now an independent nation ready to participate with other nations in fulfilling obligations under international law with respect to treaties to which this Government succeeded upon Independence. However, it is necessary to examine in depth such treaties to ascertain whether or not under customary international law any may have lapsed. Until this has been done the Government of Solomon Islands wish —

(a) that it be presumed that each treaty has been legally succeeded to by Solomon Islands; and

(b) that future action be based on the presumption in (a) above.

You will be notified in due course of those treaties this Government regards as having lapsed and those treaties which this Government wishes to terminate. Notice of lapse or termination in an appropriate form will also be given to the country or countries that is or are party to those treaties."

DEFENSE

Agreement concerning the provision of training related to defense articles under the United States International Military Education and Training (IMET) Program.

Exchange of notes at Port Moresby and Honiara June 7 and August 18, 1983.

Entered into force August 18, 1983.

35 UST 1699; TIAS 10759; 2011 UNTS 107.

Agreement concerning the status of members of the United States Forces in Solomon Islands.

Signed at Honiara July 3, 1991.

Entered into force July 3, 1991.

TIAS

ECONOMIC AND TECHNICAL COOPERATION

Economic cooperation agreement between the United States and the United Kingdom.

Signed at London July 6, 1948; applicable to Solomon Islands July 6, 1948.

62 Stat. 2596; TIAS 1795; 12 Bevans 874; 22 UNTS 263.

Amendments

January 3, 1950 (1 UST 184; TIAS 2036; 86 UNTS 304).

May 25, 1951 (2 UST 1292; TIAS 2277; 99 UNTS 308).

February 25, 1953 (4 UST 1528; TIAS 2815; 172 UNTS 332).

EXTRADITION

Extradition treaty between the United States and the United Kingdom, with protocol of signature and exchange of notes.

Signed at London June 8, 1972.

Entered into force January 21, 1977.

28 UST 277; TIAS 8468.

INTERNATIONAL CRIMINAL COURT

Agreement regarding the surrender of persons to the International Criminal Court.

Signed at Washington September 19, 2003.

Entered into force March 17, 2004.

TIAS

MUTUAL SECURITY

Agreement between the United States and the United Kingdom relating to the assurances required under the Mutual Security Act of 1951.

Exchange of notes at London January 8, 1952; applicable to Solomon Islands January 8, 1952.

3 UST 4665; TIAS 2622; 126 UNTS 307.

PEACE CORPS

Agreement concerning the program of the Peace Corps in the Solomon Islands.

Signed at Honiara November 6, 1998.

Entered into force November 6, 1998.

TIAS

POSTAL MATTERS

International express mail agreement, with detailed regulations.

Signed at Honiara and Washington April 19 and June 27, 1991.

Entered into force August 1, 1991.

TIAS 11808.

TELECOMMUNICATION

Agreement between the United States and the United Kingdom relating to the reciprocal granting of authorizations to permit licensed amateur radio operators of either country to operate their stations in the other country.

Exchange of notes at London November 26, 1965; applicable to the Solomon Islands December 11, 1969.

16 UST 2047; TIAS 5941; 561 UNTS 193.

Agreement between the United States and the United Kingdom extending to certain territories the application of the agreement relating to the reciprocal granting of authorizations to permit licensed amateur radio operators of either country to operate their stations in the other country.

Exchange of notes at London December 11, 1969.

Entered into force December 11, 1969.

20 UST 4089; TIAS 6800; 732 UNTS 334.

SOMALIA

AGRICULTURAL COMMODITIES

Agricultural commodities agreement with annex.

Signed at Washington March 15, 1968.

Entered into force March 15, 1968.

19 UST 4698; TIAS 6465; 698 UNTS 95.

Agricultural commodities agreement.

Signed at Mogadishu March 20, 1978.

Entered into force March 20, 1978.

30 UST 827; TIAS 9222.

Amendment

July 18 and August 10, 1978 (30 UST 2351; TIAS 9341; 1171 UNTS 370).

Related agreements

July 11, 1979 (34 UST 1751; TIAS 10454; 1750 UNTS 125).

June 25, 1980 (32 UST 2245; TIAS 9833).

August 14 and 17, 1980 (32 UST 2245; TIAS 9833).

January 12, 1981 (33 UST 828; TIAS 10065; 1268 UNTS 65).

June 17, 1982 (34 UST 1439; TIAS 10429).

January 30, 1983 (TIAS 10637; 1578 UNTS 29).

February 29, 1984 (35 UST 4843; TIAS 10969).

Agricultural commodities agreement.

Signed at Mogadishu March 24, 1985.

Entered into force March 24, 1985.

NP

Related agreements

February 27, 1986 (NP).

August 9, 1987 (NP).

DEFENSE

Agreement concerning the furnishing of defense articles and services to Somalia.

Exchange of notes at Mogadishu March 22 and 23 and April 19 and 29, 1978.

Entered into force April 29, 1978.

32 UST 1683; TIAS 9794.

Agreement concerning the provision of training related to defense articles under the United States International Military Education and Training (IMET) Program.

Exchange of notes at Mogadishu April 5 and June 6, 1981.

Entered into force June 6, 1981.

33 UST 2041; TIAS 10167; 1529 UNTS 477.

ECONOMIC AND TECHNICAL COOPERATION

Agreement on economic and technical cooperation.

Exchange of notes at Mogadishu June 14, October 12 and 13, 1981.

Entered into force October 13, 1981.

33 UST 3975; TIAS 10276; 1549 UNTS 325.

Agency for International Development

June 7, 1976 (29 UST 998; TIAS 8859; 1115 UNTS 59).

December 18, 1977 (29 UST 5297; TIAS 9109).

FINANCE

15 UST 6; TIAS 5512; 505 UNTS 165.

Agreement regarding the consolidation and rescheduling of certain debts owed to, guaranteed by or insured by the United States Government and its agencies, with annexes.

Signed at Washington May 9, 1985.

Entered into force June 12, 1985.

NP

Agreement regarding the consolidation and rescheduling of certain debts owed to, guaranteed by or insured by the United States Government and its agencies, with annexes.

Signed at Mogadishu January 25, 1988.

Entered into force February 26, 1988.

NP

MAPPING

Agreement concerning mapping, charting and geodesy cooperation, with annex.

Signed at Washington and Mogadishu December 31, 1984.

Entered into force December 31, 1984.

TIAS 11224.

PEACE CORPS

Agreement relating to the establishment of a Peace Corps program in the Somali Republic.

Exchange of notes at Mogadishu March 29 and April 17, 1962.

Entered into force April 17, 1962.

13 UST 499; TIAS 5016; 436 UNTS 107.

POSTAL MATTERS

International express mail agreement, with detailed regulations.

Signed at Mogadishu and Washington June 28 and July 26, 1988.

Entered into force August 15, 1988.

TIAS 11592.

SOUTH AFRICA

ATOMIC ENERGY

Agreement for cooperation concerning peaceful uses of nuclear energy, with annex and agreed minute.

Signed at Pretoria August 25, 1995.

Entered into force December 4, 1997.

TIAS 12685.

Memorandum of cooperation providing for the exchange of information and co-operation in nuclear safety, safeguards and physical security.

Signed at Vienna September 22, 2004.

Entered into force September 22, 2004.

TIAS

Arrangement for the exchange of technical information and cooperation in nuclear safety matters, with addenda.

Signed at Vienna September 28, 2005.

Entered into force September 28, 2005.

TIAS

AVIATION

Air navigation arrangement.

Exchange of notes at Pretoria March 17 and September 20, 1933.

Entered into force September 20, 1933.

48 Stat. 1828; EAS 54; 11 Bevans 462; 148 LNTS 189.

Arrangement relating to pilot licenses to operate civil aircraft.

Exchange of notes at Pretoria March 17 and September 20, 1933.

Entered into force September 20, 1933.

48 Stat. 1837; EAS 55; 11 Bevans 469; 148 LNTS 203.

Arrangement relating to certificates of airworthiness for imported aircraft.

Exchange of notes at Pretoria October 29, 1954, and February 22, 1955.

Entered into force February 22, 1955.

6 UST 657; TIAS 3200; 247 UNTS 247.

Amendment

June 7 and October 8, 1984 (TIAS 11024; 2024 UNTS 2).

Agreement on aviation security.

Exchanges of notes at Pretoria August 19, October 3, 11 and 30, 1991.

Entered into force October 30, 1991.

TIAS 11788; 2202 UNTS 283.

Air transport agreement, with annex.

Signed at Washington July 23, 1996.

Entered into force July 23, 1996.

TIAS 12785.

Memorandum of cooperation concerning mutual cooperation in the area of air navigation and air traffic control.

Signed at Washington and Pretoria May 15 and 20, 1998.

Entered into force May 20, 1998.

TIAS

CONSERVATION

Terms of reference of the Conservation, Environment and Water Committee of the South Africa-United States Binational Commission.

Signed at Pretoria December 5, 1995.

Entered into force December 5, 1995.

TIAS 12706.

CONSULS

Convention to regulate commerce (article IV) between the United States and the United Kingdom.

Signed at London July 3, 1815; effective July 3, 1815.

8 Stat. 228; TS 110; 12 Bevans 49.

DEFENSE

Agreement relating to mutual defense assistance.

Exchange of notes at Washington November 9, 1951.

Entered into force November 9, 1951.

3 UST 2565; TIAS 2424; 160 UNTS 41.

Agreement concerning the provision of training under the United States International Military Education and Training (IMET) Program.

Exchange of notes at Pretoria June 14 and July 11, 1994.

Entered into force July 11, 1994.

NP

Agreement regarding grants under the Foreign Assistance Act of 1961, as amended, and the furnishing of defense articles, related training and other defense services from the United States to South Africa.

Exchange of notes at Pretoria November 8, 1994 and October 24, 1995.

Entered into force October 24, 1995.

TIAS

Agreement concerning cooperation on defense trade controls.

Signed at Pretoria January 24, 1997.

Entered into force January 24, 1997.

TIAS 12825.

Agreement concerning security measures for the protection of classified military information.

Signed at Pretoria November 20, 1998.

Entered into force November 20, 1998.

TIAS

Agreement regarding the status of military personnel and civilian employees of the U.S. Department of Defense who may be present in the Republic of South Africa in connection with mutually agreed exercises and activities.

Exchange of notes at Pretoria April 9 and June 10, 1999.

Entered into force June 10, 1999.

NP

Acquisition and cross-servicing agreement, with annexes.

Signed at Pretoria May 8, 2001.

Entered into force May 8, 2001.

TIAS

ECONOMIC AND TECHNICAL COOPERATION

Economic, technical and related assistance agreement.

Signed at Pretoria December 5, 1995.

Entered into force December 5, 1995.

TIAS 12707.

Agency for International Development

September 26, 1995 (NP).

September 28, 1995 (NP).

September 27, 1996 (NP).

September 27, 1996 (NP).

July 31, 1997 (NP).

July 31, 1997 (NP).

July 31 and August 22, 1997 (NP).

September 29, 1997 (NP).

September 30, 1998 (NP).

September 30, 1998 (NP).

September 21, 2005 (NP).

EDUCATION

Agreement concerning the establishment of the South African-United States commission for educational exchange.

Signed at Cape Town February 17, 1997.

Entered into force February 17, 1997.

TIAS

Amendment

March 12 and July 8, 2004.

ENVIRONMENTAL COOPERATION

Agreement for cooperation in the Global Learning and Observations to Benefit the Environment (GLOBE) Program, with annexes.

Signed at Cape Town February 17, 1997.

Entered into force February 17, 1997.

TIAS

EXTRADITION

Extradition treaty.

Signed at Washington September 16, 1999.

Entered into force June 25, 2001.

TIAS

FINANCE

Investment incentive agreement.

Signed at Cape Town November 30, 1993.

Entered into force February 10, 1994.

TIAS 12169.

HEALTH

Memorandum of understanding for cooperation in the fields of public health and biomedical research.

Signed at Washington May 23, 2000.

Entered into force May 23, 2000.

TIAS

JUDICIAL ASSISTANCE

Treaty on mutual legal assistance in criminal matters.

Signed at Washington September 16, 1999.

Entered into force June 25, 2001.

TIAS

LEND-LEASE

Agreement placing all forms of mutual aid reciprocally on a cash basis.

Exchange of notes at Washington April 17, 1945.

Entered into force April 17, 1945.

60 Stat. 1576; TIAS 1511; 11 Bevans 486; 90 UNTS 267.

Agreement relating to settlement for lend-lease, reciprocal aid, surplus war property and claims.

Exchange of notes at Washington March 21, 1947.

Entered into force March 21, 1947.

61 Stat. 2640; TIAS 1593; 11 Bevans 493; 16 UNTS 47.

PACIFIC SETTLEMENT OF DISPUTES

Treaty to amend in their application to the Union of South Africa certain provisions of the treaty for the advancement of peace between the United States and the United Kingdom signed September 15, 1914.

Signed at Washington April 2, 1940.

Entered into force March 11, 1941.

55 Stat. 1130; TS 966; 11 Bevans 476.

POSTAL MATTERS

Parcel post convention.

Signed at Cape Town April 17 and at Washington June 20, 1919.

Entered into force April 12, 1919.

41 Stat. 1656; Post Office Department print.

International express mail agreement, with detailed regulations.

Signed at Pretoria and Washington May 25 and June 29, 1981.

Entered into force July 1, 1981.

33 UST 2434; TIAS 10190; 1530 UNTS 31.

Insured postal parcels agreement.

Signed at Pretoria and Washington June 19 and August 5, 1992.

Entered into force October 1, 1992.

TIAS 11869.

PROPERTY

The following conventions between the United States and the United Kingdom may be considered in force with respect to the Republic of South Africa by virtue of the adherence by the United Kingdom for the Cape Colony on February 9, 1901, and for the Orange River Colony and the Transvaal on July 24, 1902, except for Natal and Namibia:

Convention relating to tenure and disposition of real and personal property.

Signed at Washington March 2, 1899.

TS 146; 31 Stat. 1939; 12 Bevans 246.

Supplementary convention extending the time within which notifications may be given of the accession of British colonies or foreign possessions to the convention of March 2, 1899.

Signed at Washington January 13, 1902.

TS 402; 32 Stat. 1914; 12 Bevans 261.

PUBLICATIONS

Agreement relating to the exchange of official publications.

Exchange of notes at Pretoria November 16, 1949.

Entered into force November 16, 1949.

64 Stat. (3) B109; TIAS 2038; 11 Bevans 513; 73 UNTS 97.

REMOTE SENSING

Memorandum of understanding relating to the operation of the Landsat system, with annex.

Signed at Washington and Pretoria September 19 and October 19, 1983.

Entered into force October 19, 1983.

35 UST 2359; TIAS 10797; 2011 UNTS 189.

SCIENTIFIC COOPERATION

Framework agreement concerning cooperation in the scientific, technological and environmental fields, with annex.

Signed at Pretoria December 5, 1995.

Entered into force August 27, 2001.

TIAS 12772.

Memorandum of understanding concerning scientific and technical cooperation in the earth sciences.

Signed at Reston and Pretoria March 7, 2005.

Entered into force March 7, 2005.

TIAS

SEISMIC OBSERVATIONS

Agreement for cooperation regarding an integrated, real-time global seismic data acquisition system.

Signed at Pretoria December 1, 1987.

Entered into force December 1, 1987.

TIAS 11560.

TAXATION

Convention with respect to taxes on the estates of deceased persons.

Signed at Cape Town April 10, 1947.

Entered into force July 15, 1952.

3 UST 3792; TIAS 2509; 167 UNTS 211.

Protocol supplementing the estate tax convention of April 10, 1947.

Signed at Pretoria July 14, 1950.

Entered into force July 15, 1952.

3 UST 3792; TIAS 2509; 167 UNTS 228.

Convention for the avoidance of double taxation and the prevention of fiscal evasion with respect to taxes on income and capital gains.

Signed at Cape Town February 17, 1997.

Entered into force December 28, 1997.

TIAS

TELECOMMUNICATION

Agreement relating to the reciprocal granting of authorizations to permit licensed amateur radio operators of either country to operate their stations in the other country.

Exchange of notes at Pretoria March 28 and May 1, 1985.

Entered into force May 1, 1985.

TIAS 11332.

Arrangement relating to radio communications between amateur stations on behalf of third parties.

Exchange of notes at Pretoria September 13 and October 4, 1993.

Entered into force October 4, 1993.

TIAS 12509.

TRADE AND COMMERCE

Agreement relating to postwar economic settlements.

Exchange of notes at Washington April 17, 1945.

Entered into force April 17, 1945.

60 Stat. 1579; TIAS 1512; 11 Bevans 489; 90 UNTS 275.

VISAS

Agreement relating to the reciprocal issuance of passport visas to nonimmigrants.[1]

Exchange of notes at Cape Town March 28 and April 3, 1956.

Entered into force May 1, 1956.

7 UST 631; TIAS 3544; 249 UNTS 395.

Amendment

March 31, 1958 (9 UST 1023; TIAS 4076; 300 UNTS 382).

NOTE

1 Applied to Namibia.

SOUTH PACIFIC COMMISSION

TAXATION

Agreement relating to a procedure for United States income tax reimbursement.

Exchange of notes at Suva and Noumea December 21, 1981 and April 28, 1982.

Entered into force April 28, 1982; effective January 1, 1982.

34 UST 979; TIAS 10384.

SOUTH PACIFIC FORUM FISHERIES AGENCY

ECONOMIC ASSISTANCE

Agreement to promote economic development in the South Pacific region.

Signed at Majuro March 12, 2003.

Entered into force June 15, 2003.

TIAS

SPAIN

ATOMIC ENERGY

Agreement in the field of radioactive waste management.

Signed at Madrid December 16, 1992.

Entered into force December 16, 1992.

TIAS

Arrangement for the exchange of technical information and cooperation in nuclear safety matters, with addenda.

Signed at Vienna September 19, 2000.

Entered into force September 19, 2000.

TIAS

Implementing agreement in the area of nuclear safety research.

Signed at Madrid and Rockville September 3, 2002.

Entered into force September 3, 2002; effective September 21, 2001.

TIAS

Agreement on thermal-hydraulic code applications and maintenance, with addendum.

Signed at Madrid and Rockville March 12 and May 10, 2004.

Entered into force May 10, 2004; with effect from August 31, 2003.

TIAS

Arrangement for the exchange of technical information and cooperation in nuclear safety matters, with addenda.

Signed at Rockville May 23, 2005.

Entered into force May 23, 2005.

TIAS

AVIATION

Arrangement relating to certificates of airworthiness for imported aircraft.

Exchange of notes at Madrid September 23, 1957.

Entered into force September 23, 1957.

8 UST 1549; TIAS 3906; 290 UNTS 261.

Amendment

September 18 and October 13, 1978 (30 UST 750; TIAS 9217).

Air transport agreement.

Signed at Madrid February 20, 1973.

Entered into force provisionally February 20, 1973; definitively August 3, 1973.

24 UST 2102; TIAS 7725.

Amendments

May 31, 1989 (TIAS 11672; 1597 UNTS 466).

November 27, 1991 (TIAS 11946; 1722 UNTS 304).

Related agreement

February 20, March 31 and April 7, 1987 (TIAS 11297; 2177 UNTS 122).

Memorandum of agreement relating to technical assistance to Spain in civil aviation activities.

Signed at Washington and Madrid June 30 and July 22, 1982.

Entered into force July 22, 1982.

TIAS 10547.

Agreement for the promotion of aviation safety.

Signed at Washington September 23, 1999.

Entered into force September 23, 1999.

TIAS; 2084 UNTS 401.

CLAIMS

Arrangement relating to claims.

Exchange of notes at Washington August 24, 1927, and May 13 and June 20, 1929.

Entered into force June 20, 1929.

47 Stat. 2641; EAS 18; 11 Bevans 687; 120 LNTS 401.

Agreement regarding claims arising from Exercise CRISEX.

Signed at Madrid November 13, 1979.

Entered into force November 13, 1979.

31 UST 5876; TIAS 9690.

COMMERCE

Treaty of friendship and general relations.[1] [2]

Signed at Madrid July 3, 1902.

Entered into force April 14, 1903.

33 Stat. 2105; TS 422; 11 Bevans 628.

NOTES

1 Applicable to all territories.

2 Notice of termination was given by the United States of articles XXIII and XXIV, effective July 1, 1916, in accordance with the Seamen's Act (38 Stat. 1164). The notice was accepted by the Spanish Government with the understanding that only such provisions of these articles as were in conflict with the act should be terminated, and all other provisions, especially those concerning the arrest, detention, and imprisonment of deserters from war vessels, should continue in force; also on the understanding that United States consuls in Spain should not exercise the powers of which Spanish consuls in the United States were deprived by the provisions of the Act.

CONSULS

See COMMERCE

COPYRIGHT

Copyright agreement.[1]

Exchange of notes at Washington July 6 and 15, 1895.

Entered into force July 10, 1895.

TS 342-A; 11 Bevans 597.

Agreement relating to the restoration of the copyright agreement of July 6 and 15, 1895.

Exchange of notes at Madrid January 29 and November 18 and 26, 1902.

Entered into force November 26, 1902.

TS 474; 11 Bevans 639.

NOTE

1 Applicable to all Spanish territories.

CUSTOMS

Agreement regarding mutual assistance between customs services.

Signed at Madrid July 3, 1990.

Entered into force February 28, 1993.

TIAS 12120; 1717 UNTS 223.

DEFENSE

Mutual defense assistance agreement with tax relief annex and interpretative note in regard to tax relief annex.

Signed at Madrid September 26, 1953.

Entered into force September 26, 1953.

4 UST 1876; TIAS 2849; 207 UNTS 61.

Agreement confirming the bilateral arrangements for a facilities assistance program pursuant to the mutual defense assistance agreement of September 26, 1953.

Exchange of notes at Madrid April 9 and May 11 and 19, 1954.

Entered into force May 19, 1954.

5 UST 2377; TIAS 3098; 235 UNTS 87.

Supplementary agreements

May 25, 1955 (6 UST 1155; TIAS 3257; 251 UNTS 416).

September 17, 1956 (7 UST 2777; TIAS 3658; 278 UNTS 283).

Agreement relating to offshore procurement in Spain, with memorandum of understanding and standard contract attached.

Exchange of notes at San Sebastian July 30, 1954.

Entered into force July 30, 1954.

5 UST 2328; TIAS 3094; 235 UNTS 45.

Amendments

October 26, 1954 (5 UST 2357; TIAS 3094; 235 UNTS 66).

October 29 and November 11, 1958 (10 UST 344; TIAS 4196; 341 UNTS 400).

Agreement relating to the disposition of military equipment and materials furnished by the United States under the mutual defense assistance agreement.

Exchange of notes at Madrid November 27, 1956.

Entered into force November 27, 1956.

7 UST 3392; TIAS 3710; 265 UNTS 374.

Agreement concerning the grant of defense articles and services under the military assistance program.

Exchange of notes at Madrid August 30, 1979.

Entered into force August 30, 1979.

30 UST 7238; TIAS 9581; 1182 UNTS 161.

Master data exchange agreement for the mutual development of weapons systems.

Signed at Washington June 19, 1980.

Entered into force June 19, 1980.

TIAS 12376.

Cover agreement on the territorial command net, with annexes.

Signed at Madrid July 24, 1980.

Entered into force July 24, 1980.

35 UST 3745; TIAS 10880; 1577 UNTS 297.

Agreement concerning the grant of defense articles and services under the military assistance program.

Exchange of notes at Madrid August 28 and 29, 1981.

Entered into force August 29, 1981.

33 UST 3752; TIAS 10257; 1541 UNTS 121.

Agreement on friendship, defense and cooperation, with complementary agreements,[1] and exchanges of notes.

Signed at Madrid July 2, 1982.

Entered into force May 14, 1983.

TIAS 10589.

Memorandum of understanding pertaining to installation of satellite ground terminal at Rota, Spain.

Signed at Rota November 3, 1982.

Entered into force November 3, 1982.

TIAS 10566; 1871 UNTS 381.

General security of military information agreement, with protocol on security procedures for industrial operations with appendices.

Signed at Washington March 12, 1984.

Entered into force March 12, 1984.

35 UST 4639; TIAS 10962.

Agreement on defense cooperation, with annexes and related letters.

Signed at Madrid December 1, 1988.

Entered into force May 4, 1989.

TIAS

Amendment

April 10, 2002.

Memorandum of understanding concerning lease of equipment and exchange of technical information for the XXV Olympiad.

Signed at Madrid October 19, 1990.

Entered into force October 19, 1990.

TIAS

Memorandum of understanding on the exchange of service personnel between the United States Navy and the Spanish Air Force and on the general conditions which will apply to the exchange of such personnel.

Signed at Washington and Madrid July 20 and August 13, 1991.

Entered into force August 13, 1991.

NP

Memorandum of understanding on the exchange of service personnel between the United States Navy and the Spanish Navy and on the general conditions which will apply to the exchange of such personnel.

Signed at Washington and Madrid August 5 and September 5, 1991.

Entered into force September 5, 1991.

NP

Memorandum of understanding regarding the exchange of scientists and engineers, with annexes.

Signed at Madrid September 16, 1993.

Entered into force September 16, 1993.

NP

Acquisition and cross-servicing agreement.

Signed at Madrid and Patch Barracks (Germany) May 6 and 19, 1999.

Entered into force May 19, 1999.

TIAS

Agreement for research, development, test, evaluation, production and life cycle support activities for technologies and systems for AEGIS-equipped ships.

Signed at Ferrol February 28, 2002.

Entered into force February 28, 2002.

TIAS

Agreement concerning the exchange and reimbursement of marine aviation and propulsion fuels, with annexes.

Signed at Fort Belvoir and Madrid January 27 and March 8, 2005.

Entered into force March 8, 2005.

TIAS

Agreement regarding the assignment of liaison officers of its respective Marine Corps, with annex.

Signed at Madrid and Washington July 31 and September 11, 2006.

Entered into force September 11, 2006.

TIAS

NOTE

1 Complementary agreement seven concerns scientific, technological, cultural, educational and economic cooperation.

ECONOMIC AND TECHNICAL COOPERATION[1]

Economic aid agreement.

Signed at Madrid September 26, 1953.

Entered into force September 26, 1953.

4 UST 1903; TIAS 2851; 207 UNTS 93.

Agreement relating to the waiver of the counterpart deposit requirement for certain categories of AID financed commodities.

Exchange of notes at Madrid May 22, 1962.

Entered into force May 22, 1962.

13 UST 1830; TIAS 5131; 458 UNTS 304.

NOTE

1 See also complementary agreement seven to the agreement on friendship, defense and cooperation of July 2, 1982 (TIAS 10589).

EDUCATION[1]

Agreement for educational, cultural and scientific cooperation.

Signed at Madrid October 27, 1994.

Entered into force April 26, 1995.

TIAS 12577; 1872 UNTS 287.

Extension

January 20 and February 2, 2004.

NOTE

1 See also complementary agreement seven to the agreement on friendship, defense and cooperation of July 2, 1982 (TIAS 10589).

EMPLOYMENT

Agreement concerning the free pursuit of gainful employment by dependents of employees of diplomatic missions, consular posts or missions to international organizations, with exchange of notes.

Signed at Madrid July 25, 1990.

Entered into force April 1, 1991.

TIAS

ENVIRONMENTAL COOPERATION

Agreement for cooperation in the Global Learning and Observations to Benefit the Environment (GLOBE) Program, with appendices.

Signed at Madrid May 5, 1998.

Entered into force May 5, 1998.

TIAS

EXTRADITION

Treaty on extradition.[1]

Signed at Madrid May 29, 1970.

Entered into force June 16, 1971.

22 UST 737; TIAS 7136; 796 UNTS 245.

Supplementary treaty on extradition.
Signed at Madrid January 25, 1975.
Entered into force June 2, 1978.
29 UST 2283; TIAS 8938.

Second supplementary treaty on extradition.
Signed at Madrid February 9, 1988.
Entered into force July 2, 1993.
TIAS

Third supplementary extradition treaty.
Signed at Madrid March 12, 1996.
Entered into force July 25, 1999.
TIAS

NOTE
1 Applicable to all territories.

FINANCE

Agreement relating to the restitution of monetary gold looted by Germany.
Exchange of notes at Madrid April 30 and May 3, 1948.
Entered into force May 3, 1948.
62 Stat. 4071; TIAS 2123; 11 Bevans 708; 132 UNTS 155.

FRIENDSHIP AND COOPERATION

See under DEFENSE

INSULAR POSSESSIONS

Treaty for the cession to the United States of any and all islands of the Philippine Archipelago lying outside of the lines described in article III of the treaty of peace of December 10, 1898.
Signed at Washington November 7, 1900.
Entered into force March 23, 1901.
31 Stat. 1942; TS 345; 11 Bevans 623.

JUDICIAL ASSISTANCE

Agreement exempting from authentication signatures attached to letters rogatory exchanged between Puerto Rico, the Philippine Islands, and Spain.
Exchange of notes at Washington August 5, and at Manchester, Massachusetts, August 7, 1901, and declaration signed at Washington November 7, 1901.
Entered into force November 28, 1901.
TS 395; 11 Bevans 625.

Agreement on procedures for mutual assistance in connection with the Lockheed Aircraft Corporation matter, with annex.
Signed at Washington July 14, 1976.
Entered into force July 14, 1976.
27 UST 3409; TIAS 8370.

Related agreement
June 7 and July 22, 1977 (28 UST 7494; TIAS 8725).

Treaty on mutual legal assistance in criminal matters, with attachments.
Signed at Washington November 20, 1990.
Entered into force June 30, 1993.
TIAS; 1730 UNTS 113.

MAPPING

Agreement concerning technical cooperation in cartography and geodesy.
Signed at Madrid and Washington September 4 and October 27, 1986.
Entered into force October 27, 1986.
TIAS 11408; 2192 UNTS 181.

Basic exchange and technical cooperation agreement for mapping, nautical and aeronautical charting, geodesy and geophysics, digital data and related materials, with appendix and annexes.
Signed at Madrid June 29, 1992.
Entered into force June 29, 1992.
NP

NARCOTIC DRUGS

Arrangement for the direct exchange of certain information regarding the traffic in narcotic drugs.
Exchange of notes at Madrid February 3, March 10, and May 24, 1928.
Entered into force May 24, 1928.
11 Bevans 684.

Agreement on cooperation to reduce the demand for narcotic drugs.
Signed at Madrid November 25, 1991.
Entered into force May 7, 1993.
TIAS 12443.

PACIFIC SETTLEMENT OF DISPUTES

Treaty for the settlement of disputes between the two countries.
Signed at Washington September 15, 1914.
Entered into force December 21, 1914.
38 Stat. 1862; TS 605; 11 Bevans 661; 89 LNTS 427.

PATENTS

Agreement to facilitate interchange of patent rights and technical information for defense purposes.
Exchange of notes at Madrid July 13 and 21, 1960.
Entered into force July 21, 1960.
11 UST 2187; TIAS 4588; 393 UNTS 289.

PEACE TREATIES

Treaty of peace.
Signed at Paris December 10, 1898.
Entered into force April 11, 1899.
30 Stat. 1754; TS 343; 11 Bevans 615.

POSTAL MATTERS

Parcel post agreement.[1]
Signed at Madrid July 16 and at Washington August 30, 1955.
Entered into force January 1, 1956.
7 UST 451; TIAS 3530; 270 UNTS 211.

International express mail agreement, with detailed regulations.
Signed at Madrid October 18, 1982.
Entered into force April 1, 1983.
TIAS 10555; 1871 UNTS 341.

NOTE
1 Applicable to Puerto Rico, Guam, Samoa, the Virgin Islands, Andorra, and Spanish Territories of Africa.

PUBLICATIONS

Agreement relating to the exchange of official publications.
Exchange of notes at Madrid May 8, 1950.
Entered into force May 8, 1950.
1 UST 466; TIAS 2085; 98 UNTS 175.

SATELLITES

Agreement concerning a program of joint participation in intercontinental testing in connection with experimental communications satellites.
Exchange of notes at Madrid September 18, 1964 and January 26, 1965.
Entered into force January 26, 1965.
16 UST 68; TIAS 5761; 542 UNTS 81.

SCIENTIFIC COOPERATION[1]

NOTE
1 See complementary agreement seven to the agreement on friendship, defense and cooperation of July 2, 1982 (TIAS 10589).

1

Agreement on scientific and technological cooperation, with annex.
Signed at Madrid June 10, 1994.
Entered into force provisionally, June 10, 1994; definitively, January 18, 1996.
TIAS 12547; 1920 UNTS 309.

1

Memorandum of understanding on scientific and technological cooperation in the field of water resources development.
Signed at Madrid May 20, 1997.
Entered into force May 20, 1997.
TIAS

[1]

Implementing arrangement on cooperation in research on radiological evaluations.

Signed at Madrid September 15, 1997.

Entered into force September 15, 1997.

TIAS

[1]

Memorandum of understanding concerning scientific and technical cooperation in the earth sciences.

Signed at Reston and Madrid February 20 and March 5, 2004.

Entered into force March 5, 2004.

TIAS

SEISMIC OBSERVATIONS

Memorandum of understanding concerning the Sonseca Seismographic Station, with annexes.

Signed at Madrid January 18, 1996.

Entered into force January 18, 1996.

TIAS 12719; 1926 UNTS 409.

SHIPPING

Agreement relating to jurisdiction over vessels utilizing the Louisiana Offshore Oil Port.

Exchange of notes at Madrid November 5 and 22, 1983.

Entered into force October 19, 1984.

35 UST 3131; TIAS 10845.

SMUGGLING

Convention for the prevention of smuggling of alcoholic liquors.

Signed at Washington February 10, 1926.

Entered into force November 17, 1926.

44 Stat. 2465; TS 749; 11 Bevans 676; 67 LNTS 131.

SOCIAL SECURITY

Agreement on social security, with administrative arrangement.

Signed at Madrid September 30, 1986.

Entered into force April 1, 1988.

TIAS 12123.

SPACE COOPERATION

Agreement providing for a project in Spain to measure winds and temperatures at high altitudes and for continuing other cooperative space research projects.

Exchange of notes at Washington April 14, 1966.

Entered into force April 14, 1966.

17 UST 493; TIAS 5992; 586 UNTS 79.

Agreement on space cooperation.

Exchange of memoranda at Madrid August 31 and September 4, 1984.

Entered into force September 4, 1984.

TIAS 11067; 2039 UNTS 227.

Extension

March 13 and 31, 1989 (TIAS 12208).

Agreement on space cooperation.

Signed at Madrid July 11, 1991.

Entered into force May 9, 1994.

TIAS; 1785 UNTS 393.

TAXATION

Tax relief annex attached to the mutual defense assistance agreement, and interpretative note.

Signed at Madrid September 26, 1953.

Entered into force September 26, 1953.

4 UST 1876; TIAS 2849; 207 UNTS 61.

Convention for the avoidance of double taxation and the prevention of fiscal evasion with respect to taxes on income, with protocol.

Signed at Madrid February 22, 1990.

Entered into force November 21, 1990.

TIAS; 1591 UNTS 41.

TELECOMMUNICATION

Agreement relating to the reciprocal granting of authorizations to permit licensed amateur radio operators of either country to operate their stations in the other country.

Exchange of notes at Madrid December 11 and 20, 1979.

Entered into force December 20, 1979.

32 UST 517; TIAS 9721.

TRACKING STATIONS

Agreement providing for the establishment and operation of a tracking and data acquisition station.

Exchange of notes at Madrid January 29, 1964.

Entered into force January 29, 1964.

15 UST 153; TIAS 5533; 511 UNTS 61.

Extensions and amendment

October 11, 1965 (16 UST 1710; TIAS 5896; 574 UNTS 259).

February 1 and May 2, 1983 (TIAS 10717; 1607 UNTS 479).

January 19 and 22, 2001 (TIAS; 2173 UNTS 109).

TRADE AND COMMERCE

Agreement providing for consultations should exports of textiles or textile products from Spain cause market disruption in the United States.

Exchange of notes at Madrid September 23, 1976.

Entered into force September 23, 1976.

28 UST 1308; TIAS 8512.

Agreement relating to the subsidization of exports in the context of the agreement on interpretation and application of articles VI, XVI, and XXIII (subsidies code) of the General Agreement on Tariffs and Trade (TIAS 9619).

Exchange of letters at Washington April 13 and 14, 1982.

Entered into force April 14, 1982.

TIAS

Amendment

January 16 and 29, 1985.

VISAS

Agreement relating to the reciprocal waiver of visa fees for nonimmigrants.[1]

Exchange of notes at Madrid January 21, 1952.

Entered into force January 21, 1952; operative February 21, 1952.

3 UST 2927; TIAS 2471; 160 UNTS 63.

Amendment

May 11 and July 5, 1963 (14 UST 1206; TIAS 5418; 488 UNTS 236).

NOTE

1 Applicable to all territories.

SRI LANKA

Article 6 of the External Affairs Agreement between the United Kingdom and Ceylon, signed at Colombo November 11, 1947, which entered into force on February 4, 1948, provides: "All obligations and responsibilities heretofore devolving on the Government of the United Kindgom which arise from any valid international instrument shall henceforth insofar as such instrument may be held to have application to Ceylon devolve upon the Government of Ceylon. The reciprocal rights and benefits heretofore enjoyed by the Government of the United Kingdom in virtue of the application of any such international instrument to Ceylon shall henceforth be enjoyed by the Government of Ceylon."

AGRICULTURAL COMMODITIES

Agricultural commodities agreement.

Signed at Washington June 18, 1958.

Entered into force June 18, 1958.

9 UST 611; TIAS 4042; 316 UNTS 15.

Amendments

June 30, 1958 (9 UST 994; TIAS 4068; 321 UNTS 302).

August 24, 1961 (12 UST 1200; TIAS 4835; 418 UNTS 394).

Agricultural commodities agreement, with exchange of notes and related note.

Signed at Colombo March 13, 1959.

Entered into force March 13, 1959.

10 UST 749; TIAS 4211; 342 UNTS 51.

Amendments

May 28, 1959 (10 UST 1046; TIAS 4242; 346 UNTS 370).

December 1 and 8, 1959 (12 UST 1220; TIAS 4839; 418 UNTS 402).

August 24, 1961 (12 UST 1203; TIAS 4836; 418 UNTS 408).

Agricultural commodities agreement with exchange of notes.

Signed at Colombo September 30, 1960.

Entered into force September 30, 1960.

11 UST 2140; TIAS 4576; 389 UNTS 221.

Agricultural commodities agreement with exchange of notes.

Signed at Colombo July 19, 1962.

Entered into force July 19, 1962.

13 UST 1471; TIAS 5106; 454 UNTS 31.

Amendment

March 30 and June 22, 1973 (24 UST 1658; TIAS 7671).

Agricultural commodities agreement with exchange of notes.

Signed at Colombo March 12, 1966.

Entered into force March 12, 1966.

17 UST 190; TIAS 5971; 579 UNTS 117.

Amendments

August 25, 1966 (17 UST 1192; TIAS 6079; 603 UNTS 342).

June 21, 1968 (19 UST 5447; TIAS 6528; 720 UNTS 292).

Agricultural commodities agreement with annex.

Signed at Colombo October 27, 1967.

Entered into force October 27, 1967.

18 UST 3141; TIAS 6405.

Related agreements

June 21, 1968 (19 UST 5379; TIAS 6521; 719 UNTS 95).

February 19, 1969 (20 UST 512; TIAS 6658; 707 UNTS 157).

September 27, 1970 (21 UST 2191; TIAS 6968; 764 UNTS 265).

March 10, 1971 (22 UST 403; TIAS 7074; 792 UNTS 405).

April 29, 1971 (22 UST 648; TIAS 7116; 792 UNTS 408).

October 12, 1971 (22 UST 1692; TIAS 7195; 807 UNTS 355).

December 20, 1971 (22 UST 2075; TIAS 7248; 882 UNTS 295).

November 3, 1972 (23 UST 3483; TIAS 7505; 898 UNTS 340).

November 23, 1973 (24 UST 2292; TIAS 7753; 938 UNTS 417).

January 18 and February 21, 1974 (25 UST 260; TIAS 7794; 944 UNTS 400).

Agricultural commodities agreement.

Signed at Colombo March 25, 1975.

Entered into force March 25, 1975.

26 UST 1244; TIAS 8107.

Related agreements

April 9, 1976 (27 UST 1453; TIAS 8256; 1049 UNTS 133).

April 30, 1976 (27 UST 2329; TIAS 8311; 1054 UNTS 376).

October 29, 1976 (28 UST 1280; TIAS 8510).

December 15, 1976 (28 UST 1280; TIAS 8510).

January 9, 1978 (29 UST 4164; TIAS 9052; 1135 UNTS 133).

April 12, 1978 (29 UST 4177; TIAS 9052; 1135 UNTS 144).

February 22, 1979 (30 UST 3631; TIAS 9418; 1171 UNTS 187).

March 18, 1980 (32 UST 898; TIAS 9737; 1222 UNTS 153).

May 21, 1980 (32 UST 1139; TIAS 9761; 1222 UNTS 160).

May 29, 1981 (33 UST 1983; TIAS 10162).

June 30, 1982 (34 UST 2038; TIAS 10478; 1750 UNTS 457).

October 29, 1982 (TIAS 10596; 1871 UNTS 393).

April 20, 1983 (TIAS 10714; 2006 UNTS 558).

December 12, 1983 (35 UST 4125; TIAS 10910; 1578 UNTS 149).

September 28, 1984 (NP).

Agricultural commodities agreement.

Signed at Colombo October 23, 1985.

Entered into force October 23, 1985.

NP

Amendments

January 10, 1986 (NP).

August 25, 1986 (NP).

Agricultural commodities agreement.

Signed at Colombo November 13, 1986.

Entered into force November 13, 1986.

NP

Amendments

April 28, 1987 (NP).

August 12, 1987 (NP).

Related agreements

December 3, 1987 (NP).

May 20, 1988 (NP).

June 10, 1988 (NP).

September 30, 1988 (NP).

May 16, 1989 (NP).

July 26, 1989 (NP).

October 10, 1989 (NP).

July 24, 1990 (NP).

August 10, 1990 (NP).

AVIATION

Arrangement between the United States and the United Kingdom relating to pilot licenses to operate civil aircraft.

Exchange of notes at Washington March 28 and April 5, 1935.

Entered into force May 5, 1935.

49 Stat. 3731; EAS 77; 12 Bevans 513; 162 LNTS 59.

Air transport agreement, with annexes.

Signed at Washington June 11, 2002.

Entered into force November 18, 2002.

TIAS

Amendment

September 6, 2006.

CLAIMS

Agreement concerning a full and final settlement of the investment dispute between Enterprise Development International, Inc., formerly Enterprise Development Inc., and the Sri Lanka State Timber Corporation relating to Charlanka Company Ltd.

Exchange of notes at Washington October 30, 1998.

Entered into force October 30, 1998.

NP

Agreement concerning a full and final settlement of the commercial dispute between Evans International Ltd. Co. and Centrepoint Colombo Ltd. Urban Development Authority of Sri Lanka, and the Government of the Democratic Socialist Republic of Sri Lanka relating to reconstruction of the Colombo financial district.

Exchange of notes at Washington June 7, 1999.

Entered into force June 7, 1999.

NP

CONSULS

Convention to regulate commerce (article IV) between the United States and the United Kingdom.

Signed at London July 3, 1815.

Entered into force July 3, 1815.

8 Stat. 228; TS 110; 12 Bevans 49.

DEFENSE

Agreement relating to the purchase by Ceylon of certain military equipment, materials, and services.

Exchange of notes at Washington October 25 and November 2, 1956.

Entered into force November 2, 1956.

7 UST 3193; TIAS 3698; 282 UNTS 93.

Agreement regarding the status of U.S. military personnel and civilian employees of the Department of Defense who may be present in Sri Lanka for exercises or official duties.

Exchange of notes at Colombo February 9 and May 16, 1995.

Entered into force May 16, 1995.

NP

Agreement regarding grants under the Foreign Assistance Act of 1961, as amended, and the furnishing of defense articles, related training, and other defense services from the United States of America to the Government of Sri Lanka.

Exchange of notes at Colombo July 23 and August 4, 1998.

Entered into force August 4, 1998.

NP

ECONOMIC AND TECHNICAL COOPERATION

General agreement for technical cooperation.

Signed at Colombo November 7, 1950.

Entered into force November 7, 1950.

1 UST 723; TIAS 2138; 92 UNTS 125.

Agreement relating to a development assistance program in Ceylon.

Exchange of notes at Colombo April 28, 1956.

Entered into force April 28, 1956.

7 UST 751; TIAS 3554; 274 UNTS 35.

Agency for International Development

November 9, 1977 (29 UST 3472; TIAS 9023; 1124 UNTS 15).

February 28, 1978 (30 UST 1737; TIAS 9284; 1152 UNTS 127).

February 28, 1978 (29 UST 4482; TIAS 9063; 1231 UNTS 379).

August 31, 1978 (30 UST 5493; TIAS 9512; 1231 UNTS 415).

August 31, 1978 (30 UST 5571; TIAS 9516).

August 31, 1978 (30 UST 5584; TIAS 9517).

July 21, 1988 (NP).

EDUCATION

Agreement for financing certain educational exchange programs.

Signed at Colombo August 29, 1964.

Entered into force August 29, 1964.

TIAS 5645; 15 UST 1699; 531 UNTS 93.

Amendment

June 23 and August 13, 1998.

EMPLOYMENT

Agreement relating to the employment of dependents of official government employees.

Exchange of notes at Colombo December 12, 1995.

Entered into force December 12, 1995.

TIAS 12710.

ENVIRONMENTAL COOPERATION

Agreement for cooperation in the Global Learning and Observations to Benefit the Environment (GLOBE) Program, with appendices.

Signed at Colombo December 20, 1999.

Entered into force December 20, 1999.

TIAS

EXTRADITION

Extradition treaty.

Signed at Washington September 30, 1999.

Entered into force January 12, 2001.

TIAS

FINANCE

Investment incentive agreement.

Signed at Washington October 19, 1993.

Entered into force August 8, 2003.

TIAS

Agreement regarding the consolidation and rescheduling of certain debts owed to, guaranteed by, or insured by the United States Government or its agencies, with annexes.

Signed at Colombo September 30, 2005.

Entered into force November 17, 2005.

NP

INTELLECTUAL PROPERTY

Agreement on the protection and enforcement of intellectual property rights.

Signed at Colombo September 20, 1991.

Entered into force October 20, 1991.

TIAS 12436.

INTERNATIONAL CRIMINAL COURT

Agreement regarding the surrender of persons to the International Criminal Court.

Signed at Colombo November 22, 2002.

Entered into force July 4, 2003.

TIAS

INVESTMENT

Treaty concerning the encouragement and reciprocal protection of investment, with annex, protocol and exchange of letters.

Signed at Colombo September 20, 1991.

Entered into force May 1, 1993.

TIAS

PEACE CORPS

Agreement relating to the establishment of a Peace Corps program in Sri Lanka.

Exchange of notes at Colombo November 20, 1983.

Entered into force November 20, 1983.

35 UST 3124; TIAS 10844; 2014 UNTS 641.

POSTAL MATTERS

Parcel post agreement and detailed regulations.

Signed at Colombo July 18 and at Washington November 25, 1955.

Entered into force July 1, 1956.

7 UST 2871; TIAS 3670; 281 UNTS 295.

International express mail agreement, with detailed regulations.

Signed at Colombo and Washington February 1 and 14, 1990.

Entered into force March 30, 1990.

TIAS 11716.

PROPERTY

Convention between the United States and the United Kingdom relating to tenure and disposition of real and personal property.

Signed at Washington March 2, 1899; applicable to Ceylon February 9, 1901.

31 Stat. 1939; TS 146; 12 Bevans 246.

PUBLICATIONS

Agreement relating to the exchange of official publications.

Exchange of notes at Colombo January 4 and 31, 1949.

Entered into force January 31, 1949.

63 Stat. 2356; TIAS 1894; 6 Bevans 515; 88 UNTS 21.

TELECOMMUNICATION

Agreement relating to the facilities of Radio Ceylon.

Exchange of notes at Colombo May 12 and 14, 1951.

Entered into force May 14, 1951.

2 UST 1041; TIAS 2259; 141 UNTS 159.

Extensions and amendments

July 14 and August 23, 1954 (11 UST 229; TIAS 4436; 314 UNTS 297).

April 30, 1962 (13 UST 972; TIAS 5037; 445 UNTS 319).

December 9, 1983 (35 UST 3279; TIAS 10856; 2016 UNTS 4).

August 3, 1994.

TRADE AND COMMERCE

Arrangement relating to a visa system for exports of cotton, wool and man-made fiber apparel manufactured in Sri Lanka.

Exchange of letters at Colombo March 12 and 23, 1979.

Entered into force March 23, 1979.

30 UST 3859; TIAS 9428; 1171 UNTS 201.

Agreement relating to trade in textiles and textile products, with annexes.

Exchange of notes at Colombo May 23 and 24, 1988.

Entered into force May 24, 1988; effective June 1, 1988.

NP

Amendments and extensions

November 17 and December 27, 1988 (NP).

October 2 and December 14, 1992 (NP).

April 7 and July 13, 1994 (NP).

March 22 and September 5, 1995 and April 17 and 23, 1996 (NP).

Related agreement

January 13, 1994 (NP).

TRADE-MARKS

Declaration by the United States and the United Kingdom affording reciprocal protection to trade-marks.

Signed at London October 24, 1877.

Entered into force October 24, 1877.

20 Stat. 703; TS 138; 12 Bevans 198.

VISAS

Agreement providing for the reciprocal reduction of nonimmigrant visa fees and issuance of multiple-entry nonimmigrant visas.

Exchange of notes at Colombo August 25 and September 7, 1956.

Entered into force September 7, 1956; operative September 15, 1956.

8 UST 83; TIAS 3743; 280 UNTS 35.

SUDAN

AGRICULTURAL COMMODITIES

Agricultural commodities agreement with exchanges of notes.

Signed at Khartoum November 14, 1961.

Entered into force November 14, 1961.

12 UST 3107; TIAS 4910; 434 UNTS 51.

Amendment

January 12 and 18, 1966 (17 UST 311; TIAS 5976).

Agricultural commodities agreement.

Signed at Khartoum January 31, 1963.

Entered into force January 31, 1963.

14 UST 1831; TIAS 5495; 494 UNTS 119.

Amendment

January 12 and 18, 1966 (17 UST 311; TIAS 5976).

Agricultural commodities agreement with exchange of notes.

Signed at Khartoum March 2, 1964.

Entered into force March 2, 1964.

15 UST 217; TIAS 5541; 524 UNTS 217.

Agricultural commodities agreement with exchange of notes.

Signed at Khartoum April 13, 1966.

Entered into force April 13, 1966.

17 UST 502; TIAS 5994; 586 UNTS 39.

Agricultural commodities agreement with annex.

Signed at Khartoum March 18, 1973.

Entered into force March 18, 1973.

24 UST 967; TIAS 7608.

Related agreement

May 8, 1974 (25 UST 844; TIAS 7827).

Agricultural commodities agreement.

Signed at Khartoum February 21, 1977.

Entered into force July 7, 1977.

29 UST 967; TIAS 8856.

Agricultural commodities agreement.

Signed at Khartoum December 24, 1977.

Entered into force January 24, 1978.

29 UST 5873; TIAS 9157.

Related agreements

February 8, 1979 (TIAS 10660).

January 19, 1981 (33 UST 906; TIAS 10075; 1275 UNTS 139).

August 27, 1981 (33 UST 3698; TIAS 10251).

February 13, 1982 (34 UST 275; TIAS 10352).

January 20, 1983 (TIAS 10660).

February 21, 1983 (TIAS 10660).

June 13, 1983 (TIAS 10660).

December 10, 1983 (35 UST 4121; TIAS 10909).

Agricultural commodities agreement, with annexes and agreed minutes.

Signed at Khartoum December 22, 1979.

Entered into force December 22, 1979.

35 UST 1243; TIAS 10727; 2006 UNTS 297.

Amendments

August 7, 1980 (35 UST 1243; TIAS 10727; 2006 UNTS 297).

February 14, 1981 (35 UST 1243; TIAS 10727).

April 29, 1982 (35 UST 1243; TIAS 10727).

June 13, 1983 (35 UST 1243; TIAS 10727).

August 9, 1984 (35 UST 1243; TIAS 10727).

Agricultural commodities agreement.

Signed at Khartoum December 27, 1984.

Entered into force January 3, 1985.

NP

Amendments

January 9, 1985 (NP).

May 12, 1985 (NP).

August 24, 1985 (NP).

Agricultural commodities agreement, with annexes.

Signed at Khartoum January 26, 1986.

Entered into force January 26, 1986.

NP

Amendment

July 16, 1986 (NP).

Agricultural commodities agreement.

Signed at Khartoum March 12, 1987.

Entered into force March 12, 1987.

NP

Amendment

June 18, 1987 (NP).

Agricultural commodities agreement.

Signed at Khartoum February 28, 1988.

Entered into force February 28, 1988.

NP

Amendment

March 31, 1988 (NP).

Agricultural commodities agreement.

Signed at Khartoum June 8, 1989.

Entered into force June 8, 1989.

NP

Amendment

July 28, 1989 (NP).

DEFENSE

Agreement relating to the deposit by Sudan of ten percent of the value of grant military assistance furnished by the United States.

Exchange of notes at Khartoum April 27 and May 24, 1973.

Entered into force May 24, 1973.

24 UST 1740; TIAS 7677.

Mutual defense assistance agreement.

Exchange of notes at Khartoum April 8 and 22, 1981.

Entered into force April 22, 1981.

34 UST 1000; TIAS 10389; 1560 UNTS 415.

Agreement concerning the grant of defense articles and services under the military assistance program.

Exchange of notes at Khartoum August 24 and 30, 1981.

Entered into force August 30, 1981.

TIAS 10500; 1750 UNTS 171.

Amendment

August 30 and September 25, 1982 (TIAS 10500; 1750 UNTS 178).

Agreement relating to the status of United States personnel temporarily stationed in Sudan.

Exchange of letters at Khartoum November 12 and December 27, 1981.

Entered into force December 27, 1981.

33 UST 4513; TIAS 10322.

ECONOMIC AND TECHNICAL COOPERATION

Agreement providing for economic, technical and related assistance to the Sudan.

Exchange of notes at Khartoum March 31, 1958.

Entered into force March 31, 1958.

9 UST 343; TIAS 4014; 308 UNTS 105.

Understanding interpreting the agreement of March 31, 1958.

Exchange of notes at Khartoum July 1 and 12, 1958.

9 UST 1079; TIAS 4085; 335 UNTS 342.

Agency for International Development

December 31, 1979 (31 UST 5573; TIAS 9674; 1234 UNTS 73).

FINANCE

Agreement relating to investment guaranties under section 413 (b)(4) of the Mutual Security Act of 1954, as amended.

Exchange of notes at Khartoum March 17, 1959.

Entered into force March 17, 1959.

10 UST 408; TIAS 4201; 342 UNTS 13.

Amendment

March 2, 1964 (15 UST 238; TIAS 5544; 524 UNTS 318).

Agreement regarding the consolidation and rescheduling of certain debts owed to, guaranteed or insured by the United States and its agencies, with annexes.

Signed at Khartoum May 17, 1980.

Entered into force June 19, 1980.

32 UST 4373; TIAS 9952.

Agreement regarding the consolidation and rescheduling of payments due under P.L. 480 Title I agricultural commodity agreements.

Signed at Khartoum August 18, 1980.

Entered into force August 18, 1980.

32 UST 4373; TIAS 9952.

Agreement regarding the consolidation and rescheduling of certain debts owed to, guaranteed or insured by the United States Government and its agencies, with annexes.

Signed at Khartoum July 20, 1982.

Entered into force August 23, 1982.

34 UST 1567; TIAS 10437.

Agreement regarding the consolidation and rescheduling of certain debts owed to, guaranteed or insured by the United States Government and its agencies.

Signed at Khartoum January 21, 1984.

Entered into force March 27, 1984.

TIAS 10981.

Agreement regarding the consolidation and rescheduling of certain debts owed to, guaranteed by or insured by the United States Government and its agencies, with annexes.

Signed at Khartoum December 22, 1984.

Entered into force January 25, 1985.

NP

HUMANITARIAN ASSISTANCE

Agreement concerning the privileges and immunities of the International Verification and Investigation Team.

Exchange of notes at Khartoum August 29 and September 23 and 30, 2002.

Entered into force September 30, 2002.

TIAS

JUDICIAL ASSISTANCE

Agreement on procedures for mutual assistance in connection with matters relating to the Boeing Company.

Signed at Washington September 23, 1977.

Entered into force September 23, 1977.

28 UST 7482; TIAS 8723.

POSTAL MATTERS

International express mail agreement, with detailed regulations.

Signed at Khartoum and Washington October 22 and November 30, 1990.

Entered into force January 14, 1991.

TIAS 11768.

TELECOMMUNICATIONS

Agreement for the establishment of U.S. radio transmitting facilities.

Signed at Khartoum July 12, 2006.

Entered into force July 12, 2006.

TIAS

SUPREME ALLIED COMMANDER ATLANTIC (SACLANT)

DEFENSE

Acquisition and cross-servicing agreement concerning mutual logistic support, with annexes

Signed December 17 and 18, 1997.

Entered into force December 18, 1997.

TIAS

SUPREME ALLIED COMMANDER TRANSFORMATION (SACT)

DEFENSE

Implementing arrangement concerning mutual logistics support, with annexes.

Signed at Norfolk April 30 and May 12, 2005.

Entered into force May 12, 2005.

TIAS

SUPREME HEADQUARTERS ALLIED POWERS EUROPE (SHAPE)

DEFENSE

Agreement concerning support of the allied tactical operations center at Sembach Air Base, Germany, with annexes.

Signed at Heidelberg and Sembach Air Base August 28 and November 25, 1987.

Entered into force November 25, 1987; effective May 1, 1983.

TIAS

TELECOMMUNICATION

Mutual support agreement for telecommunications, with annex.

Signed at Casteau and Vaihingen January 22 and February 25, 1985.

Entered into force February 25, 1985.

TIAS 11187; 2130 UNTS 399.

SURINAME

On November 25, 1975 Suriname became an independent state. In a note dated November 29, 1975 to the Secretary-General of the United Nations, the Prime Minister made a statement reading in part as follows:

"The Government of the Republic of Surinam, conscious of the desirability of maintaining existing legal relationship, and conscious of its obligation under International Law to honour its treaty commitments, acknowledges that treaty rights and obligations of the Government of the Kingdom of the Netherlands in respect of Surinam were succeeded by the Republic of Surinam upon Independence by virtue of customary International Law.

Since, however, it is likely that by virtue of customary International Law certain treaties may have lapsed at the date of Independence of Surinam, it seems essential that each treaty should be subjected to legal examination. It is proposed after this examination has been completed, to indicate which, if any, of the treaties which may have lapsed by customary International Law the Government of the Republic of Surinam wish to treat as having lapsed.

It is desired that it be presumed that each treaty has been legally succeeded to by the Republic of Surinam and that action be based upon this presumption until a decision is reached that it should be regarded as having lapsed. Should the Government of the Republic of Surinam be of the opinion it has legally succeeded to a treaty but subsequently wish to terminate its operation, the Government will in due course give notice of termination in the terms thereof."

AVIATION

Agreement between the United States and the Netherlands providing for nonassertion of sovereign immunity from suit of air transport enterprises.

Exchange of notes at Washington June 19, 1953.

Entered into force June 19, 1953.

4 UST 1610; TIAS 2828; 212 UNTS 249.

Air transport agreement between the United States and The Netherlands.

Signed at Washington April 3, 1957.

Entered into force provisionally April 3, 1957; definitively May 31, 1957.

12 UST 837; TIAS 4782; 410 UNTS 193.

Amendment

November 25, 1969 (20 UST 4070; TIAS 6797; 732 UNTS 316).

Memorandum of agreement concerning assistance in developing and modernizing the Suriname civil aviation infrastructure, with annexes.

Signed at Washington and Paramaribo June 21 and August 27, 1990.

Entered into force August 27, 1990.

TIAS 11754; 2202 UNTS 171.

COMMERCE

Treaty of friendship, commerce and navigation, with protocol and exchange of notes between the United States and the Netherlands.

Signed at The Hague March 27, 1956; applicable to Suriname February 10, 1963.

8 UST 2043; TIAS 3942; 285 UNTS 231.

CONSULS

Convention between the United States and The Netherlands regarding consuls in the colonies of The Netherlands.[1]

Signed at The Hague January 22, 1855.

Entered into force May 25, 1855.

10 Stat. 1150; TS 253; 10 Bevans 28.

NOTE

1 American consular officers in colonies of the Netherlands have been instructed not to enforce that section of the convention relating to the arrest of deserters, as being in conflict with the Seamen's Act (38 Stat. 1164).

DEFENSE

Agreement concerning the provision of training related to defense articles under the United States International Military Education and Training (IMET) Program.

Exchange of notes at Paramaribo August 22 and 25, 1980.

Entered into force August 25, 1980.

32 UST 3741; TIAS 9916; 1267 UNTS 155.

Agreement regarding the status of U.S. Special Forces Deployment for Training Exercise Mission.

Exchange of notes at Paramaribo January 17 and February 2, 1996.

Entered into force February 2, 1996.

NP

Agreement regarding the status of United States personnel who may be temporarily present in the Republic of Suriname.

Exchange of notes at Paramaribo April 11 and October 20, 2005.

Entered into force October 20, 2005.

TIAS

ECONOMIC AND TECHNICAL COOPERATION

Economic cooperation agreement between the United States and The Netherlands.

Signed at The Hague July 2, 1948.

Entered into force July 2, 1948.

62 Stat. 2477; TIAS 1791; 10 Bevans 240; 20 UNTS 91.

Amendments

January 16 and February 2, 1950 (1 UST 665; TIAS 2126; 93 UNTS 361).

March 7 and April 3, 1951 (2 UST 1319; TIAS 2285; 141 UNTS 368).

November 28, 1952 (3 UST 5260; TIAS 2721; 173 UNTS 382).

General agreement between the United States and The Netherlands for technical cooperation for Suriname and Netherlands Antilles.

Signed at The Hague January 22, 1954.

Entered into force April 21, 1954.

5 UST 819; TIAS 2982; 190 UNTS 207.

ENVIRONMENTAL COOPERATION

Agreement for cooperation in the Global Learning and Observations to Benefit the Environment (GLOBE) Program, with appendices.

Signed at Paramaribo December 23, 1997.

Entered into force December 23, 1997.

TIAS

EXTRADITION

Convention between the United States and The Netherlands for the extradition of criminals.

Signed at Washington June 2, 1887.

Entered into force July 11, 1889.

26 Stat. 1481; TS 256; 10 Bevans 47.

Treaty extending the extradition convention of June 2, 1887, between the United States and The Netherlands to their respective island possessions and colonies.

Signed at Washington January 18, 1904.

Entered into force August 28, 1904.

33 Stat. 2257; TS 436; 10 Bevans 53.

FINANCE

Investment incentive agreement.

Signed at Paramaribo May 28, 1993.

Entered into force February 20, 1996.

TIAS 12500.

JUDICIAL ASSISTANCE

Procedures for mutual assistance in connection with matters relating to the Reynolds Metals Company.

Signed at Washington March 14, 1979.

Entered into force March 14, 1979.

30 UST 3864; TIAS 9429; 1171 UNTS 209.

MUTUAL SECURITY

Agreement between the United States and The Netherlands relating to the assurances required by the Mutual Security Act of 1951.

Exchange of notes at The Hague January 8, 1952.

Entered into force January 8, 1952.

3 UST 4633; TIAS 2615; 173 UNTS 372.

NARCOTIC DRUGS

Agreement concerning cooperation in maritime law enforcement.

Signed at Paramaribo December 31, 1998.

Entered into force August 26, 1999.

TIAS

PEACE CORPS

Agreement concerning the establishment of a Peace Corps program in Suriname.

Exchange of notes at Paramaribo October 12, 1994 and January 5, 1995.

Entered into force January 5, 1995.

TIAS 12595.

POSTAL MATTERS

Parcel post convention.

Signed at Paramaribo July 9 and at Washington August 18, 1930; operative September 1, 1930.

46 Stat. 2798; Post Office Department print; 125 LNTS 123.

REFUGEES

Agreement terminating the memorandum of understanding of August 1, 1994, for the establishment within the territory of Suriname of facilities to provide temporary protection for nationals of Haiti and transferring certain facilities and equipment to Suriname.

Exchange of notes at Paramaribo January 20 and 24, 1995.

Entered into force January 24, 1995.

TIAS 12600.

SCIENTIFIC COOPERATION

Memorandum of understanding concerning scientific and technical cooperation in the earth sciences, with annexes and related agreement.

Signed at Paramaribo March 22, 1995.

Entered into force March 22, 1995.

TIAS 12619.

TELECOMMUNICATION

Agreement relating to the reciprocal granting of authorizations to permit licensed amateur radio operators of either country to operate their stations in the other country.

Exchange of notes at Paramaribo October 3 and 12, 1978.

Entered into force October 12, 1978.

30 UST 2107; TIAS 9314.

VISAS

Agreement between the United States and the Netherlands relating to the reciprocal waiver of passport visa fees for nonimmigrants.

Exchanges of notes at The Hague January 21, February 11, and March 5 and 13, 1946.

Entered into force April 15, 1946.

61 Stat. 3834; TIAS 1728; 10 Bevans 178; 84 UNTS 3.

SWAZILAND

In a note dated October 22, 1968 to the Secretary General of the United Nations, the Minister of State of Swaziland made a statement reading in part as follows: "[F]or a period of two years with effect from September 6, 1968, the Government of the Kingdom of Swaziland accepts all treaty rights and obligations entered into prior to independence by the British Government on behalf of the Kingdom of Swaziland, during which period the treaties and international agreements in which such rights and obligations are embodied will receive examination with a view to determining, at the expiration of that period of two years, which of those rights and obligations will be adopted, which will be terminated, and which of these will be adopted with reservations in respect of particular matters." In a further note dated October 30, 1970 it was stated that the Government of the Kingdom of Swaziland shall continue to apply the terms of these treaties within Swaziland, on a basis of reciprocity, for an indefinite period of time. This provisional arrangement should be deemed to continue in each case until the depositary is notified of the decision of the Government of the Kingdom of Swaziland either to accede definitively or to terminate its further adherence to the treaty.

DEFENSE

Agreement concerning the provision of training related to defense articles under the United States International Military Education and Training (IMET) Program.

Exchange of notes at Mbabane January 10 and February 28, 1984.

Entered into force February 28, 1984.

35 UST 4505; TIAS 10952.

ECONOMIC AND TECHNICAL COOPERATION

General agreement on special development assistance.

Signed at Mbabane June 3, 1970.

Entered into force June 3, 1970.

21 UST 1412; TIAS 6898; 756 UNTS 95.

Agreement for economic, technical and related assistance.

Signed at Mbabane December 5, 1989.

Entered into force December 5, 1989.

TIAS 11733; 2202 UNTS 3.

EXTRADITION

Extradition treaty between the United States and the United Kingdom.

Signed at London December 22, 1931.

Entered into force June 24, 1935.

47 Stat. 2122; TS 849; 12 Bevans 482; 163 LNTS 59.

Agreement continuing in force between the United States and Swaziland the extradition treaty of December 22, 1931 (47 Stat. 2122), between the United States and the United Kingdom.

Exchange of notes at Mbabane May 13 and July 28, 1970.

Entered into force July 28, 1970.

21 UST 1930; TIAS 6934; 756 UNTS 103.

FINANCE

Agreement relating to investment guaranties.

Signed at Mbabane September 29, 1967.

Entered into force September 29, 1967.

18 UST 2510; TIAS 6350; 693 UNTS 167.

Agreement continuing in force the agreement of September 29, 1967 (TIAS 6350), relating to investment guaranties.

Exchange of notes at Mbabane April 3 and July 28, 1970.

Entered into force July 28, 1970.

21 UST 2006; TIAS 6944; 763 UNTS 53.

INTERNATIONAL CRIMINAL COURT

Agreement regarding the surrender of persons to the International Criminal Court.

Signed at Mbabane May 10, 2006.

Entered into force September 20, 2006.

TIAS

PEACE CORPS

Agreement relating to the establishment of a Peace Corps program in Swaziland.

Exchange of notes at Mbabane November 11, 1970.

Entered into force November 11, 1970.

21 UST 2487; TIAS 6989; 772 UNTS 173.

POSTAL MATTERS

International express mail agreement, with detailed regulations.

Signed at Mbabane and Washington March 3 and April 6, 1988.

Entered into force May 1, 1988.

TIAS 11583.

TELECOMMUNICATION

Agreement relating to establishment of a Bureau of Foreign Broadcast Information Service (FBIS) in Swaziland.

Signed at Mbabane August 3, 1981.

Entered into force August 3, 1981.

33 UST 3344; TIAS 10235.

Arrangement relating to radio communications between amateur stations on behalf of third parties.

Exchange of notes at Mbabane April 12 and May 27, 1983.

Entered into force June 26, 1983.

TIAS 10718; 1607 UNTS 131.

SWEDEN

ATOMIC ENERGY

Agreement regarding participation in the USNRC international piping integrity research group, with appendices.

Signed at Stockholm and Bethesda February 2 and March 3, 1987.

Entered into force March 3, 1987.

TIAS 12218.

Arrangement for the exchange of technical information and cooperation in the regulation of nuclear safety.

Signed at Vienna September 19, 2006.

Entered into force September 19, 2006.

TIAS

AVIATION

Arrangement relating to pilot licenses to operate civil aircraft.

Exchange of notes at Washington September 8 and 9, 1933.

Entered into force October 9, 1933.

48 Stat. 1799; EAS 48; 11 Bevans 788; 144 LNTS 171.

Agreement relating to air transport services.

Exchange of notes at Washington December 16, 1944.

Entered into force January 1, 1945.

58 Stat. 1466; EAS 431; 11 Bevans 825; 6 UNTS 397.

Amendments

August 6, 1954 (5 UST 1411; TIAS 3013; 222 UNTS 376).

June 16, 1995; (TIAS 12665).

Agreement relating to air service facilities in Sweden.

Signed at Stockholm September 30, 1946.

Entered into force September 30, 1946.

61 Stat. 3893; TIAS 1742; 11 Bevans 832; 42 UNTS 213.

Agreement relating to airworthiness certifications.

Exchange of notes at Stockholm April 24 and 26, 1973.

Entered into force April 26, 1973.

24 UST 997; TIAS 7611.

Agreement for the promotion of aviation safety.

Signed at Stockholm February 9, 1998.

Entered into force February 9, 1998.

TIAS

CONSULS

Consular convention.[1]

Signed at Washington June 1, 1910.

Entered into force March 18, 1911.

37 Stat. 1479; TS 557; 11 Bevans 730.

NOTE

1 Articles XI and XII abrogated as of March 18, 1921.

CUSTOMS

Arrangement relating to free entry, on a reciprocal basis, for goods imported by career consular representatives.

Exchange of notes at Stockholm June 23 and 29, 1931.

Entered into force July 1, 1931.

11 Bevans 771.

Arrangement for the reciprocal exemption from duty of articles imported by diplomatic officers and all other persons belonging to missions, but not including personal servants.

Exchange of notes at Washington January 5 and 17, 1933.

Entered into force January 17, 1933.

11 Bevans 776.

Agreement regarding mutual assistance in customs matters.

Signed at Washington July 8, 1987.

Entered into force May 8, 1988.

TIAS 12122.

DEFENSE

Agreement relating to the procurement of reimbursable military equipment, materials, or services.

Exchange of notes at Stockholm June 30 and July 1, 1952.

Entered into force July 1, 1952.

3 UST 2968; TIAS 2480; 187 UNTS 3.

Agreement concerning general security of military information.

Exchange of notes at Washington December 4 and 23, 1981.

Entered into force December 23, 1981.

33 UST 4400; TIAS 10309.

Memorandum of understanding relating to the principles governing mutual cooperation in the defense procurement area, with related exchange of letters.

Signed at Washington and Stockholm June 11 and July 16, 1987.

Entered into force July 16, 1987.

TIAS; 1557 UNTS 313.

Amendment

June 12 and August 11, 2003.

Memorandum of agreement concerning the exchange of engineers and scientists, with annexes.

Signed at Washington and Stockholm June 9 and 15, 1992.

Entered into force June 15, 1992.

NP

Agreement for cooperative research and development efforts in the fields of aircrew protection and performance, with annexes.

Signed at Stockholm April 23, 1993.

Entered into force April 23, 1993.

TIAS 12371.

Agreement for cooperation on environmental protection in defense matters.

Signed at Stockholm April 24, 1995.

Entered into force April 24, 1995.

TIAS 12372.

Agreement for the bilateral cooperative program in electro-magnetic effects measurement and analysis (RF Effects Program).

Signed at Washington June 2 and December 20, 1995.

Entered into force December 20, 1995.

TIAS 12373.

Agreement for technology research and development projects, with annex.

Signed at Washington and Stockholm March 10 and April 22, 1997.

Entered into force April 22, 1997.

TIAS

Agreement amending the production supplement of April 10, 1987 for development, modification and adaptation of the Hellfire Modular Missile System for Swedish coastal defense.

Signed at Stockholm and Washington May 21 and July 7, 1997.

Entered into force July 7, 1997.

NP

Agreement regarding the exchange of engineers and scientists, with annexes.

Signed at Stockholm and Washington October 7 and December 20, 1999.

Entered into force December 20, 1999.

NP

Acquisition and cross-servicing agreement, with annex.

Signed at Stuttgart and Stockholm August 28 and September 11, 2003.

Entered into force September 11, 2003.

TIAS

Memorandum of understanding regarding foreign liaison officers, with annex.

Signed at Washington and Norfolk August 25 and September 21, 2004.

Entered into force September 21, 2004.

TIAS

Agreement for cooperation in environmental protection and defense matters.

Signed at Stockholm and Washington November 23 and December 6, 2005.

Entered into force December 6, 2005.

TIAS

ECONOMIC AND TECHNICAL COOPERATION

Economic cooperation agreement.

Signed at Stockholm July 3, 1948.

Entered into force July 21, 1948.

62 Stat. 2541; TIAS 1793; 11 Bevans 855; 23 UNTS 101.

Amendments

January 5 and 17, 1950 (1 UST 181; TIAS 2034; 76 UNTS 254).

February 8 and 23, 1951 (3 UST 2800; TIAS 2448; 185 UNTS 326).

EDUCATION

Agreement for financing certain educational exchange programs.

Signed at Stockholm November 20, 1952.

Entered into force November 20, 1952.

3 UST 4812; TIAS 2653; 177 UNTS 203.

Amendments

November 20, 1959 (10 UST 1921; TIAS 4359; 360 UNTS 396).

June 28, 1963 (14 UST 985; TIAS 5389; 479 UNTS 358).

December 7, 1970 (21 UST 2732; TIAS 7018; 776 UNTS 330).

EMPLOYMENT

Arrangement relating to the employment of dependents of official government employees.

Exchange of notes at Washington October 27 and 30, 1981.

Entered into force October 30, 1981.

33 UST 4148; TIAS 10291.

ENVIRONMENTAL COOPERATION

Agreement for cooperation in the Global Learning and Observations to Benefit the Environment (GLOBE) Program, with appendices.

Signed at Stockholm August 23, 1995.

Entered into force August 23, 1995.

TIAS 12684.

EXTRADITION

Convention on extradition, with protocol.[1]

Signed at Washington October 24, 1961.

Entered into force December 3, 1963.

14 UST 1845; TIAS 5496; 494 UNTS 141.

Supplementary convention on extradition.

Signed at Stockholm March 14, 1983.

Entered into force September 24, 1984.

35 UST 2501; TIAS 10812.

NOTE

1 Protocol terminated January 1, 1965.

HIGHWAYS

Memorandum of understanding on highway management and technology.

Signed at Borlange June 15, 1992.

Entered into force June 15, 1992.

TIAS 11870.

MAPPING

Basic exchange and cooperative agreement for global geospatial information and services, with annexes.

Signed at Stockholm and Bethesda November 26 and December 14, 1998.

Entered into force December 14, 1998.

NP

MARITIME MATTERS

Arrangement relating to the reciprocal exemption of pleasure yachts from all navigation dues.

Exchange of notes at Stockholm October 22 and 29, 1930.

Entered into force October 29, 1930.

47 Stat. 2655; EAS 21; 11 Bevans 763; 109 LNTS 181.

NATIONALITY

Convention relating to exemption from military service of persons having dual nationality.

Signed at Stockholm January 31, 1933.

Entered into force May 20, 1935.

49 Stat. 3195; TS 890; 11 Bevans 778; 159 LNTS 261.

PACIFIC SETTLEMENT OF DISPUTES

Treaty for the advancement of peace.

Signed at Washington October 13, 1914.

Entered into force January 11, 1915.

38 Stat. 1872; TS 607; 11 Bevans 741.

Agreement concerning compensation for commissioners designated under the treaty for advancement of peace signed October 13, 1914.

Exchange of notes at Stockholm June 30, 1939.

Entered into force June 30, 1939.

53 Stat. 2428; EAS 154; 11 Bevans 821; 199 LNTS 203.

Treaty of arbitration.

Signed at Washington October 27, 1928.

Entered into force April 15, 1929.

46 Stat. 2261; TS 783; 11 Bevans 760; 91 LNTS 225.

PATENTS

Agreement facilitating the interchange of patent rights and technical information for defense purposes.

Exchange of notes at Washington October 4, 1962.

Entered into force October 4, 1962.

13 UST 2161; TIAS 5178; 462 UNTS 31.

Agreement approving the procedures for reciprocal filing of classified patent applications in the United States and Sweden.

Exchange of notes at Washington October 20 and November 17, 1964.

Entered into force November 17, 1964.

15 UST 2086; TIAS 5690; 532 UNTS 378.

POSTAL MATTERS

Parcel post convention.

Signed at Stockholm June 28 and at Washington July 11, 1932; operative July 1, 1932.

47 Stat. 2106; Post Office Department print.

International express mail agreement, with detailed regulations.

Signed at Stockholm and Washington August 26 and 30, 1983.

Entered into force October 1, 1983.

35 UST 2136; TIAS 10780; 2011 UNTS 115.

PUBLICATIONS

Agreement relating to exchange of official publications.

Exchange of notes at Stockholm December 16, 1947.

Entered into force December 16, 1947.

61 Stat. 3605; TIAS 1688; 11 Bevans 843; 73 UNTS 65.

SCIENTIFIC COOPERATION

Memorandum of understanding concerning scientific and technical cooperation in the earth sciences, with annexes.

Signed at Reston and Stockholm April 22 and June 1, 1994.

Entered into force June 1, 1994.

TIAS 12182.

Agreement on science and technology cooperation, with annexes.

Signed at Stockholm June 29, 2006.

Entered into force June 29, 2006.

TIAS

Memorandum of understanding concerning scientific and technical cooperation in the earth sciences, with annexes.

Signed at Reston and Stockholm December 7 and 18, 2006.

Entered into force December 18, 2006.

TIAS

SHIPPING

Agreement relating to jurisdiction over vessels utilizing the Louisiana Offshore Oil Port.

Exchange of notes at Washington August 17 and 22, 1978.

Entered into force August 22, 1978.

30 UST 1698; TIAS 9277; 1153 UNTS 145.

SMUGGLING

Convention for the prevention of smuggling of intoxicating liquors.

Signed at Washington May 22, 1924.

Entered into force August 18, 1924.

43 Stat. 1830; TS 698; 11 Bevans 750; 29 LNTS 421.

SOCIAL SECURITY

Agreement on social security, with administrative arrangement.

Signed at Stockholm May 27, 1985.

Entered into force January 1, 1987.

TIAS 11266.

SPACE COOPERATION

Memorandum of understanding for cooperative sounding rocket activities.

Signed at Washington and Stockholm May 17 and June 10, 1996.

Entered into force June 10, 1996.

TIAS 12766.

Framework agreement for cooperative activities in the exploration and use of outer space for peaceful purposes.

Signed at Stockholm October 14, 2005.

Entered into force October 14, 2005.

TIAS

TAXATION

Arrangement relating to relief from double income tax on shipping profits.

Exchange of notes at Washington March 31, 1938.

Entered into force March 31, 1938.

52 Stat. 1490; EAS 121; 11 Bevans 806; 189 LNTS 327.

Amendment

June 26 and July 24, 1987 (TIAS 11286; 2174 UNTS 379).

Convention for the avoidance of double taxation and the prevention of fiscal evasion with respect to taxes on estates, inheritances and gifts.

Signed at Stockholm June 13, 1983.

Entered into force September 5, 1984.

35 UST 2897; TIAS 10826.

Convention for the avoidance of double taxation and the prevention of fiscal evasion with respect to taxes on income, with exchange of letters.

Signed at Stockholm September 1, 1994.

Entered into force October 26, 1995.

TIAS

TELECOMMUNICATION

Agreement relating to the reciprocal granting of authorizations to permit licensed amateur radio operators of either country to operate their station in the other country.

Exchange of notes at Stockholm May 27 and June 2, 1969.

Entered into force June 2, 1969.

20 UST 773; TIAS 6690; 715 UNTS 75.

TRADE AND COMMERCE

Agreement supplementary to the general agreement on tariffs and trade to provide concession as compensation to Sweden for spring clothespins escape clause action, and exchange of notes.

Signed at Washington September 15, 1961.

Entered into force September 15, 1961.

12 UST 1271; TIAS 4847; 421 UNTS 241.

Agreement within the context of the multilateral trade negotiations concerning cheese and other agricultural products, and related letters of January 30 and February 19, 1980.

Done at Geneva June 13, July 5 and 10, 1979.

Entered into force January 1, 1980.

32 UST 5512; TIAS 10003; 1266 UNTS 49.

VISAS

Agreement relating to passport visa fees for nonimmigrants.

Exchange of notes at Washington April 10 and 30, 1947.

Entered into force April 30, 1947; operative June 1, 1947.

61 Stat. 4050; TIAS 1798; 11 Bevans 834; 84 UNTS 33.

SWITZERLAND

ATOMIC ENERGY

Agreement regarding participation in the USNRC international piping integrity research group, with appendices.

Signed at Bern and Bethesda February 3 and March 3, 1987.

Entered into force March 3, 1987.

TIAS 12219.

Agreement for cooperation concerning peaceful uses of atomic energy, with agreed minute and annexes.

Signed at Bern October 31, 1997.

Entered into force June 23, 1998.

TIAS

Arrangement for the exchange of technical information and cooperation in nuclear safety matters.

Done at Vienna September 18, 2002.

Entered into force September 18, 2002.

TIAS

AVIATION

Air service agreement relating to equipment at Cointrin Airport.

Signed at Bern April 30, 1947.

Entered into force April 30, 1947.

61 Stat. 3859; TIAS 1736; 11 Bevans 957; 42 UNTS 235.

Agreement concerning the reciprocal acceptance of certificates of airworthiness for imported aircraft.

Exchange of notes at Bern October 13, 1961.

Entered into force provisionally October 13, 1961, and definitively November 21, 1962.

13 UST 2479; TIAS 5214; 459 UNTS 219.

Amendment

January 7, 1977 (28 UST 2446; TIAS 8563).

Air transport agreement, with annexes.

Signed at Washington June 15, 1995.

Entered into force September 27, 1996.

TIAS 12662.

Agreement for promotion of aviation safety.

Signed at Washington September 26, 1996.

Entered into force September 26, 1996.

TIAS 12803.

COMMERCE

Convention of friendship, commerce and extradition.[1]

Signed at Bern November 25, 1850.

Entered into force November 8, 1855.

11 Stat. 587; TS 353; 11 Bevans 894.

NOTE

1 Articles 8-12 terminated March 23, 1900, as a result of notice given by the United States on March 23, 1899; articles 13-17 relating to extradition were superseded and expressly repealed by the extradition treaty signed May 14, 1900 (31 Stat. 1928; TS 354; 11 Bevans 904).

CONSULS

See COMMERCE

DEFENSE

Memorandum of understanding for coproduction of the M109A1B self propelled 155 MM Howitzer.

Signed at Washington July 18, 1988.

Entered into force July 18, 1988.

TIAS 11507.

Memorandum of understanding concerning defense acquisition, with annex.

Signed at Washington and Berne October 25 and November 1, 1988.

Entered into force November 1, 1988.

TIAS

Amendment

May 16 and December 10, 2001.

Agreement amending the memorandum of understanding of February 25, 1988, as amended, for the coproduction of the stinger post plus (stinger-RMP) weapon system.

Signed at Washington and Berne March 23 and May 4, 1995.

Entered into force May 4, 1995.

TIAS 12642.

Agreement on the exchange of military personnel between the U.S. Navy and the Swiss Air Force and Anti-Aircraft Command.

Signed at Bern and Washington July 5 and August 17, 1995.

Entered into force August 17, 1995.

NP

Agreement concerning acquisition and cross-servicing, with annex.

Signed at Stuttgart and Bern March 23 and December 6, 2001.

Entered into force December 6, 2001.

TIAS

ENVIRONMENTAL COOPERATION

Agreement for cooperation in the Global Learning and Observations to Benefit the Environment (GLOBE) Program, with appendices.

Signed at Berne April 22, 1998.

Entered into force April 22, 1998.

TIAS

EXTRADITION

Extradition treaty.

Signed at Washington November 14, 1990.

Entered into force September 10, 1997.

TIAS

JUDICIAL ASSISTANCE

Treaty on mutual assistance in criminal matters with related notes.

Signed at Bern May 25, 1973.

Entered into force January 23, 1977.

27 UST 2019; TIAS 8302; 1052 UNTS 61.

Related agreement

November 3, 1993 (TIAS 12514).

MAINTENANCE

Agreement for the enforcement of maintenance (support) obligations.

Signed at Washington August 31, 2004.

Entered into force September 30, 2004.

TIAS

MAPPING

Basic exchange and cooperative agreement concerning global geospatial information and services cooperation, with annexes.

Signed at Brussels June 19, 2001.

Entered into force June 19, 2001.

NP

NARCOTIC DRUGS

Arrangement for the direct exchange of certain information regarding the traffic in narcotic drugs.

Exchange of notes at Bern November 15 and 16, 1929.

Entered into force November 16, 1929.

11 Bevans 917.

NATIONALITY

Convention relative to military obligations of certain persons having dual nationality.

Signed at Bern November 11, 1937.

Entered into force December 7, 1938.

53 Stat. 1791; TS 943; 11 Bevans 936; 193 LNTS 181.

PACIFIC SETTLEMENT OF DISPUTES

Treaty of arbitration and conciliation.

Signed at Washington February 16, 1931.

Entered into force May 23, 1932.

47 Stat. 1983; TS 844; 11 Bevans 920; 129 LNTS 465.

PATENTS

Arrangement relating to reciprocal benefits under the patent laws of the two countries.

Exchange of notes at Bern January 17 and 28, 1908.

Entered into force January 28, 1908.

11 Bevans 909.

POSTAL MATTERS

Agreement concerning the exchange of parcel post, and regulations of execution.[1]

Signed at Washington April 1 and at Bern May 18, 1932; operative April 1, 1932.

47 Stat. 1997; Post Office Department print.

International express mail agreement, with detailed regulations.

Signed at Bern and Washington December 7, 1978 and January 22, 1979.

Entered into force February 1, 1979.

32 UST 5549; TIAS 10008; 1265 UNTS 131.

NOTE

1 Applicable to Liechtenstein.

PRIVILEGES AND IMMUNITIES

Agreement concerning the status, privileges, and immunities of the SALT (START) delegation in Switzerland with annex.

Exchange of notes at Bern November 21 and 22, 1972.

Entered into force November 22, 1972.

23 UST 3736; TIAS 7523.

Related agreement

June 9, 1982 (34 UST 1263; TIAS 10414).

Agreement on rights, privileges and immunities of the United States-Union of Soviet Socialist Republics Standing Consultative Commission.

Exchange of notes at Bern February 26 and March 5, 1973.

Entered into force March 5, 1973.

24 UST 772; TIAS 7582; 944 UNTS 95.

Agreement establishing rights, privileges and immunities of the delegation to the negotiations concerning theater (intermediate range) nuclear forces.

Exchange of letters at Bern October 17, 1980.

Entered into force October 17, 1980.

33 UST 610; TIAS 10056; 1265 UNTS 177.

Related agreement

November 11 and 20, 1981 (33 UST 4237; TIAS 10298).

Agreement establishing rights, privileges and immunities of the United States delegation to the negotiations on nuclear and space arms.

Exchange of notes at Bern March 1 and 5, 1985.

Entered into force March 5, 1985.

TIAS 11188; 2129 UNTS 425.

PUBLICATIONS

Agreement relating to the exchange of official publications.

Exchange of notes at Washington January 5 and February 24, 1950.

Entered into force February 24, 1950.

1 UST 396; TIAS 2058; 93 UNTS 3.

SOCIAL SECURITY

Agreement on social security, with final protocol.

Signed at Washington July 18, 1979.

Entered into force November 1, 1980.

32 UST 2165; TIAS 9830; 1252 UNTS 127.

Amendment

June 1, 1988 (TIAS 12126).

Administrative agreement for the implementation of the agreement on social security of July 18, 1979.

Signed at Bern December 20, 1979.

Entered into force November 1, 1980.

32 UST 2165; TIAS 9830; 1252 UNTS 137.

TAXATION

Convention for the avoidance of double taxation with respect to taxes on estates and inheritances.

Signed at Washington July 9, 1951.

Entered into force September 17, 1952.

3 UST 3972; TIAS 2533; 165 UNTS 51.

Convention for the avoidance of double taxation with respect to taxes on income, with protocol.

Signed at Washington October 2, 1996.

Entered into force December 19, 1997.

TIAS

TELECOMMUNICATION

Agreement relating to the reciprocal granting of authorizations to permit licensed amateur radio operators of either country to operate their stations in the other country.

Exchange of notes at Bern January 12 and May 16, 1967.

Entered into force May 16, 1967.

18 UST 554; TIAS 6264; 685 UNTS 319.

TRADE

See also COMMERCE

Agreement within the context of the multilateral trade negotiations regarding motor vehicles, and related letter of November 19, 1980.

Done at Bern April 11, 1979.

Entered into force January 1, 1980.

32 UST 5521; TIAS 10004; 1265 UNTS 181.

Arrangement within the context of the multilateral trade negotiations concerning cheeses, with exchange of letters, and related letter of November 19, 1980.

Done at Geneva and Bern April 12, 1979.

Entered into force January 1, 1980.

32 UST 5527; TIAS 10005; 1265 UNTS 151.

Commitment of Switzerland within the context of the multilateral trade negotiations concerning access to its market for beef, and related letter of November 19, 1980.

Done at Geneva and Bern April 12 and July 10, 1979.

Entered into force January 1, 1980.

32 UST 5539; TIAS 10006; 1265 UNTS 163.

Agreement within the context of the multilateral trade negotiations concerning the treatment of certain chemicals.

Exchange of letters at Geneva and Washington December 18 and 21, 1979.

Entered into force December 21, 1979.

32 UST 5545; TIAS 10007; 1265 UNTS 171.

Agreement establishing a trade and investment cooperation forum.

Signed at Washington May 25, 2006.

Entered into force May 25, 2006.

TIAS

TRADE-MARKS

Agreement relating to the registration of trade-marks.

Exchange of notes at Washington April 27 and May 14, 1883.

Entered into force May 14, 1883.

TS 471; 11 Bevans 901.

VISAS

Agreement relating to the waiver of passport visa fees for nonimmigrants.

Exchange of notes at Bern May 11, 1925.

Entered into force May 11, 1925; operative June 1, 1925.

11 Bevans 915.

Agreement relating to the waiver of passport visa fees for nonimmigrants.

Exchanges of notes at Washington October 22 and 31 and November 4 and 13, 1947.

Entered into force November 13, 1947.

6 UST 93; TIAS 3172; 251 UNTS 79.

SYRIAN ARAB REPUBLIC

AGRICULTURAL COMMODITIES

Agreement between the United States and the United Arab Republic relating to the sale of agricultural commodities to the United Arab Republic (Northern Region).

Signed at Cairo November 14, 1959.

Entered into force November 14, 1959.

10 UST 1908; TIAS 4357; 360 UNTS 311.

Agreement between the United States and the United Arab Republic relating to the sale of agricultural commodities to the United Arab Republic (Northern Region).

Signed at Cairo August 9, 1960.

Entered into force August 9, 1960.

11 UST 1994; TIAS 4551; 388 UNTS 271.

Amendment

September 17, 1960 (11 UST 2136; TIAS 4575; 389 UNTS 342).

Agricultural commodities agreement with exchange of notes.

Signed at Damascus November 9, 1961.

Entered into force November 9, 1961.

13 UST 97; TIAS 4944; 435 UNTS 75.

Amendment

February 24, 1962 (13 UST 376; TIAS 4993; 445 UNTS 389).

Agricultural commodities agreement with exchange of notes.

Signed at Damascus November 18, 1963.

Entered into force November 18, 1963.

14 UST 1864; TIAS 5497; 494 UNTS 169.

Amendment

December 28, 1963 (14 UST 1864; TIAS 5497; 494 UNTS 169).

Agricultural commodities agreement.

Signed at Damascus November 20, 1974.

Entered into force November 20, 1974.

26 UST 1576; TIAS 8119; 1006 UNTS 57.

Related agreements

April 20, 1976 (28 UST 7370; TIAS 8716).

May 11 and 16, 1976 (28 UST 7384; TIAS 8716).

June 2 and 3, 1976 (28 UST 7386; TIAS 8716).

September 28 and 29, 1976 (28 UST 7389; TIAS 8716).

March 3, 1977 (28 UST 7392; TIAS 8717).

May 3, 1978 (29 UST 5198; TIAS 9096; 1150 UNTS 47).

July 25, 1978 (29 UST 5211; TIAS 9096; 1150 UNTS 59).

May 2, 1979 (30 UST 7209; TIAS 9579).

June 23, 1979 (30 UST 7221; TIAS 9579).

CULTURAL RELATIONS

Cultural agreement.

Signed at Damascus May 12, 1977.

Entered into force May 12, 1977.

28 UST 5321; TIAS 8634.

CUSTOMS

Agreement between the United States and France relating to customs privileges for educational, religious, and philanthropic institutions in Syria and Lebanon.

Exchange of notes at Paris February 18, 1937.

Entered into force February 18, 1937.

51 Stat. 279; EAS 107; 7 Bevans 1017; 184 LNTS 479.

ECONOMIC AND TECHNICAL COOPERATION

Agreement between the United States and the United Arab Republic extending to the Syrian region of the United Arab Republic application of the general agreement for technical cooperation with Egypt of May 5, 1951, as amended, and the economic development program agreement of November 6, 1954.

Exchange of notes at Cairo April 2, 1960.

Entered into force April 2, 1960.

11 UST 1500; TIAS 4492; 376 UNTS 422.

Agency for International Development

February 27, 1975 (28 UST 575; TIAS 8477; 1068 UNTS 311).

February 27, 1975 (28 UST 809; TIAS 8482; 1068 UNTS 337).

February 27, 1975 (28 UST 595; TIAS 8478; 1068 UNTS 271).

June 30, 1975 (26 UST 3045; TIAS 8212).

June 30, 1975 (28 UST 624; TIAS 8478; 1068 UNTS 281).

July 22, 1976 (28 UST 1149; TIAS 8501; 1068 UNTS 369).

July 22, 1976 (28 UST 1174; TIAS 8502; 1068 UNTS 393).

September 30, 1976 (28 UST 3190; TIAS 8582).

September 20, 1977 (29 UST 3459; TIAS 9022; 1123 UNTS 233).

September 28, 1978 (30 UST 6296; TIAS 9554, 1234 UNTS 171).

FINANCE

Agreement relating to investment guaranties, with related letter.

Exchange of notes at Damascus August 9, 1976.

Entered into force August 13, 1977.

TIAS 8707; 28 UST 7122.

GENERAL RELATIONS

Convention between the United States and France relating to rights in Syria and Lebanon.

Signed at Paris April 4, 1924.

Entered into force July 13, 1924.

43 Stat. 1821; TS 695; 7 Bevans 925.

Agreement relating to rights of American nationals.

Exchange of notes at Damascus September 7 and 8, 1944.

Entered into force September 8, 1944.

58 Stat. 1491; EAS 434; 11 Bevans 970; 124 UNTS 251.

POSTAL MATTERS

Agreement with the United Arab Republic concerning the exchange of parcel post and regulations of execution.

Signed at Cairo December 30, 1958 and at Washington January 13, 1959.

Entered into force October 1, 1959.

10 UST 1664; TIAS 4315; 358 UNTS 3.

International express mail agreement, with detailed regulations.

Signed at Damascus and Washington September 26 and November 16, 1993.

Entered into force January 1, 1994.

NP

TELECOMMUNICATION

Agreement relating to reciprocal authorization for each Government to install and operate a lowpower radio station in the fixed service at or near its Embassy for transmission of official messages.

Exchange of notes at Washington November 13, 1974 and May 15, 1975.

Entered into force May 15, 1975.

27 UST 3292; TIAS 8363; 1068 UNTS 359.

T

TAJIKISTAN

For agreements prior to December 31, 1991, see UNION OF SOVIET SOCIALIST REPUBLICS.

DEFENSE

Agreement regarding the status of United States military and civilian personnel of the United States Department of Defense present in Tajikistan in connection with cooperative efforts in response to terrorism, humanitarian assistance and other agreed activities.

Exchange of notes at Dushanbe November 20 and 23, 2001.

Entered into force November 23, 2001.

TIAS

Acquisition and cross-servicing agreement.

Signed at Tampa and Dushanbe February 1 and March 11, 2002.

Entered into force March 11, 2002.

TIAS

Agreement on construction of a bridge between the Republic of Tajikistan and the Islamic State of Afghanistan.

Signed at Dushanbe December 31, 2003.

Entered into force December 31, 2003.

TIAS

DIPLOMATIC PROPERTIES

Agreement concerning the ownership of property for the diplomatic and consular missions of the United States and Tajikistan.

Exchange of notes at Dushanbe October 5, 2000 and January 2, 2001.

Entered into force January 2, 2001.

TIAS

ECONOMIC AND TECHNICAL COOPERATION

Agreement regarding cooperation to facilitate the provision of humanitarian and technical economic assistance.

Signed at Dushanbe September 13, 1993.

Entered into force September 13, 1993.

TIAS 12163.

EMPLOYMENT

Employment agreement concerning dependents of officials serving in both countries.

Exchange of notes at Dushanbe March 11 and August 12, 2003.

Entered into force August 12, 2003.

TIAS

FINANCE

Investment incentive agreement.

Signed at Dushanbe June 25, 1992.

Entered into force June 25, 1992.

TIAS 12461.

INTERNATIONAL CRIMINAL COURT

Agreement regarding the surrender of persons to the International Criminal Court.

Signed at Dushanbe August 26, 2002.

Entered into force June 23, 2003.

TIAS

TRADE

Agreement on trade relations, with exchanges of letters.

Signed at Dushanbe July 1, 1993.

Entered into force November 24, 1993.

TIAS

TANZANIA

On December 9, 1961 Tanganyika attained fully responsible status within the British Commonwealth. In a note dated December 9, 1961 to the Secretary-General of the United Nations from the Prime Minister, the Government of Tanganyika stated that it is willing to continue to apply, on a reciprocal basis, all such treaties validly applied or extended to it as a territory for a period of two years from the date of independence, that is to December 8, 1963, unless abrogated or modified earlier by mutual consent. On April 26, 1964 the Republic of Tanganyika and the People's Republic of Zanzibar were united as one Sovereign State under the name of the United Republic of Tanganyika and Zanzibar. In a note dated May 6, 1964 the United Republic of Tanganyika and Zanzibar informed the Secretary-General of the United Nations that "all international treaties and agreements in force between the Republic of Tanganyika or the People's Republic of Zanzibar and other States or international organizations will, to the extent that their implementation is consistent with the constitutional position established by the Articles of Union, remain in force within the regional limits prescribed on their conclusion and in accordance with the principles of international law." On October 29, 1964 the name of the Republic was changed to the United Republic of Tanzania.

AGRICULTURAL COMMODITIES

Agricultural commodities agreement.

Signed at Dar es Salaam May 23, 1975.

Entered into force May 23, 1975.

26 UST 2290; TIAS 8158.

Agricultural commodities agreement.

Signed at Dar es Salaam June 15, 1976.

Entered into force June 15, 1976.

27 UST 2314; TIAS 8310; 1055 UNTS 111.

Related agreements

March 19, 1977 (29 UST 1; TIAS 8784).

April 28, 1978 (29 UST 6078; TIAS 9170).

March 19, 1980 (32 UST 890; TIAS 9736; 1222 UNTS 171).

June 9, 1980 (32 UST 1689; TIAS 9795).

May 5, 1981 (33 UST 1779; TIAS 10146; 1529 UNTS 379).

Agricultural commodities agreement, with minutes of negotiation.

Signed at Dar es Salaam June 8, 1982.

Entered into force June 8, 1982.

TIAS 10530.

Agreement for the sale of agricultural commodities, with minutes of negotiation.

Signed at Dar es Salaam July 22, 1983.

Entered into force July 22, 1983.

35 UST 1682; TIAS 10758; 2011 UNTS 99.

CONSULS

Consular convention and protocol of signature between the United States and the United Kingdom.

Signed at Washington June 6, 1951.

Entered into force September 7, 1952.[1 2]

3 UST 3426; TIAS 2494; 165 UNTS 121.

NOTES

1 Paragraph 1 of article 7 is not applicable to Tanganyika.

2 Treaty continued in force between the United States and Tanzania by the exchange of notes of November 30 and December 6, 1965 (16 UST 2066; TIAS 5946).

ECONOMIC AND TECHNICAL COOPERATION

Agreement providing for the furnishing of economic, technical, and related assistance.

Exchange of notes at Dar es Salaam February 8, 1968.

Entered into force February 8, 1968.

19 UST 4614; TIAS 6448; 698 UNTS 67.

Agency for International Development

August 12 and 13, 1975 (29 UST 9; TIAS 8786).

April 13, 1976 (29 UST 1003; TIAS 8861).

August 15, 1977 (29 UST 5276; TIAS 9104).

April 7, 1999.

June 7, 2005 (NP).

September 26, 2005 (NP).
June 5, 2006 (NP).

ENVIRONMENTAL COOPERATION

Agreement for cooperation in the Global Learning and Observations to Benefit the Environment (GLOBE) Program, with appendices.

Signed at Dar es Salaam April 1, 1997.

Entered into force April 1, 1997.

TIAS

EXTRADITION

Extradition treaty between the United States and the United Kingdom.[1]

Signed at London December 22, 1931.

Entered into force June 24, 1935.

47 Stat. 2122; TS 849; 12 Bevans 482; 163 LNTS 59.

NOTE

1 Treaty continued in force between the United States and Tanzania by the exchange of notes of November 30 and December 6, 1965 (16 UST 2066; TIAS 5946).

FINANCE

Agreement relating to investment guaranties.

Exchange of notes at Dar es Salaam November 14, 1963.

Entered into force November 14, 1963.

14 UST 1608; TIAS 5465; 493 UNTS 75.

Agreement regarding the consolidation and rescheduling of certain debts owed to, guaranteed by or insured by the United States Government, and its agencies, with annexes.

Signed at Dar es Salaam March 18, 1987.

Entered into force April 27, 1987.

NP

Agreement regarding the consolidation and rescheduling of certain debts owed to, guaranteed by or insured by the United States Government and its agencies, with annexes.

Signed at Dar es Salaam May 4, 1989.

Entered into force June 15, 1989.

NP

Agreement regarding the consolidation and rescheduling of certain debts owed to, guaranteed by, or insured by the United States Government and its agencies, with annexes.

Signed at Dar es Salaam October 31, 1990.

Entered into force January 9, 1991.

NP

Agreement regarding the consolidation and rescheduling or refinancing of certain debts owed to, guaranteed by or insured by the United States Government and its agencies, with annexes.

Signed at Dar es Salaam September 11, 1992.

Entered into force December 3, 1992.

NP

Investment incentive agreement.

Signed at Dar es Salaam December 24, 1996.

Entered into force November 26, 1997.

TIAS 12824.

Agreement regarding the consolidation, reduction and rescheduling of certain debts owed to, guaranteed by, or insured by the United States Government and its Agency, with annexes.

Signed at Dar es Salaam January 16, 1998.

Entered into force March 27, 1998.

NP

Agreement regarding the consolidation and reduction of certain debts owed to, guaranteed by, or insured by the United States Government and its agencies, with annexes.

Signed at Dar es Salaam June 14, 2001.

Entered into force September 6, 2001.

NP

Agreement regarding the consolidation of debt owed to, guaranteed by, or insured by the United States Government, with annexes.

Signed at Dar es Salaam July 4, 2002.

Entered into force August 26, 2002.

NP

PEACE CORPS

Agreement concerning the provision of Peace Corps volunteers in Tanzania.

Signed at Dar es Salaam March 23, 1989.

Entered into force March 23, 1989.

TIAS 12110.

Extension

February 11 and March 30, 1994 (TIAS 12110).

POSTAL MATTERS

Parcel post agreement and regulations of execution.

Signed at Zanzibar October 20 and at Washington December 30, 1959.

Entered into force May 1, 1960.

11 UST 293; TIAS 4449.

International express mail agreement, with detailed regulations.

Signed at Dar es Salaam and Washington December 30, 1987 and January 25, 1988.

Entered into force February 15, 1988.

TIAS 11886.

TREATY OBLIGATIONS

Agreement continuing in force between the United States and Tanzania the extradition treaty and the consular convention between the United States and the United Kingdom.

Exchange of notes at Dar es Salaam November 30 and December 6, 1965.

Entered into force December 6, 1965; effective December 9, 1963.

16 UST 2066; TIAS 5946; 592 UNTS 53.

THAILAND

AGRICULTURAL COMMODITIES

Agricultural commodities agreement.

Signed at Bangkok June 21, 1955.

Entered into force June 21, 1955.

6 UST 1169; TIAS 3260; 262 UNTS 87.

Amendment

December 14, 1956 (7 UST 3463; TIAS 3722; 266 UNTS 436).

Agricultural commodities agreement with exchange of notes.

Signed at Bangkok March 4, 1957.

Entered into force March 4, 1957.

8 UST 317; TIAS 3777; 279 UNTS 235.

Amendment

March 12 and April 9, 1959 (10 UST 1242; TIAS 4261; 354 UNTS 416).

Agricultural commodities agreement with annex.

Signed at Bangkok March 17, 1972.

Entered into force March 17, 1972.

23 UST 657; TIAS 7330.

Amendments

May 11, 1973 (24 UST 1767; TIAS 7685).
May 23, 1974 (25 UST 1538; TIAS 7889).

ATOMIC ENERGY

Agreement for cooperation concerning civil uses of atomic energy.

Signed at Washington May 14, 1974.

Entered into force June 27, 1974.

25 UST 1181; TIAS 7850.

AVIATION

Agreement relating to air service facilities at Don Muang Airport and Bangkapi.

Signed at Bangkok May 8, 1947.

Entered into force May 8, 1947.

61 Stat. 3855; TIAS 1735; 11 Bevans 1037; 42 UNTS 241.

Air transport agreement, with annex and memorandum of understanding.

Signed at Bangkok May 8, 1996.

Entered into force May 8, 1996.

TIAS

Protocol to the air transport agreement signed at Bangkok May 8, 1996.

Signed at Bangkok October 18, 2003.

Entered into force December 9, 2003.

TIAS

Air transport agreement, with annexes.

Signed at Washington September 19, 2005.

Entered into force September 19, 2005.

TIAS

COMMERCE

Treaty of amity and economic relations with exchanges of notes.

Signed at Bangkok May 29, 1966.

Entered into force June 8, 1968.

19 UST 5843; TIAS 6540; 652 UNTS 253.

CONSULS

See COMMERCE

DEFENSE

See also MUTUAL SECURITY

Agreement respecting military assistance.

Signed at Bangkok October 17, 1950.

Entered into force October 17, 1950.

3 UST 2675; TIAS 2434; 79 UNTS 41.

Agreement relating to the disposition of military equipment and materials furnished under the military assistance agreement.

Exchange of notes at Bangkok July 6, 1955.

Entered into force July 6, 1955.

6 UST 2067; TIAS 3274; 258 UNTS 386.

Memorandum of agreement on integrated communications system, with appendix.

Signed at Bangkok January 10, 1977.

Entered into force January 10, 1977.

29 UST 591; TIAS 8837.

Memorandum of agreement relating to the storage of ammunition in Thailand.

Signed at Bangkok March 22, 1977.

Entered into force March 22, 1977.

29 UST 743; TIAS 8850.

General security of military information agreement.

Exchange of notes at Bangkok March 30 and April 5, 1983.

Entered into force April 5, 1983.

TIAS 10678; 2005 UNTS 165.

Agreement relating to a war reserve stockpile program in Thailand, with annexes.

Signed at Bangkok January 9, 1987.

Entered into force March 22, 1988.

TIAS 12604.

Amendment and extension

February 15, 1995 (TIAS 12604).

Agreement concerning measures to be taken for the transfer, security and safeguarding of technical information, software and equipment to the Ministry of Defense to enable industry to operate, maintain and expand Royal Thai Air Force air combat maneuvering instrumentation range facilities.

Signed at Washington September 30, 1993.

Entered into force September 30, 1993.

TIAS 11509.

Memorandum of agreement concerning the transfer of equipment and munitions from United States war reserve stocks to the Government of the Kingdom of Thailand, with appendices and understanding.

Signed at Bangkok November 26, 2002.

Entered into force November 26, 2002.

TIAS

Acquisition and cross-servicing agreement, with annexes.

Signed at Honolulu September 18 and 21, 2003.

Entered into force September 21, 2003.

TIAS

Agreement regarding grants under the Foreign Assistance Act of 1961, as amended, and the furnishing of defense articles, defense services, and related training, including pursuant to the United States International Military and Education Training Program (IMET), from the United States to the Government of the Kingdom of Thailand.

Exchange of notes at Bangkok December 27, 2005 and March 14, 2006.

Entered into force March 14, 2006.

NP

Amendment

March 28 and April 17, 2006.

ECONOMIC AND TECHNICAL COOPERATION

Economic and technical cooperation agreement, with exchange of notes.

Signed at Bangkok June 2, 1977.

Entered into force June 2, 1977.

28 UST 5210; TIAS 8622.

Agency for International Development

December 11, 1975 (28 UST 397; TIAS 8474).

March 31, 1976 (29 UST 5454; TIAS 9122; 1228 UNTS 247).

September 8, 1976 (28 UST 2209; TIAS 8539).

September 8, 1976 (28 UST 2214; TIAS 8540; 1071 UNTS 3).

May 31, 1977 (29 UST 1817; TIAS 8904).

May 4, 1978 (30 UST 3681; TIAS 9422; 1228 UNTS 289).

EDUCATION

Agreement for financing certain educational exchange programs.

Signed at Bangkok May 24, 1963.

Entered into force May 24, 1963.

TIAS 5355; 14 UST 770; 477 UNTS 123.

Amendment

June 9 and July 9, 1970 (TIAS 6912; 21 UST 1512; 753 UNTS 392).

ENVIRONMENTAL COOPERATION

Agreement for technical cooperation in the field of environmental protection.

Signed at Bangkok October 28, 1999.

Entered into force October 28, 1999.

TIAS

Amendment

January 7, 2004.

EXTRADITION

Treaty relating to extradition.

Signed at Washington December 14, 1983.

Entered into force May 17, 1991.

TIAS

FINANCE

Agreement relating to investment guaranties under section 413 (b)(4) of the Mutual Security Act of 1954.

Exchange of notes at Washington August 27 and September 1, 1954.

Entered into force September 1, 1954.

5 UST 2258; TIAS 3086; 237 UNTS 209.

Amendment

December 22, 1965 (16 UST 2041; TIAS 5940; 551 UNTS 292).

Agreement regarding the reduction of a certain debt owed to the Government of the United States and its agencies.

Signed at Bangkok September 19, 2001.

Entered into force September 19, 2001.

NP

HEALTH

Agreement relating to the conversion of the Southeast Asia Treaty Organization cholera research project in Thailand to a SEATO medical research laboratory.

Exchange of notes at Bangkok December 23, 1960.

Entered into force December 23, 1960.

11 UST 2683; TIAS 4665; 405 UNTS 135.

Agreement relating to the establishment and operation of a SEATO Clinical Research Center at the School of Graduate Studies of the University of Medical Sciences, with memorandum of understanding.

Exchange of notes at Bangkok April 1 and 25, 1963.

Entered into force April 25, 1963.

14 UST 459; TIAS 5340; 476 UNTS 115.

Agreement modifying and continuing the agreements of December 23, 1960 and April 1 and 25, 1963, relating to the SEATO medical research project and the SEATO clinical research centre.

Exchange of notes at Bangkok January 19 and 28, 1977.

Entered into force July 1, 1977.

29 UST 643; TIAS 8840.

INTERNATIONAL CRIMINAL COURT

Agreement regarding the surrender of persons to the International Criminal Court.

Exchange of notes at Bangkok June 3, 2003.

Entered into force June 3, 2003.

TIAS

JUDICIAL ASSISTANCE

Treaty on mutual assistance in criminal matters, with attachments.

Signed at Bangkok March 19, 1986.

Entered into force June 10, 1993.

TIAS

Agreement concerning an International Law Enforcement Academy.

Signed at Bangkok September 30, 1998.

Entered into force September 30, 1998.

TIAS

MAPPING

Agreement providing for an aerial photographic mapping survey of Thailand.

Exchange of notes at Bangkok November 8 and December 3, 1952.

Entered into force December 3, 1952.

3 UST 5893; TIAS 2759; 213 UNTS 91.

Memorandum of agreement concerning mapping, charting and geodesy.

Signed at Bangkok and Fairfax February 27 and March 15, 1990.

Entered into force March 15, 1990.

NP

MUTUAL SECURITY

Agreement relating to the assurances required by the Mutual Security Act of 1951.

Exchange of notes at Bangkok December 27 and 29, 1951.

Entered into force December 29, 1951.

3 UST 4653; TIAS 2619; 179 UNTS 113.

NARCOTIC DRUGS

Memorandum of understanding on cooperation in the narcotics field.

Signed at Washington September 28, 1971.

Entered into force September 28, 1971.

22 UST 1587; TIAS 7185; 807 UNTS 49.

PEACE CORPS

Agreement relating to the establishment of a Peace Corps program in Thailand.

Exchange of notes at Bangkok November 20 and 28, 1961.

Entered into force November 28, 1961.

12 UST 3225; TIAS 4929; 434 UNTS 77.

POSTAL MATTERS

Parcel post agreement.

Signed at Bangkok May 31 and at Washington June 7, 1962.

Entered into force October 1, 1962.

13 UST 2209; TIAS 5188; 459 UNTS 135.

International express mail agreement, with detailed regulations.

Signed at Bangkok and Washington November 14 and December 9, 1983.

Entered into force February 18, 1984.

35 UST 3142; TIAS 10847; 2015 UNTS 25.

PRISONER TRANSFER

Treaty on cooperation in the execution of penal sentences.

Signed at Bangkok October 29, 1982.

Entered into force December 7, 1988.

TIAS

PUBLICATIONS

Agreement relating to the exchange of official publications.

Exchange of notes at Bangkok September 5, 1947.

Entered into force September 5, 1947.

61 Stat. 3154; TIAS 1654; 11 Bevans 1040; 73 UNTS 57.

SCIENTIFIC COOPERATION

Memorandum of understanding concerning scientific and technical cooperation in the earth sciences, with annexes.

Signed at Reston October 28, 2005.

Entered into force October 28, 2005.

TIAS

SEISMIC OBSERVATIONS

Memorandum of understanding relating to Chiang Mai seismic research station.

Signed at Bangkok December 29, 1976.

Entered into force December 29, 1976.

28 UST 8866; TIAS 8774; 1095 UNTS 191.

TAXATION

Convention for the avoidance of double taxation and the prevention of fiscal evasion with respect to taxes on income, with exchange of notes.

Signed at Bangkok November 26, 1996.

Entered into force December 15, 1997.

TIAS

TELECOMMUNICATION

Agreement relating to the establishment of certain radio transmitting and receiving facilities in Thailand.

Exchange of notes at Bangkok August 11, 1965.

Entered into force August 11, 1965.

23 UST 1158; TIAS 7378.

Extension and amendment

February 28 and March 7, 1983 (35 UST 1620; TIAS 10751).

Agreement relating to the reciprocal granting of authorizations to permit licensed amateur radio operators of either country to operate their station in the other country.

Exchange of notes at Bangkok October 11 and 30, 1990.

Entered into force December 14, 1990.

TIAS 12421.

TRADE

See also COMMERCE

Memorandum of understanding concerning concessions and contributions to the multilateral trade negotiations, with related notes of September 28 and October 21, 1982.

Signed at Geneva April 9, 1979.

Entered into force October 21, 1982; effective January 1, 1982.

35 UST 3984; TIAS 10897.

Agreement relating to trade in textiles and textile products, with annexes.

Exchange of letters at Washington and Bangkok September 3, 1991.

Entered into force September 3, 1991; effective January 1, 1991.

NP

Amendments and extension

May 28 and June 25, 1992 (NP).

October 9 and December 17, 1992 (NP).

June 3 and July 5, 1994 (NP).

VISAS

Arrangement relating to the waiver of passport visas and visa fees for nonimmigrants.

Exchange of notes at Bangkok September 19, 1925.

Entered into force September 19, 1925.

11 Bevans 1014.

TOGO

COMMERCE

Treaty of amity and economic relations.

Signed at Lome February 8, 1966.

Entered into force February 5, 1967.

18 UST 1; TIAS 6193; 680 UNTS 159.

DEFENSE

Agreement concerning the provision of training related to defense articles under the United States International Military Education and Training (IMET) Program.

Exchange of notes at Lome March 10 and July 17, 1980.

Entered into force July 17, 1980.

32 UST 2642; TIAS 9866; 1274 UNTS 211.

Agreement concerning the loan of U.S. Government equipment and provision of logistic support services to the Economic Community of West African States (ECOWAS) and its members in support of the ECOFORCE peacekeeping operation in Cote d'Ivoire.

Exchange of notes at Lome January 22 and February 5, 2003.

Entered into force February 5, 2003.

TIAS

ECONOMIC AND TECHNICAL COOPERATION

Agreement providing for economic, technical and related assistance.

Exchange of notes at Lome December 22, 1960.

Entered into force December 22, 1960.

11 UST 2566; TIAS 4646; 401 UNTS 33.

Agency for International Development

October 12, 1977 (29 UST 5286; TIAS 9106).

FINANCE

13 UST 321; TIAS 4983; 445 UNTS 79.

Agreement regarding the consolidation and rescheduling of certain debts owed to, guaranteed or insured by the United States Government and the Export-Import Bank of the United States, with annexes.

Signed at Lome March 28, 1980.

Entered into force May 2, 1980.

32 UST 933; TIAS 9740; 1222 UNTS 225.

Agreement regarding the consolidation and rescheduling of certain debts owed to, or guaranteed by the United States Government through the Export-Import Bank of the United States, with annexes and agreed minute.

Signed at Lome September 18, 1981.

Entered into force December 7, 1981.

NP

Agreement regarding the consolidation and rescheduling of certain debts owed to, or guaranteed by the United States Government through the Export-Import Bank.

Signed at Lome November 29, 1983.

Entered into force January 31, 1984.

NP

INTERNATIONAL CRIMINAL COURT

Agreement regarding the surrender of persons to the International Criminal Court.

Signed at Lome June 13, 2003.

Entered into force January 15, 2004.

TIAS

JUDICIAL ASSISTANCE

Procedures for mutual assistance in connection with matters relating to the Gulfstream American Corporation, formerly known as Grumman American Aviation Corporation.

Signed at Washington January 30, 1979.

Entered into force January 30, 1979.

30 UST 3477; TIAS 9401; 1180 UNTS 199.

PEACE CORPS

Agreement relating to the establishment of a Peace Corps program in Togo.

Exchange of notes at Lome August 1 and September 5, 1962.

Entered into force September 5, 1962.

13 UST 2251; TIAS 5191; 461 UNTS 47.

POSTAL MATTERS

International express mail agreement, with detailed regulations.

Signed at Lome and Washington November 28, 1988 and January 6, 1989.

Entered into force January 30, 1989.

NP

SOCIAL SECURITY

Agreement relating to United States participation with respect to its eligible employees in the Togolese social security system.

Exchange of notes at Lome March 17 and 26, 1971.

Entered into force March 26, 1971.

22 UST 526; TIAS 7094; 792 UNTS 223.

TONGA

On June 4, 1970 Tonga became an independent state. In a note dated June 18, 1970 to the Secretary-General of the United Nations, the Prime Minister of Tonga stated that each treaty validly made on behalf of the Kingdom of Tonga by the Government of the United Kingdom pursuant to and within the powers of the United Kingdom derived from certain instruments entered into between the United Kingdom and the Kingdom of Tonga, continues to bind the latter until validly terminated, that it is desired that it be presumed that each treaty continues to create rights and obligations, and that action be based on this presumption until a decision is reached that the treaty should be regarded as not having been validly made for the Kingdom of Tonga or as having lapsed. Should the Government of the Kingdom of Tonga be of the opinion that it continues to be legally bound by the treaty, and wishes to terminate the operation of the treaty, it will in due course give notice of termination in the terms thereof. With respect to duly ratified treaties which were entered into by the Kingdom of Tonga before the United Kingdom undertook the responsibility for the foreign relations thereof, the Government of the Kingdom of Tonga acknowledges that they remain in force to the extent to which their provisions were unaffected in virtue of international law by certain instruments entered into between the United Kingdom and the Kingdom of Tonga or by other events.

COMMERCE

Treaty of amity, commerce, and navigation.[1]

Signed at Nuku'alofa October 2, 1886.

Entered into force September 18, 1888.

25 Stat. 1440; TS 357; 11 Bevans 1043.

NOTE

1 Entire treaty, with the exception of article VI, terminated July 28, 1920.

CONSULS

Consular convention between the United States and the United Kingdom.

Signed at Washington June 6, 1951.

Entered into force September 7, 1952.

3 UST 3426; TIAS 2494; 165 UNTS 121.

DEFENSE

Agreement concerning the provision of training related to defense articles under the United States International Military Education and Training (IMET) Program.

Exchange of notes at Suva and Nuku'alofa November 18 and 25, 1985.

Entered into force November 25, 1985.

TIAS 11101.

Agreement concerning the status of members of the United States Armed Forces in the Kingdom of Tonga.

Signed at Suva July 20, 1992.

Entered into force July 20, 1992.

TIAS 12523.

Agreement regarding grants under the Foreign Assistance Act of 1961, as amended, or successor legislation, and the furnishing of defense articles, defense services and related training, including pursuant to the United States International Military and Education Training Program (IMET), from the United States of America to the Kingdom of Tonga.

Exchange of notes at Suva and Nuku-alofa March 16 and August 24, 2006.

Entered into force August 24, 2006.

NP

EXTRADITION

Extradition treaty.

Signed at London December 22, 1931.

Entered into force June 24, 1935; applicable to Tonga August 1, 1966.

47 Stat. 2122; TS 849; 12 Bevans 482; 163 LNTS 59.

Agreement continuing in force between the United States and Tonga the extradition treaty of December 22, 1931 between the United States and the United Kingdom.

Exchange of notes at Nuku'alofa and Wellington March 14 and April 13, 1977.

Entered into force April 13, 1977.

28 UST 5290; TIAS 8628; 1087 UNTS 289.

FINANCE

Investment incentive agreement.

Exchange of notes at Suva and Nuku'alofa August 22, 1983 and November 26, 1984.

Entered into force November 26, 1984.

TIAS 11000; 2022 UNTS 125.

INTERNATIONAL CRIMINAL COURT

Agreement regarding the surrender of persons to the International Criminal Court.

Signed at Washington March 21, 2003.

Entered into force March 24, 2004.

TIAS

PEACE CORPS

Agreement relating to the establishment of a Peace Corps program in Tonga with exchange of letters.

Exchange of notes at Suva and Nuku'alofa May 17 and 27, 1968.

Entered into force May 27, 1968.

19 UST 5486; TIAS 6534; 707 UNTS 71.

TRADE-MARKS

Declaration by the United States and the United Kingdom affording reciprocal protection to trade-marks.

Signed at London October 24, 1877.

Entered into force October 24, 1877.

20 Stat. 703; TS 138; 12 Bevans 198.

TRINIDAD AND TOBAGO

On August 31, 1962 Trinidad and Tobago became independent. By an exchange of letters on August 31, 1962 between the High Commissioner for the United Kingdom in Trinidad and Tobago and the Prime Minister of Trinidad and Tobago, the Government of Trinidad and Tobago agreed to assume all obligations and responsibilities of the United Kingdom which arise from any valid international instrument (including any such instrument made by the Government of the Federation of the West Indies by virtue of authority entrusted by the Government of the United Kingdom). The rights and benefits heretofore enjoyed by the Government of the United Kingdom by virtue of application of any such international instrument to Trinidad and Tobago shall henceforth be enjoyed by the Government of Trinidad and Tobago.

AVIATION

Arrangement between the United States and the United Kingdom relating to pilot licenses to operate civil aircraft.

Exchange of notes at Washington March 28 and April 5, 1935.

Entered into force May 5, 1935.

49 Stat. 3731; EAS 77; 12 Bevans 513; 162 LNTS 59.

Air transport agreement, with annexes.

Signed at Port-of-Spain May 23, 1990.

Entered into force May 23, 1990.

TIAS 11724; 2207 UNTS 229.

CLAIMS

Agreement between the United States and the United Kingdom relating to claims for damages resulting from acts of armed forces or civilian personnel.

Exchange of notes at Washington October 23, 1946 and January 23, 1947.

Entered into force January 23, 1947; operative from June 6, 1944.

61 Stat. 2876; TIAS 1622; 12 Bevans 805; 15 UNTS 281.

CONSULS

Consular convention between the United States and the United Kingdom.

Signed at Washington June 6, 1951.

Entered into force September 7, 1952.

3 UST 3426; TIAS 2494; 165 UNTS 121.

DEFENSE

See also MUTUAL SECURITY

Agreement concerning the provision of training related to defense articles under the United States International Military Education and Training (IMET) Program, with aide memoire.

Exchange of notes at Port of Spain December 29, 1983 and November 16, 1984.

Entered into force November 16, 1984.

TIAS 10989; 2022 UNTS 123.

Agreement concerning grants under the Foreign Assistance Act of 1961, as amended, and the furnishing of defense articles, related training, and other defense services from the United States to Trinidad and Tobago for counter-narcotics purposes.

Exchange of notes at Port of Spain February 4 and 13, 1998.

Entered into force February 13, 1998.

NP

ECONOMIC AND TECHNICAL COOPERATION

Economic cooperation agreement between the United States and the United Kingdom.

Signed at London July 6, 1948; applicable, with the exception of article IV, to Trinidad and Tobago March 17, 1949.

62 Stat. 2596; TIAS 1795; 12 Bevans 874; 22 UNTS 263.

Amendments

January 3, 1950 (1 UST 184; TIAS 2036; 84 UNTS 304).

May 25, 1951 (2 UST 1292; TIAS 2277; 99 UNTS 308).

February 23, 1953 (4 UST 1528; TIAS 2815; 172 UNTS 332).

June 26 and August 20, 1959 (11 UST 2680; TIAS 4664; 405 UNTS 288).

Agreement between the United States and the United Kingdom for technical cooperation in respect of the territories for the international relations of which the Government of the United Kingdom are responsible.

Signed at London July 13, 1951; applicable to Trinidad and Tobago August 14, 1954.

2 UST 1307; TIAS 2281; 105 UNTS 71.

EMPLOYMENT

Agreement relating to the employment of dependents of official government employees.

Exchange of notes at Port of Spain May 15, 1990 and July 23, 1992.

Entered into force July 23, 1992.

TIAS 11924.

ENVIRONMENTAL COOPERATION

Agreement for cooperation in the Global Learning and Observations to Benefit the Environment (GLOBE) Program, with appendices.

Signed at Port of Spain July 16, 1996.

Entered into force July 16, 1996.

TIAS 12784.

EXTRADITION

Extradition treaty.

Signed at Port of Spain March 4, 1996.

Entered into force November 29, 1999.

TIAS

FINANCE

Agreement relating to investment guaranties.

Exchange of notes at Port-of-Spain January 8 and 15, 1963.

Entered into force January 15, 1963.

14 UST 113; TIAS 5278; 471 UNTS 141.

Agreement regarding the consolidation and rescheduling of certain debts owed to, guaranteed by, or insured by the United States Government and its agencies.

Signed at Port-of-Spain July 28, 1989.

Entered into force September 13, 1989.

NP

Agreement regarding the consolidation and rescheduling of certain debts owed to, guaranteed by, or insured by the United States Government and its agencies, with annexes.

Signed at Port-of-Spain November 26, 1990.

Entered into force January 14, 1991.

NP

INVESTMENT

Treaty concerning the encouragement and reciprocal protection of investment, with annex and protocol.

Signed at Washington September 26, 1994.

Entered into force December 26, 1996.

TIAS

JUDICIAL ASSISTANCE

Procedures for mutual assistance in the administration of justice in connection with matters relating to the investigation designated as MA-106.

Signed at Washington June 7, 1982.

Entered into force June 7, 1982.

34 UST 1271; TIAS 10416.

Treaty on mutual legal assistance in criminal matters, with forms.

Signed at Port of Spain March 4, 1996.

Entered into force November 29, 1999.

TIAS

MUTUAL SECURITY

Agreement between the United States and the United Kingdom relating to the assurances required under the Mutual Security Act of 1951.

Exchange of notes at London January 8, 1952.

Entered into force January 8, 1952.

3 UST 4665; TIAS 2622; 126 UNTS 307.

NARCOTIC DRUGS

Agreement concerning maritime counter-drug operations.

Signed at Port of Spain March 4, 1996.

Entered into force March 4, 1996.

TIAS 12732.

POSTAL MATTERS

Money order agreement.

Signed at Port-of-Spain September 18 and at Washington October 23, 1891; operative January 1, 1891.

NP

Parcel post agreement with regulations of execution.

Signed at Port-of-Spain and Washington March 9 and 18, 1968.

Entered into force May 1, 1968.

19 UST 4735; TIAS 6472; 698 UNTS 121.

International express mail agreement, with detailed regulations.

Signed at Port of Spain and Washington November 3 and December 7, 1987.

Entered into force July 1, 1988.

TIAS 11558.

PROPERTY

Convention between the United States and the United Kingdom relating to the tenure and disposition of real and personal property.

Signed at Washington March 2, 1899; applicable to Trinidad and Tobago February 9, 1901.

31 Stat. 1939; TS 146; 12 Bevans 246.

Supplementary convention relating to the tenure and disposition of real and personal property.

Signed at Washington May 27, 1936.

Entered into force March 10, 1941.

55 Stat. 1101; TS 964; 5 Bevans 140; 203 LNTS 367.

TAXATION

Convention for the avoidance of double taxation, the prevention of fiscal evasion with respect to taxes on income, and the encouragement of international trade and investment with related notes.[1]

Signed at Port-of-Spain January 9, 1970.

Entered into force December 30, 1970.

22 UST 164; TIAS 7047; 781 UNTS 99.

Agreement for the exchange of information with respect to taxes.

Signed at Port of Spain January 11, 1989.

Entered into force February 9, 1990.

TIAS 11607; 2192 UNTS 89.

NOTE

1 With reservation.

TELECOMMUNICATION

Agreement relating to the reciprocal granting of authorizations to permit licensed amateur radio operators of either country to operate their stations in the other country.

Exchange of notes at Port-of-Spain January 14 and March 16, 1967.

Entered into force March 16, 1967.

18 UST 543; TIAS 6261; 685 UNTS 93.

Arrangement relating to radio communications between amateur stations on behalf of third parties.

Exchange of notes at Port-of-Spain October 26 and November 18, 1971.

Entered into force December 18, 1971.

22 UST 2053; TIAS 7239.

TRADE AND COMMERCE

Agreement within the context of the multilateral trade negotiations, with related letter.

Signed at Washington December 19, 1979.

Entered into force January 1, 1980.

31 UST 5909; TIAS 9694; 1222 UNTS 89.

Agreement relating to trade in cotton, wool and man-made fiber textiles and textile products, with annexes and administrative visa arrangement.

Exchange of notes at Port of Spain October 15 and 23, 1986.

Entered into force October 23, 1986; effective October 1, 1986.

NP

Amendments and extension

September 8, November 18 and 30, 1988 and July 19, 1990 (NP).

December 5, 1989 and November 8 and December 14, 1990 (NP).

Agreement on removal of trade distorting practices in steel trade, with appendices and exchange of letters.

Exchange of letters at Washington and Port-of-Spain March 29 and April 12, 1990.

Entered into force April 12, 1990.

TIAS

TRADE-MARKS

Declaration by the United States and the United Kingdom affording reciprocal protection to trade-marks.

Signed at London October 24, 1877.

Entered into force October 24, 1877.

20 Stat. 703; TS 138; 12 Bevans 198.

VISAS

Agreement relating to extended validity of passports issued by Trinidad and Tobago.

Exchange of notes at Port-of-Spain October 28 and November 12, 1969.

Entered into force November 12, 1969.

21 UST 1995; TIAS 6942; 763 UNTS 9.

WEATHER STATIONS

Agreement for a cooperative meteorological observation program in Trinidad.

Exchange of notes at Port-of-Spain October 7, 1970.

Entered into force October 7, 1970; effective January 1, 1968.

21 UST 2495; TIAS 6991; 772 UNTS 163.

TUNISIA

A general convention between France and Tunisia signed June 3, 1955, provided *inter alia* (1) for recognition of the primacy of international conventions and treaties over internal law (article 3) and (2) that Tunisia would take, within the framework of its internal autonomy, measures necessary for rendering applicable treaties concerning Tunisia and for assuring their execution (article 8).

The independence of Tunisia was recognized in a protocol between France and Tunisia signed March 20, 1956, recognizing Tunisia's exercise of its responsibilities in foreign affairs and providing for organization of interdependent cooperation in external relations.

AGRICULTURAL COMMODITIES

Agreement relating to a child-feeding program for Tunisia under Title II of the Agricultural Trade Development and Assistance Act of 1954, as amended.

Exchange of notes at Tunis June 28, 1957.

Entered into force June 28, 1957.

8 UST 985; TIAS 3863; 289 UNTS 301.

Agricultural commodities agreement with exchange of notes.

Signed at Tunis February 16, 1962.

Entered into force February 16, 1962.

13 UST 229; TIAS 4965; 442 UNTS 161.

Agricultural commodities agreement with exchange of notes.

Signed at Tunis September 14, 1962.

Entered into force September 14, 1962.

13 UST 2238; TIAS 5190; 461 UNTS 31.

Amendments

September 13, 1963 (14 UST 1275; TIAS 5430; 488 UNTS 318).

December 19, 1963 (14 UST 1878; TIAS 5498; 494 UNTS 338).

Agricultural commodities agreement with exchange of notes.

Signed at Tunis April 7, 1964.

Entered into force April 7, 1964.

15 UST 300; TIAS 5556; 527 UNTS 3.

Amendment

July 7, 1964 (15 UST 1453; TIAS 5620; 529 UNTS 387).

Agricultural commodities agreement with exchange of notes.

Signed at Tunis February 17, 1965.

Entered into force February 17, 1965.

16 UST 97; TIAS 5767; 542 UNTS 125.

Amendments

November 29, 1965 (16 UST 1770; TIAS 5908; 573 UNTS 352).

April 29, 1966 (17 UST 613; TIAS 6007; 592 UNTS 271).

Agricultural commodities agreement with exchange of notes.

Signed at Tunis July 30, 1966.

Entered into force July 30, 1966.

17 UST 1108; TIAS 6067; 601 UNTS 133.

Amendment

September 19, 1966 (17 UST 1401; TIAS 6098).

Agricultural commodities agreement with annexes.

Signed at Tunis March 17, 1967.

Entered into force March 17, 1967.

18 UST 1777; TIAS 6323; 692 UNTS 155.

Related agreements

November 6, 1967 (18 UST 2929; TIAS 6385; 701 UNTS 149).

May 17, 1968 (19 UST 4925; TIAS 6498; 698 UNTS 257).

December 24, 1968 (19 UST 7832; TIAS 6616; 714 UNTS 105).

July 11, 1969 (20 UST 2673; TIAS 6725; 720 UNTS 35).

December 18, 1969 (20 UST 4132; TIAS 6811; 732 UNTS 71).

March 17, 1971 (22 UST 507; TIAS 7090; 796 UNTS 325).

November 17, 1971 (22 UST 1772; TIAS 7215).

April 19, 1972 (23 UST 1477; TIAS 7427).

June 13, 1973 (24 UST 1661; TIAS 7672).

Agricultural commodities agreement.

Signed at Tunis June 7, 1976.

Entered into force June 7, 1976.

28 UST 1233; TIAS 8506.

Amendments

July 3, 1985 (NP).

June 11, 1986 (NP).

Related agreements

January 21, 1977 (28 UST 5348; TIAS 8638; 1087 UNTS 145).

July 27 and 28, 1977 (29 UST 370; TIAS 8823; 1115 UNTS 365).

February 3, 1978 (32 UST 764; TIAS 9727; 1265 UNTS 79).

March 2, 1979 (32 UST 755; TIAS 9726; 1221 UNTS 113).

April 17, 1980 (TIAS 10527).

August 27, 1981 (34 UST 1909; TIAS 10470; 1750 UNTS 145).

May 17, 1982 (34 UST 1003; TIAS 10390).

June 4, 1983 (35 UST 1528; TIAS 10743; 2006 UNTS 329).

July 1, 1983 (35 UST 1528; TIAS 10743; 2006 UNTS 329).

June 13, 1984 (NP).

July 3, 1985 (NP).

June 11, 1986 (NP).

September 4, 1986 (NP).

January 23, 1987 (NP).

June 13, 1987 (NP).

August 25, 1987 (NP).

Agricultural commodities agreement.

Signed at Tunis March 16, 1988.

Entered into force March 16, 1988.

NP

Amendments

May 12, 1988 (NP).

July 28, 1988 (NP).

Related agreements

September 17, 1988 (NP).

May 10, 1989 (NP).

September 28, 1989 (NP).

November 1, 1990 (NP).

CONSULS

Consular convention.

Signed at Tunis May 12, 1988.

Entered into force January 15, 1994.

TIAS

DEFENSE

Agreement concerning payment to the United States of net proceeds from the sale of defense articles furnished under the military assistance program.

Exchange of notes at Tunis May 21 and June 29, 1974.

Entered into force July 1, 1974.

25 UST 1554; TIAS 7892.

Agreement relating to a program of grants of military equipment and material to Tunisia.

Exchange of notes at Tunis September 12 and October 25, 1974.

Entered into force October 25, 1974; effective July 1, 1974.

25 UST 3051; TIAS 7964.

Memorandum of understanding for cooperation in the field of military medicine.

Signed at Tunis August 14, 1985.

Entered into force August 14, 1985.

TIAS 12008.

Memorandum of understanding on the exchange of officers.

Signed at Tunis and Washington February 14 and March 12, 1992.

Entered into force March 12, 1992.

NP

Agreement concerning mutual logistic support, with annexes.

Signed at Tunis and Stuttgart-Vaihingen March 29 and April 29, 1994.

Entered into force April 29, 1994.

TIAS 12374.

ECONOMIC AND TECHNICAL COOPERATION

Agreement providing for economic, technical and related assistance.

Exchange of notes at Tunis March 26, 1957.

Entered into force March 26, 1957.

8 UST 427; TIAS 3794; 283 UNTS 117.

Agreement regarding certain assurances by Tunisia supplementing the economic, technical, and related assistance agreement of March 26, 1957.

Exchange of notes at Tunis October 8, 1958.

Entered into force October 8, 1958.

9 UST 1324; TIAS 4122; 336 UNTS 389.

Agreement relating to the commitment by the United States to Tunisia's three-year plan.

Exchange of notes at Tunis September 28 and October 29, 1962.

Entered into force October 29, 1962.

13 UST 2667; TIAS 5239; 462 UNTS 201.

Agency for International Development

December 29, 1977 (29 UST 4113; TIAS 9051; 1231 UNTS 187).

March 24, 1978 (29 UST 4557; TIAS 9068; 1231 UNTS 223).

August 31, 1978 (30 UST 6005; TIAS 9535; 1231 UNTS 249).

EDUCATION

Agreement for financing certain educational exchange programs.

Signed at Tunis November 18, 1963.

Entered into force November 18, 1963.

TIAS 5499; 14 UST 1881; 494 UNTS 193.

ENVIRONMENTAL COOPERATION

Agreement for cooperation in the Global Learning and Observations to Benefit the Environment (GLOBE) Program, with appendices.

Signed at Washington July 27, 1995.

Entered into force July 27, 1995.

TIAS 12678.

FINANCE

Investment incentive agreement.

Signed at Washington February 17, 2004.

Entered into force April 20, 2005.

TIAS

GENERAL RELATIONS

Treaty between the United States and France for the determination of their relations in Tunis.

Signed at Washington March 15, 1904.

Entered into force May 7, 1904.

33 Stat. 2263; TS 434; 7 Bevans 862.

INTERNATIONAL CRIMINAL COURT

Agreement regarding the surrender of persons to the International Criminal Court.

Exchange of notes at Tunis June 5, 2003.

Entered into force December 22, 2003.

TIAS

INVESTMENT

Treaty concerning the reciprocal encouragement and protection of investment, with protocol.

Signed at Washington May 15, 1990.

Entered into force February 7, 1993.

TIAS

MAPPING

Mapping, charting and geodesy cooperative and exchange agreement, with annexes.

Signed at Tunis December 8, 1980.

Entered into force December 8, 1980.

TIAS 10698; 2005 UNTS 97.

Amendment

July 14 and August 31, 1982 (TIAS 10698; 2005 UNTS 107).

OCEANOGRAPHIC RESEARCH

Agreement relating to the establishment and operation of a Mediterranean Marine Sorting Center in Tunisia.

Exchange of notes at Tunis September 26, 1966.

Entered into force September 26, 1966.

17 UST 1412; TIAS 6101; 616 UNTS 259.

PEACE CORPS

Agreement relating to the establishment of a Peace Corps program in Tunisia.

Exchange of notes at Tunis February 7 and 13, 1962.

Entered into force February 13, 1962.

13 UST 249; TIAS 4968; 442 UNTS 155.

POSTAL MATTERS

International express mail agreement, with detailed regulations.

Signed at Tunis and Washington November 12, 1982 and January 4, 1983.

Entered into force April 1, 1983.

TIAS 10640; 1935 UNTS 321.

Memorandum of understanding concerning the operation of the INTELPOST service, with details of implementation.

Signed at Tunis and Washington December 19, 1989 and October 3, 1991.

Entered into force February 1, 1993.

TIAS 11903.

SCIENTIFIC COOPERATION

Agreement establishing principles for cooperation between American institutions conducting basic scientific research in Tunisia under Smithsonian Institution sponsorship and appropriate Tunisian institutions, organizations or governmental agencies.

Exchange of notes at Tunis July 17, 1968.

Entered into force July 17, 1968.

19 UST 5900; TIAS 6543; 707 UNTS 127.

TAXATION

Convention for the avoidance of double taxation and the prevention of fiscal evasion with respect to taxes on income, with exchange of notes.

Signed at Washington June 17, 1985.

Entered into force December 26, 1990.

TIAS

Supplementary protocol to the convention for the avoidance of double taxation and the prevention of fiscal evasion with respect to taxes on income of June 17, 1985.

Signed at Tunis October 4, 1989.

Entered into force December 26, 1990.

TIAS

TELECOMMUNICATION

Agreement relating to the installation and operation of a radio transmitter by the Embassy of Tunisia.

Exchange of notes at Washington May 28, 1975 and May 13, 1976.

Entered into force May 13, 1976.

28 UST 2437; TIAS 8561.

VISAS

Arrangement between the United States and France for the waiver by France of visa requirements for United States citizens visiting Metropolitan France and certain French territories, and for the granting by the United States of gratis passport visas to French citizens resident in those territories who enter the United States as nonimmigrants.

Exchange of notes at Paris March 16 and 31, 1949.

Entered into force March 31, 1949.

63 Stat. 2737; TIAS 1987; 7 Bevans 1311; 84 UNTS 283.

TURKEY

AGRICULTURAL COMMODITIES

Agreement concerning lira deposits under the agricultural commodities agreements of March 12, 1956, as amended, and November 12, 1956.

Exchange of notes at Ankara November 23, 1956.

Entered into force November 23, 1956.

8 UST 1567; TIAS 3909; 290 UNTS 273.

Agricultural commodities agreement with exchange of notes.

Signed at Ankara July 29, 1961.

Entered into force July 29, 1961.

12 UST 1098; TIAS 4819; 416 UNTS 151.

Amendments

September 6, 1961 (12 UST 1628; TIAS 4874; 426 UNTS 350).

December 8, 1961 (12 UST 3215; TIAS 4926; 433 UNTS 394).

January 3, 1962 (13 UST 68; TIAS 4937; 433 UNTS 398).

January 5, 1962 (13 UST 68; TIAS 4937; 433 UNTS 402).

March 14, 1962 (13 UST 303; TIAS 4978; 445 UNTS 370).

June 21, 1962 (13 UST 1283; TIAS 5077; 459 UNTS 306).

October 11, 1962 (13 UST 2199; TIAS 5185; 459 UNTS 310).

November 21, 1962 (13 UST 2638; TIAS 5235; 462 UNTS 362).

Agricultural commodities agreement with exchange of notes.

Signed at Ankara February 21, 1963.

Entered into force February 21, 1963.

14 UST 236; TIAS 5303; 473 UNTS 311.

Amendments

April 4, 1963 (14 UST 364; TIAS 5324; 473 UNTS 326).

January 22, 1965 (16 UST 66; TIAS 5760; 542 UNTS 392).

Agricultural commodities agreement with exchange of notes.

Signed at Ankara April 2, 1966.

Entered into force April 2, 1966.

17 UST 2301; TIAS 6173; 680 UNTS 183.

Agricultural commodities agreement with annex.

Signed at Ankara February 6, 1969.

Entered into force February 6, 1969.

20 UST 438; TIAS 6645; 714 UNTS 165.

Amendment

July 22 and 24, 1969 (20 UST 2813; TIAS 6751; 724 UNTS 400).

Related agreements

Agreement on thermal-hydraulic code applications and maintenance.

Signed at Rockville and Ankara September 3 and 25, 2002.

Entered into force September 25, 2002.

TIAS

AVIATION

Air transport agreement, with annexes.

Signed at New York May 2, 2000.

Entered into force August 13, 2001.

TIAS

COMMERCE

Treaty of commerce and navigation.

Signed at Ankara October 1, 1929.

Entered into force April 22, 1930.

46 Stat. 2743; TS 813; 11 Bevans 1122; 114 LNTS 499.

Treaty of establishment and sojourn.

Signed at Ankara October 28, 1931.

Entered into force February 15, 1933.

47 Stat. 2432; TS 859; 11 Bevans 1127; 138 LNTS 345.

CUSTOMS

Agreement regarding mutual assistance between customs administrations.

Signed at Washington March 28, 1996.

Entered into force October 15, 2002.

TIAS 12773.

DEFENSE

See also MUTUAL SECURITY

Agreement relating to implementation of the agreement between the parties to the North Atlantic Treaty regarding the status of their forces of June 19, 1951 (4 UST 1792; TIAS 2846), with two minutes of understanding.

Signed at Ankara June 23, 1954.

Entered into force June 23, 1954.

5 UST 1465; TIAS 3020; 233 UNTS 189.

Agreement amending the minute of understanding on paragraph 7 of the agreement of June 23, 1954.

Exchange of notes at Ankara April 22 and July 21, 1955.

Entered into force July 21, 1955.

6 UST 2917; TIAS 3337; 265 UNTS 418.

Agreement relating to redistributable and excess equipment and materials furnished pursuant to the mutual defense assistance program.

Exchange of notes at Ankara May 26, 1955.

Entered into force May 26, 1955.

6 UST 2071; TIAS 3275; 262 UNTS 97.

Amendment

August 10, 1962 (13 UST 2628; TIAS 5232; 462 UNTS 350).

Agreement relating to a program of offshore procurement, with memorandum of understanding and model contract attached, and exchange of notes.

Exchange of notes at Ankara June 29, 1955.

Entered into force June 29, 1955.

6 UST 3729; TIAS 3372.

Agreement of cooperation.

Signed at Ankara March 5, 1959.

Entered into force March 5, 1959.

10 UST 320; TIAS 4191; 327 UNTS 293.

Agreement relating to the introduction of modern weapons into NATO defense forces in Turkey.

Exchange of notes at Ankara September 18 and October 28, 1959.

Entered into force October 28, 1959.

10 UST 1866; TIAS 4350; 360 UNTS 265.

Agreement for the establishment of a facility for repairing and rebuilding M-12 range finders in Turkey.

Exchange of notes at Ankara November 30, 1959.

Entered into force November 30, 1959.

10 UST 2027; TIAS 4372; 361 UNTS 107.

Agreement relating to a weapons production program.

Exchange of notes at Ankara March 2, 1960.

Entered into force March 2, 1960.

11 UST 1322; TIAS 4465; 372 UNTS 37.

Agreement concerning duty certificates in implementation of article VII of the agreement between the parties to the North Atlantic Treaty regarding the status of their forces.

Exchange of notes at Ankara September 24, 1968.

Entered into force September 24, 1968.

19 UST 6317; TIAS 6582; 702 UNTS 235.

Agreement concerning payment to the United States of net proceeds from the sale of defense articles furnished under the military assistance program.

Exchange of notes at Ankara October 9 and 10, 1974.

Entered into force October 10, 1974; effective July 1, 1974.

25 UST 2494; TIAS 7933.

Agreement concerning the grant of defense articles and services under the military assistance program.

Exchange of notes at Ankara August 15 and 31, 1979.

Entered into force August 31, 1979.

30 UST 7299; TIAS 9588; 1182 UNTS 93.

Amendment

August 13 and September 24, 1982 (TIAS 10502).

Agreement for cooperation on defense and economy in accordance with articles II and III of the North Atlantic Treaty, with related note; supplementary agreement number 1 on defense support; supplementary agreement number 2 on defense industrial cooperation; and supplementary agreement number 3 on installations, with implementing agreements (annexes).

Signed at Ankara March 29, 1980.

Entered into force December 18, 1980.

32 UST 3323; TIAS 9901.

Memorandum of understanding on cooperative measures for enhancing air defense capabilities of selected COBs in Turkey.

Signed at Washington and Ankara November 14 and December 26, 1984.

Entered into force December 26, 1984.

TIAS

Agreement supplementing and extending the agreement of March 29, 1980 for cooperation on defense and economy.

Exchange of letters at Washington March 16, 1987.

Entered into force March 16, 1987.

TIAS

Acquisition and cross-servicing agreement, with annexes.

Signed at Ankara and Stuttgart July 26 and August 12, 1996.

Entered into force August 12, 1996.

TIAS 12789.

Support and procedures arrangement.

Signed at Ankara December 1, 2000.

Entered into force December 1, 2000.

TIAS

Memorandum of understanding for a bilateral missile defense architecture analysis.

Signed at Washington and Ankara May 31 and June 6, 2001.

Entered into force June 6, 2001.

TIAS

Letter of agreement concerning the use of the Turkish NATO Pipeline System (TNPS), with annexes

Signed December 30 and 31, 2004.

Entered into force December 31, 2004.

TIAS

Administrative arrangement concerning accommodation, facilities, services and assistance made available to personnel of the Armed Forces of the United States of America at Headquarters NATO Rapid Deployable Corps-Turkey (NRDC-T), with annex

Signed January 5 and February 10, 2005.

Entered into force February 10, 2005.

TIAS

ECONOMIC AND TECHNICAL COOPERATION

Agreement on aid to Turkey.

Signed at Ankara July 12, 1947.

Entered into force July 12, 1947.

61 Stat. 2953; TIAS 1629; 11 Bevans 1163; 7 UNTS 309.

Economic cooperation agreement.

Signed at Ankara July 4, 1948.

Entered into force July 13, 1948.

62 Stat. 2566; TIAS 1794; 11 Bevans 1166; 24 UNTS 67.

Amendments

January 31, 1950 (1 UST 188; TIAS 2037; 76 UNTS 258).

August 16, 1951 (3 UST 54; TIAS 2392; 152 UNTS 276).

December 30, 1952 (3 UST 5348; TIAS 2742; 185 UNTS 330).

Agreement concerning economic assistance to Turkey for the acquisition of prefabricated huts to be used as facilities for primary schools.

Exchange of notes at Ankara May 26, 1959.

Entered into force May 26, 1959.

10 UST 1303; TIAS 4273; 354 UNTS 57.

Agency for International Development

December 5, 1978 (30 UST 6615; TIAS 9571; 1182 UNTS 85).

November 1, 1979 (31 UST 4704; TIAS 9634; 1202 UNTS 325).

January 28, 1980 (31 UST 5612; TIAS 9678; 1234 UNTS 285).

November 20, 1981 (33 UST 4061; TIAS 10282).

December 17, 1982 (TIAS 10631; 1935 UNTS 313).

April 22, 1983 (TIAS 10725; 1607 UNTS 113).

September 30, 1983 (TIAS 10725; 1607 UNTS 123).

December 24, 1984 (NP).

December 24, 1984 (NP).

December 29, 1986 (NP).

January 8, 1987 (NP).

EDUCATION

Agreement for the establishment of the United States Educational Commission in Turkey, and exchanges of notes.

Signed at Ankara December 27, 1949.

Entered into force March 21, 1950.

TIAS 2111; 1 UST 603; 98 UNTS 141.

Amendments

January 8, 1957 (TIAS 3737; 8 UST 41; 266 UNTS 404).

February 1, 1960 (TIAS 4458; 11 UST 399; 371 UNTS 282).

April 21 and May 30, 1961 (TIAS 4766; 12 UST 661; 409 UNTS 302).

April 26 and May 2, 1967 (TIAS 6307; 18 UST 1654; 692 UNTS 400).

EMPLOYMENT

Agreement relating to the employment of dependents of official government employees.

Exchange of notes at Ankara November 23, 1999.

Entered into force February 3, 2000.

TIAS

ENVIRONMENTAL COOPERATION

Agreement for cooperation in the Global Learning and Observations to Benefit the Environment (GLOBE) Program, with appendices.

Signed at Ankara May 5, 1995.

Entered into force May 5, 1995.

TIAS 12643.

EXTRADITION

Treaty on extradition and mutual assistance in criminal matters.

Signed at Ankara June 7, 1979.

Entered into force January 1, 1981.

32 UST 3111; TIAS 9891.

FINANCE

Agreement relating to assurances by the Government of Turkey with respect to guaranties to investors pursuant to article III of the economic cooperation agreement, as amended.

Exchange of notes at Ankara November 15, 1951.

Entered into force November 15, 1951.

3 UST 3720; TIAS 2500; 177 UNTS 315.

Amendments

January 15, 1957 (8 UST 202; TIAS 3761; 280 UNTS 79).

November 27, 1964 (15 UST 2197; TIAS 5704; 531 UNTS 322).

Agreement regarding ownership and use of local currency repayments made by Turkey to the Development Loan Fund.

Exchange of notes at Ankara September 6, 1958.

Entered into force September 6, 1958.

9 UST 1251; TIAS 4111; 336 UNTS 85.

Agreements regarding the consolidation and rescheduling of certain debts owed to, guaranteed or insured by the United States Government and its agencies, with annexes.

Signed at Washington and Ankara September 21 and December 5, 1978.

Entered into force December 7, 1978.

30 UST 2723; TIAS 9361; 1171 UNTS 3.

Agreement regarding the consolidation and rescheduling of certain debts owed to, guaranteed or insured by the United States Government and its agencies, with annexes.

Signed at Ankara December 11, 1979.

Entered into force January 14, 1980.

32 UST 1461; TIAS 9783; 1234 UNTS 273.

Implementing agreement regarding the consolidation and rescheduling of certain debts owed to the Agency for International Development.

Signed at Ankara April 22, 1980.

Entered into force April 22, 1980; effective January 14, 1980.

32 UST 1549; TIAS 9786; 1234 UNTS 293.

Agreement regarding the consolidation and rescheduling of certain debts owed to, guaranteed or insured by the United States Government and its agencies, with agreed minute and annexes.

Signed at Ankara October 24, 1980.

Entered into force November 24, 1980.

32 UST 3674; TIAS 9909; 1267 UNTS 347.

Implementing agreement regarding the consolidation and rescheduling of certain debts owed to the Agency for International Development.

Signed at Ankara February 7, 1981.

Entered into force February 7, 1981.

33 UST 1057; TIAS 10091; 1280 UNTS 437.

Agreement regarding the consolidation and rescheduling of payments due under P. L. 480 Title I agricultural commodity agreements, with annexes.

Signed at Ankara March 27, 1981.

Entered into force March 27, 1981.

33 UST 1545; TIAS 10131.

Agreement regarding the consolidation and rescheduling of certain debts owed to, guaranteed or insured by the United States Government and its agencies, with annexes and agreed minute.

Signed at Ankara September 24, 1981.

Entered into force November 2, 1981.

34 UST 1469; TIAS 10432.

Agreement regarding the consolidation and rescheduling of payments due under P.L. 480 Title I agricultural commodity agreements, with annexes.

Signed at Ankara November 25, 1981.

Entered into force November 25, 1981.

34 UST 1469; TIAS 10432.

Implementing agreement regarding the consolidation and rescheduling of certain debts owed to the Agency for International Development.

Signed at Ankara January 22, 1982.

Entered into force January 22, 1982.

34 UST 1469; TIAS 10432.

GENERAL RELATIONS

Agreement for the regularization of relations between the United States and Turkey.

Exchange of notes at Ankara February 17, 1927.

Entered into force February 17, 1927.

Foreign Relations, 1927, Vol. III, p. 794 ff.; 11 Bevans 1109.

INVESTMENT

Treaty concerning the reciprocal encouragement and protection of investments, with protocol.

Signed at Washington December 3, 1985.

Entered into force May 18, 1990.

TIAS

JUDICIAL ASSISTANCE

See EXTRADITION

LEND-LEASE

Agreement on the principles applying to aid under the Act of March 11, 1941, and exchanges of notes.

Signed at Ankara February 23, 1945.

Entered into force February 23, 1945.

59 Stat. 1476; EAS 465; 11 Bevans 1147; 121 UNTS 165.

Agreement on lend-lease and claims.

Signed at Ankara May 7, 1946.

Entered into force May 25, 1946.

60 Stat. 1809; TIAS 1541; 11 Bevans 1158; 6 UNTS 293.

MUTUAL SECURITY

Agreement relating to the assurances required by the Mutual Security Act of 1951.

Exchange of notes at Ankara January 7, 1952.

Entered into force January 7, 1952.

3 UST 4660; TIAS 2621; 179 UNTS 121.

NARCOTIC DRUGS

Arrangement for the direct exchange of certain information regarding the traffic in narcotic drugs.

Exchange of notes at Constantinople and Angora February 18 and October 3, 1928.

Entered into force October 3, 1928.

11 Bevans 1117.

PATENTS

Agreement to facilitate interchange of patent rights and technical information for purposes of defense.

Signed at Ankara May 18, 1956.

Entered into force April 2, 1957.

8 UST 597; TIAS 3809; 283 UNTS 167.

Agreement approving the procedures for reciprocal filing of classified patent applications in the United States and Turkey.

Exchange of notes at Ankara March 17 and September 16, 1959.

Entered into force September 16, 1959.

11 UST 388; TIAS 4456; 371 UNTS 314.

PEACE CORPS

Agreement relating to the establishment of a Peace Corps program in Turkey.

Exchange of notes at Ankara August 27, 1962.

Entered into force August 27, 1962.

13 UST 2263; TIAS 5193; 461 UNTS 55.

POSTAL MATTERS

Agreement concerning the exchange of parcel post, and regulations of execution.

Signed at Washington July 2 and at Ankara May 25, 1935.

Entered into force August 1, 1935.

49 Stat. 3201; 164 LNTS 125.

International express mail agreement, with detailed regulations.

Signed at Ankara and Washington October 16 and November 29, 1984.

Entered into force March 21, 1985.

TIAS 11012; 2022 UNTS 87.

Memorandum of understanding concerning the operation of the BUREAUFAX service.

Signed at Ankara and Washington February 14 and March 14, 1990.

Entered into force March 15, 1990.

TIAS 11712.

PRISONER TRANSFER

Treaty on the enforcement of penal judgments.

Signed at Ankara June 7, 1979.

Entered into force January 1, 1981.

32 UST 3187; TIAS 9892.

REFUGEES

Agreement concerning the reimbursement of costs arising from the transit of United States Government employees and their families.

Done at Ankara September 13, 1996.

Entered into force September 13, 1996.

TIAS

SCIENTIFIC COOPERATION

Agreement relating to scientific and technological cooperation, with annexes.

Signed at Ankara June 14, 1994.

Entered into force June 14, 1994.

TIAS 12185.

Extension

May 28 and June 21, 1999.

Memorandum of understanding concerning scientific and technical cooperation in the earth sciences.

Signed at Reston and Istanbul February 22 and April 2, 1999.

Entered into force April 2, 1999.

TIAS

Memorandum of understanding concerning scientific and technical cooperation in the earth sciences, with annexes.

Signed at Reston and Ankara February 7 and April 10, 2002.

Entered into force April 10, 2002.

TIAS

SEISMIC OBSERVATIONS

Agreement concerning the closure of Belbasi installation and the activation of a new seismic research station.

Signed at Ankara February 8, 2000.

Entered into force March 30, 2004.

TIAS

SHIPPING

Agreement relating to jurisdiction over vessels utilizing the Louisiana Offshore Oil Port.

Exchange of notes at Washington April 9 and 10, 1984.

Entered into force April 10, 1984.

TIAS 11239; 2174 UNTS 187.

SURPLUS PROPERTY

Agreement approving the procedures to be used in the sale of excess and/or scrap property in Turkey by the United States.

Exchange of notes at Ankara October 6 and November 13, 1959.

Entered into force November 13, 1959.

10 UST 1990; TIAS 4366; 361 UNTS 3.

TAXATION

Agreement relating to relief from Turkish taxation on expenditures made by or on behalf of the United States for common defense, with annex and minute.

Signed at Ankara June 23, 1954.

Entered into force June 23, 1954.

5 UST 1258; TIAS 2996; 222 UNTS 161.

Agreement for the avoidance of double taxation and the prevention of fiscal evasion with respect to taxes on income, with protocol.

Signed at Washington March 28, 1996.

Entered into force December 19, 1997.

TIAS

TELECOMMUNICATIONS

Arrangement relating to radio communications between amateur stations on behalf of third parties.

Exchange of notes at Ankara November 27, 1996.

Entered into force November 27, 1996.

TIAS 12818.

Agreement relating to the reciprocal granting of authorizations to permit licensed amateur radio operators of either country to operate their stations in the other country.

Exchange of notes at Ankara November 27, 1996.

Entered into force November 27, 1996.

TIAS 12819.

TRADE

See also COMMERCE

Agreement relating to subsidization of exports in the context of the agreement on interpretation and application of articles VI, XVI, and XXIII (subsidies code) of the general agreement on tariffs and trade (TIAS 9619).

Exchange of letters at Washington February 25, 1985.

Entered into force February 25, 1985.

TIAS 11322.

Visa arrangement concerning textiles and textile articles, with annex.

Exchange of letters at Washington and Ankara January 10, 1987.

Entered into force January 10, 1987; effective March 1, 1987.

NP

Amendments

November 22 and 24, 1988 (NP).

June 29 and July 17, 1989 (NP).

Agreement concerning trade in cotton and man-made fiber textiles and textile products, with annexes.

Exchange of notes at Ankara October 19 and November 16, 1988.

Entered into force November 16, 1988; effective July 1, 1988.

NP

Amendments and extensions

June 30 and July 26, 1989 (NP).

July 29 and August 6, 1991 (NP).

April 27 and May 13, 1992 (NP).

October 31 and November 30, 1994 (NP).

VISAS

Agreement relating to passport visas and visa fees.

Exchange of notes at Washington June 27, August 8, September 27, and October 11, 1955.

Entered into force October 11, 1955; operative December 1, 1955.

7 UST 337; TIAS 3508; 272 UNTS 145.

TURKMENISTAN

For agreements prior to December 31, 1991, see UNION OF SOVIET SOCIALIST REPUBLICS.

DEFENSE

Agreement concerning the provision of training related to defense articles under the United States International Military Education and Training (IMET) Program.

Exchange of notes at Ashgabat November 29, 1993 and January 3, 1994.

Entered into force January 3, 1994.

NP

Agreement regarding grants under the Foreign Assistance Act of 1961, as amended, and the furnishing of defense articles, related training, and other defense services from the United States of America to the Government of Turkmenistan.

Exchange of notes April 5 and 24, 1999.

Entered into force April 24, 1999.

NP

ECONOMIC AND TECHNICAL COOPERATION

Agreement regarding cooperation to facilitate the provision of assistance.

Signed at Ashgabat November 30, 1993.

Entered into force November 30, 1993.

TIAS 12518.

EMPLOYMENT

Agreement relating to the employment of dependents of official government employees.

Exchange of notes at Ashgabat July 15 and 20, 1999.

Entered into force July 20, 1999.

TIAS

FINANCE

Investment incentive agreement.

Signed at Ashgabat June 26, 1992.

Entered into force June 26, 1992.

TIAS 12462.

INTERNATIONAL CRIMINAL COURT

Agreement regarding the surrender of persons to the International Criminal Court.

Signed at Ashgabat December 25, 2003.

Entered into force January 30, 2004.

TIAS

PEACE CORPS

Agreement concerning the program of the Peace Corps of the United States in Turkmenistan.

Signed at Ashgabat February 26, 1993.

Entered into force February 26, 1993.

TIAS 11467.

TRADE AND COMMERCE

Agreement on trade relations, with exchanges of letters.

Signed at Washington March 23, 1993.

Entered into force October 25, 1993.

TIAS 12491.

TUVALU

On October 1, 1978, Tuvalu became an independent state. In a note dated December 19, 1978, to the Secretary-General of the United Nations, the Prime Minister of Tuvalu made a statement reading in part as follows:

"2 The Government of Tuvalu, conscious of the desirability of maintaining existing international legal relationships, and conscious of its obligations under international law to honour its treaty commitments, acknowledges that many treaty rights and obligations of the Government of the United Kingdom in respect of the Gilbert and Ellice Islands Protectorate, the Gilbert and Ellice Islands Colony and Tuvalu were succeeded to by Tuvalu upon Independence by virtue of customary international law. Since, however, it is likely that by virtue of that law certain of such treaties may be said to have lapsed at the date of Tuvalu's Independence, it seems essential that each treaty purporting or deemed to bind Tuvalu before that date should be subjected to legal examination. The Government of Tuvalu proposes after such examination has been completed to indicate which, if any, of the treaties which may be said to have lapsed by virtue of customary international law it proposes to treat as having lapsed.

3 The Government of Tuvalu desires that it should be presumed that each treaty purporting or deemed to bind Tuvalu before Independence has been legally succeeded to by Tuvalu and that action should be based on such presumption unless and until the Government of Tuvalu decides that any particular treaty should be treated as having lapsed. Should the Government of Tuvalu be of opinion that it has legally succeeded to any treaty, and wish to terminate the operation of such treaty, it will in due course give notice of termination in the terms thereof.

4 For the avoidance of doubt, the Government of Tuvalu further declares that it does not regard itself as bound by the terms of any convention creating an international organisation to the extent that such convention requires the payment of any sum by any State, by virtue only of the accession of the Government of the United Kingdom to such convention."

AVIATION

Agreement between the United States and the United Kingdom concerning air services with annexes and exchange of letters.

Signed at Bermuda July 23, 1977.

Entered into force July 23, 1977.

28 UST 5367; TIAS 8641.

Amendment

April 25, 1978 (29 UST 2680; TIAS 8965).

CONSULS

Consular convention between the United States and the United Kingdom.

Signed at Washington June 6, 1951.

Entered into force September 7, 1952.

3 UST 3426; TIAS 2494; 165 UNTS 121.

EXTRADITION

Extradition treaty between the United States and the United Kingdom, with protocol of signature and exchange of notes.

Signed at London June 8, 1972.

Entered into force January 21, 1977.

28 UST 227; TIAS 8468.

FRIENDSHIP

Treaty of friendship.

Signed at Funafuti February 7, 1979.

Entered into force September 23, 1983.

35 UST 2087; TIAS 10776; 2011 UNTS 79.

INTERNATIONAL CRIMINAL COURT

Agreement on the surrender of persons to the International Criminal Court.

Exchange of notes at Suva and Funafuti September 19, 2002 and January 9, 2003.

Entered into force February 3, 2003.

TIAS

PEACE CORPS

Agreement relating to the establishment of a Peace Corps program in Tuvalu.

Exchange of notes at Suva August 25, 1977.

Entered into force August 25, 1977.

29 UST 5428; TIAS 9119.

SCIENTIFIC COOPERATION

Memorandum of understanding concerning scientific and technical cooperation in the earth sciences, with annexes.

Signed at Reston and Funafuti August 3 and October 26, 2001.

Entered into force October 26, 2001.

TIAS

TELECOMMUNICATION

Agreement between the United States and the United Kingdom relating to the reciprocal granting of authorizations to permit licensed amateur radio operators of either country to operate their stations in the other country.

Exchange of notes at London November 26, 1965; applicable to Tuvalu December 11, 1969.

16 UST 2047; TIAS 5941; 561 UNTS 193.

Agreement between the United States and the United Kingdom extending to certain territories the application of the agreement of November 26, 1965 relating to the reciprocal granting of authorizations to permit licensed amateur radio operators of either country to operate their stations in the other country.

Exchange of notes at London December 11, 1969.

Entered into force December 11, 1969.

20 UST 4089; TIAS 6800; 732 UNTS 334.

TERRITORIAL SOVEREIGNTY

See FRIENDSHIP

TRADE-MARKS

Declaration by the United States and the United Kingdom affording reciprocal protection to trade-marks.

Signed at London October 24, 1877.

Entered into force October 24, 1877.

20 Stat. 703; TS 138; 12 Bevans 198.

TREATY OBLIGATIONS

Agreement relating to treaty obligations assumed by Tuvalu upon its independence.

Exchange of notes at Suva and Funafuti January 29 and April 25, 1980.

Entered into force April 25, 1980.

32 UST 1310; TIAS 9770; 1222 UNTS 293.

U

UGANDA

AGRICULTURAL COMMODITIES

Agricultural commodities agreement.

Signed at Kampala June 28, 1988.

Entered into force June 28, 1988.

NP

Related agreements

February 2, 1989 (NP).

April 12, 1990 (NP).

AVIATION

Memorandum of agreement for the provision of assistance in developing and modernizing the civil aviation infrastructure of Uganda.

Signed at Washington and Kampala November 10 and 11, 2003.

Entered into force November 11, 2003.

TIAS

Amendment

August 16 and September 5, 2005.

DEFENSE

Agreement concerning the provision of training related to defense articles under the United States International Military Education and Training (IMET) Program.

Exchange of notes at Kampala April 6, 1981 and June 15, 1984.

Entered into force June 15, 1984.

TIAS 10984; 2022 UNTS 121.

Agreement regarding grants under the Foreign Assistance Act of 1961, as amended, and the furnishing of defense articles, related training and other defense services from the United States to Uganda.

Exchange of notes at Kampala January 31 and March 25, 1994.

Entered into force March 25, 1994.

TIAS 11476.

Agreement regarding the status of U.S. military personnel and civilian employees of the Department of Defense temporarily in Uganda in connection with their official duties.

Exchange of notes at Kampala July 25 and August 12, 1994.

Entered into force August 12, 1994.

NP

Acquisition and cross-servicing agreement, with annexes.

Signed at Entebbe July 14, 2004.

Entered into force July 14, 2004.

TIAS

ECONOMIC AND TECHNICAL COOPERATION

Agreement relating to economic, technical and related assistance.

Exchange of notes at Kampala December 3 and 11, 1971.

Entered into force December 11, 1971.

22 UST 1848; TIAS 7229.

Agency for International Development

July 3, 1997 (NP).

August 30, 1997 (NP).

May 28, 1998 (NP).

August 28, 1998 (NP).

July 1, 1999 (NP).

August 30, 2002 (NP).

EMPLOYMENT

Agreement relating to the employment of dependents of official government employees.

Exchange of notes at Kampala October 8, 1998 and June 18, 1999.

Entered into force June 18, 1999.

TIAS

ENVIRONMENTAL COOPERATION

Agreement for cooperation on the Global Learning and Observations to Benefit the Environment (GLOBE) Program, with appendices.

Signed at Kampala November 26, 1998.

Entered into force November 26, 1998.

TIAS

FINANCE

Agreement relating to investment guaranties.

Exchange of notes at Kampala May 29, 1965.

Entered into force May 29, 1965.

16 UST 827; TIAS 5818; 546 UNTS 209.

Agreement regarding the consolidation and rescheduling of certain debts owed to, guaranteed or insured by the United States Government and its agencies, with annexes.

Signed at Kampala May 10, 1982.

Entered into force June 21, 1982.

NP

Agreements regarding the consolidation and rescheduling of certain debts owed to, or guaranteed by the United States Government and its agencies, with annexes, and implementing agreements regarding AID loans and agricultural commodity agreements.

Signed at Kampala March 31, 1983.

Entered into force May 23, 1983.

NP

Agreement regarding the consolidation and rescheduling of certain debts owed to, guaranteed by, or insured by the United States Government and its agencies, with annexes.

Signed at Kampala January 13, 1988.

Entered into force February 22, 1988.

NP

Agreement regarding the consolidation and rescheduling of certain debts owed to, guaranteed by, or insured by the United States Government and its agencies, with annexes.

Signed at Kampala December 19, 1989.

Entered into force January 26, 1990.

NP

Agreement regarding the reduction and reorganization of certain debts owed to, guaranteed by, or insured by the United States Government and its Agency, with annexes.

Signed at Kampala June 22, 1999.

Entered into force August 19, 1999.

NP

Agreement regarding the reduction of certain debts owed to, guaranteed by, or insured by the United States Government and its Agency, with annexes.

Signed at Kampala May 28, 2002.

Entered into force August 19, 2002.

NP

INTERNATIONAL CRIMINAL COURT

Agreement regarding the surrender of persons to the International Criminal Court.

Signed at Washington June 12, 2003.

Entered into force October 23, 2003.

TIAS

PEACE CORPS

Agreement relating to the establishment of a Peace Corps program in Uganda.

Exchange of notes at Kampala November 16, 1964.

Entered into force November 16, 1964.

15 UST 2433; TIAS 5735; 586 UNTS 143.

POSTAL MATTERS

International express mail agreement, with detailed regulations.

Signed at Kampala and Washington October 4 and November 3, 1988.

Entered into force December 15, 1988.

TIAS 11628.

UKRAINE

The following agreements include those between the United States and Ukraine, as well as those between the United States and the former Union of Soviet Socialist Republics that the United States and Ukraine have agreed remain in force between them. Bilateral arms limitation and related agreements between the United States and the former Union of Soviet Socialist Republics remain under review. No conclusion can be drawn from their absence from the following list.

AFGHANISTAN SETTLEMENT

Declaration between the United States and the Union of Soviet Socialist Republics on international guarantees (Afghanistan Settlement Agreement).

Signed at Geneva April 14, 1988.

Entered into force May 15, 1988.

TIAS

ARMS LIMITATION

Agreement concerning assistance to Ukraine in the elimination of strategic nuclear arms and the prevention of proliferation of weapons of mass destruction.

Signed at Kiev October 25, 1993.

Entered into force December 31, 1993.

TIAS

Extension

June 30 and July 29, 1999.

Agreement concerning development of state systems of control, accounting and physical protection of nuclear materials to promote the prevention of nuclear weapons proliferation from Ukraine.

Signed at Washington December 18, 1993.

Entered into force December 31, 1993.

TIAS

Amendment and extension

March 21, 1994.

July 7, 1999.

ATOMIC ENERGY

Memorandum of cooperation between the United States and the Union of Soviet Socialist Republics in the field of magnetic confinement fusion.

Signed at Moscow July 5, 1991.

Entered into force July 5, 1991.

TIAS

Agreement concerning operational safety enhancements, risk reduction measures and nuclear safety regulation for civilian nuclear facilities in Ukraine, with exchange of notes.

Signed at Kiev October 25, 1993.

Entered into force October 25, 1993.

TIAS

Amendment and extension

April 5 and 23, 2004.

Agreement for cooperation concerning peaceful uses of nuclear energy, with annex and agreed minute.

Signed at Kiev May 6, 1998.

Entered into force May 28, 1999.

TIAS

Agreement concerning the International Radioecology Laboratory of the International Chornobyl Center on Nuclear Safety, Radioactive Waste and Radioecology, with annex.

Signed at Kiev July 22, 1998.

Entered into force July 22, 1998.

TIAS

Agreement on cooperation on research on health and environmental effects related to the Chernobyl accident.

Signed at Washington December 8, 1999.

Entered into force December 8, 1999.

TIAS

Implementing agreement concerning the Ukraine Nuclear Fuel Qualification Project, with annex.

Signed at Kiev June 5, 2000.

Entered into force June 5, 2000.

TIAS

Extension

April 14 and June 4, 2005.

AVIATION

Agreement between the United States and the Union of Soviet Socialist Republics supplementary to the 1966 civil air transport agreement (TIAS 6135), as amended by the agreement of February 13, 1986.

Signed at Washington November 4, 1966.

Entered into force November 4, 1966.

17 UST 1936; TIAS 6135; 675 UNTS 24.

Air transport agreement, with annexes.

Signed at Kiev June 5, 2000.

Entered into force June 5, 2000.

TIAS

CONSULS

See also PRIVILEGES AND IMMUNITIES

Consular convention between the United States and the Union of Soviet Socialist Republics.

Signed at Moscow June 1, 1964.

Entered into force July 13, 1968.

19 UST 5018; TIAS 6503; 655 UNTS 213.

CULTURAL HERITAGE

Agreement on the protection and preservation of cultural heritage.

Signed at Washington March 4, 1994.

Entered into force March 4, 1994.

TIAS 11480.

CUSTOMS

Agreement regarding cooperation and mutual assistance between their customs services.

Exchange of notes at Washington November 21, 1994.

Entered into force November 21, 1994.

TIAS 12582.

DEFENSE

Agreement between the United States and the Union of Soviet Socialist Republics on the prevention of dangerous military activities, with annexes and agreed statements.

Signed at Moscow June 12, 1989.

Entered into force January 1, 1990.

TIAS

Agreement concerning the provision of training related to defense articles under the United States International Military Education and Training (IMET) Program.

Exchange of notes at Kiev May 11 and 29, 1992.

Entered into force May 29, 1992.

NP

Agreement concerning the conversion of enterprises of the military-industrial complex.

Signed at Kiev March 21, 1994.

Entered into force March 21, 1994.

TIAS

Amendments and extension

June 27, 1995.

February 12, 1996.

June 12, 1998.

January 26 and February 6, 2001.

Acquisition and cross-servicing agreement, with annexes.

Signed at Stuttgart and Kiev November 17 and 19, 1999.

Entered into force November 19, 1999.

TIAS

Implementing arrangement concerning mutual logistic support, with annexes.

Signed at Kiev and Stuttgart November 19 and December 7, 1999.

Entered into force December 7, 1999.

TIAS

Agreement concerning exchange of research and development information in the sphere of military technical cooperation, with appendix.

Signed at Washington March 31, 2000.

Entered into force July 27, 2001.

TIAS

Agreement on protection of classified defense information.

Signed at Kiev August 4, 2003.

Entered into force July 14, 2004.

TIAS

Agreement concerning the provision of equipment, training and related services under the United States International Military Education and Training (IMET) Program.

Exchange of notes at Kiev August 18, 2003 and May 5, 2004.

Entered into force May 5, 2004.

NP

ECONOMIC AND TECHNICAL COOPERATION

Agreement regarding humanitarian and technical economic cooperation.

Signed at Washington May 7, 1992.

Entered into force May 7, 1992.

TIAS 11472.

Agency for International Development

November 21, 1994 (NP).

EDUCATION

Agreement between the United States and the Union of Soviet Socialist Republics on expansion of undergraduate exchanges.

Signed at Washington June 1, 1990.

Entered into force June 1, 1990.

TIAS

EMBASSY SITES

Agreement between the United States and the Union of Soviet Socialist Republics on the reciprocal allocation for use free of charge of plots of land in Moscow and Washington with annexes and exchanges of notes.

Signed at Moscow May 16, 1969.

Entered into force May 16, 1969.

20 UST 789; TIAS 6693; 715 UNTS 33.

Agreement between the United States and the Union of Soviet Socialist Republics concerning dates for use of land for, and construction of, embassy complexes in Moscow and Washington.

Exchange of notes at Moscow March 30, 1977.

Entered into force March 30, 1977.

28 UST 5293; TIAS 8629; 1087 UNTS 67.

EMERGENCY PREPAREDNESS

Memorandum of understanding on cooperation in natural and man-made technological emergency prevention and response.

Signed at Kiev June 5, 2000.

Entered into force June 5, 2000.

TIAS

EMPLOYMENT

Agreement relating to the employment of dependents of official government employees.

Exchange of notes at Washington November 21, 1994.

Entered into force November 21, 1994.

TIAS 12196.

ENVIRONMENTAL COOPERATION

Agreement on cooperation in the field of environmental protection.

Signed at Washington May 7, 1992.

Entered into force May 7, 1992.

TIAS 11466.

Agreement concerning a regional environmental center in Ukraine.

Signed at Washington December 8, 1999.

Entered into force December 8, 1999.

TIAS

FINANCE

Investment incentive agreement.

Signed at Washington May 6, 1992.

Entered into force May 6, 1992.

TIAS 11475.

Agreement regarding the consolidation and rescheduling of certain debts owed to, guaranteed by, or insured by the United States Government and its agency, with annexes.

Signed at Kiev June 10, 2002.

Entered into force July 19, 2002.

NP

GENERAL RELATIONS

Arrangements between the United States and the Union of Soviet Socialist Republics relating to the establishment of diplomatic relations, nonintervention, freedom of conscience and religious liberty, legal protection, and claims.

Exchanges of notes at Washington November 16, 1933.

Entered into force November 16, 1933.

Department of State Publication 528; European and British Commonwealth Series 2 [new series]; Eastern European Series No. 1 [old series]; 11 Bevans 1248.

HEALTH

Agreement between the United States and the Union of Soviet Socialist Republics on cooperation in artificial heart research and development.

Signed at Moscow June 28, 1974.

Entered into force June 28, 1974.

25 UST 1331; TIAS 7867.

HOUSING

Memorandum of understanding between the United States and the Union of Soviet Socialist Republics on cooperation in housing and economic development.

Signed at Moscow July 30, 1991.

Entered into force July 30, 1991.

TIAS

INVESTMENT

Treaty concerning the encouragement and reciprocal protection of investment, with annex and exchange of letters.

Signed at Washington March 4, 1994.

Entered into force November 16, 1996.

TIAS

JUDICIAL ASSISTANCE

Agreement between the United States and the Union of Soviet Socialist Republics relating to the procedure to be followed in the execution of letters rogatory.

Exchange of notes at Moscow November 22, 1935.

Entered into force November 22, 1935.

49 Stat. 3840; EAS 83; 11 Bevans 1262; 167 LNTS 303.

Memorandum of understanding concerning cooperation in the pursuit of Nazi war criminals.

Signed at Washington August 26, 1993.

Entered into force August 26, 1993.

TIAS

Treaty on mutual legal assistance in criminal matters, with annex.

Signed at Kiev July 22, 1998.

Entered into force February 27, 2001.

TIAS

LEND–LEASE

Preliminary agreement between the United States and the Union of Soviet Socialist Republics relating to principles applying to mutual aid in the prosecution of the war against aggression, and exchange of notes.

Signed at Washington June 11, 1942.

Entered into force June 11, 1942.

56 Stat. 1500; EAS 253; 11 Bevans 1281; 105 UNTS 285.

Agreement between the United States and the Union of Soviet Socialist Republics regarding settlement of lend-lease, reciprocal aid and claims.

Signed at Washington October 18, 1972.

Entered into force October 18, 1972.

23 UST 2910; TIAS 7478; 898 UNTS 297.

Agreement between the United States and the Union of Soviet Socialist Republics regarding settlement of lend-lease accounts.

Exchange of letters at Washington June 1, 1990.

Entered into force June 1, 1990.

TIAS

MAPPING

Memorandum of understanding between the United States and the Union of Soviet Socialist Republics on cooperation in the mapping sciences, with annexes.

Signed at Moscow May 14, 1991.

Entered into force May 14, 1991.

NP

MARITIME MATTERS

Agreement between the United States and the Union of Soviet Socialist Republics on the prevention of incidents on and over the high seas.

Signed at Moscow May 25, 1972.

Entered into force May 25, 1972.

23 UST 1168; TIAS 7379; 852 UNTS 151.

Protocol between the United States and the Union of Soviet Socialist Republics to the agreement of May 25, 1972 (TIAS 7379) on the prevention of incidents on and over the high seas.

Signed at Washington May 22, 1973.

Entered into force May 22, 1973.

24 UST 1063; TIAS 7624.

Memorandum of understanding between the United States and the Union of Soviet Socialist Republics regarding marine cargo insurance.

Signed at London April 5, 1979.

Entered into force April 5, 1979.

30 UST 2194; TIAS 9326; 1171 UNTS 93.

MEDICAL ASSISTANCE

Agreement between the United States and the Union of Soviet Socialist Republics on emergency medical supplies and related assistance.

Signed at Moscow July 30, 1991.

Entered into force July 30, 1991.

TIAS

NARCOTIC DRUGS

Memorandum of understanding between the United States and the Union of Soviet Socialist Republics on cooperation to combat illegal narcotics trafficking.

Signed at Paris January 8, 1989.

Entered into force January 8, 1989.

TIAS 11436.

Agreement between the United States and the Union of Soviet Socialist Republics on a mutual understanding on cooperation in the struggle against the illicit traffic in narcotics.

Signed at Washington January 31, 1990.

Entered into force January 31, 1990.

TIAS

NORTH ATLANTIC TREATY

Agreement to treat the agreement of June 19, 1995 among the States Parties to the North Atlantic Treaty and other states participating in the Partnership for Peace regarding the status of their forces as binding between the United States and Ukraine.

Exchange of notes at Kiev May 28 and September 9, 1998.

Entered into force September 9, 1998.

TIAS

NUCLEAR MATERIAL

Implementing arrangement for cooperation in the area of prevention of illicit trafficking in nuclear and other radioactive material.

Signed at Washington and Kiev April 8 and 20, 2005.

Entered into force April 20, 2005.

TIAS

Implementing arrangement concerning cooperation to enhance the security of Ukraine's usable sources of ionizing radiation, with appendix.

Signed at Washington and Kiev June 16 and 23, 2006.

Entered into force June 23, 2006.

TIAS

NUCLEAR RISK REDUCTION

Agreement on the establishment of a secure communications link between the Nuclear Risk Reduction Center of the United States of America and the Military Cooperation and Verification Center of the General Staff of the Armed Forces of Ukraine, with annexes.

Signed at Kiev September 20, 2001.

Entered into force September 20, 2001.

TIAS

OCEANOGRAPHY

Agreement on cooperation between the United States and the Union of Soviet Socialist Republics on ocean studies, with annexes.

Signed at Washington June 1, 1990.

Entered into force June 1, 1990.

TIAS 11452.

PEACE CORPS

Agreement concerning the program of the Peace Corps of the United States in Ukraine.

Signed at Washington May 6, 1992.

Entered into force May 6, 1992.

TIAS 11510.

POSTAL MATTERS

International express mail agreement, with detailed regulations.

Signed at Kiev and Washington June 1 and November 8, 1993.

Entered into force January 1, 1994.

NP

PRISONERS OF WAR

Agreement between the United States and the Union of Soviet Socialist Republics relating to prisoners of war and civilians liberated by forces operating under Soviet command and forces operating under United States of America command.

Signed at Yalta February 11, 1945.

Entered into force February 11, 1945;

59 Stat. 1874; EAS 505; 11 Bevans 1286; 68 UNTS 175.

PRIVILEGES AND IMMUNITIES

Agreement between the United States and the Union of Soviet Socialist Republics relating to privileges and immunities of all members of the Soviet and American embassies and their families, with agreed minute.

Exchange of notes at Washington December 14, 1978.

Entered into force December 14, 1978; effective December 29, 1978.

30 UST 2341; TIAS 9340; 1171 UNTS 73.

Agreement between the United States and the Union of Soviet Socialist Republics relating to immunity of family members of consular officers and employees from criminal jurisdiction.

Exchange of notes at Washington October 31, 1986.

Entered into force October 31, 1986.

TIAS 11432.

RULES OF WARFARE

Convention between the United States and the Union of Soviet Socialist Republics relating to the rights of neutrals at sea.[1]

Signed at Washington July 22, 1854.

Entered into force October 31, 1854.

10 Stat. 1105; TS 300; 11 Bevans 1214.

NOTE

1 Declaration of accession by Nicaragua signed at Granada June 9, 1855 (7 Miller 139).

SCIENTIFIC COOPERATION

Memorandum of understanding between the United States and the Union of Soviet Socialist Republics on cooperation in the physical, chemical and engineering sciences, with annexes.

Signed at Moscow May 13, 1991.

Entered into force May 13, 1991.

TIAS

SEABED OPERATIONS

Agreement between the United States and the Union of Soviet Socialist Republics concerning the confidentiality of data on deep seabed areas, with related exchange of letters.

Exchange of notes at Moscow December 5, 1986.

Entered into force December 5, 1986.

TIAS

Agreement between the United States and the Union of Soviet Socialist Republics relating to the agreement of August 14, 1987 on the resolution of practical problems with respect to deep seabed mining areas.[1]

Exchange of notes at Moscow August 14, 1987.

Entered into force August 14, 1987.

TIAS 11438.

NOTE

1 Parties to the multilateral agreement of August 14, 1987 are Belgium, Canada, Italy, Netherlands and Union of Soviet Socialist Republics.

TAXATION

Convention for the avoidance of double taxation and the prevention of fiscal evasion with respect to taxes on income and capital, with protocol.

Signed at Washington March 4, 1994.

Entered into force June 5, 2000.

TIAS

Agreement concerning the relationship between the Taxation Convention of March 4, 1994 and the General Agreement on Trade in Services with regard to the consultation, most-favored-nation and national treatment provisions.

Exchange of notes at Washington May 26 and June 6, 1995.

Entered into force June 5, 2000.

TIAS

TECHNOLOGY TRANSFER

Agreement on technology safeguards associated with Ukrainian launch vehicles, missile equipment and technical data for the "Sea Launch" Program.

Signed at New York September 29, 1999.

Entered into force October 4, 2000.

TIAS

Extension

April 21 and September 27, 2005.

TRADE

Agreement between the United States and the Union of Soviet Socialist Republics regulating the position of corporations and other commercial associations.

Signed at St. Petersburg June 25, 1904.

Entered into force June 25, 1904.

36 Stat. 2163; TS 526; 11 Bevans 1235.

Agreement on trade relations, with related exchanges of letters.

Signed at Washington May 6, 1992.

Entered into force June 23, 1992.

TIAS

TRANSPORTATION

Agreement between the United States and the Union of Soviet Socialist Republics on cooperation in transportation science and technology, with annexes.

Signed at Moscow May 31, 1988.

Entered into force May 31, 1988.

TIAS

TREATY SUCCESSION

Agreement concerning the succession of Ukraine to bilateral treaties between the United States and the former Union of Soviet Socialist Republics, with annex.

Exchange of notes at Kiev May 10, 1995.

Entered into force May 15, 1995.

TIAS

VISAS

Agreement between the United States and the Union of Soviet Socialist Republics relating to the reciprocal issuance of multiple entry and exit visas to American and Soviet correspondents.

Exchange of notes at Moscow September 29, 1975.

Entered into force September 29, 1975.

27 UST 4258; TIAS 8448.

WEAPONS

Agreement concerning the provision of assistance to Ukraine related to the establishment of an export control system to prevent the proliferation of weapons of mass destruction from Ukraine.

Signed at Kiev December 5, 1993.

Entered into force December 31, 1993.

TIAS

Amendments and extension

March 21, 1994.

June 27, 1995.

June 12, 1998.

August 10 and 13, 1999.

Agreement concerning the provision of material, services and related training to Ukraine in connection with the elimination of strategic nuclear arms, with annexes.

Signed at Kiev December 5, 1993.

Entered into force December 31, 1993.

TIAS

Amendments and extension

December 18, 1993.

December 18, 1993.

March 21, 1994.

April 1, 1995.

June 27, 1995.

June 4, 1996.

May 1, 1997.

June 12, 1998.

July 10, 1999.

July 24 and 28, 2000.

December 1 and 4, 2000.

January 24 and 31, 2001.

August 30 and September 9, 2002.

July 24 and September 18, 2003.

Agreement concerning development of state systems of control, accounting and physical protection of nuclear materials to promote the prevention of nuclear weapons proliferation from Ukraine.

Signed at Washington December 18, 1993.

Entered into force December 31, 1993.

TIAS

Amendment

February 18 and March 23, 2004.

Agreement concerning the provision to Ukraine of emergency response equipment and related training in connection with the removal of nuclear warheads from Ukraine for destruction in the course of the elimination of strategic nuclear arms, with annex.

Signed at Washington December 18, 1993.

Entered into force December 31, 1993.

TIAS

Agreement concerning cooperation in the elimination of infrastructure for weapons of mass destruction through provision to Ukraine of material, services and related training.

Signed at Kiev June 27, 1995.

Entered into force June 27, 1995.

TIAS

Amendment and extension

June 4, 1996.

August 3 and October 30, 2001.

Agreement concerning development of state systems of control, accounting and physical protection of nuclear materials to promote the prevention of nuclear weapons proliferation from Ukraine.

Signed at Kiev June 27, 1995.

Entered into force June 27, 1995.

TIAS

Agreement on the provision of assistance to Ukraine in establishing an export control system in order to prevent the proliferation from Ukraine of weapons of mass destruction.

Signed at Kiev October 22, 2001.

Entered into force October 22, 2001; effective December 31, 1999.

TIAS

Amendments

March 15 and 26, 2004.

June 27, 2005.

August 31 and September 12, 2006.

Agreement concerning cooperation in the area of prevention of proliferation of technology, pathogens and expertise that could be used in the development of biological weapons.

Signed at Kiev August 29, 2005.

Entered into force August 29, 2005

TIAS

UNION OF SOVIET SOCIALIST REPUBLICS

The Union of Soviet Socialist Republics dissolved December 25, 1991. As stated in the Alma Ata Declaration of December 21, 1991, "... The States participating in the Commonwealth guarantee in accordance with their constitutional procedures the discharge of the international obligations deriving from treaties and agreements concluded by the former Union of Soviet Socialist Republics..." In addition, the Russian Federation has informed the United States Government by a note dated January 13, 1992, that it "... continues to perform the rights and fulfil the obligations following from the international agreements signed by the Union of the Soviet Socialist Republics..."

Section 2 of Treaties in Force covers multilateral treaties and agreements. Where a multilateral treaty action was taken prior to dissolution, "Union of Soviet Socialist Republics" is retained; where a successor state has taken action it is listed separately.

The United States is reviewing the continued applicability of the agreements listed below. Bilateral agreements subsequent to December 31, 1991, are listed under individual country headings.

AFGHANISTAN SETTLEMENT

Declaration on international guarantees (Afghanistan Settlement Agreement).

Signed at Geneva April 14, 1988.

Entered into force May 15, 1988.

TIAS

ARMS LIMITATION

See also NUCLEAR TEST LIMITATION and NUCLEAR WAR

Treaty on the limitation of anti-ballistic missile systems.

Signed at Moscow May 26, 1972.

Entered into force October 3, 1972.

23 UST 3435; TIAS 7503; 944 UNTS 13.

Protocol establishing and approving regulations governing procedures and other matters of the Standing Consultative Commission with regulations.

Signed at Geneva May 30, 1973.

Entered into force May 30, 1973.

24 UST 1124; TIAS 7637; 944 UNTS 30.

Basic principles of negotiation on the further limitation of strategic offensive arms.

Signed at Washington June 21, 1973.

Entered into force June 21, 1973.

24 UST 1472; TIAS 7653; 944 UNTS 41.

Protocol to the treaty of May 26, 1972 on the limitation of anti-ballistic missile systems.

Signed at Moscow July 3, 1974.

Entered into force May 24, 1976.

27 UST 1645; TIAS 8276.

Treaty on the limitation of underground nuclear weapon tests.

Signed at Moscow July 3, 1974.

Entered into force December 11, 1990.

TIAS

Protocol to the treaty of July 3, 1974, on the limitation of underground nuclear weapon tests.

Signed at Washington June 1, 1990.

Entered into force December 11, 1990.

TIAS

Treaty on the elimination of their intermediate-range and shorter-range missiles, with memorandum of understanding and protocols.

Signed at Washington December 8, 1987.

Entered into force June 1, 1988.

TIAS; 1657 UNTS 2.

Agreement on notifications of launches of intercontinental ballistic missiles and submarine-launched ballistic missiles.

Signed at Moscow May 31, 1988.

Entered into force May 31, 1988.

TIAS

Agreement on the conduct of a joint verification experiment, with annex.

Signed at Moscow May 31, 1988.

Entered into force May 31, 1988.

TIAS

Agreement on principles of implementing trial verification and stability measures that would be carried out pending the conclusion of the U.S.-Soviet treaty on the reduction and limitation of strategic offensive arms.

Signed at Jackson Hole, Wyoming, September 23, 1989.

Entered into force September 23, 1989.

TIAS 11459.

Memorandum of understanding regarding a bilateral verification experiment and data exchange related to prohibition of chemical weapons.

Signed at Jackson Hole, Wyoming, September 23, 1989.

Entered into force September 23, 1989.

TIAS 11460.

Agreement concerning the conduct of reciprocal demonstrations of reentry vehicle inspection procedures, with appendix.

Exchange of letters at Geneva January 22, 1990.

Entered into force March 23, 1990.

TIAS

Treaty on the reduction and limitation of strategic offensive arms, with annexes, protocols and memorandum of understanding.[1]

Signed at Moscow July 31, 1991.

Entered into force December 5, 1994.

TIAS

NOTE

1 For Protocol, see ARMS LIMITATION in multilateral section.

ATOMIC ENERGY

Memorandum of cooperation in the field of civilian nuclear reactor safety.

Signed at Washington April 26, 1988.

Entered into force April 26, 1988.

TIAS 11486.

Agreement on scientific and technical cooperation in the field of peaceful uses of atomic energy, with annex.

Signed at Washington June 1, 1990.

Entered into force June 1, 1990.

TIAS 11487.

Memorandum of cooperation in the fields of environmental restoration and waste management.

Signed at Vienna September 18, 1990.

Entered into force September 18, 1990.

TIAS

AVIATION

Agreement supplementary to the 1966 civil air transport agreement (TIAS 6135), as amended by the agreement of February 13, 1986.

Signed at Washington November 4, 1966.

Entered into force November 4, 1966.

17 UST 1936; TIAS 6135; 675 UNTS 24.

Memorandum of cooperation concerning air traffic control, with annexes.

Signed at Washington February 16, 1990.

Entered into force February 16, 1990.

TIAS 11450.

Civil air transport agreement, with annexes.

Signed at Washington June 1, 1990.

Entered into force June 1, 1990.[1]

TIAS 11461.

NOTE

1 Superseded by the agreement of January 14, 1994 as between the United States and the Russian Federation.

COMMERCE

See TRADE AND COMMERCE

CONSERVATION

Convention concerning the conservation of migratory birds and their environment.

Signed at Moscow November 19, 1976.

Entered into force October 13, 1978.

29 UST 4647; TIAS 9073; 1134 UNTS 97.

CONSULS

See also PRIVILEGES AND IMMUNITIES

Consular convention.

Signed at Moscow June 1, 1964.

Entered into force July 13, 1968.

19 UST 5018; TIAS 6503; 655 UNTS 213.

CULTURAL RELATIONS

General agreement on contacts, exchanges and cooperation in scientific, technical, educational, cultural and other fields.

Signed at Geneva November 21, 1985.

Entered into force November 21, 1985.

TIAS

Program of cooperation and exchanges for 1986-1988, with annex.

Signed at Geneva November 21, 1985.

Entered into force November 21, 1985.

TIAS

Program of cooperation and exchanges for 1989-1991, with annex.

Signed at Moscow May 31, 1988.

Entered into force May 31, 1988; effective January 1, 1989.

TIAS 11454.

DEFENSE

Agreement on the prevention of dangerous military activities, with annexes and agreed statements.

Signed at Moscow June 12, 1989.

Entered into force January 1, 1990.

TIAS 11485; 1566 UNTS 309.

ECONOMIC AND TECHNICAL COOPERATION

Long term agreement to facilitate economic, industrial, and technical cooperation.

Signed at Moscow June 29, 1974.

Entered into force June 29, 1974.

25 UST 1782; TIAS 7910.

Extension

June 15 and 27, 1984 (TIAS 11430; 2194 UNTS 257).

EDUCATION

Agreement on expansion of undergraduate exchanges.

Signed at Washington June 1, 1990.

Entered into force June 1, 1990.

TIAS

EMBASSY SITES

Agreement on the reciprocal allocation for use free of charge of plots of land in Moscow and Washington with annexes and exchanges of notes.

Signed at Moscow May 16, 1969.

Entered into force May 16, 1969.

20 UST 789; TIAS 6693; 715 UNTS 33.

Agreement on the conditions of construction of complexes of buildings of the U.S. Embassy in Moscow and the Russian Embassy in Washington with attachment.

Signed at Washington December 4, 1972.

Entered into force December 4, 1972.

23 UST 3544; TIAS 7512.

Agreement concerning dates for use of land for, and construction of, embassy complexes in Moscow and Washington.

Exchange of notes at Moscow March 30, 1977.

Entered into force March 30, 1977.

28 UST 5293; TIAS 8629; 1087 UNTS 67.

EMERGENCY PREPAREDNESS

Memorandum of understanding on cooperation in natural and man-made emergency prevention and response.

Signed at Moscow July 30, 1991.

Entered into force July 30, 1991.

TIAS 11456.

ENVIRONMENTAL COOPERATION

Agreement on cooperation in the field of environmental protection.

Signed at Moscow May 23, 1972.

Entered into force May 23, 1972.

23 UST 845; TIAS 7345.

FILMS

see HEALTH

FISHERIES

Convention regarding navigation, fishing, and trading on the Pacific Ocean and along the northwest coast of America.[1]

Signed at St. Petersburg April 17, 1824.

Entered into force January 11, 1825.

8 Stat. 302; TS 298; 11 Bevans 1205.

Agreement relating to the consideration of claims resulting from damage to fishing vessels or gear and measures to prevent fishing conflicts, with annex and protocol.

Signed at Moscow February 21, 1973.

Entered into force February 21, 1973.

24 UST 669; TIAS 7575; 938 UNTS 38.

Amendment

February 26, 1975 (26 UST 167; TIAS 8022).

Protocol to the agreement of February 21, 1973 (TIAS 7575), relating to the consideration of claims resulting from damage to fishing vessels or gear and measures to prevent fishing conflicts, with annex.

Signed at Copenhagen June 21, 1973.

Entered into force June 21, 1973.

24 UST 1588; TIAS 7663; 938 UNTS 49.

Agreement on mutual fisheries relations, with annexes.

Signed at Moscow May 31, 1988.

Entered into force October 28, 1988.

TIAS 11442; 2191 UNTS 3.

Extension

March 3, 2003 and January 30, 2004.

NOTE

1 Article 3 obsolete by virtue of Alaska cession treaty (15 Stat. 539; TS 301); article 4 expired April 17, 1834.

GENERAL RELATIONS

Arrangements relating to the establishment of diplomatic relations, nonintervention, freedom of conscience and religious liberty, legal protection, and claims.

Exchanges of notes at Washington November 16, 1933.

Entered into force November 16, 1933.

Department of State Publication 528; European and British Commonwealth Series 2 [new series]; Eastern European Series No. 1 [old series]; 11 Bevans 1248.

GRAINS

Agreement on the supply of grain.

Signed at Washington June 1, 1990.

Entered into force June 1, 1990.

TIAS

HEALTH

Agreement relating to the exchange of medical films.

Exchange of notes at Washington March 17 and September 5, 1955.

Entered into force September 5, 1955.

6 UST 3969; TIAS 3409; 256 UNTS 307.

Agreement on cooperation in the field of medical science and public health.

Signed at Moscow May 23, 1972.

Entered into force May 23, 1972.

23 UST 836; TIAS 7344.

Agreement on cooperation in artificial heart research and development.

Signed at Moscow June 28, 1974.

Entered into force June 28, 1974.

25 UST 1331; TIAS 7867.

HOUSING

Agreement on cooperation in the field of housing and other construction.

Signed at Moscow June 28, 1974.

Entered into force June 28, 1974.

25 UST 1592; TIAS 7898.

Extension

May 26 and July 11, 1989 (TIAS 11444; 2194 UNTS 250).

Memorandum of understanding on cooperation in housing and economic development.

Signed at Moscow July 30, 1991.

Entered into force July 30, 1991.

TIAS 11469.

JUDICIAL PROCEDURE

Agreement relating to the procedure to be followed in the execution of letters rogatory.

Exchange of notes at Moscow November 22, 1935.

Entered into force November 22, 1935.

49 Stat. 3840; EAS 83; 11 Bevans 1262; 167 LNTS 303.

Memorandum of understanding concerning cooperation in the pursuit of Nazi war criminals.

Signed at Moscow October 19, 1989.

Entered into force October 19, 1989.

TIAS 11462.

LEND-LEASE

Preliminary agreement relating to principles applying to mutual aid in the prosecution of the war against aggression, and exchange of notes.

Signed at Washington June 11, 1942.

Entered into force June 11, 1942.

56 Stat. 1500; EAS 253; 11 Bevans 1281; 105 UNTS 285.

Agreement relating to the disposition of lend-lease supplies in inventory or procurement in the United States.

Signed at Washington October 15, 1945.

Entered into force October 15, 1945.

7 UST 2819; TIAS 3662; 278 UNTS 151 and 315 UNTS 249.

Agreement regarding settlement of lend-lease, reciprocal aid and claims.

Signed at Washington October 18, 1972.

Entered into force October 18, 1972.

23 UST 2910; TIAS 7478; 898 UNTS 297.

Agreement regarding settlement of lend-lease accounts.

Exchange of letters at Washington June 1, 1990.

Entered into force June 1, 1990.

TIAS

MAPPING

Memorandum of understanding on cooperation in the mapping sciences, with annexes.

Signed at Moscow May 14, 1991.

Entered into force May 14, 1991.

NP

MARITIME MATTERS

Declaration concerning the admeasurement of vessels.

Signed at Washington June 6, 1884.

Entered into force August 1, 1884.

23 Stat. 789; TS 304; 11 Bevans 1223.

Agreement on the prevention of incidents on and over the high seas.

Signed at Moscow May 25, 1972.

Entered into force May 25, 1972.

23 UST 1168; TIAS 7379; 852 UNTS 151.

Protocol to the agreement of May 25, 1972 (TIAS 7379) on the prevention of incidents on and over the high seas.

Signed at Washington May 22, 1973.

Entered into force May 22, 1973.

24 UST 1063; TIAS 7624.

Memorandum of understanding regarding marine cargo insurance.

Signed at London April 5, 1979.

Entered into force April 5, 1979.

30 UST 2194; TIAS 9326; 1171 UNTS 93.

Agreement on maritime search and rescue, with exchange of letters.

Signed at Moscow May 31, 1988.

Entered into force July 3, 1989.

TIAS 11440; 2191 UNTS 115.

Agreement to abide by terms of maritime boundary agreement of June 1, 1990, pending entry into force.

Exchange of notes at Washington June 1, 1990.

Entered into force June 1, 1990; effective June 15, 1990.

TIAS 11451.

Agreement regarding certain maritime matters, with annexes.

Signed at Washington June 1, 1990.

Entered into force October 1, 1990.

TIAS 11453.

MEDICAL ASSISTANCE

Agreement on emergency medical supplies and related assistance.

Signed at Moscow July 30, 1991.

Entered into force July 30, 1991.

TIAS 11468.

NARCOTIC DRUGS

Memorandum of understanding on cooperation to combat illegal narcotics trafficking.

Signed at Paris January 8, 1989.

Entered into force January 8, 1989.

TIAS 11436; 2191 UNTS 35.

Agreement on a mutual understanding on cooperation in the struggle against the illicit traffic in narcotics.

Signed at Washington January 31, 1990.

Entered into force January 31, 1990.

TIAS

NAVIGATION

Agreement on the establishment of joint Loran-C and Chayka radionavigation systems, with annex.

Signed at Moscow May 31, 1988.

Entered into force March 2, 1989.

TIAS 11441.

NUCLEAR TEST LIMITATION

Treaty on underground nuclear explosions for peaceful purposes, with agreed minute.

Signed at Washington and Moscow May 28, 1976.

Entered into force December 11, 1990.

TIAS; 1714 UNTS 387.

Protocol to the treaty of May 28, 1976, on underground nuclear explosions for peaceful purposes.

Signed at Washington June 1, 1990.

Entered into force December 11, 1990.

TIAS; 1714 UNTS 440.

NUCLEAR WAR

Agreement on measures to reduce the risk of outbreak of nuclear war.

Signed at Washington September 30, 1971.

Entered into force September 30, 1971.

22 UST 1590; TIAS 7186; 807 UNTS 57.

Agreement on the prevention of nuclear war.

Signed at Washington June 22, 1973.

Entered into force June 22, 1973.

24 UST 1478; TIAS 7654.

Agreement on the establishment of nuclear risk reduction centers, with protocols.

Signed at Washington September 15, 1987.

Entered into force September 15, 1987.

TIAS

Agreement on reciprocal advance notification of major strategic exercises.

Signed at Jackson Hole, Wyoming, September 23, 1989.

Entered into force January 1, 1990.

TIAS 11458; 2191 UNTS 283.

PACIFIC SETTLEMENT OF DISPUTES

Treaty for the settlement of disputes.

Signed at Washington October 1, 1914.

Entered into force March 22, 1915.

39 Stat. 1622; TS 616; 11 Bevans 1239.

PASSPORTS

Agreement concerning mutual visits by inhabitants of the Bering Straits Region.

Signed at Jackson Hole, Wyoming September 23, 1989.

Entered into force July 10, 1991.

TIAS 11455.

POLLUTION

Agreement concerning cooperation in combatting pollution in the Bering and Chukchi Seas in emergency situations.

Signed at Moscow May 11, 1989.

Entered into force August 17, 1989.

TIAS 11446; 2190 UNTS 179.

POSTAL MATTERS

International express mail agreement, with detailed regulations.

Signed at Moscow March 31, 1988.

Entered into force May 1, 1988.

TIAS 11439.

Memorandum of understanding concerning the operation of the INTELPOST service, with details of implementation.

Signed at Moscow and Washington February 14 and March 9, 1989.

Entered into force April 3, 1989.

TIAS 11528.

PRISONERS OF WAR

Agreement relating to prisoners of war and civilians liberated by forces operating under Soviet command and forces operating under United States of America command.

Signed at Yalta February 11, 1945.

Entered into force February 11, 1945.

59 Stat. 1874; EAS 505; 11 Bevans 1286; 68 UNTS 175.

PRIVILEGES AND IMMUNITIES

Agreement relating to privileges and immunities of all members of the Soviet and American embassies and their families, with agreed minute.

Exchange of notes at Washington December 14, 1978.

Entered into force December 14, 1978; effective December 29, 1978.

30 UST 2341; TIAS 9340; 1171 UNTS 73.

Agreement relating to immunity of family members of consular officers and employees from criminal jurisdiction.

Exchange of notes at Washington October 31, 1986.

Entered into force October 31, 1986.

TIAS 11432.

PUBLICATIONS

Memorandum of understanding to increase distribution of the magazines "America" and "Soviet Life".

Signed at Washington June 2, 1990.

Entered into force June 2, 1990.

TIAS

REGIONAL COMMISSION

Agreement concerning the Bering Straits Regional Commission.

Signed at Jackson Hole, Wyoming September 23, 1989.

Entered into force July 10, 1991.

TIAS 11448.

RULES OF WARFARE

Convention relating to the rights of neutrals at sea.[1]

Signed at Washington July 22, 1854.

Entered into force October 31, 1854.

10 Stat. 1105; TS 300; 11 Bevans 1214.

NOTE

1 Declaration of accession by Nicaragua signed at Granada June 9, 1855 (7 Miller 139).

SCIENTIFIC COOPERATION

Agreement on cooperation in the field of basic scientific research, with annexes.

Signed at Paris January 8, 1989.

Entered into force January 8, 1989.

TIAS 11443; 2190 UNTS 419.

Memorandum of understanding on cooperation in geoscience, with annexes.

Signed at Washington and Moscow May 6, 1989.

Entered into force May 6, 1989.

TIAS

Memorandum of understanding on cooperation in the field of basic scientific research, with annexes.

Signed at Washington and Moscow May 6, 1989.

Entered into force May 6, 1989.

TIAS

Amendment

May 7 and 14, 1991.

Memorandum of understanding on cooperation in the physical, chemical and engineering sciences, with annexes.

Signed at Moscow May 13, 1991.

Entered into force May 13, 1991.

TIAS 11470.

SEABED OPERATIONS

Agreement concerning the confidentiality of data on deep seabed areas, with related exchange of letters.

Exchange of notes at Moscow December 5, 1986.

Entered into force December 5, 1986.

TIAS

Agreement relating to the agreement of August 14, 1987 on the resolution of practical problems with respect to deep seabed mining areas.[1]

Exchange of notes at Moscow August 14, 1987.

Entered into force August 14, 1987.

TIAS 11438.

NOTE

1 Parties to the multilateral agreement of August 14, 1987 are Belgium, Canada, Italy, Netherlands and Union of Soviet Socialist Republics.

SPACE COOPERATION

Agreement concerning cooperation in the exploration and use of outer space for peaceful purposes, with annex.

Signed at Moscow April 15, 1987.

Entered into force April 15, 1987.

TIAS 11433; 2192 UNTS 203.

Amendment

May 31, 1988.

Implementing agreement concerning cooperation in the space flight of a Soviet Meteor-3 satellite employing a U.S. Total Ozone Mapping Spectrometer (TOMS).

Signed at Moscow July 25, 1990.

Entered into force August 24, 1990.

TIAS

TAXATION

Convention on matters of taxation, with related letters.

Signed at Washington June 20, 1973.

Entered into force January 29, 1976; effective January 1, 1976.

27 UST 1; TIAS 8225.

TELECOMMUNICATION

Agreement on the organization of commercial radio teletype communication channels.

Signed at Moscow May 24, 1946.

Entered into force May 24, 1946.

60 Stat. 1696; TIAS 1527; 11 Bevans 1291; 4 UNTS 201.

Memorandum of understanding regarding the establishment of a direct communications ("hot-line") link, with annex.

Signed at Geneva June 20, 1963.

Entered into force June 20, 1963.

14 UST 825; TIAS 5362; 472 UNTS 163.

Agreement on measures to improve the direct communications link, with annex.

Signed at Washington September 30, 1971.

Entered into force September 30, 1971.

22 UST 1598; TIAS 7187; 806 UNTS 402.

Amendment

March 20 and April 29, 1975 (26 UST 564; TIAS 8059; 991 UNTS 442).

Agreement relating to the memorandum of understanding of June 20, 1963 (TIAS 5362) and the agreement of September 30, 1971, as amended (TIAS 7187, 8059), concerning the direct communications link.

Exchange of notes at Washington July 17, 1984.

Entered into force July 17, 1984.

TIAS 11428.

Agreement modifying the memorandum of understanding of June 20, 1963, regarding the establishment of a direct communications link.

Exchange of notes at Washington June 24, 1988.

Entered into force June 24, 1988.

TIAS

TERRITORIAL ACQUISITION

Convention ceding Alaska.

Signed at Washington March 30, 1867.

Entered into force June 20, 1867.

15 Stat. 539; TS 301; 11 Bevans 1216.

TRADE AND COMMERCE

Agreement regulating the position of corporations and other commercial associations.

Signed at St. Petersburg June 25, 1904.

Entered into force June 25, 1904.

36 Stat. 2163; TS 526; 11 Bevans 1235.

Agreement on the establishment of a U.S.-U.S.S.R. Commercial Commission.

Communique issued at Moscow May 26, 1972.

Entered into force May 26, 1972.

26 UST 1334; TIAS 8116; 1006 UNTS 17.

Protocol relating to the possibility of establishing a U.S.-U.S.S.R. Chamber of Commerce.

Signed at Washington June 22, 1973.

Entered into force June 22, 1973.

24 UST 1498; TIAS 7656.

Protocol relating to expansion and improvement of commercial facilities in Washington and Moscow.

Signed at Washington June 22, 1973.

Entered into force June 22, 1973.

24 UST 1501; TIAS 7657; 938 UNTS 127.

Protocol relating to a Trade Representation of the U.S.S.R. in Washington and a Commercial Office of the U.S.A. in Moscow.

Signed at Moscow October 3, 1973.

Entered into force October 3, 1973.

24 UST 2222; TIAS 7738; 938 UNTS 135.

Amendment

May 21 and October 7, 1974 (27 UST 2987; TIAS 8356).

Agreement relating to the status of the Commercial Office of the United States in Moscow and the Trade Representation of the Soviet Union in Washington, with annexes.

Exchange of letters at Washington June 1, 1990.

Entered into force June 1, 1990.

TIAS

TRANSPORTATION

Agreement on cooperation in transportation science and technology, with annexes.

Signed at Moscow May 31, 1988.

Entered into force May 31, 1988.

TIAS

VISAS

Agreement relating to the reciprocal waiver of visa fees to nonimmigrants.

Exchange of notes at Moscow March 26 and August 11 and 20, 1958.

Entered into force August 20, 1958.

9 UST 1413; TIAS 4134; 336 UNTS 269.

Agreement relating to the reciprocal issuance of multiple entry and exit visas to American and Soviet correspondents.

Exchange of notes at Moscow September 29, 1975.

Entered into force September 29, 1975.

27 UST 4258; TIAS 8448.

Agreement concerning diplomatic and other visas, with agreed minute and oral understanding.

Exchange of notes at Moscow July 30, 1984.

Entered into force July 30, 1984.

TIAS

Agreement modifying the agreement of July 30, 1984 concerning diplomatic and other visas.

Exchange of notes at Washington October 31, 1986.

Entered into force October 31, 1986.

TIAS

UNITED ARAB EMIRATES

AVIATION

Agreement on aviation security.

Signed at Abu Dhabi December 26, 1993 and February 17, 1994.

Entered into force February 17, 1994.

TIAS

Air transport agreement, with annexes.

Signed at Abu Dhabi March 11, 2002.

Entered into force December 11, 2002.

TIAS

DEFENSE

Agreement relating to the sale of defense articles and services to the United Arab Emirates.

Exchange of notes at Abu Dhabi June 15 and 21, 1975.

Entered into force June 21, 1975.

26 UST 1789; TIAS 8139; 1006 UNTS 251.

General security of military information agreement.

Signed at Abu Dhabi May 23, 1987.

Entered into force May 23, 1987.

TIAS

Air warfare center memorandum of understanding, with plan of operations.

Signed at Abu Dhabi February 12, 2006.

Entered into force February 12, 2006.

TIAS

ENVIRONMENTAL COOPERATION

Agreement for cooperation in the Global Learning and Observations to Benefit the Environment (GLOBE) Program, with appendices.

Signed at Abu Dhabi June 6, 1999.

Entered into force June 6, 1999.

TIAS

FINANCE

Agreement on investment guaranties.

Signed at Abu Dhabi September 29, 1991.

Entered into force April 22, 1992.

TIAS 12079.

INTERNATIONAL CRIMINAL COURT

Agreement regarding the surrender of persons to the International Criminal Court.

Exchange of notes at Abu Dhabi January 27 and February 15, 2004.

Entered into force February 15, 2004.

TIAS

MAPPING

Agreement concerning cooperation and exchange of geospatial information and related services.

Signed at Abu Dhabi and Bethesda February 24 and March 14, 2001.

Entered into force March 14, 2001.

NP

POSTAL MATTERS

Memorandum of understanding for the exchange of international express mail, with details of implementation.

Signed at Dubai and Washington December 31, 1984 and January 16, 1985.

Entered into force March 21, 1985.

TIAS 11149; 2126 UNTS 181.

SCIENTIFIC COOPERATION

Memorandum of understanding concerning scientific and technical cooperation in the earth sciences.

Signed at Abu Dhabi February 6, 1988.

Entered into force February 6, 1988.

TIAS

Extension

February 6, 2003.

TAXATION

Agreement regarding taxation of income derived from the international operation of ships or aircraft.

Exchange of notes at Abu Dhabi October 7 and December 1, 1997.

Entered into force December 1, 1997; effective January 1, 1994.

TIAS

TRADE AND COMMERCE

Administrative arrangement concerning a textile visa system.

Exchange of letters at Abu Dhabi February 4 and March 2, 1989.

Entered into force March 2, 1989.

NP

Agreement relating to trade in textiles and textile products, with annexes.

Exchange of notes at Abu Dhabi January 26 and February 5, 1991.

Entered into force February 5, 1991; effective January 1, 1989.

NP

Amendment and extension

March 29 and July 21, 1994 (NP).

December 30, 1995 and February 6, 1996 (NP).

UNITED KINGDOM

AMITY

Treaty of amity, commerce, and navigation (Jay Treaty).[1]

Signed at London November 19, 1794.

Entered into force October 28, 1795.

8 Stat. 116; TS 105; 12 Bevans 13.

Treaty for an amicable settlement of all causes of differences between the two countries (Treaty of Washington).[2]

Signed at Washington May 8, 1871.

Entered into force June 17, 1871.

17 Stat. 863; TS 133; 12 Bevans 170.

NOTES

1 Only articles 9 and 10 appear to remain in force between the United States and the United Kingdom. Article 3, so far as it relates to the right of Indians to pass across the border, appears to remain in force between the United States and Canada. But see *Akins v. U.S.*, 551 F.2d 1222 (1977).

2 Articles I-XVII and XXXIV-XLII have been executed; articles XVIII-XXV, XXX, and XXXII terminated July 1, 1885; articles XXVIII and XXIX not considered in force.

ATOMIC ENERGY

Articles of agreement governing collaboration between the authorities of the United States of America and the United Kingdom in the matter of tube alloys.

Signed at Quebec August 19, 1943.

Entered into force August 19, 1943.

5 UST 1114; TIAS 2993; 214 UNTS 341.

Agreement for cooperation on the uses of atomic energy for mutual defense purposes.

Signed at Washington July 3, 1958.

Entered into force August 4, 1958.

9 UST 1028; TIAS 4078; 326 UNTS 3.

Amendments

May 7, 1959 (10 UST 1274; TIAS 4267; 351 UNTS 458).

September 27, 1968 (20 UST 518; TIAS 6659).

October 16, 1969 (21 UST 1064; TIAS 6861).

July 22, 1974 (26 UST 110; TIAS 8014).

December 5, 1979 (31 UST 5853; TIAS 9688; 1203 UNTS 317).

June 5, 1984 (TIAS 11114).

Agreement in the field of decommissioning nuclear facilities, with appendix.

Signed at Washington March 1, 1985.

Entered into force March 1, 1985.

TIAS 11342.

Extension

February 17 and March 6, 1989.

Arrangement for the exchange of technical information and cooperation in nuclear safety matters, with addendum.

Signed at Vienna September 18, 1996.

Entered into force September 18, 1996.

TIAS

Extension

September 16, 2002.

AVIATION

Arrangement relating to pilot licenses to operate civil aircraft.[1]

Exchange of notes at Washington March 28 and April 5, 1935.

Entered into force May 5, 1935.

49 Stat. 3731; EAS 77; 12 Bevans 513; 162 LNTS 59.

Agreement relating to the transfer and maintenance of radio range and SCS 51 equipment.

Exchange of notes at London May 8 and July 31, 1946.

Entered into force July 31, 1946.

61 Stat. 4008; TIAS 1766; 12 Bevans 795; 42 UNTS 199.

Agreement relating to the reciprocal acceptance of airworthiness certifications.

Exchange of notes at London December 28, 1972.

Entered into force December 28, 1972.

23 UST 4309; TIAS 7537.

Agreement concerning air services, with annexes and exchange of letters.[2]

Signed at Bermuda July 23, 1977.

Entered into force July 23, 1977.

28 UST 5367; TIAS 8641.

Amendments

April 25, 1978 (29 UST 2680; TIAS 8965; 1124 UNTS 437).

December 4, 1980 (33 UST 655; TIAS 10059).

February 20, 1985 (TIAS 11396).

May 25, 1989 (TIAS 11674; 1584 UNTS 445).

March 27, 1997 (1986 UNTS 499).

Agreement relating to North Atlantic air fares.

Exchange of letters at Washington March 17, 1978.

Entered into force March 17, 1978.

29 UST 2676; TIAS 8964.

Extension and amendment

November 2 and 9, 1978 (30 UST 979; TIAS 9231; 1152 UNTS 473).

Memorandum of understanding concerning cooperation in the testing and development of anti-misting kerosene and related equipment, with appendix.

Signed at Washington and London June 1 and 14, 1978.

Entered into force June 14, 1978.

30 UST 1369; TIAS 9256; 1153 UNTS 49.

Agreement concerning reciprocal recognition of airline fitness and citizenship determinations.

Exchange of notes at Washington May 25, 1989.

Entered into force May 25, 1989.

TIAS 11675.

Agreement concerning settlement of the Heathrow Arbitration and the UK Arbitration and amending the air transport agreement of July 23, 1977, as amended.

Exchange of notes at Washington March 11, 1994.

Entered into force March 11, 1994.

TIAS 12536; 1882 UNTS 413.

Agreement concerning the facilitation of air navigation services.

Signed at London May 11, 1995.

Entered into force May 11, 1995.

TIAS 12645; 1913 UNTS 77.

Agreement for the promotion of aviation safety.

Signed at London December 20, 1995.

Entered into force December 20, 1995.

TIAS; 1921 UNTS 321.

NOTES

1 Applicable to American Samoa, Puerto Rico, Virgin Islands of the U.S., Bermuda, Falkland Islands and Dependencies, Gilbraltar, Turks and Caicos Islands, and the Cayman Islands, Leeward Islands, St. Helena and Ascension.

2 Applicable to all territories.

BOUNDARIES

Convention respecting fisheries, boundary, and the restoration of slaves.

Signed at London October 20, 1818.

Entered into force January 30, 1819.

8 Stat. 248; TS 112; 12 Bevans 57.

Treaty to settle and define the boundaries between the territories of the United States and the possessions of Her Britannic Majesty in North America; for the final suppression of the African slave trade, and for the giving up of criminals, fugitive from justice in certain cases (Webster-Ashburton treaty).[1]

Signed at Washington August 9, 1842.

Entered into force October 13, 1842.

8 Stat. 572; TS 119; 12 Bevans 82.

Treaty establishing the boundary in the territory on the northwest coast of America lying westward of the Rocky Mountains (Oregon Treaty).

Signed at Washington June 15, 1846.

Entered into force July 17, 1846.

9 Stat. 869; TS 120; 12 Bevans 95.

Declaration adopting maps of boundary prepared by the Joint Commission of the Northwest Boundary for surveying and marking the boundaries between the United States and British possessions on the forty-ninth parallel of north latitude, under the first article of the treaty of June 15, 1846 between the United States and the United Kingdom.

Signed at Washington February 24, 1870.

Entered into force February 24, 1870.

TS 129; 12 Bevans 157.

Protocol of a conference respecting the northwest water boundary.

Signed at Washington March 10, 1873.

Entered into force March 10, 1873.

18 Stat. (Pt. 2, Public Treaties) 369; TS 135; 12 Bevans 190.

Convention providing for the settlement of questions between the United States and the United Kingdom with respect to the boundary line between the territory of Alaska and the British possessions in North America.[2]

Signed at Washington January 24, 1903.

Entered into force March 3, 1903.

32 Stat. 1961; TS 419; 12 Bevans 263.

Acceptance of the report of the commissioners to complete the award under the convention of January 24, 1903 respecting the boundary line between Alaska and the British North American possessions.

Exchange of notes at Washington March 25, 1905.

Entered into force March 25, 1905.

TS 476; 12 Bevans 269.

Convention providing for the surveying and marking out upon the ground of the 141 degree of west longitude where said meridian forms the boundary line between Alaska and the British possessions in North America.[3]

Signed at Washington April 21, 1906.

Entered into force August 16, 1906.

34 Stat. 2948; TS 452; 12 Bevans 276.

Treaty concerning the Canadian international boundary.

Signed at Washington April 11, 1908.

Entered into force June 4, 1908.

35 Stat. 2003; TS 497; 12 Bevans 297.

Treaty relating to boundary waters and questions arising along the boundary between the United States and Canada.[4]

Signed at Washington January 11, 1909.

Entered into force May 5, 1910.

36 Stat. 2448; TS 548; 12 Bevans 319.

Treaty concerning the boundary line in Passamaquoddy Bay.

Signed at Washington May 21, 1910.

Entered into force August 20, 1910.

36 Stat. 2477; TS 551; 12 Bevans 341.

Treaty in regard to the boundary between the United States and Canada.

Signed at Washington February 24, 1925.

Entered into force July 17, 1925.

44 Stat. 2102; TS 720; 6 Bevans 7; 43 LNTS 239.

Treaty on the delimitation in the Caribbean of a maritime boundary relating to Puerto Rico/U.S. Virgin Islands and the British Virgin Islands, with annex.

Signed at London November 5, 1993.

Entered into force June 1, 1995.

TIAS; 1913 UNTS 67.

Treaty on the delimitation in the Caribbean of a maritime boundary relating to the U.S. Virgin Islands and Anguilla.

Signed at London November 5, 1993.

Entered into force June 1, 1995.

TIAS; 1913 UNTS 59.

NOTES

1 Article X terminated June 24, 1935, upon entry into force of extradition convention signed December 22, 1931 (47 Stat. 2122; TS 849).

2 Obsolete except for first paragraph of article VI.

3 Obsolete except for article II.

4 Paragraphs 3, 4, and 5 of article V terminated October 10, 1950 upon the entry into force of the treaty relating to uses of waters on the Niagara River (see under CANADA — BOUNDARY WATERS).

CANAL RIGHTS

Treaty to facilitate the construction of a ship canal.

Signed at Washington November 18, 1901.

Entered into force February 21, 1902.

32 Stat. 1903; TS 401; 12 Bevans 258.

CLAIMS

Arrangement for the disposal of certain pecuniary claims arising out of World War I.

Exchange of notes at Washington May 19, 1927.

Entered into force May 19, 1927.

TS 756; 12 Bevans 462; 64 LNTS 101.

Agreement relating to certain problems of marine transportation and litigation, and exchange of notes.

Signed at London December 4, 1942.

Entered into force December 4, 1942.

56 Stat. 1780; EAS 282; 12 Bevans 631; 205 LNTS 33.

Amendments

March 25 and May 7, 1946 (60 Stat. 1958; TIAS 1558; 12 Bevans 792; 6 UNTS 285).

June 17 and 27, 1947 (61 Stat. 3014; TIAS 1636; 12 Bevans 818; 16 UNTS 360).

Agreement relating to claims for damages resulting from acts of armed forces personnel.

Exchange of notes at London February 29 and March 28, 1944.

Entered into force March 28, 1944.

61 Stat. 2728; TIAS 1602; 12 Bevans 660; 15 UNTS 413.

Amendment

March 27, 1946 (60 Stat. 1525; TIAS 1509; 12 Bevans 745; 4 UNTS 2).

Agreement relating to mutual forbearance in claims resulting from acts of armed forces or civilian personnel.

Exchange of notes at Washington October 23, 1946 and January 23, 1947.

Entered into force January 23, 1947; operative June 6, 1944.

61 Stat. 2876; TIAS 1622; 12 Bevans 805; 15 UNTS 281.

Agreement relating to the interpretation of paragraph 6 of the agreement on settlement of intergovernmental claims of March 27, 1946 (60 Stat. 1534; TIAS 1509).

Exchange of notes at Washington February 19 and 28, 1947.

Entered into force February 28, 1947.

61 Stat. 3012; TIAS 1635; 12 Bevans 812; 89 UNTS 368.

Agreement relating to indemnities on ammunition shipments in the United Kingdom or in British ships traveling to or from the United Kingdom.

Exchange of notes at London October 27, 1966.

Entered into force October 27, 1966.

17 UST 2186; TIAS 6154, 597 UNTS 265.

COMMERCE

Convention to regulate commerce.[1]

Signed at London July 3, 1815.

Entered into force July 3, 1815.

8 Stat. 228; TS 110; 12 Bevans 49.

Convention continuing in force indefinitely the convention of July 3, 1815.

Signed at London August 6, 1827.

Entered into force April 2, 1828.

8 Stat. 361; TS 117; 12 Bevans 76.

NOTE

1 Article IV superseded from September 7, 1952 by consular convention of June 6, 1951 (3 UST 3426; TIAS 2494), including territories to which consular convention applies.

CONSULS

Consular convention and protocol of signature.[1]

Signed at Washington June 6, 1951.

Entered into force September 7, 1952.

3 UST 3426; TIAS 2494; 165 UNTS 121.

NOTE

1 Applicable to all territories over which the United States has jurisdiction or international responsibility and to all British territories.

CUSTOMS

Declaration exempting commercial travelers' samples from customs inspection.

Signed at Washington December 3 and 8, 1910.

Entered into force January 1, 1911.

TS 552; 12 Bevans 348.

Understanding relating to the importation in bulk, free from customs duties, of certain articles for the use of the diplomatic staff of United States embassy and consular officers and other employees on duty in the United Kingdom.

Exchange of notes at Washington February 16, 1949.

Entered into force February 16, 1949.

12 Bevans 928.

DEFENSE

See also MUTUAL SECURITY

Arrangement relating to naval and air bases.

Exchange of notes at Washington September 2, 1940.

Entered into force September 2, 1940.

54 Stat. 2405; EAS 181; 12 Bevans 551; 203 LNTS 201.

Protocol concerning the defense of Newfoundland.

Signed at London March 27, 1941.

Entered into force March 27, 1941.

55 Stat. 1599; EAS 235, 12 Bevans 560; 204 LNTS 70.

Mutual defense assistance agreement.[1]

Signed at Washington January 27, 1950.

Entered into force January 27, 1950.

1 UST 126; TIAS 2017; 80 UNTS 261.

Agreement concerning a long-range proving ground for guided missiles to be known as "The Bahamas Long Range Proving Ground", and exchanges of note.[2]

Signed at Washington July 21, 1950.

Entered into force July 21, 1950.

1 UST 545; TIAS 2099; 97 UNTS 193.

Amendment

July 17, 1967 (18 UST 1657; TIAS 6308; 619 UNTS 330).

Related agreements

February 24 and March 2, 1953 (4 UST 429; TIAS 2789; 172 UNTS 257).

July 11 and 22, 1955 (6 UST 3783; TIAS 3379; 218 UNTS 384).

December 6, 1956 and January 4, 1957 (8 UST 1; TIAS 3727; 266 UNTS 396).

April 1, 1957 (8 UST 493; TIAS 3803; 288 UNTS 364).

Agreement concerning the extension of the Bahamas Long Range Proving Ground by the establishment of additional sites in Ascension Island.

Signed at Washington June 25, 1956.

Entered into force June 25, 1956.

7 UST 1999; TIAS 3603; 249 UNTS 91.

Amendment

July 17, 1967 (18 UST 1657; TIAS 6308; 619 UNTS 330).

Agreement on administrative matters connected with the agreement of June 25, 1956 for the extension of the Bahamas Long Range Proving Ground by the establishment of additional sites in Ascension Island.

Exchange of notes at Washington August 24 and 25, 1959.

Entered into force August 25, 1959.

10 UST 1453; TIAS 4296; 351 UNTS 438.

Agreement relating to the disposition of equipment and material furnished by the United States under the mutual defense assistance program and found surplus to the needs of the armed forces of the United Kingdom.

Exchange of notes at London May 10 and 13, 1957.

Entered into force May 13, 1957.

8 UST 835; TIAS 3843; 291 UNTS 300.

Amendments

December 17 and 30, 1958 (9 UST 1547; TIAS 4156; 340 UNTS 342).

November 7 and 10, 1961 (12 UST 2947; TIAS 4895; 431 UNTS 288).

August 28, 1963 (14 UST 1178; TIAS 5413; 486 UNTS 398).

Agreement for the establishment of oceanographic research stations in the Bahama Islands.[2]

Signed at Washington November 1, 1957.

Entered into force November 1, 1957.

8 UST 1741; TIAS 3927; 299 UNTS 167.

Amendment

May 12, 1960 [2] (11 UST 1405; TIAS 4479; 372 UNTS 364).

Agreement relating to the supply by the United States to the United Kingdom of intermediate range ballistic missiles, with memorandum.

Exchange of notes at Washington February 22, 1958.

Entered into force February 22, 1958.

9 UST 195; TIAS 3990; 307 UNTS 207.

Agreement relating to the establishment and operation of a ballistic missile early warning station at Fylingdales Moor, with memorandum.

Exchange of notes at London February 15, 1960.

Entered into force February 15, 1960.

11 UST 156; TIAS 4425; 371 UNTS 45.

Amendment

June 18, 1979 (30 UST 6045; TIAS 9536).

Agreement concerning the establishment in the Bahama Islands of a long range aid to navigation station.[2]

Signed at Washington June 24, 1960.

Entered into force June 24, 1960.

11 UST 1587; TIAS 4502; 377 UNTS 63.

Agreement relating to rights of the United Kingdom in connection with the use of oceanographic research stations and parts of the Long Range Proving Ground.[3]

Exchange of notes at Port-of-Spain February 10, 1961.

Entered into force February 10, 1961.

12 UST 442; TIAS 4735; 409 UNTS 129.

Agreement on the setting up of a missile defense alarm system station in the United Kingdom, with memorandum.

Exchange of notes at London July 18, 1961.

Entered into force July 18, 1961.

12 UST 1058; TIAS 4809; 404 UNTS 227.

Agreement relating to a weapons production program.

Exchange of notes at London June 29, 1962.

Entered into force June 29, 1962.

13 UST 1318; TIAS 5087; 449 UNTS 286.

Agreement relating to the use of the airfield at Widewake in Ascension Island by aircraft of the Royal Air Force.

Exchange of notes at Washington August 29, 1962.

Entered into force August 29, 1962.

13 UST 1917; TIAS 5148; 449 UNTS 177.

Polaris sales agreement.

Signed at Washington April 6, 1963.

Entered into force April 6, 1963.

14 UST 321; TIAS 5313; 474 UNTS 49.

Agreement extending the Polaris sales agreement of April 6, 1963 (TIAS 5313) to cover the sale of Trident II weapon system.

Exchange of notes at Washington October 19, 1982.

Entered into force October 19, 1982.

TIAS 10549.

Agreement for the establishment of an Atlantic Undersea Test and Evaluation Center in the Bahama Islands, with agreed minutes.[2]

Signed at Washington October 11, 1963.

Entered into force October 11, 1963.

14 UST 1431; TIAS 5441; 483 UNTS 3.

Memorandum of arrangement between the United States, Australia, and the United Kingdom to cover re-entry experiments in Australia (Project Sparta).

Signed at Canberra March 30, 1966.

Entered into force March 30, 1966.

17 UST 350; TIAS 5984; 593 UNTS 261.

Agreement concerning the availability of certain Indian Ocean Islands for the defense purposes of both governments.[4]

Exchange of notes at London December 30, 1966.

Entered into force December 30, 1966.

18 UST 28; TIAS 6196; 603 UNTS 273.

Amendments

June 22 and 25, 1976 (27 UST 3448; TIAS 8376).

November 16, 1987 (1576 UNTS 179).

Agreement relating to the transfer of certain real estate on Eleuthera Island to the United States Navy with annexes.[2]

Exchange of notes at Nassau August 9, 1971 and February 17, 1972.

Entered into force February 17, 1972.

23 UST 155; TIAS 7286.

Understanding relating to the use by Bahamian organizations of certain land at the United States Navy Base, Georgetown, Great Exuma Island, with map and schedule.[2]

Exchange of notes at Nassau June 19, September 12 and November 2, 1972.

Entered into force November 2, 1972.

23 UST 3688; TIAS 7514.

Agreement relating to the lease of certain land to the United States Navy on the Island of Anegada in the British Virgin Islands for use as a drone launching facility.

Exchange of notes at Washington February 1, 1973.

Entered into force February 1, 1973.

24 UST 482; TIAS 7567.

Agreement relating to the expanded use of Ascension Island.

Exchange of notes at London March 30, 1973.

Entered into force March 30, 1973.

24 UST 918; TIAS 7602.

Arrangement relating to the status of United States forces engaged in clearance of the Suez Canal which are using British Sovereign Base areas in Cyprus.

Exchange of notes at London June 24 and July 4, 1974.

Entered into force July 4, 1974.

25 UST 2399; TIAS 7917.

Agreement concerning a United States naval support facility on Diego Garcia, British Indian Ocean Territory, with plan, related notes, and supplementary arrangement.

Exchange of notes at London February 25, 1976.

Entered into force February 25, 1976.

27 UST 315; TIAS 8230; 1018 UNTS 372.

Related agreement

December 13, 1982 (TIAS 10616; 2001 UNTS 397).

Memorandum of understanding concerning the transfer of technical data relating to the JT-10D jet engine collaboration agreement to third countries.

Signed at Washington December 30, 1976.

Entered into force December 30, 1976.

27 UST 4385; TIAS 8459; 1068 UNTS 437.

Letter of agreement concerning narrative record telecommunication interface arrangements, with appendices.

Signed at Washington and London September 2 and 21, 1977.

Entered into force September 21, 1977.

TIAS 12252.

Agreement concerning United States defense areas in the Turks and Caicos Islands, with annex, memorandum of understanding and aide-memoire.

Signed at Washington December 12, 1979.

Entered into force December 12, 1979; effective January 1, 1979.

32 UST 429; TIAS 9710.

Agreement concerning the turnover of the airfield at Grand Turk Auxiliary Air Base to the Government of the Turks and Caicos Islands and its use by the United States Government.

Exchange of notes at Washington December 12, 1979.

Entered into force December 12, 1979.

32 UST 455; TIAS 9711.

Memorandum of agreement on the exchange of personnel between the United States Coast Guard and the Royal Navy.

Signed at Washington August 29, 1980.

Entered into force August 29, 1980.

32 UST 2403; TIAS 9849; 1267 UNTS 187.

Memorandum of understanding concerning terrestrial radio site sharing, with annexes.

Signed at Mildenhall and London August 19 and September 8, 1981.

Entered into force September 8, 1981.

33 UST 3767; TIAS 10260; 1541 UNTS 157.

Memorandum of understanding regarding support to the Royal Air Force detachment at Hickam Air Force Base.

Signed at Honolulu April 21, 1981.

Entered into force April 21, 1981.

33 UST 998; TIAS 10084; 1285 UNTS 97.

Memorandum of understanding concerning the shared use of communications facilities in the northern Federal Republic of Germany, with annexes

Signed May 11 and June 2, 1981.

Entered into force June 2, 1981.

33 UST 2025; TIAS 10165; 1529 UNTS 415.

Memorandum of understanding on the exchange of personnel between the U.S. Coast Guard and the Royal Air Force.

Signed at Washington November 14 and 16, 1983.

Entered into force November 16, 1983.

35 UST 4110; TIAS 10908; 2014 UNTS 437.

Agreement regarding arrangements for continued United Kingdom access to and use of the Atlantic Undersea Test and Evaluation Centre (AUTEC) facility in The Bahamas.

Exchange of notes at Washington April 5, 1984.

Entered into force April 5, 1984.

TIAS 11059.

Memorandum of understanding concerning the provision of mutual logistic support, supplies and services, with annexes.

Signed at Vaihingen (Germany) and London October 5 and 11, 1984.

Entered into force October 11, 1984.

TIAS 11137; 2126 UNTS 229.

Amendments

June 29 and August 9, 1990 (TIAS 12198).

March 12 and April 2, 1991 (TIAS 12198).

March 15 and 18, 1996 (TIAS 12736).

Agreement concerning certain communications facilities in the defense areas in the Turks and Caicos Islands.

Exchange of notes at Washington December 18, 1984.

Entered into force December 18, 1984.

TIAS 11139.

Agreement relating to sharing facility construction costs on Ascension Island, with memoranda of agreement.

Exchange of notes at London March 25, 1985.

Entered into force March 25, 1985.

TIAS 12383; 1443 UNTS 25.

Memorandum of understanding concerning the exchange of medical cadets between the British Army Medical Services and the Uniformed Services University of the Health Sciences.

Signed at Washington and London March 25 and June 21, 1985.

Entered into force June 21, 1985.

TIAS 11109.

Memorandum of understanding concerning the exchange of medical cadets between the Royal Navy and the Uniformed Services University of the Health Sciences.

Signed at Washington and London March 25 and October 7, 1985.

Entered into force October 7, 1985.

TIAS 11225.

Memorandum of understanding for procurement of the RN ship-launched harpoon weapon system.

Signed at London October 17, 1986.

Entered into force October 17, 1986.

TIAS 11381.

Amendment

June 24 and July 9, 1996 (TIAS 12779).

Memorandum of understanding for the procurement of an airborne early warning system for the Royal Air Force, with related letter.

Signed at Washington February 25, 1987.

Entered into force February 25, 1987.

TIAS 11281.

Memorandum of understanding on the status of certain persons working for United States defense contractors in the United Kingdom, with annex.

Signed at Washington July 7, 1987.

Entered into force July 7, 1987; effective for tax years beginning on or after April 6, 1987.

TIAS 11537.

Master information exchange arrangement, with annex.

Signed at London September 6, 1988.

Entered into force September 6, 1988.

TIAS 11640.

Memorandum of understanding on the exchange of sub units.

Signed at Washington October 5, 1988.

Entered into force October 5, 1988.

TIAS 11630.

Memorandum of understanding concerning a cooperative research project in imaging of the ocean using radar, with annexes.

Signed at Arlington and London April 26 and May 5, 1989.

Entered into force May 5, 1989.

TIAS 12239.

Memorandum of understanding concerning the exchange of reserve officers.

Signed at Washington September 11, 1989.

Entered into force September 11, 1989.

TIAS 11698; 2207 UNTS 483.

Memorandum of understanding concerning cooperation in the development of a satellite communications modulator/demodulator and associated equipment resistant to electronic countermeasures and nuclear effects (Universal Modem), with annexes.

Signed at Washington and London October 25 and December 8, 1989.

Entered into force December 8, 1989.

TIAS

Memorandum of understanding concerning the establishment of a radar site in the Cayman Islands as part of the Caribbean Basin Radar Network (CBRN).

Signed at Washington February 26, 1990.

Entered into force February 26, 1990

TIAS 12240.

Memorandum of understanding concerning measures to be taken for the transfer, security and safeguarding of classified technical information, software and equipment to the Ministry of Defence to enable industry to establish a North Sea ACMI range.

Signed at Washington March 6, 1990.

Entered into force March 6, 1990.

TIAS 12248.

Memorandum of understanding covering armour technology

Signed March 9, 1990.

Entered into force March 9, 1990.

TIAS

Amendment

July 7 and 21, 2005.

Memorandum of understanding concerning the provision, trial and operation of a relocatable over the horizon radar (ROTHR) in the United Kingdom, with annex.

Signed at Washington April 20, 1990.

Entered into force April 20, 1990.

TIAS 12235.

Memorandum of understanding concerning the measures to be taken for the transfer to, and security and safeguarding of MK IV radar instrumentation system technical information, software and equipment in the United Kingdom.

Signed at Washington February 6, 1991.

Entered into force February 6, 1991.

TIAS 11834.

Memorandum of understanding concerning the establishment of a portable radar tracking station in the Cayman Islands.

Signed at Washington July 1, 1992.

Entered into force July 1, 1992.

TIAS 12241.

Agreement concerning defense cooperation arrangements.

Exchange of notes at Washington May 27, 1993.

Entered into force May 27, 1993.

TIAS 12237; 1792 UNTS 145.

Memorandum of agreement concerning the exchange of military personnel.

Signed at MacDill AFB and London September 27 and October 6, 1993.

Entered into force October 6, 1993.

NP

Memorandum of understanding for the development testing, qualification testing and unconstrained enclosure development for the intercooled recuperated (ICR) gas turbine engine, with annex.

Signed at Washington June 21, 1994.

Entered into force June 21, 1994.

TIAS 12257.

Amendments and extension

March 6 and 11, 1997.

March 28 and November 6, 2000.

Memorandum of understanding concerning the cooperative outboard logistics update project (AN/SSQ–108–V()).

Signed at London and Washington June 7 and July 1, 1994.

Entered into force July 1, 1994.

TIAS 12258.

Amendment

December 10 and 21, 2004.

Memorandum of understanding for the common affordable lightweight fighter, with annexes.

Signed at London and Washington August 5 and 9, 1994.

Entered into force August 9, 1994.

TIAS 12251.

Memorandum of understanding concerning the exchange of scientists and engineers, with annexes.

Signed at Washington and London July 27 and August 18, 1994.

Entered into force August 18, 1994.

NP

Amendment

July 2 and 28, 2004.

Memorandum of understanding concerning technology research and development projects, with annex.

Signed at Washington November 18, 1994.

Entered into force November 18, 1994.

TIAS 12250.

Memorandum of understanding concerning exchange of research and development information, with appendix.

Signed at Washington November 18, 1994.

Entered into force November 18, 1994.

TIAS 12249.

Agreement amending the agreement of November 29, 1973, as amended, to establish, operate and maintain line of communications and ancillary facilities in the United Kingdom for use under emergency conditions for logistic support of United States Armed Forces stationed in the European Command area in furtherance of the objectives of the North Atlantic Treaty.

Exchange of notes at London November 20 and December 7, 1995.

Entered into force December 7, 1995.

TIAS

Agreement regarding U.S. approval for retransfer of U.S. defense articles and services to NATO for purposes of supporting the NATO–led Implementation Force (IFOR).

Exchange of notes at Brussels December 18 and 19, 1995.

Entered into force December 19, 1995.

TIAS

Agreement amending and extending the memorandum of understanding of November 5, 1985 concerning ocean surveillance information system.

Signed at Washington and London February 21 and March 15, 1996.

Entered into force March 15, 1996; effective November 5, 1995.

TIAS 12735.

Memorandum of understanding for the cooperative development of technology upgrades to the AN/MSR-3(V) TACJAM–A Electronic Support (ES) Subsystem (Catalyst), with annexes.

Signed at Washington and London July 26 and August 15, 1996.

Entered into force August 15, 1996.

TIAS 12790.

Memorandum of understanding concerning the framework for advanced concept technology demonstration (ACTD) cooperation, with annex.

Signed at Washington and London August 12 and 16, 1996.

Entered into force August 16, 1996.

TIAS 12791.

Memorandum of understanding relating to information exchange on short range air-to-air missile technologies and systems.

Signed at Washington and Bristol September 16 and 30, 1996.

Entered into force September 30, 1996.

TIAS

Memorandum of understanding for cooperation in the development of combined arms tactical training equipment.

Signed at Alexandria and Abbey Wood December 6, 1996.

Entered into force December 6, 1996.

TIAS 12821.

Memorandum of understanding on the exchange of units between the United States Air Force and the Royal Air Force of the United Kingdom of Great Britain and Northern Ireland, with appendix.

Signed at Washington and High Wycombe July 17 and August 6, 1997.

Entered into force August 6, 1997.

NP

Memorandum of understanding concerning cooperation in the development, production and follow on support of an Armored Scout and Reconnaissance Vehicle (ASRV) system, with annexes.

Signed at Washington and Bristol February 26 and July 7, 1998.

Entered into force July 7, 1998.

TIAS

Memorandum of understanding for mission planning support to the Royal Navy Tomahawk Weapon System.

Signed at Bethesda and London November 30 and December 7, 1998.

Entered into force December 7, 1998.

TIAS

Memorandum of understanding for the production of the Universal Modem System (UMS), with annexes.

Signed at Bristol and Ft. Monmouth January 19 and 29, 1999.

Entered into force January 29, 1999.

TIAS

Memorandum of understanding for the Joint Anti-Armor Weapon System (JAAWS) Project.

Signed at Quantico and Abbey Wood September 20 and October 1, 1999.

Entered into force October 1, 1999.

TIAS

Memorandum of understanding concerning cooperative participation in research and development projects, with annexes and appendix.

Signed at Washington April 11 and 26, 2000.

Entered into force April 26, 2000.

TIAS

Memorandum of understanding concerning cooperation on the future development, operation and support of the Apache attack helicopter.

Signed at Washington May 22, 2000.

Entered into force May 22, 2000.

TIAS

Addendum to the memorandum of understanding concerning cooperative military surveys of January 4, 1996.

Signed at London August 17, 2000.

Entered into force August 17, 2000.

TIAS

Memorandum of understanding concerning the cooperative framework for engineering and manufacturing development of the Joint Strike Fighter.

Signed at Washington January 17, 2001.

Entered into force January 17, 2001.

TIAS

Amendments

February 1 and 5, 2002.

August 5, 2003.

Memorandum of understanding concerning personnel recovery, with annexes.

Signed at Washington and London September 28, 2001.

Entered into force September 28, 2001.

TIAS

Memorandum of understanding for the common missile program.

Signed at London and Washington December 4 and 7, 2001.

Entered into force December 7, 2001.

TIAS

Amendment

January 16 and February 3, 2004.

Memorandum of understanding concerning the framework for cooperation between the Defense Information Systems Agency and the Defense Communications Services Agency, with annex.

Signed at Arlington and Corsham June 13 and 17, 2002.

Entered into force June 17, 2002.

TIAS

Agreement concerning the termination of the agreement and related exchanges of notes of March 27, 1941 between the Government of the United States of America and the Government of the United Kingdom of Great Britain and Northern Ireland, as amended and supplemented, relating to the bases leased to the United States of America, with annexes.

Exchange of notes at Washington June 18, 2002.

Entered into force June 18, 2002.

TIAS; 2207 UNTS 485.

Memorandum of understanding concerning the in-service support phase of the NATO improved link eleven project, with annexes.

Signed at Koblenz, London, Rome, Ottawa, Paris and Washington June 13, 18, 20, 27 and July 2, 2002.

Entered into force July 2, 2002.

TIAS

Memorandum of understanding regarding the assignment of liaison officers, with annex.

Signed at Arlington September 18, 2002.

Entered into force September 18, 2002.

TIAS

Project arrangement to the memorandum of understanding of May 22, 2000 concerning the development and production of the Apache attack helicopter AN/APR-48A radar frequency interferometer enhanced user data module programming capability.

Signed at Huntsville and Bristol January 10, 2003.

Entered into force January 10, 2003.

TIAS

Memorandum of understanding for the cooperative development of technology upgrades to the prophet and soothsayer subsystems, with annexes and appendices.

Signed at Ft. Monmouth and Bristol May 2 and 7, 2003.

Entered into force May 7, 2003.

TIAS

Memorandum of understanding concerning ballistic missile defense, with attachment.

Signed at Brussels June 12, 2003.

Entered into force June 12, 2003.

TIAS

Memorandum of understanding concerning cooperation on the future development, interoperability and support of the Javelin Missile System (JMS), with annexes.

Signed at Troy June 17, 2003.

Entered into force June 17, 2003.

TIAS

Memorandum of understanding regarding foreign liaison officers.

Signed at Norfolk and London September 3 and 8, 2003.

Entered into force September 8, 2003.

NP

Agreement concerning the use of Wideawake Airfield on Ascension Island by civil aircraft not engaged in scheduled international air services, with annex.

Signed at Washington October 1, 2003.

Entered into force October 1, 2003.

TIAS ; 2270 UNTS 3.

Supplement number six of the memorandum of understanding of July 14, 1979 on a cooperative program for a medium multiple launch rocket system, with annexes.

Signed at Washington and Abbey Wood October 30 and December 23, 2003.

Entered into force December 23, 2003.

TIAS

Amendment

February 4 and 10, 2005.

Memorandum of understanding regarding the assignment of a missile defense liaison officer to United States strategic command, with annex.

Signed at London and Omaha February 5 and 23, 2004.

Entered into force February 23, 2004.

TIAS

Memorandum of understanding concerning the use of the United Kingdom government pipeline and storage system in the support of U.S. forces within the United Kingdom, with annexes.

Signed March 18, 2004.

Entered into force April 1, 2004.

TIAS

Amendments

April 25, 2005.

May 2 and 9, 2006.

Arrangement regarding the assignment of United Kingdom military personnel to United States strategic command, with annex and appendix.

Signed at London and Omaha May 24 and June 3, 2004.

Entered into force June 3, 2004.

TIAS

Supplement number five of the memorandum of understanding of July 14, 1979 on a cooperative program for a medium multiple launch rocket system, with annexes.

Signed at Washington and Bristol September 20 and 24, 2004.

Entered into force September 24, 2004.

TIAS

Memorandum of understanding concerning the exchange and replacement or reimbursement of marine aviation and propulsion fuels at sea and at military installations worldwide, with annexes.

Signed at Arlington September 29, 2004.

Entered into force September 29, 2004.

TIAS

Amendment

October 6, 2006.

Memorandum of understanding concerning collaboration on land battlespace systems, with annexes.

Signed at St. Louis December 15, 2004.

Entered into force December 15, 2004.

TIAS

Memorandum of understanding relating to the principles governing cooperation in research and development, production, procurement and logistics support of defense capability, with annexes

Signed December 13 and 16, 2004.

Entered into force December 16, 2004.

TIAS

Master information exchange memorandum of understanding annex concerning battlespace spectrum management.

Signed at London and Washington December 22, 2004 and March 10, 2005.

Entered into force March 10, 2005.

TIAS

Master information exchange memorandum of understanding annex concerning weather impact decision aids (WIDA).

Signed at Arlington and London March 9 and April 14, 2005.

Entered into force April 14, 2005.

TIAS

Memorandum of understanding concerning combating terrorism research and development, with annex.

Signed at Washington and London July 6 and September 1, 2005.

Entered into force September 1, 2005.

TIAS

Agreement regarding the assignment of a submarine technology liaison officer, with annex.

Signed at Washington and Abbey Wood September 20 and October 5, 2005.

Entered into force October 5, 2005.

TIAS

Annex D to the memorandum of understanding of June 17, 2002 concerning the exchange and interconnection of defense information system network and defence fixed telecommunications services, with attachment.

Signed at Arlington November 17, 2005.

Entered into force November 17, 2005.

TIAS

Memorandum of understanding for special access program coordination of research, development, and acquistion information exchange, with annexes.

Signed at Washington December 19, 2005.

Entered into force December 19, 2005.

TIAS

Arrangement regarding the assignment of a liaison officer, with annex.

Signed at Abbey Wood and Arlington January 19 and February 13, 2006.

Entered into force February 13, 2006.

TIAS

Arrangement to the agreement of April 26, 2000 concerning the network and information sciences international technology alliance project.

Signed at Washington and London March 28 and April 24, 2006.

Entered into force April 24, 2006.

TIAS

Memorandum of understanding for the loan of thermal weapon sights (TWS) for concept evaluation.

Signed at Ft. Belvoir and Bristol March 31 and May 25, 2006.

Entered into force May 25, 2006.

TIAS

Memorandum of understanding for test and evaluation program (TEP cooperation), with annexes.

Signed at Washington and London October 18 and November 7, 2006.

Entered into force November 7, 2006.

TIAS

NOTES

1 Article IV is applicable to Falkland Islands, Gibraltar, Leeward Islands, St. Helena and Western Pacific Dependencies.

2 See agreement of July 10 and 20, 1973 (TIAS 7688) between the United States and the Bahamas, under BAHAMAS — DEFENSE.

3 This agreement relates to an agreement of the same date between the United States and the short-lived Federation of the West Indies (12 UST 408; TIAS 4734).

4 See also agreement of February 25, 1976 concerning Diego Garcia, as amended (TIAS 8230, 10616).

DRUGS

See also NARCOTIC DRUGS

Agreement relating to the synthesis of penicillin.

Exchange of notes at Washington January 25, 1946.

Entered into force January 25, 1946; operative December 1, 1943.

60 Stat. 1485; TIAS 1506; 12 Bevans 713; 3 UNTS 209.

ECONOMIC AND TECHNICAL COOPERATION

Economic cooperation agreement.[1 2]

Signed at London July 6, 1948.

Entered into force July 6, 1948.

62 Stat. 2596; TIAS 1795; 12 Bevans 874; 22 UNTS 263.

Amendments

January 3, 1950 (1 UST 184; TIAS 2036; 86 UNTS 304).

May 25, 1951 (2 UST 1292; TIAS 2277; 99 UNTS 308).

February 25, 1953 (4 UST 1528; TIAS 2815; 172 UNTS 332).

June 26 and August 20, 1959 (11 UST 2680; TIAS 4664; 405 UNTS 288).

Agreement for technical cooperation in respect of the territories for the international relations of which the Government of the United Kingdom are responsible.[3]

Signed at London July 13, 1951.

Entered into force July 13, 1951.

2 UST 1307; TIAS 2281; 105 UNTS 71.

Agreement relating to the use of the counterpart aid funds alloted to the United Kingdom [4] under Section 115 (k) of the Economic Cooperation Act, as amended.

Exchange of notes at London February 25, 1953.

Entered into force February 25, 1953.

4 UST 1532; TIAS 2816;

NOTES

1 Applicable to Channel Islands, Falkland Islands, Western Pacific High Commission territories, Gibraltar, British Virgin Islands, Isle of Man, St. Helena and Dependencies.

2 Applicable, with the exception of article IV, to Turks and Caicos Islands and Cayman Islands, Montserrat, and Anguilla.

3 Applicable to British Virgin Islands, Montserrat, Anguilla, Turks and Caicos Islands and Cayman Islands.

4 Including Isle of Man.

EDUCATION

Agreement for financing certain educational and cultural exchange programs.[1]

Signed at London May 10, 1965.

Entered into force May 10, 1965.

16 UST 758; TIAS 5806; 545 UNTS 181.

Amendments

February 16, 1967 (18 UST 297; TIAS 6232; 605 UNTS 394).

June 30, 1971 (22 UST 1629; TIAS 7190).

September 11 and 23, 1992 (1723 UNTS 270).

NOTE

1 Applicable to Bermuda, British Virgin Islands, Falkland Islands, Gibraltar, Montserrat, Anguilla, St. Helena.

EMPLOYMENT

Arrangement relating to the employment of dependents of official government employees.

Exchange of notes at Washington January 14 and 15, 1981.

Entered into force January 15, 1981.

32 UST 4581; TIAS 9971; 1267 UNTS 209.

ENVIRONMENTAL COOPERATION

Memorandum of understanding concerning co-operation in the field of environmental affairs.

Signed at Washington June 2, 1986.

Entered into force June 2, 1986.

TIAS 11364.

EXTRADITION

Extradition treaty, with protocol of signature and exchange of notes.[1]

Signed at London June 8, 1972.

Entered into force January 21, 1977.

28 UST 227; TIAS 8468; 1049 UNTS 167.

Supplementary treaty to the extradition treaty of June 8, 1972, with annex.

Signed at Washington June 25, 1985.

Entered into force December 23, 1986.[2]

TIAS 12050; 1556 UNTS 369.

NOTES

1 Applicable to all U.S. territories; Channel Islands, Isle of Man, Bermuda, British Indian Ocean Territory, British Virgin Islands, Cayman Islands, Falkland Islands and Dependencies, Gibraltar, Montserrat, Pitcairn, Henderson, Ducie and Oeno Islands, Anguilla, St. Helena and Dependencies, Sovereign Base Areas of Akrotiri and Dhekelia in the Island of Cyprus, Turks and Caicos Islands.

2 With amendments.

FINANCE[1]

1

Debt funding agreement.

Signed at Washington June 18, 1923; operative December 15, 1922.

Treasury Department print; 12 Bevans 397.

1

Agreement modifying the debt funding agreement of June 18, 1923.

Signed at Washington June 4, 1932; operative July 1, 1931.

Treasury Department print; 12 Bevans 491.

1

Financial agreement.

Signed at Washington December 6, 1945.

Entered into force July 15, 1946.

60 Stat. 1841; TIAS 1545; 12 Bevans 703; 126 UNTS 13.

Amendment

March 6, 1957 (8 UST 2443; TIAS 3962; 303 UNTS 332).

1

Agreement concerning arrangements for the establishment of revolving loan funds in Uganda protectorate and Tanganyika with counterpart funds.

Exchange of letters at London June 24, 1953.

Entered into force June 24, 1953.

5 UST 160; TIAS 2909; 224 UNTS 141.

1

Agreement on behalf of the Turks and Caicos Islands relating to investment guaranties.

Signed at Washington April 20, 1999.

Entered into force April 20, 1999.

TIAS; 2076 UNTS 215.

NOTE

1 See also international fund for Ireland under FINANCE in multilateral section.

FISHERIES

Agreement adopting, with certain modifications, the rules and method of procedure recommended in the award of September 7, 1910, of the North Atlantic Coast Fisheries Arbitration.

Signed at Washington July 20, 1912.

Entered into force November 15, 1912.

37 Stat. 1634; TS 572; 12 Bevans 357.

Reciprocal fisheries agreement, with agreed minute.

Signed at London March 27, 1979.

Entered into force March 10, 1983.

TIAS 10545.

JUDICIAL ASSISTANCE

Treaty concerning the Cayman Islands relating to mutual legal assistance in criminal matters, with attachments, protocol and exchange of notes.

Signed at Grand Cayman July 3, 1986.

Entered into force March 19, 1990.

TIAS; 1648 UNTS 179.

Amendment

September 10, 2004 and February 9, 2005.

Agreement extending the application of the treaty of July 3, 1986, concerning the Cayman Islands relating to mutual legal assistance in criminal matters to Anguilla, the British Virgin Islands and the Turks and Caicos Islands.

Exchange of notes at Washington November 9, 1990.

Entered into force November 9, 1990.

TIAS 11765.

Agreement extending application of the treaty of July 3, 1986, concerning the Cayman Islands relating to mutual legal assistance in criminal matters to Montserrat.

Exchange of notes at Washington April 26, 1991.

Entered into force April 26, 1991.

TIAS 12429; 1670 UNTS 375.

Agreement for mutual assistance in administration of justice in connection with the Bank of Credit and Commerce International.

Signed at London and Washington November 15 and December 4, 1991.

Entered into force December 4, 1991.

TIAS

Treaty on mutual legal assistance in criminal matters, with appendices and related exchange of notes.

Signed at Washington January 6, 1994.

Entered into force December 2, 1996.

TIAS

Agreement concerning the application of the treaty on mutual legal assistance in criminal matters of January 6, 1994.

Exchange of notes at Washington April 30 and May 1, 2001.

Entered into force May 1, 2001.

TIAS; 2189 UNTS 468.

Agreement regarding the sharing of forfeited or confiscated assets or their equivalent funds.

Signed at Washington March 31, 2003.

Entered into force March 31, 2003.

TIAS

Agreement on the application to the Isle of Man of the treaty on mutual legal assistance in criminal matters of January 6, 1994.

Exchange of notes at London June 2 and 5, 2003.

Entered into force June 5, 2003.

TIAS

LEND-LEASE

Preliminary agreement regarding principles applying to mutual aid in the prosecution of the war against aggression.

Signed at Washington February 23, 1942.

Entered into force February 23, 1942.

56 Stat. 1433; EAS 241; 12 Bevans 603.

Agreement relating to principles applying to the provision of aid to the armed forces of the United States.

Exchange of notes at Washington September 3, 1942.

Entered into force September 3, 1942.

56 Stat. 1605; EAS 270; 12 Bevans 617.

LEND-LEASE SETTLEMENT

Joint statement regarding settlement for lend-lease, reciprocal aid, surplus war property, and claims

Dated at Washington December 6, 1945.

60 Stat. 1525; TIAS 1509; 12 Bevans 700; 4 UNTS 2.

Memorandum pursuant to joint statement of December 6, 1945, regarding settlement for lend-lease, reciprocal aid, surplus war property, and claims, with agreements annexed thereto.

Signed at Washington March 27, 1946.

Entered into force March 27, 1946.

12 Bevans 745.

Agreement relating to settlement of the lend-lease interest in future sales of surplus stores in the Middle East.

Signed at London January 7, 1948.

Entered into force January 7, 1948; operative July 15, 1947.

62 Stat. 1836; TIAS 1698; 12 Bevans 843; 89 UNTS 372.

Agreement relating to the settlement of the interests of the Government of the United States and the Government of the United Kingdom in joint installations in the Middle East.

Signed at Washington July 12, 1948.

Entered into force July 12, 1948.

62 Stat. 2027; TIAS 1769; 12 Bevans 891; 71 UNTS 199.

Agreement relating to settlement of lend-lease and reciprocal aid accounts and intergovernmental claims.

Signed at Washington July 12, 1948.

Entered into force July 12, 1948.

62 Stat. 2034; TIAS 1770; 12 Bevans 897; 71 UNTS 270.

Amendment

April 24 and 25, 1957 (8 UST 771; TIAS 3834; 284 UNTS 362).

MAPPING

Agreement relating to cooperation in mapping, charting and geodesy.

Signed at Feltham and Washington July 4 and 18, 1985.

Entered into force July 18, 1985.

TIAS 11530.

Memorandum of understanding concerning geospatial information and services cooperation, with annexes and appendices.

Signed at London April 19, 2001.

Entered into force April 19, 2001.

NP

Amendment

December 5, 2002.

METEOROLOGICAL RESEARCH

Agreement providing for a meteorological research program in Barbados.

Exchange of notes at Bridgetown January 7 and 15, 1963.

Entered into force January 15, 1963.

14 UST 109; TIAS 5276; 466 UNTS 181.

MILITARY CEMETERIES AND MONUMENTS

Agreement relating to the use of land at Madingley, near Cambridge, as a United States military cemetery.

Exchange of notes at London June 21, 1954.

Entered into force June 21, 1954.

5 UST 1404; TIAS 3011; 209 UNTS 61.

MUTUAL SECURITY

Agreement relating to the assurances required under the Mutual Security Act of 1951.[1]

Exchange of notes at London January 8, 1952.

Entered into force January 8, 1952.

3 UST 4665; TIAS 2622; 126 UNTS 307.

NOTE

1 Applicable to Falkland Islands, Gibraltar, Leeward Islands, St. Helena, Western Pacific Islands.

NARCOTIC DRUGS

See also JUDICIAL ASSISTANCE

Arrangement for the direct exchange of certain information regarding the traffic in narcotic drugs.

Exchange of notes at London December 23, 1927, and January 4 and 11, 1928.

Entered into force January 11, 1928.

12 Bevans 467.

Agreement to facilitate the interdiction by the United States of vessels of the United Kingdom suspected of trafficking in drugs.

Exchange of notes at London November 13, 1981.

Entered into force November 13, 1981.

33 UST 4224; TIAS 10296; 1285 UNTS 197.

Agreement concerning maritime and aerial operations to suppress illicit trafficking by sea in waters of the Caribbean and Bermuda.

Signed at Washington July 13, 1998.

Entered into force October 30, 2000.

TIAS

OCCUPIED TERRITORY

Agreement for the settlement of financial issues arising from the bizonal fusion agreement of December 2, 1946, as amended.

Exchange of notes at Washington June 28, 1950.

Entered into force June 28, 1950.

1 UST 540; TIAS 2098; 88 UNTS 412.

OCEANOGRAPHY

Memorandum of understanding on the participation of the United Kingdom in the ocean drilling program as a regular member, with annexes.

Signed at Swindon December 7, 1992.

Entered into force December 7, 1992; effective October 1, 1993.

TIAS

PACIFIC SETTLEMENT OF DISPUTES

Treaty for the advancement of peace.

Signed at Washington September 15, 1914.

Entered into force November 10, 1914.

38 Stat. 1853; TS 602; 12 Bevans 370.

PATENTS

Agreement to facilitate the interchange of patent and technical information for defense purposes, and exchange of notes.

Signed at London January 19, 1953.

Entered into force January 19, 1953.

4 UST 150; TIAS 2773; 161 UNTS 3.

PEACE TREATIES

Definitive treaty of peace.[1]

Signed at Paris September 3, 1783.

Entered into force May 12, 1784.

8 Stat. 80; TS 104; 12 Bevans 8.

Treaty of peace and amity.

Signed at Ghent December 24, 1814.

Entered into force February 17, 1815.

8 Stat. 218; TS 109; 12 Bevans 41.

NOTE

1 Only article 1 is in force.

POSTAL MATTERS

Agreement for the direct exchange of parcels by parcel post.

Signed at Washington October 1 and at London October 27, 1924; operative October 1, 1924.

43 Stat. 1854; Post Office Department print.

International express mail agreement, with detailed regulations.

Signed at London and Washington November 6 and December 14, 1978.

Entered into force February 12, 1979; effective January 1, 1979.

30 UST 3357; TIAS 9395; 1180 UNTS 3.

International express mail agreement, with detailed regulations.

Signed at Grand Cayman and Washington August 25 and September 9, 1986.

Entered into force November 26, 1986.

TIAS 11390.

PROPERTY

Arrangement regarding the release of property seized under the American and British Trading With the Enemy Acts.

Exchange of notes at London January 4 and February 23, 1927.

Entered into force February 23, 1927.

TS 754-A; 12 Bevans 457; 82 LNTS 17.

PROPERTY – REAL AND PERSONAL

Convention relating to tenure and disposition of real and personal property.[1]

Signed at Washington March 2, 1899.

Entered into force August 7, 1900.

31 Stat. 1939; TS 146; 12 Bevans 246.

Supplementary convention extending the time within which notifications may be given of the accession of British colonies or foreign possessions to the convention of March 2, 1899, relating to the tenure and disposition of real and personal property.

Signed at Washington January 13, 1902.

Entered into force April 2, 1902.

32 Stat. 1914; TS 402; 12 Bevans 261.

Supplementary convention providing for the accession of the Dominion of Canada to the real and personal property convention of March 2, 1899.

Signed at Washington October 21, 1921.

Entered into force June 17, 1922.

42 Stat. 2147; TS 663; 12 Bevans 390; 12 LNTS 425.

Supplementary convention relating to the tenure and disposition of real and personal property.

Signed at Washington May 27, 1936, by the United States, the United Kingdom, Australia, and New Zealand.

Entered into force March 10, 1941.

55 Stat. 1101; TS 964; 5 Bevans 140; 203 LNTS 367.

NOTE

1 Applicable to Puerto Rico, Ascension, Bermuda, Falkland Islands, Gibraltar, Leeward Islands, St. Helena.

PUBLICATIONS

Agreement for the exchange of official publications.

Exchange of notes at Washington July 13 and 30, 1951.

Entered into force July 30, 1951.

2 UST 1745; TIAS 2314; 105 UNTS 81.

SATELLITES

Agreement on cooperation in intercontinental testing in connection with experimental communications satellites.

Exchange of notes at London March 29, 1961.

Entered into force March 29, 1961.

12 UST 246; TIAS 4704; 405 UNTS 107.

Agreement confirming a memorandum of understanding concerning the furnishing of launching and associated services by NASA for United Kingdom satellites, with annexes.

Exchange of notes at Washington January 17, 1973.

Entered into force January 17, 1973.

24 UST 228; TIAS 7544; 881 UNTS 3.

Memorandum of understanding relating to a satellite-aided maritime distress alert system.

Signed at Washington July 23, 1981.

Entered into force July 23, 1981.

33 UST 3303; TIAS 10229.

SCIENTIFIC COOPERATION

Agreement concerning the Annex on Intellectual Property Rights, with attachment.

Exchange of notes at Washington November 29, 1995.

Entered into force November 29, 1995.

TIAS 12703; 1945 UNTS 295.

Agreement on cooperation in science and technology for critical infrastructure protection and other homeland/civil security matters.

Signed at London December 8, 2004.

Entered into force December 8, 2004.

TIAS

SHIPPING

Agreement relating to jurisdiction over vessels utilizing the Louisiana Offshore Oil Port.

Exchange of notes at Washington May 14 and 25, 1979.

Entered into force May 25, 1979.

30 UST 5926; TIAS 9525; 1162 UNTS 351.

SMUGGLING

Convention for the prevention of smuggling of intoxicating liquors.

Signed at Washington January 23, 1924.

Entered into force May 22, 1924.

43 Stat. 1761; TS 685; 12 Bevans 414; 27 LNTS 182.

SOCIAL SECURITY

Agreement on social security.

Signed at London February 13, 1984.

Entered into force January 1, 1985, except for Part III which entered into force January 1, 1988.

TIAS 11086.

Administrative agreement for implementation of agreement on social security.

Signed at London February 13, 1984.

Entered into force January 1, 1985.

TIAS 11086.

Supplementary agreement amending the agreement on social security of February 13, 1984 and supplementary administrative agreement amending the administrative agreement.

Done at London June 6, 1996.

Entered into force September 1, 1997.

TIAS 12776; 1995 UNTS 489.

SPACE RESEARCH

Agreement relating to the establishment of a joint program of space research.

Exchange of notes at Washington September 8, 1961.

Entered into force September 8, 1961.

12 UST 1223; TIAS 4840; 418 UNTS 53.

TAXATION

Agreement relating to relief from taxation of United States Government expenditures in the United Kingdom for the common defense effort.

Exchange of notes at London March 17 and 18, 1952.

Entered into force March 18, 1952.

3 UST 4158; TIAS 2559; 177 UNTS 33.

Convention for the avoidance of double taxation and the prevention of fiscal evasion with respect to taxes on estates of deceased persons and on gifts.[1]

Signed at London October 19, 1978.

Entered into force November 11, 1979.

30 UST 7223; TIAS 9580; 1182 UNTS 83.

Convention (on behalf of the Government of Bermuda) relating to the taxation of insurance enterprises and mutual assistance in tax matters, with exchange of notes.

Signed at Washington July 11, 1986.

Entered into force December 2, 1988.

TIAS 11676; 2192 UNTS 139.

Agreement (on behalf of the Government of Bermuda) for the exchange of information with respect to taxes.

Signed at Washington December 2, 1988.

Entered into force December 2, 1988.

TIAS 11986.

Agreement (on behalf of the Isle of Man) for the reciprocal exemption with respect to taxes on income from the international operation of ships.

Exchange of notes at Washington August 1 and 15, 1989.

Entered into force August 15, 1989.

TIAS 11678.

Convention for the avoidance of double taxation and the prevention of fiscal evasion with respect to taxes on income and on capital gains, with exchange of notes.

Signed at London July 24, 2001.

Entered into force March 31, 2003.

TIAS ; 2224 UNTS 247.

Amendment

July 19, 2002.

NOTES

1 See article 14 for the circumstances under which the convention for the avoidance of double taxation and the prevention of fiscal evasion with respect to taxes on the estates of deceased persons of April 16, 1945 (60 Stat. 1391; TIAS 1547) would continue to have effect in the United Kingdom.

TELECOMMUNICATION

Agreement on distance measuring equipment.

Signed at Washington October 13, 1947.

Entered into force October 13, 1947.

61 Stat. 3131; TIAS 1652; 12 Bevans 824; 66 UNTS 269.

Agreement relating to the reciprocal granting of authorizations to permit licensed amateur radio operators of either country to operate their stations in the other country.[1]

Exchange of notes at London November 26, 1965.

Entered into force November 26, 1965.

16 UST 2047; TIAS 5941; 561 UNTS 193.

Agreement extending to certain territories the application of the agreement of November 26, 1965 relating to the reciprocal granting of authorizations to permit licensed amateur radio operators of either country to operate their stations in the other country.[1]

Exchange of notes at London December 11, 1969.

Entered into force December 11, 1969.

20 UST 4089; TIAS 6800; 732 UNTS 334.

NOTE

1 Applicable to all territories, for whose international relations the United States is responsible and the following British territories: Bermuda, British Virgin Islands, Cayman Islands, Falkland Islands, Gibraltar, Montserrat, St. Helena, Turks and Caicos Islands.

TRACKING STATIONS

Agreement providing for the establishment of a lunar and planetary spacecraft tracking facility on Ascension Island.

Exchange of notes at London July 7, 1965.

Entered into force July 7, 1965.

16 UST 1183; TIAS 5864; 551 UNTS 221.

Agreement providing for the establishment and operation of space vehicle tracking and communications stations in the United Kingdom.

Exchange of notes at London December 28, 1966 and January 1, 1967.

Entered into force January 1, 1967.

18 UST 129; TIAS 6208; 604 UNTS 3.

Agreement concerning the establishment and operation of a space vehicle tracking and communications station on Antigua.

Exchange of notes at Washington January 17 and 23, 1967.

Entered into force January 23, 1967.

18 UST 112; TIAS 6207.

TRADE

See also COMMERCE

Agreement supplementary to the general agreement on tariffs and trade.

Signed at Washington June 27, 1957; schedule applicable June 29, 1957.

8 UST 890; TIAS 3851; 284 UNTS 75.

Agreement providing compensatory concessions under the general agreement on tariffs and trade for certain tariff actions taken by the United States.

Exchange of notes at Geneva January 26 and February 16, 1962.

Entered into force February 16, 1962.

13 UST 954; TIAS 5032.

Agreement supplementary to the general agreement on tariffs and trade to compensate for escape clause actions to increase import duties on certain carpets and glass.

Signed at Geneva December 10, 1962.

Entered into force December 10, 1962.

13 UST 3910; TIAS 5268; 471 UNTS 91.

Interim agreement relating to the renegotiation of Schedule XX (United States) to the general agreement on tariffs and trade.

Signed at Washington April 5, 1966.

Entered into force April 5, 1966.

17 UST 254; TIAS 5975; 592 UNTS 61.

Amendment

June 30, 1967 (18 UST 1753; TIAS 6318; 693 UNTS 366).

TRADE-MARKS

Declaration affording reciprocal protection to trade-marks.[1]

Signed at London October 24, 1877.

Entered into force October 24, 1877.

20 Stat. 703; TS 138; 12 Bevans 198.

NOTE

1 Applicable to all territories.

VISAS

Agreement for the waiver of the visa requirements for United States citizens traveling to the United Kingdom and for the granting of gratis passport visas to British subjects entering the United States as nonimmigrants.[1]

Exchange of notes at London November 9 and 12, 1948.

Entered into force November 12, 1948.

62 Stat. 3824; TIAS 1926; 12 Bevans 917; 84 UNTS 275.

NOTE

1 Applicable to all territories.

WEAPONS

Agreement for cooperation in research and development of weapons detection and protection-related technologies, with annex.

Signed at Washington July 3, 2002.

Entered into force July 3, 2002.

TIAS

WEATHER STATIONS

Agreement for the continuation of a cooperative meteorological program in the Cayman Islands, with memorandum of arrangement.

Exchange of notes at Washington April 6 and 13, 1976.

Entered into force April 13, 1976.

27 UST 1867; TIAS 8285.

UNITED KINGDOM (ANGUILLA)

FINANCE

Investment incentive agreement on behalf of Anguilla.

Exchange of notes at London November 9, 1987.

Entered into force November 9, 1987.

TIAS 12045; 1556 UNTS 43.

PEACE CORPS

Agreement relating to the establishment of a Peace Corps program in Anguilla.

Exchange of letters at Washington February 19 and June 24, 1981.

Entered into force June 24, 1981; effective May 1, 1981.

33 UST 2053; TIAS 10169; 1529 UNTS 429.

POSTAL MATTERS

Convention for the exchange of postal money orders with the British Colony of Saint Christopher, Nevis and Anguilla.

Signed at Basseterre, St. Kitts, June 27 and at Washington September 14, 1959.

Entered into force February 1, 1960.

11 UST 1433; TIAS 4483.

Express mail agreement, with detailed regulations.

Signed at Anguilla and Washington May 28, 1998 and January 8, 1999.

Entered into force April 15, 1999.

NP

UNITED KINGDOM (BERMUDA)

AVIATION

Agreement on preclearance for entry into the United States, with annex.

Signed at Hamilton January 15, 1974.

Entered into force January 15, 1974.

25 UST 288; TIAS 7801.

Amendment

August 28 and 29, 1979 (30 UST 7562; TIAS 9600; 1203 UNTS 365).

POLLUTION

Agreement concerning assistance to be rendered on a reimbursable basis by the United States Coast Guard in the event of major oil spills.

Signed at Hamilton July 13, 1976.

Entered into force July 13, 1976.

27 UST 3788; TIAS 8396.

POSTAL MATTERS

Parcel post agreement.

Signed at Washington December 13, 1906, and at Bermuda January 15, 1907; operative February 1, 1907.

34 Stat. 2983; Post Office Department print.

International express mail agreement, with detailed regulations.

Signed at Hamilton and Washington July 31 and August 13, 1979.

Entered into force September 1, 1979.

30 UST 6493; TIAS 9563; 1180 UNTS 47.

UNITED KINGDOM (BRITISH VIRGIN ISLANDS)

POLLUTION

Agreement concerning assistance to be rendered during discharge of oil or other hazardous and noxious substances into waters of the British Virgin Islands.

Signed at Tortola August 12, 2004.

Entered into force August 12, 2004.

TIAS

POSTAL MATTERS

Convention for the exchange of postal money orders with the Colony of British Virgin Islands.

Signed at Road Town, Tortola, February 18 and at Washington March 14, 1957.

Entered into force July 1, 1957.

11 UST 1409; TIAS 4480.

UNITED KINGDOM (GIBRALTAR)

POSTAL MATTERS

Agreement for the exchange of parcel post and detailed regulations for the execution thereof.

Signed at Gibraltar December 18, 1936, and at Washington January 5, 1937; operative January 1, 1937.

50 Stat. 1488; Post Office Department print; 177 LNTS 21.

UNITED KINGDOM (LEEWARD ISLANDS)

POSTAL MATTERS

Parcel post agreement.

Signed at Antigua May 27 and at Washington July 11, 1929; operative September 1, 1929.

46 Stat. 2321; Post Office Department print; 98 LNTS 161.

UNITED KINGDOM (MONTSERRAT)

PEACE CORPS

Agreement relating to the establishment of a Peace Corps program in Montserrat.

Exchange of letters at Bridgetown and Plymouth January 13 and February 9, 1981.

Entered into force February 9, 1981.

33 UST 1075; TIAS 10092; 1307 UNTS 415.

POSTAL MATTERS

Convention for the exchange of postal money orders with the British Colony of Montserrat.

Signed at Montserrat March 15 and at Washington June 10, 1957.

Entered into force September 1, 1957.

11 UST 1417; TIAS 4481.

UNITED KINGDOM (TURKS AND CAICOS ISLANDS)

DEFENSE

Memorandum of understanding concerning the establishment of a portable radar tracking station in the Turks and Caicos Islands.

Signed at London July 24, 1987.

Entered into force July 24, 1987.

TIAS

PEACE CORPS

Agreement relating to the establishment of a Peace Corps program in the Turks and Caicos Islands.

Exchange of letters at Washington April 17 and December 5, 1980.

Entered into force December 5, 1980.

32 UST 4235; TIAS 9945; 1267 UNTS 201.

REFUGEES

Memorandum of understanding to establish in the Turks and Caicos Islands a processing facility to determine the refugee status of boat people from Haiti, with related letter.

Signed at Grand Turk June 18, 1994.

Entered into force June 18, 1994.

TIAS

Amendment

July 13, 1994.

UNITED NATIONS

AGRICULTURAL COMMODITIES

Memorandum of understanding concerning a grant to the United Nations of Congo francs accruing to the United States under the agricultural commodities agreement of November 18, 1961 between the United States and the Republic of the Congo (Leopoldville).

Signed at New York February 13, 1962.

Entered into force February 13, 1962.

13 UST 145; TIAS 4949; 494 UNTS 213.

Amendment

August 25 and 26, 1964 (15 UST 1800; TIAS 5652; 529 UNTS 378).

ASSISTANCE

Agreement concerning the establishment of security for the United Nations Assistance Mission for Iraq.

Signed at New York December 8, 2005.

Entered into force December 8, 2005.

TIAS

DEFENSE

Agreement regarding the furnishing of defense articles and defense services by the United States to the United Nations for purposes of supporting the Rapid Reactor Force established pursuant to United Nations Security Council Resolution 998.

Exchange of notes at New York July 28, 1995.

Entered into force July 28, 1995.

TIAS 12680.

Agreement concerning the provision of services and commodities on a reimbursable basis in support of the operations of the United Nations Monitoring, Verification and Inspection Commission.

Signed at Washington and New York November 5 and 8, 2002.

Entered into force November 8, 2002.

TIAS

Agreement concerning the provision of services and commodities on a reimbursable basis in support of the operations of the United Nations Assistance Mission in Iraq.

Signed at New York December 29, 2004.

Entered into force December 29, 2004.

TIAS

DEVELOPMENT ASSISTANCE

Basic agreement governing grants by the United States to the United Nations Trust Fund for Africa.

Signed at Washington June 17, 1976.

Entered into force June 17, 1976.

28 UST 6885; TIAS 8694.

ECONOMIC AND TECHNICAL COOPERATION

Agreement concerning technical assistance for Bangladesh in the field of statistical services.

Signed at New York and Washington March 14 and May 2, 1978.

Entered into force May 2, 1978.

30 UST 1192; TIAS 9245.

HEADQUARTERS

Agreement regarding the headquarters of the United Nations.

Signed at Lake Success June 26, 1947.

Entered into force November 21, 1947.

61 Stat. 3416; TIAS 1676; 12 Bevans 956; 11 UNTS 11.

Supplemental agreement regarding the headquarters of the United Nations.

Signed at New York February 9, 1966.

Entered into force February 9, 1966.

17 UST 74; TIAS 5961; 554 UNTS 308.

Amendment

December 8, 1966 (17 UST 2319; TIAS 6176; 581 UNTS 362).

Second supplemental agreement regarding the headquarters of the United Nations.

Signed at New York August 28, 1969.

Entered into force August 28, 1969.

20 UST 2810; TIAS 6750; 687 UNTS 408.

Third supplemental agreement regarding the headquarters of the United Nations.

Signed at New York December 10, 1980.

Entered into force December 10, 1980.

32 UST 4414; TIAS 9955.

HUMANITARIAN ASSISTANCE

Memorandum of understanding for the contribution of civilian personnel to the United Nations Transitional Administration for Eastern Slavonia, Baranja and Western Sirmium, with annexes.

Signed at New York March 26, 1996.

Entered into force March 26, 1996; effective March 14, 1996.

TIAS 12737; 1918 UNTS 413.

POSTAL MATTERS

Postal agreement

Signed March 28, 1951.

Entered into force October 24, 1951.

3 UST 369; TIAS 2399; 108 UNTS 231.

Amendments

November 7 and 17, 1952 (3 UST 5164; TIAS 2711; 149 UNTS 414).

April 15 and 19, 1965 (16 UST 745; TIAS 5803; 531 UNTS 314).

June 20 and August 8, 1994 (1819 UNTS 497).

TAXATION

Agreement relating to a procedure for United States income tax reimbursement.

Exchange of letters at New York June 30 and July 12, 1978.

Entered into force July 12, 1978.

30 UST 124; TIAS 9183; 1095 UNTS 307.

TELECOMMUNICATION

Agreement to permit the exchange of third-party messages between amateur stations of the United States and amateur station 4U1VIC of the Vienna International Amateur Radio Club.

Exchange of letters at Vienna November 21 and December 3, 1985.

Entered into force January 2, 1986.

TIAS

TRUSTEESHIPS

Trusteeship agreement for the former Japanese mandated islands.

Approved by the Security Council of the United Nations April 2, 1947, and by the United States July 18, 1947.

Entered into force July 18, 1947.

61 Stat. 3301; TIAS 1665; 12 Bevans 951; 8 UNTS 189.

Agreement relating to the provision of assistance by the United Nations Development Programme to the Trust Territory of the Pacific Islands, with exchange of notes.

Signed at New York June 10, 1974.

Entered into force June 10, 1974.[1]

25 UST 1618; TIAS 7900.

NOTE

1 On December 22, 1990, the United Nations Security Council passed UNSC Resolution 683 (1990), which confirmed the termination of the Trusteeship Agreement as it applied to the Republic of the Marshall Islands, the Federated States of Micronesia, and the Commonwealth of the Northern Mariana Islands.

UNITED NATIONS CHILDREN'S FUND

ECONOMIC AND TECHNICAL COOPERATION

Agency for International Development

April 29 and May 11, 1977 (29 UST 5266; TIAS 9101).

May 4 and 11, 1977 (29 UST 5263; TIAS 9100).

March 25, 1988 (NP).

UNITED NATIONS ENVIRONMENT PROGRAMME

ENVIRONMENT

Agreement to cooperate on activities and facilities to support the UNEP division of early warning and assessment in North America.

Signed at Washington December 21, 2004.

Entered into force December 21, 2004.

TIAS

UNITED NATIONS HIGH COMMISSIONER FOR REFUGEES

ECONOMIC AND TECHNICAL COOPERATION

Agency for International Development

June 29 and 30, 1978 (30 UST 3138; TIAS 9384; 1179 UNTS 13).

MIGRATION

Agreement concerning United States and UNHCR cooperation in providing assistance to the Cuban boat people.

Exchange of letters at Washington September 29 and October 5, 1994.

Entered into force October 5, 1994.

TIAS

REFUGEE RELIEF

Grant agreement concerning assistance to displaced and uprooted persons in South Viet-Nam and Laos.

Signed at Washington and Geneva November 13 and December 2, 1974.

Entered into force December 2, 1974.

26 UST 450; TIAS 8044; 991 UNTS 386.

Amendments

December 16, 1974 (26 UST 457; TIAS 8044; 991 UNTS 392).

February 5 and 10, 1975 (26 UST 458; TIAS 8044; 991 UNTS 393).

Agreement relating to assistance with Cuban refugees.

Done at Geneva May 16 and 21, 1980.

Entered into force May 21, 1980.

TIAS

UNITED NATIONS INTERIM ADMINISTRATION MISSION IN KOSOVO

FINANCE

Agreement for investment support projects in Kosovo.

Signed at Washington and Pristina May 17 and 30, 2002.

Entered into force May 30, 2002.

TIAS

UNIVERSAL POSTAL UNION

TAXATION

Tax reimbursement agreement, with annex.

Signed at Bern January 12, 1995.

Entered into force January 12, 1995.

TIAS 12598.

URUGUAY

AGRICULTURAL COMMODITIES

Agricultural commodities agreement with exchange of notes.

Signed at Montevideo February 20, 1959.

Entered into force February 20, 1959.

10 UST 161; TIAS 4179; 341 UNTS 201.

Amendments

May 21, 1959 (10 UST 1023; TIAS 4238; 346 UNTS 358).

November 16, 1959 (10 UST 1904; TIAS 4356; 360 UNTS 428).

December 1, 1959 (10 UST 2067; TIAS 4375; 361 UNTS 372).

January 13, 1960 (11 UST 41; TIAS 4406; 368 UNTS 372).

September 13 and 16, 1960 (11 UST 2536; TIAS 4640; 401 UNTS 316).

October 14, 1960 (11 UST 2539; TIAS 4641; 401 UNTS 319).

September 18, 1961 (12 UST 1394; TIAS 4863; 433 UNTS 372).

Agricultural commodities agreement with exchanges of notes.

Signed at Montevideo April 27, 1962.

Entered into force April 27, 1962.

13 UST 1018; TIAS 5044; 452 UNTS 25.

Agricultural commodities agreement with annex.

Signed at Montevideo January 19, 1968.

Entered into force January 19, 1968.

19 UST 4534; TIAS 6445; 698 UNTS 3.

Amendments

June 13 and 27, 1968 (19 UST 6048; TIAS 6564; 702 UNTS 418).

March 4 and 18, 1970 (21 UST 1141; TIAS 6868; 745 UNTS 345).

Related agreements

May 7, 1968 (19 UST 4837; TIAS 6486; 698 UNTS 229).

July 8 and October 20, 1970 (21 UST 2256; TIAS 6976).

December 8 and 9, 1970 (21 UST 3102; TIAS 7033; 781 UNTS 356).

September 25, 1972 (23 UST 2905; TIAS 7477).

AVIATION

Air transport agreement.

Signed at Montevideo December 14, 1946.

Entered into force provisionally December 14, 1946.

15 UST 2115; TIAS 5692; 532 UNTS 87.

Amendments

July 9, 1976 and February 9, 1977 (28 UST 2442; TIAS 8562).

July 15, 1991 (TIAS 11806).

Memorandum of agreement relating to provision of Federal Aviation Administration services to the Government of Uruguay.

Signed at Washington and Montevideo March 19 and 20, 1981.

Entered into force March 20, 1981.

33 UST 1461; TIAS 10122.

Memorandum of agreement concerning assistance in developing and modernizing Uruguay's civil aviation infrastructure.

Signed at Washington and Montevideo September 25 and 30, 1997.

Entered into force September 30, 1997.

TIAS

Air transport agreement, with annexes and exchange of notes.

Signed at Montevideo October 20, 2004.

Entered into force June 16, 2006.

TIAS

CUSTOMS

Agreement providing more liberal exemptions from customs duties and related taxes for diplomatic and consular personnel.

Exchange of notes at Washington October 31 and November 12, 1952.

Entered into force November 12, 1952.

5 UST 824; TIAS 2971; 231 UNTS 145.

DEFENSE

Military assistance agreement.

Signed at Montevideo June 30, 1952.

Entered into force June 11, 1953.

4 UST 197; TIAS 2778; 207 UNTS 139.

Agreement providing for disposition of equipment and materials furnished by the United States under the military assistance agreement and no longer required by Uruguay.

Exchange of notes at Montevideo June 1 and September 16, 1955, and note of April 20, 1956.

Entered into force September 16, 1955.

7 UST 831; TIAS 3562; 273 UNTS 259.

Agreement relating to the deposit by Uruguay of ten percent of the value of grant military assistance and excess defense articles furnished by the United States.

Exchange of notes at Montevideo May 2, 1972.

Entered into force May 2, 1972; effective February 7, 1972.

23 UST 653; TIAS 7329.

Agreement relating to payment to the United States of net proceeds from the sale of defense articles furnished under the military assistance program.

Exchange of notes at Montevideo December 11 and 30, 1974.

Entered into force December 30, 1974; effective July 1, 1974.

25 UST 3181; TIAS 7985; 991 UNTS 407.

Acquisition and cross-servicing agreement, with annexes.

Signed at Montevideo March 29, 2000.

Entered into force March 29, 2000.

TIAS

Memorandum of understanding concerning the inter-American naval telecommunications network.

Signed September 13, 2006.

Entered into force September 13, 2006.

TIAS

ECONOMIC AND TECHNICAL COOPERATION

General agreement for a program of technical cooperation.

Signed at Montevideo March 23, 1956.

Entered into force March 22, 1960.

11 UST 1489; TIAS 4491; 376 UNTS 311.

Agreement concerning the establishment of an Americas Fund and Administering Commission.

Signed at Montevideo June 25, 1993.

Entered into force June 25, 1993.

TIAS 12503.

EDUCATION

Agreement for financing certain educational exchange programs.

Exchange of notes at Montevideo March 22 and May 17, 1965.

Entered into force May 17, 1965.

16 UST 872; TIAS 5825; 564 UNTS 69.

EXTRADITION

Treaty on extradition and cooperation in penal matters.

Signed at Washington April 6, 1973.

Entered into force April 11, 1984.

35 UST 3197; TIAS 10850.

FINANCE

Agreement relating to investment guaranties.

Exchange of notes at Montevideo December 15, 1982.

Entered into force July 21, 1983.

TIAS 12038.

Agreement regarding the reduction of certain debts related to foreign assistance owed to the Government of the United States and its agencies, with appendices.

Signed at Washington December 15, 1992.

Entered into force January 14, 1993.

NP

Agreement regarding the reduction of certain debts related to agriculture owed to the Government of the United States and its agencies, with appendices.

Signed at Washington December 15, 1992.

Entered into force January 14, 1993.

NP

JUDICIAL ASSISTANCE

Treaty on mutual legal assistance in criminal matters.

Signed at Montevideo May 6, 1991.

Entered into force April 15, 1994.

TIAS

MAPPING

Cooperative mapping, charting and geodesy agreement.

Signed at Montevideo and Fairfax August 27 and October 25, 1991.

Entered into force October 25, 1991.

NP

PACIFIC SETTLEMENT OF DISPUTES

Arbitration convention.

Signed at Washington January 9, 1909.

Entered into force November 14, 1913.

38 Stat. 1741; TS 583; 12 Bevans 986.

Treaty for the advancement of peace.

Signed at Washington July 20, 1914.

Entered into force February 24, 1915.

38 Stat. 1908; TS 611; 12 Bevans 988.

PEACE CORPS

Agreement relating to the establishment of a Peace Corps program in Uruguay.

Exchange of notes at Montevideo March 19 and July 31, 1963.

Entered into force July 31, 1963.

14 UST 1455; TIAS 5443; 488 UNTS 3.

POSTAL MATTERS

International express mail agreement with detailed regulations.

Signed at Washington September 22, 1983.

Entered into force February 15, 1984.

35 UST 3080; TIAS 10841; 2014 UNTS 597.

TELECOMMUNICATION

Agreement relating to radio communications between radio amateurs on behalf of third parties.

Exchange of notes at Montevideo September 12, 1961.

Entered into force September 26, 1966.

17 UST 1574; TIAS 6115; 607 UNTS 175.

Agreement relating to the reciprocal granting of authorizations to permit licensed amateur radio operators of either country to operate their stations in the other country.

Exchange of notes at Montevideo May 28, 1971.

Entered into force May 28, 1971.

22 UST 701; TIAS 7129; 797 UNTS 23.

TRADE AND COMMERCE

Convention facilitating the work of traveling salesmen.

Signed at Washington August 27, 1918.

Entered into force August 2, 1919.

41 Stat. 1663; TS 640; 12 Bevans 991.

Administrative arrangement for a visa system relating to trade in certain textile products.

Exchange of notes at Montevideo August 24 and September 13, 1984.

Entered into force September 13, 1984.

NP

Amendments

January 19 and July 11, 1988 (NP).

April 8, July 14 and October 4, 1988 (NP).

October 5, 1988 and April 25, 1989 (NP).

VISAS

Agreement relating to passport visas and fees for nonimmigrants.

Exchange of notes at Montevideo November 3 and 8, 1949.

Entered into force November 10, 1949.

64 Stat. (3) B122; TIAS 2046; 12 Bevans 1035; 82 UNTS 45.

UZBEKISTAN

For agreements prior to December 31, 1991, see UNION OF SOVIET SOCIALIST REPUBLICS.

AVIATION

Air transport agreement, with annexes.

Signed at Washington February 27, 1998.

Entered into force February 27, 1998.

TIAS

DEFENSE

Agreement concerning the provision of training under the United States International Military Education and Training (IMET) Program.

Exchange of notes at Tashkent January 25 and February 21, 1995.

Entered into force February 21, 1995.

NP

Agreement regarding grants under the Foreign Assistance Act of 1961, as amended, and the furnishing of defense articles, related training, and other defense services to the Government of Uzbekistan.

Exchange of notes at Tashkent March 18 and May 4, 1999.

Entered into force May 4, 1999.

NP

Acquisition and cross–servicing agreement, with annexes.

Signed at Tampa and Tashkent February 22 and March 26, 2003.

Entered into force March 26, 2003.

TIAS

Protocol pertaining to flights by U.S. aircraft over the territory of the Republic of Uzbekistan.

Signed at Tashkent November 14, 2006.

Entered into force November 14, 2006.

TIAS

ECONOMIC AND TECHNICAL COOPERATION

Agreement regarding cooperation to facilitate the provision of assistance.

Signed at Tashkent March 1, 1994.

Entered into force March 1, 1994.

TIAS 12534.

FINANCE

Investment incentive agreement.

Signed at Tashkent October 28, 1992.

Entered into force October 28, 1992.

TIAS

INTERNATIONAL CRIMINAL COURT

Agreement regarding the surrender of persons to the International Criminal Court.

Signed at Washington September 18, 2002.

Entered into force January 7, 2003.

TIAS

NUCLEAR MATERIAL

Agreement concerning cooperation in the area of prevention of proliferation of nuclear materials and technologies.

Signed at Washington March 12, 2002.

Entered into force March 12, 2002.

TIAS

PEACE CORPS

Agreement concerning the activity of the Peace Corps of the United States in the Republic of Uzbekistan.

Signed at Tashkent November 4, 1992.

Entered into force November 4, 1992.

TIAS 12083.

TRADE

Agreement on trade relations, with exchanges of letters.

Signed at Tashkent November 5, 1993.

Entered into force January 13, 1994.

TIAS 12515.

WEAPONS

Agreement concerning cooperation in the area of the promotion of defense relations and the prevention of proliferation of weapons of mass destruction.

Signed at Washington June 5, 2001.

Entered into force June 5, 2001.

TIAS

Agreement concerning cooperation in the area of demilitarization of biological weapons associated facilities and the prevention of proliferation of biological weapons technology.

Signed at Tashkent October 22, 2001.

Entered into force October 22, 2001.

TIAS

Amendments

June 27 and July 29, 2003.

May 6 and 17, 2004.

August 14 and September 10, 2004

April 12 and December 19, 2005.

September 29 and October 11, 2006.

V

VANUATU [1]

NOTE

1 Treaties and other agreements previously applicable to the New Hebrides are under review.

FINANCE

Millennium challenge compact, with annexes.

Signed at Port Vila March 2, 2006.

Entered into force April 28, 2006.

TIAS

PEACE CORPS

Memorandum of understanding on the establishment of a Peace Corps program in Vanuatu.

Signed at Port Vila October 2, 1989.

Entered into force October 2, 1989.

TIAS 12112.

POSTAL MATTERS

International express mail agreement, with detailed regulations.

Signed at Port Vila and Washington May 23 and June 30, 1989.

Entered into force July 31, 1989.

TIAS 11668.

VENEZUELA

AGRICULTURAL COMMODITIES

Agricultural commodities agreement with exchange of notes.

Signed at Washington May 17, 1962.

Entered into force May 17, 1962.

13 UST 1231; TIAS 5068; 456 UNTS 275.

Amendment

June 18, 1962 (13 UST 1336; TIAS 5091; 459 UNTS 348).

ATOMIC ENERGY

Agreement continuing in effect safeguards and guarantee provisions of the agreement of October 8, 1958, as amended (TIAS 4416, 6945), for cooperation concerning civil uses of atomic energy.

Exchange of notes at Caracas February 18, 1981.

Entered into force February 18, 1981.

33 UST 1111; TIAS 10097; 1281 UNTS 3.

AVIATION

Air transport agreement with exchange of notes.

Signed at Caracas August 14, 1953.

Entered into force August 22, 1953.

4 UST 1493; TIAS 2813; 213 UNTS 99.

Amendments

February 11, 1972 (24 UST 271; TIAS 7549).

September 22, 1976 (27 UST 4111; TIAS 8433).

July 19 and October 10, 1990 (TIAS 11751; 2204 UNTS 214).

Memorandum of agreement concerning the provision of technical assistance to develop and modernize Venezuela's civil aviation infrastructure, with annexes.

Signed at Washington and Caracas February 1 and 4, 1977.

Entered into force February 4, 1977.

29 UST 5300; TIAS 9110.

BOUNDARIES

Maritime boundary treaty.

Signed at Caracas March 28, 1978.

Entered into force November 24, 1980.

32 UST 3100; TIAS 9890.

COMMERCE

Treaty of peace, friendship, navigation and commerce.[1]

Signed at Caracas January 20, 1836.

Entered into force May 31, 1836.

8 Stat. 466; TS 366; 12 Bevans 1038.

NOTE

1 Articles with respect to commerce and navigation terminated January 3, 1851.

CUSTOMS

Agreement relating to duty-free entry privileges for nondiplomatic personnel.

Exchange of notes at Caracas April 7 and 17, 1959.

Entered into force April 17, 1959.

10 UST 1715; TIAS 4323; 358 UNTS 83.

DEFENSE

Agreement relating to the deposit by Venezuela of ten percent of the value of grant military assistance furnished by the United States.

Exchange of notes at Caracas July 19, 1972.

Entered into force July 19, 1972; effective February 7, 1972.

23 UST 1312; TIAS 7411.

Agreement relating to eligibility for United States military assistance and training pursuant to the International Security Assistance and Arms Export Control Act of 1976.

Exchange of notes at Caracas June 16 and 30, 1977.

Entered into force June 30, 1977.

29 UST 1884; TIAS 8907.

General security of military information agreement.

Signed at Caracas July 15, 1983.

Entered into force July 15, 1983.

35 UST 1570; TIAS 10747; 2006 UNTS 363.

Agreement regarding grants under the Foreign Assistance Act of 1961, as amended, and the furnishing of defense articles, related training and other defense services from the United States to Venezuela.

Exchange of letters at Caracas February 26 and 27, 1996.

Entered into force February 27, 1996.

TIAS 12729.

ECONOMIC AND TECHNICAL COOPERATION

Agreement relating to grants to Venezuelan nationals to facilitate their training in the United States.

Exchange of notes at Caracas May 23 and June 7, 1951.

Entered into force June 7, 1951.

2 UST 1302; TIAS 2280; 141 UNTS 273.

Amendment

December 20, 1951, and January 8 and April 8, 1952 (3 UST 4787; TIAS 2648; 205 UNTS 331).

General agreement on technical cooperation.

Exchange of notes at Caracas September 29, 1952.

Entered into force September 29, 1952.

3 UST 5096; TIAS 2700; 186 UNTS 23.

EMPLOYMENT

Agreement concerning employment of dependents of official government employees.

Exchange of notes at Caracas July 18 and 29, 1988.

Entered into force July 29, 1988, except with respect to dependents of employees of permanent missions to international organizations.

TIAS

EXTRADITION

Treaty of extradition, and additional article.

Signed at Caracas January 19 and 21, 1922.

Entered into force April 14, 1923.

43 Stat. 1698; TS 675; 12 Bevans 1128; 49 LNTS 435.

FINANCE

Agreement relating to investment guaranties.

Exchange of notes at Caracas November 26 and 29, 1962.

Entered into force November 29, 1962.

14 UST 374; TIAS 5326; 474 UNTS 107.

Swap agreement between the United States Treasury and the Central Bank of Venezuela/Government of Venezuela, with related letter.

Signed at Washington and Caracas March 10, 1989.

Entered into force March 10, 1989.

TIAS

Swap agreement among the United States Treasury and the Central Bank of Venezuela/Government of Venezuela, with memorandum of understanding.

Signed at Washington and Caracas March 16, 1990.

Entered into force March 16, 1990.

TIAS

Investment incentive agreement.

Signed at Washington June 22, 1990.

Entered into force June 22, 1990.

TIAS 12098.

Agreement supplementing the investment incentive agreement of June 22, 1990, relating to the Export-Import Bank.

Signed at Washington April 22, 1992.

Entered into force April 22, 1992.

TIAS 12098.

JUDICIAL ASSISTANCE

Agreement on procedures for mutual assistance in connection with the Boeing Company matter.

Signed at Washington May 31, 1977.

Entered into force May 31, 1977.

28 UST 5219; TIAS 8623.

Related agreement

December 6 and 8, 1978 (30 UST 2254; TIAS 9333; 1171 UNTS 105).

Agreement regarding cooperation in the prevention and control of money laundering arising from illicit trafficking in narcotic drugs and psychotropic substances, with attachment.

Signed at Washington November 5, 1990.

Entered into force January 1, 1991.

TIAS 12422.

Agreement for mutual assistance in administration of justice in connection with certain banking, financial and other institutions.

Signed at Washington March 17, 1995.

Entered into force March 17, 1995.

TIAS 12615.

MAPPING

Agreement providing for a joint program of aerial photography in Venezuela.

Exchange of notes at Caracas August 23 and September 24, 1957.

Entered into force September 24, 1957.

8 UST 1614; TIAS 3915; 293 UNTS 307.

Agreement governing cooperation in mapping, charting and geodesy.

Signed at Washington and Caracas June 18 and November 26, 1985.

Entered into force November 26, 1985.

TIAS 11209.

Basic exchange and cooperative agreement for topographic mapping, nautical and aeronautical charting and information, geodesy and geophysics, digital data and related mapping, charting and geodesy materials.

Signed at Fairfax March 20, 1996.

Entered into force March 20, 1996.

NP

MARITIME MATTERS

Agreement for exemption of merchant vessels from requirements of admeasurement by port authorities.

Signed at Caracas February 21, 1957.

Entered into force February 21, 1957.

8 UST 289; TIAS 3774; 279 UNTS 199.

MISSIONS, MILITARY

Agreement for the appointment of United States naval officers and personnel to constitute a naval mission to Venezuela.

Signed at Washington August 23, 1950.

Entered into force August 23, 1950.

1 UST 573; TIAS 2104; 92 UNTS 341.

Extension and amendment

March 31 and April 29, 1959 (10 UST 2120; TIAS 4382; 366 UNTS 392).

Agreement for appointment of an Army mission to Venezuela.

Signed at Washington August 10, 1951.

Entered into force August 10, 1951.

2 UST 1570; TIAS 2299; 140 UNTS 345.

Extension and amendment

March 31 and April 29, 1959 (10 UST 2117; TIAS 4381; 366 UNTS 405).

Agreement relating to an Air Force mission to Venezuela.

Signed at Washington January 16, 1953.

Entered into force January 16, 1953.

4 UST 97; TIAS 2766; 199 UNTS 287.

Extension and amendment

March 31 and April 29, 1959 (10 UST 2114; TIAS 4380; 361 UNTS 326).

NARCOTIC DRUGS

Agreement concerning the establishment and operation of a regional office of the Drug Enforcement Administration in Caracas.

Exchange of notes at Caracas August 26, 1974.

Entered into force August 26, 1974.

25 UST 2440; TIAS 7925.

Memorandum of understanding concerning cooperation in the narcotics field.

Signed at Caracas March 28, 1978.

Entered into force March 28, 1978.

30 UST 1012; TIAS 9235; 1152 UNTS 203.

Agreement to suppress illicit traffic in narcotic drugs and psychotropic substances by sea.

Signed at Caracas November 9, 1991.

Entered into force November 9, 1991.

TIAS 11827; 2211 UNTS 387.

Protocol to the agreement of November 9, 1991 to suppress illicit traffic in narcotic drugs and psychotropic substances by sea.

Signed at Caracas July 23, 1997.

Entered into force July 23, 1997.

TIAS

PACIFIC SETTLEMENT OF DISPUTES

Treaty for the advancement of peace.

Signed at Caracas March 21, 1914.

Entered into force February 12, 1921.

42 Stat. 1920; TS 652; 12 Bevans 1122.

PEACE CORPS

Agreement relating to the establishment of a Peace Corps program in Venezuela.

Exchange of notes at Caracas April 14 and May 28, 1962.

Entered into force May 28, 1962.

13 UST 1326; TIAS 5089; 458 UNTS 249.

POSTAL MATTERS

International express mail agreement.

Signed at Washington and Caracas August 10 and 15, 1984.

Entered into force December 1, 1984.

TIAS 11008; 2022 UNTS 89.

SCIENTIFIC COOPERATION

Memorandum of understanding concerning scientific and technical cooperation in the earth and mapping sciences.

Signed at Caracas January 15, 1992.

Entered into force January 15, 1992.

TIAS 11842.

Agreement for scientific and technological cooperation, with annexes.

Signed at Caracas October 12, 1997.

Entered into force February 17, 1998.

TIAS

TAXATION

Agreement for the avoidance of double taxation with respect to shipping and air transport.

Signed at Caracas December 29, 1987.

Entered into force August 10, 1988; effective with respect to taxable years beginning on or before January 1, 1987.

TIAS 11556; 2185 UNTS 353.

Convention for the avoidance of double taxation and the prevention of fiscal evasion with respect to taxes on income and capital, with protocol.

Signed at Caracas January 25, 1999.

Entered into force December 30, 1999.

TIAS

TELECOMMUNICATION

Arrangement for radio communications between amateur stations on behalf of third parties.

Exchange of notes at Caracas November 12, 1959.

Entered into force December 12, 1959.

10 UST 3019; TIAS 4394; 367 UNTS 81.

Agreement relating to the reciprocal granting of authorizations to permit licensed amateur radio operators of either country to operate their stations in the other country.

Exchange of notes at Caracas September 18, 1967.

Entered into force October 3, 1967.

18 UST 2499; TIAS 6348; 693 UNTS 109.

TOURISM

Agreement on the development and facilitation of tourism.

Signed at New York September 27, 1989.

Entered into force September 27, 1989.

TIAS 12402.

TRADE

See also COMMERCE

Convention facilitating the work of traveling salesmen.

Signed at Caracas July 3, 1919.

Entered into force August 18, 1920.

41 Stat. 1719; TS 648; 12 Bevans 1125.

Reciprocal trade agreement.[1]

Signed at Caracas November 6, 1939.

Entered into force provisionally December 16, 1939; definitively December 14, 1940.

54 Stat. 2375; EAS 180; 12 Bevans 1141; 203 LNTS 273.

Supplementary trade agreement.[1]

Signed at Caracas August 28, 1952.

Entered into force October 11, 1952.

3 UST 4195; TIAS 2565; 178 UNTS 51.

Agreement relating to effectiveness of the United States revised tariff schedules to the trade agreement of November 6, 1939, as supplemented.[1]

Exchange of notes at Caracas July 15 and 23, 1963.

Entered into force July 23, 1963.

14 UST 1901; TIAS 5502; 505 UNTS 316.

Agreement terminating in part the reciprocal trade agreement of November 6, 1939, as supplemented.

Exchange of notes at Caracas June 26, 1972.

Entered into force June 26, 1972.

23 UST 1213; TIAS 7387.

NOTE

1 Terminated in part June 30, 1972 by exchange of notes dated June 26, 1972.

VIETNAM, REPUBLIC OF [1]

NOTE

1 The agreements listed below were in force between the United States and the Republic of Viet-Nam (South Viet-Nam). The status of these agreements is under review.

AGRICULTURAL COMMODITIES [1]

NOTE

1 Only the basic agricultural commodities agreements are listed hereunder. Amendments and related agreements, as listed in previous editions of Treaties in Force, are on file in the Office of Treaty Affairs.

Agricultural commodities agreement with memorandum of understanding and exchange of notes.

Signed at Saigon June 17, 1958.

Entered into force June 17, 1958.

9 UST 977; TIAS 4066; 321 UNTS 35.

Agricultural commodities agreement with exchange of notes.

Signed at Saigon October 16, 1959.

Entered into force October 16, 1959.

10 UST 1868; TIAS 4351; 360 UNTS 271.

Agricultural commodities agreement.

Signed at Saigon October 28, 1960.

Entered into force October 28, 1960.

11 UST 2518; TIAS 4637; 401 UNTS 3.

Agricultural commodities agreement with exchange of notes.

Signed at Saigon March 25, 1961.

Entered into force March 25, 1961.

12 UST 350; TIAS 4722; 406 UNTS 187.

Agricultural commodities agreement with exchange of notes.

Signed at Saigon July 14, 1961.

Entered into force July 14, 1961.

12 UST 1112; TIAS 4822; 416 UNTS 133.

Agricultural commodities agreement with exchange of notes.

Signed at Saigon December 27, 1961.

Entered into force December 27, 1961.

12 UST 3169; TIAS 4920; 433 UNTS 185.

Agricultural commodities agreement with exchange of notes.

Signed at Saigon November 21, 1962.

Entered into force November 21, 1962.

13 UST 3831; TIAS 5256; 469 UNTS 101.

Agricultural commodities agreement with exchange of notes.

Signed at Saigon January 9, 1964.

Entered into force January 9, 1964.

15 UST 13; TIAS 5514; 505 UNTS 173.

Agricultural commodities agreement with exchange of notes.

Signed at Saigon September 29, 1964.

Entered into force September 29, 1964.

15 UST 1973; TIAS 5674; 531 UNTS 183.

Agricultural commodities agreement with exchange of notes.

Signed at Saigon May 26, 1965.

Entered into force May 26, 1965.

16 UST 838; TIAS 5821; 550 UNTS 3.

Agricultural commodities agreement with exchange of notes.

Signed at Saigon March 21, 1966.

Entered into force March 21, 1966.

17 UST 129; TIAS 5968; 578 UNTS 165.

Agricultural commodities agreement with exchange of notes.

Signed at Saigon December 15, 1966.

Entered into force December 15, 1966.

17 UST 2321; TIAS 6177; 681 UNTS 63.

Agricultural commodities agreement with annex.

Signed at Saigon March 13, 1967.

Entered into force March 13, 1967.

18 UST 1219; TIAS 6271; 685 UNTS 71.

Agricultural commodities agreement with annex.

Signed at Saigon July 8, 1970.

Entered into force July 8, 1970.

21 UST 2443; TIAS 6983; 775 UNTS 107.

Agricultural commodities agreement.

Signed at Saigon October 8, 1974.

Entered into force October 8, 1974.

25 UST 2891; TIAS 7952.

CLAIMS

Agreement relating to mutual waiver of government claims for damages to government property and for injury or death of members of armed services.

Exchange of notes at Saigon February 9, 1965.

Entered into force February 9, 1965.

16 UST 140; TIAS 5773; 542 UNTS 175.

COMMERCE

Treaty of amity and economic relations.

Signed at Saigon April 3, 1961.

Entered into force November 30, 1961.

12 UST 1703; TIAS 4890; 424 UNTS 137.

DEFENSE

Agreement relating to the disposition of equipment and materials furnished by the United States found surplus to the needs of the Vietnamese armed forces.

Exchange of notes at Saigon March 1 and May 10, 1955.

Entered into force May 10, 1955.

7 UST 837; TIAS 3563; 273 UNTS 157.

Agreement relating to the transfer of scrap to Viet-Nam as supplementary military assistance.

Exchange of notes at Saigon November 8 and December 14, 1972.

Entered into force December 14, 1972.

23 UST 4263; TIAS 7534.

Amendment

September 3 and October 14, 1974 (25 UST 2906; TIAS 7953).

ECONOMIC AND TECHNICAL COOPERATION

Economic cooperation agreement with exchange of notes.

Signed at Saigon September 7, 1951.

Entered into force September 7, 1951.

2 UST 2205; TIAS 2346; 174 UNTS 165.

Amendment

June 7, 1962 (13 UST 1279; TIAS 5076; 458 UNTS 300).

Agreement providing for additional direct economic assistance pursuant to the economic cooperation agreement of September 7, 1951.

Exchange of notes at Saigon February 21 and March 7, 1955.

Entered into force March 7, 1955; operative from January 1, 1955.

7 UST 2507; TIAS 3640; 277 UNTS 285.

FINANCE

Agreement relating to investment guaranties under section 413 (b)(4) of the Mutual Security Act of 1954, as amended.

Exchange of notes at Washington November 5, 1957.

Entered into force November 5, 1957.

8 UST 1869; TIAS 3932; 300 UNTS 23.

Amendment

August 8, 1963 (14 UST 1210; TIAS 5419; 488 UNTS 270).

Agreement modifying the agreement of November 5, 1957, as amended, relating to investment guaranties.

Exchange of notes at Saigon December 16, 1969 and February 12, 1970.

Entered into force February 12, 1970.

21 UST 1148; TIAS 6869; 745 UNTS 312.

INFORMATIONAL MEDIA GUARANTIES

Agreement providing for an informational media guaranty program pursuant to Section 1011 of the United States Information and Educational Exchange Act of 1948, as amended.

Exchange of notes at Saigon October 11 and November 3, 1955.

Entered into force November 3, 1955.

6 UST 3940; TIAS 3402; 239 UNTS 195.

MUTUAL SECURITY

Agreement relating to the assurances required by the Mutual Security Act of 1951.

Exchange of notes at Saigon December 18, 1951, and January 3, 16, and 19, 1952.

Entered into force January 3, 1952.

3 UST 4672; TIAS 2623; 205 UNTS 127.

PUBLICATIONS

Agreement relating to the exchange of official publications.

Exchange of notes at Saigon April 4, 1961.

Entered into force April 4, 1961.

12 UST 310; TIAS 4717; 405 UNTS 77.

RELIEF SUPPLIES AND PACKAGES

Agreement relating to duty-free entry and defrayment of inland transportation charges on relief supplies and packages.

Exchange of notes at Saigon August 20 and 26, 1954.

Entered into force August 26, 1954.

5 UST 2531; TIAS 3115; 234 UNTS 111.

SURPLUS PROPERTY

Agreement relating to the disposal of United States excess property in Viet-Nam.

Exchange of notes at Saigon November 9, 1968.

Entered into force November 9, 1968.

19 UST 6703; TIAS 6586; 702 UNTS 293.

TAXATION

Agreement regarding income tax administration.

Exchange of notes at Saigon March 31 and May 3, 1967.

Entered into force May 3, 1967.

18 UST 546; TIAS 6262; 685 UNTS 207.

TELECOMMUNICATION

Agreement relating to television broadcasting in Viet-Nam.

Exchange of notes at Saigon January 3, 1966.

Entered into force January 3, 1966.

17 UST 44; TIAS 5954; 579 UNTS 99.

TRADE-MARKS

Declaration respecting the rights of nationals concerning trademark protection, with related note.

Exchange of notes at Washington November 3, 1953, and October 25, 1954, and related note of November 22, 1954.

Entered into force October 25, 1954.

5 UST 2400; TIAS 3100; 235 UNTS 11.

VIETNAM, SOCIALIST REPUBLIC OF [1]

NOTE

1 The United States established diplomatic relations with the Socialist Republic of Vietnam on July 12, 1995.

AGRICULTURE

Memorandum of agreement on cooperation in agriculture and related fields.

Signed at Washington June 21, 2005.

Entered into force June 21, 2005.

TIAS

AVIATION

Air Transport agreement, with annexes.

Signed at Washington December 4, 2003.

Entered into force January 14, 2004.

TIAS

CHILDREN

Agreement regarding cooperation on the adoption of children.

Signed at Washington June 21, 2005.

Entered into force September 1, 2005.

TIAS

CLAIMS

Agreement concerning the settlement of certain property claims.

Signed at Hanoi January 28, 1995.

Entered into force January 28, 1995.

TIAS 12602.

COPYRIGHT

Agreement on the establishment of copyright relations.

Signed at Hanoi June 27, 1997.

Entered into force December 23, 1998.

TIAS

Amendment

December 23, 1998.

DEFENSE

Agreement concerning the provision of equipment, training and related services under the United States International Military Education and Training (IMET) Program.

Exchange of notes at Hanoi June 17, 2005.

Entered into force June 17, 2005.

NP

ECONOMIC AND TECHNICAL COOPERATION

Agreement for economic and technical cooperation.

Signed at Washington June 22, 2005.

Entered into force July 27, 2005.

TIAS

FINANCE

Agreement regarding the consolidation and rescheduling of certain debts owed to, guaranteed by, or insured by the United States Government and the Agency for International Development, with annexes.

Signed at Hanoi April 7, 1997.

Entered into force June 23, 1997.

NP

Agreement regarding the operations of the Overseas Private Investment Corporation in Vietnam.

Signed at Washington and Hanoi March 19 and 26, 1998.

Entered into force March 26, 1998.

TIAS

Project incentive agreement regarding the operations of the Export-Import Bank of the United States in Vietnam.

Signed at Hanoi December 9, 1999.

Entered into force December 9, 1999.

TIAS

HEALTH

Agreement on health and medical sciences cooperation.

Signed at Washington July 20, 2006.

Entered into force July 20, 2006.

TIAS

POSTAL MATTERS

International express mail agreement, with detailed regulations.

Signed at Seoul September 13, 1994.

Entered into force December 1, 1994.

NP

PROPERTY

Agreement concerning the transfer of diplomatic properties, with appendices and amendment.

Signed at Hanoi January 28, 1995.

Entered into force January 28, 1995.

TIAS

REFUGEES

Agreement on the implementation of the special released reeducation center detainees resettlement program, with annex.

Exchange of letters at Washington and Hanoi August 18 and 28, 1989.

Entered into force August 28, 1989.

TIAS

SCIENTIFIC COOPERATION

Agreement on scientific and technological cooperation, with annexes.

Signed at Hanoi November 17, 2000.

Entered into force March 26, 2001.

TIAS

TRADE

Agreement on trade relations, with annexes, schedules and exchange of letters.

Signed at Washington July 13, 2000.

Entered into force December 10, 2001.

TIAS

Agreement relating to trade in cotton, wool, man-made fiber, non-cotton vegetable fiber and silk blend textiles and textile products, wth annexes.

Signed at Hanoi July 17, 2003.

Entered into force July 17, 2003.

NP

Amendment

July 22, 2004.

W

WESTERN SAMOA

On January 1, 1962, Western Samoa became an independent state. In an exchange of letters dated November 30, 1962 between the Office of the High Commissioner for New Zealand and the Prime Minister of Western Samoa, the Government of Western Samoa agreed that "All obligations and responsibilities of the Government of New Zealand which arise from any valid international instrument are, from January 1, 1962, assumed by the Government of Western Samoa in so far as such instrument may be held to have application to or in respect of Western Samoa."

DEFENSE

Status of forces agreement.

Signed at Apia June 25, 1990.

Entered into force June 25, 1990.

TIAS

Agreement concerning the provision of training related to defense articles under the United States International Military Education and Training (IMET) program.

Exchange of notes at Apia December 1, 1992 and March 8, 1993.

Entered into force March 8, 1993.

NP

EMPLOYMENT

Agreement relating to the employment of dependents of official government employees.

Exchange of notes at New York and Washington February 27 and March 15, 1995.

Entered into force March 15, 1995.

TIAS 12613.

FINANCE

Investment guaranty agreement.

Signed at Wellington and Apia June 5 and July 22, 1969.

Entered into force July 22, 1969.

20 UST 2766; TIAS 6745; 720 UNTS 53.

PEACE CORPS

Agreement relating to the establishment of a Peace Corps program in Western Samoa.

Exchange of notes at Wellington October 1, 1970.

Entered into force October 1, 1970.

21 UST 2186; TIAS 6967; 764 UNTS 281.

POSTAL MATTERS

International express mail agreement, with detailed regulations.

Signed at Apia and Washington February 16 and March 18, 1993.

Entered into force May 1, 1993.

NP

WORLD FOOD PROGRAM

ECONOMIC AND TECHNICAL COOPERATION

Agency for International Development

July 9 and 23, 1976 (29 UST 1001; TIAS 8860).

WORLD HEALTH ORGANIZATION

CHEMICAL SAFETY

Memorandum of understanding regarding U.S. Environmental Protection Agency collaboration in the international program on chemical safety.

Signed at Washington and Geneva January 19 and March 19, 1981.

Entered into force March 19, 1981.

TIAS

WORLD INTELLECTUAL PROPERTY ORGANIZATION

PATENTS

Agreement regarding the functioning of the United States Patent and Trademark Office as an international searching authority and international preliminary examining authority under the Patent Cooperation Treaty, with annexes.

Signed at Geneva October 1, 1997.

Entered into force January 1, 1998.

TIAS

TAXATION

Tax reimbursement agreement, with annex.

Signed at Geneva December 5, 1988.

Entered into force December 5, 1988.

TIAS 11625; 2191 UNTS 159.

WORLD METEOROLOGICAL ORGANIZATION

TAXATION

Agreement relating to a procedure for United States income tax reimbursement, with annex.

Signed at Geneva January 23, 1987.

Entered into force January 23, 1987.

TIAS 11293; 2174 UNTS 207.

WORLD TRADE ORGANIZATION

TAXATION

Tax reimbursement agreement, with annex.

Signed at Geneva December 22, 2000.

Entered into force December 22, 2000.

TIAS

Y

YEMEN

The People's Democratic Republic of Yemen and the Yemen Arab Republic merged into a single sovereign State on May 22, 1990 called the Republic of Yemen. In a note dated May 19, 1990, to the Secretary-General of the United Nations, it was stated that ... "All treaties and agreements concluded between either the Yemen Arab Republic or the People's Democratic Republic of Yemen and other States and international organizations in accordance with international law which are in force on May 22, 1990 will remain in effect, and international relations existing on May 22, 1990 between the People's Democratic Republic of Yemen and the Yemen Arab Republic and other States will continue."....

These agreements are under review.

AGRICULTURAL COMMODITIES

Agricultural commodities agreement, with related letter.
Signed at Sanaa June 19, 1984.
Entered into force June 19, 1984.
NP

Agricultural commodities agreement.
Signed at Sanaa April 15, 1985.
Entered into force April 15, 1985.
NP

Amendment
July 30, 1985 (NP).

Agricultural commodities agreement.
Signed at Sanaa February 18, 1986.
Entered into force February 18, 1986.
NP

Amendment
July 26, 1986 (NP).

Agricultural commodities agreement.
Signed at Sanaa May 6, 1987.
Entered into force May 6, 1987.
NP

Amendments
July 2, 1987 (NP).
August 1, 1987 (NP).

Related agreements
March 9, 1988 (NP).
January 25, 1990 (NP).

Agricultural commodities agreement.
Signed at Sanaa September 29, 1988.
Entered into force September 29, 1988.
NP

COMMERCE

Agreement relating to friendship and commerce.
Exchange of notes at Sanaa May 4, 1946.
Entered into force May 4, 1946.
60 Stat. 1782; TIAS 1535; 12 Bevans 1223; 4 UNTS 165.

DEFENSE

Agreement concerning the provision of training related to defense articles under the United States International Military Education and Training (IMET) Program.
Exchange of notes at Sanaa September 9, 1986 and May 19, 1987.
Entered into force May 19, 1987.
TIAS 12015.

Agreement regarding grants under the Foreign Assistance Act of 1961, as amended, and the furnishing of defense articles, related training and other defense services from the United States to Yemen.
Exchange of notes at Sanaa June 5 and July 20, 1999.
Entered into force July 20, 1999.
NP

ECONOMIC AND TECHNICAL COOPERATION

Economic, technical, and related assistance agreement, with related letter.
Signed at Sanaa April 20, 1974.
Entered into force April 20, 1974.
25 UST 715; TIAS 7820.

Agency for International Development
March 31, 1976 (29 UST 22; TIAS 8787; 1115 UNTS 35).

FINANCE

24 UST 845; TIAS 7586.

Agreement regarding the consolidation and rescheduling of certain debts owed to, guaranteed by, or insured by the United States Government and its agencies, with annexes.
Signed at Sanaa April 8, 1997.
Entered into force May 22, 1997.
NP

Agreement regarding consolidation and rescheduling of certain debts owed to, guaranteed by, or insured by the United States Government and its agency, with annexes.
Signed at Sanaa May 19, 1998.
Entered into force August 10, 1998.
NP

Agreement regarding the reduction and reorganization of certain debts owed to, guaranteed by, or insured by the United States Government, with annexes.
Signed at Sanaa July 31, 2002.
Entered into force October 8, 2002.
NP

INTERNATIONAL CRIMINAL COURT

Arrangement regarding the surrender of persons to international tribunals.
Exchange of notes at Washington and Sanaa December 10 and 17, 2003.
Entered into force December 17, 2003.
TIAS

PEACE CORPS

Agreement relating to the establishment of a Peace Corps program in the Yemen Arab Republic.
Exchange of notes at Sanaa September 30, 1972 and January 29, 1973.
Entered into force January 29, 1973.
24 UST 853; TIAS 7588.

POSTAL MATTERS

International express mail agreement, with detailed regulations.
Signed at Sanaa and Washington June 17 and July 23, 1992.
Entered into force September 21, 1992.
TIAS 11873.

YUGOSLAVIA

Yugoslavia has dissolved. For agreements prior to dissolution, see below. Subsequent agreements are listed under individual country headings.

Section 2 of Treaties in Force covers multilateral treaties and agreements. Where a multilateral treaty action was taken prior to dissolution, "Yugoslavia" is retained; where a successor state has taken action it is listed separately.

The status of the agreements listed below is under review.

AGRICULTURAL COMMODITIES

Agricultural commodities agreement, and related letters.
Signed at Belgrade January 5, 1955.
Entered into force January 5, 1955.
6 UST 45; TIAS 3167; 251 UNTS 29.

Amendments
May 12, 1955 (6 UST 1141; TIAS 3253; 251 UNTS 422).
October 1, 1955 (6 UST 6011; TIAS 3446; 270 UNTS 408).

January 19, 1956 (7 UST 146; TIAS 3486; 268 UNTS 386).

September 10 and 11, 1958 (10 UST 155; TIAS 4177; 340 UNTS 376).

April 15, 1964 (15 UST 402; TIAS 5571; 524 UNTS 306).

Agreement providing for the furnishing of additional wheat to Yugoslavia.

Exchange of notes at Belgrade May 12, 1955.

Entered into force May 12, 1955.

6 UST 1139; TIAS 3252; 251 UNTS 331.

Agricultural commodities agreement with exchanges of notes.

Signed at Belgrade November 3, 1956.

Entered into force November 3, 1956.

7 UST 3093; TIAS 3688; 277 UNTS 119.

Amendments

January 23 and 24, 1957 (8 UST 31; TIAS 3735; 277 UNTS 128).

March 22, 1957 (8 UST 375; TIAS 3785; 279 UNTS 360).

December 27, 1957 (8 UST 2489; TIAS 3970; 307 UNTS 316).

April 15, 1964 (15 UST 402; TIAS 5571; 524 UNTS 306).

Agricultural commodities agreement with exchanges of notes.

Signed at Belgrade February 3, 1958.

Entered into force February 3, 1958.

9 UST 256; TIAS 4000; 304 UNTS 293.

Amendment

June 26, 1958 (9 UST 949; TIAS 4060; 317 UNTS 370).

Agricultural commodities agreement with exchange of notes.

Signed at Belgrade December 22, 1958.

Entered into force December 22, 1958.

9 UST 1513; TIAS 4153; 338 UNTS 243.

Amendments

July 9, 1959 (10 UST 1291; TIAS 4270; 354 UNTS 438).

April 15, 1964 (15 UST 402; TIAS 5571; 524 UNTS 306).

Agricultural commodities agreement with exchanges of notes.

Signed at Belgrade June 3, 1960.

Entered into force June 3, 1960.

11 UST 1524; TIAS 4497; 376 UNTS 243.

Amendment

July 1, 1961 (12 UST 1282; TIAS 4850; 421 UNTS 344).

Agricultural commodities agreement with exchanges of notes.

Signed at Belgrade April 28, 1961.

Entered into force April 28, 1961.

12 UST 600; TIAS 4756; 409 UNTS 171.

Amendments

July 1, 1961 (12 UST 1093; TIAS 4817; 416 UNTS 378).

April 15, 1964 (15 UST 402; TIAS 5571; 524 UNTS 306).

Agricultural commodities agreement, and exchanges of notes.

Signed at Belgrade December 28, 1961.

Entered into force December 28, 1961.

12 UST 3185; TIAS 4923; 434 UNTS 111.

Amendments

April 21, 1962 (13 UST 458; TIAS 5009; 442 UNTS 348).

April 15, 1964 (15 UST 402; TIAS 5571; 524 UNTS 306).

May 21, 1965 (16 UST 782; TIAS 5810; 546 UNTS 388).

Agricultural commodities agreement with exchange of notes.

Signed at Belgrade April 21, 1962.

Entered into force April 21, 1962.

13 UST 452; TIAS 5008; 442 UNTS 123.

Amendments

May 18, 1962 (13 UST 1097; TIAS 5053; 451 UNTS 350).

November 28, 1962 (13 UST 2562; TIAS 5222; 460 UNTS 352).

December 20, 1968 (19 UST 7844; TIAS 6620; 714 UNTS 266).

Agricultural commodities agreement with exchanges of notes.

Signed at Belgrade November 28, 1962.

Entered into force November 28, 1962.

13 UST 2578; TIAS 5224; 460 UNTS 185.

Amendments

April 19 and May 9, 1963 (14 UST 905; TIAS 5376; 479 UNTS 412).

August 19 and November 3, 1965 (16 UST 1756; TIAS 5903; 573 UNTS 336).

Agricultural commodities agreement with exchange of notes.

Signed at Belgrade April 27, 1964.

Entered into force April 27, 1964.

15 UST 372; TIAS 5566; 526 UNTS 73.

Agricultural commodities agreement with exchange of notes.

Signed at Belgrade April 27, 1964.

Entered into force April 27, 1964.

15 UST 381; TIAS 5567; 526 UNTS 89.

Amendment

December 20, 1968 (19 UST 7844; TIAS 6620; 714 UNTS 266).

Agricultural commodities agreement.

Signed at Belgrade April 28, 1964.

Entered into force April 28, 1964.

15 UST 388; TIAS 5568; 526 UNTS 103.

Amendment

December 29 and 30, 1965 (16 UST 2064; TIAS 5945; 574 UNTS 266).

Agricultural commodities agreement with exchange of notes.

Signed at Belgrade October 28, 1964.

Entered into force October 28, 1964.

15 UST 2051; TIAS 5684; 533 UNTS 3.

Agricultural commodities agreement with exchange of notes.

Signed at Belgrade October 29, 1964.

Entered into force October 29, 1964.

15 UST 2058; TIAS 5685; 533 UNTS 17.

Amendment

December 29 and 30, 1965 (16 UST 2064; TIAS 5945; 574 UNTS 266).

Agricultural commodities agreement, with exchange of notes.

Signed at Belgrade March 16, 1965.

Entered into force March 16, 1965.

16 UST 134; TIAS 5772; 542 UNTS 161.

Amendment

December 20, 1968 (19 UST 7844; TIAS 6620; 714 UNTS 266).

Agricultural commodities agreement, with exchange of notes.

Signed at Belgrade July 16, 1965.

Entered into force July 16, 1965.

16 UST 987; TIAS 5840; 549 UNTS 111.

Amendment

December 20, 1968 (19 UST 7844; TIAS 6620; 714 UNTS 266).

Agricultural commodities agreement, with exchange of notes.

Signed at Belgrade November 22, 1965.

Entered into force November 22, 1965.

16 UST 1775; TIAS 5910; 574 UNTS 211.

Amendment

January 21, 1966 (17 UST 1; TIAS 5948; 574 UNTS 224).

Agricultural commodities agreement with exchange of notes.

Signed at Belgrade April 11, 1966.

Entered into force April 11, 1966.

17 UST 771; TIAS 6031; 580 UNTS 239.

ATOMIC ENERGY

Agreement providing for a grant to assist in the acquisition of certain nuclear research and training equipment and materials.

Exchange of notes at Belgrade April 19, 1961.

Entered into force April 19, 1961.

12 UST 398; TIAS 4731; 409 UNTS 163.

AVIATION

Nonscheduled air service agreement, with annexes, and protocol.

Signed at Belgrade September 27, 1973.

Entered into force provisionally September 27, 1973; definitively April 16, 1974.

25 UST 659; TIAS 7819.

Amendments

December 15, 1977 (30 UST 4350; TIAS 9460; 1203 UNTS 369).

January 15 and July 6, 1987 (TIAS 11547).

Air transport agreement.

Signed at Washington December 15, 1977.

Entered into force provisionally December 15, 1977; definitively May 15, 1979.

30 UST 2817; TIAS 9364; 1203 UNTS 205.

Amendment

January 15 and July 6, 1987 (TIAS 11547).

CLAIMS

Agreement relating to the settlement of pecuniary claims against Yugoslavia, and accompanying aide memoire and notes.

Signed at Washington July 19, 1948.

Entered into force July 19, 1948.

62 Stat. 2658; TIAS 1803; 12 Bevans 1277; 89 UNTS 43.

Agreement regarding claims of United States nationals, with exchange of notes and minute of interpretation.

Signed at Belgrade November 5, 1964.

Entered into force January 20, 1965.

TIAS 5750; 16 UST 1; 550 UNTS 31.

COMMERCE

Treaty of commerce.

Signed at Belgrade October 2/14 1881.

Entered into force November 15, 1882.

22 Stat. 963; TS 319; 12 Bevans 1227.

CONSULS

Consular convention.

Signed at Belgrade October 2 and 14, 1881.

Entered into force November 15, 1882.

22 Stat. 968; TS 320; 12 Bevans 1233.

Arrangement providing for the taking of testimony by consular officers.

Exchange of notes at Belgrade October 17 and 24, 1938.

Entered into force October 24, 1938.

12 Bevans 1261.

CULTURAL RELATIONS

Memorandum of understanding relating to the establishment, maintenance, and operation of American reading rooms in Yugoslavia.

Signed at Belgrade June 14, 1961.

Entered into force provisionally June 14, 1961; definitively December 28, 1961.

20 UST 2826; TIAS 6753; 723 UNTS 133.

Implementing agreements

Ljubljana: June 5, 1970 (22 UST 398; TIAS 7073; 791 UNTS 293).

Skopje: April 13, 1972 (24 UST 457; TIAS 7564).

Sarajevo: July 18, 1973 (24 UST 2316; TIAS 7757).

Titograd: June 25, 1979 (31 UST 301; TIAS 9612; 1202 UNTS 173).

CUSTOMS

Agreement relating to reciprocal customs privileges for consular officers.

Exchange of notes at Washington May 21, 1956.

Entered into force July 30, 1956.

7 UST 2234; TIAS 3622; 281 UNTS 93.

Agreement regarding mutual assistance between customs administrations.

Signed at Belgrade April 11, 1990.

Entered into force November 18, 1990.

TIAS 12074.

DEFENSE

Memorandum of understanding relating to offshore procurement with standard contract and related notes.

Signed at Belgrade October 18, 1954.

Entered into force October 18, 1954.

7 UST 849; TIAS 3567; 273 UNTS 163.

Agreement relating to the termination of military assistance furnished on a grant basis by the United States to Yugoslavia and amending the memorandum of understanding of October 18, 1954 relating to offshore procurement.

Exchange of notes at Belgrade August 25, 1959.

Entered into force August 25, 1959.

10 UST 1468; TIAS 4300; 357 UNTS 77.

Agreement relating to the purchase by Yugoslavia of military equipment, materials, and services.

Exchange of notes at Belgrade August 25, 1959.

Entered into force August 25, 1959.

10 UST 1474; TIAS 4301; 357 UNTS 87.

ECONOMIC AND TECHNICAL COOPERATION

Agreement relating to publicity for distribution program of emergency food assistance.

Exchange of notes at Belgrade November 17 and 21, 1950.

Entered into force November 21, 1950.

1 UST 757; TIAS 2146; 93 UNTS 39.

Agreement governing the furnishing of assistance under the Yugoslav Emergency Relief Assistance Act of 1950.

Signed at Belgrade January 6, 1951.

Entered into force January 6, 1951.

2 UST 13; TIAS 2174; 122 UNTS 137.

Economic cooperation agreement.

Signed at Belgrade January 8, 1952.

Entered into force January 8, 1952.

3 UST 1; TIAS 2384; 152 UNTS 61.

Amendment

February 25 and March 10, 1953 (4 UST 439; TIAS 2791; 207 UNTS 360).

EDUCATION

Agreement for financing certain educational exchange programs.

Signed at Belgrade November 9, 1964.

Entered into force November 9, 1964.

15 UST 2081; TIAS 5689; 533 UNTS 39.

Amendment

January 20, 1984 (TIAS 10980).

EXTRADITION

Extradition treaty.

Signed at Belgrade October 25, 1901.

Entered into force June 12, 1902.

32 Stat. 1890; TS 406; 12 Bevans 1238.

FINANCE

Agreement relating to the funding of the indebtedness of Yugoslavia to the United States.

Signed at Washington May 3, 1926; operative June 15, 1925.

12 Bevans 1246; Treasury Department print.

Counterpart release agreement, with annex.

Signed at Belgrade April 16, 1954.

Entered into force April 16, 1954.

5 UST 2853; TIAS 3142; 237 UNTS 77.

Agreement relating to the disbursement of dinars made available for the procurement of certain agricultural commodities.

Exchange of notes at Belgrade May 12, 1955.

Entered into force May 12, 1955.

6 UST 1144; TIAS 3254; 251 UNTS 343.

Amendment

October 17, 1958 (9 UST 1499; TIAS 4150; 338 UNTS 392).

Agreement relating to the use of economic assistance funds for the financing of wheat purchases.

Exchange of notes at Belgrade May 12, 1955.

Entered into force May 12, 1955.

6 UST 1147; TIAS 3255; 251 UNTS 337.

Agreement providing for certain economic assistance on a loan basis pursuant to section 402 of the Mutual Security Act of 1954.

Exchange of notes at Belgrade January 19, 1956.

Entered into force January 19, 1956.

7 UST 149; TIAS 3487; 240 UNTS 121.

Memorandum of agreement regarding the rescheduling of certain payments under agricultural commodities agreements and various AID loans with annexes and exchange of aide memoire.

Signed at Belgrade October 15, 1971.

Entered into force March 30, 1972.

23 UST 222; TIAS 7298.

Agreement relating to investment guaranties, with aide memoire.

Exchange of notes at Belgrade January 18, 1973.

Entered into force May 30, 1973.

24 UST 1091; TIAS 7630.

Swap agreement between the U.S. Treasury and the Central Bank of the Federated Republics of Yugoslavia, with related letter.

Signed at Washington and Belgrade June 10, 1988.

Entered into force June 10, 1988.

TIAS

LEND-LEASE

Preliminary agreement regarding principles applying to mutual aid in the prosecution of the war against aggression.

Signed at Washington July 24, 1942.

Entered into force July 24, 1942.

56 Stat. 1570; EAS 263; 12 Bevans 1263; 34 UNTS 361.

Agreement regarding settlement for lend-lease, military relief, and claims.

Signed at Washington July 19, 1948.

Entered into force July 19, 1948.

62 Stat. 2133; TIAS 1779; 12 Bevans 1273; 34 UNTS 195.

MARITIME MATTERS

Agreement concerning the reciprocal recognition of tonnage certificates.

Exchange of notes at Washington June 12 and 16, 1958.

Entered into force June 16, 1958.

9 UST 709; TIAS 4047; 317 UNTS 31.

NARCOTIC DRUGS

Arrangement for the direct exchange of certain information regarding traffic in narcotic drugs.

Exchange of notes at Belgrade February 17, 1928, and May 8, 1930.

Entered into force May 8, 1930.

12 Bevans 1259.

PACIFIC SETTLEMENT OF DISPUTES

Treaty of arbitration.

Signed at Washington January 21, 1929.

Entered into force June 22, 1929.

46 Stat. 2293; TS 790; 12 Bevans 1253; 93 LNTS 307.

Treaty of conciliation.

Signed at Washington January 21, 1929.

Entered into force June 22, 1929.

46 Stat. 2297; TS 791; 12 Bevans 1256; 93 LNTS 301.

POSTAL MATTERS

Agreement concerning the exchange of parcel post and regulations of execution.

Signed at Belgrade August 14 and at Washington September 1, 1950.

Entered into force January 1, 1950.

2 UST 2079; TIAS 2336; 137 UNTS 131.

International express mail agreement, with detailed regulations.

Signed at Belgrade and Washington January 22 and March 1, 1990.

Entered into force March 30, 1990.

TIAS 11713.

PUBLICATIONS

Agreement relating to the exchange of official publications.

Exchange of letters at Belgrade June 13 and 23, 1955.

Entered into force June 23, 1955.

TIAS

RELIEF SUPPLIES AND PACKAGES

Agreement for duty-free entry and defrayment of inland transportation and related costs of relief supplies and packages, and note of December 3, 1952.

Signed at Belgrade December 3, 1952.

Entered into force December 3, 1952.

3 UST 5318; TIAS 2735; 185 UNTS 183.

TAXATION

Agreement relating to relief from taxation of United States Government expenditures in Yugoslavia for facilities, equipment, materials, or services.

Exchange of letters at Belgrade July 23, 1953.

Entered into force July 23, 1953.

4 UST 2208; TIAS 2871; 221 UNTS 365.

TELECOMMUNICATION

Agreement relating to the reciprocal granting of authorization to permit licensed amateur radio operators who are citizens of either country to operate their stations in the other country.

Exchange of notes at Belgrade October 31 and November 11, 1980.

Entered into force November 11, 1980.

32 UST 4173; TIAS 9936; 1267 UNTS 377.

TOURISM

Agreement on cooperation in the field of tourism.

Signed at Washington February 2, 1984.

Entered into force June 18, 1984.

35 UST 4517; TIAS 10954; 2019 UNTS 517.

TRADE

See also COMMERCE

Agreement providing for consultations should exports of cotton, wool, and man-made fiber textiles and apparel products from Yugoslavia cause market disruption in the United States.

Exchange of notes at Belgrade January 14, 1976.

Entered into force January 14, 1976.

27 UST 1622; TIAS 8271.

VISAS

Agreement relating to the reduction of passport visa fees for nonimmigrants.

Exchange of notes at Belgrade December 24 and 29, 1925; operative February 1, 1926.

12 Bevans 1243.

Understanding relating to entry and exit visas for American citizens visiting Yugoslavia.

Exchange of notes at Belgrade March 23 and 25, 1950.

Entered into force March 25, 1950; operative April 1, 1950.

1 UST 471; TIAS 2087; 98 UNTS 195.

Agreement for the abolition of all nonimmigrant visa fees.

Exchange of notes at Belgrade December 30, 1963, March 27 and April 4, 1964.

Entered into force April 15, 1964.

15 UST 355; TIAS 5564; 526 UNTS 47.

Z

ZAMBIA

On October 24, 1964, Zambia (former Northern Rhodesia) became an independent state. In a note dated September 1, 1965 to the Secretary General of the United Nations, the Minister of Foreign Affairs of Zambia made a Declaration reading in part as follows:

"I have the honour to inform you that the Government of Zambia, conscious of the desirability of maintaining existing legal relationships, and conscious of its obligations under international law to honour its treaty commitments acknowledges that many treaty rights and obligations of the Government of the United Kingdom in respect of Northern Rhodesia were succeeded to by Zambia upon independence by virtue of customary international law.

Since, however, it is likely that in virtue of customary international law certain treaties may have lapsed at the date of independence of Zambia, it seems essential that each treaty should be subjected to legal examination. It is proposed after this examination has been completed, to indicate which, if any, of the treaties which may have lapsed by customary international law the Government of Zambia wishes to treat as having lapsed.

The question of Zambia's succession to treaties is complicated by legal questions arising from the entrustment of external affairs powers to the former Federation of Rhodesia and Nyasaland. Until these questions have been resolved it will remain unclear to what extent Zambia remains affected by the treaties contracted by the former Federation.

It is desired that it be presumed that each treaty has been legally succeeded to by Zambia and that action be based on this presumption until a decision is reached that it should be regarded as having lapsed. Should the Government of Zambia be of the opinion that it has legally succeeded to a treaty, and wishes to terminate the operation of the treaty, it will in due course give notice of termination in the terms thereof."

AGRICULTURAL COMMODITIES

Agricultural commodities agreement.

Signed at Lusaka August 24, 1976.

Entered into force August 24, 1976.

27 UST 3451; TIAS 8377.

Agricultural commodities agreement, with minutes.

Signed at Lusaka December 3, 1976.

Entered into force December 3, 1976.

28 UST 8768; TIAS 8771; 1095 UNTS 129.

Agricultural commodities agreement.

Signed at Lusaka August 4, 1978.

Entered into force August 4, 1978.

TIAS 10590; 1871 UNTS 23.

Amendment

September 11 and 12, 1978 (TIAS 10590; 1871 UNTS 23).

Related agreements

July 19, 1979 (TIAS 10591; 1871 UNTS 25).

December 21, 1979 (TIAS 10592; 1871 UNTS 27).

July 22, 1981 (TIAS 10593; 1871 UNTS 29).

June 20, 1982 (TIAS 10594; 1871 UNTS 31).

July 16, 1982 (TIAS 10594; 1871 UNTS 31).

February 18, 1983 (TIAS 10662).

Agricultural commodities agreement.

Signed at Lusaka July 17, 1984.

Entered into force July 17, 1984.

NP

Agricultural commodities agreement.

Signed at Lusaka July 9, 1985.

Entered into force July 9, 1985.

NP

Related agreements

May 23, 1986 (NP).

July 27, 1987 (NP).

Agricultural commodities agreement.

Signed at Lusaka April 25, 1988.

Entered into force April 25, 1988.

NP

Related agreement

March 10, 1989 (NP).

AVIATION

Arrangement between the United States and the United Kingdom relating to pilot licenses to operate civil aircraft.

Exchange of notes at Washington March 28 and April 5, 1935.

Entered into force May 5, 1935.

49 Stat. 3731; EAS 77; 12 Bevans 513; 162 UNTS 59.

Agreement between the United States and the United Kingdom relating to air services.

Signed at Bermuda February 11, 1946.

Entered into force February 11, 1946.

60 Stat. 1499; TIAS 1507; 12 Bevans 726; 3 UNTS 253.

Agreement on civil aviation security.

Exchange of notes at Lusaka February 16 and March 28, 1988.

Entered into force March 28, 1988.

TIAS 11573; 2185 UNTS 299.

CONSULS

Consular convention between the United States and the United Kingdom.

Signed at Washington June 6, 1951.

Entered into force September 7, 1952.

3 UST 3426; TIAS 2494; 165 UNTS 121.

DEFENSE

Agreement concerning the provision of training related to defense articles under the United States International Military, Education and Training (IMET) Program.

Exchange of notes at Lusaka March 9, 1992.

Entered into force March 9, 1992.

NP

Agreement concerning the provision of equipment, training and related services under the United States International Military Education and Training (IMET) Program.

Exchange of notes at Lusaka February 19, 2004 and February 15, 2005.

Entered into force February 15, 2005.

NP

ECONOMIC AND TECHNICAL COOPERATION

Economic cooperation agreement between the United States and the United Kingdom.

Signed at London July 6, 1948; applicable to Zambia July 20, 1948.

62 Stat. 2596; TIAS 1795; 12 Bevans 874; 22 UNTS 263.

Amendments

January 3, 1950 (1 UST 184; TIAS 2036; 86 UNTS 304).

May 25, 1951 (2 UST 1292; TIAS 2277; 99 UNTS 308).

February 25, 1953 (4 UST 1528; TIAS 2815; 172 UNTS 332).

Agreement for technical cooperation in respect of the territories for the international relations of which the Government of the United Kingdom are responsible.

Signed at London July 13, 1951; applicable to Federation of Rhodesia and Nyasaland April 8, 1960.

2 UST 1307; TIAS 2281; 105 UNTS 71.

Agency for International Development

December 3, 1976 (28 UST 8751; TIAS 8770; 1095 UNTS 101).

March 30, 1978 (30 UST 1889; TIAS 9299; 1170 UNTS 65).

September 27, 1985 (NP).

EMPLOYMENT

Agreement relating to the employment of dependents of official government employees.

Exchange of notes at Lusaka June 26, 1989 and January 4, 1990.

Entered into force January 4, 1990.

TIAS

EXTRADITION

Extradition treaty between the United States and the United Kingdom.

Signed at London December 22, 1931.

Entered into force June 24, 1935.

47 Stat. 2122; TS 849; 12 Bevans 482; 163 LNTS 59.

FINANCE

Agreement regarding the consolidation and rescheduling of certain debts owed to, or guaranteed by the United States Government and its agencies, with annexes.

Signed at Lusaka December 19, 1983.

Entered into force February 10, 1984.

35 UST 4387; TIAS 10941.

Agreement regarding the consolidation and rescheduling of certain debts owed to, guaranteed by or insured by the United States Government and its agencies, with annexes and implementing agreement.

Signed at Lusaka December 15, 1984.

Entered into force January 22, 1985.

TIAS 11002; 2022 UNTS 75.

Agreement regarding the consolidation and rescheduling of certain debts owed to, guaranteed by or insured by the United States Government and its agencies.

Signed at Lusaka July 25, 1986.

Entered into force August 28, 1986.

NP

Agreement regarding the consolidation and rescheduling of certain debts owed to, guaranteed by or insured by the United States Government and its agencies, with annexes.

Signed at Lusaka September 14, 1990.

Entered into force November 5, 1990.

NP

Agreement regarding the consolidation and rescheduling or refinancing of certain debts owed to, guaranteed by or insured by the U.S. Government and its agencies, with annexes and addendum.

Signed at Lusaka March 23, 1993.

Entered into force August 11, 1993.

NP

Agreement regarding the consolidation, reduction, and rescheduling of certain debts owed to, guaranteed by, or insured by the United States Government and its agency, with annexes.

Signed at Lusaka September 26, 1997.

Entered into force December 3, 1997.

NP

Investment incentive agreement.

Signed at Lusaka June 23, 1999.

Entered into force July 2, 1999.

TIAS

Agreement regarding the reduction, consolidation, and rescheduling of certain debts owed to, guaranteed by, or insured by the United States Government and its Agency, with annexes.

Signed at Lusaka November 19, 1999.

Entered into force February 23, 2000.

NP

Agreement regarding the consolidation and reduction of certain debts owed to, guaranteed by, or insured by the United States Government and its agencies, with annexes.

Signed at Lusaka November 3, 2003.

Entered into force December 17, 2003.

NP

Agreement regarding the reduction of certain debts owed to, guaranteed by, or insured by the United States Government and its agencies, with annexes.

Signed at Lusaka December 30, 2005.

Entered into force February 6, 2006.

NP

INTERNATIONAL CRIMINAL COURT

Agreement regarding the surrender of persons to international tribunals.

Signed at Lusaka July 1, 2003.

Entered into force July 2, 2003.

TIAS

MUTUAL SECURITY

Agreement relating to the assurances required under the Mutual Security Act of 1951.

Exchange of notes at London January 8, 1952.

Entered into force January 8, 1952.

3 UST 4665; TIAS 2622; 126 UNTS 307.

POSTAL MATTERS

International express mail agreement, with detailed regulations.

Signed at Ndola and Washington April 25 and May 16, 1988.

Entered into force June 15, 1988.

TIAS 11589.

PROPERTY

Convention between the United States and the United Kingdom relating to tenure and disposition of real and personal property.

Signed at Washington March 2, 1899; applicable to Zambia May 29, 1947.

31 Stat. 1939; TS 146; 12 Bevans 246.

Supplementary convention relating to the tenure and disposition of real and personal property of March 2, 1899.

Signed at Washington May 27, 1936.

Entered into force March 10, 1941.

55 Stat. 1101; TS 964; 5 Bevans 140; 203 LNTS 367.

SCIENTIFIC COOPERATION

Memorandum of understanding concerning scientific and technical cooperation in the earth sciences, with annexes.

Signed at Reston and Lusaka September 9 and 23, 2002.

Entered into force September 23, 2002.

TIAS

TRADE-MARKS

Declaration by the United States and the United Kingdom affording reciprocal protection to trade-marks.

Signed at London October 24, 1877.

Entered into force October 24, 1877.

20 Stat. 703; TS 138; 12 Bevans 198.

ZIMBABWE

On April 18, 1980, Zimbabwe became an independent state. In a note dated February 24, 1981 to the Secretary General of the United Nations, the Prime Minister made a statement reading in part as follows:

"My Government will continue to apply within its territory, on the basis of the principles of reciprocity and mutual respect for sovereign independence, all bilateral treaties validly concluded or recognised by the United Kingdom Government in respect of Southern Rhodesia for a period of three years from the date of independence, i.e. 18th April, 1980, unless such treaties are terminated or modified earlier by mutual consent. It is the intention of my Government during such period to subject all bilateral treaties to full examination for the purpose of determining whether such treaties require termination, revision or renegotiation in the light of Zimbabwe's sovereign status. It is the earnest hope of my Government that during the aforementioned period the normal processes of diplomatic negotiation will enable it to reach satisfactory accord with the States concerned upon the possibility of the continuance, modification or termination of such treaties.

At the end of the three year period referred to above my Government will regard such treaties whose continuance or modification have not been agreed as having terminated.

As regards multilateral treaties validly concluded or recognised by the United Kingdom Government in respect of Southern Rhodesia, my Government proposes to review at least some of those treaties during a period of six years from the date of independence, i.e. 18th April, 1980. It will indicate to the depositaries in each case of review whether the Republic of Zimbabwe will confirm, seek to modify or terminate its obligations under the treaty concerned. During such period of review any party to a multilateral treaty which was validly applied or extended to Southern Rhodesia may, on the basis of reciprocity and respect for national independence, rely on the terms of such treaty until it is modified or terminated. At the expiration of the period of review treaties as modified, or which have not been terminated, shall continue fully in force as if they had been concluded by the Republic of Zimbabwe."

By note of April 14, 1983 to the Secretary-General of the United Nations, the Government of Zimbabwe extended the period of review of bilateral treaties to April 18, 1984. This period of review was further extended by a note dated April 11, 1984 in which the Prime Minister notified the Secretary General that "… my Government will continue to apply within its territory all such bilateral treaties until the 18th April 1985, unless terminated earlier or modified by mutual consent. Thereafter my Government will regard those treaties whose continuance or modification has not been agreed upon as having terminated."

In a further letter to the Secretary-General, received February 20, 1985, the Prime Minister stated in part:

"During the past four years my Government has reviewed all such bilateral treaties as were available to it or were brought to its attention and has also concluded a number of bilateral treaties with other governments with the effect that these instruments have superseded some of the earlier ones. It has become evident to my Government that many contracting parties prefer to enter into new arrangements with my Government rather than revive those treaties whose operations might have been suspended or terminated between 1965 and 1979 or which are now considered to be obsolete in the conduct of present-day international relations.

Whilst it has not been practicable for my Government to re-negotiate and finalise all such agreements on which a willingness to keep and maintain them in force was mutually indicated by my Government and other contracting parties, my Government has reached the stage at which it considers that legal continuity between itself and Other Contracting States has been achieved with an understanding either to revive, modify, re-negotiate, terminate or adopt such bilateral treaties and, accordingly, my Government now wishes to inform Your Excellency, and through you all Member States of the United Nations Organisation as follows:

All bilateral treaties that were validly concluded or recognised by the United Kingdom Government in respect of Southern Rhodesia and continued to be applied and respected by my Government pursuant to the declaration aforementioned will now expire on 18 April 1985, UNLESS:

(i) Either my Government has already communicated to the other contracting party its intention to maintain the continuance in force of the treaty or the process of re-negotiating its terms and provisions has been agreed upon; or

(ii) The other contracting party notifies my Government before 18 April 1985 through normal diplomatic channels of its intention either to keep and maintain the continuance in force of the treaty concerned or to re-negotiate its terms and provisions, in which case, my Government will consider itself bound by that Treaty."

The United States presented Zimbabwe by diplomatic note of April 17, 1985 a list of international agreements which the Government of the United States intended to maintain in force.

AGRICULTURAL COMMODITIES

Agricultural commodities agreement.

Signed at Harare April 1, 1985.

Entered into force April 1, 1985.

NP

AVIATION

Agreement between the United States and the United Kingdom concerning air services, with annexes and exchange of letters.

Signed at Bermuda July 23, 1977.

Entered into force July 23, 1977.

28 UST 5367; TIAS 8641.

Amendments

April 25, 1978 (29 UST 2680; TIAS 8965).

December 27, 1979 (32 UST 524; TIAS 9722).

CONSULS

Consular convention between the United States and the United Kingdom.

Signed at Washington June 6, 1951.

Entered into force September 7, 1952.

3 UST 3426; TIAS 2494; 165 UNTS 121.

DEFENSE

Agreement concerning the provision of training related to defense articles under the United States International Military Education and Training (IMET) Program.

Exchange of notes at Harare September 2 and 17, 1981.

Entered into force September 17, 1981.

35 UST 2319; TIAS 10791.

ECONOMIC AND TECHNICAL COOPERATION

General agreement for economic, technical, and related assistance.

Exchange of notes at Salisbury February 10 and March 22, 1982.

Entered into force March 22, 1982.

34 UST 194; TIAS 10348; 1557 UNTS 51.

Agency for International Development

April 7, 1982 (33 UST 4312; TIAS 10302).

EMPLOYMENT

Agreement relating to the employment of dependents of official government employees.

Exchange of notes at Harare February 7, 1991 and March 7, 1992.

Entered into force March 7, 1992.

TIAS 11857.

EXTRADITION

Extradition treaty.

Signed at Harare July 25, 1997.

Entered into force April 26, 2000.

TIAS

FINANCE

Investment incentive agreement.

Signed at Harare June 20, 1990.

Entered into force June 20, 1990.

TIAS 12097.

PEACE CORPS

Agreement relating to the establishment of a Peace Corps in Zimbabwe.

Signed at Harare March 18, 1991.

Entered into force March 18, 1991.

TIAS 12114.

POSTAL MATTERS

International express mail agreement, with detailed regulations.

Signed at Harare and Washington February 15 and March 9, 1988.

Entered into force April 1, 1988.

TIAS 11569.

PROPERTY

Convention relating to tenure and disposition of real and personal property.

Signed at Washington March 2, 1899; applicable to Southern Rhodesia July 27, 1901.

31 Stat. 1939; TS 146; 12 Bevans 246.

Supplementary convention relating to the tenure and disposition of real and personal property.

Signed at Washington May 27, 1936.

Entered into force March 10, 1941.

55 Stat. 1101; TS 964; 5 Bevans 140; 203 LNTS 367.

SCIENTIFIC COOPERATION

Agreement for scientific and technical cooperation.

Signed at Salisbury September 25, 1980.

Entered into force September 25, 1980.

32 UST 4543; TIAS 9967; 1267 UNTS 243.

TRADE-MARKS

Declaration by the United States and the United Kingdom affording reciprocal protection to trade-marks.

Signed at London October 24, 1877.

Entered into force October 24, 1877.

20 Stat. 703; TS 138; 12 Bevans 198.

CHINA (TAIWAN)

On January 1, 1979, the United States recognized the Government of the People's Republic of China as the sole legal Government of China. Within this context, the people of the United States maintain cultural, commercial and other unofficial relations with the people on Taiwan. The United States acknowledges the Chinese position that there is but one China and Taiwan is part of China. The United States does not recognize the "Republic of China" as a state or government.

Pursuant to Section 6 of the Taiwan Relations Act, (P.L. 96-8, 93 Stat. 14, 22 U.S.C. 3305) and Executive Order 12143, 44 F.R. 37191, the following agreements concluded with the Taiwan authorities prior to January 1, 1979, and any multilateral treaty or agreement relationship listed in Section 2 of this volume, are administered on a nongovernmental basis by the American Institute in Taiwan, a nonprofit District of Columbia corporation, and constitute neither recognition of the Taiwan authorities nor the continuation of any official relationship with Taiwan. The following bilateral agreements are on record as of January 1, 2007:

AGRICULTURAL COMMODITIES

Agricultural commodities agreement, with exchange of notes.

Signed at Taipei August 31, 1962.

Entered into force August 31, 1962.

13 UST 1930; TIAS 5151; 460 UNTS 247.

Amendments

January 15, 1963 (14 UST 131; TIAS 5282; 473 UNTS 380).

June 3, 1964 (15 UST 667; TIAS 5588; 526 UNTS 330).

ATOMIC ENERGY

Agreement for cooperation concerning civil uses of atomic energy.

Signed at Washington April 4, 1972.

Entered into force June 22, 1972.

23 UST 945; TIAS 7364.

Extension and amendment

March 15, 1974 (25 UST 913; TIAS 7834).

AVIATION

Memorandum of agreement relating to the provision of flight inspection services.

Signed at Washington and Taipei August 21 and October 1, 1978.

Entered into force October 1, 1978.

30 UST 273; TIAS 9197; 1150 UNTS 271.

COMMERCE

Treaty of friendship, commerce, and navigation with accompanying protocol.

Signed at Nanking November 4, 1946.

Entered into force November 30, 1948.

63 Stat. 1299; TIAS 1871; 6 Bevans 761; 25 UNTS 69.

ECONOMIC AND TECHNICAL COOPERATION

Agreement on technological advancement in connection with water resources, land utilization and various fields of irrigated agriculture.

Signed at Taipei May 12, 1972.

Entered into force May 12, 1972.

23 UST 1135; TIAS 7374.

EDUCATION

Agreement for financing certain educational and cultural exchange programs.

Signed at Taipei April 23, 1964.

Entered into force April 23, 1964.

15 UST 408; TIAS 5572; 524 UNTS 141.

FINANCE

Agreement relating to guaranties for projects in Taiwan proposed by nationals of the United States.

Exchange of notes at Taipei June 25, 1952.

Entered into force June 25, 1952.

3 UST 4846; TIAS 2657; 136 UNTS 229.

Amendment

December 30, 1963 (14 UST 2222; TIAS 5509; 505 UNTS 308).

Agreement regarding the ownership and use of local currency repayments made by China to the Development Loan Fund.

Exchange of notes at Taipei December 24, 1958.

Entered into force December 24, 1958.

10 UST 16; TIAS 4162; 340 UNTS 251.

LEND-LEASE

Preliminary agreement regarding principles applying to mutual aid in the prosecution of the war against aggression.

Signed at Washington June 2, 1942.

Entered into force June 2, 1942.

56 Stat. 1494; EAS 251; 6 Bevans 735; 14 UNTS 343.

Agreement under section 3 (c) of the Lend-Lease Act.

Signed at Washington June 28, 1946.

Entered into force June 28, 1946.

61 Stat. 3895; TIAS 1746; 6 Bevans 758; 34 UNTS 121.

Agreement on the disposition of lend-lease supplies in inventory or procurement in the United States.

Signed at Washington June 14, 1946; operative September 2, 1945.

60 Stat. 1760; TIAS 1533; 6 Bevans 753; 4 UNTS 253.

MARITIME MATTERS

Agreement relating to the loan of small naval craft to China.

Exchange of notes at Taipei May 14, 1954.

Entered into force May 14, 1954.

5 UST 892; TIAS 2979; 231 UNTS 165.

Extensions and amendments

March 22 and 31, 1955 (6 UST 750; TIAS 3215; 251 UNTS 399).

June 18, 1955 (6 UST 2973; TIAS 3346; 265 UNTS 406).

May 16, 1957 (8 UST 787; TIAS 3837; 284 UNTS 380).

October 12, 1960 (11 UST 2233; TIAS 4597; 393 UNTS 320).

August 15, 1962 (13 UST 1924; TIAS 5150; 460 UNTS 237).

February 23, 1965 (16 UST 126; TIAS 5771; 542 UNTS 361).

December 16, 1970 and January 14, 1971 (22 UST 12; TIAS 7037; 776 UNTS 334).

NARCOTIC DRUGS

Arrangement for the direct exchange of certain information regarding the traffic in narcotic drugs.

Exchanges of notes at Nanking March 12, June 21, July 28, and August 30, 1947.

Entered into force August 30, 1947.

6 Bevans 797.

PACIFIC SETTLEMENT OF DISPUTES

Treaty looking to the advancement of the cause of general peace.

Signed at Washington September 15, 1914.

Entered into force October 22, 1915. Exchange of notes signed May 11 and 19, 1916.

39 Stat. 1642; TS 619 and 619-A; 6 Bevans 711.

Treaty of arbitration.

Signed at Washington June 27, 1930.

Entered into force December 15, 1932.

47 Stat. 2213; TS 857; 6 Bevans 724; 140 LNTS 183.

POSTAL MATTERS

Parcel post convention.

Signed at Peking May 29, 1916, and at Washington July 11, 1916.

Entered into force August 1, 1916.

39 Stat. 1665; Post Office Department print.

Agreement for exchange of insured parcel post and regulations of execution.

Signed at Taipei July 30 and at Washington August 19, 1957.

Entered into force November 1, 1957.

8 UST 2031; TIAS 3941; 300 UNTS 61.

International express mail agreement, with detailed regulations.

Signed at Taipei and Washington September 11 and November 10, 1978.

Entered into force December 30, 1978; effective December 27, 1978.

30 UST 3277; TIAS 9392; 1179 UNTS 291.

RELIEF SUPPLIES AND PACKAGES

Agreement relating to duty-free entry of relief goods and relief packages and to the defrayment of transportation charges on such shipments.

Exchange of notes at Nanking November 5 and 18, 1948.

Entered into force November 18, 1948.

3 UST 5462; TIAS 2749; 198 UNTS 287.

Amendments

October 20 and December 12, 1952 (3 UST 5462; TIAS 2749; 198 UNTS 294).

July 12 and October 26, 1954 (5 UST 2930; TIAS 3151; 237 UNTS 337).

TRADE

See also COMMERCE

Agreement relating to trade in textiles with letter dated April 10, 1974.

Exchange of letters at Washington April 11, 1974.

Entered into force April 11, 1974.[1]

25 UST 720; TIAS 7821.

Agreement on trade matters, with annexes.

Exchange of letters at Washington December 29, 1978.

Entered into force December 29, 1978.

30 UST 6439; TIAS 9561; 1179 UNTS 313.

NOTES

1 Exchange of letters dated April 11, 1974 terminated January 1, 1975. Letter dated April 10, 1974 remains in force.

VISAS

Agreement prescribing nonimmigrant visa fees and validity of nonimmigrant visas.

Exchange of notes at Taipei December 20, 1955 and February 20, 1956.

Entered into force February 20, 1956; operative April 1, 1956.

7 UST 585; TIAS 3539; 275 UNTS 73.

Amendments

July 11, October 17 and December 7, 1956 (18 UST 3167; TIAS 6410; 697 UNTS 256).

May 8, June 9 and 15, 1970 (21 UST 2213; TIAS 6972; 776 UNTS 344).

Pursuant to the Taiwan Relations Act and Executive Order 12143, 44 F.R. 37191, agreements concluded after January 1, 1979 by the American Institute in Taiwan, 1700 North Moore Street, Rosslyn, Virginia 22209, with its nongovernmental Taiwan counterpart, the Taipei Economic and Cultural Representative Office, are reported to the Congress as in effect under the law of the United States. A list of such agreements appears at 65 F.R. 81898.

References

Bevans	*Treaties and Other International Agreements of the United States of America 1776-1949,* compiled under the direction of Charles I. Bevans.
EAS	*Executive Agreement Series*, issued singly in pamphlets by the Department of State (until replaced in 1945 by the TIAS).
Foreign Relations	Foreign Relations of the United States.
F.R.	*Federal Register.*
H.Doc.	House Document.
ILM	*International Legal Materials.*
LNTS	*League of Nations Treaty Series.*
Miller	*Treaties and other International Acts of the United States of America,* edited by Hunter Miller.
NP	Not Printed in *Treaties and Other International Acts Series.*
Stat.	*United States Statutes at Large.*
T. Doc.	Senate Treaty Document.
TIAS	*Treaties and Other International Acts Series,* issued singly in pamphlets by the Department of State.
TS	*Treaty Series,* issued singly in pamphlets by the Department of State (replaced in 1945 by *Treaties and Other International Acts Series*).
UNTS	*United Nations Treaty Series.*
UST	*United States Treaties and Other International Agreements* (volumes published on a calendar-year basis beginning as of January 1, 1950).

INDEX

B

C

F

G

H

I

J

K

L

M

N

O

P

Q

R

S

T

U

V

W

Y

Z